TRANSMATH™

Understanding Algebraic Expressions

Teacher Guide Volume 2

John Woodward
Mary Stroh

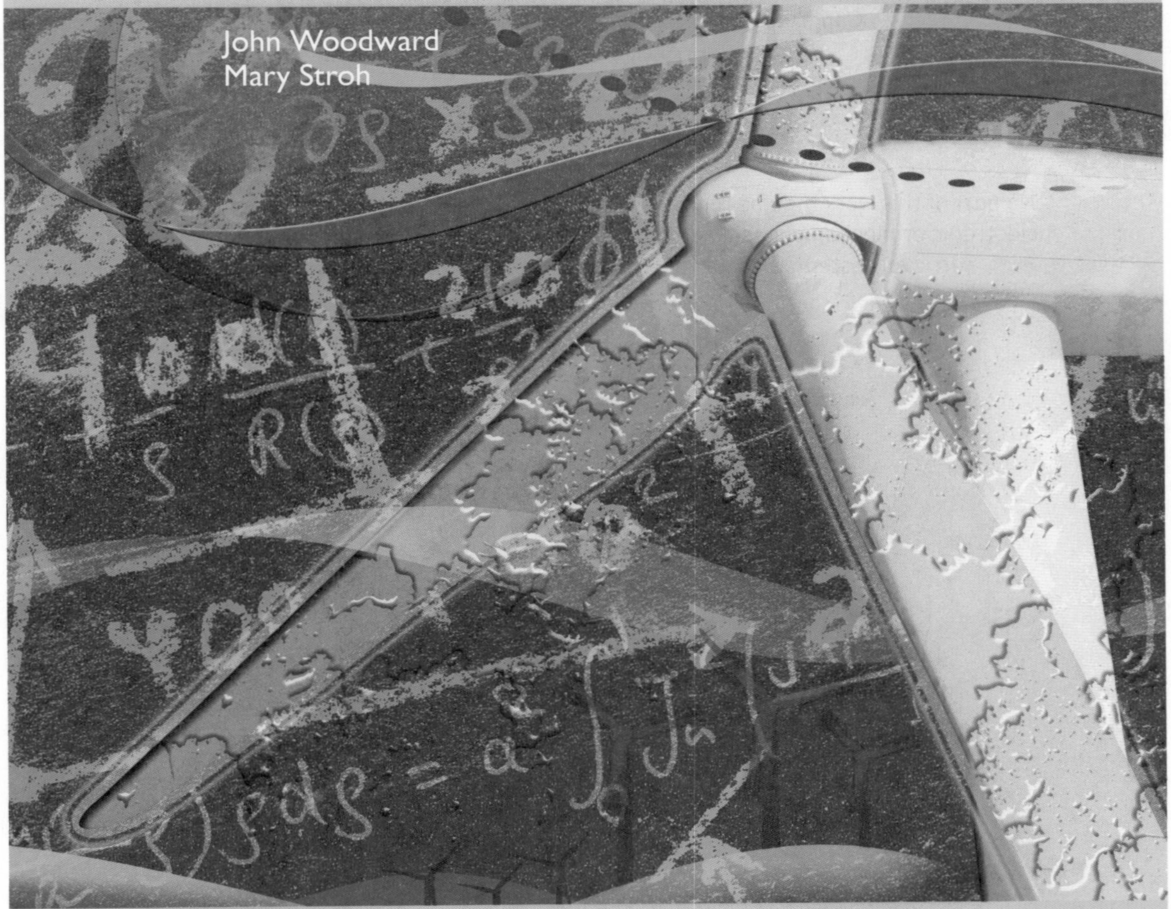

BOSTON, MA | LONGMONT, CO

13 12 11 10 09 6 5 4 3 2 1

ISBN 13: 978-160697-039-3
ISBN: 1-60697-039-9

181948/4-09

Printed in the United States of America
Published and distributed by

4093 Specialty Place • Longmont, CO 80504 • (303) 651-2829
www.sopriswest.com

TRANSMATH™

Accelerating struggling students into successful math thinkers through fewer topics and greater depth
TRANSMATH™
Developing Number Sense
Teacher Guide Volume 1
John Woodward
Mary Stroh
Cambridge Learning | Sopris West
TRANSMATH™
Making Sense of Rational Numbers
Teacher Guide Volume 1
John Woodward
Mary Stroh
Cambridge Learning | Sopris West
TRANSMATH™
Understanding Algebraic Expressions
Teacher Guide Volume 1
John Woodward
Mary Stroh
Cambridge Learning | Sopris West

Table of Contents • Volume 1

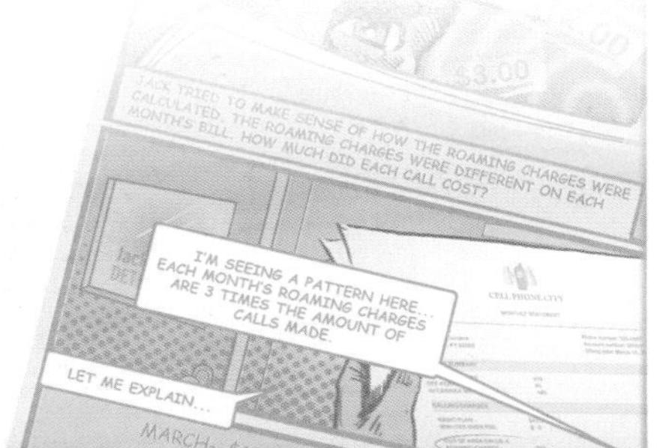

JACK TRIED TO MAKE SENSE OF HOW THE ROAMING CHARGES WERE CALCULATED. THE ROAMING CHARGES WERE DIFFERENT ON EACH MONTH'S BILL. HOW MUCH DID EACH CALL COST?
I'M SEEING A PATTERN HERE... EACH MONTH'S ROAMING CHARGES ARE 3 TIMES THE AMOUNT OF CALLS MADE.
LET ME EXPLAIN...

Unit Review
Inequalities
Problem Solving:
Working With Rates

JACK TRIED TO MAKE SENSE OF HOW THE ROAMING CHARGES WERE CALCULATED. THE ROAMING CHARGES WERE DIFFERENT ON EACH MONTH'S BILL. HOW MUCH DID EACH CALL COST?
I'M SEEING A PATTERN HERE. EACH MONTH'S ROAMING CHARGES ARE 3 TIMES THE AMOUNT OF CALLS MADE.
LET ME EXPLAIN...

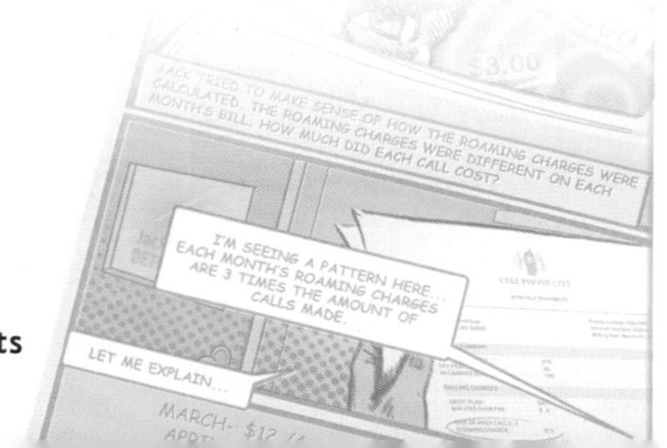

I'M SEEING A PATTERN HERE. EACH MONTH'S ROAMING CHARGES ARE 3 TIMES THE AMOUNT OF CALLS MADE.
LET ME EXPLAIN...

What is TRANSMATH™?

***TransMath* is the comprehensive mathematics intervention that provides key foundational skill-building and problem-solving experiences by targeting instruction with fewer topics, taught in greater depth.**

TransMath simultaneously teaches **foundational computation skills** while providing the **rich, grade-level, problem-solving** experiences necessary for high-stakes assessments.

Students two or more years below grade level

LEVEL 1
Number Sense

- Place Value
- Whole Numbers
- Operations
- Factors
- Multiples
- Estimation
- Fractions
- Multistep Problems
- Mean, Median, Range
- Measurement

LEVEL 2
Rational Numbers

- Fractions
- Decimal Numbers
- Percentages
- Exponents
- Negative Numbers
- Estimation
- Data and Statistics
- Two-Dimensional Geometry
- Probability

LEVEL 3
Algebraic Thinking

- Properties
- Simple Algebraic Expressions
- Inequalities
- Functions
- Square Roots
- Irrational Numbers
- Estimation
- Ratio and Proportion
- Coordinate Graphs
- Slope
- Three-Dimensional Geometry

Successful entry into Algebra

Level 1

Level 2

Level 3

According to the National Mathematics Advisory Panel's Final Report, "To prepare students for Algebra, the curriculum must simultaneously develop conceptual understanding, computational fluency, and problem-solving skills" (page 19).

Who is TRANSMATH™ for?

TransMath targets the specific learning needs of students who need immediate support.

- Students lacking the foundational skills necessary for successful entry into Algebra
- Students scoring two or more years below grade level on state standardized tests

Extensively cited by the Task Group on Instructional Practices for the National Mathematics Advisory Panel's Final Report, *TransMath* (*Transitional Mathematics*) provides comprehensive skill building by targeting instruction with fewer topics, taught in greater depth. This approach was cited as a key finding for mathematical success by the Trends in International Mathematics and Science Studies (TIMSS) and is supported by the National Council of Teachers of Mathematics (NCTM) Curriculum Focal Points.

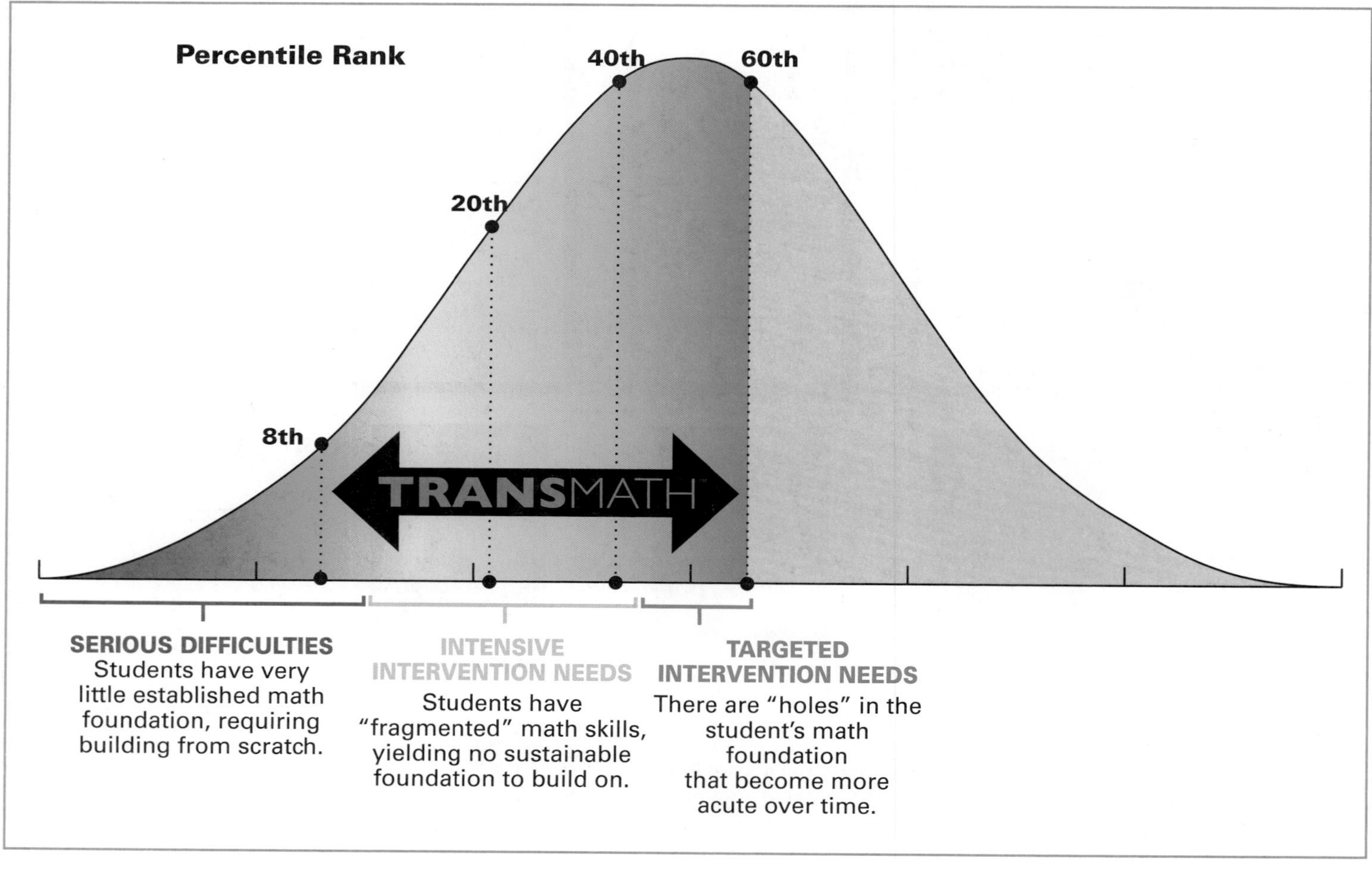

Percentile Rank
40th
60th
20th
8th
TRANSMATH
SERIOUS DIFFICULTIES
Students have very little established math foundation, requiring building from scratch.
INTENSIVE INTERVENTION NEEDS
Students have "fragmented" math skills, yielding no sustainable foundation to build on.
TARGETED INTERVENTION NEEDS
There are "holes" in the student's math foundation that become more acute over time.

Can your students solve this equation:

$10(x + 5) = 2x + 56$?

	Prerequisite skills for Algebra proficiency
$10(x + 5) = 2x + 56$	Recognize that the equation is balanced Recognize that unlike terms cannot be combined Recognize that 2 is a coefficient Be able to use the Distributive Property to delete the parentheses Know basic multiplication
$10x + 50 = 2x + 56$	Recognize that unlike terms cannot be combined
$-50 + 10x + 50 = 2x + 56 + -50$	Understand the need to maintain a balanced equation Know the property of opposites (i.e., 50 and –50)
$10x + -50 + 50 = 2x + 56 + -50$	Be able to use the Commutative Property to combine like terms Know how to add integers Know basic subtraction
$10x = 2x + 6$	Recognize that the equation is balanced
$-2x + 10x = 2x + 6 + -2x$	Understand the need to maintain a balanced equation Know the property of opposites (i.e., $2x$ and $-2x$)
$-2x + 10x = 2x + -2x + 6$	Be able to use the Commutative Property to combine like terms Know how to add integers
$8x = 0 + 6$	Recognize that the equation is balanced Know basic addition
$\frac{1}{8} \cdot 8x = 6 \cdot \frac{1}{8}$	Be able to use reciprocals Know how to multiply fractions
$\frac{8}{8}x = \frac{6}{8}$ $x = \frac{3}{4}$	Know that $1x = x$ (the "invisible coefficient") Know about fractions equal to one (i.e., $\frac{8}{8}$) Know basic multiplication Know how to simplify fractions Know about greatest common factors

Taught to Mastery in:

Level 1

Level 2

Level 3

What Makes TRANSMATH™ Work?

Dual Topics avoid cognitive overload.

Building Number Concepts:

▶ Mixed Practice With Fractions

We use models to review addition, subtraction, multiplication, and division with fractions. We also learn that when we multiply a fraction and its reciprocal, we always get 1.

Objective

Students will add, subtract, multiply, and divide fractions.

Problem Solving:

▶ Box-and-Whisker Plots

In today's lesson, students make box-and-whisker plots from a table of data. They learn that there is a difference between the median and the halfway point between the minimum and the maximum in a set of data.

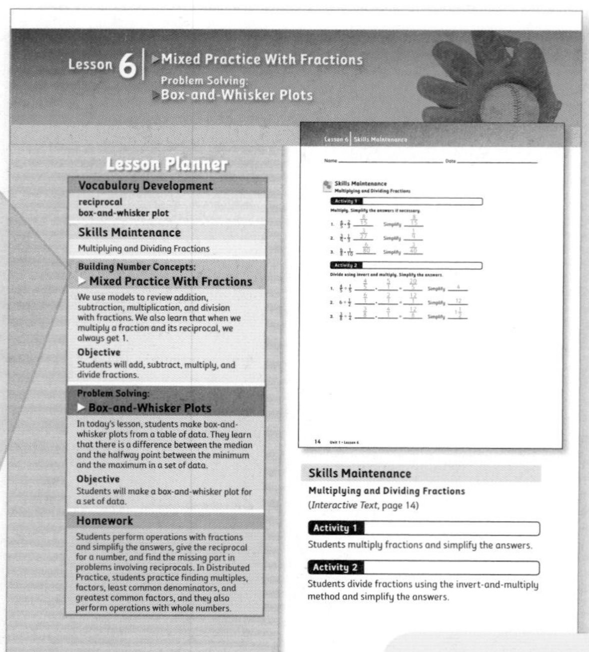
Lesson 6 | ▶Mixed Practice With Fractions
Problem Solving:
▶Box-and-Whisker Plots

Lesson Planner

Vocabulary Development
reciprocal box-and-whisker plot
Skills Maintenance
Multiplying and Dividing Fractions
Building Number Concepts: ▶ Mixed Practice With Fractions
We use models to review addition, subtraction, multiplication, and division with fractions. We also learn that when we multiply a fraction and its reciprocal, we always get 1.
Objective Students will add, subtract, multiply, and divide fractions.
Problem Solving: ▶ Box-and-Whisker Plots
In today's lesson, students make box-and-whisker plots from a table of data. They learn that there is a difference between the median and the halfway point between the minimum and the maximum in a set of data.
Objective Students will make a box-and-whisker plot for a set of data.
Homework Students perform operations with fractions and simplify the answers, give the reciprocal for a number, and find the missing part in problems involving reciprocals. In Distributed Practice, students practice finding multiples, factors, least common denominators, and greatest common factors, and they also perform operations with whole numbers.

Skills Maintenance

Multiplying and Dividing Fractions
(*Interactive Text*, page 14)

Activity 1
Students multiply fractions and simplify the answers.

Activity 2
Students divide fractions using the invert-and-multiply method and simplify the answers.

Visual Models illustrate difficult concepts.

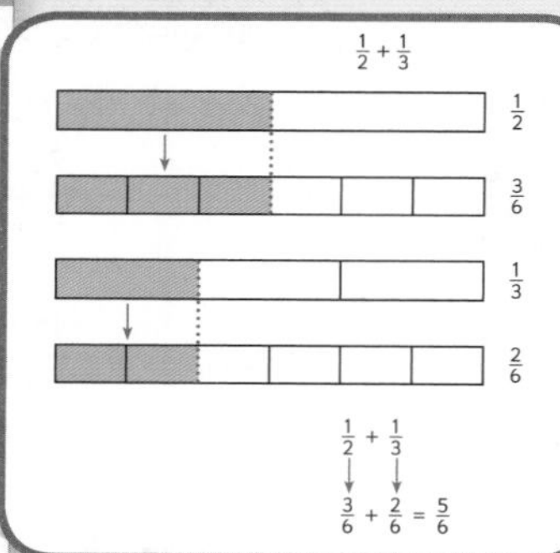

Engagement Strategies provide varied and continuous communication opportunities.

Demonstrate

Engagement Strategy: Teacher Modeling

Demonstrate how to perform different operations on fractions in one of the following ways:

 **mBook**: Use the *mBook Teacher Edition* for *Student Text*, pages 39–40. m

 **Overhead Projector**: Reproduce the problem and fraction bars on a transparency, and modify as discussed.

 **Board**: Copy the problem and fraction bars on the board, and modify as discussed.

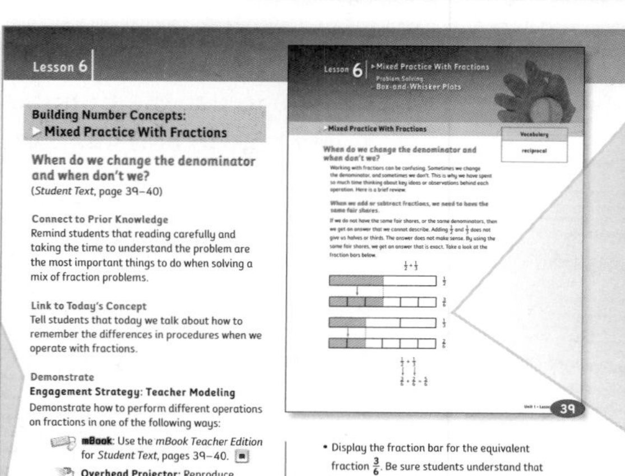
Lesson 6

Building Number Concepts:
▶ Mixed Practice With Fractions

When do we change the denominator and when don't we?
(*Student Text*, page 39–40)

Connect to Prior Knowledge
Remind students that reading carefully and taking the time to understand the problem are the most important things to do when solving a mix of fraction problems.

Link to Today's Concept
Tell students that today we talk about how to remember the differences in procedures when we operate with fractions.

Demonstrate
Engagement Strategy: Teacher Modeling
Demonstrate how to perform different operations on fractions in one of the following ways:

- Display the problem $\frac{1}{2} + \frac{1}{3}$. Remind students that we need a common denominator to add or subtract fractions.
- Display and shade the fraction bar for $\frac{1}{2}$. Label it.
- Display the fraction bar for the equivalent fraction $\frac{3}{6}$. Be sure students understand that these fractions are equivalent.
- Repeat for the equivalent fractions $\frac{1}{3}$ and $\frac{2}{6}$.
- Refer again to the addition problem. Have students tell you how to rewrite the problem with the equivalent fractions: $\frac{3}{6} + \frac{2}{6}$.
- Explain that we can now add the parts. Show $\frac{3}{6} + \frac{2}{6} = \frac{5}{6}$.

Ask:
How do we add and subtract fractions?

Listen for:
- *To find a common denominator, we can find the LCM.*
- *Once we have a common denominator, we need to add or subtract the numerator.*

60 Unit 1 • Lesson 6

Ask: questions help teachers guide discussions that assess understanding.

Ask:

How do we add and subtract fractions?

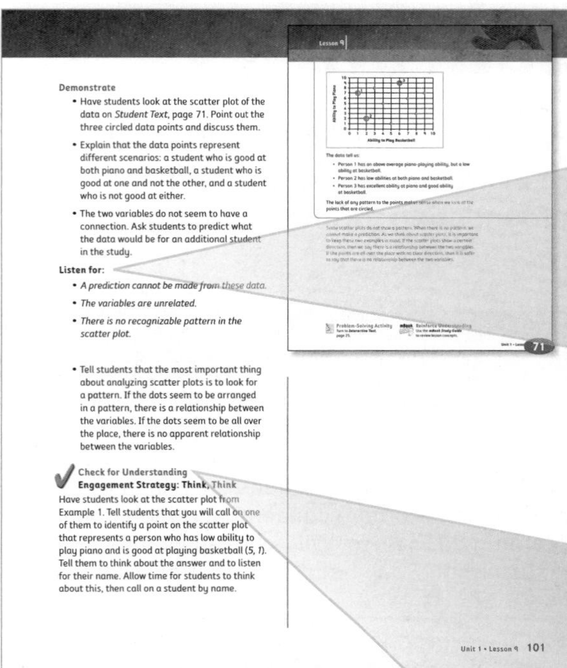

Listen for: statements guide teachers in assessing student understanding.

Listen for:

- *A prediction cannot be made from these data.*
- *The variables are unrelated.*
- *There is no recognizable pattern in the scatter plot.*

Check for Understanding provides ongoing, informal assessment in every lesson.

Check for Understanding
Engagement Strategy: Think, Think

Have students look at the scatter plot from Example 1. Tell students that you will call on one of them to identify a point on the scatter plot that represents a person who has low ability to play piano and is good at playing basketball (*5, 1*). Tell them to think about the answer and to listen for their name. Allow time for students to think about this, then call on a student by name.

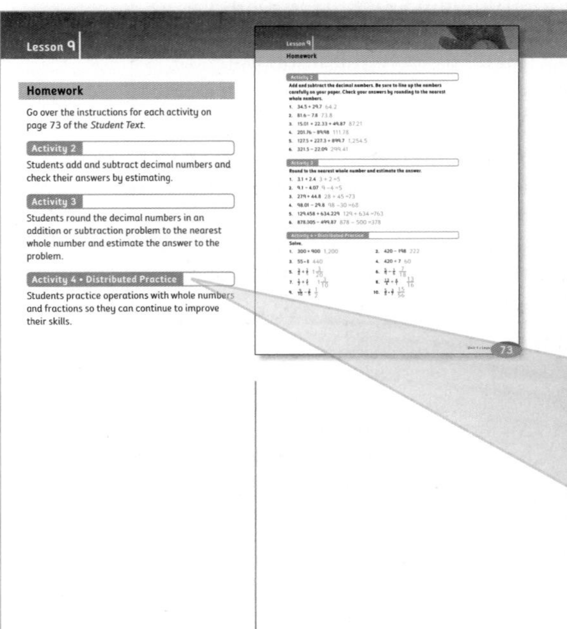

Distributed Practice in every lesson provides continued practice of previously learned skills.

Activity 4 • Distributed Practice

Students practice operations with whole numbers and fractions so they can continue to improve

Instructional Principles Are Supported by Research

A conceptually guided approach to mathematics instruction is essential to the learning needs of struggling students. The five instructional principles that best serve this population of students are the foundation for the pedagogical structure of *TransMath*.

TransMath **Instructional Principles**	**The Supporting Research**
Visual Representations	Visual representations include models, diagrams, and drawings as well as physical manipulatives. Paivio (1990) is one of many cognitive psychologists whose research supports the fact that information is stored visually as well as textually. The National Mathematics Panel Report (2008a) endorses the use of models and visual images as important ways to promote conceptual understanding, particularly in students with learning difficulties. Well-chosen visual models, in conjunction with conceptual explanations, can help students understand and remember key math concepts.
The Controlling of Cognitive Load	Many standards-based curricula have lessons that require extensive reading and contain a significant amount of mathematical as well as nonmathematical vocabulary. This is because developers want to provide authentic, or "real-world," problems for students to solve. These curricula also tend to move at a pace that is too fast for struggling students. These factors need to be addressed when standards-based curricula are adapted for struggling students (National Mathematics Panel Report 2008b). Teachers might need to summarize textual materials, and the key mathematical vocabulary needs to be highlighted and reviewed systematically (Baxter, Woodward, and Olson 2001).
Distributed Practice	Psychological and educational research emphasizes the role controlled distributed practice plays in enhancing retention as well as the overall design of curricular materials (e.g., Coyne, Kameenui, and Carnine 2007; Donovan and Radosevich 1999; Pashler, Rohrer, Cepeda, and Carpenter 2007). Too often, textbooks move from one topic or skill to the next without allowing sufficient opportunities for students to become proficient. Distributed practice on a sensible range of skills and concepts is essential to a struggling student's success in mathematics.
Varied Opportunities for Communication	Mathematical discussions can be challenging for teachers as well as students. Teachers sometimes find it difficult to interpret what some students are saying, thus interrupting the flow of the discussion. Teachers might also unintentionally favor those students who contribute the most to a discussion, leaving students with math difficulties ignored. Nonetheless, these students—like their more verbal peers—need structured opportunities to ask questions and explain their thinking. Recent research (e.g., Chapin, O'Connor, and Anderson 2003) offers important principles for conducting whole-group discussions in math classrooms.
Multiple Forms of Assessment	Ongoing or frequent assessment of students with math difficulties is a major concern in special education. This type of assessment can be seen as part of the Response to Treatment Intervention or RtI movement. At the same time, students should also experience other forms of assessment such as performance assessment and daily informal assessment (Lampert 2001; Stiggins 2005; Wiggins and McTighe 2005).

District 1

Background

To evaluate the effectiveness of *TransMath* relative to a comparison curriculum, a quasiexperimental study was conducted in two comparable middle schools in Bremerton, Washington, during the 2004–2005 school year[1].

All participating special education students had been identified for intense remedial instruction in mathematics. At the start of the study, there were no significant differences between the *TransMath* group and the comparison group on the mathematics portion of the CTB TerraNova[2] Test.

Key Details

Total Study Participants: 53

Schools: 2

Grade Level: 6

Demographics: 100% eligible for special education

Instructional Period: 2004–2005 school year

Instructional Time:

- *TransMath* group: 55 minutes per day
- Comparison group: 80 minutes per day

Measures:

- CTB TerraNova Test
- Core Concepts Test
- Attitudes Toward Math Survey

Results

The results indicated that *TransMath* students achieved higher academic outcomes than did the students in the comparison group (see Graphs 1 and 2). These results are noteworthy considering comparison students received an additional 25 minutes of instruction per day. In addition, students in the *TransMath* group demonstrated a more positive outlook on mathematics (see Graph 3).

Graph 1

CTB TerraNova Test: The data indicate that *TransMath* students showed significantly greater gains by the end of the year than comparison students.

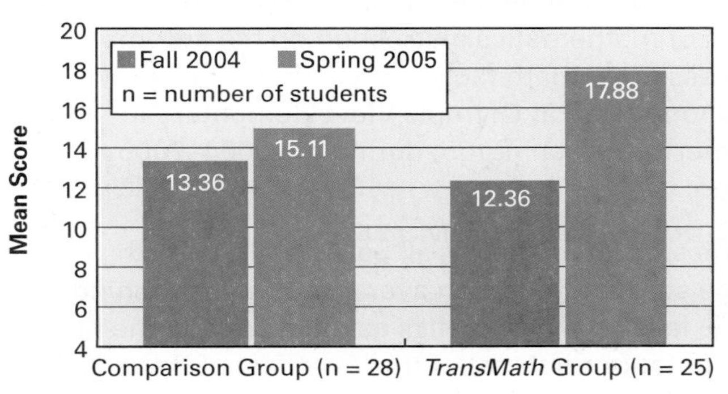

Graph 2

Core Concepts Test: On this cumulative measure of core math concepts taught across the entire year, data show that the *TransMath* group outperformed the comparison group in mathematics achievement.

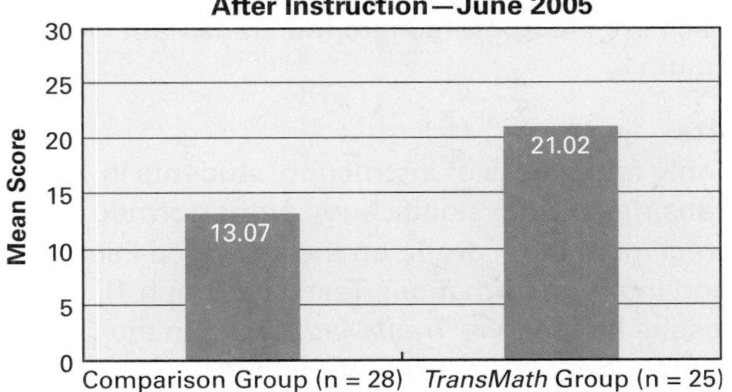

Graph 3

Attitudes Toward Math Survey: *TransMath* students developed a more positive attitude toward math, which included their self-perceptions as problem solvers.

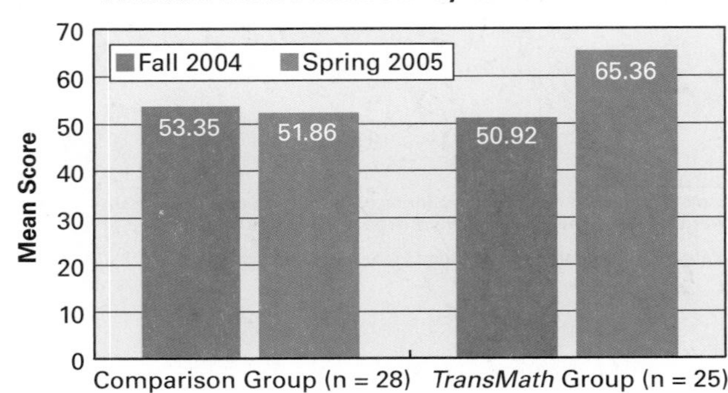

1 The complete published report in the *Journal of Special Education* (Woodward and Brown 2006) can be viewed at www.sopriswest.com/transmath.
2 McGraw-Hill. 2002. CTB TerraNova. Monterrey, Calif.: CTB McGraw-Hill.

District 2

Background

In order to examine the impact of two different kinds of mathematics instruction on the automatic processing of math facts, an experimental study was conducted at Olympic View Elementary in Bremerton, Washington, during the 2004–2005 school year[1].

At the start of the study, all participating fourth grade students were, on average, one year behind grade level in mathematics as measured by the Math Computations subtest of the Iowa Test of Basic Skills (ITBS). Random selection and assignment placed students in one of two study groups: (1) those taught by direct instruction, an approach that uses only timed practice drills, or (2) those taught using an integrated approach through a program titled *Fact Fluency and More!* which provides the foundation of whole number computations found in *TransMath*. Many of the instructional strategies in the integrated approach are incorporated into the *TransMath* curriculum.

Results

After only four weeks of instruction, students in the *TransMath* group significantly outperformed the direct instruction group on the Extended Facts Test and the Approximations Test (see Graph 1). The results favored the *TransMath* group in the development of automaticity of math facts.

Graph 1

Extended Facts Test: Results indicate that, on average, *TransMath* students were at a mastery level of performance after instruction. This was not the case for students in the direct instruction group.

Approximations Test: The results after instruction show a noticeable and significant difference, favoring the *TransMath* group.

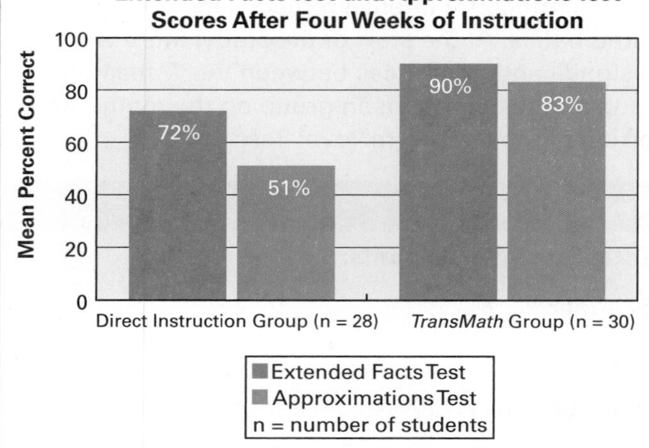

Key Details

Total Study Participants: 58

Demographics:

- 36% minority
- 20% special education for mathematics
- 57% Free/Reduced Lunch (FRL)
- 100% performed below grade level in math computation

Instructional Period: 2004–2005 school year
4 consecutive weeks

Instructional Time: 25 minutes per day focused solely on computational fluency

Measures[2]**:**

- Math Computations subtest of the Iowa Test of Basic Skills (ITBS)
- Extended Facts Test
- Approximations Test

[1] The complete published report in the *Journal of Learning Disability Quarterly* (Woodward, 2006) can be viewed at www.sopriswest.com/transmath.

[2] A complete list of measures can be found in the above published article.

What Are the TRANSMATH™ Components?

Teacher Materials	Student Materials
Teacher Guides—3 Levels Two-Volume Set at each level Level 1: 9 units Level 2: 9 units Level 3: 10 units **Teacher Placement Guide** Guides teachers in administering and scoring the placement test **Transparencies and Manipulatives** **Online Assessment System** Comprehensive data management system guides instruction and monitors change **mBook Teacher Edition** Provides online access to all teacher and student components and tools for Professional Development, Concept Modeling, and Reinforcement	**Student Text**—3 Levels Level 1: 9 units Level 2: 9 units Level 3: 10 units **Student Placement Test** Accurately places students into the curriculum **Interactive Text** Provides the in-class activities for skill application **Assessment Book** Contains all Quizzes, End-of-Unit Assessments, and Performance Assessments **mBook Study Guide** Provides online access to Student Text and Interactive Reinforcement Exercises
	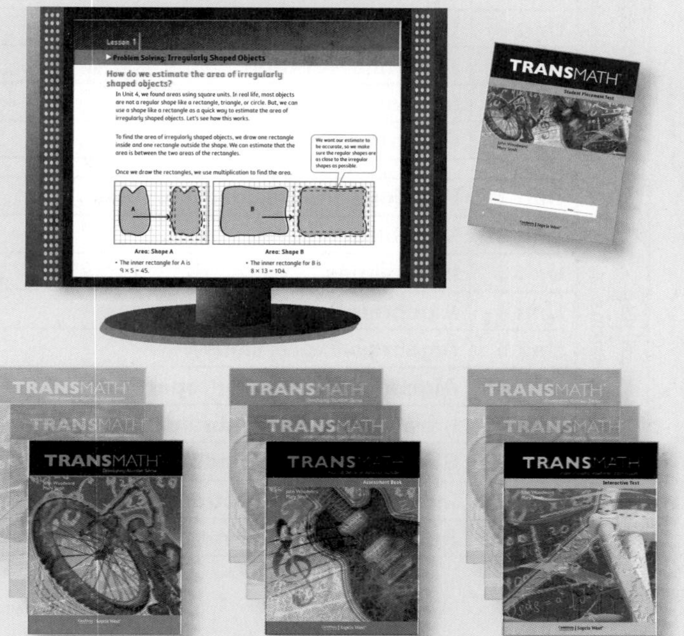

Provides a Balance of Conceptual Learning and Problem-Solving Applications

The dual-topic approach:

- Breaks learning into smaller parts
- Increases student engagement
- Addresses the issue of cognitive overload for struggling students

		Building Number Concepts	Problem Solving
Level 1: Developing Number Sense	Unit 1	Addition	Working With Data
	Unit 2	Subtraction	Working With Data
	Unit 3	Multiplication	Introduction to Measurement
	Unit 4	Division	Measuring Two-Dimensional Objects
	Unit 5	Factors, Primes, Composites	Area and Perimeter
	Unit 6	Common Factors and Number Patterns	Properties of Shapes
	Unit 7	More Number Patterns and Common Multiples	Slides, Flips, Turns, and Symmetry
	Unit 8	Concept of Fractions	Introduction to Statistics
	Unit 9	Adding and Subtracting Fractions	Converting Units of Measurement
Level 2: Making Sense of Rational Numbers	Unit 1	Review of Whole Numbers and Fractions	Working With Data
	Unit 2	Multiplication and Division of Fractions	Tools for Measurement and Construction
	Unit 3	Working With Mixed Numbers	Tessellations, Geometry, and Measurement
	Unit 4	The Concept of Decimal Numbers	Triangles and Quadrilaterals
	Unit 5	Operations on Decimal Numbers	Area of Two-Dimensional Shapes
	Unit 6	Understanding Percents	Percents in Word Problems and Graphs
	Unit 7	Scientific Notation	Probability
	Unit 8	Integers	Finding Points on a Graph
	Unit 9	Operations on Integers	Coordinate Graphs and Transformations
Level 3: Understanding Algebraic Expressions	Unit 1	Fractions and Decimal Numbers	Statistics
	Unit 2	Variables	Ratios and Proportions
	Unit 3	Inequalities	Working With Rates
	Unit 4	Algebraic Patterns	Ratios
	Unit 5	Algebraic Expressions	Surface Area of Three-Dimensional Shapes
	Unit 6	Algebraic Rules and Properties	Volume of Three-Dimensional Shapes
	Unit 7	Introduction to Algebraic Equations	Geometric Construction and Angle Measurement
	Unit 8	Solving Different Kinds of Algebraic Equations	Links and Angles
	Unit 9	Introduction to Functions	Working With Coordinate Graphs
	Unit 10	Square Roots and Irrational Numbers	Nonlinear Functions

Developing Number Sense

Level 1: Developing Number Sense

	Building Number Concepts	Problem Solving
Unit 1	**Addition** • Determine the place value of digits in a whole number. • Find sums of whole numbers with and without regrouping. • Round and estimate with whole numbers.	**Working With Data** • Read and interpret word problems. • Create, read, and interpret bar graphs. • Create pictographs.
Unit 2	**Subtraction** • Understand the relationship between basic and extended subtraction facts. • Solve whole-number subtraction problems using a variety of strategies. • Estimate the solution to problems by rounding.	**Working With Data** • Identify the question being asked in a word problem. • Read and analyze data in bar graphs and tables. • Solve word problems using whole-number subtraction.
Unit 3	**Multiplication** • Understand the relationship between basic and expanded multiplication. • Recognize and factor out powers of 10 from multiplication problems. • Estimate the solution to whole-number multiplication problems.	**Introduction to Measurement** • Measure using common objects. • Measure objects using inches and metric units. • Use a variety of measurement strategies in real-world problems.
Unit 4	**Division** • Understand the relationship between multiplication and division. • Solve problems using basic and extended division facts. • Represent whole-number division problems in a variety of ways.	**Measuring Two-Dimensional Objects** • Use square units to measure the area of shapes. • Apply the concept of area to real-world situations. • Solve word problems using whole-number division.
Unit 5	**Factors, Primes, Composites** • Factor whole numbers using a variety of methods. • Determine if a given number is prime or composite. • Find the prime factorization of a whole number.	**Area and Perimeter** • Explore the relationship between perimeter and area of shapes. • Discover and use area formulas for triangles and parallelograms. • Find the area of irregularly shaped objects.
Unit 6	**Common Factors and Number Patterns** • Find common factors for whole numbers using a variety of methods. • Identify the greatest common factor for two or more whole numbers. • Explore patterns in odd, even, and square numbers.	**Properties of Shapes** • Group shapes based on common properties. • Explore congruence and similarity of shapes. • Expand and contract shapes on a grid.
Unit 7	**More Number Patterns and Common Multiples** • Understand the relationships between triangular and square numbers. • Use exponents to show repeated multiplication. • Identify common multiples of two or more whole numbers.	**Slides, Flips, Turns, and Symmetry** • Recognize slides, flips, and turns in shapes. • Use tangrams to explore the properties of shapes. • Understand reflection and rotational symmetry.
Unit 8	**Concept of Fractions** • Recognize common fractions between whole numbers. • Represent fractions using shapes and fraction bars. • Find equivalent fractions.	**Introduction to Statistics** • Find the mean, median, and range of a set of data. • Use tables to organize data. • Read and create line plots and stem-and-leaf plots.
Unit 9	**Adding and Subtracting Fractions** • Add and subtract fractions with like and unlike denominators. • Find the least common multiple of two or more whole numbers. • Use least common multiples to find common denominators.	**Converting Units of Measurement** • Understand common units of measurement. • Convert units using a conversion table. • Measure objects to the nearest ¼ inch.

Making Sense of Rational Numbers

Level 2: Making Sense of Rational Numbers

Unit	Building Number Concepts	Problem Solving
Unit 1	**Review of Whole Numbers and Fractions** • Use place-value concepts to add and subtract whole numbers. • Use a variety of representations for fractions and decimal numbers. • Find the least common multiple of two or more whole numbers.	**Working With Data** • Read, create, and interpret bar graphs, pictographs, stem-and-leaf plots, and line graphs. • Use a bar graph to find the average of a set of data.
Unit 2	**Multiplication and Division of Fractions** • Use models to show multiplication and division of fractions. • Understand how multiplication and division of fractions is different from whole numbers. • Use the traditional methods to multiply and divide fractions.	**Tools for Measurement and Construction** • Develop an understanding of basic geometric terms. • Measure lengths and angles using a variety of tools and units. • Use a compass to complete basic geometric constructions.
Unit 3	**Working With Mixed Numbers** • Use the LAPS strategy to add, subtract, multiply, and divide mixed numbers. • Use approximations to estimate answers to problems involving fractions and mixed numbers.	**Tessellations, Geometry, and Measurement** • Recognize and use translations, reflections, and rotations of shapes. • Create and analyze tessellations.
Unit 4	**The Concept of Decimal Numbers** • Understand the relationship between fractions and decimal numbers. • Convert fractions to decimal numbers and decimal numbers to fractions. • Use strategies to round decimal numbers.	**Triangles and Quadrilaterals** • Classify triangles based on their properties. • Classify quadrilaterals based on their properties. • Understand the result of changing the dimensions of a shape.
Unit 5	**Operations on Decimal Numbers** • Demonstrate addition and subtraction of decimal numbers. • Use models to show multiplication and division of decimal numbers. • Use rounding strategies when working with decimal numbers.	**Area of Two-Dimensional Shapes** • Use formulas to find the area of rectangles, triangles, and other quadrilaterals. • Develop an understanding of the parts of a circle. • Find the circumference and area of a circle.
Unit 6	**Understanding Percents** • Understand the relationship between fractions, decimal numbers, and percents. • Convert between fractions, decimal numbers, and percents. • Use models to represent and understand percents.	**Percents in Word Problems and Graphs** • Read, create, and interpret circle graphs. • Use graphs to show percent increase or decrease. • Solve problems involving percent increase or decrease.
Unit 7	**Scientific Notation** • Understand the use of standard notation and scientific notation. • Use scientific notation to write very large and very small numbers.	**Probability** • Use fractions, decimal numbers, and percents to show probabilities. • Use models to find the probability of a single event. • Find the probability of independent and dependent events.
Unit 8	**Integers** • Use integers to represent values greater than and less than zero. • Use a number line to order and compare integers. • Use models to add and subtract integers.	**Finding Points on a Graph** • Read, create, and interpret dot graphs. • Use a coordinate grid to graph *x* and *y* coordinates. • Recognize and describe symmetry on a coordinate graph.
Unit 9	**Operations on Integers** • Use rules for integer operations to solve problems. • Use models to show multiplication and division of integers. • Use the PASS rule to multiply and divide integers.	**Coordinate Graphs and Transformations** • Use a coordinate graph to show translated and reflected shapes. • Use a coordinate graph to tell the difference between a translation and a reflection. • Use a table to show translated and reflected shapes.

Understanding Algebraic Expressions

Level 3: Understanding Algebraic Expressions	Unit	Building Number Concepts	Problem Solving
	Unit 1	**Fractions and Decimal Numbers** • Use models to show the relationship between fractions and decimal numbers. • Use a variety of methods to add, subtract, multiply, and divide rational numbers. • Use rounding and estimation strategies with rational numbers.	**Statistics** • Find the mean, median, mode, and range of a set of data. • Read, create, and interpret box-and-whisker plots and scatter plots. • Identify direct and indirect relationships in data using a scatter plot.
	Unit 2	**Variables** • Use variables to describe patterns. • Use variables to represent unknown values in formulas and equations. • Convert between equations and statements using words.	**Ratios and Proportions** • Represent part-to-whole and part-to-part relationships using ratios. • Recognize and represent proportional relationships. • Use proportions to identify similar shapes.
	Unit 3	**Inequalities** • Represent inequalities using symbols and number lines. • Represent written statements using inequalities. • Create written statements from inequalities.	**Working With Rates** • Solve rate problems using proportions. • Find unit rates using proportions. • Compare two rates using proportions.
	Unit 4	**Algebraic Patterns** • Use variables to represent numeric patterns. • Use variables to analyze patterns and make predictions. • Represent even and odd numbers and divisibility rules using algebraic equations.	**Ratios** • Represent part-to-whole and part-to-part relationships using ratios. • Solve real-world problems involving ratios. • Use percents to make comparisons.
	Unit 5	**Algebraic Expressions** • Evaluate numeric expressions using order of operations rules. • Recognize like and unlike terms in an algebraic expression. • Simplify algebraic expressions using the properties of numbers.	**Surface Area of Three-Dimensional Shapes** • Identify the attributes of three-dimensional shapes. • Use formulas to find the surface area of cylinders and prisms. • Find the surface area of pyramids and polyhedrons by breaking the shapes into familiar parts.
	Unit 6	**Algebraic Rules and Properties** • Use order of operations rules to evaluate algebraic and numeric expressions. • Use substitution to evaluate algebraic expressions. • Apply the distributive property to algebraic expressions.	**Volume of Three-Dimensional Shapes** • Use formulas to find the volume of cylinders and prisms. • Find the volume of pyramids and cones by comparing them to prisms and cylinders. • Use a formula to find the volume of a sphere.
	Unit 7	**Introduction to Algebraic Equations** • Understand the basic properties of algebraic equations. • Balance equations involving symbols or variables. • Solve problems involving algebraic equations.	**Geometric Construction and Angle Measurement** • Use a compass and straightedge to construct basic figures. • Use algebraic reasoning to find missing angle measures. • Explore the properties of triangles with congruent angles.
	Unit 8	**Solving Different Kinds of Algebraic Equations** • Use a variety of rules and properties to solve algebraic equations. • Use algebraic equations to describe a given situation. • Solve word problems involving algebraic equations using models, and check answers for how reasonable they are.	**Lines and Angles** • Use algebra to find the measures of interior angles in a polygon. • Use angle rules to solve problems involving related angles (vertical, corresponding, right, and supplementary). • Complete simple proofs involving angle measures.
	Unit 9	**Introduction to Functions** • Use word problems and tables to think about functional relationships. • Interpret the slope and *y*-intercept of a function in a real-world situation. • Use a function to make predictions in a real-world situation.	**Working With Coordinate Graphs** • Graph linear functions on a coordinate graph. • Convert functions between representations (tables, graphs, and equations). • Interpret the intersection of two functions in a real-world situation.
	Unit 10	**Square Roots and Irrational Numbers** • Solve algebraic equations and estimate answers involving square roots. • Use the Pythagorean theorem to find the lengths of sides of right triangles. • Identify and use irrational numbers.	**Nonlinear Functions** • Tell whether a function is linear or nonlinear given a table, equation, or graph. • Graph nonlinear functions on a coordinate graph. • Understand the role of the coefficient in a nonlinear function.

Establishes a Strong Math Foundation With the Building Number Concepts Strand

Students are taught concepts and skills in the order in which they need to learn them—from developing number sense to thinking algebraically.

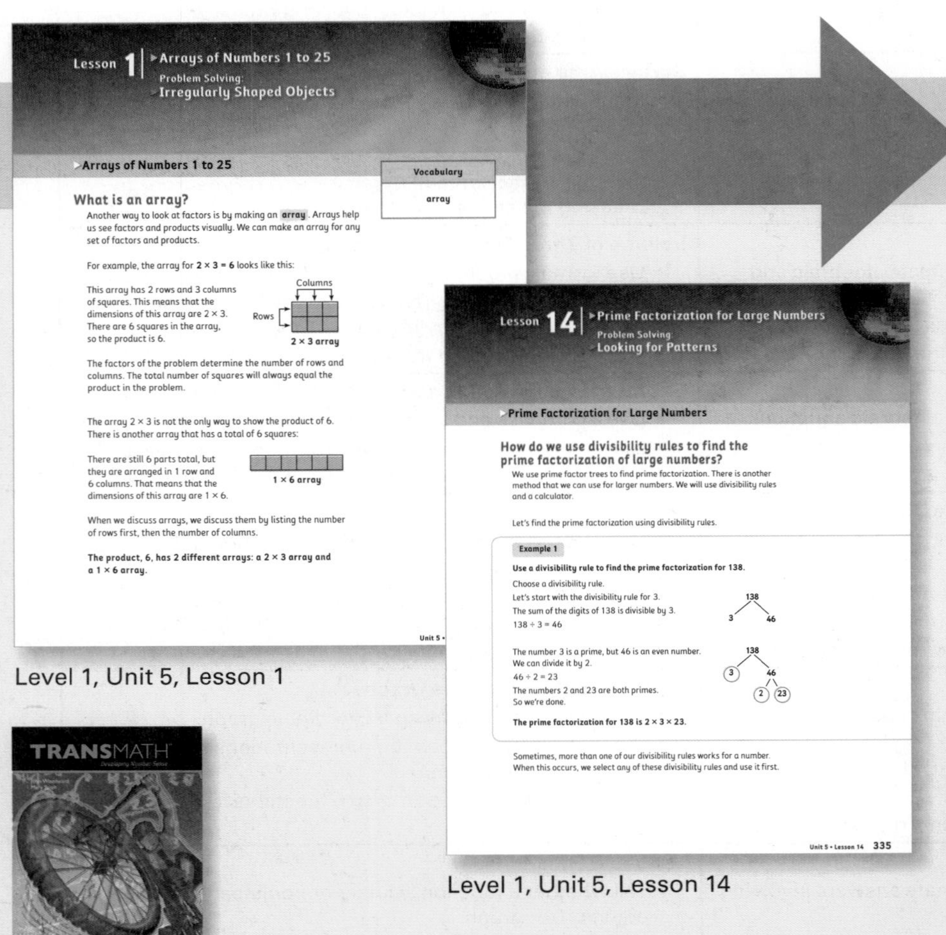

Level 1, Unit 5, Lesson 1

Level 1, Unit 5, Lesson 14

Developing Number Sense

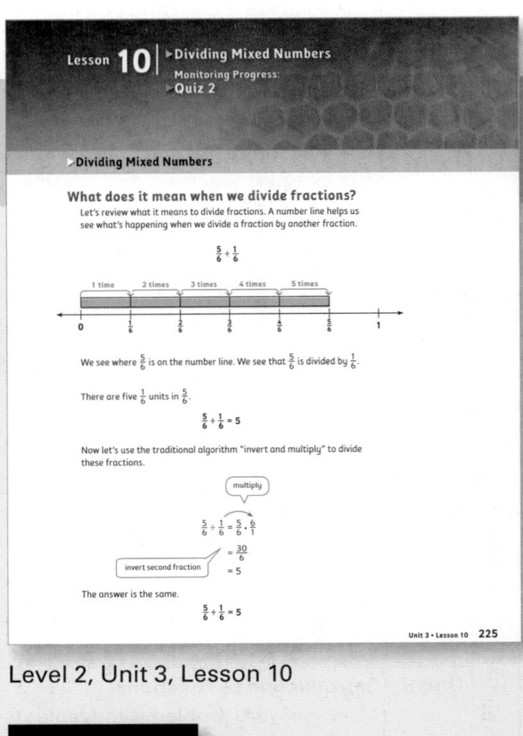

Level 2, Unit 3, Lesson 10

Making Sense of Rational Numbers

The Building Number Concepts strand encompasses:

- Whole number computation
- Factors, primes, and composites
- Rational number computation
- Comparison of fractions, decimal numbers, and percents
- Exponents and integers
- Variables and algebraic equations
- Inequalities and functions

The National Mathematics Advisory Panel's Final Report cites the three critical foundations of algebra—fluency with whole numbers, fluency with fractions, and particular aspects of geometry and measurement—as being "the most essential mathematics for students to learn thoroughly prior to algebra course work" (page 17).

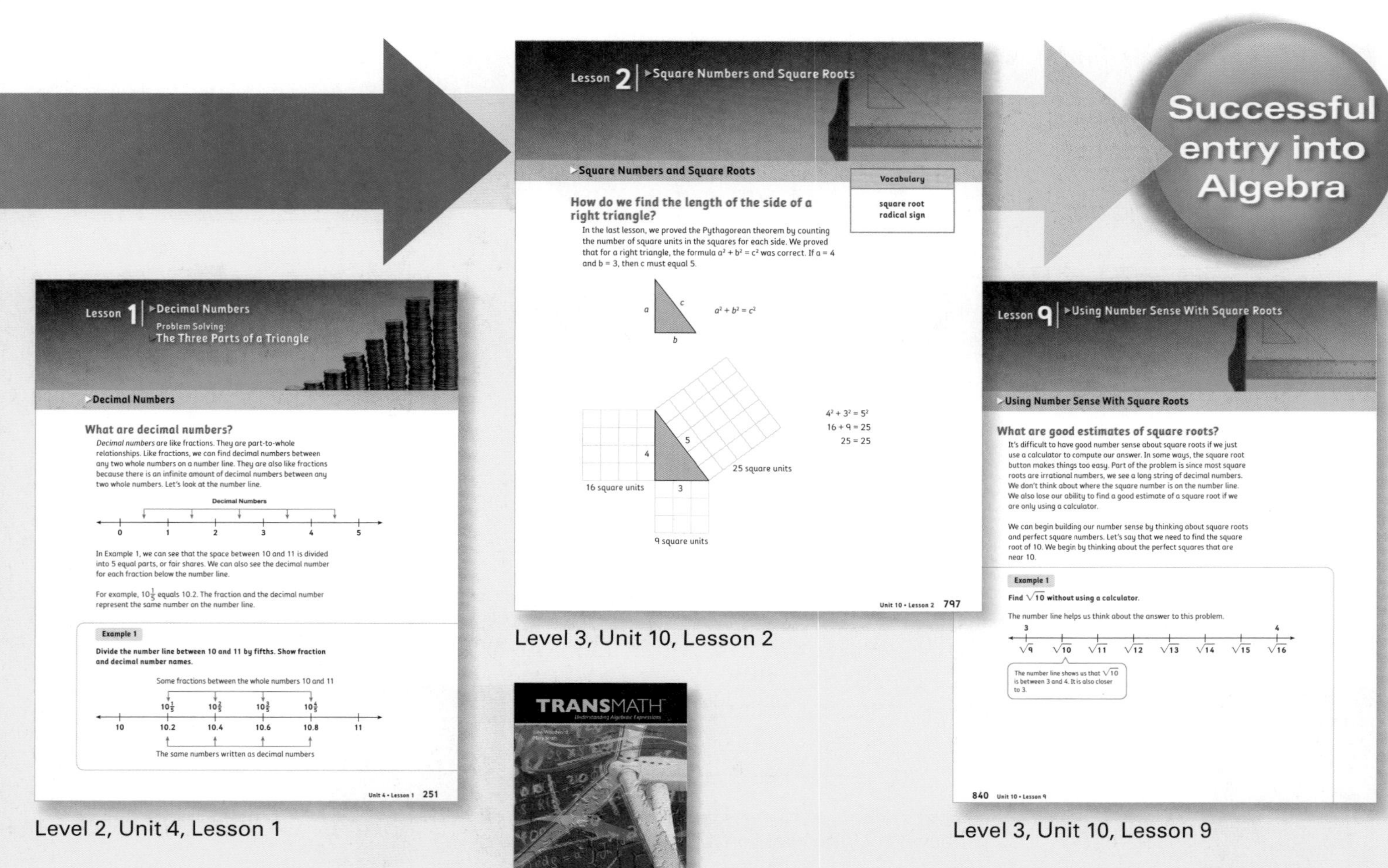

Lesson 1 | ▸Decimal Numbers
Problem Solving:
The Three Parts of a Triangle

▸Decimal Numbers

What are decimal numbers?

Decimal numbers are like fractions. They are part-to-whole relationships. Like fractions, we can find decimal numbers between any two whole numbers on a number line. They are also like fractions because there is an infinite amount of decimal numbers between any two whole numbers. Let's look at the number line.

Decimal Numbers

0 1 2 3 4 5

In Example 1, we can see that the space between 10 and 11 is divided into 5 equal parts, or fair shares. We can also see the decimal number for each fraction below the number line.

For example, $10\frac{1}{5}$ equals 10.2. The fraction and the decimal number represent the same number on the number line.

Example 1

Divide the number line between 10 and 11 by fifths. Show fraction and decimal number names.

Some fractions between the whole numbers 10 and 11

$10\frac{1}{5}$ $10\frac{2}{5}$ $10\frac{3}{5}$ $10\frac{4}{5}$

10 10.2 10.4 10.6 10.8 11

The same numbers written as decimal numbers

Unit 4 • Lesson 1 251

Level 2, Unit 4, Lesson 1

Lesson 2 | ▸Square Numbers and Square Roots

▸Square Numbers and Square Roots

Vocabulary
square root
radical sign

How do we find the length of the side of a right triangle?

In the last lesson, we proved the Pythagorean theorem by counting the number of square units in the squares for each side. We proved that for a right triangle, the formula $a^2 + b^2 = c^2$ was correct. If a = 4 and b = 3, then c must equal 5.

$a^2 + b^2 = c^2$

16 square units
9 square units
25 square units

$4^2 + 3^2 = 5^2$
$16 + 9 = 25$
$25 = 25$

Unit 10 • Lesson 2 797

Level 3, Unit 10, Lesson 2

Lesson 9 | ▸Using Number Sense With Square Roots

▸Using Number Sense With Square Roots

What are good estimates of square roots?

It's difficult to have good number sense about square roots if we just use a calculator to compute our answer. In some ways, the square root button makes things too easy. Part of the problem is since most square roots are irrational numbers, we see a long string of decimal numbers. We don't think about where the square number is on the number line. We also lose our ability to find a good estimate of a square root if we are only using a calculator.

We can begin building our number sense by thinking about square roots and perfect square numbers. Let's say that we need to find the square root of 10. We begin by thinking about the perfect squares that are near 10.

Example 1

Find $\sqrt{10}$ without using a calculator.

The number line helps us think about the answer to this problem.

$\sqrt{9}$ $\sqrt{10}$ $\sqrt{11}$ $\sqrt{12}$ $\sqrt{13}$ $\sqrt{14}$ $\sqrt{15}$ $\sqrt{16}$

The number line shows us that $\sqrt{10}$ is between 3 and 4. It is also closer to 3.

840 Unit 10 • Lesson 9

Level 3, Unit 10, Lesson 9

Understanding Algebraic Expressions

Provides Rich, Grade-Level, Problem-Solving Experiences With the Problem-Solving Strand

With *TransMath,* students apply previously learned concepts and engage in critical thinking to solve multistep problems needed for higher mathematics or the working world.

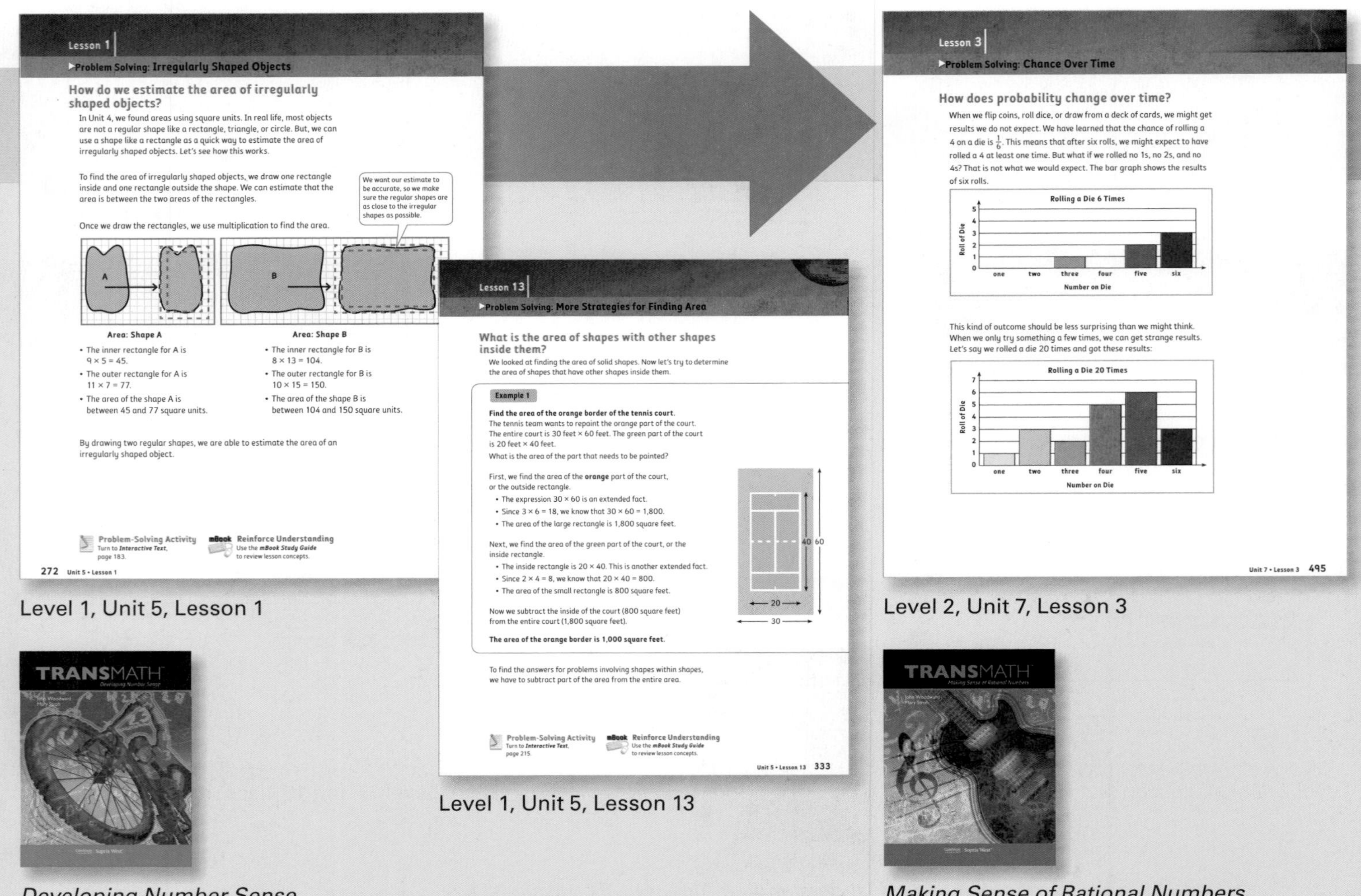

Lesson 1

▶Problem Solving: Irregularly Shaped Objects

How do we estimate the area of irregularly shaped objects?

In Unit 4, we found areas using square units. In real life, most objects are not a regular shape like a rectangle, triangle, or circle. But, we can use a shape like a rectangle as a quick way to estimate the area of irregularly shaped objects. Let's see how this works.

To find the area of irregularly shaped objects, we draw one rectangle inside and one rectangle outside the shape. We can estimate that the area is between the two areas of the rectangles.

We want our estimate to be accurate, so we make sure the regular shapes are as close to the irregular shapes as possible.

Once we draw the rectangles, we use multiplication to find the area.

Area: Shape A

- The inner rectangle for A is $9 \times 5 = 45$.
- The outer rectangle for A is $11 \times 7 = 77$.
- The area of the shape A is between 45 and 77 square units.

Area: Shape B

- The inner rectangle for B is $8 \times 13 = 104$.
- The outer rectangle for B is $10 \times 15 = 150$.
- The area of the shape B is between 104 and 150 square units.

By drawing two regular shapes, we are able to estimate the area of an irregularly shaped object.

Problem-Solving Activity Turn to ***Interactive Text,*** page 183.

mBook Reinforce Understanding Use the ***mBook Study Guide*** to review lesson concepts.

272 Unit 5 • Lesson 1

Level 1, Unit 5, Lesson 1

Lesson 13

▶Problem Solving: More Strategies for Finding Area

What is the area of shapes with other shapes inside them?

We looked at finding the area of solid shapes. Now let's try to determine the area of shapes that have other shapes inside them.

Example 1

Find the area of the orange border of the tennis court.
The tennis team wants to repaint the orange part of the court. The entire court is 30 feet × 60 feet. The green part of the court is 20 feet × 40 feet.
What is the area of the part that needs to be painted?

First, we find the area of the **orange** part of the court, or the outside rectangle.

- The expression 30×60 is an extended fact.
- Since $3 \times 6 = 18$, we know that $30 \times 60 = 1{,}800$.
- The area of the large rectangle is 1,800 square feet.

Next, we find the area of the green part of the court, or the inside rectangle.

- The inside rectangle is 20×40. This is another extended fact.
- Since $2 \times 4 = 8$, we know that $20 \times 40 = 800$.
- The area of the small rectangle is 800 square feet.

Now we subtract the inside of the court (800 square feet) from the entire court (1,800 square feet).

The area of the orange border is 1,000 square feet.

To find the answers for problems involving shapes within shapes, we have to subtract part of the area from the entire area.

Problem-Solving Activity Turn to ***Interactive Text,*** page 215.

mBook Reinforce Understanding Use the ***mBook Study Guide*** to review lesson concepts.

Unit 5 • Lesson 13 333

Level 1, Unit 5, Lesson 13

Lesson 3

▶Problem Solving: Chance Over Time

How does probability change over time?

When we flip coins, roll dice, or draw from a deck of cards, we might get results we do not expect. We have learned that the chance of rolling a 4 on a die is $\frac{1}{6}$. This means that after six rolls, we might expect to have rolled a 4 at least one time. But what if we rolled no 1s, no 2s, and no 4s? That is not what we would expect. The bar graph shows the results of six rolls.

This kind of outcome should be less surprising than we might think. When we only try something a few times, we can get strange results. Let's say we rolled a die 20 times and got these results:

Unit 7 • Lesson 3 495

Level 2, Unit 7, Lesson 3

Developing Number Sense

Making Sense of Rational Numbers

The Problem-Solving strand encompasses:

- Work with data
- One-, two-, and three-dimensional objects
- Measurement tools
- Probability
- Proportional thinking
- Properties of shapes
- Angles, transversals, and geometric transformations

For all content areas, conceptual understanding, computational fluency, and problem-solving skills are each essential and mutually reinforcing, influencing performance on such varied tasks as estimation, word problems, and computation.

—*National Mathematics Advisory Panel's Final Report, page 30.*

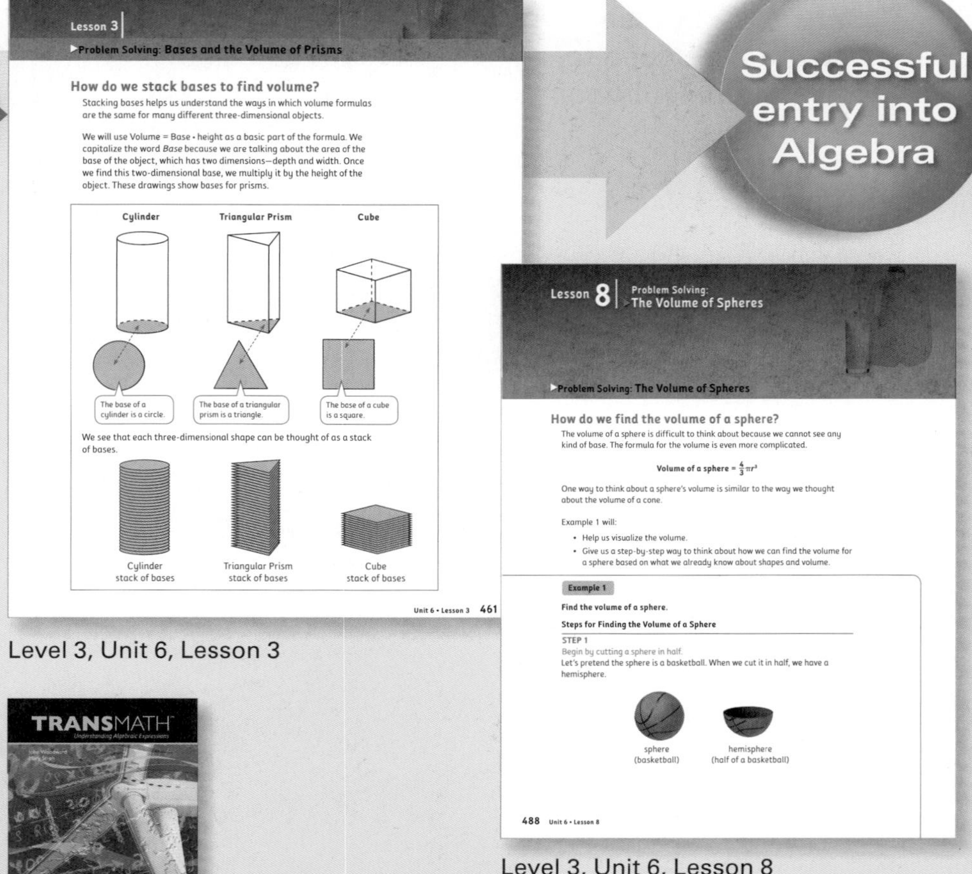

Lesson 3

▶Problem Solving: Bases and the Volume of Prisms

How do we stack bases to find volume?

Stacking bases helps us understand the ways in which volume formulas are the same for many different three-dimensional objects.

We will use Volume = Base • height as a basic part of the formula. We capitalize the word *Base* because we are talking about the area of the base of the object, which has two dimensions—depth and width. Once we find this two-dimensional base, we multiply it by the height of the object. These drawings show bases for prisms.

We see that each three-dimensional shape can be thought of as a stack of bases.

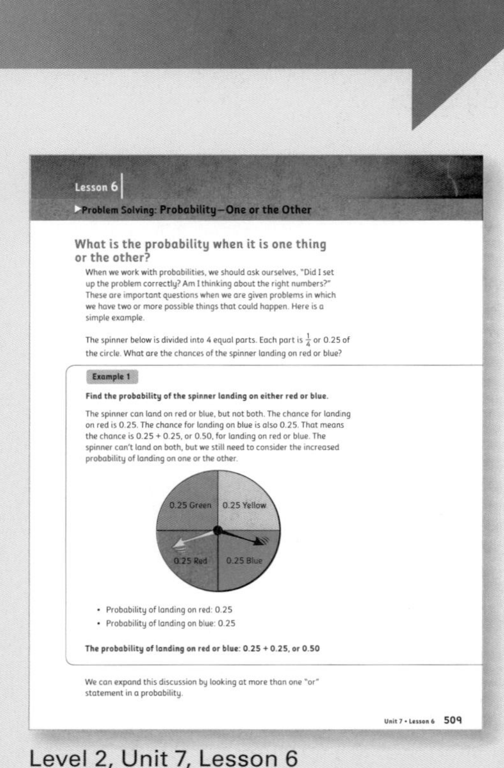

Lesson 6

▶Problem Solving: Probability—One or the Other

What is the probability when it is one thing or the other?

When we work with probabilities, we should ask ourselves, "Did I set up the problem correctly? Am I thinking about the right numbers?" These are important questions when we are given problems in which we have two or more possible things that could happen. Here is a simple example.

The spinner below is divided into 4 equal parts. Each part is $\frac{1}{4}$ or 0.25 of the circle. What are the chances of the spinner landing on red or blue?

Example 1

Find the probability of the spinner landing on either red or blue.

The spinner can land on red or blue, but not both. The chance for landing on red is 0.25. The chance for landing on blue is also 0.25. That means the chance is 0.25 + 0.25, or 0.50, for landing on red or blue. The spinner can't land on both, but we still need to consider the increased probability of landing on one or the other.

- Probability of landing on red: 0.25
- Probability of landing on blue: 0.25

The probability of landing on red or blue: 0.25 + 0.25, or 0.50

We can expand this discussion by looking at more than one "or" statement in a probability.

Unit 7 • Lesson 6 509

Level 2, Unit 7, Lesson 6

Lesson 8 | Problem Solving: The Volume of Spheres

▶Problem Solving: The Volume of Spheres

How do we find the volume of a sphere?

The volume of a sphere is difficult to think about because we cannot see any kind of base. The formula for the volume is even more complicated.

Volume of a sphere $= \frac{4}{3}\pi r^3$

One way to think about a sphere's volume is similar to the way we thought about the volume of a cone.

Example 1 will:

- Help us visualize the volume.
- Give us a step-by-step way to think about how we can find the volume for a sphere based on what we already know about shapes and volume.

Example 1

Find the volume of a sphere.

Steps for Finding the Volume of a Sphere

STEP 1

Begin by cutting a sphere in half.

Let's pretend the sphere is a basketball. When we cut it in half, we have a hemisphere.

488 Unit 6 • Lesson 8

Level 3, Unit 6, Lesson 8

Unit 6 • Lesson 3 461

Level 3, Unit 6, Lesson 3

TRANSMATH

Understanding Algebraic Expressions

Placement

***TransMath* placement is based on students' skill levels, not grade levels. Students may place into one of these three entry points:**

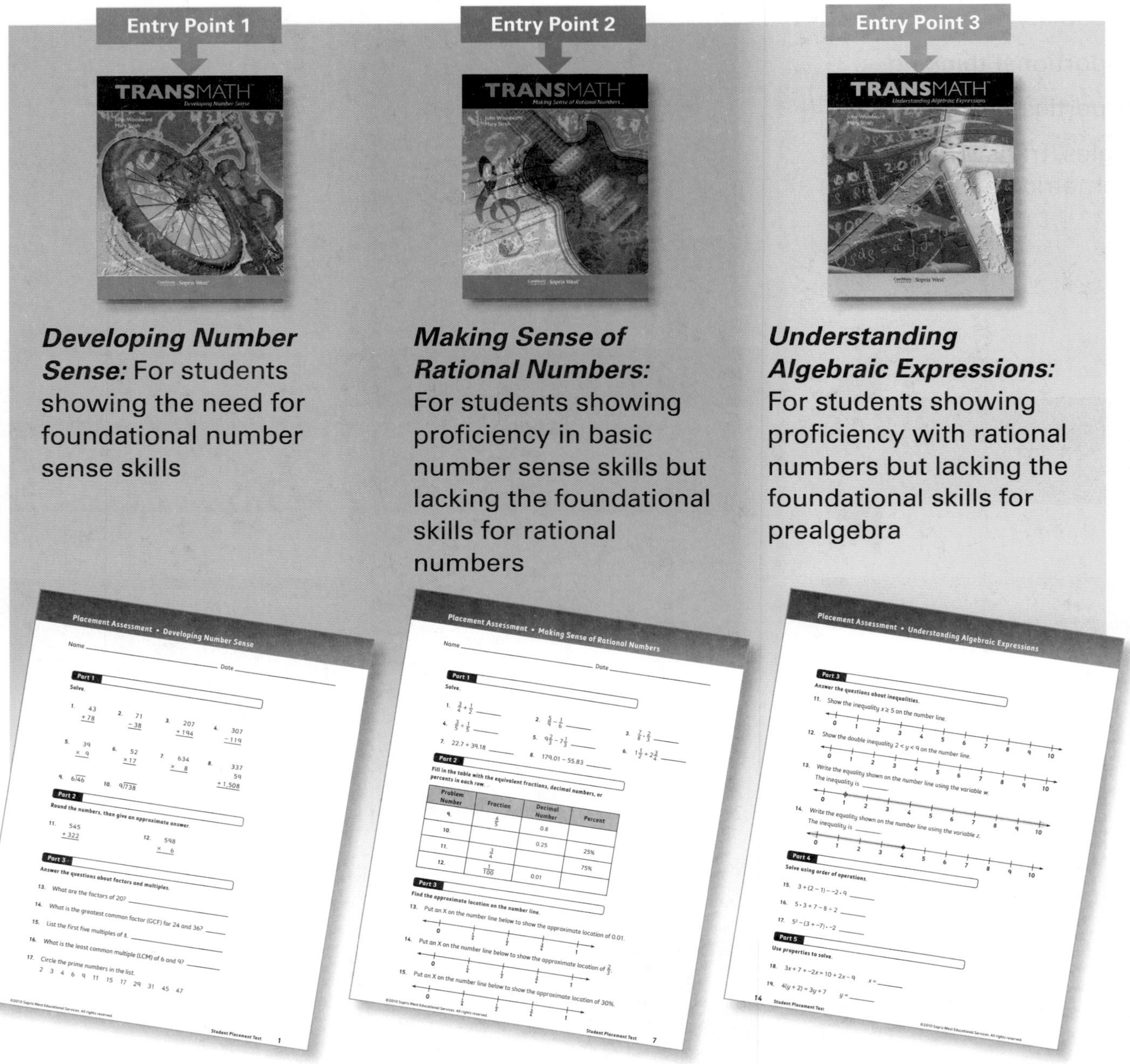

Developing Number Sense: For students showing the need for foundational number sense skills

Making Sense of Rational Numbers: For students showing proficiency in basic number sense skills but lacking the foundational skills for rational numbers

Understanding Algebraic Expressions: For students showing proficiency with rational numbers but lacking the foundational skills for prealgebra

The TRANSMATH™ Assessment System

This comprehensive assessment system provides teachers with the measures they need to accurately place students into the curriculum and to monitor their progress though the curriculum. It furnishes the teacher with the data necessary to inform instruction to ensure each student meets his or her goals.

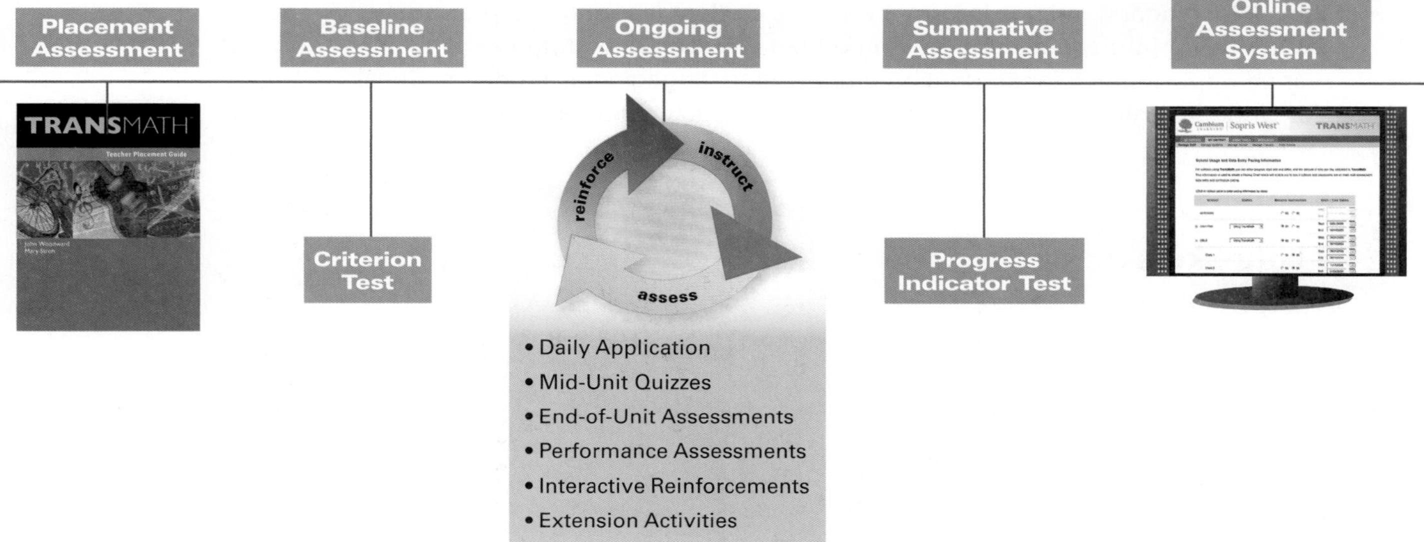

Placement
Based on students' demonstrated understanding of key mathematics concepts and skills, data from the *TransMath* placement tests accurately place students at one of the three entry points of the curriculum.

Baseline Assessments
Administered at the beginning of each book level, the Baseline Assessment establishes a starting point for measuring student's progress through the curriculum.

Ongoing Assessments
Regular assessment of student mastery of the concepts and skills taught in the curriculum ensures that teachers can adjust pacing or instruction to meet the needs of individual students.

Summative Assessments
Given at the end of each book level, the Progress Indicators measure the critical skills of mathematics through curriculum-based measures. Comparing Progress Indicators to the Baseline Assessments accurately tracks student's progress through the curriculum.

The Online Assessment System
This user-friendly database allows teachers and administrators to record, track, and report student test results. Reports can be generated at the individual, class, building, and district levels.

Ongoing Assessment

Informal Assessment

TransMath provides teachers with numerous opportunities to assess student knowledge as concepts and skills are being developed.

Check for Understanding

Check for Understandings informally assess student learning and prescribe solutions for immediate support. Embedded engagement strategies provide varied opportunities for student communication, engaging all students. Check for Understandings occur after the modeling of each major lesson concept.

Apply Skills

Apply Skills activities allow students to apply the skills they learned in the Building Number Concepts section of each lesson.

Problem-Solving Activity

Problem-Solving activities allow students to apply knowledge of the concepts from the Problem Solving section of each lesson.

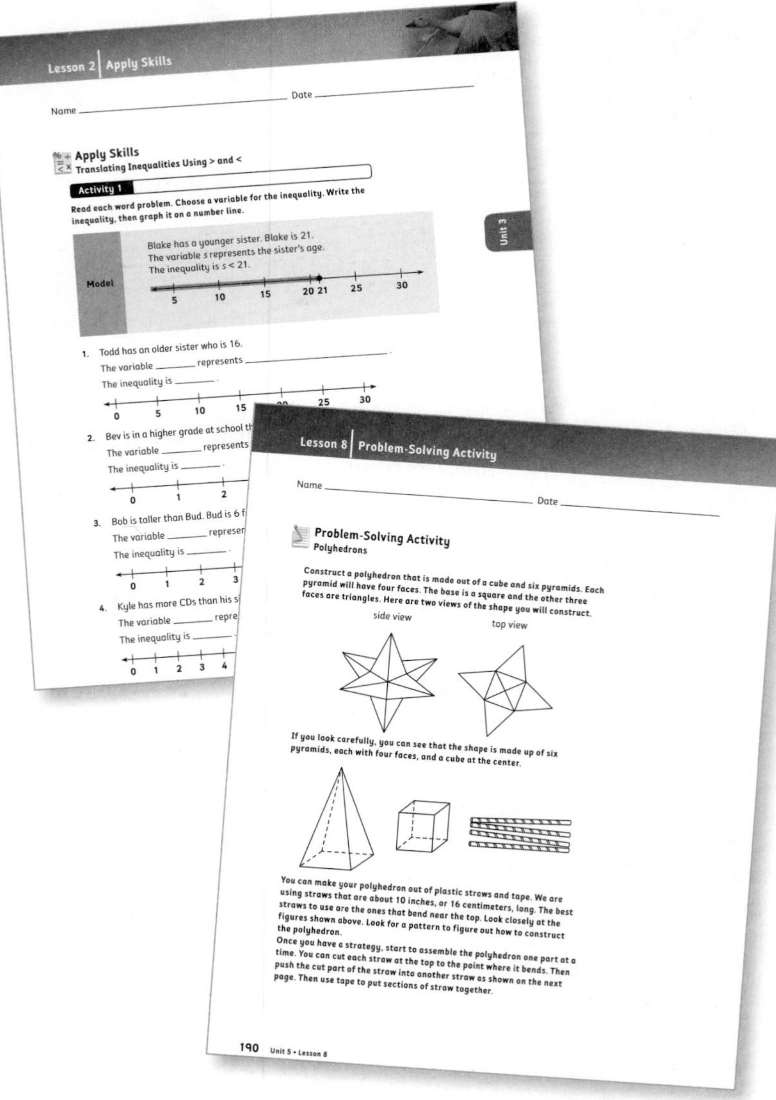

Lesson 2 | Apply Skills

Name ______ Date ______

Apply Skills
Translating Inequalities Using > and <

Activity 1

Read each word problem. Choose a variable for the inequality. Write the inequality, then graph it on a number line.

Model: Blake has a younger sister. Blake is 21. The variable *s* represents the sister's age. The inequality is $s < 21$.

1. Todd has an older sister who is 16. The variable ______ represents ______. The inequality is ______.
2. Bev is in a higher grade at school th... The variable ______ represents... The inequality is ______.
3. Bob is taller than Bud. Bud is 6 f... The variable ______ represen... The inequality is ______.
4. Kyle has more CDs than his s... The variable ______ repre... The inequality is ______.

Unit 3

Lesson 8 | Problem-Solving Activity

Name ______ Date ______

Problem-Solving Activity
Polyhedrons

Construct a polyhedron that is made out of a cube and six pyramids. Each pyramid will have four faces. The base is a square and the other three faces are triangles. Here are two views of the shape you will construct.

side view　top view

If you look carefully, you can see that the shape is made up of six pyramids, each with four faces, and a cube at the center.

You can make your polyhedron out of plastic straws and tape. We are using straws that are about 10 inches, or 16 centimeters, long. The best straws to use are the ones that bend near the top. Look closely at the figures shown above. Look for a pattern to figure out how to construct the polyhedron.

Once you have a strategy, start to assemble the polyhedron one part at a time. You can cut each straw at the top to the point where it bends. Then push the cut part of the straw into another straw as shown on the next page. Then use tape to put sections of straw together.

190 Unit 5 • Lesson 8

Formal Assessment

Each unit of *TransMath* contains multiple methods to assess student's reasoning and ability to communicate ideas. Each type of assessment serves a different purpose.

Quiz

Quizzes occur every five lessons to give teachers important feedback on student progress. Results inform instruction for differentiation days and subsequent lessons.

Students	Assess	Differentiate
	Day 1	Day 2
All	Quiz X Form A	Review Quiz
Scored 80% or Above		Extension
Scored Below 80%		Reinforcement

Day 1: Students take quiz during the second half of the lesson.

Day 2: Students work on differentiation activities based on their performance on the quiz.

End-of-Unit Assessment

The End-of-Unit Assessment measures student mastery of skills taught in the unit. Targeted support is then provided on differentiation days to reinforce difficult skills, to help students achieve mastery.

Performance Assessment

The Performance Assessment measures student's ability to reason and communicate. Students practice applying unit concepts in the context of a high-stakes test.

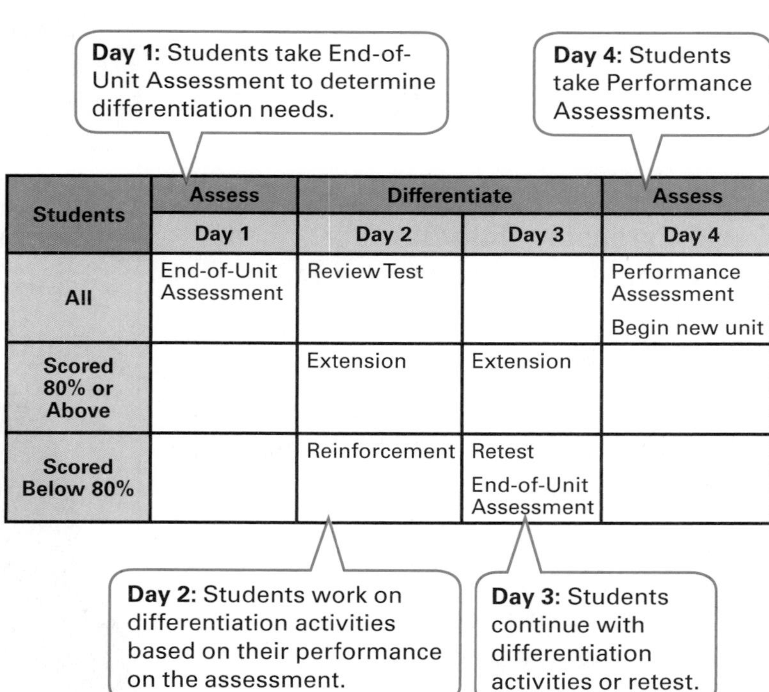
Day 1: Students take End-of-Unit Assessment to determine differentiation needs.
Day 4: Students take Performance Assessments.

Students	Assess	Differentiate		Assess
	Day 1	Day 2	Day 3	Day 4
All	End-of-Unit Assessment	Review Test		Performance Assessment Begin new unit
Scored 80% or Above		Extension	Extension	
Scored Below 80%		Reinforcement	Retest End-of-Unit Assessment	

Day 2: Students work on differentiation activities based on their performance on the assessment.
Day 3: Students continue with differentiation activities or retest.

Differentiation Informed by Data

TransMath offers multiple opportunities to assess, reinforce, and differentiate instruction:

The *TransMath* Online Assessment System

With one simple log in, teachers can access student data to inform differentiation.

mBook Teacher Edition

The *mBook Teacher Edition,* accessed through the Online Assessment System, contains a multitude of online resources to access, reinforce, and differentiate instruction:

- **Teacher-Talk Tutorials** reinforce lesson concepts using narrated, animated visual models that make the concept concrete for the student.
- **Interactive Click-Thru** slideshow presentations use visual models to concretely develop concepts.
- **On Track! Extension Activities** are multistep word problems designed for small groups to prepare students for high-stakes tests.
- **Interactive Reinforcement Exercises** are online, interactive, multiple-choice activities that provide immediate feedback.
- **Form B Retests** for Quizzes and End-of-Unit Assessments are available for downloading.

mBook Study Guide for students provides online access to:

- The entire *Student Text* to review missed concepts
- The Teacher-Talk Tutorials to reinforce difficult concepts
- The Interactive Reinforcement Exercises to review, reinforce, and practice missed concepts

Manipulative Set provides opportunities for multisensory modeling of missed concepts.

DAY 1

After administering End-of-Unit Assessment, determine differentiation by assessing student data.

- Administer assessment.
- Enter scores.
- Identify differentiation needs.
- Establish small groups.

DAY 2

Assign differentiation strategies depending on student needs.		
Student Score	80% or higher	On Track! Extension Activities
	Between 60–80%	Computer Station *mBook Study Guide* or Reinforcement Exercises
	Below 60%	Teacher Reteach

DAY 3

Students working on On Track! Activities continue while students who scored below 80% are retested.		
Student Score	80% or higher	On Track! Extension Activities
	Below 80%	Retest students that scored below 80% using End-of-Unit Assessment Form B

Pacing Guide at the Unit Level

Units are either 10 lessons or 15 lessons in length. *TransMath* lessons are designed for 50–60 minute lesson blocks per day.

10-Lesson Unit

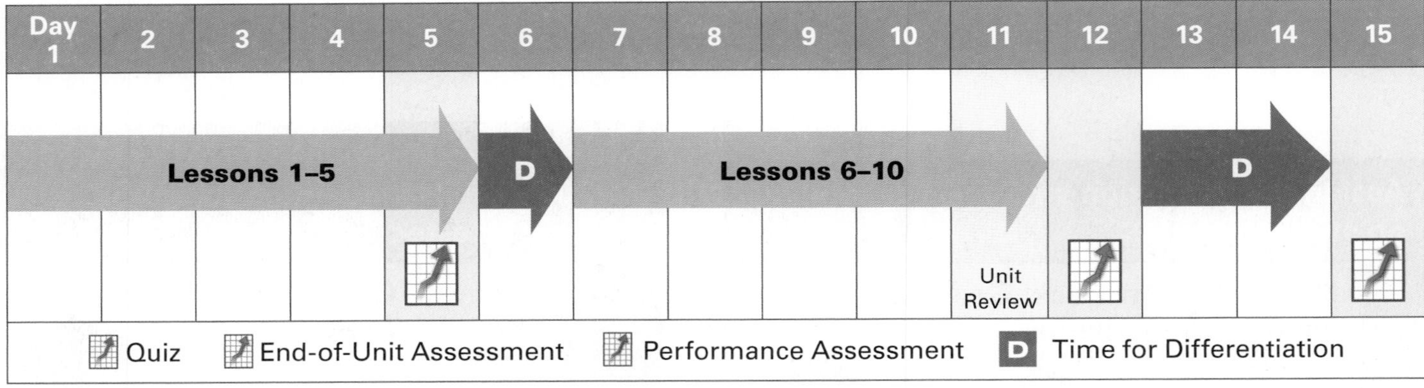

15-Lesson Unit

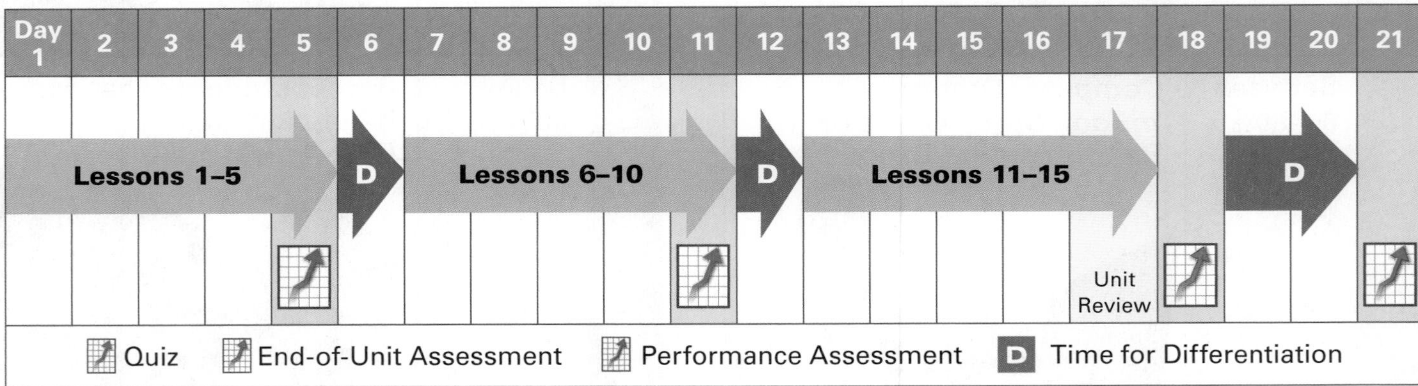

Pacing Guide at the Lesson Level

Every lesson has a predictable lesson structure. Although *TransMath* lessons are designed for 50–60 minute lesson blocks per day, adjustments can be made to fit multiple scheduling needs.

Lesson Structure	Approximate Time for a 50–60 Minute Lesson	
Skills Maintenance	Starts each lesson with distributed practice warm-ups	4–5 minutes
Building Number Concepts	Develops conceptual understanding of number, operation, and prealgebra topics through: • Teacher Modeling • Engagement Strategies • Extensive Use of Visual Models • Apply Skills Activities	20–25 minutes
Problem Solving	Develops conceptual understanding of geometry, measurement, data, and probability through: • Teacher Modeling • Engagement Strategies • Extensive Use of Visual Models • Rich, Grade-Level, Problem-Solving Activities	20–25 minutes
Homework	Provides daily, independent practice with lesson concepts and skills as well as earlier learned skills for continued distributed practice. Assignments take 15–20 minutes outside class.	5 minutes—Assign Homework

50–60 Minute Lesson

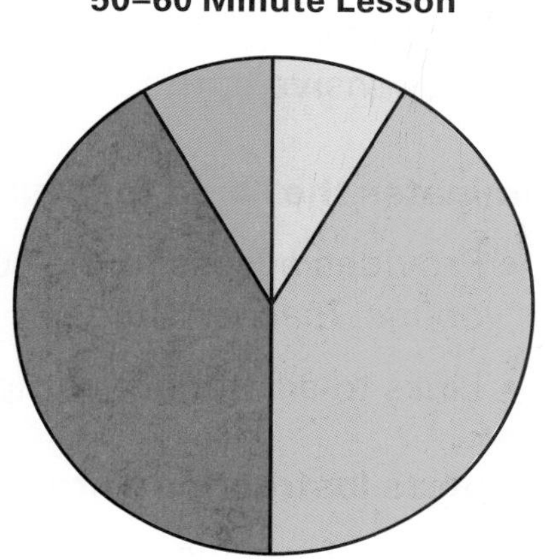

Daily Support for Teachers

Through Technology. . .

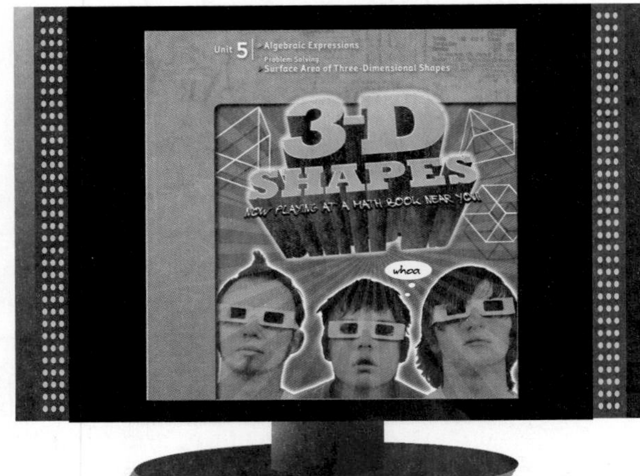

Unit 5
Algebraic Expressions
Problem Solving
Surface Area of Three-Dimensional Shapes
3-D
SHAPES
NOW PLAYING AT A MATH BOOK NEAR YOU!
whoa

The *TransMath mBook Teacher Edition* provides powerful online resources that support teachers in the successful, daily implementation of this comprehensive curriculum.

Eliminates the Need for Multiple Books

- Provides access to the complete online *Teacher Guides*
- Links to all student components—online

Supports Instruction Through Online Tools

- Allows for review of objectives and lesson plans
- Helps teachers prepare for lessons with Teacher-Talk Tutorials, which provide essential knowledge of math concepts to aid teacher modeling
- Provides Click-Thru slideshow presentations used to engage students when modeling initial lesson concepts

Individualizes Instruction With Differentiation Tools

- Reinforces concepts and skills with Interactive Reinforcement Exercises
- Extends concepts and skills with On Track! Extension Activities
- Provides alternate form Quizzes and End-of-Unit Assessments for retesting
- Provides printable *Interactive Text* pages for reinforcement opportunities

Accesses State-Specific Tools

- Correlations to state standards
- Correlations to the NCTM Curriculum Focal Points

Through Print. . .

Thought-provoking, engaging, unit openers

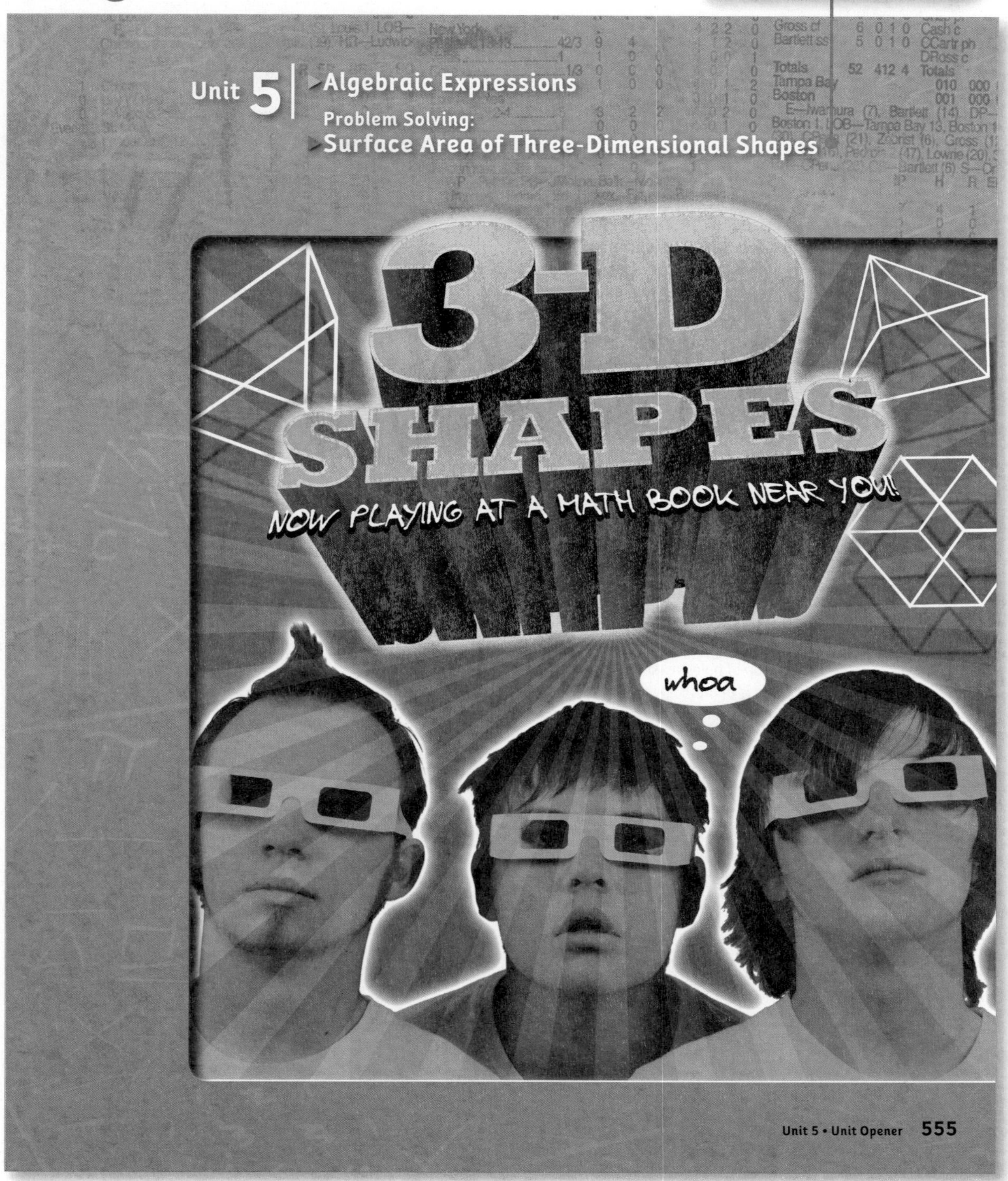

Understanding Algebraic Expressions, Teacher Guide, Unit 5

Student Text pages are showcased at point of use.

The unit opener **background information** provides real-world context to promote discussion.

Unit 5

Unit Opener: Background Information

With students, read the Unit Opener of *Student Text*, pages 371–372, then share some of these additional facts with students.

- The first 3-D film presentation occurred in New York in 1915 but flopped because of the poor filming methods available at the time. By the 1950s, improved techniques led to a 3-D craze among Hollywood filmmakers; however, audiences complained of headaches, and the fad died down.
- Pyramids take advantage of triangles, the strongest geometric shape. Of the seven wonders of the ancient world, only the great pyramids of Giza are still intact, having survived earthquakes, fires, and wars.
- The Montreal Biosphere, located in Quebec, Canada, contains a tropical forest, a replica of the St. Lawrence Seaway ecosystem, and a polar world. Originally built by Buckminster Fuller as the American pavilion for Expo 67, it is one of the largest tourist attractions in the city of Montreal.
- Architect Piet Blom designed the cube houses in Rotterdam, Holland, in 1984. Also called "pole dwellings," the cubes are built on top of poles used for storage. One of the units is open to the public for tours. Visitors note the remarkable natural light on the top floor.
- The hotel towers in Los Angeles, a designated landmark, are among the most photographed buildings in the world. They contain the Westin Bonaventure Hotel and Suites, shops, services, and more than 30 restaurants.

Understanding Algebraic Expressions, Teacher Guide, Unit 5

Unit objectives are identified for both strands.

Unit 5 Building Number Concepts: Algebraic Expressions
Problem Solving: Surface Area of Three-Dimensional Shapes

OBJECTIVES

Building Number Concepts	Problem Solving
• Evaluate numeric expressions using order of operations rules • Recognize like and unlike terms in an algebraic expression • Simplify algebraic expressions using the properties of numbers	• Identify the attributes of three-dimensional shapes • Use formulas to find the surface area of cylinders and prisms • Find the surface area of pyramids and polyhedrons by breaking the shapes into familiar parts

An overview of unit content is provided for both strands.

Overview

One reason why algebra is so difficult for students is that it involves a complex range of skills. This unit and the next help students master a set of rules and properties that become essential to solving algebraic equations.

Unit Vocabulary
expression
numeric expression
algebraic expression
evaluating the expression
order of operations
integer
absolute value
variable term
number term
coefficients
implied coefficients
commutative property
associative property
property of opposites

The Problem Solving strand investigates the relationship between two- and three-dimensional shapes. The focus is largely on the topic of surface area. Students need to know more than the area formula for a triangle or square that is a face of a three-dimensional shape. Students must unfold shapes, see patterns, and compute an overall surface area.

Vocabulary introduced in the unit is listed for each strand.

Unit Vocabulary
height
width
depth
face
edge
base
attributes
surface area
slant height

Unit 5 • Overview 557

Key questions identify **what** students need to know.

Enduring understandings explain **why** students need to know the concepts being taught.

Tools for understanding explain **how** the concepts are developed.

Unit 5 | Overview

Building Number Concepts:

Algebraic Expressions

Key Questions That Guide Student Understanding

- *What are important properties and rules for algebra?*

Enduring Understandings for Algebraic Expressions

Algebra is a gateway into more complex, or symbol-intensive, topics taught in secondary mathematics. Students need a series of rules and properties to solve equations or translate one mathematical statement into another. Rules create the foundation for consistent solutions. Key rules introduced in this unit include order of operations and the rule that "subtraction is the same as adding the opposite" applies to integers. Students also learn about the commutative property, associative property, and property of opposites.

Understanding the application of these rules and properties in algebraic problems is another fundamental concept. Whether it is simplifying expressions or solving equations, students need to be proficient in their use of rules and properties.

Tools for Understanding Algebraic Expressions

Using Models
Typical instruction often assumes definitions aid students in seeing the difference between like and unlike terms. Visual models such as Vs and Ns, however, better help students understand coefficients as well as the importance of the commutative property in simplifying expressions. Number lines enable students to see the process of adding and subtracting integers.

Using Strategies for Integer Operations
Students can remember what do when adding or subtracting integers if they remember that subtraction is the same as adding the opposite. This rule helps students solve problems such as 3 – –2 and 3 + –2.

Using Strategies for Order of Operations
The logic of order of operations, which is foundational to algebra, requires additional practice. Solving numeric equations that result in different answers helps students see why we need rules for solving numeric equations.

558 Unit 5 • Overview

Understanding Algebraic Expressions, Teacher Guide, Unit 5

Problem Solving:
▶Surface Area of Three-Dimensional Shapes

Key Questions That Guide Student Understanding

- *What are strategies for finding the surface area of a shape?*

Enduring Understandings for Surface Area of Three-Dimensional Shapes

Working with three-dimensional shapes requires the same kind of categorization that occurs with two-dimensional shapes. Many shapes, such as a cube and a cylinder, look different on the surface. However, they share common attributes that help determine surface area and, in the next unit, volume. Recognizing common attributes, which can also involve unfolding shapes into two-dimensional form, is critical in mathematics.

Once shapes like cones and pyramids or cylinders, prisms, and cubes are grouped, students can explore strategies for determining their surface areas. Congruent two-dimensional shapes are an underlying concept when determining the surface area of three-dimensional objects. Prisms, for example, can be broken into a base, top, and series of faces.

Tools for Understanding Surface Area of Three-Dimensional Shapes

Using Basic Concepts to Develop Deeper Understanding
This unit is the first of two that help students categorize different three-dimensional shapes. Seeing the relationship between two-dimensional and three-dimensional shapes provides a foundation for calculating the surface area of three-dimensional shapes.

Key questions identify **what** students need to know.

Enduring understandings explain **why** students need to know the concepts being taught.

Tools for understanding explain **how** the concepts are developed.

Unit 5 | Lesson Objectives

Building Number Concepts:
Algebraic Expressions

Lesson objectives are identified for each concept.

Lesson	Lesson Objectives—Students will:
1	• Evaluate expressions using the order of operations.
2	• Apply a new rule to the order of operations: Anything in parentheses in an expression is evaluated first.
3	• Solve expressions with exponents. • Use the acronym PEMDAS as a strategy to remember the rules of operations.
4	• Add and subtract integers.
5	
6	• Analyze the components of algebraic expressions.
7	• Simplify algebraic expressions by combining like terms.
8	• Simplify expressions using the commutative property, the associative property, and the property of opposites.
9	
10	• Review Algebraic Expressions concepts.
Unit Assessments	End-of-Unit Assessment Performance Assessment

560 Unit 5 • Lesson Objectives

Understanding Algebraic Expressions, Teacher Guide, Unit 5

Problem Solving:
▶Surface Area of Three-Dimensional Shapes

Lesson Objectives—Students will:	Assessment
• Analyze three-dimensional shapes.	
• Sort and classify shapes based on their attributes.	
• Analyze the differences in attributes to sort and classify three-dimensional shapes.	
• Apply formulas for surface area.	Quiz 1
• Find the surface area of different kinds of pyramids.	
• Analyze a polyhedron.	
• Find the surface area of polyhedrons.	
• Review Surface Area of Three-Dimensional Shapes concepts.	Unit Review
	End-of-Unit Assessment Performance Assessment

Unit 5 • Lesson Objectives 561

An **assessment** schedule is outlined for each unit.

Quizzes are administered during the second half of the lesson—every five lessons. Note that only one strand is taught on these days.

Single-strand focus provides extended instructional time for difficult concepts.

Unit Review lessons at the end of the unit reinforce student learning.

End-of-Unit Assessments and **Performance Assessments** are administered at the end of every unit.

Provides Everything Needed for Successful Implementation

Every lesson begins with an at-a-glance **Lesson Planner.**

Dual Topics provide a balance of conceptual understanding and problem-solving applications.

Skills Maintenance distributes practice across lessons and takes four to five minutes at the beginning of class.

Lesson 7 | ▶Simplifying Expressions by Combining Like Terms

Problem Solving:

▶Surface Area of Pyramids

Lesson Planner

Vocabulary Development

slant height

Skills Maintenance

Variable and Number Terms

Building Number Concepts:

▶ Simplifying Expressions by Combining Like Terms

Students learn to simplify algebraic expressions. This means combining as many parts as possible. To simplify expressions, we combine variable terms with variable terms and number terms with number terms.

Objective

Students will simplify algebraic expressions by combining like terms.

Problem Solving:

▶ Surface Area of Pyramids

Students learn how to find the surface area of pyramids. To do this, they find the area of the base and add it to the area of the faces. Students see how a coefficient represents the number of faces of a pyramid to apply the area formula.

Objective

Students will find the surface area of different kinds of pyramids.

Homework

Students select the simplified expression for each algebraic expression, simplify expressions by combining like terms, and tell the area formulas needed to find the surface area of the shapes. In Distributed Practice, students practice whole number and rational number operations in open sentences.

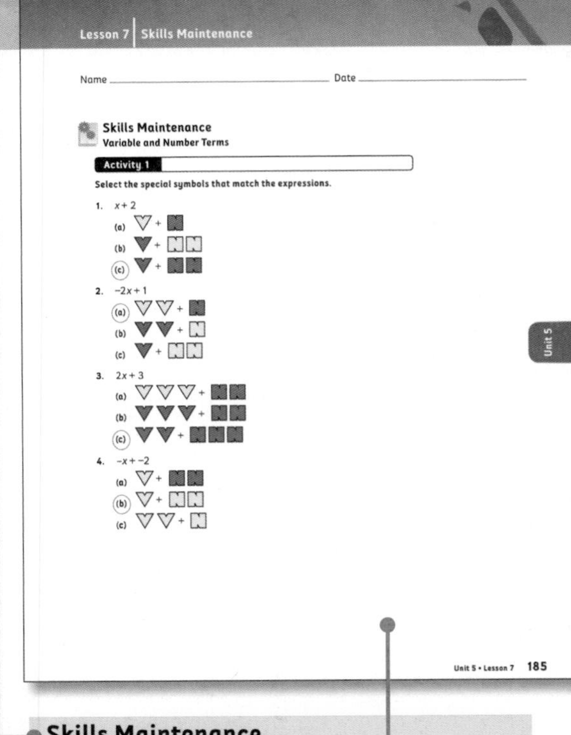
Lesson 7 | Skills Maintenance

Name ______ Date ______

Skills Maintenance
Variable and Number Terms

Activity 1

Select the special symbols that match the expressions.

1. $x + 2$
(a) (b) (c)

2. $-2x + 1$
(a) (b) (c)

3. $2x + 3$
(a) (b) (c)

4. $-x + -2$
(a) (b) (c)

Unit 5

Unit 5 • Lesson 7 185

Skills Maintenance

Variable and Number Terms

(*Interactive Text*, page 185)

Activity 1

Students select the set of special symbols that best represents the expression shown.

Modified wraparound *Teacher Guide* includes answer keys.

Understanding Algebraic Expressions, Teacher Guide, Unit 5, Lesson 7

The **Building Number Concepts** strand takes 20 to 25 minutes of the lesson, focusing on development of the concept with rich practice opportunities.

Building Number Concepts:
▶ Simplifying Expressions by Combining Like Terms

How do we simplify expressions?

(*Student Text*, pages 414–417)

Connect to Prior Knowledge

Begin by drawing these familiar two-dimensional shapes on the board or overhead:

Ask:

How do you describe the objects you see?

Listen for:

- Quantity, such as *two triangles, three circles, and three squares.*

Explain that even though we see eight shapes all together, we tend to sort them into like shapes.

Link to Today's Concept

In today's lesson, we separate like objects in algebraic expressions as well.

Demonstrate

Engagement Strategy: Teacher Modeling

Demonstrate how to simplify expressions in one of the following ways:

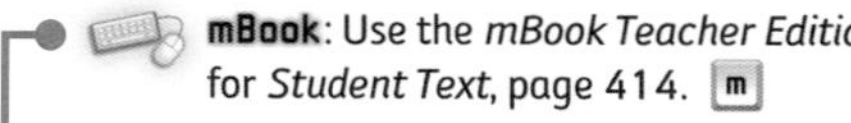

- **mBook**: Use the *mBook Teacher Edition* for *Student Text*, page 414. m
- **Overhead Projector:** Reproduce the expression on a transparency, and modify as discussed.
- **Board**: Copy the expression on the board, and modify as discussed.

- Explain that simplifying an expression means to combine variable terms with other variable terms (if they are the same variable; e.g., all *x*s) and number terms with other number terms. Point out that we cannot combine unlike terms.
- Display the expression **$2x + 3x + 2 + 1$**. m
- Walk through how to substitute the special symbols for each term of the expression. The term $2x$ is represented by two black Vs. The term $3x$ is represented by three black Vs. m
- Point out that the next term, 2, is a number term represented by two black Ns. The number 1 is represented by one black N. Show the symbols. m
- Simplify the expression by grouping like terms together. The variable terms total $5x$, represented by five black Vs. The number terms total 3, represented by three black Ns. Show the symbols. m
- Note that the simplified expression is **$5x + 3$**.

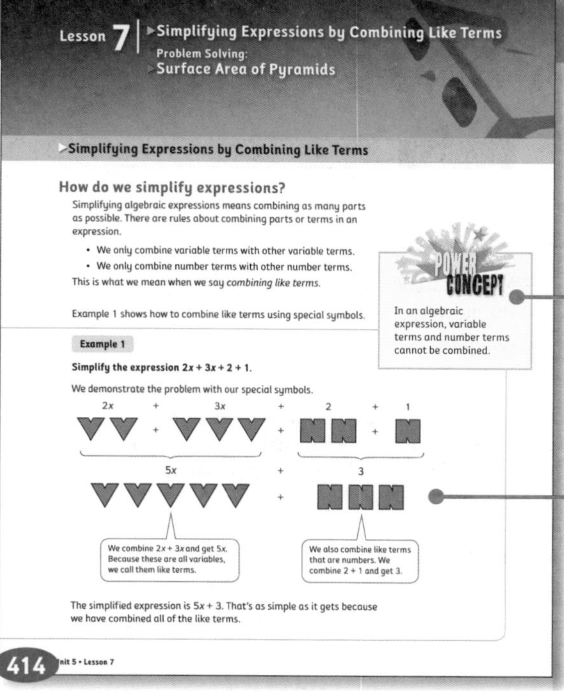

Lesson 7 | ▶Simplifying Expressions by Combining Like Terms
Problem Solving:
▶Surface Area of Pyramids

▶Simplifying Expressions by Combining Like Terms

How do we simplify expressions?

Simplifying algebraic expressions means combining as many parts as possible. There are rules about combining parts or terms in an expression.

- We only combine variable terms with other variable terms.
- We only combine number terms with other number terms.

This is what we mean when we say *combining like terms.*

POWER CONCEPT: In an algebraic expression, variable terms and number terms cannot be combined.

Example 1 shows how to combine like terms using special symbols.

Example 1

Simplify the expression $2x + 3x + 2 + 1$.

We demonstrate the problem with our special symbols.

2x + 3x + 2 + 1
5x + 3
We combine 2x + 3x and get 5x. Because these are all variables, we call them like terms.
We also combine like terms that are numbers. We combine 2 + 1 and get 3.

The simplified expression is $5x + 3$. That's as simple as it gets because we have combined all of the like terms.

414 Unit 5 • Lesson 7

Power Concepts summarize critical concepts for students.

Visual models provide a concrete representation of challenging concepts.

Icons identify the parts of instruction supported by the Click-Thru slideshow presentation.

"We do" icons identify multiple modeling strategies to demonstrate concepts.

"We do" practice provides a safe environment to monitor student understanding.

Watch for: questions help teachers recognize common misconceptions.

Students can review lesson concepts by accessing the online ***mBook Study Guide,*** which includes Teacher-Talk Tutorials.

Apply Skills

(*Interactive Text*, page 186)

Have students turn to page 186 in the *Interactive Text*, which provides students with an opportunity to practice combining like terms.

Activity 1

Students simplify expressions by combining like terms. Instruct students to write their answers with the variable terms first.

Monitor students' work as they complete the activity.

Watch for:

- Do students combine like terms only?
- If the variable term was at the end of the expression, did students rewrite the expression with the variable term in the front?

Reinforce Understanding

Remind students that they can review lesson concepts by accessing the online *mBook Study Guide*.

Lesson 7 | Apply Skills

Name ________ Date ________

Apply Skills

Simplifying Expressions by Combining Like Terms

Activity 1

Simplify the expressions by combining like terms. Use the special symbols to help you.

Model: $x + x + 2 + 3$ → $2x + 5$

1. $x + 2x + 3 + 1$ — $3x + 4$
2. $4 + 2 + 2x + 2x$ — $4x + 6$
3. $2x + 2x + 1 + 1$ — $4x + 2$
4. $4 + 2 + 3x + 2x$ — $5x + 6$

186 Unit 5 • Lesson 7

Understanding Algebraic Expressions, Teacher Guide, Unit 5, Lesson 7

The **Problem Solving** strand takes 20 to 25 minutes of the lesson for instruction and application of middle school topics in a problem-solving environment.

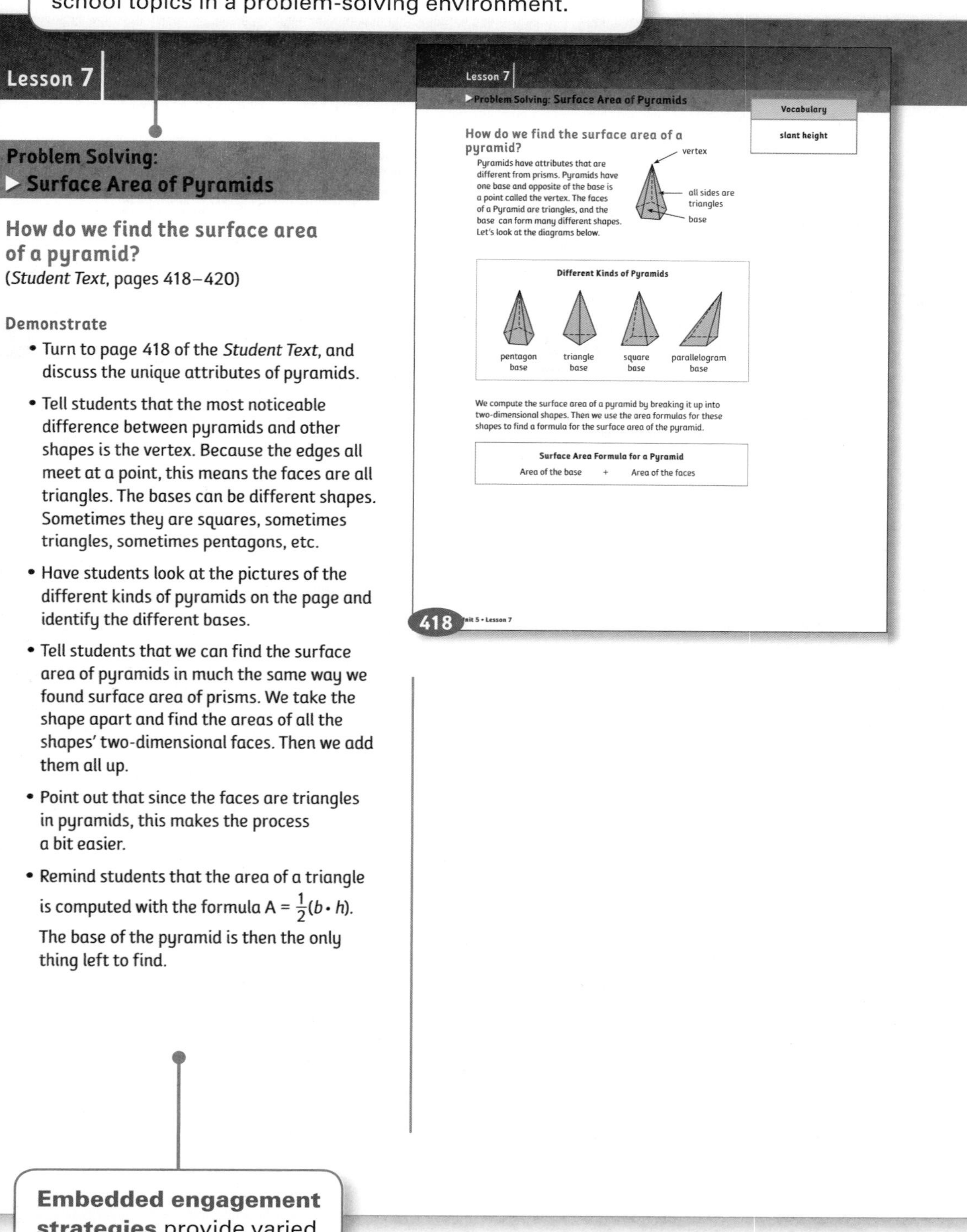

Lesson 7

Problem Solving: ▶ Surface Area of Pyramids

How do we find the surface area of a pyramid?

(*Student Text*, pages 418–420)

Demonstrate

- Turn to page 418 of the *Student Text*, and discuss the unique attributes of pyramids.
- Tell students that the most noticeable difference between pyramids and other shapes is the vertex. Because the edges all meet at a point, this means the faces are all triangles. The bases can be different shapes. Sometimes they are squares, sometimes triangles, sometimes pentagons, etc.
- Have students look at the pictures of the different kinds of pyramids on the page and identify the different bases.
- Tell students that we can find the surface area of pyramids in much the same way we found surface area of prisms. We take the shape apart and find the areas of all the shapes' two-dimensional faces. Then we add them all up.
- Point out that since the faces are triangles in pyramids, this makes the process a bit easier.
- Remind students that the area of a triangle is computed with the formula $A = \frac{1}{2}(b \cdot h)$. The base of the pyramid is then the only thing left to find.

Lesson 7

▶ Problem Solving: Surface Area of Pyramids

Vocabulary
slant height

How do we find the surface area of a pyramid?

Pyramids have attributes that are different from prisms. Pyramids have one base and opposite of the base is a point called the vertex. The faces of a Pyramid are triangles, and the base can form many different shapes. Let's look at the diagrams below.

Different Kinds of Pyramids

We compute the surface area of a pyramid by breaking it up into two-dimensional shapes. Then we use the area formulas for these shapes to find a formula for the surface area of the pyramid.

Surface Area Formula for a Pyramid		
Area of the base	+	Area of the faces

418 Unit 5 • Lesson 7

Embedded engagement strategies provide varied opportunities for student discussion.

"We do" in-class practice provides a safe environment to monitor student understanding.

Watch for: questions help teachers recognize common misconceptions.

Students can review lesson concepts by accessing the online ***mBook Study Guide***.

Problem-Solving Activity
(*Interactive Text*, page 187)

Have students turn to page 187 in the *Interactive Text*, which provides students an opportunity to practice finding the surface area of a three-dimensional figure.

Students find the surface area of a square pyramid and explain how they computed it. Be sure students have counted all of the faces and performed the calculations correctly.

Monitor students' work as they complete the activity.

Watch for:

- Can students identify the number of faces?
- Can students compute the area of the faces and multiply by how many there are?
- Can students find the sum of all the areas to come up with the surface area of the shape?
- Can students explain in writing how they got their answer?

mBook Reinforce Understanding
Remind students that they can review lesson concepts by accessing the online *mBook Study Guide*.

Lesson 7 | Problem-Solving Activity

Name ______________________ Date ______________________

Problem-Solving Activity
Surface Area of Pyramids

Find the surface area formula for a square pyramid. The base is a 4 × 4 square. The slant height of each face of the pyramid is 8 centimeters. Use your knowledge of area formulas to find the surface area of this shape. Explain how you found your answer when you are done.

Square Pyramid

8 cm

4 cm

The surface area of this square pyramid is 80 square cm.
Explanations will vary. Sample explanation: I found the area of the base: 4 • 4 = 16. Then I found the area of one face and multiplied the side by 4: 8 • 4 • 0.5 = 16; 16 • 4 = 64. Then I added both numbers together to find the surface area: 64 + 16 = 80 square cm.

Unit 5

mBook Reinforce Understanding
Use the *mBook Study Guide* to review lesson concepts.

Unit 5 • Lesson 7 187

Understanding Algebraic Expressions, Teacher Guide, Unit 5, Lesson 7

"You do" homework is designed to provide 15–20 minutes of out-of-class practice of lesson concepts and skills each day.

Activity 3

Students tell the area formulas needed to find the surface area of the shapes.

Activity 4 • Distributed Practice

Students practice whole number and rational number operations in open sentences. Sometimes this means using the inverse operation (e.g., subtraction instead of addition) when solving certain problems.

Lesson 7

Homework

Activity 3

Tell which area formulas are needed to find the surface area of each shape. Select the correct answer.

1. What area formulas do we need to find the surface area of this shape? b
   - (a) circle and rectangle
   - (b) rectangle and triangle
   - (c) triangle and circle
2. What area formulas do we need to find the surface area of this shape? c
   - (a) triangle and rectangle
   - (b) rectangle and parallelogram
   - (c) parallelogram and triangle
3. What area formulas do we need to find the surface area of this shape? b
   - (a) rectangle and triangle
   - (b) triangle and pentagon
   - (c) trapezoid and rectangle
4. What area formulas do we need to find the surface area of this shape? a
   - (a) triangle
   - (b) triangle and rectangle
   - (c) rectangle and trapezoid

Activity 4 • Distributed Practice

Solve.

1. $240 \div a = 60$ 4
2. $\frac{3}{5} \cdot \frac{1}{4} = b$ $\frac{3}{20}$
3. $12.3 \cdot 0.1 = c$ 1.23
4. $d - 80 = 70$ 150
5. $603.09 + 298.12 = e$ 901.21
6. $\frac{8}{9} - \frac{1}{3} = f$ $\frac{5}{9}$
7. $500 + g = 1{,}100$ 600
8. $\frac{5}{6} + \frac{4}{9} = h$ $1\frac{5}{18}$

422 Unit 5 • Lesson 7

Homework answers are provided at point of use.

Distributed Practice allows for continuous practice of previously learned concepts and skills.

Daily Support for Students and Parents

Through Technology. . .

TransMath is accessible to both students and parents—anytime, anywhere—through the *TransMath mBook Study Guide*. This online system provides students and parents with:

- **The complete Student Text**
  - Access to all lesson pages
  - Homework pages online—no need to take books home
- **Online Reinforcement**
  - Teacher-Talk Tutorials narrate and animate initial lesson concepts using concrete visual models to aid conceptual understanding.
  - Interactive Reinforcement Exercises provide immediate corrective feedback and track student progress.
  - Anytime, anywhere access to lesson pages to review missed content

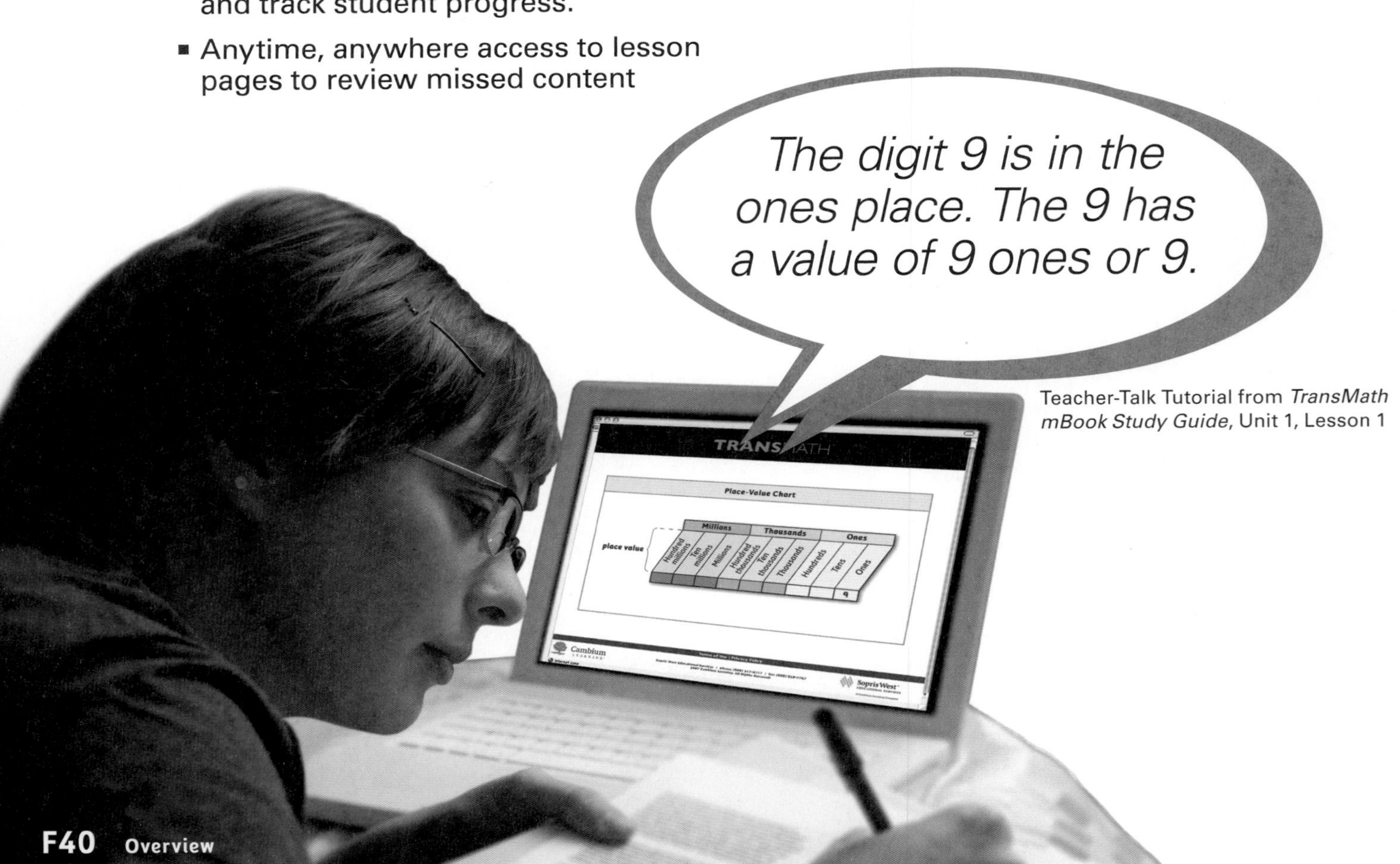

Teacher-Talk Tutorial from *TransMath mBook Study Guide*, Unit 1, Lesson 1

Engaging, **thought-provoking** openers start each unit.

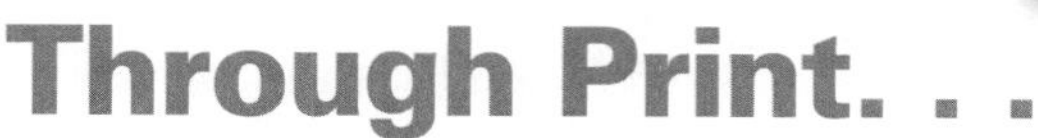

Through Print. . .

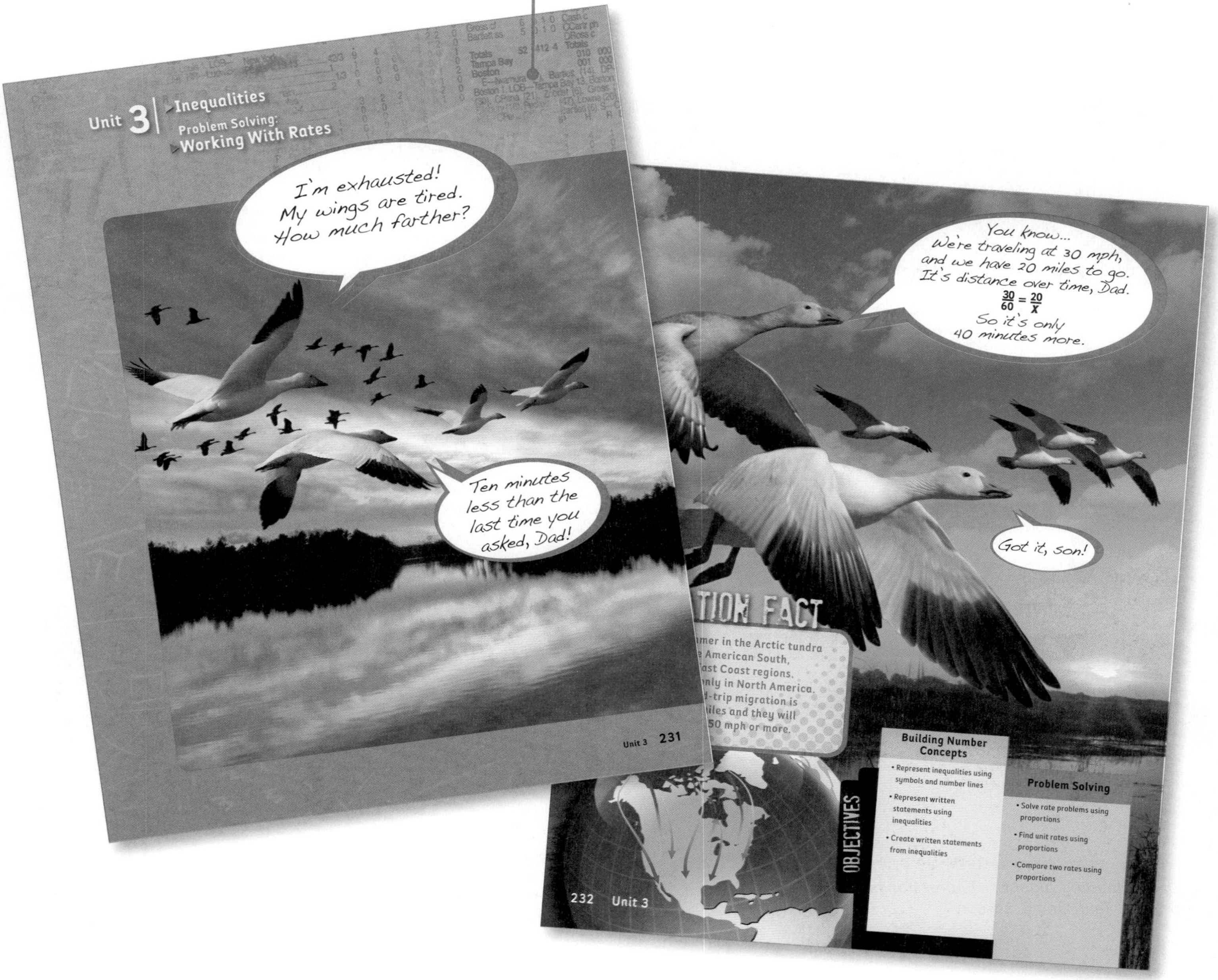

Unit 3 Inequalities
Problem Solving: Working With Rates
I'm exhausted! My wings are tired. How much farther?
Ten minutes less than the last time you asked, Dad!
Unit 3 231
You know... We're traveling at 30 mph, and we have 20 miles to go. It's distance over time, Dad. $\frac{30}{60} = \frac{20}{x}$ So it's only 40 minutes more.
Got it, son!
OBJECTIVES
Building Number Concepts
• Represent inequalities using symbols and number lines
• Represent written statements using inequalities
• Create written statements from inequalities
Problem Solving
• Solve rate problems using proportions
• Find unit rates using proportions
• Compare two rates using proportions
232 Unit 3

Provides Multiple Models and Strategies for Understanding Lesson Concepts

Daily questioning techniques establish prior knowledge and build foundational understanding.

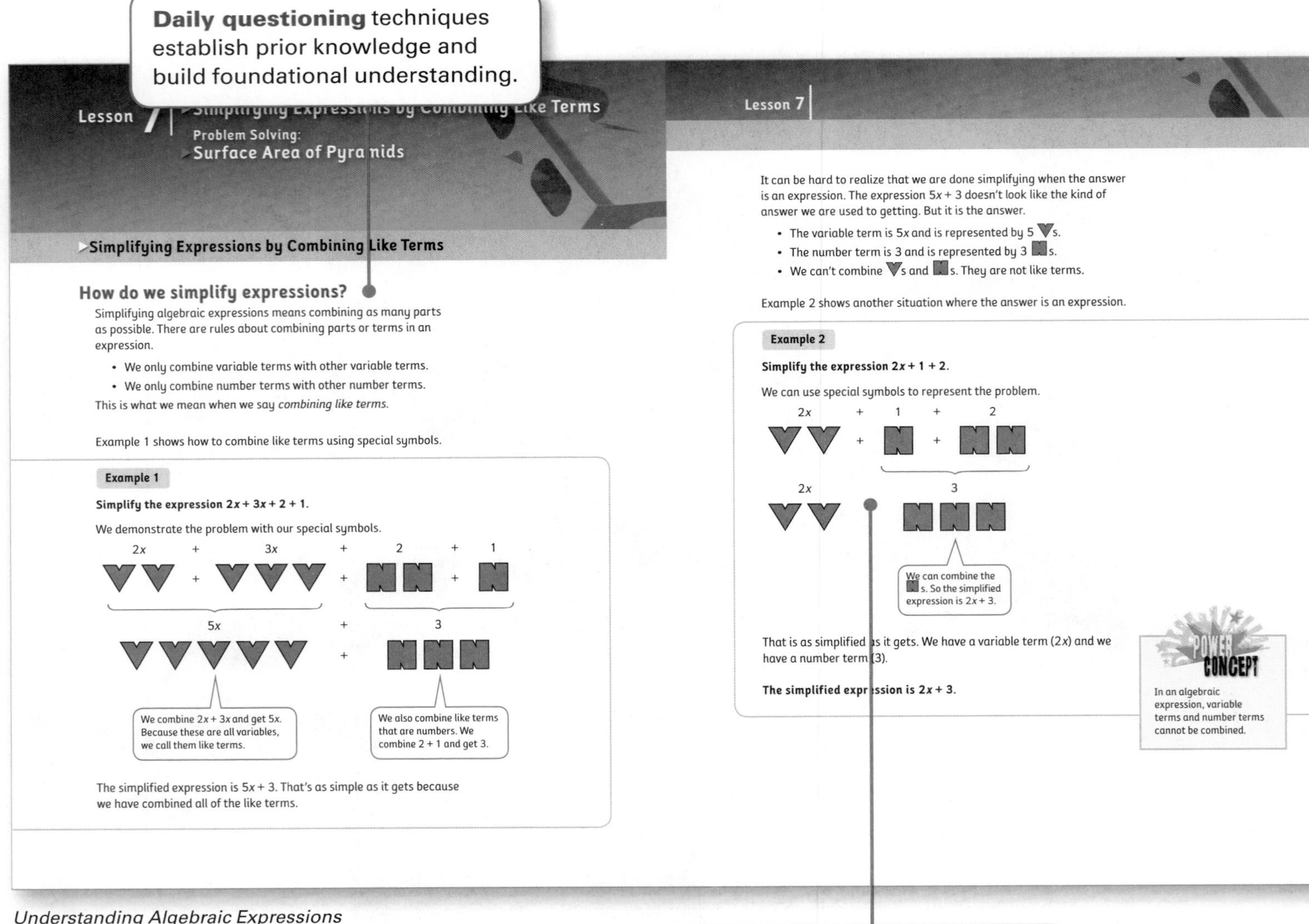

Lesson 7
Simplifying Expressions by Combining Like Terms
Problem Solving:
Surface Area of Pyramids
Simplifying Expressions by Combining Like Terms
How do we simplify expressions?
Simplifying algebraic expressions means combining as many parts as possible. There are rules about combining parts or terms in an expression.
• We only combine variable terms with other variable terms.
• We only combine number terms with other number terms.
This is what we mean when we say combining like terms.
Example 1 shows how to combine like terms using special symbols.
Example 1
Simplify the expression 2x + 3x + 2 + 1.
We demonstrate the problem with our special symbols.
2x + 3x + 2 + 1
5x + 3
We combine 2x + 3x and get 5x. Because these are all variables, we call them like terms.
We also combine like terms that are numbers. We combine 2 + 1 and get 3.
The simplified expression is 5x + 3. That's as simple as it gets because we have combined all of the like terms.
Lesson 7
It can be hard to realize that we are done simplifying when the answer is an expression. The expression 5x + 3 doesn't look like the kind of answer we are used to getting. But it is the answer.
• The variable term is 5x and is represented by 5 s.
• The number term is 3 and is represented by 3 s.
• We can't combine s and s. They are not like terms.
Example 2 shows another situation where the answer is an expression.
Example 2
Simplify the expression 2x + 1 + 2.
We can use special symbols to represent the problem.
2x + 1 + 2
2x
3
We can combine the s. So the simplified expression is 2x + 3.
That is as simplified as it gets. We have a variable term (2x) and we have a number term (3).
The simplified expression is 2x + 3.
POWER CONCEPT
In an algebraic expression, variable terms and number terms cannot be combined.

Understanding Algebraic Expressions Student Text, Unit 5, Lesson 7

Visual models take the place of extensive text explanations and provide engaging opportunities for students to build conceptual understanding.

Lessons provide meaningful applications of **problem-solving strategies** to prepare for higher-level mathematical thinking.

Studies that included visual representations along with the other components of explicit instruction tended to produce significant positive effects.

—National Mathematics Advisory Panel's Final Report, page 48.

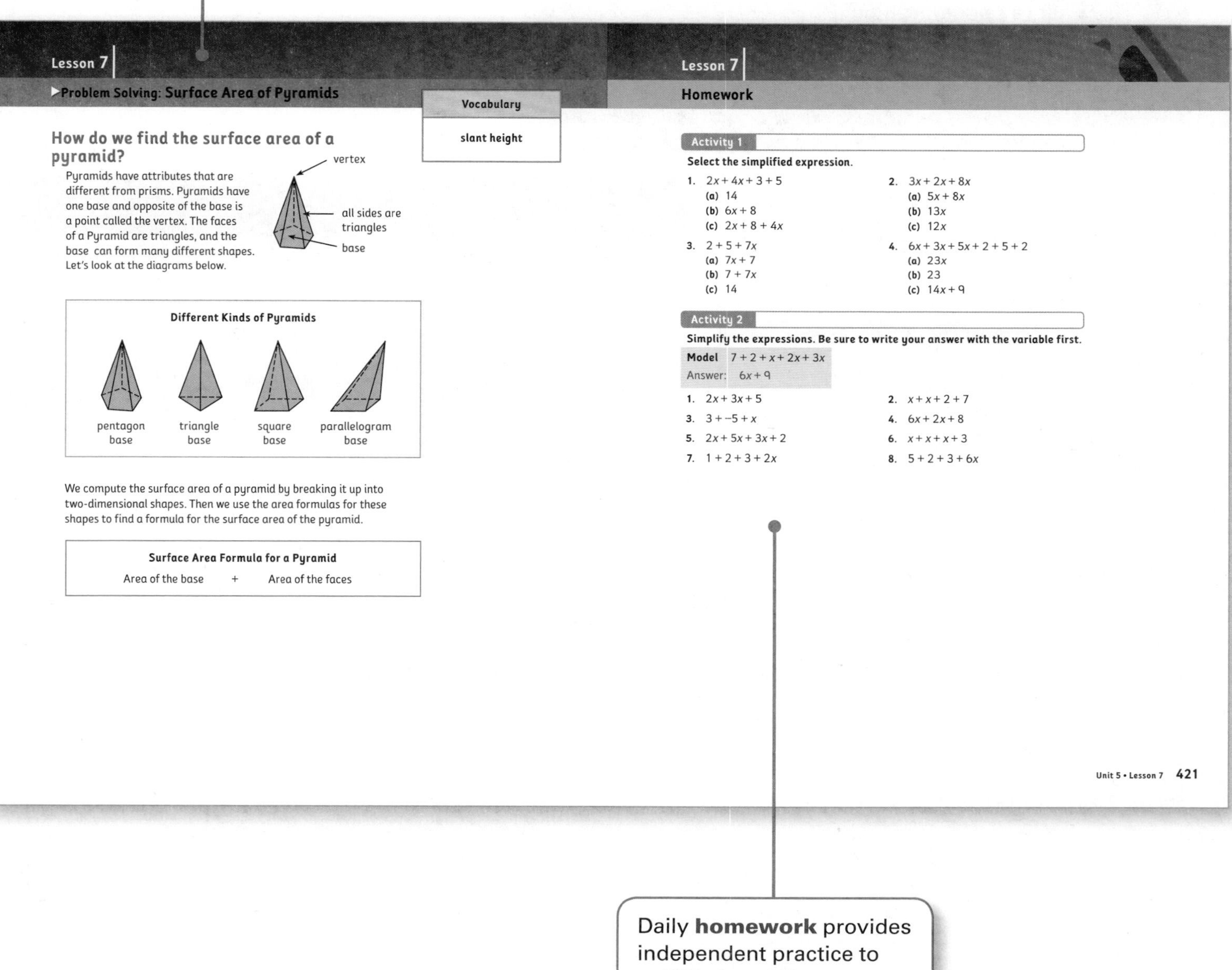

Lesson 7

▶Problem Solving: Surface Area of Pyramids

Vocabulary
slant height

How do we find the surface area of a pyramid?

Pyramids have attributes that are different from prisms. Pyramids have one base and opposite of the base is a point called the vertex. The faces of a Pyramid are triangles, and the base can form many different shapes. Let's look at the diagrams below.

Different Kinds of Pyramids

We compute the surface area of a pyramid by breaking it up into two-dimensional shapes. Then we use the area formulas for these shapes to find a formula for the surface area of the pyramid.

Surface Area Formula for a Pyramid

Area of the base + Area of the faces

Lesson 7

Homework

Activity 1

Select the simplified expression.

1. $2x + 4x + 3 + 5$
   (a) 14
   (b) $6x + 8$
   (c) $2x + 8 + 4x$
2. $3x + 2x + 8x$
   (a) $5x + 8x$
   (b) $13x$
   (c) $12x$
3. $2 + 5 + 7x$
   (a) $7x + 7$
   (b) $7 + 7x$
   (c) 14
4. $6x + 3x + 5x + 2 + 5 + 2$
   (a) $23x$
   (b) 23
   (c) $14x + 9$

Activity 2

Simplify the expressions. Be sure to write your answer with the variable first.

Model	$7 + 2 + x + 2x + 3x$
Answer:	$6x + 9$

1. $2x + 3x + 5$
2. $x + x + 2 + 7$
3. $3 + -5 + x$
4. $6x + 2x + 8$
5. $2x + 5x + 3x + 2$
6. $x + x + x + 3$
7. $1 + 2 + 3 + 2x$
8. $5 + 2 + 3 + 6x$

Unit 5 • Lesson 7 421

Daily **homework** provides independent practice to solidify key skills.

Key Concepts Consolidated in Unit Review Lessons Reinforce Student Learning

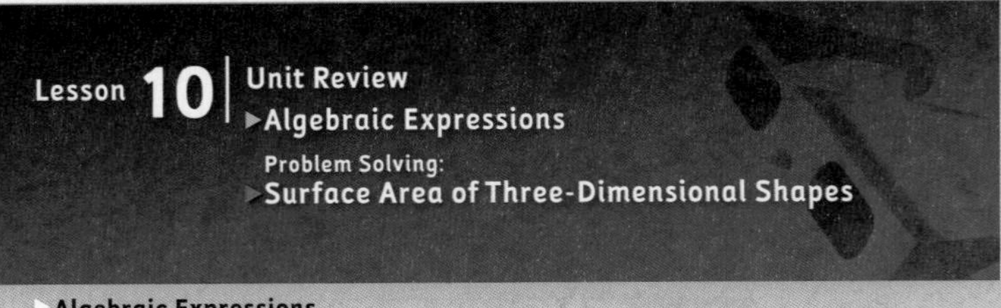

▶Algebraic Expressions

Why is PEMDAS important?

Expressions are a key part of algebra. Numeric expressions are one kind. They have just numbers. Unless we have rules for working with numeric expressions, we will get different answers. That is why mathematicians created the rules for order of operations.

One easy way to remember the rules and their order is to think PEMDAS—Please Excuse My Dear Aunt Sally.

PEMDAS—The Rules for Order of Operations		
Step 1	**P** – Parentheses	Work what is inside the parentheses.
Step 2	**E** – Exponents	Work any numbers with exponents.
Step 3	**M** – Multiplication **D** – Division	Work multiplication or division problems from left to right.
Step 4	**A** – Addition **S** – Subtraction	Last of all, work addition or subtraction problems from left to right.

Understanding Algebraic Expressions
Student Text, Unit 5, Lesson 10

Lesson 10

How do we compute with integers?

Positive and negative integers are used a lot in algebra. If we don't remember what to do when we add or subtract these numbers, we'll get the wrong answer. The most important idea to remember is: Subtraction is the same as adding the opposite. Movement on the number line also helps us remember what is going on when we add or subtract integers.

Review 1

What is happening when we add using negative numbers?

−4 + 6 = 2

We start at −4 and move 6 in the positive direction.

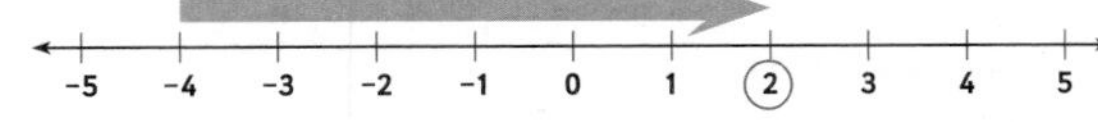

−1 + −2 = −3

We start at −1 and move 2 in the negative direction.

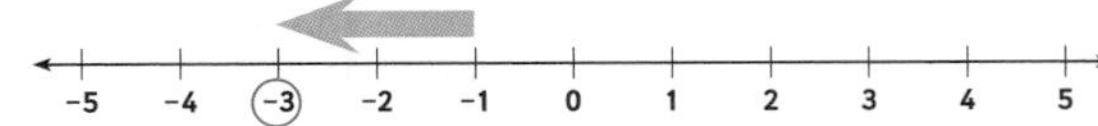

−2 − −5 Rule: Subtraction is adding the opposite.

−2 + 5 = 3

We start at −2 and move 5 in the positive direction.

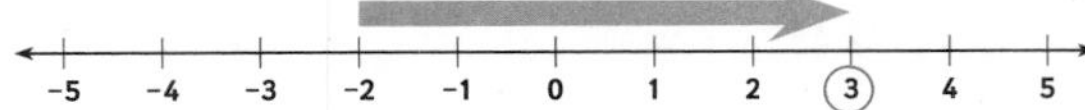

Lesson 10

▶Problem Solving: Surface Area of Three-Dimensional Shapes

What is the surface area of 3-D shapes?

Understanding the surface area of many 3-D shapes begins with sorting shapes into groups that have common attributes. In this unit, we sorted shapes into two groups.

Review 1

What are the attributes of 3-D shapes?

Group 1—Cylinder, Prisms, and Cube

cylinder

prisms

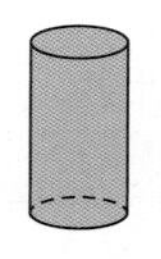
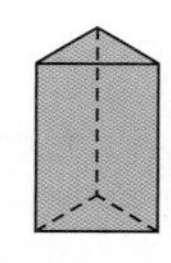
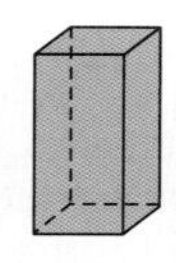
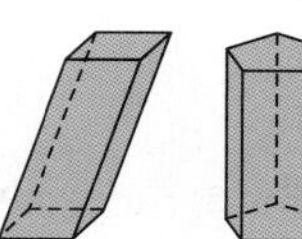
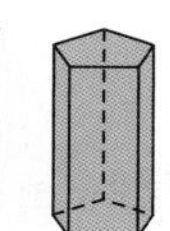
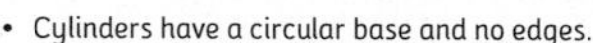

- Cylinders have a circular base and no edges.
- Cubes and prisms have edges and their tops and bottoms are parallel.
- Prisms have rectangles or parallelograms for faces.
- A cube has squares for each of its faces.
- Prisms can have many different shapes or polygons for bases.

Group 2—Cone and Pyramids

cone

pyramids

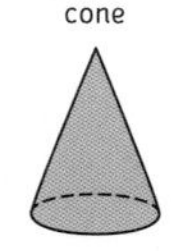
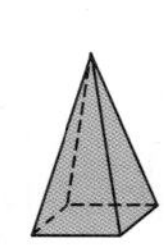
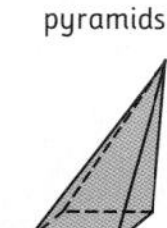
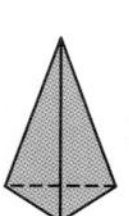

- Cones have a circular base and no edges.
- Pyramids have faces that are triangles.
- Pyramids can have many different shapes or polygons for bases.

Understanding Algebraic Expressions
Student Text, Unit 5, Lesson 10

Lesson 10

Once we separate these shapes into two groups, we start to think about ways to compute the surface area of each shape. Reviews 2 and 3 show how to think about the area of three different shapes.

Review 2

What are the formulas for the surface areas of a cylinder and triangular prism?

Formula for the Surface Area of a Cylinder

Area of two bases + Area of surface

$(2 \cdot \pi r^2) + (2\pi r \cdot h)$

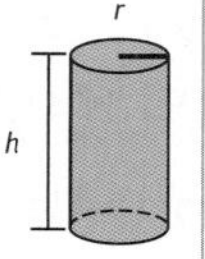

Formula for the Surface Area of a Triangular Prism

2 • (Area of triangle) + 3 • (Area of rectangle)

- The area of a triangular base is $\frac{1}{2}$ • base • height.
- We have two bases so the area is $2 \cdot \left(\frac{1}{2} \cdot \text{base} \cdot \text{height}\right)$.
- The area of a rectangular face is base • height.
- We have three rectangular faces so the area is 3 • (base • height).

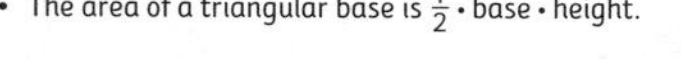
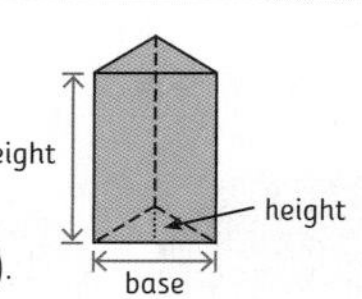

Customized Professional Development Support

At Cambium Learning®, we understand that intervention solutions don't come from programs alone. Cambium Learning Solutions is our division focused on helping educators effectively implement educational programs, including *TransMath*, through professional development services.

Our comprehensive implementation approach combines training, coaching, classroom visits, and consultation—all designed to promote higher levels of student achievement by providing opportunities for skill transfer, feedback, and practice.

With access to highly-skilled professional trainers and consultants throughout the year, Cambium Learning Solutions provides a professional development partnership that promotes ongoing success. Services include:

- Initial implementation training addressing the research foundation "Why Do" and "How To" of the particular program to be taught
- Site visits, model teaching, coaching, administrator workshops, and follow-ups
- Assessment data analysis
- Local capacity building for sustained implementation success
- Expert consultation with leaders in education

The Panel recommends that a sharp focus be placed on systematically strengthening teacher preparation, early-career mentoring and support, and ongoing professional development for teachers of mathematics at every level, with special emphasis on ways to ensure appropriate content knowledge for teaching.

—*National Mathematics Advisory Panel's Final Report, page 40.*

Professional Development

- Prepares educators to implement curriculum with fidelity
- Offers opportunities for teachers to practice what they learned
- Provides teachers with enduring understandings of math content

Unit 6 | Algebraic Rules and Properties

Problem Solving:

Volume of Three-Dimensional Shapes

Unit Opener: Background Information

After reading the Unit Opener about volume and dairy cows in *Student Text*, pages 443–444, share some of these additional facts with students.

- Cows must give birth before they can produce milk. They can make as much as 2,305 gallons of milk a year, and they need to drink two gallons of fresh water for every gallon of milk.
- The largest milk silos in the world are at the Hilmar Cheese Company in California. Each holds 200,000 gallons.
- It takes 12.5 gallons of milk to make one gallon of ice cream. Initially, ice cream was served only to the elite, such as George Washington, who enjoyed huge quantities. Later, the Welcome to America meal served to immigrants at Ellis Island included vanilla ice cream.
- The biggest ice cream sundae ever made weighed nearly 55,000 pounds. The world's largest ice cream sandwich registered 2,500 pounds.

Unit 6 | Building Number Concepts: Algebraic Rules and Properties

Problem Solving: Volume of Three-Dimensional Shapes

OBJECTIVES

Building Number Concepts	Problem Solving
• Use order of operations rules to evaluate algebraic and numeric expressions • Use substitution to evaluate algebraic expressions • Apply the distributive property to algebraic expressions	• Use formulas to find the volume of cylinders and prisms • Find the volume of pyramids and cones by comparing them to prisms and cylinders • Use a formula to find the volume of a sphere

Overview

We continue to develop the rules and properties for working with expressions and equations. Students learn how to evaluate algebraic expressions through substitution. Substitution converts an algebraic expression to a numeric expression. We also introduce the distributive property, the most complex property taught in prealgebra.

Unit Vocabulary
PASS rule **consecutive numbers** **number grid** **multiplicative** **additive** **distributive property**

The Problem Solving strand presents the volume of three-dimensional shapes. Once students analyze shapes categorically by their attributes, they can apply common formulas. These formulas are based on the logic of base and height for prisms and how many pyramids can fit within a prism of the same base and height.

Unit Vocabulary
volume **cubic inch** **cubic unit**

Building Number Concepts:

Algebraic Rules and Properties

Key Questions That Guide Student Understanding

- *What are important properties and rules for algebra?*

Enduring Understandings for Algebraic Rules and Properties

Algebra provides a foundation for more complex, or symbol-intensive, topics taught in secondary mathematics. Students must have a solid grasp on order of operations and integer rules that yield consistent solutions to problems. Keeping track of rules for different operations is challenging for many students, so we introduce the acronym PASS (**P**ositive **A**nswers Have the **S**ame **S**igns) for multiplication and division of integers. The distributive property, also introduced in this unit, is central to algebra.

Whether simplifying expressions or solving equations, students must use rules and properties proficiently. They need to be able to apply their knowledge without a great deal of mental effort or attention, so they can focus on bigger issues.

Tools for Understanding Algebraic Rules and Properties

Using Models
A simple table of numbers that shows the relationship between the step and number of items in one pattern allows students to see how we abstract an algebraic expression for the pattern.

Using Strategies for Integer Operations
As the number of rules for different integer operations increases, so does student confusion. We created a rule and a mnemonic for remembering what to do for addition, subtraction, multiplication, and division of integers. Subtraction is the same as adding the opposite, and PASS helps students recall what to do with multiplication and division.

Problem Solving:

▶Volume of Three-Dimensional Shapes

Key Questions That Guide Student Understanding

- *What are key attributes of three-dimensional shapes?*
- *What are strategies for finding the volume of a three-dimensional shape?*

Enduring Understandings for Volume of Three-Dimensional Shapes

Volume and surface area for three-dimensional shapes rely on the same categorization of shapes. Even though many shapes look different, seeing the common attributes of different shapes helps students understand several volume formulas.

Cylinders, for example, play a central role in helping students think about volume. Cylinders share common attributes with prisms and cubes. Students see that their volumes are stacks of bases, so they understand the volume formula as base • height.

We can then show students that the volume of three cones can fill a cylinder with the same base and height. Students therefore gain a better understanding of the volume formula for cones and pyramids: Volume = $\frac{1}{3}$ • base • height.

Tools for Understanding Volume of Three-Dimensional Shapes

Using Basic Concepts to Develop Deeper Understanding
This unit reinforces different categories of three-dimensional shapes. Once students classify shapes, they can apply basic concepts of base and height to determine volume. Showing that it takes three pyramids to fill a prism of the same height and base helps students remember and understand why volume formulas for pyramids have a coefficient of $\frac{1}{3}$.

Building Number Concepts:
Algebraic Rules and Properties

Lesson	Lesson Objectives—Students will:
1	• Use integer rules to solve multiplication and division problems.
2	
3	• Evaluate algebraic expressions by combining like terms and substituting values for the variables.
4	• Write algebraic expressions using variables to describe patterns of numbers.
5	
6	• Evaluate expressions using different properties of numbers.
7	• Use the distributive property to evaluate expressions.
8	
9	
10	• Review Algebraic Rules and Properties concepts.
Unit Assessments	End-of-Unit Assessment Performance Assessment

Problem Solving:

▶Volume of Three-Dimensional Shapes

Lesson Objectives—Students will:	Assessment
• Learn that volume is the measure inside a three-dimensional shape.	
• Find the volume of a rectangular prism.	
• Find the volume of three-dimensional objects by stacking the bases.	
	Quiz 1
• Find the volume of cones and pyramids.	
• Find the volume of a sphere.	
• Find the volume of complex objects.	
• Review Volume of Three-Dimensional Shapes concepts.	Unit Review
	End-of-Unit Assessment Performance Assessment

Lesson 1 ▶ Multiplication and Division of Integers

Problem Solving: Concept of Volume

Lesson Planner

Vocabulary Development

PASS rule
volume

Skills Maintenance

Integer Addition and Subtraction

Building Number Concepts:

▶ Multiplication and Division of Integers

Students learn that the main idea of integer multiplication and division can be summarized using PASS, which is an acronym for Positive Answer when the numbers have the Same Signs.

Objective

Students will use integer rules to solve multiplication and division problems.

Problem Solving:

▶ Concept of Volume

Students are introduced to the concept of volume. They learn that volume is the measurement of the inside of a three-dimensional object. Students learn the basic vocabulary related to three-dimensional objects and talk about three-dimensional objects in everyday life.

Objective

Students will learn that volume is the measure inside a three-dimensional object.

Homework

Students solve a mix of integer operations, evaluate numeric expressions using the rules for integers and PEMDAS, and answer multiple-choice questions about estimating volume. In Distributed Practice, students practice addition and subtraction of integers, PEMDAS, and operations on fractions.

Lesson 1 | Skills Maintenance

Name ______________________ Date ______________

Skills Maintenance
Integer Addition and Subtraction

Activity 1

Solve the problems involving addition and subtraction of integers.

1. −10 + 20 __10__
2. 15 − −5 __20__
3. −3 − 5 __−8__
4. −25 + −35 __−60__
5. 14 + −3 __11__
6. −20 − −10 __−10__
7. 15 + −5 __10__
8. −3 + −5 __−8__

200 Unit 6 • Lesson 1

Skills Maintenance

Integer Addition and Subtraction
(*Interactive Text*, page 200)

Activity 1

Students solve problems involving addition and subtraction of integers.

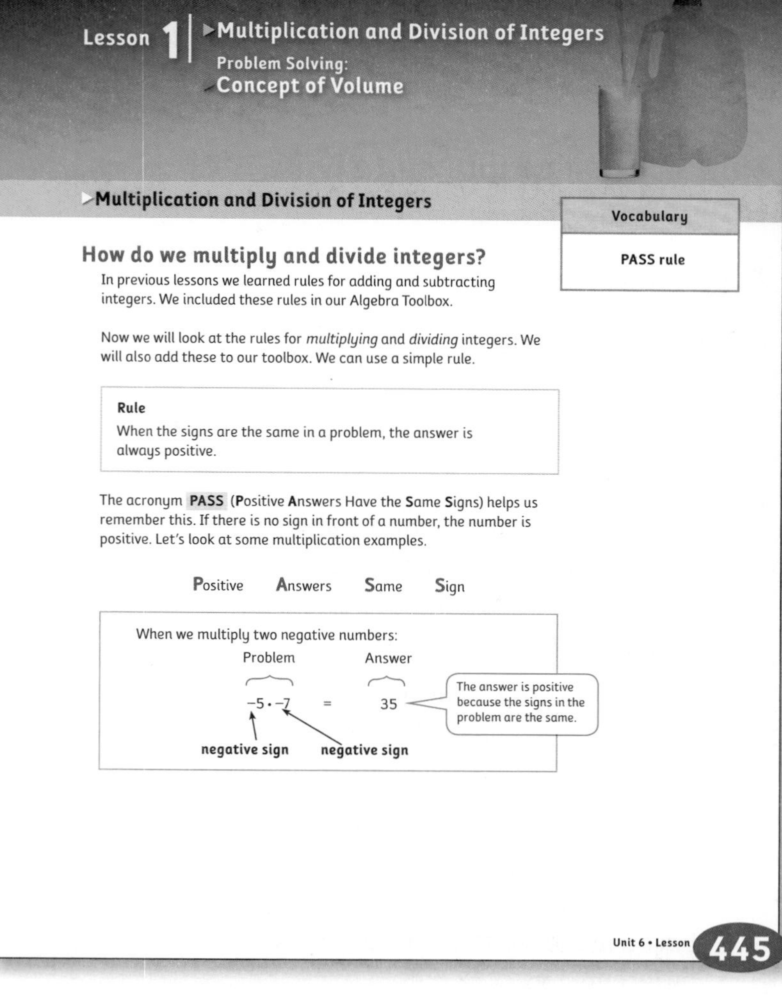

Lesson 1 | Multiplication and Division of Integers
Problem Solving:
Concept of Volume

Multiplication and Division of Integers

Vocabulary
PASS rule

How do we multiply and divide integers?

In previous lessons we learned rules for adding and subtracting integers. We included these rules in our Algebra Toolbox.

Now we will look at the rules for *multiplying* and *dividing* integers. We will also add these to our toolbox. We can use a simple rule.

> **Rule**
> When the signs are the same in a problem, the answer is always positive.

The acronym **PASS** (**P**ositive **A**nswers Have the **S**ame **S**igns) helps us remember this. If there is no sign in front of a number, the number is positive. Let's look at some multiplication examples.

Positive **A**nswers **S**ame **S**ign

> When we multiply two negative numbers:
>
> Problem = Answer
>
> $-5 \cdot -7 = 35$
>
> **negative sign** **negative sign**
>
> The answer is positive because the signs in the problem are the same.

Unit 6 • Lesson 445

Building Number Concepts: Multiplication and Division of Integers

How do we multiply and divide integers?

(*Student Text*, pages 445–447)

Connect to Prior Knowledge

Begin by discussing today's skills maintenance activity. Ask students to describe their strategies for solving these problems. Restate any misconceptions or incorrect statements using correct rules and strategies.

Link to Today's Concept

Tell students that in today's lesson, we look at the rules for multiplication and division of integers.

Demonstrate

Engagement Strategy: Teacher Modeling

Demonstrate the important terms for today's lesson in one of the following ways:

- **mBook**: Use the *mBook Teacher Edition* for *Student Text*, pages 445–446. m
- **Overhead Projector**: Reproduce the problems on a transparency, and modify as discussed.
- **Board**: Copy the problems on the board, and modify as discussed.

- Remind students that integers are positive and negative whole numbers. Review the rules for addition and subtraction of integers with students if you feel it is necessary. Use a modified number line to demonstrate the rules.
- Next tell students that multiplication and division are more difficult to show on a number line; instead we remember a simple rule: the **PASS rule**. PASS means that the answer to a problem involving multiplication or division of integers is positive if the signs of the numbers in your problem are the same. Remembering this one simple rule is really all we need to do because it implies that if the signs are different, the answer is negative. m
- Go over the model that shows when we multiply two negative numbers, $\mathbf{-5 \cdot -7 = 35}$, the answer is a positive number because the signs are the same. m

How do we multiply and divide integers? *(continued)*

Demonstrate

- Go through each of the models with students to show the variations in multiplication and division problems using integers and how to determine the sign of the answer.
- Point out the multiplication equation **−5 • 7 = −35**, and explain that the answer is negative because the signs of the two integers are different. m
- Next go over the division equation **−12 ÷ −2 = 6**, and explain that the answer is positive because both numbers have the same sign. m
- Go over the division equation **12 ÷ -2 = −6**, and explain that the answer is negative because the signs of the numbers are different. m
- Go over the division of two positive numbers with the equation **12 ÷ 2 = 6**, and explain that the answer is positive because the numbers 12 and 2 have the same sign. m

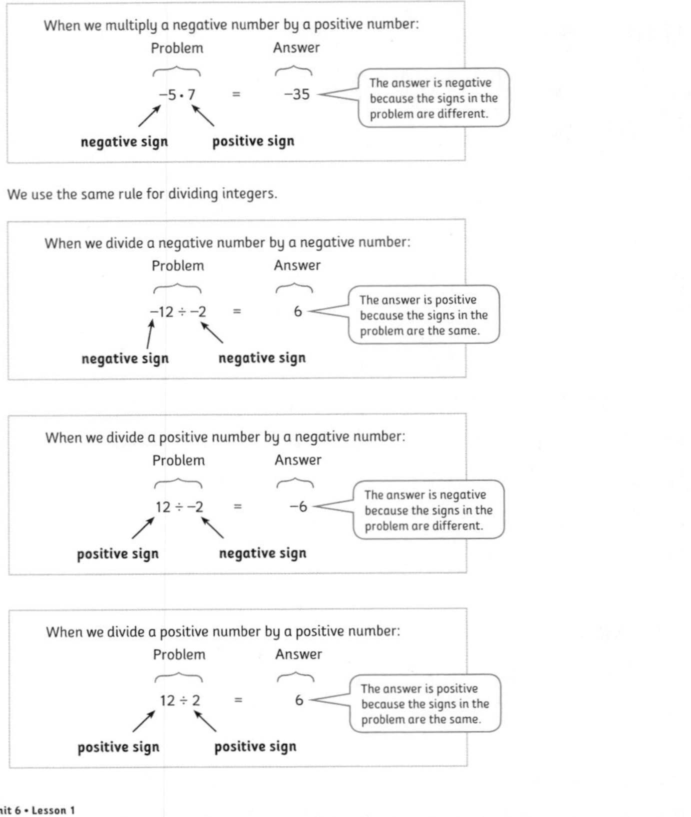
Lesson 1
When we multiply a negative number by a positive number:
Problem
Answer
−5 • 7 = −35
The answer is negative because the signs in the problem are different.
negative sign
positive sign
We use the same rule for dividing integers.
When we divide a negative number by a negative number:
Problem
Answer
−12 ÷ −2 = 6
The answer is positive because the signs in the problem are the same.
negative sign
negative sign
When we divide a positive number by a negative number:
Problem
Answer
12 ÷ −2 = −6
The answer is negative because the signs in the problem are different.
positive sign
negative sign
When we divide a positive number by a positive number:
Problem
Answer
12 ÷ 2 = 6
The answer is positive because the signs in the problem are the same.
positive sign
positive sign
446 Unit 6 • Lesson 1

Demonstrate

- Next, tell students that we are adding these rules to our algebra toolbox to complete our list of integer rules. Summarize the rules one more time to reinforce the main ideas. Explain that when evaluating complex expressions, we have to use the order of operations rules, or PEMDAS.
- Direct students to page 447 of the *Student Text* and go over **Example 1**.

STEP 1

- Look at the problem **5 + 40 ÷ −10 • −3**. Remind students that we have to use the order of operations. There are no parentheses or exponents, so we go directly to multiplication and division. We work the multiplication and division from left to right.
- Point out that we do the division operation first: **40 ÷ −10**. Point out that we are dividing two numbers that have different signs, so the answer to that portion is negative: **40 ÷ −10 is −4**.

STEP 2

- Explain that we can rewrite the problem as **5 + −4 • −3**. Next we do the multiplication. We have **−4 • −3**. Point out that because the signs are the same, the answer is positive: **−4 • −3 = 12**.

STEP 3

- Finally, we can rewrite the problem as **5 + 12**. Remind students that in PEMDAS, addition is next, and we are adding two positive numbers, so the answer is positive. **The answer is 17.**

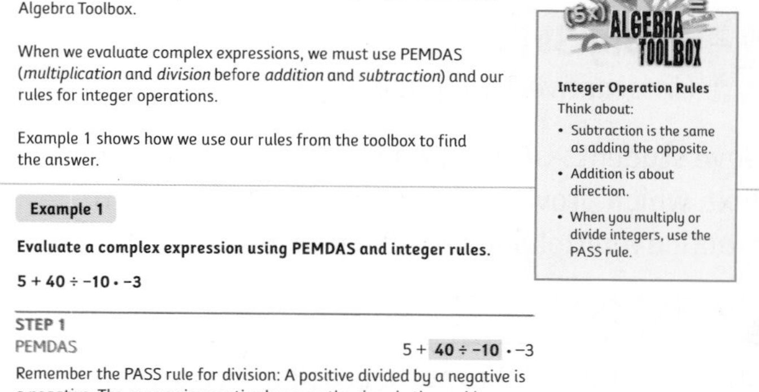

We now have the complete list of rules for integer operations in our Algebra Toolbox.

When we evaluate complex expressions, we must use PEMDAS (*multiplication* and *division* before *addition* and *subtraction*) and our rules for integer operations.

Example 1 shows how we use our rules from the toolbox to find the answer.

ALGEBRA TOOLBOX
Integer Operation Rules
Think about:
• Subtraction is the same as adding the opposite.
• Addition is about direction.
• When you multiply or divide integers, use the PASS rule.

Example 1

Evaluate a complex expression using PEMDAS and integer rules.

5 + 40 ÷ −10 • −3

STEP 1
PEMDAS — 5 + **40 ÷ −10** • −3

Remember the PASS rule for division: A positive divided by a negative is a negative. The answer is negative because the signs in the problem are different.

STEP 2
PEMDAS — 5 + **−4 • −3**

Remember the PASS rule for multiplication: A negative times a negative is a positive. The answer is positive because the signs in the problem are the same.

STEP 3
5 + 12

Remember the rule for adding integers: When we start with a positive number and move in a positive direction, we get a positive answer.

We see 17 is our answer.

Apply Skills Turn to *Interactive Text*, page 201.

Reinforce Understanding Use the *mBook Study Guide* to review lesson concepts.

Check for Understanding
Engagement Strategy: Look About

Write **8 + 20 ÷ −4 • 2** on the board. Have students evaluate the expression using PEMDAS and the PASS integer rules (*−2*). Students should write their steps and solutions in large writing on a piece of paper or a dry erase board. When students finish their work, they should hold up their answer for everyone to see.

If students are not sure about the answer, prompt them to look about at other students' solutions to help with their thinking. Review the answers after all students hold up their solutions.

Apply Skills

(*Interactive Text*, page 201)

Have students turn to page 201 in the *Interactive Text*, which provides students an opportunity to practice multiplying and dividing integers.

Activity 1

Students use PASS to solve problems involving multiplication and division of positive and negative integers.

Activity 2

Students use the rules for integer operations to solve a mix of problems.

Monitor students' work as they complete the activities.

Watch for:

- Can students remember PASS when solving multiplication and division problems involving integers?
- Can students discriminate the rules for adding and subtracting integers from the rules for multiplying and dividing integers?
- Do students get the correct answer?

mBook Reinforce Understanding

Remind students that they can review lesson concepts by accessing the online *mBook Study Guide*.

Lesson 1 | Apply Skills

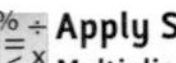

Name ______ Date ______

Apply Skills
Multiplication and Division of Integers

Activity 1

Solve the problems involving multiplication and division of integers. Remember the PASS rules.

1. $-9 \cdot -5 =$ 45
2. $45 \div -9 =$ −5
3. $-7 \cdot$ −8 $= 56$
4. $-45 \div$ 5 $= -9$
5. $-56 \div 8 =$ −7
6. $-7 \cdot$ −8 $= 56$
7. $-81 \div$ −9 $= 9$
8. 7 $\cdot -4 = -28$

Activity 2

Solve the problems involving a mix of integer operations. Remember all of the integer rules.

1. $-3 + 7 =$ 4
2. $17 - -2 =$ 19
3. $-6 \cdot -6 =$ 36
4. $28 \div -4 =$ −7
5. $-6 \cdot$ −7 $= 42$
6. $-32 \div$ −8 $= 4$
7. $-12 - 15 =$ −27
8. $18 - 25 =$ −7

Unit 6

Unit 6 • Lesson 1 201

Problem Solving: ▶ Concept of Volume

How do we measure what's inside a three-dimensional object?

(*Student Text*, pages 448–449)

Build Vocabulary

Have students turn to page 448 of the *Student Text*. Remind students of important vocabulary introduced in the last unit. Be sure students understand this vocabulary because it is critical to moving forward in the discussion of **volume**. Remind students that we worked with surface area of three-dimensional objects. Introduce the term volume as the measurement of the inside of a three-dimensional object.

Demonstrate

- Read the material on the page, and discuss the common objects shown: the coffee cup and the bottle of juice. The measurement of the coffee cup and what is in the coffee cup are the volume. The measurement of the bottle of juice and its contents are the volume.
- Be sure students see the distinction between this and the surface area, or the measurement of the outside of the objects, which we describe as the skin or the wrapping.

Lesson 1

▶Problem Solving: Concept of Volume

Vocabulary
volume

How do we measure what's inside a three-dimensional object?

In the last unit, we learned to use a number of special vocabulary terms such as *face, edge,* and *base* when we talk about *three-dimensional*, or 3-D, objects. These terms are shown below.

Basic Vocabulary for Three-Dimensional Objects

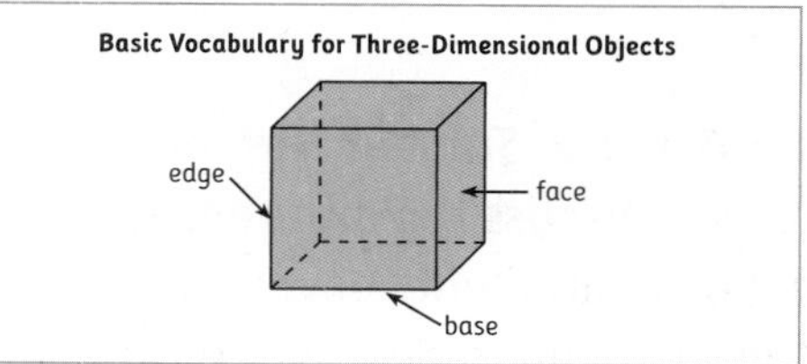

We also learned that the *surface area* of a three-dimensional object is the measurement of the outside of the object. We can think of surface area as the "skin" or "wrapping paper" on the object.

Now we will learn to find out how much space is inside a three-dimensional object. When we measure the amount of space inside a three-dimensional object, we are measuring the object's **volume**.

The volume of a 12-ounce cup of coffee

The volume of a 2-liter bottle of juice

We talk about volume all the time, but we don't use the word. Instead, we use phrases such as "a 12-ounce cup of coffee," or "a 2-liter bottle of juice." Both statements refer to the volume of the containers.

448 Unit 6 • Lesson 1

How do we measure what's inside a three-dimensional object? *(continued)*

Demonstrate

- Turn to page 449 of the *Student Text*, and read the material. Discuss the difference between exact measurements of volume and estimations. Explain that when we measure objects from the kitchen using smaller three-dimensional objects we estimate their volume.
- Go over the various fillings shown on page 449, and tell students that these help us estimate volume. Also discuss what some common three-dimensional objects are in our everyday life and how we might fill them with these fillings to estimate volume.

Check for Understanding

Engagement Strategy: Pair/Share

Put students in pairs, and have them come up with two different three-dimensional objects whose volume we use in everyday life. Then invite pairs to share their lists with the class. Give the example of a package to send in the mail.

We can accurately measure the volume of an object with tools and formulas. For example, cooks use measuring spoons and cups when they prepare meals. They use these measuring tools to make exact measurements.

However, it is also important to know how to estimate the volume of different objects. Estimation helps us understand how we get the different formulas that measure the volume of different three-dimensional objects.

Small three-dimensional cubes (such as dice or sugar cubes), and other items such as marbles, beans, packing peanuts, sand, rice, and water are different materials we can use to estimate the volume of larger three-dimensional objects.

Material for Filling Three-Dimensional Objects

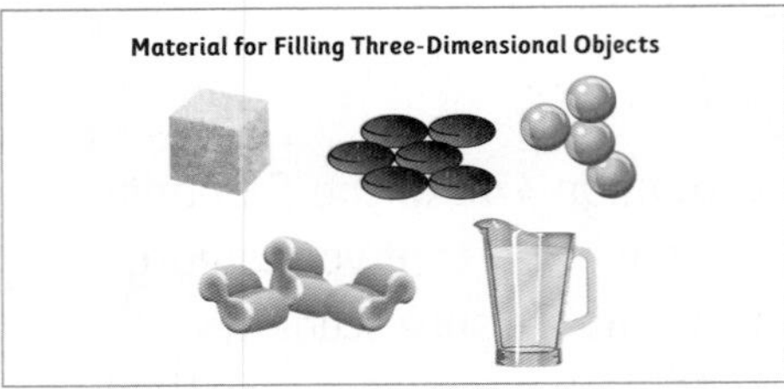

When we use these common three-dimensional objects to fill large three-dimensional objects such as the ones shown below, we are estimating volume.

Common Three-Dimensional Objects in Everyday Life

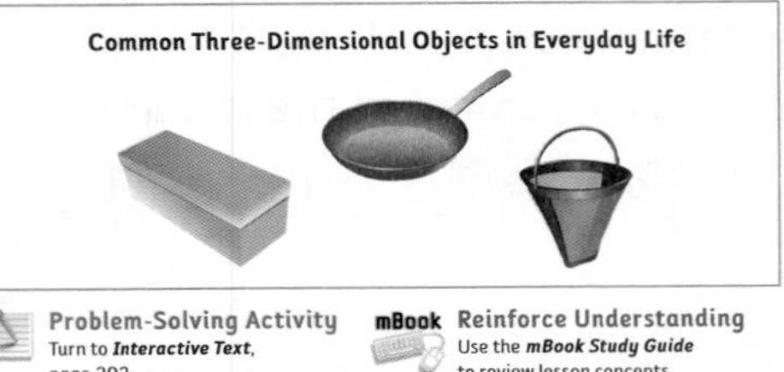

Problem-Solving Activity Turn to ***Interactive Text***, page 202.

mBook Reinforce Understanding Use the ***mBook Study Guide*** to review lesson concepts.

Problem-Solving Activity
(*Interactive Text*, page 202)

Have students turn to page 202 in the *Interactive Text*. Set up stations in the classroom for measuring the various objects and fillings you brought in. Have students get out a sheet of blank paper and create a table for entering their data, as shown in the text. Tell students to estimate the measurement of the various objects at the various stations using the fillings to fill them. Have them record their data in the tables they created on their paper.

Be sure students have adequate time to estimate the volume of the many objects at the many stations. When finished, have students compare their volume estimates for the various three-dimensional objects with other students in the class.

Monitor students' work as they complete the activity.

Watch for:

- Can students estimate the volumes of the various objects using the fillings at the various stations?
- Can students record the results of their findings in the table?
- Are students' estimates reasonable?
- Can students explain why their answers might be different from other student answers?
- Can students explain why their estimates might differ from exact measurements?
- Can students describe the units they used and how they are the same or different from others?

Lesson 1 | Problem-Solving Activity

Name ____________ Date ____________

Problem-Solving Activity
Concept of Volume

Estimate the volume of common three-dimensional objects, such as pans or boxes, using informal measuring tools like the materials shown in the *Student Text*.

On your paper, write the name of the object you are measuring and its shape. Then fill the object with one of the materials from the *Student Text* and estimate the volume by describing how much of the material you need to fill it. Write the estimate on your paper next to the object. Be sure to include the units (e.g., 2 cups of water, 10 marbles, 15 cubes, or 1 $\frac{1}{2}$ cups of rice). Make a table that looks like this on your paper and fill in your findings.

Object	Shape	Unit of Measure	Volume Estimate
Pan	Cylinder	Water	About 3 cups of water
Box	Rectangular prism	Rice	About 5 cups of rice

After you measure all the objects, compare your volume estimates for the various three-dimensional objects with other students sitting around you. Are your answers the same? Explain why or why not. How do you think your estimates compare to an exact measurements? How are the units the same? How are they different?

Answers will vary.

mBook Reinforce Understanding
Use the mBook *Study Guide* to review lesson concepts.

202 Unit 6 • Lesson 1

mBook Reinforce Understanding

Remind students that they can review lesson concepts by accessing the *mBook Study Guide* to review lesson concepts.

Homework

Go over the instructions on page 450 of the *Student Text* for each part of the homework.

Activity 1

Students solve a mix of integer operations.

Activity 2

Students evaluate numeric expressions using the rules for integers and PEMDAS.

Activity 3

Students answer multiple-choice questions about estimating volume.

Activity 4 • Distributed Practice

Students practice addition and subtraction of integers, PEMDAS, and operations on fractions.

Homework

Activity 1

Use the integer rules to solve the problems.

1. $-3 \cdot 5$ -15
2. $15 \div -3$ -5
3. $15 - 27$ -12
4. $-6 + -8$ -14
5. $-24 \div -8$ 3
6. $-5 \cdot -3$ 15
7. $5 + -7$ -2
8. $-56 \div 7$ -8

Activity 2

Use PEMDAS and integer rules to evaluate the numeric expressions. Remember to do diagnostics first, and then go to the Algebra Toolbox.

1. $5 + 2 - -3 + (3 \cdot -6)$
2. $9 \cdot (-6 + -4) + 2^2$
3. $-15 \div -3 \cdot (8 - -2)$
4. $-24 + -38 - 3^2$

See Additional Answers below.

Activity 3

Choose the material that would most likely be used for estimating the volume of the item.

1. The volume of a sauce pan is about 3 a
   (a) cups of water. (b) marbles. (c) grains of sand.
2. The volume of a shoe box is about 5 c
   (a) marbles. (b) sugar cubes. (c) cups of rice.
3. The volume of a waffle cone is about 15 b
   (a) cups of water. (b) marbles. (c) cups of beans.

Activity 4 • Distributed Practice

Solve.

1. $\frac{1}{5} \cdot \frac{5}{3} = a$ $\frac{1}{3}$
2. $-3 - 9 = b$ -12
3. $\frac{1}{12} \div \frac{1}{6} = c$ $\frac{1}{2}$
4. $3^2 + (3 \cdot 4) - 2 = d$ 19
5. $\frac{3}{4} - \frac{3}{8} = e$ $\frac{3}{8}$
6. $-9 + -9 = f$ -18
7. $(5 - 10) + 2^2 = g$ -1
8. $8 + 4 \div 2 = h$ 10

Additional Answers

Activity 2

1. $5 + 2 - -3 + (3 \cdot -6)$
   $5 + 2 - -3 + 18$
   $7 - -3 + 18$
   $10 + 18$
   28
2. $9 \cdot (-6 + -4) + 2^2$
   $9 \cdot -10 + 2^2$
   $9 \cdot -10 + 4$
   $-90 + 4$
   -86
3. $-15 \div -3 \cdot (8 - -2)$
   $-15 \div -3 \cdot 10$
   $5 \cdot 10$
   50
4. $-24 + -38 - 3^2$
   $-24 + -38 - 9$
   $-62 - 9$
   -71

Lesson 2 | Problem Solving: Measuring Volume and Cubic Units

Lesson Planner

Vocabulary Development

cubic inch
cubic unit

Skills Maintenance

Evaluating Expressions With Integers

Problem Solving:

▶ Measuring Volume and Cubic Units

Students learn that the more closely the unit of measure fits inside a three-dimensional shape without gaps, the more exact the measurement of volume. Students also learn that volume is measured in cubic units. Students learn that the formula for the volume of a rectangular prism is base times height times depth, and they see how to conceptualize the volume of a prism as a stack of bases.

Objective

Students will find the volume of a rectangular prism.

Homework

Students solve multiplication and division problems involving integers, evaluate expressions remembering the PEMDAS rules and the rules for integer operations, and select the answers to multiple-choice questions about units of measurement. In Distributed Practice, students practice addition and subtraction of integers, PEMDAS, and operations on fractions.

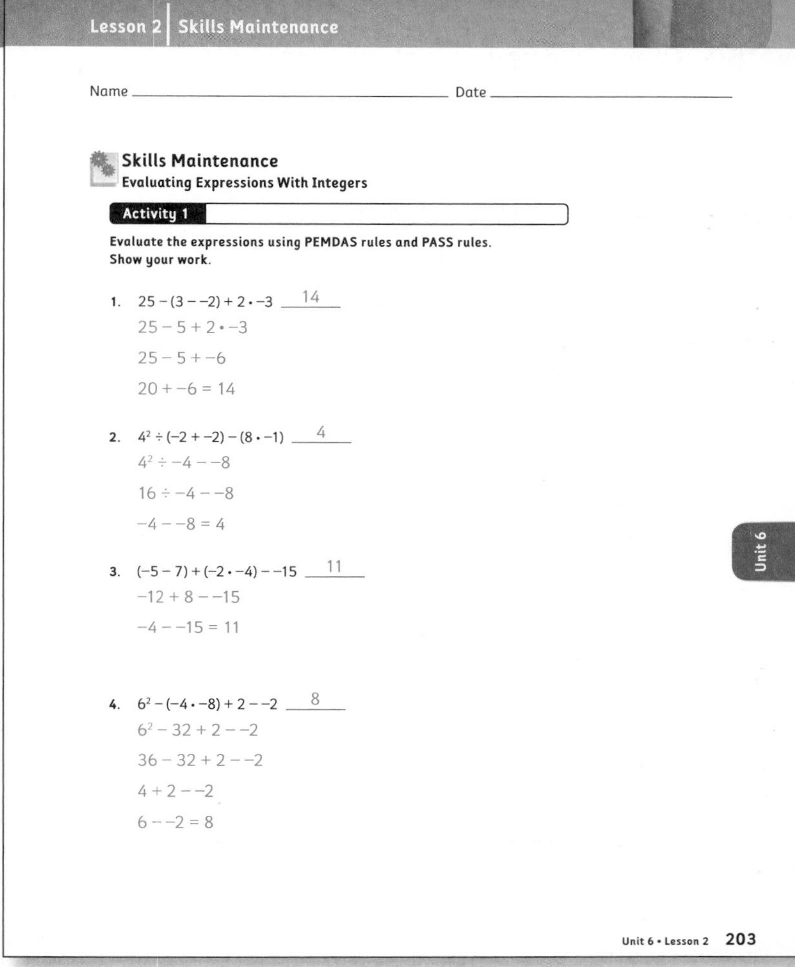
Lesson 2 | Skills Maintenance

Name ______________________ Date ______________________

Skills Maintenance
Evaluating Expressions With Integers

Activity 1

Evaluate the expressions using PEMDAS rules and PASS rules. Show your work.

1. $25 - (3 - -2) + 2 \cdot -3$ 14
   $25 - 5 + 2 \cdot -3$
   $25 - 5 + -6$
   $20 + -6 = 14$
2. $4^2 \div (-2 + -2) - (8 \cdot -1)$ 4
   $4^2 \div -4 - -8$
   $16 \div -4 - -8$
   $-4 - -8 = 4$
3. $(-5 - 7) + (-2 \cdot -4) - -15$ 11
   $-12 + 8 - -15$
   $-4 - -15 = 11$
4. $6^2 - (-4 \cdot -8) + 2 - -2$ 8
   $6^2 - 32 + 2 - -2$
   $36 - 32 + 2 - -2$
   $4 + 2 - -2$
   $6 - -2 = 8$

Unit 6

Unit 6 • Lesson 2 203

Skills Maintenance

Evaluating Expressions With Integers

(*Interactive Text*, page 203)

Activity 1

Students evaluate numeric expressions using PEMDAS rules and PASS rules for integer operations.

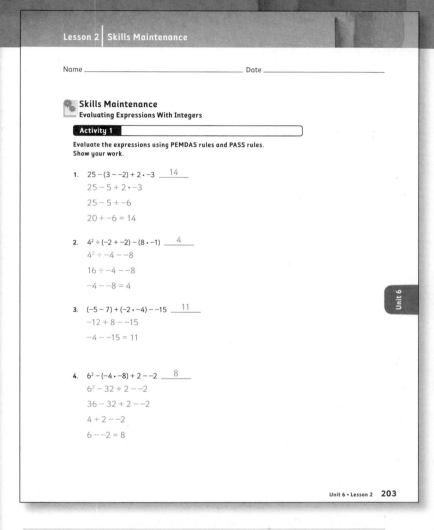

Problem Solving:
▶ Measuring Volume and Cubic Units

How do we measure volume exactly?
(*Student Text*, page 451)

Connect to Prior Knowledge
Begin by reminding students about the estimations of volume they made in the previous lesson. Ask students to describe the units of measurement and the strategies they used to estimate volume.

Listen for:

- *A discussion about filling the inside of the shapes with one of the fillings, e.g., Styrofoam shapes, marbles, rice, or water*

Ask students which of the fillings filled the shapes the best. Prompt a discussion about the size of the units of measurement.

Link to Today's Concept
Tell students that today we see how units that fill up the shape with no gaps give us the best measurement of volume.

Demonstrate
Engagement Strategy: Teacher Modeling

Demonstrate how to measure the volume of a rectangular prism in one of the following ways:

mBook: Use the *mBook Teacher Edition* for *Student Text*, pages 451–453.

Overhead Projector: Reproduce the rectangular prisms and shapes on a transparency, and modify as discussed.

Board: Copy the rectangular prisms and shapes on the board, and modify as discussed.

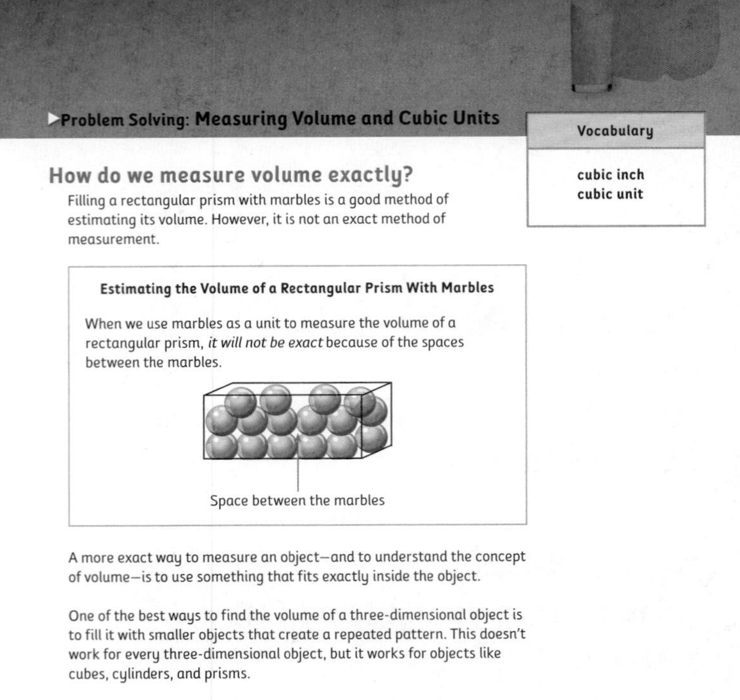
Lesson 2 | Problem Solving: Measuring Volume and Cubic Units

▶Problem Solving: Measuring Volume and Cubic Units

How do we measure volume exactly?

Filling a rectangular prism with marbles is a good method of estimating its volume. However, it is not an exact method of measurement.

Vocabulary

cubic inch
cubic unit

Estimating the Volume of a Rectangular Prism With Marbles

When we use marbles as a unit to measure the volume of a rectangular prism, *it will not be exact* because of the spaces between the marbles.

Space between the marbles

A more exact way to measure an object—and to understand the concept of volume—is to use something that fits exactly inside the object.

One of the best ways to find the volume of a three-dimensional object is to fill it with smaller objects that create a repeated pattern. This doesn't work for every three-dimensional object, but it works for objects like cubes, cylinders, and prisms.

Unit 6 • Lesson 451

- Show the rectangular prism filled with marbles. Discuss how filling a shape with marbles leaves a lot of gaps that are not measured. This makes the estimate less accurate than filling the object with something that does not produce as many gaps.
- Discuss that for some shapes, it is easiest to think about repeating a pattern inside the shape. This works for cubes, prisms, and cylinders.

How do we find the volume of a rectangular prism?

(*Student Text*, pages 452–453)

Demonstrate

- Demonstrate how to measure the volume of a rectangular prism.
- Explain that a three-dimensional shape, such as a rectangular prism, has the three dimensions of height, width, and depth. Show the rectangular prism to visualize each of these three dimensions. Point out that the dimensions for this particular prism are **5 inches** by **3 inches** by **4 inches**. m
- Next remind students that they have probably used the formula **Volume = height • width • depth** to measure volume. Demonstrate that this formula works because it is a repeated pattern of stacking the base of the object. Have students look at the picture of the rectangular prism. Then show its stacked base. m

How do we find the volume of a rectangular prism?

Before we can find the volume of a rectangular prism, we must determine the height, width, and depth. Then, to get the volume, we multiply height times width times depth. But why does that work?

Volume of a Rectangular Prism

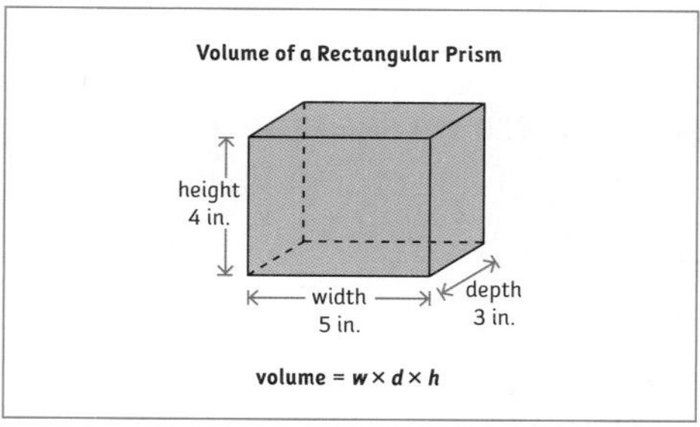

volume = $w \times d \times h$

Finding volume is like stacking cards. We stack cards from the bottom up until we reach the top. As we stack one card on top of the next card, we are creating a repeating pattern. We can think about the cards as a stack of bases.

This stack of bases helps us understand the volume formula for the rectangular prism. We find the volume by:

- Finding the area of the base.
- Multiplying the area of the base times the height.

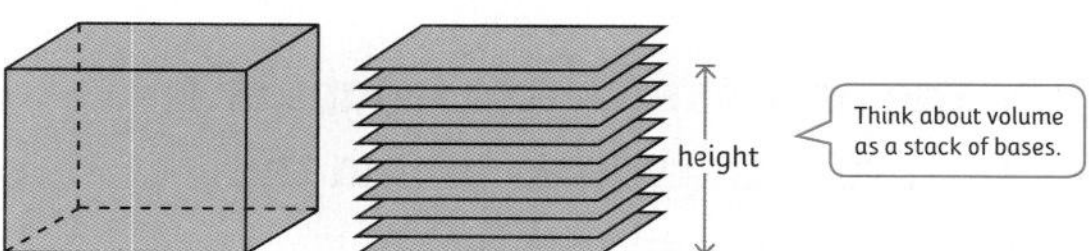

height
Think about volume as a stack of bases.

Example 1 shows how to find the volume by stacking bases.

How do we find the volume of a rectangular prism? *(continued)*

Demonstrate

- View **Example 1** where we see how to measure the volume of a rectangular prism by stacking the bases.

STEP 1

- Show the rectangular prism and its dimensions. Then demonstrate how we compute the area of the base and then stack it to the given height. m

---

STEP 2

- Show how the bases stack to a height of 4 inches. Substitute the values to find the volume of the rectangular prism. m
- Point out that this explains the formula for the rectangular prism, **Volume = height • width • depth**. Take students through the volume formula, and substitute the values for the given dimensions to get the answer of **60**. m

Check for Understanding
Engagement Strategy: Think, Think

Draw a rectangular prism with a width of **6 inches**, a depth of **2 inches**, and a height of **4 inches**. Tell students to find the volume of the shape (*48 in*^{3}). Tell students that you will call on one of them for the answer. Tell them to listen for their names. Allow time for students to compute the answer. Then call on a student. If correct, congratulate the student. Invite the student to explain the answer. If incorrect, elicit the correct answer from a volunteer.

Example 1

Find the volume of the rectangular prism.

The volume of the prism is the area of the base times the height.

Steps for Finding the Volume of a Rectangular Prism

STEP 1
Find the area of the base.
The area of the base is 5 • 3 = 15 square inches, or 15 in^2.

height 4 in.
base
width 5 in.
depth 3 in.

STEP 2
Multiply the area of the base times the height.
We can think of it as stacking these bases to a height of 4 inches.

The volume of a rectangular prism equals the area of the base times the height.

4 in.

So we multiply 15 by 4.

15 • 4 = 60

Each base has an area of 15 square inches.

This is the same as multiplying width times depth times height.

$w \times d \times h$

5 • 3 • 4 = 60

What unit do we use to measure volume?

(*Student Text,* pages 454–455)

Demonstrate

- Turn to page 454 of the *Student Text*. Point out that we have been computing volume, but we have not identified the units. Remind students that when we compute area, the units are squared units.
- Go over **Example 1**, which demonstrates the area of a rectangle measured in square units. Explain that the rectangle is a two-dimensional shape. Review how to find the area of the rectangle by multiplying the base times the height. Remind students that they can count squares to check their answer.
- Next explain that because three-dimensional objects have the added dimension of depth, volume is not measured in squared units as 2-D shapes are. We use cubic units to measure volume. Explain that the cube is the basic unit of measurement for three-dimensional objects.

Lesson 2

What unit do we use to measure volume?

We just computed the volume of the prism in the previous example as 60, but 60 what? It is not 60 square inches.

Example 1 shows how to use square units to measure a two-dimensional, or 2-D, shape such as a rectangle.

Example 1

Find the area of the rectangle.

height = 3 units
base = 5 units

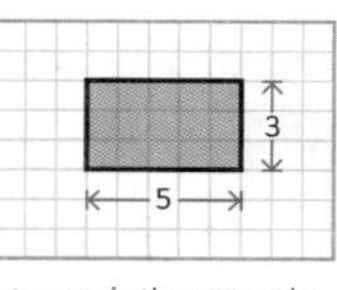

Area = 3 • 5, or 15 square units

We can check the answer by counting the squares in the rectangle.

We use *square inches* to measure two-dimensional, or 2-D, objects.

Three-dimensional objects have depth, so one way we can measure them is in **cubic inches**.

Let's use small cubes similar to dice to help us understand why the word *cubic* is in the formula for volume.

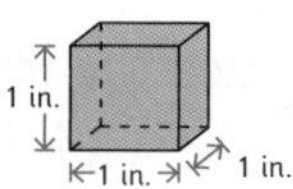

The cube is the basic unit of measurement for three-dimensional objects.

454 Unit 6 • Lesson 2

What unit do we use to measure volume? *(continued)*

Demonstrate

- Turn to page 455 of the *Student Text* and look at **Example 2**.
- Tell students that to find the volume of the prism we can find out how many cubes will fit inside it. We want to know how many **1 × 1 × 1** cubes fill a prism with the dimensions **5 × 3 × 4**.
- Help students notice the little cubes that help measure the base of the prism. If the width is 5 inches, five cubes that measure 1 × 1 × 1 can fit across. The depth is 3 inches, so three cubes that measure 1 × 1 × 1 can fit across. Explain that the base of the cube is 5 • 1 • 3, or **15 cubes**.
- Point out that to find the volume of the prism, we can stack the bases to the height. The height is four inches, so we can stack four bases to fill the prism. Explain that the volume of the prism is **5 • 3 • 4**, or **60 cubes**.
- Make sure students understand that the cube is the basic unit of measurement in a three-dimensional object. Explain that we write **cubic units**, as in^3 or cm^3.

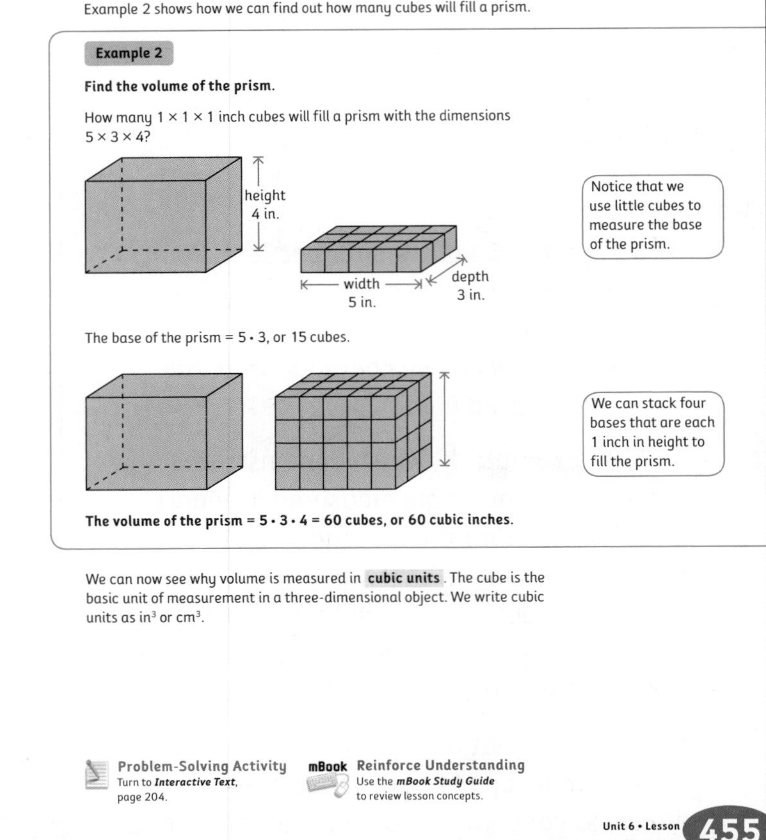
Lesson 2

Example 2 shows how we can find out how many cubes will fill a prism.

Example 2

Find the volume of the prism.

How many 1 × 1 × 1 inch cubes will fill a prism with the dimensions 5 × 3 × 4?

Notice that we use little cubes to measure the base of the prism.

The base of the prism = 5 • 3, or 15 cubes.

We can stack four bases that are each 1 inch in height to fill the prism.

The volume of the prism = 5 • 3 • 4 = 60 cubes, or 60 cubic inches.

We can now see why volume is measured in **cubic units**. The cube is the basic unit of measurement in a three-dimensional object. We write cubic units as in^3 or cm^3.

Problem-Solving Activity Turn to ***Interactive Text***, page 204.

mBook Reinforce Understanding Use the ***mBook Study Guide*** to review lesson concepts.

Unit 6 • Lesson 455

Check for Understanding
Engagement Strategy: Think, Think

Have students find the volume of a prism with the **width of 8 inches**, a **depth of 3 inches**, and a **height of 3 inches**. Tell them that you will ask questions about the volume of the prism and that you will call on one of them to answer each question after you ask it. Tell them to listen for their names. Allow time for students to think of their answers. Then call on a student.

Ask:

How many 1 × 1 × 1 cubes would fit on the base of this prism? (*24*)

How many bases can stack to fill this prism? (*3 bases*)

How many cubes or cubic inches make up the volume of this prism? (*72*)

Problem-Solving Activity

(*Interactive Text*, pages 204–205)

Have students turn to *Interactive Text*, pages 204–205.

First, students compute the volume of the cubes and rectangular prisms by using the volume formula.

Next set up stations of various-sized boxes (three or four stations) and enough sugar cubes to fill the box at each station. Divide students into groups and assign one group to each station. Rotate the groups so that students get an opportunity to fill a variety of different-sized boxes with sugar cubes.

Monitor students' work as they complete the activity.

Watch for:

- Can students substitute the dimensions into the formula?
- Can students accurately compute the volume?
- Can students carefully layer the sugar cubes in the bottom of the box to find the area of the base?
- Can students stack the sugar cubes to the height of the box to compute the volume of the shape?

Discuss the sugar cube as the cubic unit in this activity, and be sure students see how this explains the unit of measure for volume.

mBook Reinforce Understanding

Remind students that they can review lesson concepts by accessing the online *mBook Study Guide*.

Lesson 2 | Problem-Solving Activity

Name ______ Date ______

Problem-Solving Activity
Measuring Volume and Cubic Units

Use the formula Volume = height • width • depth to find the volume of the cubes and rectangular prisms.

1. The cube's volume is 64 square units.
   4 • 4 • 4 = 64
2. The rectangular prism's volume is 16 square units.
   8 • 2 • 1 = 16
3. The rectangular prism's volume is 160 square units.
   4 • 10 • 4 = 160
4. The cube's volume is 216 square units.
   6 • 6 • 6 = 216

204 Unit 6 • Lesson 2

Lesson 2 | Problem-Solving Activity

Name ______ Date ______

Problem-Solving Activity
Measuring Volume and Cubic Units

Use a cubic unit—a sugar cube—to compute the volume of a box. The sugar cube makes a good tool for measuring volume accurately since it is a unit of measure that fits neatly in the box without a lot of gaps. Once you fill the bottom of the box, record the number of sugar cubes you used. Then begin the second layer of sugar cubes, and continue until the box is filled. Record the number of layers it took to fill the box. What is the volume of the box? Is this an estimate or an exact measurement? Explain your answer.

Answers will vary. Sample answer: This is an estimate. Sugar cubes aren't all exactly the same size, and the box might not have exact measurements. There might be space for a small part of another cube, which would affect the measurements.

mBook Reinforce Understanding
Use the **mBook *Study Guide*** to review lesson concepts.

Unit 6 • Lesson 2 205

Unit 6

Homework

Go over the instructions on page 456 of the *Student Text* for each part of the homework.

Activity 1

Students solve multiplication and division problems involving integers.

Activity 2

Students evaluate expressions remembering the PEMDAS rules and the rules for integer operations.

Activity 3

Students select the answers to multiple-choice questions about units of measurement.

Activity 4 • Distributed Practice

Students continue practicing addition and subtraction of integers, PEMDAS, and operations on fractions.

Lesson 2

Homework

Activity 1

Use the integer rules for all four operations to solve the problems.

1. $-2 \cdot -3$ 6
2. $-4 + -33$ -37
3. $32 \div -8$ -4
4. $15 - -3$ 18
5. $8 \cdot -10$ -80
6. $-49 \div -7$ 7

Activity 2

Use PEMDAS and integer rules to evaluate the numeric expressions. Remember to do diagnostics first, and then go to the Algebra Toolbox.

1. $5 + (-4 + -1) - 3 \cdot -3$
2. $-3 \cdot (-2 \cdot 3) + -15$
3. $18 \div -3 \cdot 2 - 2^2$
4. $-5 + 3^2 \div -3 - -5$
5. $-12 - (-3 + -5) \cdot -2$

See Additional Answers below.

Activity 3

Select the correct measurement for each object.

1. The area of the rectangle is: b
   (a) 12 units (b) 12 units^2 (c) 12 units^3

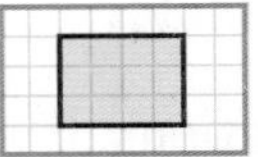

2. The length of the line is: a
   (a) 10 cm (b) 10 cm^2 (c) 10 cm^3

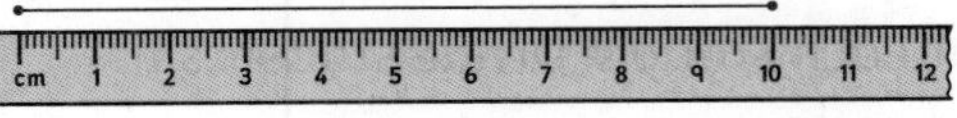

3. The volume of the cube is: c
   (a) 8 in. (b) 8 in.^{2} (c) 8 in.^{3}

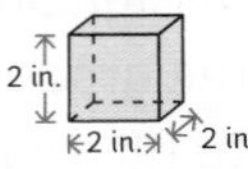

Activity 4 • Distributed Practice

Solve.

1. $-4 - -5 = a$ 1
2. $\frac{2}{3} \cdot \frac{3}{2} = b$ 1
3. $(3 \cdot 5) - 3^2 = c$ 6
4. $\frac{1}{4} \div \frac{1}{8} = d$ 2
5. $\frac{1}{4} - \frac{1}{8} = e$ $\frac{1}{8}$
6. $(8 - 12) + -3 = f$ -7
7. $-8 \div -1 = g$ 8
8. $107 + 4 \div 4 = h$ 108

456 Unit 6 • Lesson 2

Additional Answers

Activity 2

1. $5 + (-4 + -1) - 3 \cdot -3$
   $5 + -5 + -3 \cdot -3$
   $5 + -5 + 9$
   $0 + 9$
   9

2. $-3 \cdot (-2 \cdot 3) + -15$
   $-3 \cdot -6 + -15$
   $18 + -15$
   3

3. $18 \div -3 \cdot 2 - 2^2$
   $18 \div -3 \cdot 2 - 4$
   $-6 \cdot 2 + -4$
   $-12 + -4$
   -16

4. $-5 + 3^2 \div -3 - -5$
   $-5 + 9 \div -3 - -5$
   $-5 + -3 - -5$
   $-8 + 5$
   -3

5. $-12 - (-3 + -5) \cdot -2$
   $-12 - -8 \cdot -2$
   $-12 - 16$
   -28

Lesson 3 ▸ Evaluating Algebraic Expressions

Problem Solving: ▸ Bases and the Volume of Prisms

Lesson Planner

Skills Maintenance

Substitution

Building Number Concepts: ▸ Evaluating Algebraic Expressions

Students learn two different methods for evaluating algebraic equations. We begin by reminding students that only like terms can be combined. Next we introduce another method of evaluating algebraic equations by substituting values for variables to find many different instances of the pattern represented in the expression.

Objective

Students will evaluate algebraic expressions by combining like terms and by substituting values for the variables.

Problem Solving: ▸ Bases and the Volume of Prisms

Stacking bases helps students see which volume formulas are the same for different three-dimensional objects.

Objective

Students will find the volume of three-dimensional objects by stacking the bases.

Homework

Students evaluate expressions by substituting a value for the variable and then simplifying, simplify first and then substitute the value for the variable to evaluate the expression, and find the volume of the objects given the base and the height. In Distributed Practice, students continue practicing addition and subtraction of integers, PEMDAS, and operations on fractions.

Lesson 3 | Skills Maintenance

Name ______________________ Date ______________________

Skills Maintenance
Substitution

Activity 1

Substitute the value for the variable in each of the expressions, then solve the problems.

Model	Evaluate $3m$ if $m = -2$. $3 \cdot -2 = -6$

1. Evaluate $4x$ if $x = 10$. 40
2. Evaluate $-2 - w$ if $w = -5$. 3
3. Evaluate $-3a$ if $a = -2$. 6
4. Evaluate $4 - h$ if $h = -5$. 9
5. Evaluate $n \div -5$ if $n = -45$. 9

206 Unit 6 • Lesson 3

Skills Maintenance

Substitution

(*Interactive Text*, page 206)

Activity 1

Students substitute the value for the variable and evaluate the expressions.

Building Number Concepts:
▶ Evaluating Algebraic Expressions

How do we evaluate algebraic expressions?
(*Student Text*, pages 457–460)

Connect to Prior Knowledge
Begin by reminding students about the difference between numeric expressions and algebraic expressions. Put the following on the board or overhead:

$$3 - 4 + 7 - -2$$

$$3 - 4 + x - -2$$

Have students evaluate the first expression. Next ask students how they would evaluate the second expression. Point out that because there is a variable, and we do not know its value, we cannot evaluate this expression; we can only simplify it.

Link to Today's Concept
Tell students that in today's lesson, we use two methods to evaluate algebraic expressions.

Demonstrate
Engagement Strategy: Teacher Modeling
Demonstrate how to simplify the algebraic expressions in one of the following ways:

mBook: Use the *mBook Teacher Edition* for *Student Text*, pages 457–458. m

Overhead Projector: Reproduce the algebraic expressions on a transparency, and modify as discussed.

Board: Copy the algebraic expressions on the board, and modify as discussed.

- Remind students that we can only combine like terms, and explain what that means if students need clarification. Go over how to simplify the expression **$3x + 2 + 4x + 7$** in **Example 1**.

STEP 1

- Begin by using the commutative property to arrange the terms. m

STEP 2

- Combine the like terms: $3x + 4x = 7x$ and $2 + 7 = 9$. m

STEP 3

- Combine the number terms. m
- Point out that the answer **$7x + 9$** is as simple as this expression gets without knowing the value of x.

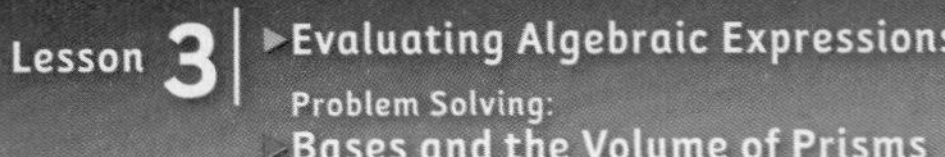
Lesson 3 | ▶Evaluating Algebraic Expressions
Problem Solving:
▶Bases and the Volume of Prisms

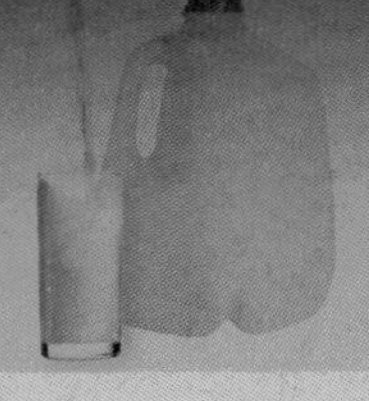

▶Evaluating Algebraic Expressions

How do we evaluate algebraic expressions?

We learned to simplify algebraic expressions by using properties such as the commutative property. When we work with these expressions, we must remember that we can only combine like terms.

Example 1 shows how we combine variable terms with variable terms, and number terms with number terms.

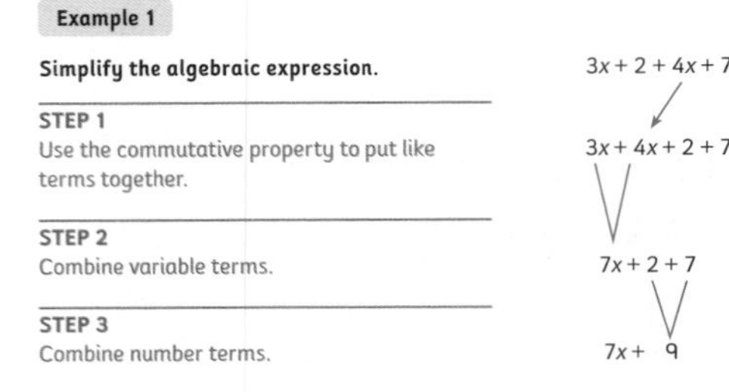
Example 1

Simplify the algebraic expression.	$3x + 2 + 4x + 7$
STEP 1 Use the commutative property to put like terms together.	$3x + 4x + 2 + 7$
STEP 2 Combine variable terms.	$7x + 2 + 7$
STEP 3 Combine number terms.	$7x + 9$

Our solution is $7x + 9$.
We cannot combine variable terms and number terms in this expression.

Unit 6 • Lesson 3 457

Demonstrate

- Remind students that we are able to substitute any value for the variable and show many different instances of the pattern.
- Go through **Example 2**, which shows how to substitute different values for *c* in the expression ***c* + 7**, and evaluate the expression for many different instances of the pattern. Remind students that this is a way to describe any number that is 7 more than *c*. m
- Go through each of the substitutions to show the different instances of the pattern. m

Check for Understanding
Engagement Strategy: Pair/Share

Put students into pairs. Write the expression ***x* + 5** on the board. Have each partner substitute two different values for *x*. Then have partners check each other's answers. Invite student volunteers to share their work. Record different answers on the board for students to see the different instances of the pattern represented by the expression.

Discuss

Call students' attention to the Power Concept, and point out that it will be helpful as they complete the activities.

When we evaluate an algebraic expression, we substitute a value for the variable.

We evaluate algebraic expressions by substituting a number for a variable.

With algebra, we can substitute any value for the variable to show the pattern represented by the expression.

Example 2 shows how to evaluate the algebraic expression $c + 7$ using different values for c.

Example 2

Evaluate the expression $c + 7$ using different values for c.

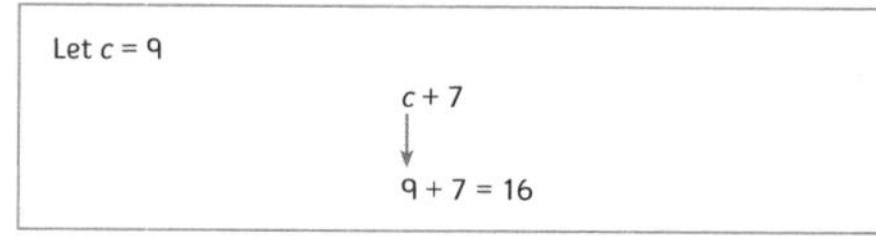

Let $c = 9$

$c + 7$

$9 + 7 = 16$

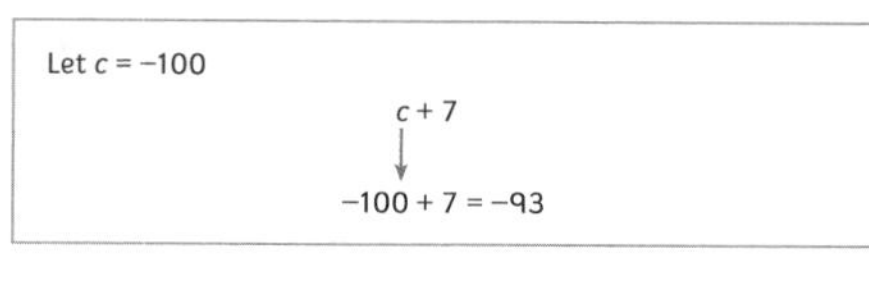

Let $c = -100$

$c + 7$

$-100 + 7 = -93$

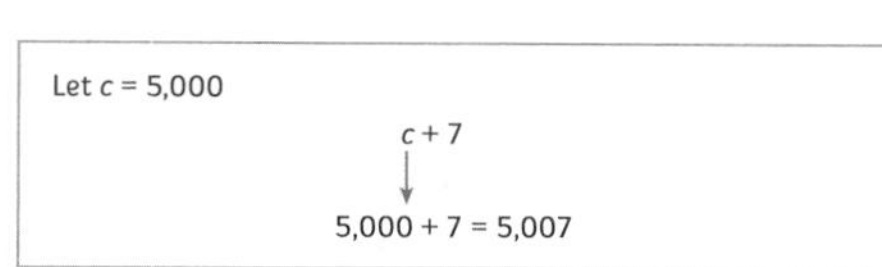

Let $c = 5{,}000$

$c + 7$

$5{,}000 + 7 = 5{,}007$

When we evaluate an algebraic expression, we substitute a value for the variable.

How do we evaluate algebraic expressions? *(continued)*

Demonstrate

- Turn to page 459 of the *Student Text,* and read through the material at the top of the page. Explain that in algebra, we have to be able to work problems in a flexible way. Some expressions are more complex and require substitution and simplification to evaluate them.
- Explain that we have choices about this in algebra. We can simplify the expression first and then substitute the value for the variable to evaluate it, or we can substitute the value for the variable and then simplify it.
- Go over **Example 3**, which demonstrates two different methods for evaluating a complex expression that requires both simplification and substitution.
- Method 1 shows how to simplify the expression **3*m* + 5 + 2*m* − 1** and then substitute the value for the variable. Walk through each of the steps of simplifying the expression by using the commutative property and then combining like terms. The simplified expression is **5*m* + 4**.
- Next substitute the value of **2** for ***m***, and use PEMDAS to solve the problem. The solution is **14**.

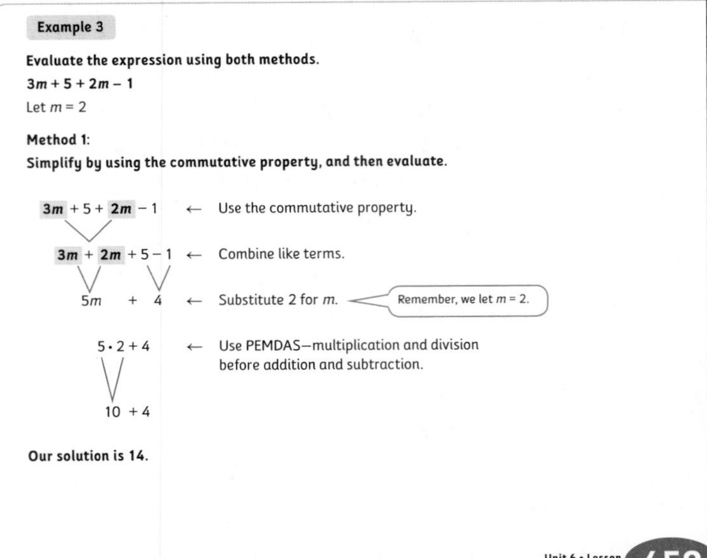

Lesson 3

We evaluated the expression in Example 2 using only one step. The expression was already simplified, so we just substituted different values.

More complicated expressions may require that we simplify the expression first and then evaluate it. Simplifying the expression first can make substitution easier when we evaluate the expression.

Example 3 shows two different ways to solve the same problem.

- In Method 1, we simplify the expression first and then substitute.
- In Method 2, we substitute and evaluate without simplifying.

We get the same answer using either method.

Example 3

Evaluate the expression using both methods.

3*m* + 5 + 2*m* − 1

Let *m* = 2

Method 1:

Simplify by using the commutative property, and then evaluate.

$3m + 5 + 2m - 1$ ← Use the commutative property.

$3m + 2m + 5 - 1$ ← Combine like terms.

$5m + 4$ ← Substitute 2 for *m*. (Remember, we let *m* = 2.)

$5 \cdot 2 + 4$ ← Use PEMDAS—multiplication and division before addition and subtraction.

$10 + 4$

Our solution is 14.

Unit 6 • Lesson 459

Demonstrate

- Turn to page 460 of the *Student Text*, and demonstrate the second method of substituting and then evaluating an expression without simplifying.
- Walk through each of the steps of substituting the value of **2** for ***m***. Then use PEMDAS to complete all the operations and get the solution of **14**. Point out that both Method 1 and Method 2 give the same answer.
- Tell students that it is important they know how to evaluate this expression in both these ways. Students need to be able to work problems in a flexible way in algebra.

Check for Understanding

Engagement Strategy: Pair/Share

Divide the class into pairs. Write the expression **$4a + 1 + 2a - 3$** on the board. Write **Let $a = 4$** on the board (*22*). Have one partner solve the problem using Method 1. Have the other partner solve the problem using Method 2. Have partners compare their answers. Invite student volunteers to explain their groupings.

Reinforce Understanding

For additional practice with the two methods of evaluating algebraic expressions, use the following:

$5x + 1 + 5 + -2x$, Let $x = 2$ (*12*)

$7 + 2n - 3$, Let $n = 5$ (*14*)

$6 - m + 8 + 4m$, Let $m = 3$ (*23*)

Method 2:
Substitute first and then evaluate.

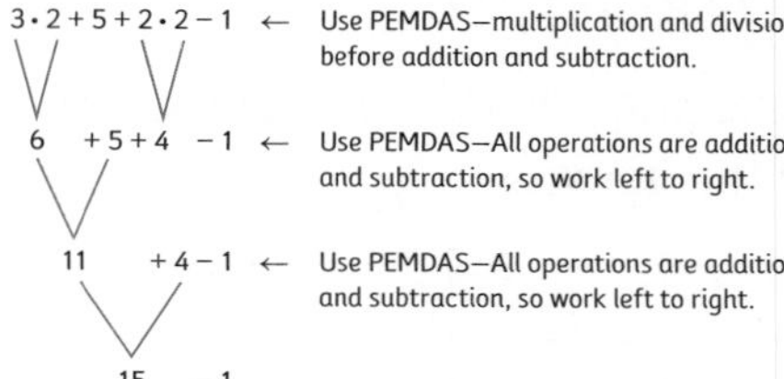

$3m + 5 + 2m - 1$ ← Substitute 2 for *m*.

$3 \cdot 2 + 5 + 2 \cdot 2 - 1$ ← Use PEMDAS—multiplication and division before addition and subtraction.

$6 + 5 + 4 - 1$ ← Use PEMDAS—All operations are addition and subtraction, so work left to right.

$11 + 4 - 1$ ← Use PEMDAS—All operations are addition and subtraction, so work left to right.

$15 - 1$

Our solution is 14.
The solution is the same using either method.

Working a math problem two different ways requires us to be flexible in our thinking. We must think about the problem and then use the right tools from the Algebra Toolbox.

Apply Skills
Turn to ***Interactive Text***, page 207.

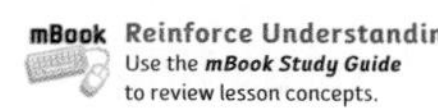
Reinforce Understanding
Use the ***mBook Study Guide*** to review lesson concepts.

Apply Skills
(*Interactive Text*, page 207)

Have students turn to page 207 in the *Interactive Text*, and complete the activity.

Activity 1

Students evaluate expressions using two different methods. Monitor students' work as they complete the activity.

Watch for:

- Can students simplify the expression and then substitute the value of the variable to evaluate it?
- Can students substitute the value for the variable in the expression and then simplify it to evaluate it?

mBook **Reinforce Understanding**
Remind students that they can review lesson concepts by accessing the online *mBook Study Guide*.

Lesson 3 | Apply Skills

Name ______________________ Date ______________

Apply Skills
Substitution and Evaluating Algebraic Expressions

Activity 1

Evaluate each of the expressions using two methods.

In Method 1, simplify and then substitute. In Method 2, substitute and then simplify.

1. Evaluate $3x + 7 + 2x + 10$ for $x = -2$.
   Method 1: Simplify and then substitute.
   Answer $5x + 17 = 5 \cdot -2 + 17 = -10 + 17 = 7$
   Method 2: Substitute and then simplify.
   Answer $3 \cdot -2 + 7 + 2 \cdot -2 + 10 = -10 + 17 = 7$
2. Evaluate $-4 - x - -3 + 2x$ for $x = 1$.
   Method 1: Simplify and then substitute.
   Answer $x - 1 = 1 - 1 = 0$
   Method 2: Substitute and then simplify.
   Answer $-4 - 1 - -3 + 2(1) = -5 - -3 + 2 = -2 + 2 = 0$
3. Evaluate $-x + 2x - 5 \cdot -3 + -x$ for $x = -1$.
   Method 1: Simplify and then substitute.
   Answer $0 - -15 = 15$
   Method 2: Substitute and then simplify.
   Answer $- -1 + 2(-1) - 5 \cdot -3 + 1 = -1 - 5 \cdot -3 + 1 = -1 + 15 + 1 = 15$

Unit 6

Unit 6 • Lesson 3 207

Problem Solving:
▶ Bases and the Volume of Prisms

How do we stack bases to find volume?

(*Student Text*, pages 461–464)

Connect to Prior Knowledge

Remind students that the bases of the three-dimensional objects are the areas of the two-dimensional shape that is at the bottom of the object.

Link to Today's Concept

In today's lesson we find the volume of prisms and cylinders.

Demonstrate

- Explain to students that we can express the volume formula for many shapes in the same way we did with cubes. We multiply the base (area of the two-dimensional shape at the base of the three-dimensional object) by the height. We write it this way: **Volume = Base • height**.
- Make sure students understand that Base (with a capital B) is the area of the base of the prism that has two dimensions. This is also called the area of the base.
- Show students the drawings of the bases of each of the prisms. Explain that the base of a cylinder is a circle, the base of a triangular prism is a prism, and the base of a cube is a square. If possible, show students everyday objects, and show the bases. For example, show a can for a cylinder, and show students that the base is a circle.
- Show students the stacks of bases that make up the volume of the three-dimensional shapes.

Lesson 3

▶Problem Solving: Bases and the Volume of Prisms

How do we stack bases to find volume?

Stacking bases helps us understand the ways in which volume formulas are the same for many different three-dimensional objects.

We will use Volume = Base • height as a basic part of the formula. We capitalize the word *Base* because we are talking about the area of the base of the object, which has two dimensions—depth and width. Once we find this two-dimensional base, we multiply it by the height of the object. These drawings show bases for prisms.

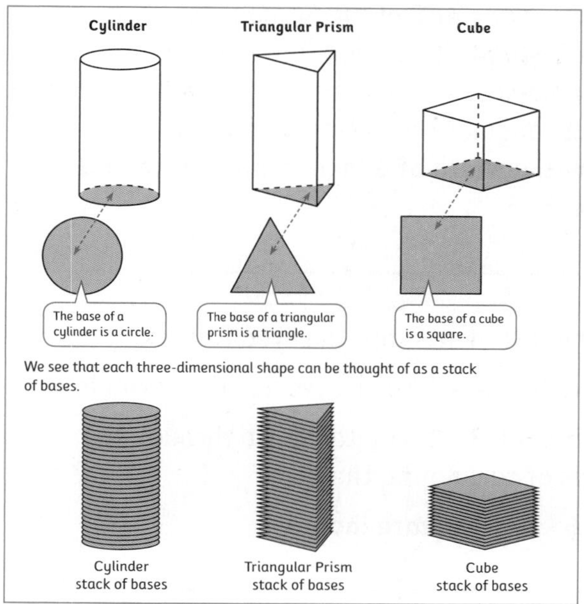

Unit 6 • Lesson 461

How do we stack bases to find volume? *(continued)*

Demonstrate

- Turn to page 462 of the *Student Text*. Use **Example 1** to show how we stack triangle-shaped bases to find the volume of a triangular prism with a **height of 12 inches**, a **width of 6 inches**, and **depth of 3 inches**.

STEP 1

- Remind students that the area formula for a triangle is $A = \frac{1}{2}(b \cdot h)$. We use this formula to find the Base (capital B). Go through the steps of calculating the Base: $\frac{1}{2} \cdot 6 \cdot 3 = 9$ **square inches.**

STEP 2

- Then multiply the Base by the height of the triangular prism: **9 • 12 = 108 cubic inches**. The volume of the triangular prism is 108 cubic inches.

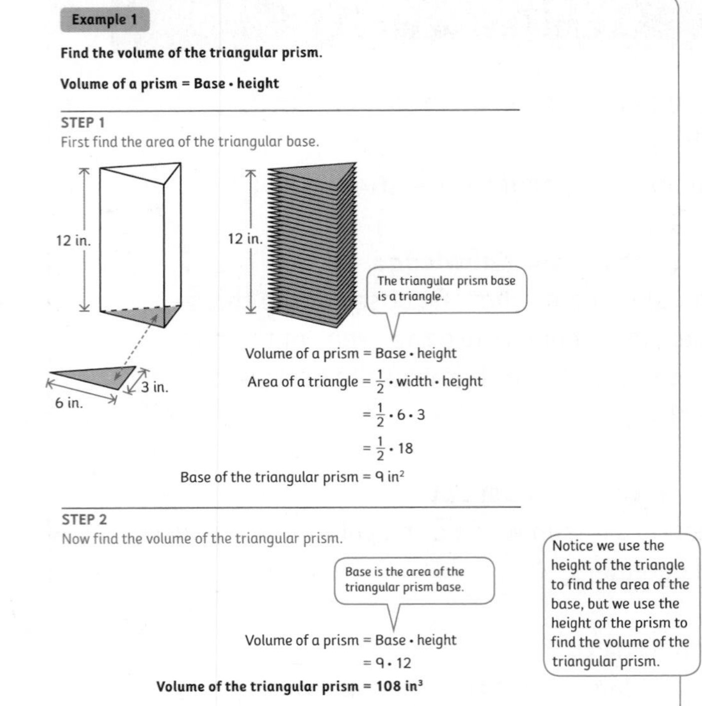

Lesson 3
We can use the same kind of thinking to find the volume of a triangular prism. We see in Example 1 that we can stack triangle-shaped bases to make the triangular prism.
Example 1
Find the volume of the triangular prism.
Volume of a prism = Base • height
STEP 1
First find the area of the triangular base.
12 in.
12 in.
6 in.
3 in.
The triangular prism base is a triangle.
Volume of a prism = Base • height
Area of a triangle = 1/2 • width • height
= 1/2 • 6 • 3
= 1/2 • 18
Base of the triangular prism = 9 in²
STEP 2
Now find the volume of the triangular prism.
Base is the area of the triangular prism base.
Volume of a prism = Base • height
= 9 • 12
Volume of the triangular prism = 108 in³
Notice we use the height of the triangle to find the area of the base, but we use the height of the prism to find the volume of the triangular prism.
462 Unit 6 • Lesson 3

Demonstrate

- Use **Example 2** on page 463 of the *Student Text* to demonstrate how to find the volume of a cylinder by finding the Base and multiplying by the height.

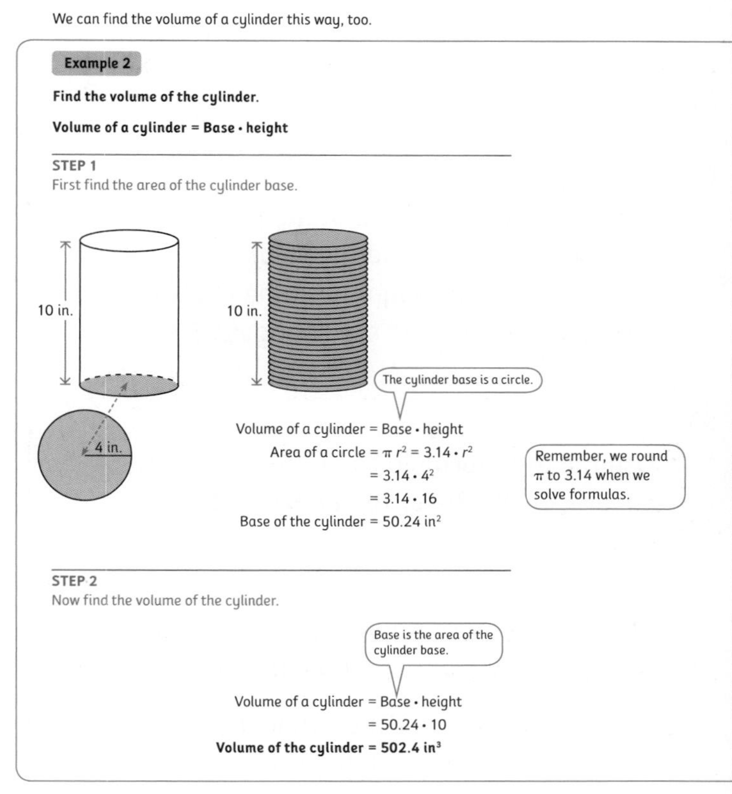

Lesson 3
We can find the volume of a cylinder this way, too.
Example 2
Find the volume of the cylinder.
Volume of a cylinder = Base • height
STEP 1
First find the area of the cylinder base.
10 in.
10 in.
4 in.
The cylinder base is a circle.
Volume of a cylinder = Base • height
Area of a circle = π r² = 3.14 • r²
= 3.14 • 4²
= 3.14 • 16
Base of the cylinder = 50.24 in²
Remember, we round π to 3.14 when we solve formulas.
STEP 2
Now find the volume of the cylinder.
Base is the area of the cylinder base.
Volume of a cylinder = Base • height
= 50.24 • 10
Volume of the cylinder = 502.4 in³
Unit 6 • Lesson
463

STEP 1

- Point out that we use the area formula for a circle ($A = \pi r^2$) to find the Base of the circle, **50.24 square inches**.

STEP 2

- Then multiply this result by the height of the cylinder to find the volume, **502.4 cubic inches**. Point out that the height of the cylinder base is different from the height of the cylinder.

How do we stack bases to find volume? *(continued)*

Demonstrate

- Turn to page 464 of the *Student Text* and use **Example 3** to find the volume of a cube. Walk students through the same process as with the cylinder and the triangular prism.

STEP 1

- Use the area formula to find the area of a square, or the Base, **16 square inches**.

STEP 2

- Multiply the Base times the height to get the volume of the cube, **64 cubic inches**.
- Be sure students see the connection between the three formulas and stacking bases.

Check for Understanding
Engagement Strategy: Think Tank

Draw a triangular prism on the board with a width of **8 inches**, depth of **2 inches**, and a height of **10 inches**.

Distribute strips of paper to students and have them write their name on their papers. Have students first find the Base (*8 square inches*) and then multiply it by the height to find the volume of the prism (*80 inches cubed*). Put all the papers into a container when students are finished. Draw a paper from the container, and share the answer with the class. Invite the student to walk through the steps of the solution.

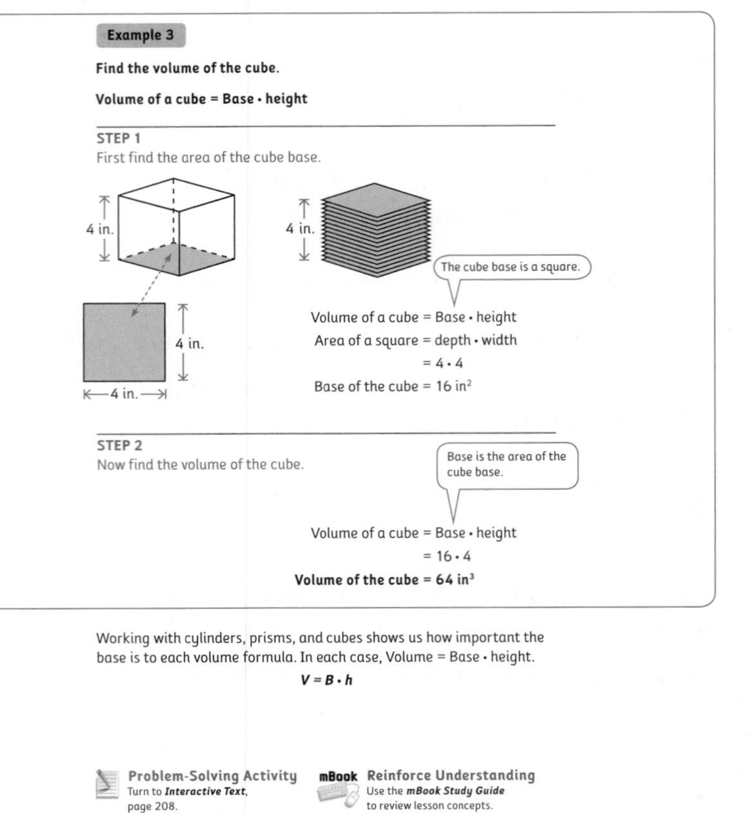

Lesson 3
Example 3
Find the volume of the cube.
Volume of a cube = Base • height
STEP 1
First find the area of the cube base.
4 in.
4 in.
The cube base is a square.
4 in.
4 in.
Volume of a cube = Base • height
Area of a square = depth • width
= 4 • 4
Base of the cube = 16 in²
STEP 2
Now find the volume of the cube.
Base is the area of the cube base.
Volume of a cube = Base • height
= 16 • 4
Volume of the cube = 64 in³
Working with cylinders, prisms, and cubes shows us how important the base is to each volume formula. In each case, Volume = Base • height.
V = B • h
Problem-Solving Activity
Turn to Interactive Text, page 208.
mBook Reinforce Understanding
Use the mBook Study Guide to review lesson concepts.
464
Unit 6 • Lesson 3

Problem-Solving Activity
(*Interactive Text*, pages 208–209)

Have students turn to pages 208–209 in the *Interactive Text*, and complete the activity. Distribute scissors and tape and have students cut out and put together the three-dimensional shapes.

Have them use a ruler to measure the dimensions of the Bases so that they can compute the areas, or the Bases. Then have them measure the height and multiply that by the Base to compute the volume.

Monitor students' work as they complete the activity.

Watch for:

- Can students build the shapes?
- Can students measure the parts of the shapes accurately to compute the volume?
- Did students compute the volume correctly?

Be sure students have adequate time to create, analyze, and compute volume for all these shapes.

Reinforce Understanding
Remind students that they can review lesson concepts by accessing the online *mBook Study Guide*.

Lesson 3 | Problem-Solving Activity

Name ______________________ Date ______________

Problem-Solving Activity
Bases and the Volume of Prisms

Use the paper models on the next page to find the area of three different prisms. When you put the prisms together, they should look like this:

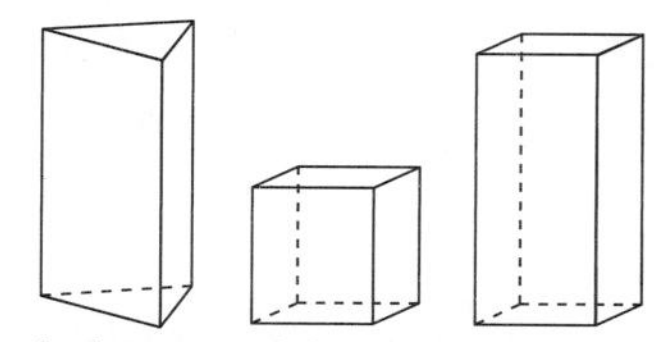

Use a metric ruler to measure the base and height of each prism. Measure the dimensions to the closest centimeter and round your measurement, if necessary. Remember to use these basic formulas for the base:
Area of a triangle = $\frac{1}{2} \cdot b \cdot h$
Area of a square or rectangle = $b \cdot h$

	Triangular Prism	Cube	Rectangular Prism
Base	4.5 sq. cm	9 sq. cm	9 sq. cm
Height	6 cm	3 cm	6 cm
Volume	27 cu. cm	27 cu. cm	54 cu. cm

208 Unit 6 • Lesson 3

Lesson 3 | Problem-Solving Activity

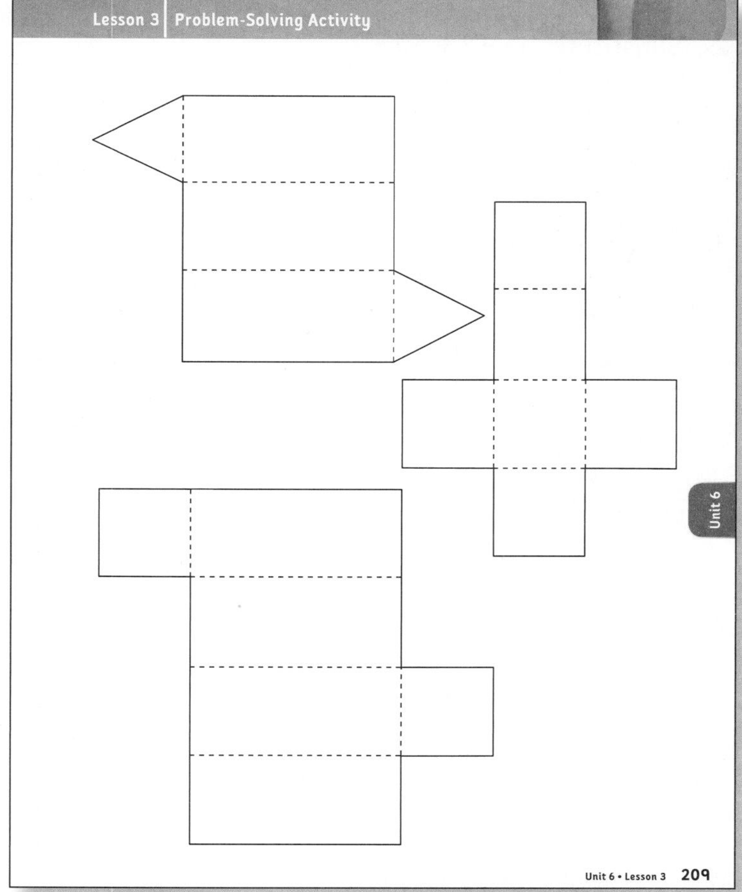

Unit 6

Unit 6 • Lesson 3 209

Homework

Go over the instructions on pages 465–466 of the *Student Text* for each part of the homework.

Activity 1

Students evaluate expressions by substituting a value for the variable and then simplifying.

Activity 2

Students simplify first and then substitute the value for the variable to evaluate the expression.

Additional Answers

Activity 1

1. Substitute: −5 + 10 + −5 + 5
   Simplify: **−5 + 10** + −5 + 5
   5 + −5 + 5
   0 + 5
   5
2. Substitute: 4 • −2 + −2 −3
   Simplify: **4 • −2** + −2 −3
   −8 + −2 −3
   −10 −3
   −13
3. Substitute: 14 + 2 • 10 + 21
   Simplify: 14 + **2 • 10** + 21
   14 + 20 + 21
   34 + 21
   55

Homework

Activity 1

Evaluate the algebraic expressions by substituting the given value for the variable and then simplifying.

Model $x + 2x + 3x$ for $x = 2$

Answer: Substitute: 2 + **2 • 2** + 3 • 2
Simplify: 2 + 4 + **3 • 2**
2 + 4 + 6
6 + 6 = 12

1. Evaluate $x + 10 + x + 5$ for $x = -5$.
2. Evaluate $4w + w - 3$ for $w = -2$.
3. Evaluate $14 + 2z + 21$ for $z = 10$.

See Additional Answers below.

Activity 2

Evaluate the expressions by simplifying them and then substituting the value for the variable.

Model $2x - x + 3 + 2x$ for $x = -1$

Answer: Simplify: $2x - x + 2x + 3$
$x + 2x + 3$
$3x + 3$
Substitute: 3 • −1 + 3
−3 + 3 = 0

1. Evaluate $2x + 3 + 4x + 5$ for $x = -5$.
2. Evaluate $w + w - 3$ for $w = -2$.
3. Evaluate $z + 3z + 8$ for $z = 10$.

1. Simplify: $2x + 4x + 3 + 5$
   $2x + 4x + 3 + 5$
   $6x + 3 + 5$
   $6x + 8$
   Substitute: 6 • −5 + 8
   −30 + 8
   −22
2. Simplify: $w + w - 3$
   $2w - 3$
   Substitute: 2 • −2 − 3
   −4 − 3
   −7
3. Simplify: $z + 3z + 8$
   $4z + 8$
   Substitute: 4 • 10 + 8
   40 + 8
   48

Homework

Go over the instructions on page 466 of the *Student Text* for each part of the homework.

Activity 3

Students find the volume of the objects given the Base and the height of each.

Activity 4 • Distributed Practice

Students practice addition and subtraction of integers, PEMDAS, and operations on fractions.

Lesson 3

Homework

Activity 3

Find the volume for each object given the Base and the height.

1. 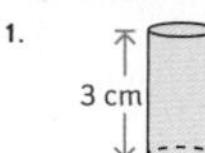

If the Base (the area of the circle) is 6 cm², what is the volume of the cylinder? 18 cm³

2. 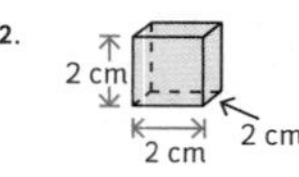

If the Base (the area of the square) is 4 cm², what is the volume of the cube? 8 cm³

3. 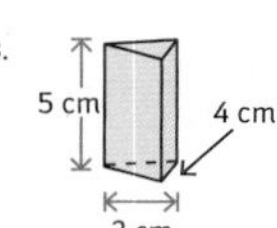

If the Base (the area of the triangle) is 6 cm², what is the volume of the triangular prism? 30 cm³

4. 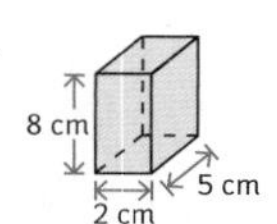

If the Base (the area of the rectangle) is 10 cm², what is the volume of the rectangular prism? 80 cm³

Activity 4 • Distributed Practice

Solve.

1. $6 - -2 = a$ 8
2. $\frac{2}{5} \cdot \frac{1}{2} = b$ $\frac{1}{5}$
3. $\frac{1}{3} \div \frac{1}{6} = c$ 2
4. $(3 \cdot 6) - 4^2 = d$ 2
5. $(8 \cdot 2) \div 4 = e$ 4
6. $\frac{1}{4} - -\frac{2}{4} = f$ $\frac{3}{4}$
7. $-7 + -1 + 7 = g$ −1
8. $16 \div 4 \div 4 = h$ 1

466 Unit 6 • Lesson 3

Lesson 4 | ▶Writing and Evaluating Expressions

Lesson Planner

Vocabulary Development

consecutive numbers
number grid

Skills Maintenance

Number Patterns With Consecutive Numbers, Volume of Common Prisms

Building Number Concepts:

▶ Writing and Evaluating Expressions

Students learn how to describe patterns of numbers using variables. Algebraic expressions are general statements about a pattern and substituting a value for the variable describes a specific instance of the pattern. We demonstrate how to use a number line and a number grid to show consecutive numbers and write algebraic expressions to represent consecutive numbers.

Objective

Students will write algebraic expressions using variables to describe patterns of numbers.

Homework

Students use properties to help them decide answers to problems, choose an example that tells the property, and tell what shape the Base is when you examine the volume of the shapes. In Distributed Practice students practice addition and subtraction of integers, PEMDAS, and operations on fractions.

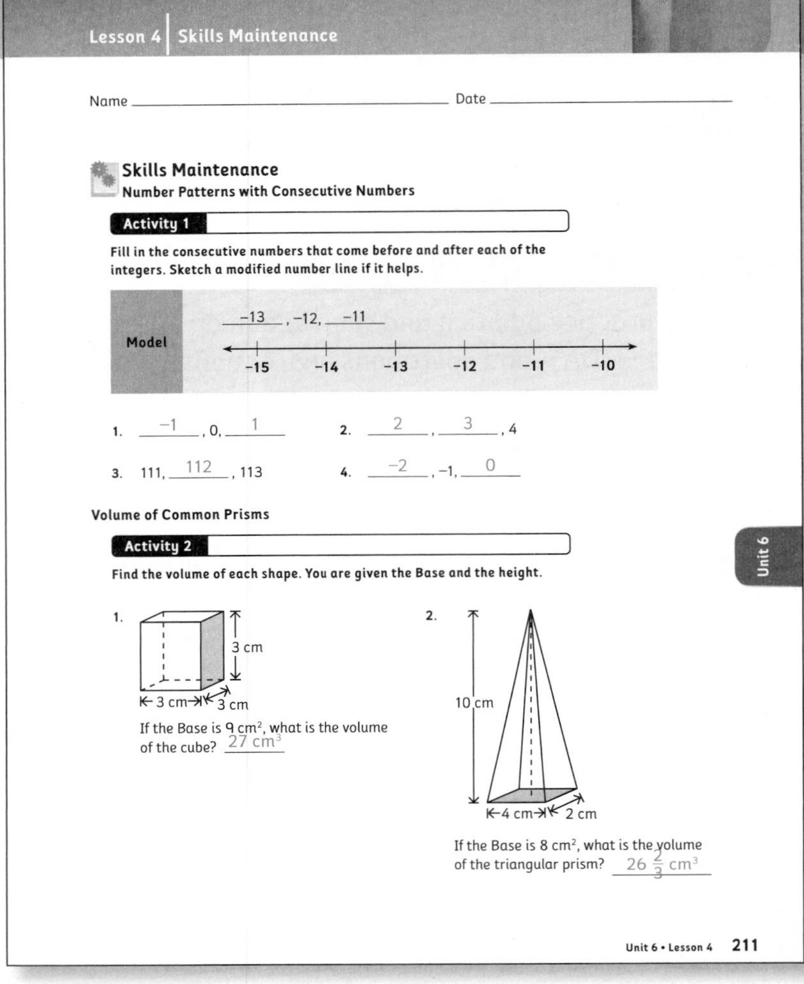

Lesson 4 | Skills Maintenance

Name ______________________ Date ______________

Skills Maintenance
Number Patterns with Consecutive Numbers

Activity 1

Fill in the consecutive numbers that come before and after each of the integers. Sketch a modified number line if it helps.

Model −13, −12, −11

−15 −14 −13 −12 −11 −10

1. −1, 0, 1
2. 2, 3, 4
3. 111, 112, 113
4. −2, −1, 0

Volume of Common Prisms

Activity 2

Find the volume of each shape. You are given the Base and the height.

1. 3 cm; 3 cm; 3 cm
If the Base is 9 cm², what is the volume of the cube? 27 cm^3

2. 10 cm; 4 cm; 2 cm
If the Base is 8 cm², what is the volume of the triangular prism? $26\frac{2}{3} \text{ cm}^3$

Unit 6

Unit 6 • Lesson 4 211

Skills Maintenance

Number Patterns With Consecutive Numbers, Volume of Common Prisms

(*Interactive Text*, page 211)

Activity 1

Students fill in the missing numbers in a series of three consecutive numbers.

Activity 2

Students find the volume of a cube and a triangular prism given the Base and the height.

Building Number Concepts:
▶ Writing and Evaluating Expressions

How do we describe patterns of numbers using variables?

(*Student Text*, pages 467–468)

Connect to Prior Knowledge

Begin by going over Activity 1 in the Skills Maintenance portion of the lesson. Remind students that **consecutive numbers** are numbers that are right next to each other on a number line.

Link to Today's Concept

Tell students that in today's lesson, we will link consecutive numbers with expressions.

Demonstrate

Engagement Strategy: Teacher Modeling

Demonstrate how to find consecutive numbers on a number line in one of the following ways:

mBook: Use the *mBook Teacher Edition* for *Student Text*, pages 467–468.

Overhead Projector: Reproduce the number line and number grid on Transparency 6, and modify as discussed.

Board: Copy the number line and number grid on the board, and modify as discussed.

- Start by discussing the idea that algebraic expressions are general statements about a pattern. When we substitute values for variables, we are finding specific instances.
- Show the number line, and point out that the numbers −2, −1, and 0 are consecutive numbers. They are next to each other on the number line. m

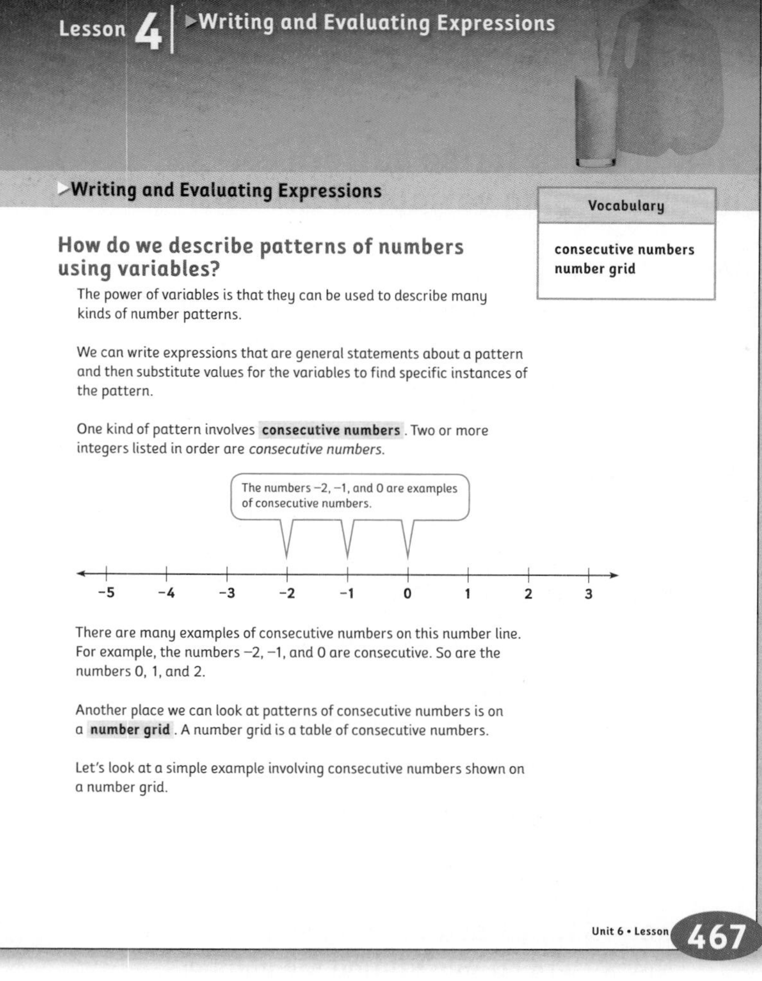

Lesson 4 | ▶Writing and Evaluating Expressions

▶Writing and Evaluating Expressions

How do we describe patterns of numbers using variables?

The power of variables is that they can be used to describe many kinds of number patterns.

We can write expressions that are general statements about a pattern and then substitute values for the variables to find specific instances of the pattern.

One kind of pattern involves **consecutive numbers**. Two or more integers listed in order are *consecutive numbers.*

The numbers −2, −1, and 0 are examples of consecutive numbers.
−5 −4 −3 −2 −1 0 1 2 3

There are many examples of consecutive numbers on this number line. For example, the numbers −2, −1, and 0 are consecutive. So are the numbers 0, 1, and 2.

Another place we can look at patterns of consecutive numbers is on a **number grid**. A number grid is a table of consecutive numbers.

Let's look at a simple example involving consecutive numbers shown on a number grid.

Vocabulary

consecutive numbers
number grid

Unit 6 • Lesson 467

- Ask students to find another set of three consecutive numbers. Some possible answers might be 0, 1, and 2 or −5, −4, and −3.
- Tell students we can also find consecutive numbers on a **number grid**. m

How do we describe patterns of numbers using variables? *(continued)*

Demonstrate

- Explain that in a number grid, we are looking at the specific instance of the pattern involving the consecutive numbers 6, 7, and 8.
- Tell students that if $x = 6$, then $x + 1 = 7$ and $x + 2 = 8$. The three consecutive numbers are represented by the series of expressions: x, $x + 1$, and $x + 2$. m
- Explain that now that we have a general statement about the relationship of three consecutive numbers, we can apply it to any three consecutive numbers.
- Point out **Example 1**, which demonstrates this pattern for two other series of three consecutive numbers: **18**, **19**, and **20** as well as **12**, **13**, and **14**. Have students check the pattern by substituting the numbers into the expressions. Be sure students see that this general pattern applies to any instances of three consecutive numbers.

Check for Understanding
Engagement Strategy: Pair/Share

Put students into pairs. Have each partner select a group of three consecutive numbers and give them to the other partner to check. Have students substitute numbers into the expressions x, $x + 1$, and $x + 2$ to check the pattern. Have partners check each other's work.

First, let's write expressions for the three consecutive numbers 6, 7, and 8, where $x = 6$.

1	2	3	4	5	6	7	8	9	10
11	12	13	14	15	16	17	18	19	20

If $x = 6$, we can write 7 as $x + 1$. That means we can write 8 as $x + 2$.

Our three consecutive numbers on a number grid can be written using the expressions:

x $x + 1$ $x + 2$ — Expressions for three consecutive numbers

When variables describe patterns, we can use the same expressions to describe three other consecutive numbers on a number grid.

Example 1 shows us that the pattern works when we substitute the variable with the value for the first of three consecutive numbers.

Example 1

Look at the three consecutive numbers in the grids. Show the pattern:

x $x + 1$ $x + 2$

In this grid, the three consecutive numbers are 18, 19, and 20.

1	2	3	4	5	6	7	8	9	10
11	12	13	14	15	16	17	18	19	20

When we substitute 18 for x, we see that the pattern works.

$x = 18$
$x + 1 = 18 + 1$, or 19
$x + 2 = 18 + 2$, or 20

In this grid, the three consecutive numbers are 12, 13, and 14.

1	2	3	4	5	6	7	8	9	10
11	12	13	14	15	16	17	18	19	20

When we substitute 12 for x, we see the pattern works with these numbers too.

$x = 12$
$x + 1 = 12 + 1$, or 13
$x + 2 = 12 + 2$, or 14

What other expressions can be used to describe the general pattern?

(*Student Text*, pages 469–470)

Demonstrate

- Turn to page 469 and read through the material at the top of the page. Tell students that the power of variables is the ability to use them flexibly and represent situations using many different expressions.
- Point out that we have been looking at series of three consecutive numbers using expressions, where x was always the first number in the series. Tell students this is just one way to represent the pattern.
- Explain that another way we represent the pattern is to make the x the middle number in the series or the last number in the series.
- Go over **Example 1**, which shows several different expressions for the same pattern by assigning the variable to a different number in the series of consecutive numbers **46**, **47**, and **48**.
- Demonstrate the first model of substituting the first number, **46**, in the set of expressions. Show that the expressions work for this set of consecutive numbers.

What other expressions can be used to describe the general pattern?

Substituting variables to make a statement about a pattern is an important tool in algebra. When we use variables, we can describe the same pattern of numbers using different expressions.

Let's look at another series of three consecutive numbers. In the last example, we used a variable to represent the first of the three numbers.

In Example 1, we will show that we can use many different expressions to describe three consecutive numbers.

Example 1

Use models to represent three consecutive numbers.

Our three consecutive numbers are 46, 47, and 48.

Model 1:

Substitute x for the first number in the series of consecutive numbers.

$x = 46$

Our expression for our three consecutive numbers is:

$x \quad x + 1 \quad x + 2$

31	32	33	34	35	36	37	38	39	40
41	42	43	44	45	46	47	48	49	50

We see that our expression works. →

$x = 46$
$x + 1 = 46 + 1$, or 47
$x + 2 = 46 + 2$, or 48

Now let's represent these three consecutive numbers another way.

What other expressions can be used to describe the general pattern? *(continued)*

Demonstrate

- Turn to page 470 of the *Student Text,* and demonstrate Model 2. We substitute the second number in the series for *x*.
- Point out that the expression now changes, but the expression still represents the consecutive numbers. Now, the expressions are $x-1$, x, and $x+1$, if $x = 47$.
- Next demonstrate the third possibility by letting *x* equal the last number in the series, **48**. The expressions change once again, but they still represent the consecutive numbers. Now the expressions are $x-2$, $x-1$, and x.
- Be sure students see that even though the expressions look different, they all represent the same pattern of numbers.

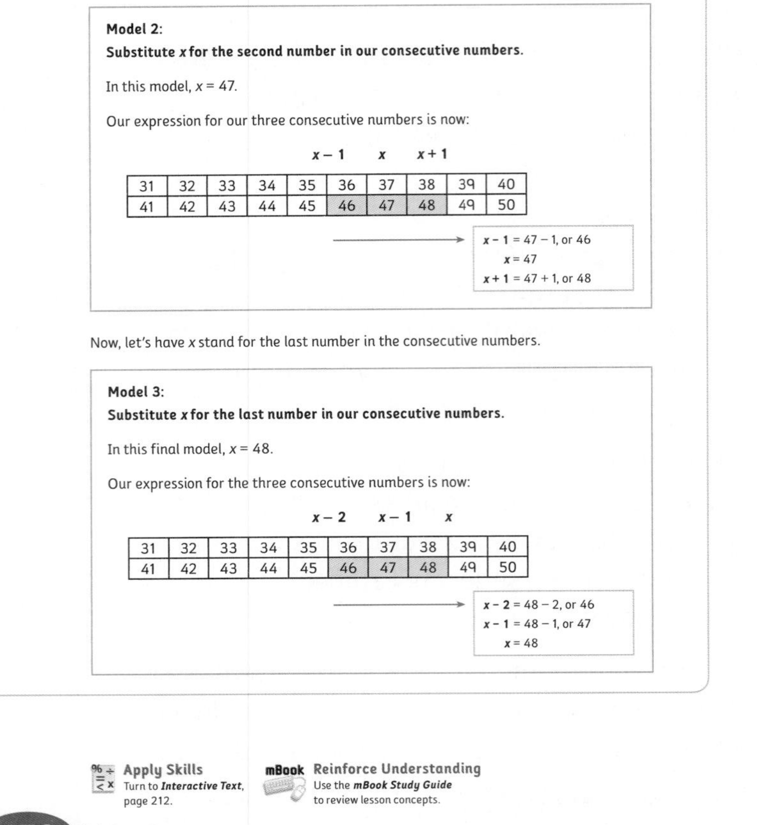

Model 2:
Substitute *x* for the second number in our consecutive numbers.

In this model, $x = 47$.

Our expression for our three consecutive numbers is now:

$x - 1$ x $x + 1$

31	32	33	34	35	36	37	38	39	40
41	42	43	44	45	46	47	48	49	50

$x - 1 = 47 - 1$, or 46
$x = 47$
$x + 1 = 47 + 1$, or 48

Now, let's have *x* stand for the last number in the consecutive numbers.

Model 3:
Substitute *x* for the last number in our consecutive numbers.

In this final model, $x = 48$.

Our expression for the three consecutive numbers is now:

$x - 2$ $x - 1$ x

31	32	33	34	35	36	37	38	39	40
41	42	43	44	45	46	47	48	49	50

$x - 2 = 48 - 2$, or 46
$x - 1 = 48 - 1$, or 47
$x = 48$

Apply Skills Turn to *Interactive Text*, page 212.

mBook Reinforce Understanding Use the *mBook Study Guide* to review lesson concepts.

Check for Understanding
Engagement Strategy: Look About

Write the consecutive numbers **21**, **22**, and **23** on the board. Have students use all three models to check the different expressions in Example 1. Students should write their steps and solutions in large writing on a piece of paper or a dry erase board. When the students finish their work, they should hold up their answer for everyone to see.

If students are not sure about the answer, prompt them to look about at the other students' solutions to help with their thinking. Review the answers after all students have held up their solutions.

Apply Skills

(*Interactive Text*, pages 212–214)

Have students turn to pages 212–214 in the *Interactive Text*, and complete the activities.

Activity 1

Students find three consecutive numbers using x, $x + 1$, and $x + 2$ on the number line and use integer rules to show that the pattern is true.

Activity 2

Students find three consecutive numbers on a number grid and show that the pattern is true.

Monitor students' work as they complete the activities.

Watch for:

- Can students find a unique set of three consecutive numbers for each part of the activity on the number line and on the number grid?
- Do students know which number to substitute into the expressions to test the general pattern?

Lesson 4 | Apply Skills

Name ______________________ Date ______________

Apply Skills

Writing and Evaluating Expressions

Activity 1

Test the general pattern for consecutive numbers represented by the expressions x, $x + 1$, and $x + 2$ by selecting three consecutive numbers from the number line. Make the first number x.

−7 −6 −5 −4 −3 −2 −1 0 1

1. Select three consecutive numbers from the number line.

   What are your three consecutive numbers? Answers will vary.

   ______, ______, ______

   Prove that the general pattern x, $x + 1$, and $x + 2$ is true for these three numbers. Answers will vary.

   x = ______ $x + 1$ = ______ $x + 2$ = ______

2. Select a different set of three consecutive numbers from the number line.

   What are your three consecutive numbers? Answers will vary.

   ______, ______, ______

   Prove that the general pattern x, $x + 1$, and $x + 2$ is true for these three numbers. Answers will vary.

   x = ______ $x + 1$ = ______ $x + 2$ = ______

212 Unit 6 • Lesson 4

Lesson 4 | Apply Skills

Name ______________________ Date ______________

Activity 2

Test the general pattern for consecutive numbers represented by the expressions x, $x + 1$, and $x + 2$ by selecting three consecutive numbers from the number grid. Make the first number x.

1	2	3	4	5	6	7	8	9	10
11	12	13	14	15	16	17	18	19	20
21	22	23	24	25	26	27	28	29	30
31	32	33	34	35	36	37	38	39	40
41	42	43	44	45	46	47	48	49	50

1. Select three consecutive numbers from the number grid.

   What are your three consecutive numbers? Answers will vary.

   ______, ______, ______

   Prove that the general pattern x, $x + 1$, and $x + 2$ is true for the three numbers you selected. Answers will vary.

   x = ______ $x + 1$ = ______ $x + 2$ = ______

2. Select a different set of three consecutive numbers from the number grid.

   What are your three consecutive numbers? Answers will vary.

   ______, ______, ______

   Prove that the general pattern x, $x + 1$, and $x + 2$ is true for these three numbers. Answers will vary.

   x = ______ $x + 1$ = ______ $x + 2$ = ______

Unit 6

Unit 6 • Lesson 4 213

Have students turn to page 214 in the *Interactive Text*. Read the instructions together.

Activity 3

Students find a set of three numbers in the shaded portion of three grids they are given. Then students write three different sets of expressions to represent these three numbers.

Monitor students' work as they complete the activities.

Watch for:

- Do students see the pattern in each grid?
- Can students show this pattern using algebraic expressions?

mBook

Reinforce Understanding

Remind students that they can review lesson concepts by accessing the online *mBook Study Guide*.

Lesson 4 | Apply Skills

Name ______________________ Date ______________

Activity 3

Select three shaded numbers from the grid. Write three different sets of expressions for these numbers.

1.

1	2	3	4	5	6	7	**8**	9	10
11	12	13	14	15	16	17	**18**	19	20
21	22	23	24	25	26	27	**28**	29	30
31	32	33	34	35	36	37	**38**	39	40
41	42	43	44	45	46	47	**48**	49	50
51	52	53	54	55	56	57	**58**	59	60
61	62	63	64	65	66	67	**68**	69	70
71	72	73	74	75	76	77	**78**	79	80
81	82	83	84	85	86	87	**88**	89	90
91	92	93	94	95	96	97	**98**	99	100

$x = 38$ Answers will vary.

$x - 10 = 28$

$x - 20 = 18$

2.

1	2	3	4	5	6	7	8	9	10
11	12	13	14	15	16	17	18	19	20
21	**22**	23	24	25	26	27	28	29	30
31	32	**33**	34	35	36	37	38	39	40
41	42	43	**44**	45	46	47	48	49	50
51	52	53	54	**55**	56	57	58	59	60
61	62	63	64	65	**66**	67	68	69	70
71	72	73	74	75	76	**77**	78	79	80
81	82	83	84	85	86	87	**88**	89	90
91	92	93	94	95	96	97	98	**99**	100

$x = 11$ Answers will vary.

$x \cdot 2 = 22$

$x \cdot 3 = 33$

mBook Reinforce Understanding
Use the **mBook** ***Study Guide*** to review lesson concepts.

214 Unit 6 • Lesson 4

Homework

Go over the instructions on pages 471–472 of the *Student Text* for each part of the homework.

Activity 1

Students tell the specific three numbers described by the expressions.

Activity 2

Students write three different expressions to represent each set of three numbers.

Lesson 4

Homework

Activity 1

Tell the three numbers described in each problem by substituting values in the expressions given to represent the pattern.

Model If $y = 4$ and the pattern is described by the expressions $y - 1$, y, and $y + 1$, what are the three numbers?
Answer: 3, 4, and 5

1. If $y = 4$ and the pattern is described by the expressions y, $y + 2$, and $y + 4$, what are the three numbers? 4, 6, and 8
2. If $z = 100$ and the pattern is described by the expressions $z - 10$, z, and $z + 10$, what are the three numbers? 90, 100, and 110
3. If $a = -5$ and the pattern is described by the expressions $a - 1$, a, and $a + 1$, what are the three numbers? −6, −5, and −4
4. If $b = 130$ and the pattern is described by the expressions $b - 2$, $b - 1$, and b, what are the three numbers? 128, 129, and 130

Activity 2

Write three different expressions to show the same general pattern for each problem.

Model 34, 35, and 36
Answer:
Method 1: If $x = 34$, the series is x, $x + 1$, and $x + 2$.
Method 2: If $x = 35$, the series is $x - 1$, x, and $x + 1$.
Method 3: If $x = 36$, the series is $x - 2$, $x - 1$, and x.

1. 10, 20, 30 2. 55, 66, 77 3. −1, 0, 1

1. Method 1: If $x = 10$, the series is x, $x + 10$, and $x + 20$.
Method 2: If $x = 20$, the series is $x - 10$, x, and $x + 10$.
Method 3: If $x = 30$, the series is $x - 20$, $x - 10$, and x.
2. Method 1: If $x = 55$, the series is x, $x + 11$, and $x + 22$.
Method 2: If $x = 66$, the series is $x - 11$, x, and $x + 11$.
Method 3: If $x = 77$, the series is $x - 22$, $x - 11$, and x.
3. Method 1: If $x = -1$, the series is x, $x + 1$, and $x + 2$.
Method 2: If $x = 0$, the series is $x - 1$, x, and $x + 1$.
Method 3: If $x = 1$, the series is $x - 2$, $x - 1$, and x.

Unit 6 • Lesson 471

Homework

Go over the instructions on page 472 of the *Student Text* for each part of the homework.

Activity 3

Students tell two sets of possible numbers that are represented by the pattern given.

Activity 4 • Distributed Practice

Students practice addition and subtraction of integers, PEMDAS, and operations on fractions.

Homework

Activity 3

Tell two different sets of numbers that may be represented by the expressions.

Model $x - 5, x, x + 5$
Answer: Set 1: 5, 10, 15
Set 2: 45, 50, 55

Answers will vary.

1. $y - 20, y - 10, y$ Set 1: 10, 20, 30 Set 2: 25, 35, 45
2. $z - 10, z, z + 10$ Set 1: 10, 20, 30 Set 2: 45, 55, 65
3. $w, w + 2, w + 4$ Set 1: 2, 4, 6 Set 2: 30, 32, 34
4. $m - 100, m, m + 100$ Set 1: 102, 202, 302 Set 2: 450, 550, 650

Activity 4 • Distributed Practice

Solve.

1. $(5 \cdot 2) \div 5 = a$ 2
2. $\frac{2}{4} \div \frac{3}{2} = b$ $\frac{1}{3}$
3. $\frac{1}{3} \div \frac{1}{3} = c$ 1
4. $4^2 + 6 \div 2 = d$ 19
5. $-4 \cdot -3 = e$ 12
6. $\frac{1}{4} \cdot \frac{1}{4} = f$ $\frac{1}{16}$
7. $-6 + -1 \cdot -6 = g$ 0
8. $5 \cdot -5 \cdot -2 = h$ 50

Lesson 5 | ▶Commonsense Algebraic Properties

Monitoring Progress: ▶Quiz 1

Lesson Planner

Vocabulary Development

multiplicative
additive

Skills Maintenance

Writing Different Expressions to Describe a Pattern, Calculating Volume

Building Number Concepts:
▶ Commonsense Algebraic Properties

Students look at several properties of numbers. These are formal rules that help evaluate expressions. Many of these properties are commonsense properties that we used informally. These are the properties that have to do with moving and grouping numbers and properties about 1 and 0.

Objective

Students evaluate expressions using different properties of numbers.

Monitoring Progress:
▶ Quiz 1

Distribute the quiz, and remind students that the questions involve material covered over the previous lessons in the unit.

Homework

Students select the multiple-choice answer that completes the example of a commonsense property, select the example that matches the property, and identify the shape that makes up the base of a three-dimensional object. In Distributed Practice students do addition and subtraction of integers, PEMDAS, and operations on fractions.

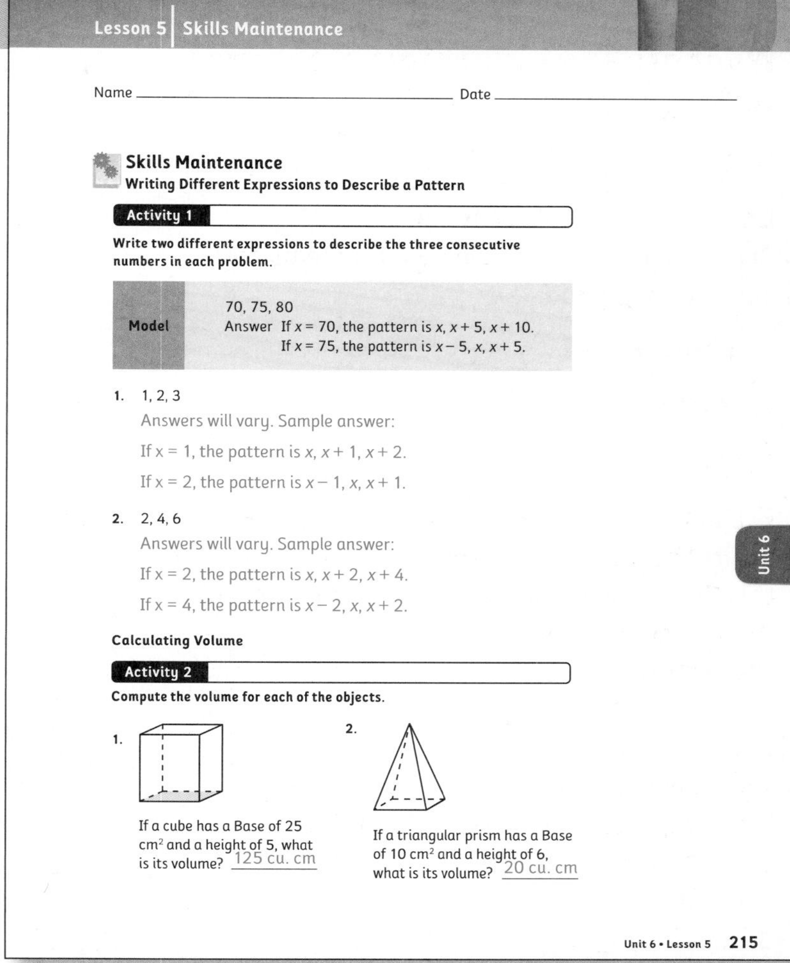
Lesson 5 | Skills Maintenance

Name ______________________ Date ______________

Skills Maintenance
Writing Different Expressions to Describe a Pattern

Activity 1

Write two different expressions to describe the three consecutive numbers in each problem.

Model	70, 75, 80 Answer If $x = 70$, the pattern is x, $x + 5$, $x + 10$. If $x = 75$, the pattern is $x - 5$, x, $x + 5$.

1. 1, 2, 3
   Answers will vary. Sample answer:
   If $x = 1$, the pattern is x, $x + 1$, $x + 2$.
   If $x = 2$, the pattern is $x - 1$, x, $x + 1$.
2. 2, 4, 6
   Answers will vary. Sample answer:
   If $x = 2$, the pattern is x, $x + 2$, $x + 4$.
   If $x = 4$, the pattern is $x - 2$, x, $x + 2$.

Calculating Volume

Activity 2

Compute the volume for each of the objects.

1. If a cube has a Base of 25 cm^2 and a height of 5, what is its volume? 125 cu. cm
2. If a triangular prism has a Base of 10 cm^2 and a height of 6, what is its volume? 20 cu. cm

Unit 6

Unit 6 • Lesson 5 215

Skills Maintenance

Writing Different Expressions to Describe a Pattern, Calculating Volume
(*Interactive Text*, page 215)

Activity 1

Students write two different expressions that describe each set of three numbers.

Activity 2

Students find the volume of a cube and a triangular prism given the dimensions.

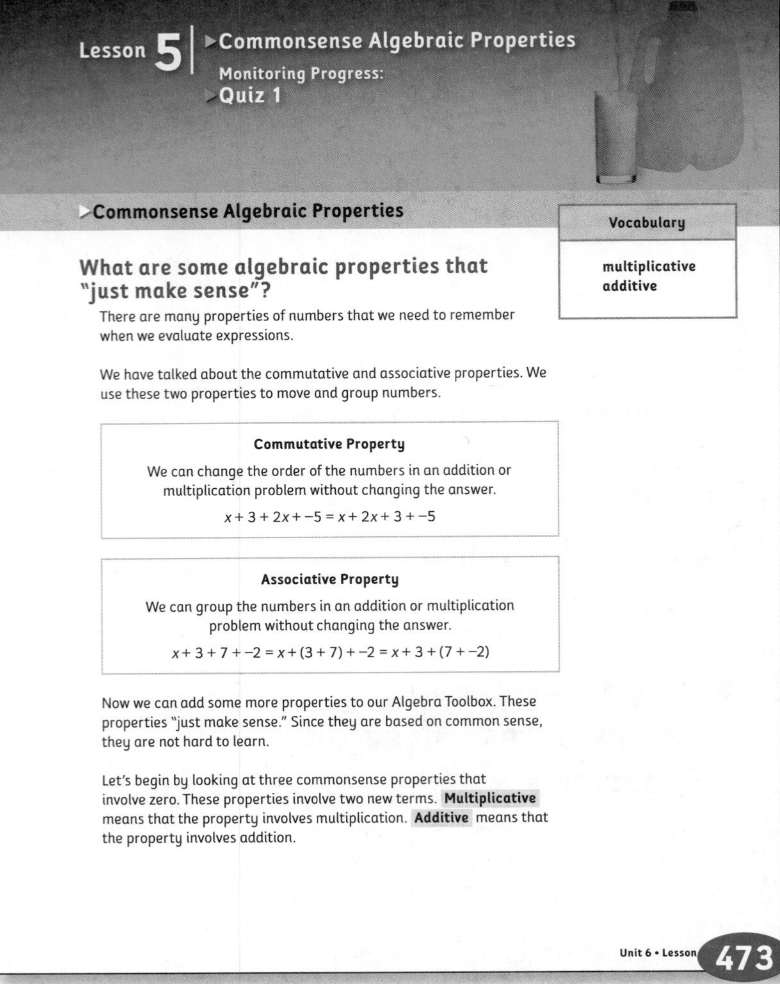

Lesson 5 ▸Commonsense Algebraic Properties

Monitoring Progress:
▸Quiz 1

▸Commonsense Algebraic Properties

Vocabulary
multiplicative **additive**

What are some algebraic properties that "just make sense"?

There are many properties of numbers that we need to remember when we evaluate expressions.

We have talked about the commutative and associative properties. We use these two properties to move and group numbers.

Commutative Property

We can change the order of the numbers in an addition or multiplication problem without changing the answer.

$x + 3 + 2x + -5 = x + 2x + 3 + -5$

Associative Property

We can group the numbers in an addition or multiplication problem without changing the answer.

$x + 3 + 7 + -2 = x + (3 + 7) + -2 = x + 3 + (7 + -2)$

Now we can add some more properties to our Algebra Toolbox. These properties "just make sense." Since they are based on common sense, they are not hard to learn.

Let's begin by looking at three commonsense properties that involve zero. These properties involve two new terms. **Multiplicative** means that the property involves multiplication. **Additive** means that the property involves addition.

Unit 6 • Lesson 473

Building Number Concepts:
▸ Commonsense Algebraic Properties

What are some algebraic properties that "just make sense"?
(*Student Text*, pages 473–475)

Connect to Prior Knowledge

Begin by putting the following problems on the board or overhead:

5,000 + 0 = ?

20,947 • 1 = ?

3,000,000 • 0 = ?

Explain that these seem like difficult problems at first because they involve large numbers, but they each have features about them that make them easy to solve. Have students solve the problems.

Link to Today's Concept

Tell students that in today's lesson, they learn important properties that have commonsense features.

Build Vocabulary

Explain to students that the new properties are **multiplicative**, meaning they involve multiplication, or **additive**, meaning they involve addition.

Demonstrate

Engagement Strategy: Teacher Modeling

Demonstrate commonsense algebraic properties in one of the following ways:

mBook: Use the *mBook Teacher Edition* for *Student Text*, pages 473–474.

Overhead Projector: Reproduce examples of commonsense algebraic properties and shapes on a transparency, and modify as discussed.

Board: Reproduce examples of commonsense algebraic properties and shapes on the board, and modify as discussed.

- Review the commutative and associative properties. Remind students that they used these properties to move and group numbers and variables when they combine like terms to simplify expressions. These properties are commonsense properties, and we use them all the time.
- Tell students that there are other commonsense properties that we will add to our Algebra Toolbox today. One group of properties that are commonsense properties have to do with the number zero.

Demonstrate

- Continue presenting the different commonsense algebraic properties.
- Point out that the next three properties all involve zero. Tell students that the names of the properties make them seem difficult because they are formal names, but the properties themselves are just common sense. Point out that it's helpful to use variables to describe the general pattern of these properties.
- Present the Identity Property of Addition (**anything plus zero is itself**), and go through the examples. m
- Emphasize the general pattern $n + 0 = n$. m
- Present the Multiplicative Property of zero (**anything times zero is zero**), and go through the examples. m
- Emphasize the general pattern $n \cdot 0 = 0$. m
- Present the Additive Inverse Property (**a number plus its opposite is zero**), and go through each example. m
- Emphasize the general pattern: $n + -n = 0$. m
- Next present commonsense properties about the number one. Tell students that the names of these properties sound formal, but the properties themselves are just common sense. As you go through the properties, stop to emphasize the example for each property that is the general pattern.
- Present the Identity Property of Multiplication (**anything times one is itself.**) m
- Emphasize the general pattern: $n \cdot 1 = n$. m
- Present the Multiplicative Inverse Property (**a number times its reciprocal is one**). m

Identity Property of Addition
Any number plus zero equals the same number.
$-3 + 0 = -3$ $\quad 0 + 5 = 5$
$\frac{1}{2} + 0 = \frac{1}{2}$ $\quad n + 0 = n$

Multiplicative Property of Zero
Any number times zero equals zero.
$-3 \cdot 0 = 0$ $\quad 0 \cdot 5 = 0$
$\frac{1}{2} \cdot 0 = 0$ $\quad n \cdot 0 = 0$

Additive Inverse Property
Any number plus its inverse equals zero.
$3 + -3 = 0$ $\quad -5 + 5 = 0$
$\frac{1}{2} + -\frac{1}{2} = 0$ $\quad n + -n = 0$

Each of these properties contains a statement that uses a variable. The statement shows the general pattern of the property.

Now let's look at two commonsense properties that have to do with the number one.

Identity Property of Multiplication
Any number times one equals itself.
$-3 \cdot 1 = -3$ $\quad \frac{1}{2} \cdot 1 = \frac{1}{2}$
$1 \cdot 5 = 5$ $\quad n \cdot 1 = n$

Multiplicative Inverse Property or Reciprocal Property
Any number times its inverse equals one.
$\frac{1}{2} \cdot \frac{2}{1} = 1$ $\quad -3 \cdot -\frac{1}{3} = 1$ $\quad \frac{1}{5} \cdot 5 = 1$
$n \cdot \frac{1}{n} = 1$ $\quad \frac{a}{b} \cdot \frac{b}{a} = 1$

- Go through each example. Emphasize the general patterns $n \cdot \frac{1}{n} = 1$ and $\frac{a}{b} \cdot \frac{b}{a} = 1$. m
- Make sure students see that there are two examples of the multiplicative inverse property because of the unique feature of the reciprocal of a whole number.

What are some algebraic properties that "just make sense"? *(continued)*

Demonstrate

- Turn to page 475 of the *Student Text*, and continue presenting the Multiplicative Inverse Property.
- Point out that any whole number can be rewritten as a fraction with 1 in the denominator. Therefore, its reciprocal is written as 1 over the number. This is worth noting as a special case of the inverse property.
- Note that this special case occurs quite frequently in algebra where we often have whole-number coefficients that we need to find the reciprocal of. For now, it is important to make the distinction and help students see that both general statements describe reciprocals.

Explain

Tell students that we now add these common-sense properties to our Algebra Toolbox because we use them very often when we evaluate or simplify expressions in algebra. They are very important tools.

Check for Understanding
Engagement Strategy: Pair/Share

Put students in pairs, and have students come up with additional examples for each of the properties. Have one partner come up with an example of the Commutative Property, and the other partner come up with an example of the Associate Property. Then have one partner come up with an example for each of the properties involving zero, and the other partner come up with an example of each of the properties involving one. Have partners check each other's work. Invite volunteers to share their examples of each of the properties. Record their answers on the board.

Lesson 5

Let's add these new properties to our Algebra Toolbox. We have grouped them in ways that are easier to remember than the properties shown in the examples.

Number Properties

Properties about moving and grouping numbers

- Commutative Property: $a + b = b + a$
  $a \cdot b = b \cdot a$
- Associative Property: $a + (b + c) = (a + b) + c$
  $a \cdot (b \cdot c) = (a \cdot b) \cdot c$

Properties about zero

- Multiplicative Property of Zero: $n \cdot 0 = 0$
- Additive Inverse Property of Zero: $n + -n = 0$
- Identity Property of Addition: $n + 0 = n$

Properties about one

- Identity Property of Multiplication: $x \cdot 1 = x$
- Reciprocal Property: $\frac{a}{b} \cdot \frac{b}{a} = 1$
  $n \cdot \frac{1}{n} = 1$

Apply Skills
Turn to ***Interactive Text***, page 216.

Reinforce Understanding
Use the ***mBook Study Guide*** to review lesson concepts.

Apply Skills
(*Interactive Text*, pages 216)

Have students turn to *Interactive Text*, page 216, and complete the activity.

Activity 1

Students are given three examples of a commonsense property, and they write the general pattern using variables and then name the property. Tell students they can look back in the *Student Text* if they do not remember the names. Monitor students' work as they complete the activity.

Watch for:

- Can students write the property using variables in a general statement?
- Can students name the property?

Reinforce Understanding
Remind students that they can review lesson concepts by accessing the online *mBook Study Guide*.

Lesson 5 | Apply Skills

Name ______________ Date ______________

Apply Skills
Commonsense Algebraic Properties

Activity 1

Write a general statement that describes the commonsense property shown by the examples in each problem. Then write the name of that property.

Model	$5 + 0 = 5$ $2.5 + 0 = 2.5$ $\frac{1}{2} + 0 = \frac{1}{2}$ General Statement $n + 0 = n$ Name of Property Additive Identity Property

1. $6 \cdot 1 = 6$ $\frac{1}{4} \cdot 1 = \frac{1}{4}$ $37.5 \cdot 1 = 37.5$
   General Statement $n \cdot 1 = n$
   Name of Property Identity Property of Multiplication
2. $3 \cdot 0 = 0$ $\frac{4}{5} \cdot 0 = 0$ $100.12 \cdot 0 = 0$
   General Statement $n \cdot 0 = 0$
   Name of Property Multiplicative Property of 0
3. $2 \cdot \frac{1}{2} = 1$ $5 \cdot \frac{1}{5} = 1$ $75 \cdot \frac{1}{75} = 1$
   General Statement $n \cdot \frac{1}{n} = 1$
   Name of Property Multiplicative Inverse Property
4. $3 + -3 = 0$ $\frac{2}{3} + -\frac{2}{3} = 0$ $1.25 + -1.25 = 0$
   General Statement $n + -n = 0$
   Name of Property Additive Inverse Property
5. $\frac{2}{3} \cdot \frac{3}{2} = 1$ $\frac{4}{5} \cdot \frac{5}{4} = 1$ $\frac{100}{200} \cdot \frac{200}{100} = 1$
   General Statement $\frac{n}{m} \cdot \frac{m}{n} = 1$
   Name of Property Multiplicative Inverse Property or Reciprocal Property

mBook **Reinforce Understanding**
Use the mBook *Study Guide* to review lesson concepts.

216 Unit 6 • Lesson 5

Monitoring Progress:
▶ Quiz 1 • Form A

Assess
Quiz 1

- Administer Quiz 1 Form A in the *Assessment Book*, pages 53–54. (If necessary, retest students with Quiz 1 Form B from the *mBook Teacher Edition* following differentiation.)

Students	Assess	Differentiate
	Day 1	Day 2
All	Quiz 1 *Form A*	
Scored 80% or above		Extension
Scored Below 80%		Reinforcement

Differentiate

- Review Quiz 1 Form A with class.
- Identify students for Extension or Reinforcement.

Extension

For those students who score 80 percent or better, provide the On Track! Activities from Unit 6, Lessons 1–5, from the *mBook Teacher Edition.*

Reinforcement

For those students who score below 80 percent, provide additional support in one of the following ways:

- Have students access the online tutorial provided in the *mBook Study Guide.*
- Have students complete the Interactive Reinforcement Exercises for Unit 6, Lessons 1–4, in the *mBook Study Guide.*
- Provide teacher-directed reteaching of unit concepts.

Name __________ Date __________

Form A

Monitoring Progress
Expressions

Part 1

Solve.

1. $5 \cdot -3$ <u>−15</u>
2. $-10 \div 5$ <u>−2</u>
3. $-6 + -2$ <u>−8</u>
4. $-3 - 1$ <u>−4</u>
5. $5 \cdot -6$ <u>−30</u>
6. $18 \div -3$ <u>−6</u>
7. $-4 \cdot -8$ <u>32</u>
8. $7 \cdot -2$ <u>−14</u>
9. $-49 \div -7$ <u>7</u>

Part 2

Use PEMDAS to evaluate the expressions.

1. $(3 + 6) \div (-1 \cdot -3)$ <u>3</u>
2. $10 \cdot 4 \div -5$ <u>−8</u>
3. $3^2 + 6 + -10 \div -2$ <u>20</u>
4. $5 + 10 - -4 \cdot -2$ <u>7</u>
5. $7 \cdot (8 + -6) + -3$ <u>11</u>

Part 3

Evaluate the expressions.

1. Let $c = 9$
   $2c + 9 - 2$
   <u>$2 \cdot 9 + 9 - 2 = 25$</u>
2. Let $r = -2$
   $4r + 2 + r$
   <u>$4 \cdot -2 + 2 + -2 = -8$</u>
3. Let $f = -5$
   $5f + -20$
   <u>$5 \cdot -5 + -20 = -45$</u>
4. Let $z = -1$
   $-3z - 5 + 6$
   <u>$-3 \cdot -1 - 5 + 6 = 4$</u>
5. Let $k = -4$
   $3k - 5$
   <u>$3 \cdot -4 - 5 = -17$</u>

Unit 6

Monitoring Progress
Volume

Part 4

Answer the questions about the three-dimensional shapes.

1. What is the volume of this cube? <u>27 inches³</u>

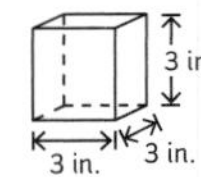

2. What is the volume of this prism? <u>15 inches³</u>

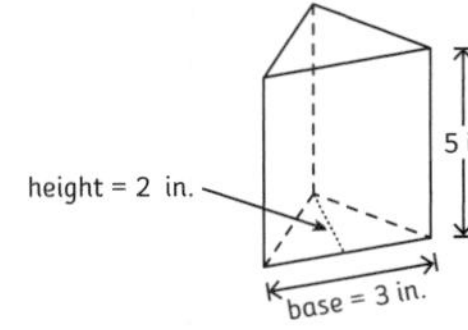

3. What is the volume of this prism? <u>160 inches³</u>

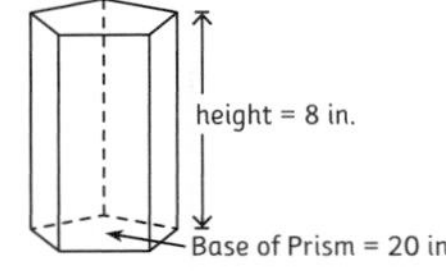

Name ______________________ Date ______________

Form B

mBook

Monitoring Progress
Expressions

Part 1

Solve.

1. 6 • −2 __−12__ 2. −14 ÷ 7 __−2__ 3. −3 + −10 __−13__
4. −3 − 5 __−8__ 5. 6 • −5 __−30__ 6. 24 ÷ −3 __−8__
7. −9 • −9 __81__ 8. 7 • −3 __−21__ 9. −36 ÷ −6 __6__

Part 2

Use PEMDAS to evaluate the expressions.

1. (5 + 20) ÷ (−5 • −2) __2.5__
2. 8 • 4 ÷ −2 __−16__
3. 2^2 + 5 + −8 ÷ −2 __13__
4. 5 + 6 − −3 • −2 __5__
5. 9 • (4 + −7) + −3 __−30__

Part 3

Evaluate the expressions.

1. Let *c* = 4
   2*c* + 6 − 2
   2 • 4 + 6 − 2 = 12
2. Let *r* = −3
   2*r* + 6 + *r*
   2 • −3 + 6 + −3 = −3
3. Let *f* = −4
   4*f* + −20
   4 • −4 + −20 = −36
4. Let *z* = −2
   −5*z* − 4 + 9
   −5 • −2 − 4 + 9 = 15
5. Let *k* = −6
   2*k* − 2
   2 • −6 − 2 = −14

Name ______________________ Date ______________

Monitoring Progress
Volume

Part 4

Answer the questions about the three-dimensional shapes.

1. What is the volume of this cube? __64 inches^3__

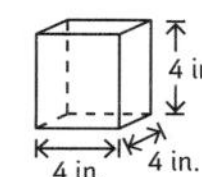

2. What is the volume of this prism? __16 inches^3__

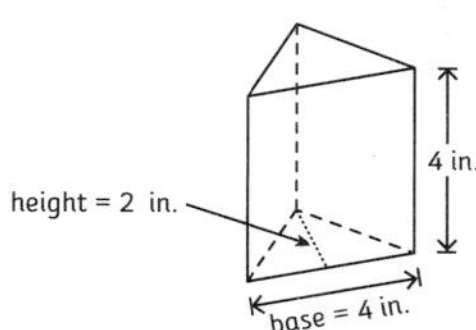

3. What is the volume of this prism? __60 inches^3__

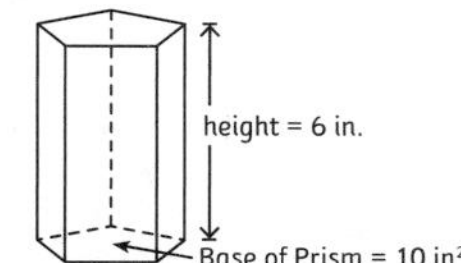

Homework

Go over the instructions on page 476 of the *Student Text* for each part of the homework.

Activity 1

Students select the multiple-choice answer that completes the example of a commonsense property.

Activity 2

Students select the example that matches the property.

Activity 3

Students identify the shape that makes up the base of the three-dimensional object.

Activity 4 • Distributed Practice

Students practice addition and subtraction of integers, PEMDAS, and operations on fractions.

Lesson 5

Homework

Activity 1

Use properties to help you decide what goes on the right side of the equal sign in each problem.

1. $3 + 4 = ?$
   (a) 0
   (b) $4 + 3$ b
   (c) $3 \cdot 4$
2. $2 \cdot 1 = ?$
   (a) 0
   (b) 1
   (c) 2 c
3. $4 \cdot 6 = ?$
   (a) $4 + 6$
   (b) $6 \cdot 4$ b
   (c) 0
4. $\frac{4}{3} \cdot \frac{3}{4} = ?$
   (a) 0
   (b) 1 b
   (c) 2
5. $5 + -5 = ?$
   (a) 0 a
   (b) 1
   (c) 2

Activity 2

Choose the example that matches the property.

1. Property of Zero
   (a) $\frac{1}{2} + 0 = \frac{1}{2}$
   (b) $\frac{1}{2} \cdot 0 = 0$ b
   (c) $\frac{1}{2} + -\frac{1}{2} = 0$
2. Property of Reciprocals
   (a) $\frac{2}{3} \cdot 1 = \frac{2}{3}$
   (b) $\frac{3}{5} + 0 = \frac{3}{5}$
   (c) $\frac{4}{6} \cdot \frac{6}{4} = 1$ c
3. Identity Property
   (a) $4 \cdot 1 = 4$ a
   (b) $4 \cdot 0 = 0$
   (c) $4 + -4 = 0$
4. Inverse Property
   (a) $3 + 0 = 3$
   (b) $3 + -3 = 0$ b
   (c) $3 \cdot 1 = 3$

Activity 3

Tell what shape the base is when you look at the volume for each of these shapes.

1. circle
2. circle
3. rectangle
4. square

Activity 4 • Distributed Practice

Solve.

1. $\frac{2}{1} \cdot \frac{1}{2} = a$ 1
2. $\frac{2}{1} \div \frac{1}{2} = b$ 4
3. $\frac{4}{3} - \frac{1}{6} = c$ $1\frac{1}{6}$
4. $4^2 + 3^2 + 2^2 = d$ 29
5. $(6 \cdot 6) \div 6 = e$ 6
6. $-3 \cdot \frac{1}{3} = f$ -1

476 Unit 6 • Lesson 5

Lesson 6 | Problem Solving: The Volume of Cones and Pyramids

Lesson Planner

Skills Maintenance

Commonsense Properties

Problem Solving:

▶ The Volume of Cones and Pyramids

Students learn that pyramids are a classification of three-dimensional shapes that are differentiated by the attribute of a vertex. They learn that the shape of the base of pyramids might vary, but all of the faces are triangular in shape. These attributes help us find the formula for calculating the volume. Then we build on this concept to show that a cone is a special case of a pyramid where the base is a circle.

Objective

Students will find the volume of cones and pyramids.

Homework

Students write a general statement that describes the property, use PEMDAS and integer rules to evaluate numeric expressions, and find the volume of a cone and a pyramid. In Distributed Practice, students practice addition and subtraction of integers, PEMDAS, and operations on fractions.

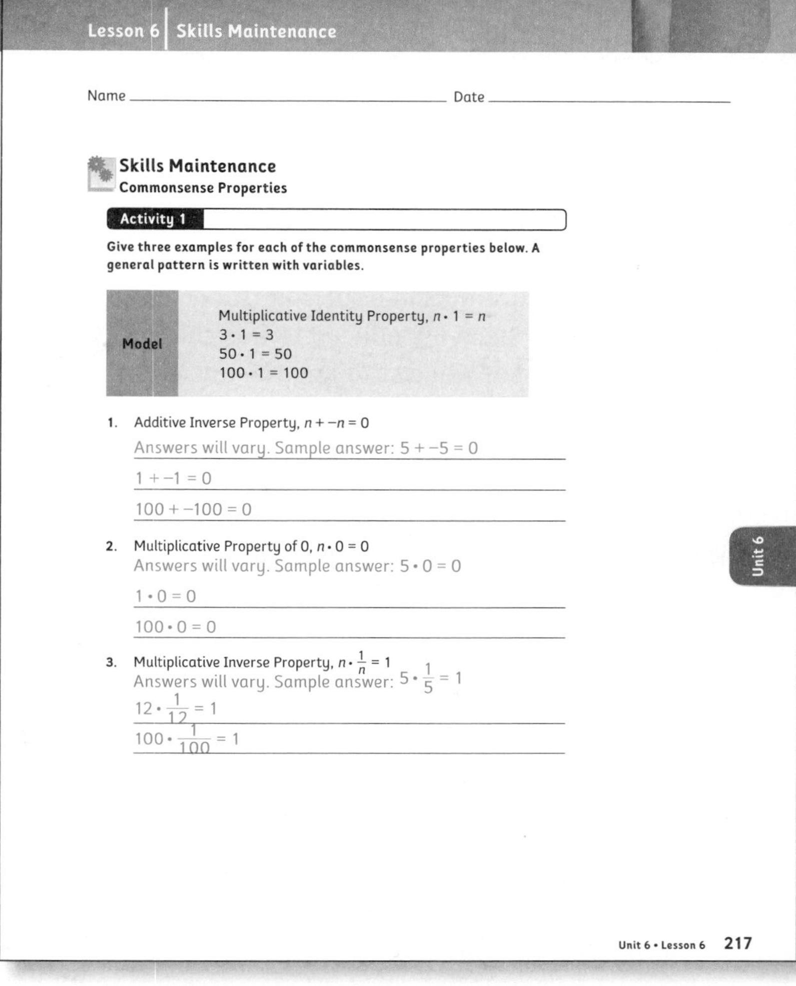
Lesson 6 | Skills Maintenance

Name ______________________ Date ______________

Skills Maintenance
Commonsense Properties

Activity 1

Give three examples for each of the commonsense properties below. A general pattern is written with variables.

Model	Multiplicative Identity Property, $n \cdot 1 = n$ $3 \cdot 1 = 3$ $50 \cdot 1 = 50$ $100 \cdot 1 = 100$

1. Additive Inverse Property, $n + -n = 0$
   Answers will vary. Sample answer: $5 + -5 = 0$
   $1 + -1 = 0$
   $100 + -100 = 0$
2. Multiplicative Property of 0, $n \cdot 0 = 0$
   Answers will vary. Sample answer: $5 \cdot 0 = 0$
   $1 \cdot 0 = 0$
   $100 \cdot 0 = 0$
3. Multiplicative Inverse Property, $n \cdot \frac{1}{n} = 1$
   Answers will vary. Sample answer: $5 \cdot \frac{1}{5} = 1$
   $12 \cdot \frac{1}{12} = 1$
   $100 \cdot \frac{1}{100} = 1$

Unit 6

Unit 6 • Lesson 6 217

Skills Maintenance

Commonsense Properties

(*Interactive Text*, page 217)

Activity 1

Students give three examples of the commonsense property in each problem. A model is provided to help students see the pattern for writing their examples.

Problem Solving:
▶ The Volume of Cones and Pyramids

What happens when we can't stack bases to find the volume?

(*Student Text*, pages 477–478)

Connect to Prior Knowledge

Begin by asking students to think about a pyramid. We saw pyramids in prior units, and they have probably been introduced to this shape in their history classes while studying the ancient pyramids. Sketch a pyramid on the board or overhead.

Ask:

What are some of the attributes of a pyramid?

Listen for:

- *A pyramid has a vertex at the top, which means that all the faces come together at one point.*
- *All of the faces of a pyramid are triangles.*
- *The base of a pyramid might be many different shapes; e.g., square, triangle, pentagon, hexagon.*

Link to Today's Concept

Tell students that in today's lesson, we look at the volume of pyramids and cones.

Demonstrate

Engagement Strategy: Teacher Modeling

Demonstrate the comparisons between cones and pyramids and their stacked base in one of the following ways:

mBook: Use the *mBook Teacher Edition* for *Student Text*, pages 477–478. [m]

Lesson 6 | Problem Solving:
▶The Volume of Cones and Pyramids

▶Problem Solving: The Volume of Cones and Pyramids

What happens when we can't stack bases to find the volume?

Our volume formula for cylinders, prisms, and cubes ($V = B \cdot h$) works because we can stack bases until we reach the top of each object.

However, we can't always stack bases to find volume. For example, the formula does not work when we try to find the volume of cones or pyramids.

In cones and pyramids, the shape at the top is not the same size as it is at the bottom because the faces of the shape come together at a single point, called the vertex.

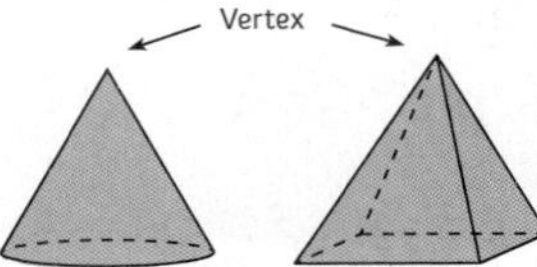

What happens when we try to stack bases for a cone to find its volume?

Let's compare a cone and the stacked circular base of the cone.

We see that if we stack circular bases we create a cylinder.

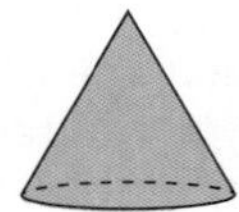

Unit 6 • Lesson 477

Overhead Projector: Reproduce the shapes and stacked bases on a transparency, and modify as discussed.

Board: Copy the shapes and stacked bases on the board, and modify as discussed.

- Remind students of the volume formulas we worked with for cylinders, prisms, and cubes: $V = B \cdot h$. This formula works for all of these shapes because they are objects that can be created by stacking the base. Tell students that we cannot always stack bases to create a three-dimensional shape.
- Show the cone and explain that when shapes have a vertex, like a cone and a pyramid, we cannot stack the base to find the volume. [m]
- Show the stack of circular bases to compare it with the cone. Point out to students that the stacked bases create a cylinder. [m]

If we draw lines on the picture of the cylinder, we can make an informal comparison of the volumes of the cone and the cylinder that is formed by the stacked bases.

The cone's volume is less than the cylinder's volume.

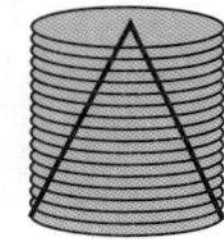

We see the same type of situation with pyramids.

Pyramids have many different shapes for bases. Let's look at what happens when we stack bases of a pyramid.

The volume of a rectangular pyramid and the volume of the shape created by stacking the bases of the pyramid are different.

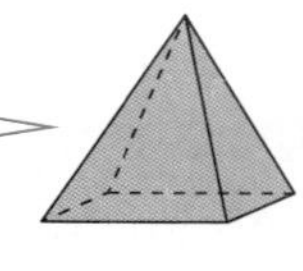

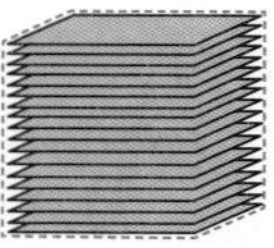

The stacked rectangular base would make a rectangular prism.

If we draw the shape of the pyramid on the picture of the rectangular prism, we can make an informal comparison of the volumes of the pyramid and the prism.

We can easily see that the volume of the pyramid is less than that of the prism.

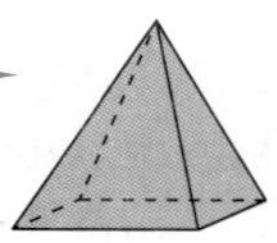

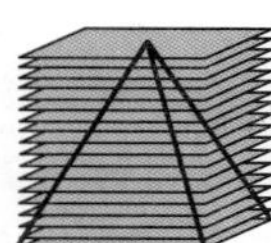

Demonstrate

- Show lines that come to a point at the top of the picture of the stacked circular bases. Explain that we can approximate the volume of the cone and make an informal visual comparison to that of the cylinder. The volume of the cone is less than the volume of the cylinder.
- Show the pyramid and explain that this situation is similar with a pyramid.
- Remind students that pyramids can have different shapes for bases. In this case, we have a rectangular base. Show the stacked bases, and point out that the stacked rectangular bases create a prism.
- Show lines on the stacked rectangular bases that come to a point at the top. Explain that we can approximate the volume of the pyramid and make an informal visual comparison to that of a prism. Point out that we can easily see that the volume of the pyramid is less than the volume of the prism.

Check for Understanding

Engagement Strategy: Think, Think

Ask students the following questions. Tell them that you will call on one of them to answer a question after you ask it. Tell them to listen for their names. After each question, allow time for students to think of the answer. Then call on a student.

Ask:

Why can't we stack bases to find the volume of a cone or pyramid? (*because the top of the cone or pyramid is not the same size as the bottom*)

If we stack the bases of a cone to make a visual comparison of volume, which has less volume? (*the cone*)

How can we use cylinders and prisms to help us find the volume formula for cones and pyramids?

(*Student Text*, pages 479–481)

Explain

Explain that when we drew our sketches of stacked bases, the volumes of the cones and pyramids were always about $\frac{1}{3}$ of the drawing.

Tell students that this is an important part of the volume formulas.

Demonstrate

- Use page 479 of the *Student Text* to demonstrate the comparison between a cone and a cylinder with the same base and height.
- Explain that it would take three cones to fill up the cylinder.
- Point out that this is an important idea to remember as we look at the volume formula for a cone.

Lesson 6

How can we use cylinders and prisms to help us find the volume formula for cones and pyramids?

In earlier illustrations, we compared cones and pyramids with drawings of their stacked bases.

When comparing the shapes, the volumes of the cones or pyramids looked like they were about $\frac{1}{3}$ the size of the stacked bases.

In fact, if we were to fill a cone with sand and pour the sand into a cylinder with the same-sized base and height, it would take exactly three cones of sand to fill it up.

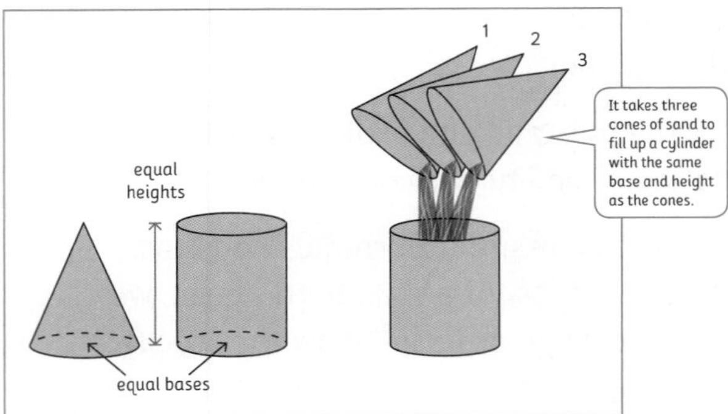

1
2
3
It takes three cones of sand to fill up a cylinder with the same base and height as the cones.
equal heights
equal bases

Now let's see how this affects the volume formula. The most important thing to notice is that we can pour the volume of three cones into a cylinder with the same base and height as each cone. This will help us remember the volume formula for a cone.

Unit 6 • Lesson 479

Demonstrate

- Continue on page 480 of the *Student Text*.
- Explain that because we can pour three cones into the cylinder, this means that the volume of the cylinder is three times the volume of the cone, or that the volume of the cone is $\frac{1}{3}$ the volume of the cylinder.
- Point out the formula for the volume of a cone: $\frac{1}{3} \cdot B \cdot h$. Remind students that the $B \cdot h$ in the formula is the volume of the cylinder.
- Go over **Example 1**, which demonstrates the volume formula for a cone. Carefully walk through the steps for computing volume. It is based on the idea that a cone is $\frac{1}{3}$ the volume of a cylinder.
- Remind students that the base of a cone is a circle, so we use the area formula for a circle, πr^2. Remind students we use 3.14 for pi. Then we can substitute 2 for the variable r to get the base of **12.56 square inches**.
- Point out that now that we have the base and height, we can substitute the information into the volume formula. We get $\frac{1}{3} \cdot 12.56 \cdot 10$.
- After multiplying, we get **41.87 inches³**. This is the volume of the cone.

Lesson 6

If we can pour three cones into the cylinder, this means the volume of the cylinder is three times the volume of the cone.

Volume of a cylinder = 3 • Volume of the cone

That means the volume of one cone is $\frac{1}{3}$ the volume of the cylinder. Now we can get our volume formula for cones. The $B \cdot h$ in the formula is the volume of the cylinder.

Volume of a cone $= \frac{1}{3} \cdot B \cdot h$

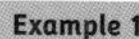
Example 1

Find the volume of the cone.

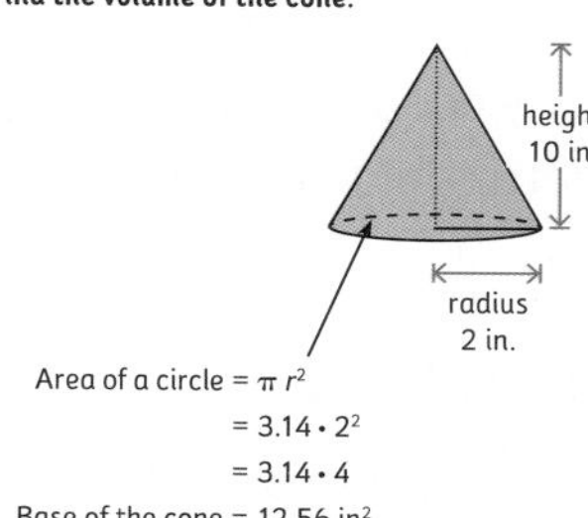

Area of a circle $= \pi r^2$
$= 3.14 \cdot 2^2$
$= 3.14 \cdot 4$
Base of the cone = 12.56 in²

Volume of a cone $= \frac{1}{3} \cdot B \cdot h$
$= \frac{1}{3} \cdot 12.56 \cdot 10$
$= 4.187 \cdot 10$

Volume of the cone = 41.87 in³

480 Unit 6 • Lesson 6

How can we use cylinders and prisms to help us find the volume formula for cones and pyramids? *(continued)*

Demonstrate

- Go over **Example 2** on page 481 of the *Student Text*. In this example, we compute the volume of a rectangular pyramid based on its relationship to a rectangular prism.
- Again point out to students that the key idea is that the volume of a pyramid is $\frac{1}{3}$ that of a prism with the same dimensions. Go through the steps carefully for computing the volume.
- Point out that because this is a rectangular pyramid, the base is a rectangle, or in this case, a square. So we use the area formula for a rectangle to get the area of **16**.
- Substitute the values into the volume formula to get $\frac{1}{3} \cdot 16 \cdot 6$. After multiplying, note that the volume of the pyramid is **32 inches**^{3}.

Check for Understanding

Engagement Strategy: Think Tank

Draw a cone on the board with a **radius of 4 inches** and a **height of 20 inches**. Distribute strips of paper and have students write their names on them. Then have students find the volume of the cone and write their answer on the strip of paper (*334.93*). When students have finished, collect their papers and put them into a container. Draw a strip of paper from the container and share the answer with the class. Invite the student to explain the solution.

This kind of thinking also works for pyramids and prisms. It doesn't matter what kind of pyramid it is, as long as we compare it to a prism with the same base and the same height.

Example 2

Find the volume of the pyramid.

height 6 in.
4 in. 4 in.
rectangular pyramid
4 in. 4 in.
rectangular prism

Area of Base = 4 • 4
Base of pyramid = 16 in²

Volume of a rectangular pyramid $= \frac{1}{3} \cdot B \cdot h$

$= \frac{1}{3} \cdot 16 \cdot 6$

$= \frac{1}{3} \cdot 96$

Notice that we used the Associative Property to multiply 16 by 6 first. It's easier to multiply $\frac{1}{3} \cdot 96$, which equals 32, than to multiply $\frac{1}{3} \cdot 16$, which equals 5.3333.

Volume of the pyramid = 32 in³

Problem-Solving Activity Turn to ***Interactive Text***, page 218.

mBook Reinforce Understanding Use the ***mBook Study Guide*** to review lesson concepts.

Problem-Solving Activity

(*Interactive Text*, pages 218–220)

Have students turn to pages 218–220 in the *Interactive Text*, which provides students an opportunity to practice these concepts on their own.

Students sketch pictures of the stacked bases of cones and pyramids. Then they draw lines on the stack of bases to make an informal visual comparison of their volumes.

Be sure students see that the volumes of the cones and pyramids are less than the volumes of the cylinders and prisms. We can see this in our informal visual representation. Point out that they are about $\frac{1}{3}$ the size.

Next students find the volume for both the original shape as well as the pyramid shape inside. Then they compare the shapes.

Monitor students' work as they complete the activities.

Watch for:

- Can students identify the base of the shape and sketch a stack of the bases?
- Can students draw lines to approximate the volume of the shape for a visual comparison of volume?
- Can students compute the volume for each of the shapes?
- Can students see the connection between the two shapes in each problem?

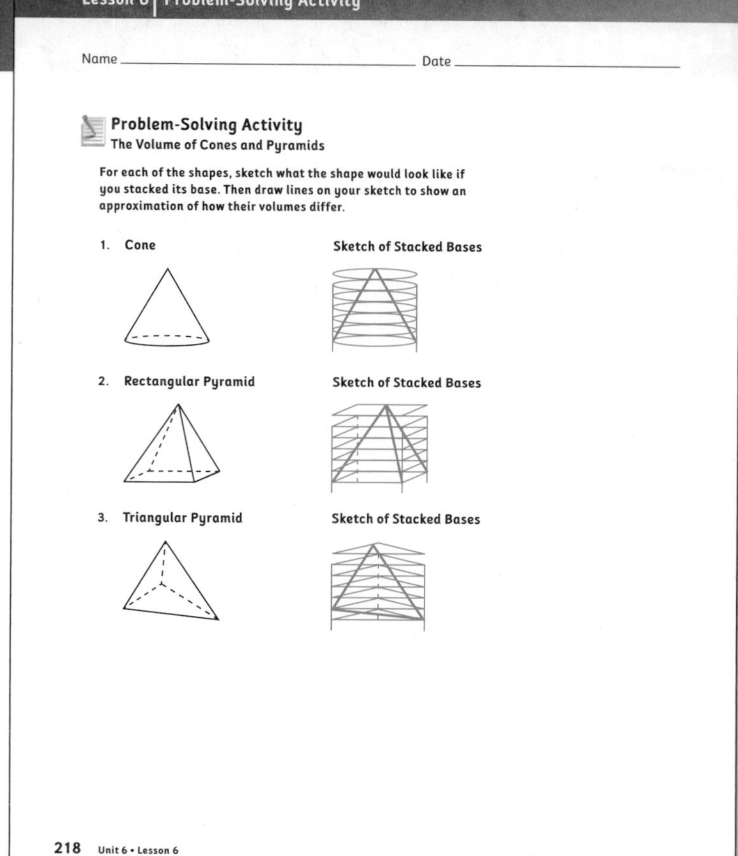

Lesson 6 | Problem-Solving Activity

Name ______ Date ______

Problem-Solving Activity
The Volume of Cones and Pyramids

For each of the shapes, sketch what the shape would look like if you stacked its base. Then draw lines on your sketch to show an approximation of how their volumes differ.

1. **Cone** — **Sketch of Stacked Bases**

2. **Rectangular Pyramid** — **Sketch of Stacked Bases**

3. **Triangular Pyramid** — **Sketch of Stacked Bases**

218 Unit 6 • Lesson 6

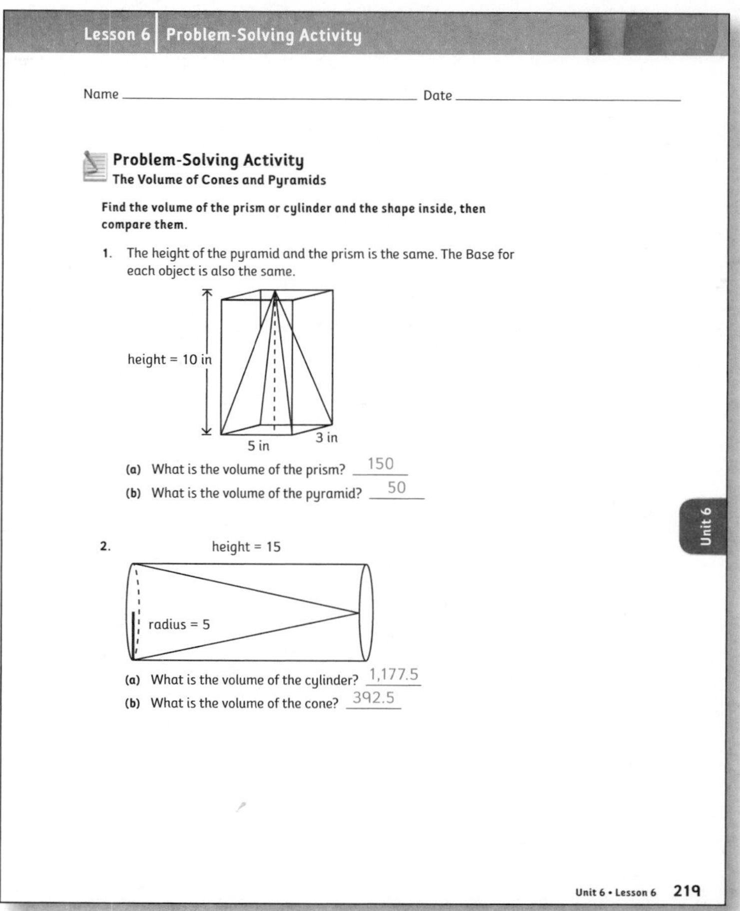

Lesson 6 | Problem-Solving Activity

Name ______ Date ______

Problem-Solving Activity
The Volume of Cones and Pyramids

Find the volume of the prism or cylinder and the shape inside, then compare them.

1. The height of the pyramid and the prism is the same. The Base for each object is also the same.

(a) What is the volume of the prism? 150
(b) What is the volume of the pyramid? 50

2.

(a) What is the volume of the cylinder? 1,177.5
(b) What is the volume of the cone? 392.5

Unit 6

Unit 6 • Lesson 6 219

mBook **Reinforce Understanding**
Remind students that they can review lesson concepts by accessing the online *mBook Study Guide.*

Name ______________________ Date ______________________

3\.

The volume of this cylinder is 300 in^3.

What is the volume of a cone with the same height and Base? 100 in^3

4\.

The volume of this pyramid is 150 in^3.

What is the volume of a prism with the same height and Base? 450 in^3

mBook **Reinforce Understanding**
Use the **mBook** ***Study Guide*** to review lesson concepts.

Homework

Go over the instructions on page 482 of the *Student Text* for each part of the homework.

Activity 1

Students write a general statement that describes the property. Examples are given so students know how to format their answer.

Activity 2

Students use PEMDAS and integer rules to evaluate numeric expressions.

Activity 3

Students find the volume of a cone and a pyramid.

Activity 4 • Distributed Practice

Students practice addition and subtraction of integers, and operations on fractions.

Lesson 6

Homework

Activity 1

Write a general statement for the properties shown.

Model Multiplicative Property of Zero

Examples: $1 \cdot 0 = 0$ $2 \cdot 0 = 0$ $3 \cdot 0 = 0$ Answer: $n \cdot 0 = 0$

1. Additive Inverse Property
   Examples:
   $5 + -5 = 0$
   $10 + -10 = 0$
   $2 + -2 = 0$ $n + -n = 0$
2. Identity Property of Addition
   Examples:
   $3 + 0 = 3$
   $\frac{2}{3} + 0 = \frac{2}{3}$
   $6{,}000 + 0 = 6{,}000$ $n + 0 = n$
3. Multiplicative Inverse Property
   Examples:
   $2 \cdot \frac{1}{2} = 1$
   $3 \cdot \frac{1}{3} = 1$
   $5 \cdot \frac{1}{5} = 1$ $n \cdot \frac{1}{n} = 1$

Activity 2

Use PEMDAS and integer rules to evaluate the numeric expressions. Remember to do diagnostics first, then go to the Algebra Toolbox.

1. $-6 \cdot -6 + -6 - 6$
2. $5 - 10 + -7$
3. $8 + -72 \div 9 - 1$
4. $-24 \div (-8 - -2) + -2$
5. $18 - 25 + 4 - -1$

Activity 3

Tell the volume of each shape.

1. height = 10 inches
   Base = 15 square inches
   $15 \cdot 10 \cdot \frac{1}{3} = 50$ in^3

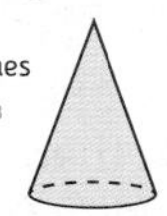

2. height = 12 inches
   Base = 21 square inches
   $21 \cdot 12 \cdot \frac{1}{3} =$
   84 in^3

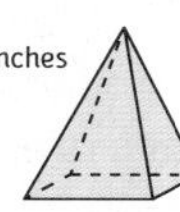

Activity 4 • Distributed Practice

Solve.

1. $2 - -2 + -2 = a$ 2
2. $4^2 + 6 - 5 = b$ 17
3. $(-3 + -1) \cdot (-5 + 4) = c$ 4
4. $\frac{6}{1} \div \frac{1}{2} = d$ 12
5. $\frac{2}{1} \cdot \frac{1}{2} = e$ 1
6. $-\frac{1}{3} \cdot \frac{1}{3} = f$ $-\frac{1}{9}$
7. $(-3 + -4) \cdot -2 = g$ 14
8. $\frac{8}{1} \cdot \frac{1}{8} = h$ 1

Activity 2
1. $-6 \cdot -6 + -6 - 6$
   $36 + -6 - 6$
   $30 - 6$
   24
2. $5 - 10 + -7$
   $-5 + -7$
   -12
3. $8 + -72 \div 9 - 1$
   $8 + -8 - 1$
   $0 - 1$
   -1
4. $-24 \div (-8 - -2) + -2$
   $-24 \div -6 + -2$
   $4 + -2$
   2
5. $18 - 25 + 4 - -1$
   $-7 + 4 - -1$
   $-3 - -1$
   -2

482 Unit 6 • Lesson 6

Lesson 7 ▶Distributive Property

Lesson Planner

Vocabulary Development

distributive property

Skills Maintenance

Commonsense Properties, Finding the Volume

Building Number Concepts:

▶ Distributive Property

Students review the commonsense properties. These properties are simple because they only involve one operation: either addition or multiplication. We introduce students to one of the most important properties in algebra, the distributive property. This property is more complex because it involves two operations: (1) addition and (2) multiplication. Students look at how to use the distributive property to evaluate expressions.

Objective

Students will use the distributive property to evaluate expressions.

Homework

Students evaluate numeric expressions to show how the distributive property works by applying the distributive property to simplify algebraic expressions and by evaluating expressions using the properties they have learned. In Distributed Practice, students practice addition and subtraction of integers, PEMDAS, and operations on fractions.

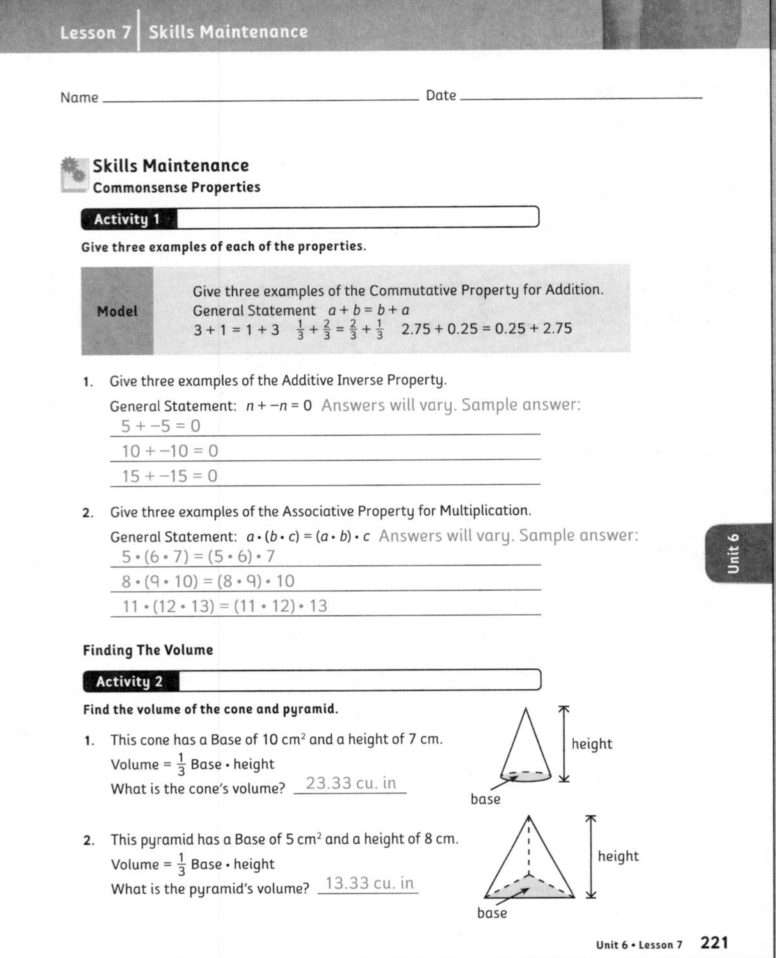

Lesson 7 | Skills Maintenance

Name ______________________ Date ______________

Skills Maintenance
Commonsense Properties

Activity 1

Give three examples of each of the properties.

Model	Give three examples of the Commutative Property for Addition. General Statement $a + b = b + a$ $3 + 1 = 1 + 3$ $\frac{1}{3} + \frac{2}{3} = \frac{2}{3} + \frac{1}{3}$ $2.75 + 0.25 = 0.25 + 2.75$

1. Give three examples of the Additive Inverse Property.
General Statement: $n + -n = 0$ Answers will vary. Sample answer:
$5 + -5 = 0$
$10 + -10 = 0$
$15 + -15 = 0$

2. Give three examples of the Associative Property for Multiplication.
General Statement: $a \cdot (b \cdot c) = (a \cdot b) \cdot c$ Answers will vary. Sample answer:
$5 \cdot (6 \cdot 7) = (5 \cdot 6) \cdot 7$
$8 \cdot (9 \cdot 10) = (8 \cdot 9) \cdot 10$
$11 \cdot (12 \cdot 13) = (11 \cdot 12) \cdot 13$

Finding The Volume

Activity 2

Find the volume of the cone and pyramid.

1. This cone has a Base of 10 cm^2 and a height of 7 cm.
Volume = $\frac{1}{3}$ Base • height
What is the cone's volume? 23.33 cu. in

2. This pyramid has a Base of 5 cm^2 and a height of 8 cm.
Volume = $\frac{1}{3}$ Base • height
What is the pyramid's volume? 13.33 cu. in

Unit 6 • Lesson 7 221

Skills Maintenance

Commonsense Properties, Finding the Volume

(*Interactive Text*, page 221)

Activity 1

Students give three examples of each of the commonsense properties.

Activity 2

Students find the volume of a cone and a pyramid given the base, the height, and the formula $V = \frac{1}{3}$ base • height. Students do not need to compute the base, as it is given in the problem.

Building Number Concepts:
▶ Distributive Property

What is the distributive property?
(*Student Text*, pages 483–485)

Connect to Prior Knowledge
Ask students to discuss how we simplify these two numeric expressions using the rules of PEMDAS:

5(3 + 2)

5 • 3 + 5 • 2

Listen for:

- *In the first problem, we add first because that is the part in parentheses. Then we multiply.*
- *In the second problem, we multiply first in order from left to right. Then we add.*

Point out to students that we got the same answer. Ask them to think of the 5 in front of the parentheses as a coefficient. Explain that if we do the part in parentheses first and then multiply by the coefficient, we get 25. But if we multiply each part in parentheses by the coefficient and then add, we also get 25.

Link to Today's Concept
In today's lesson we learn about a complex property that will help us understand why we found the same answer for the expressions.

Build Vocabulary
Introduce the term **distributive property**, and explain that this property will help us evaluate expressions.

Demonstrate
Engagement Strategy: Teacher Modeling

Demonstrate how we use the distributive property using the *Student Text* or one of the following ways:

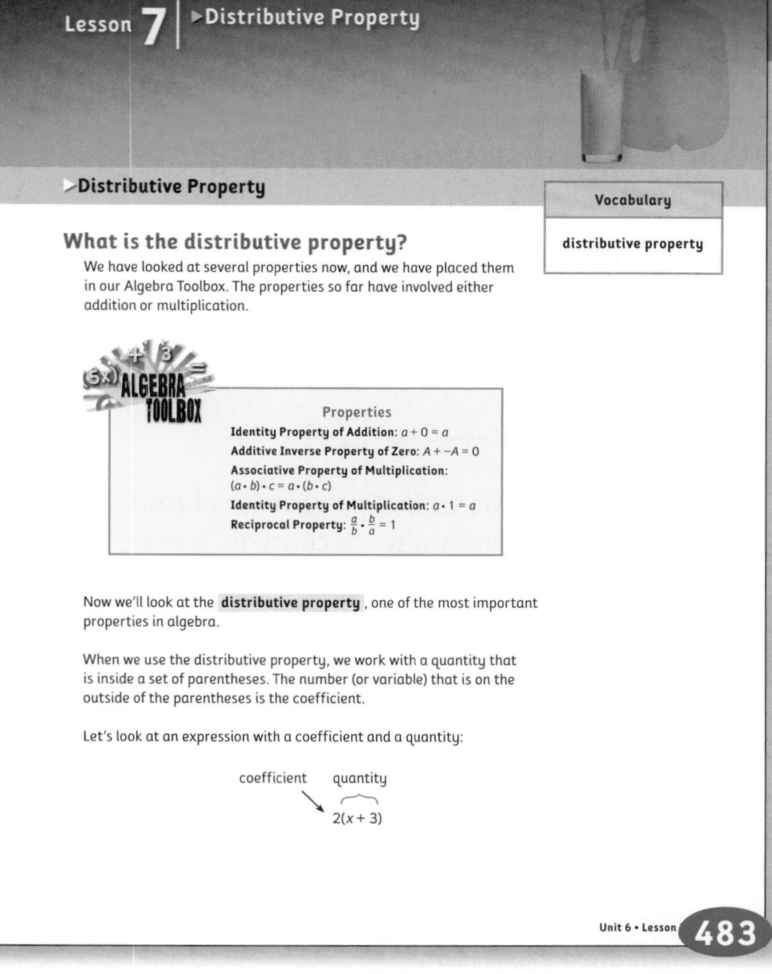

Lesson 7 | ▶Distributive Property

▶Distributive Property

Vocabulary

distributive property

What is the distributive property?

We have looked at several properties now, and we have placed them in our Algebra Toolbox. The properties so far have involved either addition or multiplication.

ALGEBRA TOOLBOX

Properties

Identity Property of Addition: $a + 0 = a$

Additive Inverse Property of Zero: $A + -A = 0$

Associative Property of Multiplication: $(a \cdot b) \cdot c = a \cdot (b \cdot c)$

Identity Property of Multiplication: $a \cdot 1 = a$

Reciprocal Property: $\frac{a}{b} \cdot \frac{b}{a} = 1$

Now we'll look at the **distributive property**, one of the most important properties in algebra.

When we use the distributive property, we work with a quantity that is inside a set of parentheses. The number (or variable) that is on the outside of the parentheses is the coefficient.

Let's look at an expression with a coefficient and a quantity:

coefficient quantity

$2(x + 3)$

Unit 6 • Lesson 483

mBook: Use the *mBook Teacher Edition* for *Student Text*, pages 483–484. m

- Review the commonsense properties we worked with so far. Tell students that one thing these all have in common is that they only involve one operation—either multiplication or addition. Go through each property in the table, providing examples as needed. m
- Tell students that the distributive property has both of these operations.
- Note that in the intro, we looked at a form of the distributive property with a numeric expression. Explain that the real power of the distributive property comes when we are simplifying expressions involving variables. Display the expression **2(*x* + 3)**, and point out that the number in front of the parentheses is the coefficient and the part in the parentheses is referred to as a quantity. m

What is the distributive property?
(*continued*)

Demonstrate

- Show **Example 1** to demonstrate the steps of using the distributive property to simplify the expression **$2(x + 3)$**. m

---

STEP 1

- Point out that we cannot combine the terms inside of the parentheses because they are not like terms. The sum involves a variable and a number.
- Explain that we first distribute the coefficient across both terms in the parentheses. m

---

STEP 2

- Point out that this gives us **$2 \cdot x$** and **$2 \cdot 3$**. When we multiply, we get **$2x + 6$**. This is the simplified expression. m
- Show how to represent the expression using the special symbols. We use two Vs to represent $2x$ and six Ns to represent the number 6. m

In Example 1 we see how to use the distributive property when evaluating an algebraic expression.

Example 1

Use the distributive property to evaluate this expression:

$$2(x + 3)$$

STEP 1
Distribute the coefficient across both terms inside the parentheses.

$2(x + 3)$

$2\ (x\ +\ 3)$

The terms inside the parentheses cannot be combined because we have a variable and a number.

$2 \cdot x$ $\quad$ $2 \cdot 3$

STEP 2
Next we simplify each term.

$2x \ + \ 6$

We have now simplified the expression using the distributive property.

Using our special symbols from the last unit, our expression looks like this:

$2x \quad + \quad 6$

V V + N N N N N N

The distributive property can be used to simplify many different kinds of expressions.

Remember to multiply, or "distribute," the coefficient across all the terms inside the parentheses.

Let's look at some other ways we can use this property.

Demonstrate

- Turn to page 485 of the *Student Text* to look at a variety of ways to apply the distributive property. Be sure students understand how we find each of the answers. Place the problems on the board or overhead to show the steps if necessary.
- Show the first expression: **2(*x* − 3)**. Explain how we distribute the coefficient across the terms *x* and 3. Then we multiply each term by 2 to get the simplified expression **2*x* − 6**.
- Go over the next expression **2(2*x* − 3)**. Again point out how to distribute the coefficient across the terms 2*x* and 3. Then we multiply each term by the coefficient to get the simplified expression **4*x* − 6**.
- Look at the expression ***x*(*x* − 3)**. Again point out how to distribute the coefficient across the terms *x* and 3. Then we multiply each term by the coefficient to get the simplified expression $\mathbf{x^2 - 3x}$.

Lesson 7

Simplified Expressions Using the Distributive Property

$2(x - 3)$

$2\ (x\ -\ 3)$

$2 \cdot x - 2 \cdot 3$

$\mathbf{2x - 6}$

$2(2x - 3)$

$2\ (2x\ -\ 3)$

$2 \cdot 2x - 2 \cdot 3$

$\mathbf{4x - 6}$

$x(x - 3)$

$x\ (x\ -\ 3)$

$x \cdot x - x \cdot 3$

$\mathbf{x^2 - 3x}$

Let's put the distributive property in our toolbox.

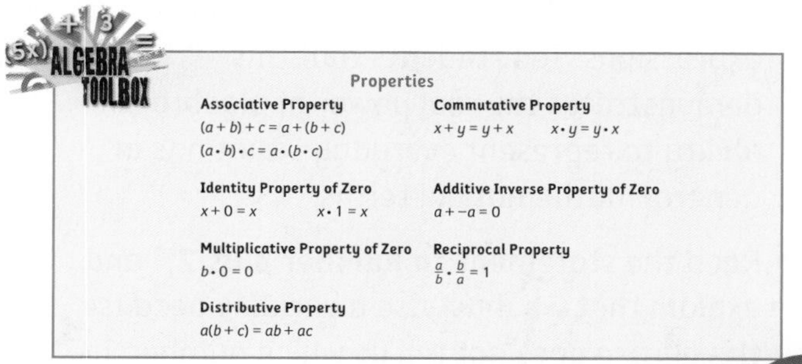
ALGEBRA TOOLBOX

Properties

Associative Property
$(a + b) + c = a + (b + c)$
$(a \cdot b) \cdot c = a \cdot (b \cdot c)$

Commutative Property
$x + y = y + x \qquad x \cdot y = y \cdot x$

Identity Property of Zero
$x + 0 = x \qquad x \cdot 1 = x$

Additive Inverse Property of Zero
$a + -a = 0$

Multiplicative Property of Zero
$b \cdot 0 = 0$

Reciprocal Property
$\frac{a}{b} \cdot \frac{b}{a} = 1$

Distributive Property
$a(b + c) = ab + ac$

Unit 6 • Lesson 7 485

Check for Understanding
Engagement Strategy: Look About

Write the following algebraic expression on the board:

4(*x* + 4)

Have students use the distributive property to simplify the expression (*4x + 16*). Students should write their work in large writing on a piece of paper or a dry erase board. When students finish their work, they should hold up their answer for everyone to see.

If students are not sure about the answer, prompt them to look about at other students' solutions to help with their thinking. Review the answers after all students have held up their solutions.

Reinforce Understanding

If students need further practice, use the following expressions:

3(2*x* − 3) (*6x − 9*)

5(*x* + 2) (*5x + 10*)

How do we translate statements into algebraic expressions?

(*Student Text*, page 486)

Explain

Turn to page 486 of the *Student Text*. Tell students that we now add the distributive property to our Algebra Toolbox, as it is a very important property that we use often in algebra.

Demonstrate

- Demonstrate how to use the variables to translate statements into algebraic expressions. Tell students that this demonstrates the real power of algebra: the ability to represent everyday situations in general mathematical terms.
- Read the statement **"a number plus 2,"** and explain that we must use a variable because the phrase does not tell us which number. In this case, we use *n*: $n + 2$.
- Point out that in each case, we use the variable ***n*** to represent an unknown number. Be sure students understand how we translate each phrase into an algebraic expression.
- Go over how phrases are translated into algebraic expressions that use the distributive property.
- For $3(n + 2)$, be sure students understand that 3 is the coefficient.

Check for Understanding
Engagement Strategy: Look About

Say the following statement aloud:

four times the sum of a number and six

Have students use a variable and translate the statement into an algebraic expression ($4(n + 6)$). Students should write their solutions in large writing on a piece of paper or a dry erase board.

Lesson 7

How do we translate statements into algebraic expressions?

Translating statements into algebraic expressions is a good way to understand any number of expressions, particularly those where we might use the distributive property.

Let's start with a simple phrase and then build up. We will use the letter *n* any time we need a variable.

"a number plus 2"

The phrase "a number plus 2" does not tell us which number. We don't have enough information, so we must use a variable. We can substitute a variable for "a number" and write the expression:

Phrase	Expression
"a number plus 2"	$n + 2$
"3 times a number"	$3 \cdot n$, or $3n$
"3 times a number plus 2"	$3n + 2$

Now let's see how we would translate a statement into an expression that has a coefficient. These are more complicated expressions. We can still use the distributive property to simplify them.

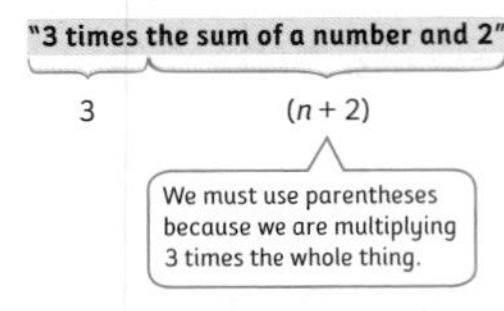
"3 times the sum of a number and 2"
3
(n + 2)
We must use parentheses because we are multiplying 3 times the whole thing.

Phrase	Expression
"3 times the sum of a number and 2"	$3(n + 2)$

Apply Skills Turn to *Interactive Text*, page 222.

mBook Reinforce Understanding Use the *mBook Study Guide* to review lesson concepts.

When students finish their work, they should hold up their answer for everyone to see.

If students are not sure about the answer, prompt them to look about at other students' solutions to help with their thinking. Review the answers after all students have held up their solutions.

Apply Skills
(*Interactive Text*, pages 222–223)

Have students turn to pages 222–223 in the *Interactive Text*, and complete the activities.

Activity 1

Students use the distributive property to simplify expressions.

Activity 2

Students translate word phrases into algebraic expressions. Some of these phrases will require the distributive property.

Monitor students' work as they complete the activities.

Watch for:

- Can students distribute the coefficient across the two terms in the parentheses?
- Are students confused by variations of the situation?
- Can students translate the word phrases into algebraic expressions, including those that involve the distributive property?

Be sure to discuss the three expressions that require the distributive property from the list of expressions (Activity 2, questions 4, 6, and 9).

mBook **Reinforce Understanding**
Remind students that they can review lesson concepts by accessing the online *mBook Study Guide*.

Lesson 7 | Apply Skills

Name ______ Date ______

Apply Skills
Distributive Property

Activity 1

Use the distributive property to simplify the expressions. Show all of your work.

1. $3(x + 2)$
   $3x + 3(2)$
   $3x + 6$
2. $4(2w - 1)$
   $8w - 4$
3. $a(a + 2)$
   $a^2 + 2a$
4. $8(3 - z)$
   $8(3) - 8z$
   $24 - 8z$
5. $4(2 + b)$
   $4(2) + 4b$
   $8 + 4b$
6. $-2(c - 4)$
   $-2c - 4(-2)$
   $-2c + 8$

222 Unit 6 • Lesson 7

Lesson 7 | Apply Skills

Name ______ Date ______

Activity 2

Read each statement carefully, then translate it into an expression. Do not simplify it. Use *h* as the variable in the expression. Here is a hint, there are only three problems where you will have an expression with a coefficient and parentheses.

1. A number minus 7 $h - 7$
2. 4 times a number plus 5 $4h + 5$
3. $\frac{1}{2}$ of a number $\frac{1}{2}h$
4. 2 times the sum of a number plus 3 $2(h + 3)$
5. 7 times a number minus 7 $7h - 7$
6. 5 times the sum of a number plus 1 $5(h + 1)$
7. A number times a number h^2
8. 3 times a number minus 2 $3h - 2$
9. 3 times the sum of a number plus −4 $3(h + -4)$
10. A number plus $\frac{3}{4}$ $h + \frac{3}{4}$

mBook **Reinforce Understanding**
Use the mBook *Study Guide* to review lesson concepts.

Unit 6

Unit 6 • Lesson 7 223

Homework

Go over the instructions on page 487 of the *Student Text* for each part of the homework.

Activity 1

Students evaluate numeric expressions two different ways to show how the distributive property works.

Activity 2

Students apply the distributive property to simplify algebraic expressions.

Activity 3

Students evaluate expressions using the properties they have learned.

Activity 4 • Distributed Practice

Students practice addition and subtraction of integers, PEMDAS, and operations on fractions.

Homework

Activity 1

Prove the distributive property works by solving these problems two ways. First distribute, then find the sum in the parentheses before distributing the coefficient.

Model $2(8+2)$

Answer: $2 \cdot 8 + 2 \cdot 2 = 16 + 4 = 20$

$2 \cdot 10 = 20$

The answers are the same.

1. $4(3+4)$ 2. $5(6+2)$ 3. $2(5+6)$ 4. $10(7+8)$

See Additional Answers below.

Activity 2

Practice using the distributive property by simplifying these algebraic expressions.

Model $3(x+5) \rightarrow 3 \cdot x + 3 \cdot 5 \quad 3x + 15$

1. $4(x+2)$ 2. $5(1+d)$ 3. $2(z+8)$
4. $a(a+7)$ 5. $-6(b+20)$

See Additional Answers below.

Activity 3

Evaluate the expression using the properties you have learned.

1. $4 + 0 = ?$
   (a) 0
   (b) 1
   (c) 4 c
2. $2 \cdot 0 = ?$
   (a) 0 a
   (b) 1
   (c) 2
3. $3 \cdot 0 = ?$
   (a) 0 a
   (b) 1
   (c) $\frac{1}{3}$
4. $5 + -5 = ?$
   (a) 0 a
   (b) 1
   (c) $\frac{1}{5}$
5. $a \cdot \frac{1}{a} = ?$
   (a) 0
   (b) 1 b
   (c) $\frac{a}{1}$

Activity 4 • Distributed Practice

Solve.

1. $\frac{2}{3} \div \frac{2}{3} = a$ 1
2. $\frac{3}{4} + \frac{1}{2} = b$ $1\frac{1}{4}$
3. $(-4 \cdot -1) \cdot (-8 \div 4) = c$ -8
4. $3^2 + 2^2 - 10 = d$ 3
5. $\frac{18}{1} \cdot \frac{1}{18} = e$ 1
6. $-\frac{1}{3} - \frac{1}{3} = f$ $-\frac{2}{3}$
7. $\frac{2}{4} + -\frac{2}{8} = g$ $\frac{1}{4}$
8. $\frac{8}{1} \cdot \frac{1}{16} = h$ $\frac{1}{2}$

Additional Answers

Activity 1

1. $4 \cdot 3 + 4 \cdot 4 = 12 + 16 = 28$; $4 \cdot 7 = 28$
2. $5 \cdot 6 + 5 \cdot 2 = 30 + 10 = 40$; $5 \cdot 8 = 40$
3. $2 \cdot 5 + 2 \cdot 6 = 10 + 12 = 22$; $2 \cdot 11 = 22$
4. $10 \cdot 7 + 10 \cdot 8 = 70 + 80 = 150$; $10 \cdot 15 = 150$

Activity 2

1. $4 \cdot x + 4 \cdot 2 = 4x + 8$
2. $5 \cdot 1 + 5 \cdot d = 5 + 5d$
3. $2 \cdot z + 2 \cdot 8 = 2z + 16$
4. $a \cdot a + a \cdot 7 = a^2 + 7a$
5. $-6 \cdot b + -6 \cdot 20 = -6b + -120$

Lesson 8 | Problem Solving: The Volume of Spheres

Lesson Planner

Skills Maintenance

Distributive Property

Problem Solving:

▶ The Volume of Spheres

Students look at a sphere as a three-dimensional version of a circle. They apply what they know about shapes and volume to help understand the volume of a sphere. We compare a sphere to a basketball and look at how we reach the volume formula of a sphere.

Objective

Students will find the volume of a sphere.

Homework

Students give a general pattern for the property by looking at the examples and writing them with variables, use PEMDAS and integer rules to evaluate numeric expressions, and find the volume of spheres. In Distributed Practice, students practice addition and subtraction of integers, PEMDAS, and operations on fractions.

Lesson 8 | Skills Maintenance

Name ______________________ Date ______________

Skills Maintenance
Distributive Property

Activity 1

Use the distributive property to simplify each problem.

1. $5(a + 2)$ $5a + 10$
2. $-2(b + 5)$ $-2b + -10$
3. $2(2 + c)$ $4 + 2c$
4. $d(d + 2)$ $d^2 + 2d$
5. $2(m - 4)$ $2m - 8$
6. $-5(2 - n)$ $-10 + 5n$

224 Unit 6 • Lesson 8

Skills Maintenance

Distributive Property

(*Interactive Text*, page 224)

Activity 1

Students apply the distributive property to simplify problems.

Problem Solving:
▶ The Volume of Spheres

How do we find the volume of a sphere?
(*Student Text*, pages 488–489)

Connect to Prior Knowledge
Begin by showing students real-world examples of spheres: a tennis ball, a ping pong ball, a basketball, a globe, etc. Tell students that we can begin thinking about these shapes by looking at a circle and spinning it. Demonstrate the optical illusion of a sphere by spinning a coin or some sort of a flat circular disk.

Link to Today's Concept
Tell students that in today's lesson, we see how our knowledge of circles and our previous work with volume helps us find the volume of a sphere.

Demonstrate
Engagement Strategy: Teacher Modeling

Demonstrate how to find the volume of a sphere in one of the following ways:

mBook: Use the *mBook Teacher Edition* for *Student Text*, pages 488–489. m

Overhead Projector: Reproduce the graphics and formulas on a transparency, and modify as discussed.

Board: Copy the graphics and formulas on the board, and modify as discussed.

- Discuss the volume formula for a sphere. Put it on the board or overhead: $V = \frac{4}{3}\pi r^3$. m
- Explain to students that this may seem complex, but if we use our knowledge of circles and our previous work with volume, we can make sense of this volume formula as well.

Lesson 8 | Problem Solving: The Volume of Spheres

▶Problem Solving: The Volume of Spheres

How do we find the volume of a sphere?

The volume of a sphere is difficult to think about because we cannot see any kind of base. The formula for the volume is even more complicated.

Volume of a sphere = $\frac{4}{3}\pi r^3$

One way to think about a sphere's volume is similar to the way we thought about the volume of a cone.

Example 1 will:

- Help us visualize the volume.
- Give us a step-by-step way to think about how we can find the volume for a sphere based on what we already know about shapes and volume.

Example 1

Find the volume of a sphere.

Steps for Finding the Volume of a Sphere

STEP 1
Begin by cutting a sphere in half.
Let's pretend the sphere is a basketball. When we cut it in half, we have a hemisphere.

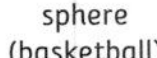
sphere (basketball)

hemisphere (half of a basketball)

488 Unit 6 • Lesson 8

- Explain that we will look at a step-by-step way of thinking about how to find the volume for a sphere. This is based on what we already know about shapes and volume. It will help us visualize volume. Go through all of the steps in the example very carefully with students.

STEP 1
- Display a sphere and have students imagine that it is a basketball. m
- Display a hemisphere and explain that if we cut a sphere in half, we get a hemisphere. m

Demonstrate

- Continue walking through the steps to find the volume of a sphere.

STEP 2

- Show a cylinder and explain that the cylinder has the same height and base as the hemisphere. The base is πr^2, and the height of the cylinder is the radius of the hemisphere.
- Show the cylinder as $\frac{2}{3}$ **full**. explain that if we fill the hemisphere with sand and then fill the cylinder with the sand from the hemisphere, the volume of the hemisphere fills $\frac{2}{3}$ of the cylinder. this means that the volume of the hemisphere is $\frac{2}{3}$ **• base • height**.
- Explain that because the height of the cylinder is the same as the radius of the hemisphere, the volume of the hemisphere is $\frac{2}{3} \cdot \pi r^2 \cdot r$, or $\frac{2}{3}\pi r^3$.

STEP 3

- Remind students that a hemisphere is half of a sphere, so we must multiply the volume of a hemisphere by 2 to get the volume of a sphere. So we get $2 \cdot \frac{2}{3} \cdot \pi r^2 \cdot r$, or $\frac{4}{3}\pi r^3$.
The volume of a sphere $= \frac{4}{3}\pi r^3$.

STEP 2

Fill the hemisphere with sand and pour it into a cylinder with the same height and base as the sphere.

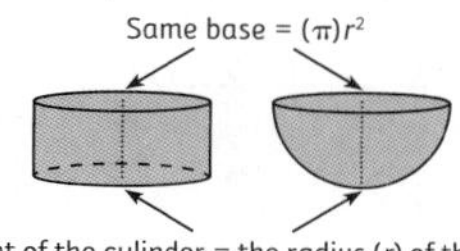

The volume of the hemisphere fills $\frac{2}{3}$ of the cylinder.

The volume of the hemisphere = $\frac{2}{3}$ • Base • height.

Remember, the height of the cylinder is the same as the radius of the hemisphere. That means the volume of the hemisphere is:

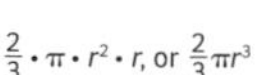

$$\frac{2}{3} \cdot \pi \cdot r^2 \cdot r, \text{ or } \frac{2}{3}\pi r^3$$

STEP 3

Multiply the volume of the hemisphere times 2 to give us the volume of a sphere.
We multiply by 2 because we know that 2 hemispheres make a sphere, as two halves make a whole.

$$2 \cdot \frac{2}{3}\pi r^3 = \frac{4}{3}\pi r^3$$

The volume of a sphere = $\frac{4}{3}\pi r^3$.

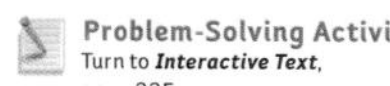
Problem-Solving Activity
Turn to *Interactive Text*, page 225.

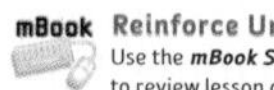
mBook Reinforce Understanding
Use the *mBook Study Guide* to review lesson concepts.

Problem-Solving Activity
(*Interactive Text*, pages 225–226)

Have students turn to pages 225–226 in the *Interactive Text*. Read all of the instructions carefully with students.

First students practice using the formula $V = \frac{4}{3}\pi r^3$. Students are given the radius of each of the spheres, then substitute this information into the formula to find the volume. Tell students to use the approximation of pi = 3.14.

Then students solve a word problem involving the volume of spheres. Be sure students have a clear understanding of what the problem is asking for, and are able to plan their strategy for solving it. Moving too quickly through a complex problem like this one sends the wrong message about our approach to problem solving. Have students look at the drawing that shows how the fruit is packed. Then tell them to complete the activity.

Monitor students' work as they complete the activities.

Watch for:

- Can students substitute the radius into the formula correctly?
- Can students accurately calculate the volume for each of the spheres?
- Can students determine the dimensions they need to solve the problem?
- Can students perform the multiple steps necessary to come up with the best solution?

mBook **Reinforce Understanding**
Remind students that they can review lesson concepts by accessing the online *mBook Study Guide*.

Lesson 8 | Problem-Solving Activity

Name ______________________ Date ______________________

Problem-Solving Activity
The Volume of Spheres

Find the volume of each sphere using this formula: $V = \frac{4}{3}\pi r^3$. Use 3.14 to estimate pi. Show your work.

1. $r = 2$
Show your work here.
$\frac{4}{3}\pi 2^3$
$\frac{4}{3}\pi 8$
$\frac{4}{3} \cdot 3.14 \cdot 8 = 33.49$
The volume is 33.49.

2. $r = 4$
Show your work here.
$\frac{4}{3}\pi 4^3$
$\frac{4}{3} \cdot 3.14 \cdot 64 = 267.95$
The volume is 267.95.

3. $r = 1$
Show your work here.
$\frac{4}{3}\pi 1^3$
$\frac{4}{3} \cdot 3.14 \cdot 1 = 4.19$
The volume is 4.19.

4. $r = 6$
Show your work here.
$\frac{4}{3}\pi 6^3$
$\frac{4}{3} \cdot 3.14 \cdot 216 = 904.32$
The volume is 904.32.

Unit 6

Unit 6 • Lesson 8 225

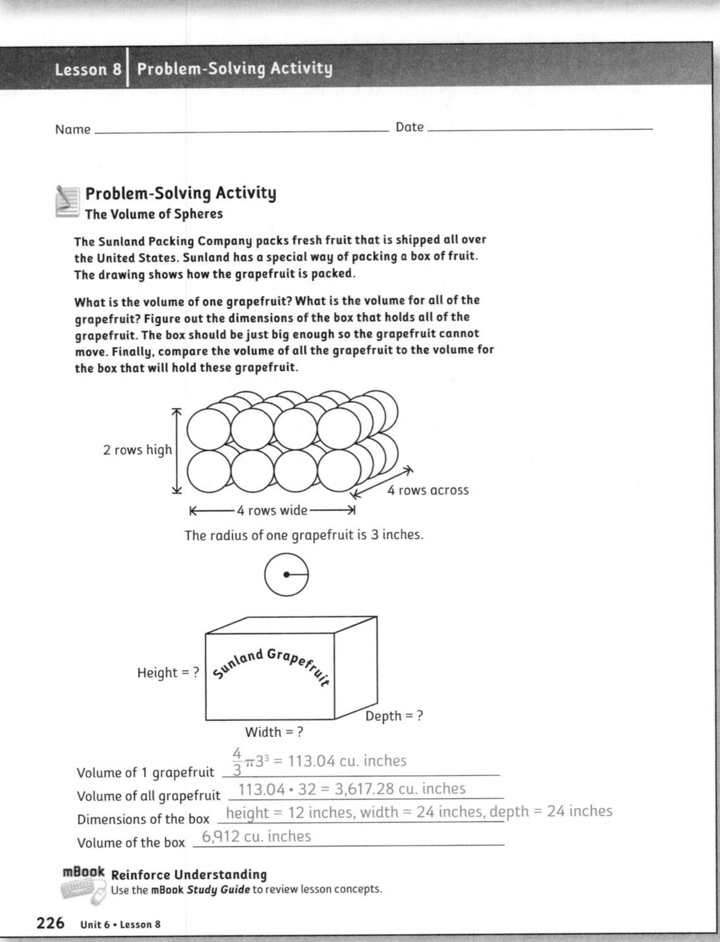

Lesson 8 | Problem-Solving Activity

Name ______________________ Date ______________________

Problem-Solving Activity
The Volume of Spheres

The Sunland Packing Company packs fresh fruit that is shipped all over the United States. Sunland has a special way of packing a box of fruit. The drawing shows how the grapefruit is packed.

What is the volume of one grapefruit? What is the volume for all of the grapefruit? Figure out the dimensions of the box that holds all of the grapefruit. The box should be just big enough so the grapefruit cannot move. Finally, compare the volume of all the grapefruit to the volume for the box that will hold these grapefruit.

The radius of one grapefruit is 3 inches.

Volume of 1 grapefruit $\frac{4}{3}\pi 3^3$ = 113.04 cu. inches
Volume of all grapefruit 113.04 • 32 = 3,617.28 cu. inches
Dimensions of the box height = 12 inches, width = 24 inches, depth = 24 inches
Volume of the box 6,912 cu. inches

mBook Reinforce Understanding
Use the mBook *Study Guide* to review lesson concepts.

226 Unit 6 • Lesson 8

Homework

Go over the instructions on page 490 of the *Student Text* for each part of the homework.

Activity 1

Students write general statements for each property by looking at the examples. They write the statements with variables.

Activity 2

Students use PEMDAS and integer rules to evaluate numeric expressions.

Activity 3

Students find the volume of spheres.

Activity 4 • Distributed Practice

Students practice addition and subtraction of integers, PEMDAS, and operations on fractions.

Additional Answers

Activity 2

1. $-8 + (-2 + -3) \cdot -7$
   $-8 + -5 \cdot -7$
   $-8 + 35$
   27
2. $15 + (-8 - -1) \cdot -2$
   $15 + -7 \cdot -2$
   $15 + 14$
   29
3. $10 - -2 \cdot -3 + -2^2$
   $10 - -2 \cdot -3 + 4$
   $10 - -2 \cdot -3 + 4$
   $10 - 6 + 4$
   $4 + 4$
   8
4. $-16 \div -4 \cdot (-1 - -8)$
   $-16 \div -4 \cdot 7$
   $4 \cdot 7$
   28

Homework

Activity 1

Write a general statement about each property below. Use the examples provided to help you.

Model Commutative Property for Multiplication
Examples: $5 \cdot 6 = 6 \cdot 5$ $3 \cdot 4 = 4 \cdot 3$ Answer: $a \cdot b = b \cdot a$

1. Associative Property
   Examples: $a + (b + c) = (a + b) + c$
   $1 + (2 + 3) = (1 + 2) + 3$
   $2 + (4 + 5) = (2 + 4) + 5$
2. Distributive Property
   Examples: $a(b + c) = ab + ac$
   $3(x + 2) = 3x + 6$
   $-2(3 + w) = -6 + -2w$
3. Multiplicative Inverse Property
   Examples:
   $\frac{2}{3} \cdot \frac{3}{2} = 1$
   $\frac{2}{1} \cdot \frac{1}{2} = 1$ $\frac{b}{c} \cdot \frac{c}{b} = 1$
4. Commutative Property for Addition $a + b = b + a$
   Examples:
   $4 + 2 = 2 + 4$
   $3 + w = w + 3$

Activity 2

Use PEMDAS and integer rules to evaluate the numeric expressions. Remember to do diagnostics first, then go to the Algebra Toolbox.

1. $-8 + (-2 + -3) \cdot -7$
2. $15 + (-8 - -1) \cdot -2$
3. $10 - -2 \cdot -3 + -2^2$
4. $-16 \div -4 \cdot (-1 - -8)$

See Additional Answers below.

Activity 3

Find the volume of each sphere. Use the formula: $V = \frac{4}{3}\pi r^3$. Use 3.14 as the approximation for pi.

1. $r = 3$ 113.04
2. $r = 0.5$ 0.523
3. $r = 1$ 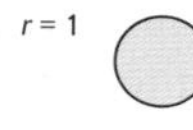 4.19

Activity 4 • Distributed Practice

Solve.

1. $\frac{2}{3} + \frac{2}{6} = a$ 1
2. $\frac{3}{4} - \frac{1}{2} = b$ $\frac{1}{4}$
3. $(-2 \cdot -2) \cdot -4 \div 4 = c$ -4
4. $4^2 - 2^2 = d$ 12
5. $\frac{6}{1} \cdot \frac{1}{6} = e$ 1
6. $-2 - -4 = f$ 2
7. $\frac{2}{4} \div \frac{2}{8} = g$ 2
8. $\frac{10}{1} \cdot \frac{1}{10} = h$ 1

Lesson 9 | Problem Solving: Finding the Volume of Complex Objects

Lesson Planner

Skills Maintenance

Properties

Problem Solving:
▶ Finding the Volume of Complex Objects

Students review the volume formulas we looked at in this unit. We remind students that the attributes of three-dimensional shapes help classify them and find their volume formulas. We build on these concepts to find the volume of more complex shapes. We begin by finding the volume of several prisms, then work towards finding the volume of polyhedrons.

Objective

Students will find the volume of complex objects.

Homework

Students select the attribute that the two shapes have in common, tell the total volume of a compound shape given the volume of each individual shape, and give a general pattern that describes the properties. In Distributed Practice, students practice addition and subtraction of integers, PEMDAS, and operations on fractions.

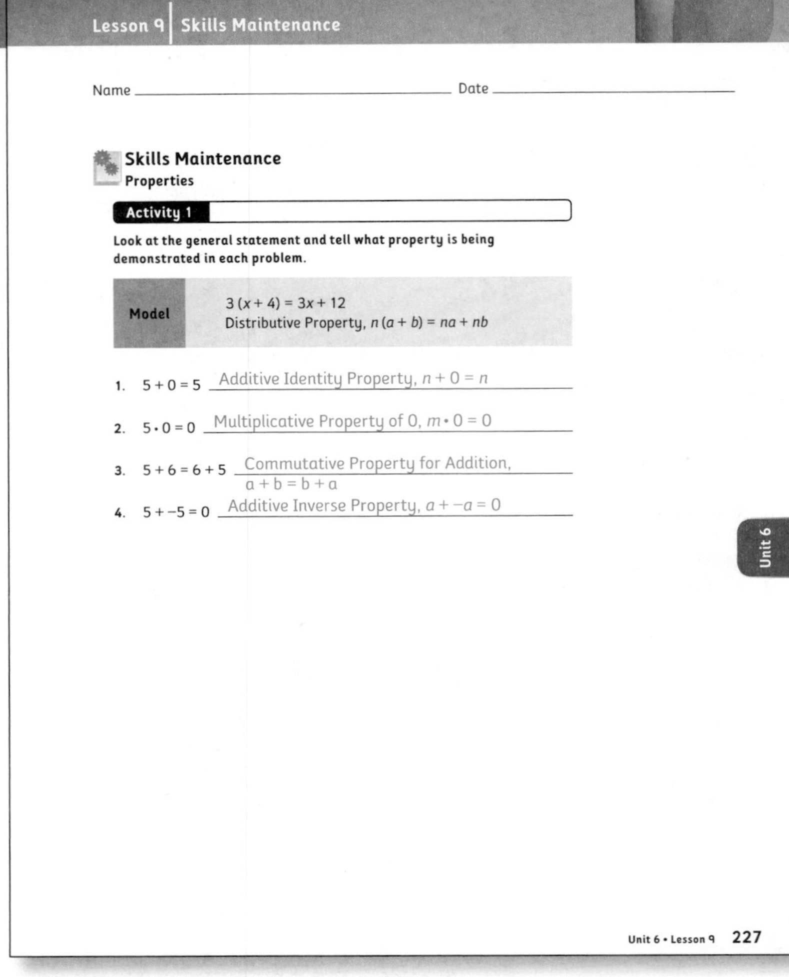

Lesson 9 | Skills Maintenance

Name ____________ Date ____________

Skills Maintenance
Properties

Activity 1

Look at the general statement and tell what property is being demonstrated in each problem.

Model	$3(x + 4) = 3x + 12$ Distributive Property, $n(a + b) = na + nb$

1. $5 + 0 = 5$ Additive Identity Property, $n + 0 = n$
2. $5 \cdot 0 = 0$ Multiplicative Property of 0, $m \cdot 0 = 0$
3. $5 + 6 = 6 + 5$ Commutative Property for Addition, $a + b = b + a$
4. $5 + -5 = 0$ Additive Inverse Property, $a + -a = 0$

Unit 6

Unit 6 • Lesson 9 227

Skills Maintenance

Properties

(*Interactive Text*, page 227)

Activity 1

Students tell what property is being demonstrated in each problem by looking at the general statement.

Problem Solving:
▶ Finding the Volume of Complex Objects

What are the key volume formulas?
(*Student Text*, pages 491–494)

Lesson 9 | Problem Solving:
▶Finding the Volume of Complex Objects

▶Problem Solving: Finding the Volume of Complex Objects

What are the key volume formulas?

In this unit we have learned to use the relationship of the height and the area of the base of an object as a way to find its volume.

Cylinders and cones are two basic types of three-dimensional objects where we use the two-dimensional base and the height to find the volume.

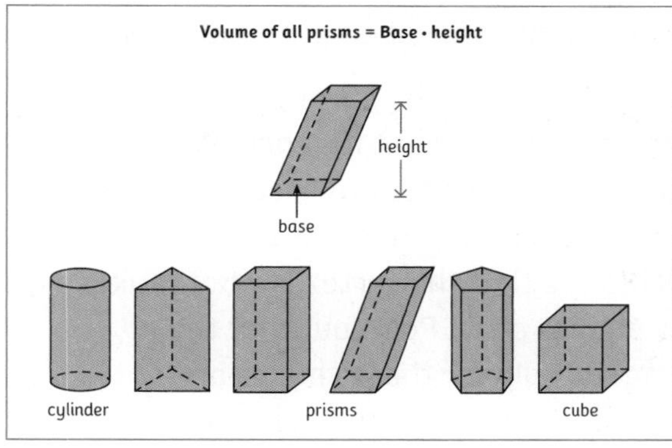

Unit 6 • Lesson 491

Connect to Prior Knowledge

Begin by telling students that we learned a lot of volume formulas in this unit. Ask students to tell you what these formulas are as you make a list on the board or overhead. If students need help with the formulas, remind them of the attributes that we use to classify the shapes. Then tell students how these attributes relate to the formulas.

Link to Today's Concept

Tell students that in today's lesson, we summarize these volume formulas. Then we learn to use them all together to find the volumes of complex shapes.

Demonstrate

Engagement Strategy: Teacher Modeling

Demonstrate the different objects and volume formulas we looked at in one of the following ways:

mBook: Use the *mBook Teacher Edition* for *Student Text*, pages 491–492.

Overhead Projector: Reproduce the objects and formulas on a transparency, and modify as discussed.

Board: Copy the objects and formulas on the board, and modify as discussed.

- Show the cylinder, prisms, and cube. Point out that the cylinder is a special case of the prism with a circular base. Be sure students see that the top and bottom of these shapes are what make them alike, even though they all look different.
- Remind students of the volume formula they learned for prisms: **Base • height**. Display a prism, and label the base and height.

What are the key volume formulas?
(continued)

Demonstrate

- Discuss the volume formula for cones and pyramids $\left(\frac{1}{3} \cdot \textbf{Base} \cdot \textbf{height}\right)$, and discuss how we classify shapes as pyramids. m
- Show the cone and the pyramid, and point out the base and height for each. Remind students that the cone is a special case of a pyramid with a circular base. Be sure students see that the vertex is what makes these shapes alike. Point out that the volume formula for these shapes are connected to their unique physical attributes. m
- Review the formula for the volume of spheres: $\frac{4}{3}\pi r^3$. Show a sphere and point out the radius. m
- Tell students that knowing the volume of these basic objects helps us when we have to compute the total volume of a more complex object.

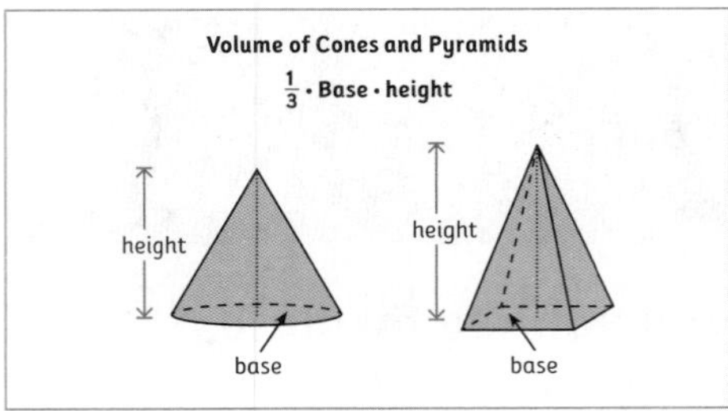

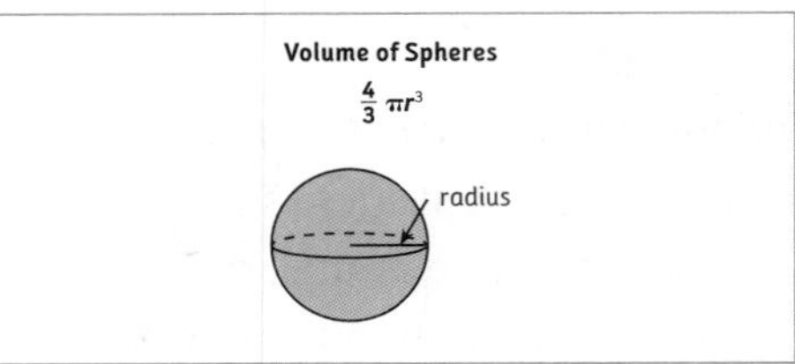

Knowing the volume of these basic objects helps us when we have to compute the total volume of a more complex object.

Example 1 shows us how to find the volume of a complex object made of three cans. If we look closely, we see three cylinders. We can combine the volume of each cylinder to get a total volume of the object.

Demonstrate

- Turn to page 493 of the *Student Text* to go over **Example 1**. In this example, we combine the volume of each cylinder to get a total volume for all three cans.
- Point out that each can has the same radius: **2 inches**. This tells us that the cans all have the same base. Use the steps to demonstrate how we find the total volume of the three cans.

STEP 1

- Walk through the calculations to find the Base of the cans, using the area formula for a circle to get the area of **12.56 square inches**.

STEP 2

- Explain that we can now find the volume of each can. We start with the first can, which has a height of 8 inches. We substitute this number into the formula with the Base value of 12.56 to get the volume of **100.48 inches^3**.

Example 1

What is the volume of the three cans?

We have two small cans of tomato sauce and one large can of tomato sauce. We need to find the volume of all three cans.

To find the total volume, we:

- find the volume of each of the cylinders.
- add the volume of each of the cylinders together.

The radius for the taller can is 2 inches. Each of the shorter cans also has a radius of 2 inches. So we know each can has the same area for the base.

STEP 1

First, find the area of the base of the cans.

Area of a circle $= \pi r^2$

$= 3.14 \cdot r^2$

$= 3.14 \cdot 2^2$

$= 3.14 \cdot 4$

The area of each base = 12.56 in^2.

STEP 2

Find the volume of the taller can of tomato sauce.

Volume of a cylinder = Base · height

$= 12.56 \cdot 8$

The volume of the taller can = 100.48 in^3.

Unit 6 • Lesson 9 493

What are the key volume formulas?
(*continued*)

Demonstrate

- Continue going over Example 1 on page 494 of the *Student Text*.

STEP 3

- Explain that we can find the volume of one of the shorter cans, with a height of 4 inches, using the same Base because we already know that all of the cans have the same radius. We use the volume formula to get **50.24 inches^3**. We only need to find the volume of one of the remaining two cans, since they have the same base and height.

STEP 4

- Explain that to find the total volume of the cans, we find the sum of the volume of the three cans: 50.24 + 50.24 + 100.48 = 200.96. **The total volume is 200.96 inches^3.**

Check for Understanding
Engagement Strategy: Pair/Share

Draw two cylinders, one with a **height of 10 inches** and a **radius of 3 inches**, and the other with a **height of 5 inches** and a **radius of 1 inch**. Have students partner with another student. Explain that they are to find the total volume of the cylinders. Have one partner find the volume of the taller cylinder (*282.6 in^3*), and the other partner find the volume of the shorter cylinder (*15.7 in^3*). Then have them add the volumes together to get the total volume of the two (*298.3 in^3*). When students have finished, review the answers with the class and invite pairs to explain their solutions.

STEP 3
Next we must find the volume of a shorter can of tomato sauce.

We know the area of the base of the shorter can is the same as the area of the base of the taller can. So the base of each of the cans is 12.56 in^2.

$$\text{Volume of a cylinder} = \text{Base} \cdot \text{height}$$
$$= 12.56 \cdot 4$$

The volume of the shorter can = 50.24 in^3.

STEP 4
Now we can add the volume of the cans to find the total volume of all three cans.

50.24 + 50.24 + 100.48 = 200.96

The total volume of the cans = 200.96 in^3.

How do we find the volume of polyhedrons?

(*Student Text*, pages 495–496)

Explain

Remind students of the polyhedron they created for Unit 5, where they found its surface area. Tell students that if we want, we can go back and find the volume of that same polyhedron with the strategy we are about to learn.

Demonstrate

- Turn to page 495 of the *Student Text* to look at the polyhedron on the page.
- Point out that it is difficult to see all of the parts of the polyhedron when it is drawn on paper.
- Remind students that the polyhedron is formed by a pattern of pyramids that go around the center.
- Explain that it is easier to see the parts of the polyhedron if we break it apart into familiar shapes. This will help us find the total volume of the polyhedron.
- Have students look at the disassembled polyhedron.

Ask:

What are the different shapes that make up the polyhedron?

Listen for:

- *There are six pyramids.*
- *There is a cube in the center.*

How do we find the volume of polyhedrons?

We studied polyhedrons in the last unit when we were working on surface area.

It is difficult to see all of the parts of the polyhedron shown because it is a three-dimensional object drawn on paper.

However, if we think about the pattern of pyramids that go around the center, we see that there are six pyramids in the drawing.

It is easier to see the parts of this polyhedron if we break it apart into familiar shapes. This will help us find the volume of the whole polyhedron.

How do we find the volume of polyhedrons? *(continued)*

Demonstrate

- Continue on page 496 of the *Student Text* to look at the cube and the pyramid.
- Explain that we need to look at one of the pyramids to see the dimensions of its height and base. We also need to look at the dimensions of the cube.
- Explain that with these dimensions, we have all the measurements we need to figure out the volume of the polyhedron. Use the steps to demonstrate how we find its volume.

STEP 1

- Explain that we start by finding the volume of one pyramid. We know that **Volume** = $\frac{1}{3}$ • **Base • height**.

STEP 2

- Remind students that we need to find the volume of the cube in the center of the polyhedron. We know that we use the formula **Volume of a cube = depth • Base • height**.

STEP 3

- Explain that we add the volumes of the six pyramids and the one cube to find the total volume.

Let's look at one of the pyramids so that we can see the height and dimensions of the base. We also need to look at the cube to see its dimensions.

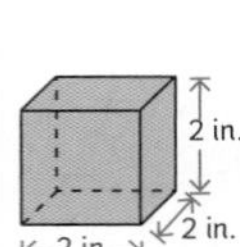

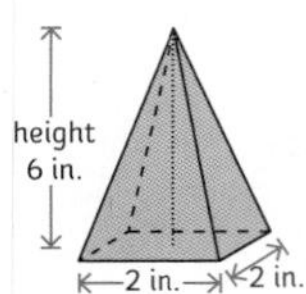

The measurements for the pyramid and the cube are all that we need to figure out the volume of the polyhedron.

Steps for Finding the Volume of the Polyhedron

STEP 1
Find the volume of one pyramid.
Remember, Volume = $\frac{1}{3}$ • Base • height

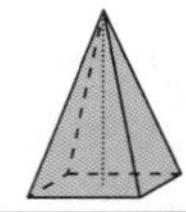

STEP 2
Find the volume of the cube in the center.
Volume of a cube = depth • width • height

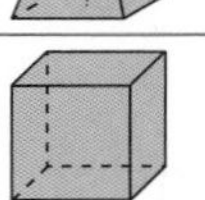

STEP 3
Add the volumes of six pyramids and the cube to find the total volume.

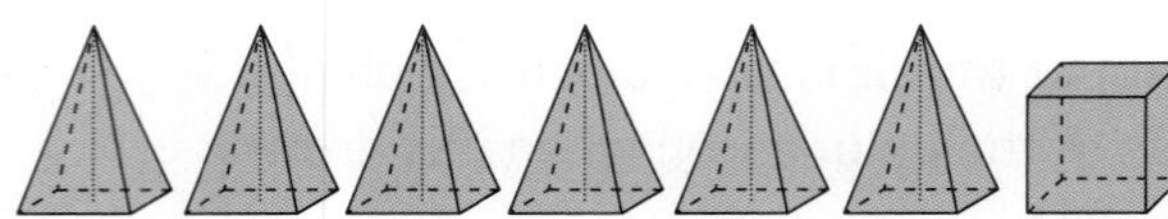

Problem-Solving Activity
Turn to ***Interactive Text***, page 228.

mBook Reinforce Understanding
Use the ***mBook Study Guide*** to review lesson concepts.

Problem-Solving Activity
(*Interactive Text*, pages 228–230)

Have students turn to pages 228–230 in the *Interactive Text*. Read the instructions carefully with students.

First students circle the volume formula for each of the shapes and compute their volumes.

Lesson 9 | Problem-Solving Activity

Name ______________________ Date ______________

Problem-Solving Activity
Finding the Volume of Complex Objects

Look at each of the shapes and select the correct volume formula for it. Then find the volume.

1. What is this shape's volume formula? (circle one)
(a) $V =$ Base • height (circled)
(b) $V = \frac{1}{3}$ Base • height
(c) $V = \frac{4}{3}\pi r^3$
Compute the volume of this shape if it has a Base of 4 cm² and a height of 10cm. 40 cu. cm
Show your work here.
$\frac{1}{3} \cdot 4 \cdot 10$

2. What is this shape's volume formula? (circle one)
(a) $V =$ Base • height
(b) $V = \frac{1}{3}$ Base • height (circled)
(c) $V = \frac{4}{3}\pi r^3$
Compute the volume of this shape if it has a Base of 2 cm² and a height of 6 cm. 4 cu. cm
Show your work here.
$\frac{1}{3} \cdot 2 \cdot 6$

228 Unit 6 • Lesson 9

Lesson 9 | Problem-Solving Activity

Name ______________________ Date ______________

3. What is this shape's volume formula? (circle one)
(a) $V =$ Base • height (circled)
(b) $V = \frac{1}{3}$ Base • height
(c) $V = \frac{4}{3}\pi r^3$
Compute the volume of this shape if it has a Base of 8 cm² and a height of 7 cm. 56 cu. cm
Show your work here.
$8 \cdot 7$

4. What is this shape's volume formula? (circle one)
(a) $V =$ Base • height
(b) $V = \frac{1}{3}$ Base • height (circled)
(c) $V = \frac{4}{3}\pi r^3$
Compute the volume of this shape if it has a Base of 4 cm² and a height of 11 cm. $14\frac{2}{3}$ cu. cm
Show your work here.
$\frac{1}{3} \cdot 4 \cdot 11$

Unit 6

Unit 6 • Lesson 9 229

Next students sketch a picture of a compound shape by combining two or more of the shapes they just worked with. Then they compute the volume of the compound shape. They are to use the same dimensions and measurements given on pages 228–229 of the *Interactive Text* for computing the volume.

Monitor students' work as they complete the activities.

Watch for:

- Can students identify the correct volume formula for the shapes?
- Can students apply the formula and compute the volume of the shape?
- Do students sketch a compound shape with two or more of the shapes from pages 228–229?
- Do students add the volumes of each individual part to come up with the total volume of the compound shape?
- Can students describe what strategies they used to find the total volume?

Reinforce Understanding
Remind students that they can review lesson concepts by accessing the online *mBook Study Guide*.

Lesson 9 | Problem-Solving Activity

Name ____________ Date ____________

Problem-Solving Activity
Finding the Volume of Complex Objects

Sketch a picture of a polyhedron that uses two or more of the shapes from Questions 1–4. Find the volume of the polyhedron using the dimensions and measurements you know.

Sketch your compound shape here. Answers will vary.

Find your shape's volume. Make sure to look for a pattern when you determine the total volume. Think carefully about the parts of the polyhedron that you cannot see. Make sure that you can explain how you figured out the volume of the polyhedron. Be able to describe what strategies you used to find the volume.

What is its volume? Answers will vary.

mBook **Reinforce Understanding**
Use the mBook *Study Guide* to review lesson concepts.

230 Unit 6 • Lesson 9

Homework

Go over the instructions on pages 497–498 of the *Student Text* for each part of the homework.

Activity 1

Students select the attribute that the two shapes have in common.

Activity 2

Students add the volumes of shapes to find the total volume of a compound shape.

Lesson 9

Homework

Activity 1

Select the attribute that the two shapes have in common.

1. 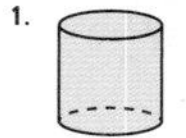 
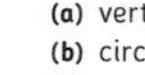 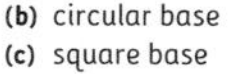
(a) vertex
(b) circular base b
(c) square base

2. 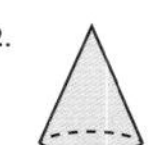 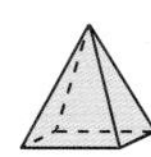
(a) vertex a
(b) circular base
(c) square base

3.  
(a) vertex
(b) a base b
(c) circular base

4. 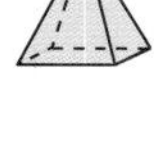 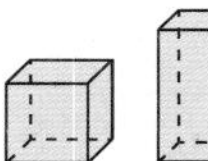
(a) vertex
(b) circular base
(c) square base c

Activity 2

Add together all of the volumes of the compound shapes to find the total volume of the shape.

1. The volume of the cube is 10 cm^3. The volume of each rectangular prism is 12 cm^3. What is the total volume?
34 cm^3

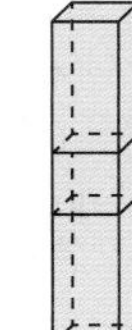

2. The volume of the cylinder is 30 cm^3. The volume of each cone is 10 cm^3. What is the total volume?
50 cm^3

Lesson 9

Homework

Go over the instructions on page 498 of the *Student Text* for each part of the homework.

Activity 3

Students give a general pattern that describes the properties. Examples of the properties are given to help them.

Activity 4 • Distributed Practice

Students practice addition and subtraction of integers, PEMDAS, and operations on fractions.

Lesson 10

Homework

Activity 3

Give a general pattern for each of the properties named below. An example of the property is provided to help you.

1. Distributive Property, $4(n + 3) = 4n + 12$ $g(n + b) = gn + gb$
2. Multiplicative Inverse Property, $5 \cdot \frac{1}{5} = 1$ $p \cdot \frac{1}{p} = 1$
3. Identity Property of Addition, $100 + 0 = 100$ $y + 0 = y$
4. Identity Property of Multiplication, $5 \cdot 1 = 5$ $t \cdot 1 = t$
5. Multiplicative Property of Zero, $25 \cdot 0 = 0$ $q \cdot 0 = 0$
6. Commutative Property for Addition, $2.5 + 3.7 = 3.7 + 2.5$ $d + e = e + d$

Activity 4 • Distributed Practice

Solve.

1. $-5 \div 5 + 7 - 2 = a$ 4
2. $\frac{3}{6} \div \frac{1}{2} = b$ 1
3. $-6 + 6 = c$ 0
4. $3^2 - (3 \cdot 3) = d$ 0
5. $3^2 - (-3 \cdot 3) = e$ 18
6. $9 - -8 = f$ 17
7. $\frac{2}{3} \div \frac{2}{3} = g$ 1
8. $\frac{3}{1} \cdot \frac{1}{3} = h$ 1

498 Unit 6 • Lesson 10

Lesson 10 | Unit Review ▶Algebraic Rules and Properties

Problem Solving:

▶Volume of Three-Dimensional Shapes

Lesson Planner

Vocabulary Development

PASS rule
consecutive numbers
number grid
multiplicative
additive
distributive property
volume
cubic inch
cubic unit

Skills Maintenance

Using Properties With Integers

Building Number Concepts:

▶ Algebraic Rules and Properties

Students are reminded that integer rules are used constantly in algebraic expressions and equations. We review the order of operations for evaluating expressions.

Algebraic expressions can be written to represent consecutive numbers in a number grid. We also review how the distributive property allows us to multiply the terms inside of the parentheses by a coefficient.

Problem Solving:

▶ Volume of Three-Dimensional Shapes

Student review three-dimensional shapes which can be grouped based on attributes. Grouping helps us understand volume formulas.

Cylinders, prisms, and cubes have common attributes. We can find their volumes by multiplying base times height. Cones and pyramids have common attributes. The volume of three cones fills a cylinder with the same base and height. The same is true of pyramids.

Lesson 10 | Skills Maintenance

Name ______________________ Date ______________________

Skills Maintenance
Using Properties With Integers

Activity 1

Use the properties and rules you know to simplify the problems.

1. $3(m - 4) + 10 \div 2$
   $3m - 12 + 5$
   $3m - 7$

2. $15 \div -3 + 10(9 \div 3) \cdot 2x$
   $15 \div -3 + 10 \cdot 3 \cdot 2x$
   $-5 + 10 \cdot 3 \cdot 2x$
   $-5 + 30 \cdot 2x$
   $25 \cdot 2x$

3. $4(4 + k) + k(k - 15)$
   $16 + 4k + k^2 - 15k$

Unit 6

Unit 6 • Lesson 10 231

Skills Maintenance

Using Properties With Integers
(*Interactive Text*, page 231)

Activity 1

Students use the properties and rules they learned to simplify the problems.

Building Number Concepts:
▶ Algebraic Rules and Properties

What rules help us evaluate algebraic expressions?

(*Student Text*, pages 499–502)

Discuss

Begin by writing the following numeric equation on the board:

$$-4 + (6 \cdot -2) \div 2^2$$

Ask students how you would start if you were going to evaluate this expression. Make sure you ask them what integer rules they would use.

Listen for:

- *You start inside of the parentheses.*
- *You need to use PASS when you multiply 6 • −2. The answer is negative.*
- *You need to compute the exponent next.*
- *You add the −4 last.*

Work through the expression with students. Ask them to perform the operations and discuss their reasons with the class.

Demonstrate

- Turn to *Student Text*, page 499, and demonstrate the rules for operations with integers and the order of operations.
- Discuss the importance of integer rules and PEMDAS. These rules make sure that the solution to equations like the one we just looked at result in the same solution.
- Show the table in **Review 1** to students to go over the addition and subtraction rules of integers. Remind students that subtraction is the same as adding the opposite. We see this in the examples **9 − −2 = 9 + 2** and **9 − 2 = 9 + −2**.

Lesson 10 | Unit Review
▶Algebraic Rules and Properties
Problem Solving:
▶Volume of Three-Dimensional Shapes

▶Algebraic Rules and Properties

What rules help us evaluate algebraic expressions?

To get the same answer every time we evaluate an algebraic expression, we need rules that we can depend on.

Review 1

What are the rules we use when working with algebraic expressions?

Mathematicians have created two major rules that we can use with algebraic expressions.

The first major rule involves adding, subtracting, multiplying, and dividing integers. We use these rules all the time when we work with algebraic expressions and equations.

Addition/Subtraction	Multiplication/Division
Remember, subtraction is the same as adding the opposite. 9 − −2 = 9 + 2 9 − 2 = 9 + −2	Remember PASS: **P**ositive **A**nswers Have the **S**ame **S**igns 8 • −5 = −40 −8 • −5 = 40

The second major rule involves the order of operations. The acronym PEMDAS helps us think about how we evaluate numeric expressions.

Unit 6 • Lesson 10 499

- Then go over the multiplication and division rules. Remind students of PASS: Positive Answers Have the Same Signs. Show the example **8 • −5 = −40**. In this case, the numbers being multiplied do not have the same signs. The answer is negative.
- Then show the second example: **−8 • −5 = 40**. Point out that all of the numbers being multiplied have the same sign, in this case negative, so the answer is positive.
- You may consider having students give you problems where they have to remember PASS and that subtraction is adding the opposite.

Demonstrate

- Have students turn to page 500 of the *Student Text* to review the second major rule in algebra: the order of operations.
- Go over the table to look at each step of PEMDAS. When you go over PEMDAS, remind students about the different levels. That is, if there is just multiplication/division or addition/subtraction, you work each expression from left to right. Otherwise, follow the steps in PEMDAS.
- Explain that these major rules give us all of the information we need to evaluate expressions.
- Go over **Review 2** to demonstrate how we apply the rules for integers and PEMDAS to evaluate the expression $\mathbf{10 \cdot 4 \div -2 - 3^2}$.
- Show how we follow the order of operations to solve the exponent first, since there are no parentheses in the expression.
- Solve the multiplication and division from left to right. Start with $10 \cdot 4$ to get **40**. Then divide $40 \div -2$ to get **−9**. PASS tells us that this answer will be negative. So we rewrite the expression as **−20 + −9**.
- Explain that there are no more multiplication or division operations, so we move to addition and subtraction. We subtract 9 from −20 to get **−29**.
- Make sure students have a thorough understanding of why each step is performed.

Explain

Review the term evaluate. Remind students that we substitute for the variable. This means we are turning an algebraic expression into a numeric expression.

PEMDAS—The Rules for Order of Operations		
Step 1	**P**—Parentheses	Work what is inside the parentheses.
Step 2	**E**—Exponents	Work any numbers with exponents.
Step 3	**M**—Multiplication **D**—Division	Work multiplication or division problems from left to right.
Step 4	**A**—Addition **S**—Subtraction	Last of all, work addition or subtraction problems from left to right.

These two major rules give us all the information we need to evaluate expressions like the ones shown in Review 2.

Review 2

How do we use rules for integers and PEMDAS to evaluate expressions?

$\mathbf{10 \cdot 4 \div -2 - 3^2}$

$10 \cdot 4 \div -2 - 3^2$ ← Work with exponents.

$\mathbf{10 \cdot 4} \div -2 - 9$ ← Multiplication/division: Work left to right and use PASS.

$\mathbf{40 \div -2} - 9$ ← Multiplication/division: Work left to right and use PASS.

$-20 + -9$ ← Add the opposite.

$\mathbf{-29}$ ← Solution.

What rules help us evaluate algebraic expressions? *(continued)*

Demonstrate

- Look at **Review 3** on page 501 of the *Student Text*.
- Demonstrate how to substitute **10** for the variable ***j***. Show how to rewrite the expression as a numeric expression: $\mathbf{-3 \cdot 10 + 8 - 10}$.
- Make sure students understand that operations at a level like multiplication/division or addition/subtraction are done left to right. In other words, if an expression has only multiplication and division operations, we simply work left to right.
- Show how we first multiply $\mathbf{-3 \cdot 10}$ and use PASS to determine that the product is negative.
- Point out that there are no more multiplication or division operations, so we move to addition and subtraction. Again we work from left to right. Remind students that subtraction is the same as adding the opposite.
- Once we complete the addition and subtraction, we get the solution **−32**.

Lesson 10

We can also evaluate algebraic expressions that use variables if we know the value of the variable. We just have to substitute the value and then evaluate.

Review 3

How do we use substitution to evaluate expressions?

$\mathbf{-3j + 8 - j}$

Let $j = 10$

$-3j + 8 - j$ ← Substitute 10 for j.

$\mathbf{-3 \cdot 10} + 8 - 10$ ← Multiplication/division: Work left to right and use PASS.

$\mathbf{-30} + 8 - 10$ ← Addition/subtraction: Work left to right and use subtraction (same as adding the opposite).

$-22 + -10$

$\mathbf{-32}$ ← Solution.

Finally, we look at the distributive property, which is one of the most important properties we will use in beginning algebra.

Demonstrate

- Use *Student Text*, page 502, to review the distributive property. Remind students that with this property, we distribute the coefficients across all of the terms inside the parentheses. The coefficient means we multiply by each of the terms in the parentheses.
- Go over **Review 4**. Begin by pointing out that the terms inside the parentheses in each problem cannot be combined because they are unlike terms.
- Next remind students that the number outside of the parentheses is a coefficient. That means the number is multiplied by each number or variable inside of the parentheses. So we multiply each term by the coefficient. Another way of saying this is that the coefficient is being distributed across the terms inside the parentheses.

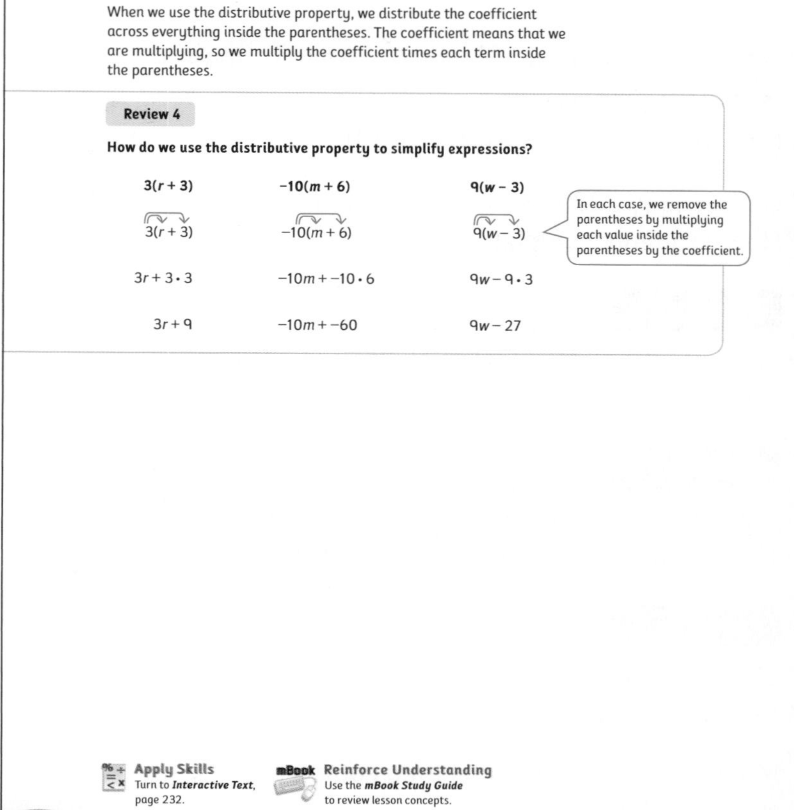

Lesson 10
When we use the distributive property, we distribute the coefficient across everything inside the parentheses. The coefficient means that we are multiplying, so we multiply the coefficient times each term inside the parentheses.
Review 4
How do we use the distributive property to simplify expressions?
3(r + 3)
−10(m + 6)
9(w − 3)
3(r + 3)
−10(m + 6)
9(w − 3)
In each case, we remove the parentheses by multiplying each value inside the parentheses by the coefficient.
3r + 3 • 3
−10m + −10 • 6
9w − 9 • 3
3r + 9
−10m + −60
9w − 27
Apply Skills
Turn to Interactive Text, page 232.
mBook Reinforce Understanding
Use the mBook Study Guide to review lesson concepts.
502 Unit 6 • Lesson 10

Unit Review: More Algebraic Rules and Properties

(*Interactive Text*, pages 232–233)

Go to pages 232–233 in the *Interactive Text*. Have students complete the activities.

Activity 1

Students use PEMDAS to evaluate expressions with integers.

Activity 2

Students substitute numbers for the variables. They should use the PASS rules to help them.

Activity 3

Students use the distributive property to simplify the expressions.

Monitor students' work as they complete the activities.

Watch for:

- Are students able to use PEMDAS and integer operation rules?
- Do students use the correct operation after they have substituted a number for a variable?
- Can students distribute the coefficient across both terms?
- Do students understand they are simplifying the expressions, not solving them?

Once students have finished, discuss any difficulties that you noticed.

mBook Reinforce Understanding

Remind students that they can review lesson concepts by accessing the online *mBook Study Guide*.

Lesson 10 | Unit Review

Name ______ Date ______

Unit Review
More Algebraic Rules and Properties

Activity 1

Use PEMDAS to evaluate these expressions with integers.

1. $-4 \cdot 3 \div (6 + -2)$
   $-4 \cdot 3 \div 4$
   $-12 \div 4 = -3$
2. $-25 \div -5 + -3$
   $5 + -3 = 2$
3. $(20 + 10) \div 2 \cdot -3$
   $30 \div 2 \cdot -3$
   $15 \cdot -3 = -45$
4. $4^2 + -6 - -3$
   $16 + -6 - -3$
   $10 - -3 = 13$
5. $6 \cdot (-8 \div -4)$
   $6 \cdot 2 = 12$

Activity 2

Use substitution to evaluate the expressions. Remember the PASS rules.

1. Let $f = -2$ $3f + 6 - 5$
   $3(-2) + 6 - 5$
   $-6 + 6 - 5 = -5$
2. Let $m = 9$ $3m - -4$
   $3(9) - -4$
   $27 - -4 = 31$
3. Let $v = -1$ $4v + 10 + -6v$
   $4(-1) + 10 + -6(-1)$
   $-4 + 10 + 6$
   $6 + 6 = 12$
4. Let $z = 10$ $-2z + 5$
   $-2(10) + 5$
   $-20 + 5 = -15$
5. Let $y = 5$ $3y - (2 \cdot 10)$
   $3(5) - 20$
   $15 - 20 = -5$

232 Unit 6 • Lesson 10

Lesson 10 | Unit Review

Name ______ Date ______

Activity 3

Use the distributive property to simplify these expressions.

1. $-2(v + 7)$ $-2v + -14$
2. $-3(b - 5)$ $-3b + 15$
3. $6(e + 6)$ $6e + 36$
4. $2(-w + 10)$ $-2w + 20$
5. $5(g - 5)$ $5g - 25$

Unit 6

Unit 6 • Lesson 10 233

Problem Solving: ▶ Volume of Three-Dimensional Shapes

What is the volume of three-dimensional shapes?

(*Student Text*, pages 503–508)

Discuss

Discuss with students the attributes of the Bases of objects. Talk about why the word Base is capitalized.

Ask:

> **What is the importance of Base and height when finding the volume of three-dimensional shapes?**

Listen for:

- *Base is the bottom of most three-dimensional shapes.*
- *You can stack bases to find the volume for prisms.*
- *The base of a two-dimensional shape is different from the base of a three-dimensional shape.*
- *Base • height is part of most volume formulas.*

Demonstrate

- Turn to page 503 of the *Student Text* to review the different groupings of shapes. Make sure students understand how we sort the shapes based on attributes. Go over each of the numbered points to discuss how we group cylinders, prisms, and cubes together.
- Then discuss the second group: cones and pyramids. Read through each of the numbered points to show why these objects are grouped together.

Lesson 10

▶Problem Solving: Volume of Three-Dimensional Shapes

What is the volume of three-dimensional shapes?

When we studied surface area in the last unit, we sorted three-dimensional shapes based on attributes. This sorting helps us think about volume formulas. Here are the two groups of shapes that we used.

Group 1

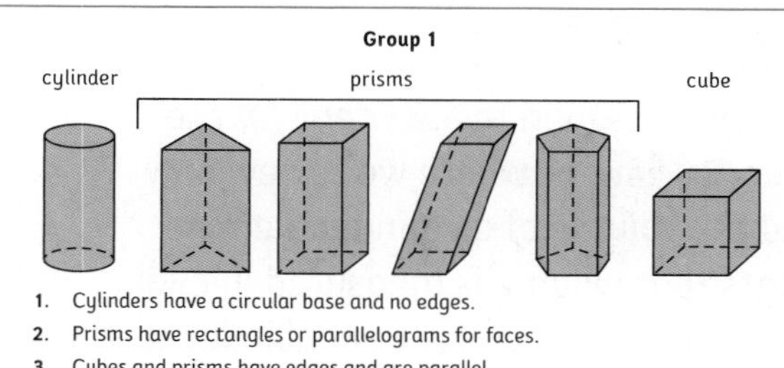

1. Cylinders have a circular base and no edges.
2. Prisms have rectangles or parallelograms for faces.
3. Cubes and prisms have edges and are parallel.
4. A cube has squares for each of its faces.
5. Prisms can have many different shapes, including polygons, for bases.

Group 2

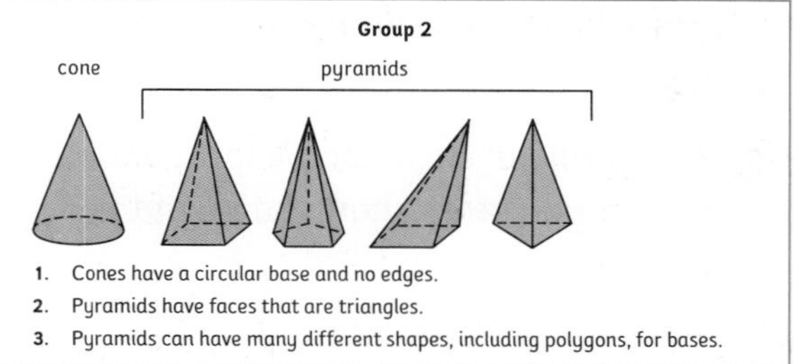

1. Cones have a circular base and no edges.
2. Pyramids have faces that are triangles.
3. Pyramids can have many different shapes, including polygons, for bases.

Now let's review different volume formulas. First let's look at finding the volume for cylinders.

Unit 6 • Lesson 10 503

What is the volume of three-dimensional shapes? *(continued)*

Demonstrate

- Turn to page 504 in the *Student Text* to go over **Review 1**, where we review how to find the volume of a cylinder. Remind students that volume is measured in cubic units. In this example, we use cubic inches.
- Review the formula for the volume of a cylinder: **Volume = Base • height**. Then have students look at the dimensions of the cylinder.
- Emphasize the role of Base and height, and make sure that you stress how the height is just a stack of bases.
- Show how to find the Base of the cylinder by finding the area of the circle. We plug in the value of the radius, in this case 2, and compute to get the Base of **12.56 square inches**.
- Then show how to find the volume using the volume formula: **Base • height**. We put in 12.56 for the Base and 5 for the height. We get the volume of **62.8 cubic inches**.

Lesson 10

We will use Volume = Base • height as a basic part of the formula to find the volume of three-dimensional shapes. We capitalize the word Base because we are talking about the area of the base of the object, which has two dimensions—depth and width. Once we find this two-dimensional base, we multiply it by the height of the object.

Review 1

How do we find the volume of a cylinder?

Volume of a Cylinder
Volume = Base • height

5 in.

radius = 2 in.

Base of a cylinder = Area of a circle
$= \pi r^2$
$= 3.14 \cdot 2^2$
$= 3.14 \cdot 4$
Base of the cylinder = 12.56 in^2.

Now we can find the volume of the cylinder.

Volume of a cylinder = Base • height
= 12.56 • 5

Base is the area of the cylinder base.

Volume of the cylinder = 62.8 in^3.

504 Unit 6 • Lesson 10

Demonstrate

- Turn to page 505 of the *Student Text* to go over **Review 2**. Here we find the volume of a prism.
- Again emphasize the role of base and height, and make sure that you highlight how the height is just a stack of bases.
- Show how we find the Base by using the area formula of a parallelogram to get the Base of **6 in^2**.
- Point out that now we can find the volume using the volume formula for a prism: **Base • height**. We get **36 inches^3**.

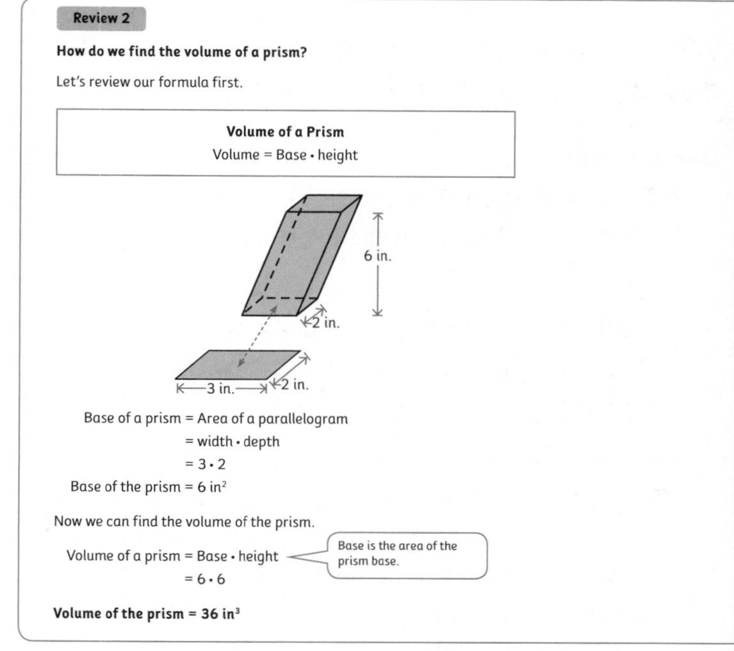

Lesson 10
Review 2
How do we find the volume of a prism?
Let's review our formula first.
Volume of a Prism
Volume = Base • height
6 in.
2 in.
3 in.
2 in.
Base of a prism = Area of a parallelogram
= width • depth
= 3 • 2
Base of the prism = 6 in²
Now we can find the volume of the prism.
Volume of a prism = Base • height
= 6 • 6
Base is the area of the prism base.
Volume of the prism = 36 in³
Unit 6 • Lesson 1
505

What is the volume of three-dimensional shapes? *(continued)*

Demonstrate

- Turn to **Review 3** on page 506 of the *Student Text* to go over how to find the volume of a cube.
- Again point out the role of base and height, and make sure that you stress how the height is just a stack of bases.
- Show how we find the Base by using the area formula of a square to get the Base of **4 in^2**. You may also point out that only one dimension needs to be given for a cube. The definition of a cube is that all of the edges are of equal length.
- Show how to find the volume, using the volume formula for a cube: **Base • height**. We get **8 inches^3**.

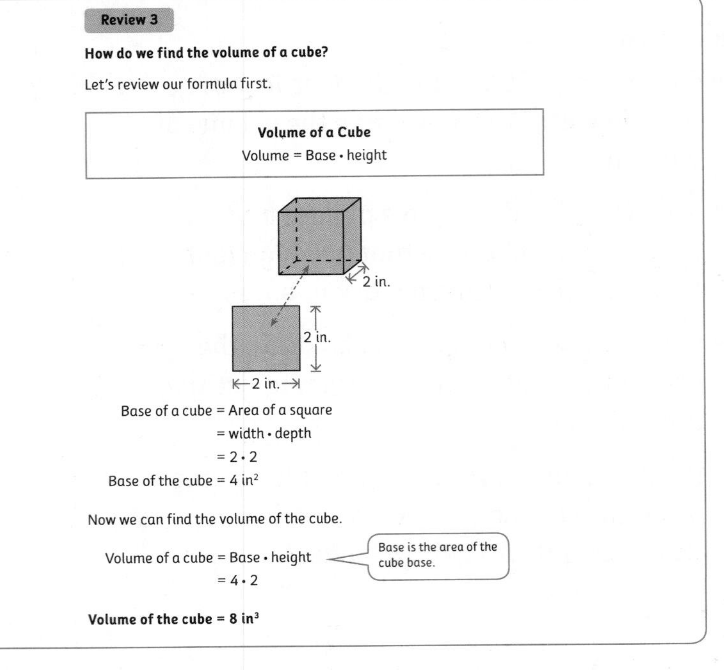
Lesson 10

Review 3

How do we find the volume of a cube?

Let's review our formula first.

Volume of a Cube
Volume = Base • height

Base of a cube = Area of a square
= width • depth
= 2 • 2
Base of the cube = 4 in^2

Now we can find the volume of the cube.

Volume of a cube = Base • height
= 4 • 2

Base is the area of the cube base.

Volume of the cube = 8 in^3

506 Unit 6 • Lesson 10

Demonstrate

- Before going over **Review 4** on page 507 of the *Student Text*, remind students that the contents of three cones fill a cylinder with the same base and height. This is an easy way to think about the volume formula for a cone or pyramid.
- Go through the example to review how we find the volume of a cone. Point out the volume formula: $\frac{1}{3}$ **• Base • height**.
- Show how we find the Base by using the area formula of a circle, as we did for the cylinder, to get the Base of **28.26 in²**.
- Show how to find the volume using the volume formula for a cone: $\frac{1}{3}$ • Base • height. We get **56.52 in³**.

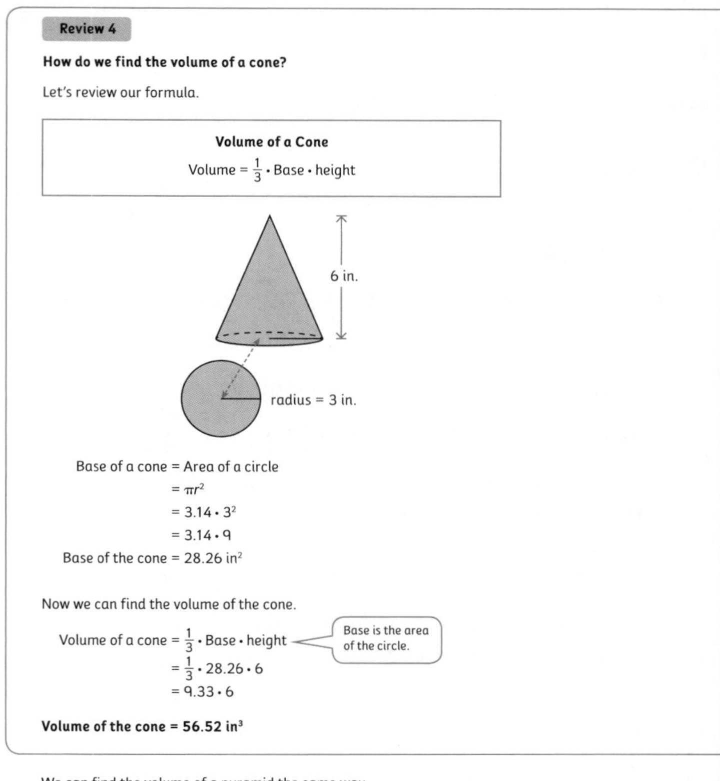
Lesson 10

Review 4

How do we find the volume of a cone?

Let's review our formula.

Volume of a Cone

Volume = $\frac{1}{3}$ • Base • height

Base of a cone = Area of a circle
= πr^2
= $3.14 \cdot 3^2$
= $3.14 \cdot 9$
Base of the cone = 28.26 in²

Now we can find the volume of the cone.

Volume of a cone = $\frac{1}{3}$ • Base • height
= $\frac{1}{3} \cdot 28.26 \cdot 6$
= $9.33 \cdot 6$

Base is the area of the circle.

Volume of the cone = 56.52 in³

We can find the volume of a pyramid the same way.

Unit 6 • Lesson 10 507

What is the volume of three-dimensional shapes? *(continued)*

Demonstrate

- Turn to page 508 of the *Student Text* to go over **Review 5**.
- Go through the example to review how to find the volume of a cone. Point out the volume formula: $\frac{1}{3}$ • **Base • height**.
- Show how we find the Base by using the area formula of a square to get the Base of **9 inches²**.
- Show how to find the volume using the volume formula for a pyramid: $\frac{1}{3}$ • Base • height. We get **12 in³**.

Review 5

How do we find the volume of a pyramid?

Let's review our formula.

Volume of a Pyramid
Volume = $\frac{1}{3}$ • Base • height

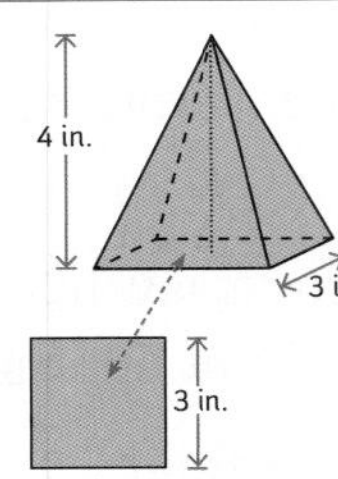

Base of a pyramid = Area of a square
= width • depth
= 3 • 3
Base of the pyramid = 9 in²

Now we can find the volume of the pyramid.

Volume of a pyramid = $\frac{1}{3}$ • Base • height
= $\frac{1}{3}$ • 9 • 4
= 3 • 4

Base is the area of the square.

Volume of the pyramid = 12 in³

Problem-Solving Activity Turn to ***Interactive Text***, page 234.

mBook Reinforce Understanding Use the ***mBook Study Guide*** to review lesson concepts.

Unit Review: Volume of Three-Dimensional Shapes

(*Interactive Text*, page 234)

Go to page 234 in the *Interactive Text*. Go over directions with students before they begin the activity.

Activity 1

Students find the volume of a pyramid, a cylinder, and a rectangular prism. The area formulas are provided for students, and they may use a calculator.

Monitor students' work as they complete the activity.

Watch for:

- Do students know what area formulas to use for each problem?
- Do students confuse the term Base when they compute the volume?
- Do students know how to use πr^2 and $2\pi r$ to find the volume of a cylinder?
- Do students accurately compute the two-dimensional base for each object?

Once students have finished, discuss any difficulties that you noticed.

mBook

Reinforce Understanding

Remind students that they can review lesson concepts by accessing the online *mBook Study Guide*.

Lesson 10 | Unit Review

Name ______________ Date ______________

Unit Review

Volume of Three-Dimensional Shapes

Activity 1

Use a calculator to find the volume of each shape. Use these important area formulas:

Area of a circle = πr^2
Area of a triangle = $\frac{1}{2} \cdot b \cdot h$
Area of a square or rectangle = $b \cdot h$
Volume of a prism = $B \cdot h$
Volume of a cylinder = $B \cdot h$
Volume of a pyramid = $\frac{1}{3} \cdot B \cdot h$

1. What is the volume of this pyramid? 12 in^3

6 in.
3 in.
2 in.

2. What is the volume of this cylinder? 28.26 in^3

10 in.
radius = 3 in.

3. What is the volume of this prism? 72 in^3

6 in.
4 in.
3 in.

mBook Reinforce Understanding
Use the mBook *Study Guide* to review lesson concepts.

234 Unit 6 • Lesson 10

Unit 6 | Monitoring Progress: ▶Unit Assessments

Assessment Planner

Students	Assess	Differentiate		Assess
	Day 1	Day 2	Day 3	Day 4
All	End-of-Unit Assessment *Form A*			Performance Assessments Unit 7 Opener
Scored 80% or above		Extension	Extension	
Scored Below 80%		Reinforcement	Retest	

Assessment Objectives

Building Number Concepts:
▶ More Algebraic Rules and Properties

- Use order of operations rules to evaluate algebraic and numeric expressions
- Use substitution to evaluate algebraic expressions
- Apply the distributive property to algebraic expressions

Problem Solving:
▶ Volume of Three-Dimensional Shapes

- Use formulas to find the volume of cylinders and prisms
- Find the volume of pyramids and cones by comparing them to prisms and cylinders
- Use a formula to find the volume of a sphere

Monitoring Progress: ▶ Unit Assessments

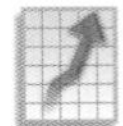

Assess
End-of-Unit Assessment

- Administer End-of-Unit Assessment Form A in the *Assessment Book*, pages 55–56.

Differentiate

- Review End-of-Unit Assessment Form A with class.
- Identify students for Extension or Reinforcement.

Extension
For those students who score 80 percent or better, provide the On Track! Activities from Unit 6, Lessons 6–10, from the *mBook Teacher Edition*.

Reinforcement
For those students who score below 80 percent, provide additional support in one of these ways:

- Have students access the online tutorial provided in the *mBook Study Guide*.
- Have students complete the Interactive Reinforcement Exercises for Unit 6, in the *mBook Study Guide*.
- Provide teacher-directed reteaching of unit concepts.

Retest
Administer End-of Unit Assessment Form B from the *mBook Teacher Edition* to those students who scored below 80 percent on Form A.

Assess
Performance Assessments

- Guide students through the Performance Assessment Model on *Assessment Book*, page 57. Then, administer the Performance Assessments on pages 58–59.

Form A

Monitoring Progress
Algebraic Rules and Properties

Part 1

Use PEMDAS to evaluate the expressions.

1. $10 \div -2 \cdot -3$ $-5 \cdot -3 = 15$
2. $-5 + 2^2 + -6$ $-5 + 4 + -6 = -7$
3. $3 \cdot 6 \div (-1 + 2)$ $3 \cdot 6 \div 1$; $18 \div 1 = 18$
4. $-100 + 90 + -7 + -2$ $-100 + 90 + -7 + -2 = -19$
5. $7 \cdot (-4 + -6)$ $7 \cdot -10 = -70$

Part 2

Evaluate the expressions.

1. Let $s = -4$
   $2s + 5 - 2$
   $2 \cdot -4 + 5 - 2 = -5$
2. Let $b = 7$
   $3b + -4$
   $3 \cdot 7 + -4 = 17$
3. Let $g = -2$
   $5g + -20 + -5g$
   $5 \cdot -2 + -20 + -5 \cdot -2 = -20$
4. Let $t = 10$
   $-3t - 5$
   $-3 \cdot 10 - 5 = -35$

Part 3

Use the distributive property to simplify the expressions.

1. $3(x + 7)$ $3x + 21$
2. $-5(r - 6)$ $-5r + 30$
3. $2(z + 3)$ $2z + 6$
4. $4(-m + 5)$ $-4m + 20$
5. $10(c - 10)$ $10c - 100$

Unit 6

Monitoring Progress
Volume of Three-Dimensional Shapes

Part 4

Use a calculator to solve.

Area of a circle = πr^2
Area of a triangle = $\frac{1}{2} \cdot b \cdot h$
Area of a square or rectangle = $b \cdot h$

1. What is the volume of this pyramid?
   15 inches³

2. What is the volume of this prism?
   160 inches³

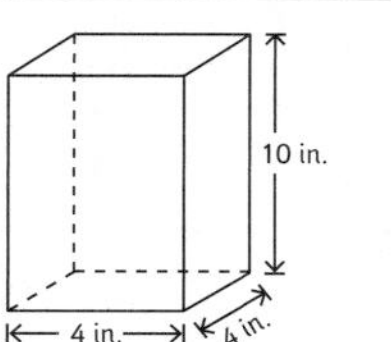

3. What is the volume of this cone?
   150.72 inches³

4. What is the volume of this cylinder?
   678.24 inches³

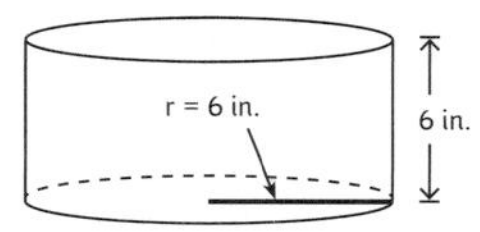

Name ______________________ Date ______________

Form B

mBook

Monitoring Progress
Algebraic Rules and Properties

Part 1

Use PEMDAS to evaluate the expressions.

1. $16 \div -2 \cdot -2$ $-8 \cdot -2 = 16$
2. $-6 + 3^2 + -4$ $-6 + 9 + -4 = -1$
3. $3 \cdot 5 \div (-1 + -4)$ $3 \cdot 5 \div -5 = -3$
4. $-80 + 90 + -4 + -4$ $10 + -4 + -4 = 2$
5. $5 \cdot (-3 + 6)$ $5 \cdot 3 = 15$

Part 2

Evaluate the expressions.

1. Let $s = -3$
   $4s + 4 - 2$
   $4 \cdot -3 + 4 - 2 = -10$
2. Let $b = 6$
   $2b + -4$
   $2 \cdot 6 + -4 = 8$
3. Let $g = -5$
   $3g + -10 + -2g$
   $3 \cdot -5 + -10 + -2 \cdot -5 = -15$
4. Let $t = 6$
   $-2t - 8$
   $-2 \cdot 6 - 8 = -20$

Part 3

Use the distributive property to simplify the expressions.

1. $2(x + 5)$ $2x + 10$
2. $-3(r - 4)$ $-3r + 12$
3. $4(z + 2)$ $4z + 8$
4. $5(-m + 6)$ $-5m + 30$
5. $9(c - 9)$ $9c - 81$

Name ______________________ Date ______________

Monitoring Progress
Volume of Three-Dimensional Shapes

Part 4

Use a calculator to solve.

Area of a circle = πr^2
Area of a triangle = $\frac{1}{2} \cdot b \cdot h$
Area of a square or rectangle = $b \cdot h$

1. What is the volume of this pyramid?
   18 inches²

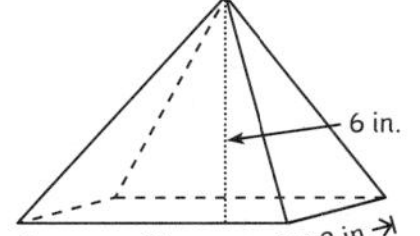

2. What is the volume of this prism?
   20 inches³

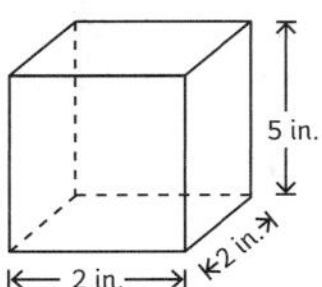

3. What is the volume of this cone?
   56.52 inches³

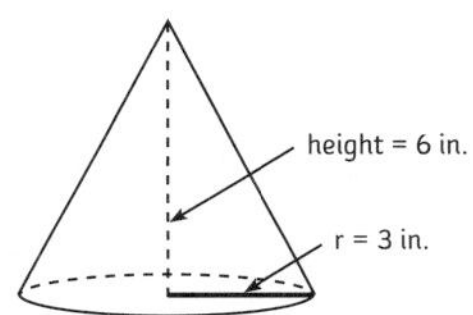

4. What is the volume of this cylinder?
   200.96 inches³

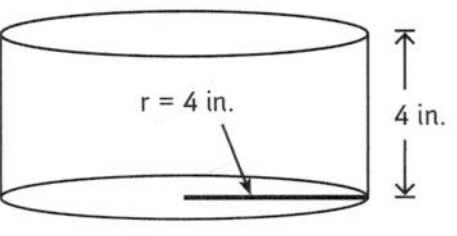

Name ______________________ Date ______________________

Monitoring Progress
Practice Problem 3-6

Solve the Problem

How many cubes are needed to fill in the entire shape?

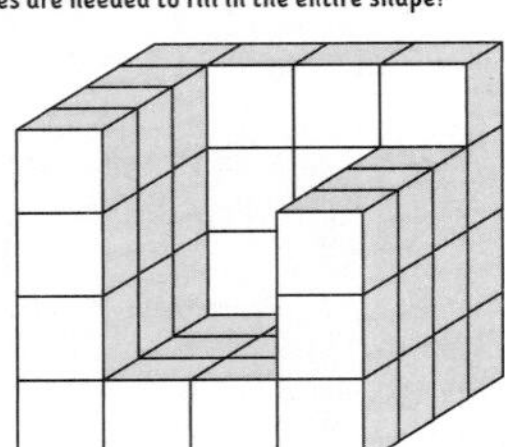

(a) 21
(b) 18
(c) 15
(d) 12

(The answer is a.)

Monitoring Progress
Problem 3-6-A

Solve the Problem

How many cubes are needed to fill in the entire shape?

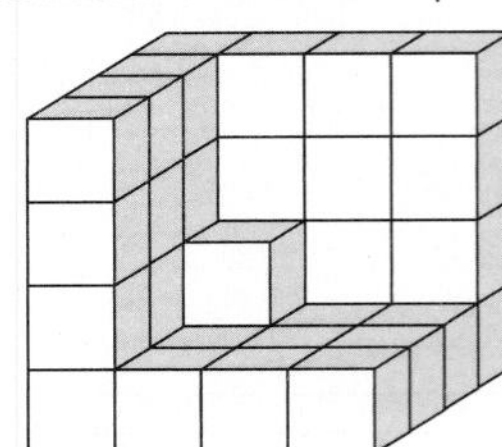

(a) 24
(b) 26
(c) 64
(d) 27

Name ______________________ Date ______________________

Monitoring Progress
Problem 3-6-B

Solve the Problem

Ace Packing Company packs books into boxes. The books for one job are all the same size—9 inches by 12 inches by 1 inch. The available boxes are 12 inches by 18 inches by 12 inches. How many books can be packed into each box? Draw a picture to help you solve the problem.

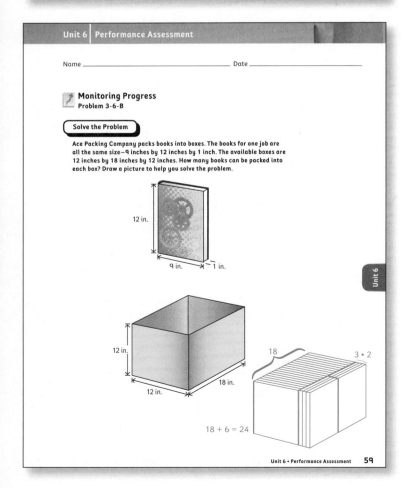

12 in.
9 in.
1 in.

12 in.
12 in.
18 in.

18
3 • 2
18 + 6 = 24

Unit 7 | Introduction to Algebraic Equations

Problem Solving:

Geometric Construction and Angle Measurement

$r = D \div t$!!!
45°?!!

What's he saying?

Unit Opener: Background Information

Read about snowboards, rate, and distance in the Unit Opener in *Student Text*, pages 509–510. Then share some of these additional facts with students.

- The equation $r = d \div t$ is read "rate equals distance divided by time." Forty-five degrees refers to the angle of the slope. In a jump, a ramp of 45 degrees is halfway to vertical, or 90 degrees.
- Snowboarding got its start in the 1960s and 1970s among people who enjoyed skiing, skateboarding, and surfing. In fact, they called themselves "snurfers" for snow surfers.
- Olympic gold medalist Shaun White said in an interview with the *Los Angeles Times* that snowboarding is "just math"—a 180, 360 (full circle), 1080, 1260. But snowboarders who catch a lot of air (or airdogs) have invented many more tricks than spinning in the air one or more times. An alley oop is a trick in which the snowboarder rotates forward to backward or backward to forward. For an eggplant, the snowboarder plants a hand on the lip of the halfpipe wall and rotates a half turn. Snowboarders who "stomp that McTwist" land one-and-a-half rotations (540 degrees) with a front flip. But if they are "rolling down the windows," it means they are flailing their arms wildly to regain balance.
- The highest speed recorded on a snowboard is 125.56 mph by Australian Darren Powell at Les Arcs, France.

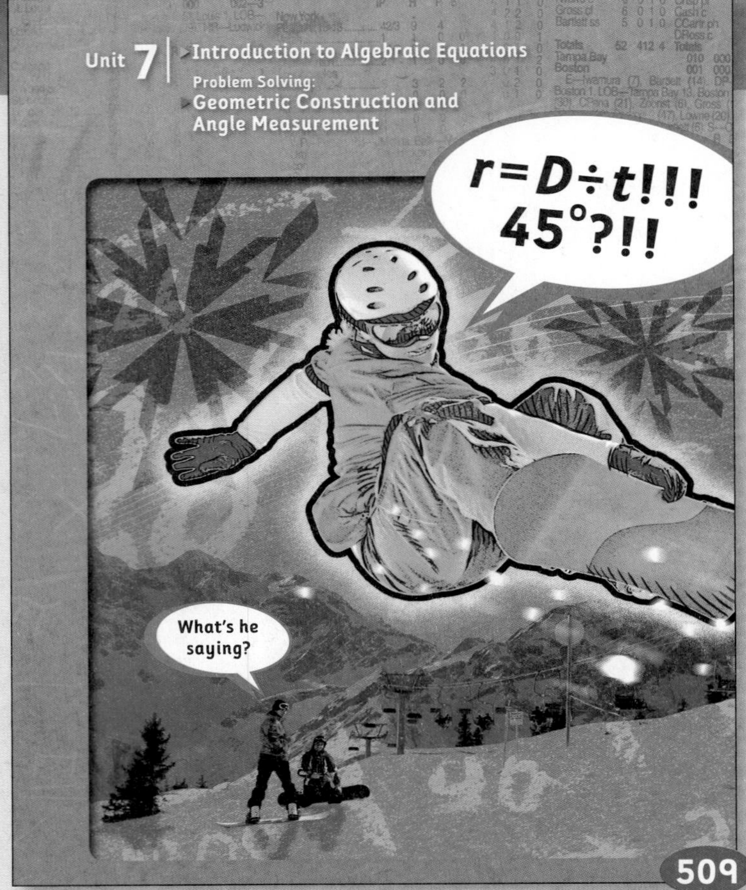

Unit 7 Building Number Concepts: Introduction to Algebraic Equations

Problem Solving: Geometric Construction and Angle Measurement

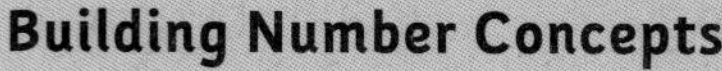

OBJECTIVES

Building Number Concepts	Problem Solving
• Understand the basic properties of algebraic equations • Balance equations involving symbols or variables • Solve problems involving algebraic equations	• Use a compass and straightedge to construct basic figures • Use algebraic reasoning to find missing angle measures • Explore the properties of triangles with congruent angles

Overview

This unit introduces students to algebraic equations and places an emphasis on how and why we balance equations. Equations in this unit are limited to one-step equations. We focus on how rules and properties from the toolbox help two equations remain balanced even though they do not look the same.

Unit Vocabulary
equation **balanced** **property of equality** **coefficient** **reciprocal**

As students move further into secondary mathematics, they work increasingly with angles and measurement. The Problem Solving strand reviews basic geometry terms related to lines and angles. Students begin to connect algebraic equations and angle measurement.

Unit Vocabulary
line segment **arc** **perpendicular** **right angle** **midpoint** **parallel** **constructions** **bisect** **supplementary angles**

Building Number Concepts:

Introduction to Algebraic Equations

Key Questions That Guide Student Understanding

- *Why is the concept of balance important to understanding algebraic equations?*

Enduring Understandings for Algebraic Equations

Many concepts in higher mathematics are built around the idea that we can transform expressions in equations to show equivalency between a new expression and an expression used in the beginning of a proof. Balancing equations—doing the same thing on both sides of the equal sign—is at the center of this process. Expressions remain balanced at each step.

Students best focus on the balance between the two expressions in an equation when exposed to a variety of visual representations. Balance scales, symbolic objects on the scales, and the special symbols that we used in previous units help students see how variables and numbers are manipulated at each step when solving an equation.

Tools for Understanding Algebraic Equations

Using Models
The balance beam is a traditional visual used to remind students that what is done to an expression on one side of an equation should also be done to the other side. To extend this image, we have students balance shapes, not just numbers and variables. Shapes that equal different quantities help students see the need to balance equations at the conceptual level. The Vs and Ns also show how we can balance equations.

Problem Solving:

Geometric Construction and Angle Measurement

Key Questions That Guide Student Understanding

- *How does an algebraic equation help us determine an unknown value?*

Enduring Understandings for Geometric Construction and Angle Measurement

One use of algebraic equations is to determine the value of a variable. When we apply algebra to geometry and angle measurement, we often use properties of angles or shapes to help us determine the value of variables.

For example, we can use what we know about the sum of a triangle's angles as the basis for creating an equation where 180 is on one side of the equal sign (e.g., $x + 45 = 180$). Solving such equations not only reminds students of the basic properties of geometric shapes but allows them to connect three topics: algebra, geometry, and measurement. These kinds of exercises help students learn how to make inferences, which is central to secondary geometry.

Tools for Understanding Geometric Construction and Angle Measurement

Using Tools
Compasses are essential tools for drawing geometric shapes. In this unit, we show how compasses can replace protractors to draw lines and angles.

Using Algebra to Measure Angles
We can determine the measure of angles based on the properties of lines and triangles. In doing so, we make an inference based on what is known and let the variable stand for what is unknown. The result is an equation like $180 = 20 + x + 75$.

Building Number Concepts:
Introduction to Algebraic Equations

Lesson	Lesson Objectives—Students will:
1	• Examine algebraic equations
2	• Balance equations with only half the information.
3	• Use substitution of different shapes to balance the scale.
4	• Use the property of equality to solve simple algebraic equations. • Check their answers using substitution.
5	• Solve problems with coefficients.
6	• Use reciprocals to solve problems with coefficients.
7	• Solve equations with negative numbers.
8	• Use algebra to solve rate problems.
9	• Translate word statements into algebraic equations.
10	• Review Introduction to Algebraic Equation concepts.
Unit Assessments	End-of-Unit Assessment Performance Assessment

Problem Solving:
Geometric Construction and Angle Measurement

Lesson Objectives—Students will:	Assessment
• Make geometric constructions to explore different geometric terms.	
• Make geometric constructions involving bisected angles.	
• Solve algebraic equations to find the measurement of an unknown angle.	
	Quiz 1
• Find the measure of two angles.	
• Use algebra to find the missing angle in triangles.	
• Find the measurement of angles in triangles with congruent angles.	
• Write algebraic equations for word problems, then solve.	
• Review Geometric Construction and Angle Measurement concepts.	Unit Review
	End-of-Unit Assessment Performance Assessment

Lesson 1 | Introduction to Algebraic Equations

Problem Solving: Geometric Construction and Angle Measurement

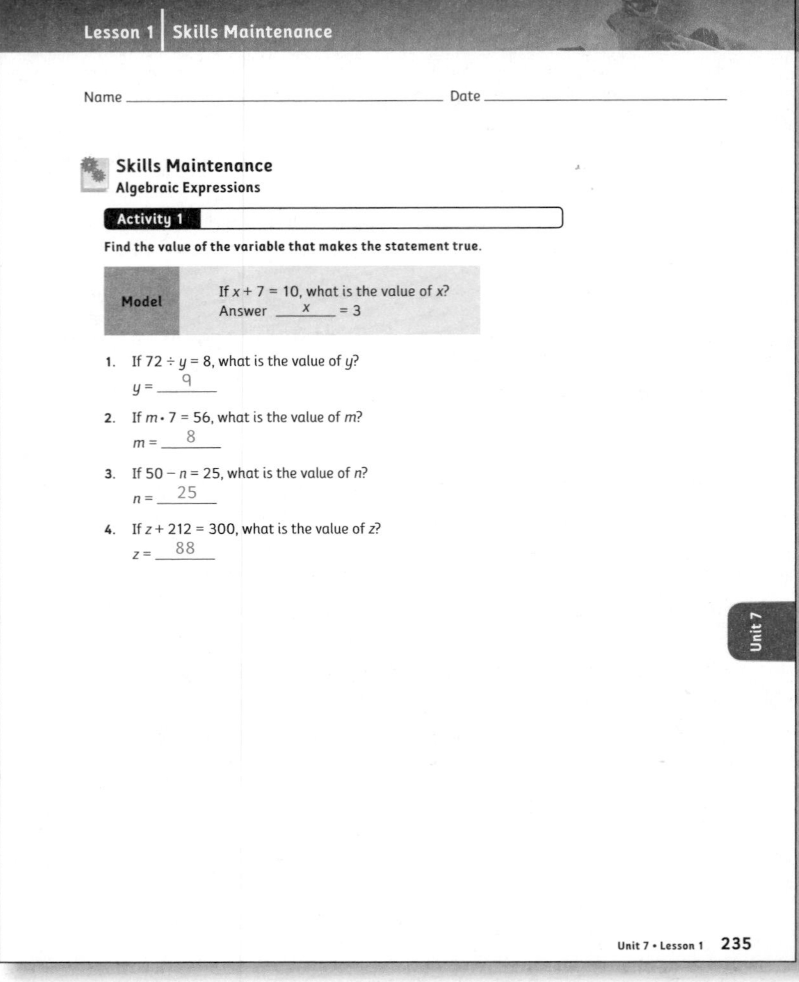
Lesson 1 | Skills Maintenance

Name ______ Date ______

Skills Maintenance
Algebraic Expressions

Activity 1

Find the value of the variable that makes the statement true.

Model	If $x + 7 = 10$, what is the value of x? Answer $x = 3$

1. If $72 \div y = 8$, what is the value of y? $y =$ 9
2. If $m \cdot 7 = 56$, what is the value of m? $m =$ 8
3. If $50 - n = 25$, what is the value of n? $n =$ 25
4. If $z + 212 = 300$, what is the value of z? $z =$ 88

Unit 7

Unit 7 • Lesson 1 235

Lesson Planner

Vocabulary Development

equation
balanced
line segment
arc
perpendicular
right angle
midpoint
parallel

Skills Maintenance

Algebraic Expressions

Building Number Concepts:

▶ Introduction to Algebraic Equations

Students are introduced to the concept of algebraic equations. They learn that if an equation is true, the two expressions on either side of the equal sign must be equal.

Objective

Students will examine algebraic equations.

Problem Solving:

▶ Geometric Construction and Angle Measurement

Students learn the importance of making geometric constructions to understand geometric terms.

Objective

Students will make geometric constructions to explore different geometric terms.

Homework

Students identify balanced equations and identify geometric figures. In Distributed Practice, students solve problems that include operations on fractions and integers, PEMDAS, and the distributive property.

Skills Maintenance

Algebraic Expressions

(*Interactive Text*, page 235)

Activity 1

Students find the value for the variable that makes the statement true.

Building Number Concepts:
▶ Introduction to Algebraic Equations

What are algebraic equations?
(*Student Text*, pages 511–513)

Connect to Prior Knowledge

Write the statement **7 = 7** on the board or overhead. Explain that we can write many other expressions that mean the same thing as 7. Write **5 + 2 = 7** under 7 = 7. Below that, write **5 + 2 = 10 − 3**. Tell students that the two sides of the equation look different, but they are still equal.

Link to Today's Concept

Tell students that in today's lesson, we look at a math statement called an **equation** and evaluate the two sides to see if they are equal.

Demonstrate

Engagement Strategy: Teacher Modeling

Demonstrate how to create a balanced equation in one of the following ways:

mBook: Use the *mBook Teacher Edition* for *Student Text*, page 511. m

Overhead Projector: Display Transparency 16, and modify as discussed.

Board: Copy the scale on the board, and modify as discussed.

- Tell students that in equations, when both sides of the equal sign are the same, the equation is **balanced**. Explain that sometimes this is hard to see because the two sides might look very different. m
- Show the equation **3 (4 • 2) = 26 − 2**. Explain that each side of the equation is an expression. To be balanced, they must be equal to each other. m

Lesson 1 | ▶Introduction to Algebraic Equations
Problem Solving:
▶Geometric Construction and Angle Measurement

▶Introduction to Algebraic Equations

Vocabulary
equation balanced

What are algebraic equations?

In this unit, we will start working with equations. An **equation** is a math statement that shows that one expression is equal to another expression.

The following statements are equations. The expressions on each side of the equal sign do not look the same, but they are equal. The sides have to be equal to make it an equation. When the expression on one side of an equation equals the expression on the other side, we say the equation is **balanced**.

equation

expression

3 (4 • 2) = 26 − 2

$n + 25 = 30$

$52 = 4c$

$3x + 1 = x + 16$

POWER CONCEPT

When the expression on one side of an equation equals the expression on the other side, the equation is balanced.

Unit 7 • Lesson 1 511

- Simplify each side of the equation: 3 (4 • 2) = 3 • 8, which equals 24, and 26 − 2 = 24; so **24 = 24**.
- Look at the other three scales. Point out the expressions in each equation. Explain the difference between algebraic equations and numeric equations. Be sure students see the inclusion of variables in the algebraic equations. m

Discuss

Call students' attention to the Power Concept, and point out that it will be helpful as they learn more about algebraic equations.

When the expression on one side of an equation equals the expression on the other side, the equation is balanced.

What are algebraic equations?
(*continued*)

Demonstrate

- Turn to page 512 of the *Student Text*. Read the material at the top of the page. Use **Example 1** to demonstrate how to prove that the two sides of the equation are balanced by simplifying each side. Walk though the outlined steps to simplify the equation **3(4 + 3) − 1 = 2 • 2 • 2 • 2 + 2 + 2**.
- Tell students that it does not matter which side you simplify first. In this example, we simplify the right side of the equation first. We simplify the expression using PEMDAS.
- We solve the multiplication first from left to right: **2 • 2 • 2 • 2 = 16**. Then we add left to right: **16 + 2 + 2 = 20**. Next we simplify the left side of the equation by completing the operation in parentheses first: **4 + 3 = 7**. Next we do the multiplication: **3 • 7 = 21**. Then we complete the subtraction: **21 − 1 = 20**. Now we have **20 = 20**; both sides of the equation are equal. They are balanced.
- Explain to students that we could have started on either side of the equation.

We learned that both sides of an equation are equal even though they do not look the same in the beginning. Let's explore this concept further. The examples use numeric equations to show that the two expressions are equal. We can solve the equation in Example 1 by starting on either side of the equal sign.

Example 1

Show that the expressions are equal by simplifying.

3(4 + 3) − 1 = 2 • 2 • 2 • 2 + 2 + 2

Start on the right side of the equal sign and use PEMDAS.

3(4 + 3) − 1 = 2 • 2 • 2 • 2 + 2 + 2
3(4 + 3) − 1 = 4 • 2 • 2 + 2 + 2
3(4 + 3) − 1 = 8 • 2 + 2 + 2
3(4 + 3) − 1 = 16 + 2 + 2
3(4 + 3) − 1 = 18 + 2
3(4 + 3) − 1 = 20

PEMDAS
Parentheses first
Exponent next
Multiplication and
Division (left to right)
Addition and
Subtraction (left to right)

Now go to the left side of the equal sign and use PEMDAS.

3(4 + 3) − 1 = 20
3(7) − 1 = 20
21 − 1 = 20
20 = 20

Now it is clear that both sides are equal. They are balanced.

We could have solved the problem in Example 1 by starting on the left side of the equal sign. We would find the same answer, 20 = 20. The main idea with numeric equations is that the two sides are the same, or balanced. We prove they are the same by simplifying each expression.

Demonstrate

- Go over **Example 2** on page 513 of the *Student Text*. In this example, we start on the left.
- Point out that again we use our Algebra Toolbox to help us simplify the expressions on either side of the equal sign. In this example, we have parentheses, exponents, and multiple operations. We use our PEMDAS rules to help us simplify the expressions in the right order.
- Walk through each of the steps, starting first with the operations in parentheses: $\mathbf{4 - 3 = 1}$. Next we divide: $\mathbf{6 \div 2 = 3}$, and then multiply: $\mathbf{3(1) = 3}$. Finally complete the addition: $\mathbf{3 + 3 = 6}$.
- Next simplify the right-hand side of the equation. First complete the operation inside the parentheses: $\mathbf{2 + 1 = 3}$. Then solve for the exponent: $\mathbf{3^2 = 9}$. Next complete the multiplication $\mathbf{5(3) = 15}$. Finally complete the subtraction: $\mathbf{15 - 9 = 6}$. It is clear now that both sides equal 6. The equation is balanced.
- Explain to students that we use these skills to balance numeric equations later, when we look at other types of equations.

Lesson 1

Now let's explore how we can start on the left side first and show that the two expressions are equal. We follow the PEMDAS rules for each step.

Example 2

Solve the equation starting with the left side.

Use PEMDAS and start inside the parentheses.

$6 \div 2 + 3(4 - 3) = 5(2 + 1) - 3^2$

$6 \div 2 + 3(1) = 5(2 + 1) - 3^2$

$6 \div 2 + 3 = 5(2 + 1) - 3^2$

$3 + 3 = 5(2 + 1) - 3^2$

$6 = 5(2 + 1) - 3^2$

Now go to the right side and use PEMDAS.

$6 = 5(2 + 1) - 3^2$

$6 = 5(3) - 3^2$

$6 = 5(3) - 9$

$6 = 15 - 9$

$\mathbf{6 = 6}$

Now it is clear that both sides are equal. They are balanced.

PEMDAS
Parentheses first
Exponent next
Multiplication and
Division (left to right)
Addition and
Subtraction (left to right)

We can see if both sides of a numeric equation are balanced by simplifying the expressions. This is helpful later on when we look at different kinds of equations.

Apply Skills
Turn to ***Interactive Text***, page 236.

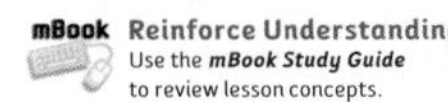
Reinforce Understanding
Use the ***mBook Study Guide*** to review lesson concepts.

Unit 7 • Lesson 513

Check for Understanding
Engagement Strategy: Think Tank

Distribute pieces of paper to students and have them write their names on them. Write the equation $\mathbf{4^2 + 2(2 - 1) = 3^2 \cdot 4 \div 2}$ on the board. Have students show that the expressions are equal by simplifying (*18 = 18*). Remind students that they can start on either side of the equation, and they should use PEMDAS to help them simplify the expressions in the right order. When students are finished, collect the papers and put them into a container. Draw an answer and share it with the class. Invite the student to walk through the steps they used to find the answer.

Apply Skills

(*Interactive Text*, pages 236–237)

Have students turn to pages 236–237 in the *Interactive Text*, and complete the activity.

Activity 1

Students simplify the two sides of the equations and determine whether they are equal. Go over the model so that students see how to solve the problems and how to show their work. Remind students that they can start on either side of the equation. We started on the left in the example, but we could have started on the right.

Monitor students' work as they complete the activity.

Watch for:

- Can students simplify the expressions on either side of the equal sign, using PEMDAS?
- Can students show that the two sides are equal?
- Do students show their work and use the algebra tools correctly?

mBook **Reinforce Understanding**

Remind students that they can review lesson concepts by accessing the online *mBook Study Guide*.

Lesson 1 | Apply Skills

Name ______ Date ______

Apply Skills

Introduction to Algebraic Equations

Activity 1

Decide whether the two sides of each equation are equal by simplifying the expressions on either side.

Model

$27 - 14 + 8 \cdot 2 = 3^2 + 4^2 + 2^2$

Solving on the left
$27 - 14 + \mathbf{8 \cdot 2} = 3^2 + 4^2 + 2^2$
$\mathbf{27 - 14} + 16 = 3^2 + 4^2 + 2^2$
$\mathbf{13 + 16} = 3^2 + 4^2 + 2^2$
$29 = 3^2 + 4^2 + 2^2$

Solving on the right
$29 = \mathbf{3^2} + 4^2 + 2^2$
$29 = 9 + \mathbf{4^2} + 2^2$
$29 = 9 + 16 + \mathbf{2^2}$
$29 = 9 + 16 + 4$
$29 = \mathbf{9 + 16} + 4$
$29 = \mathbf{25 + 4}$
$29 = 29$

Both of the sides equal 29.

1. $54 - 30 + 40 = 8^2$

Show your work here.
Left: $24 + 40 = 64$ Right: $8 \cdot 8 = 64$
Left: 64 Right: 64
Both of the sides equal 64.

236 Unit 7 • Lesson 1

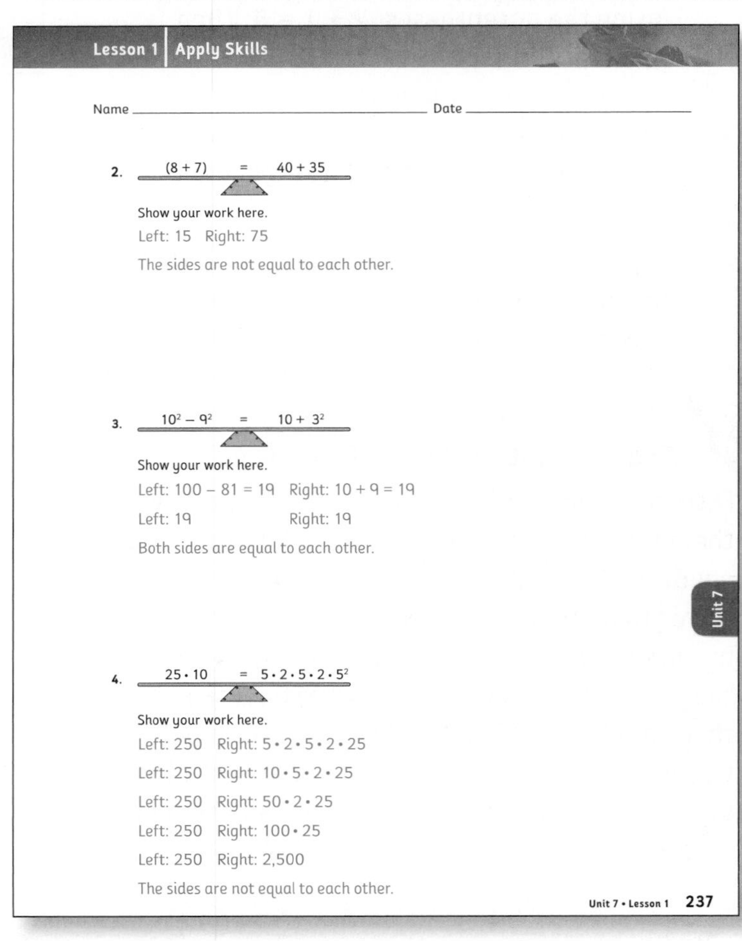

Lesson 1 | Apply Skills

Name ______ Date ______

2. $(8 + 7) = 40 + 35$

Show your work here.
Left: 15 Right: 75
The sides are not equal to each other.

3. $10^2 - 9^2 = 10 + 3^2$

Show your work here.
Left: $100 - 81 = 19$ Right: $10 + 9 = 19$
Left: 19 Right: 19
Both sides are equal to each other.

4. $25 \cdot 10 = 5 \cdot 2 \cdot 5 \cdot 2 \cdot 5^2$

Show your work here.
Left: 250 Right: $5 \cdot 2 \cdot 5 \cdot 2 \cdot 25$
Left: 250 Right: $10 \cdot 5 \cdot 2 \cdot 25$
Left: 250 Right: $50 \cdot 2 \cdot 25$
Left: 250 Right: $100 \cdot 25$
Left: 250 Right: 2,500
The sides are not equal to each other.

Unit 7

Unit 7 • Lesson 1 237

Problem Solving: ▶ Geometric Construction and Angle Measurement

What terms are important in geometric construction?
(*Student Text*, pages 514–518)

Explain

Have students turn to page 514 of the *Student Text*. Explain that they will learn a lot of important terms in this lesson, and it is important to learn and know these terms rather than just memorize them. Explain that the lessons in this unit provide opportunities for them to do this. For today's lesson, we use a ruler and a compass.

Demonstrate

- Walk through the steps of making a **line segment** in **Example 1**. Have students get out a ruler and a compass and work through the steps as you go over them.

STEP 1

- Draw a line segment and label its endpoints A and B. Remind students that line segments have a definite length. They do not go on forever.

STEP 2

- Follow the directions to make an **arc** by putting the point of the compass on an endpoint and making an arc above the line segment. Tell students that an arc is a part of a circle.

STEP 3

- Repeat Step 2 with the other endpoint, making sure the arcs intersect. Point out that you did not change the width of the compass.

Lesson 1

▶Problem Solving: Geometric Construction and Angle Measurement

What terms are important in geometric construction?

Vocabulary is an important part of geometry. It is one thing to memorize the terms, and it is another thing to use them. We are going to use our vocabulary terms as we make parallel and perpendicular lines using just a compass and a ruler or straightedge.

Vocabulary

line segment
arc
perpendicular
right angle
midpoint
parallel

Example 1

Steps for Making a Perpendicular Line Segment

STEP 1

Draw a line segment with endpoints A and B.
A **line segment** is a part of a line that has a definite length.

A B

Practice using the terms you learn in geometry as you are drawing and using your compass.

STEP 2

Put the sharp end of the compass at one endpoint and stretch the compass to create an arc above the center of the segment.
An **arc** is a part of a circle.

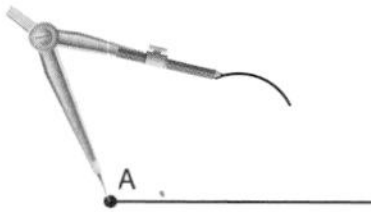

STEP 3

Do the same thing from the other endpoint so that the two arcs intersect.

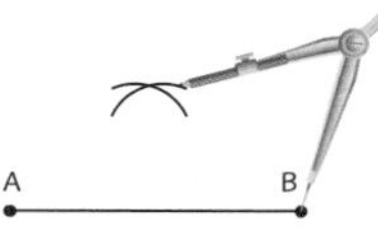

514 Unit 7 • Lesson 1

What terms are important in geometric construction? *(continued)*

Demonstrate

- Have students turn to page 515 of the *Student Text*. Continue walking through the steps in Example 1.

STEP 4

- Draw another set of arcs below the line segment. Point out again that you did not change the width of your compass.

STEP 5

- Use a ruler or straightedge and draw a line through the point where the arcs intersect, as shown.
- Explain that the two line segments that you drew are **perpendicular**. Perpendicular lines create a **right angle**. Right angles measure 90 degrees. Note the point where the two lines intersect. Explain that this is the **midpoint** of the lines.

STEP 4

Draw another set of arcs on the opposite side of the line segment. Make sure not to change the width of the compass.

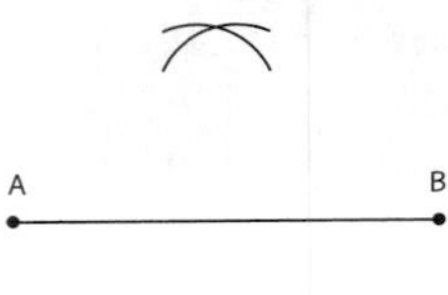

STEP 5

Finally, use a ruler or straightedge to draw a line segment that crosses through the two points where the arcs intersect.

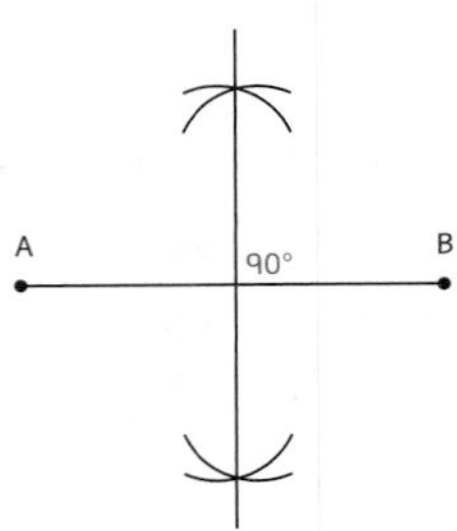

The two line segments are **perpendicular** to each other. This means the line segments form a **right angle** where the line segments intersect. A right angle is an angle whose measure is 90 degrees. The place where they intersect is the **midpoint** on the lines.

Demonstrate

- Turn to page 516 of the *Student Text*. Go over how to make a **parallel** line segment in **Example 2**. Explain that parallel lines never intersect.
- Have students work through the steps of the construction with a ruler and compass as you discuss them together.

STEP 1

- Draw a line segment as shown.

STEP 2

- Draw a point and label it **A** above the line segment, then draw a diagonal line through it as shown.

STEP 3

- Draw an arc as shown. The arc should go through both lines, and intersect the line about halfway to point A. Point out that you do not change the width of the compass.

Lesson 1

We make a parallel line segment by following the steps shown in Example 2.

Example 2

Steps for Making a Parallel Line Segment

STEP 1
Draw a line segment.

STEP 2
Make point A above the line segment and draw a diagonal line through point A.

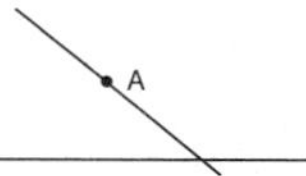

STEP 3
Draw an arc through both lines about halfway to point A. Do not change the width of the compass.

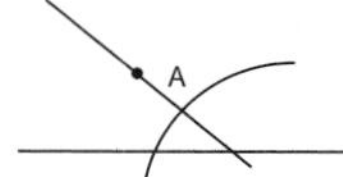

516 Unit 7 • Lesson 1

What terms are important in geometric construction? *(continued)*

Demonstrate

- Continue walking through the steps in Example 2 on page 517 of the *Student Text*.

STEP 4

- Show students how to make another arc above point A by putting the sharp end of the compass on point A and drawing the arc. Remember not to change the width of the compass from the previous step. Label point B at the intersection of the line and the second arc.

STEP 5

- Follow the instructions in Step 5 to measure the distance between the points on the arc where the diagonal line and the horizontal line intersect. Keep the compass at this width for the next step.

STEP 6

- Show students how to draw an arc as shown by putting the sharp end of the compass on point B. The new arc is connected to point B's arc.

Lesson 1

STEP 4

Put the sharp end of the compass on point A and make another arc above point A. Label the intersection of the arc and the line point B.

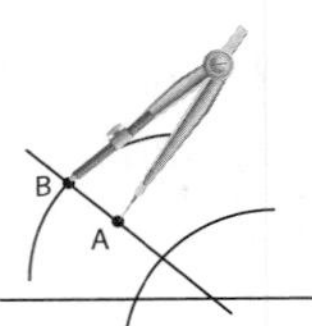

STEP 5

Put the sharp end of the compass on the point where the first arc and the horizontal line meet. Use your compass to measure the distance to the point where the first arc and the diagonal line intersect. Do not change the width of the compass after measuring.

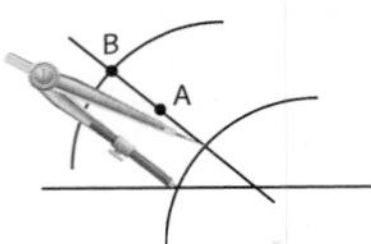

STEP 6

Put the sharp end of your compass on point B. Draw an arc as shown below.

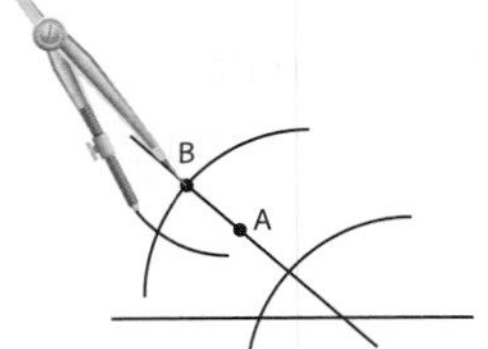

Demonstrate

- Walk through the final step in Example 2 on page 518 of the *Student Text*.

STEP 7

- Draw a horizontal line segment with a straightedge or ruler through the intersecting arcs and point A, as shown.
- Point out that the new line segment is parallel to the original line segment. Reiterate to students that parallel lines will never intersect.

STEP 7

Use your straightedge or ruler to draw a line segment through the intersecting arcs and point A.

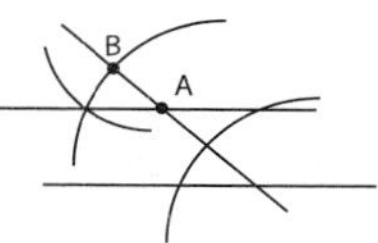

The new line segment is **parallel** to the original line segment. Parallel lines are lines that will never intersect.

Problem-Solving Activity Turn to ***Interactive Text***, page 238.

mBook **Reinforce Understanding** Use the ***mBook Study Guide*** to review lesson concepts.

Problem-Solving Activity

(*Interactive Text*, page 238)

Have students turn to page 238 in the *Interactive Text*. Read the directions with students.

Students construct another perpendicular line segment and another parallel line segment. Explain that they should follow the same steps as shown in Examples 1 and 2 of the *Student Text*. When they are done, have them exchange papers and explain their work to a classmate, using the geometric terms they learned.

Monitor students' work as they complete the activity.

Watch for:

- Can students follow the steps and accurately construct a set of perpendicular lines and parallel lines independently?
- Can students describe their construction using appropriate geometric terms?

Be sure students have adequate time to complete their constructions and discuss them with classmates. The use of terms in geometry is very important as a part of problem-solving activities. Students should be able to recognize and apply the terms, rather than having them simply memorized.

mBook **Reinforce Understanding**

Remind students that they can review lesson concepts by accessing the online *mBook Study Guide*.

Lesson 1 | Problem-Solving Activity

Name ____________________ Date ____________________

Problem-Solving Activity

Geometric Construction and Angle Measurement

Follow the instructions for each problem and make a set of perpendicular line segments and parallel lines. Explain your constructions and use as many of the geometric terms you learned as possible.

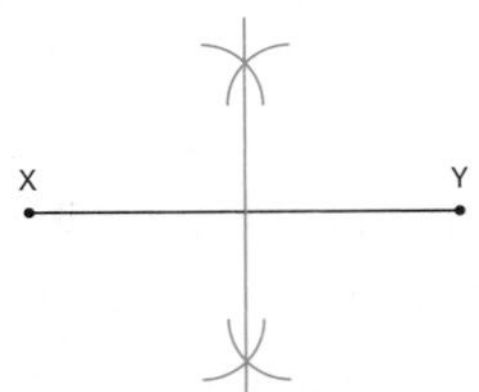

1. **Using line segment XY, draw perpendicular lines with a ruler and compass.**

   Answers will vary. Sample answer: I used each point to make intersecting arcs above and below the segment. Then I drew a line that went through both intersecting arcs. The line and segment formed four right angles.

2. **Using line segment LM, draw a line that is parallel to the segment.**

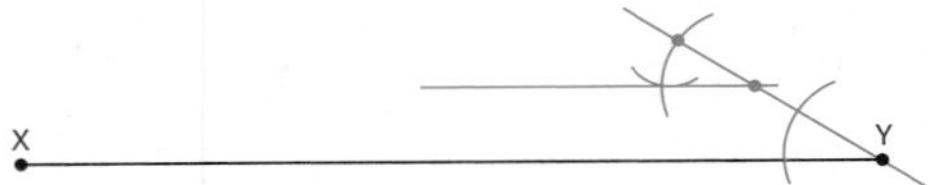

   Answers will vary. Sample answer: First I picked a point and drew a line through it from Y. Then I made two arcs the same size from Y and my point. I measured the distance from the line to my line and made the arc the same size from B. Then I connected the intersection and my first point to make a parallel line.

238 Unit 7 • Lesson 1

Homework

Go over the instructions on page 519 of the *Student Text* for each part of the homework.

Activity 1

Students simplify each side of equations and identify whether the equations are balanced or not balanced.

Activity 2

Students identify the geometric terms that were used in the lesson by looking at simple drawings.

Activity 3 • Distributed Practice

Students practice operations on fractions and integers, PEMDAS, and the distributive property.

Lesson 1

Homework

Activity 1

Simplify the sides of each equation and tell if the equation is balanced.

1. $5 + 2 \cdot 3 = 21 - 5 + 6$ not balanced
2. $2 \cdot 2 \cdot 2 \cdot 2 + 3 + 4 = 5^2 - 1 \cdot 1 - 1$ balanced
3. $27 = (4 + 5) \cdot (2 + 1)$ balanced
4. $3 + 2 \cdot 6 = 10 + 10 + 10$ not balanced

Activity 2

Select the geometric term that matches each of the following.

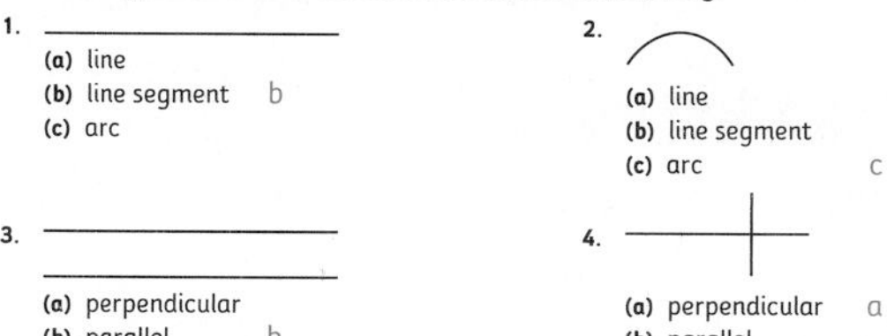

1. (a) line (b) line segment (c) arc — b
2. (a) line (b) line segment (c) arc — c
3. (a) perpendicular (b) parallel (c) arc — b
4. (a) perpendicular (b) parallel (c) arc — a

Activity 3 • Distributed Practice

Solve.

1. $\frac{1}{3} \cdot \frac{3}{1}$ 1
2. $-4 - 2$ -6
3. $-4 \cdot -2$ 8
4. $-4 \div -2$ 2
5. $\frac{3}{4} \div \frac{1}{8}$ 6
6. $3^2 + (6 - -3)$ 18
7. $(6 - -3) + 3^2$ 18
8. Simplify using the distributive property: $3(x + 2)$ $3x + 6$

Unit 7 • Lesson 519

Lesson 2 ▶ Balancing an Equation
Problem Solving: ▶ Bisecting Angles

Lesson Planner

Vocabulary Development

constructions
bisect

Skills Maintenance

Balanced Equations

Building Number Concepts: ▶ Balancing an Equation

In this lesson, students learn to balance an equation when given only half of the information. Students already learned that the expressions on either side of an equation do not have to look alike to be equal. For an equation to be true, both sides of the equation have to be equal.

Objective

Students will balance equations with only half of the information.

Problem Solving: ▶ Bisecting Angles

Students are introduced to the concept of bisecting angles. Students again use their compass and ruler to bisect angles.

Objective

Students will make geometric constructions involving bisected angles.

Homework

Students simplify the two sides of an equation, complete an expression that balances the equation, and tell the measurement of one of the angles of a bisected angle. In Distributed Practice, students practice operations on fractions and integers, PEMDAS, and the distributive property.

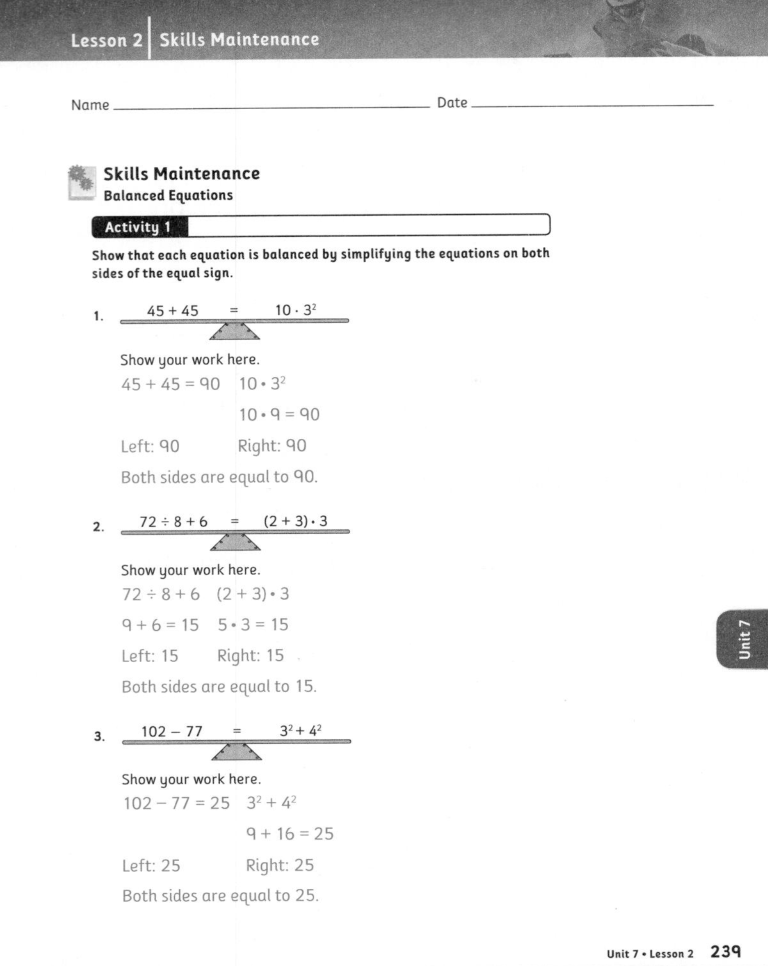
Lesson 2 | Skills Maintenance

Name ____________ Date ____________

Skills Maintenance
Balanced Equations

Activity 1

Show that each equation is balanced by simplifying the equations on both sides of the equal sign.

1. $45 + 45 = 10 \cdot 3^2$

Show your work here.
$45 + 45 = 90$ $10 \cdot 3^2$
$10 \cdot 9 = 90$
Left: 90 Right: 90
Both sides are equal to 90.

2. $72 \div 8 + 6 = (2 + 3) \cdot 3$

Show your work here.
$72 \div 8 + 6$ $(2 + 3) \cdot 3$
$9 + 6 = 15$ $5 \cdot 3 = 15$
Left: 15 Right: 15
Both sides are equal to 15.

3. $102 - 77 = 3^2 + 4^2$

Show your work here.
$102 - 77 = 25$ $3^2 + 4^2$
$9 + 16 = 25$
Left: 25 Right: 25
Both sides are equal to 25.

Unit 7

Unit 7 • Lesson 2 239

Skills Maintenance

Balanced Equations

(*Interactive Text*, page 239)

Activity 1

Students show that the two sides of the equations are balanced by simplifying each side.

Building Number Concepts:
▶ Balancing an Equation

How do we balance an equation with only half the information?

(*Student Text*, pages 520–521)

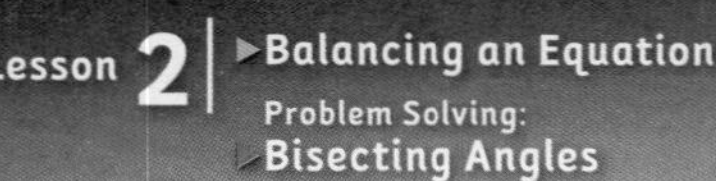

Lesson 2 | ▶Balancing an Equation
Problem Solving:
▶Bisecting Angles

▶**Balancing an Equation**

How do we balance an equation with only half the information?

We proved that a numeric equation is balanced by simplifying each expression. We ended up with two numbers that were the same.

What happens when we want to balance an equation, but only have half the information? The illustration shows how we have an expression on only one side. Once we simplify it, we can create another expression that is different from the first one to balance the equation.

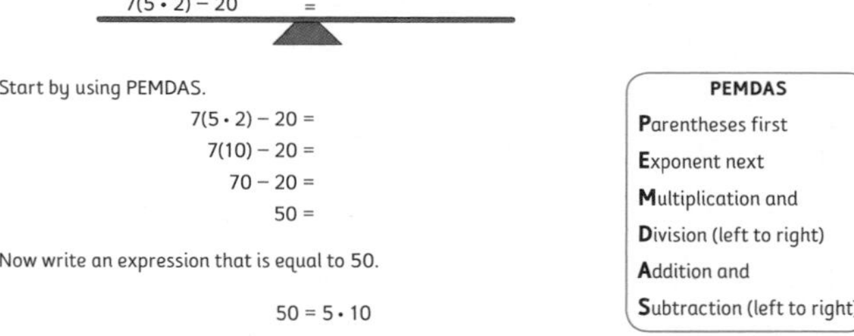

Start by using PEMDAS.

7(5 • 2) − 20 =
7(10) − 20 =
70 − 20 =
50 =

PEMDAS
Parentheses first
Exponent next
Multiplication and
Division (left to right)
Addition and
Subtraction (left to right)

Now write an expression that is equal to 50.

50 = 5 • 10

Finally, put this expression on the right side of the equal sign to balance the equation.

7(5 • 2) − 20 = 5 • 10

These expressions do not look the same, but they are equal. When we simplify them, we know that 50 = 50.

520 Unit 7 • Lesson 2

Connect to Prior Knowledge

Begin with the same activity used to introduce Lesson 1, but use different numbers: **20 = 20**.

Ask:

> **What are some different expressions to represent the number 20 and show them as balanced equations?**

Listen for:

- Any expression with any operation equal to 20, such as 10 + 10, 4 • 5, 25 − 5, 40 ÷ 2

Link to Today's Concept

Tell students that in today's lesson, we look at just one side of the equation and we fill in the other side with an equivalent expression.

Demonstrate

Engagement Strategy: Teacher Modeling

Demonstrate how to simplify an expression and create a new expression in one of the following ways:

mBook: Use the *mBook Teacher Edition* for *Student Text*, pages 520–521. m

Overhead Projector: Display Transparency 16, and modify as discussed.

Board: Copy the scale on the board, and modify as discussed.

- Show the expression **7(5 • 2) − 20** on the scale. Explain that we only have half of the information, but because this is an equation, we can use what we know to find an equal expression. m
- Show how to simplify the expression. Point out that there are mixed operations and we use PEMDAS to simplify. Walk through each step of the simplification to get the number **50**. m
- After simplifying, explain that to balance the equation, we need to find an expression that equals 50 for the other side of the equation. Write **50 = 5 • 10**, and explain that there are many possible answers other than this one. m
- Show **5 • 10** on the right side of the scale. Explain that this balances the equation, because both expressions are equal. Be sure students see the importance of checking the answer at the end by simplifying the two expressions and confirming that they are equal. m

How do we balance an equation with only half the information? *(continued)*

Demonstrate

- Turn to on page 521 of the *Student Text* to find a different expression that is equal to **7(5 • 2) − 20**.
- Explain that 5 • 10 is not the only possible answer. Explain that the expression 5 • 2 • 5 is also equal to 50, so we can balance the equation in another way: 50 = 5 • 2 • 5. Show **5 • 2 • 5** on the right side of the scale. m
- If time allows, elicit from students other expressions that equal 50 that also balance the equation.

Listen for:

- Any expression with any operation equal to 50, such as 25 + 25, 25 • 2, 100 − 50, 100 ÷ 2

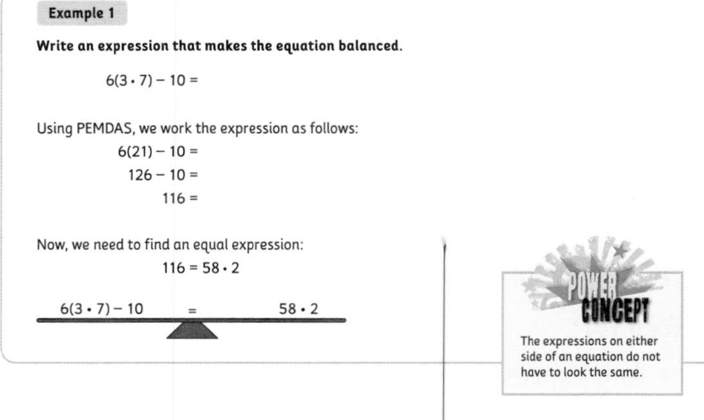

- Next look at **Example 1**. Walk through the steps to create an expression that balances the equation **6(3 • 7) − 10**. Explain that we want to write an equivalent expression to go on the other side of the equal sign for an expression. Remind students to simplify the side we know first, then write an expression that is equivalent.
- Walk through each of the PEMDAS steps, pointing out the order of operations. The expression simplifies to **116**, so explain that we need to find an equal expression. One possible expression is **58 • 2**. Point out that it is written on the other side of the equal sign to balance the equation.
- Be sure students see the importance of checking the answer at the end by simplifying the two expressions and making sure they are equal.

Discuss

Call students' attention to the Power Concept, and point out that it will be helpful as they complete the activity.

The expressions on either side of an equation do not have to look the same.

Check for Understanding

Engagement Strategy: Pair/Share

Divide the class into pairs. Have partners each come up with a different expression equal to the expression **6(3 • 7) − 10** from Example 1. Have students check each others' answers. Then invite student volunteers to share their different expressions with the class. Record students' answers on the board, and compare the different expressions.

Apply Skills
(*Interactive Text*, pages 240–241)

Have students turn to pages 240–241 in the *Interactive Text*, which provides students an opportunity to practice balancing equations on their own.

Activity 1

Students fill in the missing side of an equation by writing an equivalent expression. Tell them to follow the steps we practiced in the *Student Text*: simplify one of the sides, think of an expression that is equal, and write the expression in the diagram. Tell them to check their work by simplifying both sides to be sure they are equal.

Monitor students' work as they complete the activity.

Watch for:

- Can students correctly simplify the side of the equation they are given?
- Can students come up with a different, yet equivalent expression to write on the other side?
- Do students know to check their work at the end to be sure the two sides are equal?

mBook **Reinforce Understanding**
Remind students that they can review lesson concepts by accessing the online *mBook Study Guide*.

Lesson 2 | Apply Skills

Name ______________________ Date ______________

Apply Skills
Balancing an Equation

Activity 1

Write an expression on the blank side of the scale that is equal to the other equation. Your expression should include one operation or more and more than one term. Then show that the two sides are balanced.

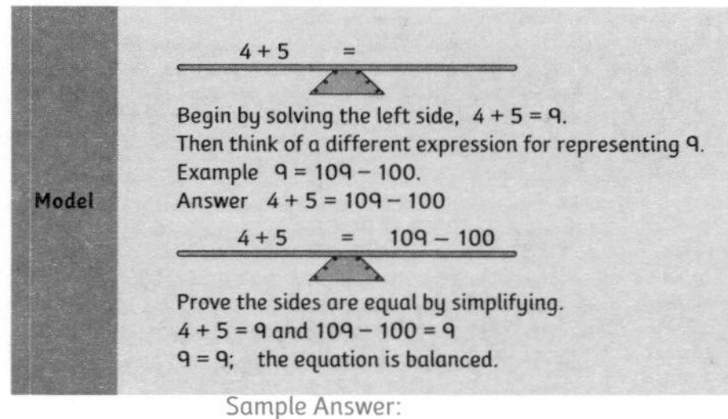
Model

$4 + 5 =$

Begin by solving the left side, $4 + 5 = 9$.
Then think of a different expression for representing 9.
Example $9 = 109 - 100$.
Answer $4 + 5 = 109 - 100$

$4 + 5 = 109 - 100$

Prove the sides are equal by simplifying.
$4 + 5 = 9$ and $109 - 100 = 9$
$9 = 9$; the equation is balanced.

1. $2^2 + 45 =$ Sample Answer: $50 - 1$
   (a) Simplify the left side. $2^2 + 45 = 49$
   (b) Think of a different expression for representing the same thing and write it above.
   (c) Prove the equation is balanced by simplifying both sides. Show your work here.
   $4 + 45 = 49$ and $50 - 1 = 49$
   The equation is balanced.

240 Unit 7 • Lesson 2

Name ______________________ Date ______________

2. Sample Answer: $80 - 30 = 5^2 + 6^2 - 11$
   (a) Simplify the right side. $25 + 36 - 11 = 50$
   (b) Think of a different expression for representing the same thing and write it above.
   (c) Prove the equation is balanced by simplifying both sides. Show your work here.
   $80 - 30 = 50$ and $25 + 36 - 11 = 50$
   The equation is balanced.

3. $5(8 + 2) =$ Sample Answer: $25 \cdot 2$
   (a) Simplify the left side. $5(10) = 50$
   (b) Think of a different expression for representing the same thing and write it above.
   (c) Prove the equation is balanced by simplifying both sides. Show your work here.
   $5(10) = 50$ and $25 \cdot 2 = 50$
   The equation is balanced.

4. Sample Answer: $6 \cdot 6 = 900 \div (3 \cdot 10) + 6$
   (a) Simplify the right side. $900 \div 30 + 6 = 36$
   (b) Think of a different expression for representing the same thing and write it above.
   (c) Prove the equation is balanced by simplifying both sides. Show your work here.
   $6 \cdot 6 = 36$ and $900 \div (3 \cdot 10) + 6 = 36$
   The equation is balanced.

Unit 7

Unit 7 • Lesson 2 241

Problem Solving: ▶ Bisecting Angles

How do we bisect angles?

(*Student Text*, pages 522–524)

Build Vocabulary

Have students turn to the material on page 522 of the *Student Text*. Discuss the importance of angles in higher level mathematics. The angle measurements of shapes tell us a lot about the shapes.

Have students look at the diagram of common angles shown on the page. Tell them that these are common benchmark angles that they should memorize so they can use them to compare other angles.

Next tell students that we use a compass and a straightedge to make geometric items, or **constructions**. These tools will help us **bisect** an angle, or cut it exactly in half. Explain that we do this by using properties of angles to measure the angles without using a protractor.

Lesson 2

▶Problem Solving: Bisecting Angles

Vocabulary
constructions **bisect**

How do we bisect angles?

Angles and their measurements will become increasingly important in your study of mathematics. In this unit, we use what we know about angles and shapes like triangles to figure out the measurement of an unknown angle. The diagram shows common measurements for angles.

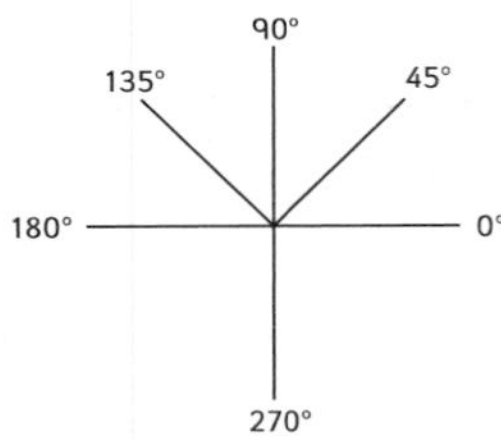

We can learn a lot about an angle by just using a ruler or a straightedge and a compass. **Constructions** are the drawing of geometric items, such as lines and circles, using only a compass and a straightedge. They allow us to **bisect**, or split in half, an angle without using a protractor.

522 Unit 7 • Lesson 2

Demonstrate

- Turn to page 523 of the *Student Text*. Demonstrate how to make and bisect an angle in **Example 1**.
- Have students take out a ruler and a compass and work through the steps in the problem as you go over the example in class. Tell them to pay close attention, as they will need to use these skills for the problem-solving activity.

STEP 1

- Point out to students that they need to use a ruler or straightedge to draw an angle.

STEP 2

- Explain that we draw an arc across the sides of the angle by putting the sharp end of the compass on the vertex of the angle, as shown.

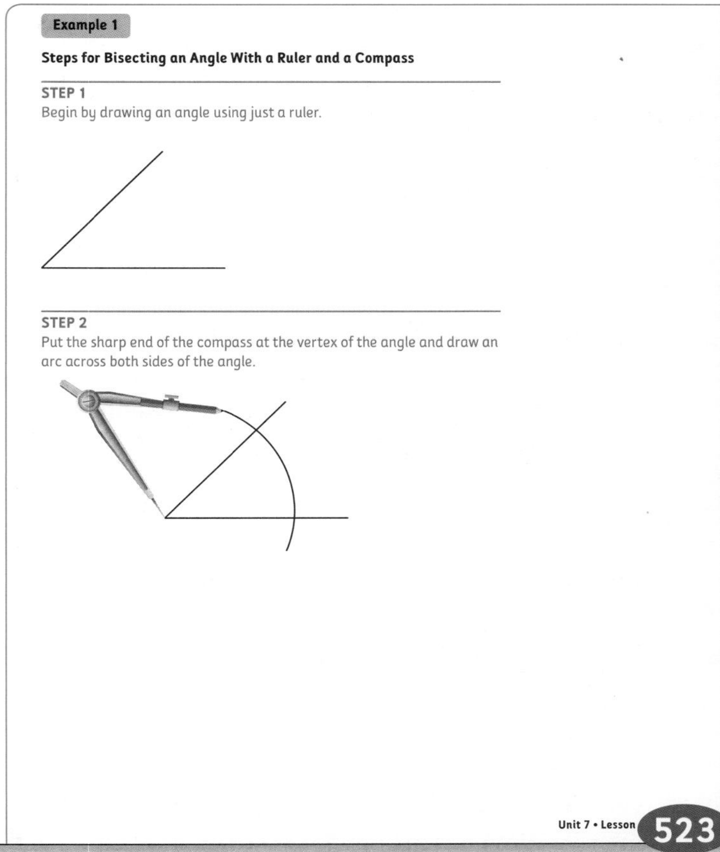

Lesson 2

Example 1

Steps for Bisecting an Angle With a Ruler and a Compass

STEP 1

Begin by drawing an angle using just a ruler.

STEP 2

Put the sharp end of the compass at the vertex of the angle and draw an arc across both sides of the angle.

Unit 7 • Lesson 523

How do we bisect angles? *(continued)*

Demonstrate

- Continue walking through the steps in Example 1 on page 524 of the *Student Text.*

STEP 3

- Tell students to put the sharp end of the compass where the arc and one side of the angle intersect. They make an arc between the two lines, as shown.

STEP 4

- Explain to students that without changing the width of the compass, they should put the sharp end on the other point where the arc intersects with the other side of the angle. Have students draw another arc. Then use a ruler to draw a line from the vertex through the intersection of the two arcs, as shown. This line bisects the angle.
- Explain to students that we can use a protractor to check that the measurements of the angles are equal.

STEP 3
Now, put the sharp end of the compass at the point where the arc crosses one side of the angle. Make another arc in between the two lines near the middle.

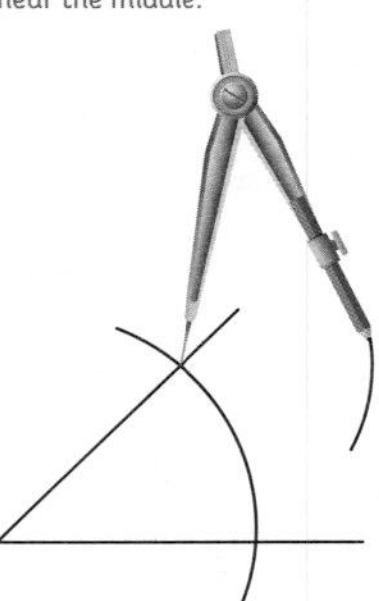

STEP 4
Next, put the sharp end of the compass on the other point where the arc crosses the side of the angle. Draw another arc. Now we can draw a line from the vertex through the point where the two arcs cross. Our line bisects the angle. We can check this by measuring the angles with our protractor.

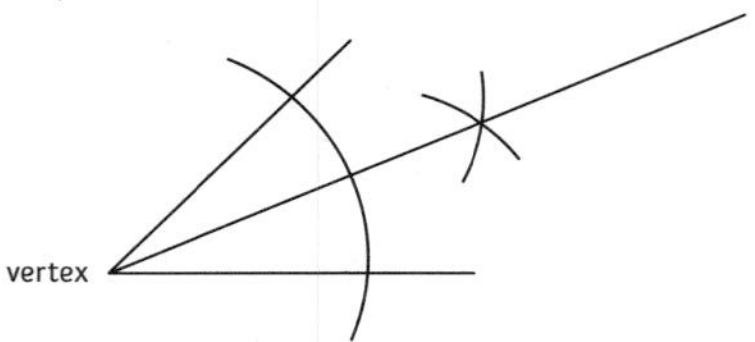

Problem-Solving Activity Turn to *Interactive Text*, page 242.

mBook Reinforce Understanding Use the *mBook Study Guide* to review lesson concepts.

Problem-Solving Activity
(*Interactive Text*, page 242)

Have students turn to page 242 in the *Interactive Text*, and complete the activity.

Students use just a ruler or straight edge and a compass to construct the following angles: 45°, 135°, 225°, and 315°.

Monitor students' work as they complete the activity.

Watch for:

- Can students construct perpendicular lines and use that angle as a benchmark for 90 degrees?
- Do students recognize how to use the 90 degree angle to help them make the measurements of 45 degrees (bisected on the upper right), 135 degrees (bisected on the upper left) and 225 degrees (bisected on the lower left)?

Be sure students have adequate time to work on this activity, as it is an important way for them to learn and apply important geometric concepts.

Reinforce Understanding
Remind students that they can review lesson concepts by accessing the online *mBook Study Guide*.

Lesson 2 | Problem-Solving Activity

Name ______________________ Date ______________________

Problem-Solving Activity
Bisecting Angles

Use what you learned about creating a perpendicular line. Then use a ruler or straight edge and a compass to construct each angle.

1. An angle that measures 45°

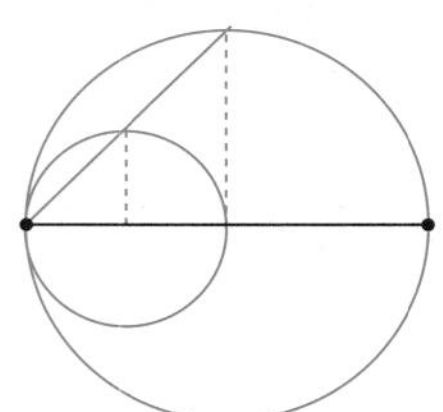

2. An angle that measures 135°

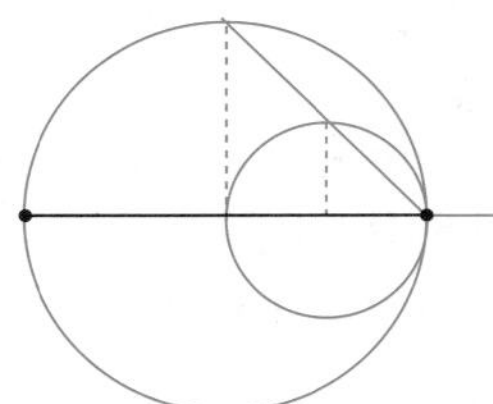

3. An angle that measures 225°

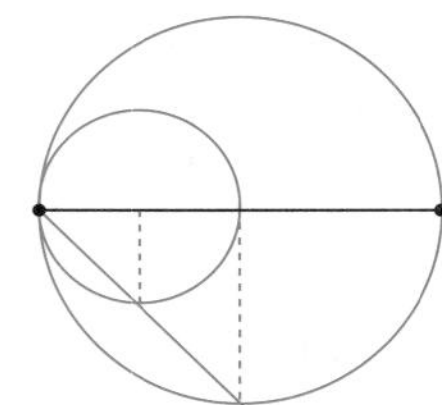

4. An angle that measures 315°

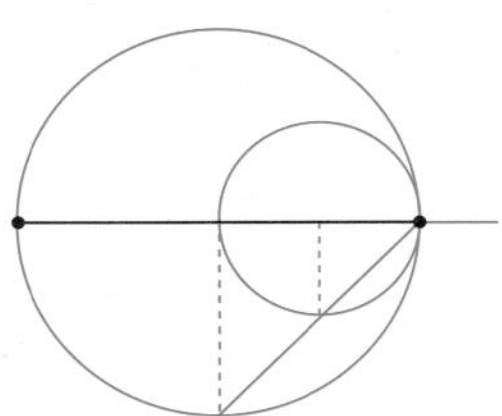

Reinforce Understanding
Use the mBook ***Study Guide*** to review lesson concepts.

242 Unit 7 • Lesson 2

Homework

Go over the instructions on pages 525–526 of the *Student Text* for each part of the homework.

Activity 1

Students simplify the two sides of an equation and prove they are equal.

Activity 2

Students complete an expression that balances the scale. They must simplify the expression that is given to them, then find the remaining part of the expression on the other side. Tell students that it needs to be a different expression than the one given, but still equal to the same number.

Additional Answers

Activity 1

1. $8 + 5 \cdot 2 = 6 \cdot 3$
   $8 + 10 = 18$
   $18 = 18$
2. $2 \cdot 5 + 1 + 1 = 3 + 7 + 2$
   $10 + 1 + 1 = 3 + 7 + 2$
   $12 = 12$
3. $9^2 - 5 + 2 = 40 + 41 + -3$
   $81 - 5 + 2 = 40 + 41 + -3$
   $76 + 2 = 81 + -3$
   $78 = 78$
4. $1 + 2 + 3 - 1 = 40 \div (9 - 1)$
   $1 + 2 + 3 - 1 = 40 \div 8$
   $1 + 2 + 3 - 1 = 5$
   $6 - 1 = 5$
   $5 = 5$

Lesson 2

Homework

Activity 1

Prove that the sides of the equations are equal by simplifying.

1. $8 + 5 \cdot 2 = 6 \cdot 3$
2. $2 \cdot 5 + 1 + 1 = 3 + 7 + 2$
3. $9^2 - 5 + 2 = 40 + 41 + -3$
4. $1 + 2 + 3 - 1 = 40 \div (9 - 1)$

See Additional Answers below.

Activity 2

Write an expression that will balance the right side of the equation with the left side. Use the operation given.

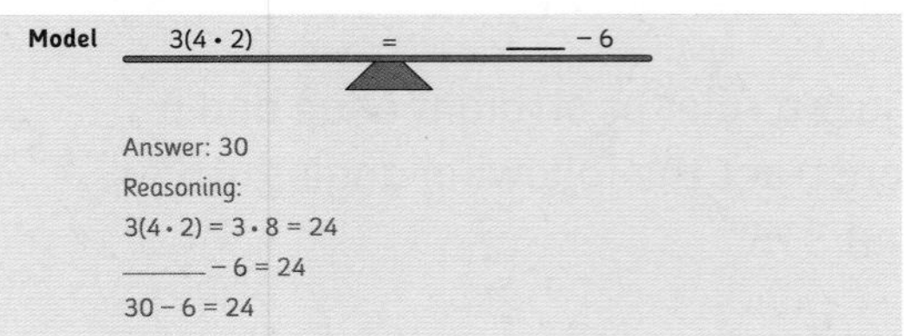

Model
3(4 • 2)
=
___ − 6
Answer: 30
Reasoning:
3(4 • 2) = 3 • 8 = 24
___ − 6 = 24
30 − 6 = 24

1. $25 \div (2 + 3)$ = $17 - \underline{12}$
2. $8 + 9 - 7$ = $100 \div \underline{10}$
3. $37 - 3 \cdot 3$ = $\underline{7} \cdot 4$

Unit 7 • Lesson 525

Activity 3

Students tell the measurement of each bisected angle. Students are given the original angle measurement.

Activity 4 • Distributed Practice

Students practice operations on fractions and integers, PEMDAS, and the distributive property.

Homework

Activity 3

Tell the measurement of each bisected angle.

1. If the large angle is 90 degrees, what is the measure of $\angle a$? $\angle a = 45°$

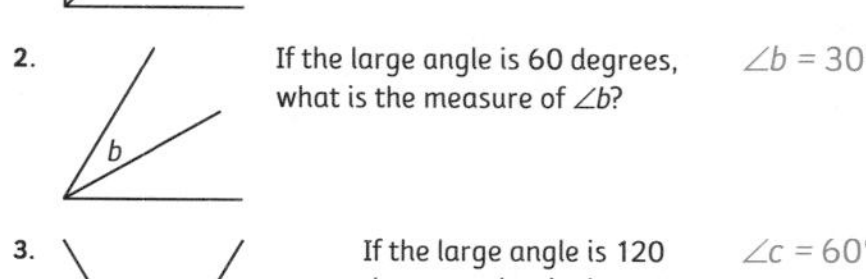

2. If the large angle is 60 degrees, what is the measure of $\angle b$? $\angle b = 30°$
3. If the large angle is 120 degrees, what is the measure of $\angle c$? $\angle c = 60°$
4. If the large angle is 20 degrees, what is the measure of $\angle d$? $\angle d = 10°$

Activity 4 • Distributed Practice

Solve.

1. $\frac{2}{3} - \frac{1}{9}$ $\frac{5}{9}$
2. $\frac{2}{3} \div \frac{1}{9}$ 6
3. $-8 - -5$ -3
4. $(6 \div 3) + 6 \cdot 2$ 14
5. $4^2 - 3^2$ 7
6. $2^2 \cdot 1^2$ 4
7. $(-6 + -3) + (4 \cdot -2)$ -17
8. Simplify using the distributive property: $4(x - 1)$ $4x - 4$

Lesson 3 ▶Another Way to Think About Balancing Equations

Lesson Planner

Skills Maintenance

Geometric Constructions

Building Number Concepts:

▶ Another Way to Think About Balancing Equations

In this lesson, students continue to explore balanced equations by thinking of balanced scales. Students learn that substitution allows us to replace some shapes with equivalent shapes to balance the scale. Balance scales are a good way to think about balanced algebraic equations.

Objective

Students will use substitution of different shapes to balance the scale.

Homework

Students tell if the scales are balanced and use cancellation to find the value of the symbol. In Distributed Practice, students practice operations on fractions and integers.

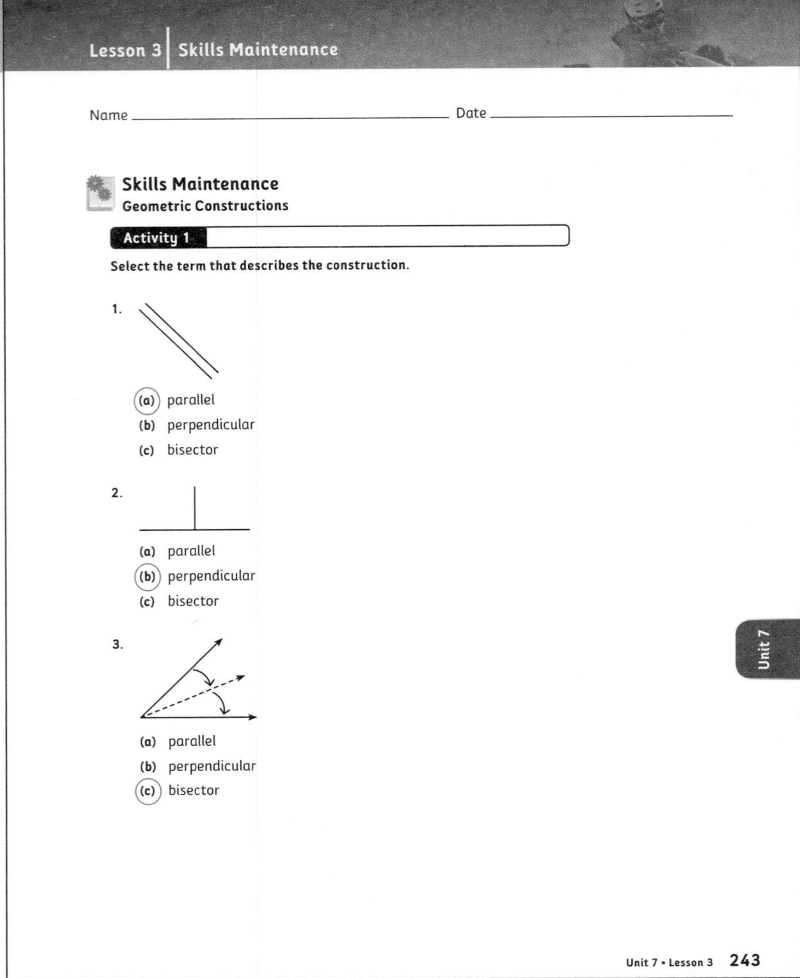
Lesson 3 | Skills Maintenance

Name ______________________ Date ______________

Skills Maintenance
Geometric Constructions

Activity 1

Select the term that describes the construction.

1.
(a) parallel
(b) perpendicular
(c) bisector

2.
(a) parallel
(b) perpendicular
(c) bisector

3.
(a) parallel
(b) perpendicular
(c) bisector

Unit 7

Unit 7 • Lesson 3 243

Skills Maintenance

Geometric Constructions

(*Interactive Text*, page 243)

Activity 1

Students identify the term that matches the geometric constructions.

Building Number Concepts:
▶ Another Way to Think About Balancing Equations

How do the weights of different-shaped objects help us understand equations?
(*Student Text*, pages 527–529)

Connect to Prior Knowledge
Tell students that we worked with balance scales and numeric equations on scales in prior lessons. Now we look at physical objects on a scale. If you have the materials available, show how various physical items impact a balance scale. Use common items such as paper clips, pencils, and erasers. Show that when you add one to one side, you have to add one to the other side to balance the scale. If you do not have a scale available, discuss this situation by drawing a balance scale. Discuss the impact of the addition of common items to one side or the other, or both.

Link to Today's Concept
Tell students that in today's lesson, we use substitution to add shapes to the sides of a balance scale to make it equal, or balanced. Tell students that this is similar to the moving and substituting we do when we work with algebraic equations.

Demonstrate
Engagement Strategy: Teacher Modeling

Demonstrate how to balance an equation in one of the following ways:

mBook: Use the *mBook Teacher Edition* for *Student Text*, pages 527–529. m

Overhead Projector: Display Transparency 16, and modify as discussed.

Lesson 3 | ▶Another Way to Think About Balancing Equations

▶Another Way to Think About Balancing Equations

How do the weights of different-shaped objects help us understand equations?

So far, we have worked with equations involving numeric expressions. We have learned that even though the expressions do not look the same, they need to be equal if they are going to be used in an equation.

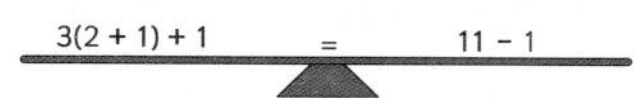

To be balanced, expressions need to be equal to each other.

When we start including variables in equations, it is even harder to remember that both expressions are equal and that the equation is balanced.

We can use shapes to represent the numbers in an equation. This makes it easier to see the relationships between the numbers. Moving and substituting shapes to balance the scale is a lot like moving and substituting numbers when we work with algebraic equations.

Unit 7 • Lesson 527

Board: Copy the scale on the board, and modify as discussed.

- Show **3(2+1) + 1 = 11 − 1**. Display the scale, and remind students that an equation is balanced when both sides are equal. m
- Next point out that the numeric expressions on either side of the equation have to be equal. Have students compute each expression to see that they are both equal to 10. m

How do the weights of different-shaped objects help us understand equations? *(continued)*

Demonstrate

- Turn to page 528 of the *Student Text*, and look at **Example 1**. Go through the shapes and make sure students understand the equivalencies of each of the shapes. m
- Show the shapes on a balanced scale. Then show how to make substitutions on either side of the balance scale to show the sides are equal. Go through each of the steps carefully. m
- Point out that we substituted three triangles for the circle to keep the scale balanced. Be sure students understand how each of the substitutions is made, and how this leads to equal sides and balance. m

Example 1 helps us think about balancing equations. It shows how substitution can prove that both sides are equal. We use three shapes of different weights to show that the scale is balanced, even though the two sides do not look the same.

Example 1

Balance the scale with the same shapes on each side using substitution.

The relative weight for each shape is shown here.

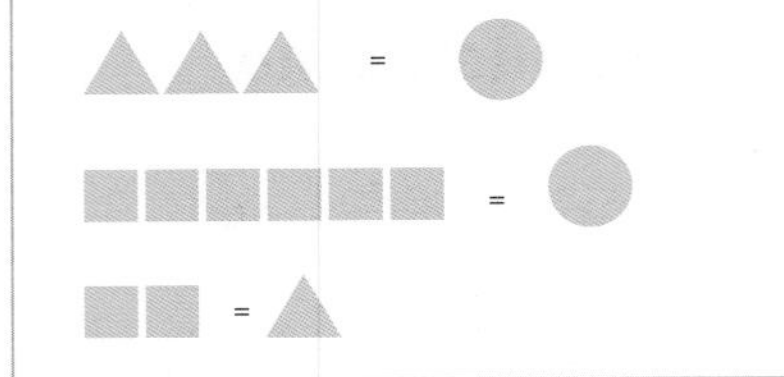

We begin with the shapes below on a balanced scale.

We can substitute on the right side. We trade three triangles for the circle that was there.

Demonstrate

- Continue substituting shapes in Example 1. Show how to make the substitution of one triangle for two squares that were there. The scale is balanced. m

Speaking of Math

- Read through each of the points with students to make sure they understand the steps of balancing equations. Tell students that this is a good checklist of strategies to check their work.

Check for Understanding

Engagement Strategy: Pair/Share

Divide the class into pairs. Have partners each come up with a different combination of shapes to substitute into the equation in Example 1. Have students check each others' answers to make sure that the equation is balanced. Then invite student volunteers to share their solutions with the class. Record students' answers on the board, and compare the different substitutions.

Next, we can substitute on the left side. We trade one triangle for two of the squares that were there. We now see that both sides are equal. They have exactly the same shapes on each side. The scale is balanced.

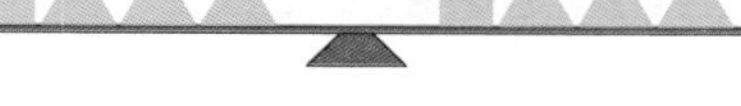

Speaking of Math

Here is how you can explain your thinking when balancing equations.

- *First, I look for things that are equivalent.*
- *Then, I substitute for equivalent values.*
- *Finally, I check both sides to see that they are the same, or balanced.*

How do we use substitution to balance the weight of different objects?

(*Student Text*, pages 530–531)

Explain

Have students turn to page 530 of the *Student Text*. Discuss how we can use two different scales to help us determine the weight of one of the objects. We use the weight of one shape to figure out the weight of another shape.

Demonstrate

- Go over **Example 1**, and point out the two scales in the first part of the example. Explain to students that we can figure out the weight of the triangle by using information from the scale on the right. Tell them that we can then substitute two circles for one square and change the scale on the left.
- Next point out that we can substitute two triangles for six circles. Then we substitute one triangle for three circles. Explain that **one triangle weighs the same as three circles**.

Lesson 3

How do we use substitution to balance the weight of different objects?

There is another way to think about shapes and balance scales. We can look at balancing as a problem-solving activity, where it is important to figure out the weight of one shape based on another shape. Example 1 shows how we use information from two different balance scales to figure out the weight of the triangle.

Example 1

Find the weight of one triangle using substitution.

We can figure out the weight of the triangle by using information from the scale on the right. We see that we can take the square from the scale on the left and substitute it with two circles.

Now we see that there are two triangles for six circles. This is the same as one triangle for three circles.

or

We can say that one triangle weighs the same as three circles.

530 Unit 7 • Lesson 3

Explain

Turn to page 531 in the *Student Text.* Explain to students that there is another strategy for solving these types of problems. Explain that sometimes we can just cancel out the same shapes on each side of the same balance scale.

Demonstrate

- Go over **Example 2**. Show the first scale, with the shapes in balance. In this example, we figure out how much one circle weighs by canceling out boxes and circles on each side of the scale.
- Next explain that we can cross out a square from each side and a circle from each side. Explain that we are left with one circle on one side and two squares on the other side. We cannot cancel these shapes out. So one circle weighs the same as two squares.

Check for Understanding

Engagement Strategy: Look About

Draw a balanced scale as follows:

Tell students that they are going to find out the value of one circle (*1 circle = 2 squares*) with the help of the whole class. Students should copy the scale and cross out the shapes on either side of the scale that are equal to each other. They should do this in large writing on a piece of paper or a dry erase board. When students finish their work, they should hold up their answer for everyone to see.

If students are not sure about the answer, prompt them to look about at other students' solutions to help with their thinking. Review the answers after all students have held up their solutions.

Sometimes we can solve these kinds of problems by using another strategy. We just cancel out the same shapes on each side of the same balance scale. In Example 2, we can figure out how much one circle weighs by canceling out squares and circles on each side of the scale.

Example 2

Figure out the weight of the circle by cancelling out the same shapes on each side.

First, we cross out those shapes on either side of the scale that are equal to each other.

We end up with one circle on the left side and two squares on the right. The scale is still balanced because we began with a balanced scale and crossed out equally on both sides.

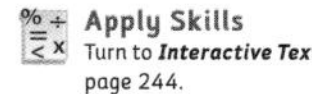

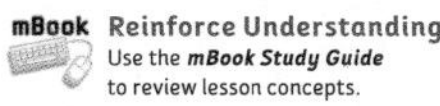

We can say that one circle weighs the same as two squares.

Apply Skills Turn to ***Interactive Text***, page 244.

mBook Reinforce Understanding Use the ***mBook Study Guide*** to review lesson concepts.

Apply Skills

(*Interactive Text*, pages 244–245)

Have students turn to pages 244–245 in the *Interactive Text*, and complete the activities.

Activity 1

Students substitute equivalent shapes until both sides of the equation are the same.

Activity 2

Students substitute and cancel out shapes to make the scales balanced.

Monitor students' work as they complete the activities.

Watch for:

- Can students make the appropriate substitutions to balance the scales?
- Can students make the appropriate cancellations to balance the scales?
- Do students understand that they need to find the relative weight of a shape, (i.e., what shapes does one shape equal)?

mBook **Reinforce Understanding**
Remind students that they can review lesson concepts by accessing the online *mBook Study Guide*.

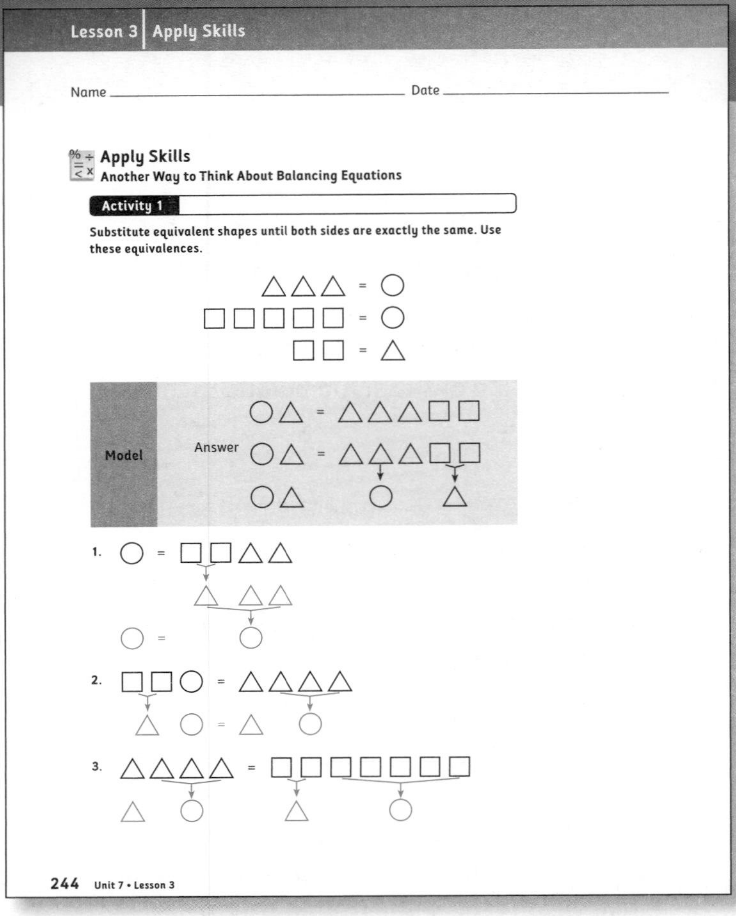

Lesson 3 | Apply Skills

Name ______________________ Date ______________

Apply Skills
Another Way to Think About Balancing Equations

Activity 1

Substitute equivalent shapes until both sides are exactly the same. Use these equivalences.

△△△ = ○
□□□□□ = ○
□□ = △

Model

○△ = △△△□□

Answer ○△ = △△△□□

○△ ○ △

1. ○ = □□△△

△ △△

○ = ○

2. □□○ = △△△△

△ ○ = △ ○

3. △△△△ = □□□□□□□

△ ○ △ ○

244 Unit 7 • Lesson 3

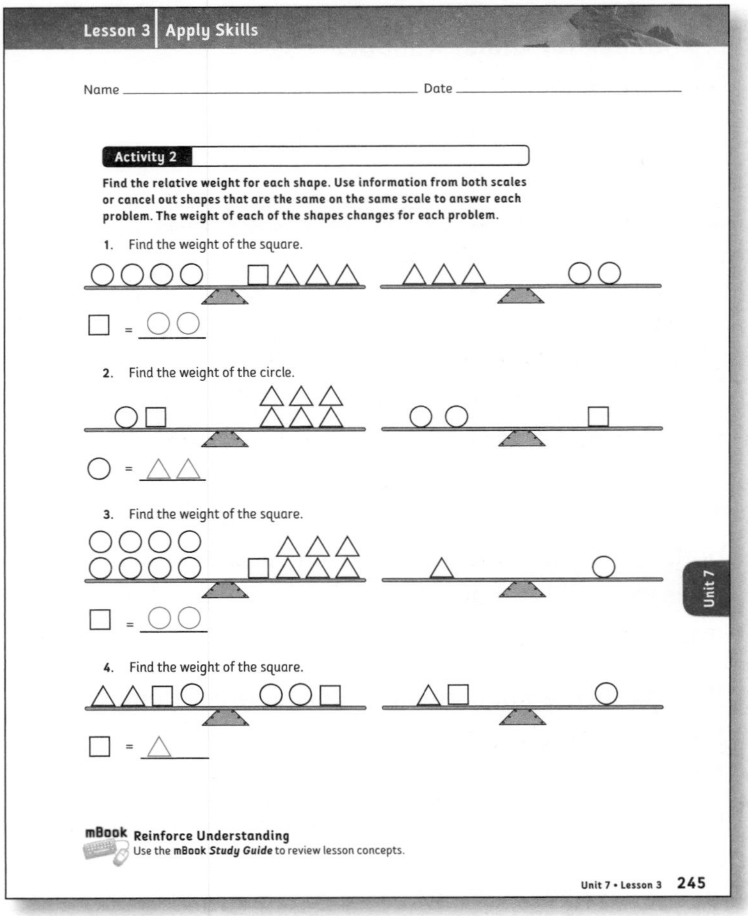

Lesson 3 | Apply Skills

Name ______________________ Date ______________

Activity 2

Find the relative weight for each shape. Use information from both scales or cancel out shapes that are the same on the same scale to answer each problem. The weight of each of the shapes changes for each problem.

1. Find the weight of the square.

○○○○ □△△△ | △△△ ○○

□ = ○○

2. Find the weight of the circle.

○□ △△△△△△ | ○○ □

○ = △△

3. Find the weight of the square.

○○○○○○○○ □△△△△△△ | △ ○

□ = ○○

4. Find the weight of the square.

△△□○ ○○□ | △□ ○

□ = △

mBook Reinforce Understanding
Use the mBook *Study Guide* to review lesson concepts.

Unit 7 • Lesson 3 245

Unit 7

Homework

Go over the instructions on page 532 of the *Student Text* for each part of the homework.

Activity 1

Students tell if the scales are balanced. Have them write yes or no on their papers.

Activity 2

Students use cancellation to find the value of the symbol.

Activity 3 • Distributed Practice

Students practice operations on fractions and integers.

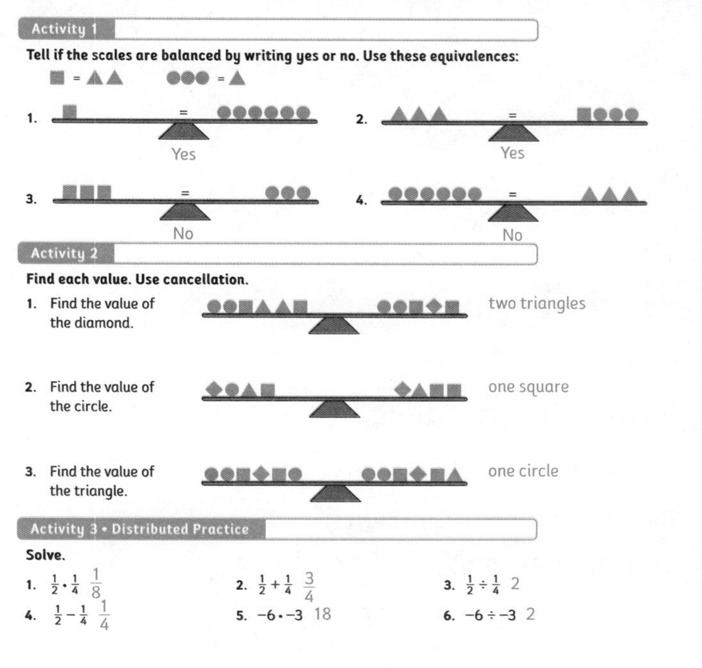

Lesson 3

Homework

Activity 1

Tell if the scales are balanced by writing yes or no. Use these equivalences:

1. Yes
2. Yes
3. No
4. No

Activity 2

Find each value. Use cancellation.

1. Find the value of the diamond. two triangles
2. Find the value of the circle. one square
3. Find the value of the triangle. one circle

Activity 3 • Distributed Practice

Solve.

1. $\frac{1}{2} \cdot \frac{1}{4}$ $\frac{1}{8}$
2. $\frac{1}{2} + \frac{1}{4}$ $\frac{3}{4}$
3. $\frac{1}{2} \div \frac{1}{4}$ 2
4. $\frac{1}{2} - \frac{1}{4}$ $\frac{1}{4}$
5. $-6 \cdot -3$ 18
6. $-6 \div -3$ 2

532 Unit 7 • Lesson 3

Lesson 4 ▶Equations With Variables

Problem Solving:

▶Determining Measurements of Angles

Lesson Planner

Vocabulary Development

property of equality

Skills Maintenance

Balanced Scales

Building Number Concepts:

▶ Equations With Variables

Students learn to solve simple algebraic equations. They learn the property of equality, which states that when we do something to one side of the equation, we must do the same thing to the other side of the equation.

Students use special symbols to solve for the variable. Then students use substitution to check their answers.

Objectives

Students will use the property of equality to solve simple algebraic equations.
Student will check their answers using substitution.

Problem Solving:

▶ Determining Measurements of Angles

Students apply what they know about solving algebraic equations to find the measurement of an unknown angle.

Objective

Students will solve algebraic equations to find the measurement of an unknown angle.

Homework

Students solve simple equations using properties and substitution, check to see if the answers are correct for problems using substitution, and tell the measure of the missing angle. In Distributed Practice, students practice operations on fractions and integers, and the distributive property.

Lesson 4 | Skills Maintenance

Name ______________ Date ______________

Skills Maintenance
Balanced Scales

Activity 1

Use cancellation and the balance scales to find the value of a certain shape in each problem.

Model What is the value of △ in the scale?

△◇○□ ◇○□□

△◇̸○̸□̸ ◇̸○̸□̸□

△ = □

1. What is the value of △ in the scale?

△◇ ◇○

△ = ○

2. What is the value of ○ in the scale?

△◇ ◇○

○ = △

3. What is the value of □ in the scale?

△◇○○□ △◇○□□

□ = ○

246 Unit 7 • Lesson 4

Skills Maintenance

Balanced Scales

(*Interactive Text*, page 246)

Activity 1

Students use cancellation to answer questions about the value of shapes. There is a model for students to reference if they need help getting started.

Building Number Concepts: Equations With Variables

How do we solve simple equations?

(*Student Text*, pages 533–535)

Connect to Prior Knowledge

Remind students that special symbols represent expressions with variables. Write the symbols **N N N + V V + N + V V** on the board. Remind students that we can only combine like terms.

Ask:

> **How would we simplify this expression? What does it look like as an algebraic expression?**

Listen for:

- *Move like terms next to each other: N N N + N + V V + V V.*
- *Combine like terms: N N N N + V V V V.*
- *Write it as an expression using numbers and variables: 4 + 4x.*

Link to Today's Concept

Tell students that in today's lesson, we use the special symbols to look at like terms, but we use them in equations rather than expressions.

Demonstrate

Engagement Strategy: Teacher Modeling

Demonstrate how to solve for *x* in an equation in one of the following ways:

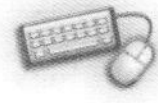

mBook: Use the *mBook Teacher Edition* for *Student Text*, pages 533–534. m

Overhead Projector: Reproduce the equation on a transparency, and modify as discussed.

Board: Copy the equation on the board, and modify as discussed.

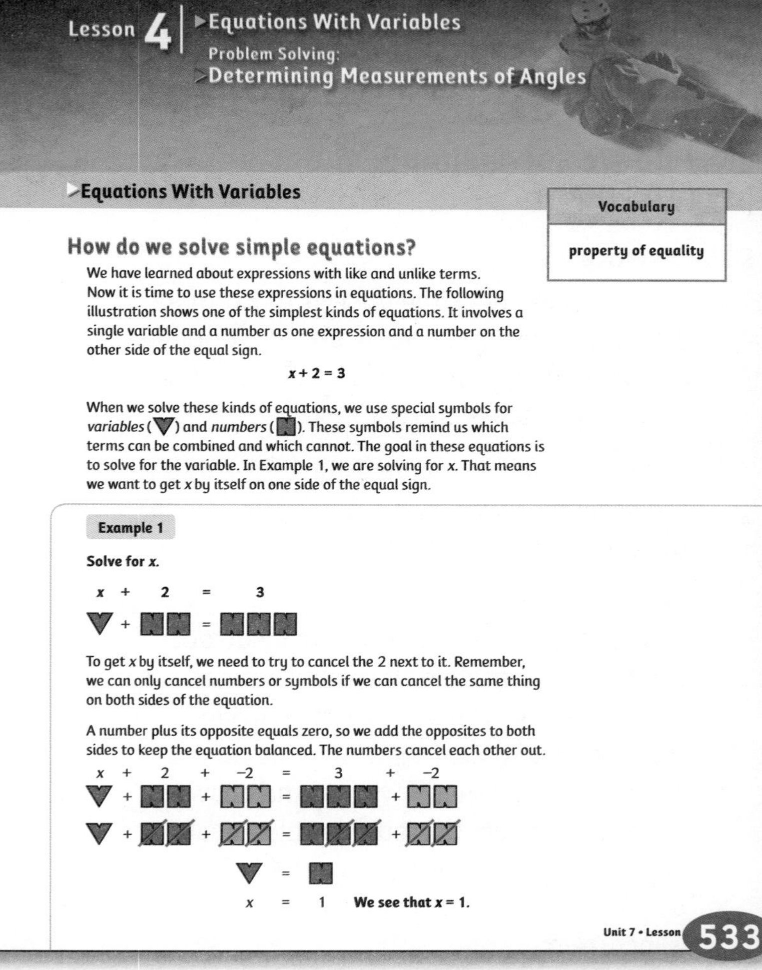

Lesson 4 | Equations With Variables
Problem Solving: Determining Measurements of Angles

Equations With Variables

Vocabulary
property of equality

How do we solve simple equations?

We have learned about expressions with like and unlike terms. Now it is time to use these expressions in equations. The following illustration shows one of the simplest kinds of equations. It involves a single variable and a number as one expression and a number on the other side of the equal sign.

$x + 2 = 3$

When we solve these kinds of equations, we use special symbols for *variables* (▼) and *numbers* (■). These symbols remind us which terms can be combined and which cannot. The goal in these equations is to solve for the variable. In Example 1, we are solving for *x*. That means we want to get *x* by itself on one side of the equal sign.

Example 1

Solve for *x*.

$x + 2 = 3$

To get *x* by itself, we need to try to cancel the 2 next to it. Remember, we can only cancel numbers or symbols if we can cancel the same thing on both sides of the equation.

A number plus its opposite equals zero, so we add the opposites to both sides to keep the equation balanced. The numbers cancel each other out.

$x + 2 + -2 = 3 + -2$

$x = 1$ We see that $x = 1$.

Unit 7 • Lesson 533

- Show $x + 2 = 3$, and explain to students that this simple equation involves variables and numbers. m
- Show the equation with special symbols. The *x* is a positive variable term, so it is represented with a black **V**. The 2 and the 3 are both positive numeric terms, so they are represented with black **N**s. m
- Explain that we need to get *x* by itself. We have to cancel out the 2. The opposite of 2 is –2, so add a –2 to both sides of the equation, and add 2 red **N**s to both sides of the special symbols equation. Remind students red symbols represent negative numbers. m
- Cross out 2 red Ns and 2 black Ns on each side of the equation. m
- Point out that once we have a value for the variable, we have solved the problem: $x = 1$. m

How do we solve simple equations?
(continued)

Demonstrate

- Show how to check the answer to Example 1 by substituting the value into the original equation. If the equation is true, the value for the variable is correct.
- In this example, we substitute 1 for x into the original equation, $\mathbf{x + 2 = 3}$. We end up with $\mathbf{3 = 3}$. This is a true statement; our answer is correct. m
- Explain that if we substitute an incorrect value for the variable, we would not get a balanced, or true statement. Provide students with an example of an incorrect answer. Explain that if we had the answer $x = 4$ and we substituted this value in our original equation, we would get $4 + 2 = 3$, or $6 = 3$. That statement is false—the answer is incorrect.

Lesson 4

How do we check to see if the answer is correct? We substitute 1 for x in the original equation.

$x + 2 = 3$
$1 + 2 = 3$ ← Substitute 1 for x.
$3 = 3$

This problem used a new property from the toolbox. Notice that we got the variable by adding the opposite of the number to each side. We added −2 to 2 and −2 to 3. This property is the **property of equality**. It reminds us that when we do something to one side of the equation, we have to do the same thing to the other side. We use the same kind of thinking when we begin an equation with a negative number. This property is demonstrated in Example 2.

Property of equality
When we do something to one side of the equation, we have to do the same thing to the other.

Example 2

Solve the equation involving negative numbers. Use the property of equality.

$x - 2 = 1$

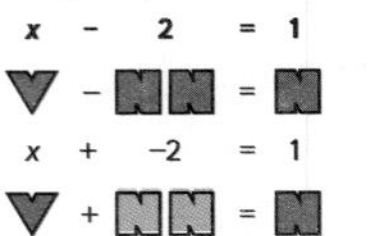

$x + -2 = 1$

Subtraction is the same as adding the opposite.

$x + -2 + 2 = 1 + 2$

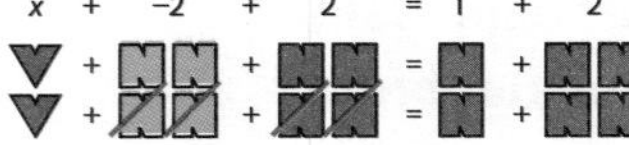

We add the opposites to both sides to keep the equation balanced. A number plus its opposite equals zero, so the numbers cancel each other out. On the right side, we add the like terms and we have our answer.

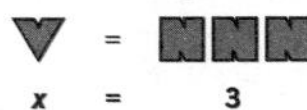

$x = 3$

Build Vocabulary

Next explain that the reason for adding the opposite of 2 in Example 1 comes from the **property of equality**. Tell students that as long as we do the same thing to each side of the equation, it remains balanced. When we add −2 to both sides in Example 1, the equation remains the same. Tell students the reason we use −2 is because it helps cancel out one of the terms in the problem, and gets the variable term alone on one side of the equation.

Demonstrate

- Use **Example 2** to show how this property works for negative numbers. In the equation $\mathbf{x - 2 = 1}$, we have subtraction. Remind students that all subtraction can be rewritten as addition by adding the opposite.
- Rewrite the equation as $\mathbf{x + -2 = 1}$ on the board. Then represent the equation with symbols. Point out that the red Ns mean the number is negative.
- Apply the property of equality by adding 2 to each side of the equation, so that we can cancel out the −2 on the left. Cross out the Ns that cancel each other out. This will leave x by itself on one side of the equation, for the answer of $\mathbf{x = 3}$.

Discuss

Direct students' attention to the Algebra Toolbox, and explain that it will be helpful as they complete the activity.

Property of equality
When we do something to one side of the equation, we have to do the same thing to the other.

Demonstrate

- Walk through the steps to check the answer to Example 2 on *Student Text*, page 535. We do this with substitution. When we substitute 3 into the original equation, the statement is true: **3 − 2 = 1**.

Improve Your Skills

- Read the material with students for a situation where a student solved the equation $\boldsymbol{x + 5 = 7}$. The student made an error, because he got the answer of $\boldsymbol{x = 12}$. When the student substituted 12 into the original equation, the statement **17 = 7** was false. Ask students if they see the error.
- Explain that the student only subtracted 5 from the left side of the equation to cancel it out. Because of the property of equality, he should have also subtracted 5 from the right side of the equation to keep the equation balanced. The answer is $\boldsymbol{x = 2}$, and when substituted into the equation, **7 = 7** is true. Therefore, the answer is correct.

Check for Understanding

Engagement Strategy: Pair Share

Divide the class into pairs. Write these equations on the board:

$\mathbf{3 + x = 9}$ $(x = 6)$

$\mathbf{y - 6 = 11}$ $(y = 17)$

Have each partner solve one of the equations. Then have partners switch papers and substitute the answer into the original equation to check the answer. If the partners find an error in the answer and the statement is false, they should find where the error is and correct it.

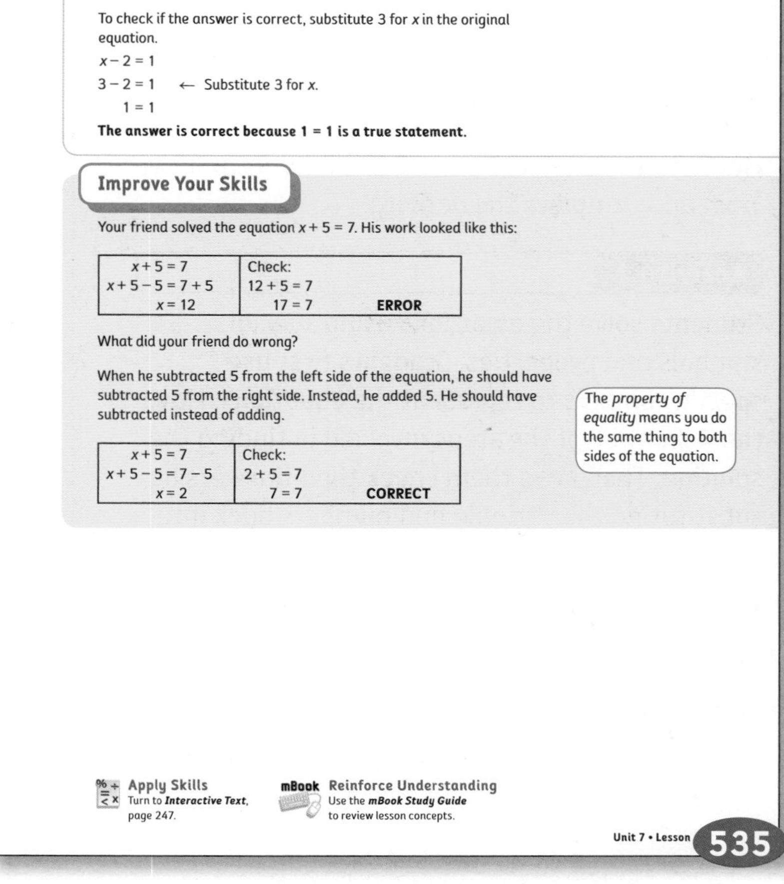

Lesson 4

To check if the answer is correct, substitute 3 for x in the original equation.

$x - 2 = 1$

$3 - 2 = 1$ ← Substitute 3 for x.

$1 = 1$

The answer is correct because 1 = 1 is a true statement.

Improve Your Skills

Your friend solved the equation $x + 5 = 7$. His work looked like this:

$x + 5 = 7$ $x + 5 - 5 = 7 + 5$ $x = 12$	Check: $12 + 5 = 7$ $17 = 7$ **ERROR**

What did your friend do wrong?

When he subtracted 5 from the left side of the equation, he should have subtracted 5 from the right side. Instead, he added 5. He should have subtracted instead of adding.

The *property of equality* means you do the same thing to both sides of the equation.

$x + 5 = 7$ $x + 5 - 5 = 7 - 5$ $x = 2$	Check: $2 + 5 = 7$ $7 = 7$ **CORRECT**

Apply Skills
Turn to *Interactive Text*, page 247.

mBook Reinforce Understanding
Use the *mBook Study Guide* to review lesson concepts.

Reinforce Understanding

For additional practice, use these equations:

$\mathbf{x - 2 = 8}$ $(x = 10)$

$\mathbf{y - -3 = 6}$ $(y = 3)$

$\mathbf{3 - n = 4}$ $(n = -1)$

Apply Skills

(*Interactive Text*, page 247)

Have students turn to page 247 in the *Interactive Text*, and complete the activity.

Activity 1

Students solve the equations using special symbols and properties. Students first use special symbols to represent the equations. Have them show all of the steps involved in finding the solution. Then have them check their answers by substituting the variable and numbers back into the original equation.

Monitor students' work as they complete the activity.

Watch for:

- Can students solve the equation correctly, using the special symbols and the properties?
- Do students remember to check their answers by substituting them back into the original equation?
- If the answer did not check out, can students evaluate their work to find the correct answer?

It is important that students use the check step to correct their own mistakes. This might require some guidance from you. Make sure students show all their work so errors are easier to find.

mBook **Reinforce Understanding**

Remind students that they can review lesson concepts by accessing the online *mBook Study Guide*.

Lesson 4 | Apply Skills

Name ____________ Date ____________

Apply Skills

Equations With Variables

Activity 1

Solve the equations using special symbols and properties. Check your answer by substituting the value of the variable into the original equation. Gray symbols represent negatives.

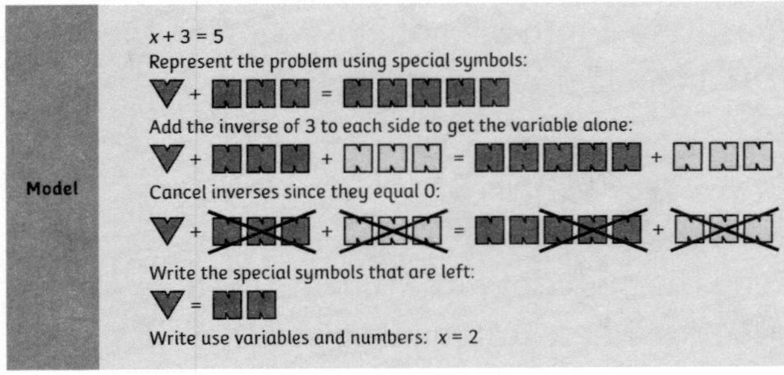

Model
$x + 3 = 5$
Represent the problem using special symbols:
Add the inverse of 3 to each side to get the variable alone:
Cancel inverses since they equal 0:
Write the special symbols that are left:
Write use variables and numbers: $x = 2$

1. $y - 5 = 4$ Show your work here:

   $y = 9$

   Check your answer here: $9 - 5 = 4$

2. $z + 3 = -2$ Show your work here:

   $Z = -5$

   Check your answer here: $-5 + 3 = -2$

Unit 7

Unit 7 • Lesson 4 247

Problem Solving:
▶ Determining Measurements of Angles

How do we find the measure of an unknown angle?

(*Student Text*, pages 536–537)

Connect to Prior Knowledge

Have students turn to the material on page 536 of the *Student Text*. Explain that we know the measure of the two angles shown because they are common benchmark angles we memorized.

Look at Figure A. Explain that a straight line or a straight angle always has an angle measurement of 180 degrees. Look at Figure B, and point out that a right angle always has an angle measurement of 90 degrees.

Link to Today's Concept

Tell students that this basic knowledge can help us solve problems involving angles we do not know. We can use algebraic equations to figure out the measures of unknown angles.

How do we find the measure of an unknown angle?

We know a lot about the properties of angles and lines based on what they look like. Even though the pictures below have no angle measures given, we can determine the measurements just by looking at them. They are based on common benchmarks we learned earlier.

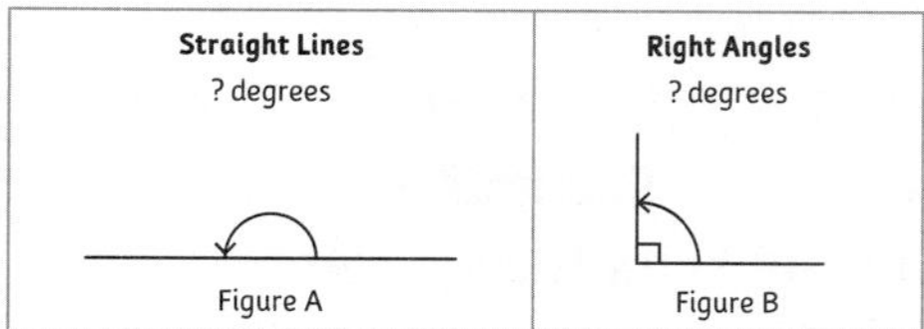

In Figure A, we know that straight lines always measure 180 degrees.
In Figure B, we know that right angles always measure 90 degrees. The small box in Figure B is a symbol that tells us that it is a right angle.

What happens when we are given only some of the information about the measure of an angle? How do we figure out the measure of the angle that has a variable? We can use the same kind of algebraic equation that we learned earlier in the lesson.

How do we find the measure of an unknown angle? *(continued)*

Demonstrate

- Turn to page 537 of the *Student Text*. Have students look at **Example 1**. In this example, we do not know the measure of angle *c*, but we can easily find it out by using the properties we do know. Tell students we can use algebra to find the measure of the missing angle. Go through the steps for finding the measure of the missing angle.
- Explain that we know the right angle has a measure of **90 degrees**, and we are told that the adjacent angle has a measure of **20 degrees**. Point out to students that the diagram refers to the measurement of the angle we do not know as *x* degrees. Explain that we know that the measure of a straight line is 180 degrees. All of the angles in the diagram add up to **180 degrees**.
- Write $\mathbf{x + 90 + 20 = 180}$ on the board. Explain that now that we have an equation, we can apply what we learned to solve for *x*.
- In the next step, we combine like terms to get $\mathbf{x + 110 = 180}$. Then we want to isolate the *x* on the left side of the equation, so we use the property of equality and add the opposite on both sides of the equation. Write $\mathbf{x + 110 - 110 = 180 - 110}$ on the board to illustrate this step.
- Next we cancel out the opposite numbers, and we are left with $\mathbf{x = 70}$. The measure of angle **c** is **70 degrees**. Be sure students understand each of the steps.
- Walk through the steps to substitute 70 into the original equation. The answer is correct.

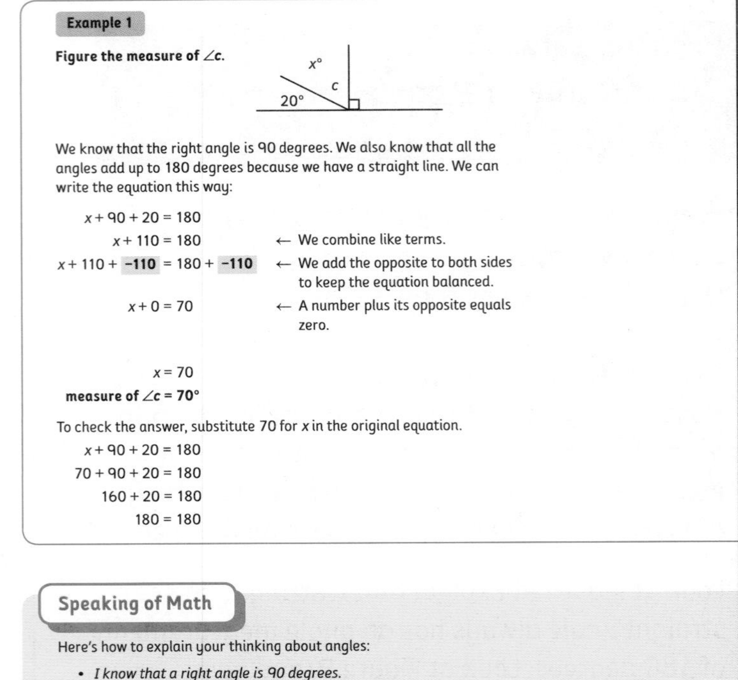
Lesson 4

Example 1

Figure the measure of ∠*c*.

We know that the right angle is 90 degrees. We also know that all the angles add up to 180 degrees because we have a straight line. We can write the equation this way:

$x + 90 + 20 = 180$

$x + 110 = 180$ ← We combine like terms.

$x + 110 + -110 = 180 + -110$ ← We add the opposite to both sides to keep the equation balanced.

$x + 0 = 70$ ← A number plus its opposite equals zero.

$x = 70$

measure of ∠*c* = 70°

To check the answer, substitute 70 for *x* in the original equation.

$x + 90 + 20 = 180$

$70 + 90 + 20 = 180$

$160 + 20 = 180$

$180 = 180$

Speaking of Math

Here's how to explain your thinking about angles:

- *I know that a right angle is 90 degrees.*
- *I know that a straight line is 180 degrees.*
- *When using equations to find what degree an angle is, I add the opposite to both sides to keep the equation balanced.*

Problem-Solving Activity Turn to ***Interactive Text***, page 248.

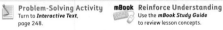

mBook Reinforce Understanding Use the ***mBook Study Guide*** to review lesson concepts.

Unit 7 • Lesson 537

Speaking of Math

Read through the tips at the bottom of the page. Tell students that these strategies will help them when they are thinking about angles.

Problem-Solving Activity
(*Interactive Text*, pages 248–249)

Have students turn to pages 248–249 in the *Interactive Text*. Read through the directions with students.

Students find the measure of missing angles using the properties and information they are given about the other angles in the problem. Make sure students show their work.

Monitor students' work as they complete the activity.

Watch for:

- Can students set up the algebraic equation needed to find the measure of the missing angle?
- Can students recall important benchmark angles, such as right angles (90°) and straight angles (180°)?

Be sure students have adequate time to explore the properties of the angles and set up the equations properly before solving. Remember the important message we want to send to students about problem solving—we work slowly and carefully.

Reinforce Understanding
Remind students that they can review lesson concepts by accessing the online *mBook Study Guide*.

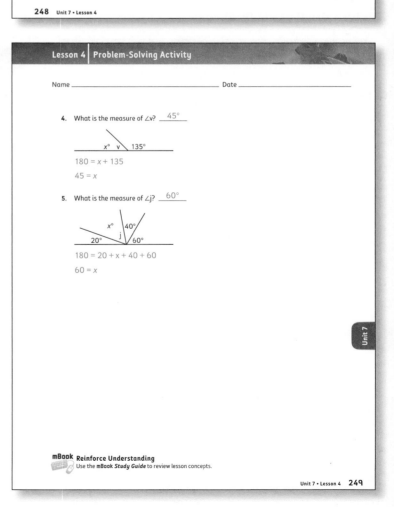

Lesson 4 | Problem-Solving Activity

Name ______________ Date ______________

Problem-Solving Activity
Determining Measurements of Angles

Use algebraic equations to find the missing angle measurements in each problem. Be sure to show all your work.

1. What is the measure of ∠b? 80°

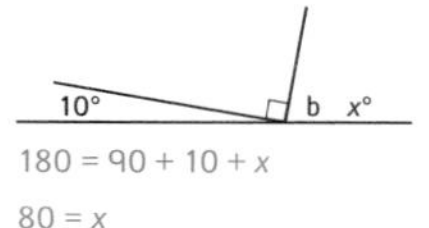

$180 = 90 + 10 + x$

$80 = x$

2. What is the measure of ∠r? 120°

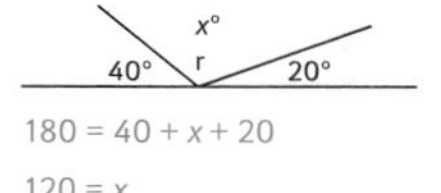

$180 = 40 + x + 20$

$120 = x$

3. What is the measure of ∠c? 75°

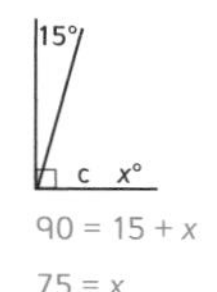

$90 = 15 + x$

$75 = x$

248 Unit 7 • Lesson 4

Lesson 4 | Problem-Solving Activity

Name ______________ Date ______________

4. What is the measure of ∠v? 45°

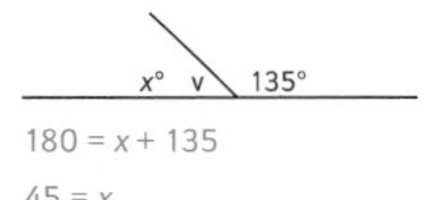

$180 = x + 135$

$45 = x$

5. What is the measure of ∠j? 60°

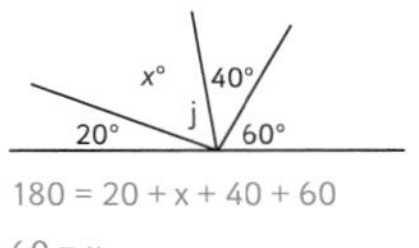

$180 = 20 + x + 40 + 60$

$60 = x$

mBook Reinforce Understanding
Use the mBook *Study Guide* to review lesson concepts.

Unit 7 • Lesson 4 249

Homework

Go over the instructions on page 538 of the *Student Text* for each part of the homework.

Activity 1

Students solve simple equations for the variables using integer rules and check their results using substitution.

Activity 2

Students check to see if the answers are correct using substitution.

Activity 3

Students tell the measure of the missing angle in a series of adjacent angles. They use their knowledge of benchmark angles and given information in the problem.

Activity 4 • Distributed Practice

Students practice operations on fractions and integers, and the distributive property.

Lesson 4

Homework

Activity 1

Solve the equations. Be sure to show all your work and check your answers at the end.

1. $3 + x = 12$ $x = 9$
2. $y - 4 = 3$ $y = 7$
3. $1 + w = -5$ $w = -6$
4. $z - -5 = -2$ $z = -7$
5. $-4 + a = -2$ $a = 2$
6. $3 - 4 = n$ $n = -1$

Activity 2

Tim got the following answers for each equation. Substitute Tim's answer in each equation to see if it is correct. If he was correct, write "correct." If Tim got the answer wrong, write "incorrect."

Model $z + 5 = 12$ $6 + 5 = 12$
Answer: $z = 6$ $11 = 12$
6 is not correct

1. $x - -4 = 1$ Answer: $x = 5$ Incorrect
2. $-3 + z = 2$ Answer: $z = 5$ Correct
3. $w + 7 = -4$ Answer: $w = -11$ Correct
4. $12 - n = 2$ Answer: $n = -10$ Incorrect

Activity 3

Tell the measure of the missing angle in each problem.

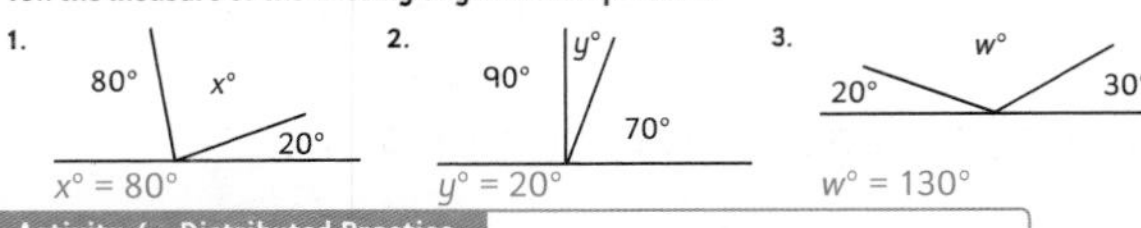

$x° = 80°$ $y° = 20°$ $w° = 130°$

Activity 4 • Distributed Practice

Solve.

1. $4 - -3$ 7
2. $4 - 3$ 1
3. $4 \cdot -3$ −12
4. $\frac{1}{2} \cdot \frac{1}{2}$ $\frac{1}{4}$
5. $\frac{1}{2} \cdot \frac{2}{1}$ 1
6. $\frac{1}{2} \div \frac{1}{2}$ 1
7. Simplify using the distributive property: $5(2x + 2)$ $10x + 10$

538 Unit 7 • Lesson 4

Lesson 5 ▶Equations With Coefficients

Monitoring Progress: Quiz 1

Lesson Planner

Vocabulary Development

coefficient

Skills Maintenance

Solving Simple Equations

Building Number Concepts:

▶ Equations With Coefficients

In today's lesson, students solve problems that involve coefficients. We review the concept of coefficients, and then we explore how coefficients change the way we solve equations.

Objective

Students will solve problems with coefficients.

Monitoring Progress:

▶ Quiz 1

Distribute the quiz, and remind students that the questions involve material covered over the previous lessons in the unit.

Homework

Students use special symbols to find the value of *x*. Then they find the measure of the missing angle. In Distributed Practice, students practice operations with integers, PEMDAS, and the distributive property.

Lesson 5 | Skills Maintenance

Name ______________________ Date ______________

Skills Maintenance
Solving Simple Equations

Activity 1

Use the rules and properties you learned to solve the algebraic equations. Then check the answers by substituting the value of the variable into the original equations.

1. $x - 2 = 4$

   Show your work here.

   $x - 2 = 4$

   $x - 2 + 2 = 4 + 2$

   $x = 6$

   Check your work here. $6 - 2 = 4$

2. $3 + y = -1$

   Show your work here.

   $3 + y = -1$

   $3 + y - 3 = -1 - 3$

   $y = -4$

   Check your work here. $3 + -4 = -1$

3. $z - -5 = -2$

   Show your work here.

   $z - -5 = -2$

   $z + 5 - 5 = -2 - 5$

   $z = -7$

   Check your work here. $-7 - -5 = -2$

250 Unit 7 • Lesson 5

Skills Maintenance

Solving Simple Equations

(*Interactive Text*, page 250)

Activity 1

Students use rules and properties to solve algebraic equations. They check their answers by substituting the value into the original equation.

Building Number Concepts: ▶ Equations With Coefficients

How do coefficients change the way we work equations?

(*Student Text*, pages 539–541)

Connect to Prior Knowledge

Review the term **coefficient** with students. Tell students that a coefficient is a number that is multiplied by an unknown quantity, or a variable. Write the following expressions on the board or overhead and have students identify which expressions have a coefficient:

$2x$ **$-x$**   **$510x$**   **12**   **x**

Link to Today's Concept

Tell students that in today's lesson, we explore equations with coefficients and see how they change the way we solve different equations.

Demonstrate

Engagement Strategy: Teacher Modeling

Demonstrate how to solve equations with coefficients in one of the following ways:

mBook: Use the *mBook Teacher Edition* for *Student Text*, page 539. m

Overhead Projector: Reproduce the equation on a transparency, and modify as discussed.

Board: Copy the equation on the board, and modify as discussed.

- Show $x + x + x = 3x$. Explain that the special symbols for the expression $3x$ are just a series of 3 Vs. Explain that there is no combining or moving necessary. m
- Explain that these 3 Vs all represent just one term, $3x$, where x is the variable and 3 is the coefficient. m

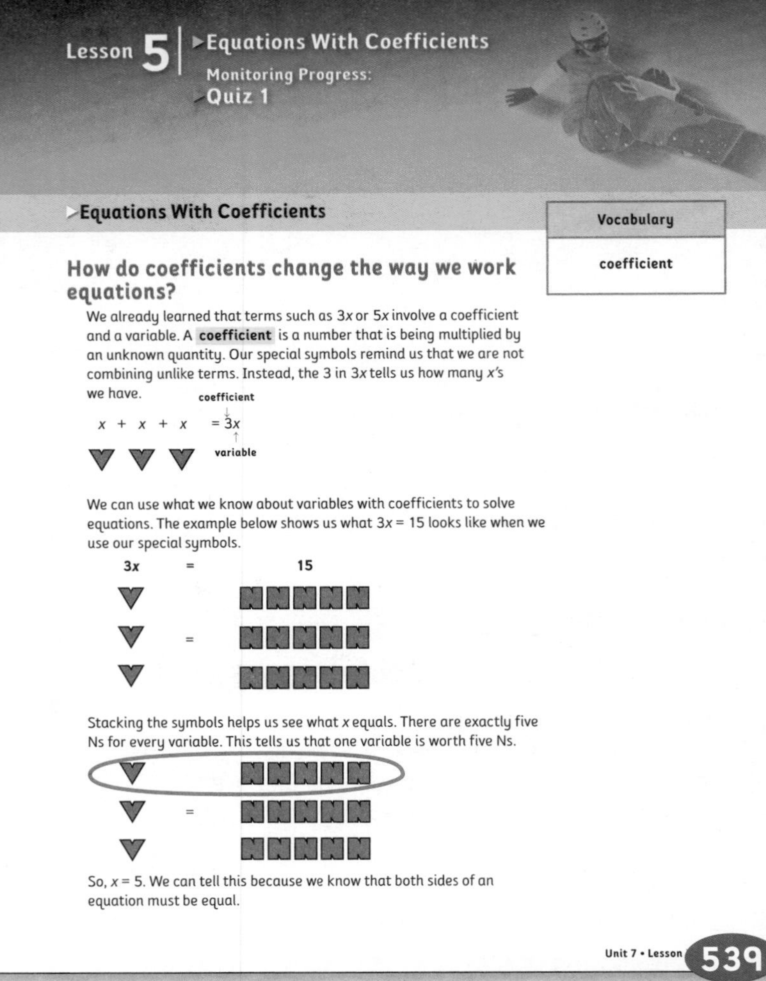

Lesson 5 ▶Equations With Coefficients
Monitoring Progress: Quiz 1

▶Equations With Coefficients

Vocabulary
coefficient

How do coefficients change the way we work equations?

We already learned that terms such as $3x$ or $5x$ involve a coefficient and a variable. A **coefficient** is a number that is being multiplied by an unknown quantity. Our special symbols remind us that we are not combining unlike terms. Instead, the 3 in $3x$ tells us how many x's we have.

$x + x + x = 3x$ (coefficient, variable)

We can use what we know about variables with coefficients to solve equations. The example below shows us what $3x = 15$ looks like when we use our special symbols.

$3x = 15$

Stacking the symbols helps us see what x equals. There are exactly five Ns for every variable. This tells us that one variable is worth five Ns.

So, $x = 5$. We can tell this because we know that both sides of an equation must be equal.

Unit 7 • Lesson 539

- Tell students that we now look at an equation with coefficients. Show $3x = 15$. m
- Show the symbols that are under the equation. Point out the unique way we used the special symbols to show this equation. It is important for students to look at the symbols vertically to understand how it represents the equation. m
- Circle the first row of special symbols. Then tell students to look at the problem horizontally by looking at the circled portion. m
- Explain that the circled portion helps us see what one x is equal to: $x = 5$. m
- Remind students that to check the answer, we can substitute the 5 back in the original equation, and we find the true statement, **15 = 15**.

Explain

Read the text at the top of page 540 of the *Student Text*. Make sure students understand that the value of x will not always be equal to 5, even if some of the numbers in the equation are the same. Explain that we always want to solve for the variable.

Demonstrate

- Have students look at **Example 1**. Explain that in this example, we want to find x in the equation $\mathbf{3x = 30}$.
- Demonstrate how to set up the special symbols, placing the Vs in one column, one V for each x. We divided the Vs into three groups because we want to know the value of one x. Tell students that the coefficient, 3, tells you how many Xs there are.
- Then point out the symbols for the number 30. Explain that we divide the 30 into three groups as well. Point out that all three rows have exactly 10 Ns. These three rows of 10 Ns represent the number 30. Explain that we want to know the value of one variable, which is represented in the circled row. In this case, $\mathbf{x = 10}$.

Lesson 5

Let's see how the coefficient helps us solve many different equations.

A variable is an unknown quantity, so its value can be different in different equations. In the equation $3x = 15$, x is equal to 5. But the variable x will not always be equal to 5, even if some of the numbers in the equation are the same. Let's look at some more equations. Our goal is to solve for x.

Example 1

Find the value of x in the equation.

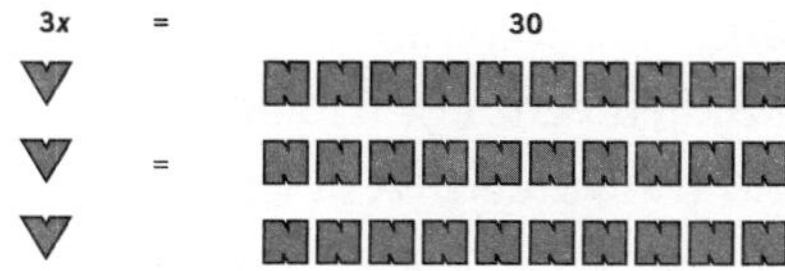

We divided the 30 from the right side of the equal sign into three groups. Since we want to know the value of x, we only need to look at the first row.

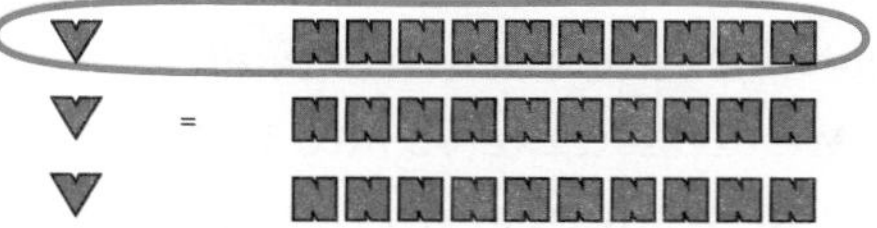

There are three groups of exactly ten Ns.

In this case, $x = 10$.

540 Unit 7 • Lesson 5

How do coefficients change the way we work equations? *(continued)*

Demonstrate

- Have students look at **Example 2** on page 541 of the *Student Text*. Explain that in this example, we use a different coefficient, **5**. We want to find the value of x in the equation $\mathbf{5x = 15}$.
- Demonstrate how to set up the special symbols, placing the Vs in one column, because we use one V for each x. Explain that this time, we divided the Vs into five groups because we want to know the value of one x. Tell students that the coefficient, 5, tells us there are 5 *X*s.
- Then point out the symbols for the number 15. Explain that we divide 15 into five groups as well. Point out that all five rows have exactly 3 Ns. These five rows of 3 Ns represent the number 15. Explain that we want to know the value of one variable, which is represented in the circled row. In this case, $\mathbf{x = 3}$.

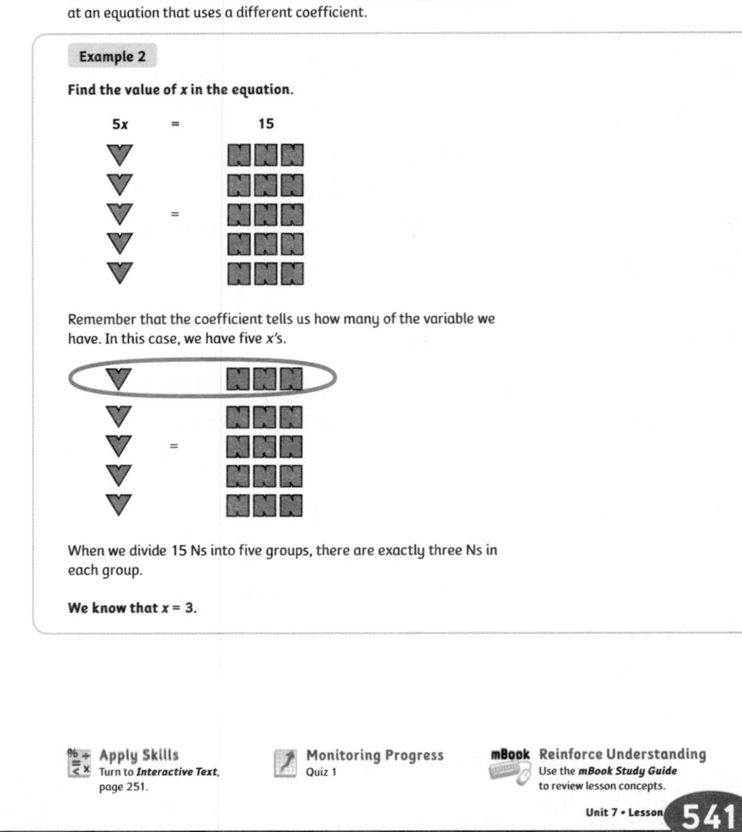

Lesson 5
We have seen the number 3 used as a coefficient twice. Now let's look at an equation that uses a different coefficient.
Example 2
Find the value of x in the equation.
5x = 15
Remember that the coefficient tells us how many of the variable we have. In this case, we have five x's.
When we divide 15 Ns into five groups, there are exactly three Ns in each group.
We know that x = 3.
Apply Skills
Turn to Interactive Text, page 251.
Monitoring Progress
Quiz 1
mBook Reinforce Understanding
Use the mBook Study Guide to review lesson concepts.
Unit 7 • Lesson
541

Check for Understanding

Engagement Strategy: Look About

Write the equation $\mathbf{6x = 18}$ on the board. Tell students that they are going to find out the value of x ($x = 3$) with the help of the whole class. Students should use special symbols to find the value of x, as in Examples 1 and 2. Then they should circle the symbols that represent the value of x in their diagram. They should do this in large writing on a piece of paper or a dry erase board. When students finish their work, they should hold up their answer for everyone to see.

If students are not sure about the answer, prompt them to look about at other students' solutions to help with their thinking. Review the answers after all students have held up their solutions.

Apply Skills
(*Interactive Text*, page 251)

Have students turn to *Interactive Text*, page 251, and complete the activity.

Activity 1

Students solve simple equations involving coefficients. Have students use special symbols to represent the equations, and make sure they show their work. Students should check their work by substituting the value of the variable into the original equation.

Monitor students' work as they complete the activity.

Watch for:

- Can students represent the equation accurately with special symbols?
- Do students use the coefficient to determine how many rows of special symbols to set up?
- Do students substitute the variable into the original equation correctly to check their answer?

Reinforce Understanding

Remind students that they can review lesson concepts by accessing the online *mBook Study Guide.*

Lesson 5 | Apply Skills

Name ______ Date ______

Apply Skills
Equations With Coefficients

Activity 1

Use special symbols to solve the simple equations.

1. $3x = 18$ Show your work here.

   $x =$ 6 Check your work here: $3(6) = 18$

2. $\frac{1}{2}y = 4$ Show your work here.

   $y =$ 8 Check your work here: $\left(\frac{1}{2}\right)8 = 4$

3. $6w = 54$ Show your work here.

   $w =$ 9 Check your work here: $6 \cdot 9 = 54$

4. $\frac{1}{5}a = 5$ Show your work here.

   $a =$ 25 Check your work here. $\left(\frac{1}{5}\right)25 = 5$

mBook **Reinforce Understanding**
Use the **mBook *Study Guide*** to review lesson concepts.

Unit 7 • Lesson 5 251

Unit 7

Monitoring Progress:
▶ Quiz 1 • Form A

Assess
Quiz 1

- Administer Quiz 1 Form A in the *Assessment Book*, pages 61–62. (If necessary, retest students with Quiz 1 Form B from the *mBook Teacher Edition* following differentiation.)

Students	Assess	Differentiate
	Day 1	Day 2
All	Quiz 1 *Form A*	
Scored 80% or above		Extension
Scored Below 80%		Reinforcement

Differentiate

- Review Quiz 1 Form A with class.
- Identify students for Extension or Reinforcement.

Extension

For those students who score 80 percent or better, provide the On Track! Activities from Unit 7, Lessons 1–5, from the *mBook Teacher Edition.*

Reinforcement

For those students who score below 80 percent, provide additional support in one of the following ways:

- Have students access the online tutorial provided in the *mBook Study Guide.*
- Have students complete the Interactive Reinforcement Exercises for Unit 7, Lessons 1–4, in the *mBook Study Guide.*
- Provide teacher-directed reteaching of unit concepts.

Unit 7 | Quiz 1 • Form A

Name ______ Date ______

Form A

Monitoring Progress
Algebraic Equations

Part 1

Use PEMDAS to prove that both sides are equal. Show all of your work.

1. $6 \cdot 3 + 3 \cdot -3 = 3^2 + 1^2 - 1$
   $6 \cdot 3 + 3 \cdot -3 = 9 + 1 - 1$
   $18 + -9 = 9 + 1 - 1$
   $9 = 9$

2. $5 + 4 \div 2 + 4^2 = 7(2 + 1) + 2$
   $5 + 4 \div 2 + 4^2 = 7(3) + 2$
   $5 + 4 \div 2 + 16 = 7(3) + 2$
   $5 + 2 + 16 = 21 + 2$
   $23 = 23$

3. $6 \div 2 + 12 \div 6 + 20 \div 5 = 3^2$
   $6 \div 2 + 12 \div 6 + 20 \div 5 = 9$
   $3 + 2 + 4 = 9$
   $9 = 9$

4. $9 - -3 + 4(3) = 2 \cdot 2 \cdot 2 \cdot 2 + 2 \cdot 2 \cdot 2$
   $9 - -3 + 12 = 2 \cdot 2 \cdot 2 \cdot 2 + 2 \cdot 2 \cdot 2$
   $9 - -3 + 12 = 16 + 8$
   $24 = 24$

Part 2

Solve the equations with variables. Show all of your work.

1. $x + 3 = 15$
   $x = 15 - 3$
   $x = 12$

2. $m + 4 + 9 = 14 - 4$
   $m + 13 = 10$
   $m = 10 - 13$
   $m = -3$

3. $5 + t - 4 = 16 + 9$
   $1 + t = 25$
   $t = 25 - 1$
   $t = 24$

4. $10 + b + 10 = 35$
   $20 + b = 35$
   $b = 35 - 20$
   $b = 15$

Unit 7

Unit 7 • Quiz 1 • Form A 61

Unit 7 | Quiz 1 • Form A

Monitoring Progress
Measurement of Angles

Part 3

Find the measure of the missing angle. Show all of your work.

1. What is the measure of angle d?

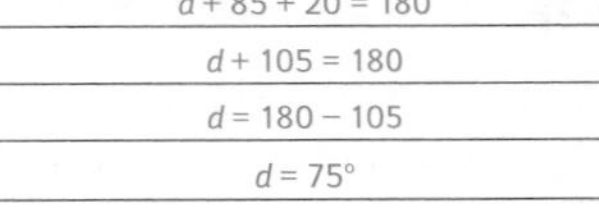

   $d + 85 + 20 = 180$
   $d + 105 = 180$
   $d = 180 - 105$
   $d = 75°$

2. What is the measure of angle e?

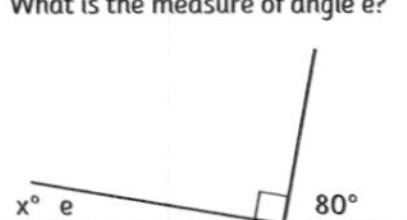

   $e + 90 + 80 = 180$
   $e + 170 = 180$
   $e = 180 - 170$
   $e = 10°$

3. What is the measure of angle f?

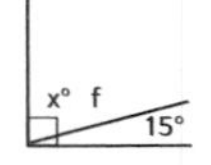

   $f + 15 = 90$
   $f = 90 - 15$
   $f = 75°$

4. What is the measure of angle c?

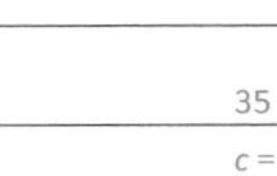

   $35 + c = 180$
   $c = 180 - 35$
   $c = 145°$

5. What is the measure of angle w?

   $25 + 55 + 40 + w = 180$
   $120 + w = 180$
   $w = 180 - 120$
   $w = 60°$

62 Unit 7 • Quiz 1 • Form A

Name ____________________ Date ____________________

Form B

mBook

Monitoring Progress
Algebraic Equations

Part 1

Use PEMDAS to prove that both sides are equal. Show all of your work.

1. $6 \cdot 3 + 1 = 4^2 + 2^2 - 1$
   $6 \cdot 3 + 1 = 16 + 4 - 1$
   $18 + 1 = 16 + 4 - 1$
   $19 = 19$

2. $4 + 4 \div 2 + 4^2 = 5(3 + 1) + 2$
   $4 + 4 \div 2 + 4^2 = 5(4) + 2$
   $4 + 4 \div 2 + 16 = 5(4) + 2$
   $4 + 2 + 16 = 20 + 2$
   $22 = 22$

3. $27 \div 3 + 18 \div 6 + 16 \div 4 = 4^2$
   $27 \div 3 + 18 \div 6 + 16 \div 4 = 16$
   $9 + 3 + 4 = 16$
   $16 = 16$

4. $9 - -3 + 2(1) = 2 \cdot 2 \cdot 2 + 3 \cdot 2 \cdot 1$
   $9 - -3 + 2 = 2 \cdot 2 \cdot 2 + 3 \cdot 2 \cdot 1$
   $9 - -3 + 2 = 8 + 6$
   $14 = 14$

Part 2

Solve the equations with variables. Show all of your work.

1. $x + 6 = 16$
   $x + 6 - 6 = 16 - 6$
   $x = 10$

2. $m + 4 + 5 = 14 - 2$
   $m + 9 = 12$
   $m + 9 - 9 = 12 - 9$
   $m = 3$

3. $6 + t - 2 = 16 + 12$
   $t + 4 = 28$
   $t + 4 - 4 = 28 - 4$
   $t = 24$

4. $10 + b + 20 = 45$
   $b + 30 = 45$
   $b + 30 - 30 = 45 - 30$
   $b = 15$

Name ____________________ Date ____________________

Monitoring Progress
Measurement of Angles

Part 3

Find the measure of the missing angle. Show all of your work.

1. What is the measure of angle d?

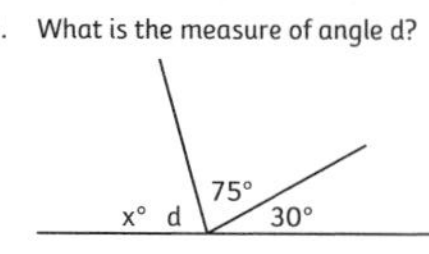

   $d + 75 + 30 = 180$
   $d + 105 = 180$
   $d + 105 - 105 = 180 - 105$
   $d = 75°$

2. What is the measure of angle e?

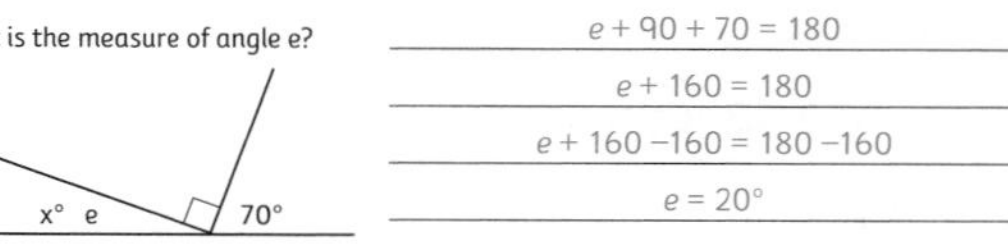

   $e + 90 + 70 = 180$
   $e + 160 = 180$
   $e + 160 - 160 = 180 - 160$
   $e = 20°$

3. What is the measure of angle f?

   $f + 20 = 90$
   $f + 20 - 20 = 90 - 20$
   $f = 70°$

4. What is the measure of angle c?

   $45 + c = 180$
   $45 - 45 + c = 180 - 45$
   $c = 135°$

5. What is the measure of angle w?

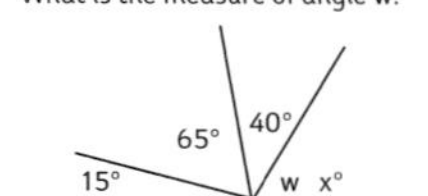

   $15 + 65 + 40 + w = 180$
   $120 + w = 180$
   $120 - 120 + w = 180 - 120$
   $w = 60°$

Homework

Go over the instructions on page 542 of the *Student Text* for each part of the homework.

Activity 1

Students use special symbols to find the value of x.

Activity 2

Students find the measure of the missing angle.

Activity 3 • Distributed Practice

Students practice operations on integers, PEMDAS, and the distributive property.

Homework

Activity 1

Use the special symbols to find the value of x.

1. $2x = 10$ $x = 5$
2. $4x = 12$ $x = 3$
3. $3x = 9$ $x = 3$
4. $5x = 10$ $x = 2$

Activity 2

Find the measure of the missing angle in each problem.

1. 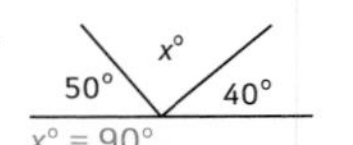

$x° = 90°$

2. 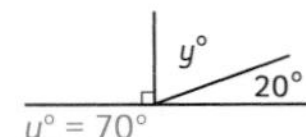

$y° = 70°$

3. 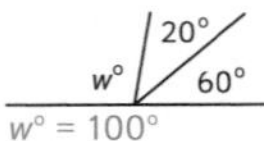

$w° = 100°$

Activity 3 • Distributed Practice

Solve.

1. $4 \div -2$ -2
2. $-4 \div -2$ 2
3. $-2 - -6$ 4
4. $-2 + -6$ -8
5. $5 + (6 \cdot 5) - 5$ 30
6. $2 \cdot -6$ -12
7. $(3^2 + 2) - 9$ 2
8. Simplify using the distributive property: $2(-x + 1)$ $-2x + 2$

Lesson 6 | More Equations With Coefficients

Problem Solving: Finding the Measure of Two Angles

Lesson Planner

Vocabulary Development

reciprocal
supplementary angles

Skills Maintenance

Finding the Missing Angle, Simple Equations

Building Number Concepts: More Equations With Coefficients

Students learn to use the multiplicative inverse property (also called property of reciprocals) to solve problems that involve coefficients. When we solve equations involving coefficients using the properties of reciprocals and equality, the main goal is to get a coefficient of one.

Objective

Students will use reciprocals to solve problems with coefficients.

Problem Solving: Finding the Measure of Two Angles

Students learn to find the measure of two angles. They look at the relationship between straight lines and supplementary angles. Students use this relationship to set up equations to find the measure of the angles.

Objective

Students will find the measure of two angles.

Homework

Students solve one-step equations involving coefficients, find the measures of the missing angles, and solve proportions. In Distributed Practice, students practice operations on integers, PEMDAS, and the distributive property.

Lesson 6 | Skills Maintenance

Name ____________ Date ____________

Skills Maintenance
Finding the Missing Angle

Activity 1

Make algebraic expressions to find the missing angle in each of the triangles. Remember the sum of the interior angles of a triangle is 180 degrees.

1. 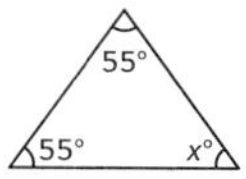

Write your equation here.
$180° - 55° - 55° = 70°$

Show your work here.
$180 = 55 + 55 + x$
$180 = 110 + x$
$x = 70$

The missing angle, x, has a measurement of 70°

2. 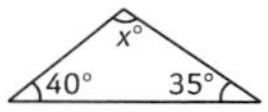

Write your equation here.
$180° - 40° - 35° = 105°$

Show your work here.
$180 = 40 + 35 + x$
$180 = 75 + x$
$x = 105$

The missing angle, x, has a measurement of 105°

Simple Equations

Activity 2

Find the missing number to complete the equations.

1. $\frac{1}{3} \cdot 3 =$ 1
2. $3 \cdot$ $\frac{1}{3}$ $= 1$
3. 3 $\cdot \frac{1}{3} = 1$
4. $\frac{2}{3} \cdot \frac{3}{2} =$ 1
5. $\frac{3}{2} \cdot$ $\frac{2}{3}$ $= 1$
6. $\frac{3}{2}$ $\cdot \frac{2}{3} = 1$

252 Unit 7 • Lesson 6

Skills Maintenance

Finding the Missing Angle, Simple Equations
(*Interactive Text*, page 252)

Activity 1

Students find the missing angle measure in triangles, using their knowledge of properties of triangles.

Activity 2

Students solve multiplication problems involving reciprocals to prepare for today's lesson on coefficients.

Building Number Concepts:
▶ More Equations With Coefficients

How do we solve equations with coefficients?

(*Student Text*, pages 543–544)

Connect to Prior Knowledge

Begin by reviewing expressions with coefficients. Put these examples on the board:

$3x$ $-2x$ x $17x$ $-x$

Have students tell you the coefficient in each. Pay special attention to the expressions x and $-x$ and be sure students understand their coefficients are 1 and −1, respectively.

Link to Today's Concept

Tell students that in today's lesson, we look at equations with coefficients and learn new properties involving them.

Demonstrate

Engagement Strategy: Teacher Modeling

Demonstrate how to solve an equation with coefficients in one of the following ways:

mBook: Use the *mBook Teacher Edition* for *Student Text*, pages 543–544. m

Overhead Projector: Reproduce the equation on a transparency, and modify as discussed.

Board: Copy the equation on the board, and modify as discussed.

- Show the equation $\mathbf{4x = 12}$. Remind students how we use the special symbols. For the expression $4x$, we draw a series of 4 Vs; for 12, we draw a series of 12 Ns. Point out the unique way we use the special symbols to show this equation. m

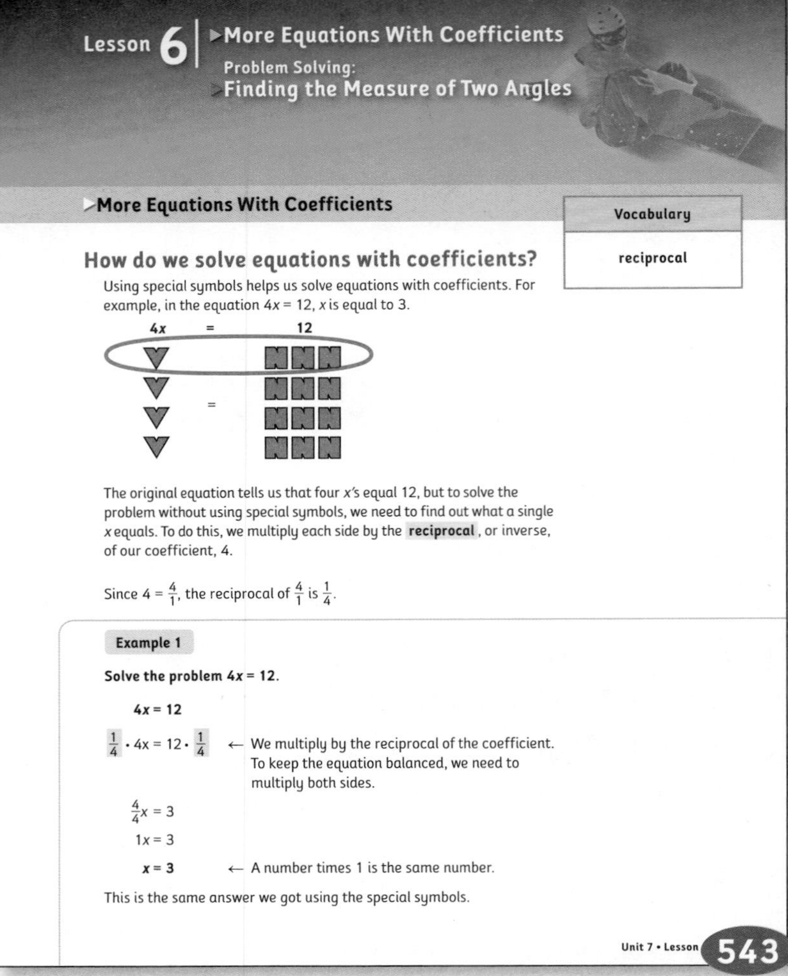

Lesson 6 ▶More Equations With Coefficients
Problem Solving:
▶Finding the Measure of Two Angles

▶More Equations With Coefficients

Vocabulary
reciprocal

How do we solve equations with coefficients?

Using special symbols helps us solve equations with coefficients. For example, in the equation $4x = 12$, x is equal to 3.

The original equation tells us that four x's equal 12, but to solve the problem without using special symbols, we need to find out what a single x equals. To do this, we multiply each side by the **reciprocal**, or inverse, of our coefficient, 4.

Since $4 = \frac{4}{1}$, the reciprocal of $\frac{4}{1}$ is $\frac{1}{4}$.

Example 1

Solve the problem $4x = 12$.

$4x = 12$

$\frac{1}{4} \cdot 4x = 12 \cdot \frac{1}{4}$ ← We multiply by the reciprocal of the coefficient. To keep the equation balanced, we need to multiply both sides.

$\frac{4}{4}x = 3$

$1x = 3$

$x = 3$ ← A number times 1 is the same number.

This is the same answer we got using the special symbols.

Unit 7 • Lesson 543

- Circle the first row of symbols. This helps us see what one x is equal to: $\mathbf{x = 3}$. m
- Explain that we can solve the equation the traditional way. This involves a new property: the multiplicative inverse property.
- Remind students that $\mathbf{4 = \frac{4}{1}}$. The **reciprocal** of $\frac{4}{1}$ is $\frac{1}{4}$. We can solve the problem by multiplying each side by the reciprocal of the coefficient. m
- Refer to the original expression $\mathbf{4x = 12}$. Show that by multiplying the equation by $\frac{1}{4}$ on both sides, we can find what just one x is equal to. This is because $4 \cdot \frac{1}{4} = 1$. This is also a property of equality. m
- Walk through the operation to get $\mathbf{\frac{4}{4}x = 3}$. Remind students that $\frac{4}{4} = 1$, so we get $\mathbf{1x = 3}$, or $\mathbf{x = 3}$. m

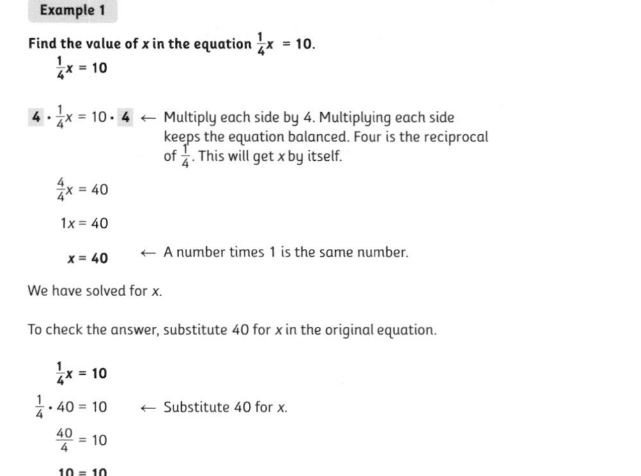

Lesson 6

To check our answer, substitute 3 for x in the original equation.

$4x = 12$

$4 \cdot 3 = 12$ ← Substitute 3 for x.

$12 = 12$

How do we solve equations when the coefficients are fractions?

Example 1 shows what happens when we have a fraction for a coefficient. The steps are almost the same. Once again, we use a coefficient to get x by itself.

Example 1

Find the value of x in the equation $\frac{1}{4}x = 10$.

$\frac{1}{4}x = 10$

$4 \cdot \frac{1}{4}x = 10 \cdot 4$ ← Multiply each side by 4. Multiplying each side keeps the equation balanced. Four is the reciprocal of $\frac{1}{4}$. This will get x by itself.

$\frac{4}{4}x = 40$

$1x = 40$

$x = 40$ ← A number times 1 is the same number.

We have solved for x.

To check the answer, substitute 40 for x in the original equation.

$\frac{1}{4}x = 10$

$\frac{1}{4} \cdot 40 = 10$ ← Substitute 40 for x.

$\frac{40}{4} = 10$

$10 = 10$

544 Unit 7 • Lesson 6

Demonstrate

- Continue going through Example 1. Explain that if we substitute the 3 back into the original equation, we can check the answer. m
- Once we solve the multiplication, we see that **12 = 12**. Our answer is correct. m

How do we solve equations when the coefficients are fractions?

(*Student Text*, page 544)

Demonstrate

- Direct attention to **Example 1**. In this example, the coefficient is a fraction: $\frac{1}{4}x = 10$.
- Go through each step of the problem with students, and be sure they see that multiplying $\frac{1}{4}$ by 4 results in a coefficient of 1. This is what we are working towards. We want to know the value of just one x. Be sure students understand this important goal when we are solving equations involving coefficients.
- In this example, we see that $x = 40$. Again, point out that we can check the answer by substituting 40 for x in the original equation. After substituting and multiplying, we get $\frac{40}{4} = 10$. When we simplify, we get **10 = 10**. The answer is correct.

Check for Understanding

Engagement Strategy: Pair/Share

Divide the class into pairs. Write the expression $3x = 15$ on the board. Have pairs find the value of x ($x = 5$). Explain that one partner will use the special symbols to solve for x, and the other will use the reciprocal of the coefficient to solve for x. When students have finished, have partners compare their answers. Then have them substitute the value of x back into the original expression to check the answer. Invite student volunteers to share their answers with the class.

How do proportions relate to algebra?

(*Student Text*, pages 545–546)

Explain

Have students turn to the material on page 545 of the *Student Text*. Discuss the way we solved proportion problems in the past by finding equivalent fractions. Tell students that we can solve these problems using a shortcut, now that we have learned how to solve algebraic equations. The shortcut is called cross multiplying.

Demonstrate

- Go over **Example 1**. Read the problem with students, make sure students understand what the problem is asking.
- Point out the information that we know from the problem: **2 inches** on the map equals **500 yards**, and Latisha has to walk the equivalent of 4 inches on the map. We need to find out how many yards 4 inches is on the map.
- Point out how we set up the proportion $\frac{2}{500} = \frac{4}{x}$, where x is the number of yards Latisha has to walk. Show students how we write the equation using cross multiplication.
- Be sure students see that we create the equation by multiplying the numerator, 2, of the first number by the denominator of the second number in the proportion, in this case the variable x. Then we multiply the denominator, 500, of the first number by the numerator, 4, of the second number. We make these two expressions equal to one another to get the equation $\mathbf{2x = 500 \cdot 4}$. Now that we know how to solve equations, we can solve this problem using our properties and rules.

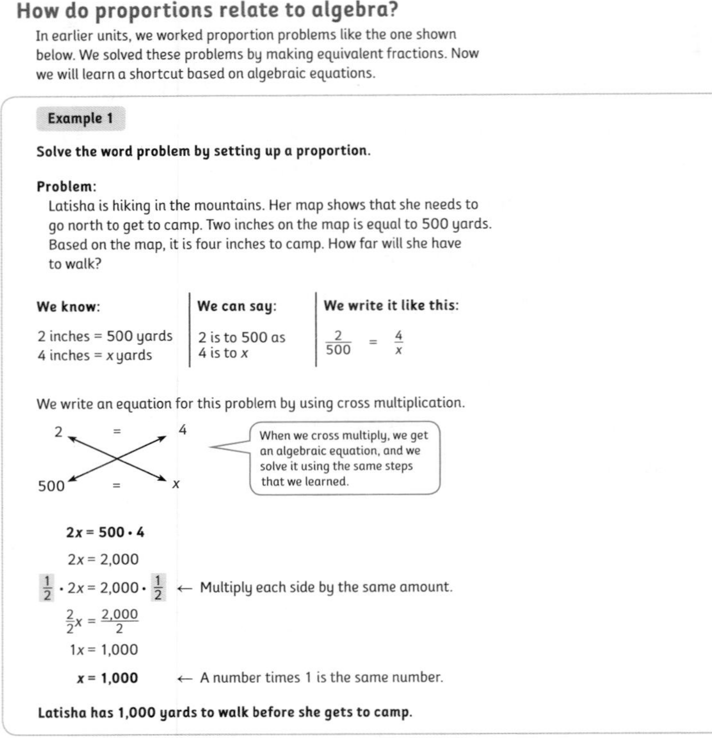

- Go through each step of the problem carefully with students. Remind students to multiply each side by $\frac{1}{2}$, the reciprocal of 2, to get a coefficient of 1. So $\mathbf{x = 1{,}000}$. **Latisha has to walk 1,000 yards.**

Improve Your Skills

- Direct students to page 546 of the *Student Text*. Here we see three solutions to **$3n = 21$**, found by three different students. Have students look at each student's steps to analyze the errors and the correct answer.
- Point out that Lena did not use the reciprocal $\frac{1}{3}$ to solve the equation, so her answer was incorrect. Forest did not write the entire expression on the left side. He forgot to include the coefficient, 3.
- Then have students look at Rianna's solution. She correctly multiplied both sides by the reciprocal of the coefficient to get the solution **$n = 7$**.

Improve Your Skills

Ms. Case asked three students to find the value of n when $3n = 21$. Rianna found the correct answer. What mistakes did her friends Lena and Forest make?

Lena: **ERROR**

$3n = 21$

$3 \cdot 3n = 21 \cdot 3$ ← Lena multiplied the coefficient by 3 instead of $\frac{1}{3}$. She did not use the reciprocal to solve the equation.

$n = 63$

Forest: **ERROR**

$3n = 21$

$\frac{1}{3} \cdot n = 21 \cdot \frac{1}{3}$ ← Forest did not write the entire expression on the left side of the equal sign. He wrote $\frac{1}{3} \cdot n$ instead of $\frac{1}{3} \cdot 3n$. He left off the coefficient 3.

$\frac{1}{3}n = 7$

$3 - \frac{1}{3}n = 7 \cdot 3$

$n = 21$

Rianna: **CORRECT**

$3n = 21$

$\frac{1}{3} \cdot 3n = 21 \cdot \frac{1}{3}$ ← Rianna multiplied both sides by the reciprocal of the coefficient.

$\frac{3}{3}n = 7$

$n = 7$

It is important to multiply by the reciprocal on both sides of the equation.

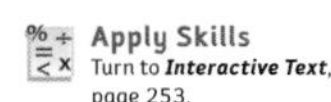

Apply Skills
Turn to *Interactive Text*, page 253.

Reinforce Understanding
Use the *mBook Study Guide* to review lesson concepts.

Apply Skills

(*Interactive Text*, page 253)

Have students turn to page 253 in the *Interactive Text*, and complete the activity.

Activity 1

Students solve the problems by setting up a proportion, and then use cross multiplication to write and solve an algebraic equation. Monitor students' work as they complete the activity.

Watch for:

- Can students identify the proportion in the problem?
- Can students use cross multiplying to set up the equation for solving the problem?
- Can students solve the algebraic equation?

Be sure students have adequate time to work through these problems. This is a very complex activity with many steps. It is important that students have time to work through all of the parts of each problem carefully.

mBook Reinforce Understanding

Remind students that they can review lesson concepts by accessing the online *mBook Study Guide*.

Lesson 6 | Apply Skills

Name ______________________ Date ______________

Apply Skills
More Equations With Coefficients

Activity 1

Set up each problem as a proportion. Then use the cross-multiplying strategy to solve the problems. Be sure to show all of your work.

1. Johnson's Furniture Store gets deliveries of new sofas every month. The delivery truck carries 10 sofas. This month Johnson is having a big sale, so 3 delivery trucks will be coming to the store. How many sofas will they deliver?
$\frac{1}{10} = \frac{3}{x}$ $x = 30$

2. There are 10 shelves of shoes in the back room of The Sports Center. Each shelf has the same number of shoes. There are 80 shoes on the 10 shelves. How many shoes are on one shelf?
$\frac{10}{80} = \frac{1}{s}$ $s = 8$

3. Carmen is playing wheelchair basketball. You have to stay in the wheelchair the whole time you play the game. Carmen can roll her wheelchair down the court 12 feet in 2 seconds. How far can she go in 6 seconds?
$\frac{12}{2} = \frac{r}{6}$ $r = 36$

4. The cost of gasoline is hitting record prices. It costs $4 for a gallon of gas during the summer when everyone wants to travel. How much will it cost to buy 15 gallons of gas?
$\frac{1}{4} = \frac{15}{g}$ $g = \$60$

5. Ramon's Music Store will buy used CDs from you at the price of 3 CDs for $10. You want to sell the store 12 CDs. What will they pay you?
$\frac{3}{10} = \frac{12}{c}$ $c = \$40$

Unit 7

Unit 7 • Lesson 6 253

Problem Solving:
▶ Finding the Measure of Two Angles

How do we use algebra to find the measure of angles?

(*Student Text*, pages 547–549)

Connect to Prior Knowledge

Tell students that we look at connecting our past knowledge of lines and angles to help us find measures of angles with less and less information given to us.

Link to Today's Concept

In today's lesson we use the relationship between the angles and lines, as well as our knowledge of algebra, to help us find the measure of angles.

Demonstrate

- Go over **Example 1** on page 547 of the *Student Text*. In this example, we review how to use algebraic equations to find one missing angle measure. Remind students that the sum of the angles in a straight line is 180 degrees. We know the measurements of two of the angles: **20 degrees** and **75 degrees**.
- Point out that we can set up the equation as $x + 20 + 75 = 180$, where x equals the measurement of the missing angle. When we do the addition, we get $x + 95 = 180$. We subtract 95 from each side of the equation to get $x = 85$. **The measure of angle *a* is 85 degrees**.

▶Problem Solving: Finding the Measure of Two Angles

Vocabulary
supplementary angles

How do we use algebra to find the measure of angles?

We have worked on problems where we found the measure of the angle by using what we know about the measure of straight lines. We have also created a simple equation to solve the problem.

As we read through the next example, think about the rules for the properties used at each step.

Example 1

Find the measure of one unknown angle.

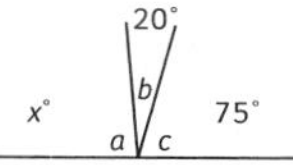

$x + 20 + 75 = 180$ ← The sum of the angles in a straight line is 180°.

$x + 95 = 180$

$x + 95 + -95 = 180 + -95$ ← Add −95 to both sides of the equation to get x by itself.

$x + 0 = 85$

$x = 85$

The measure of $\angle a$ = 85°.

How do we use algebra to find the measure of angles? *(continued)*

Build Vocabulary

Direct students to page 548 of the *Student Text*. Tell students that we can find more than one missing angle measure using our knowledge of angles, straight lines, and their relationship.

Have students look at the angles on the page. Remind them that we know that a straight line is 180 degrees. In this case, we know that angle *a* and angle *b* add up to 180 degrees. Explain that angles that add up to 180 degrees are called **supplementary angles**.

Demonstrate

- Explain that we know the relationship between the two angles in the problem. One angle is twice the size of the other angle. We can represent this algebraically with the terms $\boldsymbol{x}$ and $\mathbf{2}\boldsymbol{x}$. Point out that since all straight angles equal 180, we can write an equation for finding the missing angles: $\boldsymbol{x + 2x = 180}$.
- Point out to students that it is very important to keep what we are solving for in our equation straight. Explain that in this example, x is the measure of angle b and $2x$ is the measure of angle a. Confusing the two would result in an incorrect answer. Tell students that keeping this information straight is critical to finding the correct answer to the problem.

We are now able to solve more complicated problems with angles. In these cases, we have more than one angle that is unknown. At first, the problem does not look like it can be solved because we are not given the measurement for the two angles. However, we can use algebra and what we know about the measurement of straight lines to solve this problem.

- We know that a straight line is 180 degrees.
- So we know that angle *a* and angle *b* add up to 180 degrees.

Angles that add up to 180 degrees are called **supplementary angles**.

- So we know that angles *a* and *b* are *supplementary angles.*

$x°$ $2x°$
a *b*

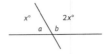

Since we know that the two angles added together equal 180 degrees, we write the equation like this:

$x + 2x = 180$

Then we solve for x.

$\boldsymbol{x + 2x = 180}$

$3x = 180$ ← Combine like terms.

$\frac{1}{3} \cdot 3x = 180 \cdot \frac{1}{3}$ ← We want x by itself, so we need to multiply by $\frac{1}{3}$. Also, we multiply both sides by $\frac{1}{3}$ to keep the equation balanced.

$\frac{3}{3}x = \frac{180}{3}$

$1x = 60$

$\boldsymbol{x = 60}$ ← A number times 1 is the same number.

Since $x = 60$, that means the measure of $\angle a = 60°$ and the measure of $\angle b = 2 \cdot 60$ or $120°$.

- Go through the steps for solving the equation x + 2x = 180. Point out that we can combine like terms to get $\mathbf{3}\boldsymbol{x} \mathbf{= 180}$. We multiply both sides by the reciprocal, $\frac{1}{3}$, to get a coefficient of 1. So $\boldsymbol{x = 60}$. Since we know that $x = 60$, **the measure of angle $\boldsymbol{a}$ = 60 degrees**. Since the measure of angle b is $2x$, we substitute x with 60 to get **120 degrees**.

Demonstrate

- Go over **Example 2** on page 549 of the *Student Text.*

Ask:

What information do we know from looking at the problem?

Listen for:

- *Angles f and g are supplementary angles. They add up to 180 degrees.*
- *Angle g is three times angle f.*

- Show how to set up the equation $\mathbf{x + 3x = 180}$ using the information we gathered. Then explain how to solve for x. Combine like terms to get $\mathbf{4x = 180}$. Then multiply each side by $\frac{1}{4}$ to get a coefficient of 1. So $\mathbf{x = 45}$.
- Then show students how to substitute the value of x to find the angle measurements. The measure of angle $f = x$, so $\mathbf{f = 45}$. The measure of angle $g = 3x$, so angle $\mathbf{g = 135}$.

Example 2

Find the measure of the angles.

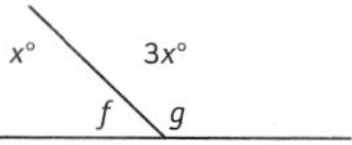

We know that f and g are supplementary angles.
We know we can set the equation up like this:

$x + 3x = 180$

Then we solve for x:

$\mathbf{x + 3x = 180}$.

$4x = 180$ ← Combine like terms.

 $\frac{1}{4} \cdot 4x = 180 \cdot \frac{1}{4}$ ← Multiply both sides of the equation by $\frac{1}{4}$ to get x by itself.

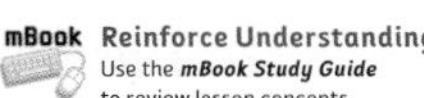

$1x = 45$

$\mathbf{x = 45}$ ← A number times 1 is the same number.

Now we can use the value of the variable to find all of the angle measurements.

$x° = 45°$ and $3x° = 3 \cdot 45$ or $135°$

The measure of $\angle f = 45°$.
The measure of $\angle g = 135°$.

We use algebra to help us solve many different problems involving angles.

Problem-Solving Activity Turn to ***Interactive Text***, page 254.

mBook Reinforce Understanding Use the ***mBook Study Guide*** to review lesson concepts.

Problem-Solving Activity

(*Interactive Text*, pages 254–255)

Have students turn to pages 254–255 in the *Interactive Text*, and complete the activity.

Students write algebraic expressions to find the missing measures of angles, based on their knowledge of angles and the relationship between the angles.

Monitor students' work as they complete the activity.

Watch for:

- Can students identify the algebraic equation needed to find the missing measures of angles?
- Can students solve the equation to find the measure of *x*? Can students determine the other angles measures based on the measure of *x*?

mBook **Reinforce Understanding**

Remind students that they can review lesson concepts by accessing the online *mBook Study Guide*.

Lesson 6 | Problem-Solving Activity

Name ______________________ Date ______________

Problem-Solving Activity

Finding the Measure of Two Angles

Write algebraic expressions to find the missing measures of the angles.

1. What is the measure of each angle? d = 75°, c = 15°

   $90 = 6x$ $(5x + x)$

   $x = 15$

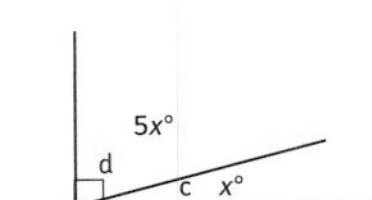

2. What is the measure of each angle? c = 45°, b = 90°, a = 45°

   $180 = 4x$ $(x + 2x + x)$

   $x = 45$

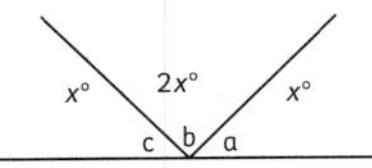

254 Unit 7 • Lesson 6

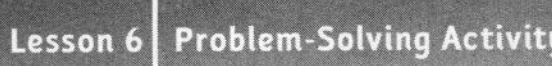

Lesson 6 | Problem-Solving Activity

Name ______________________ Date ______________

3. All of the angles measure *x*°. What is the measure of each angle?

   each angle = 30° $180 = 6x$

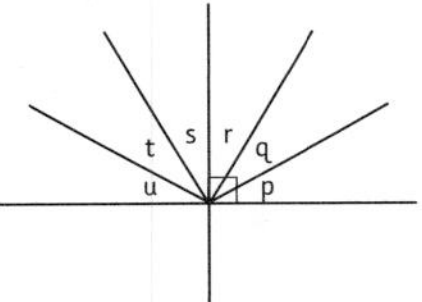

4. What is the measure of ∠j? 30°

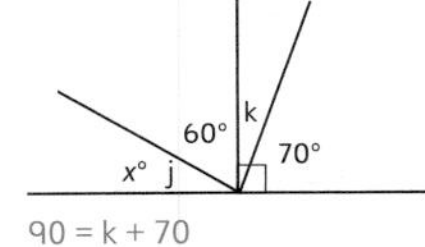

   $90 = k + 70$

   $90 = j + 60$

Unit 7

mBook **Reinforce Understanding**

Use the **mBook** ***Study Guide*** to review lesson concepts.

Unit 7 • Lesson 6 255

Homework

Go over the instructions on page 550 of the *Student Text* for each part of the homework.

Activity 1

Students solve one-step equations involving coefficients by using properties of equality and reciprocals.

Activity 2

Students find the measures of the missing angles.

Activity 3

Students solve proportions by using cross multiplication.

Activity 4 • Distributed Practice

Students practice operations on integers, PEMDAS, and the distributive property.

Homework

Activity 1

Solve each equation by using properties of equality and reciprocals.

1. $3x = 24$ $\quad \frac{1}{3} \cdot 3x = \frac{1}{3} \cdot 24$ $\quad x = 8$
2. $5y = 15$ $\quad \frac{1}{5} \cdot 5y = \frac{1}{5} \cdot 15$ $\quad y = 3$
3. $2w = 6$ $\quad \frac{1}{2} \cdot 2w = \frac{1}{2} \cdot 6$ $\quad w = 3$
4. $\frac{1}{3}z = 4$ $\quad 3 \cdot \frac{1}{3}z = 3 \cdot 4$ $\quad z = 12$
5. $\frac{1}{2}a = 6$ $\quad 2 \cdot \frac{1}{2}a = 2 \cdot 6$ $\quad a = 12$
6. $\frac{2}{3}b = 1$ $\quad \frac{3}{2} \cdot \frac{2}{3}b = \frac{3}{2} \cdot 1$ $\quad b = 1\frac{1}{2}$

Activity 2

Find the measures of the missing angles.

1. What is the measure of $\angle c$?

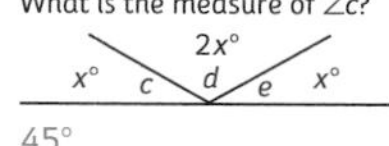

45°

2. What is the measure of $\angle a$?

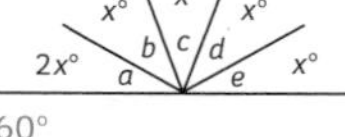

60°

Activity 3

Solve the proportions by using cross multiplication.

1. $\frac{3}{4} = \frac{x}{6}$
2. $\frac{w}{5} = \frac{8}{10}$
3. $\frac{2}{5} = \frac{12}{z}$
4. $\frac{1}{a} = \frac{5}{15}$

1.	2.	3.	4.
$4 \cdot x = 3 \cdot 6$	$10 \cdot w = 5 \cdot 8$	$2 \cdot z = 5 \cdot 12$	$a \cdot 5 = 1 \cdot 15$
$4x = 18$	$10w = 40$	$2z = 60$	$5a = 15$
$\frac{1}{4} \cdot 4x = \frac{1}{4} \cdot 18$	$\frac{1}{10} \cdot 10w = \frac{1}{10} \cdot 40$	$\frac{1}{2} \cdot 2z = \frac{1}{2} \cdot 60$	$\frac{1}{5} \cdot 5a = \frac{1}{5} \cdot 15$
$x = 4\frac{1}{2}$	$w = 4$	$z = 30$	$a = 3$

Activity 4 • Distributed Practice

Solve.

1. $4 + -2$ $\quad 2$
2. $-4 + -2$ $\quad -6$
3. $-2 \cdot -6$ $\quad 12$
4. $-2 \cdot 6$ $\quad -12$
5. $5 \cdot (6 - 5) - 5$ $\quad 0$
6. $(3^2 - 2) + 9$ $\quad 16$
7. Simplify using the distributive property: $2(-x + 1)$ $\quad -2x + 2$

550 Unit 7 • Lesson 6

Lesson 7 ▶ Equations With Negative Numbers

Problem Solving:

▶ Missing Angles in Triangles

Lesson Planner

Skills Maintenance

Equations With Coefficients

Building Number Concepts:

▶ Equations With Negative Numbers

In this lesson, students learn that negative numbers require careful consideration when we solve equations. We review the rules for working with integers and look at how the rules can help us when dealing with negative numbers in equations.

Objective

Students will solve equations with negative numbers.

Problem Solving:

▶ Missing Angles in Triangles

Students build on the previous lesson to find the missing angle of a triangle. We use the properties of triangles to help set up algebraic equations to find the missing angle. With information about two angles, students learn to use a variable to find the missing angle.

Objective

Students will use algebra to find the missing angle in triangles.

Homework

Students simplify expressions by combining like terms, solve equations involving negative terms, and find the missing measures of angles. In Distributed Practice, students practice operations on fractions and integers, PEMDAS, and the distributive property.

Lesson 7 | Skills Maintenance

Name ______________________ Date ______________

Skills Maintenance
Equations With Coefficients

Activity 1

Solve the problems with coefficients by using properties of equality and reciprocals.

1. $6a = 42$ $a = 7$
2. $7b = 49$ $b = 7$
3. $8c = 56$ $c = 7$
4. $9d = 81$ $d = 9$

Activity 2

Find the missing integers to complete the equations.

1. $-6 \cdot -9 =$ 54
2. $-27 = -3 \cdot$ 9
3. −1 $+ -12 = -13$
4. $17 -$ −10 $= 27$
5. $56 \div -8 =$ −7
6. $-100 +$ −50 $= -150$

256 Unit 7 • Lesson 7

Skills Maintenance

Equations With Coefficients

(*Interactive Text*, page 256)

Activity 1

Students solve equations involving coefficients.

Activity 2

Students solve a mix of integer operations by finding the missing integer. This prepares them for the concepts in today's lesson.

Building Number Concepts:
▶ Equations With Negative Numbers

How do we work with negative numbers in an equation?

(*Student Text*, pages 551–553)

Connect to Prior Knowledge

Begin by reminding students that we had to think about operations differently when they involved negative numbers. Go over Activity 2 of the Skills Maintenance, which students just completed.

Ask:

How do negative numbers impact addition, subtraction, multiplication, and division?

Listen for:

- *When you add negative numbers, you move in a different direction on the number line.*
- *When you subtract negative numbers, you rewrite the problem by adding the opposite.*
- *When you multiply or divide two negatives, the answer is positive. When you multiply or divide a negative and a positive, you get a negative.*

Be sure to emphasize that negative numbers add another layer of complexity to problems.

Link to Today's Concept

Tell students that today we look at how to work with negative numbers in an equation.

Demonstrate

Engagement Strategy: Teacher Modeling

Demonstrate the rules for working with integers in one of the following ways:

mBook: Use the *mBook Teacher Edition* for *Student Text*, page 551.

Lesson 7 | ▶Equations With Negative Numbers
Problem Solving:
Missing Angles in Triangles

▶Equations With Negative Numbers

How do we work with negative numbers in an equation?

Sometimes equations with a lot of negative numbers can be confusing. When we work with these difficult equations, it is important to remember the rules for integers.

Rules for Working With Integers		
Rule	**Example**	
Addition and Subtraction		
Subtraction is the same as adding the opposite.	$4 - 1$ is the same as $4 + -1$	
When adding two numbers with the same sign, the sign on the answer is always the same.	• $4 + 3 = 7$ • $-6 + -2 = -8$	
When the signs are different, the sign of the answer depends on the values in the problem.	• $-2 + 6 = 4$ • $2 + -6 = -4$	
Multiplication and Division		
PASS: Positive answers have the same signs in multiplication and division.	• $-6 \cdot -3 = 18$ • $6 \cdot 3 = 18$	• $-6 \div -3 = 2$ • $6 \div 3 = 2$
When the amount of negative numbers being multiplied or divided is an odd number, the answer is negative.	• $2 \cdot -1 \cdot 3 \cdot 4 = -24$ • $6 \div -3 = -18$	
When the amount of negative numbers being multiplied or divided is an even number, the answer is positive.	• $2 \cdot -1 \cdot -3 \cdot 4 = 24$	

Unit 7 • Lesson 551

Overhead Projector: Reproduce the table on a transparency, and modify as discussed.

- Explain that we have to consider negative numbers carefully in equations, whether they are part of variable terms or number terms. Knowing the rules for integers can help us.
- Show the first half of the table to review the rules for working with integers. Go over each of the addition and subtraction rules and examples carefully. Pay particular attention to negative numbers and how to deal with them.
- Then go over each of the multiplication and division rules, reminding students of the PASS strategy. Again make special note of how we deal with the negative numbers.

How do we work with negative numbers in an equation? *(continued)*

Explain

Turn to page 552 of the *Student Text*. Remind students that in algebra, it is important to understand the rules for operation on integers. Emphasize the need for slowing down and working carefully, especially when working with negative numbers.

Demonstrate

- Go over **Example 1**. We are still working with one-step equations, but we now include negative numbers. Point out that there are negative numbers in the problem $-3 + x - 2 = 8$. Walk through the steps carefully with students.
- Remind students of the subtraction rule. Since subtraction is the same as adding the opposite, we can add -2 instead of subtracting 2. So we can rewrite the problem as $-3 + x + -2 = 8$.
- Remind students of the property of commutation. We can move numbers in addition problems without changing the answer. So $x + -3 + -2 = 8$.
- Explain that we combine the like terms: $x + -5 = 8$. To cancel out the -5 on the left side of the equation, we add 5 to both sides to keep the equation balanced. We get $x + 0 = 13$. When we add 5 and -5 together, we get 0. So the answer is $x = 13$.
- Remind students that we can check the answer at the end by substituting the value of x back into the original equation. When we substitute 13 for x and complete the operations, we get $8 = 8$. The answer is correct.

A good understanding of rules for operation on integers is important to being successful in algebra. We use these rules all the time.

Examples 1 and 2 show how important these rules are when we work the kinds of equations that we have seen in this unit. Whenever we see negative signs, it is important to slow down and remember the integer rules in the toolbox.

Example 1

Use the rules for integers to solve the equation $-3 + x - 2 = 8$.

$$-3 + x - 2 = 8$$

$-3 + x + -2 = 8$ ← Subtraction is the same as adding the opposite. Instead of subtracting 2, we will be adding a -2.

$x + -3 + -2 = 8$ ← We commute so that we can combine the same terms.

$x + -5 = 8$

$x + -5 + 5 = 8 + 5$ ← We add 5 to both sides to get x by itself. We have added 5 on both sides to keep the equation balanced.

$x + 0 = 13$

$x = 13$

Check to make sure the answer is correct with substitution.

13 ↓

$-3 + x - 2 = 8$

$-3 + 13 - 2 = 8$

$-3 + 13 + -2 = 8$

$10 + -2 = 8$

$8 = 8$

Check for Understanding

Engagement Strategy: Look About

Write $-3 + x - 3 = 9$ on the board. Tell students that they are going to solve the equation with the help of the whole class ($x = 15$). Students should write their steps and solutions in large writing on a piece of paper or a dry erase board. When students finish their work, they should hold up their answer for everyone to see.

If students are not sure about the answer, prompt them to look about at other students' solutions to help with their thinking. Review the answers after all students have held up their solutions.

Reinforce Understanding

If students need further practice, use these problems:

$-5 + -4 + x = 15$ ($x = 24$)

$6 + x + -4 = 24$ ($x = 22$)

Explain

Explain that we can use the rules for integers to help us solve equations with variables that have coefficients.

Demonstrate

- Turn to page 553 of the *Student Text* to go over **Example 2**. We are still working with one-step equations, but this example also involves negative numbers, including a negative coefficient.
- Guide students through the steps for solving the problem $-5x = -30$. Emphasize the need to slow down and work carefully using the rules and properties that apply to algebra, and specifically negative numbers. Remind students to think about PASS when working with multiplication and division.
- Elicit the reciprocal for −5. Point out that the reciprocal $-\frac{1}{5}$ has the same sign. The number −5 is negative, so its reciprocal is also negative.
- Show how we multiply both sides by $-\frac{1}{5}$, reminding students that we need to keep the equation balanced. Point out that PASS rule works for both numbers. We divide a negative by a negative. We get the coefficient of 1, so $x = 6$.
- Remind students that they can always use substitution to check their answers. Tell them that the check step requires rules for working with negative numbers as well, so it is a little more complex.

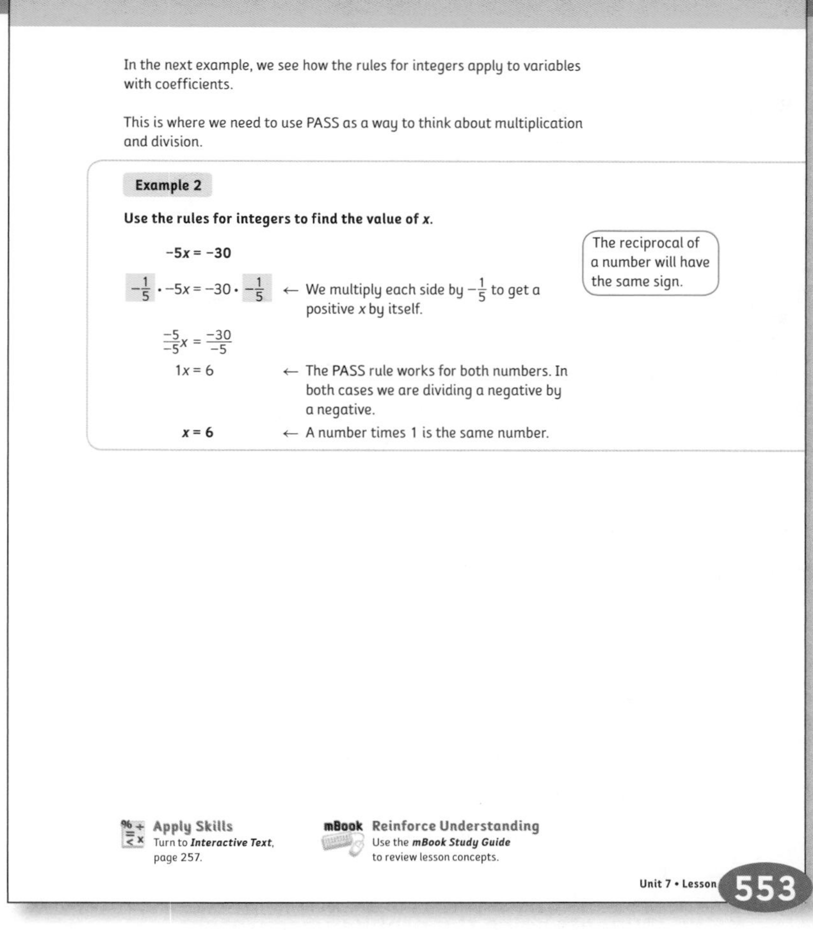

Lesson 7

In the next example, we see how the rules for integers apply to variables with coefficients.

This is where we need to use PASS as a way to think about multiplication and division.

Example 2

Use the rules for integers to find the value of *x*.

$-5x = -30$

$-\frac{1}{5} \cdot -5x = -30 \cdot -\frac{1}{5}$ ← We multiply each side by $-\frac{1}{5}$ to get a positive x by itself.

$\frac{-5}{-5}x = \frac{-30}{-5}$

$1x = 6$ ← The PASS rule works for both numbers. In both cases we are dividing a negative by a negative.

$x = 6$ ← A number times 1 is the same number.

The reciprocal of a number will have the same sign.

Apply Skills Turn to ***Interactive Text***, page 257.

Reinforce Understanding Use the ***mBook Study Guide*** to review lesson concepts.

Unit 7 • Lesson 553

Check for Understanding

Engagement Strategy: Think Tank

Write $-7x = -56$ on the board. Distribute strips of paper and have students write their names on them. Tell students that they are going to find the value of x (*8*) using the rules for integers. Have students write their steps and solution on their papers. When they have finished, collect the strips in a container. Draw out an answer and read it aloud. If it is correct, congratulate the student and invite him or her to explain the answer. Review the solution with the class. If there is time, have students substitute the value of x into the original equation to check the answer.

Apply Skills

(*Interactive Text*, page 257)

Have students turn to page 257 in the *Interactive Text*, and complete the activity.

Activity 1

Students solve a mix of equations involving negative variable terms and number terms. Then students use the check step to make sure their answer is correct. Monitor students' work as they complete the activity.

Watch for:

- Can students identify the rules and properties for working with negative numbers?
- Can students identify the rules and properties for the algebra involved in solving the equations, and adjust as needed for negative numbers?
- Can students solve the problem accurately and use substitution for their answers?

mBook **Reinforce Understanding**

Remind students that they can review lesson concepts by accessing the online *mBook Study Guide*.

Lesson 7 | Apply Skills

Name ______________________ Date ______________

Apply Skills
Equations With Negative Numbers

Activity 1

Solve the equations involving negative variables and/or number terms. Be sure to check your answers when you are finished using substitution.

1. $-5 - x + 5 + 5x = 12$ $x = 3$

   Show your work here.

   Check your answer here: $4x = 12$

2. $x - 2 + -4 = -5$ $x = -1$

   Show your work here.

   Check your answer here: $x - -6 = -5$

3. $-10 + x - -5 = 10$ $x = 15$

   Show your work here.

   Check your answer here: $-5 + x = 10$

4. $3x - 4 - -4 + 2x = -15$ $x = -3$

   Show your work here.

   Check your answer here. $5x = 15$

Unit 7

Unit 7 • Lesson 7 257

Problem Solving:
▶ Missing Angles in Triangles

Lesson 7

▶Problem Solving: Missing Angles in Triangles

What are important properties of triangles?

We have studied four common types of triangles. Each of these triangles share a common property. Their interior angles all add up to 180 degrees.

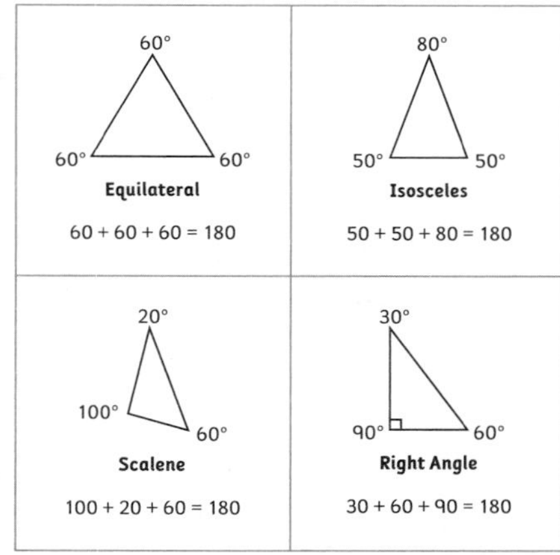

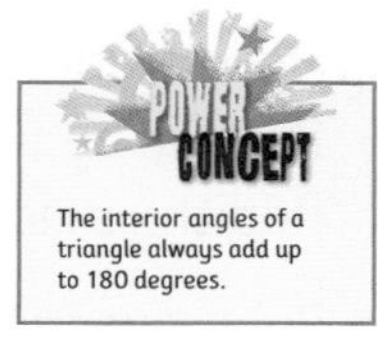

A simple way to prove that the interior angles of any of these triangles add up to 180 degrees is to tear off the corners and put them side by side. The picture below shows us that when the triangles are put together, the bottom forms a straight line, or 180 degrees.

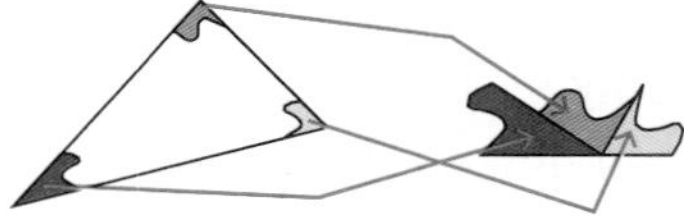

554 Unit 7 • Lesson 7

What are important properties of triangles?

(*Student Text*, page 554)

Explain

Go to page 554 in the *Student Text*, and use the material to discuss the important properties of triangles. Remind students that the interior angles of a triangle add up to 180 degrees.

Demonstrate

- Go over each type of triangle shown.
- Point out the angles in each triangle, and have students add the angle measures up to see that the three angles add to 180 degrees in each case.

Ask:

What are the properties of each type of triangle?

Listen for

- *The sides of an equilateral triangle are the same length. Each interior angle is 60 degrees.*
- *An isosceles triangle has two sides that are the same length. Two of its angles are equal.*
- *A scalene triangle has no equal sides and no equal angles.*
- *A right triangle has one angle that is 90 degrees.*

- Point out that we can prove that the interior angles of any triangle add up to 180 degrees by tearing off the corners and putting them side by side. The bottom will form a straight line. Have students look at the visualization of this idea at the bottom of the page.

Discuss

Call students' attention to the Power Concept, and point out that it will be helpful as they complete the activity.

The interior angles of a triangle always add up to 180 degrees.

How do we use algebra when working with triangles?

(*Student Text*, page 555)

Demonstrate

- Go to page 555 of the *Student Text* to look at how to use algebra to work with triangles. Have students look at **Example 1**. Explain that we can use an algebraic equation to find the measure of angle *e*.
- Point out that we know the measure of two angles: 65 degrees and 45 degrees. We know that all of the interior angles add up to 180 degrees. So we can write an algebraic equation: $x + 65 + 45 = 180$.
- Show students how to solve the problem. We combine like terms to get $x + 110 = 180$. We add opposites to isolate *x* on one side. Remind students that a number plus its opposite is zero. In this case, we add −110 to both sides. So $x = 70$. **The measure of angle *e* is 70 degrees.**
- Again remind students that we can substitute the value of *x* into our original equation to check the answer. In this case, we substitute 70. When we complete the operations, we get **180 = 180**. The answer is correct.

How do we use algebra when working with triangles?

We use the information about the interior angles of triangles to figure out the measure of unknown angles. Example 1 shows how we figure out the measure of the unknown angle *e*. We use an algebraic equation to find the measure of angle *e*.

Example 1

Find the measure of the missing angle.

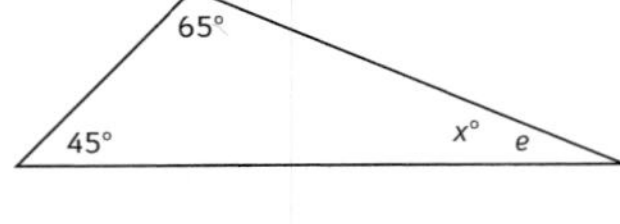

$x + 65 + 45 = 180$

$x + 110 = 180$ ← Combine like terms.

$x + 110 + \mathbf{-110} = 180 + \mathbf{-110}$ ← Add −110 to both sides of the equation to get *x* by itself.

$x + 0 = 70$

$x = 70$

The measure of ∠*e* is 70°.

Check to see if the answer is correct by substituting.

70
↓
$x + 65 + 45 = 180$

$70 + 65 + 45 = 180$

$135 + 45 = 180$

$180 = 180$

Problem-Solving Activity Turn to ***Interactive Text***, page 258.

mBook Reinforce Understanding Use the ***mBook Study Guide*** to review lesson concepts.

Problem-Solving Activity
(*Interactive Text*, pages 258–259)

Direct students to *Interactive Text*, pages 258–259, and read the instructions together.

Students use what they know about the measure of common angles to solve the problems. Then students write algebraic equations with a variable to find the values of the angles.

Monitor students' work as they complete the activity.

Watch for:

- Can students identify the algebraic equation needed to find the missing measures of angles?
- Can students solve the equation to find the measure of *x*? Can students determine the other angle measures based on *x*?
- Can students answer correctly the questions about the measures of the various angles?

mBook **Reinforce Understanding**
Remind students that they can review lesson concepts by accessing the online *mBook Study Guide.*

Name ______________________ Date ______________

Problem-Solving Activity
Missing Angles in Triangles

Use what you know about the measures of common angles to solve the problems. Write algebraic equations to find each solution and be sure to show your work. Think about each problem before you try to solve it. Some problems require different strategies.

1. What are the measurements of ∠f, ∠g *and* ∠h?
   $f = 90°$, $g = 45°$, $h = 45°$ $x = 45$ $2x = 90$

2. What are the measurements of ∠h, ∠j, and ∠k?
   $h = 48°$, $j = 24°$, $k = 108°$ $x = 12$ $2x = 24$ $4x = 48$

Name ______________________ Date ______________

3. What are the measurements of ∠k, ∠l, and ∠m?
   each angle = 60° $3x = 180$ $x = \frac{180}{3}$ $x = 60$

4. What are the measurements of ∠b, ∠m, and ∠x?
   $b = 90°$, $m = 45°$, $x = 45°$ $4x = 180$ $x = \frac{180}{4}$ $x = 45$

mBook Reinforce Understanding
Use the **mBook** ***Study Guide*** to review lesson concepts.

Homework

Go over the instructions on page 556 of the *Student Text* for each part of the homework.

Activity 1

Students simplify expressions by combining like terms. Remind students that they do not solve for the variable.

Activity 2

Students solve equations by using the rules for integers. Then they use substitution to check their answers.

Activity 3

Students find the missing measures of angles in triangles.

Activity 4 • Distributed Practice

Students continue practicing operations on fractions and integers, PEMDAS, and the distributive property.

Lesson 7

Homework

Activity 1

Simplify each expression by combining like terms.

1. $-5x + x + -4x$ $-8x$
2. $x - 4 - 3$ $x - 7$
3. $2x - -3 + 4 - x$ $x + 7$
4. $7x + -2 + -7 + -6x$ $x + -9$

Activity 2

Solve the equations using the rules for integers. Check your answer at the end using substitution.

1. $-4 + -3 + x = 14$ $x = 21$ $-4 + -3 + 21 = 14$
2. $2x - 5 + 5 - x = 12$ $x = 12$ $2 \cdot 12 - 5 + 5 - 12 = 12$
3. $x - -4 - 3 = 1$ $x = 0$ $0 - -4 - 3 = 1$
4. $-2 + 2x - -2 + 3x = 20$ $x = 4$ $-2 + 2 \cdot 4 - -2 + 3 \cdot 4 = 20$

Activity 3

Find the missing angles in each of the triangles.

1. What are the measures of $\angle x$ and $\angle y$ in the equilateral triangle?

x
60°   y
60° for both

2. What is the measure of $\angle x$?

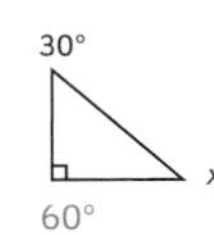

60°

3. What is the measure of $\angle x$?

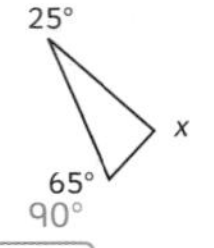

90°

Activity 4 • Distributed Practice

Solve.

1. $\frac{1}{4} \div \frac{1}{2}$ $\frac{1}{2}$
2. $\frac{1}{4} \cdot \frac{1}{2}$ $\frac{1}{8}$
3. $-2 \cdot -6$ 12
4. $4^2 \div 2 + 6$ 14
5. $2 \cdot 4^2 + 3$ 35
6. $(-5 \cdot -2) - 6$ 4
7. Simplify using the distributive property: $2(3x + 2)$ $6x + 4$

556 Unit 7 • Lesson 7

Lesson 8 ▶Rate Problems and Algebra

Problem Solving: ▶Triangles With Congruent Angles

Lesson Planner

Skills Maintenance

Solving Proportions

Building Number Concept: ▶ Rate Problems and Algebra

In this lesson, students learn that a good strategy for solving rate problems is setting up a proportion and solving it using cross multiplication.

Students learn the distance formula to solve rate problems. Students learn to identify information in a rate problem that can be substituted into the formula.

Objective

Students will use algebra to solve rate problems.

Problem Solving: ▶ Triangles With Congruent Angles

Today we focus on missing angle measures in triangles with congruent angles, and isosceles and equilateral triangles. Students use their knowledge of these triangles and angles to find the measurement of angles using an algebraic equation.

Objective

Students will find the measurement of angles in triangles with congruent angles.

Homework

Students use cross multiplication to solve simple proportion problems, find the measure of the missing angle, and use the distance formula to solve simple distance problems. In Distributed Practice, students practice operations on fractions and integers, PEMDAS, and the distributive property.

Lesson 8 | Skills Maintenance

Name ______________________ Date ______________________

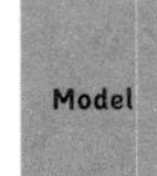

Skills Maintenance
Solving Proportions

Activity 1

Use cross multiplication to solve the proportions.

Model	$\frac{4}{x} = \frac{2}{4}$ $2x = 16$ $x =$ 8

1. $\frac{3}{4} = \frac{12}{w}$ $w =$ 16
   Show your work here.
   $3w = 48$
   $w = 16$

2. $\frac{5}{x} = \frac{15}{18}$ $x =$ 6
   Show your work here.
   $15x = 90$
   $x = 6$

3. $\frac{z}{8} = \frac{27}{72}$ $z =$ 3
   Show your work here.
   $72z = 216$
   $z = 3$

260 Unit 7 • Lesson 8

Skills Maintenance

Solving Proportions

(*Interactive Text*, page 260)

Activity 1

Students solve proportion problems using cross multiplication. A model is provided to remind them of the steps.

Building Number Concepts:
▶ Rate Problems and Algebra

How do we convert proportion rate problems?

(*Student Text*, pages 557–559)

Connect to Prior Knowledge

Begin by reminding students about the concept of rate. Tell them miles per hour are an example of a rate. Then elicit a few more examples of rate from students.

Be sure students understand that rate involves the comparison of two different units.

Link to Today's Concept

Tell students that in today's lesson, we use algebra to help us solve rate problems.

Demonstrate

Engagement Strategy: Teacher Modeling

Demonstrate how to convert a proportion rate problem into an algebraic expression in one of the following ways:

mBook: Use the *mBook Teacher Edition* for *Student Text*, page 557. m

Overhead Projector: Reproduce the problem on a transparency, and modify as discussed.

Board: Copy the problem on the board, and modify as discussed.

- Show the word problem. m
- Help students identify the information that we know: the ball traveled 30 yards every 2 seconds. We want to know how many seconds it took for the ball to go 60 yards. Point out how we say this: **2 is to 30 as *g* is to 60**. m
- Explain that the solution strategy involves setting up a proportion for the rate expressed in the problem. Show how to set up the proportion. Be sure students understand that *g* stands for the number of seconds it took the ball to go 60 yards. Show $\frac{2}{30} = \frac{g}{60}$. m
- Next go over the steps for cross multiplying. Draw arrows to point out that we multiply 30 by *g*, and 2 by 60 to get the equation $30 \cdot g = 2 \cdot 60$. m
- Show how to simplify the problem as $30g = 120$. m
- Remind students that we multiply by the reciprocal of 30, $\frac{1}{30}$, on each side to get $\frac{30}{30}g = \frac{120}{30}$. m
- Point out that $\frac{30}{30} = 1$ and $\frac{120}{30} = 4$, so we get $1g = 4$, which is the same as $g = 4$. So it took the ball 4 seconds to go 60 yards. m

---

Lesson 8 ▶ Rate Problems and Algebra
Problem Solving:
▶ Triangles With Congruent Angles

▶ Rate Problems and Algebra

How do we convert proportion rate problems?

We have learned to use algebra to solve proportion problems. One kind of proportion involves rate. Let's see how we convert a rate problem from proportions into a simple algebraic equation.

Problem:
In the last play of the football game, Quentin threw a long pass that went more than half the distance of the field. It traveled 30 yards every 2 seconds. How long did it take for the ball to go 60 yards?

We know:	We can say:	We write it like this:
2 seconds = 30 yards *g* seconds = 60 yards	2 is to 30 as *g* is to 60.	$\frac{2}{30} = \frac{g}{60}$

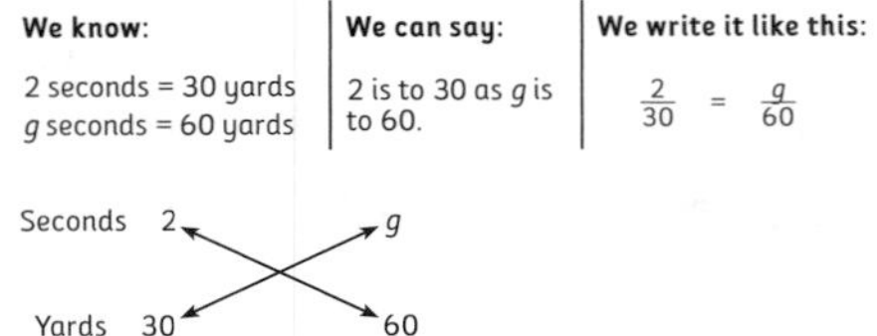

We write an equation for this problem by using cross multiplication.

$30 \cdot g = 2 \cdot 60$ ← When we cross multiply, we get this equation. We simplify the problem this way.

$30g = 120$ ← We simplify the problem this way.

$\frac{1}{30} \cdot 30g = 120 \cdot \frac{1}{30}$ ← We multiply each side by $\frac{1}{30}$ to get *x* by itself.

$\frac{30}{30}g = \frac{120}{30}$

$1g = 4$

$g = 4$ ← A number times 1 is the same number.

It took the ball 4 seconds to go 60 yards.

Unit 7 • Lesson 557

Explain

Have students turn to the material on page 558 of the *Student Text*. Discuss that often in algebra, rate problems are expressed using the distance formula: $D = rt$. Point out that r stands for rate and t stands for time.

Demonstrate

- Go over **Example 1** with students to show them how to apply the distance formula.
- Read the problem and help students identify the information that we know: Josie can run **20 feet per second**. This is the rate. The distance is 60 feet. Point out that the problem is asking how long it will take, which is the amount of time.
- Show how we substitute the information we know into the formula to get $\mathbf{60 = 20 \cdot t}$. This looks like any other algebraic equation.
- We isolate the t by multiplying each side by the reciprocal of 20, $\frac{1}{20}$, to get $\mathbf{3 = 1t}$. So $\mathbf{3 = t}$. Remind students that t is the time, in this case, in seconds. **It takes Josie 3 seconds to run 60 feet.**

Using proportions and cross multiplication is just one way to solve a rate problem. Another way is to substitute for variables using an algebraic formula.

We can use a formula called the *distance formula*, or $D = rt$. The D stands for *distance*, the r stands for *rate*, and the t stands for *time*.

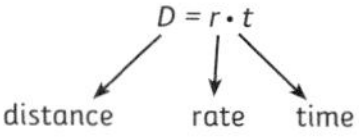

distance rate time

Example 1

Find the distance using the distance formula.

Problem:
Josie is the fastest player on her basketball team. She can run 20 feet per second. If she runs 60 feet, how long does it take?

We know:

- The rate is 20 feet per second, so $r = 20$.
- The distance is 60 feet, so $D = 60$.

The question is asking "how long," or the amount of time, it will take. When we substitute what we know into the formula, we have an algebraic equation.

$D = r \cdot t$

$60 = 20 \cdot t$

We now treat this like any other algebra problem.

$60 = 20t$

$\frac{1}{20} \cdot 60 = 20t \cdot \frac{1}{20}$ ← We multiply both sides of the equation by $\frac{1}{20}$ to get t by itself.

$3 = 1t$

$3 = t$ ← A number times 1 is the same number.

It takes Josie 3 seconds to run 60 feet.

Check for Understanding

Engagement Strategy: Think, Think

Write the distance formula $\boldsymbol{D = rt}$ on the board. Present this situation: The winning frog of the County Fair's Frog Race jumped **40 feet per minute**. How long would it take the winning frog to jump **120 feet**?

Ask students the following questions. Tell them that you will call on one of them to answer a question after you ask it. Tell them to listen for their names. After each question, allow time for students to think of the answer. Then call on a student.

Ask:

What is this problem asking us to find? (*time*)

What is the rate in this problem? (*40 feet per minute*)

What is the distance we are discussing in this problem? (*120 feet*)

What will the algebraic equation look like when we substitute what we know into the formula? ($120 = 40 \cdot t$)

If time permits, work through the solution with the class ($t = 3$; *It would take 3 minutes*).

How do we convert proportion rate problems? *(continued)*

Demonstrate

- Next have students look at **Example 2** on page 559 of the *Student Text*. In this example, we use the distance formula to find rate.
- Have students read the problem and identify what we know: the distance is **1,000 yards** and the time is **50 seconds**. Make sure students understand that we are trying to find rate.
- Show students how to reverse the equation so that the variable is on the left. Then remind students that we substitute the values we know. In this case, $r \cdot 50 = 1{,}000$.
- Point out that we use the commutative property to change $r \cdot 50$ to $50r$. Remind students that we multiply each side by the reciprocal of 50, $\frac{1}{50}$. When we complete the operations, we get $r = 20$. **The rate is 20 yards per second**.

Check for Understanding
Engagement Strategy: Think, Think

Present the following situation: Lucia can cycle **20 miles in 60 minutes**. How long would it take her to cycle 15 miles? (*45 minutes*)

Tell students that you will call on one of them give the answer to the question. Tell them to listen for their names. Allow time for students to solve the problem. Then call on a student to answer and explain the solution.

The distance formula allows us to use algebra to find rate, time, or distance. In the next example, let's find the rate.

Example 2

Find the rate using the distance formula.

Problem:
Roxy is a serious snowboarder. She won the final race with her best time. She completed a 1,000-yard course in 50 seconds. What was her rate of speed?

We know:

- She traveled 1,000 yards, so $D = 1{,}000$.
- It took her 50 seconds, so $t = 50$.

The question asks for the rate. In this case, we want to know yards per second. Now we can substitute the information we know into the formula.

$r \cdot t = D$ ← This time we reverse the equation so the variable is on the left.

$r \cdot 50 = 1{,}000$

$50r = 1{,}000$ ← We use the commutative property to change $r \cdot 50$ into $50r$.

 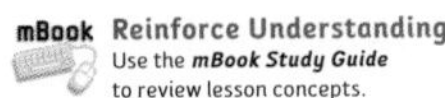

$\frac{1}{50} \cdot 50r = 1{,}000 \cdot \frac{1}{50}$ ← We multiply each side by $\frac{1}{50}$ to get r by itself.

$1r = 20$

$r = 20$ ← A number times 1 is the same number.

Roxy traveled at a rate of 20 yards per second.

Apply Skills Turn to ***Interactive Text***, page 261.

mBook Reinforce Understanding Use the ***mBook Study Guide*** to review lesson concepts.

Apply Skills

(*Interactive Text*, pages 261–262)

Have students turn to pages 261–262 in the *Interactive Text*, and complete the activity.

Activity 1

Students write a proportion to represent a rate problem and use cross multiplication to solve it. Monitor students' work as they complete the activity.

Watch for:

- Do students have difficulty reading the word problem?
- Do students have difficulty with any of the steps needed to solve the problem?
- Can students set up the correct proportion?
- Can students solve the proportion using cross multiplication?
- Can students identify the correct answer to the correct question once they have solved the proportion?

mBook **Reinforce Understanding**

Remind students that they can review lesson concepts by accessing the online *mBook Study Guide*.

Lesson 8 | Apply Skills

Name ______________________ Date ______________

Apply Skills
Rate Problems and Algebra

Activity 1

Write a proportion to represent each of the rate problems. Use cross multiplication to solve the proportions. Be sure you are answering the question that the problem asks.

1. If it takes Jonah 15 minutes to run a mile, how long will it take him to run 3 miles at the same rate?
   Write the proportion. $\frac{1}{15} = \frac{3}{x}$
   Solve the proportion. $x = 45$
   What is the answer to the problem?
   45 minutes to run 3 miles

2. If it takes Becca 10 minutes to read one page of her book, how long will it take her to read 5 pages at the same rate?
   Write the proportion. $\frac{1}{10} = \frac{5}{x}$
   Solve the proportion. $x = 50$
   What is the answer to the problem?
   It will take her 50 minutes to read 5 pages.

3. If Eli can earn 100 points in 5 minutes on his video game, how many points can he earn in 20 minutes at the same rate?
   Write the proportion. $\frac{5}{100} = \frac{20}{x}$
   Solve the proportion. $x = 400$
   What is the answer to the problem?
   He will earn 400 points in 20 minutes.

Unit 7

Unit 7 • Lesson 8 261

Lesson 8 | Apply Skills

Name ______________________ Date ______________

4. Marshall's Shipping Service moves goods up and down the East Coast. Their truck drivers work at night when there are fewer people on the freeway. Bill usually drives at 65 miles per hour, and he drives for 6 hours before he stops. How far does he drive before he stops?
   Write the proportion. $\frac{1}{65} = \frac{6}{x}$
   Solve the proportion. $x = 390$
   What is the,answer to the problem? He drives 390 miles before he stops.

5. One night Juanita was driving from New York to Boston when she ran into bad weather. She averaged 50 miles per hour and she stopped for coffee and something to eat after 250 miles. How long did she drive?
   Write the proportion. $\frac{1}{50} = \frac{x}{250}$
   Solve the proportion. $x = 5$
   What is the answer to the problem?: She drove for 5 hours.

6. Marshall's also uses trains to ship goods long distances. Trains average a slower speed than trucks. They average 50 miles per hour, but trains don't stop as often as trucks. The train to Pittsburgh goes 12 hours before it stops. How many miles does it travel?
   Write the proportion. $\frac{1}{50} = \frac{12}{x}$
   Solve the proportion. $x = 600$
   What is the answer to the problem?: It travels 600 miles.

7. When a train goes through the mountains, the speed drops even further. It can take 10 hours to go 300 miles. What is the rate of speed?
   Write the proportion: $\frac{10}{300} = \frac{1}{x}$
   Solve the proportion: $x = 30$
   What is the answer to the problem?: It moves 30 miles per hour.

262 Unit 7 • Lesson 8

Problem Solving:
▶ Triangles With Congruent Angles

What do we need to know about triangles to solve difficult problems?
(*Student Text*, pages 560–561)

Connect to Prior Knowledge
Begin by asking students to recall the different types of triangles we learned in Lesson 7. Ask them to describe the characteristics of these triangles.

Listen for:

- *An equilateral has three equal sides and three equal angles.*
- *An isoceles has two equal sides and two equal angles.*
- *A scalene has no equal sides or angles.*
- *A right triangle has one right angle.*

Link to Today's Concept
In today's lesson, we use what we know about traingles to find the measure of angles in a triangle.

Demonstrate
- Turn to page 560 of the *Student Text* to discuss the material on the page. Explain that it is helpful to remember properties of triangles to help us solve difficult problems involving triangles and angles.
- Review the properties of isosceles and equilateral triangles by looking at the diagrams. Make sure students see the two equal sides and two equal angles.
- Have students identify properties of an equilateral triangle in the diagram. Remind students that an equilateral triangle has three equal sides and three equal angles.

Lesson 8

▶Problem Solving: Triangles With Congruent Angles

What do we need to know about triangles to solve difficult problems?

When we are not given a lot of information in a problem, it can be difficult to solve. We know that isosceles triangles have two equal sides and two equal angles. We also know that all sides and all angles are equal in an equilateral triangle. The triangles below have marks that show the congruent sides and angles.

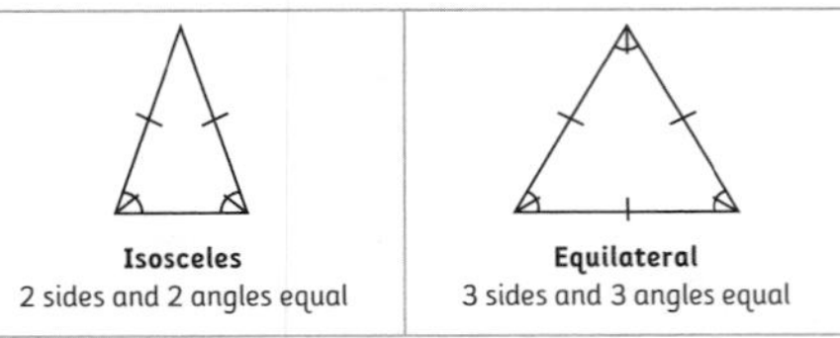

Isosceles 2 sides and 2 angles equal	**Equilateral** 3 sides and 3 angles equal

This information is useful in solving the problem on the next page. Notice that only the measure of one of the angles is given.

560 Unit 7 • Lesson 8

- Point out the marks on the triangles that show the congruent sides and angles.

Demonstrate

- Move to page 561 of the *Student Text* to go over **Example 1**. In this example, we find the measure of angle k in an isosceles triangle.
- Point out the information we know about the triangle: the two angles at the bottom each measure 50 degrees. We know this because the marks indicate that the two angles are congruent.
- Remind students that the sum of the interior angles of any triangle is 180 degrees. Using this information, we can write an equation: $\mathbf{x + 50 + 50 = 180}$.
- Walk through the steps as outlined to find the value of x. Remind students to combine like terms. Then point out how to add opposites to both sides to isolate the x. We find that $\mathbf{x = 80}$. **The measure of angle k is 80 degrees.**
- Remind students that we can check our answers by substituting 80 into the original equation.

Speaking of Math

- Go through each of the bullet points at the bottom of the page. Tell students that these points are a good way to explain their thinking when finding the measurement of an angle in a triangle.
- Refer to Example 1 as you go through each of the points to show how each point applies to solving a problem.

Example 1

Find the measure of $\angle k$ in this isosceles triangle.

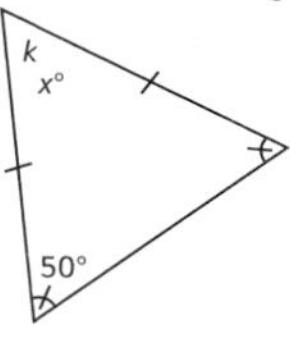

We know that the angles at the bottom measure 50 degrees because the marks on the angles show they are congruent.

Now we can write and solve an equation.

$$x + 50 + 50 = 180$$
$$x + 100 = 180 \quad \leftarrow \text{Combine like terms.}$$
$$x + 100 + -100 = 180 + -100 \quad \leftarrow \text{Add } -100 \text{ to both sides.}$$
$$x + 0 = 80$$
$$x = 80$$

The measure of $\angle k$ = 80°

Speaking of Math

Here's how you can explain your thinking when you find the measurement of an angle in a triangle.

- *First, I look at the triangle to see what I know.*
- *Next, I look for congruent sides and angles.*
- *Then, I label the triangle with the information I learned based on the congruent sides and angles.*
- *Last, I write and solve my equation.*

Problem-Solving Activity Turn to ***Interactive Text***, page 263.

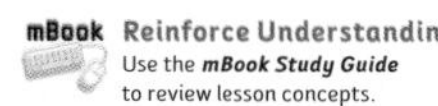

mBook Reinforce Understanding Use the ***mBook Study Guide*** to review lesson concepts.

Problem-Solving Activity

(*Interactive Text*, page 263)

Have students turn to page 263 in the *Interactive Text*. Read the instructions with students.

Students decide if triangles have congruent sides or angles. Then they use algebraic expressions to find the measurements of all the angles in each triangle.

Monitor students' work as they complete the activity.

Watch for:

- Can students identify congruent sides and angles?
- Do students label the triangles with the information they know based on the congruent sides and angles?
- Can students write the algebraic expressions to solve the equations?

mBook **Reinforce Understanding**
Remind students that they can review lesson concepts by accessing the online *mBook Study Guide*.

Name ____________________ Date ____________________

Problem-Solving Activity
Triangles With Congruent Angles

Decide if the triangles have congruent sides or angles. Use algebraic expressions to find the measurements of all the angles.

1.

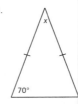

Algebraic expression:
$x + 70 + 70 = 180 \quad x = 40$

2.

Algebraic expression:
$3x = 180 \quad x = 60$

3.

Algebraic expression:
$x + 45 + 90 = 180 \quad x = 45$

4.

Algebraic expression:
$67 + 67 + x = 180 \quad x = 46$

mBook **Reinforce Understanding**
Use the **mBook** ***Study Guide*** to review lesson concepts.

Homework

Go over the instructions on page 562 of the *Student Text* for each part of the homework.

Activity 1

Students use cross multiplication to solve simple proportion problems.

Activity 2

Students find the measure of the missing angle. Remind students to write an algebraic equation.

Activity 3

Students use the distance formula to solve simple distance problems using algebra.

Activity 4 • Distributed Practice

Students practice operations on fractions and integers, PEMDAS, and the distributive property.

Lesson 8

Homework

Activity 1

Solve the proportions using cross multiplication.

1. $\frac{1}{3} = \frac{12}{f}$ $1f = 36$ $f = 36$
2. $\frac{10}{2} = \frac{15}{v}$ $10v = 30$ $\frac{1}{10} \cdot 10v = \frac{1}{10} \cdot 30$ $v = 3$
3. $\frac{t}{4} = \frac{6}{3}$ $3t = 24$ $\frac{1}{3} \cdot 3t = \frac{1}{3} \cdot 24$ $t = 8$
4. $\frac{10}{5} = \frac{m}{3}$ $5m = 30$ $\frac{1}{5} \cdot 5m = \frac{1}{5} \cdot 30$ $m = 6$

Activity 2

Find the missing angle.

1. What is the measure of $\angle b$? 70°

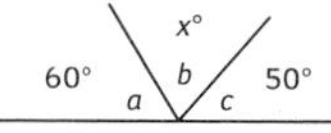

Activity 3

Use the distance formula $D = r \cdot t$ to solve these problems.

1. A baseball travels through the air at 100 feet per second. How far does it travel in 4 seconds? 400 feet ($100 \cdot 4 = 400$)
2. It takes 30 seconds for a diver to rise from under water. She travels 5 feet per second. How far does she travel in 30 seconds? 150 feet ($5 \cdot 30 = 150$)
3. Snow is sliding down the side of the mountain at the rate of 50 feet per second. It travels 300 feet before it stops. How long did it take the snow to travel the 300 feet? 6 seconds ($50 \cdot 6 = 300$)

Activity 4 • Distributed Practice

Solve.

1. $\frac{4}{5} - \frac{1}{2}$ $\frac{3}{10}$
2. $\frac{4}{5} \cdot \frac{5}{4}$ 1
3. $4^2 \div (2 + 6)$ 2
4. $(3 \cdot -6) \div 2$ −9
5. $4^2 \div 2^2$ 4
6. $6 \cdot 3 + 3$ 21
7. $-5 \cdot -2 + 10$ 20
8. Simplify using the distributive property: $3(-2x + 1)$ $-6x + 3$

562 Unit 7 • Lesson 8

Lesson 9 ▶ Writing Equations From Words

Problem Solving: ▶ Word Problems and Algebra

Skills Maintenance

Missing Angles

Building Number Concepts: ▶ Writing Equations From Words

In this lesson, students learn that algebra is important because we use it to translate word statements into algebraic expressions or equations. By doing this, we can solve problems in a systematic way, using commonly agreed upon rules and properties.

Objective

Students will translate word statements into algebraic equations.

Problem Solving: ▶ Word Problems and Algebra

Students continue to look at how we translate word statements into algebraic equations. We extend this to full word problems. Students learn to write equations for problems and solve for the value of a variable to answer the question.

Objective

Students will write algebraic equations for word problems, then solve.

Homework

Students write algebraic expressions for the phrases given, translate words into algebraic equations, and solve word problems using algebraic equations. In Distributed Practice, students continue practicing operations on fractions and integers, PEMDAS, and the distributive property.

Lesson 9 | Skills Maintenance

Name ______________________ Date ______________

Skills Maintenance
Missing Angles

Activity 1

Use your knowledge of angles, properties, and algebraic expressions to find the missing angles.

1. What is the measure of angle a? $20°$

   $2x°$, a, $4x°$, b, c, $3x°$

   $9x = 90$

   $x = 10$

2. What is the measure of angle m? $150°$

   $5x°$, m, n, $x°$

   $6x = 180$

   $x = 30$

3. What is the measure of angle h? $60°$

   $x°$, $x°$, $x°$, f, g, h

   $3x = 180$

   $x = 60$

264 Unit 7 • Lesson 9

Skills Maintenance

Missing Angles

(*Interactive Text*, page 264)

Activity 1

Students find the missing angles using their knowledge of angles, properties, and algebraic equations.

Building Number Concepts:
▶ Writing Equations From Words

How do we write algebraic equations from word statements?
(*Student Text*, pages 563–564)

Connect to Prior Knowledge

Begin by going over the Skills Maintenance activity that students just completed. Ask for volunteers to come to the board and share their answers and describe their strategies for finding missing angles measurements. Write the key points of their strategies adjacent to their work on the board or overhead.

Link to Today's Concept

Tell students that today's lesson brings together our knowledge of translation strategies and algebraic expressions and equations to solve word problems.

Demonstrate

Engagement Strategy: Teacher Modeling

Demonstrate how we solve a typical algebraic equation in one of the following ways:

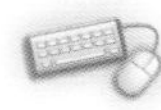

mBook: Use the *mBook Teacher Edition* for *Student Text*, page 563. m

Overhead Projector: Reproduce the equation on a transparency, and modify as discussed.

Board: Copy the equation on the board, and modify as discussed.

- Show students the equation $3x + x = 19 + 1$ from **Example 1**. m
- Remind students that we add like terms together on both sides of the equation. The terms $3x$ and x are alike; 19 and 1 are alike. So we can rewrite the equation as $4x = 20$. m
- Then remind students that we multiply each side by the reciprocal of 4, $\frac{1}{4}$. So $\frac{1}{4} \cdot 4x = 20 \cdot \frac{1}{4}$ to get x alone on one side. m
- When we multiply, we get $\frac{4}{4}x = \frac{20}{4}$. m
- Remind students that $\frac{4}{4} = 1$, and $\frac{20}{4} = 5$. So our equation becomes $1x = 5$. m
- Remind students that 1 times a number is the same number, so $x = 5$. m

---

Lesson 9 | ▶Writing Equations From Words
Problem Solving:
▶Word Problems and Algebra

▶Writing Equations From Words

How do we write algebraic equations from word statements?

Much of this unit has involved solving algebraic equations. We have learned to solve for x by using properties and rules from our toolbox. Let's review the steps in solving a typical equation.

Example 1

Solve the equation $3x + x = 19 + 1$.

$3x + x = 19 + 1$

$4x = 20$ ← We add like terms on both sides of the equation.

$\frac{1}{4} \cdot 4x = 20 \cdot \frac{1}{4}$ ← We multiply each side by $\frac{1}{4}$ to get x by itself.

$\frac{4}{4}x = \frac{20}{4}$

$1x = 5$

$x = 5$ ← A number times 1 is the same number.

Sometimes we are given an equation using words instead of variables. Let's look at how we change words into equations.

Unit 7 • Lesson 563

How do we write algebraic equations from word statements? *(continued)*

Explain

Direct students to page 564 of the *Student Text.* Tell students that algebra is important because we use it to translate words and real-world situations into algebraic equations.

Demonstrate

- Have students look at **Example 2**. Discuss the steps for translating words into an algebraic expression.

STEP 1

- Read the statement aloud, then read the first half of the statement again. Point out that we identify what we know and do not know. In this case, we do not know the number. We represent this unknown with the variable *n*.
- The statements says three times a number. Tell students that we can write this part of the statement as $3 \cdot n$ or $3n$.

STEP 2

- Read the second half of the statement again. This part is easier to translate. We use the = sign for the part of the statement that says "is equal to." We can write the rest of the statement as $= 8 + 1$.

STEP 3

- Explain that the last step is to put the two parts together to make the entire equation: $3n = 8 + 1$. Reread the whole statement aloud so that students can see the relationship between the words and the equation.
- Be sure students understand which words are translated as variables, which are translated as operators, and which are translated as the equal sign. Tell students that the words are not always the same as what we saw in this example, and it takes a lot of practice to learn how to translate them.

We need to be able to translate words into numbers and variables. It is trickier than it seems, because we have to read the problem carefully and put the numbers and symbols in the right order. Example 2 demonstrates this.

Example 2

Translate this statement into an equation.

Statement: *Three times a number is equal to eight plus one.*

STEP 1
Begin with the first part of the statement: "Three times a number..."
We do not know what the number is. That means we are working with an unknown, or a variable. We write this part of the statement using a variable. In this case, we will use *n*.

$3 \cdot n$ or $3n$

STEP 2
Translate the rest of the sentence. The rest of the sentence is easier to translate: "...is equal to eight plus one."
The phrase "is equal to" is the same as =. We translate this part of the statement this way:

$= 8 + 1$

STEP 3
Put the equation together.
Now we have the entire statement.

$3n = 8 + 1$

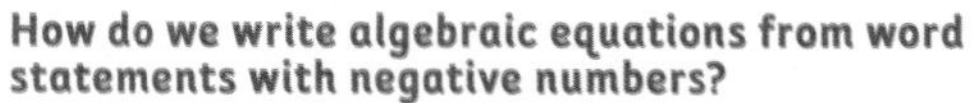

How do we write algebraic equations from word statements with negative numbers?

(*Student Text*, page 565)

Explain

Tell students that when we translate word statements into equations, we need to pay careful attention to the symbols we use.

Demonstrate

- Go over **Example 1** on page 565 of the *Student Text*. In this example, we include negatives in the word statement. Tell students that the translation strategies are the same, but the problem solving is more complex with negatives.
- Walk through each of the steps with students.

How do we write algebraic equations from word statements with negative numbers?

Translating negative numbers in statements can be difficult. Example 1 shows how we have to pay extra attention to the symbols that we use.

Example 1

Translate this statement with negative numbers into an equation.

Statement: *A number plus negative three is equal to nine minus five.*

STEP 1

Begin with the first part of the statement: "A number plus negative three..."

We do not know what the number is. That means we are working with an unknown, or a variable. We write this part of the statement using a variable. In this case, we will use *v*.

$v + -3$

STEP 2

Translate the rest of the statement. The rest of the statement is easier to translate: "...is equal to nine minus five."

The phrase "is equal to" is the same as =. We translate this part of the statement this way:

$= 9 - 5$

STEP 3

Put the equation together.

Now we have the entire statement.

$v + -3 = 9 - 5$

Give extra care and attention when working with negative numbers.

Apply Skills Turn to ***Interactive Text***, page 265.

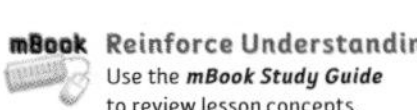

Reinforce Understanding Use the ***mBook Study Guide*** to review lesson concepts.

Unit 7 • Lesson 565

STEP 1

- Read the statement aloud, then reread the first part of the statement. Help students identify what is known and unknown. Point out that the unknown is represented by a variable, in this case, *v*. We know this unknown number is plus negative three, we write $\mathbf{v + -3}$.

STEP 2

- Reread the second part of the statement. Elicit from students the symbol we use for the part of the statement that says "is equal to," and how we write the numbers and operation symbol. We can translate this part of the statement as $= \mathbf{9 - 5}$.

STEP 3

- Remind students that the last step is to put the equation together. So $\mathbf{v + -3 = 9 - 5}$. Reread the whole statement aloud so that students can see the relationship between the words and the equation.

Check for Understanding

Engagement Strategy: Look About

Read this statement aloud: **Two times a number is equal to nine plus eleven**. Tell students that they are going to translate the statement into an equation with the help of the whole class ($2n = 9 + 11$). Students should write their equations in large writing on a piece of paper or a dry erase board. When students finish their work, they should hold up their answer for everyone to see.

If students are not sure about the answer, prompt them to look about at other students' answers to help with their thinking. Review the equations after all students have held up their answers.

Apply Skills

(*Interactive Text*, page 265)

Have students turn to page 265 in the *Interactive Text*, and complete the activities.

Activity 1

Students write algebraic expressions for each of the word statements. Make sure students realize they are also dealing with inequalities.

Activity 2

Students write algebraic equations for each of the word statements, then solve them.

Monitor students' work as they complete the activities.

Watch for:

- Can students translate the word statements into algebraic expressions and equations?
- Do students recognize the phrases that refer to inequalities (e.g., a number less than three, a number more than three)?
- Can students set up the equation correctly, then solve it?

mBook **Reinforce Understanding**

Remind students that they can review lesson concepts by accessing the online *mBook Study Guide*.

Lesson 9 | Apply Skills

Name ______________________ Date ______________________

Apply Skills
Writing Equations From Words

Activity 1

Write algebraic expressions for each of the word statements. Use any of the four operations or inequality signs to write your expressions.

1. three times a number $3x$
2. three more than a number $x + 3$
3. a number less than 3 $x < 3$
4. the sum of 3 and a number times three $(3 + x) \cdot 3$
5. a number greater than 3 $x > 3$

Activity 2

Write algebraic equations for each of the word statements, then solve them.

1. Three times a number equals 180.
   Equation $3x = 180$
   Solve $x = 60$
2. A number minus four equals twelve.
   Equation $x - 4 = 12$
   Solve $x = 16$
3. Two times a number equals negative ten.
   Equation $2x = -10$
   Solve $x = -5$
4. A number minus negative three equals negative seven.
   Equation $x - -3 = -7$
   Solve $x = -10$

Unit 7

Unit 7 • Lesson 9 265

Problem Solving:
▶ Word Problems and Algebra

How do we translate word problems?
(*Student Text*, pages 566–567)

Explain

Explain that we can also translate word problems into algebraic equations. However, these types of problems can be more complex and require us to carefully double-check our work.

Demonstrate

- Have students turn to **Example 1** on page 566 of the *Student Text*. Explain that once we translate the word statements correctly, it is important to be able to use our algebraic equation to answer questions.
- Read the problem with students, then go over the steps carefully. Explain that these types of problems are complex, but not difficult to solve if we slow down and work carefully. Show students how to organize their work as demonstrated by the example to break it into manageable steps.

Lesson 9

▶Problem Solving: Word Problems and Algebra

How do we translate word problems?

Word problems require even more translation than simple statements for algebraic equations. It is important to check and double-check our work as we work through the problem. Example 1 shows how we have to think about the relationship first before we write the equation.

Example 1

Translate the word problem and solve.

Zach is three times older than his sister Rebecca. Zach is 15 years old. How old is Rebecca?

STEP 1

Think about what we know and what we don't know in the problem.

We know:

- Zach is three times older than Rebecca.
- Zack is 15 years old.

We don't know:

- Rebecca's age

STEP 2

Figure out what the variable is.

We do not know Rebecca's age, so that is the unknown. Let's use t to represent Rebecca's age.

t = Rebecca's age

We have a variable for Rebecca's age, and we know that Zach is three times older than Rebecca.

Zach's age = $3 \cdot t$, or $3t$

STEP 3

Write the equation.

Now we can use the two things we know about Zach to write the equation. We can write the equation because the two sides are balanced.

$3t = 15$

566 Unit 7 • Lesson 9

STEP 1

- Remind students to identify what we know and do not know. This helps us determine what the problem is asking, and figure out the parts of the equation that we know.
- After going through the word problem, we see that we know Zack's age, and that he is three times older than Rebecca. We don't know Rebecca's age.

STEP 2

- We need to determine the variable, in this case Rebecca's age. We use the variable t to represent her age. This is what we are trying to find out. We know Zach is three times older than Rebecca, so we can represent Zach's age as $\mathbf{3 \cdot t}$ or $\mathbf{3t}$.

STEP 3

Now we can write the equation. We know Zach is 15 years old. So, $\mathbf{3t = 15}$.

How do we translate word problems? *(continued)*

Demonstrate

- Continue looking at Example 1 and walking through the steps on page 567 of the *Student Text*.

STEP 4

- Explain that we can now solve the problem, using the equation that we wrote. Walk through the steps to find the value of t.
- Remind students to multiply both sides of the equation by $\frac{1}{3}$ to get a coefficient of 1. Then remind students that any number times 1 is the number itself, so we get $\boldsymbol{t = 5}$. Remind students that the variable t represents Rebecca's age, so **Rebecca is 5 years old**.
- Remind students to check answers by substituting the value, in this case 5, back into the original equation. When we substitute into the equation and complete the operations, we see that **15 = 15**, so the answer is correct.

STEP 4

Solve the problem.

Now that we have written the problem, we know how to solve it.

$3t = 15$

$\frac{1}{3} \cdot 3t = 15 \cdot \frac{1}{3}$ ← Multiply both sides of the equation by $\frac{1}{3}$ to get t by itself.

$\frac{3}{3}t = \frac{15}{3}$

$1t = 5$

$t = 5$ ← A number times 1 is the same number.

Rebecca is five years old.

We can check our answer by substituting in the original equation.

5

↓

$3t = 15$

$3 \cdot 5 = 15$

$\mathbf{15 = 15}$

Problem-Solving Activity Turn to ***Interactive Text***, page 266.

mBook Reinforce Understanding Use the ***mBook Study Guide*** to review lesson concepts.

Problem-Solving Activity
(*Interactive Text*, page 266)

Direct students to *Interactive Text*, page 266, and read the instructions together.

Students solve word problems by setting them up as algebraic equations to answer the question asked in the problem.

Monitor students' work as they complete the activity.

Watch for:

- Can students translate the word statements into algebraic expressions?
- Can students solve the algebraic equations using the properties and rules for algebra?
- Do students recognize the answer when they are finished solving the algebraic equation?

Reinforce Understanding
Remind students that they can review lesson concepts by accessing the online *mBook Study Guide*.

Lesson 9 | Problem-Solving Activity

Name ______________________ Date ______________________

Problem-Solving Activity
Word Problems and Algebra

Translate each word problem into an algebraic expression and solve.

1. John makes three times as much as Allen per hour. Allen makes $7 per hour. How much does John make?
   if h = John's wage, $3 \cdot 7 = h$; $h = 21$
2. Randy's pet store carries two times less feed brands than Mandy's store. Randy has 14 kinds of feed. How many kinds does Mandy carry?
   if m = Mandy's feed, $2 \cdot 14 = m$; $m = 28$
3. Rich can run three times as far as Mike in 4 hours. Rich can run 12 miles. How far can Mike run?
   if r = how far Mike can run, $3r = 12$; $r = 4$
4. Lulu goes to the movie theater 17 times per month. Her friend Sarah goes to the movie theater 16 less time a month than Lulu. How many times does Sarah go to the movie theater per month?
   if l = how many times Sarah goes to the theater, $17 - 16 = l$; $l = 1$
5. Train trips that go from the East Coast to the middle of the country can take a long time because of delays. A recent trip averaged 45 miles per hour, and it traveled 900 miles. How long did this trip take?
   if m = hours, $m = \frac{45}{900} = m$; $m = 20$ hours
6. Your friend and you are racing to see who can drive the 730 miles from Boston, Massachusetts to Raleigh, North Carolina first. It takes you 15 hours to get there. Your friend gets to Raleigh twice as fast. How long does it take your friend to get to Raleigh?
   if b = how many hours it takes your friend to get to Raleigh; $b = 7.5$ hours
   $2b = 15 \quad \left(\frac{1}{2}\right)2b = 15\left(\frac{1}{2}\right) \quad \frac{2}{2}b = \frac{15}{2}$

Reinforce Understanding
Use the **mBook** ***Study Guide*** to review lesson concepts.

266 Unit 7 • Lesson 9

Homework

Go over the instructions on page 568 of the *Student Text* for each part of the homework.

Activity 1

Students write algebraic expressions for the phrases. Tell students they may use any of the four operation symbols, as well as the symbols > and < to write each of the expressions.

Activity 2

Students translate word statements into algebraic equations.

Activity 3

Students solve word problems using algebraic equations.

Activity 4 • Distributed Practice

Students continue practicing operations on fractions and integers, PEMDAS, and the distributive property.

Lesson 9

Homework

Activity 1

Write algebraic expressions for each of the phrases. Use any of the four operation symbols as well as > and < to write your expressions.

1. a number times five $5x$
2. three less than a number $x - 3$
3. four more than a number $x + 4$
4. a number greater than six $x > 6$
5. seven more than three times a number $3x + 7$
6. eleven is more than a number $11 > x$

Activity 2

Write algebraic equations for each of the phrases. You do not need to solve the equation.

1. a number plus seven equals fourteen $x + 7 = 14$
2. twenty minus a number equals three times two $20 - x = 3 \cdot 2$
3. four hundred divided by a number equals negative four $400 \div x = -4$

Activity 3

Set the word problems up as algebraic equations and then solve.

1. Joanna earns $8 for every hour she works at her mom's store, plus $5 for cleaning the floors. Yesterday she made $37 at her mom's store. How many hours did she work? 4 hours
2. Blake has a CD case that holds the same number of CDs on each page. He has enough CDs to fill 6 full pages, plus put 2 more CDs on the next page. He has 62 CDs in all. How many CDs fit on a full page? 10 CDs
3. You can make $2 for every program you sell at the game, plus $5 for helping at the food stand. How many programs did you sell at the game if you made $55? 25 programs

Activity 4 • Distributed Practice

Solve.

1. $\frac{6}{5} - \frac{1}{5}$ 1
2. $\frac{6}{5} \cdot \frac{5}{6}$ 1
3. $4^2 \div (2^2 - 2)$ 8
4. $3 \cdot -4 \div 2$ -6
5. $4^2 \div 2 - 3$ 5
6. Simplify using the distributive property: $-2(-2x + 4)$ $4x - 8$

568 Unit 7 • Lesson 9

Lesson 10 | Unit Review ▶ Introduction to Algebraic Equations

Problem Solving: ▶ Geometric Construction and Angle Measurement

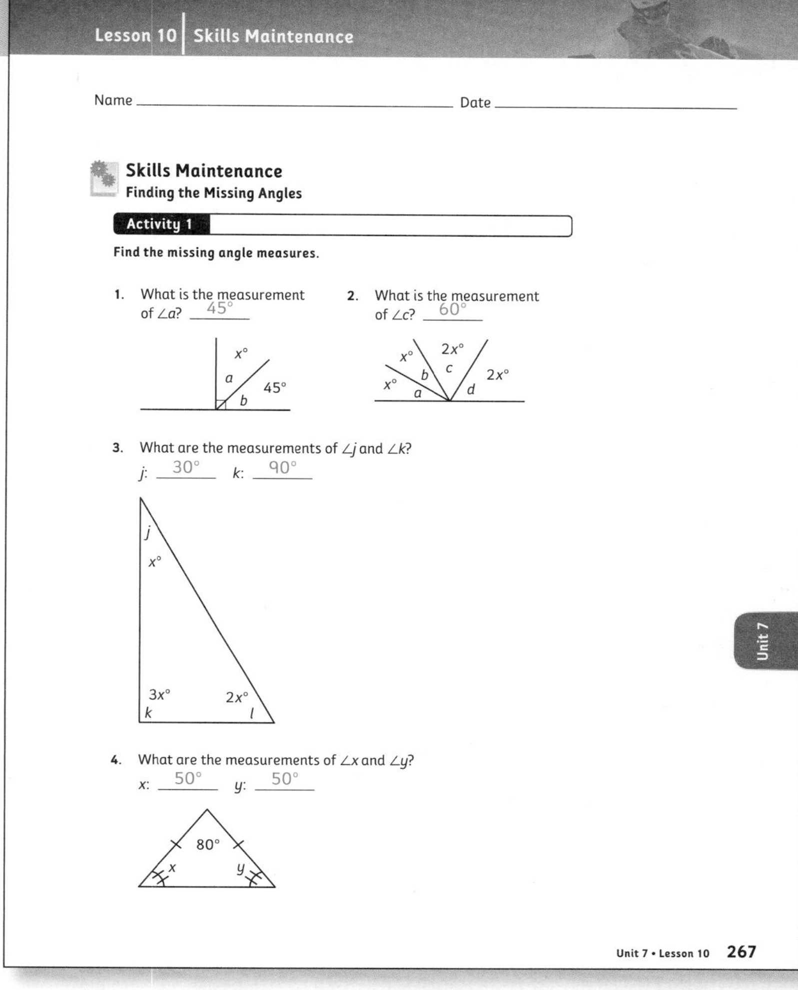

Lesson 10 | Skills Maintenance
Name
Date
Skills Maintenance
Finding the Missing Angles
Activity 1
Find the missing angle measures.
1. What is the measurement of ∠a? 45°
x°
a
45°
b
2. What is the measurement of ∠c? 60°
x°
2x°
b
c
2x°
x°
a
d
3. What are the measurements of ∠j and ∠k?
j: 30° k: 90°
j
x°
3x°
k
2x°
l
4. What are the measurements of ∠x and ∠y?
x: 50° y: 50°
80°
x
y
Unit 7
Unit 7 • Lesson 10 267

Lesson Planner

Vocabulary Development

equation
balanced
property of equality
coefficient
reciprocal
line segment
arc
perpendicular
right angle
midpoint
parallel
constructions
bisect
supplementary angles

Skills Maintenance Review

Finding the Missing Angles

Building Number Concepts:

▶ Introduction to Algebraic Equations

Students review the important ideas associated with algebraic equations. Equations are mathematical statements that show that one expression is equal to another expression. When we work with equations, we need to keep them balanced.

Problem Solving:

▶ Geometric Construction and Angle Measurement

Students review key concepts of geometric constructions and angle measurement. Once we work with angles and shapes like triangles, we can use what we know about their properties to determine the measurement of an angle. Algebraic equations can be used to find the measure of unknown angles.

Skills Maintenance

Finding the Missing Angles

(*Interactive Text*, page 267)

Activity 1

Students find the missing angle measurements.

Building Number Concepts: ▸ Introduction to Algebraic Equations

How do we work with equations?

(*Student Text*, pages 569–571)

Discuss

Begin by writing the following numeric equation on the board:

$4 \cdot 5 + 2 = 12 \cdot 2 - 2$

Work through the first steps on both sides involving multiplication so that the equation looks like this:

$20 + 2 = 24 - 2$

Ask:

Are both sides of the equation balanced, and if so, what makes them balanced?

Listen for:

- *Yes, 20 + 2 is 22 and 24 − 2 is 22.*
- *The expression on one side is equal to the expression on the other side.*

Discuss the importance of balanced equations throughout the steps of solving equations. Emphasize that each side of the equal sign contains an expression, and that these expressions do not look alike. That is the nature of algebraic equations; the expressions do not look the same, but they have to be equivalent to be an equation.

Demonstrate

- Review the concept of balanced equations on page 569 of the *Student Text*. Recall the comparison to a scale to remind students of the importance of balanced equations. Look at the scale and write the expression **4(6 ÷ 2)** on the left side.

Lesson 10 | Unit Review ▸Introduction to Algebraic Equations

Problem Solving: ▸Geometric Construction and Angle Measurement

▸Introduction to Algebraic Equations

How do we work with equations?

Throughout this unit we balanced equations. We defined an equation as a math statement that shows one expression is equal to another expression. These two expressions usually do not look the same, but that doesn't matter. If it is an equation, the two expressions must be equal. All of the equations below are balanced.

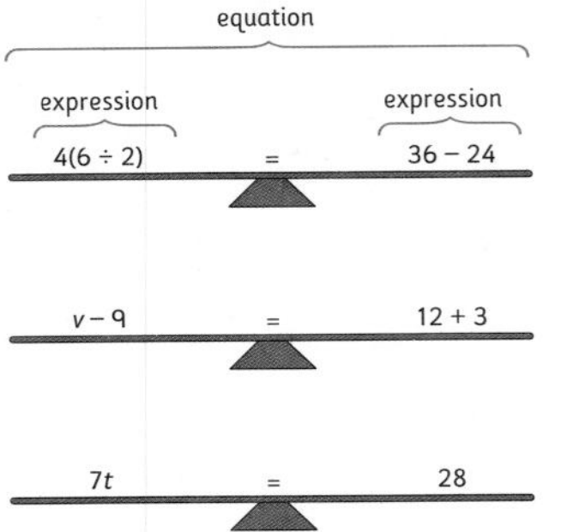

Unit 7 • Lesson 1 569

- Point out the equal sign in the center. Remind students that both sides of the equal sign must be equal in an equation. Point out the expression **36 − 24** on the right side.
- Look at the labels expression and equation, then remind students that an equation is a math statement that shows that one expression is equal to another.
- Have students solve the two expressions to see that they are equal.
- Go through the other two equations, $v - 9 = 12 + 3$ and $7t = 28$, in the same way to show that the equations are balanced.

Demonstrate

- Have students turn to page 570 of the *Student Text* to look at **Review 1**. Remind students about the rules for operations on integers. In this case, remind students that subtraction is the same as adding the opposite.
- Show how to rewrite the equation using addition. As you walk through the process, discuss how each part of the process is used to solve for the value of the variable, and how the same actions on each side of the equal sign keep the equation balanced.
- Remind students that in this case, we add −1 to both sides to isolate x. Point out that −1 is the opposite of 1, so when we add them together, we get zero.
- Remind students that we can check our answer of $\boldsymbol{x = 26}$ by substituting 26 into the original equation. Show how to substitute the value and complete the operations. We get **27 = 27**. The answer is correct.

The goal in working with equations is to solve for the variable. We use properties and rules from our toolbox to find the value of the variable.

Review 1

How do we keep equations balanced when solving?
When we solve an equation, we need to remember to do the same thing to each side of the equation. This keeps the equation balanced.

$\mathbf{5 + x - 4 = 27}$

$5 + x + -4 = 27$ ← Subtraction is the same as adding the opposite.

$x + 5 + -4 = 27$ ← We commute so that we combine the same terms.

$x + 1 = 27$

$x + 1 + -1 = 27 + -1$ ← We add −1 to both sides to get x by itself.

$x + 0 = 26$

$\mathbf{x = 26}$

We check this answer to make sure it is correct by using substitution.

26
↓
$5 + x - 4 = 27$

$5 + 26 - 4 = 27$

$5 + 26 + -4 = 27$

$31 + -4 = 27$

$\mathbf{27 = 27}$

Our answer was correct.

How do we work with equations?
(*continued*)

Discuss

Turn to page 571 of the *Student Text*. Remind students that we need to pay careful attention when working with negative numbers. Remembering the rules from our toolbox can help us solve equations correctly.

Demonstrate

- Have students look at the equation **$-2x = 16$** in **Review 2**. This example shows how to solve equations with negative numbers.
- Walk carefully through each of the steps as outlined. Remind students that we multiply by the reciprocal of −2: $-\frac{1}{2}$. Remind students of the property of equality. We must multiply $-\frac{1}{2}$ on each side of the equation to keep the equation balanced.
- Review the PASS rules with students and point out that it works for both numbers. Point out the two negative signs on the left side of the equation. Remind students that the answer is positive when dividing a negative by a negative. Point out the negative on the right side, and remind students that that we are dividing a negative by a positive, so the answer is negative. We get **$1x = -8$**. The coefficient 1, which means we multiply x by 1. So **$x = -8$**.
- Again remind students that we can check our answer by substituting the value of x with −8. We get **16 = 16**, so the answer is correct.

Sometimes balancing equations with negative numbers is difficult. We need to remember the rules from our toolbox that involve operations on integers. Knowing the PASS rules and remembering that subtraction is adding the opposite helps us make sure we solve the equation correctly.

Review 2

How do we solve equations that contain negative numbers?
When we solve equations that have negative numbers in them, we need to use the rules for integers.

$$-2x = 16$$

$$-\frac{1}{2} \cdot -2x = 16 \cdot -\frac{1}{2}$$ ← We multiply each side by $-\frac{1}{2}$ to get x by itself.

$$\frac{-2}{-2}x = \frac{16}{-2}$$

$$1x = -8$$ ← The PASS rule works for both numbers.

On the left side of the equal sign, we are dividing a negative by a negative. Both numbers have the same signs, which means that the answer is positive.

On the right side of the equal sign, we are dividing a positive by a negative number. The signs are different, which means the answer is negative.

$$x = -8$$ ← A number times 1 is the same number.

We always check our work. We can substitute −8 for x.

−8
↓
$-2x = 16$
$-2 \cdot -8 = 16$
$16 = 16$

How do we solve distance problems using algebra?

(Student Text, pages 572–573)

Discuss

Turn to page 572 of the *Student Text*. Remind students that one of the advantages of algebra is that it can provide a great shortcut for solving proportion problems. We can cross multiply.

Demonstrate

- Have students look at **Review 1**. Read the problem with students. Elicit the information needed to set up the proportion. In this case, we set up the proportion using inches and miles.
- Point out that we use the variable ***x*** to represent the number of miles from Los Angeles to Denver. Our proportion is $\frac{3}{500} = \frac{6}{x}$.
- Remind students that we cross multiply by multiplying the numerator from the first number by the denominator from the second number. In this case, we get 3*x*. Then we multiply the denominator of the first number by the numerator of the second number. In this case, we get the problem **500 • 6**.
- Now we can write the equation: **3*x* = 500 • 6**. Walk through the process for finding the value of *x*, reminding students to keep the equation balanced as we isolate *x*. We get the answer ***x* = 1,000. It is about 1,000 miles from Los Angles to Denver**.

Lesson 10

How do we solve distance problems using algebra?

One of the big advantages of algebra is that it gives us a general way to represent and solve word problems.

Proportions are a good example of how we can solve a problem quickly using algebra. All we need to do is cross multiply.

Review 1

How do we solve proportion problems using algebra?

Problem:

A map shows 3 inches for every 500 miles. The distance on the map between Los Angeles and Denver is about 6 inches. How many miles is it from Los Angeles to Denver?

We begin by setting up the proportion. In this case, the proportion is $\frac{3}{500} = \frac{6}{x}$.

We then cross multiply to create an algebraic equation.

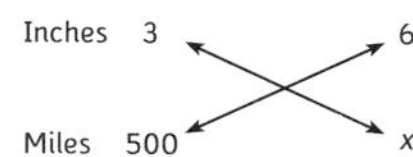

Now we can solve our equation to find the value of *x*.

$3x = 500 \cdot 6$

$3x = 3{,}000$

$\frac{1}{3} \cdot 3x = 3{,}000 \cdot \frac{1}{3}$ ← We multiply both sides of the equation by $\frac{1}{3}$ to get *x* by itself.

$\frac{3}{3}x = \frac{3{,}000}{3}$

$1x = 1{,}000$

$x = 1{,}000$ ← A number times 1 is the same number.

It is about 1,000 miles from Los Angeles to Denver.

572 Unit 7 • Lesson 10

How do we solve distance problems using algebra? *(continued)*

Discuss

Remind students that the cross-multiplication method works for any proportion problem. Remind students that we also learned the distance formula. This formula allows us to plug in, or substitute, information that we know from a problem and solve for the unknown variable.

Ask:

What is the distance formula?

Listen for:

- *Distance = rate • time,* or $D = rt$

Demonstrate

- Have students look at **Review 2** on page 573 of the *Student Text*, where we solve a rate problem using the distance formula.
- Have students read the problem. Make sure they understand what the problem is asking. Have them identify what we know from the problem. We know the rate, 175 feet per second, and the distance, 875 feet, but we do not know the time.
- Point out that the question asks how long it will take. This is the clue that tells us we are trying to find the time.
- Show how we substitute the known values into the equation to get **875 = 175*t***. Now we solve as with any other algebra problem. We isolate the variable, *t*. We divide 175 from both sides to get **5 = 1*t***, so ***t* = 5**. Remind students that t represents time in seconds, so **it takes about 5 seconds for a person to fall 875 feet.**

We also use algebra to solve rate problems. We learned a formula for distance: $D = r \cdot t$. This formula is more efficient and flexible than setting up each problem as a ratio. Let's look at an example.

Review 2

How do we solve rate problems using algebra?

Problem:
When a person jumps out of a plane with a parachute, they can fall as fast as 175 feet per second. How long does it take to fall 875 feet?

We know:

- Rate = 175 ft./sec.
- Time is unknown.
- Distance = 875 ft.

Now we substitute our values into the equation.

875 175
↓ ↓
$D = r \cdot t$

$875 = 175t$

$\frac{875}{175} = \frac{175}{175}t$

$5 = 1t$

$t = 5$

It takes about 5 seconds for a person to fall 875 feet.

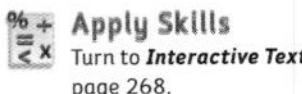
Apply Skills
Turn to ***Interactive Text***, page 268.

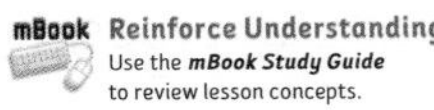
Reinforce Understanding
Use the ***mBook Study Guide*** to review lesson concepts.

Unit Review: Introduction to Algebraic Equations

(*Interactive Text*, page 268)

Go to page 268 in the *Interactive Text*. Have students complete Activities 1–2.

Activity 1

Students balance the equations and solve for the variable.

Activity 2

Students solve word problems by making algebraic equations that represent the information in the problems.

Monitor students' work as they complete the activities.

Watch for:

- Do students use tools and properties accurately?
- Do students check their work by evaluating the equation?
- Do students have difficulties translating proportion and rate word problems into algebraic form?

Once students have finished, discuss any difficulties you noticed.

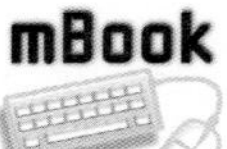

Reinforce Understanding
Remind students that they can review unit concepts by accessing the online *mBook Study Guide*.

Lesson 10 | Unit Review

Name ______________________ Date ______________________

Unit Review
Introduction to Algebraic Expressions

Activity 1

Solve the problems by making sure each side of the equation is balanced. Be sure to show your work.

1. $x + 10 = 23 + 9$ $x = 22$
2. $3 + b - 8 = 15$ $b = 20$
3. $-4 + c + -6 = -20$ $c = -10$
4. $3 \cdot 5 + s = 4 \cdot 2 + 16$ $s = 9$
5. $4d = 60$ $d = 15$
6. $-3f = 15$ $f = -5$
7. $-5x = -20$ $x = 4$
8. $4v = 28 - 4 + 8$ $v = 8$

Activity 2

Solve the word problems using algebra. Be sure to show all of your work.

1. A recipe for cake calls for 2 cups of flour and 4 eggs. You want to make a cake that uses 12 eggs. How much flour should you use?
   $\frac{2}{4} = \frac{f}{12}$ $4f = 24$ $f = 6$ cups of flour
2. Your teacher is passing out tests and pencils for an exam. She wants there to be 3 pencils for every 1 exam. If she passes out 98 tests, how many pencils does she need?
   $\frac{3}{1} = \frac{x}{98}$ $x = 294$ pencils
3. Katie and Ali and running to see who can get to their car first. Katie runs the 500 meters in 20 seconds. If Ali gets there twice as fast, how many seconds will it take her?
   $2a = 20$ $a = 10$ seconds

268 Unit 7 • Lesson 10

Problem Solving:
▶ Geometric Construction and Angle Measurement

What are constructions?
(*Student Text*, page 574)

Discuss

Begin this part of the lesson by reviewing constructions and the related vocabulary. Remind students that constructions are ways to draw angles without needing to measure them with a protractor. Also remind them that parallel lines never meet, so they never create an angle.

Demonstrate

- Have students look at **Review 1** on page 574 of the *Student Text* to look at how to construct a perpendicular line that bisects a segment.
- Then have them look at **Review 2** to look at how to bisect an angle.

Ask:

How do you know if line segments are perpendicular?

How do you know that a perpendicular line bisects a line segment?

How do you know if an angle is bisected?

Listen for:

- *Line segments are perpendicular if they form right angles where they intersect.*
- *We know a perpendicular line bisects a line segment if the arcs cross at an equal distance from each end point. That means the line goes through the line segment at the midpoint.*
- *The arc that goes through each side of the angle is the same distance from the vertex. The arcs that cross are an equal distance from each side. That means the line from the vertex through the crossed arcs is an equal distance from each side.*

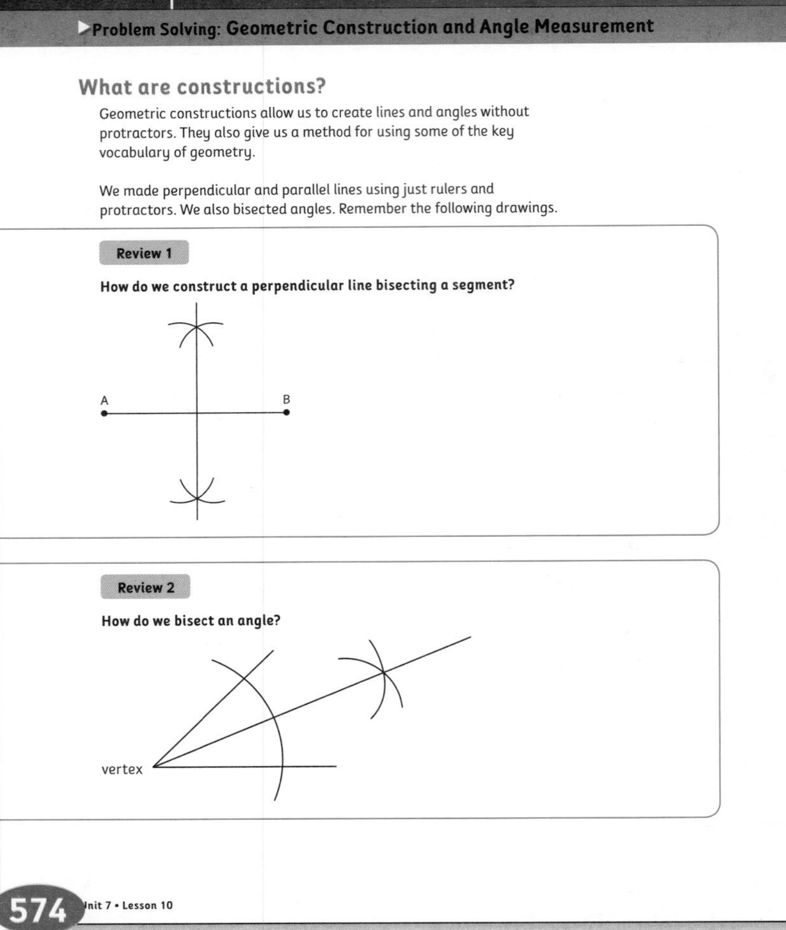
Lesson 10

▶Problem Solving: Geometric Construction and Angle Measurement

What are constructions?

Geometric constructions allow us to create lines and angles without protractors. They also give us a method for using some of the key vocabulary of geometry.

We made perpendicular and parallel lines using just rulers and protractors. We also bisected angles. Remember the following drawings.

Review 1

How do we construct a perpendicular line bisecting a segment?

Review 2

How do we bisect an angle?

574 Unit 7 • Lesson 10

How do we measure angles using algebra?

(*Student Text*, pages 575–576)

Discuss

Remind students that geometry is much more than knowing vocabulary terms. There are times when you have to figure out, or make inferences, about angles or geometric relationships. Remind students about the relationship between lines, angles, and triangles.

Discuss how supplementary angles are angles that add up to 180 degrees. Remind students that likewise, the interior angles of a triangle all add up to 180 degrees. These properties can help us to figure out the measure of missing angles.

Demonstrate

- Go over **Review 1** on page 575 of the *Student Text*, where we solve for the measure of angles in an isosceles triangle.
- Draw attention to the symbols showing that angle *a* and angle *b* are equal. Also mention that the sum of the interior angles is not mentioned anywhere in the drawing of the triangle. Nonetheless, that information is essential in making the algebraic equation. We know that the sum is 180 degrees.
- Show students how to set up the equation and use the variable x for the measure of angle c: $\mathbf{65 + 65 + x = 180}$. Make sure students know where each number and variable comes from.
- Then walk through each of the steps to solve for x. We find that $\mathbf{x = 50}$. So **the measure of angle *c* is 50 degrees**.
- Remind students that we can check the answer by substituting 50 for x in the equation.

Lesson 10

How do we measure angles using algebra?

Once we begin working with angles, we see the connection to algebraic equations. The equations help us figure out the measure of unknown angles. If we know certain properties of angles, we can set up simple algebraic equations to solve different kinds of problems.

Review 1

How do we solve for the measure of angles in a triangle?

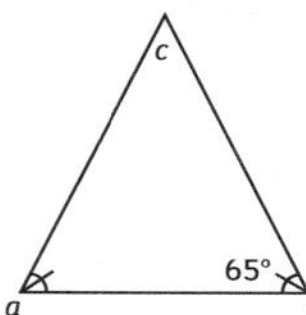

The marks tell us that $\angle a$ and $\angle b$ are equal. We also know that the measure of the interior angles on all triangles totals 180 degrees.

We can set up our equation using x for the measure of $\angle c$.

$$65 + 65 + x = 180$$

$$130 + x = 180 \quad \leftarrow \text{Combine like terms.}$$

$$-130 + 130 + x = 180 + -130 \quad \leftarrow \text{Add } -130 \text{ to both sides of the equation.}$$

$$0 + x = 50$$

$$x = 50$$

The measure of $\angle c$ = 50°

Unit 7 • Lesson 1 575

How do we measure angles using algebra? *(continued)*

Demonstrate

- Finally have students look at **Review 2** on page 576 of the *Student Text*. Note that no angle measurements are given, but we can still figure out, or infer, the measure of each angle using algebra. Mention that this kind of problem solving involving algebra will continue in the next unit.
- Remind students that using what we know about the properties of triangles and the information given, we can write an equation: $x + 3x + x = 180$. Once we write the equation, we can solve for x.
- Walk through each of the steps with students, making sure they see how we combine like terms, balance the equation, and isolate the variable to get $x = 36$. Now that we know the value of x, we can find the measure of each x by substituting the value for each variable.

Lesson 10

Review 2

How do we find the measure of more than one angle in a triangle?

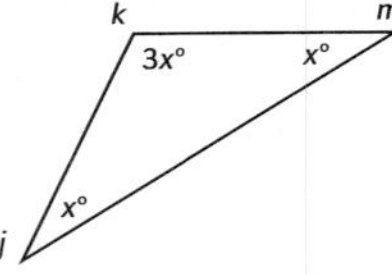

We know that the interior angles on all triangles total 180 degrees. That means all of the angles have to total 180 degrees. We set up the equation this way:

$x + 3x + x = 180$

Then we solve.

$x + 3x + x = 180$

$4x + x = 180$ ← Combine like terms.

$5x = 180$

$\frac{1}{5} \cdot 5x = 180 \cdot \frac{1}{5}$ ← Multiply both sides of the equation by $\frac{1}{5}$.

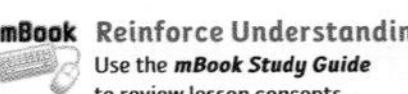

$\frac{5}{5}x = \frac{180}{5}$

$1x = 36$

$x = 36$ ← A number times 1 is the same number.

We can now substitute to find the measure of each angle.

- **If $\angle j = x$, then the measure of $\angle j = 36°$**
- **If $\angle k = 3x$, then the measure of $\angle k = 3 \cdot 36$, or 108°**
- **If $\angle m = x$, then the measure of $\angle m = 36°$**

Problem-Solving Activity Turn to *Interactive Text*, page 269.

mBook Reinforce Understanding Use the *mBook Study Guide* to review lesson concepts.

Unit Review: Geometric Construction and Angle Measurement

(*Interactive Text*, pages 269–271)

Go to pages 269–270 in the *Interactive Text*. Have students work Activities 1–2.

Activity 1

Students use a ruler and a compass to construct perpendicular lines, then bisect an angle.

Activity 2

Students use their knowledge of properties and angles to find the missing angle measurements in each triangle. They write algebraic expressions to solve each problem.

Monitor students as they complete the activities.

Lesson 10 | Unit Review

Name ______ Date ______

Unit Review
Geometric Construction and Angle Measurement

Activity 1

Use a compass and a ruler to construct a perpendicular line, then bisect the angle.

1. Use line segment FG to create a perpendicular line segment.

F G

2. Bisect this angle.

Unit 7

Unit 7 • Lesson 10 269

Lesson 10 | Unit Review

Name ______ Date ______

Activity 2

Use this information and your knowledge of angle properties to find the missing angle in each problem. Answer the problem using an algebraic equation. Show all of your work.

1. What is the measure of ∠v? 70°

80° 30° v

Show your work here:
$180 = 30 + 80 + y \quad y = 70$

2. What is the measure of ∠g? 50°

40° g

Show your work here:
$180 = 90 + 40 + g \quad g = 50$

3. What is the measure of ∠m? 70°

m 55°

Show your work here:
$180 = 55 + 55 + m \quad m = 70$

270 Unit 7 • Lesson 10

Go to page 271 in the *Interactive Text* to complete Activity 2.

Watch for:

- Are students comfortable using a compass and a ruler to draw lines?
- Do students remember how to bisect an angle?
- Do students have difficulty translating the information into an algebraic equation?
- Are students able to draw on information not shown in the problem (e.g., the sum of the angles for a triangle is 180 degrees)?
- Do students clearly state the measure of each angle once they have solved for the variable?

Once students have finished, discuss any difficulties you noticed.

mBook **Reinforce Understanding**
Remind students that they can review unit concepts by accessing the online *mBook Study Guide*.

Name ______________________ Date ______________________

4. What is the measure of ∠t? 55°

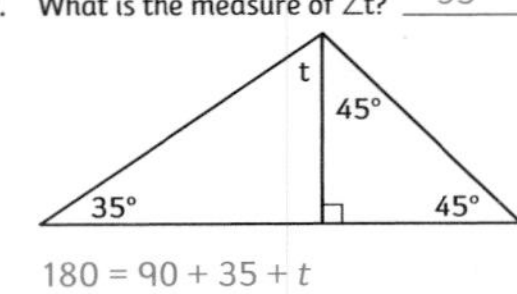

$180 = 90 + 35 + t$

$t = 55$

5. What is the measure of ∠z? 30°

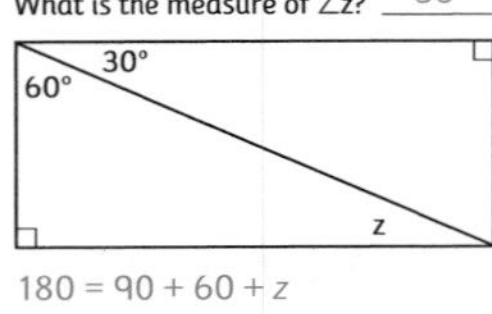

$180 = 90 + 60 + z$

$z = 30$

6. What is the measure of ∠f? What is the measure of ∠g?
f 45° g 135°

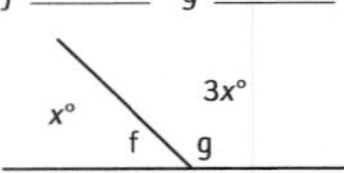

Unit 7

Assessment Planner

Students	Assess	Differentiate		Assess
	Day 1	Day 2	Day 3	Day 4
All	End-of-Unit Assessment *Form A*			Performance Assessments Unit 8 Opener
Scored 80% or above		Extension	Extension	
Scored Below 80%		Reinforcement	Retest	

Assessment Objectives

Building Number Concepts
▶ Introduction to Algebraic Equations

- Understand the basic properties of algebraic equations
- Balance equations involving symbols or variables
- Solve problems involving algebraic equations

Problem Solving
▶ Geometric Construction and Angle Measurement

- Use a compass and straightedge to construct basic figures
- Use algebraic reasoning to find missing angle measures
- Explore the properties of triangles with congruent angles

Monitoring Progress:
▶ Unit Assessments

Assess
End-of-Unit Assessment

- Administer End-of-Unit Assessment Form A in the *Assessment Book*, pages 63–64.

Differentiate

- Review End-of-Unit Assessment Form A with class.
- Identify students for Extension or Reinforcement.

Extension

For those students who score 80 percent or better, provide the On Track! Activities from Unit 7, Lessons 6–10, from the *mBook Teacher Edition.*

Reinforcement

For those students who score below 80 percent, provide additional support in one of these ways:

- Have students access the online tutorial provided in the *mBook Study Guide.*
- Have students complete the Interactive Reinforcement Exercises for Unit 7, in the *mBook Study Guide.*
- Provide teacher-directed reteaching of unit concepts.

Retest

Administer End-of Unit Assessment Form B from the *mBook Teacher Edition* to those students who scored below 80 percent on Form A.

Assess
Performance Assessments

- Guide students through the Performance Assessment Model on *Assessment Book*, page 65. Then, administer the Performance Assessments on pages 66–67.

Form A

Name ______________________ Date ______________________

Monitoring Progress
Introduction to Algebraic Equations

Part 1

Solve the equations. Show all of your work.

1. $m + 50 = 90 + 10$
   $m + 50 = 100$
   $m = 100 - 50$
   $m = 50$

2. $7 + f - 8 = 20$
   $-1 + f = 20$
   $f = 20 + 1$
   $f = 21$

3. $5c = -25$
   $c = -25 \div 5$
   $c = -5$

4. $-3n = 12$
   $n = 12 \div -3$
   $n = -4$

Part 2

Solve the word problems using algebra. Show all of your work.

1. The police are concerned about speeding on Wayman Boulevard. In two hours, they used radar to catch 20 speeders. How many speeders would you expect them to catch in five hours?
   2 hr 5 hr
   20 x
   $2x = 100$
   $x = 100 \div 2$ $x = 50$

2. Mt. Cosmos is a volcano in a small island in the Pacific. It is an active volcano, and it has been erupting about six times every three days. How many times would you expect it to erupt in eight days?
   6 eruptions 3 days
   x 8 days
   $3x = 48$
   $x = 48 \div 3$ $x = 16$

Unit 7

Monitoring Progress
Geometric Construction and Angle Measurement

Part 3

Use algebra to find the angle measurements.

1. What is the measure of angle c?

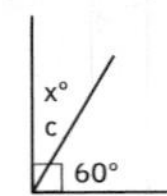

   $c + 60 = 90$
   $c = 90 - 60$
   $c = 30°$

2. What is the measure of angle h?

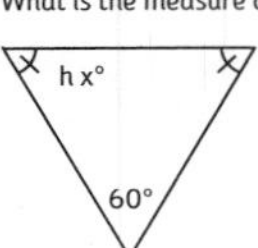

   $60 + h + h = 180$
   $2h = 180 - 60$
   $h = 120 \div 2$
   $h = 60°$

3. What are the measures of a, b and c?

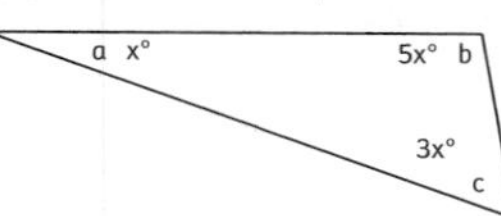

   $x + 5x + 3x = 180$
   $9x = 180$
   $x = 180 \div 9$
   $x = 20$
   $a = 20°$ $b = 100°$ $c = 60°$

4. What is the measure of angle s? What is the measure of angle t?

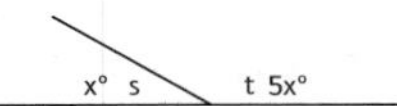

   $x + 5x = 180$
   $6x = 180$
   $x = 180 \div 6$
   $x = 30°$ $s = 30°$ $t = 150°$

Form B

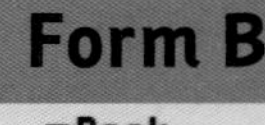

Name ______________________ Date ______________________

Monitoring Progress
Introduction to Algebraic Equations

Part 1

Solve the equations. Show all of your work.

1. $m + 20 = 70 + 25$
   $m + 20 = 95$
   $m + 20 - 20 = 95 - 20$
   $m = 75$

2. $9 + f - 2 = 15$
   $7 + f = 15$
   $7 - 7 + f = 15 - 7$
   $f = 8$

3. $4c = -36$
   $4c \div 4 = -36 \div 4$
   $c = -9$

4. $-5n = 25$
   $-5n \div -5 = 25 \div -5$
   $n = -5$

Part 2

Solve the word problems using algebra. Show all of your work.

1. The police are concerned about speeding on Wayman Boulevard. In four hours, they used radar to catch 40 speeders. How many speeders would you expect them to catch in five hours?
   4 hr 40
   5 hr x
   $200 = 4x$ $x = 50$ speeders

2. Mt. Cosmos is a volcano in a small island in the Pacific. It is an active volcano, and it has been erupting about 10 times every five days. How many times would you expect it to erupt in eight days?
   5 days 10 times
   8 days x times
   $5x = 80$ $x = 16$ eruptions

Name ______________________ Date ______________________

Monitoring Progress
Geometric Construction and Angle Measurement

Part 3

Use algebra to find the angle measurements.

1. What is the measure of angle c?

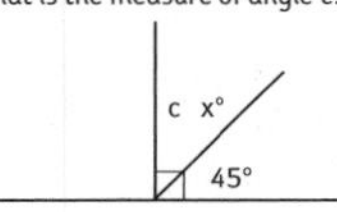

   $c + 45 = 90$
   $c + 45 - 45 = 90 - 45$
   $c = 45°$

2. What is the measure of angle h?

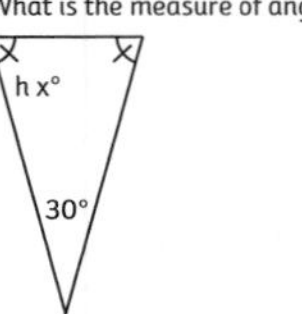

   $30 + h + h = 180$
   $30 + 2h = 180$
   $30 - 30 + 2h = 180 - 30$
   $2h = 150$
   $h = 75°$

3. What are the measures of a, b, and c?

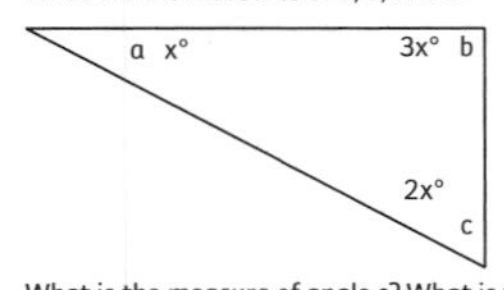

   $x + 3x + 2x = 180$
   $6x = 180$
   $6x \div 6 = 180 \div 6$
   $x = 30$
   $a = 30°$ $b = 90°$ $c = 60°$

4. What is the measure of angle s? What is the measure of angle t?

   x° s t 8x°

   $x + 8x = 180$
   $9x = 180$
   $9x \div 9 = 180 \div 9$
   $x = 20$
   $s = 20$ $t = 160$

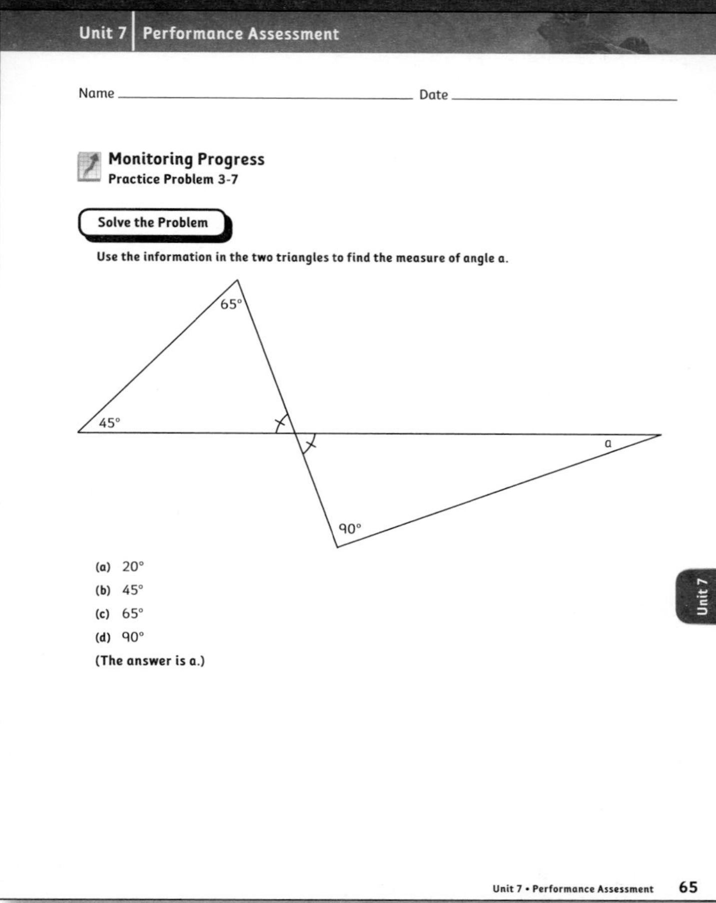

Unit 7 | Performance Assessment

Name ______________________ Date ______________________

Monitoring Progress
Practice Problem 3-7

Solve the Problem

Use the information in the two triangles to find the measure of angle a.

(a) 20°
(b) 45°
(c) 65°
(d) 90°

(The answer is a.)

Unit 7 • Performance Assessment 65

Unit 7 | Performance Assessment

Monitoring Progress
Problem 3-7-A

Solve the Problem

Use the information in the two triangles to find the measure of angle d.

45°
50°
d
35°

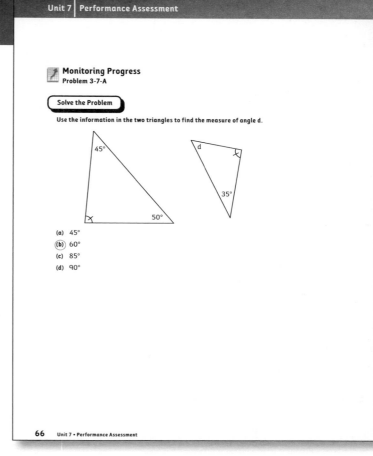

(a) 45°
(b) 60°
(c) 85°
(d) 90°

66 Unit 7 • Performance Assessment

Unit 7 | Performance Assessment

Name ______________________ Date ______________________

Monitoring Progress
Problem 3-7-B

Solve the Problem

Use the information in the two triangles to find the measure of angle m.

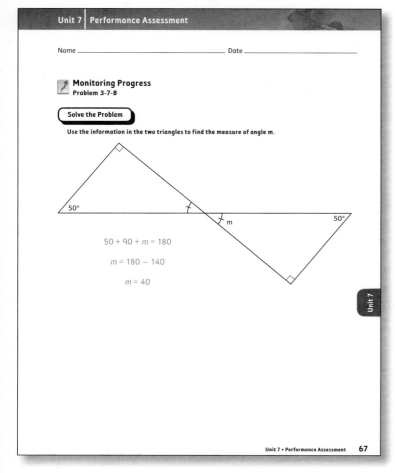

50°
m
50°

$50 + 90 + m = 180$

$m = 180 - 140$

$m = 40$

Unit 7 • Performance Assessment 67

Unit 8 Solving Different Kinds of Algebraic Equations

Problem Solving: Lines and Angles

WHAT DO YOU GET IF YOU CROSS TWO TRACKS WITH ONE TRACK?

Unit Opener: Background Information

With students, look carefully at the pictures showing transversals—lines that cross at least two other lines—in the Unit Opener of *Student Text*, pages 577–578. Then share some of this additional information.

- Airport runways often include transversals. Runways are built to align with the prevailing winds. If there were only one runway, planes would encounter dangerous crosswinds when the wind shifted from its prevailing direction. Airports often build additional runways that cross the main runways so pilots can safely land airplanes in winds coming from different directions.
- We've mentioned before that triangles are one of the strongest shapes. Look at the cross brace (the transversal) running diagonally on the barn door. Diagonal braces are often used in engineering to add strength to a rectangular structure. To demonstrate why diagonals are strong, take a drinking straw, and cut it into three pieces. Thread a piece of string through all three pieces, and tie the ends in a tight knot to create a triangle. Then repeat with four pieces of straw to create a rectangle. Hold each figure, and press down on the top. The triangle does not change its shape, but the rectangle collapses.

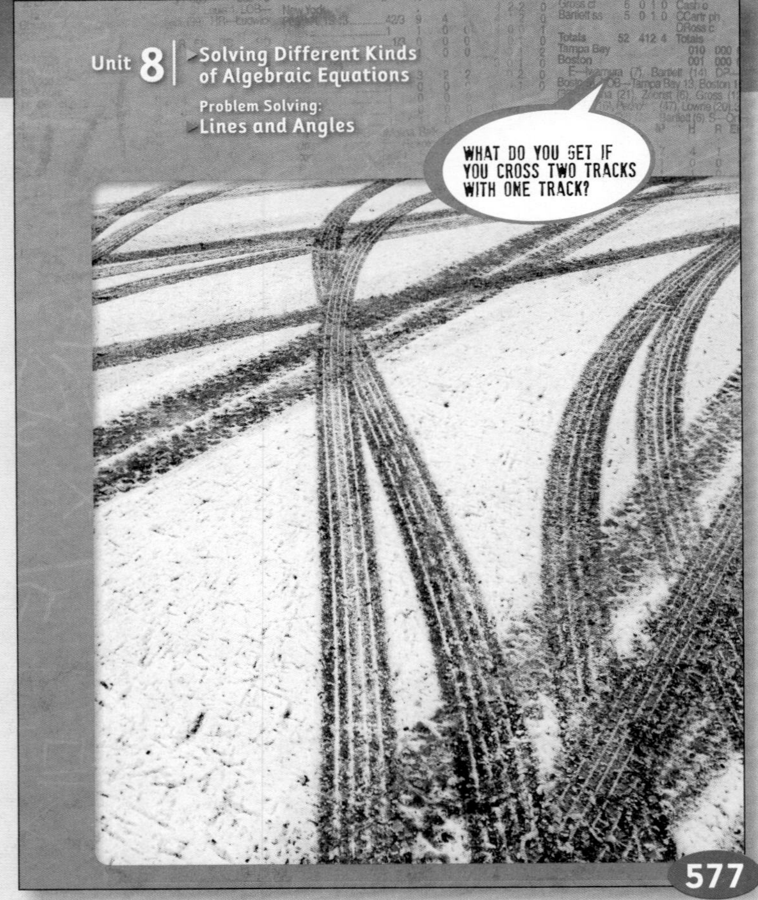

Unit 8 | Building Number Concepts: Solving Different Kinds of Algebraic Equations

Problem Solving: Lines and Angles

OBJECTIVES

Building Number Concepts	Problem Solving
• Use a variety of rules and properties to solve algebraic equations • Use algebraic equations to describe a given situation • Solve word problems involving algebraic equations that use models, and check answers for what is reasonable	• Use algebra to find the measures of interior angles in a polygon • Use angle rules to solve problems involving related angles (vertical, corresponding, right, and supplementary) • Complete simple proofs involving angle measures

Overview

Algebraic equations are filled with all kinds of little differences. This unit stresses that students should not become confused by small changes. Instead they should look for what might be new or different in an equation, then apply rules and properties that they already know.

The Problem Solving strand focuses on measurement of angles, which affords an excellent opportunity for students to apply the basic algebraic equations they used in other lessons. Simple word problems involving age, coins, and rate provide another context for translating and using these equations.

Unit Vocabulary
proof **transitive property** **transversal**

Building Number Concepts:

Solving Different Kinds of Algebraic Equations

Key Questions That Guide Student Understanding

- *What does it mean to be proficient when solving algebraic equations?*

Enduring Understandings for Solving Different Kinds of Algebraic Equations

Success in solving mathematical equations depends on a mastery of rules and properties. A command of rules and properties allows students to pay closer attention to new or different parts of an equation. Competence in algebra also requires a disposition where students look at the entire equation and search for parts of the equation that might be new or different.

For example, students might work a series of equations where the variable is on the right side. A new equation has variables on both sides. Students need a flexible understanding of how to apply rules and properties so that they can plan how to solve the equation and evaluate the solution.

Tools for Understanding Solving Different Kinds of Algebraic Equations

Using Strategies for Algebraic Equations

To prevent students from developing a fragmented approach for solving equations, we must remind students of a consistent, overarching framework. Even though the equation might have a small change, such as a fraction for a coefficient, what students know at this stage of algebra is sufficient for solving a range of equations. The Algebra Toolbox provides the central framework for processing how to solve equations.

Problem Solving:

Lines and Angles

Key Questions That Guide Student Understanding

- *How do we represent relationships in word problems using algebra?*
- *How do we make inferences in geometry?*

Enduring Understandings for Lines and Angles

Mathematical thinking often requires the ability to take an everyday context and represent it symbolically. With algebra, this means the use of variables. Simple word problems involving coins, ages, and rate enable students to abstract from a simple context and use variables to represent the relationship between two or more quantities. Although the word problems might be contrived, the skill in abstracting from these contexts is not. Abstraction is a key way for students to learn how to use variables, expressions, and equations.

Analyzing the properties of two-dimensional shapes is another context for applying algebra. Inferring what is unknown from certain information is characteristic of many dimensions of secondary mathematics.

Tools for Understanding Lines and Angles

Using Models
Algebraic word problems require a significant level of abstraction. Students can use drawings or diagrams as effective models to represent the relationship between different quantities. We encourage students to use models as the first step in translating word problems into algebraic equations.

Using Algebra to Measure Angles
We can determine the measure of angles based on the properties of quadrilaterals. In doing so, we make inferences based on what is known and let the variable stand for what is unknown. The result is an equation like $360 = 2x + 80 + 40$.

We can also take properties of intersecting lines, parallel lines, and transversals and use algebra to determine the measurement of an unknown angle.

Building Number Concepts:
Solving Different Kinds of Algebraic Equations

Lesson	Lesson Objectives—Students will:
1	• Use steps to evaluate algebraic equations.
2	• Solve equations with coefficients of 1 or −1.
3	• Solve multistep equations.
4	• Translate numbers into algebraic equations.
5	
6	• Solve equations with negative coefficients.
7	• Solve equations with variables on both sides of the equal sign.
8	• Use the distributive property to solve equations.
9	• Use different methods to solve algebra problems.
10	• Find the missing dimension of a two-dimensional shape when given partial information.
11	• Use different methods to solve algebra problems.
12	• Evaluate which method is most efficient, and solve equations with fractions as coefficients.
13	• Analyze fractions with a variable in the numerator to solve equations.
14	• Solve problems with negative numbers.
15	• Review Solving Different Kinds of Algebraic Equations concepts.
Unit Assessments	End-of-Unit Assessment Performance Assessment

Problem Solving:
Lines and Angles

Lesson Objectives—Students will:	Assessment
• Write equations for the measure of interior angles of regular polygons.	
• Find the measure of exterior angles of regular polygons.	
• Find the angle measurements of irregular polygons.	
• Find the measure of angles in quadrilaterals.	Quiz 1
• Use drawings to help solve word problems.	
• Use drawings to solve rate problems.	
• Use the properties of angles and intersecting lines to find the measure of missing angles.	
• Analyze relationships of angles created by intersecting lines.	
	Quiz 2
• Use inferences to justify proofs in geometry.	
• Find the measure of unknown angles by making inferences.	
• Use drawings to help solve word problems that involve a person's age.	
• Solve algebra problems involving coins.	
• Review Lines and Angles concepts.	Unit Review
	End-of-Unit Assessment Performance Assessment

Lesson 1 | Thinking About Algebraic Equations

Problem Solving:

Interior Angle Measurement of Regular Polygons

Lesson Planner

Skills Maintenance

Solving Equations

Building Number Concepts:

Thinking About Algebraic Equations

Students learn the importance of evaluating algebraic equations carefully before solving them. A slight difference in the problem can result in a much different answer. We introduce four steps to help students think about how to approach equations in a systematic way.

Objective

Students will use steps to evaluate algebraic equations.

Problem Solving:

Interior Angle Measurement of Regular Polygons

In this lesson, we review some important properties of regular polygons. Students learn that we can make inferences about measures of angles in regular polygons because they have predictable patterns that can be computed using algebraic equations.

Objective

Students will write equations for the measure of interior angles of regular polygons.

Homework

Students tell the difference in each pair of figures, tell the difference in each pair of equations, and use their knowledge of angles to answer questions about the measure of angles in regular polygons. In Distributed Practice, students practice order of operations, integer operations, and one-step equations.

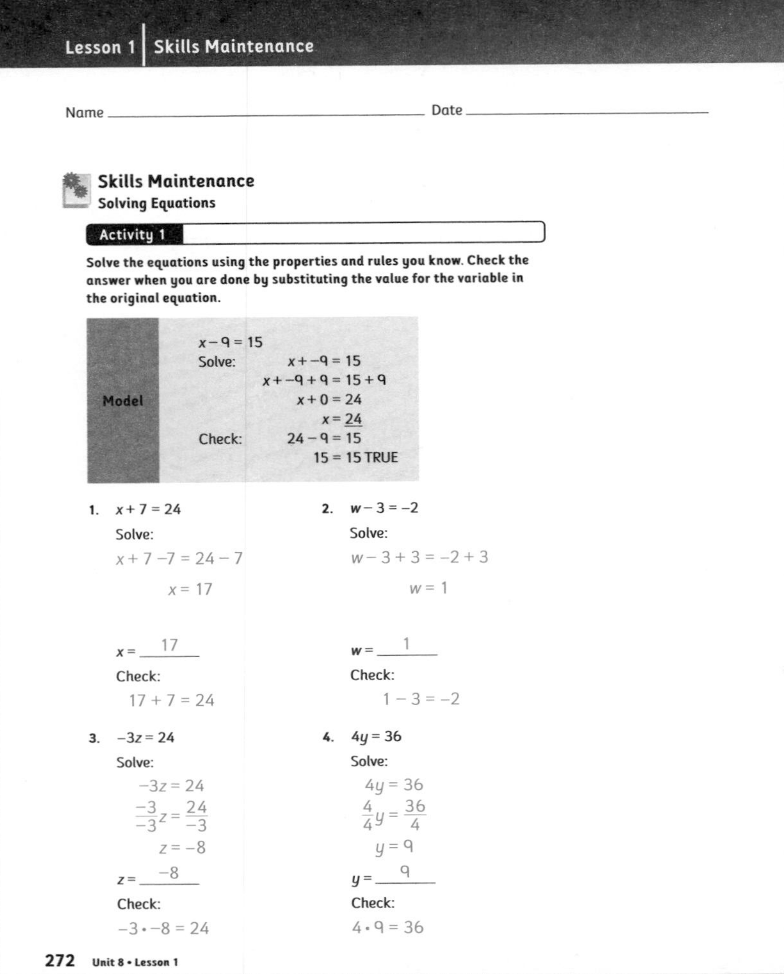

Lesson 1 | Skills Maintenance

Name ________________ Date ________________

Skills Maintenance

Solving Equations

Activity 1

Solve the equations using the properties and rules you know. Check the answer when you are done by substituting the value for the variable in the original equation.

Model	
	$x - 9 = 15$
	Solve: $x + -9 = 15$
	$x + -9 + 9 = 15 + 9$
	$x + 0 = 24$
	$x = \underline{24}$
	Check: $24 - 9 = 15$
	$15 = 15$ TRUE

1. $x + 7 = 24$
   Solve:
   $x + 7 - 7 = 24 - 7$
   $x = 17$
   $x =$ 17
   Check:
   $17 + 7 = 24$

2. $w - 3 = -2$
   Solve:
   $w - 3 + 3 = -2 + 3$
   $w = 1$
   $w =$ 1
   Check:
   $1 - 3 = -2$

3. $-3z = 24$
   Solve:
   $-3z = 24$
   $\frac{-3}{-3}z = \frac{24}{-3}$
   $z = -8$
   $z =$ −8
   Check:
   $-3 \cdot -8 = 24$

4. $4y = 36$
   Solve:
   $4y = 36$
   $\frac{4}{4}y = \frac{36}{4}$
   $y = 9$
   $y =$ 9
   Check:
   $4 \cdot 9 = 36$

272 Unit 8 • Lesson 1

Skills Maintenance

Solving Equations

(*Interactive Text*, page 272)

Activity 1

Students solve one-step equations and check their answers by substituting the value for the variable in the original equation.

Building Number Concepts:
▶ Thinking About Algebraic Equations

What are the four steps for solving algebraic equations?

(*Student Text*, pages 579–583)

Connect to Prior Knowledge

Begin by going over the Skills Maintenance activity. Ask for volunteers to come up to the board or overhead and demonstrate their strategies for solving these problems.

Link to Today's Concept

Tell students that we move beyond these one-step equations in this unit and solve more complex equations. Explain that the rules and properties are all the same, but we combine more of them within one problem.

Demonstrate

Engagement Strategy: Teacher Modeling

Demonstrate the four steps for solving algebraic equations in one of the following ways:

mBook: Use the *mBook Teacher Edition* for pages 579–581 of the *Student Text*. m

Overhead Projector: Reproduce pages 579–581 on a transparency.

- Show each step for solving equations as you discuss.

STEP 1

- Tell students that we have to look carefully at the entire equation.
- Explain that while our first instinct is to solve from left to right, it is important to adjust our thinking. m

Lesson 1 ▶Thinking About Algebraic Equations
Problem Solving:
▶Interior Angle Measurement of Regular Polygons

▶Thinking About Algebraic Equations

What are the four steps for solving algebraic equations?

As algebraic equations become more complex, it's easier to make mistakes. Sometimes we don't know where to start to solve the problem.

Here is a way to think about how we approach equations:

Steps for Solving Equations

STEP 1
Look at the entire equation.

STEP 2
Look for the **parts** of the equation that seem different.

STEP 3
Remember the goal: Solve the equation so that we have a **positive variable on one side**.

STEP 4
Use the rules or properties we need to reach our goal.

Use the following exercise as a reminder to think about the first two steps.

Unit 8 • Lesson 1 579

STEP 2

- Point out that there may be differences in the problems that cause us to adjust our strategy.
- Tell students to analyze all of the parts of the problem before beginning to solve it. m

STEP 3

- Explain that this step is especially important when we have a coefficient that is negative.
- Explain that we must remember that $-x$ has a coefficient of -1, and we need to get a coefficient of positive 1 to solve for the variable. m

STEP 4

- Point out that we use many different properties and rules in different combinations to solve algebraic equations. m

What are the four steps for solving algebraic equations? *(continued)*

Demonstrate

- Tell students that differences between equations may be very subtle and hard to see.
- Show **Figures 1** and **2** and ask students to describe the difference between the two figures. Explain that they will have to look carefully at both figures and go back and forth to find the difference. Give students an opportunity to find it.
- Make sure students see that the difference occurs in the first row, fourth column.
- Explain that unless we look carefully and think about what we are seeing, we might think that Figure 1 is exactly like Figure 2.
- Discuss how this relates to algebraic equations. Show **Equation 1** and **Equation 2**. Explain that the equations contain a slight difference that is hard to see at first glance.
- Have students identify the difference. Then point out that there is a −15 in Equation 1 and 15 in Equation 2.
- Explain to students that this is the reason we keep reminding them to work slowly and analyze the whole problem before they begin solving it.

Lesson 1

Let's look at Figure 1 and Figure 2.

- Are they the same?
- If there is a change from one figure to the next, where is it?

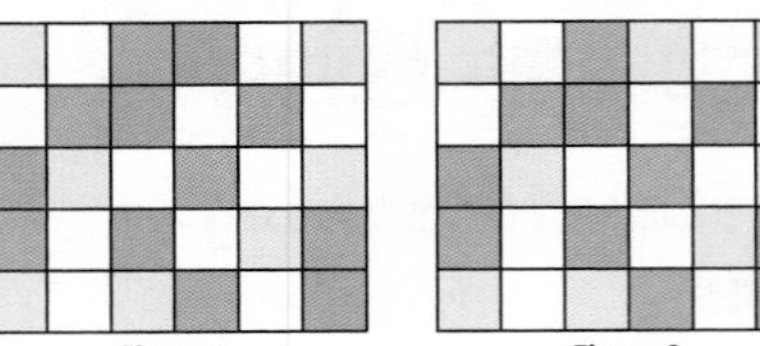

Figure 1 **Figure 2**

There is a difference, but it is a very small one. To find it, we look carefully at both figures and go back and forth. The change is in the top row.

Let's start on the top row of Figure 1 and count across four boxes. This box is blue. The color in the same box in Figure 2 is a little lighter. Unless we look carefully and think about what we are seeing, we'd think that Figure 1 was exactly like Figure 2.

So how does this apply to algebraic equations? Let's look at these equations. Are they the same, or is there a difference?

$3x = 25 + 3 + -15 + -1$	$3x = 25 + 3 + 15 + -1$
Equation 1	**Equation 2**

There is one difference between the two equations. There is a −15 in Equation 1 and 15 in Equation 2.

$3x = 25 + 3 + -15 + -1$	$3x = 25 + 3 + 15 + -1$
Equation 1	**Equation 2**

Demonstrate

- Discuss **Example 1**. Show the two equations and explain that we will solve each equation to show how much of a difference this little change makes. m
- Focus on Equation 1: $\mathbf{3x = 25 + 3 + -15 + -1}$. m
- Explain that when we add 25 + 3 we get 28, and when we add −15 and −1, we get −16. So now our equation is $\mathbf{3x = 28 + -16}$. m
- Show how we add the terms on the right side to get $\mathbf{3x = 12}$. m
- Point out that we multiply each side by $\frac{1}{3}$, which is the reciprocal of 3, to get $\mathbf{x = 4}$. m
- Tell students that next we focus on Equation 2: $\mathbf{3x = 25 + 3 + 15 + -1}$. m
- Explain that when we add 25 and 3, we get 28. In this equation we add 15 and −1. We get 14. So now our equation is $\mathbf{3x = 28 + 14}$. m
- Then show how we add the terms on the right side to get $\mathbf{3x = 42}$. m
- We multiply each side by the reciprocal $\frac{1}{3}$ to get $\mathbf{x = 14}$. m

  Make sure students see the difference in the two answers, emphasizing that the small change of a negative sign completely changes the answer.

Improve Your Skills

- Direct attention to the two equations on page 581 of the *Student Text*. Go over the student's error.
- Point out that there is a difference in the two equations. Make sure students see that in **Equation 2**, the coefficient x is negative, not positive as it is in **Equation 1**.

Example 1 shows how much of a difference this little change can make.

Example 1

Solve each equation.

Equation 1	**Equation 2**
$3x = 25 + 3 + -15 + -1$	$3x = 25 + 3 + 15 + -1$
$3x = 28 + -16$	$3x = 28 + 14$
$3x = 12$	$3x = 42$
$\mathbf{x = 4}$	$\mathbf{x = 14}$

The answers to the equations are entirely different.

Improve Your Skills

A student looked for the difference between two equations.

$2x = 14 + 10$	$-2x = 14 + 10$
Equation 1	**Equation 2**

He says that there is no difference. **ERROR**

There is a difference between the two equations. In Equation 2, the coefficient x is negative instead of positive. **CORRECT**

What are the four steps for solving algebraic equations? *(continued)*

Demonstrate

- Turn to **Example 2** on page 582 of the *Student Text* to look at how to apply the four steps to solve the equation. Go over each step as outlined.

STEP 1

- Remind students that we **look** at both sides of the equation.

STEP 2

- Point out **parts** of the equation that seem different. We have a negative number, –2, on the left side of the equation. This means we need to pay attention to this when we solve the problem.

STEP 3

- Remind students that the goal is to solve for **positive *x***.

STEP 4

- Point out that we can now **use the rules and properties** we know to solve the problem.
- Show how we first add like terms: 14 and 10.
- Remind students that we multiply by the reciprocal, $\frac{1}{2}$, to get *x* by itself.
- Remind students that we need to multiply by $\frac{1}{2}$ on both sides to keep the equation balanced.

Lesson 1

Let's see how we use the four steps we learned earlier to solve an equation.

Example 2

Use the four steps for solving equations. $-2x = 14 + 10$

STEP 1
Look at the entire equation.
Look at both sides of the equation. $-2x = 14 + 10$

STEP 2
Look for the **parts** of the equation that seem different.
We have a negative number: $-2x$. We need to pay attention to this when solving the problem. $-2x = 14 + 10$

STEP 3
Remember the goal: Solve the equation so that we have a **positive variable on one side**.
We need to solve for positive *x*. $-2x = 14 + 10$

STEP 4
Use the rules or properties we need to reach our goal.
We add like terms. → $-2x = 14 + 10$

$-2x = 24$

We multiply each side by $-\frac{1}{2}$ so that we will end up with *x* by itself. We multiply each side by $-\frac{1}{2}$ to keep the equation balanced. → $-\frac{1}{2} \cdot -2x = 24 \cdot -\frac{1}{2}$

$\frac{-2}{-2}x = \frac{24}{-2}$

582 Unit 8 • Lesson 1

Demonstrate

- Continue on page 583 of the *Student Text*.
- Point out that now we use our integer rules for division. We know that a negative number divided by a negative number is a positive number, so **−2 ÷ −2 = 1**.
- Remind students that a positive number divided by a negative number is a negative number, so **24 ÷ −2 = −12**.
- Remind students that 1 times a number is the same number, so $1 \cdot x = x$. The answer is $\mathbf{x = -12}$.

Check for Understanding

Engagement Strategy: Look About

Write $\mathbf{-4x = 12 + 10}$ on the board. Have students solve the equation using the four steps. Students should write their steps and solutions in large writing on a piece of paper or a dry erase board. When students finish their work, they should hold up their answer for everyone to see ($x = -\frac{11}{2}$, *or* $x = -5\frac{1}{2}$).

If students are not sure about the answer, prompt them to look about at the other students' solutions to help with their thinking. Review the answers after all students have held up their solutions.

Lesson 1

We use integer rules for division:

A negative number divided by a negative number is a positive number.	→ $\frac{-2}{-2} = 1$
A positive number divided by a negative number is a negative number.	→ $\frac{24}{-2} = -12$
One times a number is the same number.	→ $\mathbf{x = -12}$

We use the same properties and rules that we learned before to solve for *x*.

We did not have to solve the equation in an entirely different way. We just had to look at the whole equation first and find something that might be different.

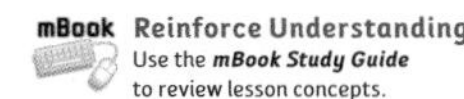

Apply Skills
Turn to ***Interactive Text***, page 273.

mBook Reinforce Understanding
Use the ***mBook Study Guide*** to review lesson concepts.

Apply Skills

(*Interactive Text*, page 273)

Have students turn to page 273 in the *Interactive Text*, and complete the activities.

Activity 1

Students identify what is different about the two equations and circle the difference. Tell students they do not need to solve these problems any further.

Activity 2

Students solve pairs of equations with slight differences. Tell them to compare the answers when they are finished.

Monitor students' work as they complete the activities.

Watch for:

- Can students identify the part of the pairs of equations where there is a difference?
- Can students solve the equations?
- Do students compare the answers and make sense of them? For instance, if we are adding a 2 in one of the equations and subtracting a 2 from the other equation, how do the two answers compare to one another? Does this make sense?

Reinforce Understanding

Remind students that they can review lesson concepts by accessing the online *mBook Study Guide*.

Lesson 1 | Apply Skills

Name ______ Date ______

Apply Skills

Thinking About Algebraic Equations

Activity 1

Look at the pairs of equations. There is a slight difference in each of them. Circle the part that is different.

Model	$3x + 2 - 3 + 5 = 10$ $3x + 2 - 3 - 5 = 10$

1. $x + 2 + -3 + 5 = 20$ / $x + 2 + 3 + 5 = 20$
2. $24 = 3x + 5 - -3 - x$ / $24 = 3x + 5 - -3 + x$
3. $3x - 9 + 2 = 35$ / $-3x - 9 + 2 = 35$
4. $-17 = -x - 3 - 5 - -2$ / $-17 = -x - 3 + 5 - -2$

Activity 2

There is a slight difference between the two equations in each pair. Solve each equation and be ready to compare and discuss the answers. Show your work.

1. $3x - x + 2x = 8$ and $-3x - x + 2x = 8$
   $2x + 2x = 8$ | $-4x + 2x = 8$
   $4x = 8$ | $-2x = 8$
   $x = 2$ | $x = -4$
2. $-5 + x - 7 = 24$ and $5 + x - 7 = 24$
   $-12 + x = 24$ | $-2 + x = 24$
   $x = 36$ | $x = 26$
3. $-17 + x + 17 + -1 = 2$ and $-17 + x + 17 + 1 = 2$
   $x + -1 = 2$ | $x + 1 = 2$
   $x = 3$ | $x = 1$

Unit 8

Unit 8 • Lesson 1 273

Problem Solving:
▶ Interior Angle Measurement of Regular Polygons

How do we write equations for the measure of interior angles of regular polygons?

(*Student Text*, pages 584–585)

Demonstrate

- Have students turn to page 584 of the *Student Text* to discuss the terms regular polygons and interior angles, or the angles inside the shape.
- Remind students that regular polygons have all the same side and angle measures.
- Explain that we can see an interesting pattern that happens with regular polygons in the table.
- Go over each shape in the table and note the pattern that we see in the number of sides, the total measure of the interior angles and the measure of each interior angle. For example, a regular triangle has three sides that are the same length. The total measure of its interior angles is 180 degrees. The three angles each measure 60 degrees.
- Note that in a regular rectangle, all of the sides are the same length and all of the angles are 90 degree angles. The total measure of the interior angles is 360 degrees. Point out that this type of rectangle is also a square.
- Go over the pentagon and hexagon in the same way.
- Tell students these observations about attributes of shapes help us form more complex rules and properties about geometry.

How do we write equations for the measure of interior angles of regular polygons?

Regular polygons are shapes where the measure of each angle is the same. There is an interesting pattern that happens with regular polygons.

Look at the table. Notice what is happening to the total measure of the interior angles as we add one more side to a polygon. Remember that interior angles are the angles inside the shape. When we talk about the total measure of these angles, we mean their sum when we add them all up.

Table of Measures for Regular Polygons

Shape	Number of Sides	Total Measure of the Interior Angles	Measure of Each Interior Angle
Triangle	3	180°	60°
Square	4	360°	90°
Pentagon	5	540°	108°
Hexagon	6	720°	120°

The total measure of the interior angles increases 180 degrees each time we add a side to a polygon. Why does this happen?

Let's look at the shapes below. We can make a new triangle each time we add a side to a polygon.

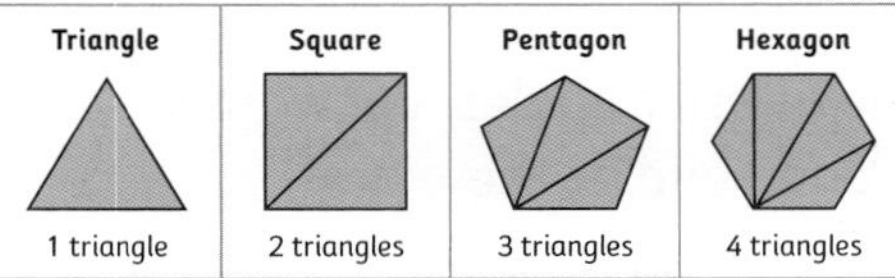

Each triangle has a sum of 180 degrees. That is how we get to the pattern.

- Be sure students understand the total angle measure and each of the interior angle measures for each shape. Then have students look at the shapes at the bottom of the page.
- Point out that each time we add a new side to a polygon we can make a new triangle. Each triangle has a sum of 180 degrees. This is how we discover the pattern.

How do we write equations for the measure of interior angles of regular polygons? *(continued)*

Demonstrate

- Turn to page 585 of the *Student Text* to go over **Example 1**. Demonstrate how to write algebraic equations for the relationship between the angle measure, the number of angles, and the total measure of the interior angles.
- Point out the first equation is written when we know one angle measure and the total measure of the interior angles. We want to find out how many angles there are.
- Explain that the variable x represents the number of angles in a square.
- Explain that the second equation is written when we know how many angles there are and the measure of each angle. In this case, we want to know the total measure of the interior angles.
- Explain that here the variable x represents the total measure of the interior angles.
- Explain that the third equation is a little different. In this equation we use the fact that every regular polygon may be decomposed into a series of triangles.
- Explain that since the total angle measure of a triangle is 180, we multiply by how many triangles there are in the shape to find the total angle measure of the polygon.
- Tell students that they can break a shape into two or more triangles. In this case, the variable x represents the total number of triangles in the square.

Lesson 1

We can write three different algebraic equations based on the angles of regular polygons. Example 1 shows the equations we write for a square.

Example 1

Write different algebraic equations for a square.

Equation based on the measure of one angle.

Let x = the number of angles in a square.

$90x = 360$

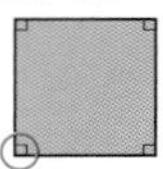

Equation based on the total measure of the interior angles.

Let x = the total measure of the interior angles.

$x = 4 \cdot 90$

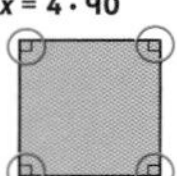

Equation based on the number of triangles in the shape.

Let x = the total number of triangles in the square.

$180x = 360$

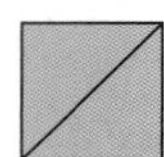

Problem-Solving Activity Turn to *Interactive Text*, page 274.

mBook Reinforce Understanding Use the *mBook Study Guide* to review lesson concepts.

Problem-Solving Activity
(*Interactive Text*, pages 274–275)

Have students turn to pages 274–275 in the *Interactive Text*, and complete the activity.

Students use the pattern in the Table of Measures for Regular Polygons on *Student Text*, page 584, to solve the problems. They write three equations for each of the shapes.

Monitor students' work as they complete the activity.

Watch for:

- Can students use their knowledge of algebra and geometry to write an equation that helps them find out the measure of each angle in the polygon?
- Can students use their knowledge of algebra and geometry to write an equation that helps them find out the total measure of the interior angles in a shape?

Reinforce Understanding
Remind students that they can review lesson concepts by accessing the online *mBook Study Guide*.

Lesson 1 | Problem-Solving Activity

Name ______ Date ______

Problem-Solving Activity
Interior Angle Measurement of Regular Polygons

Use the pattern in the *Table of Measures for Regular Polygons* in the *Student Text* to solve the problems. In some cases, you will have to draw triangles in the shape in order to find out how many there are. Then write three equations for each shape.

1. Hexagon

Three algebraic equations for a hexagon

$120 \cdot x = 720$

$x = 6 \cdot 120$

$180 \cdot x = 720$

2. Octagon

Three algebraic equations for an octagon

$135x = 1{,}080$

$x = 8 \cdot 135$

$180x = 1{,}080$

274 Unit 8 • Lesson 1

Lesson 1 | Problem-Solving Activity

Name ______ Date ______

3. Pentagon

Three algebraic equations for a pentagon

$108x = 540$

$x = 5 \cdot 108$

$180x = 540$

4. Nonagon

Three algebraic equations for a nonagon

$140x = 1{,}260$

$x = 9 \cdot 140$

$180x = 1{,}260$

Unit 8

mBook **Reinforce Understanding**
Use the mBook *Study Guide* to review lesson concepts.

Unit 8 • Lesson 1 275

Homework

Go over the instructions on page 586 of the *Student Text* for each part of the homework.

Activity 1

Students tell the difference in each pair of figures.

Activity 2

Students tell the difference in each pair of equations.

Activity 3

Students use their knowledge of angles to answer questions about the measure of angles in regular polygons.

Activity 4 • Distributed Practice

Students practice order of operations, integer operations, and one-step equations.

Lesson 1

Homework

Activity 1

Look at Figures 1 and 2. One is slightly different than the other. Tell the difference on your own sheet of paper.

1. 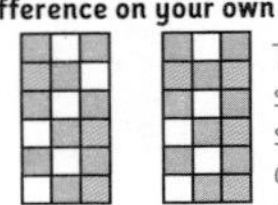
Figure 1 Figure 2
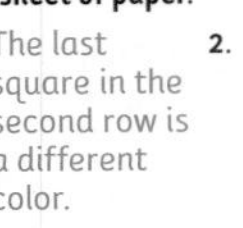
The last square in the second row is a different color.

2. 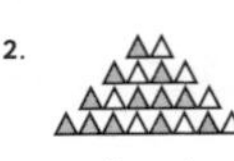 
Figure 1 Figure 2
The bottom right-hand triangle is a different color.

3. 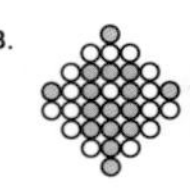
Figure 1 Figure 2
The middle circle in the third row from the bottom is a different color.

Activity 2

Look at each pair of equations labeled (a) and (b). One is slightly different than the other. Tell the difference.

1. (a) $2x + 3 = 7$ (b) $2x + -3 = 7$
Equation b has a negative 3.
2. (a) $-x + y = 10$ (b) $x + y = 10$
Equation a has a negative x.
3. (a) $y = -5 + x$ (b) $y = -5 + -x$
Equation b has a negative x.

Activity 3

Use the formula to answer the question about the shape.

1. $3m = 180$
What is the measure of one angle in a triangle?
60 degrees
2. $4 \cdot 90 = y$
What is the total measure of all the angles in a square?
360 degrees

Activity 4 • Distributed Practice

Solve.

1. $\frac{1}{x} = \frac{3}{6}$ 2
2. $-3 + -7 = y$ −10
3. $2x = x + 7$ 7
4. $\frac{3}{5} \cdot \frac{z}{3} = 1$ 5
5. $w = -2 - -8$ 6
6. $3^2 \cdot 8 + 5 = w$ 77

586 Unit 8 • Lesson 1

Lesson 2 ▶Invisible Coefficients

Problem Solving:

▶Exterior Angle Measurement of Regular Polygons

Lesson Planner

Skills Maintenance

Multiplying Integers

Building Number Concepts:

▶ Invisible Coefficients

Coefficients of 1 and −1 can be difficult for students to see in an equation. Students need to be aware of these invisible coefficients and learn how to solve equations involving them. We pay close attention to equations involving these types of coefficients and use the four steps for solving equations that we introduced in the last lesson.

Objective

Students will solve equations with coefficients of 1 or −1.

Problem Solving:

▶ Exterior Angle Measurement of Regular Polygons

In the last lesson, we looked at the angle patterns for regular polygons, focusing on the interior angle measurements. In this lesson, we demonstrate that if the sides of a polygon are extended, exterior angles are created. We discuss the properties and rules about angles and how they apply to exterior angles as well. Exterior angles give us even more information about polygons that we can use when we analyze situations involving them.

Objective

Students will find the measure of exterior angles of regular polygons.

Homework

Students tell the coefficient in each equation, solve equations, and answer questions about interior and exterior angles. In Distributed Practice, students practice order of operations, integer operations and one-step equations.

Lesson 2 | Skills Maintenance

Name ______________ Date ______________

Skills Maintenance
Multiplying Integers

Activity 1

Complete the equations. Remember the PASS rules.

1. $-1 \cdot 3 = \underline{-3}$
2. $4 \cdot \underline{-1} = -4$
3. $-7 = \underline{7} \cdot -1$
4. $-2 \cdot -1 = \underline{2}$
5. $-1 \cdot \underline{8} = -8$
6. $-12 = \underline{-1} \cdot 12$

276 Unit 8 • Lesson 2

Skills Maintenance

Multiplying Integers

(*Interactive Text*, page 276)

Activity 1

Students solve multiplication problems involving −1.

Building Number Concepts:
▶ Invisible Coefficients

What is difficult to see in an algebraic equation?

(*Student Text*, pages 587–589)

Connect to Prior Knowledge

Begin by writing **−4 • 4** and **−4 • −4** on the board. Tell students that little changes like the negative sign in the second expression are the kinds of things that we sometimes miss. Looking for little differences, and then using the right rules or properties, is essential to success in algebra.

Link to Today's Concept

Tell students that today we look at details that are sometimes difficult to see in algebraic equations.

Demonstrate

Engagement Strategy: Teacher Modeling

Demonstrate how to deal with invisible coefficients in one of the following ways:

mBook: Use the *mBook Teacher Edition* for *Student Text*, page 587. m

Overhead Projector: Display Transparency 6 and the equations on a transparency, and modify as discussed.

Board: Copy the number lines and equations onto the board, and modify as discussed.

- Explain that when we look at a negative number, it is easy to think of it as a number on the number line. Show **−6** on the number line. m
- Show the equation **−6 = −1 • 6**. Explain that a negative number is the product of −1 times a positive number. m

Lesson 2 ▶Invisible Coefficients
Problem Solving:
▶Exterior Angle Measurement of Regular Polygons

▶Invisible Coefficients

What is difficult to see in an algebraic equation?

Let's think about negative numbers. When we look at a number like −6, it is easy to think of it as any other number on the number line.

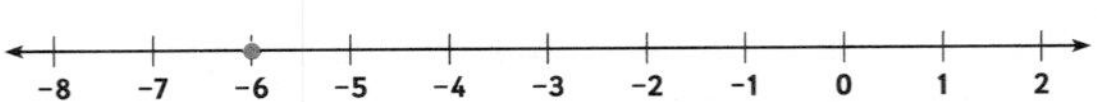

Now that we know about rules for operations on integers, there is another way to think about negative numbers: They are the product of −1 times a positive number.

Think of −1 as an invisible coefficient.

$-6 = -1 \cdot 6$

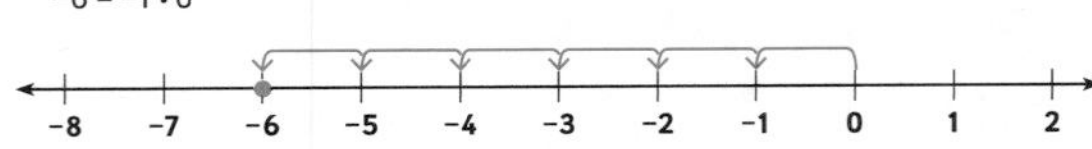

$-10 = -1 \cdot 10$

$-540 = -1 \cdot 540$

$-77 = -1 \cdot 77$

Unit 8 • Lesson 587

- Explain to students that like the problems they solved in the Skills Maintenance activity, this problem involves multiplication with −1. Tell students that the impact of multiplying by −1 is the opposite. Display the arrows on the number line to show the multiplication of −1 and 6. m
- Have students look at each of the problems at the bottom of the page. Point out that in each case, the negative number is the product of −1 and a positive number. m

Demonstrate

- Next review the steps for solving algebraic equations on page 588 of the *Student Text*.

STEP 1

- Remind students to first **look** at the entire equation.

STEP 2

- Remind students of the importance of looking for **parts** of the equation that seem different.

STEP 3

- Point out that we need a **positive variable on one side**. This is the step that is most important in today's lesson.

STEP 4

- Tell students that in the last step we **use our rules and properties** to reach the goal.
- Show the two equations $\boldsymbol{n} = \mathbf{80}$ and $\boldsymbol{-n} = \mathbf{80}$. Explain to students that the first equation, $n = 80$, is already solved. The coefficient for the variable n is 1. This is one of our invisible or, more formally, implied coefficients.
- Remind students of the identity rule for multiplication: anything times 1 is itself. We know the value for the positive variable n is 80.
- Explain that the second equation, $-n = 80$, is not solved because there is a negative sign in front of the variable. Remind students that the goal is to have a positive variable on one side of the equation.

Lesson 2

This kind of understanding is important when it comes to certain kinds of algebraic equations. Let's review the four steps for solving equations.

Steps for Solving an Equation

STEP 1
Look at the entire equation.

STEP 2
Look for the **parts** of the equation that seem different.

STEP 3
Remember the goal: Solve the equation so that we have a **positive variable on one side**.

STEP 4
Use the rules or properties we need to reach our goal.

Let's look at the following equations. There is one difference between them.

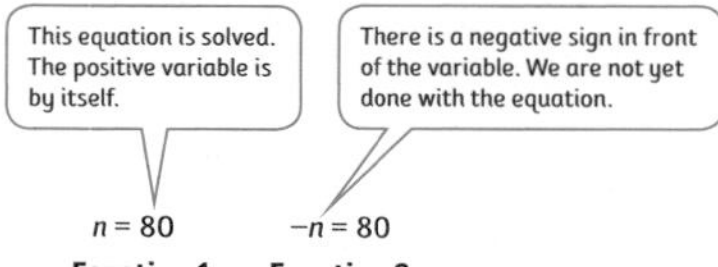

This equation is solved. The positive variable is by itself.
There is a negative sign in front of the variable. We are not yet done with the equation.

$n = 80$ — **Equation 1**

$-n = 80$ — **Equation 2**

Example 1 shows what rules we use to make the variable positive and solve the equation.

588 Unit 8 • Lesson 2

What is difficult to see in an algebraic equation? *(continued)*

Demonstrate

- Move to **Example 1** on page 589 of the *Student Text* which shows students how to solve the second equation, $-n = 80$.
- Point out that the coefficient in this equation is −1. We can write the equation as $-1 \cdot n = 80$.
- Work through the equation to show how we get a positive coefficient of 1 in front of the variable. By multiplying each side by −1, we keep the equation balanced, and we eliminate the negative sign in front of the variable, or in other words, we find the opposite of −1 which is 1.
- Point out to students that we have now solved the problem. The answer is $n = -80$. We have found the value for a positive value of *n*.

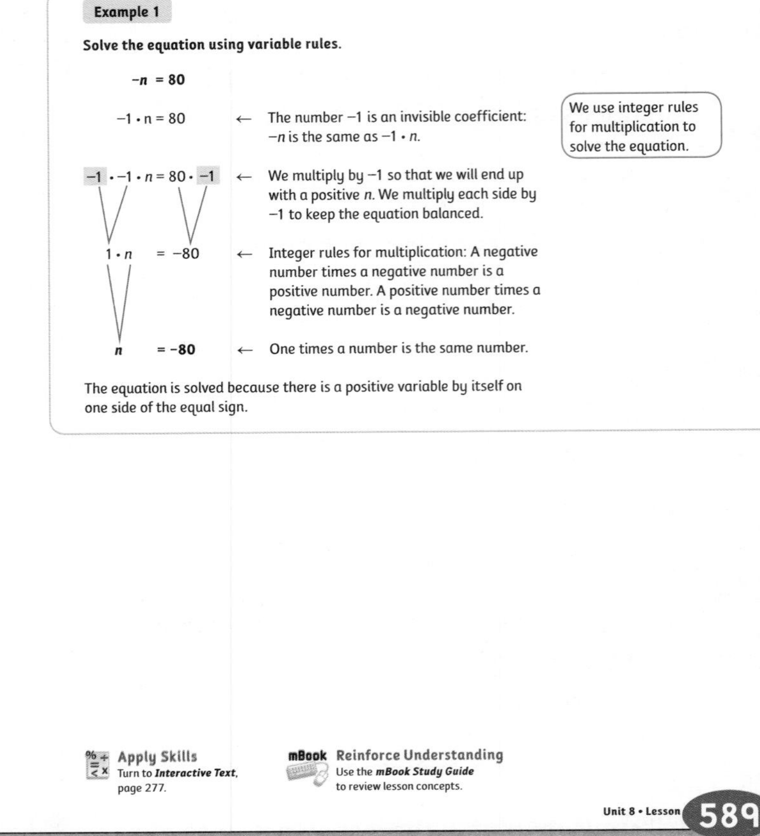

Lesson 2

Example 1

Solve the equation using variable rules.

$-n = 80$

$-1 \cdot n = 80$ ← The number −1 is an invisible coefficient: $-n$ is the same as $-1 \cdot n$.

$-1 \cdot -1 \cdot n = 80 \cdot -1$ ← We multiply by −1 so that we will end up with a positive *n*. We multiply each side by −1 to keep the equation balanced.

$1 \cdot n = -80$ ← Integer rules for multiplication: A negative number times a negative number is a positive number. A positive number times a negative number is a negative number.

$n = -80$ ← One times a number is the same number.

The equation is solved because there is a positive variable by itself on one side of the equal sign.

We use integer rules for multiplication to solve the equation.

Apply Skills Turn to *Interactive Text*, page 277.

mBook Reinforce Understanding Use the *mBook Study Guide* to review lesson concepts.

Unit 8 • Lesson 589

Check for Understanding

Engagement Strategy: Pair/Share

Write the equation $-1 \cdot v = 25$ on the board. Have students solve the equation using the four steps ($v = -25$). Then divide the class into pairs and have partners check each other's work and compare answers. Invite student volunteers to walk through their answers.

Apply Skills

(*Interactive Text*, page 277)

Have students turn to page 277 in the *Interactive Text*, and complete the activity.

Activity 1

Students solve problems involving invisible coefficients. Monitor students' work as they complete the activity.

Watch for:

- Do students realize that variables must have a positive coefficient of 1 in front of them for the problem to be solved?
- Can students go through the steps of multiplying by −1 in order to get a positive coefficient of 1?
- Do students remember the properties of equality and to multiply both sides of the equation by −1 to keep it balanced?

mBook **Reinforce Understanding**

Remind students that they can review lesson concepts by accessing the online *mBook Study Guide*.

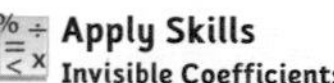

Lesson 2 | Apply Skills

Name ____________________ Date ____________________

Apply Skills
Invisible Coefficients

Activity 1

Solve the equations involving invisible coefficients. Show all of your work so you can analyze the steps later if you make a mistake.

1. $-a = -25$

   Show your work here:

   $-1 \cdot -a = -25 \cdot -1$

   $a = 25$

2. $b - 2b = 12$

   Show your work here:

   $-b = 12$

   $-1 \cdot -b = 12 \cdot -1$

   $b = -12$

3. $-27 = -3c + -6c$

   Show your work here:

   $-27 = -9c$

   $\frac{-27}{-9} = \frac{-9}{-9}c$

   $3 = c$

4. $-d = 5 + -5$

   Show your work here:

   $-d = 0$

   $-1 \cdot -d = 0 \cdot -1$

   $d = 0$

5. $e + 2e + -4e = -5$

   Show your work here:

   $3e + -4e = -5$

   $-e = -5$

   $-1 \cdot -e = -5 \cdot -1$

   $e = 5$

Unit 8

Unit 8 • Lesson 2 277

Problem Solving:
▶ Exterior Angle Measurement of Regular Polygons

How do we find the measures of exterior angles?

(*Student Text*, pages 590–592)

Connect to Prior Knowledge

Review the concept of exterior angles. Remind students that in the last lesson, we looked at the measure of the interior angles of regular polygons.

Link to Today's Concept

In today's lesson, we learn that if we extend the line segments that make up the sides of a polygon, we see how they form angles on the outside of the shape. We call these angles exterior angles.

Demonstrate

- Have students look at the three shapes that demonstrate the concept of exterior angles on page 590 of the *Student Text*.
- Point out that for each shape, the variable for each angle is the same. Explain that this means the measure of the angles is the same.
- Explain that the interior angle and exterior angle are adjacent angles that add up to 180 degrees, otherwise known as supplementary angles.
- Point out to students that even though we have not been given any of the angles in the pictures, we can figure them out from what we know about properties of angles and polygons.

How do we find the measures of exterior angles?

In the last lesson, we looked at the interior angles of regular polygons. These are the angles inside the shape. A polygon also has exterior angles, as we see in the following illustration. These angles are on the outside of the shape.

Each exterior angle in the illustration is labeled with a variable.

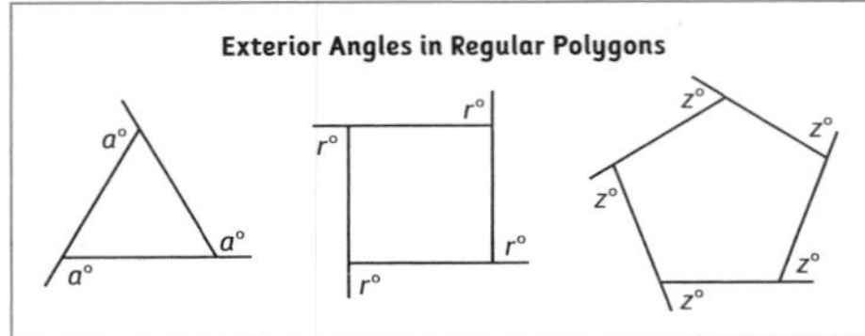

In each polygon, the variable for each angle is the same. That means each angle has the same measure.

How do we figure out the measure of the exterior angles for each polygon? We need to remember what we know about angles and straight lines to answer this question.

Let's look closely at just one part of the triangle. Example 1 takes a close-up look at the lower right-hand corner of the triangle. We have labeled the angles:

Angle s is the interior angle.
Angle t is the exterior angle.

We can tell a lot about these angles by remembering what we learned about the properties of angles and lines.

- Read the material at the bottom of the page to discuss the triangle before moving to the example.

Demonstrate

- Turn to **Example 1** on page 591 of the *Student Text* to demonstrate the properties of a regular triangle.
- Explain that we know that all the angles of a regular triangle are the same. We also know that the sum of their angles is 180.
- Remind students that the interior angle of a regular triangle is **60** degrees. Because we know the interior angle, we can now find the value of the exterior angle.
- Point out that the interior angle and exterior angle must add up to **180** because together they form a straight line.
- Explain that we can write an equation: $\boldsymbol{n} + \mathbf{60} = \mathbf{180}$, where n is the measure of angle t.
- Walk through how to solve the equation by adding −60 to both sides of the equation to get $\boldsymbol{n} = \mathbf{120}$. All of the exterior angles of a regular triangle are 120, so t equals **120 degrees**.
- Explain that we can check the answer by adding the measure of $\angle s$, 60 degrees, and $\angle t$, 120 degrees, to make sure they add up to 180 degrees.

Example 1

Use what we know about the measure of angles in a regular triangle to find the measure of exterior $\angle t$.

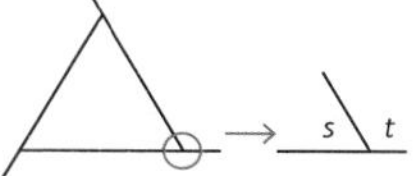

- We know that a straight line measures 180 degrees.
- We know from the last lesson that the interior angle of a regular triangle measures 60 degrees.

Let n = the measure of $\angle t$.

We write an algebraic equation this way:

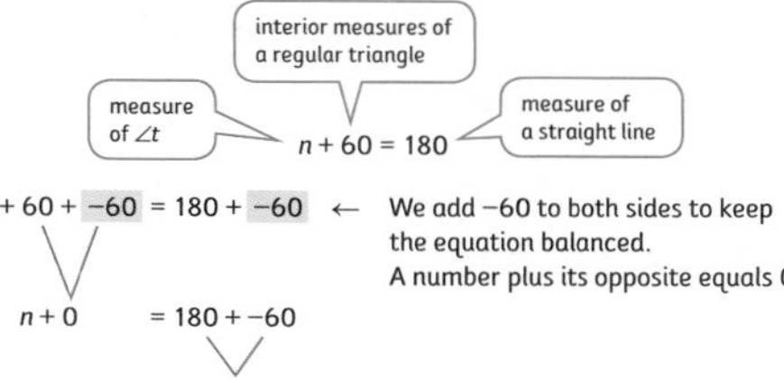

$n + 60 + -60 = 180 + -60$ ← We add −60 to both sides to keep the equation balanced. A number plus its opposite equals 0.

$n + 0 = 180 + -60$

$n = 120$

The measure of $\angle t$ = 120 degrees.

We can check our work by adding the measure of $\angle s$ and $\angle t$ to make sure they add up to 180 degrees.

$60 + 120 = 180$

That means the measure of all the exterior angles for a regular triangle is 120 degrees.

How do we find the measures of exterior angles? *(continued)*

Demonstrate

- Explain that we need to think about straight lines when we think about exterior angles.
- Look at **Example 2** on page 592 of the *Student Text*. In this example, we use the information we computed in Example 1 to help us find the sum of the exterior angles.
- Explain that to write an equation, we let ***z*** equal the sum of the measures of the exterior angles for a regular triangle.
- Show students how to write the equation: $\boldsymbol{z = 3 \cdot 120}$. The sum of the exterior angles is **360 degrees**.
- Explain to students that while this might not seem important at this point, all of this deduction and inference about angles and polygons will help us a lot in higher-level mathematics.

We need to think about straight lines when we think about exterior angles. We use this information to write an equation for the sum of the exterior angle measurements.

Example 2

Write an equation to find the sum of the measures of the exterior angles for a regular triangle.

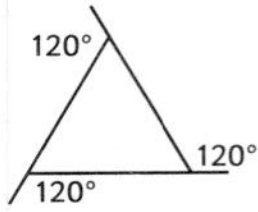

Let z = the sum of the measures of the exterior angles for a regular triangle. We write the equation this way:

$$z = 3 \cdot 120$$
$$z = 360$$

The sum of the measures of the exterior angles is 360 degrees.

We will explore other shapes to show that the sum of the exterior angles is always 360°.

Problem-Solving Activity Turn to ***Interactive Text***, page 278.

mBook Reinforce Understanding Use the ***mBook Study Guide*** to review lesson concepts.

Problem-Solving Activity
(*Interactive Text*, pages 278–279)

Have students turn to pages 278–279 in the *Interactive Text*, and complete the activity.

Students use their knowledge of angles and polygons, as well as a table of information, to answer questions about the angles of polygons.

Monitor students' work as they complete the activity.

Watch for:

- Can students determine the measure of one exterior angle?
- Can students write two different equations that represent some relationship about the polygon?
- Do students use existing knowledge, the table of measures given to them, and good problem-solving skills to complete this activity?

Have students share the equations they have written for this activity. There are different possible correct answers for these problems so it is important to demonstrate the variety of equations that the class came up with.

mBook **Reinforce Understanding**

Remind students that they can review lesson concepts by accessing the online *mBook Study Guide*.

Name ______________________ Date ______________

Problem-Solving Activity

Exterior Angle Measurement of Regular Polygons

In the *Table of Measures for Regular Polygons* you will find the measure of interior angles for different regular polygons. Use this information to solve the problems. Find the sum of the measure of exterior angles for different polygons. You will also write two equations:

1. An equation for the exterior angle.
2. An equation for the sum of the exterior angles.

Table of Measures for Regular Polygons			
Shape	Number of Sides	Total Measure of the Interior Angles	Measure of Each Angle
triangle	3	180°	60°
square	4	360°	90°
pentagon	5	540°	108°
hexagon	6	720°	120°
octagon	8	1,080°	135°

1. Hexagon

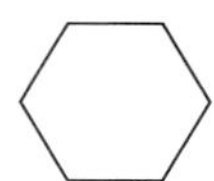

Write an equation for the exterior angle of a hexagon.

$n + 120 = 180$

$n =$ 60

Write an equation for the sum of the exterior angles of a hexagon.

$6 \cdot 60 = n$

$n =$ 360

2. Octagon

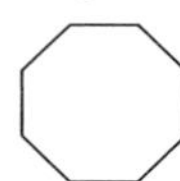

Write an equation for the exterior angle of an octagon.

$n + 135 = 180$

$n =$ 45

Write an equation for the sum of the exterior angles of an octagon.

$8 \cdot 45 = c$

$c =$ 360

Name ______________________ Date ______________

3. Pentagon

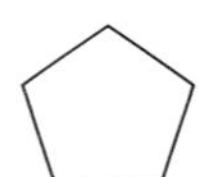

Write an equation for the exterior angle of a pentagon.

$n + 108 = 180$

$n =$ 72

Write an equation for the sum of the exterior angles of a pentagon.

$5 \cdot 72 = j$

$j =$ 360

4. Square

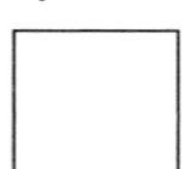

Write an equation for the exterior angle of a square.

$n + 90 = 180$

$n =$ 90

Write an equation for the sum of the exterior angles of a square.

$4 \cdot 90 = s$

$s =$ 360

mBook **Reinforce Understanding**
Use the **mBook *Study Guide*** to review lesson concepts.

Homework

Go over the instructions on page 593 of the *Student Text* for each part of the homework.

Activity 1

Students tell the coefficient in each equation.

Activity 2

Students solve equations.

Activity 3

Students answer questions about interior and exterior angles.

Activity 4 • Distributed Practice

Students practice order of operations, integer operations, and one-step equations.

Homework

Activity 1

Tell the coefficient in each question.

1. $-x = 7$ −1
2. $y = 7$ 1
3. $w = 12$ 4
4. $-12 = z$ 1
5. $3 + -m = 14$ −1
6. $y = 17$ 1

Activity 2

Solve the equations.

1. $2c + 12 = c$ −12
2. $-a = -10$ 10
3. $-b = 4$ −4

Activity 3

Answer the questions about interior and exterior angles.

1. The measure of one interior angle of a triangle is 60 degrees. What is the total measure of all the interior angles? 180 degrees
2. The measure of one interior angle of a pentagon is 108 degrees. What is the measure of one exterior angle? 72 degrees
3. The total measure of the interior angles of a square is 360 degrees. What is the measure of one interior angle, and what is the measure of one exterior angle?
Both are 90 degrees.

Activity 4 • Distributed Practice

Solve.

1. $4 - 2 \cdot 3 = w$ −2
2. $2z + 7 = 21$ 7
3. $4a = -12$ −3
4. $5d = -30$ −6
5. $\frac{2}{b} = \frac{6}{15}$ 5
6. $-4 \cdot -\frac{1}{4} = c$ 1

Lesson 3 ▶ Multistep Equations

Problem Solving: ▶ Angle Measurements of Irregular Polygons

Lesson Planner

Skills Maintenance

Evaluating Expressions

Building Number Concepts: ▶ Multistep Equations

Students build upon their understanding of one-step equations to solve multistep equations. Once again, we refer to the four steps to solve algebraic equations, which helps students to approach increasingly complex equations.

Objective

Students will solve multistep equations.

Problem Solving: ▶ Angle Measurements of Irregular Polygons

Students review what they know about exterior angles. They learn that not all shapes are regular polygons. Often in real-world situations, shapes are irregular. In this lesson, we look at how to find important information about irregular shapes and how to use multistep equations to find angle measurements.

Objective

Students will find the angle measurements of irregular polygons.

Homework

Students tell which step is first for each problem, solve equations, and use properties and rules to find the missing angles. In Distributed Practice, students practice order of operations, integer operations, and one-step equations.

Lesson 3 | Skills Maintenance

Name ______________________ Date ______________

Skills Maintenance
Evaluating Expressions

Activity 1

Evaluate the expressions. Select the correct answer.

1. $3 + -2 \cdot 5$
   (a) −7 (circled)
   (b) 7
   (c) 6
2. $-1 \cdot 4 + 7$
   (a) −11
   (b) 3 (circled)
   (c) 11
3. $-7 - 42 \div 7$
   (a) 7
   (b) −13 (circled)
   (c) −7
4. $4 - 8 + 4$
   (a) −8
   (b) 16
   (c) 0 (circled)

280 Unit 8 • Lesson 3

Skills Maintenance

Evaluating Expressions

(*Interactive Text*, page 280)

Activity 1

Students evaluate expressions and choose the correct answer.

Building Number Concepts: ▶ Multistep Equations

Where do we start with multistep equations?

(*Student Text*, pages 594–596)

Connect to Prior Knowledge

Begin by going over the answers to the Skills Maintenance section with students. Write the answers to the expressions on the board or overhead as equations.

$3 + -2 \cdot 5 = -7$ $-1 \cdot 4 + 7 = 3$

$-7 - 42 \div 7 = -13$ $4 - 8 + 4 = 0$

Have students replace both 4s in Problem 4 with the variable y: $y - 8 + y = 0$. Explain to students that we now have a different type of problem to solve. It involves multiple steps.

Link to Today's Concept

Tell students that we practice these kinds of multistep equations in today's lesson.

Demonstrate

Engagement Strategy: Teacher Modeling

Demonstrate the two ways students learned to solve equations so far in one of the following ways:

mBook: Use the *mBook Teacher Edition* for *Student Text*, pages 594–595. m

Overhead Projector: Reproduce the equations and steps on a transparency, and modify as discussed.

Board: Copy the equations and steps on the board, and modify as discussed.

- Demonstrate examples of the multiplicative, or reciprocal property, and the additive inverse property. m

Lesson 3 ▶Multistep Equations
Problem Solving:
▶Angle Measurements of Irregular Polygons

▶Multistep Equations

Where do we start with multistep equations?

Until now, we have worked with relatively simple equations. Solving the equations usually means that we used a reciprocal to change the coefficient so that it equals 1. Other times, we added an opposite so that a single variable was by itself.

Example 1 shows how we solve each of these types of equations.

Example 1

Solve a simple equation.

Use a Reciprocal

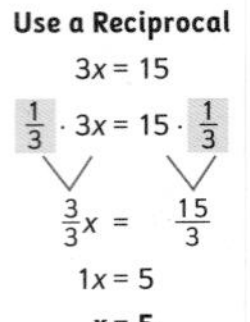

$3x = 15$

$\frac{1}{3} \cdot 3x = 15 \cdot \frac{1}{3}$

$\frac{3}{3}x = \frac{15}{3}$

$1x = 5$

$\mathbf{x = 5}$

Add the Opposite

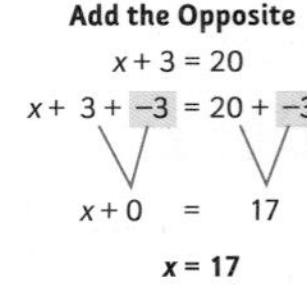

$x + 3 = 20$

$x + 3 + -3 = 20 + -3$

$x + 0 = 17$

$\mathbf{x = 17}$

Now let's look at equations where we have to change the coefficient and add the opposite. This is the first of many kinds of complex, multistep equations we will work on. Solving these kinds of equations takes a little more time.

We will use the four steps we learned for solving equations.

594 Unit 8 • Lesson 3

- Go through the process for solving the equation $\mathbf{3x = 15}$ using the reciprocal, as shown in **Example 1**. m
- Remind students that we want to get a positive x by itself on one side, so we multiply by the reciprocal, $\frac{1}{3}$, on both sides of the equation. m
- Walk through the simplification to get $\mathbf{x = 5}$. m
- Then review how to solve equations by adding the opposite. Use the equation $\mathbf{x + 3 = 20}$. m
- Remind students that the goal is still to get x alone on one side, so we add the opposite of 3, −3, on both sides to keep the equation balanced. m
- Walk through the simplification to get $\mathbf{x = 17}$. m

Demonstrate

- Tell students that we will combine these two types of problems. Review the steps for solving algebraic equations. m

---

STEP 1

- Remind students to **look** at the entire equation. m

STEP 2

- Remind students to look for the **parts** of the equation that seem different. m

---

STEP 3

- Make sure students remember the goal is to have a **positive variable on one side**. m

---

STEP 4

- Remind students to **use the rules or properties** we need to reach the goal. m

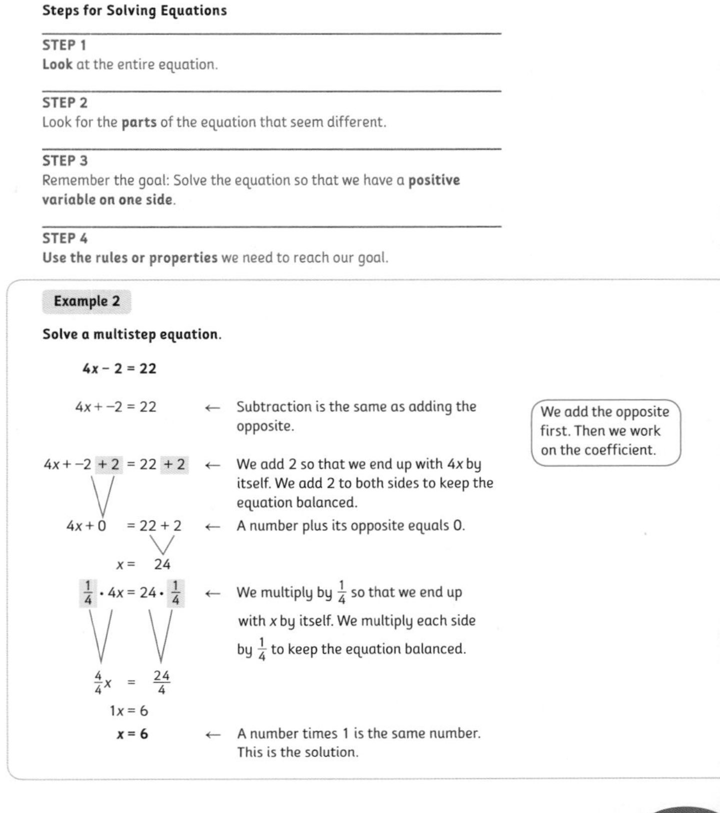
Lesson 3

Steps for Solving Equations

STEP 1
Look at the entire equation.

STEP 2
Look for the **parts** of the equation that seem different.

STEP 3
Remember the goal: Solve the equation so that we have a **positive variable on one side**.

STEP 4
Use the rules or properties we need to reach our goal.

Example 2

Solve a multistep equation.

$\mathbf{4x - 2 = 22}$

$4x + -2 = 22$ ← Subtraction is the same as adding the opposite.

$4x + -2 + 2 = 22 + 2$ ← We add 2 so that we end up with $4x$ by itself. We add 2 to both sides to keep the equation balanced.

$4x + 0 = 22 + 2$ ← A number plus its opposite equals 0.

$x = 24$

$\frac{1}{4} \cdot 4x = 24 \cdot \frac{1}{4}$ ← We multiply by $\frac{1}{4}$ so that we end up with x by itself. We multiply each side by $\frac{1}{4}$ to keep the equation balanced.

$\frac{4}{4}x = \frac{24}{4}$

$1x = 6$

$\mathbf{x = 6}$ ← A number times 1 is the same number. This is the solution.

We add the opposite first. Then we work on the coefficient.

Unit 8 • Lesson 595

- Show students **Example 2**, which is a multistep problem. Be sure to emphasize the two parts of the problem as you work through the steps together.
- Display the equation $\mathbf{4x - 2 = 22}$, and remind students that subtraction is the same as adding the opposite. So we can rewrite the expression as $\mathbf{4x + -2 = 22}$. m
- Point out that to get $4x$ alone on one side, we add the opposite of –2, which is 2, to both sides of the equation. m
- Show students how to simplify the equation to get $\mathbf{4x = 24}$. m
- Explain that now we want to get x alone on one side, so we multiply by the reciprocal of the coefficient 4, $\frac{1}{4}$, on both sides of the equation. m
- Walk through the remainder of the process to simplify the equation to get $\mathbf{x = 6}$. m

Where do we start with multistep equations? *(continued)*

Demonstrate

- Next go over **Example 3** on page 596 of the *Student Text*. This problem is the same as the problem in Example 2, but it is addition rather than subtraction.
- As you walk through the example, point out how the steps are slightly different for this problem.
- Show students that in this case, we add −2 to end up with $4x$ by itself.
- Complete the addition. We get $\mathbf{4x = 20}$.
- Point out that as in Example 2, we multiply by the reciprocal, $\frac{1}{4}$, on both sides of the equation to isolate x.
- When we complete the multiplication and division, we get $\boldsymbol{x = 5}$.

Check for Understanding
Engagement Strategy: Think Tank

Write the equation $\mathbf{2x + 4 = 12}$ on the board. Distribute strips of paper and have students write their names on them. Then have students solve the equation ($x = 4$), reminding them to write out each step. When students have finished, collect the strips of paper in a container. Draw an answer to read aloud. If the answer is correct, congratulate the student and invite the student to explain the solution.

Reinforce Understanding

If students need further practice, use these equations:

$\mathbf{3x - 7 = 14}$ ($x = 7$)

$\mathbf{5x + 7 = 27}$ ($x = 4$)

Let's look at the equation in Example 3. We will use the equation from the previous example, but we will change the −2 to 2.

We use our Algebra Toolbox to solve the equation.

Example 3

Solve a multistep equation.

$\mathbf{4x + 2 = 22}$

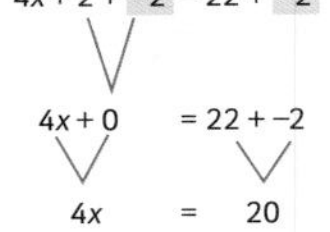

$4x + 2 + -2 = 22 + -2$ ← We add −2 so that we will end up with $4x$ by itself. We add −2 to both sides to keep the equation balanced.

$4x + 0 = 22 + -2$

$4x = 20$ ← A number plus its opposite equals 0.

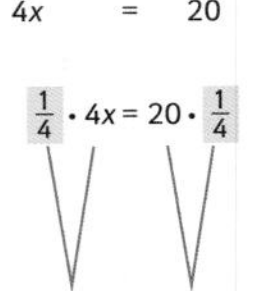

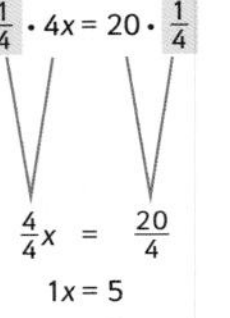

$\frac{1}{4} \cdot 4x = 20 \cdot \frac{1}{4}$ ← We multiply by $\frac{1}{4}$ so that we end up with x by itself. We multiply each side by $\frac{1}{4}$ to keep the equation balanced.

$\frac{4}{4}x = \frac{20}{4}$

$1x = 5$

$\boldsymbol{x = 5}$ ← A number times 1 is the same number. This is the solution.

Apply Skills
Turn to ***Interactive Text***, page 281.

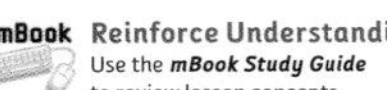

Reinforce Understanding
Use the ***mBook Study Guide*** to review lesson concepts.

Apply Skills
(*Interactive Text*, page 281)

Have students turn to page 281 in the *Interactive Text*, and complete the activity.

Activity 1

Students solve multistep equations. Students are to show all of the steps they use, then check their answers using substitutions. Monitor students' work as they complete the activity.

Watch for:

- Can students identify the additive inverse and solve that step of the problem?
- Can students identify the reciprocal and solve that step of the problem?
- Do students get the correct answer?
- Do students check their answers using substitution?

mBook **Reinforce Understanding**
Remind students that they can review lesson concepts by accessing the online *mBook Study Guide*.

Lesson 3 | Apply Skills

Name ____________ Date ____________

Apply Skills
Multistep Equations

Activity 1

Solve the equations. Show all of the steps involved. Check your work by substituting the value for the variable back into the original equation.

1. $3x + 9 = 27$
   Show your work here:
   $3x = 18$
   $x = 6$
   $x =$ 6
   Check your work here:
   $3(6) + 9 = 27$
   $27 = 27$

2. $4x - 12 = 24$
   Show your work here:
   $4x = 36$
   $x = 9$
   $x =$ 9
   Check your work here:
   $4(9) - 12 = 24$
   $36 - 12 = 24$
   $24 = 24$

3. $-3 + -4 + 6x = 35$
   Show your work here:
   $-7 + 6x = 35$
   $6x = 42$
   $x = 7$
   $x =$ 7
   Check your work here:
   $-3 + -4 + 6(7) = 35$
   $35 = 35$

4. $-2x - 3 + 5 = -10$
   $-2x + 2 = -10$
   $-2x = -12$
   $x = 6$
   $x =$ 6
   Check your work here:
   $-2(6) - 3 + 5 = -10$
   $-10 = -10$

Unit 8

Unit 8 • Lesson 3 281

Problem Solving:
▶ Angle Measurement of Irregular Polygons

What do we know about the measurement of exterior angles?

(*Student Text*, page 597)

Connect to Prior Knowledge

Begin by reminding students that when we found the measure of exterior angles in Lesson 2, we noticed that the exterior angles of the triangle added up to 360°.

Link to Today's Concept

In today's lesson we continue to study exterior angles in polygons.

Demonstrate

- Have students turn to page 597 of the *Student Text* to discuss exterior angles. Explain that the sum of the exterior angles of polygons is always 360 degrees.
- Have students look at the shapes, which demonstrate why the exterior angles of a regular polygon all add up to 360 degrees.
- Discuss with students that a circle is made of 360 degrees. We can draw a circle around the shape and show the different angles that add up to 360 degrees.

Lesson 3

▶Problem Solving: Angle Measurements of Irregular Polygons

What do we know about the measurement of exterior angles?

We learned an important idea about exterior angles in the last lesson. It doesn't matter what kind of polygon it is, the sum of the exterior angles is always 360 degrees.

The illustrations below show why this is true. Even if we shrink each shape, the sum of the exterior angles always adds up to 360 degrees.

Exterior Angles of Polygons

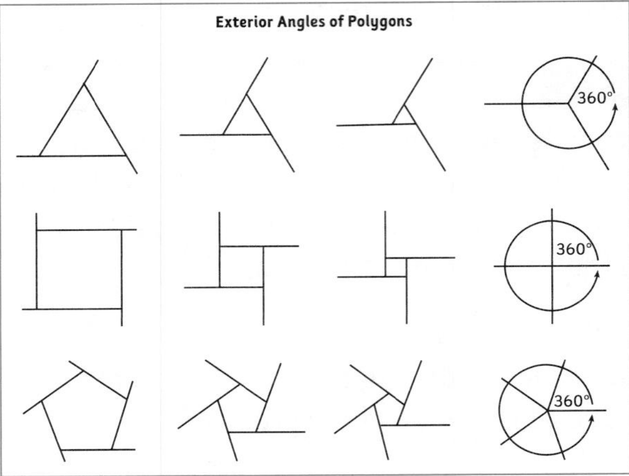

Unit 8 • Lesson 597

How do we use multistep equations to find angle measurements?

(*Student Text*, pages 598–599)

Demonstrate

- Turn to page 598 of the *Student Text*. Tell students that not all shapes are regular polygons—some are irregular polygons.
- Go over the table that shows Polygons and the Sums of the Measures of Interior and Exterior Angles.
- Explain to students that the information in the table should give them a good idea of how to analyze the shapes.
- Go over **Example 1**. In this example, we are given a triangle with the three angles: x, x, and $x + 30$. We know the sum of the interior angles is 180 degrees.
- Tell students that knowing these pieces of information gives us enough information to write and solve an algebraic equation. With this information, we can write the equation as $\boldsymbol{x + x + x + 30 = 180}$.
- Show students how we combine like terms to get $\boldsymbol{3x + 30 = 180}$.

How do we use multistep equations to find angle measurements?

The following table shows information about polygons.

Polygons and the Sums of the Measures of Interior and Exterior Angles			
Shape	Number of Sides	Sum of Interior Angles	Sum of Exterior Angles
Triangle	3	180°	360°
Quadrilateral	4	360°	360°
Pentagon	5	540°	360°
Hexagon	6	720°	360°
Octagon	8	1,080°	360°

We can use this information to solve angle problems using algebraic equations. In Example 1, we use the sum of the interior angles for a triangle to write an algebraic equation.

Example 1

Show the measure of each interior angle.

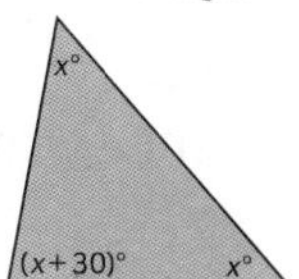

We know that the sum of the interior angles of a triangle is 180 degrees. That means we can set up the equation this way.

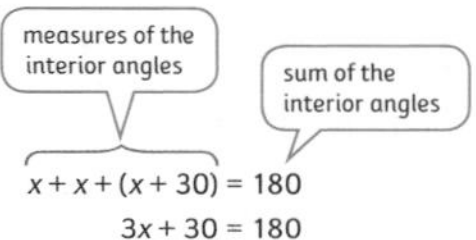

$$x + x + (x + 30) = 180$$
$$3x + 30 = 180$$

How do we use multistep equations to find angle measurements? *(continued)*

Demonstrate

- Continue going over Example 1 on page 599 of the *Student Text.*
- Remind students how to add the opposite to isolate 3*x*. In this case, we add –30 to both sides of the equation to get **3*x* = 150**.
- Point out that we multiply by $\frac{1}{3}$, which is the reciprocal of the coefficient, 3, to get *x* by itself.
- Show how we simplify to get ***x* = 50**.
- Explain that once we find the value of *x*, we can substitute the value in the triangle and get the measures of each of the interior angles. We see that the angles are 50, 80, and 50 degrees.
- Point out that we can check the answer by adding together the measure of three angles to make sure they add up to 180.

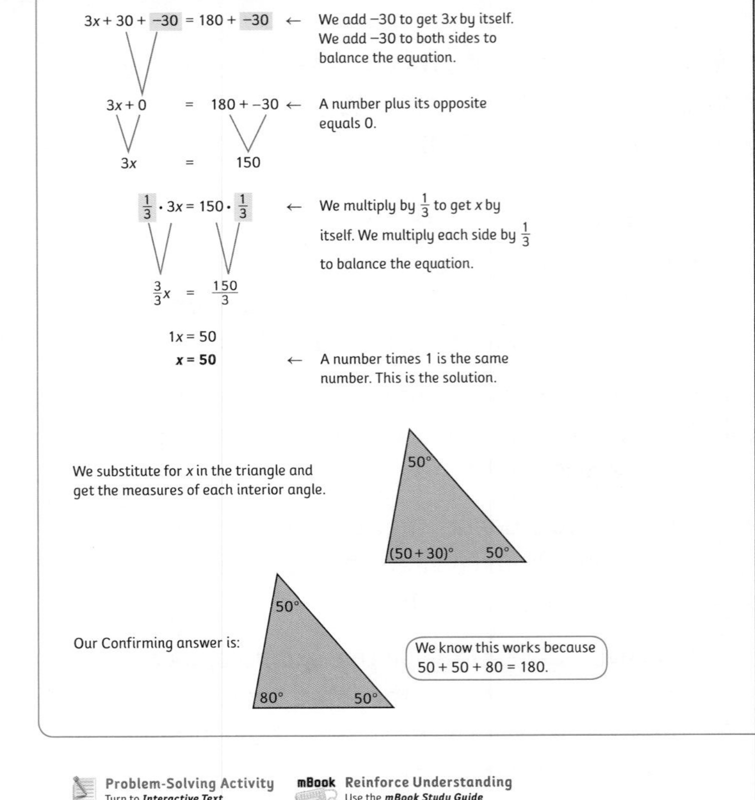

Lesson 3
3x + 30 + −30 = 180 + −30
We add −30 to get 3x by itself. We add −30 to both sides to balance the equation.
3x + 0 = 180 + −30
A number plus its opposite equals 0.
3x = 150
1/3 · 3x = 150 · 1/3
We multiply by 1/3 to get x by itself. We multiply each side by 1/3 to balance the equation.
3/3x = 150/3
1x = 50
x = 50
A number times 1 is the same number. This is the solution.
We substitute for x in the triangle and get the measures of each interior angle.
50°
(50 + 30)°
50°
Our Confirming answer is:
50°
80°
50°
We know this works because 50 + 50 + 80 = 180.

Problem-Solving Activity
Turn to *Interactive Text*, page 282.

mBook Reinforce Understanding
Use the *mBook Study Guide* to review lesson concepts.

Unit 8 • Lesson 599

Problem-Solving Activity
(*Interactive Text*, page 282)

Have students turn to page 282 in the *Interactive Text*, and complete the activity.

Students find the missing angles in polygons using properties and rules. They write algebraic expressions to solve each problem.

Monitor students' work as they complete the activity.

Watch for:

- Can students identify appropriate rules about interior angles and use them to solve the problem?
- Can students identify appropriate rules about interior angles and use them to solve the problem?
- Do students use the table as a reference?
- Can students write an equation that represents the problem?

Go over student answers after they have completed the activity. Help students find errors if they did not get the correct angle measures.

mBook Reinforce Understanding
Remind students that they can review lesson concepts by accessing the online *mBook Study Guide*.

Lesson 3 | Problem-Solving Activity

Name ______________ Date ______________

Problem-Solving Activity
Angle Measurement of Irregular Polygons

Use the table *Polygons and the Sums of the Measures of Interior and Exterior Angles* from the *Student Text* to solve the problems. Make sure you write an algebraic equation to solve each problem.

1.

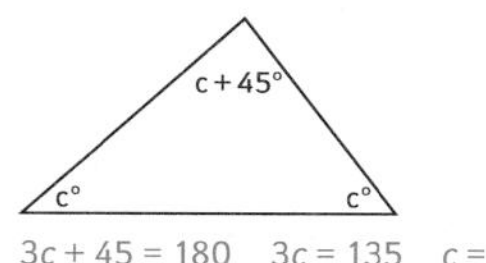

$3c + 45 = 180 \quad 3c = 135 \quad c = 45$

2.

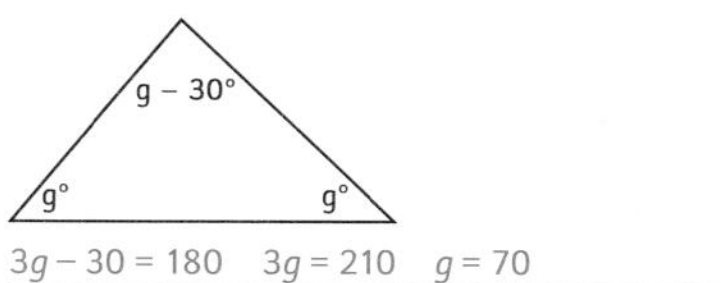

$3g - 30 = 180 \quad 3g = 210 \quad g = 70$

3.

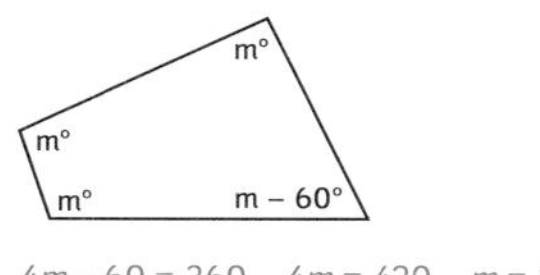

$4m - 60 = 360 \quad 4m = 420 \quad m = 105$

mBook Reinforce Understanding
Use the mBook *Study Guide* to review lesson concepts.

282 Unit 8 • Lesson 3

Homework

Go over the instructions on page 600 of the *Student Text* for each part of the homework.

Activity 1

Students tell which step is first for each problem.

Activity 2

Students solve algebraic equations with coefficients.

Activity 3

Students use properties and rules to find the missing angles in different shapes.

Activity 4 • Distributed Practice

Students practice order of operations, integer operations, and one-step equations to solve for the variable.

Lesson 3

Homework

Activity 1

In each problem, tell what step is first.

1. $3x + 12 = 24$ b
   (a) Multiply each side by $\frac{1}{3}$.
   (b) Add −12 to each side.
   (c) Multiply each side by 12.
2. $4x = 16$ c
   (a) Add −4 to each side.
   (b) Add −16 to each side.
   (c) Multiply each side by $\frac{1}{4}$.

Activity 2

Solve the equations.

1. $4z + 14 = 26$ 3
2. $w + -7 = -12$ −5
3. $-16 = -x + -4$ 12
4. $27 = 8y + 3$ 3
5. $8a + -3 = 5$ 1
6. $-3 + -b = 1$ −4

Activity 3

Find the measurements of the interior angles for each shape.

1. What is the measure of each angle?
   40, 40, and 100 degrees

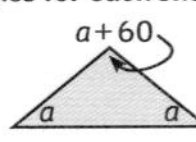

2. What is the measure of each angle?
   80, 80, 80, and 120 degrees

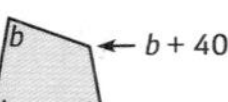

3. What is the measure of each angle?
   50, 60, and 70 degrees

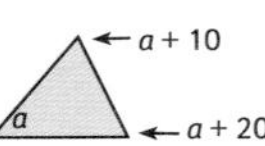

Activity 4 • Distributed Practice

Solve.

1. $\frac{x}{12} = \frac{2}{6}$ 4
2. $-4 = \frac{12}{y}$ −3
3. $9w = -81$ −9
4. $-54 + z = -60$ −6
5. $4^2 + 2 \cdot -3 = b$ 10
6. $5 + x = 0$ −5

600 Unit 8 • Lesson 3

Lesson 4 ▶Translating Numbers Into Equations

Lesson Planner

Skills Maintenance

Multistep Equations

Building Number Concepts:

▶ Translating Numbers Into Equations

Students now know how to translate numeric equations into algebraic equations. In this lesson, students learn that we can use one or more variables in an equation to represent a number pattern. When we know the relationship between two variables, we can state it using an equation with just one variable. Students also apply the use of variables to word problems.

Objective

Students will translate numbers into algebraic equations.

Homework

Students choose the equation that shows the general pattern shown by the numeric examples, translate the words to expressions using just one variable, and solve word problems by writing an equation. In Distributed Practice, students practice order of operations, integer operations, and one-step equations.

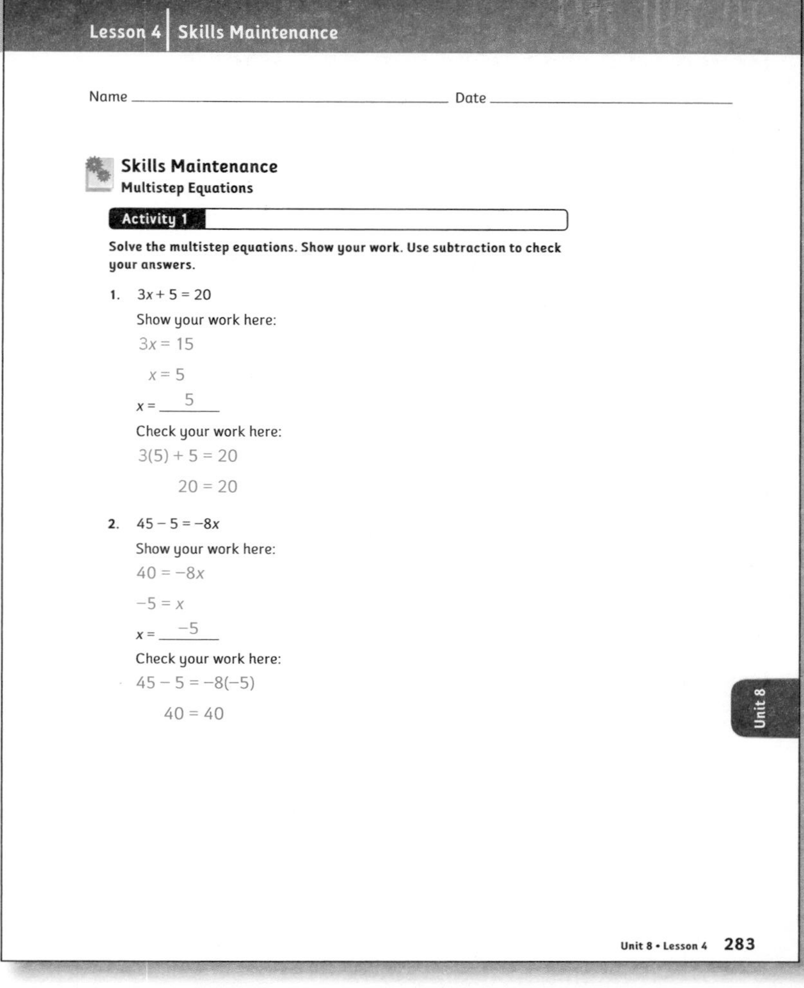
Lesson 4 | Skills Maintenance

Name ______________________ Date ______________________

Skills Maintenance
Multistep Equations

Activity 1

Solve the multistep equations. Show your work. Use subtraction to check your answers.

1. $3x + 5 = 20$

   Show your work here:

   $3x = 15$

   $x = 5$

   $x =$ 5

   Check your work here:

   $3(5) + 5 = 20$

   $20 = 20$

2. $45 - 5 = -8x$

   Show your work here:

   $40 = -8x$

   $-5 = x$

   $x =$ −5

   Check your work here:

   $45 - 5 = -8(-5)$

   $40 = 40$

Unit 8

Unit 8 • Lesson 4 283

Skills Maintenance

Multistep Equations

(*Interactive Text*, page 283)

Activity 1

Students practice solving multistep equations. Remind students to show all of their work and to check the answer at the end by substituting the value for the variable back into the original equation.

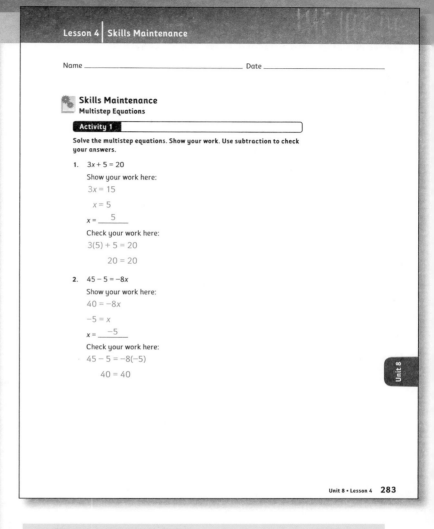

Building Number Concepts:
▶ Translating Numbers Into Equations

How do we translate simple numeric equations using variables?
(*Student Text*, page 601)

Connect to Prior Knowledge
Begin by reminding students that with algebra, we can write one statement that summarizes an entire pattern. For instance, $\mathbf{1{,}000{,}000 \cdot 1 = 1{,}000{,}000}$ and $\mathbf{4 \cdot 1 = 4}$ can both be generalized by the pattern $\boldsymbol{a \cdot 1 = a}$.

Link to Today's Concept
Tell students that in today's lesson, we look at how we translate numbers into equations.

Demonstrate
Engagement Strategy: Teacher Modeling

Demonstrate how to translate numeric patterns using variables in one of the following ways:

mBook: Use the *mBook Teacher Edition* for *Student Text*, page 601.

Overhead Projector: Reproduce the equations on a transparency, and modify as discussed.

Board: Copy the equations on the board, and modify as discussed.

- Show the first set of equations, and ask students if they see a pattern.

Listen for:

- *Zero plus a number equals the number itself.*

- Explain that we can write this pattern using variables: $\mathbf{0 + y = y}$. Explain that the variable y represents any number.
- Show the second set of equations, and ask students if they see a pattern.

Lesson 4 ▶Translating Numbers Into Equations

▶Translating Numbers Into Equations

How do we translate simple numeric equations using variables?

We learned to translate numeric equations into algebraic equations. In these kinds of problems, we looked for a pattern in the numeric equations, then substituted a variable for the part of the equation that kept changing. Let's look at three different patterns.

$0 + 7 = 7$
$0 + 82 = 82$
$0 + 9.99 = 9.99$

What is the general pattern? $\mathbf{0 + y = y}$

$55 - 55 = 0$
$0.9 - 0.9 = 0$
$\frac{3}{4} - \frac{3}{4} = 0$

What is the general pattern? $\mathbf{h - h = 0}$

$44 + 22 = 22 + 44$
$0.6 + 0.3 = 0.3 + 0.6$
$694 + 255 = 255 + 694$

What is the general pattern? $\mathbf{m + r = r + m}$

In the first two patterns, we ask the question, "What is the same and what is changing?" The variable is used to represent what is changing.

In the third pattern, both numbers on each side of the equal sign keep changing. That is why we use two variables to represent that pattern.

Unit 8 • Lesson 4 601

Listen for:

- *A number minus itself equals zero.*

- Show this pattern using variables: $\mathbf{h - h = 0}$.
- Show the last set of equations, and ask students if they see a pattern.

Listen for:

- *We can change the order of the numbers being added and the expressions are equal.*

- Show this pattern using variables: $\mathbf{m + r = r + m}$.
- Point out that some patterns required one variable and others, two. Explain that the key is to determine what stays the same and what changes.

How do we use variables in word problems?

(*Student Text*, pages 602–604)

Demonstrate

- Turn to page 602 of the *Student Text*. Explain that one important way we use variables and equations is in solving word problems.
- Read the problem in **Example 1**. Point out that our first instinct with a problem like this one is to use two variables, x and y, to get $x + y = 50$.
- Tell students that the drawback to this strategy is that we cannot solve it algebraically. We have to use guess and check.
- Tell students that if we describe the relationship between the two numbers in a more specific way, we can solve it algebraically.
- Demonstrate how we use just one variable to describe the relationship.
- Explain that we will let x be the smaller number and $x + 6$ will be the larger number. This way we can solve the problem algebraically.
- Point out that we can now write the equation as $\boldsymbol{x + x + 6 = 50}$.

How do we use variables in word problems?

Another way to use variables to represent numbers is in word problems.

Example 1

Solve the word problem by using variables.

Problem:

Two numbers add up to 50. The larger number is 6 greater than the smaller number. What are the two numbers?

What happens if we use two variables to try to solve the problem?

- Let x = the smaller number.
- Let y = the larger number.
- $x + y = 50$

In this equation, the variables x and y stand for the two different numbers. But there is no way to solve this problem using what we know about algebraic equations. The only way to solve this problem is to use the guess-and-check method.

The key to solving a problem like this is to think about the relationship between the two numbers.

- Instead of using x and y, we use just one variable.
- If we let x = the smaller number, then $x + 6$ = the larger number.

Now we have a way of solving this kind of problem.

	smaller number		larger number		
	x	+	y	=	50
becomes →	$\boldsymbol{x}$	**+**	$\boldsymbol{x + 6}$	**=**	**50**

How do we use variables in word problems? *(continued)*

Demonstrate

- Turn to page 603 in the *Student Text* to continue working through Example 1. Go over the process for solving the equation.
- Show students how to combine like terms to get $\mathbf{2x + 6 = 50}$.
- Remind students that we add the opposite, in this case −6, to get $2x$ by itself. Point out that we must add −6 on both sides to keep the equation balanced.
- Explain that once we get $\mathbf{2x = 44}$, we must multiply both sides by $\frac{1}{2}$ to get x by itself. We find the answer is $\mathbf{x = 22}$.
- Remind students that x equals the smaller number, and in this case, **the smaller number is 22**.
- Point out that the larger number is $x + 6$, so we need to substitute 22 into x. We add **22** and **6** to get **28**.
- Remind students that we can check our answer by substituting the numbers back into the original equation. We get **22 + 28 = 50**, which is **50 = 50**. The answer is correct.

Lesson 4

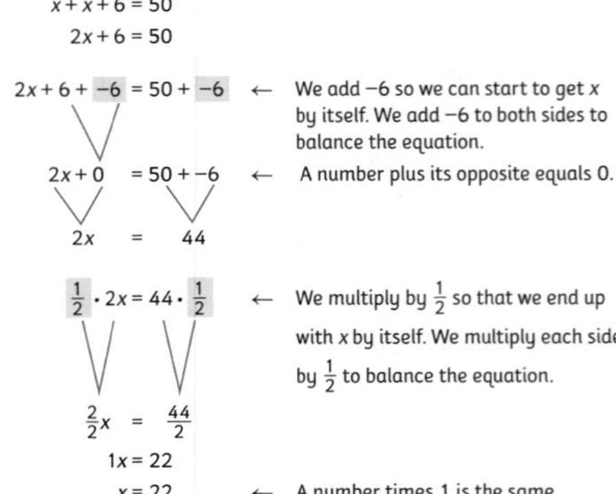

$x + x + 6 = 50$

$2x + 6 = 50$

$2x + 6 + -6 = 50 + -6$ ← We add −6 so we can start to get x by itself. We add −6 to both sides to balance the equation.

$2x + 0 = 50 + -6$ ← A number plus its opposite equals 0.

$2x = 44$

$\frac{1}{2} \cdot 2x = 44 \cdot \frac{1}{2}$ ← We multiply by $\frac{1}{2}$ so that we end up with x by itself. We multiply each side by $\frac{1}{2}$ to balance the equation.

$\frac{2}{2}x = \frac{44}{2}$

$1x = 22$

$x = 22$ ← A number times 1 is the same number. This is the solution.

That means:

- **The smaller number is 22.**
- **The larger number is 22 + 6 or 28.**

We check if this is correct by substituting the numbers 22 and 28 into the original equation.

22

↓ ↓

$x + x + 6 = 50$

$22 + 22 + 6 = 50$

$50 = 50$

It is important to think about the problem and the relationship between the numbers. We do this by substituting our answer into the original equation.

This step proves that we answered the problem correctly.

These word problems look simple because they are just a couple of sentences, but they are more complicated than we might think.

Demonstrate

- Turn to page 604 of the *Student Text* to look at **Example 2**, which shows another word problem that can be solved using an equation with just one variable.
- Read the problem. Point out that even though the relationship is different than the one in the previous example, we can still express it using just one variable.
- Explain that the two unknown numbers in this problem are $\boldsymbol{y}$ and $\mathbf{3}\boldsymbol{y}$, since one of the numbers is three times bigger than the other number.
- Point out that we write the equation as $\boldsymbol{y + 3y = 80}$.
- Go through each step of the problem with students as outlined, reminding students to combine like terms, multiply by the reciprocal, and simplify.
- Remind students that the goal is to get the variable, y, by itself on one side of the equal sign. In this case, $\boldsymbol{y = 20}$.
- Point out that since y equals 20, we know the smaller number is 20. The larger number is 3 times y, so it is **60**.
- Show students how to check the answer by substituting the numbers 20 and 60 back into the original equation. In this case, **20 + 60 = 80**, or **80 = 80**. The answer is correct.

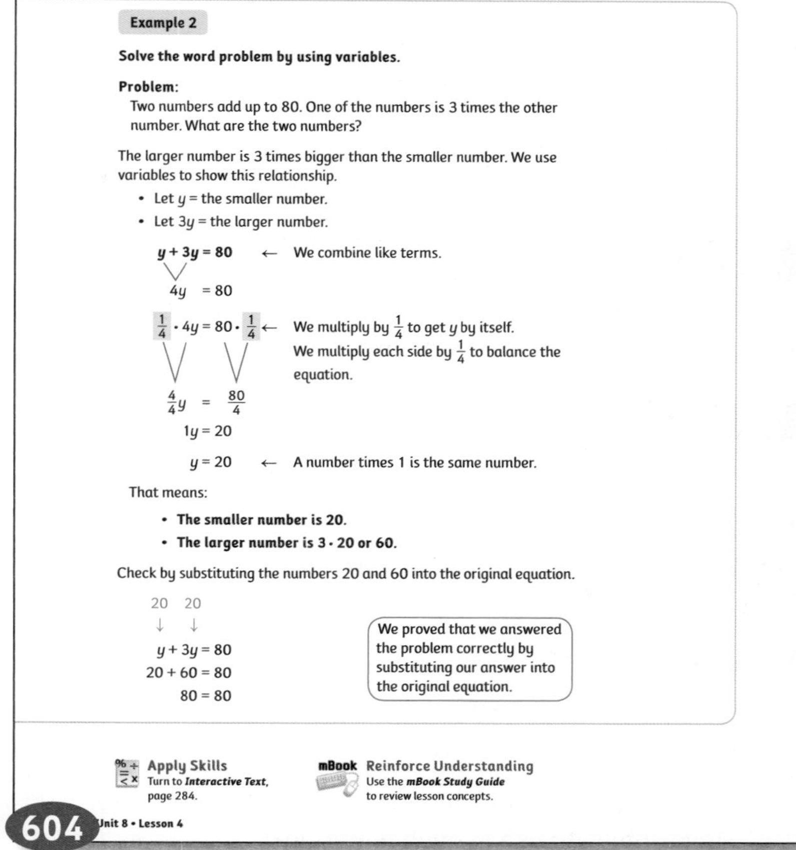

Lesson 4
Example 2
Solve the word problem by using variables.
Problem:
Two numbers add up to 80. One of the numbers is 3 times the other number. What are the two numbers?
The larger number is 3 times bigger than the smaller number. We use variables to show this relationship.
• Let y = the smaller number.
• Let 3y = the larger number.
y + 3y = 80 ← We combine like terms.
4y = 80
1/4 · 4y = 80 · 1/4 ← We multiply by 1/4 to get y by itself. We multiply each side by 1/4 to balance the equation.
4/4 y = 80/4
1y = 20
y = 20 ← A number times 1 is the same number.
That means:
• The smaller number is 20.
• The larger number is 3 · 20 or 60.
Check by substituting the numbers 20 and 60 into the original equation.
20 20
y + 3y = 80
20 + 60 = 80
80 = 80
We proved that we answered the problem correctly by substituting our answer into the original equation.
Apply Skills
Turn to Interactive Text, page 284.
mBook Reinforce Understanding
Use the mBook Study Guide to review lesson concepts.
604
Unit 8 • Lesson 4

Check for Understanding

Engagement Strategy: Pair/Share

Write the following problem on the board:

> **Two numbers add up to 50. One number is 16 greater than the other number. What are the two numbers?**

Put students into pairs. Have the pairs work together to write an equation using one variable (*y + y + 16 = 50*). Once the pairs have come up with an equation, have each partner solve the equation and find the two numbers (*17, 33*). When each has found the two numbers, have pairs check each other's answers by substituting the numbers back into the original equation (*17 + 33 = 50*). When pairs have finished, review the answers with the class and invite volunteers to share their steps and work.

Apply Skills

(*Interactive Text*, pages 284–285)

Have students turn to pages 284–285 in the *Interactive Text*, and complete the activities.

Activity 1

Students write an equation that represents the patterns shown in the numeric examples.

Activity 2

Students write equations to help them solve word problems.

Monitor students' work as they complete the activities.

Watch for:

- Can students determine what parts of the numeric patterns are variables?
- Can students determine the correct number of variables to use in each equation?
- Can students write the correct equation that represents the general pattern?
- Can students identify the relationship between the two numbers?
- Can students use just one variable to represent the relationship?
- Can students solve the multistep equation after they set it up?

mBook Reinforce Understanding

Remind students that they can review lesson concepts by accessing the online *mBook Study Guide*.

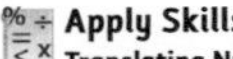
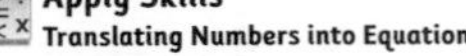

Lesson 4 | Apply Skills

Name ______ Date ______

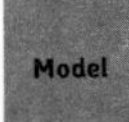

Apply Skills
Translating Numbers into Equations

Activity 1

Write the number patterns using algebraic equations. You may need two variables.

Model The numeric pattern is:
$3 + -3 = 0 \quad 4 + -4 = 0 \quad 5 + -5 = 0$
Write the equation. $x + -x = 0$

1. The numeric pattern is:
$5 \cdot -1 = -5$
$6 \cdot -1 = -6$
$7 \cdot -1 = -7$
Write the equation.
$x \cdot -1 = -x$

2. The numeric pattern is:
$0 = -5 \cdot 0$
$0 = 27 \cdot 0$
$0 = 1{,}437.5 \cdot 0$
Write the equation.
$0 = n \cdot 0$

3. The numeric pattern is:
$3 \cdot 4 = 4 \cdot 3$
$100 \cdot 10 = 10 \cdot 100$
$-5 \cdot -4 = -4 \cdot -5$
Write the equation.
$x \cdot y = y \cdot x$

4. The numeric pattern is:
$5(3 + 2) = 5 \cdot 3 + 5 \cdot 2$
$-2(7 + 1) = -2 \cdot 7 + -2 \cdot 1$
$18(1 + 2) = 18 \cdot 1 + 18 \cdot 2$
Write the equation.
$x(y + z) = xy + xz$

5. The numeric pattern is:
$3 + 5 + -5 = 3 + 0$
$4 + 6 + -6 = 4 + 0$
$17 + 22 + -22 = 17 + 0$
Write the equation.
$y + x + -x = y + 0$

6. The numeric pattern is:
$-3 \cdot -1 = 3$
$-100 \cdot -1 = 100$
$-4.5 \cdot -1 = 4.5$
Write the equation.
$-x \cdot -1 = x$

284 Unit 8 • Lesson 4

Lesson 4 | Apply Skills

Name ______ Date ______

Activity 2

Think about the relationship between numbers as you answer the problems. Make sure to check your answer by substituting the values into the original equation.

1. Two numbers add up to 100. The larger number is three times greater than the smaller number. What are the two numbers? 25, 75
$100 = x + 3x$
$100 = 4x$
$x = 25$

2. Two numbers add up to 56. The larger number is 10 greater than the smaller number. What are the two numbers? 23, 33
$56 = x + x + 10$
$56 = 2x + 10$
$46 = 2x$
$x = 23$

3. Two numbers add up to 30. One number is 4 less than the other number. What are the two numbers? 13, 17
$30 = x + x - 4$
$30 = 2x - 4$
$34 = 2x$
$x = 17$

4. Two numbers add up to 90. One number is 5 times greater than the other number. What are the two numbers? 15, 75
$90 = x + 5x$
$90 = 6x$
$x = 15$

5. Three numbers add up to 70. The first number is 10 more than the second number. The second number is the same as the third number. What are the three numbers? 30, 20, 20
$70 = x + x + x + 10$
$70 = 3x + 10$
$60 = 3x$
$x = 20$

mBook Reinforce Understanding
Use the **mBook *Study Guide*** to review lesson concepts.

Unit 8

Unit 8 • Lesson 4 285

Homework

Go over the instructions on page 605 of the *Student Text* for each part of the homework.

Activity 1

Students choose the equation that shows the general pattern shown by the numeric examples.

Activity 2

Students translate the words to expressions using just one variable.

Activity 3

Students solve word problems by writing an equation.

Activity 4 • Distributed Practice

Students practice order of operations, integer operations, and one-step equations.

Lesson 4

Homework

Activity 1

Tell the general pattern for each property shown.

1. $12 + 0 = 12$ b
   $\frac{1}{2} + 0 = \frac{1}{2}$
   $-7 + 0 = -7$
   (a) $12 + x = 12$
   (b) $x + 0 = x$
   (c) $x + y = z$
2. $-5 + 5 = 0$ c
   $-\frac{1}{3} + \frac{1}{3} = 0$
   $-7.2 + 7.2 = 0$
   (a) $-5 + \frac{1}{5} = 0$
   (b) $-\frac{1}{3} + \frac{1}{3} = x$
   (c) $-x + x = 0$

Activity 2

Translate the words into expressions.

1. 5 more than a number $n + 5$
2. a number minus 6 $n - 6$
3. a number plus 7 $x + 7$
4. 17 minus a number $17 - y$
5. 4.7 divided by a number $\frac{4.7}{x}$
6. 3 less than a number $n - 3$

Activity 3

Write the word problems using algebra, then solve.

1. The sum of two numbers is 130. One of the numbers is 50 more than the other number. What are the two numbers? $x + x + 50 = 130$; 40 and 90
2. The sum of three numbers is 60. The smallest number is 10 less than the middle number. The biggest number is 10 more than the middle number. What are the three numbers? $x - 10 + x + x + 10 = 60$; 10, 20, and 30

Activity 4 • Distributed Practice

Solve.

1. $25 = 4 + 3z$ 7
2. $4h = -40$ −10
3. $\frac{3}{5} = \frac{9}{a}$ 15
4. $16 = 2(-2 + x)$ 10
5. $b = -3 + 5$ 2
6. $c + -\frac{1}{2} = 0$ $\frac{1}{2}$

Unit 8 • Lesson 605

Lesson 5 | Problem Solving: Angles of Quadrilaterals

Monitoring Progress: Quiz 1

Lesson Planner

Skills Maintenance

Writing Equations to Solve Word Problems

Problem Solving:

▶ Angles of Quadrilaterals

Students use their knowledge about the interior angles of quadrilaterals (the sum of the interior angles equals 360) to help them find missing angle measures. They learn that we need certain information about the angles to apply the properties of interior angles of quadrilaterals.

Objective

Students will find the measure of angles in quadrilaterals.

Monitoring Progress:

▶ Quiz 1

Distribute the quiz, and remind students that the questions involve material covered over the previous lessons in the unit.

Homework

Students solve equations, write equations for word problems, and find missing angle measurements. In Distributed Practice, students practice order of operations, integer operations, and one-step equations.

Lesson 5 | Skills Maintenance

Name ______________________ Date ______________

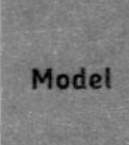

Skills Maintenance
Writing Equations to Solve Word Problems

Activity 1

Write the equation that you would use to solve each of the word problems. You do not need to solve the problem.

Model	If the difference between two numbers is 60 and one number is 4 times bigger than the other number, what are the two numbers? Write the equation. $4x - x = 60$

1. If the sum of two numbers is 150 and one number is 20 more than the other number, what are the two numbers?
   Write the equation. $x + x + 20 = 150$
2. If the sum of four numbers is 100 and each of the numbers is the same, what are the four numbers?
   Write the equation. $4x = 100$ or $x + x + x + x = 100$
3. If the difference of two numbers is 500 and one number is three times greater than the other number, what are the two numbers?
   Write the equation. $3x - x = 500$

286 Unit 8 • Lesson 5

Skills Maintenance

Writing Equations to Solve Word Problems

(*Interactive Text*, page 286)

Activity 1

Students write algebraic equations for solving word problems. They do not need to solve the problems.

Problem Solving:
▶ Angles of Quadrilaterals

How do we use algebra to find the measure of each angle?
(*Student Text*, pages 606–608)

Connect to Prior Knowledge

Begin by reminding students about the table of Polygons and Sums of the Measures of Interior and Exterior angles in Lesson 3. Put the table on the board or overhead with some parts left blank, and ask students to fill in the missing parts.

Link to Today's Concept

Tell students that we use this information again in today's lesson. We demonstrate ways to use algebra to find the measure of each angle in different polygons.

Demonstrate

Engagement Strategy: Teacher Modeling

Demonstrate how to find the measure of angles in polygons in one of the following ways:

mBook: Use the *mBook Teacher Edition* for *Student Text*, pages 606–609. m

Overhead Projector: Reproduce the polygons and equations on a transparency, and modify as discussed.

Board: Reproduce the polygons and equations on the board, and modify as discussed.

- Discuss how the sum of interior angles of any quadrilateral is 360 degrees. Point out that this is demonstrated in the table we created at the beginning of the lesson.
- Next discuss common properties and attributes of some quadrilaterals.

Lesson 5 
Problem Solving:
▶ Angles of Quadrilaterals
Monitoring Progress:
▶ Quiz 1

▶ **Problem Solving: Angles of Quadrilaterals**

How do we use algebra to find the measure of each angle?

We studied different types of quadrilaterals. One fact that we learned about quadrilaterals is that the sum of the interior angles is always 360 degrees.

Some quadrilaterals, such as squares, rectangles, and parallelograms, have consistent properties. For example, squares and rectangles always have angle measurements that are 90 degrees. The little square at each angle tells us this.

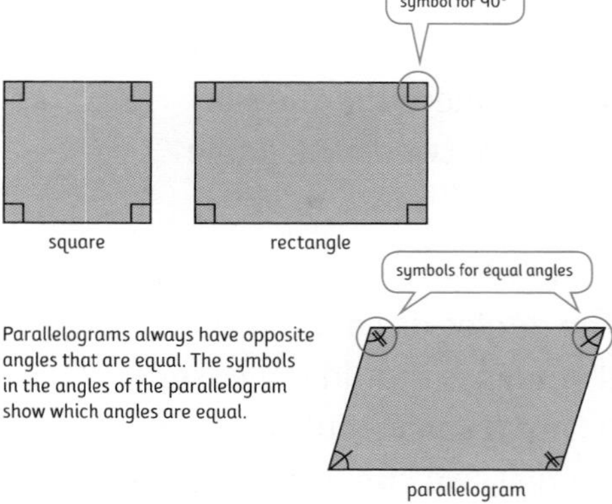

Parallelograms always have opposite angles that are equal. The symbols in the angles of the parallelogram show which angles are equal.

Other quadrilaterals might have a pair of angles that are the same and two others that are different.

606 Unit 8 • Lesson 5

- Show the picture of the square and rectangle. Be sure students see that they have right angles. Point out the symbol that denotes a right angle. m
- Show the parallelogram. Be sure students see that the parallelogram has opposite angles that are equal. m

How do we use algebra to find the measure of each angle? *(continued)*

Demonstrate

- Show the kite and point out that it has two angles that are equal, angles *d* and *f*. Point out the symbol that shows that these two angles are equal. m
- Explain to students that some quadrilaterals might have angles where there is no consistent pattern between the angle measures.
- Show the next quadrilateral on the page where all of the angles are a different measure. Tell students that in the cases where there is not a consistent relationship between the angles, we can use algebra to find missing angle measures. m
- Go over **Example 1**, which shows how to use algebra to find the measure of the missing angles.
- Show the kite, and point out the important information. We know that $\angle b$ is 70 degrees, $\angle d$ is 40 degrees, and $\angle a$ and $\angle c$ are equal. Tell students that we will use the variable *x* to represent the measure of each unknown angle. m
- Remind students that the sum of the interior angles for all quadrilaterals is 360 degrees. Explain that we have enough information to set up an equation: $\mathbf{x + x + 70 + 40 = 360}$. m

Let's look at a kite. This shape has only two angles that are equal. ($\angle d = \angle f$).

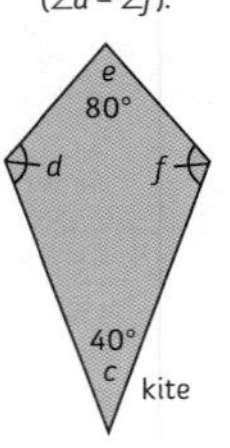

Some quadrilaterals have different measures for each angle, like the shape in this illustration.

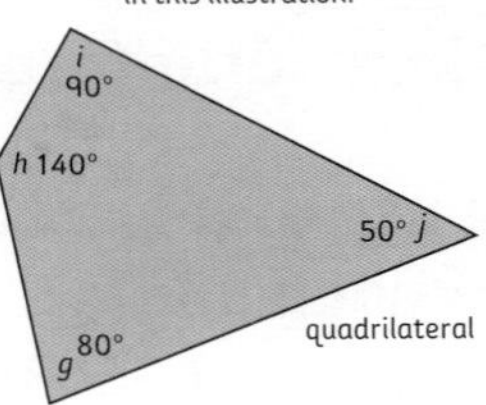

Algebra helps us find the measure of each angle when we create equations. Example 1 shows how to find the measure of angles using an algebraic equation.

Example 1

Find the measure of each angle in the kite.

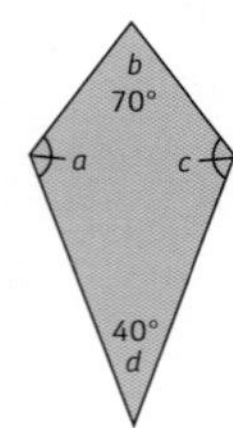

The symbols show that $\angle a$ and $\angle c$ are equal.
Let x = the measure of each unknown angle.

We also know that the sum of the interior angles for all quadrilaterals is 360 degrees.

We set up the equation this way:
$x + x + 70 + 40 = 360$

Demonstrate

- Continue with Example 1. Work through the process of solving the equation.
- Show how to combine like terms to get $\mathbf{2x + 110 = 360}$.
- Remind students that we want to get $2x$ by itself on one side, so we add -110 to both sides of the equation.
- Walk through the addition to get $\mathbf{2x = 250}$.
- Remind students that the goal is to get x alone on one side. We need to multiply both sides by $\frac{1}{2}$, which is the reciprocal of the coefficient, 2.
- Walk through the multiplication and division to get $\mathbf{x = 125}$. Explain that since we know the value of x, we know that $\angle \mathbf{a} = \mathbf{125}$ and $\angle \mathbf{c} = \mathbf{125}$.
- Remind students that we can check our answer by substituting the values back into the original equation to see that **360 = 360**. The values are correct.

Check for Understanding
Engagement Strategy: Pair/Share

Draw a kite on the board with the following angles: $\angle \mathbf{a} = \mathbf{x}$; $\angle \mathbf{b} = \mathbf{80}$, $\angle \mathbf{c} = \mathbf{x5}$, $\angle \mathbf{d} = \mathbf{40}$. Have students set up an equation to find the missing angle measurements (*5x + x + 80 + 40 = 360*). Review the equations with the class before moving on. Then have students use the equation to find the missing values (*x = 40; 5x = 200*). When students have finished, have students pair up with another student to check each other's answers by substituting the values back into the original equation (*5 • 40 + 40 + 80 + 40 = 360*). When all pairs have finished, review the solutions with the class.

$\mathbf{x + x + 70 + 40 = 360}$ ← We add like terms to simplify the equation.

$2x + 110 = 360$

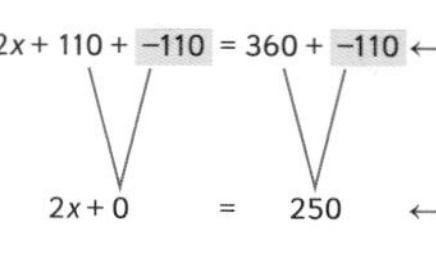

$2x + 110 + -110 = 360 + -110$ ← We add -110 so that we will end up with $2x$ by itself. We add -110 to both sides to balance the equation.

$2x + 0 = 250$ ← A number plus its opposite equals 0.

$2x = 250$

$\frac{1}{2} \cdot 2x = 250 \cdot \frac{1}{2}$ ← We multiply by $\frac{1}{2}$ so that we get x by itself. We multiply each side by $\frac{1}{2}$ to balance the equation.

$\frac{2}{2}x = \frac{250}{2}$

$1x = 125$

$\mathbf{x = 125}$ ← A number times 1 is the same number. **That means the measure of $\angle a = 125$ and $\angle c = 125$.**

We substitute these values into the original equation to check our answer.

125 ↓ ↓

$x + x + 70 + 40 = 360$

$125 + 125 + 70 + 40 = 360$

$250 + 70 + 40 = 360$

$320 + 40 = 360$

$360 = 360$

We cannot solve angle measurement problems if we are not given enough information.

When isn't it possible to find the measurement of an angle?

(*Student Text*, page 609)

Demonstrate

- Explain to students that some angle measurement problems cannot be solved because we do not have enough information.
- Tell students that it is important to know when you have enough information and when you do not.
- Have students look at the quadrilateral, which shows a situation where we do not have enough information to solve the problem. Tell students that we can see this because we do not know enough about the relationship between the two missing angles and the two angles that are given. m
- Explain that we can make some good guesses, but we do not know exact measures.
- Be sure students understand that in this case, we would need more information about one or the other of the missing angles and/or their relationships to the other angles in order to use algebra to find the missing measures.

When isn't it possible to find the measurement of an angle?

Look at the quadrilateral. The measures for $\angle r$ and $\angle u$ are not given.

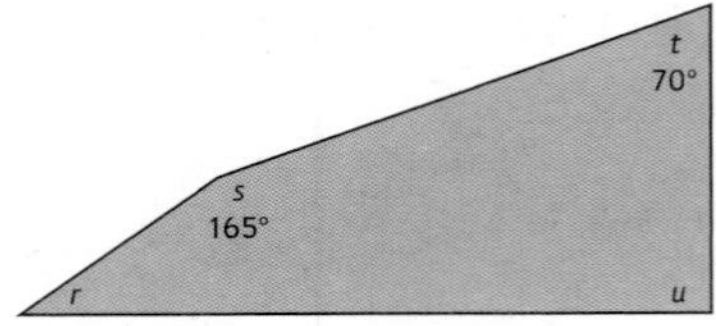

There are no symbols that show the angles are equal, so we cannot figure out their measurement.

Problem-Solving Activity Turn to ***Interactive Text***, page 287.

Monitoring Progress Quiz 1

Reinforce Understanding Use the ***mBook Study Guide*** to review lesson concepts.

Problem-Solving Activity

(*Interactive Text*, page 287)

Have students turn to *Interactive Text*, page 287, and complete the activity.

Students first determine if there is enough information to find the missing angle measures. If there is enough information, they are to use algebra to find the measures of the angles.

Monitor students' work as they complete the activity.

Watch for:

- Can students determine if there is enough information?
- Can students write the algebraic equation for finding the missing angle measure?
- Do students remember that the sum of the angles is always 360?
- Do students find the correct angle measure?

mBook Reinforce Understanding

Remind students that they can review lesson concepts by accessing the online *mBook Study Guide*.

Lesson 5 | Problem-Solving Activity

Name ________________ Date ________________

Problem-Solving Activity
Angles of Quadrilaterals

Tell if there is enough information to find the missing angle measures. If there is enough information, use algebra to find the missing angle measures.

1. (Figure angles: 70°, 120°, x°, 60°)
Is there enough information to find the measure of x?
(circle) YES or NO — YES circled
If there is enough information, write the equation.
$60 + 120 + 70 + x = 360$
Solve the equation. $250 + x = 360$
$x = 110$
What is the measure of angle x? 110°

2. (Figure angles: x°, 130°, y°, z°)
Is there enough information to find the measure of angle z?
(circle) YES or NO — NO circled
If there is enough information, write the equation.
Solve the equation.
What is the measure of angle z? ______

3. (Figure angles: $x + 10$°, $x + 100$°, $x + 110$°, x°)
Is there enough information to find the measure of angle x?
(circle) YES or NO — NO circled
If there is enough information, write the equation.
Solve the equation.
What is the measure of angle x?

Unit 8

Unit 8 • Lesson 5 287

Monitoring Progress: ▶ Quiz 1 • Form A

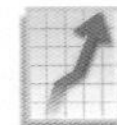

Assess Quiz 1

- Administer Quiz 1 Form A in the *Assessment Book*, pages 69–70. (If necessary, retest students with Quiz 1 Form B from the *mBook Teacher Edition* following differentiation.)

Students	Assess	Differentiate
	Day 1	Day 2
All	Quiz 1 *Form A*	
Scored 80% or above		Extension
Scored Below 80%		Reinforcement

Differentiate

- Review Quiz 1 Form A with class.
- Identify students for Extension or Reinforcement.

Extension

For those students who score 80 percent or better, provide the On Track! Activities from Unit 8, Lessons 1–5, from the *mBook Teacher Edition.*

Reinforcement

For those students who score below 80 percent, provide additional support in one of the following ways:

- Have students access the online tutorial provided in the *mBook Study Guide.*
- Have students complete the Interactive Reinforcement Exercises for Unit 8, Lessons 1–4, in the *mBook Study Guide.*
- Provide teacher-directed reteaching of unit concepts.

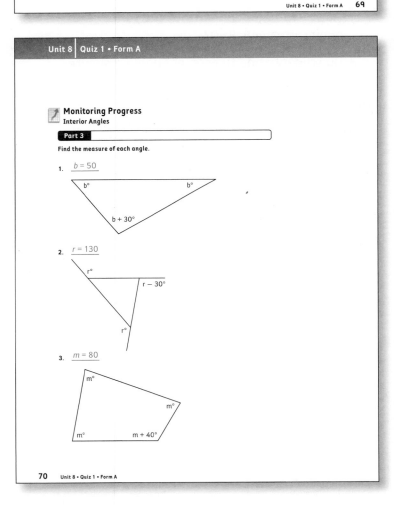

Unit 8 | Quiz 1 • Form A

Name ______ Date ______

Form A

Monitoring Progress
Algebraic Equations

Part 1

Solve the equations.

1. $-3x = 36$ $x = -12$
2. $4a = -24$ $a = -6$
3. $-5c = -45$ $c = 9$
4. $-d = 75$ $d = -75$
5. $3v - 2 = 16$ $v = 6$
6. $11 = 2x + 5$ $x = 3$
7. $-y = 55$ $y = -55$
8. $3n + 1 = 16$ $n = 5$
9. $6c = -24$ $c = -4$
10. $4k - 1 = 15$ $k = 4$

Part 2

Translate the word problems into equations, then solve them.

1. Two numbers add up to 50. One number is four times as big as the other number. What are the two numbers?
   $4n + n = 50$; $n = 10$; 10 and 40
2. Two numbers add up to 25. One number is five greater than the other number. What are the two numbers?
   $x + (x + 5) = 25$; $x = 10$; 10 and 15
3. Two numbers add up to 75. One number is two times as big as the other number. What are the two numbers?
   $s + 2s = 75$; $s = 25$; 25 and 75

Unit 8

Unit 8 • Quiz 1 • Form A 69

Unit 8 | Quiz 1 • Form A

Monitoring Progress
Interior Angles

Part 3

Find the measure of each angle.

1. $b = 50$

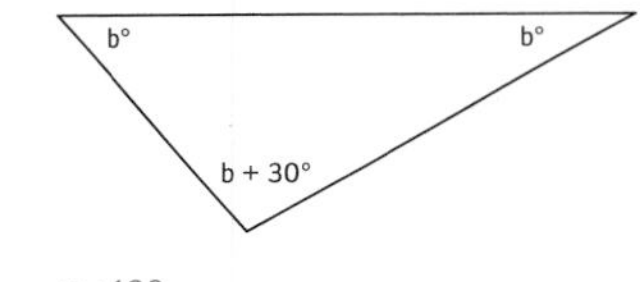

2. $r = 130$

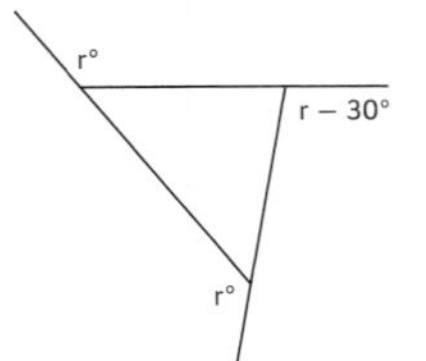

3. $m = 80$

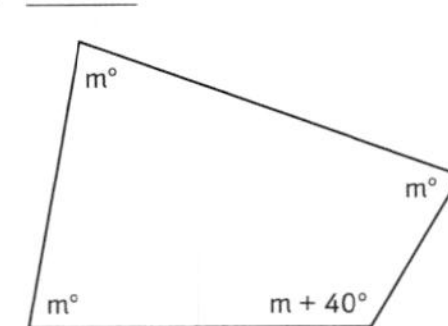

70 Unit 8 • Quiz 1 • Form A

Name ______________________ Date ______________________

Form B

mBook

Monitoring Progress
Algebraic Equations

Part 1

Solve the equations.

1. $-3x = 24$ $x = -8$
2. $2a = -20$ $a = -10$
3. $-4c = -36$ $c = 9$
4. $-d = 30$ $d = -30$
5. $2v - 2 = 16$ $v = 9$
6. $13 = 2x + 7$ $x = 3$
7. $-y = 23$ $y = -23$
8. $4n + 3 = 15$ $n = 3$
9. $2c = -100$ $c = -50$
10. $2k - 1 = 15$ $k = 8$

Part 2

Translate the word problems into equations, then solve them.

1. Two numbers add up to 60. One number is four times the size of the other number. What are the two numbers?
   $x + 4x = 60$; $x = 12$; 12 and 48
2. Two numbers add up to 15. One number is five times the size of the other number. What are the two numbers?
   $f + 5f = 15$; $f = 2.5$; 2.5 and 12.5
3. Two numbers add up to 45. One number is twice the size of the other number. What are the two numbers?
   $p + 2p = 45$; $p = 15$; 15 and 30

Name ______________________ Date ______________________

Monitoring Progress
Interior Angles

Part 3

Find the measure of each angle.

1. $b = 40$

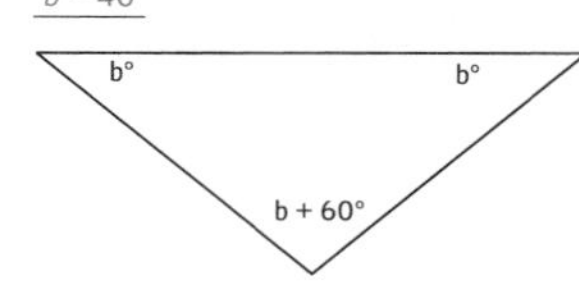

2. $r = 140$

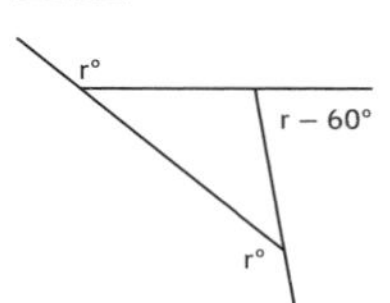

3. $m = 75$

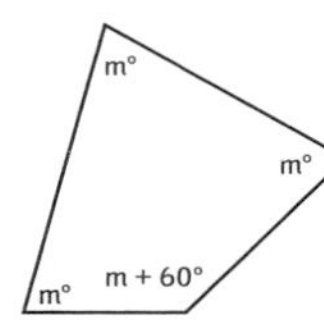

Homework

Go over the instructions on page 610 of the *Student Text* for each part of the homework.

Activity 1

Students solve algebraic equations. Point out that the equations represent angle measures in quadrilaterals.

Activity 2

Students write an equation for the word problems. They do not need to solve the problems.

Activity 3

Students find the missing angle measurements.

Activity 4 • Distributed Practice

Students practice order of operations, integer operations, and one-step equations.

Lesson 5

Homework

Activity 1

Solve.

1. $30 + 60 + x = 180$ 90
2. $45 + 40 + 35 + w = 360$ 240
3. $z = 3 \cdot 60$ 180
4. $4 \cdot m = 360$ 90

Activity 2

Write an equation for each of the word problems. You do not need to solve it.

1. If the sum of the interior angles of a square is 360, write an equation to show the measurement of one interior angle. $x = \frac{360}{4}$
2. If a triangle has angles with measures of 90 and 30 degrees, write an equation to show the measurement of the third angle. $x = 180 - 90 - 30$

Activity 3

Tell the missing angle measures.

1. What are the measures of $\angle a$ and $\angle b$?
   120 degrees

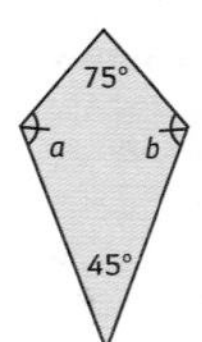

2. What is the measure of $\angle x$?
   40 degrees

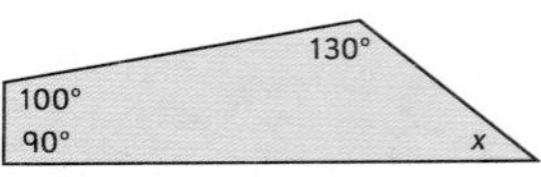

Activity 4 • Distributed Practice

Solve.

1. $\frac{12}{24} = \frac{x}{6}$ 3
2. $2(a + 6) = -24$ −18
3. $7b = -49$ −7
4. $-22 + x + -9 = -50$ −19
5. $\frac{1}{4} \cdot g = 1$ 4
6. $d + -4 = 0$ 4

610 Unit 8 • Lesson 5

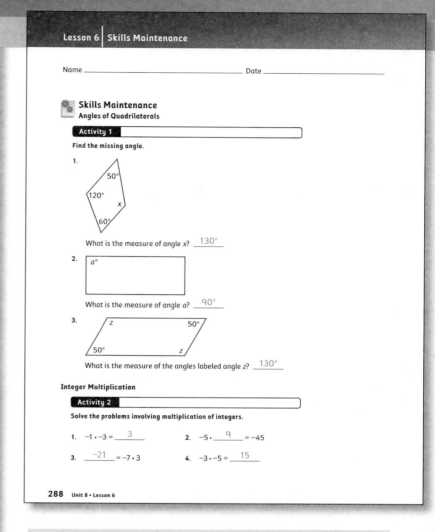

Lesson 6 ▶ Negative Coefficients

Problem Solving:

▶ Using Drawings to Solve Problems

Lesson Planner

Skills Maintenance

Angles of Quadrilaterals, Integer Multiplication

Building Number Concepts:

▶ Negative Coefficients

Students examine the difference that a negative makes in an equation and learn to solve equations that have negative coefficients. Students need to pay close attention to a negative when it is in the coefficient.

Objective

Students will solve equations with negative coefficients.

Problem Solving:

▶ Using Drawings to Solve Problems

Solving algebra word problems can be difficult for students. Students learn that sometimes drawings can help them to better understand the problem. In this lesson, students work with problems involving money and learn to start with a drawing to figure out how to use a variable.

Objective

Students will use drawings to help solve word problems.

Homework

Students tell the next step to solve each problem, solve two-step equations that involve negative numbers, and solve word problems using algebra and drawing pictures. In Distributed Practice, students practice order of operations, integer operations, and one-step equations.

Lesson 6 | Skills Maintenance

Name ______________________ Date ______________

Skills Maintenance
Angles of Quadrilaterals

Activity 1

Find the missing angle.

1.

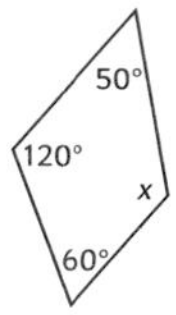

What is the measure of angle x? 130°

2.

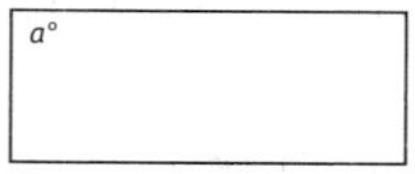

What is the measure of angle a? 90°

3.

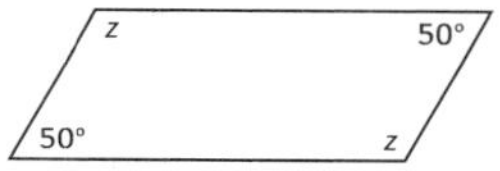

What is the measure of the angles labeled angle z? 130°

Integer Multiplication

Activity 2

Solve the problems involving multiplication of integers.

1. $-1 \cdot -3 =$ 3
2. $-5 \cdot$ 9 $= -45$
3. −21 $= -7 \cdot 3$
4. $-3 \cdot -5 =$ 15

288 Unit 8 • Lesson 6

Skills Maintenance

Angles of Quadrilaterals, Integer Multiplication
(*Interactive Text*, page 288)

Activity 1

Students find the measure of the missing angle in each problem.

Activity 2

Students solve integer multiplication problems.

Building Number Concepts:
Negative Coefficients

What difference does a negative coefficient make?

(*Student Text*, pages 611–612)

Connect to Prior Knowledge

Begin by discussing with students how they might approach these two equations differently: **$2x + 5 = 15$** and **$2x = 5 + 15$**. Explain that the small difference changes where we start, how we solve the equation, and the answer we get.

Link to Today's Concept

Tell students that in today's lesson, we look at the small but important difference a negative coefficient can make in an equation.

Demonstrate

Engagement Strategy: Teacher Modeling

Demonstrate the difference a negative coefficient makes in one of the following ways:

mBook: Use the *mBook Teacher Edition* for *Student Text*, page 611. m

Overhead Projector: Reproduce the equations on a transparency, and modify as discussed.

Board: Copy the equations on the board, and modify as discussed.

- Explain that slight changes can be the most difficult to find.
- Display the two equations: **$3x + 5 = 14$** and **$-3x + 5 = 14$** and have students identify that the difference is a negative and positive coefficient. m
- Tell students that a negative coefficient has a major impact on the result of the problem.

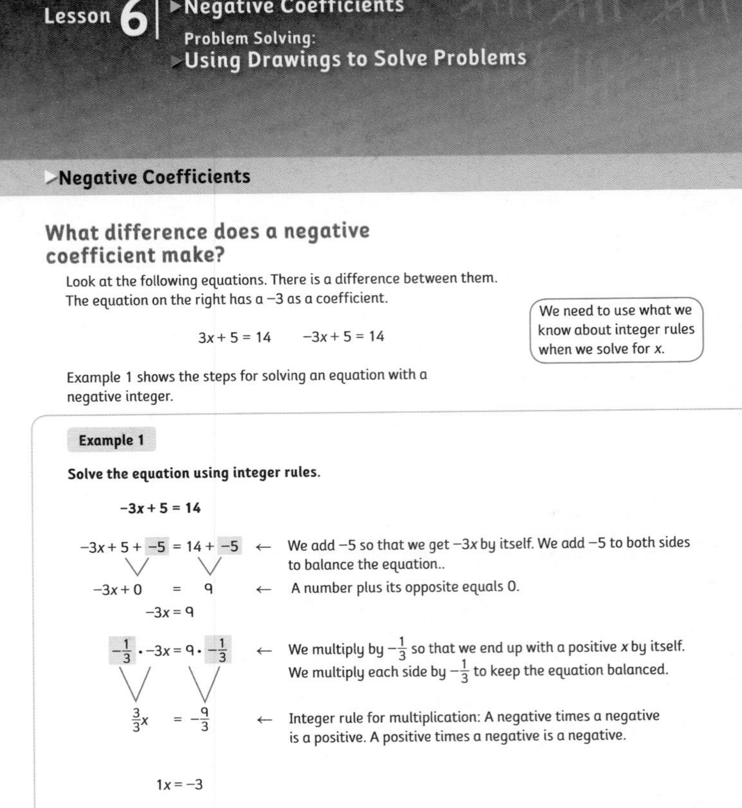
Lesson 6 | Negative Coefficients
Problem Solving:
Using Drawings to Solve Problems

Negative Coefficients

What difference does a negative coefficient make?

Look at the following equations. There is a difference between them. The equation on the right has a −3 as a coefficient.

$3x + 5 = 14$ $\quad -3x + 5 = 14$

We need to use what we know about integer rules when we solve for x.

Example 1 shows the steps for solving an equation with a negative integer.

Example 1

Solve the equation using integer rules.

$-3x + 5 = 14$

$-3x + 5 + -5 = 14 + -5$ ← We add −5 so that we get $-3x$ by itself. We add −5 to both sides to balance the equation..

$-3x + 0 = 9$ ← A number plus its opposite equals 0.

$-3x = 9$

$-\frac{1}{3} \cdot -3x = 9 \cdot -\frac{1}{3}$ ← We multiply by $-\frac{1}{3}$ so that we end up with a positive x by itself. We multiply each side by $-\frac{1}{3}$ to keep the equation balanced.

$\frac{3}{3}x = -\frac{9}{3}$ ← Integer rule for multiplication: A negative times a negative is a positive. A positive times a negative is a negative.

$1x = -3$

$x = -3$ ← A number times 1 is the same number. This is the solution.

Unit 8 • Lesson 611

- Show students how to solve the equation **$-3x + 5 = 14$** in **Example 1**. Explain that we solve the equation similarily to solving a problem with all positives, but we need slightly different mechanics.
- Point out that we want to get $-3x$ by itself, so we add −5 to both sides. m
- Walk through the addition to get **$-3x = 9$**. m
- Point out the coefficient, 3, and remind students that we multiply by its reciprocal, $\frac{1}{3}$, to get x by itself. m
- Walk through the multiplication and division to get **$x = -3$**. m
- Explain that it is always a good idea to substitute the value back in the original equation to check it.

Demonstrate

- Next turn to page 612 of the *Student Text* and look at the two equations at the top of the page.

What happens when we make one more small change? Look at the following equations. Do you see the difference between them?

$-3x + 6 = 18 \qquad -3x - 6 = 18$

The equation on the right uses subtraction in one of the expressions. Subtraction is the same as adding the opposite. Example 2 shows the steps in solving this type of equation.

Example 2

Solve the equation using what we know about rules.

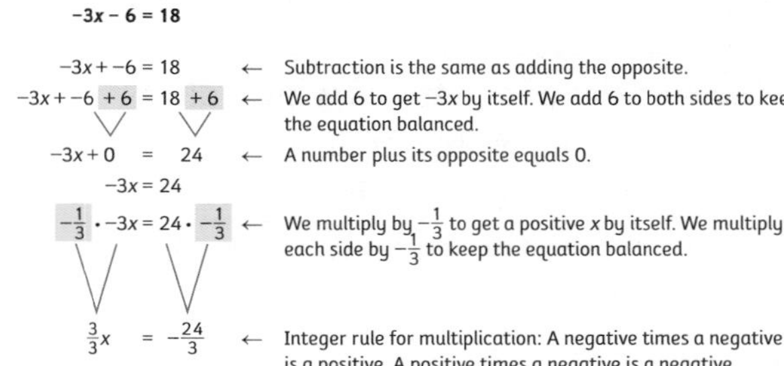

$\mathbf{-3x - 6 = 18}$

$-3x + -6 = 18$ ← Subtraction is the same as adding the opposite.

$-3x + -6 + 6 = 18 + 6$ ← We add 6 to get $-3x$ by itself. We add 6 to both sides to keep the equation balanced.

$-3x + 0 = 24$ ← A number plus its opposite equals 0.

$-3x = 24$

$-\frac{1}{3} \cdot -3x = 24 \cdot -\frac{1}{3}$ ← We multiply by $-\frac{1}{3}$ to get a positive x by itself. We multiply each side by $-\frac{1}{3}$ to keep the equation balanced.

$\frac{3}{3}x = -\frac{24}{3}$ ← Integer rule for multiplication: A negative times a negative is a positive. A positive times a negative is a negative.

$1x = -8$

$\mathbf{x = -8}$ ← A number times 1 is the same number. This is the solution.

-8

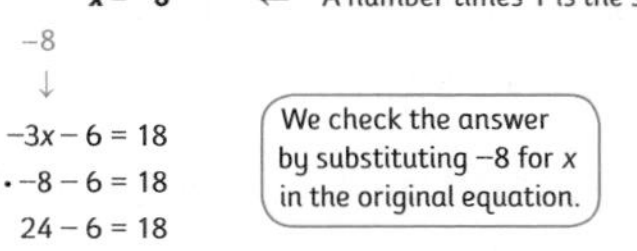

$-3x - 6 = 18$

$-3 \cdot -8 - 6 = 18$

$24 - 6 = 18$

$18 = 18$

We check the answer by substituting -8 for x in the original equation.

Apply Skills
Turn to ***Interactive Text***, page 289.

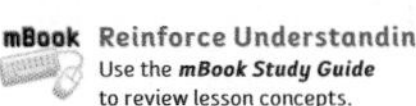

Reinforce Understanding
Use the ***mBook Study Guide*** to review lesson concepts.

Ask:

What is the difference in the two equations?

Listen for:

- *One equation uses addition; the other uses subtraction.*

- Move to **Example 2** to show how to solve the second equation.
- Remind students that subtraction is the same as adding the opposite, so we can rewrite the equation with addition.
- Remind students that we want to get $-3x$ by itself, so we add 6 to both sides of the equation.
- Walk through the addition, and remind students that a number plus its opposite is zero.
- Remind students that the goal is to get a positive variable, in this case x, alone on one side of the equal sign. We need to multiply each side of the equation by $-\frac{1}{3}$, which is the reciprocal of the coefficient.
- Walk through the multiplication and division to get $\mathbf{x = -8}$.
- Explain that we can check the answer by substituting -8 back into the original equation. We see that **18 = 18**, so our answer is correct.

Check for Understanding

Engagement Strategy: Look About

Write the equation $\mathbf{-2x + 4 = 22}$ on the board. Tell students that they will solve the equation ($x = -9$) with the help of the whole class. Students should write their work in large writing on a piece of paper or a dry erase board. When students finish their work, they should hold up their answer for everyone to see.

If students are not sure about the answer, prompt them to look about at the other students' solutions to help with their thinking. Review the answers after all students have held up their solutions.

Reinforce Understanding

For additional practice solving equations with negative coefficients, use these equations:

$\mathbf{-4x - 2 = 30}$ ($x = -8$)

$\mathbf{-5x + 10 = 40}$ ($x = -6$)

Apply Skills

(*Interactive Text*, pages 289–290)

Have students turn to pages 289–290 in the *Interactive Text*, and complete the activity.

Activity 1

Students solve pairs of equations with slight differences. Then they write about the differences in the solutions and in the steps for solving them. Monitor students' work as they complete the activity.

Watch for:

- Can students solve each problem, carefully adjusting for the negative sign?
- Can students compare and write about the differences in the steps they use?
- Can students compare and write about the differences?

Reinforce Understanding
Remind students that they can review lesson concepts by accessing the online *mBook Study Guide*.

Lesson 6 | Apply Skills

Name ______ Date ______

Apply Skills
Negative Coefficients

Activity 1

Solve each pair of equations. Pay close attention to the negative signs. Compare the answers. Write about the different steps that you used because of the negative sign. Write about the difference in the answers.

1. Solve the two equations: $2x = 6$ $-2x = 6$

 Show your work here:

 $2 \cdot 3 = 6$

 $-2 \cdot -3 = 6$

 Compare the steps you used to solve each. How are they alike and how are they different?

 Answers will vary. Sample answer: When I divided to get the variable alone, I first divided by a positive 2 and then a negative 2.

 Compare answers. What is the difference in the answer?

 Answers will vary. Sample answer: The variable x is the same number, but one is positive and one is negative.

Unit 8

Unit 8 • Lesson 6 289

Lesson 6 | Apply Skills

Name ______ Date ______

2. Solve the two equations: $x + 5 = 14$ $-x + 5 = 14$

 Show your work here:

 $9 + 5 = 14$

 $-(-9) + 5 = 14$

 Compare the steps you used to solve each. How are they alike and how are they different?

 Answers will vary. Sample answer: I subtracted both sides of each equation by 5. I divided the first equation by a positive 1 and the second equation by a negative 1.

 Compare answers. What is the difference in your answer?

 Answers will vary. Sample answer: The variable x is the same number, but one is positive and one is negative. The double negative cancels itself out so both equations have the same answer.

3. Solve the two equations: $2x + 4 = 20$ $-2x - 4 = 20$

 Show your work here:

 $2 \cdot 8 + 4 = 20$

 $-2 \cdot -12 - 4 = 20$

 Compare the steps you used to solve each. How are they alike and how are they different?

 Answers will vary. Sample answer: Because there are two different negatives in the second problem, I found a different number for x in each problem.

 Compare answers. What is the difference in the answer?

 Answers will vary. Sample answer: The second problem has a negative coefficient, but it also has a different value for x.

290 Unit 8 • Lesson 6

Problem Solving:
▶ Using Drawings to Solve Problems

Why are drawings important for problem solving?

(*Student Text*, pages 613–614)

Demonstrate

- Use page 613 in the *Student Text* to discuss the strategy of drawing a picture to help solve problems.
- Tell students that it is very common for people in all types of careers to use this strategy for solving complex problems in their jobs. When engineers are designing cars, a picture is usually the beginning of a complicated process.
- Explain that we can use drawings to help us solve algebra word problems. Have students look at **Example 1**. Read through the problem, then walk through the steps to solve the problem.

STEP 1

- Show how we draw the three jars from the word problem. This helps us identify what we know and what we do not know.
- Explain that we know that Jar 1 has some money, Jar 2 has twice as much money as Jar 1, and Jar 3 has 3 times as much money as Jar 1. We also know the total amount of money Latisha has from the three jars is 60 dollars.

Why are drawings important for problem solving?

Algebra word problems can be difficult to solve. Sometimes a drawing helps us better understand the problem. In this lesson, we are going to work problems involving money. We will see how to:

- start with a drawing.
- figure out how to use a variable.

Example 1

Figure out how much money is in the first jar.

Problem:

Latisha puts extra money into three jars in the kitchen.

- The second jar has twice as much money as the first jar.
- The third jar has three times as much money as the first jar.
- Latisha counted all of her money yesterday, and she has $60.

How can we use a drawing to figure out how much money is in each jar?

STEP 1

Begin with a drawing.

Draw three jars and label each one.

What do we know? We know how much money she has.

What don't we know? How much money is in each jar.

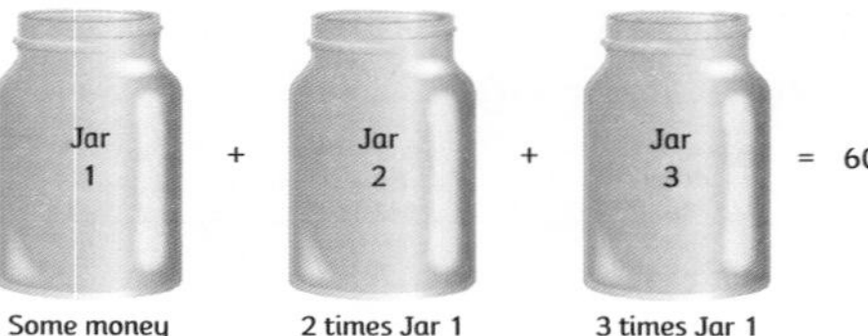

Why are drawings important for problem solving? *(continued)*

Demonstrate

- Continue going over the steps in Example 1 on page 614 of the *Student Text*.

STEP 2

- Explain that the next step is to figure out the variable.
- Point out that we do not know how much money is in each jar. We use w to represent the amount of money in Jar 1.
- Show how we set up the equation using the drawing: $\mathbf{w + 2w + 3w = 60}$.

STEP 3

- Tell students that now we can solve the equation.
- Walk through the steps to solve the equation: combining like terms, multiplying both sides by the reciprocal, and then simplifying to get $\mathbf{w = 10}$.

STEP 4

- Point out that we now have the information needed to answer the question.
- Explain that we have to substitute 10 for w in the original equation to find out the amount of money in each jar. We see that Jar 1 has **$10**, Jar 2 has **$20**, and Jar 3 has **$30**. This adds up to the total of **$60**.

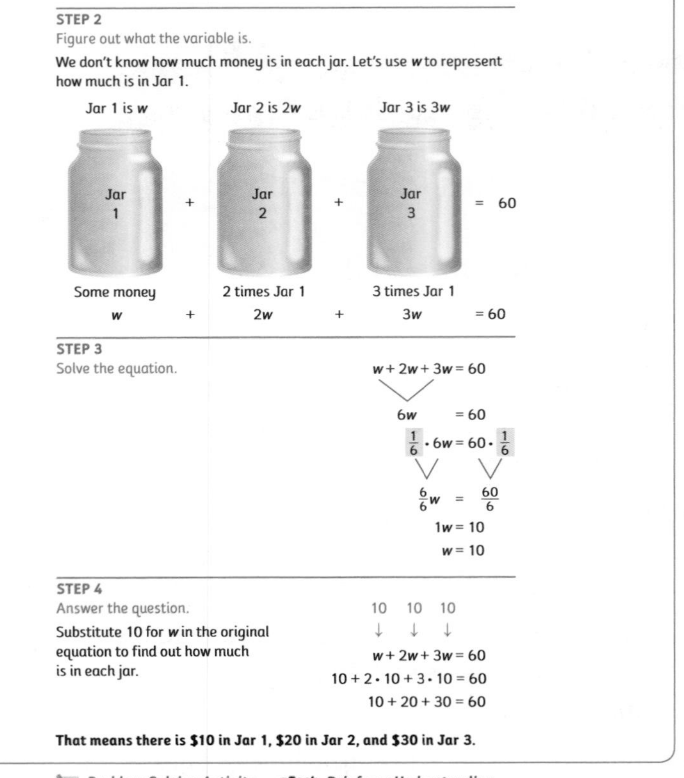

Lesson 6
STEP 2
Figure out what the variable is.
We don't know how much money is in each jar. Let's use w to represent how much is in Jar 1.
Jar 1 is w
Jar 2 is 2w
Jar 3 is 3w
Jar 1
Jar 2
Jar 3
= 60
Some money
2 times Jar 1
3 times Jar 1
w + 2w + 3w = 60
STEP 3
Solve the equation.
w + 2w + 3w = 60
6w = 60
1/6 · 6w = 60 · 1/6
6/6 w = 60/6
1w = 10
w = 10
STEP 4
Answer the question.
Substitute 10 for w in the original equation to find out how much is in each jar.
w + 2w + 3w = 60
10 + 2 · 10 + 3 · 10 = 60
10 + 20 + 30 = 60
That means there is $10 in Jar 1, $20 in Jar 2, and $30 in Jar 3.
Problem-Solving Activity
Turn to Interactive Text, page 291.
mBook Reinforce Understanding
Use the mBook Study Guide to review lesson concepts.
614
Unit 8 • Lesson 6

Problem-Solving Activity

(*Interactive Text*, pages 291–292)

Have students turn to pages 291–292 in the *Interactive Text*, and complete the activity.

Students solve problems by drawing a picture to clarify what they are solving. Then they follow the steps to solve the problem and write an algebraic expression for each problem.

Monitor students' work as they complete the activity.

Watch for:

- Can students draw an accurate picture of the problem?
- Can students write an equation for solving the problem?
- Can students solve the problem correctly?

mBook **Reinforce Understanding**

Remind students that they can review lesson concepts by accessing the online *mBook Study Guide*.

Lesson 6 | Problem-Solving Activity

Name ____________ Date ____________

Problem-Solving Activity
Using Drawings to Solve Problems

Use drawings to set up the problems. Then follow the steps to solve each problem. Make sure that you answer what the problem is asking for.

1. There are three stacks of dollar bills on the counter. The second stack has 5 times the number of bills as the first stack. The third stack has 2 times the number of bills as the first stack. When you count all of the money, the total amount is $160. How much money is in each stack?

   Stack 1: $20; Stack 2: $100; Stack 3: $40

   $x + 5x + 2x = 160$

   $8x = 160$

   $x = 20$

2. It is time to pay bills. Carmen writes three checks. The second check is 4 times the amount of the first check. The third check is 3 times the amount of the first check. The total amount for all three checks is $200. How much is written on each check?

   Check 1: $25; Check 2: $100; Check 3: $75

   $x + 4x + 3x = 200$

   $8x = 200$

   $x = 25$

3. Hector's younger sister saves pennies in jars. She has two jars with pennies. The first jar has 10 times more pennies than the second jar. Combined, she has 55 pennies. How many pennies are in each jar?

   Jar 1: 50 pennies; Jar 2: 5 pennies

   $x + 10x = 55$

   $11x = 55$

   $x = 5$

Unit 8

Unit 8 • Lesson 6 291

Lesson 6 | Problem-Solving Activity

Name ____________ Date ____________

4. Laura and Dana are both working as servers in a restaurant. At the end of the shift, they count their tips. Laura has 2 times minus $5 as much money in tips than Dana. Combined they have $40. How much money does each one have in tips?

   Laura: $25; Dana: $15

   $x + 2x - 5 = 40$

   $3x = 45$

   $x = 15$

5. There are two cash registers in the store. The second cash register has 3 times the amount of money as the first cash register plus $10. The total amount of money in the two cash registers is $90. How much money is in each cash register?

   Register 1: $20; Register 2: $70

   $x + 3x + 10 = 90$

   $4x = 80$

   $x = 20$

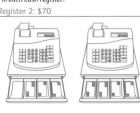

mBook **Reinforce Understanding**
Use the **mBook *Study Guide*** to review lesson concepts.

292 Unit 8 • Lesson 6

Homework

Go over the instructions on page 615 of the *Student Text* for each part of the homework.

Activity 1

Students tell the next step to solve each problem.

Activity 2

Students solve two-step equations that involve negative numbers.

Activity 3

Students use algebra and draw pictures to solve word problems.

Activity 4 • Distributed Practice

Students practice order of operations, integer operations, and one-step equations.

Lesson 6

Homework

Activity 1

Tell the next step to solve each problem.

1. $-3x + 11 = 20$
   $-3x + 11 + -11 = 20 + -11$
   $-3x = 9$
   What is the next step? Multiply each side by $-\frac{1}{3}$.

2. $-2x + 2 = 16$
   $-2x + 2 + -2 = 16 + -2$
   $-2x = 14$
   What is the next step? Multiply each side by $-\frac{1}{2}$.

Activity 2

Solve.

1. $-4x + 10 = 50$ -10
2. $-6x + -2 = -20$ 3
3. $-2x - 4 = 20$ -12

Activity 3

Write the word problems using algebra, then solve. Draw a picture to help you understand the problem better.

1. Maria saves baseball cards. She has two boxes of cards. The first box has 4 times as many cards as the second box. Altogether, she has 75 cards. How many cards does she have in each box? $x + 4x = 75$; The first box has 60 cards and the second box has 15 cards.
2. Penny and Sheldon are both working as servers in a restaurant. At the end of the evening, they count their tips. Penny has $10 less than 3 times as much money in tips as Sheldon. Altogether they have $74. How much money does each one have in tips? $x + 3x - 10 = 74$; Sheldon has $21 and Penny has $53 in tips.

Activity 4 • Distributed Practice

Solve.

1. $3(x + 4) = 12$ 0
2. $\frac{4}{5} = \frac{w}{10}$ 8
3. $5 + w = 0$ -5
4. $-100 \div a = 25$ -4
5. $\frac{1}{5} \cdot z = 1$ 5
6. $4(x - 3) = 4$ 4

Unit 8 • Lesson 615

Lesson 7 ▸Variables on Both Sides of the Equal Sign

Problem Solving: ▸Rate Problems

Lesson Planner

Skills Maintenance

Equations With Integers, Angles of Quadrilaterals

Building Number Concepts:

▸ Variables on Both Sides of the Equal Sign

Sometimes the variable in an equation appears on both sides of the equal sign. This requires additional steps to get the variable alone on just one side of the equation. We look at how to solve equations with variables on both sides of the equal sign.

Objective

Students will solve equations with variables on both sides of the equal sign.

Problem Solving:

▸ Rate Problems

We build on the previous lesson and continue to look at how drawings and pictures help us solve all kinds of problems. In this lesson, we look at rate problems.

Objective

Students will use drawings to solve rate problems.

Homework

Students select the two different ways to start solving the problems, solve equations, and solve rate problems. In Distributed Practice, students practice order of operations, integer operations, and one-step equations.

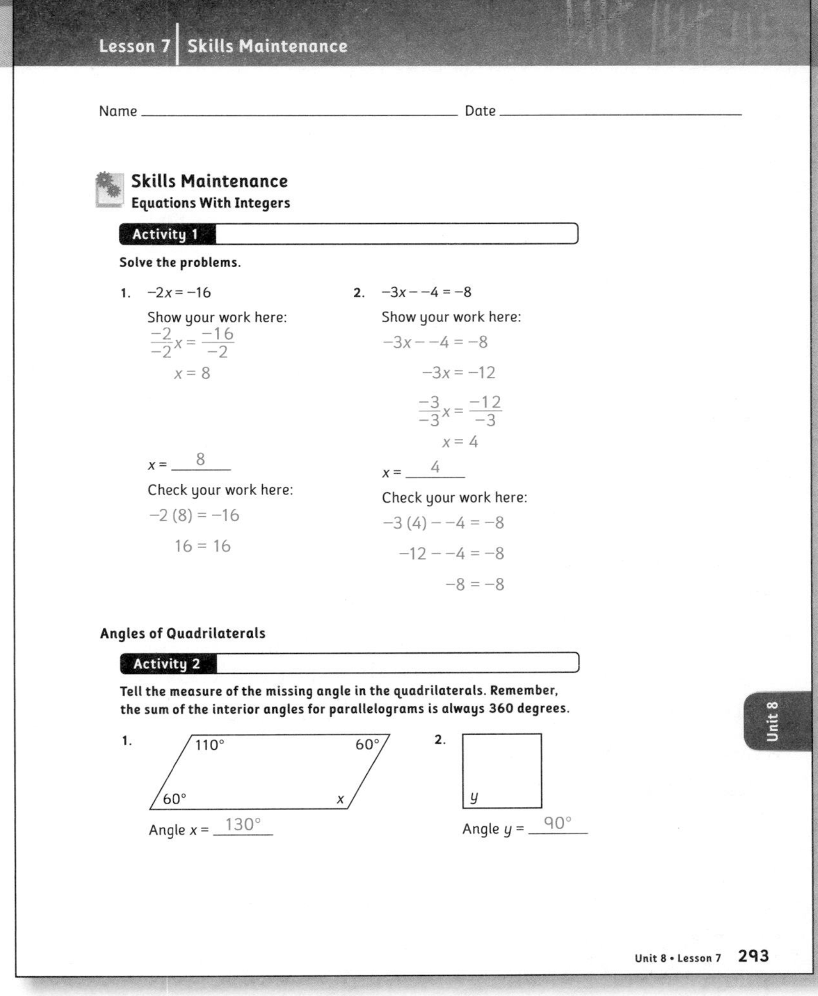

Lesson 7 | Skills Maintenance

Name ______________________ Date ______________________

Skills Maintenance
Equations With Integers

Activity 1

Solve the problems.

1. $-2x = -16$

Show your work here:

$\frac{-2}{-2}x = \frac{-16}{-2}$

$x = 8$

$x =$ 8

Check your work here:

$-2(8) = -16$

$16 = 16$

2. $-3x - -4 = -8$

Show your work here:

$-3x - -4 = -8$

$-3x = -12$

$\frac{-3}{-3}x = \frac{-12}{-3}$

$x = 4$

$x =$ 4

Check your work here:

$-3(4) - -4 = -8$

$-12 - -4 = -8$

$-8 = -8$

Angles of Quadrilaterals

Activity 2

Tell the measure of the missing angle in the quadrilaterals. Remember, the sum of the interior angles for parallelograms is always 360 degrees.

1. 110°, 60°, 60°, x

Angle $x =$ 130°

2. y

Angle $y =$ 90°

Unit 8

Unit 8 • Lesson 7 293

Skills Maintenance

Equations With Integers, Angles of Quadrilaterals
(*Interactive Text*, page 293)

Activity 1

Students solve equations with negative numbers and coefficients.

Activity 2

Students find the measure of the missing angle. Remind students that a quadrilateral's interior angles add up to 360 degrees.

Building Number Concepts:
▶ Variables on Both Sides of the Equal Sign

What do we do about variables in each expression?
(*Student Text*, pages 616–617)

Connect to Prior Knowledge
Begin by writing this statement on the board or overhead: **3 + 2 = 2 + 2 + 1**.

Ask students to check if the statement is true. Be sure they see that the statement simplifies to 5 = 5, and it is a true statement.

Substitute the variable *x* for every 2 in the equation to get: $\mathbf{3 + x = x + x + 1}$. Ask students if the statement is still true. Allow students to share their conjectures about this. Point out that there are variables on both sides of the equation, which is a departure from what we saw with equations in the past.

Link to Today's Concept
Tell students that in today's lesson, we look at equations with variables on both sides of the equal sign and learn how to solve the equations.

Demonstrate
Engagement Strategy: Teacher Modeling

Demonstrate how to solve equations with variables in both expressions in one of the following ways:

mBook: Use the *mBook Teacher Edition* for *Student Text*, page 616. m

Overhead Projector: Reproduce the equations on a transparency, and modify as discussed.

Board: Copy the equations on the board, and modify as discussed.

Lesson 7 ▶Variables on Both Sides of the Equal Sign
Problem Solving: Rate Problems

▶Variables on Both Sides of the Equal Sign

What do we do about variables in each expression?

Look at the following equations. There is a difference between them.

$$2x - 3 = 17 \qquad 2x - 3 = x + 17$$

The second equation has a variable to the right of the equal sign. Remember our goal. We want to have a positive *x* by itself on the left side of the equal sign.

Example 1

Solve the equation using what we know about opposites.

$\mathbf{2x - 3 = x + 17}$

$2x + -3 = x + 17$ ← Subtraction is the same as adding the opposite.

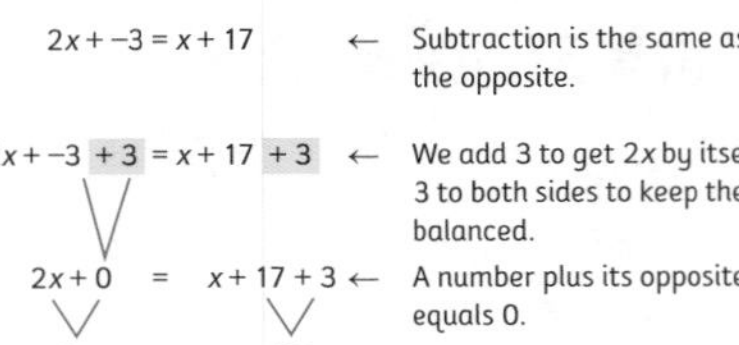
$2x + -3 + 3 = x + 17 + 3$ ← We add 3 to get 2*x* by itself. We add 3 to both sides to keep the equation balanced.

$2x + 0 = x + 17 + 3$ ← A number plus its opposite equals 0.

$2x = x + 20$

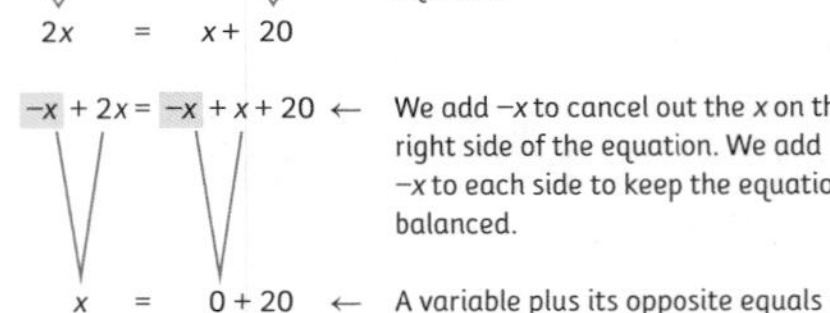
$-x + 2x = -x + x + 20$ ← We add −*x* to cancel out the *x* on the right side of the equation. We add −*x* to each side to keep the equation balanced.

$x = 0 + 20$ ← A variable plus its opposite equals 0.

$\mathbf{x = 20}$

616 Unit 8 • Lesson 7

- Display the two equations: $\mathbf{2x - 3 = 17}$ and $\mathbf{2x - 3 = x + 17}$. Note that the second equation has a variable on both sides of the equation. m
- Move to **Example 1** to show how to solve $\mathbf{2x - 3 = x + 17}$. Tell students that we solve this kind of problem just like we solved any other problem; it just takes more steps. m
- Remind students that subtraction is adding the opposite, so we can rewrite the equation: $\mathbf{2x + -3 = x + 17}$. m
- Explain that we want to get 2x by itself, so we add 3 to both sides of the equation. m
- Walk through the addition to get $\mathbf{2x = x + 20}$. m
- Explain that we want to cancel out the *x* on the right side of the equation, so we add −*x* to both sides of the equation to keep it balanced. m
- Walk through the addition to get $\mathbf{x = 20}$. m

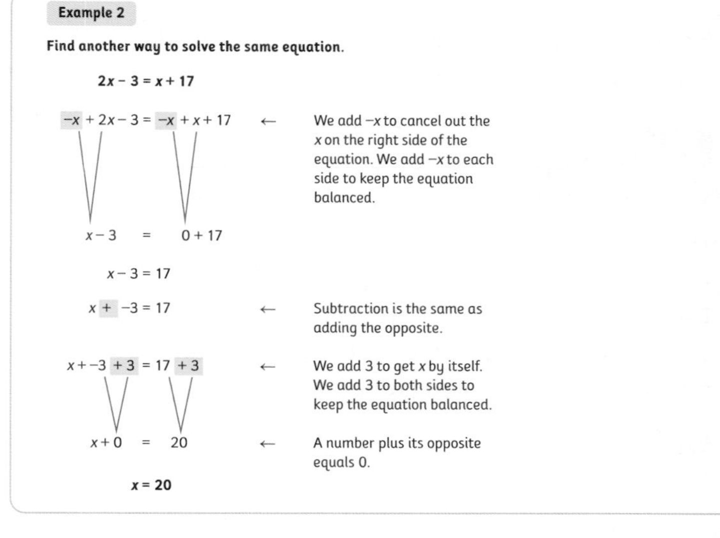
Lesson 7

Sometimes, equations like the one in Example 1 can be solved in more than one way. In fact, it is important in algebra to be flexible.

Example 2 uses the same equation. This time we start by cancelling out the x on the right side. We end up with the same answer.

Example 2

Find another way to solve the same equation.

$$2x - 3 = x + 17$$

$-x + 2x - 3 = -x + x + 17$ ← We add $-x$ to cancel out the x on the right side of the equation. We add $-x$ to each side to keep the equation balanced.

$x - 3 = 0 + 17$

$x - 3 = 17$

$x + -3 = 17$ ← Subtraction is the same as adding the opposite.

$x + -3 + 3 = 17 + 3$ ← We add 3 to get x by itself. We add 3 to both sides to keep the equation balanced.

$x + 0 = 20$ ← A number plus its opposite equals 0.

$$x = 20$$

Apply Skills Turn to ***Interactive Text***, page 294.

mBook Reinforce Understanding Use the ***mBook Study Guide*** to review lesson concepts.

Unit 8 • Lesson 617

Demonstrate

- Next turn to page 617 of the *Student Text* and tell students that there is more than one way to solve the problem from Example 1.
- Explain that we approached the solution by adjusting the number terms first (e.g., adding + 3 to both sides).
- Tell students that we could have begun by manipulating the variable terms first. We could add $-x$ to each side as our initial step.
- Go over **Example 2**, which demonstrates how to solve the problem by adding $-x$ as the first step.
- Show students how we first add $-x$ to cancel out the x on the right side. Remind them that we need to add $-x$ to both sides to keep the equation balanced.
- Walk through the addition to get $\mathbf{x - 3 = 17}$.
- Point out that subtraction is the same as adding the opposite, so we rewrite the equation with addition.
- Explain that now we need to get x by itself, so we add 3 to both sides of the equation.
- Walk through the addition to get $\mathbf{x = 20}$.
- Be sure students understand that the steps are the same as in Example 1; we are just performing them in a different order.

Check for Understanding
Engagement Strategy: Pair/Share

Write the equation $\mathbf{2x + 4 = x + 2}$ on the board. Divide the class into pairs. Tell students that one partner will solve the equation by first subtracting 4 from both sides of the equation. The other partner will solve the equation by first cancelling out the x on the right side of the equation. Allow students time to solve the equation ($x = -2$). Then have partners compare their answers and work. They should see that they both have the same answer, regardless of the first step they used. Have partners explain to each other the steps they took to solve the equation. Review the solutions with the class.

Apply Skills

(*Interactive Text*, pages 294–295)

Have students turn to pages 294–295 in the *Interactive Text*, and complete the activity.

Activity 1

Students solve equations where there are variable terms on both sides of the equation. Students should show every step of their work, then substitute their answer back into the original problem to check the answer. Monitor students' work as they complete the activity.

Watch for:

- Can students determine the steps for getting one x alone on one side of the equation?
- Do students show their work by writing out each step that is justifiable by a property or rule, then write about the differences?
- Do students check the answer at the end by substituting the value for the variable in the original equation?

mBook **Reinforce Understanding**
Remind students that they can review lesson concepts by accessing the online *mBook Study Guide*.

Lesson 7 | Apply Skills

Name ______________________ Date ______________

Apply Skills
Variables on Both Sides of the Equal Sign

Activity 1

Solve the equations that have variables on both sides of the equal sign. Show all of your work. Check your answer by substituting the value back into the original equation.

Model

$3x - 6 = x + 8$
$-x + 3x - 6 = -x + x + 8$
$2x - 6 = 8$
$2x - 6 + 6 = 8 + 6$
$2x = 14$
$x = 7$

1. $4x + -2 = -2x + 4$
Show your work here:
$4x + -2 + 2 = -2x + 4 + 2$
$4x + 2x = -2x + 2x + 6$
$6x = 6$
$x =$ 1
Check your work here:
$4(1) + -2 = -2(1) + 4$
$2 = 2$

2. $3 + x = -2 + x + x$
Show your work here:
$3 + x = -2 + 2x$
$3 + x + -x = -2 + 2x + -x$
$3 + 2 = -2 + 2 + x$
$5 = x$
$x =$ 5
Check your work here:
$3 + 5 = -2 + 5 + 5$
$8 = 8$

294 Unit 8 • Lesson 7

Lesson 7 | Apply Skills

Name ______________________ Date ______________

3. $6x - 4 = -4x + 36$
Show your work here:
$6x = -4x$
$+ 40$
$10x = 40$
$x = 4$
$x =$ 4
Check your work here:
$24 - 4 = -16 + 36$
$20 = 20$

4. $-2 - 6 - x = -2x - 6$
Show your work here:
$-8 - x = -2x - 6$
$-2 - x = -2x$
$-2 = -x$
$2 = x$
$x =$ 2
Check your work here:
$-2 - 6 - 2 = -2(2) - 6$
$-10 = -10$

Unit 8

Unit 8 • Lesson 7 295

Problem Solving:
▶ Rate Problems

How do we use drawings to solve rate problems?

(*Student Text*, pages 618–620)

Connect to Prior Knowledge

Use the top of page 618 in the *Student Text* to remind students about the rate formula. It is $r \cdot t = d$ where r = rate, t = time, and d = distance.

Link to Today's Concept

In today's lesson students learn that it often helps to make a drawing of these types of problems.

Demonstrate

- Have students look at **Example 1**. Read the problem with students, then walk through the four steps to solve the problem.

STEP 1

- Show how we can draw two planes from the word problem and the rate. This helps us identify what we know and what we do not know.
- We know that Plane 1 is flying 150 miles per hour and Plane 2 is flying 350 miles per hour.

Lesson 7

▶Problem Solving: Rate Problems

How do we use drawings to solve rate problems?

In the previous unit we learned how to do simple rate problems. The formula used in a simple rate problem is this equation:

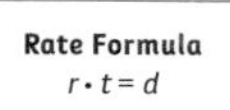

Rate Formula
$r \cdot t = d$

r = rate t = time d = distance

A rate problem can be more complicated than the one where we just substitute for one of the unknown variables.

To solve a complicated problem, it often helps to make a drawing to represent what is going on in the problem.

Let's use the four steps to solve a problem.

Example 1

Use a drawing to solve the problem.

Problem:

Two planes take off from an airport at the same time going opposite directions. One plane is flying 150 miles per hour. The second plane is flying 350 miles per hour. How long will it take them to be 1,000 miles apart?

STEP 1

Begin with a drawing.

618 Unit 8 • Lesson 7

How do we use drawings to solve rate problems? *(continued)*

Demonstrate

- Continue discussing the steps in Example 1 on page 619 of the *Student Text.*

STEP 2

- Explain that the next step is to figure out the variable. Remind students that we use a variable for what we do not know. In this case, we do not know the time. We will use k to represent the time.
- Show how we set up the equation using the variable, what we know, and the basic rate formula. We know that Plane 1 and Plane 2 will be flying for the same amount of time. So our equation is **150*k* + 350*k* = 1,000**.

Lesson 7

STEP 2

Figure out what the variable is.

We use a variable for something we don't know. The question asks how long it will take the planes to be 1,000 miles apart. That means we do not know the time.

Let's use the variable k to represent the time.

Both planes will be flying for the same amount of time, so we use the variable to show rate times time.

	$r \cdot t$
Plane 1	$150k$
Plane 2	$350k$

We put this information into the basic rate equation: $r \cdot t = d$.

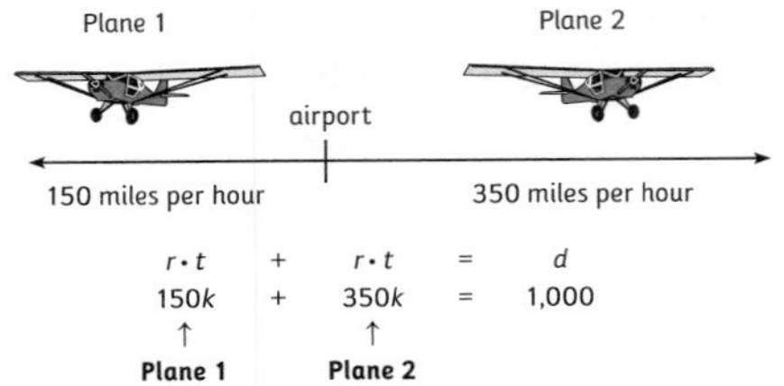

$r \cdot t$	+	$r \cdot t$	=	d
$150k$	+	$350k$	=	1,000
↑ **Plane 1**		↑ **Plane 2**		

Demonstrate

- Continue discussing the steps in Example 1 on page 620 of the *Student Text*.

STEP 3

- Point out that now we can solve the equation. Walk through the steps to solve the equation: combine like terms, multiply both sides by the reciprocal, and then simplify to get $\boldsymbol{k} = \mathbf{2}$.

STEP 4

- Point out that we now have the information needed to answer the question. Explain that we have to substitute 2 for k in the original equation to check the answer and to answer the equation.
- Show how to substitute the answer into the original equation, then work through the multiplication and division to see that **1,000 = 1,000**.
- Explain that the answer to the word problem is that **the planes will be 1,000 miles apart after 2 hours**.

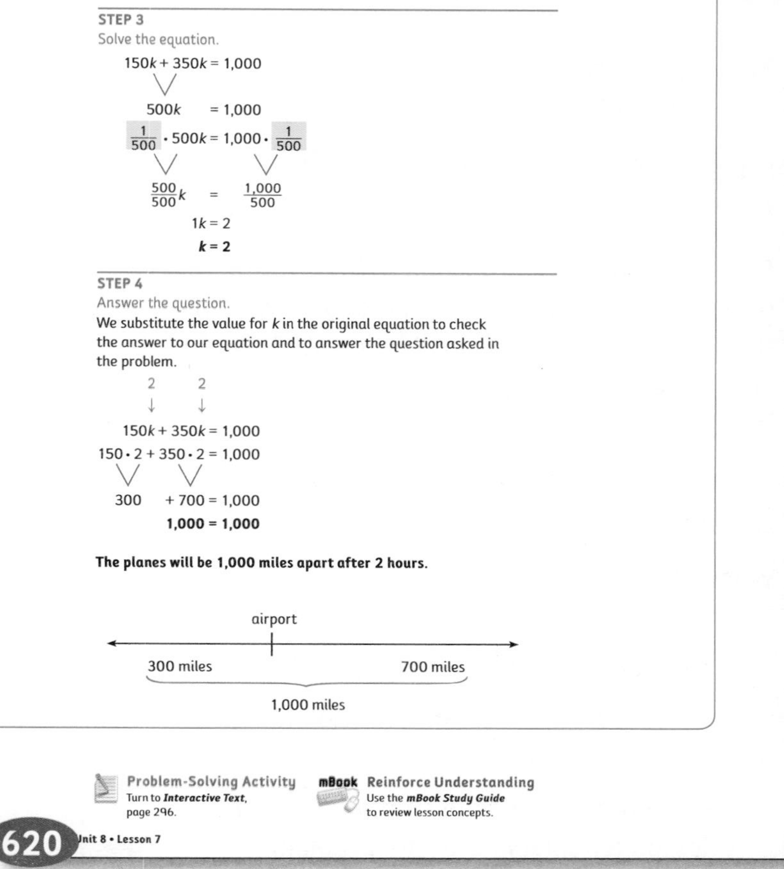

Problem-Solving Activity

(*Interactive Text*, pages 296–297)

Have students turn to pages 296–297 in the *Interactive Text*, and complete the activity.

Students solve rate problems. They draw pictures to represent the problem, then follow the steps they learned in this lesson. Remind students to check their answer by substituting their answer into the original problem.

Monitor students' work as they complete the activity.

Watch for:

- Can students draw a picture representing the relationship in the rate problem?
- Can students write the equation for solving the rate problem?
- Can students use the steps outlined in the lesson for solving the rate problem?
- Do students check the answer at the end using substitution?

mBook **Reinforce Understanding**

Remind students that they can review lesson concepts by accessing the online *mBook Study Guide*.

Lesson 7 | Problem-Solving Activity

Name ______________________ Date ______________________

Problem-Solving Activity
Using Drawings to Solve Rate Problems

Draw pictures to help you set up the problems. Then follow the steps you learned in this lesson to solve each problem. Remember that these problems are based on the formula $r \cdot t = d$. Make sure that you answer what the problem is asking.

1. Two cars start out in two different cities. The cities are 270 miles apart. The cars are driving toward each other on the same road. The first car's speed is 50 miles per hour. The second car's speed is 40 miles per hour. How long before they meet? 3 hours

$270 = 40k + 50k$

$270 = 90k$

$k = 3$

2. Jing and Maya are riding their bikes. They start at Jing's house, but they go opposite directions. Both are going the same speed and they ride for 2 hours. At the end of that time, they are 40 miles apart. How fast are they riding (in miles per hour)? 10 mph

$40 = 2 \cdot 2x$

$40 = 4x$

$x = 10$

296 Unit 8 • Lesson 7

Lesson 7 | Problem-Solving Activity

Name ______________________ Date ______________________

3. Bill and Carl are running a race for cancer. Each person gets $3 for every mile he runs. Bill is running 8 miles per hour and Carl is running 12 miles per hour. How long will they have to run before they run a total of 60 miles between the two of them? 3 hours

$60 = 8c + 12c$

$60 = 20c$

$c = 3$

4. Two space satellites are going to crash into each other in their next orbit around Earth. They are now 5,000 miles apart. The first satellite is traveling 200 miles per minute and the second satellite is traveling 300 miles per minute. How many minutes until they crash? 10 minutes

$5{,}000 = 200s + 300s$

$5{,}000 = 500s$

$s = 10$

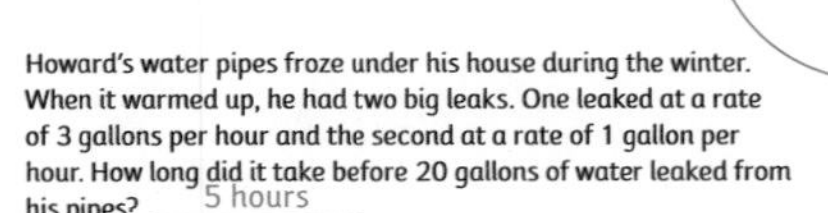

5. Howard's water pipes froze under his house during the winter. When it warmed up, he had two big leaks. One leaked at a rate of 3 gallons per hour and the second at a rate of 1 gallon per hour. How long did it take before 20 gallons of water leaked from his pipes? 5 hours

$3k + k = 20$

$4k = 20$

$k = 5$

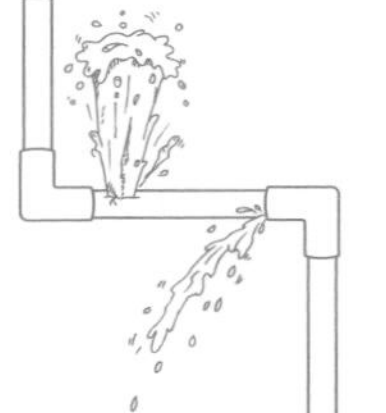

mBook Reinforce Understanding
Use the **mBook *Study Guide*** to review lesson concepts.

Unit 8

Unit 8 • Lesson 7 297

Homework

Go over the instructions on page 621 of the *Student Text* for each part of the homework.

Activity 1

Students choose the multiple choice answers that demonstrate the two different ways to start solving the problems.

Activity 2

Students solve equations with variables on both sides of the equal sign.

Activity 3

Students solve rate problems.

Activity 4 • Distributed Practice

Students practice order of operations, integer operations, and one-step equations.

Lesson 7

Homework

Activity 1

For each problem, select the two different ways you could start solving them (choose two answers).

1. $2x + 7 = -x + 5$ a and b
   (a) Add x to each side.
   (b) Add −5 to each side.
   (c) Divide each side by 7.
   (d) Multiply each side by 2.
2. $y - 8 = 12 + 2y$ b and c
   (a) Multiply each side by 2.
   (b) Add 8 to each side.
   (c) Add $-y$ to each side.
   (d) Add 12 to each side.

Activity 2

Solve.

1. $a + 10 = 2a - 2$ 12
2. $4 - 2b = b + 1$ 1
3. $-3 - c = c + 2$ −2.5
4. $x - 4 = 3x + 8$ −6

Activity 3

Solve the rate problems using the formula $r \cdot t = d$.

1. Raj's family was traveling at about 60 mph to visit cousins living 100 miles away. About how long will it take them to get there? $1\frac{2}{3}$ hours or 1 hour and 40 minutes
2. If a satellite is 4,000 miles away from its target and it is traveling 200 miles per minute, how many minutes before it reaches its target? 20 minutes

Activity 4 • Distributed Practice

Solve.

1. $-5 - -2 = y$ −3
2. $-18 + w = 2$ 20
3. $\frac{1}{3} \cdot z = 1$ 3
4. $\frac{5}{7} = \frac{h}{42}$ 30
5. $4{,}000 = 200t$ 20
6. $12 = 3(a + 2)$ 2

Unit 8 • Lesson 621

Lesson 8 ▶The Distributive Property in Equations

Problem Solving:
▶Angles and Intersecting Lines

Lesson Planner

Skills Maintenance

Equations With Variables on Both Sides

Building Number Concepts:
▶ The Distributive Property in Equations

Students review that the distributive property allows us to distribute the coefficient across each term in parentheses in an expression. In this lesson, students build on what they know about the distributive property and apply it to solving equations.

Objective

Students will use the distributive property to solve equations.

Problem Solving:
▶ Angles and Intersecting Lines

We examine the relationship between angles and intersecting lines. Students learn that intersecting lines create angles which have unique properties. Learning these properties helps students understand them better and allows them to use assumptions that help find the measures of missing angles.

Objective

Students will use the properties of angles and intersecting lines to find the measure of missing angles.

Homework

Students decide if the terms inside the parentheses can be combined, solve problems using the distributive property, and tell the measure of the missing angles. In Distributed Practice, students practice order of operations, integer operations, and one-step equations.

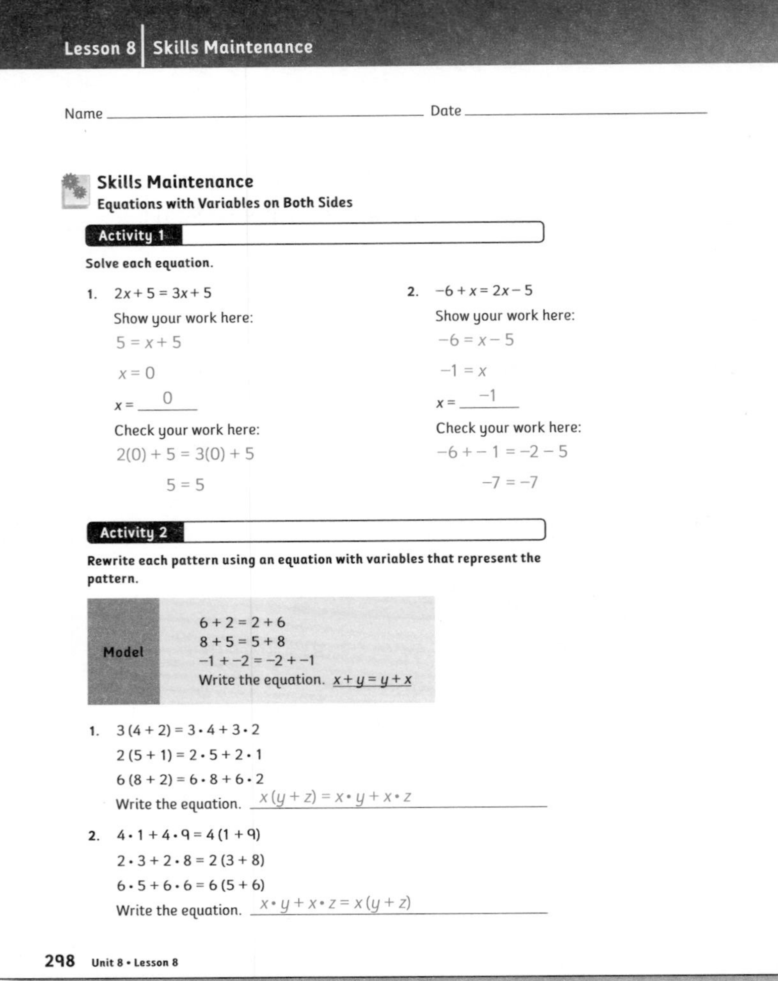

Lesson 8 | Skills Maintenance

Name ______ Date ______

Skills Maintenance
Equations with Variables on Both Sides

Activity 1

Solve each equation.

1. $2x + 5 = 3x + 5$
   Show your work here:
   $5 = x + 5$
   $x = 0$
   $x =$ 0
   Check your work here:
   $2(0) + 5 = 3(0) + 5$
   $5 = 5$

2. $-6 + x = 2x - 5$
   Show your work here:
   $-6 = x - 5$
   $-1 = x$
   $x =$ −1
   Check your work here:
   $-6 + -1 = -2 - 5$
   $-7 = -7$

Activity 2

Rewrite each pattern using an equation with variables that represent the pattern.

Model	$6 + 2 = 2 + 6$ $8 + 5 = 5 + 8$ $-1 + -2 = -2 + -1$ Write the equation. $x + y = y + x$

1. $3(4 + 2) = 3 \cdot 4 + 3 \cdot 2$
   $2(5 + 1) = 2 \cdot 5 + 2 \cdot 1$
   $6(8 + 2) = 6 \cdot 8 + 6 \cdot 2$
   Write the equation. $x(y + z) = x \cdot y + x \cdot z$

2. $4 \cdot 1 + 4 \cdot 9 = 4(1 + 9)$
   $2 \cdot 3 + 2 \cdot 8 = 2(3 + 8)$
   $6 \cdot 5 + 6 \cdot 6 = 6(5 + 6)$
   Write the equation. $x \cdot y + x \cdot z = x(y + z)$

298 Unit 8 • Lesson 8

Skills Maintenance

Equations With Variables on Both Sides
(*Interactive Text*, page 298)

Activity 1

Students solve equations with variables on each side.

Activity 2

Students write an equation that shows a general pattern based on the three numeric examples.

Building Number Concepts: ▶ The Distributive Property in Equations

How does the distributive property work in equations?

(*Student Text*, pages 622–625)

Connect to Prior Knowledge

Begin by reminding students of the difference parentheses make in an expression. Write the two expressions on the board:

$\mathbf{2x + 3}$ and $\mathbf{2(x + 3)}$.

Explain that the seemingly small difference of the parentheses makes a big difference in the way we approach the expression. In the first case, the expression cannot be simplified further. In the second case, the distributive property can be used to simplify it.

Link to Today's Concept

Tell students that in today's lesson, we look at how to use the distributive property in equations.

Demonstrate

Engagement Strategy: Teacher Modeling

Demonstrate how to use the distribute property in equations in one of the following ways:

mBook: Use the *mBook Teacher Edition* for *Student Text*, pages 622–624. m

Overhead Projector: Reproduce the expressions and equations on a transparency, and modify as discussed.

Board: Copy the expressions and equations on the board, and modify as discussed.

Lesson 8 ▶The Distributive Property in Equations
Problem Solving:
▶Angles and Intersecting Lines

▶The Distributive Property in Equations

How does the distributive property work in equations?

Look at the following equations. There is a difference between them.

$2x + 4 = 18 \qquad 2(x + 4) = 18$

The equation on the right contains parentheses.

We learned about expressions with parentheses when we worked with the distributive property. Let's stop and think about how to approach expressions like these.

What we know:

- We cannot combine terms that are different or unlike terms. In this case, we cannot combine the $2x$ and the 4.

$2x + 4$

The Distributive Property and Expressions

- We can "distribute" the 2 to each term when we simplify the expression. We multiply 2 times both terms inside of the parentheses.

$2(x + 4)$
$2x + 8$

622 Unit 8 • Lesson 8

- Show the two expressions $\mathbf{2x + 4 = 18}$ and $\mathbf{2(x + 4) = 18}$ and discuss how they are slightly different in the way they look, but quite different in the way we solve them. m
- Point out that the equation with the parentheses is another example of the distributive property.
- Remind students about the general patterns they wrote in the Skills Maintenance activity, which were examples of the distributive property.
- Review the bulleted points and then show how we use the distributive property with the expression $\mathbf{2(x + 4) = 18}$. m
- Show students how the 2 is distributed across the two terms in parentheses to get $\mathbf{2x + 8}$. m

How does the distributive property work in equations? *(continued)*

Demonstrate

- Go over **Example 1**. Refer again to the equation $\mathbf{2(x + 4) = 18}$ and remind students that we use the distributive property to distribute the 2 across the two terms in the parentheses: $\mathbf{2x + 8 = 18}$.
- Explain that now we can solve the equation as we always have. First we add −8 on the left side of the equation to cancel out the 8. We need to do this on both sides to keep the equation balanced. Walk through the addition to get $\mathbf{2x = 10}$.
- Remind students that we multiply by the reciprocal $\frac{1}{2}$ to get x by itself. We need to do this on both sides to keep the equation balanced.
- Walk through the multiplication and division to get $\mathbf{x = 5}$.

Now let's use what we know about the distributive property to help solve equations.

Once we use the property, all we have to do is use the other rules and properties in our Algebra Toolbox.

Example 1

Use the distributive property to solve the equation.

$\mathbf{2(x + 4) = 18}$

$2x + 8 = 18$ ← The distributive property: $2 \cdot x = 2x$ and $2 \cdot 4 = 8$.

$2x + 8 + -8 = 18 + -8$ ← We add −8 to cancel out the 8 on the left side of the equation. We add −8 to each side to keep the equation balanced.

$2x + 0 = 10$

$2x = 10$

$\frac{1}{2} \cdot 2x = 10 \cdot \frac{1}{2}$ ← We multiply by $\frac{1}{2}$ to get x by itself. We multiply each side by $\frac{1}{2}$ to keep the equation balanced.

$\frac{2}{2}x = \frac{10}{2}$

$1x = 5$

$\mathbf{x = 5}$ ← A number times 1 is the same number.

Notice what happens when we substitute for x in the original equation. We can add inside of the parentheses because both terms are the same. They are like terms.

Demonstrate

- Continue looking at Example 1 to explain that we can substitute the answer for x in the original equation to check our work. m
- Display the new equation: **2(5 + 4) = 18.** Point out that now we can combine the terms inside the parentheses because they are like terms; they are both numeric terms. m
- Explain that this makes it a little easier to solve. Be sure students understand we cannot combine terms if one of the terms is a variable and one is a number. m
- Show how to multiply to get **18 = 18.** m
- Next go over **Example 2**, which provides students with another example of how the distributive property works when solving equations.
- Point out the equation **5(2*x* − 1) = 25.** Discuss how we distribute the 5 outside the parentheses across the terms inside the parentheses to get **10*x* − 5 = 25.**
- Explain that now we solve the equation like any other equation. In this case we rewrite the equation as addition because subtraction is the same as adding the opposite.
- Show how we cancel out the −5 on the left by adding 5. Remind students that we need to do this on both sides to keep the equation balanced.
- Walk through the addition to get **10*x* = 30.**

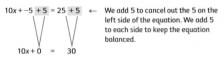

$2(x + 4) = 18$ (5 ↓ above x)	←	We substitute 5 for x.
$2(5 + 4) = 18$	←	We add 5 + 4 because they are like terms.
$2(9) = 18$	←	The equation 2(9) is the same as 2 • 9.
$2 \cdot 9 = 18$	←	The numbers are the same.
18 = 18		

We see two important ideas in Example 1:

- First, we begin by checking what is inside of the parentheses. If they are like terms, we combine them. If they are unlike terms, we cannot do anything.
- Second, we have to distribute the term on the outside across all terms that are inside of the parentheses.

Let's look at another example.

Example 2

Use the distributive property to solve the equation.

5(2*x* − 1) = 25

$10x - 5 = 25$	←	The distributive property: $5 \cdot 2x = 10x$ and $5 \cdot 1 = 5$.
$10x + -5 = 25$	←	Subtraction is the same as adding the opposite.
$10x + -5 + 5 = 25 + 5$	←	We add 5 to cancel out the 5 on the left side of the equation. We add 5 to each side to keep the equation balanced.
$10x + 0 = 30$		
10*x* = 30		

How does the distributive property work in equations? *(continued)*

Demonstrate

- Continue looking at Example 2 on page 625 of the *Student Text.*
- Remind students that we want to get x by itself, so we multiply by the reciprocal of 10, $\frac{1}{10}$. We do this on both sides to balance the equation.
- Walk through the multiplication and division to get $\boldsymbol{x = 3}$.
- Remind students that we can check by substituting the value back into the original equation.
- Show students how to substitute 3 into the original equation. In 5(6 − 1) = 25, we can combine the terms to get 5 because they are like terms.
- Walk through the multiplication to see that **25 = 25**.

Check for Understanding
Engagement Strategy: Think Tank

Write $\mathbf{3(x + 2) = 12}$ on the board. Distribute strips of paper and have students write their names on them. Then have them solve the equation. Encourage students to write out their steps. When students finish, collect the strips of paper in a container. Draw out an answer to read aloud. If the answer is correct, congratulate the student and invite the student to explain the solution. If the answer is incorrect, ask for a student to explain the correct answer ($x = 2$).

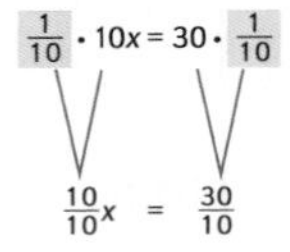

Lesson 8

$\frac{1}{10} \cdot 10x = 30 \cdot \frac{1}{10}$ ← We multiply by $\frac{1}{10}$ to get x by itself. We multiply each side by $\frac{1}{10}$ to keep the equation balanced.

$\frac{10}{10}x = \frac{30}{10}$

$1x = 3$

$\boldsymbol{x = 3}$ ← A number times 1 is the same number.

Remember what happens when we substitute for x in the original equation. We can add inside of the parentheses because both terms are now the same. They are like terms.

$5(2x - 1) = 25$ (3 substituted for x)

$5(6 - 1) = 25$ ← We substitute 3 for x and $3 \cdot 2 = 6$.

$5(5) = 25$ ← We subtract 6 − 1 because they are like terms.

$5 \cdot 5 = 25$ ← The equation 5(5) is the same as $5 \cdot 5$.

25 = 25 ← The numbers are the same.

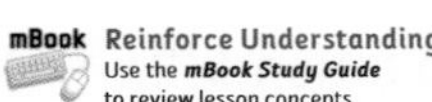

Apply Skills Turn to ***Interactive Text***, page 299.

mBook Reinforce Understanding Use the ***mBook Study Guide*** to review lesson concepts.

Unit 8 • Lesson 625

Apply Skills
(*Interactive Text*, page 299)

Have students turn to page 299 in the *Interactive Text*, and complete the activity.

Activity 1

Students solve equations using the distributive property. Monitor students' work as they complete the activity.

Watch for:

- Can students use the distributive property to distribute the number outside the parentheses across the two terms inside the parentheses?
- Can students get the correct answer for x?
- Do students remember to check the answer at the end using substitution?

mBook **Reinforce Understanding**
Remind students that they can review lesson concepts by accessing the online *mBook Study Guide* to review lesson concepts.

Name ____________________ Date ____________________

Apply Skills
The Distributive Property in Equations

Activity 1

Solve the equations using the distributive property. Be sure to show your work and check your answers.

1. $3(x + 5) = 30$

   Show your work here:
   $3x + 15 = 30$
   $3x = 15$
   $x = 5$
   $x =$ 5

   Check your work here:
   $3(10) = 30$
   $30 = 30$

2. $2(x + 10) = 40$

   Show your work here:
   $2x + 20 = 40$
   $2x = 20$
   $x = 10$
   $x =$ 10

   Check your work here:
   $2(20) = 40$
   $40 = 40$

3. $-2(-x + -1) = -12$

   Show your work here:
   $2x + 2 = -12$
   $2x = -14$
   $x = -7$
   $x =$ −7

   Check your work here:
   $-2(6) = -12$
   $-12 = -12$

Unit 8

Problem Solving:
▶ Angles and Intersecting Lines

What is the relationship between angles and intersecting lines?

(*Student Text*, page 626)

Connect to Prior Knowledge

Begin by reviewing the properties of a rectangle with students. Ask students to share what they know about rectangles.

Listen for:

- *Opposite sides are equal in length.*
- *Opposite sides are parallel.*
- *All the interior angles measure 90 degrees.*

- Turn to page 626 of the *Student Text* and read the material about the properties of a rectangle.

Link to Today's Concept

Tell students that today we use what we know about rectangles to see the relationship between angles and intersection lines.

Demonstrate

- Have students look at the diagram of the rectangle. Point out the symbol that represents a right angle, or 90°.
- Have students look at what happens when we extend the sides of the rectangle.
- Point out that angles 2, 3, and 4 are exterior angles to the rectangle.

Lesson 8

▶Problem Solving: Angles and Intersecting Lines

What is the relationship between angles and intersecting lines?

Let's look at the properties of a rectangle.

Properties of a Rectangle

- Not all of the sides are equal in length.
- The opposite sides of rectangle are parallel.
- Every interior angle measures 90 degrees. That is what the little square stands for in each angle.

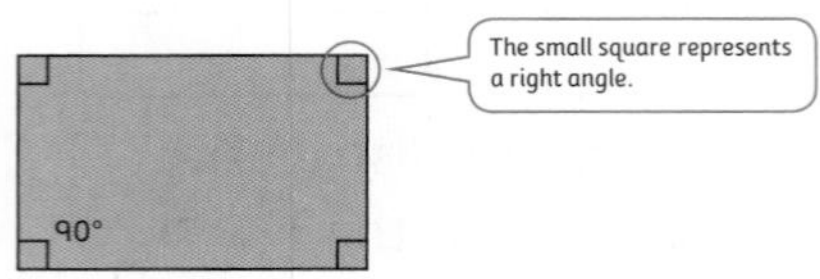
The small square represents a right angle.
90°

What happens when we extend the sides of a rectangle as shown in the next figure?

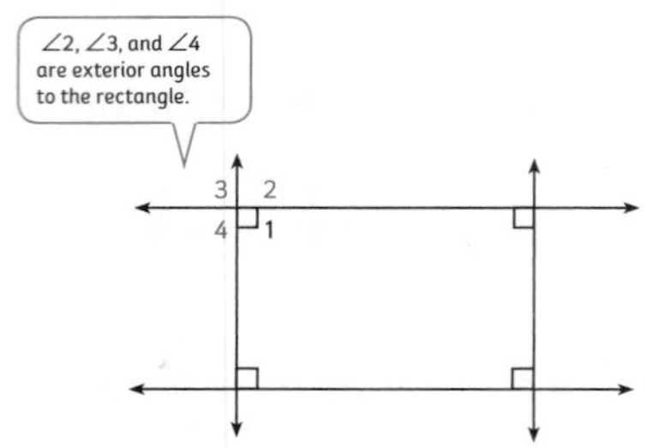
∠2, ∠3, and ∠4 are exterior angles to the rectangle.
3
2
4
1

626 Unit 8 • Lesson 8

How do we find the measure of exterior angles?
(*Student Text*, pages 627–631)

Demonstrate

- Turn to page 627 of the *Student Text*. Go over the material that discusses the properties of straight lines.
- Remind students that straight lines have an angle measure of 180 degrees.
- Have students look at the diagram of the corner of the rectangle where we see the intersecting lines. Point out the labels for the lines.
- Next look at **Example 1** and explain that we will find the measures of angles **2**, **3**, and **4**.

Lesson 8

How do we find the measure of exterior angles?

By extending the sides of the rectangle, we created exterior angles. How do we find the measures of the exterior angles 2, 3, and 4?

We need to remember one important property of straight lines to answer this question:

- The measure of any straight line is 180 degrees.

Let's look closely at the corner of the rectangle and especially at the intersecting lines. We added labels to the line segments so that we can talk about them.

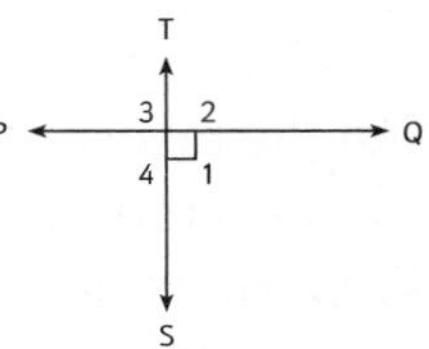

Example 1 shows how we find the measures of the exterior angles.

Example 1

Find the measures of ∠2, ∠3, and ∠4.

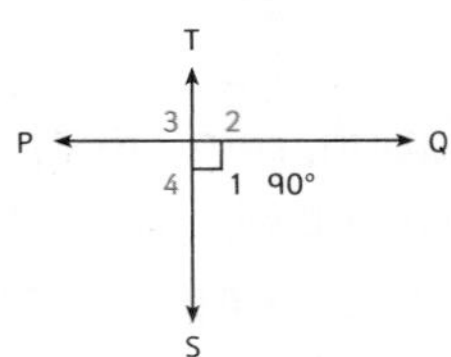

Unit 8 • Lesson 627

How do we find the measure of exterior angles? *(continued)*

Demonstrate

- Continue to look at Example 1 on page 628 of the *Student Text*.
- Demonstrate how to find the measure of angle **2**. Explain that we know that angle 1 is 90 degrees and we know that a line—in this case line ST—measures 180 degrees.
- Show how we set up the equation with the variable x representing the measure of angle 2.
- Walk through the equation, reminding students of the steps to get x by itself. We find that $x = 90$ degrees. So **angle 2 is 90 degrees**.
- Show how to find the measure of angle **3**. Walk through the steps in the same way to find that **angle 3 is also 90 degrees**.

First, what is the measure of ∠2?

The vertical line ST has ∠1 and ∠2.

- We know that ∠1 = 90 degrees.
- We also know that line ST measures 180 degrees.
- Let x = the measure of ∠2.

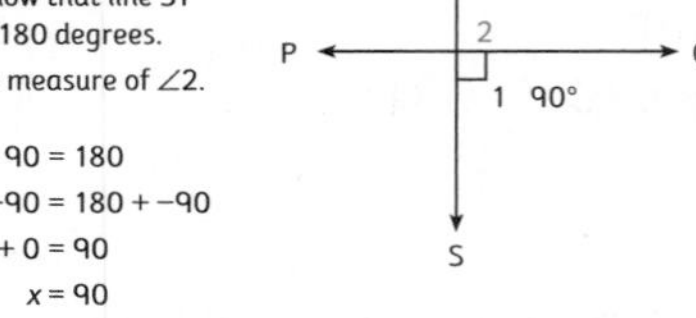

$$x + 90 = 180$$
$$x + 90 + -90 = 180 + -90$$
$$x + 0 = 90$$
$$x = 90$$

The measure of ∠2 = 90°

What is the measure of ∠3?

- We know that ∠2 = 90 degrees.
- We know the line PQ is straight so it measures 180 degrees.
- Let y = the measure of ∠3.

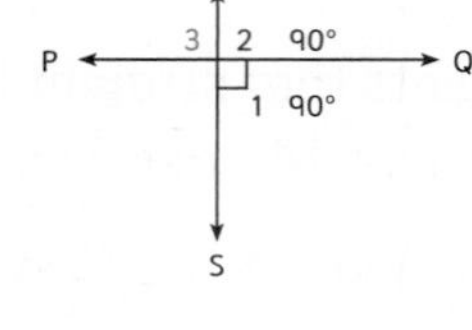

$$y + 90 = 180$$
$$y + 90 + -90 = 180 + -90$$
$$y + 0 = 90$$
$$y = 90$$

The measure of ∠3 = 90°

Demonstrate

- Continue with Example 1 on page 629 of the *Student Text*. Show how to find the measure of angle **4**.
- Point out that we can use either line PQ or line ST to figure out the measure of angle 4.
- Explain that we already know that angle 1 and angle 2 are 90 degrees, and we know that a line measures 180 degrees.
- Tell students that we can take the equation $\mathbf{x + 90 = 180}$ that we used to find the other angles. We know that $x = 90$, so **angle 4 is also 90 degrees**.
- Direct students' attention to the diagram at the bottom of the page. Explain that this diagram shows the corner of a trapezoid whose sides have been extended. Point out the labeled angles and lines.

What is the measure of $\angle 4$?

- We can use either line PQ or line ST to figure out the measure of $\angle 4$.
- If we add angles 1, 2, and 3 we get 270 degrees.
- We know that the sum of the measurements of angles 1, 2, 3, and 4 is 360 degrees.
- Let's see why the measure of $\angle 4$ is 90 degrees. We know that the measure of $\angle 4$ must be $360° - 270° = 90°$.

T
90° 3 | 2 90°
P Q
4 | 1 90°
S

When we extend the sides of a trapezoid, the same thing happens. We create exterior angles. In the picture below, the exterior angles are labeled $\angle 2$, $\angle 3$, and $\angle 4$.

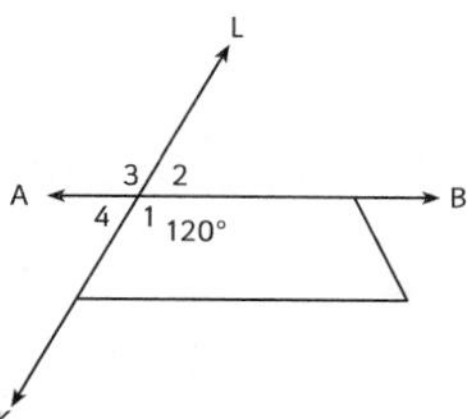

How do we find the measure of exterior angles? *(continued)*

Demonstrate

- Turn to page 630 of the *Student Text* to go over **Example 2**. Point out that since we know one angle, we can use our knowledge of straight lines and angles to figure out all the rest of the angles.
- Remind students that lines AB and KL each measure 180 degrees because they are straight lines.
- Show how to find the measure of angle **2** by writing an equation. Tell students that we will use the variable x to represent the measure of angle 2.
- Explain that with the information we have, we can set up the equation as $\mathbf{x + 120 = 180}$. Tell students that now we can solve for x.
- Show how we subtract 120 from both sides to get x all by itself. When we complete the subtraction and addition, we get $x = 60$. This means that **angle 2 is 60 degrees**.

In Example 2 we find the measures of the exterior angles for the upper left corner of a trapezoid.

Example 2

Find the measures of ∠2, ∠3, and ∠4.

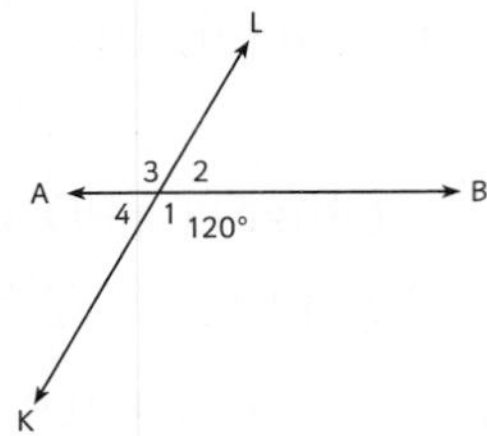

We know that lines AB and KL are straight lines. That means these lines measure 180 degrees.

What is the measure of ∠2?

Let x = the measure of ∠2.

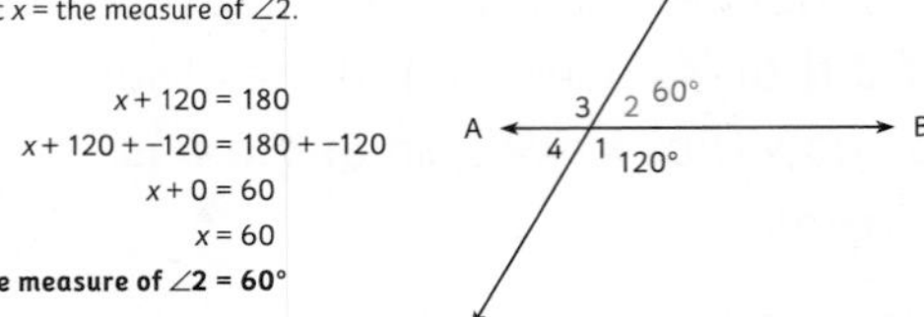

$$x + 120 = 180$$
$$x + 120 + -120 = 180 + -120$$
$$x + 0 = 60$$
$$x = 60$$

The measure of ∠2 = 60°

Demonstrate

- Turn to page 631 of the *Student Text* to continue with Example 2. Show how to find the measure of angle **4**.
- Explain that we repeat the process. Point out that we can use either line AB or line KL to figure out the measure for angle 4.
- Explain that we know the measure of **angle 4 is 60 degrees** because the sum of angles 1, 2, and 3, equal 300. So angle 4 must equal 60 degrees to make a sum of 360 degrees for all the angles.

Check for Understanding
Engagement Strategy: Look About

Draw two intersecting lines, labeled AB and ST. Label the angles 1, 2, 3, and 4. Label angle 1 as 110 degrees. Tell students that they will find the measure for angles 2, 3, and 4 with the help of the whole class. Students should write their solutions in large writing on a piece of paper or a dry erase board. When the students finish their work, they should hold up their answer for everyone to see ($\angle 2 = 70°$, $\angle 3 = 110°$, $\angle 4 = 70°$).

If students are not sure about the answer, prompt them to look about at the other students' solutions to help with their thinking. Review the answers after all students have held up their solutions.

What is the measure of $\angle 3$?

- Let y = the measure of $\angle 3$.
- We know that $\angle 2 = 60°$.

$$y + 60 = 180$$
$$y + 60 + -60 = 180 + -60$$
$$y + 0 = 120$$
$$y = 120$$

The measure of $\angle 3$ = 120°

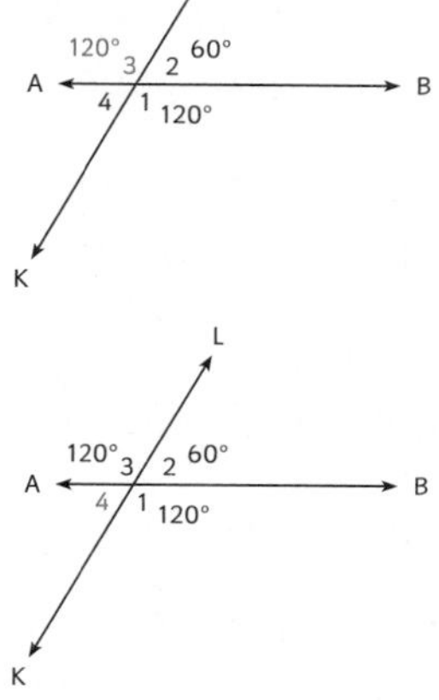

What is the measure of $\angle 4$?

Repeating the process will help us figure out the measure of $\angle 4$.

We know that $\angle 2 = 60°$ and that $\angle 3 = 120°$.

- We can use either line AB or line KL to figure out the measure of $\angle 4$.
- We know that the measure of $\angle 4 = 60$ degrees because $\angle 1 + \angle 2 + \angle 3 = 300$.

$300 + 60 = 360$

Problem-Solving Activity Turn to *Interactive Text*, page 300.

mBook Reinforce Understanding Use the *mBook Study Guide* to review lesson concepts.

Problem-Solving Activity

(*Interactive Text*, pages 300–301)

Have students turn to pages 300–301 in the *Interactive Text*, and complete the activity.

Students use their knowledge of the properties of angles to find missing angles in various shapes.

Monitor students' work as they complete the activity.

Watch for:

- Can students use the information in the picture to find the measure of the missing angles?
- Can students use their knowledge of the properties of angles to help them find the measure of the missing angles?
- Can students correctly identify the measures of each of the angles?

mBook **Reinforce Understanding**

Remind students that they can review lesson concepts by accessing the online *mBook Study Guide* to review lesson concepts.

Lesson 8 | Problem-Solving Activity

Name ______________________ Date ______________

Problem-Solving Activity
Angles and Intersecting Lines

Use algebra to find the total measurement of the exterior angles for each figure. Look for a pattern in the measures of these angles. Can you make a general statement about the measure of angles in straight lines that intersect?

1. What are the measures of ∠2, ∠3, and ∠4?

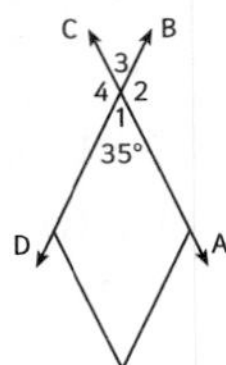

∠2 = 145°, ∠3 = 35°, and ∠4 = 145°

2. What are the measures of ∠1, ∠2, and ∠3?

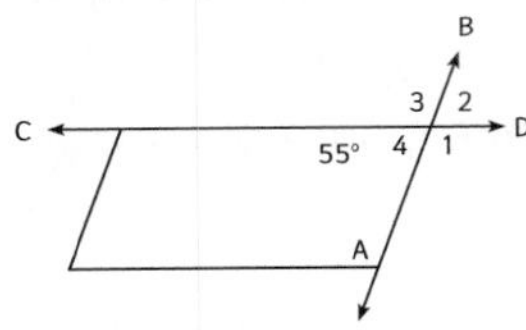

∠1 = 125°, ∠2 = 55°, and ∠3 = 125°

300 Unit 8 • Lesson 8

Lesson 8 | Problem-Solving Activity

Name ______________________ Date ______________

3. What are the measures of ∠2, ∠3, and ∠4?

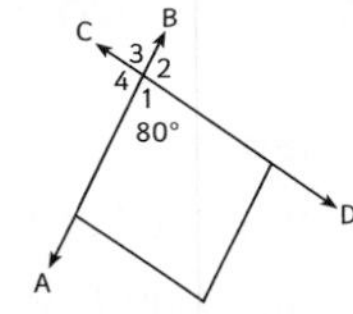

∠2 = 100°, ∠3 = 80°, and ∠4 = 100°

4. What are the measures of ∠1, ∠2, and ∠3?

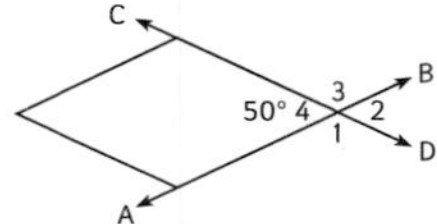

∠1 = 130°, ∠2 = 50°, and ∠3 = 130°

Unit 8

mBook Reinforce Understanding
Use the mBook *Study Guide* to review lesson concepts.

Unit 8 • Lesson 8 301

Homework

Go over the instructions on page 632 of the *Student Text* for each part of the homework.

Activity 1

Students decide if the terms inside the parentheses can be combined or not.

Activity 2

Students solve problems using the distributive property.

Activity 3

Students tell the measures of the angles.

Activity 4 • Distributed Practice

Students practice order of operations, integer operations, and one-step equations.

Homework

Activity 1

For each problem, answer "yes" if you can combine the terms inside the parentheses and "no" if you cannot.

1. $2(x + 4) = 6$ No
2. $4x = 3(4 + 5)$ Yes
3. $3(x + 2x) = 12$ Yes
4. $15 = 3(x + 3)$ No
5. $20 = 2(4 + w)$ No
6. $2(2 + 4) = 2x$ Yes

Activity 2

Solve.

1. $2(a + 1) = 6$ 2
2. $24 = 3(b + 1)$ 7
3. $25 = 5(1 + x)$ 4
4. $-2(-z - 3) = 18$ 6

Activity 3

Find the missing angles using the diagram.

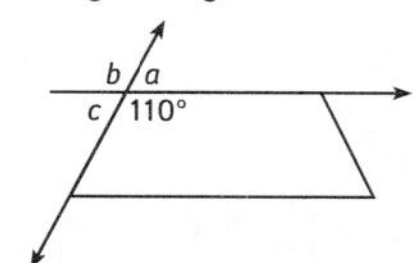

1. **What is the measure of $\angle a$?** 70 degrees
2. **What is the measure of $\angle b$?** 110 degrees
3. **What is the measure of $\angle c$?** 70 degrees

Activity 4 • Distributed Practice

Solve.

1. $\frac{a}{2} = \frac{10}{4}$ 5
2. $2(2 - y) = -12$ 8
3. $x + 5 = 0$ −5
4. $y = -12 + -17$ −29
5. $-12 = 2t$ −6
6. $-5 + w = -12$ −7

Lesson 9 | Flexibility and the Distributive Property

Problem Solving: Angles and Parallel Lines

Lesson Planner

Skills Maintenance

Distributive Property

Building Number Concepts

▶ Flexibility and the Distributive Property

Students look at different ways to solve algebra problems. It is important to be flexible when solving equations and to choose the method that provides the easiest computations.

Objective

Students will use different methods to solve algebra problems.

Problem Solving:

▶ Angles and Parallel Lines

Students learn that intersecting lines create angles that have unique relationships. We can use inference to determine the measures of these angles. Students are introduced to the vertical angle rule that vertical angles are equal, and the corresponding angle rule, that corresponding angles are equal.

Objective

Students analyze relationships of angles created by intersecting lines.

Homework

Students select two different ways to solve problems, solve equations using the distributive property and the reciprocal, and find missing angle measures. In Distributed Practice, students practice order of operations, integer operations, and one-step equations.

Lesson 9 | Skills Maintenance

Name ______________________ Date ______________________

Skills Maintenance
Distributive Property

Activity 1

Solve the equations using the distributive property. Be sure to show your work and check your answers.

1. $2(-x - 4) = 16$
   Show your work here:
   $-2x - 8 = 16$
   $-2x = 24$
   $x = -12$
   $x =$ <u>-12</u>
   Check your work here:
   $2(8) = 16$
   $16 = 16$

2. $-x(3 + 4) = 14$
   Show your work here:
   $-3x + -4x = 14$
   $-7x = 14$
   $x = -2$
   $x =$ <u>-2</u>
   Check your work here:
   $2(7) = 14$
   $14 = 14$

Activity 2

Solve the multiplication problems with fractions.

1. $\frac{1}{3} \cdot 3 = \underline{1}$
2. $\frac{3}{5} \cdot \underline{\frac{5}{3}} = 1$
3. $\frac{4}{5} \cdot \frac{5}{4} = \underline{1}$
4. $1 = \frac{2}{3} \cdot \underline{\frac{3}{2}}$
5. $\underline{\frac{3}{1}} \cdot \frac{1}{3} = 1$
6. $\frac{1}{2} \cdot \underline{\frac{2}{1}} = 1$
7. $8 \cdot \underline{\frac{1}{8}} = 1$
8. $\frac{11}{12} \cdot \frac{12}{11} = \underline{1}$

302 Unit 8 • Lesson 9

Skills Maintenance

Distributive Property

(*Interactive Text*, page 302)

Activity 1

Students solve equations using the distributive property.

Activity 2

Students solve problems involving reciprocals.

Building Number Concepts:
▶ Flexibility and the Distributive Property

What is another way to solve an algebra equation?
(*Student Text*, pages 633–635)

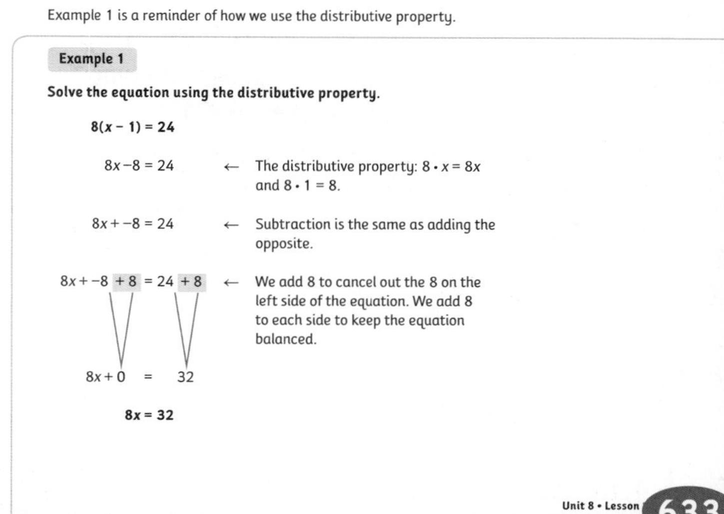
Lesson 9 ▶Flexibility and the Distributive Property
Problem Solving:
▶Angles and Parallel Lines

▶Flexibility and the Distributive Property

What is another way to solve an algebra equation?

In the last lesson, we learned how to solve equations using the distributive property. Two ideas were important:

- We cannot combine terms inside of the parentheses if they are not like terms.
- We must distribute what is outside of the parentheses over both terms inside the parentheses.

Example 1 is a reminder of how we use the distributive property.

Example 1

Solve the equation using the distributive property.

$8(x - 1) = 24$

$8x - 8 = 24$ ← The distributive property: $8 \cdot x = 8x$ and $8 \cdot 1 = 8$.

$8x + -8 = 24$ ← Subtraction is the same as adding the opposite.

$8x + -8 + 8 = 24 + 8$ ← We add 8 to cancel out the 8 on the left side of the equation. We add 8 to each side to keep the equation balanced.

$8x + 0 = 32$

$8x = 32$

Unit 8 • Lesson 633

Connect to Prior Knowledge

Begin by reminding students about the distributive property. Put $3(4 + 2) = x$ on the board or overhead. Have students solve the problem two different ways. The first way is to distribute the 3 across the two terms in parentheses. The second way is to find the sum of the two numbers in parentheses and then multiply.

Link to Today's Concept

Tell students that today we look at another way to solve problems using the distributive property.

Demonstrate

Engagement Strategy: Teacher Modeling

Demonstrate how we solve an equation using the distributive property in one of the following ways:

mBook: Use the *mBook Teacher Edition* for pages 633–634 of the *Student Text*. m

Overhead Projector: Reproduce the equation on a transparency, and modify as discussed.

Board: Copy the equation on the board, and modify as discussed.

- Display and read the points about the distributive property. m
- Explain that we solve $8(x - 1) = 24$ from **Example 1** using the distributive property in the traditional way. m
- Remind students that we cannot add the terms inside the parentheses because one is a variable term and one is a number. In this example, we avoid that by using the distributive property. Explain that 8 is actually the coefficient of the number in the parentheses, and $8(x - 1)$ is the same as $8x - 8$. m
- Go through each step with students and be sure they understand the justification for each one. m
- Then go through the steps of adding 8 to both sides of the equation to get x by itself until you get $8x = 32$. m

What is another way to solve an algebra equation? *(continued)*

Demonstrate

- Go through the steps of multiplying both sides of the equation **8x = 32** by $\frac{1}{8}$ and then simplifying to find ***x* = 4.**
- Tell students that distributing the number on the outside of the parentheses is one way to solve the problem. Use **Example 2** to explain that there is another way to solve the problem using properties other than the distributive property.
- Start with the same problem: **8(*x* − 1) = 24.**
- Explain that we can multiply each side of the equation by the reciprocal so that the coefficient in front of the parentheses is 1. Explain that this is just like taking the parentheses away.
- Go through each step of solving the same equation by multiplying both sides first by $\frac{1}{8}$. This gets *x* by itself on the left side of the equation, and balances the equation when multiplied to the right side of the equation.
- Continue solving the equation, and show students that we get the same answer, ***x* = 4**, using this method as we did using the distributive property.

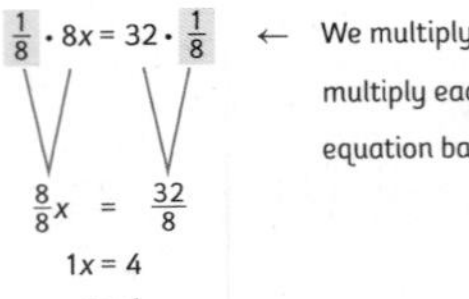

$\frac{1}{8} \cdot 8x = 32 \cdot \frac{1}{8}$ ← We multiply by $\frac{1}{8}$ to get *x* by itself. We multiply each side by $\frac{1}{8}$ to keep the equation balanced.

$\frac{8}{8}x = \frac{32}{8}$

$1x = 4$

$\mathbf{x = 4}$

Distributing the number outside of the parentheses is one way to solve this problem. But we can also solve it another way.

To get the same solution, we use the rules and properties in our Algebra Toolbox.

Example 2

Use rules and properties other than the distributive property to solve the equation.

$\mathbf{8(x - 1) = 24}$

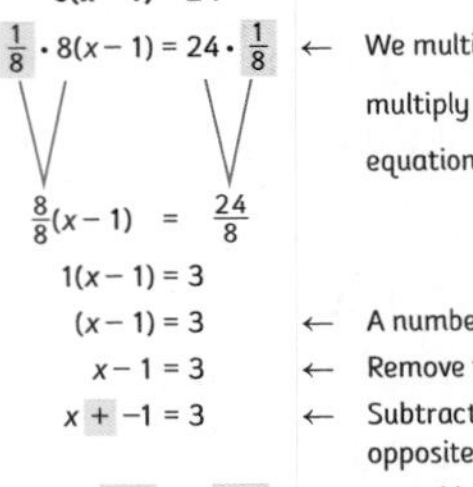

$\frac{1}{8} \cdot 8(x - 1) = 24 \cdot \frac{1}{8}$ ← We multiply by $\frac{1}{8}$ to get *x* by itself. We multiply each side by $\frac{1}{8}$ to keep the equation balanced.

$\frac{8}{8}(x - 1) = \frac{24}{8}$

$1(x - 1) = 3$

$(x - 1) = 3$ ← A number times 1 is the same number.

$x - 1 = 3$ ← Remove the parentheses.

$x + -1 = 3$ ← Subtraction is the same as adding the opposite.

$x + -1 + 1 = 3 + 1$ ← We add 1 to cancel out the −1 on the left side of the equation. We add 1 to each side to keep the equation balanced.

$x + 0 = 4$

$\mathbf{x = 4}$

Demonstrate

- Turn to page 635 of the *Student Text*. Remind students what a coefficient is.
- Have students look at the diagram which shows the coefficient in the problem **$8(x - 1) = 24$** in front of the parentheses, just as the 5 in $5a$ is a coefficient.
- Explain that the reciprocal of the coefficient can be used to change it to 1.

Check for Understanding
Engagement Strategy: Pair/Share

Write the problem **$6(x + 3) = 36$** on the board. Divide the class into pairs. Have one partner solve the equation using the distributive property. Have the other partner solve the equation by multiplying both sides of the equation by the reciprocal of the coefficient. When partners are finished, have them check that their answers are the same ($x = 3$). Invite student volunteers to explain their answers for each method.

Reinforce Understanding
For additional practice, use these equations:

$2x - 12 = 14$ ($x = 13$)

$3x + 15 = 30$ ($x = 5$)

$5x - 20 = 5$ ($x = 5$)

Lesson 9

This is the same answer we got in Example 1.

Example 2 reminds us that the 8 outside of $(x - 1)$ is a coefficient. This means it is like the 5 in $5a$.

That means we can use its reciprocal to change it to 1.

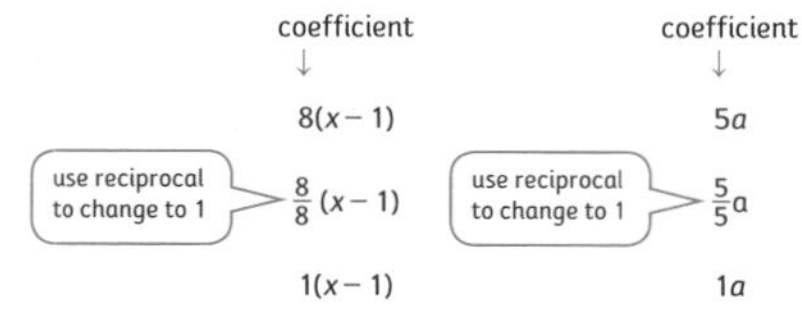

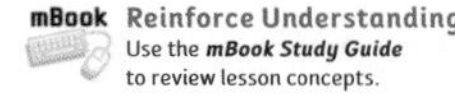

Apply Skills Turn to ***Interactive Text***, page 303.

Reinforce Understanding Use the ***mBook Study Guide*** to review lesson concepts.

Apply Skills

(*Interactive Text*, pages 303–304)

Have students turn to pages 303–304 in the *Interactive Text*, which provide students an opportunity to solve equations using the distributive property.

Activity 1

Students solve the problems one way.

Activity 2

Students solve the same problems in a different way and write how the steps are different.

Monitor students' work as they complete the activities.

Watch for:

- Can students solve the problem by distributing the coefficient across the two terms inside the parentheses?
- Can students solve the problems by multiplying each side by the reciprocal?
- Do students get the correct answer? Did students check their answers using substitution?

Reinforce Understanding

Remind students that they can review lesson concepts by accessing the online *mBook Study Guide* to review lesson concepts.

Lesson 9 | Apply Skills

Name ______________________ Date ______________

Apply Skills
Flexibility and the Distributive Property

Activity 1

Solve the equations. Show your work and check your answers.

1. $-2(3 + x) = 12$
   Show your work here:
   $-\frac{1}{2} \cdot -2(3 + x) = 12 \cdot -\frac{1}{2}$
   $1(3 + x) = -6$
   $x = -9$
   $x =$ -9
   Check your work here:
   $-2(-6) = 12$
   $12 = 12$

2. $3(-z - 1) = -12$
   Show your work here:
   $\frac{1}{3} \cdot 3(-z - 1) = -12 \cdot \frac{1}{3}$
   $1(-z - 1) = -4$
   $-z = -3$
   $z =$ 3
   Check your work here:
   $3(-4) = -12$
   $-12 = -12$

3. $4(y - 1) = 16$
   Show your work here:
   $\frac{1}{4} \cdot 4(y - 1) = 16 \cdot \frac{1}{4}$
   $y - 1 = 4$
   $y = 5$
   $y =$ 5
   Check your work here:
   $4(4) = 16$
   $16 = 16$

Unit 8 • Lesson 9 303

Lesson 9 | Apply Skills

Name ______________________ Date ______________

Activity 2

For each of the problems on the previous page, select a different strategy to solve the equations again. Explain how the steps are different.

1. Solve $-2(3 + x) = 12$ in a different way than you solved it in Activity 1.
   Show your work here: $-2(3 + x) = 12$ $-6 + -2x = 12$ $-2x = 18$ $x = -9$
   $x =$ -9
   Check your work here: $-2(-6) = 12$ $12 = 12$
   Tell how the steps are different:
   Answers will vary. Sample answer: Instead of multiplying by the inverted coefficient, I distribute the coefficient inside of the parentheses.

2. Solve $3(-z - 1) = -12$ in a different way than you solved it in Activity 1.
   Show your work here: $3(-z - 1) = -12$ $-3z - 3 = -12$ $-3z = -9$
   $z =$ 3
   Check your work here: $3(-4) = -12$ $-12 = -12$
   Tell how the steps are different:
   Answers will vary. Sample answer: Instead of multiplying by the inverted coefficient, I distribute the coefficient inside of the parentheses.

3. Solve $4(y - 1) = 16$ using a different method.
   Show your work here: $4(y - 1) = 16$ $4y - 4 = 16$ $4y = 20$ $y = 5$
   $y =$ 5
   Check your work here: $4(4) = 16$ $16 = 16$
   Tell how the steps are different:
   Answers will vary. Sample answer: Instead of multiplying by the inverted coefficient, I distribute the coefficient inside of the parentheses.

304 Unit 8 • Lesson 9

Problem Solving:
▶ Angles and Parallel Lines

How do parallel lines help us understand angles?
(*Student Text*, pages 636–639)

Connect to Prior Knowledge
Begin by discussing how we extended the lines of shapes in the last lesson so we could see they were intersecting lines.

Link to Today's Concept
Explain to students that today we use our knowledge of angles to look at how parallel lines affect them.

Demonstrate

- Have students look at the pictures on *Student Text*, page 636. Define the terms vertical angles and supplementary angles.
- Be sure students understand that vertical angles are angles that are opposite from one another and have sides that are opposite rays.
- Note that the vertical angle rule tells us that vertical angles are equal.
- Have students look at the diagram of supplementary angles. Make sure they see that the sum of supplementary angles is 180 degrees.
- Explain that when we combine the supplementary angles, they form a straight line.

Lesson 9

▶Problem Solving: Angles and Parallel Lines

How do parallel lines help us understand angles?

In the previous lesson, we worked with different kinds of quadrilaterals. We extended lines from the sides of quadrilaterals so that we could find properties of intersecting lines. Let's review what we learned and look at some important definitions and rules.

Vertical Angles	Supplementary Angles
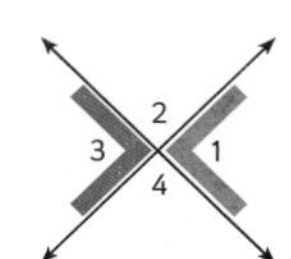	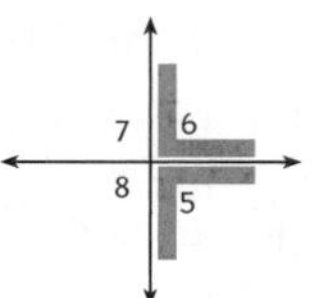
Two angles whose sides are opposite rays.	**The sum of two angles is 180 degrees.**
$\angle 1 = \angle 3$ $\angle 2 = \angle 4$	$\angle 6 = \angle 8$ $\angle 5 = \angle 7$
Angle 1 and angle 3 are vertical angles because the point of intersection makes rays for each angle. They are opposite each other.	Angle 5 and angle 6 are supplementary. When we combine the angles, they form a straight line. We know a straight line measures 180 degrees.

Vertical Angles Rule
The measures of vertical angles are equal.

We proved this in the previous lesson using algebra.

636 Unit 8 • Lesson 9

How do parallel lines help us understand angles? *(continued)*

Demonstrate

- Turn to page 637 of the *Student Text* to look at the extended lines of a parallelogram.
- Go over the angles in the diagram and point out which angles have the same measure.
- Explain that when a straight line intersects parallel lines, the angles in the same position are equal.

Lesson 9

Let's look at parallelograms.

This quadrilateral has opposite sides that are parallel. Working with this shape helps us see how to make inferences about angles on parallel lines.

We begin by extending lines along each side of the parallelogram.

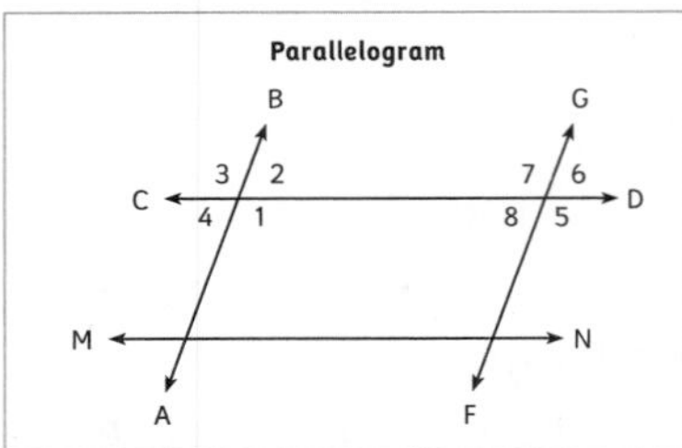

Lines AB and FG are parallel. That means we could move AB over and put it on top of FG and it would be at the same line. If that is true, then ∠1, ∠2, ∠3, and ∠4 would fit on top of ∠5, ∠6, ∠7, and ∠8.

This means that when we have parallel lines and a straight line that intersects the two lines, the angles that are in the same position are equal.

In this case,

- measure of ∠1 = measure of ∠5
- measure of ∠2 = measure of ∠6
- measure of ∠3 = measure of ∠7
- measure of ∠4 = measure of ∠8

Demonstrate

- Turn to page 638 of the *Student Text* to look at the properties of the angles in this diagram.
- Define the term corresponding angles. Tell students that corresponding angles are angles that appear in the same location at each corner of the parallelogram.
- Be sure students understand that the corresponding angles are in the same position, and are created by a line crossing two parallel lines.

Check for Understanding

Ask:

What are some of the corresponding angles in the parallelogram?

Listen for:

- *Angles 1 and 5*
- *Angles 4 and 8*
- *Angles 3 and 7*
- *Angles 2 and 6*

When two lines are crossed by another line, like CD on the previous page, they form angles that match or are in the same position.

Because ∠1 and ∠5 below are corresponding angles, we know that the measure of angle 1 = the measure of angle 5.

Parallelogram
corresponding angles

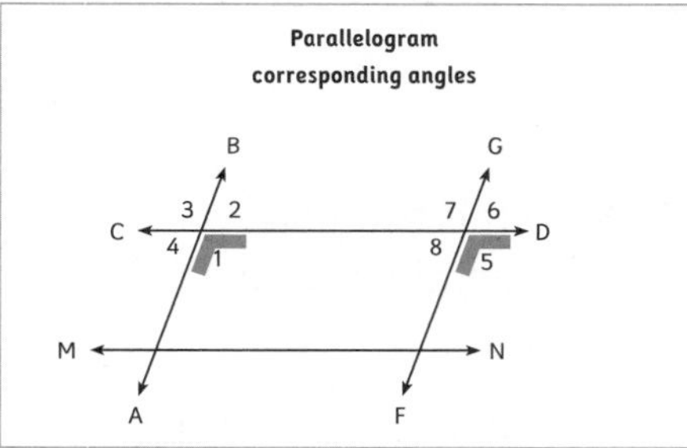

Corresponding Angle Rule

When two parallel lines (like AB and FG) are crossed by another line (like CD), the angles formed have equal measurement.

We use this understanding to make inferences. We figure out the measure of one angle based on another angle in a different position. Example 1 shows us how this is done.

How do parallel lines help us understand angles? *(continued)*

Demonstrate

- Turn to page 639 of the *Student Text*, and look at **Example 1**. In this example, we show students how to identify the vertical and corresponding angles.
- Point out that lines AB and FG are parallel. The straight line that crosses lines AB and FG creates angles 1 through 8.
- Walk through each point of the explanation and explain to students that the information we are given helps us make inferences about the measures of the angles, based on the rules.
- Point out that we know that the measure of angle 3 is 110 degrees.
- Explain that according to the vertical angle rule, the measure of angle 3 and angle 1 is the same. Angle 1 measures 110 degrees.
- Direct students' attention to angle 5. Explain that because of the corresponding angle rule, angle 5 has the same measure as angle 1. Help students to notice that angles 1 and 5 are in the same position.
- Point out to students that if angle 3 is equal to angle 1, and angle 1 is equal to angle 5, then angle 3 is also equal to angle 5. **Angle 5 measures 110 degrees.**

Check for Understanding
Engagement Strategy: Look About

Have students use the diagram in Example 2 to make inferences about the measure of angles 2, 4, 6, and 8, using what they have learned. Students should write their inferences in large writing on a piece of paper or a dry erase board. When the students finish their work, they should hold up their answer for everyone to see.

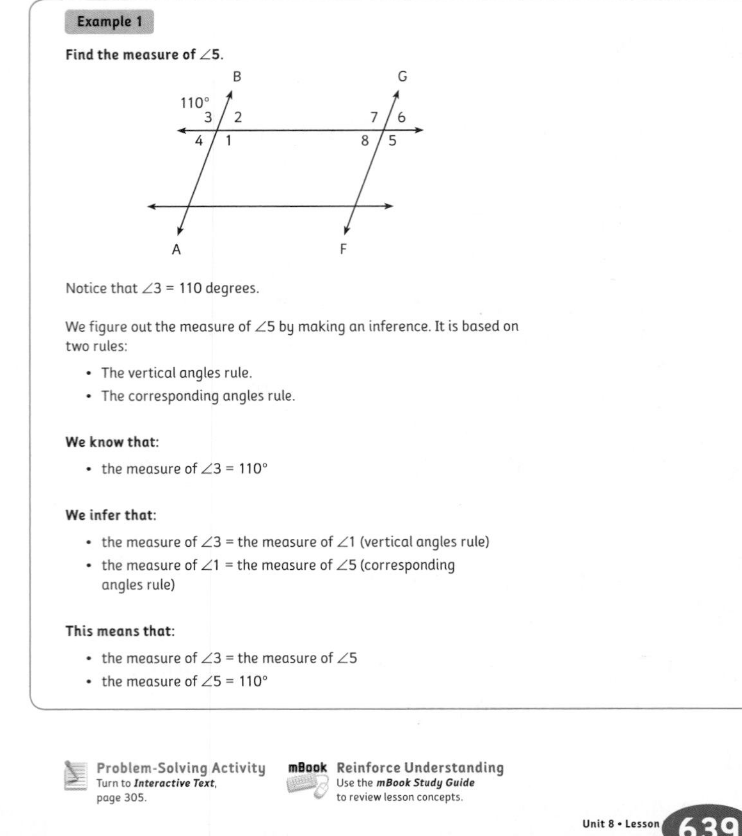

Lesson 9

Example 1

Find the measure of ∠5.

Notice that ∠3 = 110 degrees.

We figure out the measure of ∠5 by making an inference. It is based on two rules:

- The vertical angles rule.
- The corresponding angles rule.

We know that:

- the measure of ∠3 = 110°

We infer that:

- the measure of ∠3 = the measure of ∠1 (vertical angles rule)
- the measure of ∠1 = the measure of ∠5 (corresponding angles rule)

This means that:

- the measure of ∠3 = the measure of ∠5
- the measure of ∠5 = 110°

Problem-Solving Activity Turn to ***Interactive Text***, page 305.

mBook Reinforce Understanding Use the ***mBook Study Guide*** to review lesson concepts.

Unit 8 • Lesson 639

If students are not sure about the answer, prompt them to look about at other students' solutions to help with their thinking. After all students have finished, ask them to discuss their answers.

Listen for:

- *Angle 2 is equal to Angle 4 because of the vertical angle rule.*
- *Angle 2 is equal to Angle 6 because of the corresponding angle rule.*
- *Angles 2, 4, 6, and 8, are all equal.*
- *The measure of angles 2, 4, 6, and 8 is 70 degrees.*

Problem-Solving Activity

(*Interactive Text*, pages 305–306)

Have students turn to pages 305–306 in the *Interactive Text*, and complete the activity.

Students use inferences based on the rules for vertical and corresponding angles to find the measures of the missing angles.

Monitor students' work as they complete the activity.

Watch for:

- Can students identify the vertical and corresponding angles?
- Can students apply the rules for vertical and corresponding angles to find the measure of the missing angles?
- Can students use algebra and other computations to find the measure of the angles after they have made the appropriate inferences?

mBook **Reinforce Understanding**

Remind students that they can review lesson concepts by accessing the online *mBook Study Guide* to review lesson concepts.

Lesson 9 | Problem-Solving Activity

Name ______________________ Date ______________

Problem-Solving Activity
Angles and Parallel Lines

Use what you have learned about vertical angles and corresponding angles to solve the problems. All lines in the problems are parallel.

1. What is the measure of ∠6? 90°

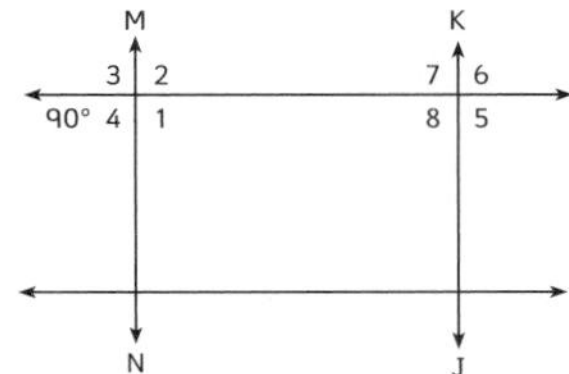

2. What is the measure of ∠8? 80°

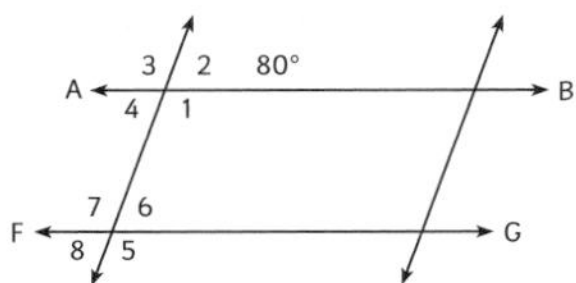

Unit 8

Unit 8 • Lesson 9 305

Lesson 9 | Problem-Solving Activity

Name ______________________ Date ______________

3. What is the measure of ∠2? 70°

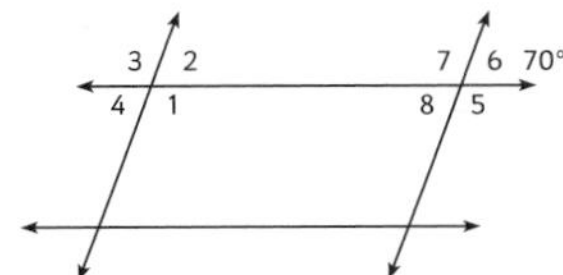

4. What is the measure of ∠3? 120°

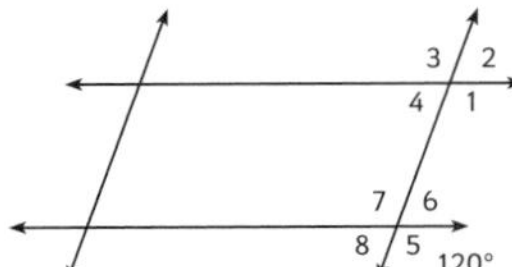

mBook **Reinforce Understanding**
Use the **mBook** ***Study Guide*** to review lesson concepts.

306 Unit 8 • Lesson 9

Homework

Go over the instructions on page 640 of the *Student Text* for each part of the homework.

Activity 1

Students select two different ways to solve problems.

Activity 2

Students solve equations using the distributive property and reciprocals.

Activity 3

Students find the missing angle measures.

Activity 4 • Distributed Practice

Students practice order of operations, integer operations, and one-step equations.

Additional Answers

Activity 2

1. $3a + 3 = 9$
   $3a + 3 - 3 = 9 - 3$
   $3a = 6$
   $\frac{1}{3} \cdot 3a = \frac{1}{3} \cdot 6$
   $a = 2$

2. $35 = 5b + 5$
   $35 - 5 = 5b + 5 - 5$
   $30 = 5b$
   $\frac{1}{5} \cdot 30 = \frac{1}{5} \cdot 5b$
   $b = 6$

3. $30 = 5 + 5x$
   $30 - 5 = 5 - 5 + 5x$
   $25 = 5x$
   $\frac{1}{5} \cdot 25 = \frac{1}{5} \cdot 5x$
   $x = 5$

4. $2z - -6 = -14$
   $2z + 6 = -14$
   $2z + 6 - 6 = -14 - 6$
   $2z = -20$
   $\frac{1}{2}\, 2z = \frac{1}{2} -20$
   $z = -10$

Homework

Activity 1

Select two different ways you could start solving the problems (choose two answers).

1. $-2(x + 4) = 6$ b and c
   (a) Add $\frac{1}{6}$ to each side.
   (b) Multiply each side by $-\frac{1}{2}$.
   (c) Distribute to get $-2x + -8$.
   (d) Multiply each side by $\frac{1}{4}$.

2. $8 = 4(y - 2)$ a and c
   (a) Distribute to get $4y - 8$.
   (b) Add $\frac{1}{8}$ to both sides.
   (c) Multiply each side by $\frac{1}{4}$.
   (d) Multiply each side by $-\frac{1}{4}$.

Activity 2

Solve the problems. Use the distributive property for problems 1 and 2. Use the reciprocal for problems 3 and 4.

1. $3(a + 1) = 9$
2. $35 = 5(b + 1)$
3. $30 = 5(1 + x)$
4. $-2(-z - 3) = -14$

See Additional Answers below.

Activity 3

Find the missing angles using the diagram.

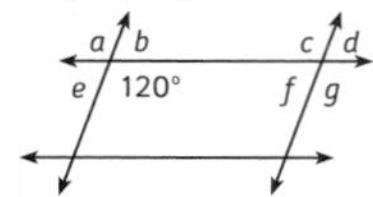

1. What is the measure of $\angle a$? 120 degrees
2. What is the measure of $\angle c$? 120 degrees
3. What is the measure of $\angle f$? 60 degrees

Activity 4 • Distributed Practice

Solve.

1. $2w = 6{,}000$ 3,000
2. $\frac{a}{10} = \frac{2}{5}$ 4
3. $\frac{1}{5} \cdot b = 1$ 5
4. $0 = 4 + x$ −4
5. $-15 \div z = 5$ −3
6. $3(x + 1) = 27$ 8

Lesson 10 ▶ Area Formulas and Algebraic Equations

Monitoring Progress: ▶ Quiz 2

Lesson Planner

Skills Maintenance

Vertical and Corresponding Angles

Building Number Concepts: ▶ Area Formulas and Algebraic Equations

Students learn how to use simple algebraic formulas in geometry. We use the area formulas of two-dimensional shapes to help us figure out the missing information when given partial information about a shape.

Objective

Students will find the missing dimension of a two-dimensional shape when given partial information.

Monitoring Progress: ▶ Quiz 2

Distribute the quiz, and remind students that the questions involve material covered over the previous lessons in the unit.

Homework

Students solve equations, find the missing dimension in the shape, and use the area formula for a triangle to solve problems. In Distributed Practice, students practice order of operations, integer operations, and one-step equations.

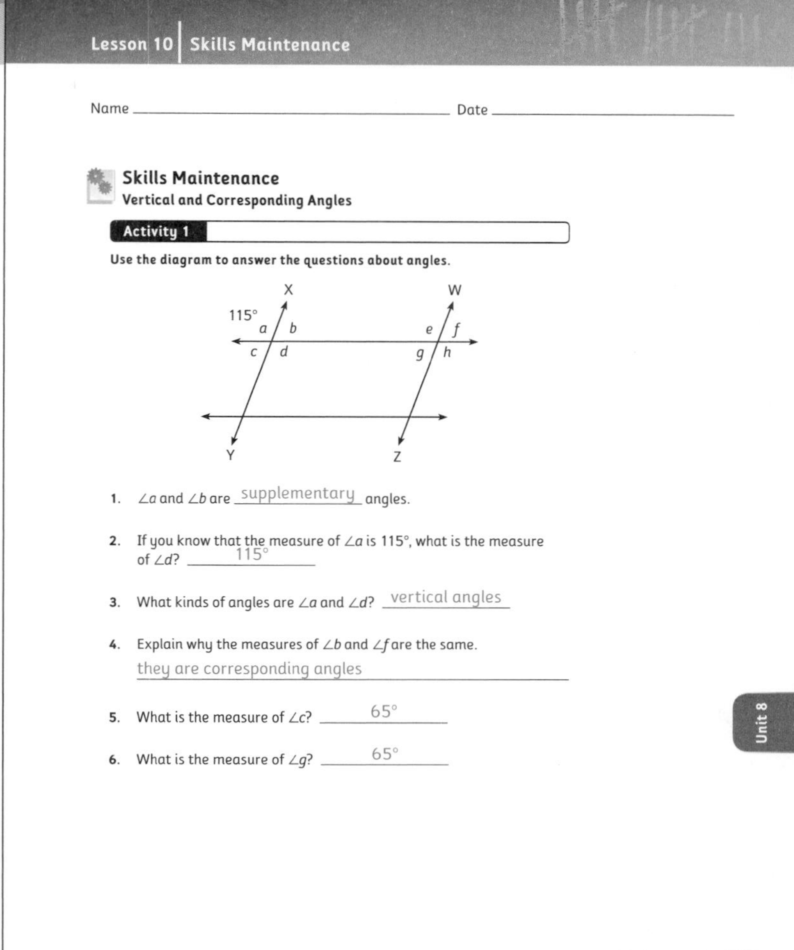
Lesson 10 | Skills Maintenance

Name ______ Date ______

Skills Maintenance
Vertical and Corresponding Angles

Activity 1

Use the diagram to answer the questions about angles.

1. $\angle a$ and $\angle b$ are supplementary angles.
2. If you know that the measure of $\angle a$ is 115°, what is the measure of $\angle d$? 115°
3. What kinds of angles are $\angle a$ and $\angle d$? vertical angles
4. Explain why the measures of $\angle b$ and $\angle f$ are the same. they are corresponding angles
5. What is the measure of $\angle c$? 65°
6. What is the measure of $\angle g$? 65°

Unit 8 • Lesson 10 307

Unit 8

Skills Maintenance

Vertical and Corresponding Angles

(*Interactive Text*, page 307)

Activity 1

Students answer questions about vertical and corresponding angles using rules, properties, and inference.

Building Number Concepts:
▶ Area Formulas and Algebraic Equations

How do we use the distributive property in geometry?
(*Student Text*, pages 641–646)

Connect to Prior Knowledge

Begin by asking students to review the area formulas they remember. Here are a few of the most common ones:

Triangle

$A = \frac{1}{2}\, b \cdot h$

Square

$A = s^2$

Rectangle

$A = b \cdot h$

Parallelogram

$A = b \cdot h$

Tell students that they have been using these formulas in their math classes for several years. These formulas represent some of the first uses of algebra and variables for most students.

Link to Today's Concept

Explain that in today's lesson we use variables and algebra to solve more complex problems involving area. In these problems, we are only given partial information about shapes' dimensions.

Demonstrate

Engagement Strategy: Teacher Modeling

Demonstrate solving simple algebra equations with the area formulas for a triangle, rectangle, and parallelogram in one of the following ways:

Lesson 10 ▶Area Formulas and Algebraic Equations

Monitoring Progress:

▶Quiz 2

▶Area Formulas and Algebraic Equations

How do we use the distributive property in geometry?

Simple algebraic formulas are used to describe the area of two-dimensional shapes.

The three shapes below use base and height to calculate area.

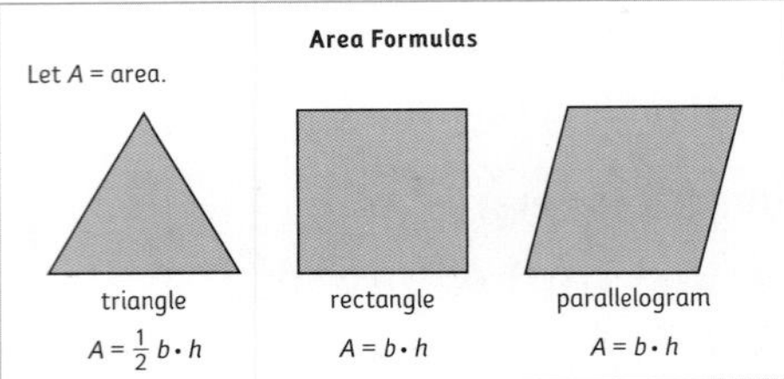

Area Formulas
Let A = area.
triangle
A = 1/2 b • h
rectangle
A = b • h
parallelogram
A = b • h

Now that we know how to solve simple algebra equations, we can find more than just the area of two-dimensional shapes using base and height.

Example 1 and Example 2 show that for a two-dimensional object, we can find:

- the base if we know the height and area.
- the height if we know the base and area.
- the area if we know the base and height.

Unit 8 • Lesson 10 641

mBook: Use the *mBook Teacher Edition* for pages 641–642 of the *Student Text*. m

Overhead Projector: Reproduce the area formulas on a transparency, and modify as discussed.

Board: Reproduce the area formulas on the board, and modify as discussed.

- Display the pictures of the three shapes, along with their area formulas. m
- Explain to students that the formula can help us find the area of the shapes. They also can help us find base and height. m

Demonstrate

- Display the triangle. Demonstrate how we use algebra to find the missing measure. m
- Explain that we can find the measure of the base of the triangle when we know the height or altitude of the triangle and its area. m
- Walk through the steps of substituting the area and the height into the area formula. m
- Next, take students through each step of solving for *b*, to find the length of the base of the triangle. **The base of the triangle is 4 inches.** m

Example 1

Find the base of the triangle if the area of the triangle is 24 in².

$h = 12$ in

b

We know:

- the height of the triangle is 12 inches.
- the area of the triangle is 24 square inches.
- $A = \frac{1}{2}b \cdot h$.

We begin by substituting the information we are given.

$$A = \frac{1}{2}b \cdot h \quad (A \to 24,\ h \to 12)$$

$$24 = \frac{1}{2}b \cdot 12$$

$$24 = \frac{1}{2} \cdot 12 \cdot b$$ ← We use the commutative property to reorder the equation so we can combine $\frac{1}{2}$ and 12.

$$24 = 6b$$

$$\frac{1}{6} \cdot 24 = \frac{1}{6} \cdot 6b$$ ← We multiply by $\frac{1}{6}$ to get b by itself. We multiply each side by $\frac{1}{6}$ to keep the equation balanced.

$$\frac{24}{6} = \frac{6}{6}b$$

$$4 = 1b$$

$$4 = b$$

The base of the triangle = 4 inches.

How do we use the distributive property in geometry? *(continued)*

Demonstrate

- Turn to *Student Text*, page 643, and walk through **Example 2**.
- Demonstrate how to find the measure of the height of the parallelogram when we know its base and its area. Point out that the base is **10 inches**, and the area is **80 square inches**.
- Remind students of the area formula of a parallelogram: $A = b \cdot h$.
- Walk through the example, starting with substituting the information that we know into the area formula.
- Solve for h by multiplying both sides of the equation by the reciprocal, $\frac{1}{10}$, to get h alone on one side and to balance the equation. Simplify to get the height of **8 inches**.
- Tell students that sometimes in the real world, when we are working with area, we only know partial information about dimensions of shapes. We use algebra to help us find what we need to know.

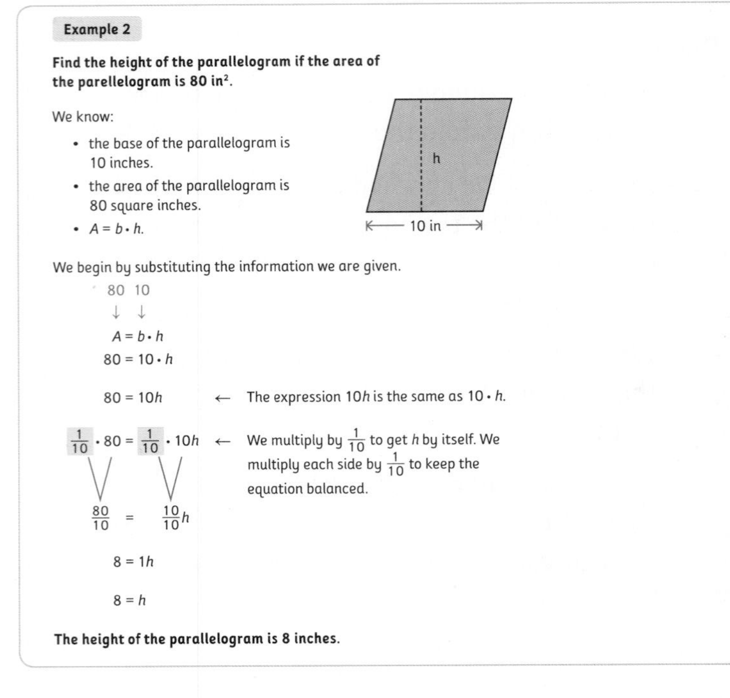

Lesson 10

Example 2

Find the height of the parallelogram if the area of the parellelogram is 80 in².

We know:

- the base of the parallelogram is 10 inches.
- the area of the parallelogram is 80 square inches.
- $A = b \cdot h$.

We begin by substituting the information we are given.

$A = b \cdot h$ (80 → A, 10 → b)

$80 = 10 \cdot h$

$80 = 10h$ ← The expression $10h$ is the same as $10 \cdot h$.

$\frac{1}{10} \cdot 80 = \frac{1}{10} \cdot 10h$ ← We multiply by $\frac{1}{10}$ to get h by itself. We multiply each side by $\frac{1}{10}$ to keep the equation balanced.

$\frac{80}{10} = \frac{10}{10}h$

$8 = 1h$

$8 = h$

The height of the parallelogram is 8 inches.

Unit 8 • Lesson 1 643

Check for Understanding
Engagement Strategy: Think Tank

Draw a parallelogram on the board with the following dimensions:

- **Base: 6 inches**
- **Area: 30 square inches**

Distribute strips of paper to students and have them write their name on their papers. Have students use the area formula for parallelograms to find the missing measure, the height (*5 inches*). Put all the papers into a container when students are finished. Draw a paper from the container, and share the answer with the class. Invite the student to walk through the steps of the solution.

Reinforce Understanding

For additional practice, draw the following shapes with the given measures on the board and have students find the missing measure.

- Triangle with **height of 5 inches** and **area of 40 square inches** (*b = 16 inches*)
- Parallelogram with area of **18 square inches** and base of **9 inches** (*h = 2 inches*)

Demonstrate

- Turn to *Student Text*, page 644, and use **Example 3** to show how we use algebra to find the area of the compound shape.
- Help students see that the rectangle is a compound shape made of two smaller rectangles.
- Point out that we know the dimensions of the left rectangle. Its base is **7** inches, and its height is **4** inches.
- Explain that by looking at the diagram, we can make inferences about the shape of the rectangle on the right, but we need to use algebra to find the area of the entire shape.
- Point out to students that the base of the compound shape can be represented by the expression $\mathbf{7 + x}$. Tell them that we substitute this into our area formula for a.
- Explain that to find the area, we need to multiply the whole quantity of $(7 + x)$ by the height, 4.
- Tell students that this equation is similar to the equations we have been solving with the distributive property.

Rectangles present another way to use what we have learned about algebra.

Example 3 shows a rectangle broken into two parts. We are given the measure for only part of the base. We must use the distributive property to find the length of the right part of the base.

Example 3

Find the base length of the rectangle by first finding the base length of the right side of the rectangle. The area of the rectangle is 40 in².

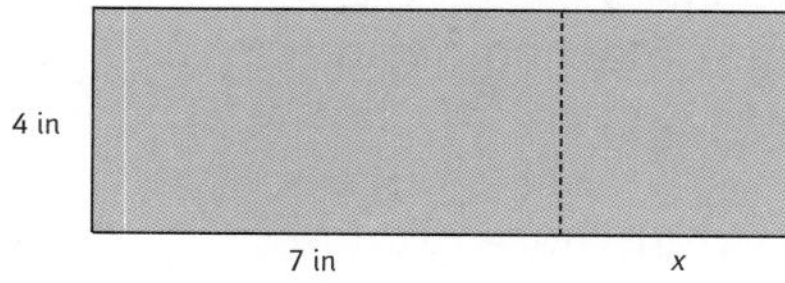

We know:

- the area of the rectangle is 40 square inches.
- the height is 4 inches.
- the base is $7 + x$ inches.
- $A = b \cdot h$.

So that we do not make a mistake in the order of operations, we put the base in parentheses.

We begin by substituting the information we are given.

$$\begin{array}{ccccc} 40 & & (x+7) & & 4 \\ \downarrow & & \downarrow & & \downarrow \\ A & = & b & \cdot & h \\ 40 & = & (x+7) & & 4 \end{array}$$

There are two methods we can use to figure out the base of the rectangle.

- Method 1 uses the commutative property.
- Method 2 uses the distributive property.

How do we use the distributive property in geometry? *(continued)*

Demonstrate

- Turn to *Student Text*, page 645, and demonstrate the first method of finding the base of the rectangle.
- Explain to students that there are two different ways to solve the problem. First, we solve it using the commutative property.
- Walk through each of the steps, making sure students understand the justifications of each of the steps as you go through the example.
- Show students that the commutative property allows us to move the coefficient in front of the parentheses.
- Explain that we multiply both sides of the equation by $\frac{1}{4}$ to get x by itself and keep the equation balanced.
- Next tell students we simplify and remove the parentheses.
- Explain that we add **−7** to both sides of the equation to get the x alone. Point out that after simplifying we find that **3 =** $\boldsymbol{x}$.
- Tell students that we are not yet finished, because x represents the base of the rectangle on the right. We need to find the base of the compound shape, which is **3 + 7, or 10 inches**.

Lesson 10

Method 1: Using the Commutative Property

$40 = (x + 7)4$

$40 = 4(x + 7)$ ← We use the commutative property so that the coefficient is in front of the parentheses.

$\frac{1}{4} \cdot 40 = \frac{1}{4} \cdot 4(x + 7)$ ← We multiply by $\frac{1}{4}$ so that we get x by itself. We multiply each side by $\frac{1}{4}$ to keep the equation balanced.

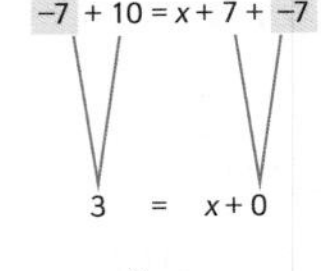

$\frac{40}{4} = \frac{4}{4}(x + 7)$

$10 = 1(x + 7)$

$10 = (x + 7)$ ← A number times 1 is the same number.

$10 = x + 7$ ← Remove the parentheses.

$-7 + 10 = x + 7 + -7$ ← We add −7 to cancel out the 7 on the right side of the equation. We add −7 to each side to keep the equation balanced.

$3 = x + 0$

$3 = x$

The missing part of the base for the rectangle is 3 inches. Remember what the question is asking for. We need to find the base.

The base of the rectangle is 3 + 7 or 10 inches.

Unit 8 • Lesson 10 645

Demonstrate

- Turn to *Student Text*, page 646, and demonstrate the second method of finding the base of the compound shape.

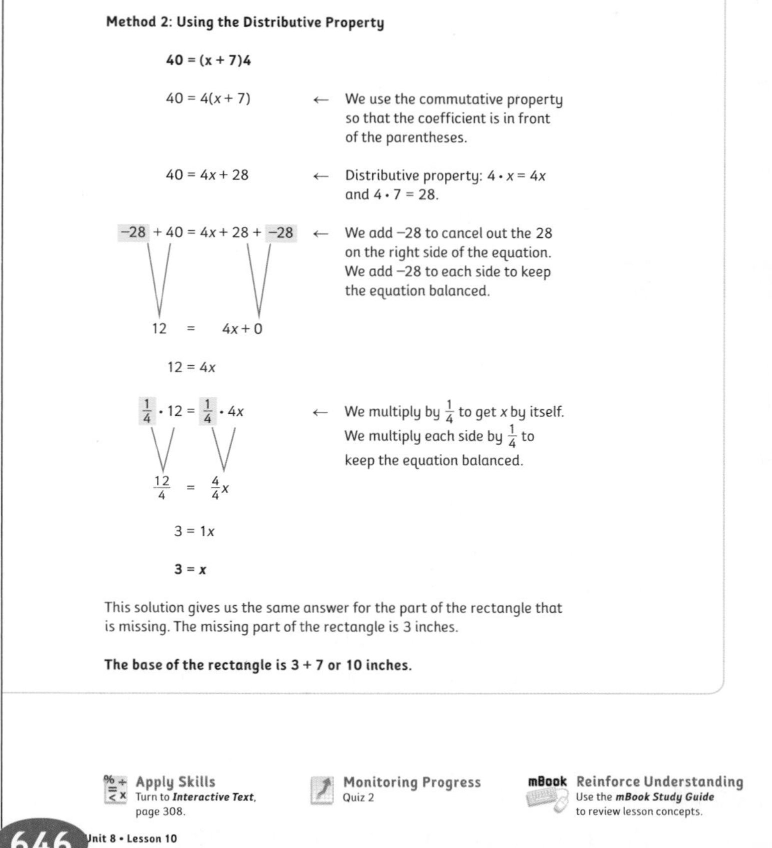

Lesson 10

Method 2: Using the Distributive Property

$\mathbf{40 = (x + 7)4}$

$40 = 4(x + 7)$ ← We use the commutative property so that the coefficient is in front of the parentheses.

$40 = 4x + 28$ ← Distributive property: $4 \cdot x = 4x$ and $4 \cdot 7 = 28$.

$-28 + 40 = 4x + 28 + -28$ ← We add −28 to cancel out the 28 on the right side of the equation. We add −28 to each side to keep the equation balanced.

$12 = 4x + 0$

$12 = 4x$

$\frac{1}{4} \cdot 12 = \frac{1}{4} \cdot 4x$ ← We multiply by $\frac{1}{4}$ to get x by itself. We multiply each side by $\frac{1}{4}$ to keep the equation balanced.

$\frac{12}{4} = \frac{4}{4}x$

$3 = 1x$

$\mathbf{3 = x}$

This solution gives us the same answer for the part of the rectangle that is missing. The missing part of the rectangle is 3 inches.

The base of the rectangle is 3 + 7 or 10 inches.

Apply Skills: Turn to *Interactive Text*, page 308.

Monitoring Progress: Quiz 2

mBook Reinforce Understanding: Use the *mBook Study Guide* to review lesson concepts.

646 Unit 8 • Lesson 10

- Go through each of the steps of using the distributive property to solve the problem. Make sure students understand the justification for each of these steps.
- Start by substituting the dimensions that we know into the area formula, as we did in the first method.
- This time, use the distributive property: $\mathbf{40 = 4x + 28}$.
- Proceed through the steps by adding **−28** to both sides of the equation to cancel out 28 on the right side and get x alone, and to keep the equation balanced.
- Simplify until we get $\mathbf{12 = 4x}$.
- Point out that we want to get x alone on one side. To make the coefficient 1, we have to multiply by the reciprocal, $\frac{1}{4}$. Simplify to get the answer of $\mathbf{3 = x}$.
- Make sure students see that they need to keep in mind what the problem is asking. Be sure in this example that they see that the problem is asking for the measure of the base.
- Refer to the diagram of the compound rectangle, and point out we want to find the base, which is $x + 7$. We now know that $x = 3$, so **the base is 3 + 7, or 10 inches**.

Check for Understanding
Engagement Strategy: Look About

Draw a shape made of two smaller rectangles on the board. Label the height of the shape **5 inches**. Label the base of one of the rectangles **8 inches**. Tell students the area of the whole shape is **60 square inches**. Ask students to find the base of the compound shape, using one of the methods from Example 3 (*base = 12*). Students should write their steps and solutions in large writing on a piece of paper or a dry erase board. When students finish their work, they should hold up their answer for everyone to see.

If students are not sure about the answer, prompt them to look about at other students' solutions to help with their thinking. Review the answers after all students have held up their solutions.

Apply Skills
(*Interactive Text*, page 308)

Have students turn to *Interactive Text*, page 308, and complete the activity.

Activity 1

Students find missing dimensions of compound shapes. Monitor students' work as they complete the activity.

Watch for:

- Can students write an equation that represents the dimensions of the shape using the area formula?
- Do students know what the problem is asking and answer that particular question using algebra?

mBook **Reinforce Understanding**
Remind students that they can review lesson concepts by accessing the online *mBook Study Guide*.

Lesson 10 | Apply Skills

Name ______________________ Date ______________

Apply Skills
Area Formulas and Algebra Equations

Activity 1

Find the missing measure in each shape using area formulas and the distributive property.

1. If the area of this shape is 32 square units, what is the measure of its base? 8

   4, x, 2

   Show your work here:

   $32 = (x + 2) \cdot 4$

   $32 = 4x + 8$

   $24 = 4x \quad x = 6$

   If the base is represented with the expression $x + 2$, what is the measure of x? 6

2. If the area of this shape is 24 square units, what is the measure of its base? 8

   3, 6, x

   Show your work here:

   $24 = (6 + x) \cdot 3$

   $24 = 18 + 3x$

   $6 = 3x \quad x = 2$

   If the base is represented with the expression $6 + x$, what is the measure of x? 2

3. If the area of this shape is 48 square units, what is the measure of the height? 12

   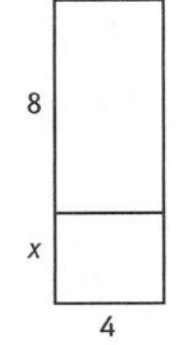

   Show your work here:

   $48 = 4(x + 8)$

   $\frac{1}{4} \cdot 48 = x + 8$

   $12 = x + 8 \quad x = 4$

   If the height is represented with the expression $8 + x$, what is the measure of x? 4

308 Unit 8 • Lesson 10

Monitoring Progress:
▶ Quiz 2 • Form A

Assess
Quiz 2

- Administer Quiz 2 Form A in the *Assessment Book*, pages 71–72. (If necessary, retest students with Quiz 2 Form B from the *mBook Teacher Edition* following differentiation.)

Students	Assess	Differentiate
	Day 1	Day 2
All	Quiz 2 *Form A*	
Scored 80% or above		Extension
Scored Below 80%		Reinforcement

Differentiate

- Review Quiz 2 Form A with class.
- Identify students for Extension or Reinforcement.

Extension

For those students who score 80 percent or better, provide the On Track! Activities from Unit 8, Lessons 6–10, from the *mBook Teacher Edition.*

Reinforcement

For those students who score below 80 percent, provide additional support in one of the following ways:

- Have students access the online tutorial provided in the *mBook Study Guide.*
- Have students complete the Interactive Reinforcement Exercises for Unit 8, Lessons 5–9, in the *mBook Study Guide.*
- Provide teacher-directed reteaching of unit concepts.

Unit 8 | Quiz 2 • Form A

Name ______________ Date ______________

Form A

Monitoring Progress
Algebraic Equations

Part 1

Solve the equations.

1. $-3x - 5 = 22$ $x = -9$
2. $-8a = -64$ $a = 8$
3. $6s = s + 40$ $s = 8$
4. $3(y - 3) = 18$ $y = 9$
5. $-9p + 3 = 21$ $p = -2$
6. $7x = 2x + 5$ $x = 1$
7. $-g = 44$ $g = -44$
8. $3y + 1 = 2y + 9$ $y = 8$
9. $2(x + 3) = 20$ $x = 7$
10. $17 = 2t + 5$ $t = 6$

Part 2

Translate the word problems into equations, then solve them.

1. Trina and her brothers, James and Marcus, put all of their money on the kitchen table. James had two times as much money as Trina. Marcus also had two times as much money as Trina. The total amount of money on the table was $100. How much money did each person have?
$2x + 2x + x = 100$; $x = 20$; Trina = $20, James = $40, Marcus = $40
2. There are two jars of water in the refrigerator. The larger jar has twice as much water as the smaller jar. The total water in both jars is 15 ounces. How much water is in each jar?
$x + 2x = 15$; $x = 5$; 5 and 10
3. Two friends start driving from two different cities. The cities are 330 miles apart. The friends are in cars driving toward each other. The first car is going 50 miles per hour. The second car is going 60 miles per hour. How long before the friends meet?
$60x + 50x = 330$; $x = 3$ hours

Unit 8

Unit 8 • Quiz 2 • Form A 71

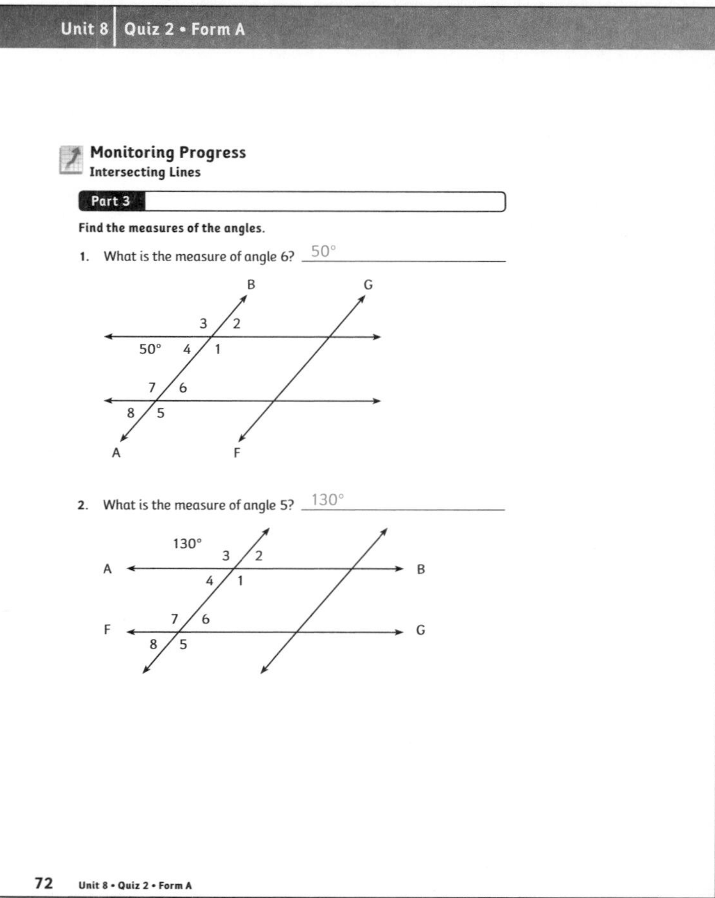
Unit 8 | Quiz 2 • Form A

Monitoring Progress
Intersecting Lines

Part 3

Find the measures of the angles.

1. What is the measure of angle 6? 50°

2. What is the measure of angle 5? 130°

72 Unit 8 • Quiz 2 • Form A

Name ______________ Date ______________

Form B

mBook

Monitoring Progress
Algebraic Equations

Part 1

Solve the equations.

1. $-2x - 5 = 21$ $x = -13$
2. $-8a = -36$ $a = 4.5$
3. $6s = s + 50$ $s = 10$
4. $3(y - 1) = 18$ $y = 7$
5. $-5p + 3 = 23$ $p = -4$
6. $12x = 2x + 5$ $x = 0.5$
7. $-g = 34$ $g = -34$
8. $3y + 1 = 2y + 6$ $y = 5$
9. $2(x + 5) = 30$ $x = 10$
10. $21 = 2t + 5$ $t = 8$

Part 2

Translate the word problems into equations, then solve them.

1. Trina and her brothers, James and Marcus, put all of their money on the kitchen table. James had two times as much money as Trina. Marcus also had two times as much money as Trina. The total amount of money on the table was $80. How much money did each person have?
   $2x + 2x + x = 80$; $x = 16$; Trina had $16, and her brothers each had $32.
2. There are two jars of water in the refrigerator. The larger jar has two times as much water as the smaller jar. The total water in both jars is 21 ounces. How much water is in each jar?
   $2x + x = 21$; $x = 7$; the small jar holds 7 ounces and the large jar holds 14 ounces
3. Two friends start driving from two different cities. The cities are 220 miles apart. The friends are in cars driving toward each other. The first car is going 50 miles per hour. The second car is going 60 miles per hour. How long before the friends meet?
   $50x + 60x = 220$; $x = 2$ hours

Name ______________ Date ______________

Monitoring Progress
Intersecting Lines

Part 3

Find the measures of the angles.

1. What is the measure of angle 6? 50°

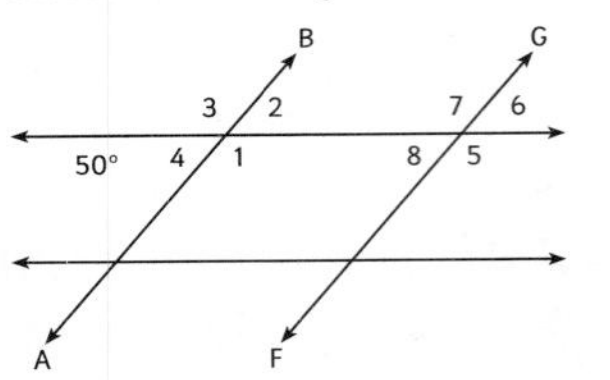

2. What is the measure of angle 5? 100°

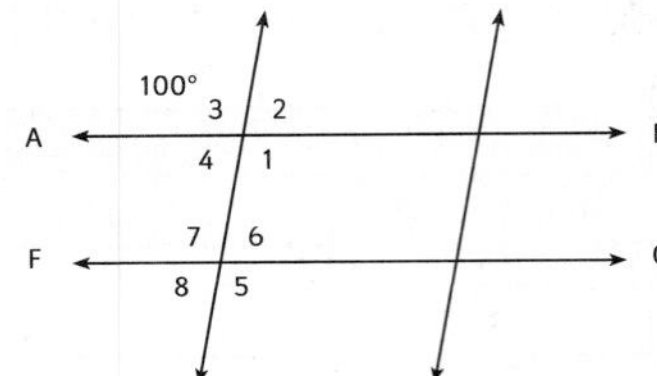

Homework

Go over the instructions on page 647 of the *Student Text* for each part of the homework.

Activity 1

Students solve equations.

Activity 2

Students find the missing dimension in the compound shape where one of the dimensions is represented as an expression.

Activity 3

Students find the missing dimension in the area of a triangle.

Activity 4 • Distributed Practice

Students practice order of operations, integer operations, and one-step equations.

Lesson 10

Homework

Activity 1

Solve.

1. $A = 5 \cdot 7$ 35
2. $P = 2 \cdot 4 + 2 \cdot 8$ 24
3. $A = \frac{1}{2} \cdot 3 \cdot 2$ 3
4. $5^2 = A$ 25
5. $A = 2(x + 2)$ $2x + 4$
6. $A = 4 \cdot 6$ 24

Activity 2

Use the area formula for a rectangle, $A = b \cdot h$, to solve the problems.

1. What is the length of the base of this rectangle if its area is 20 square inches? 10 in.

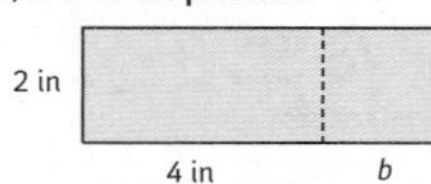

2. What is the height of this rectangle if its area is 40 square inches? 4 in.

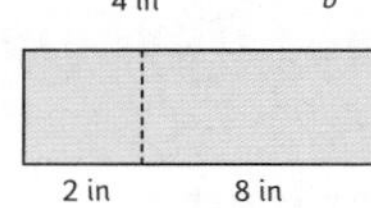

Activity 3

Use the area formula for a triangle, $A = \frac{1}{2} \cdot b \cdot h$, to solve the problems.

1. What is the length of the base of this triangle if its area is 10 square units? 4 units

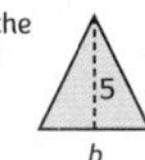

2. What is the height of this triangle if its area is 12 square units? 8 units

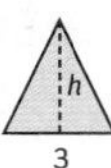

Activity 4 • Distributed Practice

Solve.

1. $\frac{2}{a} = \frac{4}{6}$ 3
2. $-54 \div y = -6$ 9
3. $\frac{2}{3} \cdot c = 1$ $1\frac{1}{2}$
4. $-\frac{1}{2} + w = 0$ $\frac{1}{2}$
5. $-4 + z = -8$ -4
6. $14 = 2(x + 6)$ 1

Unit 8 • Lesson 10 647

Lesson 11 ▶ Commutative and Associative Properties

Problem Solving: ▶ Proving Angles Are Equal

Lesson Planner

Vocabulary Development

proof
transitive property
transversal

Skills Maintenance

Area Formulas and Algebra

Building Number Concepts

▶ Commutative and Associative Properties

Students learn that even though some algebra problems look complex, if we break the problems into manageable parts, we have everything we need to solve them. Having a flexible approach to solving problems works better than memorization.

Objective

Students will use different methods to solve algebra problems.

Problem Solving:

▶ Proving Angles Are Equal

Students are introduced to geometric proofs. A proof in geometry is a series of steps that are justifiable by formal properties and rules. Students also learn the transitive property: if a = b and b = c then a = c. This property proves angles are equal.

Objective

Students will use inferences to justify proofs in geometry.

Homework

Students combine like terms using the commutative and associative properties, solve equations, and prove that pairs of angles are equal. In Distributed Practice, students practice order of operations, integer operations, and one-step equations.

Lesson 11 | Skills Maintenance

Name ______________________ Date ______________

Skills Maintenance
Area Formulas and Algebra

Activity 1

Use algebra and common area formulas to solve the problems.

1. What is the area of this triangle? The formula is $A = \frac{1}{2} \cdot b \cdot h$ ___12___

6, 4

2. What is the measure of the base of this rectangle if its area is 20 square units? The formula is $A = b \cdot h$ ___5___

4, x

3. What is the measure of the height of this rectangle if the area is 27 square units? ___9___

8, x, 3

Unit 8

Unit 8 • Lesson 11 309

Skills Maintenance

Area Formulas and Algebra

(*Interactive Text*, page 309)

Activity 1

Students solve problems involving algebra and area.

Building Number Concepts: Commutative and Associative Properties

What do we do when equations look complicated?

(*Student Text*, pages 648–649)

Connect to Prior Knowledge

Begin by putting this statement on the board or overhead:

10 • 357 • 149 • 100 • 5,555 • −7,080 • 0

Tell students that this might seem like a very complex equation, but if we analyze it carefully, we can solve it quickly and easily. Ask students if anyone sees the reason this is actually easy to solve. Listen for the rule anything times 0 is 0. It helps to look at the entire equation first and see the 0 at the end.

Link to Today's Concept

Tell students that in today's lesson we look for shortcuts and ways to simplify equations to make complex equations easier to solve.

Demonstrate

Engagement Strategy: Teacher Modeling

Demonstrate the four main steps to solving algebraic equations in one of the following ways:

mBook: Use the *mBook Teacher Edition* for pages 648–649 of the *Student Text*. m

Overhead Projector: Reproduce the steps and equations on a transparency and modify as discussed.

- Display and read the four steps for solving equations with students. Explain that it is especially important to remember these steps when solving complex equations.

Lesson 11 | Commutative and Associative Properties
Problem Solving:
Proving Angles Are Equal

Commutative and Associative Properties

What do we do when equations look complicated?

It's important to have a flexible approach for solving algebraic equations. Often, we try to memorize just one way to solve an equation, then get stuck when we run into an equation that is slightly different.

Here are the four main steps we use.

Steps for Solving Equations

STEP 1
Look at the entire equation.

STEP 2
Look for the **parts** of the equation that seem different.

STEP 3
Remember the goal: Solve the equation so that we have a **positive variable on one side**.

STEP 4
Use the rules or properties we need to reach our goal.

The equation in Example 1 looks complicated because the expression on the left side is long. We use the commutative property to change the equation and make it easier to solve.

648 Unit 8 • Lesson 11

STEP 1

- Explain that the first step is to **look** at the entire equation. m

STEP 2

- Explain that the second step is to look for **parts** of the equation that seem different. m

STEP 3

- Tell students that the third step is to remember the goal. We solve the equation to have a **positive variable on one side**. m

STEP 4

- Tell students that the fourth step is to **use the rules or properties** we need to reach our goal. m

What do we do when equations look complicated? *(continued)*

Demonstrate

- Demonstrate how to use the commutative property to make the problem easier to solve.
- Show the problem $\mathbf{2x + 3 + 5x - 4 = 13}$. m
- Use the commutative property to put like terms next to each other. m
- Explain that subtraction is the same as adding the opposite, so subtracting 4 is the same as adding −4. m
- Continue walking through each of the steps to get x alone on one side of the equation, until you get $\mathbf{7x = 14}$. m
- Demonstrate how to multiply both sides of the equation by the reciprocal $\frac{1}{7}$ to get one positive x by itself, and the answer of $\mathbf{x = 2}$. m

Check for Understanding
Engagement Strategy: Think, Think

Write the equation $\mathbf{4x + 1 + 3x - 2 = 27}$ on the board. Tell students to use the commutative property to solve the equation (*x = 4*). Tell them that you will call on one of them to answer a question after you ask it. Tell them to listen for their names. Allow time for students to solve the problem. Then call on a student.

Example 1

Use the commutative property to make it easier to solve the equation.

$\mathbf{2x + 3 + 5x - 4 = 13}$

$2x + 5x + 3 - 4 = 13$ ← We use the commutative property to put like terms next to each other.

$2x + 5x + 3 + -4 = 13$ ← Subtraction is the same as adding the opposite.

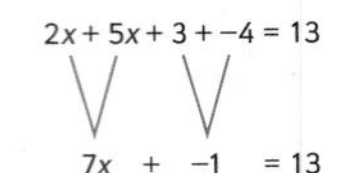

$7x + -1 = 13$ ← We combine like terms.

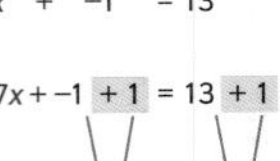

$7x + -1 + 1 = 13 + 1$ ← We add 1 to cancel out the −1 on the left side of the equation. We add 1 to each side to balance the equation.

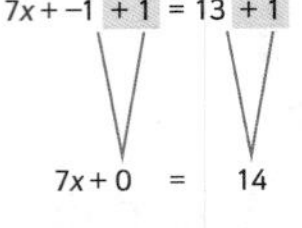

$7x + 0 = 14$

$7x = 14$

$\frac{1}{7} \cdot 7x = \frac{1}{7} \cdot 14$ ← We multiply by $\frac{1}{7}$ to get x by itself. We multiply each side by $\frac{1}{7}$ to balance the equation.

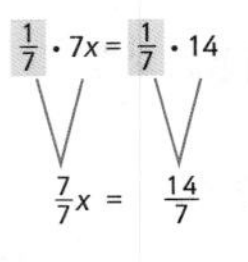

$\frac{7}{7}x = \frac{14}{7}$

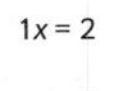

$1x = 2$

$\mathbf{x = 2}$

Apply Skills Turn to ***Interactive Text***, page 310.

Reinforce Understanding Use the ***mBook Study Guide*** to review lesson concepts.

Apply Skills

(*Interactive Text*, page 310)

Have students turn to page 310 in the *Interactive Text*, and complete the activity.

Activity 1

Students solve complex equations by simplifying them first. Monitor students' work as they complete the activity.

Watch for:

- Can students simplify the equation using the commutative property?
- Can students solve the simplified equation?
- Do students get the correct answer? Did students check their answers?

mBook **Reinforce Understanding**

Remind students that they can review lesson concepts by accessing the online *mBook Study Guide*.

Lesson 11 | Apply Skills

Name ______________ Date ______________

Apply Skills

Commutative and Associative Properties

Activity 1

Solve the problems using the properties you learned to simplify your work.

1. $2x - 4 + 7 - 8 + x + 3x + 4 = -7$

   Simplify the equation here:

   $6x - 1 = -7$

   Solve the simplified equation here:

   $6x = -6$

   $x = -1$

   $x =$ $\underline{-1}$

   Check your work here:

   $-2 - 4 + 7 - 8 + -1 + -3 + 4 = -7$

   $-7 = -7$

2. $-2 = 3 + x + 4 + -x + x - 4$

   Simplify the equation here:

   $-2 = 3 + x$

   Solve the simplified equation here:

   $-5 = x$

   $x =$ $\underline{-5}$

   Check your work here:

   $-2 = 3 + -5 + 4 + 5 + -5 - 4$

   $-2 = -2$

3. $2x + 4 = -5 + x + 7 + 2x + -2 - 1$

   Simplify the equation here:

   $2x + 4 = -1 + 3x$

   Solve the simplified equation here:

   $5 = x$

   $x =$ $\underline{5}$

   Check your work here:

   $10 + 4 = -5 + 10 + 7 + 10 + -2 - 1$

   $14 = 14$

4. $4 + 5 - 3 - 1 + 2x - 4 = x + 1$

   Simplify the equation here:

   $1 + 2x = x + 1$

   Solve the simplified equation here:

   $2x = x$

   $x = 0$

   $x =$ $\underline{0}$

   Check your work here:

   $4 + 5 - 3 - 1 + 0 - 4 = 0 + 1$

   $1 = 1$

310 Unit 8 • Lesson 11

Problem Solving:
▶ Proving Angles Are Equal

What does it mean to prove something in geometry?
(*Student Text*, page 650)

Demonstrate

- Have students turn to the material on page 650 of the *Student Text*. Discuss the concept of a formal **proof** in geometry.
- Explain to students that we have already done a lot of proof-like work when we solve algebraic equations, as they are a series of steps with justifications of properties and rules.
- Discuss the **transitive property** with students. This property helps us prove angles are equal. Write this general statement on the board or overhead: **If $a = b$ and $b = c$, then $a = c$.**
- Go through the real-world example of Cara, Gabriella, and Ramon in the textbook. Explain that Cara is as tall as Gabriella, and Ramon is as tall as Gabriella. The transitive property tells us that Cara is as tall as Ramon.
- Give students additional real-world examples of the use of the transitive property in everyday life. Some possibilities are:
  - If a student is in the marching band, and the marching band is part of the music department, then the student is in the music department.
  - If a tomato is a fruit, and a fruit is a food, than a tomato is a food.
  - If a dog is a pet, and a pet is an animal, then a dog is an animal.

Lesson 11

▶Problem Solving: Proving Angles Are Equal

Vocabulary

proof
transitive property
transversal

What does it mean to prove something in geometry?

Throughout this unit we have been following a series of steps to solve algebraic equations.

The previous example showed how we solved an equation. For most of the steps, we described the rule or property from the Algebra Toolbox that explains the reason behind the step.

We can do something similar in geometry, and the process is called a **proof**. When we do a proof, we show the steps we use to make an inference about something.

Another property we need to learn to help us do this is the **transitive property**. This property is an easy way to show how different objects are related to each other.

Let's imagine three people: Cara, Gabriella, and Ramon. Let's say we know that Cara is the same height as Gabriella, and Gabriella is the same height as Ramon. We use this information to say that Cara and Ramon are the same height. The transitive property looks like this.

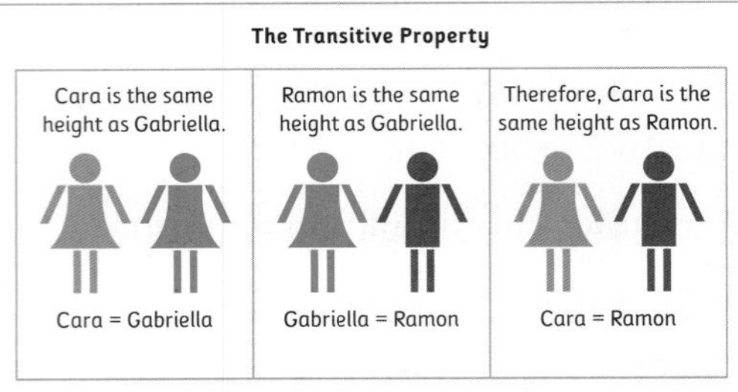

The Transitive Property
Cara is the same height as Gabriella.
Ramon is the same height as Gabriella.
Therefore, Cara is the same height as Ramon.
Cara = Gabriella
Gabriella = Ramon
Cara = Ramon

How do we use inferences in proofs?
(*Student Text*, pages 651–652)

Demonstrate

- Turn to page 651 of the *Student Text*, and look at **Example 1**. Explain that a line that cuts across two parallel lines is called a **transversal**. Point out that a transversal can cut across the lines at any angle.
- Walk through Example 1 to show how we prove that two angles are equal.
- Point out that we do not use any measurements. Explain to students that we do not need to use measurements because of our rules and properties.
- Go through each step, and be sure students understand that a rule or property justifies each step.
- Explain that due to the Vertical Angles Rule, angles 2 and 4 are equal.
- Point out that because of the Corresponding Angles Rule, angles 4 and 8 are equal.
- Finally point out that because of the Transitive Property, angles 2 and 8 are equal.

Lesson 11

How do we use inferences in proofs?

Example 1 shows a line that cuts across two parallel lines. This line is called a **transversal**. The transversal can cut across the lines at any angle. We can prove that the angles created by the transversal line are equal by using the rules we have learned in previous lessons.

No measurements are given in Example 1. However, we can make inferences to prove that details about the angles are true. We don't need to use numbers. We will just use rules and properties.

Example 1

Use an inference to prove that ∠2 and ∠8 are equal.

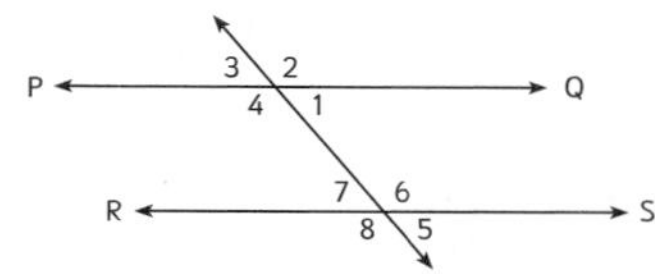

Proof	
Steps	**Reasons**
measure of ∠2 = measure of ∠4	Vertical Angles Rule
measure of ∠4 = measure of ∠8	Corresponding Angles Rule
measure of ∠2 = measure of ∠8	Transitive Property

Remember the example of Cara, Gabriella, and Ramon when using the transitive property.

Unit 8 • Lesson 1[1] 651

How do we use inferences in proofs?
(continued)

Demonstrate

- Turn to page 652 of the *Student Text*, and look at **Example 2**.
- Explain that this is a slightly more complex problem where we are proving that two angles are equal. Go through each step and be sure students understand the justification for each.
- Point out that the rules and properties that we have learned allow us to make inferences about the angles.
- Point out that angles 1 and 3 are equal because of the Vertical Angles Rule.
- Make sure students understand that angles 3 and 7 and angles 7 and 11 are equal due to the Corresponding Angles Rule.
- Help students observe that angles 1 and 11 are equal, due to the Transitive Property.

We can extend our thinking to more complicated problems. Example 2 shows how we make inferences to prove that different angles on a parallelogram are equal.

Example 2

Use an inference to prove that ∠1 and ∠11 are equal.

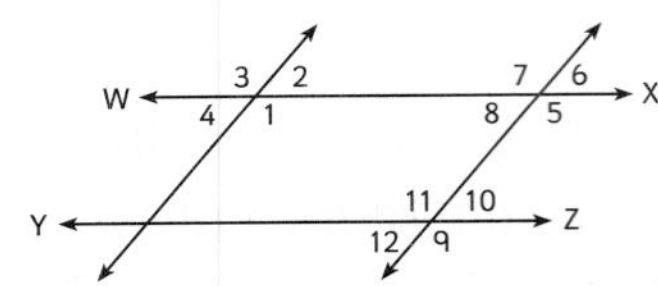

Proof	
Steps	**Reasons**
measure of ∠1 = measure of ∠3	Vertical Angles Rule
measure of ∠3 = measure of ∠7	Corresponding Angles Rule
measure of ∠7 = measure of ∠11	Corresponding Angles Rule
measure of ∠1 = measure of ∠11	Transitive Property

Problem-Solving Activity Turn to ***Interactive Text***, page 311.

mBook Reinforce Understanding Use the ***mBook Study Guide*** to review lesson concepts.

Problem-Solving Activity

(*Interactive Text*, pages 311–312)

Have students turn to pages 311–312 in the *Interactive Text*, and read the instructions together.

Students use the vertical and corresponding angles rules, as well as the transitive property, to prove that two angles are equal. Tell them to be sure to write justifications for each step as they work through their proof.

Monitor students' work as they complete the activity.

Watch for:

- Can students identify the steps and write justifications for them?
- Can students use the properties and rules effectively for justifying the steps?
- Can students prove the angles are equal in the most direct way (e.g., minimum number of steps)?

mBook Reinforce Understanding

Remind students that they can review lesson concepts by accessing the online *mBook Study Guide*.

Lesson 11 | Problem-Solving Activity

Name ______________________ Date ______________

Problem-Solving Activity
Proving Angles Are Equal

Use the vertical and corresponding angles rules, as well as the transitive property, to solve the problems. Be sure to write the reasons for each step in your proof.

1. Lines PQ and XY are parallel. Prove that ∠3 and ∠5 are equal.
   Angle 3 and angle 1 are equal because of the vertical angle rule, and angle 1 and 5 are equal because of the transitive property.

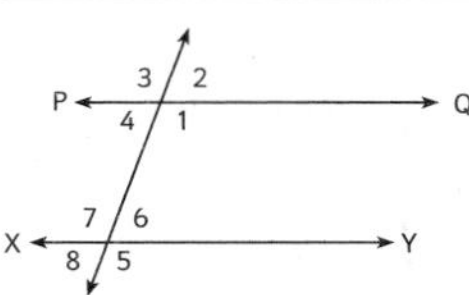

2. Lines RS and TU are parallel. Prove that ∠4 and ∠6 are equal.
   Angle 4 is equal to 2 because of the vertical angle property, so angle 4 is equal to angle 6 because of the transitive property.

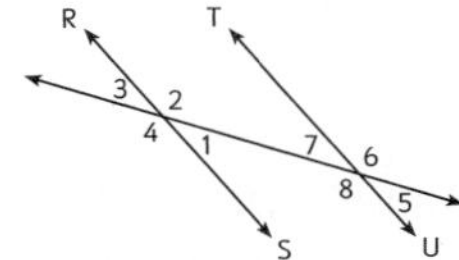

Unit 8 • Lesson 11 311

Lesson 11 | Problem-Solving Activity

Name ______________________ Date ______________

3. Lines RS and TU are parallel. Lines WX and YZ are parallel. Prove that ∠1 and ∠7 are equal.
   Angle 1 is equal to 3 because of the vertical angle rule, so is equal to angle 10 because they are corresponding angles.

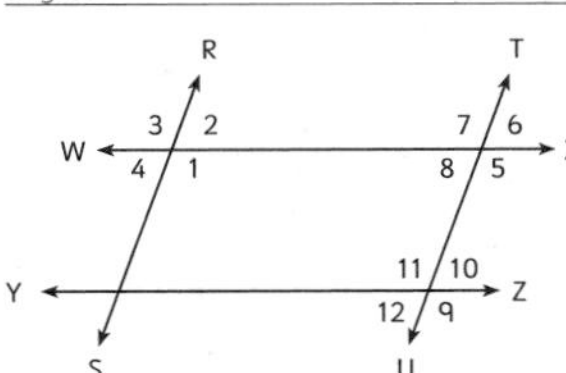

4. Lines EF and KM are parallel. Lines WX and YZ are parallel. Prove that ∠4 and ∠10 are equal.
   They are equal because of the vertical angle rule.

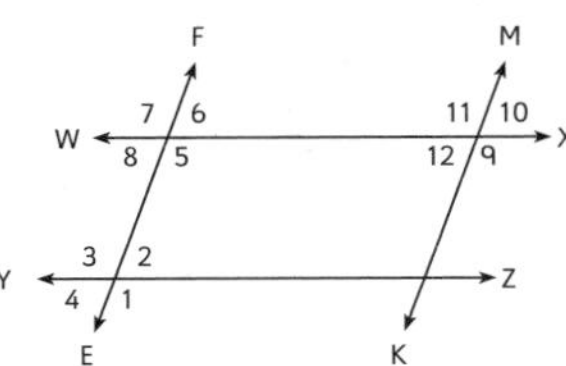

mBook Reinforce Understanding
Use the mBook *Study Guide* to review lesson concepts.

312 Unit 8 • Lesson 11

Homework

Go over the instructions on page 653 of the *Student Text* for each part of the homework.

Activity 1

Students combine like terms using the commutative and associative properties in expressions.

Activity 2

Students solve equations.

Activity 3

Students prove that pairs of angles are equal. Tell students to show all their work including justifications for each step.

Activity 4 • Distributed Practice

Students practice order of operations, integer operations, and one-step equations.

Lesson 11

Homework

Activity 1

Combine like terms using the commutative and associative properties in the expressions.

1. $x + 7 + x$ $2x + 7$
2. $-4 + y + -8$ $y + -12$
3. $-w + 11 + 2w$ $w + 11$
4. $6 + -a - 3$ $-a + 3$
5. $-2m + 4 + -3m + 6$ $-5m + 10$
6. $8 + n + 2 + -3$ $n + 7$

Activity 2

Solve.

1. $18 = 2x + -3 + -2x + 3x$ 7
2. $3 + w + -7 = 21$ 25
3. $a + 2a + -3 + a = 20$ $5\frac{3}{4}$
4. $4 + b + -2 + 2b = 8 + b$ 3

Activity 3

Tell the reasons for each of the steps proving that $\angle 1$ and $\angle 11$ are equal.

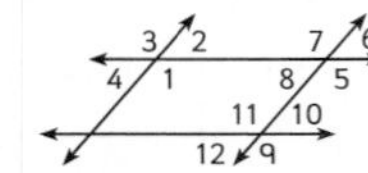

Proof	
Steps	**Reasons**
1. measure of $\angle 1$ = measure of $\angle 3$	vertical angles rule
2. measure of $\angle 3$ = measure of $\angle 7$	corresponding angles rule
3. measure of $\angle 7$ = measure of $\angle 11$	corresponding angles rule
4. measure of $\angle 1$ = measure of $\angle 11$	transitive property

Activity 4 • Distributed Practice

Solve.

1. $x \cdot \frac{4}{3} = 1$ $\frac{3}{4}$
2. $-9 \cdot -8 = m$ 72
3. $a + -1.2 = 0$ 1.2
4. $\frac{z}{15} = \frac{3}{5}$ 9
5. $-27 + b = 30$ 57
6. $15 = 3(m + 1)$ 4

Unit 8 • Lesson 11 653

Lesson 12 ▸ Fractions as Coefficients

Problem Solving: ▸ Making Inferences in Geometry

Lesson Planner

Skills Maintenance

Solving Complex Equations

Building Number Concepts:

▸ Fractions as Coefficients

Students learn how to solve problems when the coefficient is a fraction. It is important that students understand these problems might look difficult, but they are really not that complicated. The problems are solved using the rules and properties that students have already studied.

Objective

Students will evaluate which method is most efficient and solve equations with fractions as coefficients.

Problem Solving:

▸ Making Inferences in Geometry

Students learn that we use rules, properties, and inferences to solve complex problems involving measures of angles. These inferences will help us figure out the measure of unknown angles.

Objective

Students will find the measure of unknown angles by making inferences.

Homework

Students change coefficients to 1 using reciprocals, solve equations where there are fractional coefficients, and find the missing angle measures using rules, properties, and inferences. In Distributed Practice, students practice order of operations, integer operations, and one-step equations.

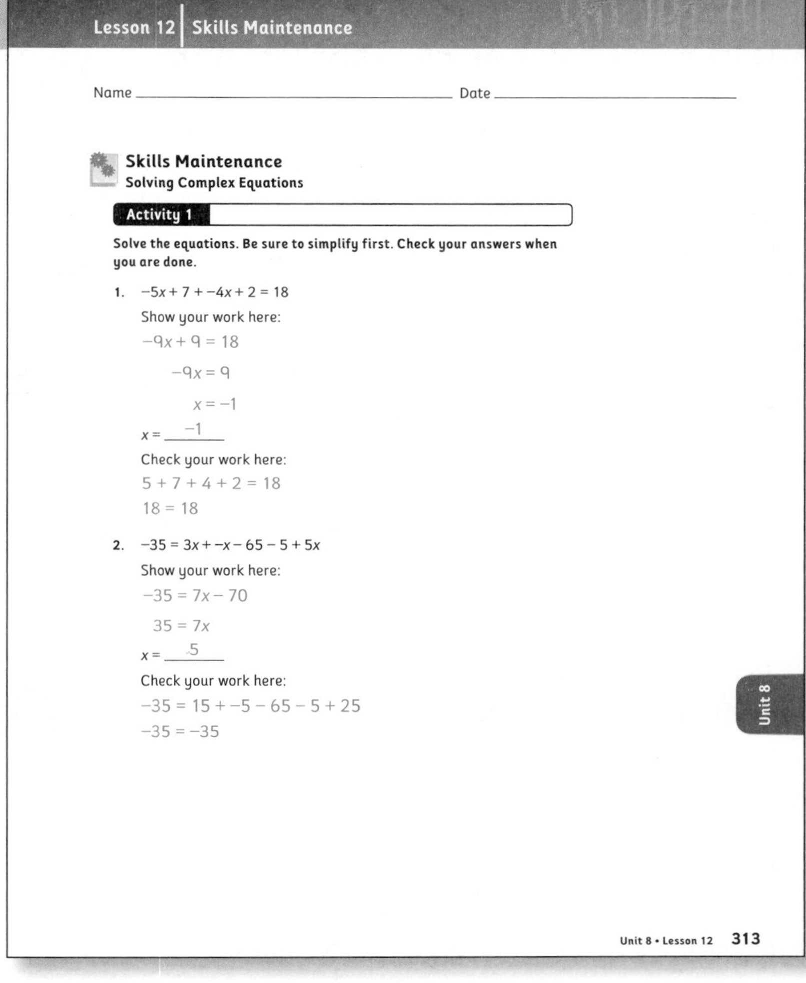

Lesson 12 | Skills Maintenance

Name ______________________ Date ______________________

Skills Maintenance
Solving Complex Equations

Activity 1

Solve the equations. Be sure to simplify first. Check your answers when you are done.

1. $-5x + 7 + -4x + 2 = 18$

   Show your work here:

   $-9x + 9 = 18$

   $-9x = 9$

   $x = -1$

   $x =$ __−1__

   Check your work here:

   $5 + 7 + 4 + 2 = 18$

   $18 = 18$

2. $-35 = 3x + -x - 65 - 5 + 5x$

   Show your work here:

   $-35 = 7x - 70$

   $35 = 7x$

   $x =$ __5__

   Check your work here:

   $-35 = 15 + -5 - 65 - 5 + 25$

   $-35 = -35$

Unit 8

Unit 8 • Lesson 12 313

Skills Maintenance

Solving Complex Equations

(*Interactive Text*, page 313)

Activity 1

Students solve complex equations. Remind students to simplify the equation first by combining like terms.

Building Number Concepts: ▶ Fractions as Coefficients

How do we solve an equation when the coefficient is a fraction?

(*Student Text*, pages 654–655)

Connect to Prior Knowledge

Begin by writing these two equations on the board:

$$\frac{1}{4} \cdot d = 1 \text{ and } \frac{1}{4} \div e = 1$$

Have students solve the problems mentally. Discuss the role reciprocals play in working with fractions. Also stress that the difference between d and $e\left(\frac{4}{1} \text{ and } \frac{1}{4}\right)$ remind us that multiplication and division are inverse operations.

Link to Today's Concept

Tell students that in today's lesson, we apply what we know about reciprocals to solve equations with fractions as coefficients.

Demonstrate

Engagement Strategy: Teacher Modeling

Demonstrate solving an equation with a fraction as the coefficient in one of the following ways:

mBook: Use the *mBook Teacher Edition* for page 654 of the *Student Text*. m

Overhead Projector: Reproduce the problems on a transparency, and modify as discussed.

Board: Draw the problems on the board, and modify as discussed.

- Show the two equations $2x + 4 = 20$ and $\frac{1}{2}x + 4 = 20$. m
- Ask students to describe how the equations are different. Tell students that while having a fraction as a coefficient might make the equation seem more complex, it is no different than a whole number coefficient in terms of how we solve it.
- Remind students that the reciprocal property helps us get a coefficient of 1.
- Go through the steps in **Example 1** to solve $\frac{1}{2}x + 4 = 20$. m
- Explain that we need to get x by itself, so we add −4 to both sides of the equation. Remind students that we have to add −4 to the right side to keep the equation balanced. m
- Simplify to get $\frac{1}{2}x = 16$. m
- Then multiply both sides by 2 to get x by itself. Remind students that $\frac{2}{1}$ is the reciprocal of $\frac{1}{2}$, and the goal is for a coefficient of 1. m
- Simplify to get the answer $x = 32$. m

Lesson 12 ▶Fractions as Coefficients
Problem Solving:
▶Making Inferences in Geometry

▶Fractions as Coefficients

How do we solve an equation when the coefficient is a fraction?

Let's look at the following two equations. There is a difference between them.

$$2x + 4 = 20 \qquad \frac{1}{2}x + 4 = 20$$

The equation on the right has a fraction as a coefficient. This might look like a big change, but it doesn't make that much of a difference. We use the same rules and properties from our Algebra Toolbox to solve for x.

Example 1

Solve each equation.

$\frac{1}{2}x + 4 = 20$

$\frac{1}{2}x + 4 + -4 = 20 + -4$ ← We add −4 to get x by itself. We add −4 to both sides to keep the equation balanced.

$\frac{1}{2}x + 0 = 16$

$\frac{1}{2}x = 16$

$2 \cdot \frac{1}{2}x = 16 \cdot 2$ ← We multiply by 2 to get a positive x by itself. We multiply each side by 2 to keep the equation balanced.

$\frac{2}{2}x = 32$

$1x = 32$

$x = 32$

654 Unit 8 • Lesson 12

Demonstrate

- Turn to page 655 of the *Student Text* and use **Example 2** to demonstrate how to solve a slightly more difficult equation, $\mathbf{\frac{4}{3}(x + 1) = 8}$.
- Tell students that in this problem, we have a coefficient that is in front of an expression in parentheses.
- Point out to students that while we could distribute the $\frac{4}{3}$ across the terms using the distributive property, it is much easier to multiply by the reciprocal.
- Remind students that this gives us a coefficient of 1 and then we do not have to worry about solving a bunch of fraction computations.
- Go through each step with students and be sure they understand the justification for each.
- Begin by multiplying each side of the equation by the reciprocal, $\mathbf{\frac{3}{4}}$.
- Simplify to get a coefficient of 1. This makes a much easier problem: $\mathbf{(x + 1) = 6}$.
- Walk through the rest of the problem to solve for x: $\mathbf{x = 5}$.

Check for Understanding
Engagement Strategy: Think Tank

Distribute pieces of paper to students and have them write their names on them. Write the equation $\mathbf{\frac{5}{2}(x + 3) = 25}$ on the board. Have students think about which method would make the equation easier to solve. Then have students solve the equation on the piece of paper and check their work by substituting the value back into the equation. Collect the papers in a container and draw a piece of paper. Share the answer with the class. If correct, congratulate the student and invite the student to explain the answer ($x = 7$).

Be sure to discuss with students that while using the distributive property in this case is not incorrect, it is not the most efficient way to solve the problem.

Watch for:

- Students choose the reciprocal method.
- Students multiply both sides of the equation by the reciprocal, $\frac{2}{5}$.
- Students simplify correctly.
- Students compute correctly when they check their answer.

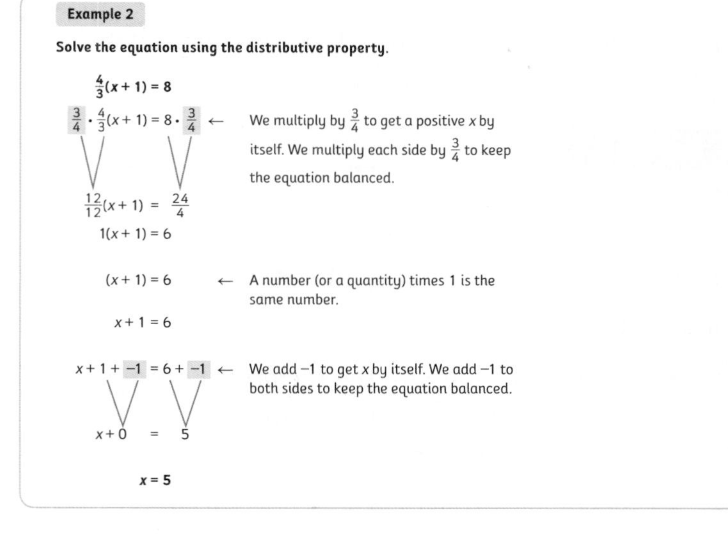

Lesson 12

We use the same kind of thinking when we work equations that involve the distributive property.

We get rid of the fraction coefficient by using a reciprocal. This method makes solving the equation much easier.

Example 2

Solve the equation using the distributive property.

$\frac{4}{3}(x + 1) = 8$

$\frac{3}{4} \cdot \frac{4}{3}(x + 1) = 8 \cdot \frac{3}{4}$ ← We multiply by $\frac{3}{4}$ to get a positive x by itself. We multiply each side by $\frac{3}{4}$ to keep the equation balanced.

$\frac{12}{12}(x + 1) = \frac{24}{4}$

$1(x + 1) = 6$

$(x + 1) = 6$ ← A number (or a quantity) times 1 is the same number.

$x + 1 = 6$

$x + 1 + -1 = 6 + -1$ ← We add −1 to get x by itself. We add −1 to both sides to keep the equation balanced.

$x + 0 = 5$

$x = 5$

Apply Skills: Turn to *Interactive Text*, page 314.

mBook Reinforce Understanding: Use the *mBook Study Guide* to review lesson concepts.

Unit 8 • Lesson 12 655

Apply Skills

(*Interactive Text*, page 314)

Have students turn to page 314 in the *Interactive Text*, and complete the activity.

Activity 1

Students solve equations involving fractional coefficients, then check their work. Monitor students' work as they complete the activity.

Watch for:

- Can students identify the reciprocal of each coefficient and multiply by that reciprocal to get a coefficient of 1?
- Can students solve the equation once they have simplified the coefficient to 1?
- Do students remember to use the rule for reciprocals rather than the distributive property when appropriate?
- Do students compute correctly when they check their answers?

Be sure to discuss with students that while using the distributive property for every problem is not incorrect, it is not always the most efficient way to solve the problem.

Explain to students that we teach these different solution strategies so that they know the options for solving equations. Point out the importance of analyzing the equation first before selecting a strategy so as to choose the most efficient method for solving.

mBook **Reinforce Understanding**
Remind students that they can review lesson concepts by accessing the online *mBook Study Guide*.

Lesson 12 | Apply Skills

Name ______________ Date ______________

Apply Skills
Fractions as Coefficients

Activity 1

Solve the equations that have fractions as coefficients.

1. $\frac{1}{2}x + 34 = 48$

Show your work here:

$\frac{1}{2}x = 14$

$2 \cdot \frac{1}{2}x = 14 \cdot 2$

$x = 28$

$x =$ 28

Check your work here:

$\frac{1}{2}(28) = 14$

$14 = 14$

2. $\frac{1}{3}(x + 3) = 9$

Show your work here:

$3 \cdot \frac{1}{3}(x + 3) = 9 \cdot 3$

$x + 3 = 27$

$x = 24$

$x =$ 24

Check your work here:

$\frac{1}{3}(27) = 9$

$9 = 9$

3. $40 = \frac{2}{3}x + -34$

Show your work here:

$74 = \frac{2}{3}x$

$\left(\frac{3}{2}\right)74 = \left(\frac{3}{2}\right)\frac{2}{3}x$

$x = 111$

$x =$ 111

Check your work here:

$40 = \frac{2}{3}(111) + -34$

$74 = 74$

314 Unit 8 • Lesson 12

Problem Solving:
▶ Making Inferences in Geometry

How do we figure out the measure of unknown angles?

(*Student Text*, pages 656–659)

Connect to Prior Knowledge

Begin by reminding students that we use rules and properties to make inferences in geometry.

Link to Today's Concept

In today's lesson we use the rules we know to find the measure of unknown angles.

Demonstrate

- Be sure students understand what each rule does and how it helps us in our proofs.
- Review the Right Angles Rule, that the measure of a right angle is 90 degrees. Point out the symbol used to show a right angle.
- Go over the Supplementary Angles Rule, that when two angles form a straight line, they are supplementary angles.
- Refer to the diagram and remind students that the measure of a straight line is 180 degrees.

How do we figure out the measure of unknown angles?

We learned about proof and inference in geometry. We learned about rules and properties that help us make inferences in geometry.

Let's review two other ideas about the measures of angles.

Right Angles Rule

The measure of a right angle is 90 degrees.

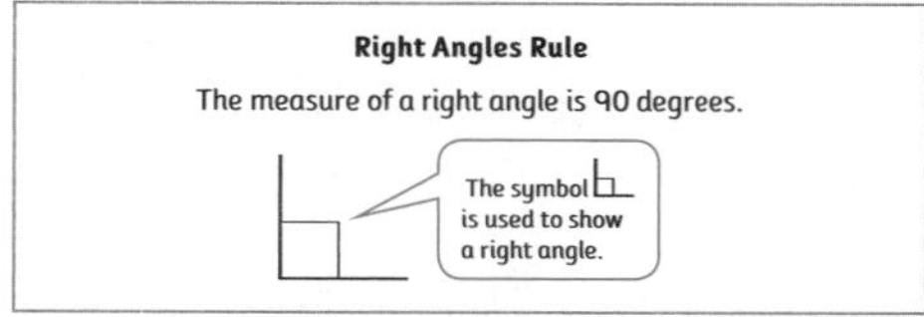
The symbol ∟ is used to show a right angle.

Supplementary Angles Rule

When we combine two angles to form a straight line, we have supplementary angles.

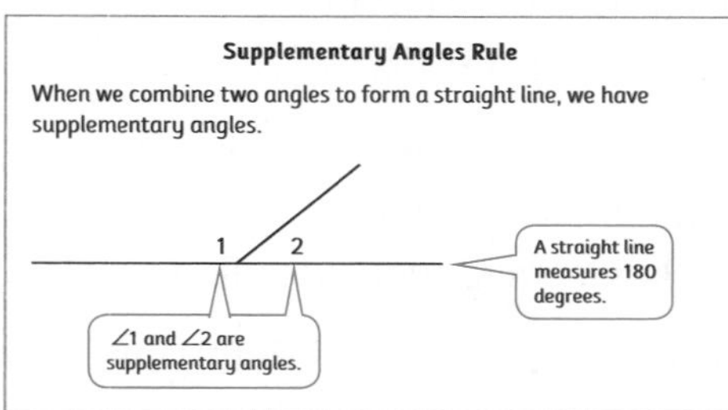
1
2
A straight line measures 180 degrees.
∠1 and ∠2 are supplementary angles.

How do we figure out the measure of unknown angles? *(continued)*

Demonstrate

- Turn to page 657 of the *Student Text* and discuss the material.
- Go over the Vertical Angles Rule, that vertical angles have sides that are opposite rays.
- Refer to the diagram and point out the vertical angles. Remind students that vertical angles have equal measurement.
- Review the Corresponding Angles Rule, that when two parallel lines are crossed by a transversal, the angles that are in the same position are corresponding angles. They have equal measurement.
- Refer to the diagram and point out the corresponding angles.

Lesson 12

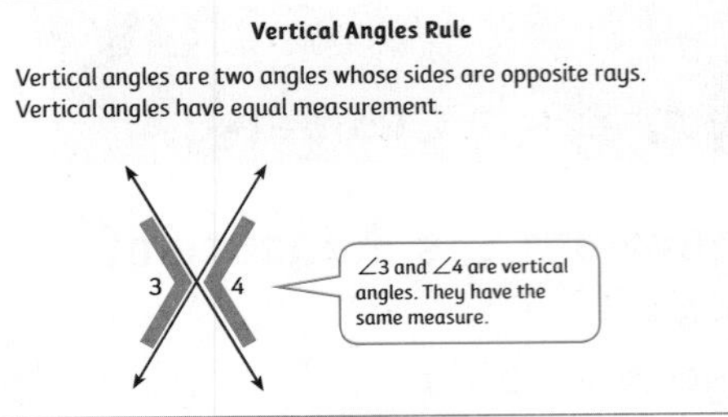
Vertical Angles Rule

Vertical angles are two angles whose sides are opposite rays. Vertical angles have equal measurement.

3
4
∠3 and ∠4 are vertical angles. They have the same measure.

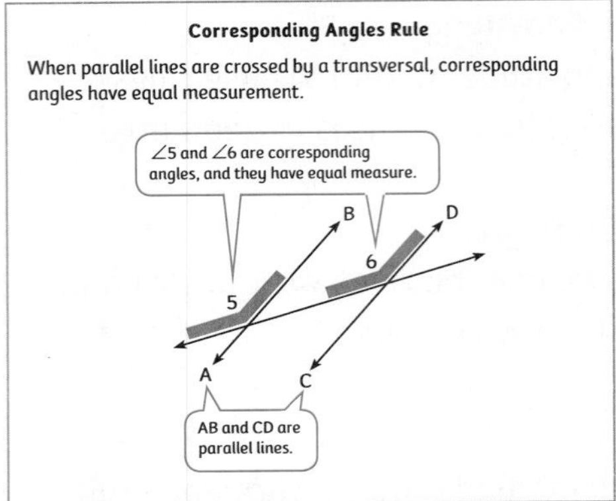
Corresponding Angles Rule

When parallel lines are crossed by a transversal, corresponding angles have equal measurement.

∠5 and ∠6 are corresponding angles, and they have equal measure.
B
D
6
5
A
C
AB and CD are parallel lines.

Unit 8 • Lesson 1 657

Demonstrate

- Turn to page 658 of the *Student Text* and review the Transitive Property Rule, that if $a = b$ and $b = c$, then $a = c$. Use the diagram to reinforce understanding.
- Explain to students that we can use all these ideas to solve more complex geometry problems.
- Direct students' attention to **Example 1** and have them study the diagram. Then explain that we use what we know to find the measure of angle 15.
- Start by pointing out the information that we do know, based on the diagram.
- Point out the right angle symbol in angle 2. We know that angle 2 measures 90 degrees.
- Point out that angle 8 measures 60 degrees.
- Remind students that the sum of the interior angles of a quadrilateral equals 360 degrees.

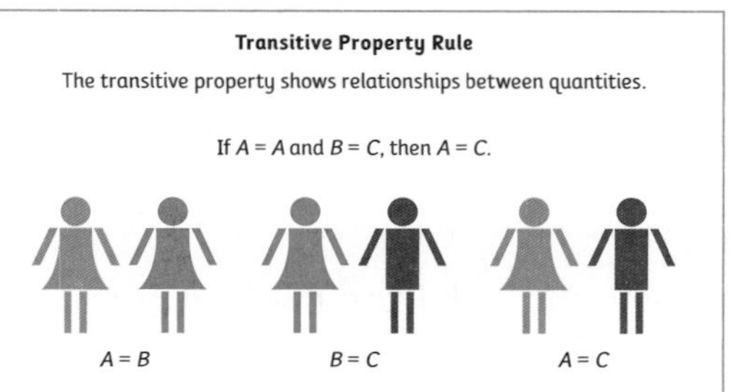

Transitive Property Rule
The transitive property shows relationships between quantities.
If A = A and B = C, then A = C.
A = B
B = C
A = C

We use these ideas to solve complex problems involving angles. Let's look at the problem in Example 1.

Example 1

Use interior angles to find the measure of ∠15.

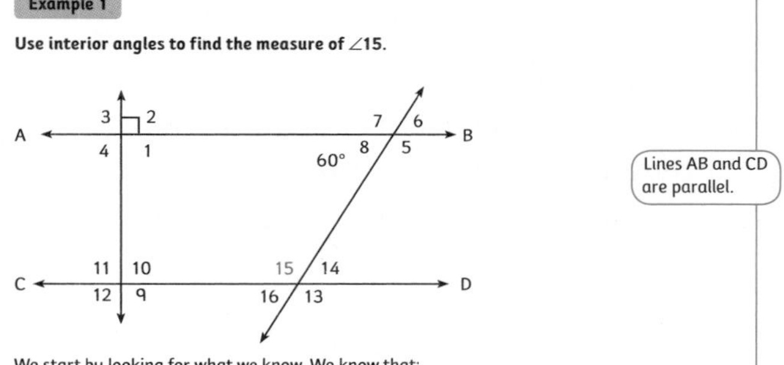

Lines AB and CD are parallel.

We start by looking for what we know. We know that:

- ∠2 = 90°
- ∠8 = 60°
- the sum of the interior angles of a quadrilateral = 360°

How do we figure out the measure of unknown angles? *(continued)*

Demonstrate

- Continue going through Example 1 on page 659 of the *Student Text*.
- Explain to students that once we have a list of things we know about angles in a diagram, we can make inferences.
- Go through each of the inferences that will help us find the measure of angle 15. Point out that angles 2 and 10 are corresponding angles whose measures are 90 degrees.
- Point out that angles 2 and 1 make up a straight line, so they are supplementary angles. Because we know the measure of angle 2 and the measure of a straight line, we can find the measure of angle 1.
- Demonstrate how to find the measure of angle 1 by writing **$90 + x = 180$** on the board. Point out that 90 is the measure of angle 2, and 180 is the measure of a straight line. The variable x represents the measure of angle 1. Solve for x to get the measure of angle 1, 90 degrees.
- Point out that we now have the information necessary to find the measure of angle 15.
- Demonstrate how to substitute the angle measures into the equation for the values that we know. If y is the measure of angle 15, we solve for y. Walk through the steps for solving the equation: **$y = 120$ degrees**.
- Tell students that problem solving can require many steps. What we have learned will help us make inferences to find the measures of unknown angles.

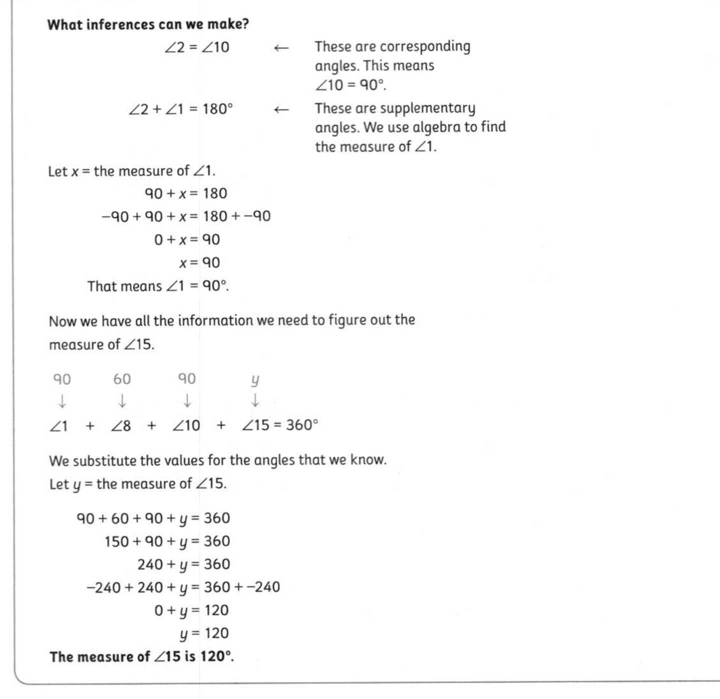

Lesson 12

What inferences can we make?

$\angle 2 = \angle 10$ ← These are corresponding angles. This means $\angle 10 = 90°$.

$\angle 2 + \angle 1 = 180°$ ← These are supplementary angles. We use algebra to find the measure of $\angle 1$.

Let x = the measure of $\angle 1$.

$$90 + x = 180$$
$$-90 + 90 + x = 180 + -90$$
$$0 + x = 90$$
$$x = 90$$

That means $\angle 1 = 90°$.

Now we have all the information we need to figure out the measure of $\angle 15$.

$$\underset{90}{\angle 1} + \underset{60}{\angle 8} + \underset{90}{\angle 10} + \underset{y}{\angle 15} = 360°$$

We substitute the values for the angles that we know.
Let y = the measure of $\angle 15$.

$$90 + 60 + 90 + y = 360$$
$$150 + 90 + y = 360$$
$$240 + y = 360$$
$$-240 + 240 + y = 360 + -240$$
$$0 + y = 120$$
$$y = 120$$

The measure of $\angle 15$ is 120°.

What we have learned about angles helps us make the inferences we need to solve this kind of problem.

Problem-Solving Activity
Turn to ***Interactive Text***, page 315.

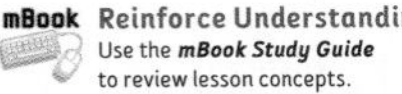

Reinforce Understanding
Use the ***mBook Study Guide*** to review lesson concepts.

Unit 8 • Lesson 1 659

Check for Understanding
Engagement Strategy: Think, Think

Ask students the following questions about the rules and properties that help us make inferences in geometry. Tell students that you will call on one of them to answer a question after you ask it. Tell them to listen for their names. After each question, call on a student for an answer.

Ask:

Which rule talks about two angles forming a straight line? (*Supplementary Angles Rule*)

Which rule states that the measure of a right angle is 90 degrees? (*Right Angle Rule*)

Which rule states that when parallel lines are crossed by a transversal, the angles in the same position have the same measurement? (*Corresponding Angles Rule*)

Problem-Solving Activity

(*Interactive Text*, pages 315–316)

Have students turn to pages 315–316 in the *Interactive Text,* and complete the activity.

Students find missing angle measures by using the information given in the problem as well as rules, properties, and inferences.

Monitor students' work as they complete the activity.

Watch for:

- Can students identify the necessary rules and properties for finding the missing angle?
- Can students make the appropriate inferences for finding the missing angle?

Be sure students have adequate time to work on the problems in this activity. You want to send the right message about working carefully and slowly through this type of complex problem solving.

mBook Reinforce Understanding

Remind students that they can review lesson concepts by accessing the online *mBook Study Guide*.

Lesson 12 | Problem-Solving Activity

Name ______________________ Date ______________

Problem-Solving Activity
Making Inferences in Geometry

Use what you know about the measure of angles, shapes, and the rules and properties described below to solve the problems.

Right angles—this symbols shows that an angle is always a right angle. The measure of a right angle is 90°.

Supplementary angles—When you combine two angles to form a straight line, you have supplementary angles. A straight line measures 180°.

Vertical angles rule—These are two angles whose sides are opposite rays. Vertical angles have equal measurement.

Corresponding angle rule—When parallel lines are crossed by a transversal, corresponding angles have equal measurement.

Transitive property—This is a property that shows relationships between quantities. If A = B and B = C, then A = C.

1. Find the measure of ∠15. 120°

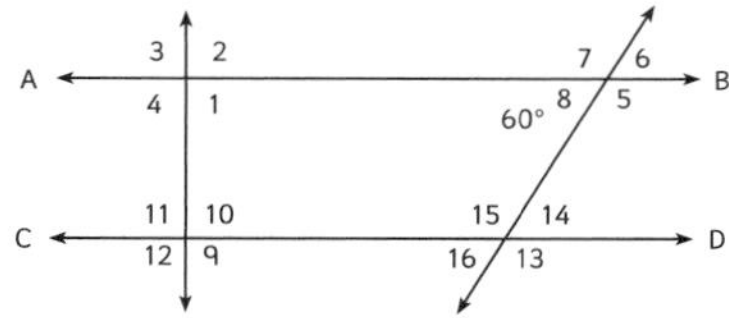

2. Find the measure of ∠2. 45°

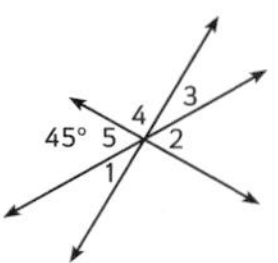

Unit 8 • Lesson 12 315

Unit 8

Lesson 12 | Problem-Solving Activity

Name ______________________ Date ______________

3. Find the measure of ∠16. 120°
Lines AB and CD are parallel

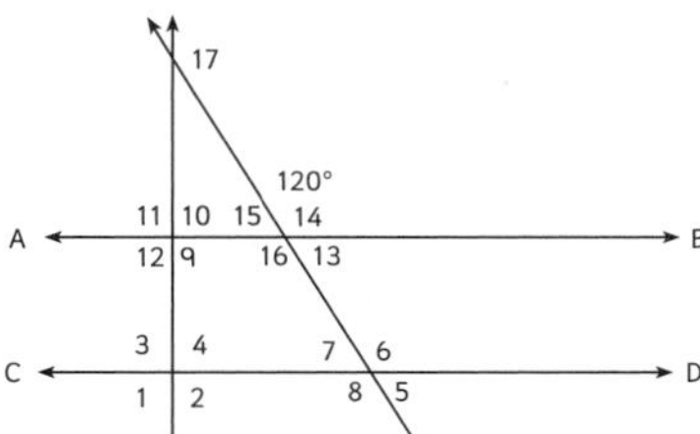

4. Find the measure of ∠14. 60°
Lines JK and LM are parallel

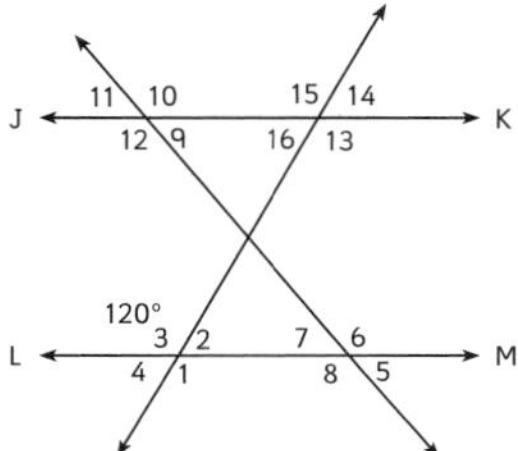

mBook Reinforce Understanding
Use the **mBook** ***Study Guide*** to review lesson concepts.

316 Unit 8 • Lesson 12

Homework

Go over the instructions on page 660 of the *Student Text* for each part of the homework.

Activity 1

Students solve problems involving reciprocals.

Activity 2

Students solve equations where there are fractional coefficients.

Activity 3

Students find the missing angle measures using rules, properties, and inferences.

Activity 4 • Distributed Practice

Students practice order of operations, integer operations, and one-step equations.

Lesson 12

Homework

Activity 1

For each expression, tell what you would multiply by to change the coefficient in front of the variable to 1.

1. $\frac{2}{3}x$ $\frac{3}{2}$
2. $2x$ $\frac{1}{2}$
3. $-x$ -1
4. $\frac{1}{3}x$ 3
5. $\frac{4}{5}x$ $\frac{5}{4}$
6. $-3x$ $-\frac{1}{3}$

Activity 2

Solve.

1. $\frac{2}{3}z = 8$ 12
2. $6 = \frac{1}{5}w$ 30
3. $\frac{1}{2}x + 4 = 10$ 12
4. $\frac{1}{4}y - 4 = 2$ 24

Activity 3

Find the missing angle measures using the diagram. Lines AB and CD are parallel.

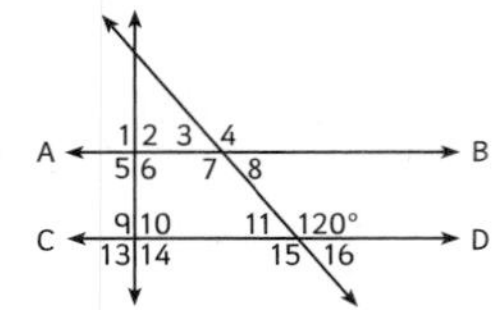

1. What is the measure of $\angle 10$? 90 degrees
2. What is the measure of $\angle 6$? 90 degrees
3. What is the measure of $\angle 3$? 60 degrees
4. What is the measure of $\angle 15$? 120 degrees

Activity 4 • Distributed Practice

Solve.

1. $\frac{3}{4} = \frac{b}{24}$ 18
2. $2w = -8$ -4
3. $1 = \frac{5}{4} \cdot d$ $\frac{4}{5}$
4. $a + -10 = 0$ 10
5. $2(x + 5) = 3$ -3.5
6. $-100 = -30 + x$ -70

660 Unit 8 • Lesson 12

Lesson 13 | ▶More Fractions as Coefficients

Problem Solving:
▶Word Problems

Lesson Planner

Skills Maintenance

Reciprocals, Inferences About Angles

Building Number Concepts:
▶ More Fractions as Coefficients

Students learn that when a variable appears as the numerator of a fraction, we decompose the problem into a fractional coefficient and the variable.

Objective

Students will analyze fractions with a variable in the numerator to solve equations.

Problem Solving:
▶ Word Problems

Students learn that drawing pictures can help make sense of complex word problems.

Objective

Students will use drawings to help solve word problems that involve a person's age.

Homework

Students solve equations that have variables in either their numerators or denominators and use pictures to solve word problems. In Distributed Practice, students practice integer operations and one-step equations.

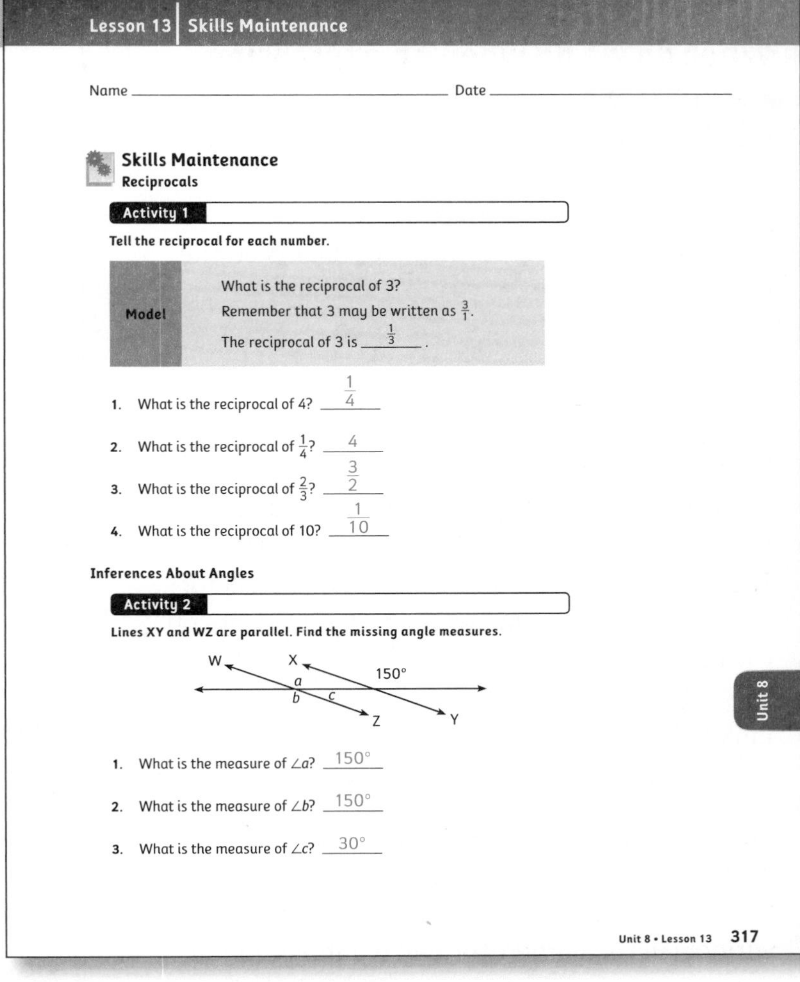
Lesson 13 | Skills Maintenance

Name ______________ Date ______________

Skills Maintenance
Reciprocals

Activity 1

Tell the reciprocal for each number.

Model	What is the reciprocal of 3? Remember that 3 may be written as $\frac{3}{1}$. The reciprocal of 3 is $\frac{1}{3}$.

1. What is the reciprocal of 4? $\frac{1}{4}$
2. What is the reciprocal of $\frac{1}{4}$? 4
3. What is the reciprocal of $\frac{2}{3}$? $\frac{3}{2}$
4. What is the reciprocal of 10? $\frac{1}{10}$

Inferences About Angles

Activity 2

Lines XY and WZ are parallel. Find the missing angle measures.

1. What is the measure of $\angle a$? 150°
2. What is the measure of $\angle b$? 150°
3. What is the measure of $\angle c$? 30°

Unit 8

Unit 8 • Lesson 13 317

Skills Maintenance

Reciprocals, Inferences About Angles

(*Interactive Text*, page 317)

Activity 1

Students tell the reciprocal for each number.

Activity 2

Students use properties, rules, and inferences to find the missing angle measures.

Building Number Concepts: ▶ More Fractions as Coefficients

What do we do when an expression includes a fraction?

(*Student Text*, pages 661–663)

Connect to Prior Knowledge

Begin by putting the following problems on the board or overhead:

$\frac{3}{1} \cdot \frac{1}{4} \left(\frac{3}{4}\right)$

$\frac{4}{1} \cdot \frac{1}{5} \left(\frac{4}{5}\right)$

Remind students that when we multiply fractions, we multiply across: numerator by numerator and denominator by denominator. Then have students solve the problems. Ask for volunteers to show and explain their answers on the board or overhead.

Link to Today's Concept

Write the problem $\frac{x}{1} \cdot \frac{1}{2}$ on the board. Point out that this is a different kind of fraction than what we are used to. Tell students that in today's lesson, we look at this type of fraction with a variable in the numerator and a number in the denominator and learn how to break it down to solve the equation.

Demonstrate

Engagement Strategy: Teacher Modeling

Demonstrate how to think about equations involving expressions with fractions in one of the following ways:

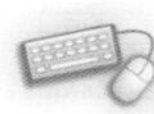

mBook: Use the *mBook Teacher Edition* for pages 661–662 of the *Student Text*. m

Overhead Projector: Reproduce the problems on a transparency, and modify as discussed.

Lesson 13 ▶More Fractions as Coefficients
Problem Solving:
▶Word Problems

▶More Fractions as Coefficients

What do we do when an expression includes a fraction?

Let's look at the two equations below. There is a difference between them.

$x = 20 \qquad \frac{x}{2} = 20$

The equation on the right looks different from anything we have solved before because it includes a fraction.

But it is less challenging than we might think. We just have to remember rules about multiplication of fractions.

Let's look at the following patterns.

$\frac{3}{4} = \frac{1}{4} \cdot 3$ because $\frac{1}{4} \cdot \frac{3}{1} = \frac{3}{4}$

$\frac{7}{5} = \frac{1}{5} \cdot 7$ because $\frac{1}{5} \cdot \frac{7}{1} = \frac{7}{5}$

$\frac{x}{2} = \frac{1}{2} \cdot x$ because $\frac{1}{2} \cdot \frac{x}{1} = \frac{x}{2}$

A number or variable divided by 1 is the same number or variable.

One way to work problems like $\frac{x}{2} = 20$ is to convert the expression $\frac{x}{2}$ into $\frac{1}{2} \cdot x$ or $\frac{1}{2}x$.

Example 1 shows how to solve these kinds of equations.

Unit 8 • Lesson 13 661

Board: Write the problems on the board, and modify as discussed.

- Show the two equations $x = 20$ and $\frac{x}{2} = 20$.

  Point out that the equation on the left is like the ones we saw in Lesson 12. Explain that the equation on the right is not difficult to solve, even though it looks different than any of the equations we have solved in the past. m

- Remind students of the problems we solved at the beginning of this lesson. Then display and discuss over the problems that show that fractions can be rewritten as the product of 1 over the denominator and the numerator over 1. m

Demonstrate

- Demonstrate how to solve the equation $\frac{x}{2} = 20$ in **Example 1**. Begin by converting $\frac{x}{2}$ to $\frac{1}{2} \cdot x$.
- Explain that we need to get x by itself, and our goal is to get the coefficient equal to 1. So we multiply both sides of the equation by 2. On the left side, this makes the coefficient 1, and on the right side, it keeps the equation balanced.
- Simplify to get $1x = 40$. Remind students that 1 times any number is the same number, so the answer is $x = 40$.
- Read the text at the bottom of the page. Explain to students that sometimes unlike terms appear in the numerator.
- Tell students that the key to solving these problems is to think about the numerator. We will solve the problem on the next page.

Example 1

Solve an equation that includes a fraction.

$\frac{x}{2} = 20$

$\frac{1}{2} \cdot x = 20$ ← The fraction $\frac{x}{2}$ is the same as $\frac{1}{2} \cdot x$.

$2 \cdot \frac{1}{2}x = 20 \cdot 2$ ← We multiply by 2 to get x by itself. We multiply each side by 2 to keep the equation balanced.

$\frac{2}{2}x = 40$

$1x = 40$

$x = 40$

The process is a little more complicated with expressions like the following one. There are two unlike terms in the numerator.

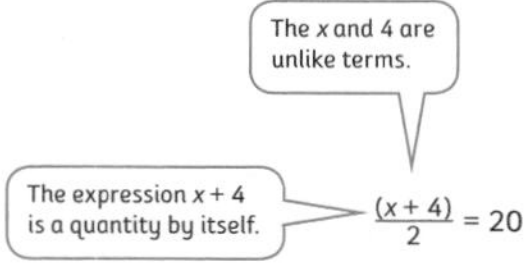

The x and 4 are unlike terms.
The expression x + 4 is a quantity by itself.
(x + 4) / 2 = 20

When we pull out the $\frac{1}{2}$, we need to remember that:

- we are multiplying the entire $x + 4$ by $\frac{1}{2}$.
- we must use order of operations to make sure that this happens.
- we do not want to multiply $\frac{1}{2}$ times either x or 4 by itself.

We use a similar process to solve the equation in Example 2. The key idea is to think about the numerator.

What do we do when an expression includes a fraction? *(continued)*

Demonstrate

- Have students turn to *Student Text*, page 663, and look at **Example 2**.
- Explain that in this example we show how to rewrite the fraction as 1 over the denominator and the numerator (an expression) over 1. We use parentheses to show this.
- In this case, tell students that the coefficient is $\frac{1}{2}$ and the rest of the problem is the expression $\boldsymbol{x + 4}$, which we write it in parentheses. This should look familiar to students because we have solved these equations using the distributive property in the past.
- Go over the steps of the problem. Be sure students understand the justification for each.
- Begin by converting $\frac{(x + 4)}{2}$ to $\frac{1}{2} \cdot (x + 4)$.
- Multiply both sides by 2 to get x by itself and keep the equation balanced.
- Simplify the equation to get $\boldsymbol{(x + 4) = 40}$.
- Add -4 to both sides to get x by itself and keep the equation balanced.
- Point out that $\boldsymbol{x = 36}$.

Check for Understanding
Engagement Strategy: Look About

Tell students that they will solve a problem involving a fractional coefficient with the help of the whole class. Write the problem $\frac{(x + 6)}{3} = 4$ on the board. Have students write out the steps to solving the problem in large writing on a piece of paper or a dry erase board. When students finish their work, they should hold up their answer for everyone to see ($x = 6$).

If students are not sure about the answer, prompt them to look about at other students' solutions to help with their thinking. Review the answers after all students have held up their solutions.

Lesson 13

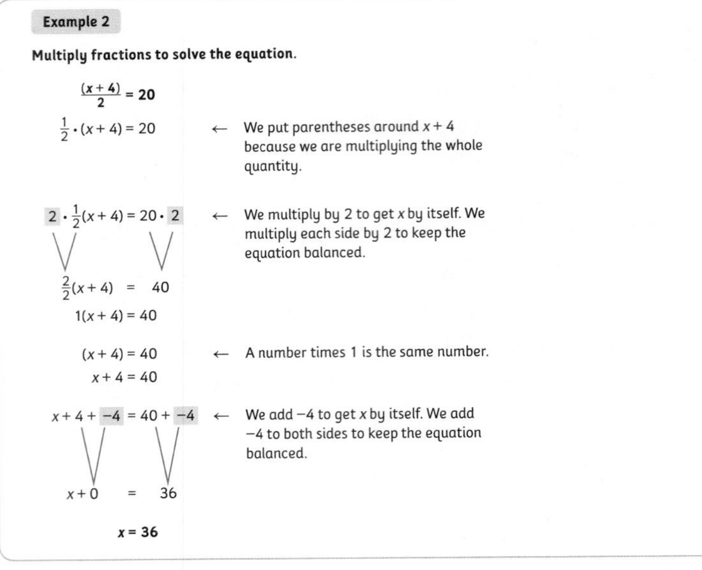

Example 2

Multiply fractions to solve the equation.

$\frac{(x + 4)}{2} = 20$

$\frac{1}{2} \cdot (x + 4) = 20$ ← We put parentheses around $x + 4$ because we are multiplying the whole quantity.

$2 \cdot \frac{1}{2}(x + 4) = 20 \cdot 2$ ← We multiply by 2 to get x by itself. We multiply each side by 2 to keep the equation balanced.

$\frac{2}{2}(x + 4) = 40$

$1(x + 4) = 40$

$(x + 4) = 40$ ← A number times 1 is the same number.

$x + 4 = 40$

$x + 4 + -4 = 40 + -4$ ← We add -4 to get x by itself. We add -4 to both sides to keep the equation balanced.

$x + 0 = 36$

$x = 36$

When we have an expression in fractional form like the ones shown in Examples 1 and 2, we need to think, "What is the coefficient in front of the variable?" Once we have identified the coefficient, we work the equation using the rules and properties from the Algebra Toolbox just like any other equation.

Apply Skills
Turn to ***Interactive Text***, page 318.

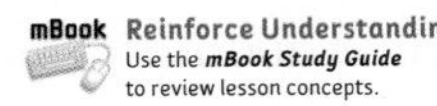

Reinforce Understanding
Use the ***mBook Study Guide*** to review lesson concepts.

Unit 8 • Lesson 13 663

Apply Skills

(*Interactive Text*, pages 318–320)

Have students turn to pages 318–320 in the *Interactive Text*, and complete the activities.

Activity 1

Students decompose the fractions into the product of 1 over the denominator and the numerator over 1.

Name ______ Date ______

Apply Skills

More on Fractions as Coefficients

Activity 1

Convert each of the fractions by writing them as a product of 1 over the denominator and the numerator over 1.

Model	$\frac{3}{2} = \frac{1}{2} \cdot \frac{3}{1}$

1. $\frac{4}{5} = \frac{1}{5} \cdot \frac{4}{1}$
2. $\frac{2}{3} = \frac{1}{3} \cdot \frac{2}{1}$
3. $\frac{8}{9} = \frac{1}{9} \cdot \frac{8}{1}$
4. $\frac{3}{4} = \frac{1}{4} \cdot \frac{3}{1}$

Activity 2

Students solve equations that involve fractions with a variable or an expression with a variable in the numerator.

Monitor students' work as they complete the activities.

Watch for:

- Can students decompose the fraction into the product of 1 over the denominator and the numerator over 1?
- Can students solve the problem once they have decomposed it?
- Do students remember when to use the rule for reciprocals rather than the distributive property?
- Do students use the distributive property to solve the problems where the numerator is an expression?

mBook **Reinforce Understanding**
Remind students that they can review lesson concepts by accessing the online *mBook Study Guide*.

Name ________________ Date ________________

Activity 2

Solve the equations. Rewrite the fraction as the product of 1 over the denominator and the numerator over 1.

Model	
	$\frac{x+1}{2} = 12$
Answer	$\frac{1}{2}(x+1) = 12$
	$2 \cdot \frac{1}{2}(x+1) = 12 \cdot 2$
	$x + 1 = 24$
	$x + 1 - 1 = 24 - 1$
	$x + 0 = 23$
	$x = 23$
Check	$\frac{23+1}{2} = 12 \rightarrow \frac{24}{2} = 12 \rightarrow 12 = 12$ TRUE

1. $\frac{x}{5} = 5$

Rewrite the problem as 1 over the denominator and the numerator over 1:
$\frac{1}{5} \cdot \frac{x}{1} = 5$

Solve the equation. Show your work here:
$5 \cdot \frac{1}{5}\left(\frac{x}{1}\right) = 5 \cdot 5$
$\frac{x}{1} = 25$

$x =$ 25

Check your work here:
$\frac{25}{5} = 5$

2. $\frac{x+1}{2} = 2$

Rewrite the problem as 1 over the denominator and the numerator over 1:
$\frac{1}{2} \cdot \frac{x+1}{1} = 2$

Solve the equation. Show your work here:
$2 \cdot \frac{1}{2}(x + 1) = 2 \cdot 2$
$x + 1 = 4$
$x = 3$

$x =$ 3

Check your work here:
$\frac{3+1}{2} = 2$
$\frac{4}{2} = 2$
$2 = 2$

Lesson 13 | Apply Skills

Name ________________ Date ________________

3. $\frac{y+6}{6} = 3$

Rewrite the problem as 1 over the denominator and the numerator over 1:
$\frac{1}{6} \cdot \frac{y+6}{1} = 3$

Solve the equation. Show your work here:
$\frac{1}{6}(y + 6) = 3$
$6 \cdot \frac{1}{6}(y + 6) = 3 \cdot 6$
$y + 6 = 18$
$y = 12$

$y =$ 12

Check your work here:
$\frac{12+6}{6} = 3$
$\frac{18}{6} = 3$
$3 = 3$

4. $\frac{z+3}{4} = 10$

Rewrite the problem as 1 over the denominator and the numerator over 1:
$\frac{1}{4} \cdot \frac{z+3}{1} = 10$

Solve the equation. Show your work here:
$4 \cdot \frac{1}{4}(z + 3) = 10 \cdot 4$
$z + 3 = 40$
$z = 37$

$z =$ 37

Check your work here:
$\frac{37+3}{4} = 10$
$\frac{40}{4} = 10$
$10 = 10$

Problem Solving: ▶ Word Problems

Why are drawings helpful for solving a word problem that involves a person's age?

(*Student Text*, pages 664–666)

Demonstrate

- Have students turn to page 664 of the *Student Text*. Read the steps for using a drawing to help solve an equation.
- Point out that we do not always have to use drawings, but sometimes they help us better see what is going on in a problem.

STEP 1

- Explain that the first step is to create a drawing of a word problem.

STEP 2

- Explain that the next step is to figure out what the variable is.

STEP 3

- Tell students that once we have a drawing and know what the variable is, we solve the equation.

STEP 4

- Tell students that the last step is to make sure we have answered what the question is asking.

- Read through the problem in **Example 1** and go through the first step.

Lesson 13

▶Problem Solving: Word Problems

Why are drawings helpful for solving a word problem that involves a person's age?

Problems involving ages are like the money problems and rate problems we have solved before. We use drawings to help us understand what is going on in the problem.

Steps for Using Drawings to Help Solve Equations

We don't always need a drawing, but sometimes it helps.

STEP 1
Begin with a drawing.

STEP 2
Figure out what the variable is.

STEP 3
Solve the equation.

STEP 4
Make sure to answer what the question is asking for.

Here is an example of a problem involving different ages.

Example 1

Find the ages of the three sisters.

Problem:
Amanda, Joanna, and Emily are sisters. Emily is the youngest, Joanna is in the middle, and Amanda is the oldest. Joanna is 2 years older than Emily. Amanda is 5 years older than Emily. When you add up their ages, it totals 67. How old is each sister?

STEP 1
Begin with a drawing.

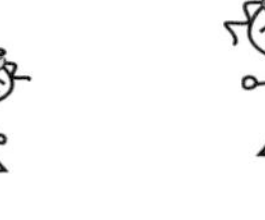

Emily | Joanna: 2 years older than Emily | Amanda: 5 years older than Emily

664 Unit 8 • Lesson 13

STEP 1

- Remind students that the first step is to draw a picture of the problem. Point out the drawings of the three sisters to show their ages in relation to one another.

Why are drawings helpful for solving a word problem that involves a person's age? *(continued)*

Demonstrate

- Turn to page 665 of the *Student Text* and continue walking through the steps to solve the word problem about the ages of sisters Emily, Joanna, and Amanda.

STEP 2

- Explain that now that we have a picture, we have to find out what the variable is. We know each sister's age in relation to one another, but we do not know their ages. We know their combined age is 67.
- Point out that we can use b to represent Emily's age. We know that Joanna is two years older than Emily, or $b + 2$, and Amanda is five years older than Emily, or $b + 5$.
- Demonstrate how to set up the equation with the information we know:

  $b + (b + 2) + (b + 5) = 67$.

STEP 3

- Explain that now that we have an equation, we can solve it. Go through the steps of using the commutative property to combine like terms, and then simplify: $b = 20$.

Lesson 13

STEP 2

Figure out what the variable is.

We use variables for what we don't know. We don't know how old each sister is.

Let's use b to represent Emily's age. If we do that, then we can represent the age difference of the other two sisters.

Emily b | Joanna $b + 2$ | Amanda $b + 5$

We set up the equation this way:

$b + (b + 2) + (b + 5) = 67$

STEP 3

Solve the equation.

$\mathbf{b + b + 2 + b + 5 = 67}$

$b + b + b + 2 + 5 = 67$ ← We use the commutative property so that like terms are next to each other. Combine like terms.

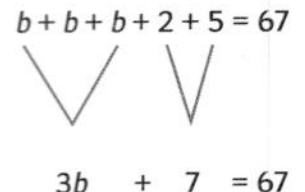

$3b + 7 = 67$

$3b + 7 + -7 = 67 + -7$ ← We add −7 to get b by itself. We add −7 to both sides to keep the equation balanced.

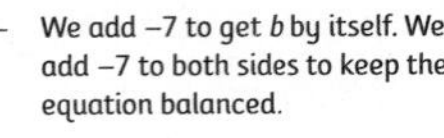

$3b + 0 = 60$

$3b = 60$

$\frac{1}{3} \cdot 3b = \frac{1}{3} \cdot 60$ ← We multiply by $\frac{1}{3}$ to get b by itself. We multiply each side by $\frac{1}{3}$ to keep the equation balanced.

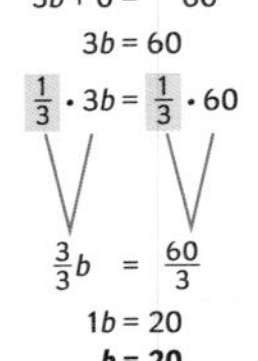

$\frac{3}{3}b = \frac{60}{3}$

$1b = 20$

$\mathbf{b = 20}$

Demonstrate

- Turn to page 666 and finish solving the word problem.

STEP 4

- Remind students that the last step to solving word problems is to make sure we have answered what the question is asking.
- Point out that in the last step, we found that $b = 20$. This is not the answer to the problem, because we want to find the ages of all three of the sisters.
- Demonstrate substituting the value in to the original equations to find the age of each sister: Emily = 20, Joanna = 20 + 2, or **22**, and Amanda = 20 + 5, or **25**.
- Explain that we have to check our work to make sure everything adds up. So, we add the sisters' ages together and get **67**. Our answer is correct.

Lesson 13

STEP 4

Make sure to answer what the question is asking for.

We check our answer to make sure it is correct by using substitution.

Substitute the value for b in the original equation to find the age of each sister.

Emily = 20
Joanna = 20 + 2 or 22
Amanda = 20 + 5 or 25

$$\begin{array}{ccccccc} 20 & & 20 & & 20 & & \\ \downarrow & & \downarrow & & \downarrow & & \\ b & + & b+2 & + & b+5 & = & 67 \\ 20 & + & 22 & + & 25 & = & 67 \\ & & 42 & + & 25 & = & 67 \\ & & & & \mathbf{67} & = & \mathbf{67} \end{array}$$

Problem-Solving Activity Turn to *Interactive Text*, page 321.

mBook Reinforce Understanding Use the ***mBook Study Guide*** to review lesson concepts.

666 Unit 8 • Lesson 13

Problem-Solving Activity
(*Interactive Text*, pages 321–322)

Have students turn to pages 321–322 in the *Interactive Text*. Read the instructions with students.

Students solve problems that lend themselves to drawing a picture.

Monitor students' work as they complete the activity.

Watch for:

- Can students draw a picture that represents the problem?
- Can students select an appropriate problem-solving strategy?
- Can students solve the problem correctly?

mBook Reinforce Understanding
Remind students that they can review lesson concepts by accessing the online *mBook Study Guide*.

Lesson 13 | Problem-Solving Activity

Name ______________________ Date ______________

Problem-Solving Activity
Word Problems

Solve the age problems. Use these four steps to help you solve each problem:

1. **Begin with a drawing.**
2. **Figure out how to use a variable.**
3. **Solve the equation.**
4. **Make sure the answer is what the question is asking for.**

1. Niki is 2 years younger than her brother Michael. When you combine their ages, it totals 38. How old are Niki and Michael?
   Niki = 18, Michael = 20
   $38 = x + x - 2$
   $38 = 2x - 2$
   $40 = 2x \quad x = 20$

2. Jordan is Randall's father. Jordan is 4 times older than Randall. When you add their ages together, it is 50. How old are Jordan and Randall?

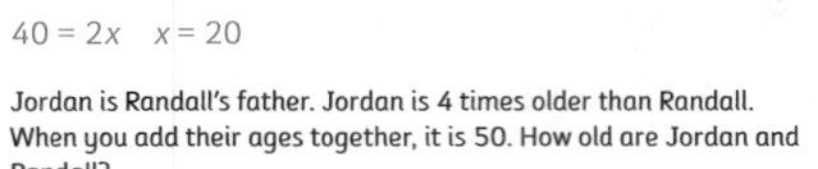

   Jordan = 40, Randall = 10
   $50 = x + 4x$
   $50 = 5x$
   $x = 10$

3. Sherilyn has a much older cousin, Alisa, who lives in another city. Alisa is twice as old as Sherilyn. When you combine their ages it totals 24. How old are Sherilyn and Alisa?
   Sherilyn = 8, Alisa = 16
   $24 = x + 2x$
   $24 = 3x$
   $x = 8$

Unit 8

Unit 8 • Lesson 13 321

Lesson 13 | Problem-Solving Activity

Name ______________________ Date ______________

4. Kara is 8 years older than Leah. In 10 more years, the total of their ages will be 28. How old are Kara and Leah?
   Kara = 13, Leah = 5
   $28 - 10 = x + x + 8$
   $18 = 2x + 8$
   $10 = 2x \quad x = 5$

5. Robert is 5 years older than Josh. Danny is 8 years older than Josh. Their total age is 43. How old are Robert, Josh, and Danny?
   Robert = 15, Josh = 10, Danny = 18
   $43 = x + x + 5 + x + 8$
   $43 = 3x + 13$
   $30 = 3x \quad x = 10$

mBook Reinforce Understanding
Use the **mBook *Study Guide*** to review lesson concepts.

322 Unit 8 • Lesson 13

Homework

Go over the instructions on page 667 of the *Student Text* for each part of the homework.

Activity 1

Students decompose fractions into the product of 1 over the denominator and the numerator over 1 to solve problems.

Activity 2

Students solve equations involving fractions with variables in the numerator or denominator.

Activity 3

Students use a drawing to help solve word problems.

Activity 4 • Distributed Practice

Students practice order of operations, integer operations, and one-step equations.

Lesson 13

Homework

Activity 1

Solve.

1. $\frac{x}{2} = 10$ 20
2. $\frac{10}{y} = -5$ −2
3. $\frac{12}{z} = 6$ 2
4. $\frac{a}{9} = 3$ 27
5. $-\frac{27}{b} = -3$ 9
6. $\frac{c}{3} = -9$ −27

Activity 2

Solve.

1. $\frac{(m+4)}{2} = 4$ 4
2. $\frac{(n+2)}{3} = 6$ 16
3. $\frac{1}{(g+1)} = 2$ $-\frac{1}{2}$
4. $\frac{1}{(2z)} = 3$ $\frac{1}{6}$

Activity 3

Use a drawing to help solve the problems.

1. Teri is 4 years younger than her brother Christopher. When you combine their ages, it totals 24. How old are Teri and Christopher? Teri is 10 and Christopher is 14.
2. Matt is Ava's father. Matt is 5 times older than Ava. When you add their ages together, it is 60. How old are Matt and Ava? Matt is 50 and Ava is 10.

Activity 4 • Distributed Practice

Solve.

1. $-\frac{36}{h} = -9$ 4
2. $4 + -12 = x$ −8
3. $g \div -8 = -9$ 72
4. $-\frac{4}{5} \cdot c = 1$ $-\frac{5}{4}$
5. $0 = 500 + d$ −500
6. $-112 - -399 = e$ 287

Unit 8 • Lesson 1 667

Lesson 14 ▶Negative Numbers
Problem Solving: ▶Coin Problems

Lesson Planner

Skills Maintenance

Values of Coins as Equations, Missing Angle Measures

Building Number Concepts: ▶ Negative Numbers

Students learn that negative numbers in equations require special consideration. Although problems with negative numbers seem complicated, students just need to remember operations on integers to solve them.

Objective

Students will solve problems with negative numbers.

Problem Solving: ▶ Coin Problems

Students learn that coin problems make good algebra problems because the coefficient is the value of the coin. We use the four-step process and pictures to help solve them.

Objective

Students will solve algebra problems involving coins.

Homework

Students solve equations involving negative numbers, solve more complex equations involving negative numbers, and solve word problems involving coins. In Distributed Practice, students practice order of operations, integer operations, and one-step equations.

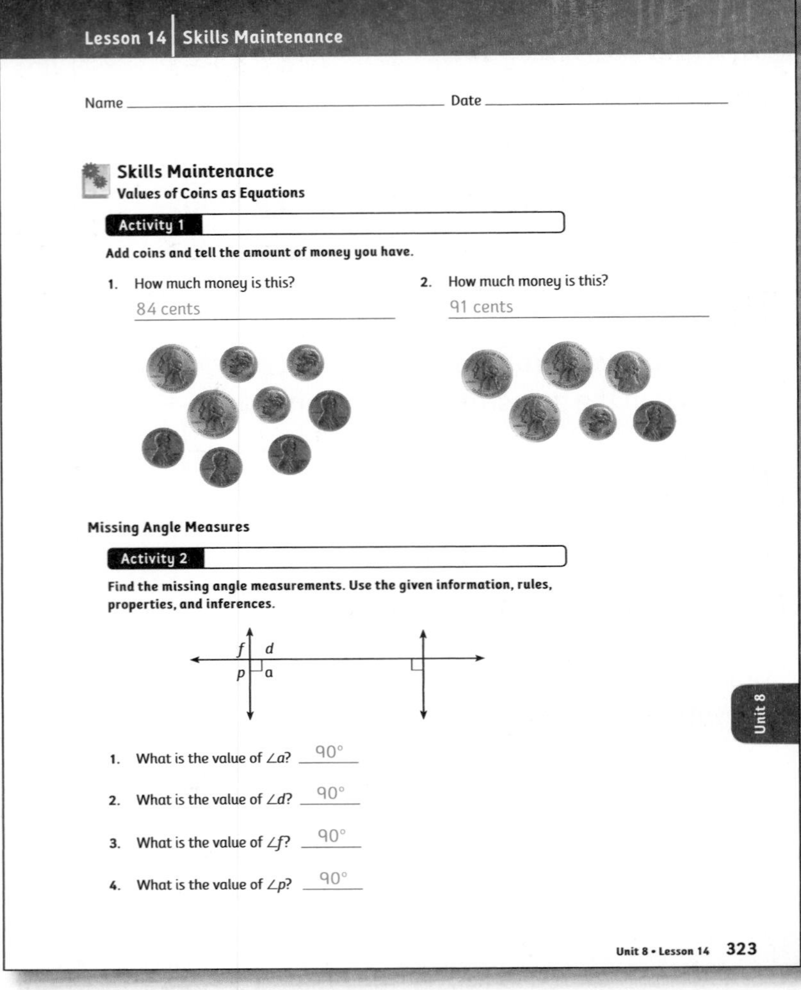

Skills Maintenance

Values of Coins as Equations, Missing Angle Measures

(*Interactive Text*, page 323)

Activity 1

Students tell the sum of the coins.

Activity 2

Students find the missing angle measures.

Building Number Concepts:
▶ Negative Numbers

What do we do when an expression contains a negative number?
(*Student Text*, pages 668–669)

Connect to Prior Knowledge

Review operations on integers. Put the following problems on the board and walk students through the steps in using what they know from the toolbox about operations on integers.

−1 − −1 + 1 (*1*)

−1 • −1 • −1 (*−1*)

−1 ÷ −1 ÷ −1 (*−1*)

Link to Today's Concept

Tell students that in today's lesson, we use operations on integers to solve equations with negative numbers.

Lesson 14 ▶Negative Numbers
Problem Solving:
▶Coin Problems

▶Negative Numbers

What do we do when an expression contains a negative number?

Let's look at the following equations. There is a difference between them.

$3x + 3 = 18 \qquad -3x - 3 = -18$

The equation on the right is different because of the negative numbers. While this looks like a big change, it isn't. We just need to remember the rules about operations on integers.

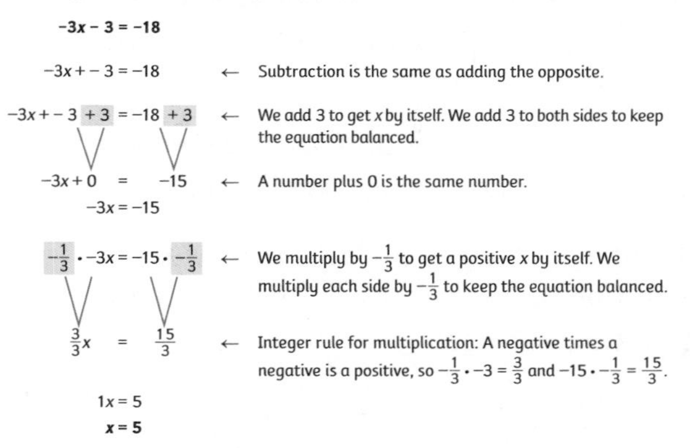

Example 1

Solve an equation that contains negative numbers.

$\mathbf{-3x - 3 = -18}$

$-3x + -3 = -18$ ← Subtraction is the same as adding the opposite.

$-3x + -3 + 3 = -18 + 3$ ← We add 3 to get x by itself. We add 3 to both sides to keep the equation balanced.

$-3x + 0 = -15$ ← A number plus 0 is the same number.

$-3x = -15$

$-\frac{1}{3} \cdot -3x = -15 \cdot -\frac{1}{3}$ ← We multiply by $-\frac{1}{3}$ to get a positive x by itself. We multiply each side by $-\frac{1}{3}$ to keep the equation balanced.

$\frac{3}{3}x = \frac{15}{3}$ ← Integer rule for multiplication: A negative times a negative is a positive, so $-\frac{1}{3} \cdot -3 = \frac{3}{3}$ and $-15 \cdot -\frac{1}{3} = \frac{15}{3}$.

$1x = 5$

$\mathbf{x = 5}$

668 Unit 8 • Lesson 14

Demonstrate

Engagement Strategy: Teacher Modeling

Demonstrate how to solve the equations in one of the following ways:

mBook: Use the *mBook Teacher Edition* for page 668 of the *Student Text*. m

Overhead Projector: Reproduce the problems on a transparency, and modify as discussed.

Board: Draw the problems on the board, and modify as discussed.

- Show the equations **$3x + 3 = 18$** and **$-3x - 3 = -18$**. Point out that the terms in one equation are all positive, and the terms in the other equation are all negative. Tell students that the equation with negative numbers looks more complex, but we have all the tools necessary to solve it. m
- Go over **Example 1** and be sure students understand the justification for each step. m
- Start by rewriting **−3** as **+ −3** and remind students that subtraction is the same as adding the opposite. m
- Demonstrate how to get x by itself and keep the equation balanced by adding 3 to both sides of the equation. m
- Simplify until you get **$-3x = -15$**. m
- Multiply both sides of the equation by the reciprocal of the coefficient to get a positive x by itself. Remind students that because −3 is negative, the coefficient, $-\frac{1}{3}$, should be negative to get a positive answer. m
- Walk through the steps of simplifying and solving for the answer: **$x = 5$**. m

What do we do when an expression contains a negative number? *(continued)*

Demonstrate

- Turn to page 669 of the *Student Text* and demonstrate how to solve the equation $-\frac{x}{5} + 6 = 31$ in **Example 2**. Explain that in this example, there is a negative fraction.
- Point out that while this might seem complex, we have all the tools necessary to solve it.
- Go over all the steps and be sure students understand the justification for each.
- Begin by adding −6 to both sides of the equation to get *x* by itself and keep the equation balanced.
- Simplify to get $-\frac{x}{5} = 25$.
- Remind students that $-\frac{x}{5}$ is the same as $-\frac{1}{5}x$.
- Demonstrate how to get a positive *x* on one side of the equation by multiplying by the reciprocal of the coefficient, or −5.
- Remind students of the integer rules that a negative times a negative is a positive.
- Multiply the other side of the equation by −5 to keep the equation balanced.
- Simplify to get the answer: $x = -125$.

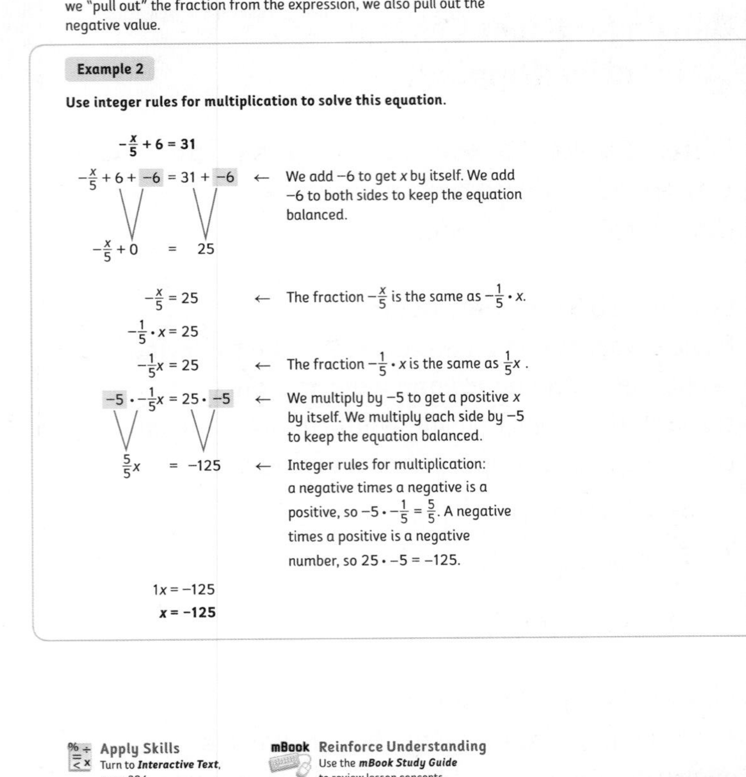

Lesson 14

Integer rules apply to expressions that contain fractions, too. When we "pull out" the fraction from the expression, we also pull out the negative value.

Example 2

Use integer rules for multiplication to solve this equation.

$-\frac{x}{5} + 6 = 31$

$-\frac{x}{5} + 6 + -6 = 31 + -6$ ← We add −6 to get *x* by itself. We add −6 to both sides to keep the equation balanced.

$-\frac{x}{5} + 0 = 25$

$-\frac{x}{5} = 25$ ← The fraction $-\frac{x}{5}$ is the same as $-\frac{1}{5} \cdot x$.

$-\frac{1}{5} \cdot x = 25$

$-\frac{1}{5}x = 25$ ← The fraction $-\frac{1}{5} \cdot x$ is the same as $\frac{1}{5}x$.

$-5 \cdot -\frac{1}{5}x = 25 \cdot -5$ ← We multiply by −5 to get a positive *x* by itself. We multiply each side by −5 to keep the equation balanced.

$\frac{5}{5}x = -125$ ← Integer rules for multiplication: a negative times a negative is a positive, so $-5 \cdot -\frac{1}{5} = \frac{5}{5}$. A negative times a positive is a negative number, so $25 \cdot -5 = -125$.

$1x = -125$

$\mathbf{x = -125}$

Apply Skills
Turn to *Interactive Text*, page 324.

mBook Reinforce Understanding
Use the *mBook Study Guide* to review lesson concepts.

Unit 8 • Lesson 1[4] 669

Check for Understanding
Engagement Strategy: Look About

Tell students that they will solve a problem involving negative numbers with the help of the whole class. Write the problem $-\frac{x}{3} + 5 = -4$ on the board. Have students write out the steps to solving the problem in large writing on a piece of paper or a dry erase board. When students finish their work, they should hold up their answer for everyone to see ($x = 27$).

If students are not sure about the answer, prompt them to look about at other students' solutions to help with their thinking. Review the answers after all students have held up their solutions.

Apply Skills
(*Interactive Text*, page 324)

Have students turn to page 324 in the *Interactive Text*, and complete the activity.

Activity 1

Students solve equations involving negative numbers. Monitor students' work as they complete the activity.

Watch for:

- Can students identify the ways the problem needs to change because of negative numbers?
- Can students apply the rules for negative numbers correctly?
- Did students find the correct answer?

Reinforce Understanding
Remind students that they can review lesson concepts by accessing the online *mBook Study Guide*.

Lesson 14 | Apply Skills

Name ______ Date ______

Apply Skills
Negative Numbers

Activity 1

Solve the equations. Pay close attention to the negative numbers.

1. $-3 + -x = -12$

   Show your work here:

   $-x = -9$

   $x = 9$

   $x =$ 9

   Check your answer here:

   $-3 + -9 = -12$

   $-12 = -12$

2. $-x - -5 = -7$

   Show your work here:

   $-x + 5 = -7$

   $-x = -12$

   $x = 12$

   $x =$ 12

   Check your answer here:

   $-12 - -5 = -7$

   $-7 = -7$

3. $-2x - 4 + 8 = 12$

   Show your work here:

   $-2x + 4 = 12$

   $-2x = 8$

   $x = -4$

   $x =$ −4

   Check your answer here:

   $8 - 4 + 8 = 12$

   $12 = 12$

4. $-4 - 7x = -32$

   Show your work here:

   $-7x = -28$

   $x = 4$

   $x =$ 4

   Check your answer here:

   $-4 - 28 = -32$

   $-32 = -32$

324 Unit 8 • Lesson 14

Problem Solving:
▶ Coin Problems

How do we solve word problems with coins?

(*Student Text*, pages 670–674)

Demonstrate

- Have students turn to page 670 of the *Student Text* and discuss how coin problems work well with algebra because the coin values become the coefficients.
- Explain that the coefficient for pennies is 1, the coefficient for nickels is 5, the coefficient for dimes is 10, and the coefficient for quarters is 25.
- Read the example about representing the value of different coins in an algebraic expression.
- Note that if we have an unknown number of quarters, we use the value of the coin, 25, and a variable, y, to represent the total value of the coins, $25y$.
- Remind students of the problems in the Skills Maintenance where they added up the coins.
- Tell students that now that we know algebra, we can solve more complex problems involving coins.
- Take a few moments to remind students of the steps of using drawing to help solve equations, which they learned in the previous lesson.
- Point out that using drawings of coins in algebra problems will help them visualize the problem.

Lesson 14

▶Problem Solving: Coin Problems

How do we solve word problems with coins?

Algebra word problems that involve coins are a lot like rate, number, and age problems. We still follow the four steps for setting up and solving the equations.

Coin problems are different because we know the value of common coins. We know that a quarter equals 25 cents and a dime equals 10 cents.

The value of the coin is important because we use it as part of an equation.

How do we represent the value of different coins in an expression?

Steps for Using Drawings to Help Solve Equations

STEP 1
Begin with a drawing.

STEP 2
Figure out what the variable is.

STEP 3
Solve the equation.

STEP 4
Make sure to answer what the question is asking for.

Let's say we have some quarters, but we don't know how many quarters we have. Because the number of quarters is unknown, we use a variable.

Let y = the number of quarters.
The expression for the total value is:

value of the coin → $25y$ ← number of quarters

Let's use this kind of thinking to solve a coin problem. We need to remember the value of the coin when we represent the problem.

670 Unit 8 • Lesson 14

STEP 1

- Explain that the first step is to create a drawing of a word problem.

STEP 2

- Explain that the next step is to figure out what the variable is.

STEP 3

- Tell students that once we have a drawing and know what the variable is, we solve the equation.

STEP 4

- Tell students that the last step is to make sure we have answered what the question is asking.

Demonstrate

- Turn to page 671 of the *Student Text* and have students look at **Example 1**. Read the word problem and walk through each of the steps of using drawings to help solve the problem.

STEP 1

- Start with a drawing. We know that we have four dimes. We know we have some quarters, but we do not know how many.
- Tell students we can use a picture of a quarter and a question mark to represent the unknown number of quarters.

STEP 2

- Remind students that now that we have a picture, we have to find out what the variable is.
- Note that we do not know the number of quarters, so we let ***h*** represent the number of quarters. We know we have four dimes, and each dime is worth 10 cents. So we know we have at least 40 cents. We also know that the total amount of coins we have is worth 90 cents.
- Explain that we write the equation as $\mathbf{25h + 40 = 90}$.

Example 1

Find the number of quarters in the coin problem.

Problem:

In my pocket are some quarters and four dimes. The amount of money in my pocket is 90 cents. How many quarters do I have?

STEP 1

Begin with a drawing.

?

quarters dimes

STEP 2

Figure out what the variable is.

- We don't know the number of quarters, so let h = the number of quarters.
- We do know the number of dimes. I have 4 dimes and each dime is worth 10 cents.

$4 \cdot 10 = 40$ cents

?

↓

quarters dimes

$25h + 40 = 90$

How do we solve word problems with coins? *(continued)*

Demonstrate

- Turn to page 672 of the *Student Text* and finish solving the coin problem.

STEP 3

- Explain that now that we have an equation, we can solve it. Go through the steps of getting the h by itself on one side of the equation and then solving for h.
- Remind students that any operation they do on the left side of the equation must be done to the right side of the equation in order to keep the equation balanced.
- Simplify until you find the answer of $\boldsymbol{h = 2}$. We have two quarters.

STEP 4

- Remind students that the last step to solving word problems is to make sure we have answered what the question is asking.
- Demonstrate substituting the value of h, 2, into the original equations to make sure everything is correct.
- Explain that we will change the problem slightly. Let's suppose we do not know the number of dimes.
- Remind students to think carefully about the different coins. Point out that we can still solve problems where the number of coins is unknown.

STEP 3

Solve the equation.

$$25h + 40 = 90$$
$$25h + 40 + -40 = 90 + -40$$
$$25h + 0 = 50$$
$$25h = 50$$
$$\frac{1}{25} \cdot 25h = 50 \cdot \frac{1}{25}$$
$$\frac{25}{25}h = \frac{50}{25}$$
$$1h = 2$$
$$h = 2$$

I have two quarters.

STEP 4

Make sure to answer what the question is asking for.

We check to see if two quarters is correct by substituting for the variable in the original equation.

$$\overset{2}{\downarrow}$$
$$25h + 40 = 90$$
$$25 \cdot 2 + 40 = 90$$
$$50 + 40 = 90$$
$$\mathbf{90 = 90}$$

Let's change this problem slightly. Suppose we don't know the number of dimes we have. Can we still solve the problem?

We need to think carefully about the different coins. But we can still solve problems where the number of coins is unknown.

Demonstrate

- Turn to page 673 of the *Student Text* and set up **Example 2**. Explain that in this example, we solve an even more complex problem involving coins because we do not know how many of each coin we have.
- Read the problem with students and go over each step. Be sure students understand the justification of each step.

STEP 1

- Start with a drawing. We do not know how many dimes or quarters we have. We can use a picture of a quarter, a picture of a dime and question marks to represent the unknown number of quarters and dimes.

STEP 2

- Remind students that now that we have a picture, we have to find out what the variable is. We do not know the number of quarters or dimes, but we do know that we have twice as many dimes as we do quarters.
- Point out that if we let ***v*** equal the number of quarters, the number of dimes is **2*v***, because we have two times as many dimes as we have quarters. Make sure students see how you identified dimes as 2*v*.
- We have to remember the value of each coin. Quarters are worth 25 cents, so we write **25*v***, and dimes are worth 10 cents, so we write **10 • 2*v*** to represent the value of dimes we have. We write an equation: **25*v* + 10 • 2*v* = 90**.

Lesson 14

Example 2

Find the number of quarters and dimes in the coin problem.

Problem:

I have some quarters and dimes in my pocket. I have twice as many dimes as I have quarters. The total amount of money in my pocket is 90 cents. How many quarters and dimes do I have?

STEP 1

Begin with a drawing.

? ?

quarters dimes

2 times as many dimes as quarters

STEP 2

Figure out what the variable is.

- We don't know the number of quarters or dimes.
- There are two times as many dimes as quarters.

Let v = the number of quarters.

That means the number of dimes is $2v$. We need to show the value for each coin.

quarter = v

dime = $2v$

There are 2 times as many dimes as quarters.

$25v + 10 \cdot 2v = 90$

quarters dimes

Unit 8 • Lesson 14 673

How do we solve word problems with coins? *(continued)*

Demonstrate

- Turn to page 674 of the *Student Text* and finish solving the coin problem.

STEP 3

- Explain that now that we have an equation, we can solve it. Remind students to use the order of operations to make $\mathbf{10 \cdot 2v = 20v}$.
- Go through the steps of getting the v by itself on one side of the equation and then solving for v.
- Remind students that any operation they do on the left side of the equation must be done to the right side of the equation in order to keep the equation balanced.
- Simplify until you find the answer: $\mathbf{v = 2}$. We have two quarters.
- Explain that if there are two times as many dimes as there are quarters, and there are two quarters, we have four dimes.

STEP 4

- Remind students that the last step to solving word problems is to make sure we have answered what the question is asking.
- Demonstrate substituting the value of v, 2, into the original equation to make sure everything is correct.

STEP 3

Solve the equation.

$$25v + 10 \cdot 2v = 90$$

$$25v + 20v = 90 \quad \leftarrow \text{We use order of operations to make } 10 \cdot 2v = 20v$$

$$45v = 90$$

$$\frac{1}{45} \cdot 45v = 90 \cdot \frac{1}{45}$$

$$\frac{45}{45}v = \frac{90}{45}$$

$$1v = 2$$

$$v = 2$$

If I have two times as many dimes as quarters, that means I have $2 \cdot 2$ or 4 dimes.

I have 2 quarters and 4 dimes.

STEP 4

Make sure to answer what the question is asking for.

We check to see if two quarters is correct by substituting for the variable in the original equation.

$$\begin{array}{c} 2 \quad\quad 2 \\ \downarrow \quad\quad \downarrow \\ 25v + 10 \cdot 2v = 90 \end{array}$$

$$25 \cdot 2 + 10 \cdot 2 \cdot 2 = 90$$

$$50 + 10 \cdot 4 = 90$$

$$50 + 40 = 90$$

$$\mathbf{90 = 90}$$

Problem-Solving Activity Turn to *Interactive Text*, page 325.

mBook Reinforce Understanding Use the *mBook Study Guide* to review lesson concepts.

Problem-Solving Activity
(*Interactive Text*, pages 325–326)

Have students turn to pages 325–326 in the *Interactive Text*. Read the instructions with students.

Students use algebra to solve problems involving coins.

Monitor students' work as they complete the activity.

Watch for:

- Can students apply the correct coefficient for the coins involved in the problem?
- Can students write the equation for solving the problem?
- Can students solve the problem correctly?

Reinforce Understanding
Remind students that they can review lesson concepts by accessing the online *mBook Study Guide*.

Lesson 14 | Problem-Solving Activity

Name ______ Date ______

Problem-Solving Activity
Coin Problems

Solve the coin problems using the four steps. Remember that you need to use the value of each coin when you make an equation. This is what makes coin problems a little different from other kinds of algebraic word problems.

1. **Begin with a drawing.**
2. **Figure out how to use a variable.**
3. **Solve the equation.**
4. **Make sure the answer is what the question is asking for.**

1. I have 3 nickels and some dimes in the pants that I left on the floor of my bedroom. I remember that I had 85 cents in the pocket of those pants. How many dimes did I have? 7

$85 = 3(5) + 10d$

$85 = 15 + 10d$

$70 = 10d$

$d = 7$

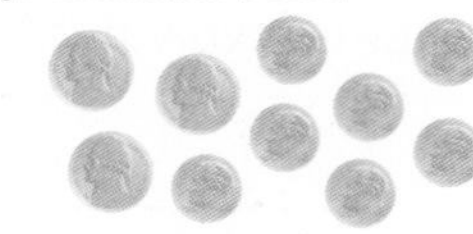

2. I thought that I took all of the money out of my desk drawer but I found 28 cents in it yesterday. I had 3 pennies and some nickels. How many nickels did I have? 5

$28 = 3 + 5n$

$25 = 5n$

$n = 5$

3. It turns out that I counted wrong when I looked in my desk drawer. I only had 22 cents. I had twice as many nickels as I had pennies. How many nickels and pennies did I have?

4 nickels and 2 pennies

$22 = 1p + 2p \cdot 5$

$22 = 11p$

$p = 2$

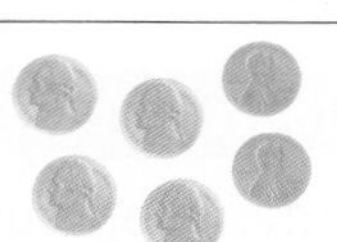

Unit 8

Unit 8 • Lesson 14 325

Lesson 14 | Problem-Solving Activity

Name ______ Date ______

4. I needed to borrow some money for lunch from a friend at school. He gave me all of the change in his pocket. When I counted it, the total was 53 cents. There was one quarter, one dime, one nickel, and a bunch of pennies. How many pennies were there? 13

$53 = 25 + 10 + 5 + p$

$53 = 40 + p$

$13 = p$

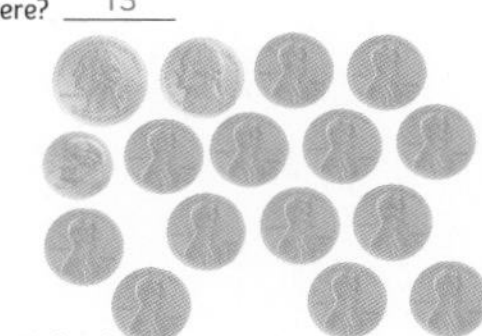

5. Your turn. Make your own word problem using coins. Write the equation that goes along with the problem.

Answers will vary. Sample answer: I want to buy an ice-cream sandwich that costs 95 cents. In my wallet, I have $1.02 that is comprised of 2 quarters, 1 dime, and a handful of pennies. How many pennies do I have? 42

$102 = 50 + 10 + p$

$102 = 60 + p$

$42 = p$

mBook Reinforce Understanding
Use the **mBook** ***Study Guide*** to review lesson concepts.

326 Unit 8 • Lesson 14

Homework

Go over the instructions on page 675 of the *Student Text* for each part of the homework.

Activity 1

Students solve problems involving negative numbers.

Activity 2

Students solve more complex problems involving negative numbers.

Activity 3

Students solve word problems using coins.

Activity 4 • Distributed Practice

Students practice order of operations, integer operations, and one-step equations.

Lesson 14

Homework

Activity 1

Solve.

1. $-5x = 10$ -2
2. $-24 = -4y$ 6
3. $-\frac{1}{2}x = 4$ -8
4. $-72 = -9z$ 8
5. $-3m = 12$ -4
6. $-\frac{2}{3}z = -1$ $\frac{3}{2}$

Activity 2

Solve.

1. $-5x + 6 = 16$ -2
2. $-2(3 + x) = -22$ 8
3. $-32 = -4x - 8$ 6
4. $1 - x + 8 + -5x = -x + 7$ $\frac{2}{5}$

Activity 3

Solve the word problems involving coins.

1. Donny reached in his pocket and pulled out 75 cents, all in dimes and nickels. He had twice as many dimes as he had nickels. How many nickels did he have? How many dimes did he have? 6 dimes and 3 nickels
2. Trinity needed to borrow some money for lunch. She asked Cassandra for money. Cassandra gave her all the change in her pocket. It was a total of 57 cents. There was one quarter, one dime, seven pennies, and the rest were nickels. How many nickels were there? 3 nickels

Activity 4 • Distributed Practice

Solve.

1. $\frac{2}{5} = \frac{h}{35}$ 14
2. $3(x + 1) = 30$ 9
3. $-15 + -27 = m$ -42
4. $1 = \frac{1}{3} \cdot z$ 3
5. $-5{,}000 = -5x$ $1{,}000$
6. $0 = 1{,}000 + x$ $-1{,}000$

Unit 8 • Lesson 14 675

▶ Solving Different Kinds of Algebraic Equations

Problem Solving:

▶ Lines and Angles

Lesson Planner

Vocabulary Development

proof
transitive property
transversal

Skills Maintenance

Solving Complex Equations

Building Number Concepts:

▶ Solving Different Kinds of Algebraic Equations

Students review key concepts of solving different kinds of algebraic equations. It is important for students to realize that success in solving equations means looking at the whole equation and looking for small changes or differences when solving an equation.

Students remember to evaluate problems and use the properties and rules in the Algebra Toolbox to solve equations.

Problem Solving:

▶ Lines and Angles

Students review two-dimensional shapes, which can be examined based on their interior and exterior angles. The exterior measure of all polygons is 360 degrees, and the sum of the measures of interior angles for a polygon depends upon the type of polygon. In each case, we can think about the measure of these angles by using basic algebraic equations.

A further look at parallel lines and transversals allows us to make inferences and prove that angles are equal, based on the properties of straight lines, parallel lines, and transversals.

Also, simple word problems are another context for seeing algebraic equations and can be a tool for representing everyday situations.

Lesson 15 | Skills Maintenance

Name ______________________ Date ______________________

Skills Maintenance
Solving Complex Equations

Activity 1

Solve the equations. Be sure to simplify first, and then solve the simplified equation. Check your answers when you are done.

1. $4x - 2 + 6 - 5x = 10 + -3 + 2x$ $x =$ <u>-1</u>

Show your work here:

$-x + 4 = 7 + 2x$
$4 = 7 + 3x$
$-3 = 3x$
$x = -1$

Check your work here:

$4(-1) - 2 + 6 - 5(-1) = 10 + -3 + 2(-1)$
$-4 - 2 + 6 + 5 = 10 + -3 - 2$
$5 = 5$

2. $5 + -6 - 3x = 10x + 15 + 3x$ $x =$ <u>-1</u>

Show your work here:

$-1 - 3x = 13x + 15$
$-3x = 13x + 16$
$-16x = 16$
$x = -1$

Check your work here:

$5 + -6 + 3 = -10 + 15 - 3$
$2 = 2$

Unit 8

Unit 8 • Lesson 15 327

Skills Maintenance

Solving Complex Equations
(*Interactive Text*, page 327)

Activity 1

Students use the properties and rules they learned to solve complex equations. Make sure students simplify the original equation, then check their work when they are done.

Building Number Concepts:
▶ Solving Different Kinds of Algebraic Equations

What is important when we solve different algebraic equations?

(*Student Text*, pages 676–677]

Discuss

Begin by writing the equation **$3x - 3 = 15$** on the board. Next, write the equation **$3x - 3 = x + 15$** below it. Ask students what is different about the two equations. Also ask them if they need any new properties or rules to solve the second equation.

Listen for:

- *You added an x on the other side.*
- *It will take you longer to solve the second equation.*
- *You don't need any more properties. You can just subtract an x from both sides.*

Discuss how equations may change, and note that it is important to see these kinds of small differences. However, we can still use the properties and rules in the Algebra Toolbox to solve these equations.

If time permits, work through the two equations on the board, asking students about each step and what properties and rules apply to each step.

Demonstrate

- Turn to *Student Text*, page 676.
- Explain that sometimes when equations look different, we might think we have not seen this type of equation before. Remind students that we learned the rules and properties we need to solve the equations.
- Review the steps for solving equations with students.

Lesson 15 | Unit Review
▶Solving Different Kinds of Algebraic Equations
Problem Solving:
▶Lines and Angles

▶Solving Different Kinds of Algebraic Equations

What is important when we solve different algebraic equations?

Sometimes we get confused when we move from one equation to the next. The equations look different, and we might think, "I haven't seen this before. I don't know where to start."

Throughout this unit we learned the rules and properties we need to solve these equations. They are in our Algebra Toolbox. We keep in mind the four steps for working equations.

Steps for Solving Equations

STEP 1
Look at the entire equation.

STEP 2
Look for the **parts** of the equation that seem different.

STEP 3
Remember the goal: Solve the equation so that we have a **positive variable on one side**.

STEP 4
Use the rules or properties we need to reach our goal.

We use similar properties in the two equations in Review 1. The equations are slightly different from one another, but most of the properties and rules are the same.

676 Unit 8 • Lesson 15

STEP 1

- Remind students that the first step is to **look** at the entire equation.

STEP 2

- Remind students that the next step is to look for **parts** of the equation that seem different.

STEP 3

- Then remind students that the next step is to remember that the goal of solving an equation is to get a **positive variable on one side** of the equation.

STEP 4

- Remind students that the last step is to **use the rules and properties** we need to reach the goal.

Demonstrate

- Have students turn to page 677 of the *Student Text* and work through the two equations in **Review 1**.
- Point out that the same properties from the Algebra Toolbox apply, and the ongoing goal is to keep the equation balanced.
- Start with the equation $\mathbf{5x + 4 = 54}$. Walk through the steps of getting x by itself by first adding −4 to each side of the equation. Simplify, then multiply each side of the equation by $\frac{1}{5}$. We get $\mathbf{x = 10}$.
- Go over the second equation: $\mathbf{\frac{x}{5} + 4 = 54}$.
- Remind students that $\frac{x}{5}$ is the same as $\frac{1}{5}x$, so the problem is not as complicated as it may look at first glance. We just have to multiply each side of the equation by 5.
- Walk through each step of solving the equation, making sure students see that when we do an operation on one side of the equation, we must do the same operation on the other side of the equation to keep the equation balanced.

Lesson 15

Review 1

How do we use rules and properties to solve equations?

Equation 1:

$\mathbf{5x + 4 = 54}$

$5x + 4 + -4 = 54 + -4$ ← We add −4 to get x by itself. We add −4 to both sides to keep the equation balanced.

$5x + 0 = 50$

$5x = 50$

$\frac{1}{5} \cdot 5x = 50 \cdot \frac{1}{5}$ ← We multiply by $\frac{1}{5}$ to get a positive x by itself. We multiply each side by $\frac{1}{5}$ to keep the equation balanced.

$\frac{5}{5}x = \frac{50}{5}$

$1x = 10$ ← A number times 1 is the same number.

$\mathbf{x = 10}$

Equation 2:

$\mathbf{\frac{x}{5} + 4 = 54}$

$\frac{x}{5} + 4 + -4 = 54 + -4$ ← We add −4 so that we will end up with x by itself. We add −4 to both sides to keep the equation balanced.

$\frac{x}{5} + 0 = 50$ ← A number plus 0 is the same number.

$\frac{x}{5} = 50$ ← The fraction $\frac{x}{5}$ is the same as $\frac{1}{5} \cdot x$.

$\frac{1}{5} \cdot x = 50$ ← The fraction $\frac{1}{5} \cdot x$ is the same as $\frac{1}{5}x$.

$\frac{1}{5}x = 50$

$5 \cdot \frac{1}{5}x = 50 \cdot 5$ ← We multiply by 5 to get x by itself. We multiply each side by 5 to keep the equation balanced.

$\frac{5}{5}x = 250$

$1x = 250$

$\mathbf{x = 250}$

Unit 8 • Lesson 1 677

How do we solve algebra word problems?

(*Student Text*, pages 678–681)

Demonstrate

- Turn to page 678 of the *Student Text* and explain to students that this part of the lesson reviews how we use variables to help us solve word problems.
- Point out that algebra allows us to represents a wide range of situations.
- Direct students' attention to **Review 1**. Tell students that we use the four steps of using a drawing to help solve the problems.
- As you go through each problem, stress the use of each step. The first two steps are particularly important because representations like drawings and thinking about how to use a variable are at the heart of this kind of problem solving.
- Read the first problem. Two planes pass each other when flying between Chicago and Los Angeles.

STEP 1

- Remind students to begin the problem by drawing a picture.
- Refer to the picture of the two airplanes, and then point out that the information we know from the problem about each plane is written under them.

STEP 2

- Remind students that the next step is to find out what the variable is. Review the information that we know: the distance formula, the total distance of 1,800 miles, and the rates of 550 mph and 350 mph for each plane.

Lesson 15

How do we solve algebra word problems?

We have looked at different types of algebra word problems in this unit. These problems are important because they show us how variables are used to represent unknown quantities.

Algebra also shows us that we can use equations to describe different situations. By using variables and equations, we can represent a wide range of problems.

Review 1 presents two types of problems that we have studied. Let's see how we use the four steps as we solve each problem.

Review 1

How do we use a drawing to solve problems?

Problem:

Every day, planes fly between Chicago and Los Angeles. A jet plane takes off from Los Angeles at 8 AM, flying to Chicago at 550 miles per hour. Another jet takes off from Chicago, flying to Los Angeles. It is up against strong winds, so it can only go 350 miles per hour.

The distance is about 1,800 miles between Chicago and Los Angeles. When will the two planes pass each other?

STEP 1

Begin with a drawing.

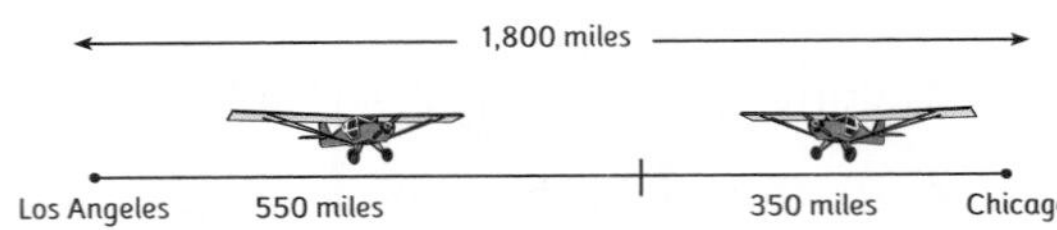

STEP 2

Figure out what the variable is.

We know:

- the formula for rate is $r \cdot t$ = distance.
- the distance is 1,800 miles.
- the rate for each plane: 550 mph and 350 mph.

Demonstrate

- Turn to page 679 of the *Student Text* and continue discussing the steps for solving the word problem.

STEP 2

- Explain that we do not know the amount of time that the planes are flying.
- Tell students that if we let p = the time that the planes are flying, the plane from Los Angeles is $550p$, and the plane from Chicago is $350p$. We know the total number of miles is 1,800, so we can write the equation: **$550p + 350p = 1{,}800$**.

STEP 3

- Tell students that now that we know the equation, we can solve it. Walk through the process as outlined to solve the problem.
- Make sure you point out the operations that are done to each side of the equation to keep it balanced.
- Simplify until you get the answer **$p = 2$**. Tell students that the planes will be in the air for two hours before they pass each other.

STEP 4

- Remind students that the final step is to make sure that we answered what the question is asking.
- Substitute the value we found for p into the original equation to make sure the answer is correct.
- Walk through each step to confirm the answer.

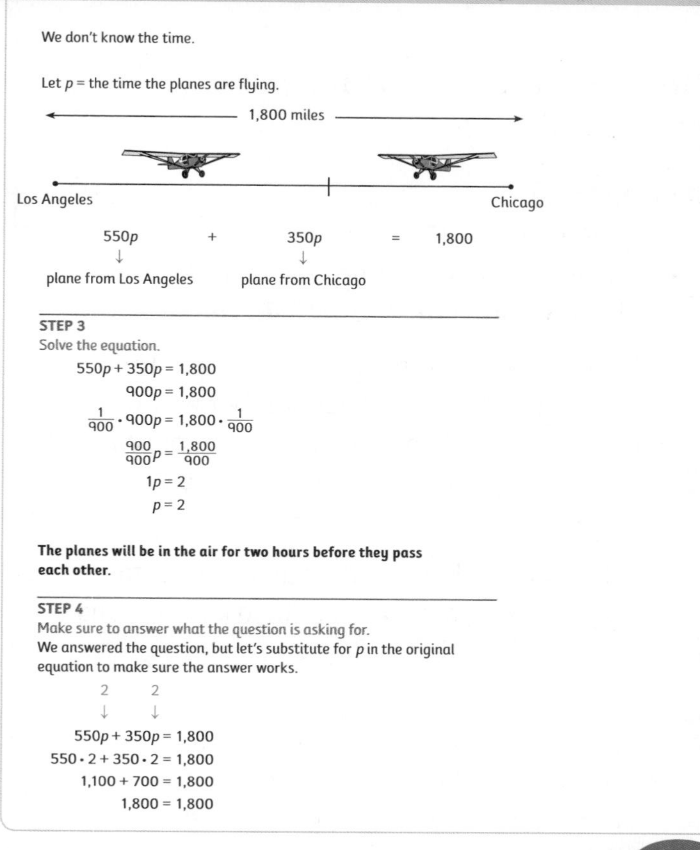

Lesson 15
We don't know the time.
Let p = the time the planes are flying.
1,800 miles
Los Angeles
Chicago
550p + 350p = 1,800
plane from Los Angeles
plane from Chicago
STEP 3
Solve the equation.
550p + 350p = 1,800
900p = 1,800
1/900 · 900p = 1,800 · 1/900
900/900 p = 1,800/900
1p = 2
p = 2
The planes will be in the air for two hours before they pass each other.
STEP 4
Make sure to answer what the question is asking for.
We answered the question, but let's substitute for p in the original equation to make sure the answer works.
550p + 350p = 1,800
550 · 2 + 350 · 2 = 1,800
1,100 + 700 = 1,800
1,800 = 1,800
679

How do we solve algebra word problems? *(continued)*

Demonstrate

- Turn to page 680 of the *Student Text* and continue demonstrating how to solve algebra word problems with **Review 2**.
- Read the word problem, and point out that we do not know either number but we have enough information about the relationship between the two numbers to be able to solve the equation.
- Tell students that we will again use the four steps of using a drawing to help us write and solve the equation.

STEP 1

- Tell students that we again start with a drawing. Here we do not know the two numbers, but we do know that the first number is 4 less than 2 times the second number.

STEP 2

- Next we figure out the variable. We do not know the numbers, but we do know they add up to 32.
- Tell students that the first number depends on the second number. If we let *w* equal the second number, we have to translate the first number.
- Tell students that 4 less than 2 times w means 2w – 4. Point out the equation: $\mathbf{2w - 4 + w = 32}$.

Review 2

How do we use a drawing to solve problems?

Problem:
I am thinking of two numbers. The first number is 4 less than 2 times the second number. Both numbers add up to 32. What are the two numbers?

STEP 1
Begin with a drawing.

first number

second number

We know that the first number is 4 less than 2 times the second number.

STEP 2
Figure out what the variable is.
We do not know either number, but we do know they add up to 32.

Figuring out the first number depends on the second number. Let w = the second number. That means we have to translate the first number.

Four less than 2 times w means $2w - 4$.

?
$2w - y$

?
w

Now we write an equation.

$\mathbf{2w - 4 + w = 32}$

Demonstrate

- Turn to page 681 of the *Student Text* and continue demonstrating how to solve algebra word problems in Review 2.

STEP 3

- Tell students that now that we know the equation, so we can solve it. Walk through each of the steps as outlined to solve the problem.
- Make sure you point out the operations that are done to each side of the equation to keep it balanced.
- Simplify until you get the answer of $\mathbf{w = 12}$. Tell students that this is one of the numbers.

STEP 4

- Remind students that the final step is to make sure that we have answered what the question is asking.
- Make sure students understand that w represents the second number, so the second number is 12.
- Refer to the expression you wrote to represent the first number in Step 2: $2w - 4$. Then substitute the 12 into the expression to get the first number, **20**.
- Add 20 and 12 together to check that the answer is **32**. The answer is correct, so the first number is 20, and the second number is 12.

STEP 3

Solve the equation.

$$2w - 4 + w = 32$$
$$2w + -4 + w = 32$$
$$2w + w + -4 = 32$$
$$3w + -4 = 32$$
$$3w + -4 + 4 = 32 + 4$$
$$3w + 0 = 36$$
$$3w = 36$$
$$\frac{1}{3} \cdot 3w = 36 \cdot \frac{1}{3}$$
$$\frac{3}{3}w = \frac{36}{3}$$
$$1w = 12$$
$$\mathbf{w = 12}$$

STEP 4

Make sure to answer what the question is asking for.
The question asks what the two numbers are.

w = the second number
$w = 12$

$2w - 4$ = the first number
$2 \cdot 12 - 4 = 24 - 4$ or 20

First number = 20
Second number = 12
20 + 12 = 32

Apply Skills
Turn to ***Interactive Text***, page 328.

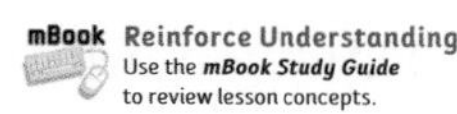
Reinforce Understanding
Use the ***mBook Study Guide*** to review lesson concepts.

Unit Review: Solving Different Kinds of Algebraic Expressions

(*Interactive Text*, pages 328–330)

Have students turn to pages 328–330 in the *Interactive Text*, and complete Activities 1–2.

Activity 1

Students solve algebraic equations, and show all of their work. Tell students to be alert for negative coefficients and fractional coefficients. Monitor students' work as they complete the activity.

Watch for:

- Do students use appropriate tools and properties, particularly involving negative numbers?
- Are students able to work equations successfully when there is a variable on each side of the equal sign?

Lesson 15 | Unit Review

Name ______________________ Date ______________

Unit Review
Solving Different Kinds of Algebraic Expressions

Activity 1

Solve the algebraic expressions. Some problems involve fractions with variables. Show all of your work.

1. $4x + 5 = 65$ $x =$ 15

   Show your work here:
   $4x = 60$
   $x = 15$

   Check your answer here:
   $4(15) + 5 = 65$
   $60 + 5 = 65$

2. $-3x - 7 = 20$ $x =$ −9

   Show your work here:
   $-3x = 27$
   $x = -9$

   Check your work here:
   $-3(-9) - 7 = 20$
   $27 - 7 = 20$

3. $2x - 3 = x + 7$ $x =$ 10

   Show your work here:
   $x - 3 = 7$
   $x = 10$

   Check your work here:
   $2(10) - 3 = 10 + 7$
   $20 - 3 = 17$

4. $\frac{1}{3}x = 10$ $x =$ 30

   Show your work here:
   $3 \cdot \frac{1}{3}x = 10 \cdot 3$
   $x = 30$

   Check your work here:
   $\frac{1}{3}(30) = 10$
   $10 = 10$

328 Unit 8 • Lesson 15

Lesson 15 | Unit Review

Name ______________________ Date ______________

5. $\frac{x}{2} + 1 = 9$ $x =$ 16

   Show your work here:
   $\frac{x}{2} = 8$
   $\frac{1}{2}x = 8$
   $2 \cdot \frac{1}{2}x = 8 \cdot 2$
   $x = 16$

   Check your work here:
   $\frac{16}{2} + 1 = 9$
   $9 = 9$

6. $-\frac{x}{2} + 1 = 9$ $x =$ −16

   Show your work here:
   $-\frac{x}{2} = 8$
   $-\frac{1}{2}x = 8$
   $-2 \cdot -\frac{1}{2}x = 8 \cdot -2$
   $x = -16$

   Check your work here:
   $\frac{16}{2} + 1 = 9$
   $9 = 9$

7. $9x - 3 = 15$ $x =$ 2

   Show your work here:
   $9x = 18$
   $x = 2$

   Check your work here:
   $9(2) - 3 = 15$
   $18 - 3 = 15$

8. $3x - 5 = -23$ $x =$ −6

   Show your work here:
   $3x = -18$
   $x = -6$

   Check your work here:
   $3(-6) - 5 = -23$
   $-18 - 5 = -23$

Unit 8

Unit 8 • Lesson 15 329

Activity 2

Students write algebraic equations to solve word problems. Students may draw pictures to help them, but it is not required.

Monitor students' work as they complete the activity.

Watch for:

- Do students need to use drawings as a way to begin representing word problems?
- Are there difficulties translating word problems into algebraic equations?
- Do students go through all of the steps to solve the equations?

Once students have finished, discuss any difficulties you noticed.

mBook 

Reinforce Understanding

Remind students that they can review unit concepts by accessing the online *mBook Study Guide.*

Lesson 15 | Unit Review

Name ________________ Date ________________

Activity 2

Solve the algebra word problems. Write an equation with a variable for each problem. Draw a picture if you need to.

1. Two numbers add up to 80. The larger number is three times greater than the smaller number. What are the two numbers?

   20; 60

   $80 = x + 3x$

   $80 = 4x$

   $x = 20$

2. Two cars are traveling across the Nevada desert on the same road. They are driving toward each other. One car starts in Reno driving at 50 miles per hour. The other car starts in Las Vegas driving at 60 miles per hour. It is about 440 miles between the two cities. How long until they meet?

   4 hours

   $440 = 60x + 50x$

   $440 = 110x$

   $x = 4$

3. Howard, Jamal, and Michael are brothers. Howard is the youngest. Michael is the oldest. Jamal is 3 years older than Howard. Michael is 7 years older than Howard. Their combined ages are 40. How old is each brother?

   Howard is 10, Jamal is 13, and Michael is 17

   $40 = x + x + 3 + x + 7$

   $40 = 3x + 10$

   $30 = 3x$

   $x = 10$

330 Unit 8 • Lesson 15

Problem Solving:
▶ Lines and Angles

What do we know about lines and angles?

(*Student Text*, pages 682–684)

Discuss

Turn to page 682 of the *Student Text* to review the measures of the interior angles of different shapes. Discuss the standard rules we learned about angle measurements:

- The interior angles of a triangle always measure 180 degrees.
- A rectangle has 360 degrees, and a pentagon has 540 degrees.
- The total of exterior angles is always 360 degrees.

We can use information about exterior and interior angles to solve a range of algebra problems. Remind students that the symbol we use to show equal angles helps us see which angles have the same measure.

Demonstrate

- Direct students' attention to **Review 1**. Explain that once again, we have the opportunity to show how algebra can be used to make inferences and solve problems.
- If necessary, remind students why angles *w* and *y* are equal. Discuss each step in the problem and how once we recognize that this is a quadrilateral (and that the interior angles of any quadrilateral total 360 degrees), we can create the algebraic equation: $\boldsymbol{a + a + 80 + 50 = 360}$.

▶Problem Solving: Lines and Angles

What do we know about lines and angles?

We learned that the total measure of the interior angles of different shapes is not the same.

- A triangle always has a total measure of 180 degrees for its interior angles.
- A rectangle has 360 degrees.
- A pentagon has 540 degrees.

But the total of the exterior angles is always 360 degrees.

We use information about interior and exterior angles to solve a range of algebra problems. The symbols we use to show that angles are equal give us a clue about what angles have the same measure.

Review 1

Find the measure of $\angle w$ and $\angle y$.

Let a = the measure of each unknown angle.

We know that the sum of the interior angles for all quadrilaterals is 360 degrees.

$$a + a + 80 + 50 = 360$$
$$2a + 130 = 360$$
$$2a + 130 + -130 = 360 + -130$$
$$2a + 0 = 230$$
$$2a = 230$$
$$\frac{1}{2} \cdot 2a = 230 \cdot \frac{1}{2}$$
$$\frac{2}{2}a = \frac{230}{2}$$
$$1a = 115$$
$$a = 115$$

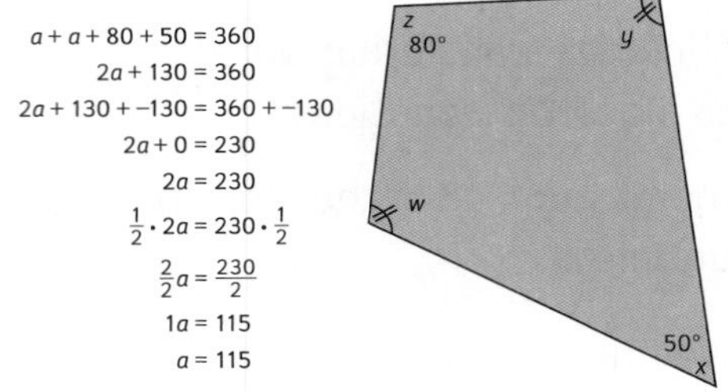

The measure of $\angle w$ is 115° and the measure of $\angle y$ is 115°.

- Be sure to review the properties used in each step in solving the equation and how the value for the variable of the unknown angle, *a*, can be substituted for angles *w* and *y*. If necessary, add **80 + 50 + 115 + 115** to show that it totals 360 degrees.

Demonstrate

- Turn to page 683 of the *Student Text*, and review the information in the box on Key Ideas, Rules, and Properties.
- Go through all of the rules and properties. If necessary, explain that the transitive property is something that we use all of the time, and that it gives us another way to think about geometry and angle measurement.
- Ask student volunteers to come to the board and draw supplementary angles, vertical angles, and corresponding angles.

Watch for:

- Supplementary angles make a straight line.
- Vertical angles have sides that are opposite rays.
- Corresponding angles are created by a transversal crossing two parallel lines.

Ask:

What do we know about the measures of the angles?

Listen for:

- *The measures of supplementary angles add up to 180 degrees.*
- *Vertical angles are equal.*
- *Corresponding angles are in the same position and are equal.*

We also learned how to solve more complex problems using a set of rules and properties. This information helps us prove the measure of an angle or how angles are equal.

Key Ideas, Rules, and Properties
Right Angle Rule The symbol ∟ in the corner of an angle shows that the angle is a right angle. The measure of a right angle is 90 degrees.
Supplementary Angles Rule When we combine two angles to form a straight line, we have supplementary angles. A straight line measures 180 degrees.
Vertical Angles Rule These are two angles whose sides are opposite rays. Vertical angles have equal measurement.
Corresponding Angles Rule When parallel lines are crossed by a transversal, corresponding angles have equal measurement.
Transitive Property This is a property that shows relationships between quantities. If $A = B$ and $B = C$, then $A = C$.

We can use this information to solve a complex problem like the one in Review 2.

What do we know about lines and angles? *(continued)*

Demonstrate

- Turn to *Student Text*, page 684, and discuss **Review 2**.
- Describe the rules used for most of the steps as you go through the example. Also point out how algebra is an exact way of helping us find the angle measurement that we are looking for.
- Start by having students study the diagram. Tell them that Lines *HJ* and *PQ* are parallel.
- Point out that angles 8 and 12 are equal because of the corresponding angle rule. This means that the measure of angle 8, 120 degrees, is the same measure of angle 12.
- Point out that angles 11 and 12 form a straight line. They measure 180 degrees, according to the supplementary angle rule.
- Tell students that if we want to find the measure of angle 11, we substitute 120 degrees for angle 12.
- Explain that we know that the measure of angle 11 plus the measure of angle 12 should equal 180 degrees because they form a straight line.
- Tell students that we let x = the measure of angle 11. Then write the equation $\mathbf{x + 120 = 180}$.
- Walk through solving for x. Make sure students understand each step.
- Solve the equation: $\mathbf{x = 60}$. The measure of angle 11 is 60 degrees.

Lesson 15

Review 2

How do we use angle rules to solve problems?
Lines HJ and PQ are parallel.

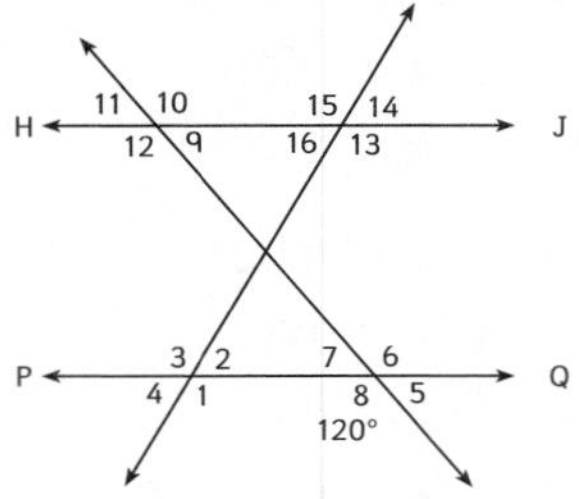

$\angle 8 = \angle 12$ ← Corresponding angle rule.
$\angle 12 = 120°$

$\angle 11 + \angle 12 = 180°$ ← These are supplementary angles.

- Let x = the measure of $\angle 11$.
- Substitute 120° for $\angle 12$.

$$x + 120 = 180$$
$$x + 120 + -120 = 180 + -120$$
$$x + 0 = 60$$
$$x = 60$$

The measure of $\angle 11$ = 60°.

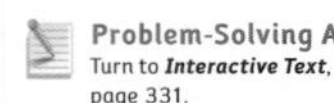

Problem-Solving Activity
Turn to ***Interactive Text***, page 331.

mBook Reinforce Understanding
Use the ***mBook Study Guide*** to review lesson concepts.

Unit Review: Lines and Angles

(*Interactive Text*, pages 331–332)

Have students turn to pages 331–332 in the *Interactive Text*, and complete the activity.

Activity 1

Students write algebraic equations to find the measures of the angles. They look at quadrilaterals and intersecting lines. Monitor students' work as they complete the activity.

Watch for:

- Do students know that the figure in Problem 1 is a quadrilateral?
- Can students verbalize rules that allow them to work the problems?
- Do students use informal strategies to solve the problems?
- Are students overwhelmed by the amount of information in any of the problems?

Once students have finished, discuss any difficulties you noticed.

mBook **Reinforce Understanding**

Remind students that they can review unit concepts by accessing the online *mBook Study Guide*.

Lesson 15 | Unit Review

Name ______________________ Date ______________

Unit Review
Lines and Angles

Activity 1

Find the measurement of each angle in the quadrilaterals.

1. $a =$ 80; 3 angles are 80°, 1 angle is 120°

$360 = 4a + 40$

$320 = 4a$

$a = 80$

$a°$ $a°$ $a°$ $a° + 40°$

2. What are the measures of ∠1, ∠3, and ∠4?

C A B D 3 2 60° 4 1

Angle 1 is 120°, Angle 3 is 120°, and Angle 4 is 60°

What rules or properties did you use to find the angle measurements?

Vertical and Corresponding angle rules

Unit 8 • Lesson 15 331

Unit 8

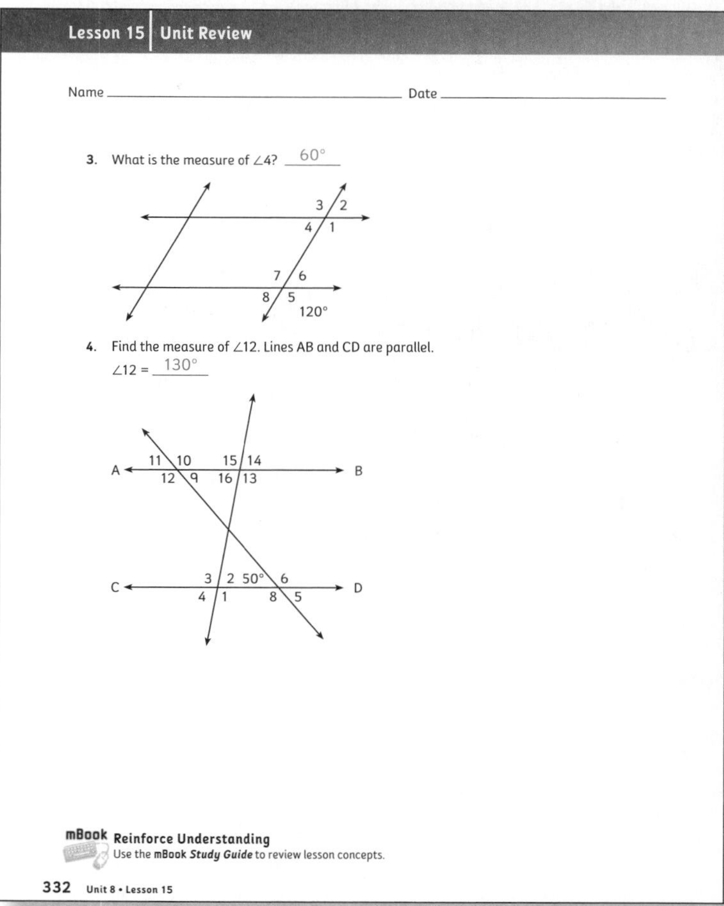

Lesson 15 | Unit Review

Name ______________________ Date ______________

3. What is the measure of ∠4? 60°

4. Find the measure of ∠12. Lines AB and CD are parallel.

∠12 = 130°

mBook Reinforce Understanding
Use the **mBook** ***Study Guide*** to review lesson concepts.

332 Unit 8 • Lesson 15

Assessment Planner

Students	Assess	Differentiate		Assess
	Day 1	Day 2	Day 3	Day 4
All	End-of-Unit Assessment *Form A*			Performance Assessments Unit 9 Opener
Scored 80% or above		Extension	Extension	
Scored Below 80%		Reinforcement	Retest	

Assessment Objectives

Building Number Concepts:

▶ Solving Different Kinds of Algebraic Equations

- Use a variety of rules and properties to solve algebraic equations
- Use algebraic equations to describe a given situation
- Solve word problems involving algebraic equations using models and check if answers are reasonable

Problem Solving:

▶ Lines and Angles

- Use algebra to find the measures of interior angles in a polygon
- Use angle rules to solve problems involving related angles (vertical, corresponding, right, and supplementary)
- Complete simple proofs involving angle measures

Monitoring Progress: ▶ Unit Assessments

Assess
End-of-Unit Assessment

- Administer End-of-Unit Assessment Form A in the *Assessment Book*, pages 73–74.

Differentiate

- Review End-of-Unit Assessment Form A with class.
- Identify students for Extension or Reinforcement.

Extension
For those students who score 80 percent or better, provide the On Track! Activities from Unit 8, Lessons 11–15, from the *mBook Teacher Edition.*

Reinforcement
For those students who score below 80 percent, provide additional support in one of these ways:

- Have students access the online tutorial provided in the *mBook Study Guide.*
- Have students complete the Interactive Reinforcement Exercises for Unit 8, in the *mBook Study Guide.*
- Provide teacher-directed reteaching of unit concepts.

Retest
Administer End-of Unit Assessment Form B from the *mBook Teacher Edition* to those students who scored below 80 percent on Form A.

Assess
Performance Assessments

- Guide students through the Performance Assessment Model on *Assessment Book*, page 75. Then, administer the Performance Assessments on pages 76–77.

Name ______________________ Date ______________________

Form A

Monitoring Progress
Solving Different Kinds of Algebraic Equations

Part 1

Solve the equations.

1. $\frac{1}{2}x + 3 = 13$ $x = 20$
2. $4(m + 1) = 24$ $m = 5$
3. $-6f + 4 = 40$ $f = -6$
4. $\frac{1}{3}y - 5 = 13$ $y = 54$
5. $-2z - 5 = -17$ $z = 6$
6. $7(w - 1) = 28$ $w = 5$
7. $-x = -100$ $x = 100$
8. $4g + 2 = 3g + 7$ $g = 5$
9. $15 = 5h + 5$ $h = 2$
10. $\frac{1}{4}b - 2 = 26$ $b = 112$

Part 2

Write an equation for each word problem, then solve it.

1. Randi is two years older than her sister, Myle. When you combine their ages, they total 46. How old are Randi and Myle?
   $x + x + 2 = 46$; $x = 22$; Myle is 22, Randi is 24
2. When I got home, I took the change out of my pocket. I had 39 cents. I had four pennies and some nickels. How many nickels did I have?
   $39 = 4 + 5x$; $x = 7$ nickels
3. Two numbers add up to 100. The larger number is four times the size of the smaller number. What are the two numbers?
   $x + 4x = 100$; $x = 20$; 20 and 80

Unit 8

Monitoring Progress
Lines and Angles

Part 3

Find the measures of the angles.

1. Lines AB and CD are parallel. What is the measure of ∠ 3? 110°

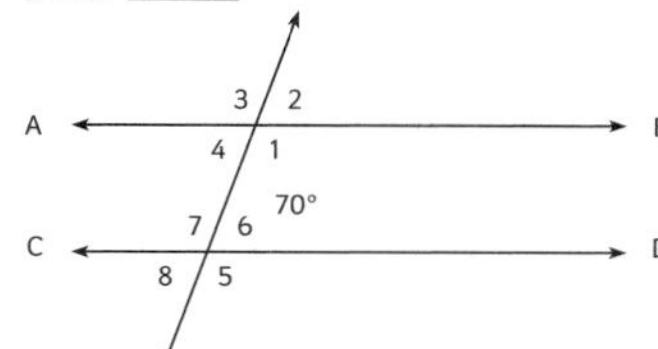

2. Lines RS and TU are parallel. Lines WX and YZ are parallel. What is the measure of ∠ 2? 60°

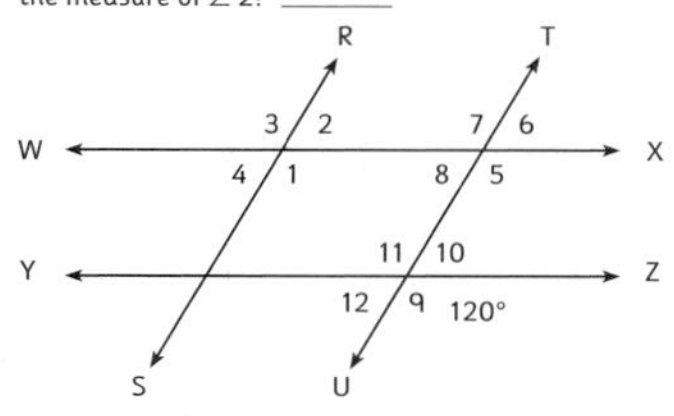

3. What is the measure of ∠ 1? 45°

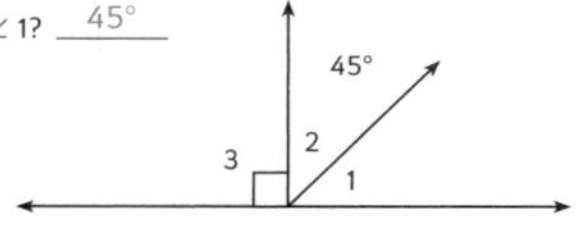

Name ______________________ Date ______________________

Form B

mBook

Monitoring Progress
Solving Different Kinds of Algebraic Equations

Part 1

Solve the equations.

1. $\frac{1}{4}x + 1 = 13$ $x = 48$
2. $4(m + 2) = 24$ $m = 4$
3. $-6f + 2 = 38$ $f = -6$
4. $\frac{1}{2}y - 7 = 13$ $y = 40$
5. $-2z - 7 = -17$ $z = 5$
6. $7(w + 2) = 28$ $w = 2$
7. $-x = -60$ $x = 60$
8. $3g + 2 = 2g + 6$ $g = 4$
9. $25 = 5h + 10$ $h = 3$
10. $\frac{1}{4}b - 2 = 14$ $b = 64$

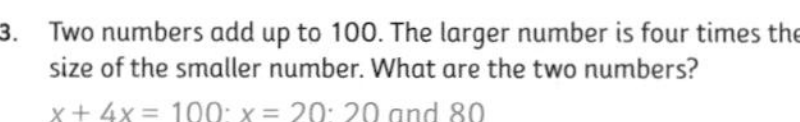

Part 2

Write an equation for each word problem, then solve it.

1. Randi is 2 years older than her sister, Myle. When you combine their ages, they total 48. How old are Randi and Myle?
   $2x + 2 = 48$; $x = 23$; Myle is 23, Randi is 25
2. When I got home, I took the change out of my pocket. I had 49 cents. I had four pennies and some nickels. How many nickels did I have?
   $49 = 4 + 5x$; $x = 9$ nickels
3. Two numbers add up to 90. The larger number is four times the size of the smaller number. What are the two numbers?
   $x + 4x = 90$; $x = 18$; 18 and 72

Name ______________________ Date ______________________

Monitoring Progress
Lines and Angles

Part 3

Find the measures of the angles.

1. Lines AB and CD are parallel. What is the measure of ∠ 3? 100°

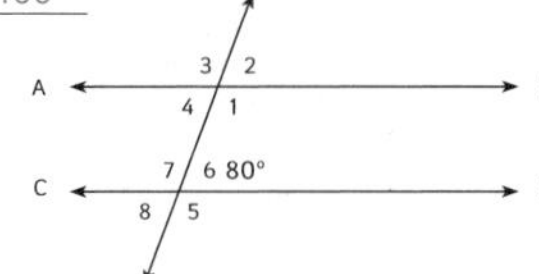

2. Lines RS and TU are parallel. Lines WX and YZ are parallel. What is the measure of ∠ 2? 60°

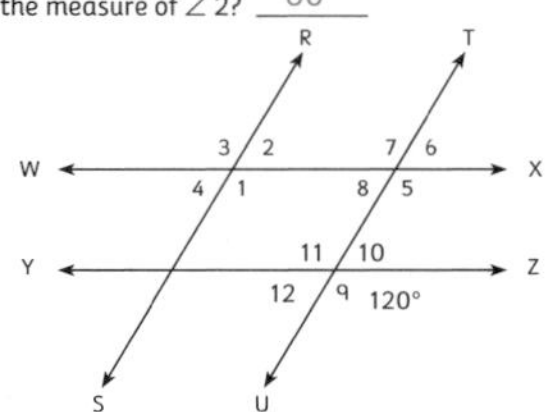

3. What is the measure of ∠ 4? 35°

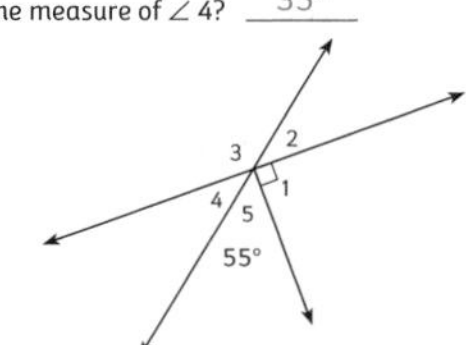

Name ______________________ Date ______________________

Monitoring Progress
Practice Problem 3-8

Solve the Problem

The Ride Into Nowhere motorcycle race is a race across the desert. The course is over hills and riverbeds, and it is 200 miles long. Each racer starts one at a time, and the goal is to have the fastest time on the course. Eric is first. He is riding at 40 miles per hour. One hour later Sonia takes off. She is riding at 60 miles per hour. She thinks she can catch Eric before the end of the course. How long will it take her to catch up to him?

(a) 1 hour

(b) 2 hours

(c) 4 hours

(d) She will not catch him before the end of the race.

(The answer is b.)

Monitoring Progress
Problem 3-8-A

Solve the Problem

Andrea and Marti are sisters. They each have their own cars. On Saturday they are driving from San Diego to Los Angeles for a concert. They have to leave at different times. Andrea leaves first. She is driving 50 miles per hour. When Marti leaves, Andrea is 30 miles ahead of her. Marti is driving 60 miles per hour. How long will it take for Marti to be at the same point as Andrea?

(a) 1 hour

(b) 2 hours

(c) 3 hours

(d) 5 hours

Name ______________________ Date ______________________

Monitoring Progress
Problem 3-8-B

Solve the Problem

Albuquerque, New Mexico, has a balloon festival every fall. Part of the festival includes a balloon race. Hector and Amelia each have a balloon and plan to race each other. Both are ready to start, but Hector realizes that he doesn't have all of his equipment. When the race starts, Amelia takes off, and she is traveling 15 miles per hour. By the time Hector gets his equipment, Amelia is 10 miles ahead. But Hector has a faster balloon. He is traveling 20 miles per hour. How long will it take Hector to catch up with Amelia?

2 hours

Unit 9 Introduction to Functions

Problem Solving: Working With Coordinate Graphs

In 1962, President John F. Kennedy said . . .

We choose to go to the moon in this decade..., not because [it is] easy, but because [it is] hard.

Unit Opener: Background Information

After reading through the Unit Opener of *Student Text*, pages 685–686, share with students some additional information about the *Apollo 11* mission.

- In 1957, the former Soviet Union launched Sputnik (which means traveler in Russian), the first artificial satellite. From that point, the United States and the Soviet Union competed in what has been called the Space Race to be the first to reach the Moon. U.S. astronauts set foot on the Moon six months before the end of the 1960s.
- *Apollo 11* missed its landing coordinates for several reasons. First, computer alarms went off because some of the input were not as predicted in the premission calculations. In addition, as they approached the Moon's surface, Neil Armstrong saw they were headed for a crater almost the size of a football field. He had to steer the spacecraft to a safer landing site. Given the unknown landing area, the dust rising from the rockets and obscuring the astronauts' vision and the computer alarms constantly buzzing, it is no wonder that Armstrong's heart rate increased from a normal 77 to 156 beats per minute on landing!
- The *Apollo 11* astronauts stayed on the Moon's surface for more than 21 hours. They left a plaque that reads, "Here Men From Planet Earth First Set Foot Upon the Moon. July 1969 A.D. We Came In Peace For All Mankind."

Unit 9 Building Number Concepts: Introduction to Functions
Problem Solving: Working With Coordinate Graphs

Building Number Concepts	Problem Solving
• Use word problems and tables to think about functional relationships • Interpret the slope and y-intercept of a function in a real-world situation • Use a function to make predictions in a real-world situation	• Graph linear functions on a coordinate graph • Convert functions between representations (tables, graphs, and equations) • Interpret the intersection of two functions in a real-world situation

Overview

Students learn about functions when they are introduced to algebra. In some cases, the line between algebra equations and functions can be unclear, especially if functions are presented only through symbols and graphs. This unit uses word problems, tables, and symbols to present an integrated treatment of the topic.

Unit Vocabulary
function **systematic relationship** **independent variable** **dependent variable** **slope** **run** **rise** **positive slope** **negative slope** **rate of change** ***y*-intercept**

The Problem Solving strand begins with a brief review of coordinate graphs and a discussion of locating points. It also reviews methods for plotting and transforming simple two-dimensional shapes on the graph. The majority of this unit involves the connection of functions as lines on graphs to word problems, tables, and symbols.

Unit Vocabulary
coordinate graph **coordinates** ***x*-axis** ***y*-axis** ***x*-coordinate** ***y*-coordinate** **point of origin** **linear functions** **zero slope**

Building Number Concepts:

Introduction to Functions

Key Questions That Guide Student Understanding

- *Why is a function a dependency relationship?*

Enduring Understandings for Functions

Once students become proficient in their ability to manipulate symbols, they tend to look at early algebra topics in the same way. Consequently, solving an equation like $3x + 20 = 50$ seems much like $y = 3x + 20$. Functions allow students to represent everyday problems in meaningful ways. This unit stresses the dependent nature of functions. Thinking about the relationship between what is on each side of the equal sign as "one depends on the other" helps students see that functions are systematic or predictable relationships. This understanding allows students to create a potentially infinite x/y table based on even the simplest function.

Tools for Understanding Functions

Using Word Problems, Tables, and Graphs

Current thought about introducing functions suggests students learn best with an integrated understanding of functions. This means using common contexts for word problems and linking them to tables and graphs as a way of showing functional relationships.

Problem Solving:
▸Working With Coordinate Graphs

Key Questions That Guide Student Understanding

- *What do functions look like on a coordinate graph?*
- *How do functions help us model real-world events?*

Enduring Understandings for Working With Coordinate Graphs

Throughout the remainder of secondary mathematics, functions become increasingly complex, and they often appear on coordinate graphs. At this stage, students are able to see the connection between a relatively simple symbolic representation of a function and its appearance as a line. They can apply what they know about components of the formula for linear functions ($y = mx + b$) to understand concepts of slope and y-intercept.

This understanding allows students to move back and forth between coordinate graphs and symbolic representations of functions without creating tables. Functions on coordinate graphs are also concise ways to understand concepts like rate of change, the intersection of two functions, and the comparison of one function to another over time.

Tools for Understanding Working With Coordinate Graphs

Using Graphs

The coordinate graph is the foundation for presenting functions visually. Students can use tables to plot lines and then adjust lines based on changes in slope. Intersections of lines on coordinate graphs help students see when different functions produce the same result.

Building Number Concepts:
▶Introduction to Functions

Lesson	Lesson Objectives—Students will:
1	• Define the functional relationship between input and output.
2	• Put values into function tables to analyze relationships.
3	• Analyze dot graphs to state the relationship of variables.
4	• Use tables and graphs to analyze functional relationships in everyday data.
5	• Examine the data in an *x*/*y* table. • Write functions based on the relationship between *x* and *y*.
6	• Write functions algebraically.
7	• Determine the slope of a line.
8	• Analyze different kinds of slopes.
9	• Solve rate of change problems.
10	• Analyze graphs of linear functions that do not go through the origin.
11	• Use the slope to plot an intercept form function on a coordinate graph.
12	• Use algebraic equations to solve word problems.
13	• Create *x*/*y* tables from graphs.
14	• Create equations from a graph.
15	• Review Introduction to Functions concepts.
Unit Assessments	End-of-Unit Assessment Performance Assessment

Problem Solving:

▶Working With Coordinate Graphs

Lesson Objectives—Students will:	Assessment
• Graph linear functions on a coordinate graph.	
• Translate shapes on a coordinate graph.	
• Reflect shapes on a coordinate graph.	
	Quiz 1
• Graph functions on coordinate graphs.	
• Use the slope to draw lines.	
• Identify the function represented by a graph.	
• Examine the disadvantages of using lines to make comparisons.	
	Quiz 2
• Graph linear equations.	
• Graph linear equations.	
• Find where two functions intersect on a graph.	
• Use functions to figure out the best deal.	
• Review Working With Coordinate Graphs concepts.	Unit Review
	End-of-Unit Assessment Performance Assessment

Lesson 1 ▶Introduction to Functions

Problem Solving: ▶Coordinate Graphs

Lesson Planner

Vocabulary Development

function
coordinate graph
coordinates
***x*-axis**
***y*-axis**
***x*-coordinate**
***y*-coordinate**
point of origin

Skills Maintenance

Solving Algebraic Equations

Building Number Concepts: ▶ Introduction to Functions

Students learn that functions are systematic relationships between two variables. Students learn about functions through the concepts of input and output. Students begin to see the difference between a function and other kinds of algebraic equations.

Objective

Students will define the functional relationship between input and output.

Problem Solving: ▶ Coordinate Graphs

Students learn to graph linear functions on a coordinate graph. A linear function's graph is a straight line.

Objective

Students will graph linear functions on a coordinate graph.

Homework

Students tell what part of each statement depends on another part of the statement, tell the rule for the function machines, and answer questions about the coordinate graph. In Distributed Practice, students solve one- and two-step equations.

Lesson 1 | Skills Maintenance

Name ______________________ Date ______________________

Skills Maintenance
Solving Algebraic Equations

Activity 1

Evaluate the algebraic expressions.

1. Evaluate $5w$ if $w = -5$.
   $5 \cdot -5 = -25$
2. Evaluate $-x + 7$ if $x = -2$.
   $2 + 7 = 9$
3. Evaluate $-6z$ if $z = 7$.
   $-6 \cdot 7 = -42$
4. Evaluate $3 - m$ if $m = 12$.
   $3 - 12 = -9$
5. Evaluate $7n$ if $n = -8$.
   $7 \cdot -8 = -56$

Unit 9

Unit 9 • Lesson 1 333

Skills Maintenance

Solving Algebraic Equations
(*Interactive Text*, page 333)

Activity 1

Students evaluate expressions for the given value of the variable.

Building Number Concepts:
▶ Introduction to Functions

What is a function?
(*Student Text*, pages 687–688)

Connect to Prior Knowledge
Begin by putting the following expressions on the board or overhead:

$x + 3 \qquad y - 9 \qquad 7 \cdot w$

Ask students to give you a value for each of the variables and evaluate the expressions for the value given. Walk through the answers. Then ask students to describe the difference between the problems we start with and how we express the answers.

Listen for:

- *We start with expressions. When we substitute a value for the variable and solve it, we write an equation.*

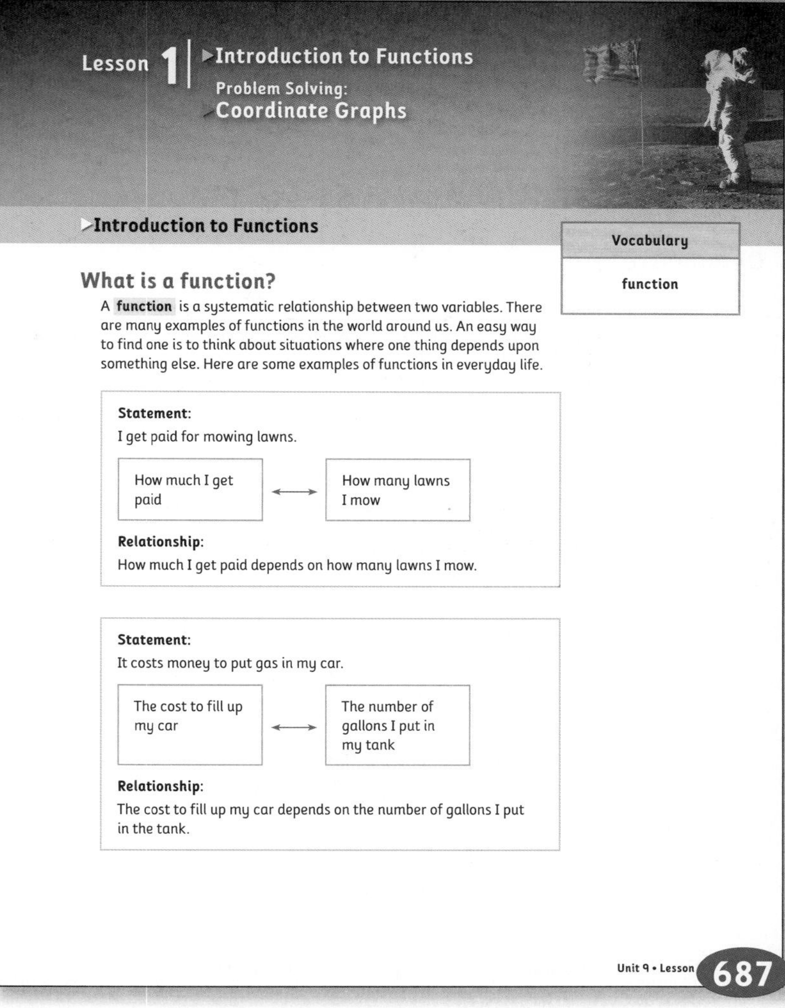

Lesson 1 ▶Introduction to Functions
Problem Solving:
▶Coordinate Graphs

▶Introduction to Functions

Vocabulary
function

What is a function?

A **function** is a systematic relationship between two variables. There are many examples of functions in the world around us. An easy way to find one is to think about situations where one thing depends upon something else. Here are some examples of functions in everyday life.

Statement:
I get paid for mowing lawns.

How much I get paid ⟷ How many lawns I mow

Relationship:
How much I get paid depends on how many lawns I mow.

Statement:
It costs money to put gas in my car.

The cost to fill up my car ⟷ The number of gallons I put in my tank

Relationship:
The cost to fill up my car depends on the number of gallons I put in the tank.

Unit 9 • Lesson 1 687

Link to Today's Concept
Tell students that expressions and equations are closely linked. When we evaluate expressions for a particular value of the variable, we do so by writing an equation. In today's lesson we look at these situations as we define the term **function**.

Demonstrate
Engagement Strategy: Teacher Modeling

Demonstrate examples of everyday functions in one of the following ways:

- **mBook**: Use the *mBook Teacher Edition* for pages 687–688 of the *Student Text*. m
- **Overhead Projector**: Reproduce the functions on a transparency, and modify as discussed.
- **Board**: Copy the functions on the board, and modify as discussed.

- Explain to students that a function is a systematic relationship between two variables in an equation. We usually use ***x*** and ***y*** to describe the function. m
- Read through the examples of real-world situations that can be written as functions. Be sure students understand that each one represents the relationship between two variables.
- Start with the first statement about mowing lawns. Explain that how much a person get paid depends on how many lawns he or she mows. m
- Read through the example of filling up the gas tank. Explain that the cost to fill up the car depends on how many gallons of gas we put in the tank. m

What is a function? *(continued)*

Demonstrate

- Continue showing everyday functions. Explain that how easy it is to move a rock in the garden depends on how heavy the rock is. m
- Next direct students' attention to **Example 1**. Tell students that a good way to visualize functions is with a table and a function machine. In a function machine, we discuss input and we discuss output. The function is the rule that you apply to the input to get the output.
- Go over the function in Example 1. In this example, we demonstrate the function $y = 5x$.
- Go through each input and output. Be sure students understand that the y values, or the output, are always five times the x values, or the input.

Check for Understanding

Engagement Strategy: Think, Think

Tell students that you will give them the following input numbers for the function from Example 1, $y = 5x$. Have students listen for their name and give you the output number when you call on them. Allow students time to think of their answer for each input number, then call on a student by name. If correct, congratulate the student.

Ask:

What is the output if 3 is the input? (*15*)

What is the output if 5 is the input? (*25*)

What is the output if 100 is the input? (*500*)

Statement:
The big rocks in the yard were hard to move.

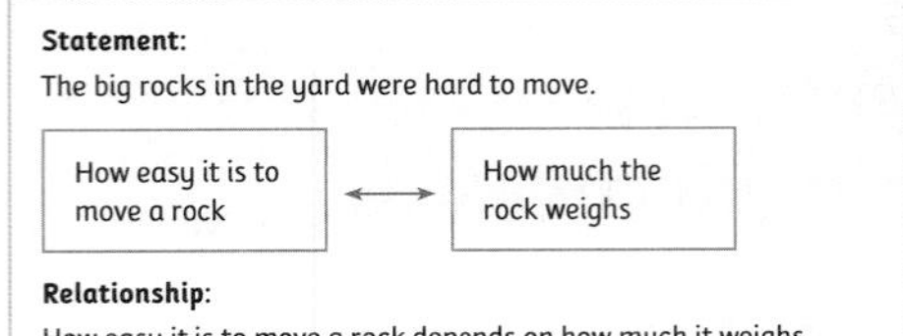

Relationship:
How easy it is to move a rock depends on how much it weighs.

One way to show a functional relationship is with a table. These number machines also represent functions because they show a systematic relationship between the input and the output.

In Example 1, the functional relationship between the input and the output is that the output is always five times the input. The value of the output depends on the value of the input.

Example 1

Define the functional relationship between the input and the output.

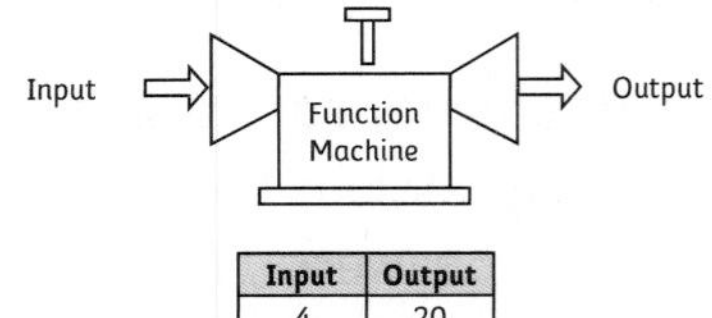

Input	Output
4	20
10	50
2	10
6	30

The functional relationship between the input and the output can be stated this way: We multiply the input by 5 to get the output.

Apply Skills Turn to *Interactive Text*, page 334.

mBook Reinforce Understanding Use the *mBook Study Guide* to review lesson concepts.

Apply Skills

(*Interactive Text*, pages 334–336)

Have students turn to pages 334–336 in the *Interactive Text*, which provide students an opportunity to practice these skills on their own.

Activity 1

Students describe the part of the statement that depends on another part of the statement. Tell students they do not need to solve these problems.

Lesson 1 | Apply Skills

Name ______ Date ______

Apply Skills
Introduction to Functions

Activity 1

Find the relationship between the two parts of each statement.

Model

Lisa gets paid $10 per hour for babysitting.

Amount Lisa Makes ↔ Number of Hours Lisa Works

The amount Lisa makes depends on how many hours she works.

1. Gas costs $4 per gallon.

   Total Cost of Gas ↔ Number of Gallons of Gas

   Write a statement describing the function.

   The total cost of gas depends on the number of gallons purchased.

2. Tina makes $8 per hour for her waitress job.

   How Much Tina Makes ↔ How Many Hours Tina Works

   Write a statement describing the function.

   How much Tina makes depends on how many hours Tina works.

3. Strawberries cost $5 per pound.

   Amount Paid for Strawberries ↔ Number of Pounds

   Write a statement describing the function.

   The total cost of strawberries depends on how many pounds purchased.

4. There is a $1 processing fee for each ticket purchased.

   Total Processing Fees ↔ Number of Tickets Purchased

   Write a statement describing the function.

   The total processing fee depends on the number of tickets purchased.

334 Unit 9 • Lesson 1

Activity 2

Students tell the rules for each of the function machines. Tell them to analyze the input and output carefully in order to determine the rules. They should state the rule using words like plus five, minus ten, times three, etc.

Monitor students' work as they complete the activities.

Watch for:

- Can students identify the part of the statement that depends on the other part of the statement?
- Can students identify the rule that matches the input and output for the function machines and write it in words?

Reinforce Understanding

Remind students that they can review lesson concepts by accessing the online *mBook Study Guide*.

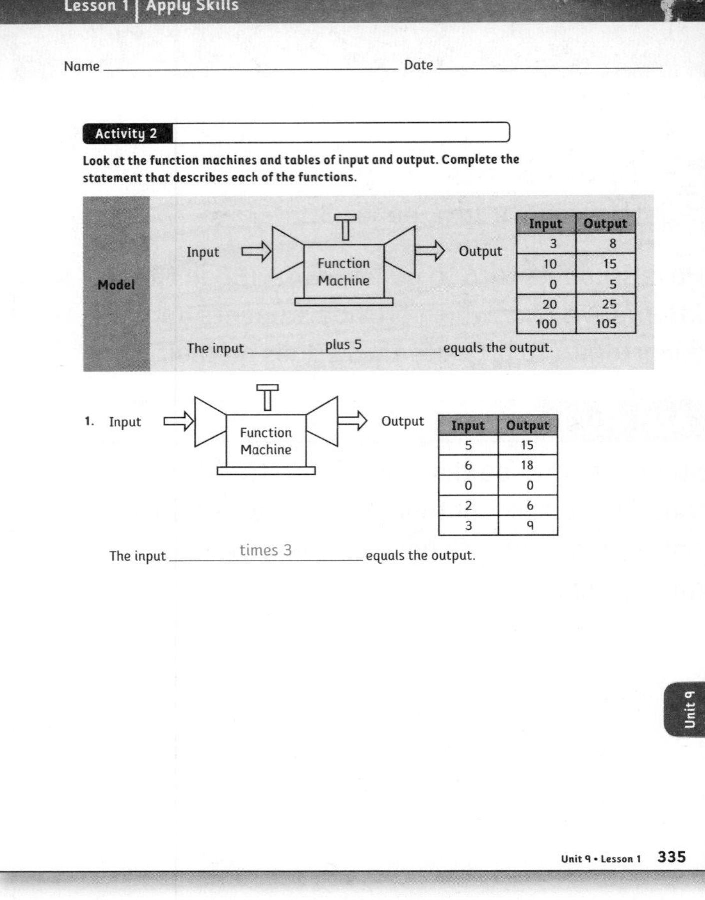

Lesson 1 | Apply Skills

Name ______________________ Date ______________________

Activity 2

Look at the function machines and tables of input and output. Complete the statement that describes each of the functions.

Model

Input ⇨ Function Machine ⇨ Output

Input	Output
3	8
10	15
0	5
20	25
100	105

The input ___plus 5___ equals the output.

1. Input ⇨ Function Machine ⇨ Output

Input	Output
5	15
6	18
0	0
2	6
3	9

The input ___times 3___ equals the output.

Unit 9

Unit 9 • Lesson 1 335

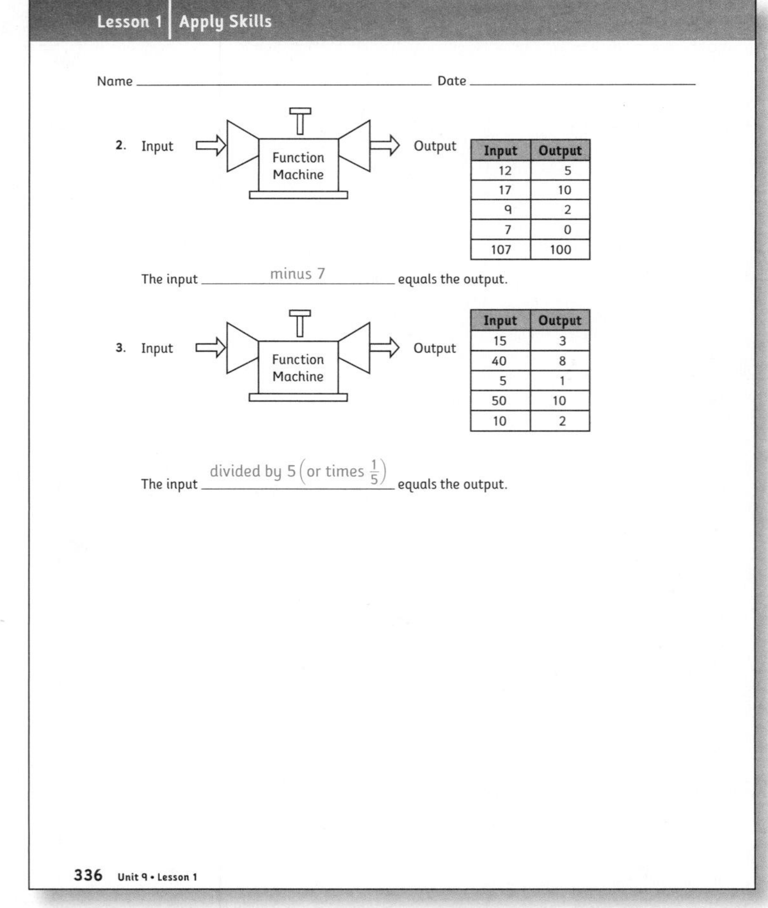

Lesson 1 | Apply Skills

Name ______________________ Date ______________________

2. Input ⇨ Function Machine ⇨ Output

Input	Output
12	5
17	10
9	2
7	0
107	100

The input ___minus 7___ equals the output.

3. Input ⇨ Function Machine ⇨ Output

Input	Output
15	3
40	8
5	1
50	10
10	2

The input ___divided by 5 $\left(\text{or times } \frac{1}{5}\right)$___ equals the output.

336 Unit 9 • Lesson 1

Problem Solving: ▶ Coordinate Graphs

What should we remember about coordinate graphs?

(*Student Text*, pages 689–690)

Explain

Have students turn to page 689 of the *Student Text* and review the important parts of a coordinate graph. Explain to students that a coordinate graph is an important tool we use to help us understand functions.

Demonstrate

- Point out the x- and y-axes, the origin, and the four quadrants on the coordinate graph in the textbook.
- Explain to students that it is a standard in mathematics to write the names of the quadrants using Roman numerals—I, II, III, and IV.
- Have students pay special attention to the information in the four corners of the graph about the signs of the coordinates in each of the quadrants.

▶Problem Solving: Coordinate Graphs

Vocabulary

- **coordinate graph**
- **coordinates**
- ***x*-axis**
- ***y*-axis**
- ***x*-coordinate**
- ***y*-coordinate**
- **point of origin**

What should we remember about coordinate graphs?

Coordinate graphs are used a great deal when we study algebra. Let's review some of the basic properties of coordinate graphs.

Properties of Coordinate Graphs

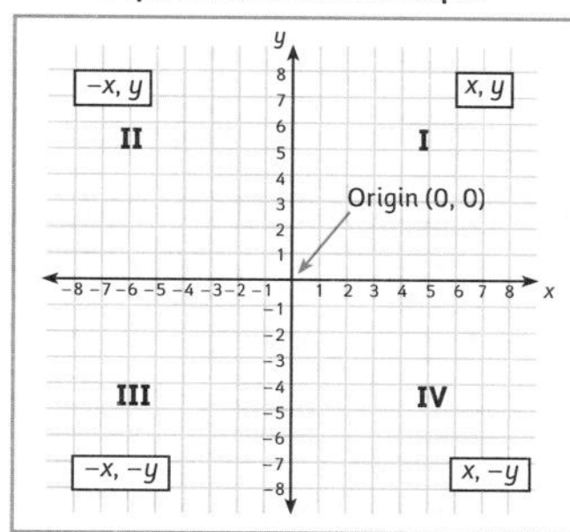

We use **coordinates** to describe the location of points on the coordinate graph. The first number in the coordinate tells us our location on the **x-axis**, or horizontal axis. The second number tells us our location on the **y-axis**, or vertical axis.

The pair of x and y coordinates in each quadrant tells us something about the value of the points that are plotted in that quadrant. The **x-coordinates** to the right of the y-axis are positive and those to the left are negative. The **y-coordinates** above the x-axis are positive and those below it are negative.

The point where the x-axis and y-axis intersect is called the **point of origin**. The coordinates of this point are (0, 0).

What should we remember about coordinate graphs? *(continued)*

Demonstrate

- Turn to page 690 of the *Student Text* and go over **Example 1**, which shows a rectangle drawn on the coordinate graph so that each of the four vertices of the rectangle appears in a different quadrant.
- Make sure students note the sign of each of the coordinates of the four vertices and relate that information to their knowledge of the four quadrants.
- Remind students of how to find each coordinate point on the coordinate graph by counting along the x- and y-axes.

Check for Understanding

Engagement Strategy: Pair/Share

Put students in pairs and have each partner draw a rectangle that has a vertex in each of the quadrants on a coordinate graph, without labeling the vertices of the rectangle. Then have partners switch papers and label the vertices of their partner's rectangle and name the quadrant that each vertex appears in. Ask pairs to present their rectangles to the class.

Lesson 1

Example 1 shows a rectangle that cuts through all the quadrants. Each vertex of the rectangle has different x- and y-coordinates based on the quadrant. For example, the vertex in Quadrant III has the coordinates (−2, −3) because all coordinates in that quadrant are negative.

Example 1

Identify the coordinates in each quadrant.

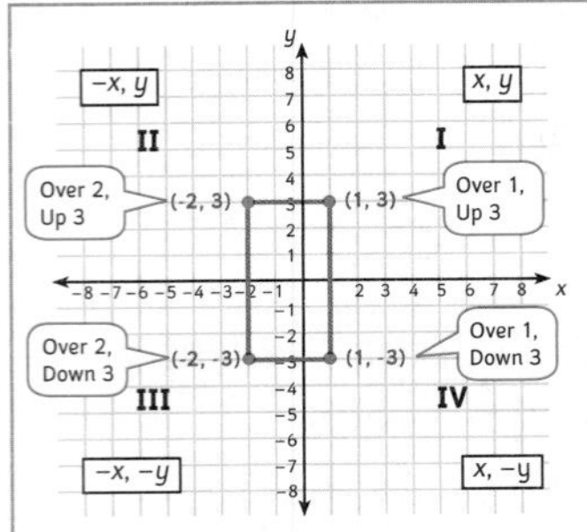

Problem-Solving Activity Turn to ***Interactive Text***, page 337.

mBook Reinforce Understanding Use the ***mBook Study Guide*** to review lesson concepts.

690 Unit 9 • Lesson 1

Problem-Solving Activity
(*Interactive Text*, pages 337–338)

Have students turn to pages 337–338 in the *Interactive Text*, which provide students an opportunity to practice these skills on their own.

Have students follow the directions in the text for drawing rectangles on the coordinate graph.

Monitor students' work as they complete the activity.

Listen for:

- Can students draw a rectangle that lies only in Quadrants I and II?
- Can students draw a triangle that lies only in Quadrants III and IV?
- Can students the L-shaped object so that it lies only in Quadrants I, II, and IV?
- Can students correctly identify the coordinates of the vertices of all of these shapes?

mBook Reinforce Understanding
Remind students that they can review lesson concepts by accessing the online *mBook Study Guide*.

Name ______________________ Date ______________

Problem-Solving Activity
Coordinate Graphs

Follow the directions to draw shapes on the graph. Make sure that each drawing uses the correct quadrants. Label the coordinates for each vertex of the shape.

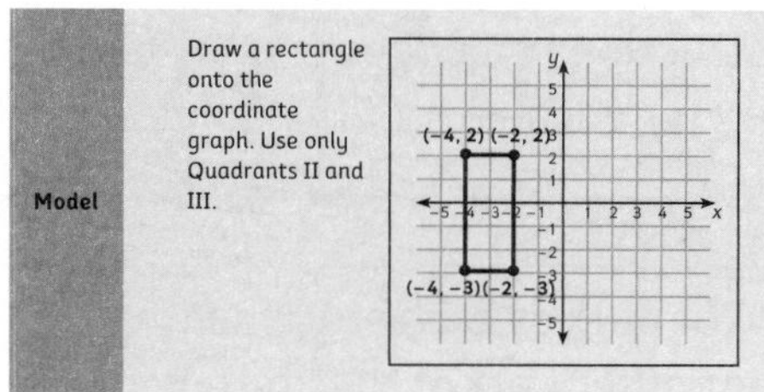

1. Draw a rectangle onto the coordinate graph. Use only Quadrants I and II.

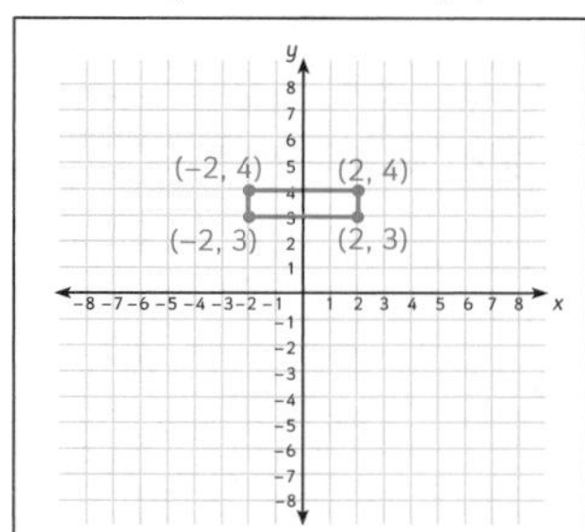

Answers will vary.

Name ______________________ Date ______________

2. Draw a triangle onto the coordinate graph. Use only Quadrants III and IV.
3. Draw an L shape onto the coordinate graph. Use Quadrants I, II, and IV.

Answers will vary.

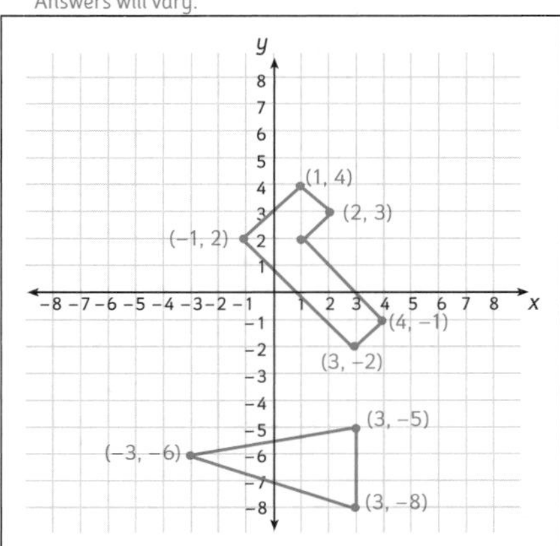

mBook Reinforce Understanding
Use the **mBook** *Study Guide* to review lesson concepts.

Homework

Go over the instructions on pages 691–693 of the *Student Text* for each part of the homework.

Activity 1

Students tell what part of each statement depends on what other part of the statement.

Activity 2

Students tell the rule for the function machines.

Homework

Activity 1

In each of the statements, tell what part of the statement depends on another part.

1. Patricia makes $7 per hour for pulling weeds. ______ depends on ______
   How much Patricia makes depends on how long she works.
2. The cost of gas is $5 per gallon. ______ depends on ______
   The total cost depends on how many gallons are bought.
3. The heavier rocks are harder to move. ______ depends on ______
   How hard the rocks are to move depends on their weight.

Activity 2

Look at the function machines and their inputs and outputs. Tell the relationship each one represents.

Model The input minus 4 equals the output.

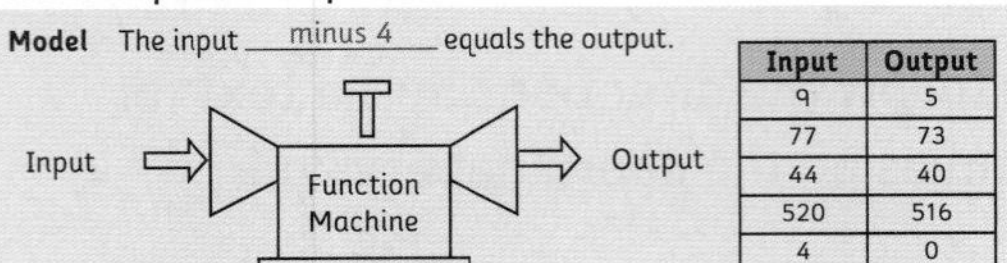

Input	Output
9	5
77	73
44	40
520	516
4	0

1. The input plus one equals the output.

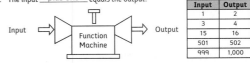

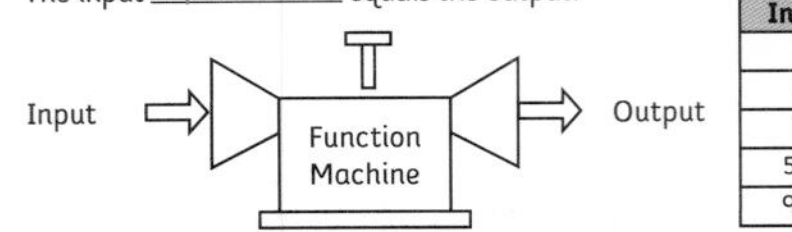

Input	Output
1	2
3	4
15	16
501	502
999	1,000

2. The input times 2 equals the output.

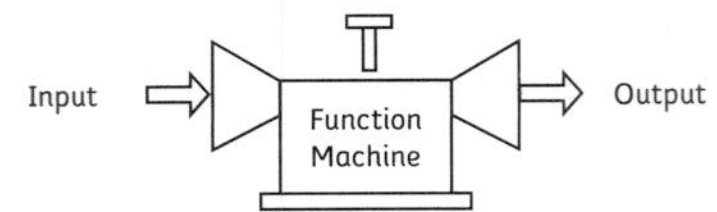

Input	Output
2	4
3	6
4	8
100	200
50	100

Homework

Go over the instructions on page 692 of the *Student Text* for the homework.

Activity 3

Students answer questions about the coordinate graph. Tell students to use the letter labels on the graph to identify the parts in the questions.

3. The input divided by 11 equals the output.

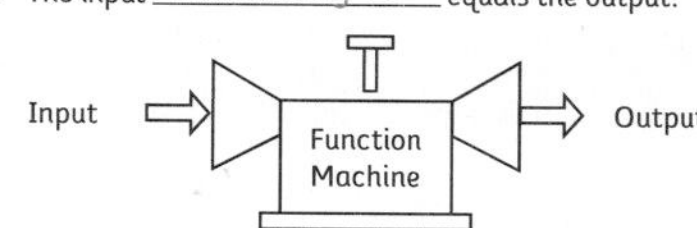

Input	Output
99	9
88	8
11	1
22	2
33	3

Activity 3

Identify the parts of the coordinate grid by selecting the word or phrase that describes it. Write a, b, or c on your paper.

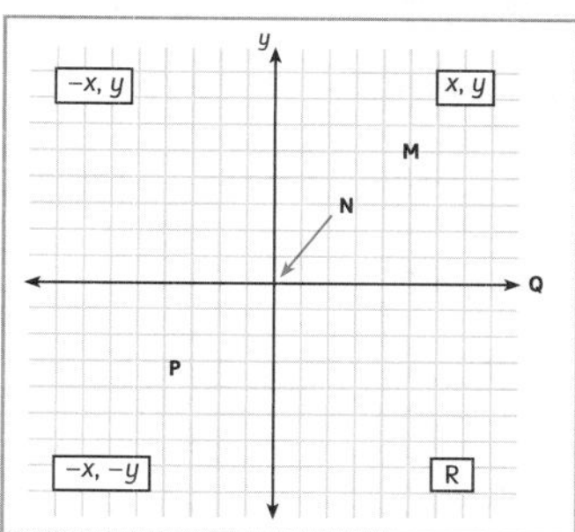

1. The section of the graph labeled **M** is called: b
   (a) Quadrant III
   (b) Quadrant I
   (c) the origin

2. The section of the graph labeled **N** is called: c
   (a) $(x, -y)$
   (b) Quadrant I
   (c) the origin

Homework

Go over the instructions on page 693 of the *Student Text* for the homework.

Activity 4 • Distributed Practice

Students solve one- and two-step equations.

Homework

3. The part of the graph that is labeled **R** should say: a
   (a) $(x, -y)$
   (b) Quadrant I
   (c) the x-axis

4. The section of the graph labeled **P** is called: a
   (a) Quadrant III
   (b) Quadrant I
   (c) the origin

5. The section of the graph labeled **Q** is called: c
   (a) $(x, -y)$
   (b) Quadrant I
   (c) the x-axis

Activity 4 • Distributed Practice

Solve.

1. $9 = 3x$ 3
2. $2x + 3 = 7$ 2
3. $3(x + 2) = 15$ 3
4. $3x + 2x + 1 = 26$ 5
5. $36 + 2x = 4 + 6x$ 8
6. $-54 = -9x$ 6
7. $-2x + 5 = -x + -2$ 7
8. $x + 10 = 20$ 10

Lesson 2 ▶ Functions From Everyday Life

Problem Solving: Translations on a Coordinate Graph

Lesson Planner

Vocabulary Development

systematic relationship

Skills Maintenance

Solving Algebraic Equations

Building Number Concepts:

▶ Functions From Everyday Life

We continue our exploration of functions in everyday life. There are many everyday situations that have systematic relationships between two variables. In this lesson, we use tables to help us analyze the relationships.

Objective

Students will put values into function tables to analyze relationships.

Problem Solving:

▶ Translations on a Coordinate Graph

Students learn that a geometric translation on a coordinate graph is a slide horizontally left or right or a slide vertically up or down. Students then learn that the coordinates of the vertices change in a predictable way as the shape is translated on the coordinate graph.

Objective

Students will translate shapes on a coordinate graph.

Homework

Students create a table of values for given input, answer specific questions about the tables they created, and tell the coordinates of the vertices of a translated rectangle. In Distributed Practice, students practice using order of operations and properties, as well as rules for performing operations on integers.

Lesson 2 | Skills Maintenance

Name ______________________ Date ______________________

Skills Maintenance
Solving Algebraic Equations

Activity 1

Use mental math to solve the algebraic equations.

1. $27 = 9w$ What is the value of w? 3
2. $9 = 36 \div z$ What is the value of z? 4
3. $5y = 45$ What is the value of y? 9
4. $15 - x = 12$ What is the value of x? 3
5. $20 = 12 + a$ What is the value of a? 8

Unit 9

Unit 9 • Lesson 2 339

Skills Maintenance

Solving Algebraic Equations

(*Interactive Text*, page 339)

Activity 1

Students solve algebraic equations using mental math.

Building Number Concepts:
▶ Functions From Everyday Life

How do we create a function from an everyday situation?

(*Student Text*, pages 694–695)

Connect to Prior Knowledge

Begin by reviewing the concept of a function from the previous lesson. Remind students that a function is a **systematic relationship** between two variables. Ask students for some examples, either from the previous lesson or from everyday experiences.

Listen for:

- Accurate descriptions of one variable depending on another

Link to Today's Concept

Tell students we continue our discussion about everyday functions in today's lesson. We put values in a function table to help us analyze the relationships.

Demonstrate

Engagement Strategy: Teacher Modeling

Demonstrate how to put data in a function table and state the relationship in one of the following ways:

mBook: Use the *mBook Teacher Edition* for pages 694–695 of the *Student Text*. m

Overhead Projector: Reproduce the tables on a transparency, and modify as discussed.

Board: Copy the tables on the board, and modify as discussed.

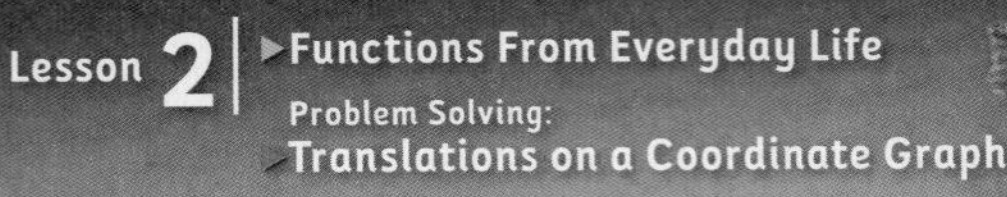

Lesson 2 ▶Functions From Everyday Life

Problem Solving:

▶Translations on a Coordinate Graph

▶Functions From Everyday Life

Vocabulary
systematic relationship

How do we create a function from an everyday situation?

In the last lesson, we learned that functions show a **systematic relationship** between two variables. This means the change in one variable leads to a predictable change in another variable. This happens often in the world around us.

Example 1 shows two real-life examples of systematic relationships. In each case, we use a table to show the relationship between one variable and another variable.

Example 1

Show the function in a table and state the relationship.

Problem 1: Going Up in a Balloon

There are people who like to fly in hot air balloons. We often see the people in these balloons wearing jackets. Why? There is an interesting relationship between elevation and the temperature of the air. For every 500 meters up in the air, the temperature drops 6 degrees. Let's say it is 60 degrees on the ground when a balloon takes off. What is the change in temperature as the balloon goes up?

Height or Altitude (in meters)	Air Temperature (in degrees)
0	60
500	54
1,000	48
1,500	42
2,000	36

694 Unit 9 • Lesson 2

- Remind students that in functions, the change in one variable leads to a predictable change in another variable. This is called a systematic relationship.
- Explain to students that functions occur around us all of the time. We will see how to represent the relationships in a function table.
- Go over **Example 1**, which shows two problems that are everyday uses of functions and how you represent the relationships in a function table.
- In Problem 1, we show the relationship between how high a hot air balloon rises and the temperature of the air. m
- Go through each of the different heights and temperatures in the table. Tell students that the height and the temperature chart represents input and output in the function. m

Demonstrate

- Summarize the functional relationship by pointing out that higher the balloon goes, the lower the temperature becomes. m
- Look at Problem 2, which shows the number of quarts of oil a car needs and the cost of an oil change.
- Go through each number of quarts and costs in the table. Point out that the total cost of the oil depends on the number of quarts necessary for the car. m
- Explain to students that a table is a good tool to use to help us understand a functional relationship.

Check for Understanding

Engagement Strategy: Look About

Copy the following question and chart on the board. Tell students that they will complete a chart and answer the question. Explain to students that they will do this with the help of the whole class. Students should copy and complete the chart, and write their statement in large writing on a piece of paper or a dry erase board. When the students finish their work, they should hold up their answer for everyone to see.

If students are not sure about the answer, prompt them to look about at other students' solutions to help with their thinking. Review the answers after all students have held up their solutions.

Ask:

Suppose that grapes cost $2 per pound. How much do 4 pounds of grapes cost? ($*8*)

Pounds	Cost

Lesson 2

By the time the balloon gets to 2,000 meters, or about 6,500 feet, the air is 36 degrees.

How do we state the relationship?

The higher you rise in the balloon, the lower the temperature falls.

Problem 2: Changing the Oil

Vroom Oil Change changes oil for all kinds of cars. It charges different amounts depending on the size of the car's engine. Larger engines usually take more quarts of oil. The business charges $6 a quart to change oil. What would this look like on a table?

Number of Quarts	Total Cost
2	$12
3	$18
4	$24
5	$30

How do we state the relationship?

The total cost depends on the number of quarts.

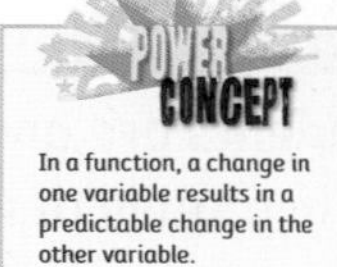

In a function, a change in one variable results in a predictable change in the other variable.

Understanding functions means seeing the relationship between two variables in many different situations. Tables help us see this relationship between variables.

Apply Skills Turn to *Interactive Text*, page 340.

mBook Reinforce Understanding Use the *mBook Study Guide* to review lesson concepts.

Discuss

Call students' attention to the Power Concept, and point out that it will be helpful as they complete the activity.

In a function, a change in one variable results in a predictable change in the other variable.

Apply Skills
(*Interactive Text*, pages 340–341)

Have students turn to pages 340–341 in the *Interactive Text*, and complete the activity.

Activity 1

Students are given a common function, and they fill in a table of input and output. Point out to students that they will need to read the whole problem first, including the question, so they know what values to include in the table. The table will help them answer the question.

Monitor students' work as they complete the activity.

Watch for:

- Can students complete the table?
- Do students include the information from the question in the table of input and output?
- Can students answer the question correctly?

mBook **Reinforce Understanding**
Remind students that they can review lesson concepts by accessing the online *mBook Study Guide*.

Name ______ Date ______

Apply Skills
Functions From Everyday Life

Activity 1

Look at the everyday functions. Make a table of input and output that demonstrates the function. Be sure your input and output include the answer to the question that is asked. Then answer the question.

1. Suppose strawberries cost $3 per pound. How much does it cost for 5 pounds of strawberries? $15

Pounds	Cost
1	3
2	6
3	9
4	12
5	15

2. A gas station charges $4 per gallon for gas. How much does it cost for 10 gallons of gas? $40

Gallon	Cost
1	4
2	8
4	16
8	32
10	40

Name ______ Date ______

3. Elizabeth makes $10 per hour for babysitting. If Elizabeth works 6 hours, how much does she make? $60

Hours	Payment
1	10
2	20
4	40
6	60
8	80

4. The ticket agency charges a $5 processing fee for every ticket that you purchase. If you buy 4 tickets, how much will you need to pay as a processing fee? $20

Ticket	Processing Fee
1	5
2	10
3	15
4	20
5	25

Problem Solving:
▶ Translations on a Coordinate Graph

How do we make translations on a coordinate graph?

(*Student Text*, pages 696–697)

Explain

Remind students that a geometric translation is when we slide a shape either vertically or horizontally on a graph.

Tell students that we can learn a lot by looking at the coordinates of the vertices of an object that we translate on a graph.

Demonstrate

- Have students look at **Example 1** on page 696 of the *Student Text*. Explain that this graph shows a shape that is translated from Quadrant I to Quadrant II.
- Point out the coordinates of the shape in its starting position, and then point out the coordinates for the image.
- Tell students there are predictable patterns. Have students examine the changes in the coordinates of the vertices very carefully. Also point out the marks that tell us that the shape has been moved on the graph.
- Point out that when we slide a shape horizontally, only the x-coordinates change.

Lesson 2

▶Problem Solving: Translations on a Coordinate Graph

How do we make translations on a coordinate graph?

Translating shapes on a coordinate graph means sliding them either vertically or horizontally. It's important to keep track of the coordinates of a shape when we translate it. The patterns we see can help us learn more about geometry and movement on a coordinate graph.

Example 1 shows how we translate a trapezoid from Quadrant I to Quadrant II. The table shows how we move a distance of 9 on the graph.

Example 1

Translate the trapezoid by subtracting 9 from each x-coordinate.

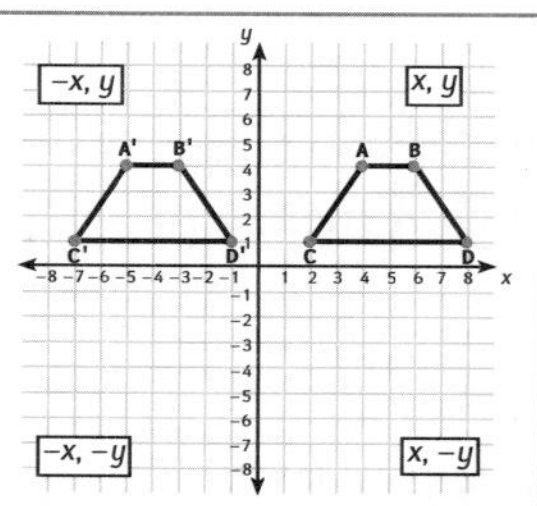

Subtract 9 from each x-coordinate.

Notice that the coordinates of the translated shape are A', B', C', and D'. This is the way mathematicians write the coordinates of a translated shape.

Start		End	
Vertices	Coordinates	Vertices	Coordinates
A	(4, 4)	A′	(−5, 4)
B	(6, 4)	B′	(−3, 4)
C	(2, 1)	C′	(−7, 1)
D	(8, 1)	D′	(−1, 1)

The change is only in the x-coordinates. Why is that? Since we are moving horizontally, we only see a change in the x-coordinate.

Unit 9 • Lesson 2

How do we make translations on a coordinate graph? *(continued)*

Demonstrate

- Turn to page 697 of the *Student Text*, and have students look at the translated shape in **Example 2**.
- Explain that this graph shows how a shape is translated vertically from Quadrant I to Quadrant IV.
- Point out that the y-coordinates all change. We subtract 6 from the starting coordinates to get the ending coordinates. Have students study the coordinates carefully and make sure that they see that when we slide a shape vertically, only the y-coordinates change.
- Remind students that the tic mark is used to label the vertices after the shape has been moved.

In each case, we end up with negative x-coordinates. The graph in Example 2 shows how the trapezoid is translated from Quadrant I to Quadrant IV.

Example 2

Translate the trapezoid by subtracting 6 from each y-coordinate.

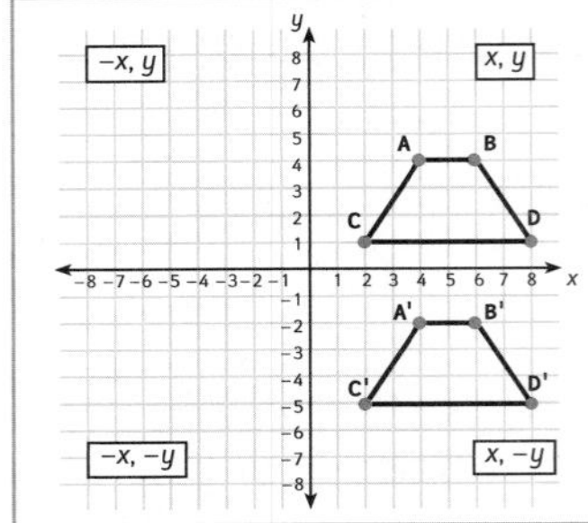

Subtract 6 from each y-coordinate.

Start		End	
Vertices	Coordinates	Vertices	Coordinates
A	(4, 4)	A′	(4, −2)
B	(6, 4)	B′	(6, −2)
C	(2, 1)	C′	(2, −5)
D	(8, 1)	D′	(8, −5)

Because we are moving vertically, we only see a change in the y-coordinate.

Problem-Solving Activity
Turn to *Interactive Text*, page 342.

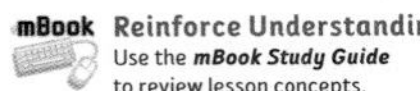

Reinforce Understanding
Use the ***mBook Study Guide*** to review lesson concepts.

Check for Understanding
Engagement Strategy: Look About

Have students copy the starting shape on the coordinate graph from Examples 1 and 2. Then tell students that they will translate the shape with the help of the whole class. Have students translate the shape by subtracting 8 from each y-coordinate. Have students draw the translated shape and make a table of the coordinates of the vertices. Students should draw their translated shape and write the coordinates in a table in large writing on a piece of paper or a dry erase board. When the students finish their work, they should hold up their answer for everyone to see.

If students are not sure about the answer, prompt them to look about at other students' solutions to help with their thinking. Review the answers after all students have held up their solutions.

Watch for:

- The shape moves vertically.
- The shape moves from Quadrant I to Quadrant IV.
- The y-coordinates of the vertices change, but the x-coordinates stay the same.

Problem-Solving Activity

(*Interactive Text*, pages 342–343)

Have students turn to pages 342–343 in the *Interactive Text*, and complete the activity.

Students are given the starting points of different shapes. Students fill out a table with the ending points, then draw the shape in its end position.

Monitor students' work as they complete the activity.

Watch for:

- Can students fill out the table?
- Can students draw the translated shape in the end position?
- Can students label the coordinates of the vertices?

mBook **Reinforce Understanding**

Remind students that they can review lesson concepts by accessing the online *mBook Study Guide*.

Lesson 2 | Problem-Solving Activity

Name ______________________ Date ______________

Problem-Solving Activity
Translations on a Coordinate Graph

Translate each shape. Each problem shows the shape in its start position. Fill out the table first, then draw the shape in its end position. Make sure you label your coordinates on the graph.

1.

Starting Points		Ending Points	
Vertices	**Coordinates**	**Vertices**	**Coordinates**
A	(−8, 6)	A'	(2, 6)
B	(−4, 6)	B'	(6, 6)
C	(−8, 2)	C'	(2, 2)
D	(−4, 2)	D'	(6, 2)

Move the square a distance of 10 from Quadrant II to Quadrant I.

2.

Starting Points		Ending Points	
Vertices	**Coordinates**	**Vertices**	**Coordinates**
A	(4, −1)	A'	(4, 4)
B	(1, −4)	B'	(1, 1)
C	(7, −4)	C'	(7, 1)

Move the triangle a distance of 5 from Quadrant IV to Quadrant I.

3.

Starting Points		Ending Points	
Vertices	**Coordinates**	**Vertices**	**Coordinates**
A	(−6, 6)	A'	(−6, −2)
B	(−4, 6)	B'	(−4, −2)
C	(−8, 4)	C'	(−8, −4)
D	(−2, 4)	D'	(−2, −4)

Move the trapezoid a distance of 8 from Quadrant II to Quadrant III.

342 Unit 9 • Lesson 2

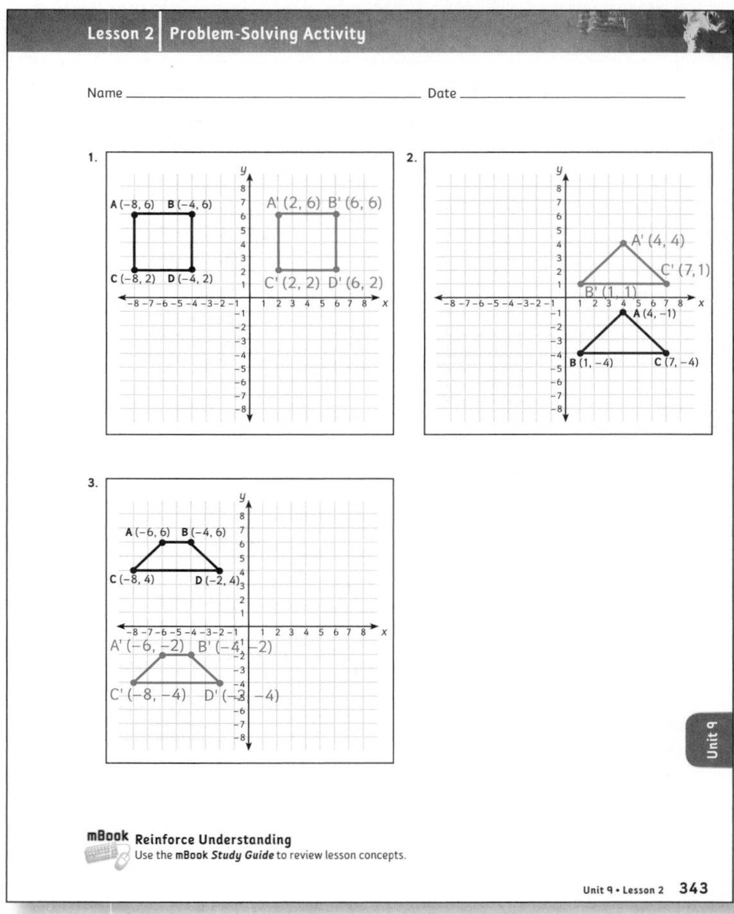
Lesson 2 | Problem-Solving Activity

Name ______________________ Date ______________

mBook Reinforce Understanding
Use the mBook *Study Guide* to review lesson concepts.

Unit 9 • Lesson 2 343

Homework

Go over the instructions on pages 698–699 of the *Student Text* for each part of the homework.

Activity 1

Students create a table of values for input that represent the function they given.

Activity 2

Students answer specific questions about the tables they created for Activity 1.

Homework

Activity 1

Create the input/output table for each everyday function below. Then state the relationship between the input and output.

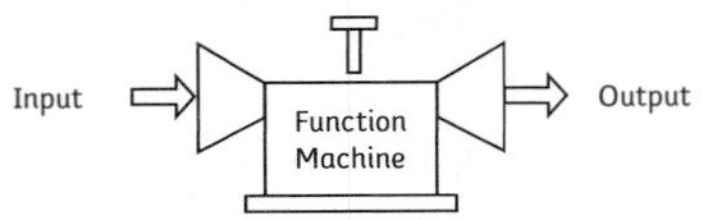

1. A gallon of gas costs $5.
2. There is a $5 processing fee for each ticket.
3. It takes Michael 10 minutes to read one page in his book.

See Additional Answers below.

Activity 2

Use the information from the tables in Activity 1 to answer the questions.

1. How many pages does Michael read in 30 minutes? Three pages
2. How many tickets did you buy if you paid $25 in processing fees? Five tickets
3. If you paid $40 for gas, how many gallons did you buy? Eight gallons
4. How long did it take Michael to read 5 pages? 50 minutes

Additional Answers

Activity 1

1.

Gallons	Cost in Dollars
1	5
2	10
3	15
4	20

Cost increases $5 for every gallon put in.

2.

Ticket	Processing Fee
1	5
2	10
3	15
4	20

Cost increases $5 for each ticket.

3. It takes Michael 10 minutes to read one page in his book.

Pages	Time Spent Reading
1	10
2	20
3	30
4	40

Time increases by 10 minutes for every page read.

Homework

Go over the instructions on page 699 of the *Student Text* for each part of the homework.

Activity 3

Students tell the change in the coordinates of the vertices of the rectangle when it is translated one unit to the right.

Activity 4 • Distributed Practice

Students practice using order of operations and properties, as well as rules for performing operations on integers.

Homework

Activity 3

Tell the coordinates of the shape if you translate it one unit to the right.

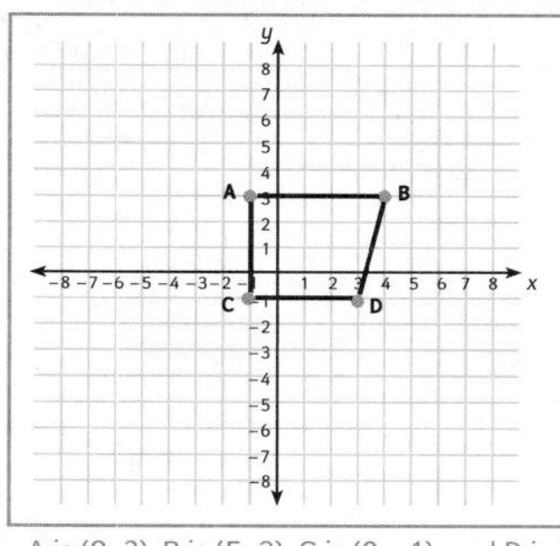

A is (0, 3), B is (5, 3), C is (0, −1), and D is (4, −1)

Activity 4 • Distributed Practice

Evaluate the numeric expressions using the order of operations.

1. $-3 \cdot (4 + 3) + 10$ −11
2. $5 - -2 + 7 - 11$ 3
3. $5^2 - 4 \cdot 5 + -5$ 0
4. $(3 + -4) \cdot (11 - -9)$ −20
5. $9^2 \div 3^2 \cdot 7 - 5$ 58
6. $-1 \cdot -1 \cdot -1 \cdot -1 \cdot -1$ −1
7. $8 + -13 - 4 \cdot 8 + 10^2$ 63
8. $1^2 + 2^2 + 3^2 + 4^2 \cdot 0$ 14

Lesson 3 ▶Graphing Functional Relationships

Problem Solving: ▶Reflections on a Coordinate Graph

Lesson Planner

Skills Maintenance

Coordinate Graphs

Building Number Concepts:

▶ Graphing Functional Relationships

Students learned that tables are a good way to see functions. In this lesson, students learn that a graph is another representation of a function. Each axis is labeled with one of the variables, then we plot the relationship on the graph to see how the variables are related.

Objective

Students will analyze dot graphs to state the relationship of variables.

Problem Solving:

▶ Reflections on a Coordinate Graph

We continue our study of predictable patterns in the coordinates of the vertices of a shape that moves. This time, we look at reflected shapes and how their coordinates change when they are flipped across a line of symmetry.

Objective

Students will reflect shapes on a coordinate graph.

Homework

Students write function tables for functional relationships, draw dot graphs that represent each of the function tables from Activity 1, and answer questions about the coordinates of a reflected shape. In Distributed Practice, students write a general statement that describes the property in each problem.

Lesson 3 | Skills Maintenance

Name ______________________ Date ______________

Skills Maintenance
Coordinate Graphs

Activity 1

Plot the points on the graph. Label each point with the letter next to it.

A (3, 2) B (−1, −1) C (2, −1) D (−1, 1)
E (1, 0) F (−2, 3) G (0, 0) H (0, 1)

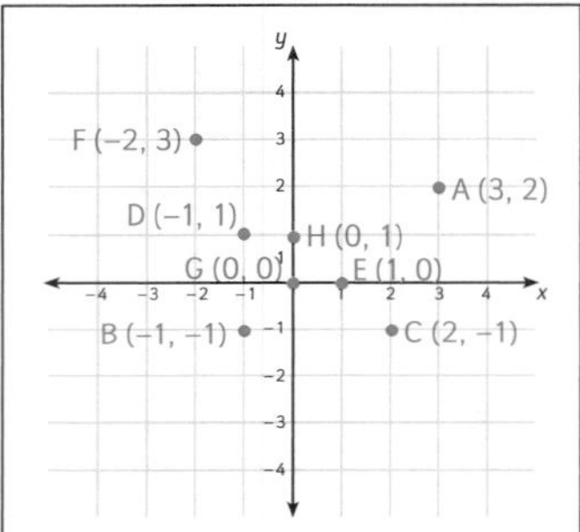

344 Unit 9 • Lesson 3

Skills Maintenance

Coordinate Graphs

(*Interactive Text*, page 344)

Activity 1

Students plot and label points on a coordinate graph.

Building Number Concepts: ▶ Graphing Functional Relationships

What does the graph of a function look like?

(*Student Text*, pages 700–702)

Connect to Prior Knowledge

Begin by asking students to tell you ways we represent functions.

Listen for:

- *We can write the function using an equation with two variables, x and y.*
- *We can write functions using words telling what the relationship is between the two variables.*
- *We can use a function table to tell the input and the output.*

Link to Today's Concept

Tell students that in today's lesson, we look at another way of representing functions: graphing functions.

Demonstrate

Engagement Strategy: Teacher Modeling

Demonstrate how to show functions in tables and graphs in one of the following ways:

mBook: Use the *mBook Teacher Edition* for *Student Text*, pages 700–701. m

Overhead Projector: Reproduce the functions on a transparency, and modify as discussed.

Board: Copy the functions on the board, and modify as discussed.

- Show the function machine and review the concepts of input and output with students. m

Lesson 3 | ▶Graphing Functional Relationships

Problem Solving: ▶Reflections on a Coordinate Graph

▶Graphing Functional Relationships

What does the graph of a function look like?

Function machines and tables are great ways to see functions. When we look at the input and output of a function machine or the two columns in a table, we see the systematic relationship between two variables.

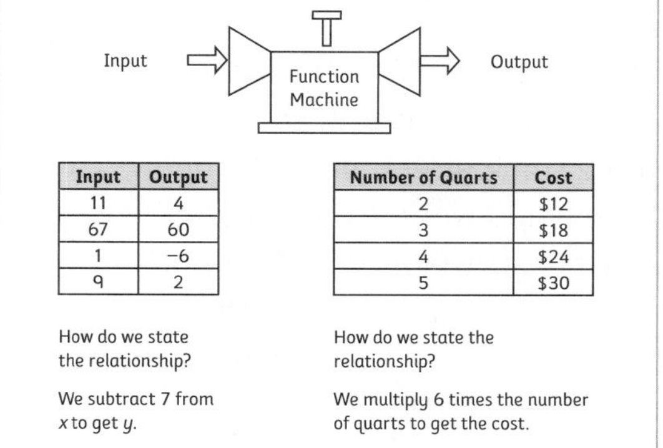

Input	Output
11	4
67	60
1	−6
9	2

How do we state the relationship?

We subtract 7 from *x* to get *y*.

Number of Quarts	Cost
2	\$12
3	\$18
4	\$24
5	\$30

How do we state the relationship?

We multiply 6 times the number of quarts to get the cost.

Another way to show a systematic relationship is to use a graph. We label each axis with the variables, then draw the relationship.

- Point out the functional relationships demonstrated by the two function tables. Go through the first function table and explain how to state the relationship of *x* to *y*. m
- Show the second function table. It tells the number of quarts of oil related to the cost. Point out how we state this relationship. We multiply 6 times the number of quarts to get the cost. m
- Tell students that we can also look at a table and a graph to see a relationship.

What does the graph of a function look like? *(continued)*

Demonstrate

- Display **Example 1**. Here we demonstrate the function using a dot graph.
- Read the problem with students and explain that in this example, both of the variables move in the same direction. Go through each of the hours worked and amount paid in the chart of six weeks that Tina worked. Make sure students understand the amount of money she earns depends on the number of hours she works.
- Demonstrate how to draw the graph by plotting the points. Point out the input value is represented by the *x*-axis, or hours worked, and the output is represented by the *y*-axis, or amount paid. Demonstrate how to plot the first point of week 1: **30 hours worked and 300 dollars earned**.
- Continue plotting all of the dots on the graph.
- Point out that the graph shows that as Tina works more hours, the more money she gets paid. Tell students this is one pattern in a functional relationship.

Example 1 shows the relationship between the number of hours worked and how much Tina made at the restaurant. The graph makes the relationship clearer than the table does. Each dot on the graph shows the relationship between input and output.

Example 1

Use a graph to solve the word problem.

Problem:

Tina works in the kitchen at Big Tom's Restaurant. She makes $10 an hour. The table shows how many hours she worked per week for six weeks and how much money she made. What is the relationship between how much she works and how much she gets paid?

Week	Hours Worked	Amount Paid
1	30	$300
2	25	$250
3	22	$220
4	35	$350
5	29	$290
6	38	$380

Let's draw a graph to show the relationship between hours worked and pay. In this graph, we find the first point on the graph by going over 30 (the input value) and going up 300 (the output value). Then we plot the remaining data from the table.

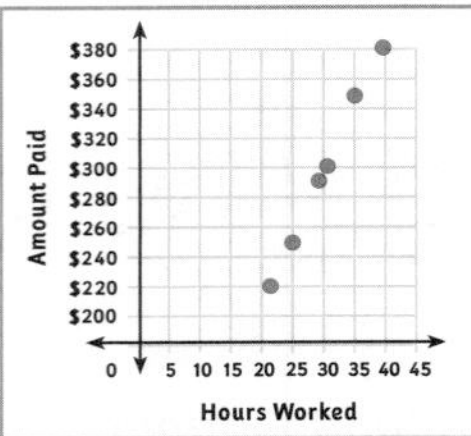

How do we state the relationship?

The more hours you work, the more you get paid.

Demonstrate

- Turn to page 702 of the *Student Text* and explain to students that there are other patterns in graphs. Sometimes the dots on graphs go in the other direction.
- Look at **Example 2** to demonstrate a graph of a function that goes in the other direction.
- Explain that sometimes when one variable goes up, the other goes down. Remind students of the hot air balloon and the temperature. When the balloon rose higher, the temperature went down.
- Point out the location of each point on the graph.
- Have students look at the graph and state the relationship: As the balloon rises, the temperature drops. Therefore, as one variable goes up, the other variable goes down.
- Be sure students see how these two types of functions are graphed using dots on a dot graph and how we can predict, or determine, the nature of the relationships by looking at the graph.

Check for Understanding
Engagement Strategy: Pair/Share

Divide the class into pairs. Tell students to draw a dot graph to represent the cost of oil per quart table on page 700 of the *Student Text*. Then have students analyze their graph and state the relationship between quarts of oil and cost. (*The more quarts of oil you need, the higher the cost.*) Invite student volunteers to share their graph with the class.

The pattern on graphs can go the other direction too. In other words, one variable increases while the other decreases. We saw in the last lesson that as you go higher in elevation, the temperature gets lower.

Example 2

Use a graph to find the relationship between the temperature and the height of the balloon.

Height or Altitude (in meters)	Temperature
0	60°F
500	54°F
1,000	48°F
1,500	42°F
2,000	36°F

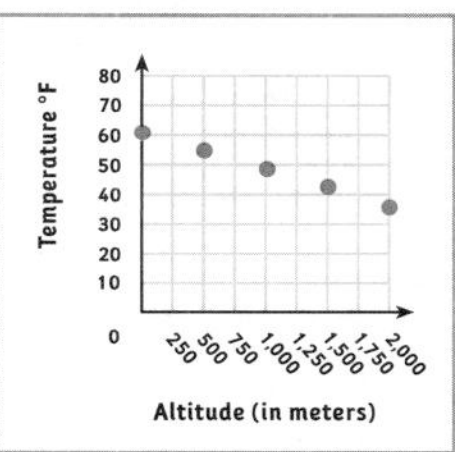

How do we state the relationship?

The higher you go in the balloon, the lower the temperature gets.

Graphing a function helps us see the relationship between the variables.

In each case, the graph helps us see the relationship between the variables. The graph also helps us make predictions about variables that are not in the table. This is one reason why functions are very important tools in mathematics.

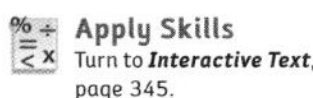

Apply Skills
Turn to ***Interactive Text***, page 345.

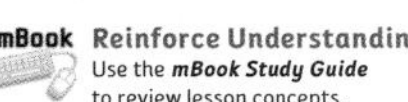

Reinforce Understanding
Use the ***mBook Study Guide*** to review lesson concepts.

Discuss

Call students' attention to the Power Concept, and point out that it will be helpful as they complete the activity.

Graphing a function helps us see the relationship between the variables.

Apply Skills
(*Interactive Text*, page 345)

Have students turn to page 345 in the *Interactive Text*, and complete the activity.

Activity 1

Students make a dot graph by plotting the points from the function table. Then they describe each function in words.

Monitor students' work as they complete the activity.

Watch for:

- Can students plot the points correctly?
- Can students analyze the dot graph and describe the relationship between the two variables?

mBook **Reinforce Understanding**
Remind students that they can review lesson concepts by accessing the online *mBook Study Guide*.

Name ______________________ Date ______________________

Apply Skills
Graphing Functional Relationships

Activity 1

Plot each of the points from the input/output tables to make a dot graph that represents the function. Then write a sentence that describes the function.

1. Strawberries cost $6 per pound.

Pounds	Cost
1	$6
2	$12
3	$18
4	$24

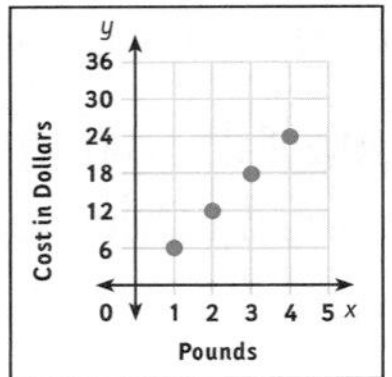

Describe the function in words.
The cost is 6 times the amount of pounds.

2. Gas costs $4 per gallon.

Gallons	Cost
1	$4
2	$8
3	$12
4	$16

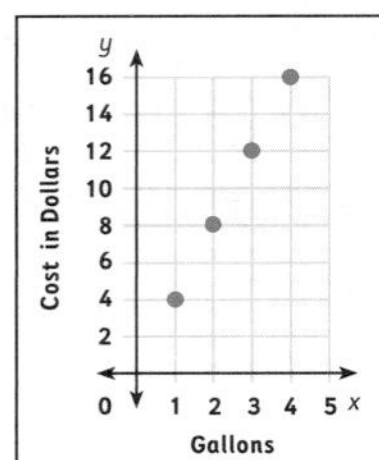

Describe the function in words.
The cost is the amount of gallons times 4.

Problem Solving:
▶ Reflections on a Coordinate Graph

How do we reflect a shape on a coordinate graph?

(*Student Text*, pages 703–704)

Explain

Have students turn to page 703 of the *Student Text* and discuss the meaning of geometric reflections. Tell students that it has a lot to do with the concept of symmetry.

Explain that when we reflect a shape, it is like flipping it over the line of symmetry.

Demonstrate

- Have students look at the table and shapes in **Example 1**.
- Point out that the triangle is flipped over the y-axis. Point out that in this example, the y-axis is the line of symmetry.
- Go over the changes in the coordinates for each vertex in the reflected shape.

How do we reflect a shape on a coordinate graph?

One way to think about a reflected line or shape is to think about a line of symmetry. When we reflect something, it flips across the line of symmetry an equal distance from the line.

Example 1 shows a reflected right triangle. We begin with a table of coordinates that shows the change from Quadrant II to Quadrant I. We are using the y-axis as a line of symmetry.

Example 1

Use the table to reflect the triangle from Quadrant II to Quadrant I.

Start		End	
Vertices	**Coordinates**	**Vertices**	**Coordinates**
A	(−1, 5)	A′	(1, 5)
B	(−4, 1)	B′	(4, 1)
C	(−1, 1)	C′	(1, 1)

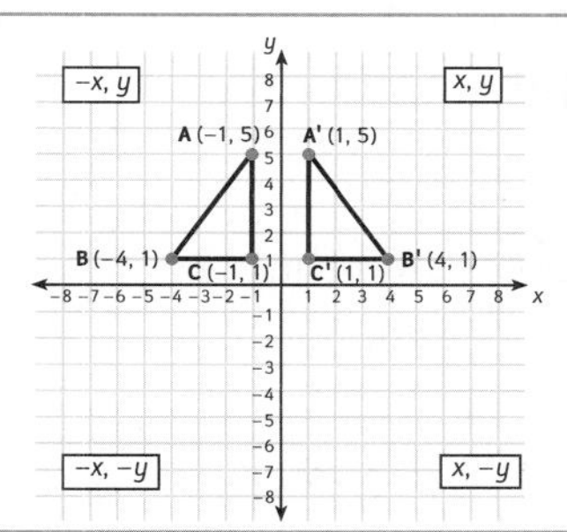

How do we reflect a shape on a coordinate graph? *(continued)*

Discuss

Turn to page 704 of the *Student Text* and read the material with students. Refer to the reflected triangle and table to make sure students see the patterns involved in this geometric transformation.

Point out that the x-coordinates are opposites and the y-coordinates are the same for the shape and its reflection.

Make sure that students understand that the changes in coordinates are more than just going from a negative to a positive number. Each coordinate is the same distance from the y-axis.

Ask:

> **How do you think the coordinate would change if we reflect a shape across the x-axis?**

Listen for:

- *The x-coordinates stay the same.*
- *The y-coordinates are opposites.*
- *The coordinates are the same distance from the x- or y-axis.*

Lesson 3

When we look at the coordinates in the reflected triangle, we see a pattern. We are reflecting the triangle across the y-axis. This means that the only changes are in the x-coordinates.

The x-coordinates are opposites. For example, the x-coordinate in Quadrant II is −4, but it changes to 4 in Quadrant I. This change is more than just going from a negative to a positive number. It shows how each coordinate is the same distance from the y-axis.

When we reflect shapes on a coordinate graph, we think about which signs we are changing. We also need to remember that these changes show that each coordinate is the same distance from the x- or y-axis.

Problem-Solving Activity Turn to ***Interactive Text,*** page 346.

mBook Reinforce Understanding Use the ***mBook Study Guide*** to review lesson concepts.

Problem-Solving Activity
(*Interactive Text*, pages 346–347)

Have students turn to pages 346–347 in the *Interactive Text*, and complete the activity.

Students fill in a table to find the coordinates of a reflected shape. Then they show a reflection of each of the shapes on a coordinate graph around the specified line of symmetry.

Monitor students' work as they complete the activity.

Watch for:

- Can students identify the coordinates of the reflected shape?
- Can students reflect the shape around the correct line of symmetry?

mBook **Reinforce Understanding**
Remind students that they can review lesson concepts by accessing the online *mBook Study Guide*.

Lesson 3 | Problem-Solving Activity

Name ______________________ Date ______________

Problem-Solving Activity
Reflections on a Coordinate Graph

Reflect the shapes on the coordinate graphs in each problem. Begin by using the tables and filling in the coordinates before drawing the reflected shape. Label each vertex of the reflected shape.

1. Reflect the triangle from Quadrant II to Quadrant III.

Starting Points		Ending Points	
Vertices	Coordinates	Vertices	Coordinates
A	(–4, 4)	A'	(–4, –4)
B	(–6, 1)	B'	(–6, –1)
C	(–2, 1)	C'	(–2, –1)

2. Reflect the parallelogram from Quadrant III to Quadrant IV.

Starting Points		Ending Points	
Vertices	Coordinates	Vertices	Coordinates
A	(–6, –1)	A'	(6, –1)
B	(–2, –1)	B'	(2, –1)
C	(–8, –3)	C'	(8, –3)
D	(–4, –3)	D'	(4, –3)

3. Reflect the trapezoid from Quadrant IV to Quadrant I.

Starting Points		Ending Points	
Vertices	Coordinates	Vertices	Coordinates
A	(4, –2)	A'	(4, 2)
B	(6, –2)	B'	(6, 2)
C	(2, –5)	C'	(2, 5)
D	(6, –5)	D'	(6, 5)

346 Unit 9 • Lesson 3

Lesson 3 | Problem-Solving Activity

Name ______________________ Date ______________

1.

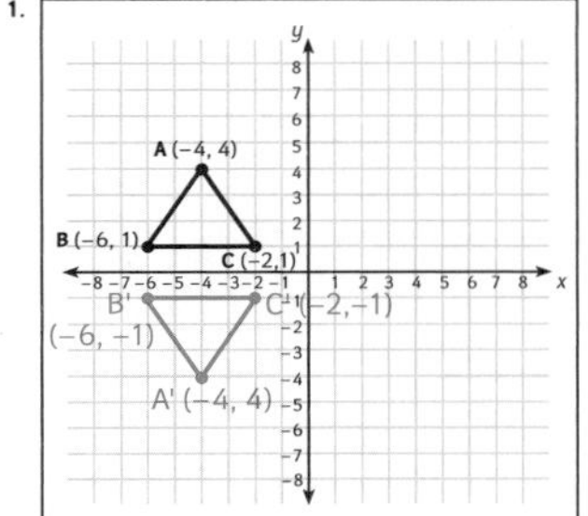

2.

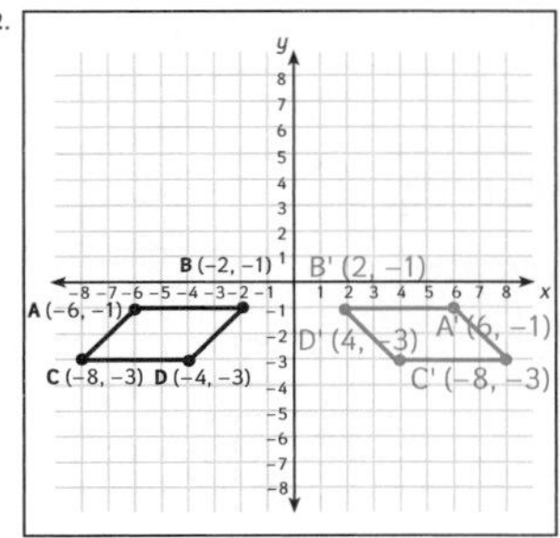

3.

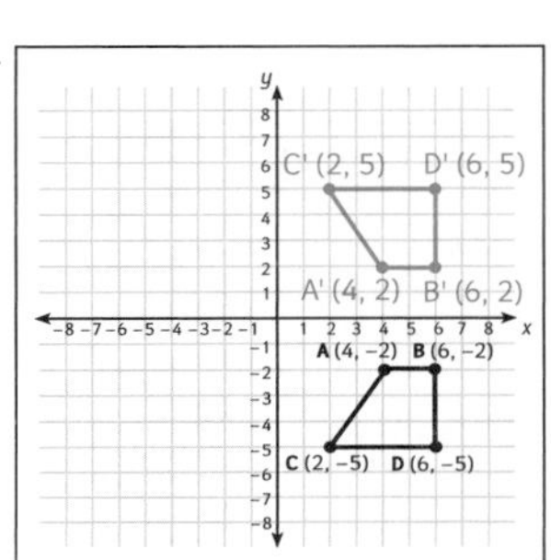

mBook **Reinforce Understanding**
Use the mBook *Study Guide* to review lesson concepts.

Unit 9 • Lesson 3 347

Unit 9

Homework

Go over the instructions on pages 705–706 of the *Student Text* for each part of the homework.

Activity 1

Students write the function tables for each functional relationship.

Activity 2

Students draw dot graphs that represent each function table from Activity 1. Then they answer questions about the graphs.

Homework

Activity 1

Create function tables for each problem.

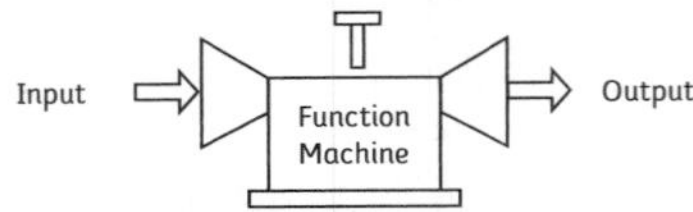

1. In basketball, each basket is worth 2 points.
2. At the Candy Shoppe in the mall, the price of a bag of candy is $5 per pound.

See Additional Answers below.

Activity 2

Draw a dot graph for each of the problems in Activity 1 on graph paper. Be sure to label the axes of your graph and use an appropriate scale. Use the graph to answer the following questions.

1. How many pounds of candy can you buy for $10?
2. How many points do you get for shooting 5 baskets?
3. What does it cost for 3 pounds of candy?
4. If you scored 6 points, how many baskets did you make?

See Additional Answers below.

Additional Answers

Activity 1

1.

Basket	Points
1	2
2	4
3	6
4	8
5	10
6	12

2.

Pound	Price
1	5
2	10
3	15
4	20
5	25
6	30

Activity 2

Graph 1:

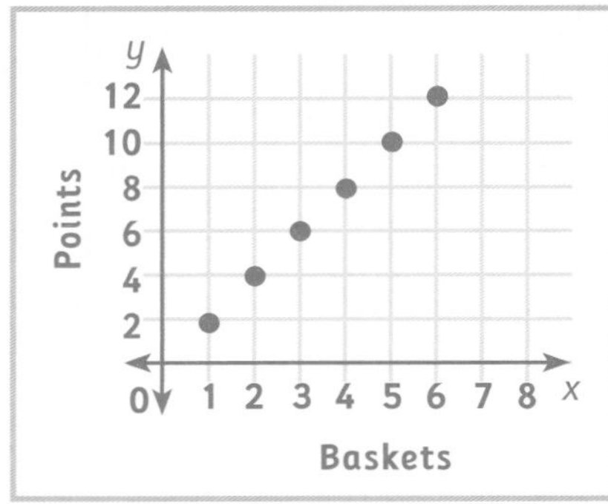

Graph 2:

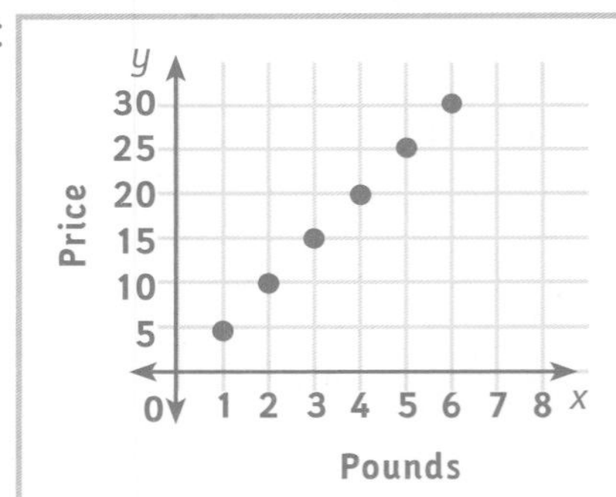

1. 2 pounds
2. 10 points
3. $15
4. 3 baskets

Homework

Go over the instructions on page 706 of the *Student Text* for each part of the homework.

Activity 3

Students tell the coordinates of the vertices when the shape is reflected over the specified axis.

Activity 4 • Distributed Practice

Students write a general statement that shows the property in each example.

Lesson 3

Homework

Activity 3

Write the coordinates of all the vertices of the reflected triangles below. Use the letters to label your answers. Then answer the questions about the triangles.

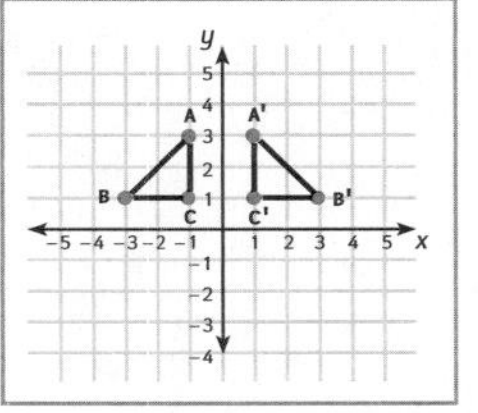

A (−1, 3)
B (−3, 1)
C (−1, 1)
A′ (1, 3)
B′ (3, 1)
C′ (1, 1)

1. Look at the coordinates for A and A′. Do you see a pattern? Write a statement that tells the pattern. They are the same except the *x*-coordinates are opposite.
2. Do you see the same pattern for B and B′? How about C and C′? There is the same pattern.

Activity 4 • Distributed Practice

Write a general statement that shows the property being used in each example.

1. Write a general statement using the variables *a*, *b*, and *c* to demonstrate the distributive property. $a(b + c) = a \cdot b + a \cdot c$
   Examples: $3(4 + 5) = 3 \cdot 4 + 3 \cdot 5$ $\quad 2(-1 + -2) = 2 \cdot -1 + 2 \cdot -2$
2. Write a general statement using the variables *x* and *y* to demonstrate the commutative property for multiplication. $x \cdot y = y \cdot x$
   Examples: $4 \cdot 3 = 3 \cdot 4$ $\quad -1 \cdot 2 = 2 \cdot -1$
3. Write a general statement using the variable *w* to demonstrate the multiplicative property of 0. $w \cdot 0 = 0$
   Examples: $4 \cdot 0 = 0$ $\quad -\frac{4}{5} \cdot 0 = 0$
4. Write a general statement using the variable *z* to demonstrate the additive inverse property. $0 = z + -z$
   Examples: $0 = 6 + -6$ $\quad 0 = 15 + -15$

706 Unit 9 • Lesson 3

Lesson Planner

Skills Maintenance

Plotting Points

Building Number Concepts:

▶ Analyzing Functional Relationships in a Set of Data

Students look for functional relationships in everyday data. They again see how to use tables to collect data and graphs to represent the functional relationship. Then students analyze the relationship based on trends in the data.

Objective

Students will use tables and graphs to analyze functional relationships in everyday data.

Homework

Students tell the systematic relationship shown by the data, if the functions are systematic relationships or not, and tell the new coordinates of the translated or reflected shape. In Distributed Practice, students practice operations on integers.

Lesson 4 | Skills Maintenance

Name ______________________ Date ______________

Skills Maintenance
Plotting Points

Activity 1

Plot the points on the coordinate graph. Use the letters to label the points.

A (0, 1) B (3, 1) C (2, −1) D (−2, −1)
E (−1, 1) F (0, 0) G (−1, −2) H (2, 0)

348 Unit 9 • Lesson 4

Skills Maintenance

Plotting Points

(*Interactive Text*, page 348)

Activity 1

Students plot and label points on a coordinate graph.

Building Number Concepts:
▶ Analyzing Functional Relationships in a Set of Data

How do we find functions in everyday data?

(*Student Text*, pages 707–708)

Connect to Prior Knowledge

Begin by selecting four students from the class to come to board. Put a sticky note directly above each student's head with their name on it. Have the students return to their seats. Discuss with the class if there is a systematic relationship in the heights of the four students.

Link to Today's Concept

Tell students that sometimes analysis of data will reveal a relationship and sometimes it will not. In today's lesson, we look at the data gathered from an experiment where there is a systematic relationship.

Demonstrate

Engagement Strategy: Teacher Modeling

Demonstrate how to graph the results of an experiment in one of the following ways:

mBook: Use the *mBook Teacher Edition* for *Student Text*, pages 707–708. m

Overhead Projector: Reproduce the data tables and graphs on a transparency, and modify as discussed.

Board: Copy the data tables and graphs onto the board, and modify as discussed.

- Explain that the data we look at in this lesson all have to do with functional relationships.

Lesson 4 ▶Analyzing Functional Relationships in a Set of Data

▶Analyzing Functional Relationships in a Set of Data

How do we find functions in everyday data?

Every spring Mr. Raster's science class conducts an experiment outside the school cafeteria. Mr. Raster's students climb a ladder and measure the bounces of three different kinds of balls: a rubber ball, a tennis ball, and a golf ball. They drop each ball from different heights to see how the height of the bounce changes based on the type of ball. The students carefully measure each height where the ball is dropped. They also measure how high it returns after the bounce.

Example 1 shows the results of the experiment.

Example 1

Graph how high each ball bounces.

All heights are measured in inches.

Rubber Ball	
Drop Height	**Bounce Height**
24	19
30	24
36	29
40	32
50	40
60	48
70	56
80	64
90	72
100	80

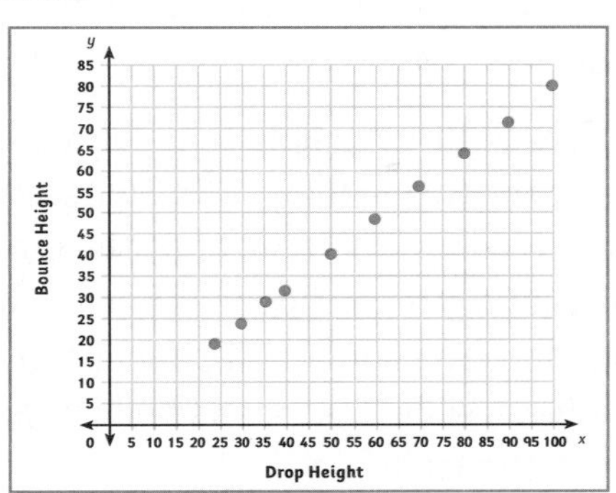

Unit 9 • Lesson 707

- Display the blank tables and the graph, then read the introduction about Mr. Raster's class. Explain that the pieces of information the class collected are called data. We analyze data to draw conclusions about occurrences. For example, Mr. Raster's class dropped three different kinds of balls from different heights and recorded the data. m
- Tell students that we need to determine if we have a systematic relationship or a function from these data.
- Record each set of data in the table. As you present each drop height and bounce height, plot the corresponding point on the graph. Review how to plot points if necessary. m

How do we find functions in everyday data? *(continued)*

Demonstrate

- Continue presenting the data from Mr. Raster's class experiment.
- Discuss the data and the graph for the tennis ball. Show students how to plot each drop height and bounce height on the graph. m
- Repeat the process with the data for the golf ball. m
- Show all three graphs, side by side. Ask students if they see a systematic relationship. Point out that the data show us that each ball bounces back to different heights. The super ball bounces the highest, while the tennis ball bounces back the least. m
- Explain that the data can show us how variables are related.

Tennis Ball	
Drop Height	Bounce Height
24	12
30	15
36	18
40	20
50	25
60	30
70	35
80	40
90	45
100	50

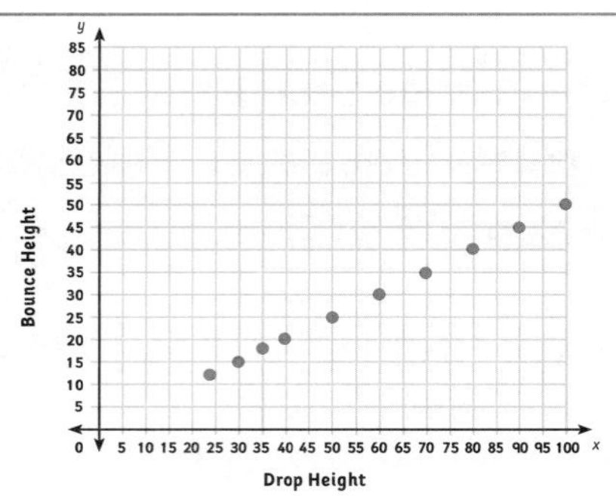

Golf Ball	
Drop Height	Bounce Height
24	18
30	23
36	27
40	30
50	38
60	45
70	52.5
80	60
90	67.5
100	75

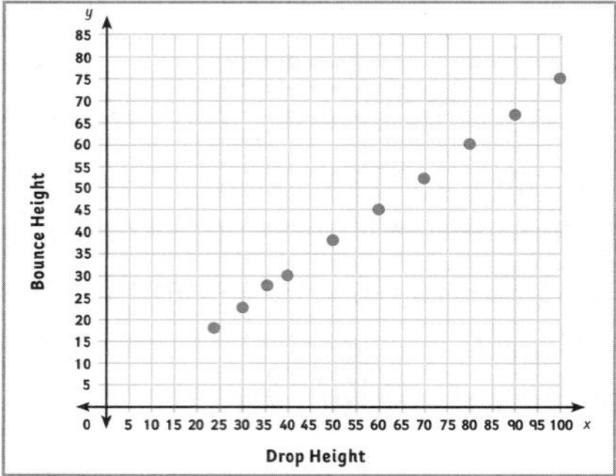

We see the relationship between the drop height and how high the ball bounces back up. We also see that each ball bounces back to different heights. The rubber ball bounces back the highest. That is why the trend in the graph is steeper than the other two. The tennis ball bounces back the least. Its trend is the flattest.

How do we collect our own data to analyze functions?

(*Student Text*, page 709)

Demonstrate

- Have students turn to page 709 of the *Student Text* and review the experiments described in the first part of the lesson.
- Remind students to look for predictable patterns in the relationship between two variables when we perform these experiments. In Mr. Raster's class, we saw a predictable pattern in the relationship between the height the ball was dropped and the height of the bounce after it hit the floor.
- Point out that all the data were collected before an analysis was made about the pattern of the relationship.

Check for Understanding

Engagement Strategy: Think, Think

Ask students the following questions about collecting data and finding functions in a data set. Tell students that you will call on one of them to answer a question after you ask it. Tell them to listen for their names. After each question, allow students time to think. Then call on a student for an answer.

Ask:

In Mr. Raster's class, what were the two variables that the students collected data on? (*drop height and bounce height*)

How can graphs help us understand data involving functions? (*We can see the relationship between a change in one variable and a change in the other variable.*)

Lesson 4

How do we collect our own data to analyze functions?

Classroom experiments involving functions work when we can see the relationship between a change in one variable and a change in the other variable.

In Mr. Raster's class, taking the ball to different heights was one variable. How far the ball bounced back was the other variable. At each step, his class collected data on how high the ball was before it was dropped and then measured, as carefully as they could, how high it bounced back up.

All of this information was added to a table before drawing a graph.

Rubber Ball	
Drop Height	**Bounce Height**
24	19
30	24
36	29
40	32
50	40
60	48
70	56
80	64
90	72
100	80

Apply Skills
Turn to ***Interactive Text***, page 349.

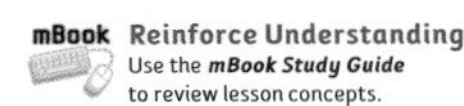

Reinforce Understanding
Use the ***mBook Study Guide*** to review lesson concepts.

Unit 9 • Lesson 709

Lesson 4

Apply Skills

(*Interactive Text*, pages 349–350)

Have students turn to pages 349–350 in the *Interactive Text*, and complete the activities.

Activity 1

Students write a scale and create a dot graph from data in a table. Then they write a statement about the relationship between the data.

Activity 2

Brainstorm ideas with students for an experiment that is some variation of the example given involving Mr. Raster's class. Keep the experiment relatively simple and guide students towards selecting an event where one variable depends on another, with predictable outcomes.

Monitor students' work as they complete the activities.

Watch for:

- Can students choose an appropriate scale for the graph?
- Can students create a dot graph that represents the problem?
- Can students write a statement about the relationship that is evident from the data?
- Can students collect the appropriate data for analyzing the relationship between the two variables?
- Can students determine the function by identifying the predictable relationship between the two variables?

Reinforce Understanding
Remind students that they can review lesson concepts by accessing the online *mBook Study Guide*.

Name ____________ Date ____________

Apply Skills
Analyzing Functional Relationships in a Set of Data

Activity 1

Create a dot graph of the data. These data were collected from crash tests.

Speed of Car at Time of Crash	How Much the Car Length Changed as a Result of the Crash
20 mph	1 inch
40 mph	2 inches
60 mph	3 inches
80 mph	4 inches
100 mph	5 inches

The two parts of the functional relationship are:

Speed of Car ↔ Change in Car Length

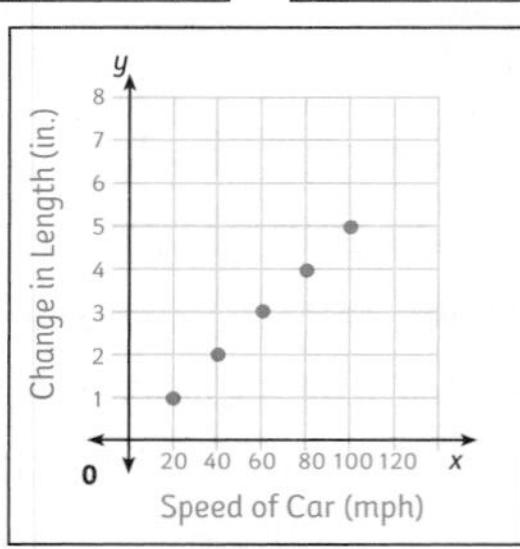

What is the relationship evident in this data?

The speed of the car at the time of the crash is 20 times the amount of inches the car shortened.

Name ____________ Date ____________

Activity 2

Analyze the data you collected in class that shows systematic relationship between two variables. Make a chart that shows the relationship between the functions. Then plot the functions on the blank graph. Remember to label all parts of the graph.

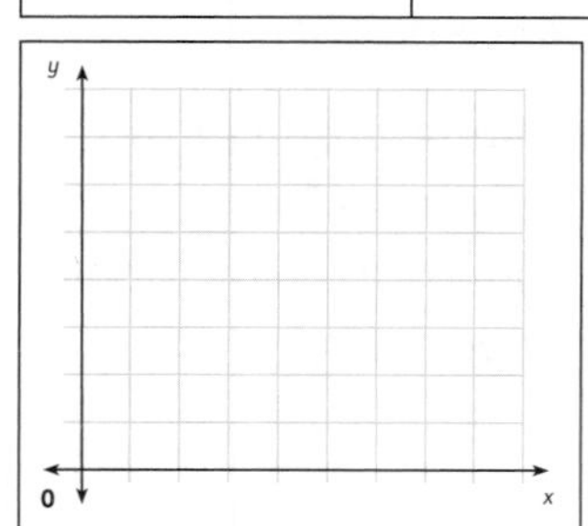

Answers will vary.

Reinforce Understanding
Use the mBook *Study Guide* to review lesson concepts.

Homework

Go over the instructions on pages 710–711 of the *Student Text* for each part of the homework.

Activity 1

Students select the functional relationship shown in tables of data by choosing from a multiple choice list.

Activity 2

Students tell if the functions are systematic relationships by answering yes or no.

Homework

Activity 1

Select the statement that best describes the functional relationships shown in the tables. Write a, b, or c on your paper.

1.

Input	Output
2	4
5	10
10	20
25	50

(a) times 2 a
(b) plus 2
(c) plus 25

2.

Input	Output
12	4
9	3
24	8
3	1

(a) minus 8 b
(b) divided by 3
(c) times 3

3.

Input	Output
27	22
17	12
7	2
37	32

(a) minus 7 c
(b) divided by 3
(c) plus −5

Activity 2

Tell if there is a systematic relationship shown by the table of data in each problem. Answer yes or no.

1.

x	y
5	2
7	9
11	15
2	−5

Does this data represent a systematic relationship? No

2.

x	y
1	4
2	8
3	12
4	16

Does this data represent a systematic relationship? Yes

3.

x	y
1	5
2	10
3	15
4	20
5	25

Does this data represent a systematic relationship? Yes

Homework

Go over the instructions on page 711 of the *Student Text* for each part of the homework.

Activity 3

Students tell the new coordinates of the translated and reflected shape.

Activity 4 • Distributed Practice

Students practice integer operations.

Homework

Activity 3

Tell the coordinates of the new shape.

1. Translate the rectangle one unit to the left.

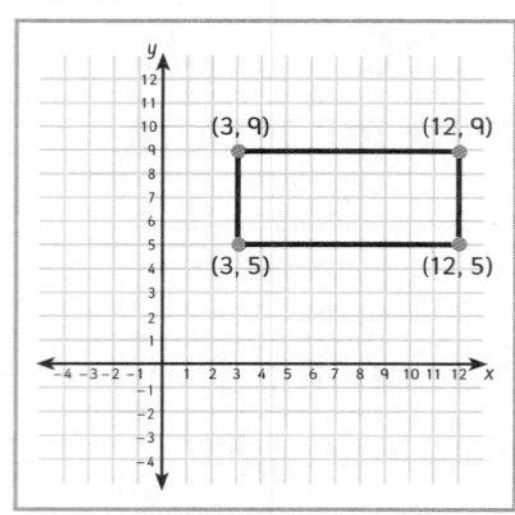

(2, 9), (11, 9), (2, 5), and (11, 5)

2. Reflect the triangle across the y-axis.

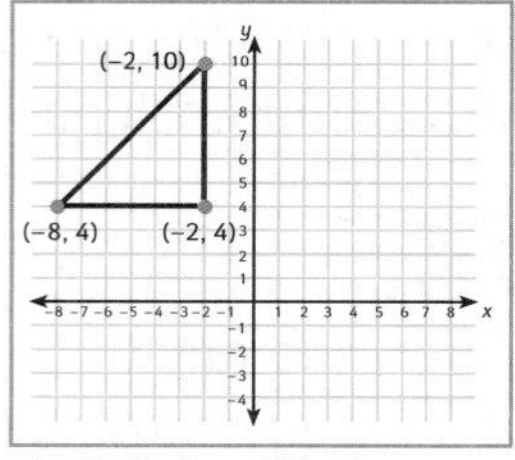

(2, 10), (8, 4), and (2, 4)

Activity 4 • Distributed Practice

Solve.

1. −25 − −15 −10
2. 270 ÷ −30 −9
3. 17 + −25 −8
4. −80 • −3 240
5. 7 − 22 −15
6. −100 ÷ −5 20
7. −125 + −125 −250
8. −70 • −7 490

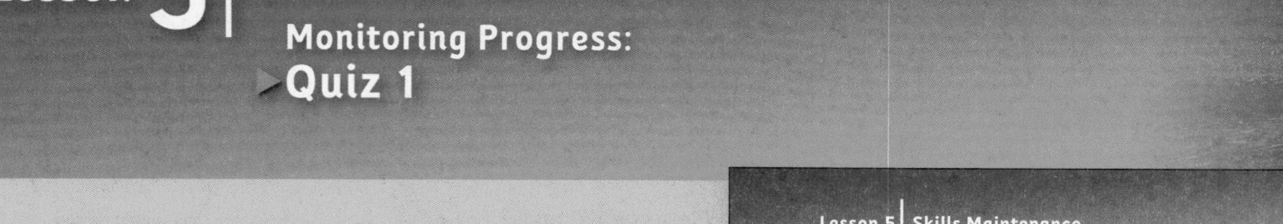

Lesson 5 ▸ The *X*/*Y* Table and Functions

Monitoring Progress: ▸ Quiz 1

Lesson Planner

Vocabulary Development

independent variable
dependent variable

Skills Maintenance

Solving Proportions, Substitution

Building Number Concepts:

▸ The *X*/*Y* Table and Functions

Students learn that one way to represent a function is an x/y table. This is the formal name for the function tables we have been working with where the input is referred to as x and the output is referred to as y. The x/y table helps us write functions in algebraic form based on the relationships between the two variables.

Objectives

Students will examine the data in an x/y table.
Students will write functions based on the relationship between x and y.

Monitoring Progress:

▸ Quiz 1

Distribute the quiz, and remind students that the questions involve material covered over the previous lessons in the unit.

Homework

Students solve proportions, write a function using x and y to describe the values shown in the x/y tables, and answer questions about a dot graph. In Distributed Practice, students solve one- and two- step equations.

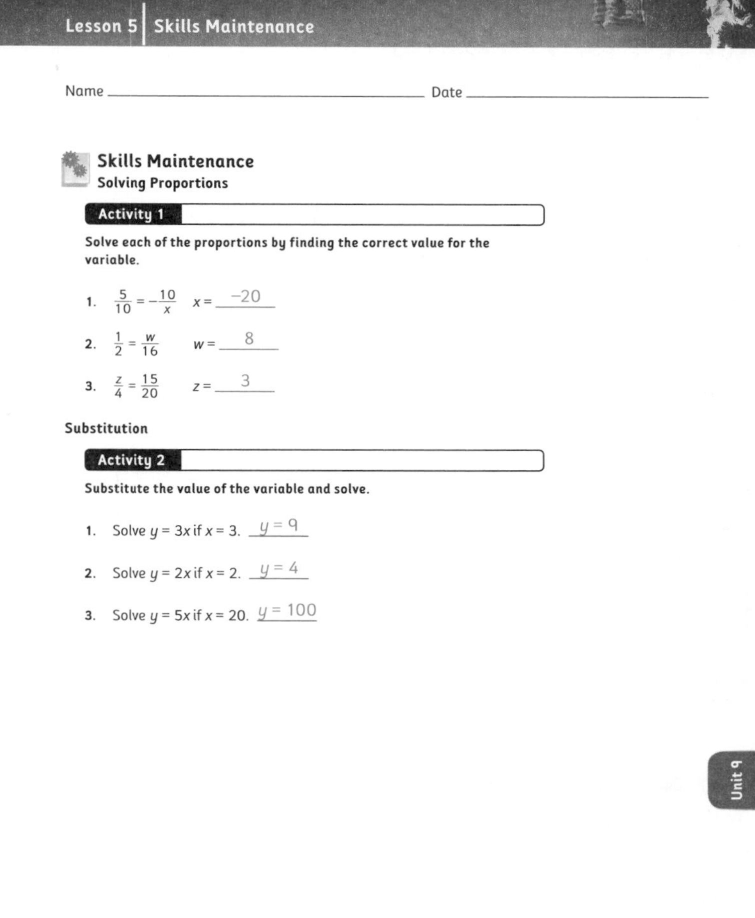

Lesson 5 | Skills Maintenance

Name ____________ Date ____________

Skills Maintenance
Solving Proportions

Activity 1

Solve each of the proportions by finding the correct value for the variable.

1. $\frac{5}{10} = -\frac{10}{x}$ $x =$ −20
2. $\frac{1}{2} = \frac{w}{16}$ $w =$ 8
3. $\frac{z}{4} = \frac{15}{20}$ $z =$ 3

Substitution

Activity 2

Substitute the value of the variable and solve.

1. Solve $y = 3x$ if $x = 3$. $y = 9$
2. Solve $y = 2x$ if $x = 2$. $y = 4$
3. Solve $y = 5x$ if $x = 20$. $y = 100$

Unit 9

Unit 9 • Lesson 5 351

Skills Maintenance

Solving Proportions, Substitution

(*Interactive Text*, page 351)

Activity 1

Students solve the proportions by finding the correct value for each variable.

Activity 2

Students substitute the value for each variable and solve the equations.

Building Number Concepts
▶ The *X/Y* Table and Functions

What is an *X/Y* table?
(*Student Text*, pages 712–713)

Connect to Prior Knowledge
Begin by reminding students of function tables. We call the left column input and the right column output. Ask students to give you input and output for the function $y = \frac{1}{2}x$. Record students' answers on the board or overhead. It should look like this:

Input	Output
2	1
4	2
6	3
10	5
100	50

Lesson 5 ▶The *X/Y* Table and Functions

Monitoring Progress:
▶Quiz 1

▶The *X/Y* Table and Functions

What is an *x/y* table?

We worked with tables and function machines to look at systematic relationships between variables. We described these variables as inputs and outputs.

We will now switch to a more algebraic form and write the variables as *x* and *y*. We will use Tina, who works at Big Tom's Restaurant, as the context. We learned in an earlier lesson that she earns $10 per hour, but the amount of time she works every week varies. The table shows how many hours she worked while she was going to school.

Week	Hours Worked	Amount Paid
1	5	$50
2	15	$150
3	8	$80
4	12	$120
5	10	$100

Vocabulary
independent variable dependent variable

712 Unit 9 • Lesson 5

Link to Today's Concept
Tell students it is important to begin thinking of input as *x* and output as *y*. In today's lesson, we give these tables their formal algebraic name: *x/y* tables.

Demonstrate
Engagement Strategy: Teacher Modeling

Demonstrate how to make an *x/y* table in one of the following ways:

mBook: Use the *mBook Teacher Edition* for *Student Text*, pages 712–713. m

Overhead Projector: Reproduce the tables on a transparency, and modify as discussed.

Board: Reproduce the tables on the board, and modify as discussed.

- Remind students about the function table we created for Tina, who worked at a restaurant. Go over the table with students and be sure they see what input is, what output is, and what the predictable relationship is between the two. From looking at the table we can see that the amount Tina is paid depends on the amount of hours she works. m

Demonstrate

- Continue discussing input and output tables.
- Go over **Example 1**, where we transition the data from the function table to the more formal *x/y* table.
- Tell students that an input and output table is formally called an *x/y* table in algebra. Point out that they look very much the same, but the *x/y* table specifically associates the data with one variable or the other. **m**
- Also point out that the equation $y = 10x$ is the formal way in algebra of describing the relationship between the hours Tina worked and amount she gets paid. In the past, we used words to describe the function: Multiply the input by 10 to get the output. Point out that the format is represented in the function. **m**

We can take the data from the table and put it in an *x/y* table. If that is all we did, it wouldn't be that much of a change. However, we describe all the data in the table using a simple equation. What is so important about functions is they let us summarize the systematic relationship between the two variables, usually represented by *x* and *y*, with an equation.

Example 1

Make an *x/y* table and a function from these data.

We will use the same data but just change the headings. Let x = the number of hours worked and y = the amount paid.

Hours Worked	Amount Paid
5	$50
15	$150
8	$80
12	$120
10	$100

x	*y*
5	50
15	150
8	80
12	120
10	100

The variable *x* represents the input data and *y* represents the output data. We said that Tina gets paid $10 per hour. We describe the relationship between the hours worked and the amount she gets paid this way:

$y = 10x$

What is the value of using an equation?

(*Student Text*, pages 714–715)

Explain

Turn to *Student Text*, page 714 and read the material. Refer to the function $y = 10x$. Explain that y depends on what we substitute for x. This is why y is the **dependent variable** and x is the **independent variable**.

Point out that there are three things to notice in the equation we created from the x/y table.

First explain that there are two different variables in these equations: x is the unknown, y is the answer appearing on the left. Tell students that this is the standard for writing functions in algebra. Second, explain that one variable depends on the other variable. That is, our output depends on what number we input; what we get for y depends on what value we have for x.

Third, point out that an important part of functions is that we get a predictable value of y for every value of x we substitute in the equation. Explain that the x/y values have a proportional relationship.

Demonstrate

- Walk through the explanation of the proportional relationship between x and y. Remind students that proportional relationships are all about multiplication. If we multiply the input, or the x variable, by the same constant number, we get the output, or the y variable.
- Remind students that we get proportions when we have two ratios that are equal to one another. They are formed by multiplying both of the numbers in a ratio by the same number.

What is the value of using an equation?

The value of using an equation is that it gives us a simple, general statement about a function that works for any data we are interested in.

There are three things to notice in the equation we created from the x/y table.

$$y = 10x$$

- First, we now have two different variables in the equation, x and y. This is different from the equations we studied in the last unit.
- Second, we write the equation starting with y on the left side of the equal sign. One way of talking about this function is to say, "What we get for y depends on what we substitute for x." We say that y depends on x. That is why x is called the **independent variable** and y is called the **dependent variable**.

The importance of functions is that we can substitute any value for x and get a predictable value for y.

- Third, there is a connection between the relationship of x and y and proportions. The variables x and y have a proportional relationship. The proportion is $\frac{x}{y} = \frac{1}{10}$. Let's see how this is true.

The relationship between each set of x/y data is proportional.

$\frac{x}{y}$	$\frac{5}{50}$ ↓	$\frac{8}{80}$ ↓	$\frac{10}{100}$ ↓	$\frac{12}{120}$ ↓	$\frac{15}{150}$ ↓
$\frac{x}{y}$	$\frac{5}{50} = \frac{1}{10}$	$\frac{8}{80} = \frac{1}{10}$	$\frac{10}{100} = \frac{1}{10}$	$\frac{12}{120} = \frac{1}{10}$	$\frac{15}{150} = \frac{1}{10}$

This means that each pair of data is proportional to any other pair of x/y data. The x value is $\frac{1}{10}$ of the y value. We can also say it this way: The value of y is always 10 times the value of x.

That's where we get the function $y = 10x$.

Demonstrate

- Turn to page 715 of the *Student Text*. Go over **Example 1**, which shows another function with a predictable relationship.
- Have students look at the table. Explain how those values in the table lead us to the function $\boldsymbol{y = -3x}$.
- Be sure students see that each of the rows of values in the table come from substituting the x into the function $y = -3x$ and result in y.
- Tell students that you can always check to see if you have the right function by substituting the x/y pairs back into the equation. Walk through the example of substituting 5 in for x and seeing if we get the same answer that is in the y column of the x/y table. Our answer is $\boldsymbol{y = -15}$. This matches the number in the table.
- Tell students that our equation is correct.

Lesson 5

Here is another function that shows a systematic relationship. We write an equation with two variables to show how x relates to y.

Example 1

Find the functional relationship between x and y.

x	y
3	−9
5	−15
−2	6
−4	12
10	−30

We get each y by multiplying x by −3. We write the function for the relationship this way:

$$y = -3x$$

A way to check the equation is to put a value in the x column and see if we get the correct value in the y column.

$$\begin{gathered} 5 \\ \downarrow \\ y = -3x \\ y = -3 \cdot 5 \\ y = -15 \end{gathered}$$

The y value of −15 is associated with 5 in the x column. The equation is correct.

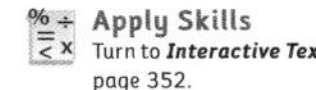

Apply Skills
Turn to ***Interactive Text***, page 352.

Monitoring Progress
Quiz 1

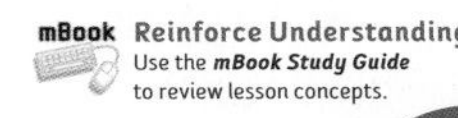

Reinforce Understanding
Use the ***mBook Study Guide*** to review lesson concepts.

Unit 9 • Lesson 715

Apply Skills
(*Interactive Text*, pages 352–353)

Have students turn to *Interactive Text*, pages 352–353, and complete the activity.

Activity 1

Students tell what functional relationship is represented by each *x*/*y* table. Then they check their work by substituting the values into the equation.

Monitor students' work as they complete the activity.

Watch for:

- Can students determine what the functional relationship is?
- Do students check the function by substituting in each *x* value from the table and confirming that the answer is the associated *y* value?

mBook **Reinforce Understanding**
Remind students that they can review lesson concepts by accessing the online *mBook Study Guide*.

Name ______________________ Date ______________

Apply Skills
The *X*/*Y* Table and Functions

Activity 1

Write a function for each problem using the variables *x* and *y* to describe the data in the *x*/*y* tables. Remember to put the *y* on the left. Check your answer by substituting in one of the *x*-values to make sure you get the corresponding *y*-value.

1. What is the function? $y = 8x$

x	*y*
3	24
7	56
10	80
6	48
2	16

Check the answer here:
Answers will vary.
Sample answer: $y = 8 \cdot 7$
$x = 7$, $y = 56$

2. What is the function? $y = 2x$

x	*y*
3	6
4	8
10	20
100	200
2	4

Check the answer here:
Answers will vary.
Sample answer: $y = 2 \cdot 4$
$x = 4$, $y = 8$

Name ______________________ Date ______________

3. What is the function? $y = 3x$

x	*y*
4	12
10	30
30	90
100	300
1	3

Check the answer here:
Answers will vary.
Sample answer: $y = 3 \cdot 10$
$x = 10$, $y = 30$

4. What is the function? $y = 10x$

x	*y*
10	100
2	20
300	3,000
1	10
50	500

Check the answer here:
Answers will vary.
Sample answer: $y = 10 \cdot 60$
$x = 60$, $y = 600$

Unit 9

mBook Reinforce Understanding
Use the **mBook** ***Study Guide*** to review lesson concepts.

Monitoring Progress: ▶ Quiz 1

Assess Quiz 1

- Administer Quiz 1 Form A in the *Assessment Book*, pages 79–80. (If necessary, retest students with Quiz 1 Form B from the *mBook Teacher Edition* following differentiation.)

Students	Assess	Differentiate
	Day 1	Day 2
All	Quiz 1 *Form A*	
Scored 80% or above		Extension
Scored Below 80%		Reinforcement

Differentiate

- Review Quiz 1 Form A with class.
- Identify students for Extension or Reinforcement.

Extension

For those students who score 80 percent or better, provide the On Track! Activities from Unit 9, Lessons 1–5, from the *mBook Teacher Edition.*

Reinforcement

For those students who score below 80 percent, provide additional support in one of the following ways:

- Have students access the online tutorial provided in the *mBook Study Guide.*
- Have students complete the Interactive Reinforcement Exercises for Unit 9, Lessons 1–4, in the *mBook Study Guide.*
- Provide teacher-directed reteaching of unit concepts.

Unit 9 | Quiz 1 • Form A

Name ______________________ Date ______________

Form A

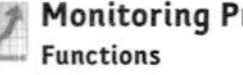

Monitoring Progress
Functions

Part 1

Fill in the function tables.

1.

x	y
1	6
5	30
3	18
4	24
10	60

2.

x	y
1	10
9	90
2	20
5	50
7	70

Part 2

Plot each of the points from the input/output table to make a dot graph representing the function.

1. The people putting on the concert are giving away T-shirts to the fans. There is one T-shirt for every five fans at the concert.

T-shirts	Fans
1	5
2	10
3	15
4	20

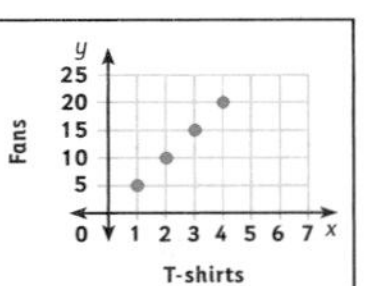

Unit 9 • Quiz 1 • Form A 79

Unit 9 | Quiz 1 • Form A

Monitoring Progress
Coordinate Graphs

Part 3

Draw a shape on the coordinate graph based on the instructions. Be sure to label the coordinates for each vertex of the shape.

1. Draw a rectangle onto the coordinate graph. Use only Quadrants III and IV.

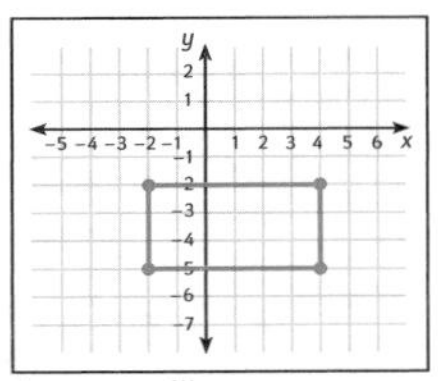

2. Draw a triangle onto the coordinate graph. Use only Quadrants II and III.

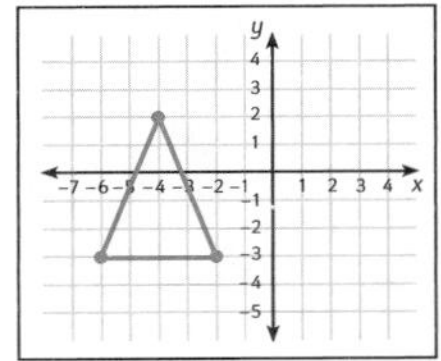

Answers will vary.

Part 4

Use the table to reflect the triangle from Quadrant II to Quadrant I. Fill in the coordinates in the table, then draw the reflected triangle.

Start		End	
Vertices	Coordinates	Vertices	Coordinates
A	(−4, 4)	A'	(4, 4)
B	(−6, 1)	B'	(6, 1)
C	(−2, 1)	C'	(2, 1)

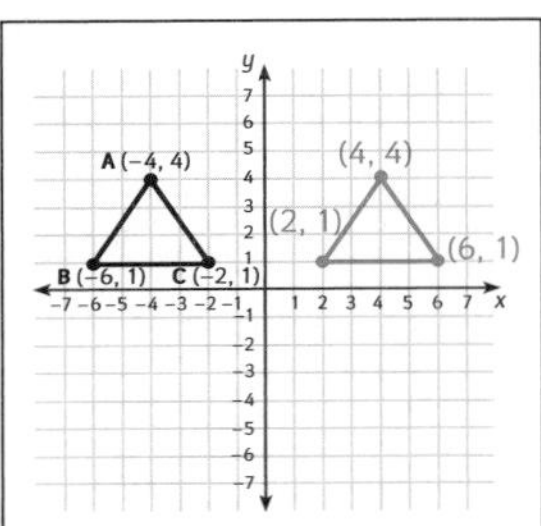

80 Unit 9 • Quiz 1 • Form A

Name ______________________ Date ______________________

Form B
mBook

Monitoring Progress
Functions

Part 1

Fill in the function tables.

1.

x	y
1	4
7	28
4	16
5	20
9	36

2.

x	y
1	5
9	45
2	10
5	25
7	35

Part 2

Plot each of the points from the input/output table to make a dot graph representing the function.

1. The people putting on the concert are giving away T-shirts to the fans. There is one T-shirt for every three fans at the concert.

T-shirts	Fans
1	3
2	6
3	9
4	12

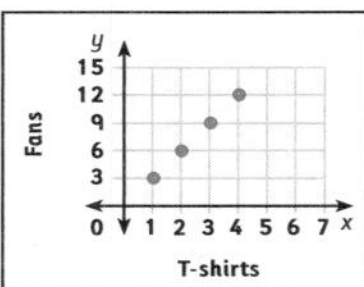

Name ______________________ Date ______________________

Monitoring Progress
Coordinate Graphs

Part 3

Draw a shape on the coordinate graph based on the instructions. Be sure to label the coordinates for each vertex of the shape.

1. Draw a rectangle onto the coordinate graph. Use only Quadrants II and III.

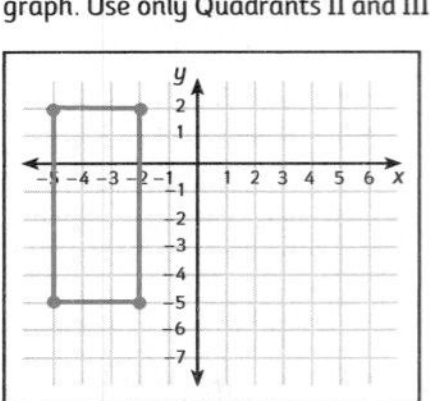

Answers will vary.

2. Draw a triangle onto the coordinate graph. Use only Quadrants III and IV.

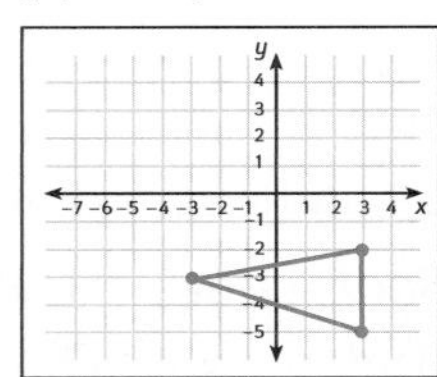

Part 4

Use the table to reflect the triangle from Quadrant II to Quadrant I. Fill in the coordinates in the table, then draw the reflected triangle.

Start		End	
Vertices	Coordinates	Vertices	Coordinates
A	(−3, 3)	A'	(3, 3)
B	(−4, 1)	B'	(4, 1)
C	(−2, 1)	C'	(2, 1)

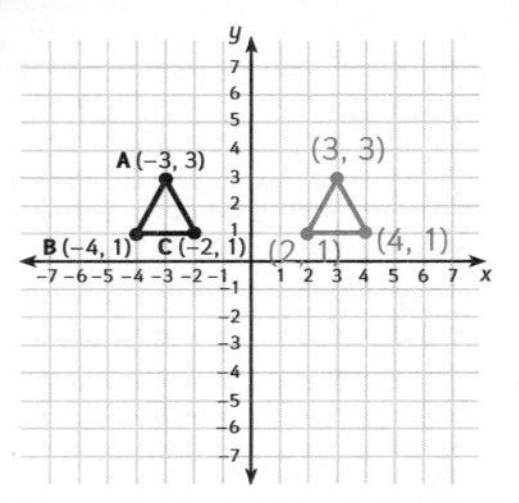

Homework

Go over the instructions on pages 716–717 of the *Student Text* for each part of the homework.

Activity 1

Students solve proportions by finding the value of each variable.

Activity 2

Students write a function using the variables x and y to describe the values shown in the x/y tables.

Activity 3

Students look at a dot graph and answer questions about the functional relationship it represents.

Lesson 5

Homework

Activity 1

Solve the proportions by finding the value of the variable.

1. $\frac{y}{3} = \frac{6}{9}$ 2
2. $\frac{2}{5} = \frac{z}{20}$ 8
3. $\frac{3}{8} = \frac{27}{w}$ 72
4. $\frac{4}{n} = \frac{24}{54}$ 9

Activity 2

Use the x/y tables to write an equation.

1. What is this function?

x	y
2	4
5	10
10	20
25	50

$y = 2x$

2. What is this function?

x	y
1	5
2	10
3	15
10	50

$y = 5x$

3. What is this function?

x	y
4	36
7	63
3	27
8	72

$y = 9x$

Activity 3

The dot graph shows the functional relationship between how much Tina gets paid and how much she works. Answer the questions using the graph.

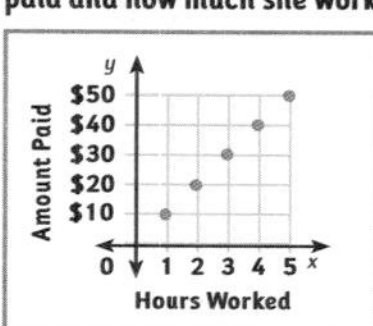

1. How much does Tina get paid for working 5 hours? $50
2. How many hours does Tina work if she gets paid $40? 4 hours
3. How much does Tina get paid per hour? $10
4. If Tina worked 8 hours, how much would she get paid? $80

716 Unit 9 • Lesson 5

Homework

Go over the instructions on page 717 of the *Student Text* for the homework.

Activity 4 • Distributed Practice

Students solve for the variable solve one- and two-step equations.

Homework

Activity 4 • Distributed Practice

Solve.

1. $3x + 2 = 14$ $x = 4$
2. $-5z = 15$ $z = -3$
3. $-27 = 3y$ $y = -9$
4. $a + 16 = 17$ $a = 1$
5. $15 = b - 2$ $b = 17$
6. $3c = -24$ $c = -8$
7. $5d + 10 = 25$ $d = 3$
8. $-6e - 18 = -24$ $e = 1$

Lesson 6 ▶Writing Functions for Everyday Situations

Problem Solving: Graphing Linear Functions

Lesson Planner

Vocabulary Development

linear function

Skills Maintenance

Writing Functions

Building Number Concepts:

▶ Writing Functions for Everyday Situations

Students learn that there are many functional relationships in our lives. We can solve-real world problems by writing these functions algebraically. We continue to look at different ways to represent functions.

Objective

Students will write functions algebraically.

Problem Solving:

▶ Graphing Linear Functions

So far we have four ways to represent functions. They are: (1) in words, (2) as an equation, (3) in an x/y table, and (4) as a graph. We look at linear functions on a graph and learn that we can make predictions with functions.

Objective

Students will graph functions on coordinate graphs.

Homework

Students create x/y tables, write functions for x/y tables, and graph linear functions. In Distributed Practice, students evaluate numeric expressions.

Lesson 6 | Skills Maintenance

Name __________ Date __________

Skills Maintenance
Writing Functions

Activity 1

Write the function for each x/y table. Be sure to use the correct form with y on the left. Check your work by substituting in the values of x and making sure you get the correct value for y.

1. What is the function? $y = 2x$

x	y
2	4
3	6
4	8
5	10

Check your work here:

$y = 3 \cdot 4$

$x = 4, y = 12$

2. What is the function? $y = 6x$

x	y
1	6
2	12
3	18
4	24

Check your work here:

$y = 6 \cdot 3$

$x = 3, y = 18$

354 Unit 9 • Lesson 6

Skills Maintenance

Writing Functions

(*Interactive Text*, page 354)

Activity 1

Students tell the function represented by each x/y table. Remind them to use the correct form with y on the left. Have them check their answers using substitution.

Building Number Concepts: ▶ Writing Functions for Everyday Situations

How do we write a function about an everyday situation?
(*Student Text*, pages 718–719)

Connect to Prior Knowledge
Begin by putting the function $y = 2x$ on the board or overhead. Ask students to think about everyday situations where they might encounter this function. If they struggle, tell them it means one variable is double the other variable. Here are some sample answers:

- *You wear a pair of shoes on your feet. One pair = two shoes.*
- *You wear a pair of contacts to help you see better. One pair = two contact lenses.*
- *You get two points for every field goal in basketball. One basket = two points.*

Link to Today's Concept
Tell students that in today's lesson, we look at everyday functions and practice writing them algebraically.

Demonstrate
Engagement Strategy: Teacher Modeling
Demonstrate how to write a function algebraically in one of the following ways:

mBook: Use the *mBook Teacher Edition* for *Student Text*, pages 718–719. m

Overhead Projector: Reproduce the steps on a transparency, and modify as discussed.

Board: Copy the steps on the board, and modify as discussed.

Lesson 6 ▶Writing Functions for Everyday Situations
Problem Solving: Graphing Linear Functions

▶Writing Functions for Everyday Situations

How do we write a function about an everyday situation?

Functions are everywhere around us. They describe a systematic relationship between two things, or variables. Let's see how to make a function from an everyday situation.

Situation:
Sunshine Bakery makes a lot of muffins every day. They send the muffins to stores and supermarkets around the city. They cook muffins on large trays. One tray makes 40 muffins at a time.

Steps for Writing Functions for Everyday Situations

STEP 1
Turn the situation into a function.
Based on the information, we know that 1 tray will make 40 muffins. That means 2 trays will make 80 muffins and 3 trays will make 120 muffins.

There is a relationship between the number of trays and the number of muffins.

We create an x/y table this way:

x = the number of trays
y = the total amount of muffins

x	y
1	40
2	80
3	120
4	160

718 Unit 9 • Lesson 6

- Explain that functions are around us everywhere. Read the situation about a function from the Sunshine Bakery. m

STEP 1

- Direct students to turn the situation into a function. m
- Explain that the functional relationship we are focusing on in this example is the number of muffins on a tray. Explain that we put the values in an x/y table, where x is the number of trays, and y is the total amount of muffins. m
- Discuss each of the values in the table. m

Demonstrate

- Continue demonstrating how to write the function algebraically.

STEP 2

- Describe the function. Make sure students see how the values in the table help us see the systematic relationship, which is a proportional relationship.
- Explain to students that our understanding of the relationship leads us to the function written in algebraic form: $\boldsymbol{y = 40x}$. Be sure they understand that y represents the total number of muffins and x represents the number of trays. m
- Then guide students as they substitute the value of **10** in the equation to check if the function works. Make sure students understand we can check the equation with any number, but we are using 10 in this instance. m
- Tell students it is important to remember what the variables stand for when writing functions for everyday situations and solving problems using the functions.
- Explain that the difference between this lesson and previous lessons is that we are now demonstrating how to use formal representations to describe everyday functions.

Speaking of Math

- Read the information to help students explain their thinking when writing an equation to represent a function. Tell students that this can serve as a helpful checklist when writing functions.

STEP 2

Write the equation for the function.

We multiply 40 times the number of trays to get the total amount of muffins. If we have 3 trays, then we have $40 \cdot 3 = 120$ muffins. We use variables to make this equation:

$$y = 40x$$

Now we can check to see if the equation makes sense. Let's try a value for x and see if it works. Let's use 10 trays of muffins.

$$10$$
$$\downarrow$$
$$y = 40x$$
$$y = 40 \cdot 10$$
$$y = 400$$

Sunshine Bakery can make 400 muffins using 10 trays.

Speaking of Math

Here's how you can explain your thinking when you are writing an equation to represent a function.

- *First, I look for a relationship in the information.*
- *Next, I create a table so I can see the relationship.*
- *Then, I write an equation to represent the function. I start writing on the left side of the equal sign. The equation involves two variables that have a proportional relationship.*

It is important to know how to explain your thinking about functions.

Apply Skills Turn to ***Interactive Text***, page 355.

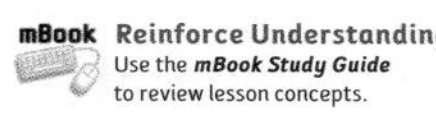
Reinforce Understanding Use the ***mBook Study Guide*** to review lesson concepts.

Check for Understanding
Engagement Strategy: Look About

Present the following situation to students: **Katie charges $8 per hour to babysit.** Tell students that they will write a function about how many hours worked and how much Katie gets paid with the help of the whole class. Students should write their function in large writing on a piece of paper or a dry erase board ($y = 8x$). When students finish their work, they should hold up their answer for everyone to see.

If students are not sure about the answer, prompt them to look about at other students' solutions to help with their thinking. Review the answers after all students have held up their solutions.

Apply Skills
(*Interactive Text*, page 355)

Have students turn to page 355 in the *Interactive Text*, which provides students an opportunity to practice writing functions as equations.

Activity 1

Students write everyday situations as functions. Then they use the function they have written to answer additional questions about the everyday situation. Monitor students' work as they complete the activity.

Watch for:

- Can students write the function correctly?
- Can students answer the questions using the function they wrote?
- Do students check their work using substitution?

Reinforce Understanding
Remind students that they can review lesson concepts by accessing the online *mBook Study Guide*.

Name ______________________ Date ______________________

Apply Skills
Writing Functions for Everyday Situations

Activity 1

Write a function for each everyday situation. Then use the function to answer the questions about the situation.

1. Micah works at a bakery. His specialty is donuts. He bakes 12 donuts on a tray. Write a function that describes the relationship between the number of donuts and the number of trays. $y = 12x$

   Questions

   (a) If Micah makes five trays of donuts, how many donuts has he baked?
   60; $y = 12 \cdot 5$

   (b) How many trays would Micah need to make to get 100 donuts? 9

2. Elijah rides his bike in the evenings to prepare for a bike race. It takes him an hour to ride five miles. Write a function that describes the relationship between the number of miles and the number of hours. $y = 5x$

   Questions

   (a) How far can Elijah ride in two hours?
   10 miles; $y = 5 \cdot 2$

   (b) How many miles would Elijah travel if he rode his bike for four hours?
   20 miles; $y = 5 \cdot 4$

3. Katarina gets paid $10 per hour for math tutoring. Write a function that describes how much she gets paid and how many hours she works. $y = 10x$

   Questions

   (a) If Katarina earned $50 in a day, how many hours of tutoring did she do?
   5 hours; $y = 10 \cdot 5$

   (b) How much does Katarina earn if she tutors for three hours?
   $30; $y = 10 \cdot 3$

4. Raj makes a pitcher of iced tea each morning. He gets four 8-ounce glasses of tea from the pitcher. Write a function that describes the relationship between the number of pitchers and the number of glasses of tea. $y = 4x$

   Questions

   (a) If Raj makes three pitchers of tea, how many 8-oz glasses of tea is that?
   12 glasses; $y = 4 \cdot 3$

   (b) If Raj drank six glasses of tea one day, how many pitchers did he need to make that day?
   2 pitchers; $y = 4 \cdot 2$

Unit 9

Problem Solving:
▶ Graphing Linear Functions

What does the function look like on a graph?
(*Student Text*, pages 720–721)

Build Vocabulary
Have students turn to the material on page 720 of the *Student Text* and discuss the term **linear function**. Tell students that it means the function has a graph that is a line.

Demonstrate
- Have students look at **Example 1**, which demonstrates the graph for the function ***y* = 40*x***.
- Review how to plot the points, then draw a line through the coordinates.
- Explain that this is the graph for the linear function that represents how many muffins fit on a tray. Forty muffins can fit on one tray.

Discuss
Call students' attention to the Power Concept, and point out that it will be helpful as they complete the activity.

The graph of a linear function is a straight line.

Lesson 6

▶Problem Solving: Graphing Linear Functions

What does the function look like on a graph?

When we show functions like $y = 40x$ on a graph, we use a line instead of a series of dots. This is why we call them **linear functions**—linear refers to the use of lines.

In Example 1, we draw a function on a coordinate graph and do not use labels for the axes. We just have the x- and y-axes.

Vocabulary
linear function

Example 1

Show the linear function $y = 40x$ on a coordinate graph.

We get values for y by substituting different values for x. This lets us make a simple x/y table so that we can draw a line on the graph.

x	y
0	0
1	40
2	80

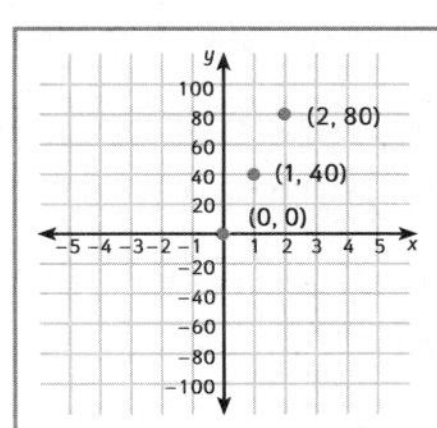

If we draw a line through these coordinates, we get a graph that shows a linear function.

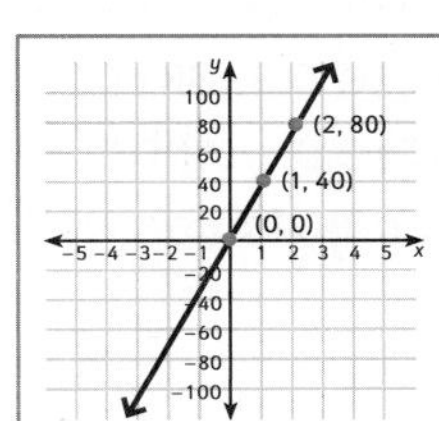

POWER CONCEPT

The graph of a linear function is a straight line.

720 Unit 9 • Lesson 6

What does the function look like on a graph? *(continued)*

Demonstrate

- Turn to *Student Text*, page 721 and go over **Example 2** with students.
- Explain that in this example, we change the function slightly. It is the function we used for the bakery, but we changed it to represent the situation where there are only 25 muffins on a tray.
- Point out the important data we can find on the graph if we look at certain points. Tell students we can make predictions beyond what is shown on the graph as well.

Lesson 6

Example 2 shows what happens when Sunshine Bakery cuts back on the number of muffins for each tray. Rather than putting 40 muffins on each tray, they only put 25 muffins on a tray.

Example 2

Graph a linear function to show the number of muffins made per tray.

The number of muffins per tray is now 25.

Let x = the number of trays and y = the total amount of muffins.

x	y
1	25
2	50
3	75
4	100

Function: $y = 25x$

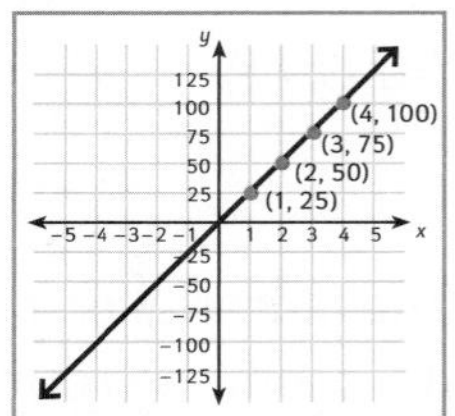

The line in a linear function extends beyond what we can see in the graph on the page. Because of this, we can make predictions about other instances of this function.

Unit 9 • Lesson 721

How do we make predictions with functions?

(*Student Text*, page 722)

Demonstrate

- Turn to page 722 of the *Student Text* and read the material. Show students the graph of the function of the number of muffins per tray at the Sunshine Bakery.
- Demonstrate how to use the line to make a prediction about how many muffins the bakery will make with five trays.
- Explain that we use number sense to make predictions based on the table and the graph. To predict how many muffins the bakery will make with five trays by looking at the graph, we locate the 5 on the x-axis.
- Demonstrate how to move over to the 5 and then up to where the line meets the 5. Explain that we can see that the coordinates for five trays are **(5,125)**
- Explain that based on the coordinates, we can predict that five trays make 125 muffins.

Check for Understanding

Engagement Strategy: Think, Think

Copy the graph onto the board and extend the axes and the line. Label the intervals. Tell students that you will call out a number of trays, and they should use the graph to predict how many muffins the bakery will make, based on where the line meets the number of trays.

Tell students that you will call on them by name for an answer. Pause after you call out each number of trays to allow students time to think of an answer. Then call on a student by name. Go over the answers with the class by demonstrating how to find each coordinate point and make each prediction of number of muffins.

Lesson 6

How do we make predictions with functions?

In the last example, we used the line to predict how many muffins the bakery could make with 5 trays, 10 trays, or even 100 trays. All we need to do is look closely at the table and the graph and use number sense to extend the information we see there.

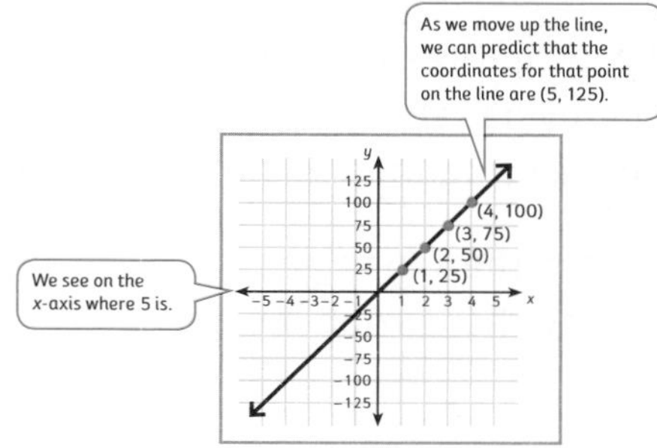

That means the number of muffins for 5 trays will be 125. We can't see 10 or 100 on the graph, but we can make predictions based on what we know about the relationships.

Problem-Solving Activity Turn to *Interactive Text*, page 356.

mBook Reinforce Understanding Use the ***mBook Study Guide*** to review lesson concepts.

722 Unit 9 • Lesson 6

Ask:

How many muffins will 7 trays make? (*175*)

How many muffins will 8 trays make? (*200*)

How many muffins will 11 trays make? (*275*)

Problem-Solving Activity

(*Interactive Text*, pages 356–357)

Have students turn to pages 356–357 in the *Interactive Text*, which provides students an opportunity to write and draw functions.

Students look at the data in the *x*/*y* table. They write the function and then graph it on a coordinate graph.

Monitor students' work as they complete the activity.

Watch for:

- Can students identify the function?
- Can students write the function using the correct form?
- Can students graph the function?

mBook **Reinforce Understanding**

Remind students that they can review lesson concepts by accessing the online *mBook Study Guide*.

Lesson 6 | Problem-Solving Activity

Name ______________________ Date ______________

Problem-Solving Activity

Graphing Linear Functions

You are given a situation and an *x*/*y* table in each problem. Use the data in the tables to write the functions, then draw them on the coordinate graphs.

1. Each quarter gives you time on the parking meter. The more quarters you put into the meter, the more time you get.

   Let x = the number of quarters and y = the total amount you put in the meter.

x	y
1	\$0.25
2	\$0.50
3	\$0.75
4	\$1.00
5	\$1.25

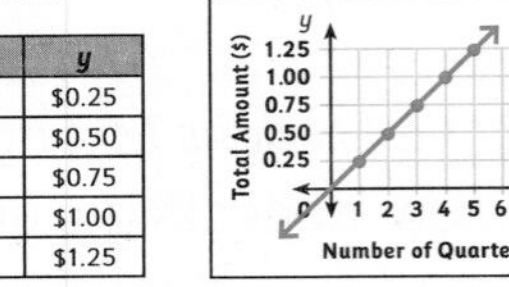

$y = \frac{1}{4}x$ or $y = 0.25x$

2. The price of hamburger in the store is \$4 per pound. Hamburger is sold in different sized packages, and what you pay depends on how much the package weighs.

   Let x = the number of pounds and y = the total cost of the hamburger.

x	y
1	\$4
2	\$8
3	\$12
4	\$16
5	\$20
6	\$24

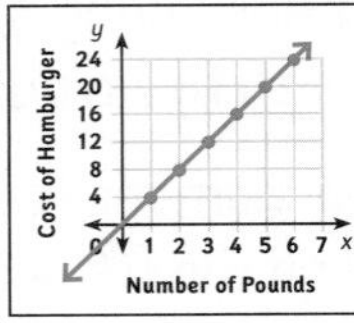

$y = 4x$

356 Unit 9 • Lesson 6

Lesson 6 | Problem-Solving Activity

Name ______________________ Date ______________

3. As gas prices get higher, people buy more small cars. Some small cars get 40 miles per gallon of gasoline. This information helps you plan how far you can drive on the number of gallons of gas in your car.

   Let x = the number of gallons of gas and y = the total miles you can drive.

x	y
5	200
6	240
7	280
8	320

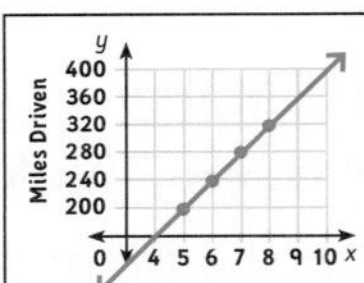

$y = 40x$

Unit 9

mBook **Reinforce Understanding**

Use the **mBook *Study Guide*** to review lesson concepts.

Unit 9 • Lesson 6 357

Homework

Go over the instructions on pages 723–724 of the *Student Text* for each part of the homework.

Activity 1

Students create *x/y* tables from equations of functions.

Activity 2

Students write equations from an *x/y* table of values.

Additional Answers

Activity 1

1.

x	y
−1	−5
0	0
1	5
2	10

2.

x	y
−1	−3
0	0
1	3
2	6

3.

x	y
−1	−20
0	0
1	20
2	40

Homework

Activity 1

Create an x/y table on your paper for each of the functions. Use −1, 0, 1, and 2 for the x values in the table. Then solve for y and fill in the y values.

Model $y = 2x$

Answer: The x/y table looks like this:

x	y
−1	−2
0	0
1	2
2	4

1. $y = 5x$
2. $y = 3x$
3. $y = 20x$

See Additional Answers below.

Activity 2

Write the functions for each of the following x/y tables with an equation. Use x and y and put y on the left of the equal sign.

1.

x	y
−1	−2
0	0
1	2
2	4

$y = 2x$

2.

x	y
2	8
10	40
−2	−8
20	80

$y = 4x$

3.

x	y
27	54
−2	−4
2	4
50	100

$y = 2x$

4.

x	y
40	400
3	30
200	2,000
6	60

$y = 10x$

5.

x	y
3	18
5	30
−7	−42
2	12

$y = 6x$

6.

x	y
16	80
−5	−25
4	20
25	125

$y = 5x$

Homework

Go over the instructions on page 724 of the *Student Text* for each part of the homework.

Activity 3

Students graph linear functions on a separate piece of paper.

Activity 4 • Distributed Practice

Students evaluate numeric expressions using order of operations.

Additional Answers

Activity 3

1.

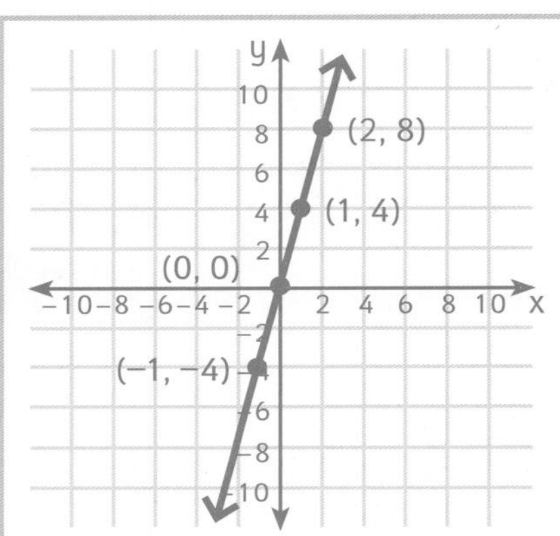

2.

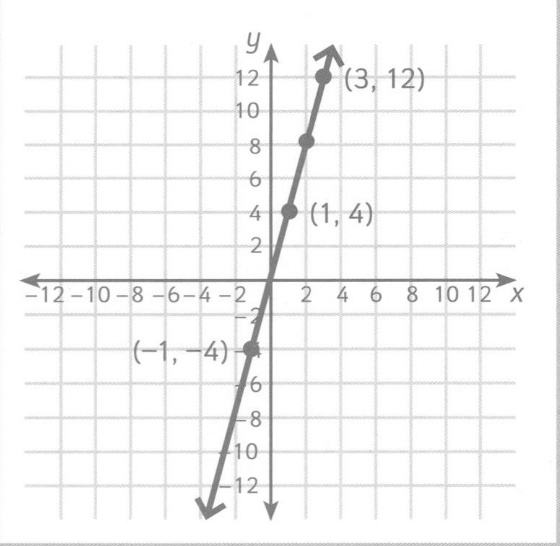

Homework

Activity 3

Look at the functions shown by the equations and tables. Graph each on a sheet of graph paper. Label each point and connect them to show the line.

$y = 2x$

x	y
−1	−2
0	0
1	2
2	4

$y = 4x$

x	y
−1	−4
1	4
3	12
2	8

See Additional Answers below.

Activity 4 • Distributed Practice

Evaluate the numeric expressions using order of operations.

1. $-4 \cdot 8 \cdot -1 + 10$ 42
2. $(3 + 17) \cdot (-4 + -5)$ −180
3. $25 \div 5^2 + 10 - 15$ −4
4. $17 - 25 + 45 - 3^2$ 28
5. $3 \cdot (49 \div -7) + 40$ 19
6. $-6 + -8 - -5 \cdot -8$ −54
7. $(45 \div 3^2) - 5 + 15 - 10$ 5
8. $-7 \cdot 6 \cdot -1 \cdot \frac{1}{6}$ 7

Lesson 7 ▶Slope and Linear Functions

Problem Solving: ▶Drawing Lines

Lesson Planner

Vocabulary Development

slope
run
rise

Skills Maintenance

Drawing Graphs of Functions

Building Number Concepts:

▶ Slope and Linear Functions

We introduce the concept of the slope of a line. We can determine the slope of a line from an equation by looking at the coefficient in front of x. If there is no coefficient, it is assumed to be 1. We can determine the slope of a line from a graph by looking at rise over run.

Objective

Students will determine the slope of a line.

Problem Solving:

▶ Drawing Lines

Students learn to draw a line when given a point and the slope of the function.

Objective

Students will use the slope to draw lines.

Homework

Students tell the slope by looking at the equation of linear functions, tell the slope by looking at graphs of linear functions, and draw lines on graph paper, given a point and the slope. In Distributed Practice, students identify the property represented by general statements.

Lesson 7 | Skills Maintenance

Name ______________________ Date ______________________

Skills Maintenance
Drawing Graphs of Functions

Activity 1

Use the equation and x/y table to graph the function. Fill in the scale on the graph to help plot the points and draw the line.

$y = 3x$ The x/y table is:

x	y
−1	−3
0	0
1	3
2	6
3	9

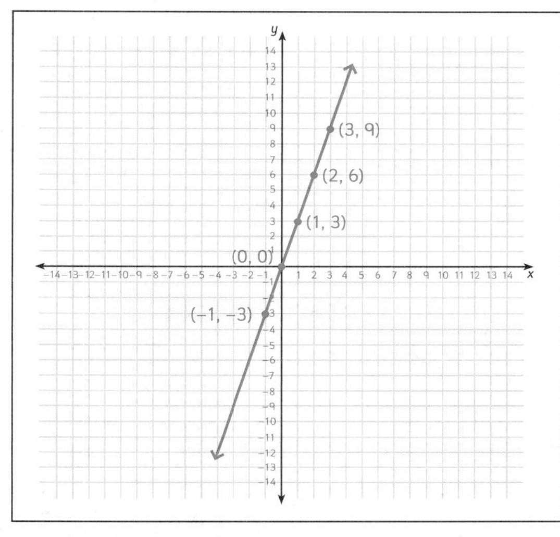

358 Unit 9 • Lesson 7

Skills Maintenance

Drawing Graphs of Functions

(*Interactive Text*, page 358)

Activity 1

Students use an equation and x/y table to graph the function.

Building Number Concepts: ▶ Slope and Linear Functions

What is slope?

(*Student Text*, page 725)

Connect to Prior Knowledge

Begin by sketching linear graphs on the board or overhead with different slopes. Tell students that they are all linear functions, but they look different. Ask students to describe how they are different from one another. Guide students to a discussion about the steepness of the lines.

Link to Today's Concept

Tell students that in today's lesson, we discuss the steepness of lines and formally introduce the concept of **slope**.

Demonstrate

Engagement Strategy: Teacher Modeling

Demonstrate how to recognize the slope of a line in one of the following ways:

mBook: Use the *mBook Teacher Edition* for *Student Text*, page 725. m

Overhead Projector: Reproduce the table on Transparency 17, and modify as discussed.

Board: Copy the table and graph on the board, and modify as discussed.

- Show the first x/y table. Be sure students see that the systematic relationship in the x/y table can be represented as the function $\boldsymbol{y = 4x}$. m
- Tell students that an important feature of linear functions is the slope. The slope is the steepness of the line.
- Have students look at the function $\boldsymbol{y = 4x}$ on a graph. m

Lesson 7 | ▶Slope and Linear Functions

Problem Solving: Drawing Lines

▶Slope and Linear Functions

Vocabulary
slope run rise

What is slope?

In the last lesson, we wrote functions based on x/y tables. Look at the function below. The relationship between x and y is the linear function $y = 4x$. That means we multiply the value of x times 4 to get the value of y.

x	y
1	4
2	8
3	12
4	16
5	20

What is the linear function?

$y = 4x$

Let's look at this function on a coordinate graph. It's important to notice the slant of the line. We use the word **slope** to describe the steepness or slant of a function. When we look at the equation for a linear function, the slope is the coefficient in front of the variable x. In this case, the slope is 4.

A Function With a Slope of 4

x	y
1	4
2	8
3	12
4	16
5	20

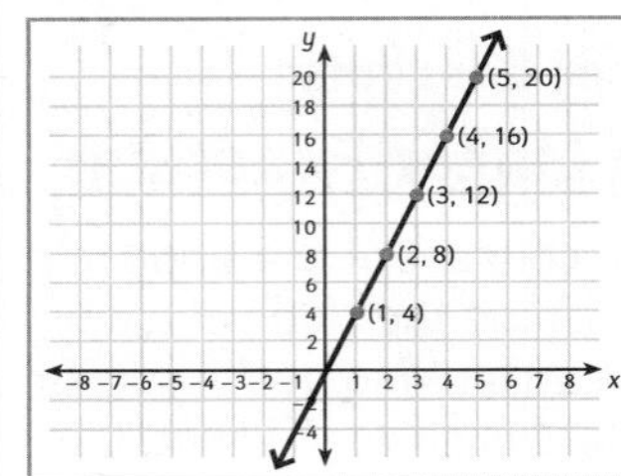

What is the slope for this line?

It is 4.

Unit 9 • Lesson 7 725

- Ask students what feature of the line on the graph represents the slope. Listen for a discussion about the slant of the line. Point out that the coefficient in front of x in the equation (in this function, it is 4) is the slope of the line. m

How do we determine the slope of a linear function?

(*Student Text*, pages 726–727)

Explain

Go to page 726 of the *Student Text* and tell students we can tell the slope of a linear function just by looking at a graph.

Demonstrate

- Have students look at the coordinate graph in **Example 1**.
- Make sure students can see that **run** is horizontal and **rise** is vertical. Explain that a good way to understand slope is by looking at the graph of a function and using a method called rise over run.
- Refer to the graph of the linear function $y = 4x$ and show how the line has a **rise of 4** and a **run of 1**. Show how the slope is written as rise/run. This is the slope.

Discuss

Call students' attention to the Power Concept, and point out that it will be helpful as they complete the activities.

The slope tells us how steep or slanted the graph of a function is.

How do we determine the slope of a linear function?

We can also determine the slope of a linear function just by looking at the line on a graph.

Example 1 shows part of the graph we just made. This section shows how we describe horizontal movement on the graph as the **run** and vertical movement as the **rise**. We use the formula "rise over run" to calculate the slope.

Example 1

Show the formula rise over run.

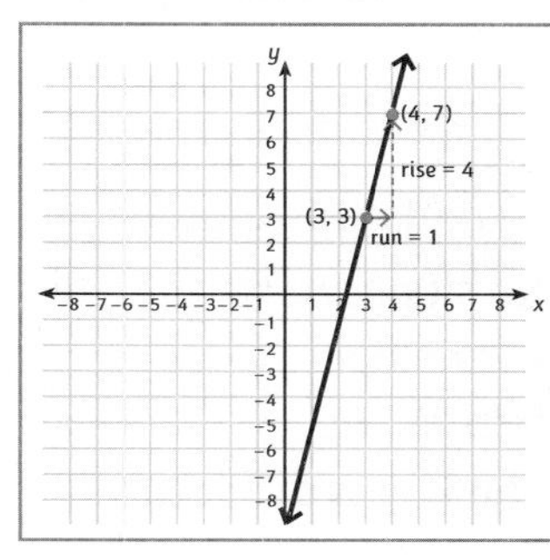

Slope = $\frac{\text{rise}}{\text{sun}} = \frac{4}{1} = 4$

The slope tells us how steep or slanted the graph of a function is.

How do we determine the slope of a linear function? *(continued)*

Demonstrate

- Turn to **Example 2** on page 727 of the *Student Text* where we examine a function with a fractional slope.
- Point out the rise and the run on this graph.
- Ask students if they notice any differences in functions with fractional slopes versus functions with whole number slopes. Students should recognize that the steepness of the slant of the line is different.
- Note we will discuss this more formally in the next lesson, but point out that the line with the slope of 4 is steeper than the line with the slope of $\frac{2}{3}$.

Check for Understanding
Engagement Strategy: Pair/Share

Divide students into pairs. Write the following linear functions on the board:

$$y = 3x$$

$$y = \frac{1}{3}x$$

Assign each partner one of the linear functions. Have each partner create an *x*/*y* table of values, then plot two points on a graph and draw the line through the coordinates on a piece of grid paper. Then have partners exchange papers and identify the slope of the line using the rise/run method. Have partners check the slope by looking at the equation. Invite pairs to present their answers.

Reinforce Understanding

If students need further practice plotting functions on a coordinate graph, use these linear functions:

$$y = 5x$$

$$y = \frac{1}{5}x$$

Slope doesn't always have to be a whole number. It can also be a fraction. Example 2 shows representations for a function that has a fraction as its slope. Notice in the *x*/*y* table that we multiply each *x* value by $\frac{2}{3}$ to get the *y* value. On the graph the rise is 2 and the run is 3.

Example 2

Find the slope of the line.

Here is the *x*/*y* table:

x	*y*
3	2
6	4
9	6
12	8
15	10

Here is the graph of the linear function $y = \frac{2}{3}x$:

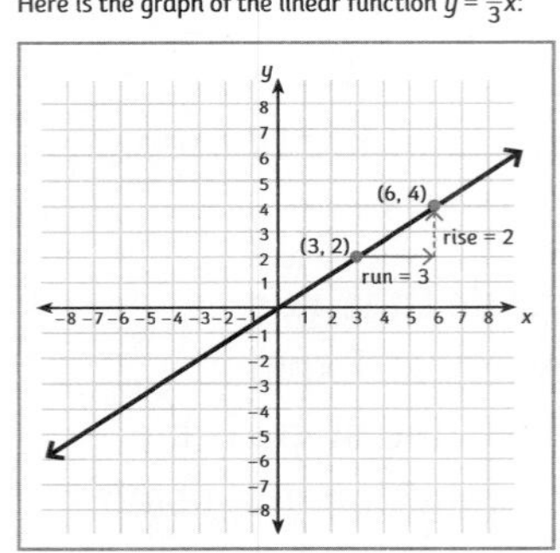

Slope = $\frac{\text{rise}}{\text{run}} = \frac{2}{3}$

The slope of this function is $\frac{2}{3}$.

Apply Skills
Turn to *Interactive Text*, page 359.

mBook Reinforce Understanding
Use the *mBook Study Guide* to review lesson concepts.

Apply Skills

(*Interactive Text*, pages 359–360)

Have students turn to pages 359–360 in the *Interactive Text*, which provides students an opportunity to identify slopes in functions.

Activity 1

Students tell the slope of a line just by looking at the equation of the function.

Activity 2

Students determine the slope of functions from graphs of lines. Remind students to examine the rise and the run. Students also write the function. If you feel this step is too complex for your students, you might omit this step of the process.

Monitor students' work as they complete the activities.

Watch for:

- Can students identify the slope from the equation?
- Can students identify the slope using rise over run on a graph?
- Can students write the equation from the graph using the slope?
- Can students identify the function with a slope of 1 as the equation $y = x$?

Be sure to discuss the functions and their slopes when students are done with Activity 2. Give special attention to the function $y = x$, which has a slope of 1. Remind students of invisible or implied coefficients.

Reinforce Understanding

Remind students that they can review lesson concepts by accessing the online *mBook Study Guide.*

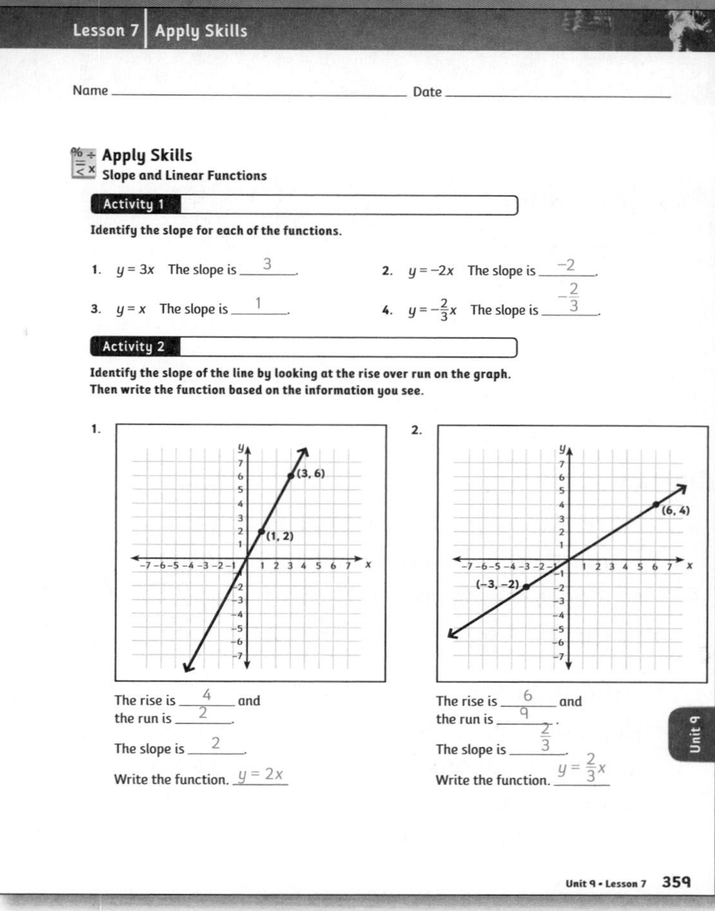

Lesson 7 | Apply Skills

Name ______ Date ______

Apply Skills
Slope and Linear Functions

Activity 1

Identify the slope for each of the functions.

1. $y = 3x$ The slope is 3.
2. $y = -2x$ The slope is -2.
3. $y = x$ The slope is 1.
4. $y = -\frac{2}{3}x$ The slope is $-\frac{2}{3}$.

Activity 2

Identify the slope of the line by looking at the rise over run on the graph. Then write the function based on the information you see.

1. (3, 6) (1, 2)

The rise is 4 and the run is 2.

The slope is 2.

Write the function. $y = 2x$

2. (6, 4) (−3, −2)

The rise is 6 and the run is 9.

The slope is $\frac{2}{3}$.

Write the function. $y = \frac{2}{3}x$

Unit 9 • Lesson 7 359

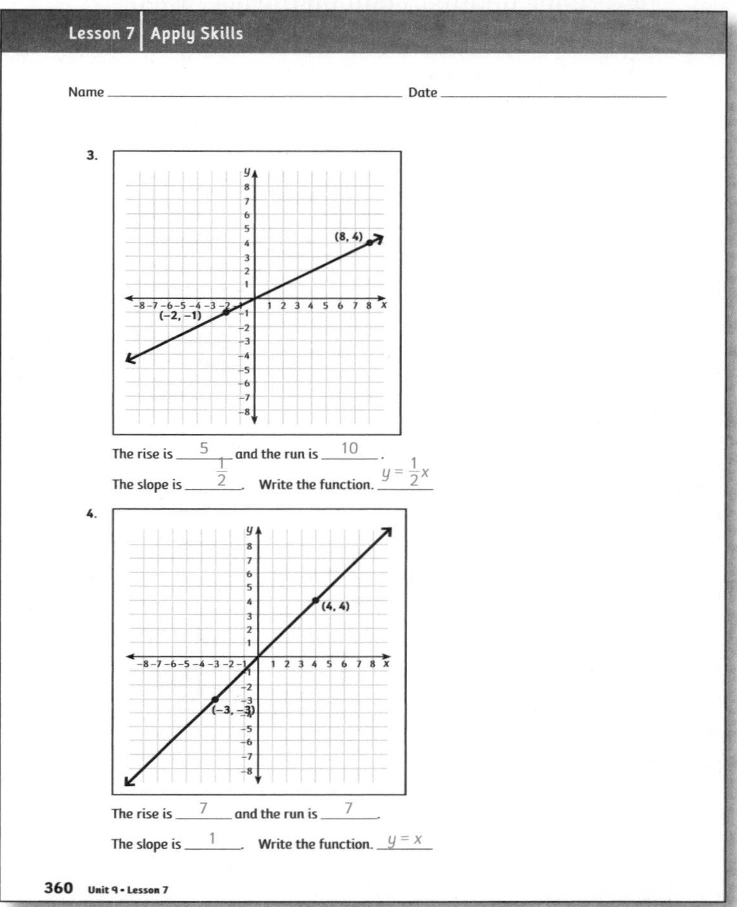

Lesson 7 | Apply Skills

Name ______ Date ______

3. (8, 4) (−2, −1)

The rise is 5 and the run is 10.

The slope is $\frac{1}{2}$. Write the function. $y = \frac{1}{2}x$

4. (4, 4) (−3, −3)

The rise is 7 and the run is 7.

The slope is 1. Write the function. $y = x$

360 Unit 9 • Lesson 7

Problem Solving:
▶ Drawing Lines

How do we use slope to help us draw a line?

(*Student Text*, page 728)

Demonstrate

- Have students turn to page 728 of the *Student Text*. Discuss another situation students might encounter with respect to slope.
- Point out that sometimes we are given the slope and one point on the line, then we have to draw the line. Go over **Example 1**, where we draw a line with the slope of 2 that goes through the point (1, 2).
- Show students how we use rise over run to determine another point on the line. Then we draw the line. Explain that we only need two points to draw a line.

Lesson 7

▶Problem Solving: Drawing Lines

How do we use slope to help us draw a line?

We saw how to figure out slope by looking at the rise over run of a line on a graph. We use the same idea to create a line with a slope from just one point on the graph. Example 1 shows how this works.

Example 1

Create a line with a slope of 2 that contains the point (1, 2).

We begin by plotting the point (1, 2) on the graph. We think about the rise and the run for a slope of 2.

Slope = $\frac{\text{Rise}}{\text{Run}}$ = 2 or $\frac{2}{1}$

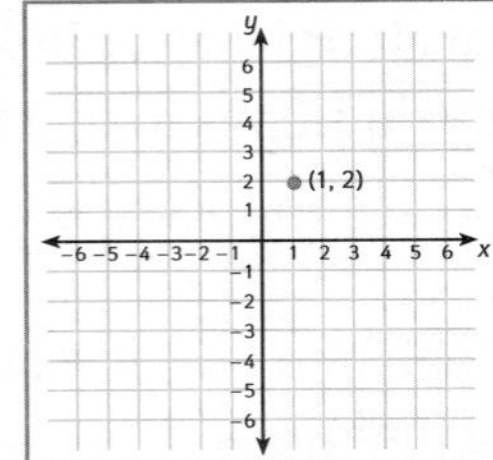

That means we move horizontally 1 for run and vertically 2 for rise.

We put a second point and then draw a line.

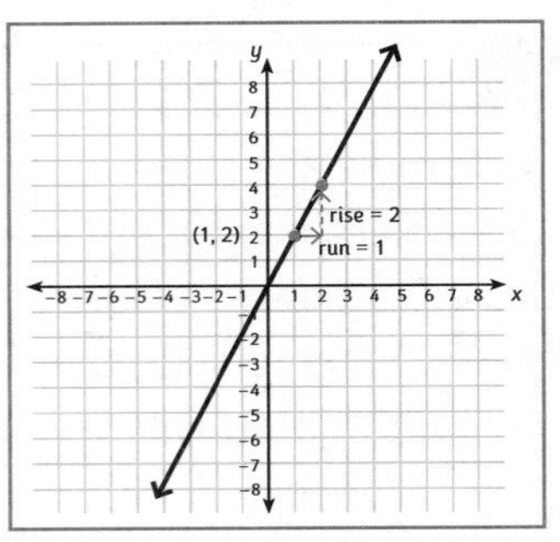

Problem-Solving Activity Turn to *Interactive Text*, page 361.

mBook Reinforce Understanding Use the *mBook Study Guide* to review lesson concepts.

728 Unit 9 • Lesson 7

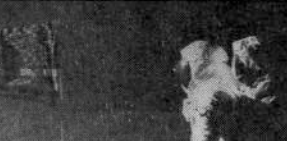

Problem-Solving Activity
(*Interactive Text*, page 361)

Have students turn to page 361 in the *Interactive Text*, and complete the activity.

Students are to draw lines based on certain conditions. They are given the slope and one point.

Monitor students' work as they complete the activity.

Watch for:

- Do students begin by plotting the point on the line?
- Can students find another point on the line by using rise over run, generated from the given slope?
- Can students draw the line from the two points plotted on the graph?

mBook Reinforce Understanding
Remind students that they can review lesson concepts by accessing the *mBook Study Guide.*

Name ______________________ Date ______________

Problem-Solving Activity
Drawing Lines

For each problem, graph a line based on the slope. Use rise over run.

1. Draw the line with the slope $\frac{1}{2}$ that goes through the point (4, 2).

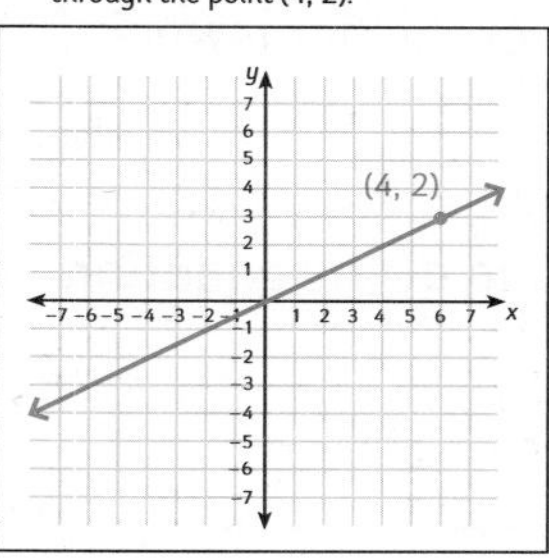

2. Draw the line with the slope −1 that goes through the point (2, −2).

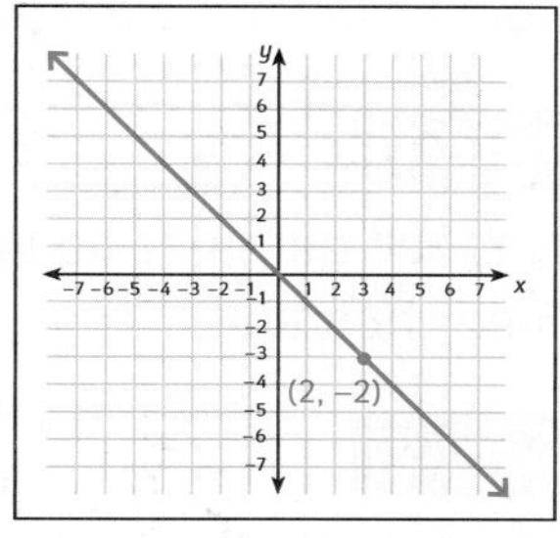

3. Draw the line with the slope 2 that goes through the point (1, 2).

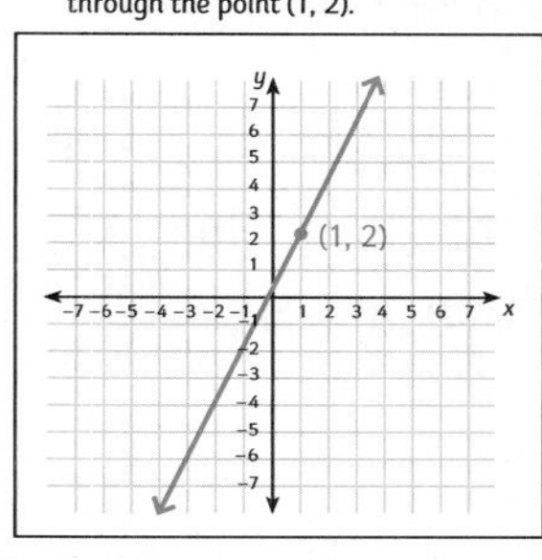

4. Draw the line with the slope $\frac{2}{3}$ that goes through the point (3, 2).

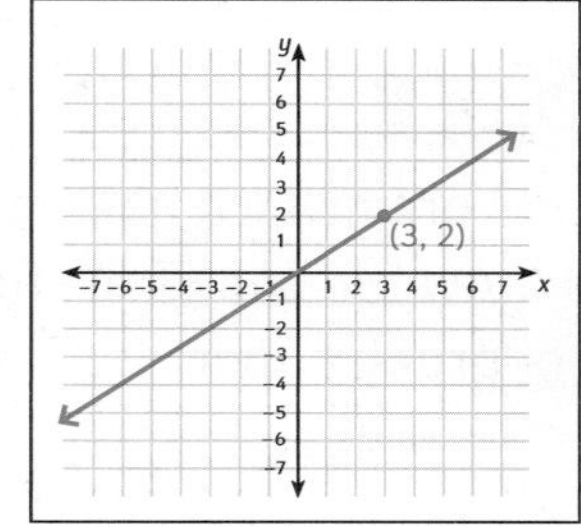

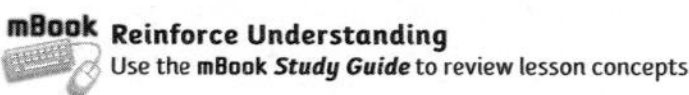

mBook Reinforce Understanding
Use the **mBook *Study Guide*** to review lesson concepts.

Homework

Go over the instructions on pages 729–730 of the *Student Text* for each part of the homework.

Activity 1

Students tell the slope by looking at the equation of a linear function.

Activity 2

Students tell the slope by looking at the graph of a linear function and using rise over run.

Activity 3

Students are given a point and the slope. They are to draw the line of the function on a separate piece of graph paper.

Homework

Activity 1

Tell the slope by looking at the function written as an equation.

1. $y = 2x$ 2
2. $y = \frac{1}{5}x$ $\frac{1}{5}$
3. $y = 6x$ 6
4. $y = x$ 1
5. $y = \frac{2}{3}x$ $\frac{2}{3}$

Activity 2

Tell the slope of the function by looking at rise over run on the graph of the function.

1. 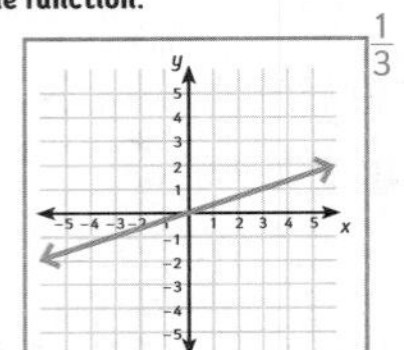 $\frac{1}{3}$

2. 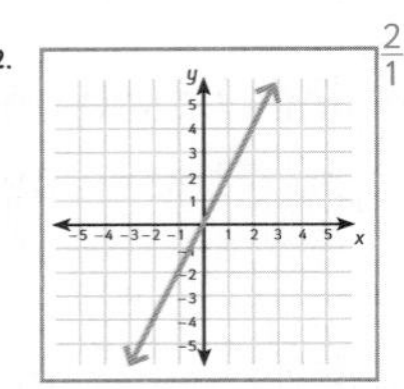 $\frac{2}{1}$

3. 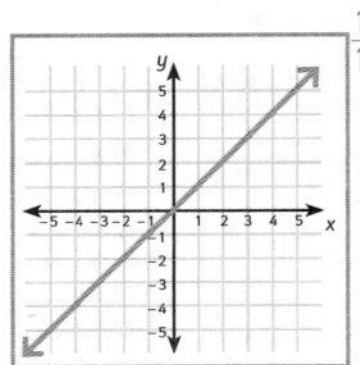 $\frac{1}{1}$

Activity 3

Draw the lines on graph paper. Be sure the line has the given slope and goes through the given point.

1. Draw a line with a slope of $\frac{1}{4}$ that goes through the point (4, 1).
2. Draw a line with a slope of −2 that goes through the point (1, −2).
3. Draw a line with a slope of $\frac{1}{3}$ that goes through the point (3, 1).

See Additional Answers below.

(*Additional Answers continue on Appendix, page A5.*)

Homework

Go over the instructions on page 730 of the *Student Text*.

Activity 4 • Distributed Practice

Students identify the property that is represented by general statements.

Homework

Activity 4 • Distributed Practice

Select the correct answer.

1. Select the name of the property represented by this general statement: $a + b = b + a$ c
   (a) Distributive Property
   (b) Identity Property of Addition
   (c) Commutative Property of Addition
2. Select the name of the property represented by this general statement: $a + 0 = a$ b
   (a) Distributive Property
   (b) Identity Property of Addition
   (c) Commutative Property of Addition
3. Select the name of the property represented by this general statement: $a + (b + c) = (a + b) + c$ a
   (a) Associative Property for Addition
   (b) Distributive Property
   (c) Identity Property of Addition
4. Select the name of the property represented by this general statement: $a(b + c) = ab + ac$ a
   (a) Distributive Property
   (b) Identity Property of Addition
   (c) Inverse Property of Addition
5. Select the name of the property represented by this general statement: $a + -a = 0$ c
   (a) Distributive Property
   (b) Identity Property of Addition
   (c) Inverse Property of Addition
6. Select the name of the property represented by this general statement: $\frac{a}{b} \cdot \frac{b}{a} = 1$ a
   (a) Inverse Property of Multiplication
   (b) Identity Property of Addition
   (c) Inverse Property of Addition

Lesson 8 ▸Positive and Negative Slopes

Problem Solving: ▸Using Slopes to Analyze Functions

Lesson Planner

Vocabulary Development

positive slope
negative slope

Skills Maintenance

Translations and Reflections

Building Number Concepts: ▶ Positive and Negative Slopes

We continue looking at slopes of lines. Students learn about the relationship between the slope of a line and its steepness.

Students are also introduced to the concept of positive and negative slope of a line, and which quadrants the line appears in on a coordinate graph.

Objective

Students will analyze different kinds of slopes.

Problem Solving: ▶ Using Slopes to Analyze Functions

It is important that students become familiar with the impact of different slopes when analyzing a function. In this lesson, they use the properties of graphs of lines and their slopes to determine the function.

Objective

Students will identify the function represented by a graph.

Homework

Students tell the slope of each function, tell which direction the line goes by looking at the slope, and tell which line is steeper by looking at the functions. In Distributed Practice, students practice integer operations.

Lesson 8 | Skills Maintenance

Name ____________________ Date ____________________

Skills Maintenance
Translations and Reflections

Activity 1

Translate or reflect the shapes and find the coordinates of the vertices of the new shape.

1. Translate the triangle 3 units up. Draw the new triangle and label the coordinates of its vertices.

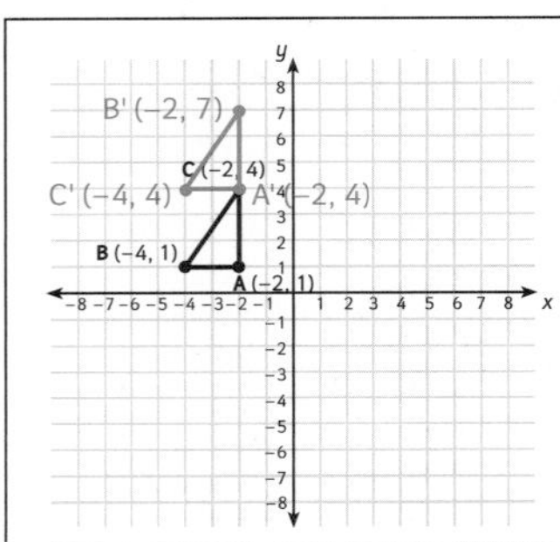

2. Reflect the square across the x-axis. Draw the new square and label the coordinates of its vertices.

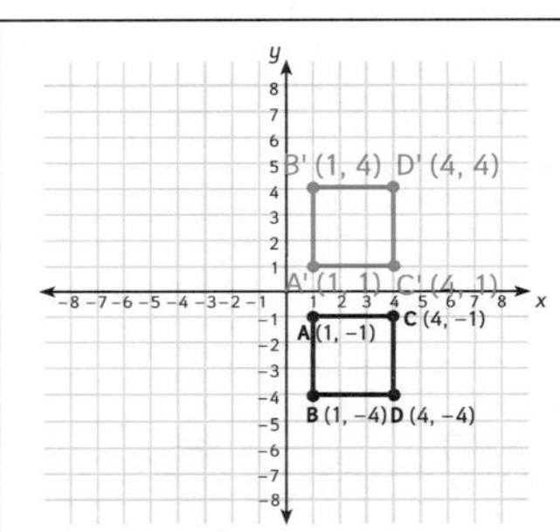

362 Unit 9 • Lesson 8

Skills Maintenance

Translations and Reflections

(*Interactive Text*, page 362)

Activity 1

Students translate and reflect shapes on a coordinate graph and give the coordinates of the vertices of the new shape.

Building Number Concepts:
▶ Positive and Negative slopes

What are some different kinds of slopes?

(*Student Text*, pages 731–733)

Connect to Prior Knowledge

Remind students about lines we looked at in prior lessons. Ask for students to discuss steepness and the directions that lines can go.

Link to Today's Concept

Tell students that in today's lesson, we learn how different slopes impact steepness and direction in the graphs of functions.

Demonstrate

Engagement Strategy: Teacher Modeling

Demonstrate how to recognize different slopes of lines in one of the following ways:

mBook: Use the *mBook Teacher Edition* for *Student Text*, pages 731–732. m

Overhead Projector: Display Transparency 17, and modify as discussed.

Board: Copy the graphs on the board, and modify as discussed.

- Tell students that the slope of a line impacts how steep the line will be and what direction the line will go.
- Call attention to **Example 1** and explain that in this example, we compare three functions with different slopes.
- Show the equation and graph of $y = \frac{2}{3}x$.

  Point out the characteristics of the graph, the quadrants that the line is in, the steepness of the line, and the direction that the line goes. m

Lesson 8 | ▶Positive and Negative Slopes
Problem Solving:
▶Using Slopes to Analyze Functions

▶Positive and Negative Slopes

Vocabulary
positive slope negative slope

What are some different kinds of slopes?

In the last lesson, we learned about the slope of a line. We know that the slope tells us how steep the line will be. Let's look at the functions graphed in Example 1 and see how the different slopes impact the graph of the line.

Example 1

Compare the slopes of the functions $y = \frac{2}{3}x$, $y = 2x$, and $y = 6x$.

How do the different slopes impact the graph of the line?

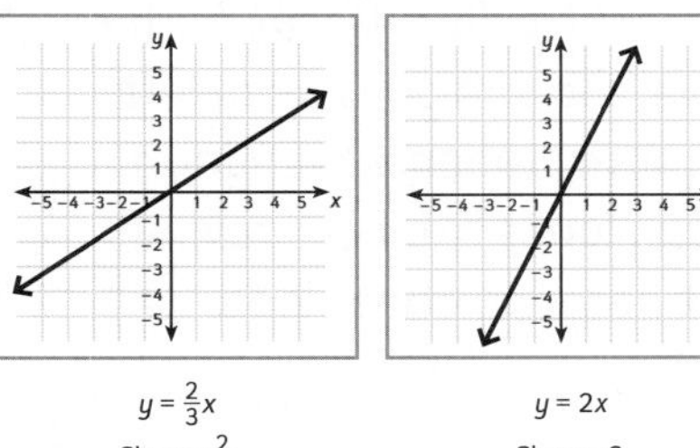

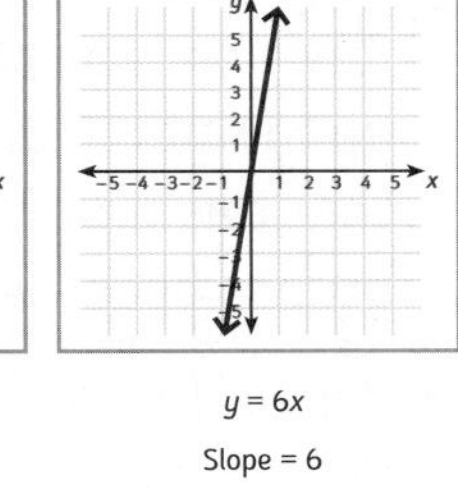

$y = \frac{2}{3}x$ Slope = $\frac{2}{3}$ | $y = 2x$ Slope = 2 | $y = 6x$ Slope = 6

The bigger the slope, the steeper the line.

The comparison in Example 1 involves slopes that are all **positive slopes**. These slopes are all greater than zero.

Unit 9 • Lesson 731

- Repeat with $y = 2x$ and $y = 6x$. m
- Tell students that all of the graphs and functions in this example represent **positive slopes**. Help students see that the equations all have slopes that are greater than zero, so the graphs have positive inclines that go up from left to right.
- Tell students that slope impacts the steepness of the graph. Explain that steepness has to do with the way the line is angled. Tell students they probably look at steepness in everyday life in the form of skateboard ramps, uphill sidewalks, escalators, etc. Point out that the bigger the slope, the steeper the line. m

What are some different kinds of slopes? *(continued)*

Demonstrate

- Present the next three functions and their graphs. In this example, students see the impact of a **negative slope**.
- Show the first function, $y = x$, and point out the characteristics of the line. Because the function is positive, the line goes from left up to right. Make sure students recognize that this first graph looks like the previous graphs because it has a positive slope. m
- Repeat for the functions $y = -x$ and $y = -2x$. Point out the characteristics of the lines. m
- Explain that positive slopes go up from left to right, and negative slopes go down from left to right.
- Point out that the graph of a function with a negative slope is in Quadrants II and IV. This is different than functions with a positive slope. Their graphs are in Quadrants I and III.

Another kind of slope is a **negative slope**. A negative slope is less than zero. Example 2 shows what a negative slope looks like as a line on a coordinate graph.

Example 2

Compare the graphs of the functions $y = x$, $y = -x$, and $y = -2x$.

What does the negative slope look like on the graph?

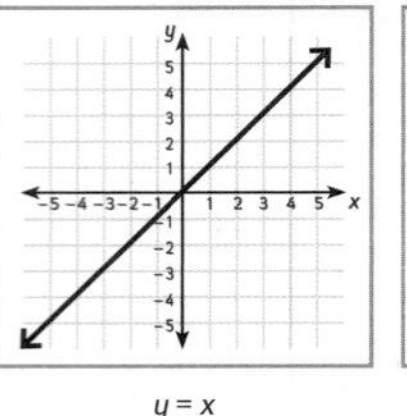
$y = x$
Slope = 1

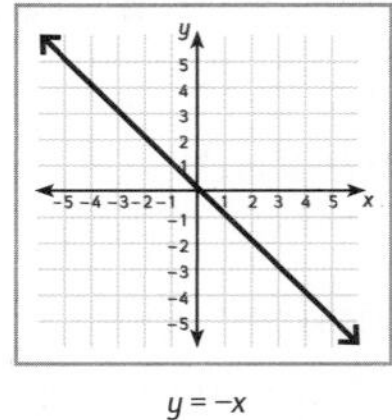
$y = -x$
Slope = −1

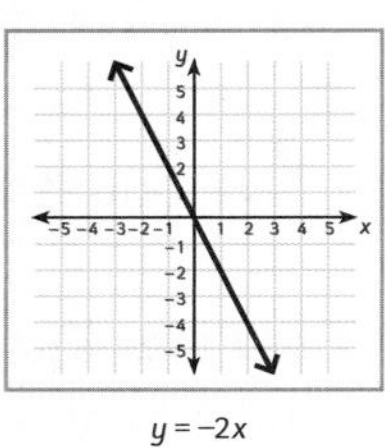
$y = -2x$
Slope = −2

The graphs of these functions show that positive slopes go up from left to right and negative slopes go down from left to right.

Negative slopes are the opposite of positive slopes when we think about steepness. With positive slopes, the bigger the number, the steeper the slope. In the case of negative slopes, the smaller the number, the steeper the slope. For example, a slope of −2 is steeper than a slope of −1 even though $-1 > -2$.

Example 3 shows the relative steepness of negative slopes.

Demonstrate

- Turn to **Example 3** on page 733 of the *Student Text*, where we compare the steepness of graphs with negative slopes.
- Show each of the functions: $y = -x$, $y = -\frac{1}{2}x$, and $y = -2x$ and their graphs. Point out the characteristics of the lines.
- Compare the steepness of the slopes. This is shown by comparing -1, $-\frac{1}{2}$, and -2. The line with a slope of -1 is steeper than the line with a slope of -2. We know that $-1 < -2$. The line with a slope of $-\frac{1}{2}$ is steeper than both of the other lines. The slope $-\frac{1}{2} < -1$ and -2.
- Point out that negative slopes work the opposite from positive slopes. Tell students that when comparing functions with negative slopes, the smaller the number, the steeper the slope.

Example 3

Compare the coordinate graphs of the following lines with negative slopes:

$y = -x$, $y = -\frac{1}{2}x$, and $y = -2x$.

How does the size of the negative slope impact the graph of the line?

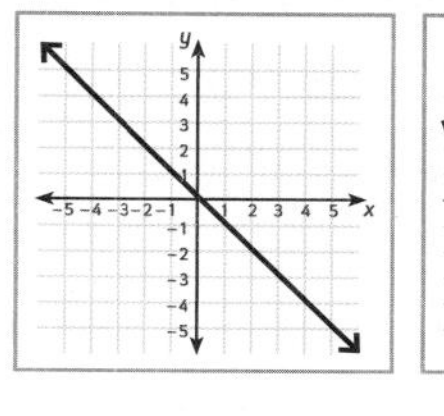

$y = -x$
Slope = -1

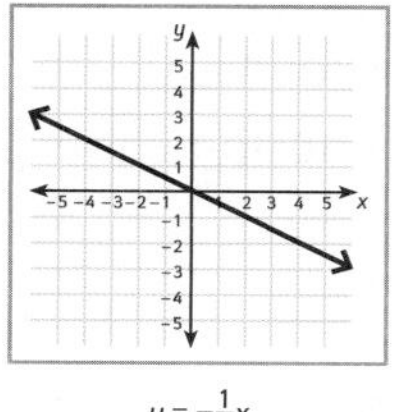

$y = -\frac{1}{2}x$
Slope = $-\frac{1}{2}$

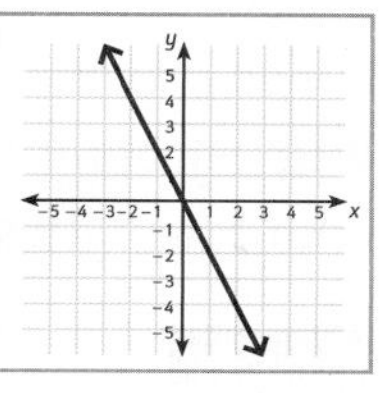

$y = -2x$
Slope = -2

When a slope is negative, the smaller the slope, the steeper the line.

It's important to become familiar with these different types of slopes and how slopes affect lines on the graph. This information helps us make even better analyses of functions.

- For positive slopes, bigger numbers mean steeper slopes.
- For negative slopes, smaller numbers mean steeper slopes.

Turn to *Interactive Text*, page 363.

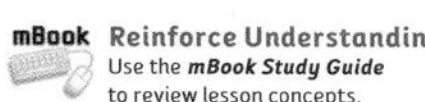

Reinforce Understanding
Use the *mBook Study Guide* to review lesson concepts.

Explain

Tell students that it is important to understand these different features of lines with various slopes. It helps us analyze functions in a different way and helps us build number sense about the coordinate graph.

Discuss

Call students' attention to the Power Concept, and point out that it will be helpful as they complete the activities.

- For positive slopes, bigger numbers mean steeper slopes.
- For negative slopes, smaller numbers mean steeper slopes.

Check for Understanding

Engagement Strategy: Think, Think

Write these functions on the board:

$$y = -3x \qquad y = -\frac{1}{3}x \qquad y = -x$$

Ask students the following questions about the functions and their slopes. Tell students that you will call on one of them to answer a question after you ask it. Tell them to listen for their names. After each question, call on a student for an answer.

Ask:

Just by looking at the equations, are the slopes of these lines positive or negative? (*negative*)

What direction will these lines go on a graph? (*down from left to right*)

Just by looking at the equations, which line has the steepest slope? ($y = -3x$)

Apply Skills

(*Interactive Text*, page 363)

Have students turn to page 363 in the *Interactive Text*, which provides students an opportunity to practice graphing functions and identifying their characteristics.

Activity 1

Students graph four functions with different slopes on a coordinate graph. Make sure students label each of the lines.

Activity 2

Students write about the steepness of the lines and what quadrants the lines fall in.

Monitor students' work as they complete the activities.

Watch for:

- Can students graph each of the functions?
- Can students identify the slope using rise over run on a graph?
- Can students see the difference in the graphs based on the slopes?
- Can students write about the differences in the graphs based on the slopes and quadrants?

mBook Reinforce Understanding

Remind students that they can review lesson concepts by accessing the online *mBook Study Guide*.

Name ______________________ Date ______________________

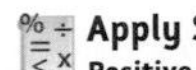

Apply Skills

Positive and Negative Slopes

Activity 1

Draw a line for each of the functions on the coordinate graph. Use the letters to label the lines.

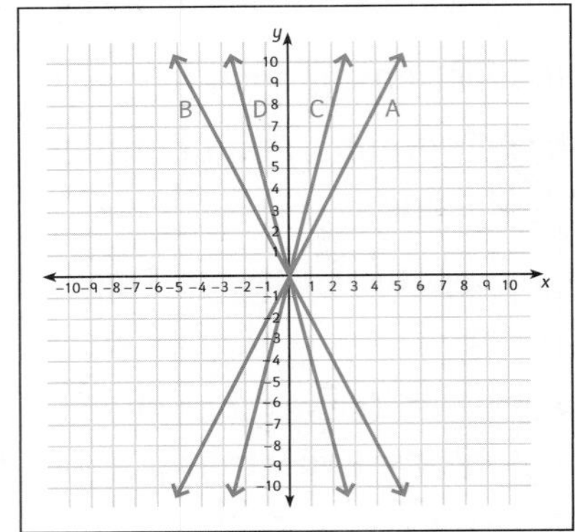

Line A: $y = 2x$ Line B: $y = -2x$ Line C: $y = 4x$ Line D: $y = -4x$

Activity 2

Write about the lines you drew in Activity 1. Tell about where the lines fall in quadrants. Describe the steepness of the lines.

Answers will vary. Sample answer: Lines A and B were steep, but not as steep as lines C and D. Lines A and C were in quadrants I and III, and lines B and D went through quadrants II and IV and have negative slopes.

Problem Solving: ▶ Using Slopes to Analyze Functions

How do we use slopes to analyze functions?

(*Student Text*, page 734)

Discuss

Have students turn to page 734 of the *Student Text* and discuss how we can tell a lot about the slope of a line by looking at the graph.

Demonstrate

- Go over **Example 1**. Demonstrate how to look at a graph and see what type of function is associated with it just by looking at the quadrants, the line, and the slant of the line.
- Point out that in this case, the line is in Quadrants II and IV. That means the slope is negative.
- Of the choices for the equation of the function, there is only one function that has a negative slope. The function $y = -x$ is associated with this graph.

▶Problem Solving: Using Slopes to Analyze Functions

How do we use slopes to analyze functions?

Now that we understand different types of slopes, we can analyze functions. Sometimes we are given problems with incomplete information and we have to make assumptions about a function. Example 1 shows such a case.

Example 1

Tell the function represented by the graph.

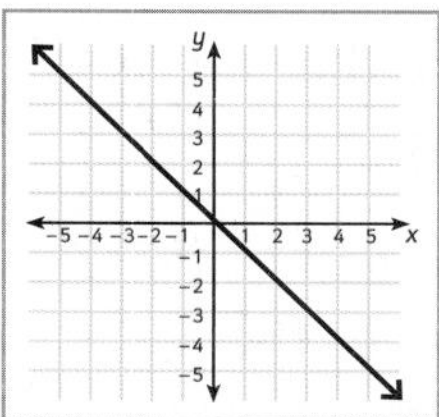

Which function is represented by this graph?

(a) $y = -x$
(b) $y = x$
(c) $y = 10x$

The answer is (a) $y = -x$.

This is the only answer that fits the graph since the line goes down from left to right. Only graphs with negative slopes have this characteristic. The other choices in the problem are positive slopes, which go up from left to right.

Problem-Solving Activity Turn to ***Interactive Text***, page 364.

mBook Reinforce Understanding Use the ***mBook Study Guide*** to review lesson concepts.

Problem-Solving Activity

(*Interactive Text*, pages 364–365)

Have students turn to pages 364–365 in the *Interactive Text*, which provide students an opportunity to practice identifying the characteristics of graphs of functions.

Students analyze each graph, then select the multiple choice answer that matches the function. Then students write a statement that describes how they decided on the answer.

Monitor students' work as they complete the activity.

Watch for:

- Can students select the function that matches the graph?
- Do students use what they learned about slopes to help choose their answers?
- Can students explain how they made their selection?

Be sure students have adequate time to write about their strategies for selecting the matching functions. Look for explanations that describe the quadrants where the function appears and the steepness of the line.

mBook **Reinforce Understanding**
Remind students that they can review lesson concepts by accessing the online *mBook Study Guide*.

Name ______________________ Date ______________

Problem-Solving Activity
Using Slopes to Analyze Functions

Select the function that matches the graph. Use your knowledge about types of slopes to help you make your decision. Then write a statement explaining how you know this is the function represented by the graph.

1. Which function is represented by this graph?

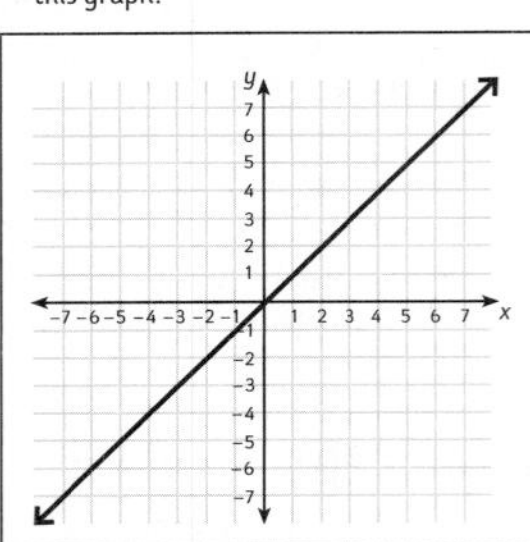

(a) $y = -x$
(b) $y = x$ (circled)
(c) $y = 10x$

Explain your answer.
Sample answer: The rise and run are the same.

2. Which function is represented by this graph?

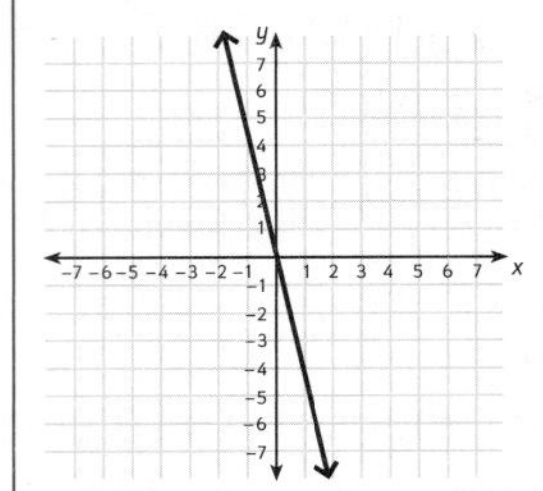

(a) $y = -\frac{1}{2}x$
(b) $y = 10x$
(c) $y = -10x$ (circled)

Explain your answer.
Sample answer: The rise is much greater than the run, and the line goes down.

Name ______________________ Date ______________

3. Which function is represented by this graph?

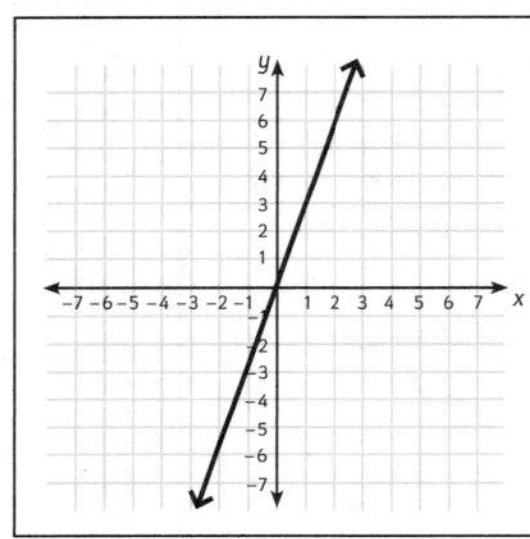

(a) $y = -10x$
(b) $y = x$
(c) $y = 10x$ (circled)

Explain your answer.
Sample answer: The rise is much greater than the run, and the lines go up.

4. Which function is represented by this graph?

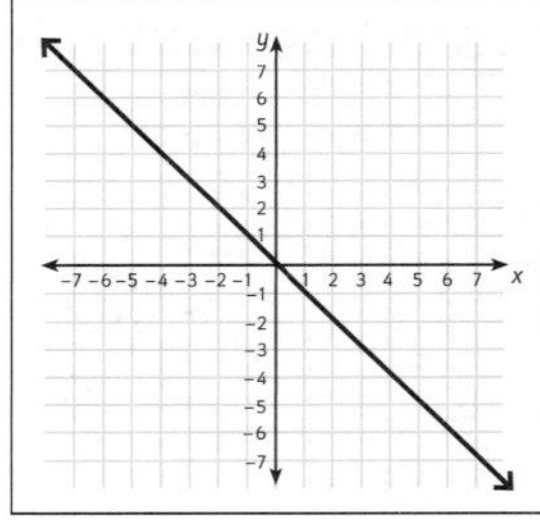

(a) $y = -x$ (circled)
(b) $y = x$
(c) $y = -10x$

Explain your answer.
Sample answer: The rise and run are the same, and lines go down.

Unit 9

mBook Reinforce Understanding
Use the mBook *Study Guide* to review lesson concepts.

Homework

Go over the instructions on page 735 of the *Student Text* for each part of the homework.

Activity 1

Students tell the slope of each function.

Activity 2

Students look at the slopes in functions and tell the direction of lines.

Activity 3

Students tell which line is steeper in pairs of functions.

Activity 4 • Distributed Practice

Students practice integer operations.

Lesson 8

Homework

Activity 1

Tell the slope of each function.

1. $y = 3x$ 3
2. $y = 4x$ 4
3. $y = \frac{1}{4}x$ $\frac{1}{4}$
4. $y = -x$ −1
5. $y = x$ 1
6. $y = \frac{1}{3}x$ $\frac{1}{3}$

Activity 2

For each of the functions, look at the slope and tell whether the line on the graph will go up or down from left to right.

1. $y = -5x$ down
2. $y = \frac{2}{3}x$ up
3. $y = 10x$ up
4. $y = -x$ down
5. $y = -\frac{1}{2}x$ down

Activity 3

For each pair of functions, tell which line is steeper.

1. Line A: $y = -\frac{1}{2}x$ B
   Line B: $y = -x$
2. Line A: $y = 3x$ A
   Line B: $y = \frac{1}{3}x$
3. Line A: $y = -2x$ A
   Line B: $y = -x$
4. Line A: $y = \frac{5}{6}x$ B
   Line B: $y = 4x$

Activity 4 • Distributed Practice

Solve.

1. −27 + −35 −62
2. −8 − 15 −23
3. −5 • −20 100
4. −540 ÷ 60 −9
5. 12 − −35 47
6. 17 + −100 −83
7. −20 • 4 −80
8. −54 ÷ −6 9

Unit 9 • Lesson 735

Lesson 9 | ▶Rate of Change

Problem Solving: The Advantages of Lines

Lesson Planner

Vocabulary Development

rate of change

Skills Maintenance

Analyzing Slope

Building Number Concepts:

▶ Rate of Change

Students learn that we can use our knowledge of slopes to help us solve everyday problems involving rate of change. We look at a situation involving salary, and how the rate of change can help us predict how long it takes to reach a goal.

Objective

Students will solve rate of change problems.

Problem Solving:

▶ The Advantages of Lines

Students learn that we can get much more information about a function by seeing it as a line on a graph than by solving equations. This is because the line shows us many characteristics of the function at once.

Objective

Students will examine the advantages of using lines to make comparisons.

Homework

Students look at three lines on a coordinate graph and identify the equation that goes with each line, compare pairs of functions and tell which function has the steepest line, and make comparisons of two lines on a graph. In Distributed Practice, students practice solving one- and two-step equations.

Lesson 9 | Skills Maintenance

Name ______________________ Date ______________________

Skills Maintenance
Analyzing Slope

Activity 1

Look at the pairs of functions and think about how they look on a graph. Which of the lines is steeper? Circle the correct answer.

1. Line A: $y = 2x$
   Line B: $y = 3x$
   Which line has the steeper slope? (circle one) A or (B)
2. Line A: $y = -2x$
   Line B: $y = -3x$
   Which line has the steeper slope? (circle one) A or (B)
3. Line A: $y = \frac{1}{2}x$
   Line B: $y = 3x$
   Which line has the steeper slope? (circle one) A or (B)

Activity 2

Tell which quadrants the line appears in on a coordinate graph. Circle the correct answer.

1. Where is the line $y = -x$?
   (circle one) (Quadrants II & IV) or Quadrants I & III
2. Where is the line $y = \frac{1}{2}x$?
   (circle one) Quadrants II & IV or (Quadrants I & III)
3. Where is the line $y = -\frac{3}{4}x$?
   (circle one) (Quadrants II & IV) or Quadrants I & III

366 Unit 9 • Lesson 9

Skills Maintenance

Analyzing Slope

(*Interactive Text*, page 366)

Activity 1

Students tell which line is steeper by looking at the equations of two functions.

Activity 2

Students tell which quadrants contain the line for each of the functions described.

Building Number Concepts:
▶ Rate of Change

How do we use slope to compare everyday functions?

(*Student Text*, pages 736–738)

Connect to Prior Knowledge

Begin by discussing the Skills Maintenance activities. Tell students that the rules about slopes they already learned are helpful concepts as they begin to look at other uses of functions.

Link to Today's Concept

Explain that in today's lesson, we look at rates of change. The slope of the line becomes very important in analyzing this kind of function.

Demonstrate

Engagement Strategy: Teacher Modeling

Demonstrate how to use slope to compare everyday functions in one of these ways:

mBook: Use the *mBook Teacher Edition* for pages 736–737 of the *Student Text*. m

Overhead Projector: Reproduce the table on Transparency 17, and modify as discussed.

Board: Copy the table and graph on the board, and modify as discussed.

- Remind students about the two ways we found the slope of a line. One way is to describe the relationship between x and y from an x/y table. Another way is to examine the rise and run on a graph. m
- Refer to the table and be sure students see that the function described by the table is $\boldsymbol{y = 3x}$. This is because we multiply each of the x values by 3 to get the y values. We see that the slope is **3**. m

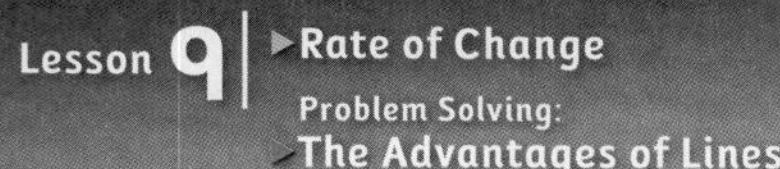

▶Rate of Change

Vocabulary
rate of change

How do we use slope to compare everyday functions?

We have learned two ways to figure out the slope of a function.

The first is with an x/y table. We analyze the relationship between the x and y values in the table, then state it using words. Then we use the words to write an equation using x and y. The coefficient in front of x is the slope.

The second way to figure out the slope of a function is using the formula for rise over run of a line on a coordinate graph.

Both strategies give us the same function.

x	y
1	3
2	6
3	9
4	12

Look at the x/y table for a pattern. If we multiply each x by 3, we get y. We use this pattern to write the function $y = 3x$. The slope is 3.

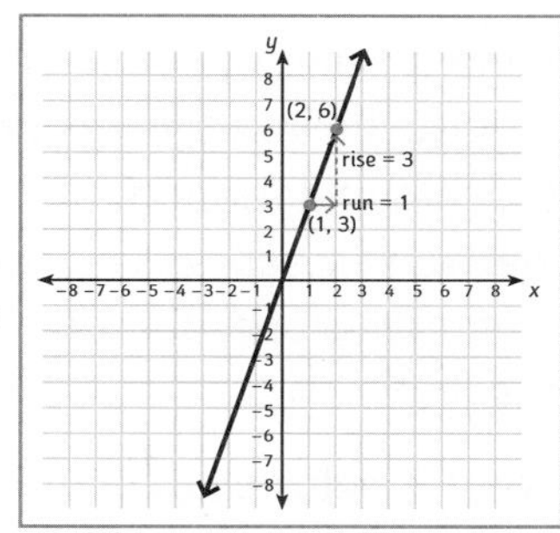

We also find the equation for the function by measuring rise and run on the coordinate graph.

$$\text{Slope} = \frac{\text{rise}}{\text{run}} = \frac{3}{1} = 3$$

The slope is 3. We write the function $y = 3x$.

736 Unit 9 • Lesson 9

- Then refer to the graph and point out that the rise is 3 and the run is 1 on the graph of the function. This means our slope is $\frac{3}{1}$, or **3**. The function is $\boldsymbol{y = 3x}$. m
- Explain that both of these ways are acceptable ways of computing slope. Often the situation determines which method we use because we are given one representation or the other: an x/y table or a graph.

How do we use slope to compare everyday functions? *(continued)*

Demonstrate

- Have a discussion with students about the importance of analyzing the steepness of a line. We talked about steepness of lines in the last lesson, but we did not discuss the value of this information in practical situations.
- Go over the general rules about slope. Read through each of the bulleted points and make sure students understand the relationship between steepness and slope, positive and negative slope, and the direction of the lines. m
- Tell students that it helps us to analyze the **rate of change** in a problem, which is the steepness of slope of the entire line. This is common in problems where we want to reach a certain goal in the minimum amount of time.

In the last lesson, we looked at how to tell the steepness or direction of a line just by looking at the slope. We were able to discuss these general rules about slope:

> **Lines With Positive Slopes:**
> - The bigger the slope, the steeper the line.
> - Lines with positive slopes go up from left to right.
>
> **Lines With Negative Slopes:**
> - The smaller the slope, the steeper the line.
> - Lines with negative slopes go down from left to right.

Looking at the steepness, or slope, of the line tells us something else that is very important. It tells us about the **rate of change**. The rate of change tells us how quickly a function is increasing or decreasing.

Example 1 shows why rate of change is important. We use it in everyday life when we think about how long it takes to reach a goal. In this example, Tina, who works at Big Tom's Restaurant, wants to make $60 to pay for college textbooks. Tina used to earn $10 per hour, then she got a raise to $15 per hour.

Demonstrate

- Direct students to page 738 of the *Student Text* and go over **Example 1**, which shows how we can use slope, or steepness, to determine when someone reaches a certain earning goal. Explain that in this example, we compare Tina's old salary with her new one in terms of which one gets her to an earning goal of **$60**.
- Explain that we will let x equal the number of hours, and y equal the dollars she gets per hour.
- Show the first x/y table, which shows data for Tina's old salary of $10 per hour. Go over this table carefully with students.
- Go over the second x/y table, which shows data for Tina's new salary of $15 per hour.
- Display the graph and plot the function for Tina's old salary of $10 per hour. Explain that the function is $\boldsymbol{y = 10x}$.
- Plot the function for Tina's new salary of $15 per hour and explain that the function is $\boldsymbol{y = 15x}$.
- Make sure students see that Tina gets to $60 faster if she makes $15 per hour.
- Explain to students that this information is very simple if we just look at the problem: $15 per hour is more pay than $10 per hour.
- Tell students that we are using this example to point out the value of a graph when comparing and analyzing more complex problems. We use the steepness, or slope, of the graph to determine when we arrive at $60. We compare this with two functions.
- Explain that that with more complex functions in algebra, the ability to see rates of change on a graph to determine which function meets the goal first is very helpful.

The tables and graph show two different functions for how Tina can earn $60.

Example 1

Show how Tina's old wage compares to her new wage using slopes.

Let x = the number of hours worked and y = dollars paid.

$10 per hour	
x	y
1	10
2	20
3	30
4	40
5	50
6	60

Function: $y = 10x$

$15 per hour	
x	y
1	15
2	30
3	45
4	60
5	75
6	90

Function: $y = 15x$

We compare the two lines. One line is steeper than the other. The $y = 15x$ line is steeper. Both lines get to $60, but the $y = 15x$ line gets there faster.

This means that Tina gets to the goal of $60 faster when she is paid $15 per hour. That is because the rate of change is larger. The rate of change helps us see how Tina gets to her goal faster when she earns $15 per hour.

One of the best ways to compare two functions is to compare their slopes. Slope tells us about the rate of change. This is important data for making comparisons.

Apply Skills Turn to ***Interactive Text***, page 367.

mBook Reinforce Understanding Use the ***mBook Study Guide*** to review lesson concepts.

Check for Understanding
Engagement Strategy: Think, Think

Ask students these questions. Tell them that you will call on one of them to answer a question after you ask it. Tell them to listen for their names. After each question, allow time for students to think of the answer. Then call on a student.

Ask:

If a line goes up from left to right, does it have a positive or negative slope? (*positive*)

For a line with a positive slope, is the line steeper if the slope is bigger or smaller? (*bigger*)

Which type of line goes down from left to right? (*a line with a negative slope*)

For a line with a negative slope, is the line steeper if the slope is bigger or smaller? (*smaller*)

Apply Skills

(*Interactive Text*, page 367)

Have students turn to page 367 in the *Interactive Text*, which provides students an opportunity to practice analyzing different rates of change.

Activity 1

Students fill in *x*/*y* tables and draw graphs for everyday functions. Then they are to tell which function meets the goal first. Monitor students' work as they complete the activity.

Watch for:

- Can students complete the *x*/*y* table for the function?
- Can students draw the lines of the functions?
- Can students tell which function meets the goal first based on the *x*/*y* table, the graph, and the rate of change they observe on the graph (e.g., steepness)?

mBook **Reinforce Understanding**
Remind students that they can review lesson concepts by accessing the online *mBook Study Guide.*

Lesson 9 | Apply Skills

Name ______________________ Date ______________________

Apply Skills
Rate of Change

Activity 1

Tell who reached their goal first by completing the *x*/*y* tables and graphing the functions.

1. The goal is to score 60 points. Marcus scores 15 points per level and Liza scores 20 points per level.
   Complete the *x*/*y* tables. The *x* stands for level and the *y* stands for points.

Marcus's Points		Liza's Points	
x	*y*	*x*	*y*
1	15	1	20
2	30	2	40
3	45	3	60

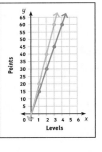

Graph the functions. Who reached the goal first? Liza

2. The goal is to make $30 babysitting. Hannah makes $6 per hour and Ali makes $5 per hour.
   Complete the *x*/*y* tables. The *x* stands for hours and the *y* stands for earnings.

Hannah's Earnings		Ali's Earnings	
x	*y*	*x*	*y*
1	6	1	5
2	12	2	10
3	18	3	15
4	24	4	20
5	30	5	25
6	36	6	30

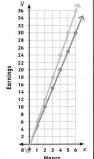

Graph the functions. Who reached the goal first? Hannah

Unit 9

Unit 9 • Lesson 9 367

Problem Solving:
▶ The Advantages of Lines

What are the advantages of using lines to make comparisons?

(*Student Text*, pages 739–740)

Explain

Have students turn to the material on page 739 of the *Student Text*. Discuss the fact that there is more than one way to solve a problem involving rate of change, besides examining it on a graph.

Explain to students that in the example we looked at with Tina's salary, we could have solved the equations and found out which function reached $60 first. Point out to students that the advantage of a graph is that it lets us make comparisons at many different points in time.

Demonstrate

- Direct students' attention to **Example 1**. In this example, we describe two different companies that wash windows of big buildings.
- Read through the problem, then have students look at the *x*/*y* tables that compare the rate that the windows are washed at many different points in time. Explain that x equals the hours and y equals the number of windows cleaned.
- Point out that from the *x*/*y* tables, we write the functions: $\boldsymbol{y = 3x}$ and $\boldsymbol{y = 2x}$.

▶ Problem Solving: The Advantages of Lines

What are the advantages of using lines to make comparisons?

In the previous example, we compared how long it would take Tina to earn $60 based on two different rates of pay. In one case, the linear function showed her original rate of $10 per hour. In the other case, the linear function showed what she was earning after her raise to $15 per hour.

When we solve an equation, we can only find one value at a time. The advantage of a coordinate graph is that it lets us make comparisons at many different points in time.

Let's look at Example 1. The problem describes two different companies that wash windows on tall buildings. It shows different rates for washing windows. We can compare how many windows have been washed at different points in time.

Example 1

Use a graph to solve the word problem.

Problem:

Ajax Window Workers is trying to get contracts to wash windows for the buildings downtown. It is trying to beat Wonder Washers by advertising that it can do the job faster. Based on the data in the tables, which company washes windows faster?

Here are *x*/*y* tables for the two companies. The number of windows cleaned depends on the time they have to clean them.

Let x = hours and y = the number of windows cleaned.

Ajax	
x	y
1	3
2	6
3	9
4	12
5	15

Function: $y = 3x$

Wonder Washers	
x	y
1	2
2	4
3	6
4	8
5	10

Function: $y = 2x$

What are the advantages of using lines to make comparisons? *(continued)*

Demonstrate

- Turn to page 740 of the *Student Text* and continue going over Example 1.
- Next explain that we draw a graph of the functions. Point out to students that the graph allows us to compare the functions to see which company washes more windows in less time. Be sure students see from the graph that it is clearly Ajax. They wash the same number of windows in less time than Wonder Washers.
- Point out the tables and go over the information in each table to confirm what the graph shows.
- Explain that this kind of comparison helps us make decisions, in this case about which company is more efficient.

Lesson 9

We make comparisons on the graph where the lines intersect points on the grid. We see three different comparisons.

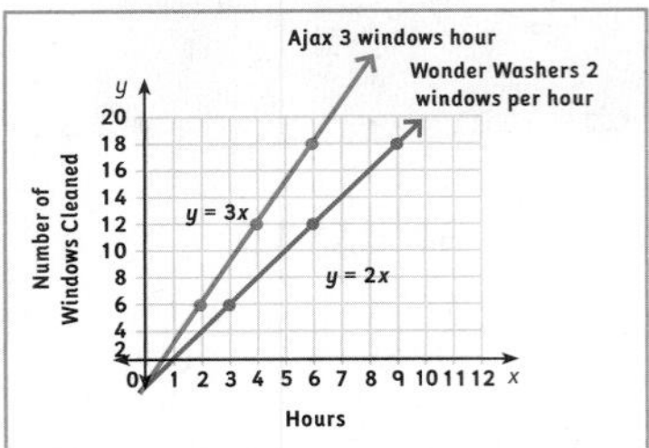

Ajax
6 windows in 2 hours
12 windows in 4 hours
18 windows in 6 hours

Wonder Washers
6 windows in 3 hours
12 windows in 6 hours
18 windows in 9 hours

We make our decision about these two companies by looking at which washes more windows in less time. Ajax washes the same number of windows in less time than Wonder Washers. That makes it the faster window-washing company.

Problem-Solving Activity Turn to *Interactive Text*, page 368.

mBook Reinforce Understanding Use the *mBook Study Guide* to review lesson concepts.

Problem-Solving Activity

(*Interactive Text*, pages 368–369)

Have students turn to pages 368–369 in the *Interactive Text*, which provide students an opportunity to solve problems that involve a comparison.

Students are given a coordinate graph in each problem to examine, and a corresponding situational word problem. Then they interpret the graph based on two functions and answer questions about rate of change involving the graphs.

Monitor students' work as they complete the activity.

Watch for:

- Can students read the problem carefully to find all the relevant information for solving it?
- Can students use the coordinate graph to compare the two functions and answer the question?

mBook **Reinforce Understanding**

Remind students that they can review lesson concepts by accessing the online *mBook Study Guide*.

Lesson 9 | Problem-Solving Activity

Name ______________ Date ______________

Problem-Solving Activity
The Advantage of Lines

In each of the problems, interpret the graph based on two functions. Use what you know about coordinate graphs to answer the questions.

1. Janelle and her sister Tanya are leaving their house in two different cars. They are both driving on the same road, and they are going on a long trip. Janelle is driving at 40 miles per hour and Tanya is driving at 50 miles per hour. How much farther ahead will Tanya be after 4 hours? What about after 6 hours?

   40 miles; 60 miles

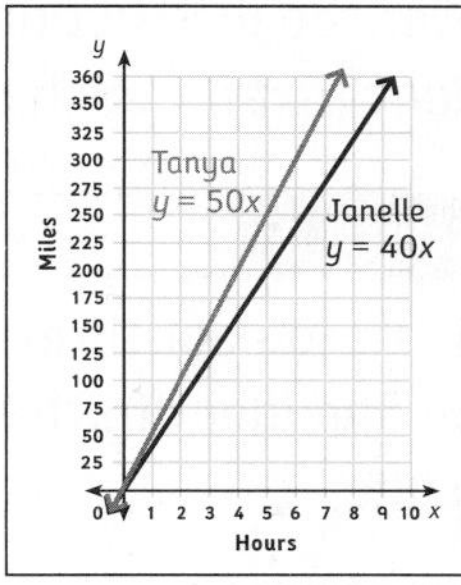

2. Satellites move around the Earth in space. They travel at different speeds. Some are faster than others. At noon a TV satellite and a spy satellite are next to each other in space. The spy satellite is going 80 miles per minute and the TV satellite is going 60 miles per minute. How much farther will the spy satellite be after 8 minutes? What about after 12 minutes?

   160 miles; 240 miles

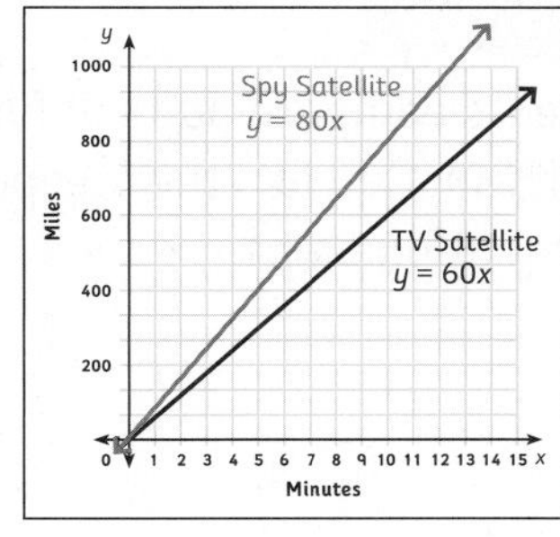

Lesson 9 | Problem-Solving Activity

Name ______________ Date ______________

3. Two gears are part of a large machine that makes dog food. If the gears didn't turn, there would be no dog food. Gear A makes 5 turns a minute and Gear B makes 7 turns a minute. When you turn on the machine, the gears are in the same starting place. How many more turns will Gear B make after 4 minutes? What about 8 minutes?

   8; 16

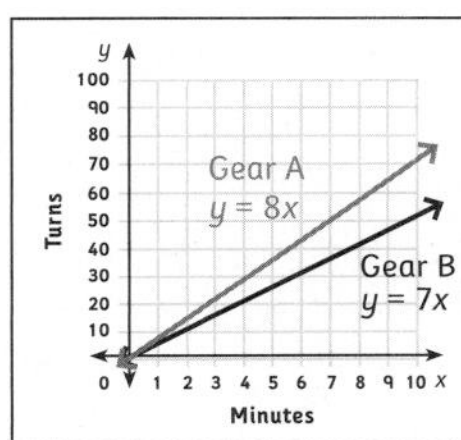

4. Two other machines in the factory pour the dog food into sacks and seal each one of them. They're ready to be put in boxes after that. The large machine pours and seals 15 sacks per minute. The small machine pours and seals 10 sacks per minute. How many more sacks will the large machine pour and seal after 3 minutes? What about after 8 minutes?

   15; 40

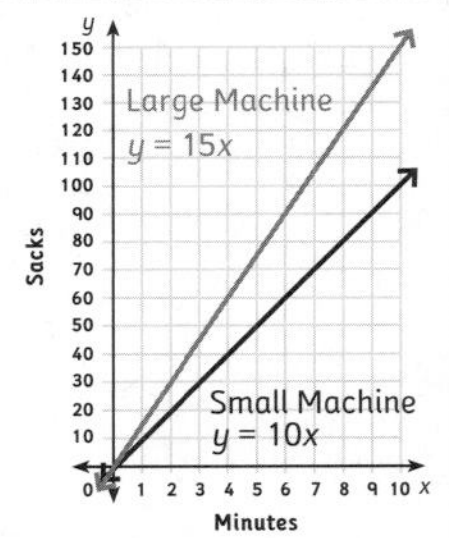

Unit 9

mBook Reinforce Understanding
Use the mBook *Study Guide* to review lesson concepts.

Homework

Go over the instructions on pages 741–742 of the *Student Text* for each part of the homework.

Activity 1

Students look at three lines on a coordinate graph and identify the equation that goes with each line.

Activity 2

Students compare pairs of functions and tell which function has the steepest graph just from the equation alone.

Homework

Activity 1

Look at the three lines on the graph and select the equation that matches each line. Use your knowledge of slope and steepness to help you.

1. Which equation matches Line A? b
   (a) $y = 2x$
   (b) $y = x$
   (c) $y = \frac{1}{2}x$

2. Which equation matches Line B? c
   (a) $y = 2x$
   (b) $y = x$
   (c) $y = \frac{1}{2}x$

3. Which equation matches Line C? a
   (a) $y = 2x$
   (b) $y = x$
   (c) $y = \frac{1}{2}x$

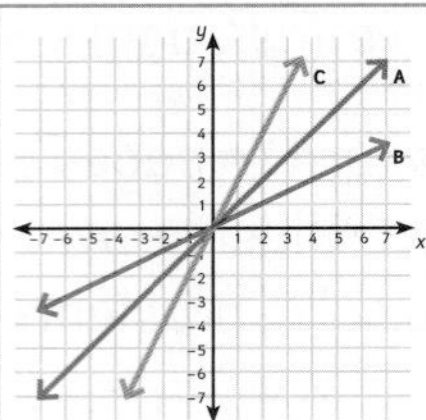

Activity 2

Tell which line is steeper by comparing slopes. Write a or b on your paper.

1. Which line is steeper? a
   (a) $y = 3x$
   (b) $y = \frac{1}{3}x$

2. Which line is steeper? b
   (a) $y = \frac{1}{2}x$
   (b) $y = 2x$

3. Which line is steeper? b
   (a) $y = 2x$
   (b) $y = 3x$

4. Which line is steeper? b
   (a) $y = \frac{2}{3}x$
   (b) $y = x$

Homework

Go over the instructions on page 742 of the *Student Text* for each part of the homework.

Activity 3

Students look at two lines on a graph and make comparisons to answer the questions.

Activity 4 • Distributed Practice

Students practice solving one- and two-step equations.

Lesson 9

Homework

Activity 3

Look at the two lines on the graph. They show that Marcus earns $10 per hour at the restaurant and Elizabeth earns $12 per hour. Answer the questions using the graph.

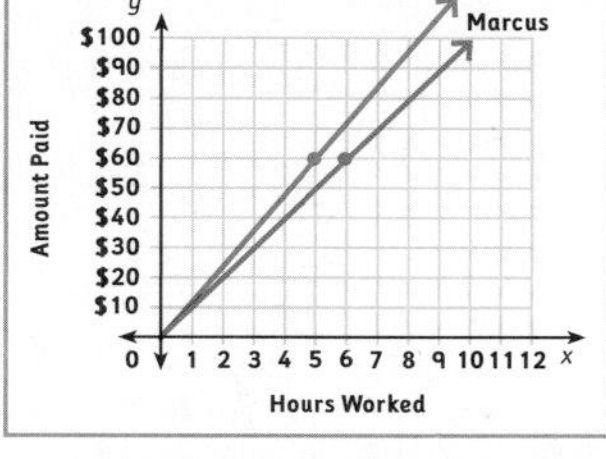

1. How many hours does Marcus have to work to earn $60?
   6 hours
2. How many hours does Elizabeth have to work to earn $60?
   5 hours
3. If the goal was to see who was first to earn $120, who would reach the goal faster, Elizabeth or Marcus? Elizabeth

Activity 4 • Distributed Practice

Solve.

1. $3x = -24$ -8
2. $-4x + 5 = -27$ 8
3. $72 = 9x$ 8
4. $-6 + -6y = 36$ -7
5. $x - 13 = 13$ 26
6. $-6x + 1 = -5$ 1
7. $170 = x + 80$ 90
8. $210 = -30y$ -7

Lesson 10 ▶ The *Y*-Intercept

Monitoring Progress: ▶ Quiz 2

Lesson Planner

Vocabulary Development

y-intercept

Skills Maintenance

Solving Equations With Variables

Building Number Concepts: ▶ The *Y*-Intercept

Students learn that not all functions cross the *y*-axis at the point (0, 0). They learn that the point where the line crosses the *y*-axis is called the *y*-intercept. We look at real-life situations to show functions that do not cross the *y*-axis at the (0, 0) point.

Objective

Students will analyze graphs of linear functions that do not go through the origin.

Monitoring Progress: ▶ Quiz 2

Distribute the quiz, and remind students that the questions involve material covered over the previous lessons in the unit.

Homework

Students select the correct *y*-intercept for each function, select the correct equation for each function, and compare slopes of two functions and tell which one is steeper. In Distributed Practice, students practice solving one- and two-step equations, practice using order of operations and properties, and apply rules for performing operations on integers.

Lesson 10 | Skills Maintenance

Name ______________________ Date ______________

Skills Maintenance
Solving Equations With Variables

Activity 1

Solve the equations by substituting the value for the variable.

1. Solve $y = 2x + 1$ if $x = 2$. $y = 5$
   $y = 2 \cdot 2 + 1$
2. Solve $y = -x + 5$ if $x = -3$. $y = 8$
   $y = -(-3) + 5$
3. Solve $y = x + 7$ if $x = 10$. $y = 17$
   $y = 10 + 7$
4. Solve $y = \frac{1}{2}x + 10$ if $x = 6$. $y = 13$
   $y = \frac{1}{2} \cdot 6 + 10$

370 Unit 9 • Lesson 10

Skills Maintenance

Solving Equations With Variables

(*Interactive Text*, page 370)

Activity 1

Students solve equations by substituting values for the variables.

Building Number Concepts:
▶ The *Y*-Intercept

What about lines that don't go through the origin?
(*Student Text*, pages 743–747)

Connect to Prior Knowledge
Remind students about graphs of functions they saw in previous lessons. Tell them that most lines went through the origin, which is the point (0, 0). Draw an example on the board or overhead if you need to.

Link to Today's Concept
Explain that in today's lesson, we look at graphs of functions that do not cross the *y*-axis at the point of origin. Introduce the term ***y*-intercept**, and explain that it is the point where the line crosses the *y*-axis.

Demonstrate
Engagement Strategy: Teacher Modeling

Demonstrate lines that do and do not go through the origin in one of the following ways:

mBook: Use the *mBook Teacher Edition* for *Student Text*, pages 743–745. m

Overhead Projector: Reproduce the tables on Transparency 17, and modify as discussed.

Board: Reproduce the graphs and tables on the board, and modify as discussed.

- Discuss the kinds of lines we have been graphing. Point out that all of them have gone through the point of origin at (0, 0).
- Have students look at the graphs of ***y* = 2*x*** and ***y* = −3*x***, and identify the point (0, 0) for each. m

Lesson 10 | ▶The *Y*-Intercept
Monitoring Progress:
▶Quiz 2

▶The *Y*-Intercept

Vocabulary
y-intercept

What about lines that don't go through the origin?

Every linear function we have looked at so far has gone through the point of origin, or where the *x*- and *y*-axes intersect. The graph shows two different kinds of linear functions. Each one goes through the point of origin.

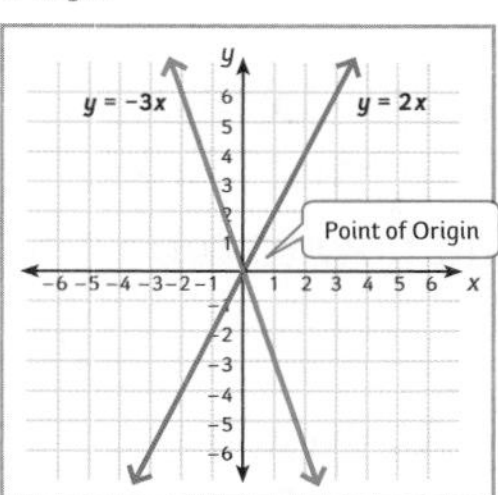

Some linear functions pass through the *y*-axis at some point other than (0, 0). The point where the line crosses the *y*-axis is called the ***y*-intercept**. We can see how a line crosses the *y*-axis at a point other than (0, 0) when we create a graph for a function such as the price Vroom Oil Change charges for an oil change.

Unit 9 • Lesson 10 743

- Tell students that not all graphs go through this point. Explain that sometimes graphs cross the *y*-axis at a different point.

What about lines that don't go through the origin? *(continued)*

Demonstrate

- Go over **Example 1**, which is about Vroom Oil Change. m
- Display the table showing the quarts, oil cost, recycling charge, and total cost. Make sure that students understand how to read the table. m
- Explain that we can put this into an x/y table, where ***x* equals the number of quarts** and ***y* equals the total cost.** m

Example 1 shows a table for the cost of oil based on the number of quarts a customer needs. Notice that Vroom Oil Change charges $3 to recycle the old oil from a car. We see that the line passes through (0, 3) on the y-axis of the graph.

The point (0, 3) on the graph means 0 quarts of oil and $3 to recycle the oil. This could happen if somebody changed their own oil and brought the used oil to Vroom Oil Change for recycling.

Example 1

Use a table, equation, and graph to solve the word problem.

Problem:
Vroom Oil Change charges $6 per quart to change oil. It charges $3 to recycle the old oil from your car. It doesn't matter how much oil you have, the recycling charge is always the same.

Here is a table showing all the charges. How much does it cost to recycle oil if Vroom doesn't change the oil?

Number of Quarts	Cost for Oil	Recycling Charge	Total Cost
1	$6	$3	$9
2	$12	$3	$15
3	$18	$3	$21
4	$24	$3	$27
5	$30	$3	$33

When we put this into an x/y table, we need to figure out the equation that will give us the total cost. Here is the x/y table showing quarts and total cost.

Let x = the number of quarts and y = the total cost.

x	y
1	9
2	15
3	21
4	27
5	33

Demonstrate

- Continue going over Example 1.
- Explain that we can find the total cost by multiplying 6 times the number of quarts and adding \$3. This means that the function is **$y = 6x + 3$**. m
- Tell students that we can check this by substituting one of the x values into the function to see if it gives us the correct value. Substitute **4** into the x value and walk through the calculations to see that **$y = 27$**. m
- Show students the graph of the linear functions. Point out that the function crosses the y-axis at a different place than the origin, in this case at (0, 3), so **the y-intercept is 3**. m
- If there is a \$3 recycling that is added to the bill no matter how many ounces of oil purchased, that causes the graph of the function to move from the origin to a different point on the y-axis.

We find the cost by multiplying 6 times the number of quarts and adding \$3. That means our function is:

$$y = 6x + 3$$

We can check this by substituting one of the x values in the function to see if it gives us the correct y value.

$$\overset{4}{\downarrow}$$
$$y = 6x + 3$$
$$y = 6 \cdot 4 + 3$$
$$y = 24 + 3$$
$$y = 27$$

Here is what the graph looks like for this linear function.

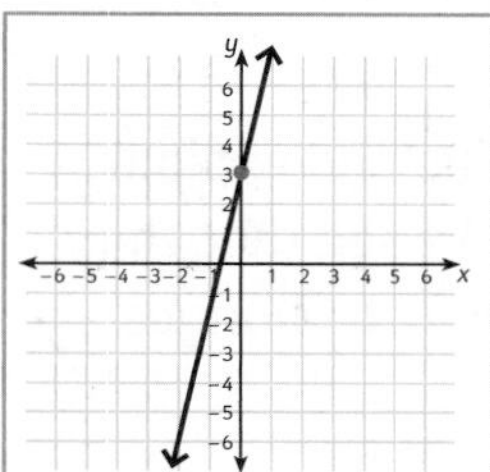

The function crosses the y-axis at (0, 3). The y-intercept for this function is 3.

What happens if Vroom Oil Change decides to change the price it charges for recycling the oil? Let's say that it now charges \$4 to recycle the oil.

Example 2 shows the change from the old charge of \$3 to the new charge of \$4. The slope of the line does not change. The line has just moved up one unit on the y-axis. The lines are parallel because they have the same slope.

Check for Understanding

Engagement Strategy: Think Tank

Draw a coordinate graph on the board and plot a positive line that has coordinates of **(0, 4)**. Distribute strips of paper to students and have them write their name on their papers. Have students write the y-intercept on the paper.

Put all the papers into a container when students are finished. Draw a paper from the container and share the answer. If the answer is correct, congratulate the student. If the answer is incorrect, invite a volunteer to share the correct answer.

What about lines that don't go through the origin? *(continued)*

Demonstrate

- Turn to *Student Text*, page 746 to walk through **Example 2**. This example shows the change from the old recycling charge of $3 to the new charge of $4.
- Have students look at the table and explain how the table has changed. We see that the recycling charge is now $4, which changes the total cost by $1.
- Show students how we create the x/y table by letting x equal the number of quarts and y equal the total cost.
- Then explain that the function is now $\boldsymbol{y = 6x + 4}$.
- Go over the graph and point out that the slope does not change; only the location where the line crosses the y-axis is a different point.
- Tell students that adding 3 in Example 1 and adding 4 in Example 2 are examples of y-intercept. Tell them we are adding a constant to the functional relationship, which we call the y-intercept. Remind students that a constant is a term in an algebraic equation that is a number.
- Explain that when we add a constant to linear functions, we move the y-intercept up the y-axis. Tell students that a similar thing happens when we subtract a constant.

Lesson 10

Example 2

Use a table, function, and graph to solve the word problem.

Problem:

Vroom Oil Change still charges $6 per quart to change oil. But it now charges $4 to recycle the old oil from your car. How does the function change?

Number of Quarts	Cost for Oil	Recycling Charge	Total Cost
1	$6	$4	$10
2	$12	$4	$16
3	$18	$4	$22
4	$24	$4	$28
5	$30	$4	$34

When we put this into an x/y table, we need to figure out the equation that will give us the total cost. Here is the x/y table showing quarts and total cost.

Let x = the number of quarts and y = the total cost.

x	y
1	10
2	16
3	22
4	28
5	34

What is our function?

$y = 6x + 4$

Here is what the graph looks like for this function. The y-intercept is now 4. The line has shifted up one unit.

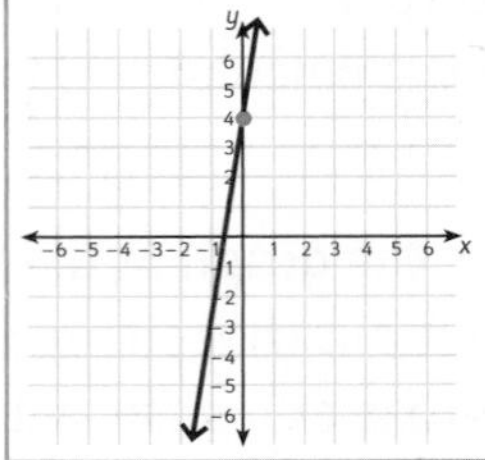

By adding a constant to linear functions, we move the y-intercept up the y-axis. A similar thing happens when we subtract a constant.

746 Unit 9 • Lesson 10

Demonstrate

- Turn to *Student Text*, page 747, and read through the scenario about Al's Auto Repair.
- Go over **Example 3**, which demonstrates what happens when we subtract a constant. This example demonstrates a problem where customers get a $5 discount. This, in effect, is subtracting a constant.
- Go over the first table and point out the $5 discount in this case.
- Point out how we create the *x*/*y* table to get the function $y = 6x - 5$.
- Then have students look at the graph. Point out the place where the line crosses the *y*-axis. Help students notice that the line has shifted down the *y*-axis.

Check for Understanding
Engagement Strategy: Think, Think

Ask students the following questions about the Al's Auto Repair scenario. Tell them that you will call on one of them to answer a question after you ask it. Tell them to listen for their names. After each question, allow time for students to think of the answer. Then call on a student.

Ask:

What will happen to the *y*-intercept if Al reduces the discount to $4? (*The y-intercept will be −4.*)

How will the graph change? (*The line will move up on the y-axis.*)

What will happen to the *y*-intercept if Al increases the discount to $6? (*The y-intercept will be −6.*)

How will the graph change? (*The line will move down on the y-axis.*)

Let's imagine that Al's Auto Repair wants to get into the oil changing business. Al decides to change oil for $6 a quart, but he will not charge for recycling the oil.

Al has a big opening day celebration. On opening day, he will give everyone a discount of $5 off an oil change for coming to his shop. In this case, we are subtracting 5 in the function. This means the line intersects the *y*-axis at (0, −5).

Example 3

Use a table, equation, and graph to show the $5 discount.

Number of Quarts	Cost for Oil	Discount	Total Cost
1	$6	$5	$1
2	$12	$5	$7
3	$18	$5	$13
4	$24	$5	$19
5	$30	$5	$25

When we put this into an *x*/*y* table, we need to figure out the equation that will give us the total cost.

Let x = the number of quarts and y = the total cost.

x	*y*
1	1
2	7
3	13
4	19
5	25

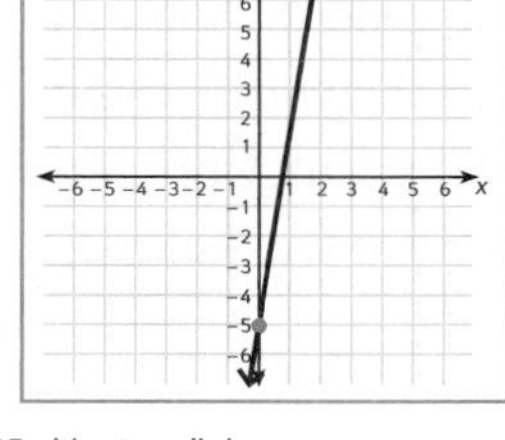

What is our function?

$y = 6x - 5$

The graph for this function tells us that the *y*-intercept is −5. However, in real life we could not walk into Al's shop and get $5 without an oil change.

Apply Skills
Turn to ***Interactive Text***, page 371.

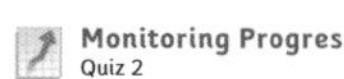
Monitoring Progress
Quiz 2

mBook Reinforce Understanding
Use the ***mBook Study Guide*** to review lesson concepts.

Apply Skills

(*Interactive Text*, pages 371–372)

Have students turn to *Interactive Text*, pages 371–372, which provide students the opportunity to practice identifying the y-intercept.

Activity 1

Students use what they just learned about adding or subtracting a constant to a function to draw a graph. Each problem describes a situation and provides a table of data. First students label the x- and y-axes based on the information in the problem. Next they draw the line on the graph. Finally they write the function. Monitor students' work as they complete the activity.

Watch for:

- Can students identify the labels for the x- and y-axes?
- Can students draw the line?
- Can students write the function?

Be sure to go over the problems when students have completed the activity. It is important that they see how the y-intercept impacts the table, the coordinate graph, and the equation of the function.

Reinforce Understanding

Remind students that they can review lesson concepts by accessing the online *mBook Study Guide*.

Lesson 10 | Apply Skills

Name ______________________ Date ______________

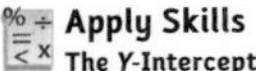

Apply Skills
The Y-Intercept

Activity 1

Find the functions for each problem. Each problem describes a situation and provides a table of data. Your job is to:
(a) Label the x- and y-axes based on the information in the problem.
(b) Draw the line on the graph.
(c) Write the function.

1. Watch It Tonight! is a local video store that rents movies. They have a plan where you pay $10 per month, and then $2 per movie. This way you can watch as many movies as you want for the month for just $2 each. The table shows the total cost to rent movies (up to 5).

Number of Movies	Cost for Videos	Monthly Charge	Total Cost
0	0	10	10
1	2	10	12
2	4	10	14
3	6	10	16
4	8	10	18
5	10	10	20

Write the function. $y = 2x + 10$

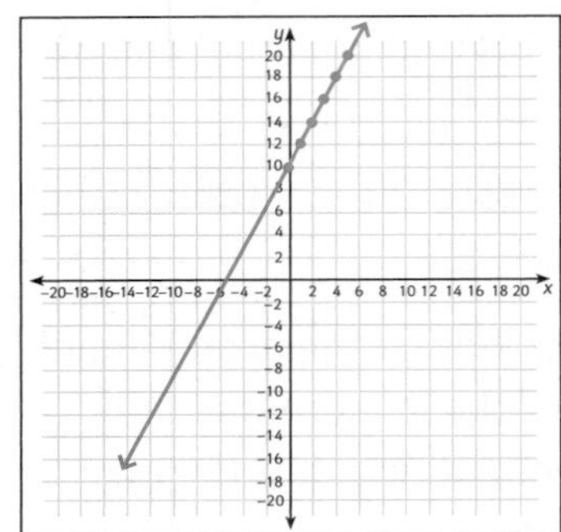

Unit 9

Lesson 10 | Apply Skills

Name ______________________ Date ______________

2. Watch It Tonight! decided that it was not getting enough business by charging $10 per month, so it dropped its monthly charge to $7 per month. Here is a new table that shows the cost of renting up to five videos per month.

Number of Movies	Cost for Videos	Monthly Charge	Total Cost
0	0	7	7
1	2	7	9
2	4	7	11
3	6	7	13
4	8	7	15
5	10	7	17

Write the function. $y = 2x + 7$

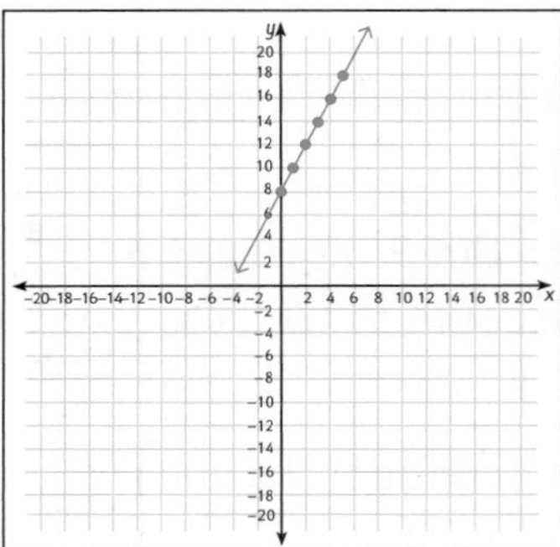

mBook **Reinforce Understanding**
Use the **mBook *Study Guide*** to review lesson concepts.

Monitoring Progress:
▶ Quiz 2

Assess
Quiz 2

- Administer Quiz 2 Form A in the *Assessment Book*, pages 81–82. (If necessary, retest students with Quiz 2 Form B from the *mBook Teacher Edition* following differentiation.)

Students	Assess	Differentiate
	Day 1	**Day 2**
All	Quiz 2 *Form A*	
Scored 80% or above		Extension
Scored Below 80%		Reinforcement

Differentiate

- Review Quiz 2 Form A with class.
- Identify students for Extension or Reinforcement.

Extension

For those students who score 80 percent or better, provide the On Track! Activities from Unit 9, Lessons 6–10, from the *mBook Teacher Edition.*

Reinforcement

For those students who score below 80 percent, provide additional support in one of the following ways:

- Have students access the online tutorial provided in the *mBook Study Guide.*
- Have students complete the Interactive Reinforcement Exercises for Unit 9, Lessons 5–9, in the *mBook Study Guide.*
- Provide teacher-directed reteaching of unit concepts.

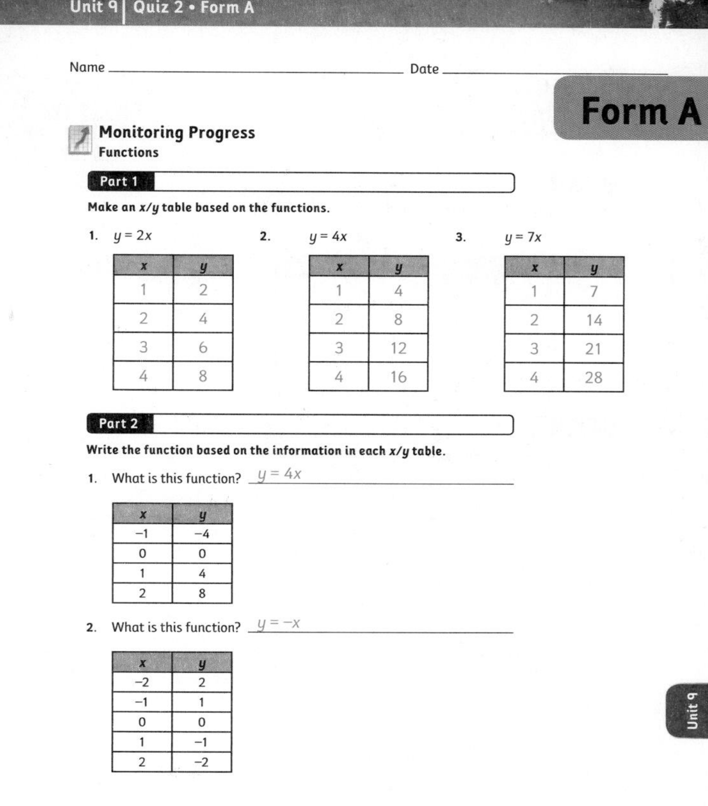

Unit 9 | Quiz 2 • Form A

Name ______ Date ______

Form A

Monitoring Progress
Functions

Part 1

Make an *x*/*y* table based on the functions.

1. $y = 2x$

x	y
1	2
2	4
3	6
4	8

2. $y = 4x$

x	y
1	4
2	8
3	12
4	16

3. $y = 7x$

x	y
1	7
2	14
3	21
4	28

Part 2

Write the function based on the information in each *x*/*y* table.

1. What is this function? $y = 4x$

x	y
−1	−4
0	0
1	4
2	8

2. What is this function? $y = -x$

x	y
−2	2
−1	1
0	0
1	−1
2	−2

Unit 9

Unit 9 • Quiz 2 • Form A 81

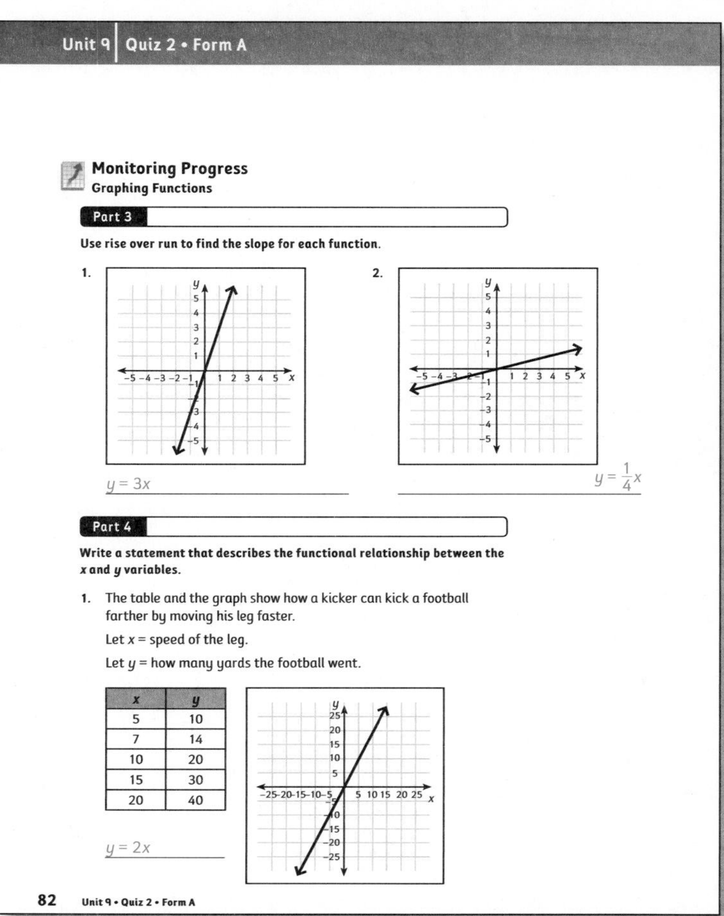

Unit 9 | Quiz 2 • Form A

Monitoring Progress
Graphing Functions

Part 3

Use rise over run to find the slope for each function.

1. $y = 3x$

2. $y = \frac{1}{4}x$

Part 4

Write a statement that describes the functional relationship between the *x* and *y* variables.

1. The table and the graph show how a kicker can kick a football farther by moving his leg faster.
   Let x = speed of the leg.
   Let y = how many yards the football went.

x	y
5	10
7	14
10	20
15	30
20	40

$y = 2x$

82 Unit 9 • Quiz 2 • Form A

Name ______________________ Date ______________

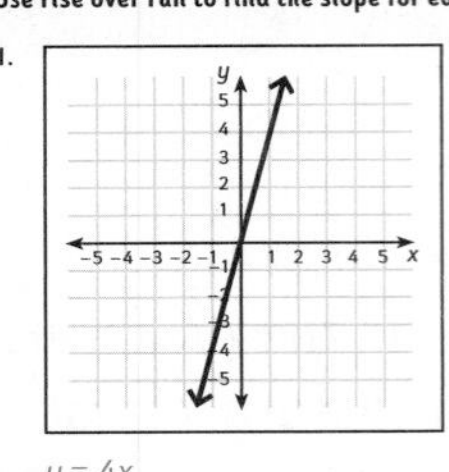

Monitoring Progress
Functions

Part 1

Make an *x/y* table based on the functions.

1. $y = 3x$

x	y
1	3
2	6
3	9
4	12

2. $y = 5x$

x	y
1	5
2	10
3	15
4	20

3. $y = 2x$

x	y
1	2
2	4
3	6
4	8

Part 2

Write the function based on the information in each *x/y* table.

1. What is this function? $y = 3x$

x	y
−1	−3
0	0
1	3
2	6

2. What is this function? $y = x$

x	y
−2	−2
−1	−1
0	0
1	1
2	2

Name ______________________ Date ______________

Monitoring Progress
Graphing Functions

Part 3

Use rise over run to find the slope for each function.

1. $y = 4x$

2. $y = \frac{1}{3}x$

Part 4

Write a statement that describes the functional relationship between the *x* and *y* variables.

1. The table and the graph show how a batter can hit a baseball farther by swinging faster.

Let x = speed of the bat.

Let y = how many feet the baseball went.

x	y
10	20
15	30
20	40
30	60
40	80

$y = 2x$

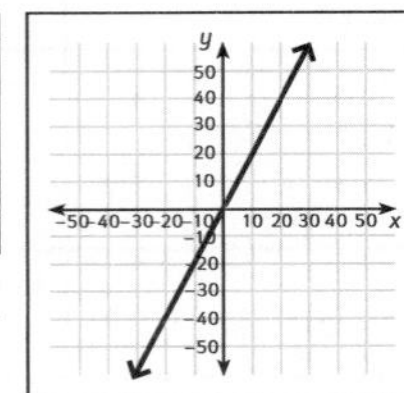

Homework

Go over the instructions on pages 748–749 of the *Student Text* for each part of the homework.

Activity 1

Students select the correct y-intercept for each function from possible multiple choice answers.

Activity 2

Students select the correct equation for each function on the coordinate graphs.

Homework

Activity 1

Identify the y-intercept for each graph.

1. 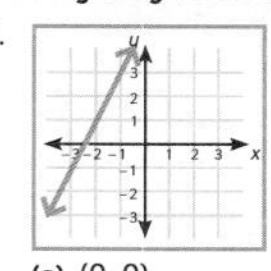 c
(a) (0, 0)
(b) (0, 2)
(c) (0, 5)
(d) (0, 10)

2. b
(a) (0, 2)
(b) (0, −2)
(c) (−2, 2)
(d) (−2, 0)

3. 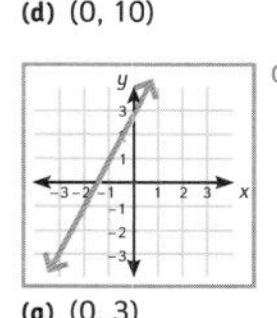 a
(a) (0, 3)
(b) (3, 0)
(c) (2, 3)
(d) (3, 2)

4. 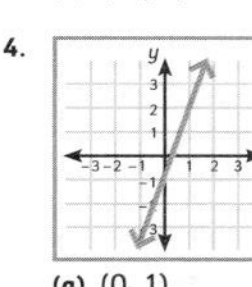 b
(a) (0, 1)
(b) (0, −1)
(c) (1, 0)
(d) (−1, 0)

Activity 2

Look at the graphs. Select the equation that matches each function. Use your knowledge of slope and steepness to help you.

1. 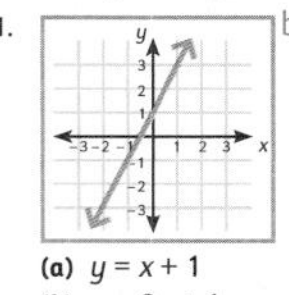 b
(a) $y = x + 1$
(b) $y = 2x + 1$
(c) $y = 3x + 1$
(d) $y = 4x + 1$

2. 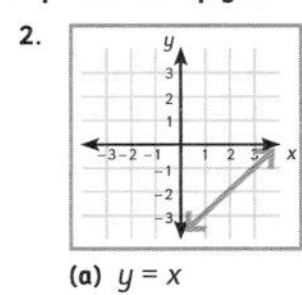 d
(a) $y = x$
(b) $y = x - 1$
(c) $y = x - 2$
(d) $y = x - 4$

3. 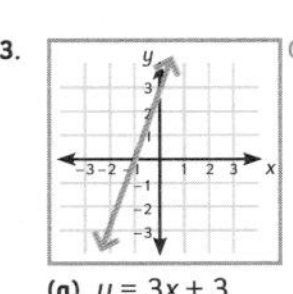 a
(a) $y = 3x + 3$
(b) $y = 2x + 3$
(c) $y = x + 3$
(d) $y = -x + 3$

Homework

Go over the instructions on page 749 of the *Student Text* for each part of the homework.

Activity 3

Students compare slopes of two functions and tell which one is steeper.

Activity 4 • Distributed Practice

Students practice solving one- and two-step equations, practice using order of operations and properties, and apply rules for performing operations on integers.

Homework

Activity 3

Tell which line is steeper by comparing slopes. Write a or b on your paper.

1. Which line is steeper? a
   (a) $y = x$
   (b) $y = \frac{1}{2}x$
2. Which line is steeper? a
   (a) $y = 3x$
   (b) $y = x$
3. Which line is steeper? a
   (a) $y = 5x$
   (b) $y = 2x$
4. Which line is steeper? b
   (a) $y = \frac{2}{3}x$
   (b) $y = 2x$

Activity 4 • Distributed Practice

Solve.

1. $-3 + 2 \cdot -8 + 100$ 81
2. $5^2 - (8 + 2) \cdot 2$ 5
3. $100 \div 50 + 7 - 4$ 5
4. $100 \div 5^2 + 7 - 4$ 7
5. $20 \cdot 8 \cdot 0 - 100$ −100
6. $-15 + -30 - -8 \cdot 10$ 35
7. $24 \div (8 - 4) + -12$ −6
8. $-8 \cdot -8 \div 32 + (2 - 9)$ −5

Lesson 11 | Slope-Intercept Form: $y = mx + b$

Problem Solving: Graphing Linear Equations

Lesson Planner

Vocabulary Development

zero slope

Skills Maintenance

Solving Equations With Variables

Building Number Concepts:

▶ Slope-Intercept Form: $y = mx + b$

Students learn that the formal way to write a function is using the slope-intercept form: $y = mx + b$. They learn that m is the slope and b is the y-intercept.

Students learn to substitute values for x in a function to find the value of y. Then they create an x/y table to find coordinates to plot on a graph.

Objective

Students will use the slope-intercept form to plot a function on a coordinate graph.

Problem Solving:

▶ Graphing Linear Equations

Students look at what $y = mx + b$ looks like with no slope. They examine how different choices can lead to different kinds of graphs.

We look at a real-life scenario and show how to put each choice into a function and graph it on a line.

Objective

Students will graph linear equations.

Homework

Students tell the slope and y-intercept for the functions, write the equation for a function, and create an x/y table and a graph for each of the functions. In Distributed Practice, students write the general pattern for each of the properties.

Lesson 11 | Skills Maintenance

Name ______________________ Date ______________________

Skills Maintenance
Solving Equations With Variables

Activity 1

Solve the equations by substituting the value for the variable.

1. Solve $y = 2x + 3$ for $x = -1$. $y = 1$
   $y = 2 \cdot -1 + 3$
2. Solve $y = 3x - 1$ for $x = -2$. $y = -7$
   $y = 3 \cdot -2 - 1$
3. Solve $y = 2x + 5$ for $x = 1$. $y = 7$
   $y = 2 \cdot 1 + 5$
4. Solve $y = \frac{1}{2}x + 10$ for $x = 8$. $y = 14$
   $y = \frac{1}{2} \cdot 8 + 10$

Unit 9

Unit 9 • Lesson 11 373

Skills Maintenance

Solving Equations With Variables

(*Interactive Text*, page 373)

Activity 1

Students solve equations by substituting the value for the variable.

Building Number Concepts: ▶ Slope-Intercept Form: $y = mx + b$

What is the equation for a linear function?

(*Student Text*, pages 750–751)

Connect to Prior Knowledge

Begin by writing the following equation on the board or overhead:

$y = 3x + 7$

Ask students to describe the function that is represented by this equation.

Listen for:

- *slope*
- *y-intercept*
- *x/y coordinates*
- *steepness*
- *quadrants*
- *any of the things discussed so far in this unit as a way of describing the function*

Link to Today's Concept

Tell students that in today's lesson we look at the formal representation of a function: $y = mx + b$ form, the slope-intercept form.

Demonstrate

Engagement Strategy: Teacher Modeling

Demonstrate how to interpret the slope-intercept form in one of the following ways:

mBook: Use the *mBook Teacher Edition* for pages 750–751 of the *Student Text.* m

Overhead Projector: Reproduce the functions, table, and graph, and modify as discussed.

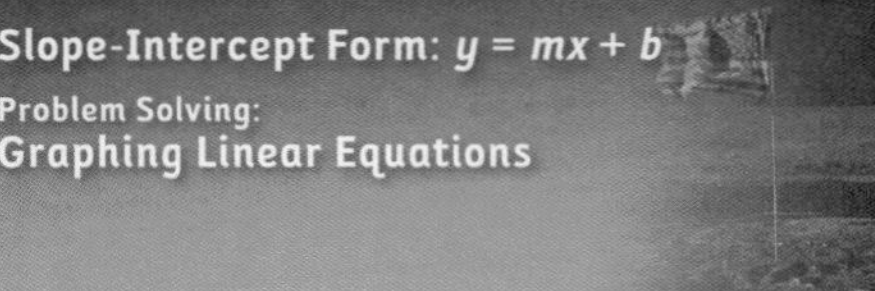

▶Slope-Intercept Form: $y = mx + b$

What is the equation for a linear function?

We are now ready to start working with the traditional equation for a linear function, which is $y = mx + b$. Each part of the equation shows what we have already learned in previous lessons. Let's look at each part of the equation for a linear function.

The value of y depends on $mx + b$.

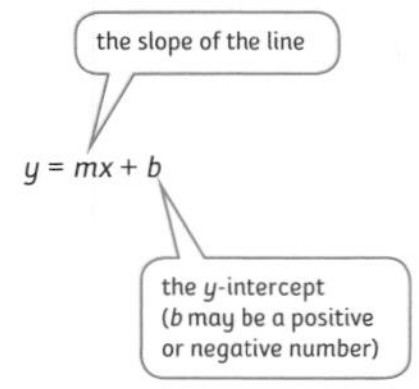

We use this equation to create a table of data and then draw a line on a coordinate graph. All that we have to do is substitute a value for x and then solve the equation just like any other equation. Example 1 shows what this process looks like.

750 Unit 9 • Lesson 11

Board: Copy the functions, table, and graph, and modify as discussed.

- Present the equation $\boldsymbol{y = mx + b}$ and explain that this is the formal representation of a function. m
- Be sure students understand that m is the slope and b is the y-intercept. m
- Explain that the relationship between x and y can be determined from an x/y table.

Demonstrate

- Go over **Example 1**, which shows how to create the *x*/*y* table and graph for the function $y = 2x - 3$.
- Go over each step with students for graphing the function.

STEP 1

- Show how to substitute the values for *x* to create the *x*/*y* table.
- Start with **0** and show how we **substitute 0 for *x*** to get $y = 2 \cdot 0 - 3$.
- Walk through the calculations to get $y = -3$ and show **−3** in the first row of the *y* column of the table.
- Repeat the process to substitute **1**, **2**, and **3** for *x* to get the *y* values **−2**, **1**, and **3**.

STEP 2

- Explain that we can now use the table to plot a line on the coordinate graph.
- Tell students that we can check to see if our line is correct by looking at the function $y = 2x - 3$.
- Be sure students see that the **slope is 2** (rise = 2 over run = 1) and the **y-intercept is −3** (0, −3) when they analyze the graph.

Check for Understanding
Engagement Strategy: Pair/Share

Write the following function on the board:

$y = 4x - 2$

Have students work with a partner to create an *x*/*y* table by substituting the values **0**, **1**, **2**, and **3** for *x*. Then review the *x*/*y* tables with the class. Next have pairs plot the line on a coordinate graph using the table. Have students check that they drew the lines correctly by looking at the rise and run.

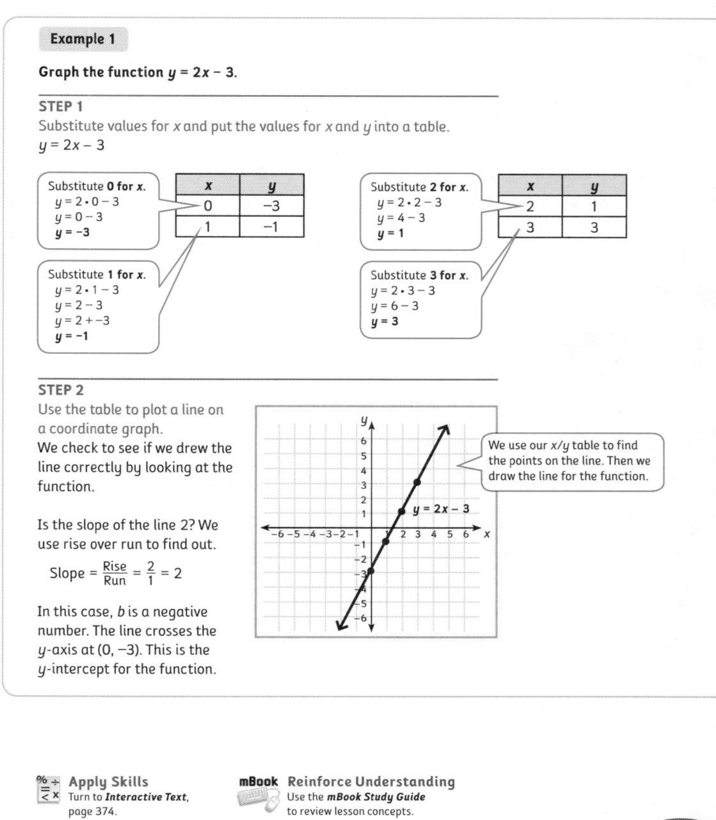

Lesson 11

Example 1

Graph the function $y = 2x - 3$.

STEP 1
Substitute values for *x* and put the values for *x* and *y* into a table.
$y = 2x - 3$

Substitute **0 for *x*.** $y = 2 \cdot 0 - 3$, $y = 0 - 3$, $y = -3$

Substitute **1 for *x*.** $y = 2 \cdot 1 - 3$, $y = 2 - 3$, $y = 2 + -3$, $y = -1$

x	*y*
0	−3
1	−1

Substitute **2 for *x*.** $y = 2 \cdot 2 - 3$, $y = 4 - 3$, $y = 1$

Substitute **3 for *x*.** $y = 2 \cdot 3 - 3$, $y = 6 - 3$, $y = 3$

x	*y*
2	1
3	3

STEP 2
Use the table to plot a line on a coordinate graph.
We check to see if we drew the line correctly by looking at the function.

Is the slope of the line 2? We use rise over run to find out.

Slope = $\frac{\text{Rise}}{\text{Run}} = \frac{2}{1} = 2$

In this case, *b* is a negative number. The line crosses the *y*-axis at (0, −3). This is the *y*-intercept for the function.

$y = 2x - 3$
We use our *x*/*y* table to find the points on the line. Then we draw the line for the function.

Apply Skills
Turn to *Interactive Text*, page 374.

mBook Reinforce Understanding
Use the *mBook Study Guide* to review lesson concepts.

Unit 9 • Lesson 11 751

Apply Skills

(*Interactive Text*, pages 374–375)

Have students turn to pages 374–375 in the *Interactive Text*, which provide students an opportunity to practice interpreting slope-intercept form.

Activity 1

Students fill in an x/y table and create a graph from the function given in slope-intercept form. Then they are to tell the slope and the y-intercept. Monitor students' work as they complete the activity.

Watch for:

- Can students fill in the x/y table for the function?
- Can students graph the function?
- Can students tell the slope and y-intercept? Can they find this information in the graph? Can they find this information in the equation?

Reinforce Understanding
Remind students that they can review lesson concepts by accessing the online *mBook Study Guide*.

Lesson 11 | Apply Skills

Name ______________ Date ______________

Apply Skills
Slope Intercept Form: $y = mx + b$

Activity 1

Fill in the x/y table and make a graph for each of the functions written in slope-intercept form.

1. Function: $y = 2x + 2$

x	y
1	4
2	6
3	8
4	10

Draw the graph.
What is the slope? 2
What is the y-intercept? 2

2. Function: $y = x - 2$

x	y
1	–1
2	0
3	1
4	2

Draw the graph.
What is the slope? 1
What is the y-intercept? –2

374 Unit 9 • Lesson 11

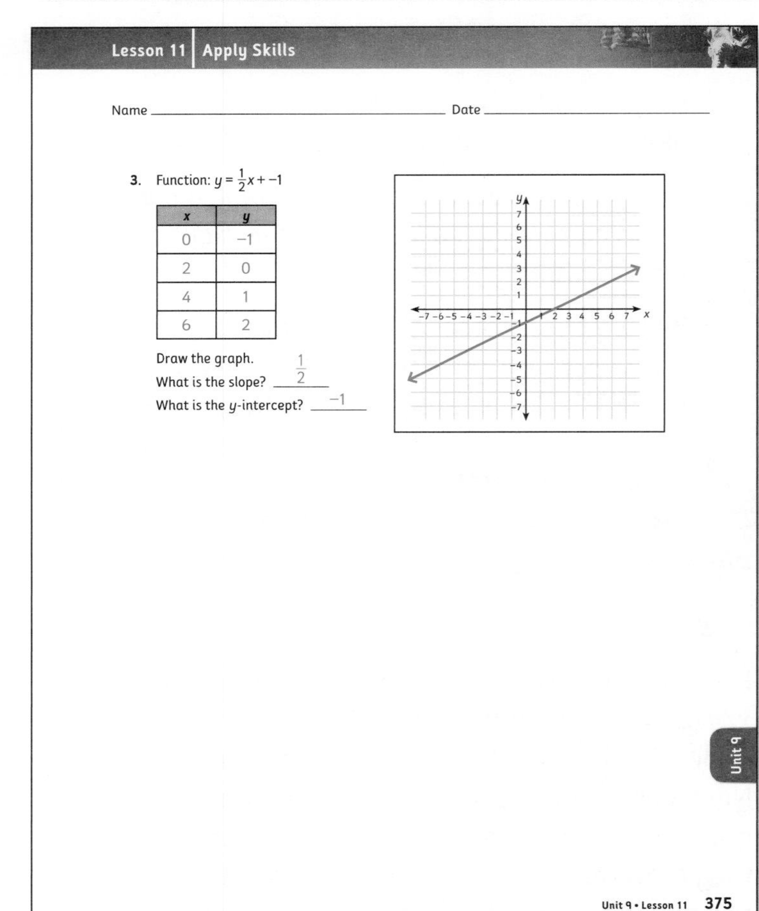
Lesson 11 | Apply Skills

Name ______________ Date ______________

3. Function: $y = \frac{1}{2}x + -1$

x	y
0	–1
2	0
4	1
6	2

Draw the graph.
What is the slope? $\frac{1}{2}$
What is the y-intercept? –1

Unit 9

Unit 9 • Lesson 11 375

Problem Solving: ▶ Graphing Linear Equations

What does $y = mx + b$ look like with no slope?

(*Student Text*, pages 752–755)

Explain

Have students turn to the material on page 752 of the *Student Text* and discuss positive and negative slopes. Have students look at the picture of both kinds of slopes.

Next discuss what happens when the slope of a line is zero. In this instance, the line is horizontal on the graph. Introduce the term **zero slope**. Tell students that an example is the best way to think about this type of slope. We will look at an example of zero slope on page 755.

Demonstrate

- Go over **Example 1**, which is a traditional rental car problem. Tell students you can either pay so much per mile plus a flat rate or you can just pay a flat rate regardless of how many miles you drive.
- Explain that we put each choice into a function, $\mathbf{y = 0.10x + 20}$, and graph it on a line.
- Have students look at Choice #1 and the function $y = mx + b$. Make sure students see that m represents the rate per mile, in this case \$0.10, and b equals the basic rate, in this case \$20.
- Remind students that the slope is the variable that can change, but the y-intercept is what stays the same.

Lesson 11

▶Problem Solving: Graphing Linear Equations

Vocabulary
zero slope

What does $y = mx + b$ look like with no slope?

We looked at two different kinds of slopes in this unit: positive and negative slopes. They go in opposite directions.

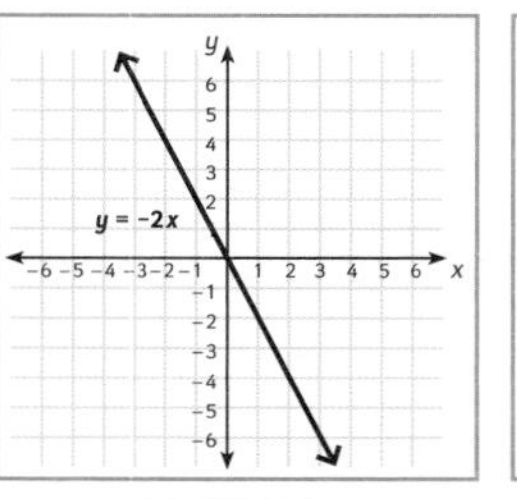

negative slope

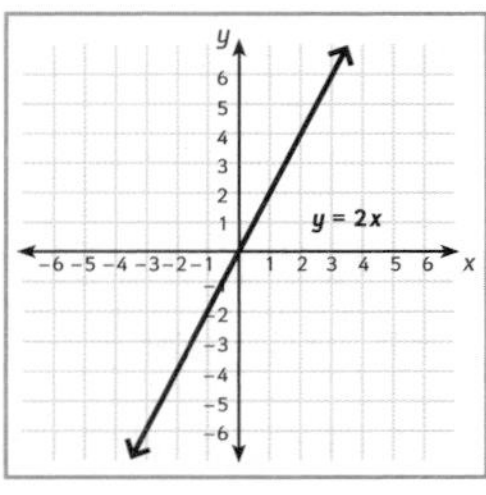

positive slope

There is one other kind of slope we need to know about— **zero slope**.

Example 1 shows how two different choices can lead to different kinds of graphs.

Example 1

Compare the graphs of the rental car choices.

Dented Rental Car Company has two rental choices.

Choice 1: Pay \$20 a day for the car, and then 10 cents (or \$0.10) for every mile driven.

Choice 2: Pay \$25 a day for the car, and drive an unlimited number of miles for no extra charge.

We put each choice into a function, then graph it on a line.

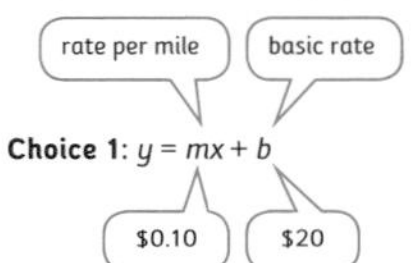

The function is $y = 0.10x + 20$.

752 Unit 9 • Lesson 11

What does $y = mx + b$ look like with no slope? *(continued)*

Demonstrate

- Turn to page 753 of the *Student Text* to continue with Example 1.
- Go over the table we make based on the function. Make sure students understand how the table was created. Have students notice that the y-intercept appears in the table and does not change.
- Have students look at the x/y table. Tell students that **x equals the number of miles driven** and **y equals the total cost**. Be sure students understand how to transfer the information from the first table to the x/y table.
- Then have students look at the graph. Point out that the graph is a positive function.

Lesson 11

We make a table based on the function.

Number of Miles Driven	Cost for Miles Driven	Basic Charge	Total Charge
0	$0	$20	$20
10	$1	$20	$21
20	$2	$20	$22
30	$3	$20	$23
40	$4	$20	$24
50	$5	$20	$25

Then we place the information in an x/y table.
Let x = number of miles driven and y = total cost.

x	y
0	$20
10	$21
20	$22
30	$23
40	$24
50	$25

Finally, our graph is a positive function that looks like this.

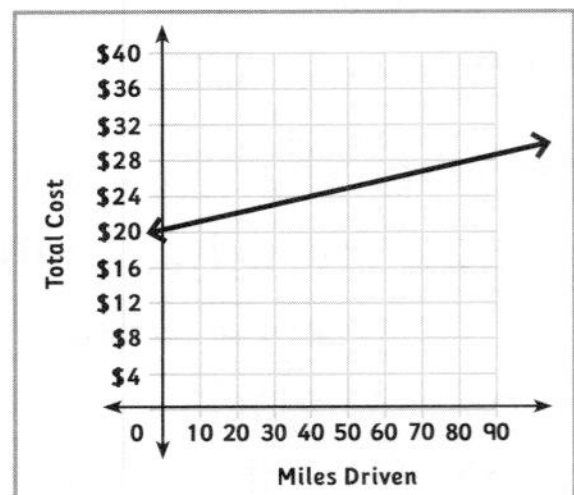

Demonstrate

- Continue with Example 1 on page 754 of the *Student Text*.
- Now have students look at the function for Choice #2. Point out that the rate per mile in this case is \$0 and the basic rate is \$25, so our function is $\boldsymbol{y = 0x + 25}$, or $\boldsymbol{y = 25}$.
- Go over the tables and make sure students understand how we transfer the data from the first table to the values of the x/y table. Point out that **x equals the number of miles driven** and **y equals the total cost**.

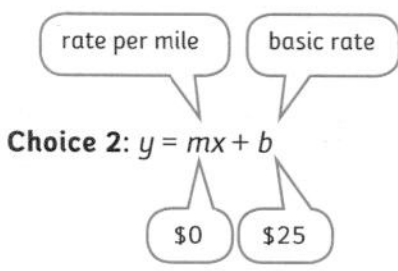

Choice 2: $y = mx + b$

The function is $y = 0x + 25$ or $y = 25$.

We make a table based on the function.

Number of Miles Driven	Cost for Miles Driven	Basic Charge	Total Charge
0	\$0	\$25	\$25
10	\$0	\$25	\$25
20	\$0	\$25	\$25
30	\$0	\$25	\$25
40	\$0	\$25	\$25
50	\$0	\$25	\$25

Then we place the information in an x/y table.
Let x = number of miles driven and y = total cost.

x	y
0	\$25
10	\$25
20	\$25
30	\$25
40	\$25
50	\$25

What does $y = mx + b$ look like with no slope? *(continued)*

Demonstrate

- Continue with Example 1 on page 755 of the *Student Text.*
- Have students look at the graph. Be sure students see that the function that represents the flat rate is a straight line.
- Point out that straight lines do not have any slant to them. Make sure students see that this is the same as a zero slope.
- Explain that it makes sense if we think about slope in terms of rate of change. There is no change in a flat rate. It is the same rate if we drive five miles or 105 miles.

Our graph is a positive linear function that looks like this.

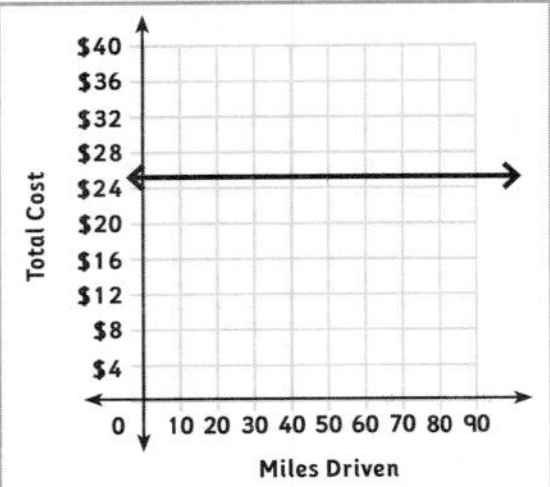

The slope of the second line is zero. It is a horizontal line that keeps going on and on. It doesn't matter how many miles we drive that day, the charge for the rental car will still be $25. This is a linear function with zero slope.

If we compare the two graphs, we see that Choice 1 is a better deal if we are going to drive less than 50 miles a day. If we are going to drive more than 50 miles a day, then Choice 2 is the better deal.

Problem-Solving Activity Turn to ***Interactive Text***, page 376.

mBook Reinforce Understanding Use the ***mBook Study Guide*** to review lesson concepts.

Problem-Solving Activity
(*Interactive Text*, pages 376–377)

Have students turn to pages 376–377 in the *Interactive Text*, which provide students an opportunity to practice graphing functions with different types of slopes.

Remind students about the three kinds of slopes they have learned about—positive, negative, and zero. In today's activity, students match the equation of a function with the appropriate graph of the function. Then students explain what feature on the graph helped them make their decision.

Monitor students' work as they complete the activity.

Watch for:

- Can students identify the function that goes with each graph?
- Can students explain the feature of the graph that helped them make their choice?

Be sure students have adequate time to evaluate each graph and explain their answers.

Reinforce Understanding
Remind students that they can review lesson concepts by accessing the online *mBook Study Guide*.

Lesson 11 | Problem-Solving Activity

Name ______________________ Date ______________

Problem-Solving Activity
Graphing Linear Equations

You learned about three kinds of slopes:
- **Positive slope**
- **Negative slope**
- **Zero slope**

Match the functions with the graphs in each problem. Think about the direction of the line and rise-over-run when you figure out which function goes with what graph.

Functions:

$y = -2x + 3$ $y = 4x - 1$ $y = 0x + 3$ $y = -4x + 1$ $y = 0x - 1$

1. Which function goes with this graph?
$y = 0x + 3$

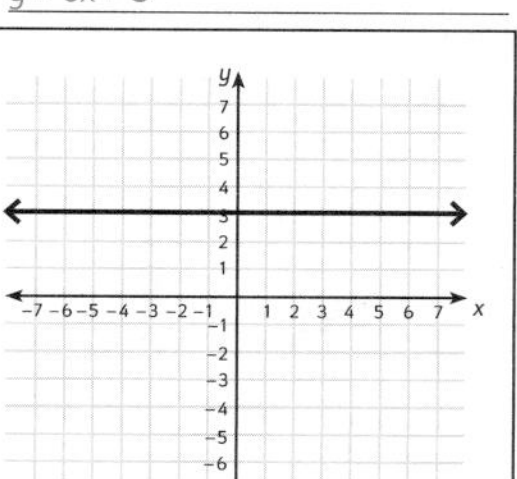

Explain the feature of the graph that helped you make this choice.
Answers will vary. Sample answer: There is no slope and the y-intercept is 3.

2. Which function goes with this graph?
$y = 0x - 1$

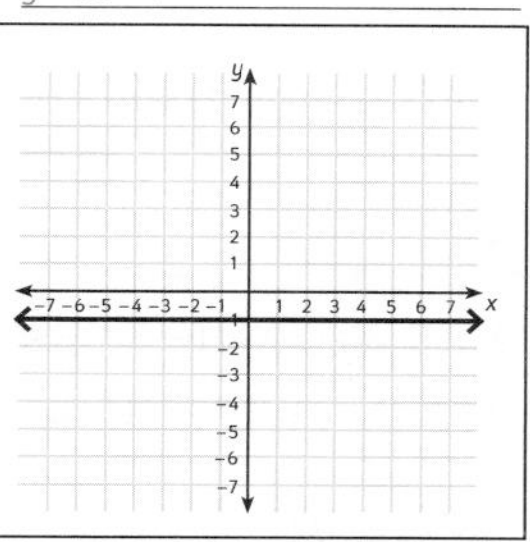

Explain the feature of the graph that helped you make this choice.
Answers will vary. Sample answer: There is no slope and the y-intecept is −1.

376 Unit 9 • Lesson 11

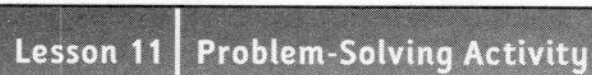

Lesson 11 | Problem-Solving Activity

Name ______________________ Date ______________

3. Which function goes with this graph?
$y = -2x + 3$

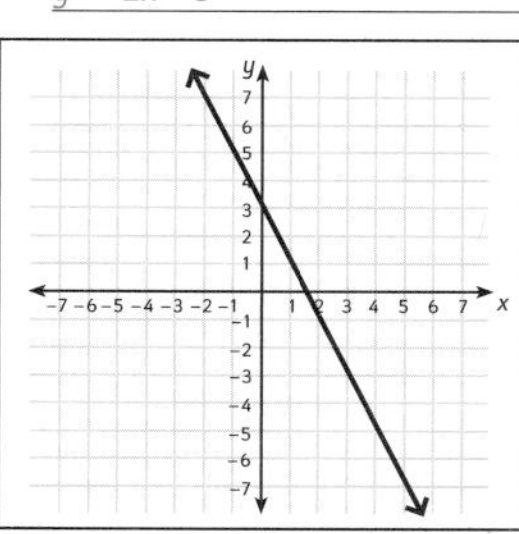

Explain the feature of the graph that helped you make this choice.
Answers will vary. Sample answer: The slope is in Quadrants II and IV with a mild slope and the y-intercept was 3.

4. Which function goes with this graph?
$y = -4x + 1$

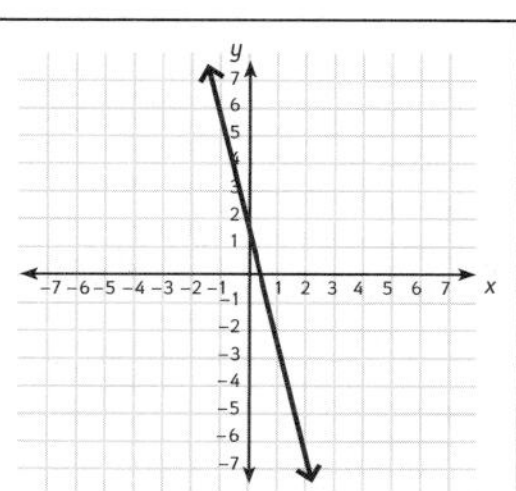

Explain the feature of the graph that helped you make this choice.
Answers will vary. Sample answer: It had a steep negative slope and the y-intercept is 1.

5. Which function goes with this graph?
$y = 4x - 1$

Explain the feature of the graph that helped you make this choice.
Answers will vary. Sample answer: It was a steep slope and was In Quadrant I and III, and the y-intercept was −1.

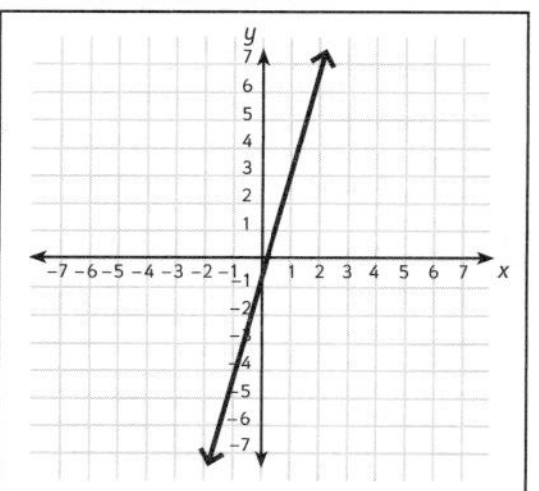

Unit 9

Unit 9 • Lesson 11 377

Homework

Go over the instructions on pages 756–757 of the *Student Text* for each part of the homework.

Activity 1

Students tell the slope and y-intercept for the functions given in equation form.

Activity 2

Students write the slope-intercept form for a function given the slope and y-intercept.

Activity 3

Students create an x/y table and a graph for each of the functions.

Lesson 11

Homework

Activity 1

Each of the functions is written in $y = mx + b$ form. Tell the slope and the y-intercept in each function.

1. $y = 2x + 3$
   (a) What is the slope? 2
   (b) What is the y-intercept? 3
2. $y = \frac{1}{2}x + 4$
   (a) What is the slope? $\frac{1}{2}$
   (b) What is the y-intercept? 4
3. $y = 3x$
   (a) What is the slope? 3
   (b) What is the y-intercept? 0
4. $y = 4$
   (a) What is the slope? 0
   (b) What is the y-intercept? 4

Activity 2

Write the equation for each of the functions using $y = mx + b$ form.

1. Write the function whose slope is –1 and y-intercept is 5. $y = -x + 5$
2. Write the function whose slope is 0 and y-intercept is 2. $y = 2$
3. Write the function whose slope is 1 and y-intercept is 0. $y = x$

Activity 3

Create an x/y table and a graph for each of the functions you wrote in Activity 2.

See Additional Answers below.

756 Unit 9 • Lesson 11

Additional Answers

Activity 3

1.

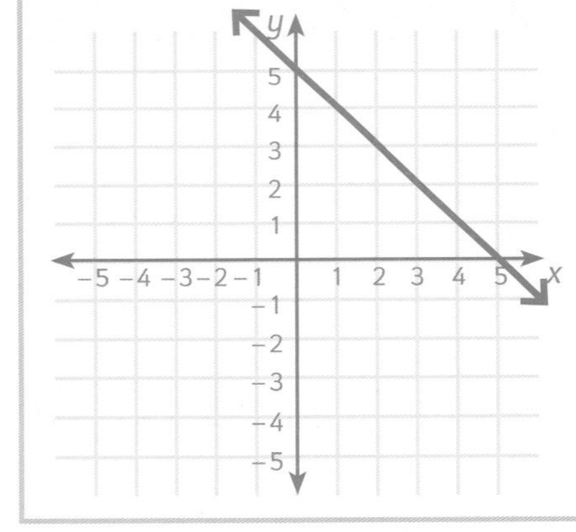

x	y
−1	6
0	5
1	4
2	3

2.

x	y
−1	2
0	2
1	2
2	2

3.

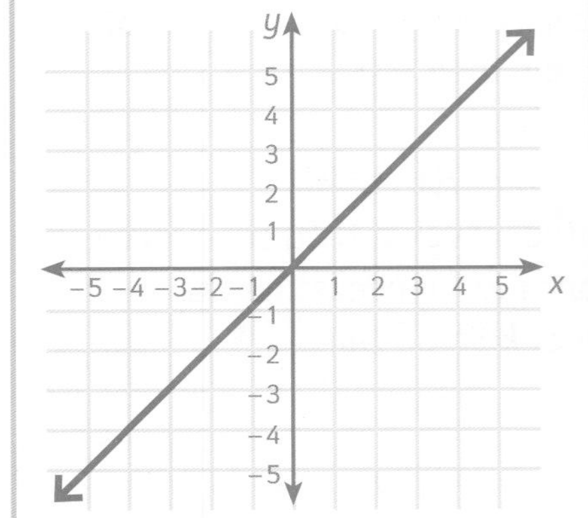

x	y
−1	−1
0	0
1	1
2	2

Homework

Go over the instructions on page 757 of the *Student Text*.

Activity 4 • Distributed Practice

Students write the general pattern for each of the properties.

Lesson 11

Homework

Activity 4 • Distributed Practice

Write the general pattern for each of the properties. You are given examples to help you.

1. Additive Identity Property $m + 0 = m$
   $3 + 0 = 3$
   $-\frac{1}{2} + 0 = -\frac{1}{2}$
   $2.3 + 0 = 2.3$
   Write the general pattern using the variable *m*.
2. Multiplicative Inverse (reciprocal) Property $\frac{a}{b} \cdot \frac{b}{a} = 1$
   $\frac{2}{3} \cdot \frac{3}{2} = 1$
   $\frac{4}{3} \cdot \frac{3}{4} = 1$
   $\frac{2}{1} \cdot \frac{1}{2} = 1$
   Write the general pattern using the variables *a* and *b*.
3. Distributive Property $y(x + z) = yx + yz$
   $2(x + 5) = 2x + 10$
   $3(x + 7) = 3x + 21$
   $4(x + 9) = 4x + 36$
   Write the general pattern using the variables *x*, *y*, and *z*.

Unit 9 • Lesson 11 757

Lesson 12 ▸ Algebraic Equations and Functions

Problem Solving: ▸ More Graphs of Linear Functions

Lesson Planner

Skills Maintenance

$y = mx + b$

Building Number Concepts: ▸ Algebraic Equations and Functions

Students learn that in more complex problems, they need to combine what they know about functions with tools from the Algebra Toolbox. Students look at how to apply what they learned about solving equations to working with functions. They learn that solving equations helps find an exact point in the relationship between two variables.

Objective

Students will use algebraic equations to solve word problems.

Problem Solving: ▸ More Graphs of Linear Functions

Students learn that it is important to think carefully about the parts of the equation $y = mx + b$ when using it to solve complex problems. They learn that we have to think about what changes and what stays the same when we assign the parts of the equation $y = mx + b$ in a problem-solving situation.

Objective

Students will graph linear equations.

Homework

Students use algebra to solve functions, write equations for each function using car rental contracts, and write equations that represent everyday functions. In Distributed Practice, students solve integer operations.

Lesson 12 | Skills Maintenance

Name ____________________ Date ____________________

Skills Maintenance
$y = mx + b$

Activity 1

Use the form $y = mx + b$ to write a function for each problem. Remember, m is the slope and b is the y-intercept.

1. Write the equation for the function where the slope is –2 and the y-intercept is 5.
   $y = -2x + 5$
2. Write the equation for the function where the slope is –1 and the y-intercept is 0.
   $y = -1x + 0$
3. Write the equation for the function where the slope is 1 and the y-intercept is 1.
   $y = 1x + 1$
4. Write the equation for the function where the slope is 0 and the y-intercept is 2.
   $y = 0x + 2$

378 Unit 9 • Lesson 12

Skills Maintenance

$y = mx + b$

(*Interactive Text*, page 378)

Activity 1

Students write the equation when given the slope and the y-intercept.

Building Number Concepts:
▶ Algebraic Equations and Functions

How do we use what we learned about solving equations when working with functions?

(*Student Text*, pages 758–759)

Connect to Prior Knowledge

Begin by discussing the rental car problems from the last lesson. Ask students to think about the problems and tell what part of the problem stayed the same.

Listen for:

- A discussion about the number of miles that a person drove in the rental car.

Next ask students about the parts that stayed the same.

Listen for:

- A discussion about the rate per mile and the amount that was charged as a basic fee.

Link to Today's Concept

Tell students that in today's lesson we go over the assignment of parts in the equation $y = mx + b$ in problem-solving situations. Explain that this is the most important part of solving functions algebraically—setting up the problem correctly.

Demonstrate

Engagement Strategy: Teacher Modeling

Demonstrate how to use an algebraic equation to solve the word problem in one of the following ways:

mBook: Use the *mBook Teacher Edition* for pages 758–759 of the *Student Text.* m

Overhead Projector: Reproduce the equation on Transparency 17, and modify as discussed.

Lesson 12 | ▶Algebraic Equations and Functions
Problem Solving:
▶More Graphs of Linear Functions

▶Algebraic Equations and Functions

How do we use what we learned about solving equations when working with functions?

We have learned a lot about how to solve algebraic equations. We have created an Algebra Toolbox. It is filled with properties and rules that help us solve equations step-by-step.

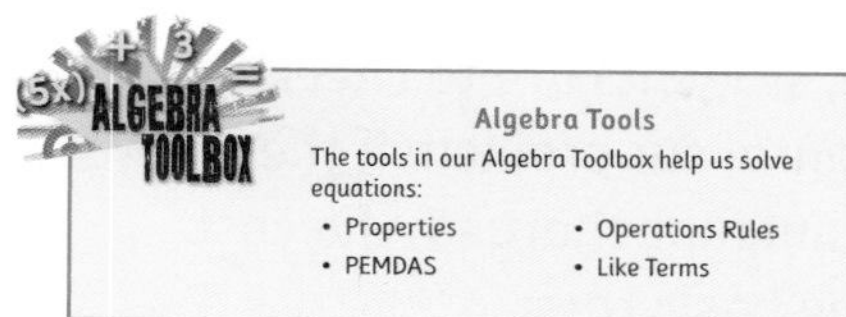

ALGEBRA TOOLBOX
Algebra Tools
The tools in our Algebra Toolbox help us solve equations:
• Properties
• PEMDAS
• Operations Rules
• Like Terms

Knowing how to solve equations is very important when we work with functions. While functions help us see a predictable, systematic relationship between two variables, solving equations helps us find an exact point in that relationship. It is easiest to see that point when we graph a function.

Let's go back to the rental car example in the last lesson. We can rent the car for one day and pay \$20 plus 10 cents (or \$0.10) for every mile that we drive.

Example 1 shows the graph of the function. But let's say that we turn in the car, and the rental charge is \$28. How many miles did we drive? We can look closely at the graph or use algebra to answer this question. Example 1 shows how we can do this.

758 Unit 9 • Lesson 12

Board: Copy the graph and equation on the board, and modify as discussed.

- Remind students about the Algebra Toolbox from previous units. Tell students that in more complex problems, we need to combine what we know about functions with the tools from the Algebra Toolbox. m
- Remind students about the rental car problems they solved in previous lessons. Tell students we can use rules and properties as well as knowledge of functions to solve more complex problems involving the rental car scenario.

How do we use what we learned about solving equations when working with functions? *(continued)*

Demonstrate

- Direct students' attention to **Example 1**. In this example, students are to check the mileage for a rental car problem if they know the total amount charged, the cost per mile, and the basic rate.
- Read through the problem and explain that we will let ***x* equal the number of miles driven** and ***y* equal the total cost**. The function is ***y* = 0.10*x* + 20**. m
- Go over the graph of the function and point out the answer, **80 miles**. m
- Explain that we can also solve the problem by using an algebraic expression. Explain that we will substitute the total cost, **$28**, for ***y***. Go over the algebra problem carefully and be sure students understand the justification for each step. m
- Tell students that the advantage of using algebra to solve the problem is that we might not always have a graphical representation for the problem. It also takes a long time to create one.

Check for Understanding
Engagement Strategy: Look About

Present students with the following situation:

You rented a car again from Dented Rental, using Choice #1. This time by total bill was $50. You still pay $20, plus $0.10 per mile. How far did you drive?

Have students use an algebraic equation to solve the problem (*300 miles*). Students should write their work in large writing on a piece of paper or a dry erase board. When the students finish their work, they should hold up their answer for everyone to see.

If students are not sure about the answer, prompt them to look about at other students' solutions to help with their thinking. Review the answers after all students have held up their solutions.

Example 1

Use an algebraic equation to solve the word problem.

Problem:
I rented a car from Dented Rental Car Company, and I decided to use Choice 1. That means I pay $20 a day plus $0.10 per mile. That day, I drive from Baltimore to Washington, D.C., and back again. My total bill from Dented Rental is $28. How far did I drive?

Let x = number of miles driven and y = total cost.

The function is $y = 0.10x + 20$.

The graph shows a line. To find out exactly how many miles were driven, we start by finding $28 on the y-axis. Then we go across the graph until we reach the line to determine where this intersects with the x-axis. If we look closely, we see it is 80 miles.

Another way to solve this problem is to use an algebraic expression.

We know that the total cost is $28 and y = the total cost. All we have to do is substitute for y.

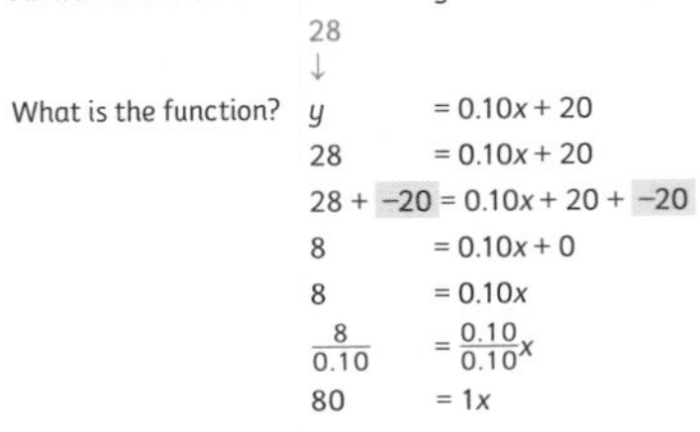

28 ↓

What is the function? $y = 0.10x + 20$

$28 = 0.10x + 20$

$28 + -20 = 0.10x + 20 + -20$

$8 = 0.10x + 0$

$8 = 0.10x$

$\frac{8}{0.10} = \frac{0.10}{0.10}x$

$80 = 1x$

$80 = x$

I drove 80 miles. We get the same answer using algebra.

The advantage of using algebra is we often do not have the function on a graph. This means that we need to use algebra to solve the problem.

Apply Skills
Turn to *Interactive Text*, page 379.

mBook Reinforce Understanding
Use the ***mBook Study Guide*** to review lesson concepts.

Apply Skills
(*Interactive Text*, page 379)

Have students turn to page 379 in the *Interactive Text*, which provides students an opportunity to practice solving functions in slope-intercept form.

Activity 1

Students solve problems involving rental car agreements. In each problem, they use algebra to tell how many miles were driven.

Monitor students' work as they complete the activity.

Watch for:

- Can students solve the problem algebraically?
- Can students come up with the correct number of miles for the answer?

mBook **Reinforce Understanding**
Remind students that they can review lesson concepts by accessing the online *mBook Study Guide*.

Name ______________________ Date ______________________

Apply Skills
Algebraic Equations and Functions

Activity 1

Suppose you rent a car from Dented Rentals. The base charge is $20, plus 25 cents per mile. The equation for this function looks like this: $y = 0.25x + 20$. Each problem gives you a total charge amount for different scenarios. Find the amount of miles you have to drive to reach each amount.

1. The total amount you owe Dented Rentals is $140. Here is the equation: $140 = 0.25x + 20$. How many miles did you travel?
   480 miles
   Show your work here:
   $140 - 20 = 0.25x + 20 - 20$
   $120 \div 0.25 = 0.25x \div 0.25$
   $480 = x$

2. The total amount you owe Dented Rentals is $200. Here is the equation: $200 = 0.25x + 20$. How many miles did you travel?
   720 miles
   Show your work here:
   $200 - 20 = 0.25x + 20 - 20$
   $180 \div 0.25 = 0.25x \div 0.25$
   $720 = x$

3. The total amount you owe Dented Rentals is $380. Here is the equation: $380 = 0.25x + 20$. How many miles did you travel?
   1,440 miles
   Show your work here:
   $380 - 20 = 0.25x + 20 - 20$
   $360 \div 0.25 = 0.25x \div 0.25$
   $1{,}440 = x$

Problem Solving: ▶ More Graphs of Linear Functions

How do we know what changes and what stays the same in a function?

(*Student Text*, pages 760–763)

Demonstrate

- Have students turn to the material on page 760 of the *Student Text*. Discuss how to solve problems involving functional relationships using algebraic equations.
- Tell students that we first need to think carefully about what the variables are to stand for.
- Explain to students that we need to analyze what changes and what stays the same. Next we have to determine what part of the problem represents the slope, the y-intercept, and any extra information.
- Remind students of the rental car problem. Explain that the amount that was changing was the number of miles. The person could have driven more miles or fewer miles.
- Tell students that this is the part that changes, and we use x to represent this in the equation of the form $y = mx + b$.
- Tell students that in the rental car scenario, the part that stayed the same was the amount charged per mile. That becomes m in the $y = mx + b$ equation.
- Next tell students that we have to think about if there are any basic fees or flat rates. Explain to students that this is the y-intercept, or the b part of the equation. This is the part of the equation that stays the same.

How do we know what changes and what stays the same in a function?

Functions help us think about the systematic relationship between two variables. We have used equations involving x and y to represent each variable. We have also learned that the traditional way of showing a function is to use the equation $y = mx + b$.

When we solve an equation of a function algebraically, we need to think carefully about what each variable in the equation stands for. A good way to begin is to think about what is changing and what is staying the same.

In the rental car example, the amount that was changing was the number of miles. In Choice 2, we could have driven 10 miles or 50 miles. That part could have changed. What stayed the same was the basic cost of the rental car, which was always going to be $25 no matter how many miles were driven. When we look at the equation for the function, we see which parts are changing and which parts stay the same. The y-intercept, which we call b, is a constant. It stays the same.

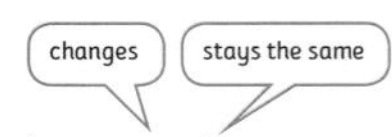

Equation for a function: $y = mx + b$

Let's look at how to take a simple function and turn it into an algebraic equation we can solve. Example 1 shows how we translate it into an equation.

- Tell students that once we identify all the parts that change and all the parts that are constant, we can translate the problem into an algebraic equation that represents the function.

Demonstrate

- Have students turn to the page 761 of the *Student Text* to look at **Example 1**. We look again at Tina, who works at Big Tom's Restaurant.
- Read through the word problem and go over each step to solve it.

STEP 1

- Explain that we first have to decide what is changing and what is staying the same. In this case, the **$50** in the bank is not changing. What changes is the number of hours Tina works.
- Point out how this relates to the equation for a function.

STEP 2

- Tell students that now we can find out what the variables represent. In this case, ***x* equals the number of hours Tina works** and ***y* equals the total amount Tina has saved**.
- Explain that variable *b* does not change because that is the $50 in the bank.

STEP 3

- Show how we substitute the variables into the function. We substitute **350 for *y***, the total amount; **15 for *m***, the rate per hour; and **50 for *b***, the amount in the bank.

Example 1

Use algebra to solve the word problem.

Problem:

Tina is working at Big Tom's Restaurant and is paid $15 an hour. She has $50 in the bank, and she needs $350 to pay her rent this month. How many hours will she have to work until she has $350 to pay her rent?

STEP 1

Decide what is changing and what is staying the same.

The $50 Tina has in the bank is not changing. It stays there. What changes is the number of hours she is going to work.

Equation for a function: $y = mx + b$

STEP 2

Find what the variables represent in the function.

Let x = the number of hours she works and y = the total amount she has saved. The variable b does not change. That is the $50 Tina has in the bank. We use this to understand what y, x, and b stand for in the function equation.

STEP 3

Substitute for the variables in the function. This will give us a simple algebraic equation.

350 15 50

Equation for a function: $y = mx + b$

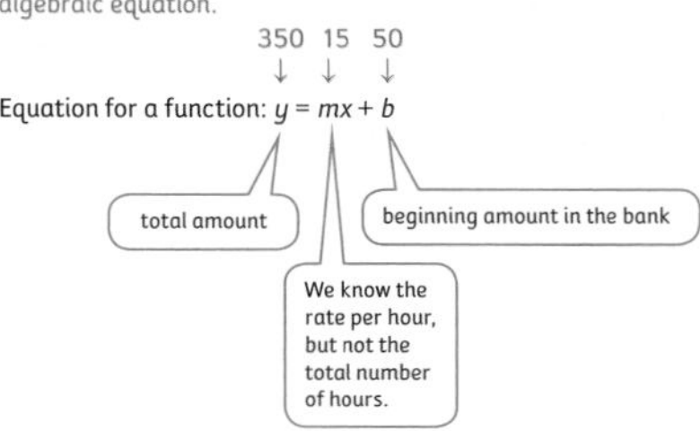

How do we know what changes and what stays the same in a function? *(continued)*

Demonstrate

- Continue with Example 1 on page 762 of the *Student Text*

STEP 4

- Explain that after we substitute the values we know for the variables, our equation is now **350 = 15*x* + 50**. Now we can solve the equation.
- Walk through equation, and be sure students understand the justification for each step.
- Explain that because *x* equals 20, this means that **Tina will have to work 20 hours to save a total of $350**.
- Remind students that it is a good idea to use substitution to check our answer.
- Walk through the calculations to see that **350 = 350**. The answer is correct.
- Then move to **Example 2**, which is another problem that requires algebra to solve. Read through the word problem about Tina's cell phone plan.

Lesson 12

STEP 4
Solve the equation.
The equation is: $350 = 15x + 50$

Solution:

$$350 = 15x + 50$$
$$350 + -50 = 15x + 50 + -50$$
$$300 = 15x + 0$$
$$300 = 15x$$
$$\frac{300}{15} = \frac{15}{15}x$$
$$20 = 1x$$
$$20 = x$$

Tina will have to work 20 hours to save a total of $350.

We substitute to check if we are correct.

20
↓
$$350 = 15x + 50$$
$$350 = 15 \cdot 20 + 50$$
$$350 = 300 + 50$$
$$350 = 350$$

Let's look at another problem using the equation $y = mx + b$. Tina also has a cell phone. She pays $30 a month and an additional $8 for every hour she talks on the phone each month. Example 2 shows how our function changes and how we solve it.

Example 2

Use algebra to solve the word problem.

Problem:
Tina has an inexpensive cell phone plan. She pays a monthly charge of $30, but has to pay an additional $8 for every hour she talks on the phone. The company just charges by the hour, not by the minute. Last month her bill was $54. How many hours did she talk on the phone?

762 Unit 9 • Lesson 12

Demonstrate

- Continue with Example 2 on page 763 of the *Student Text.*

STEP 1

- Remind students that we first have to decide what is changing and what is staying the same. In this case, the **$30** that Tina pays each month does not change. What changes is the number of hours she talks on the phone.
- Be sure students understand each part of the $y = mx + b$ equation.

STEP 2

- Tell students that now we can find out what the variables represent. In this case, ***x* equals the number of hours Tina talks on the phone** and ***y* equals the total amount of her bill**.
- Explain that variable b does not change because that is the $30 a month for the phone.

STEP 3

- Show how we substitute the variables into the function. We substitute **54 for *y***, the total amount of the bill; **8 for *m***, the rate per hour; and **30 for *b***, the monthly charge.

STEP 4

- Explain that after substitution, our equation is now **54 = 8*x* + 30**. Now we can solve the equation.
- Walk through equation, and be sure students understand the justification for each step.
- Explain that because x equals 3, this means that **Tina talked for 3 hours on the phone**.

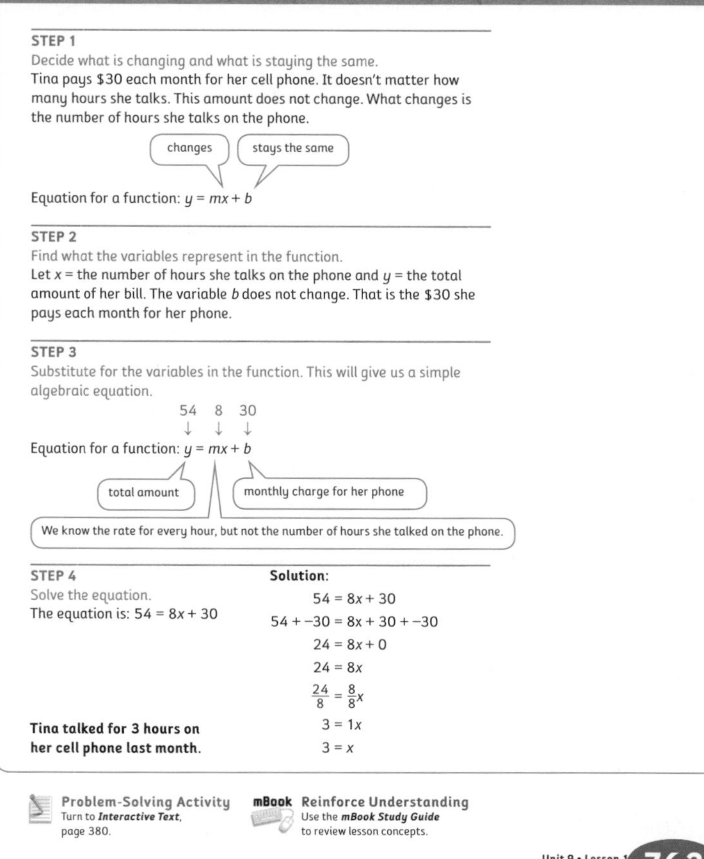

Lesson 12

STEP 1
Decide what is changing and what is staying the same.
Tina pays $30 each month for her cell phone. It doesn't matter how many hours she talks. This amount does not change. What changes is the number of hours she talks on the phone.

changes | stays the same

Equation for a function: $y = mx + b$

STEP 2
Find what the variables represent in the function.
Let x = the number of hours she talks on the phone and y = the total amount of her bill. The variable b does not change. That is the $30 she pays each month for her phone.

STEP 3
Substitute for the variables in the function. This will give us a simple algebraic equation.

54 ↓ 8 ↓ 30 ↓

Equation for a function: $y = mx + b$

total amount | monthly charge for her phone

We know the rate for every hour, but not the number of hours she talked on the phone.

STEP 4
Solve the equation.
The equation is: $54 = 8x + 30$

Solution:

$$54 = 8x + 30$$
$$54 + -30 = 8x + 30 + -30$$
$$24 = 8x + 0$$
$$24 = 8x$$
$$\frac{24}{8} = \frac{8}{8}x$$
$$3 = 1x$$
$$3 = x$$

Tina talked for 3 hours on her cell phone last month.

Problem-Solving Activity Turn to ***Interactive Text***, page 380.

mBook Reinforce Understanding Use the ***mBook Study Guide*** to review lesson concepts.

Unit 9 • Lesson 1 763

Check for Understanding
Engagement Strategy: Look About

Remind students that it is a good idea to use substitution to check our answer. Tell them that they will substitute the value of x, 3, into the equation to check the answer. Students should write their solutions in large writing on a piece of paper or a dry erase board. When the students finish their work, they should hold up their answer for everyone to see.

If students are not sure about the answer, prompt them to look about at other students' solutions to help with their thinking. Review the answers after all students have held up their solutions.

Problem-Solving Activity
(*Interactive Text*, page 380)

Have students turn to page 380 in the *Interactive Text*, which provides students an opportunity to practice solving word problems with functions.

Tell students they are going to work on word problems that involve functions using algebra. Review the four steps on the board or overhead:

Step 1: What is changing and what is staying the same?

Step 2: Find what the variables represent in the function.

Step 3: Substitute for the variables in the function.

Step 4: Solve the equation.

Monitor students' work as they complete the activity.

Watch for:

- Can students figure out what information in the problem goes with each part of the $y = mx + b$ equation?
- Can students follow the four steps to solve the equations?
- Can students find the correct answer?
- Do students check the answer?

mBook **Reinforce Understanding**
Remind students that they can review lesson concepts by accessing the online *mBook Study Guide*.

Lesson 12 | Problem-Solving Activity

Name ______________ Date ______________

Problem-Solving Activity
More Graphs of Linear Functions

Write the word problems in $y = mx + b$ form, then solve algebraically. Remember the four steps for solving these kinds of problems:
Step 1: Decide what is changing and what is staying the same.
Step 2: Find what each variable represents in the function.
Step 3: Substitute numbers for the variables in the function.
Step 4: Solve the equation.

1. Juliana sells programs at baseball games. She makes $5 per night and $2 for every program she sells. At the end of Thursday night, she made $37. How many programs did she sell?
   She sold 16.
   $37 = 2x + 5$ $\quad 37 - 5 = 2x + 5 - 5$ $\quad \frac{32}{2} = \frac{2x}{2}$
   $16 = x$

2. A carpet cleaning service charges a base fee of $10 to clean carpets, then $2 for every square yard. The bill to clean the house was $58. How many square yards did the service clean?
   They cleaned 24 square yards.
   $58 = 2x + 10$ $\quad 58 - 10 = 2x + 10 - 10$ $\quad \frac{48}{2} = \frac{2x}{2}$
   $24 = x$

3. A wagon is used to move boxes around the warehouse. The wagon weighs 40 pounds and each box weighs 5 pounds. After Cesar stacked the wagon with boxes, the wagon and the boxes weighed 95 pounds. How many boxes did Cesar stack on the wagon?
   He stacked 9 boxes on the wagon.
   $95 = 5x + 40$ $\quad 95 - 40 = 5x + 40 - 40$ $\quad \frac{45}{5} = \frac{5x}{5}$
   $9 = x$

mBook **Reinforce Understanding**
Use the **mBook** ***Study Guide*** to review lesson concepts.

380 Unit 9 • Lesson 12

Homework

Go over the instructions on page 764 of the *Student Text* for each part of the homework.

Activity 1

Students use algebra to solve functions.

Activity 2

Students write equations for each function using car rental contracts.

Activity 3

Students write equations that represent everyday functions. Point out that they do not need to solve the problems; just write the correct equations for the functions.

Activity 4 • Distributed Practice

Students solve integer operations.

Lesson 12

Homework

Activity 1

Use algebra to solve the functions.

1. $y = 0.10x + 20$ for $y = 360$ $x = 3{,}400$
2. $y = 0.20x + 10$ for $y = 210$ $x = 1{,}000$
3. $y = 0.50x + 40$ for $y = 140$ $x = 200$
4. $y = 0.30x + 30$ for $y = 930$ $x = 3{,}000$

Activity 2

Write an equation for each function using the car rental contracts.

Model A rental car costs $50 plus 20 cents per mile. Write the equation that describes this function.
Answer: $y = 0.20x + 50$

1. A rental car costs $25 plus 10 cents per mile. Write the equation. $y = 0.10x + 25$
2. A rental car costs $100 plus 5 cents per mile. Write the equation. $y = 0.05x + 100$
3. A rental car costs $20 plus 30 cents per mile. Write the equation. $y = 0.30x + 20$
4. A rental car company only charges per mile. The rate is $1 per mile. Write the equation. $y = x$

Activity 3

For each of the everyday functions, write the equation that describes the function. Use $y = mx + b$ form.

1. Todd is a busboy at a popular restaurant. He gets paid $8 per hour and $50 per night he works. Write an equation that describes this function. $y = 8x + 50$
2. Loretta has a babysitting business and she charges $10 per hour and a flat fee of $5 per job. Write an equation that shows this function. $y = 10x + 5$
3. The tickets for the baseball game cost $30 per ticket plus a $10 processing fee for each group purchasing tickets. Write an equation that shows this function. $y = 30x + 10$

Activity 4 • Distributed Practice

Solve.

1. $-24 + -18 + -14$ -56
2. $27 - 4 - 8$ 15
3. $-18 \div 9$ -2
4. $-9 \cdot -8$ 72
5. $-170 - -90$ -80
6. $417 - 503$ -86

764 Unit 9 • Lesson 12

Lesson 13 ▸ Creating an *X*/*Y* Table From a Graph

Problem Solving: ▸ The Point Where Functions Intersect on a Graph

Lesson Planner

Skills Maintenance

Identifying Coordinates on a Graph

Building Number Concepts:

▸ Creating an *X*/*Y* Table From a Graph

In this lesson, students learn how to identify coordinates of points on a graph and use those coordinates to create an *x*/*y* table. We can then use the table to write the function in $y = mx + b$ form.

Objective

Students will create *x*/*y* tables from graphs.

Problem Solving:

▸ The Point Where Functions Intersect on a Graph

Students learn that sometimes linear functions help us make important decisions, often when we are given a choice and do not know which to pick. We look at how to compare two functions to see where they meet algebraically by making the two equations equal by seeing where the two lines intersect on the graph.

Objective

Students will find where two functions intersect on a graph.

Homework

Students create *x*/*y* tables from graphs of lines, write the equation for the function that is represented in the *x*/*y* tables, and tell the point where two lines intersect on a graph. In Distributed Practice, students solve one- and two-step equations.

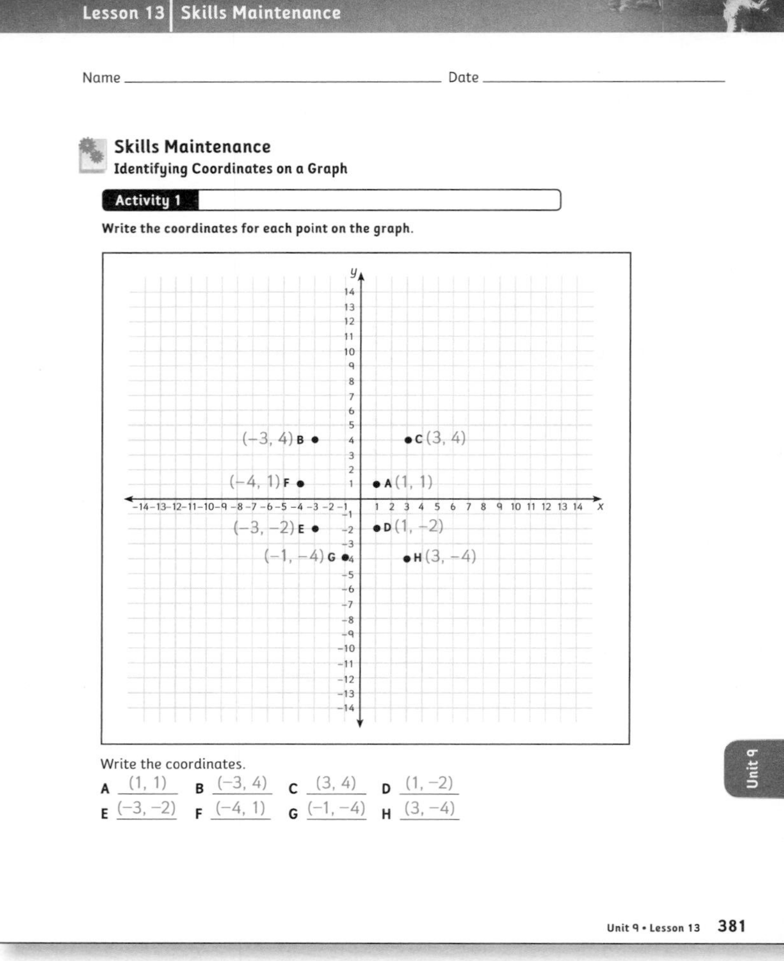
Lesson 13 | Skills Maintenance

Name ______________ Date ______________

Skills Maintenance
Identifying Coordinates on a Graph

Activity 1

Write the coordinates for each point on the graph.

Write the coordinates.

A (1, 1) B (−3, 4) C (3, 4) D (1, −2)
E (−3, −2) F (−4, 1) G (−1, −4) H (3, −4)

Unit 9

Unit 9 • Lesson 13 381

Skills Maintenance

Identifying Coordinates on a Graph

(*Interactive Text*, page 381)

Activity 1

Students identify the coordinates of points on a coordinate graph.

Building Number Concepts:
▶ Creating an *X/Y* Table From a Graph

How do we create tables from a graph?

(*Student Text*, page 765)

Connect to Prior Knowledge

Begin by putting these equations on the board or overhead:

$$12 = 3x \qquad 12 = 2x + 4$$

Tell students that since both equations have a 12 on the left, we can make the equations equal to each other to find the value of *x*. The equation looks like this:

$$3x = 2x + 4$$

Next have students solve the equation, then substitute the value of the variable (4) into the original equations to be sure it works.

Link to Today's Concept

Tell students that we use this concept to solve problems in today's lesson.

Demonstrate

Engagement Strategy: Teacher Modeling

Demonstrate how to create tables from a graph in one of the following ways:

mBook: Use the *mBook Teacher Edition* for page 765 of the *Student Text.* m

Overhead Projector: Reproduce the graph and table on a transparency, and modify as discussed.

Board: Copy the graph and table on the board, and modify as discussed

- Discuss the way we have been solving functions. Most of the time, we have taken the *x/y* coordinates from an *x/y* table and plotted them on a graph.

Lesson 13 | ▶Creating an *X/Y* Table From a Graph
Problem Solving:
▶The Point Where Functions Intersect on a Graph

▶Creating an *X/Y* Table From a Graph

How do we create a table from a graph?

Up until now, we have been given functions and then plotted them on a coordinate graph. What happens when we reverse this process?

Example 1 shows how we can create a table by looking at points on a graph.

Example 1

Make an *x/y* table from the graph of a function.

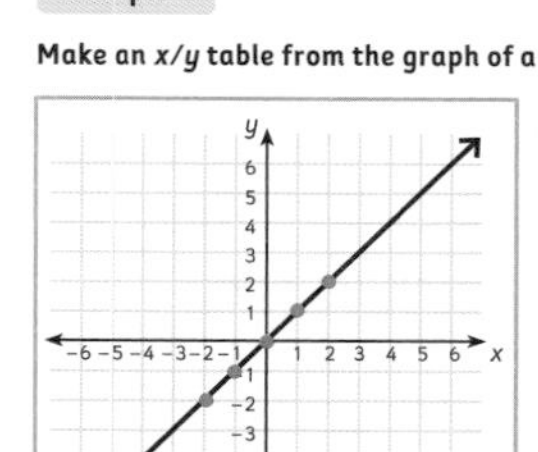

If we identify the coordinates of the points on this graph, we see *x* and *y* values for the function. The coordinates of the points are: (0, 0), (1, 1), (2, 2), (−1, −1), and (−2, −2). We just take the *x* and *y* values from these coordinates and put them in a table.

x	*y*
−2	−2
−1	−1
0	0
1	1
2	2

An *x/y* table shows the *x* values and *y* values for a function. These are very easily translated from (*x*, *y*) coordinates to *x* and *y* values in a table. This is also a way to find the equation of a function shown on a graph because once we show it in a table, it is easy to analyze the relationship between *x* and *y*. For the function shown in Example 1, the equation is $y = x$. Every input value is the same as every output value.

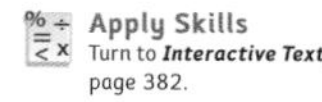

Apply Skills
Turn to *Interactive Text*, page 382.

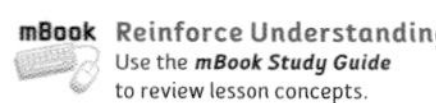

Reinforce Understanding
Use the *mBook Study Guide* to review lesson concepts.

Unit 9 • Lesson 13 765

- Tell students that we can also do the reverse. We can look at the graph of a line, pull out the *x/y* coordinates, and write them in a table. From this form, we can write the equation of the function.
- Go over **Example 1**, which shows students how to do this. Show the graph of the line and explain that we analyze it to determine the coordinates of the points on the line. m
- Next tell students that we create an *x/y* table to put these values in so that we can analyze their relationship more closely. We use the coordinates of the points and take the *x* and *y* values from the coordinates and put them in a table. m
- Show how we can determine the relationship between *x* and *y* and write the equation for the function, $y = x$.

Apply Skills
(*Interactive Text*, page 382)

Have students turn to page 382 in the *Interactive Text*, which provides students an opportunity to practice these concepts on their own.

Activity 1

Students create *x*/*y* tables from the coordinates on a graph. Then they write the function in slope-intercept form. Monitor students' work as they complete the activity.

Watch for:

- Can students identify coordinates of points shown on the graph?
- Can students transfer this information into an x/y table?
- Can students write the equation in $y = mx + b$ form?

mBook **Reinforce Understanding**
Remind students that they can review lesson concepts by accessing the online *mBook Study Guide*.

Lesson 13 | Apply Skills

Name ______________________ Date ______________________

Apply Skills
Creating an *X*/*Y* Table From a Graph

Activity 1

Create an *x*/*y* table for each problem. Then tell the function in $y = mx + b$ form.

1.

x	y
1	3
2	6
3	9
4	12

$y = 3x$

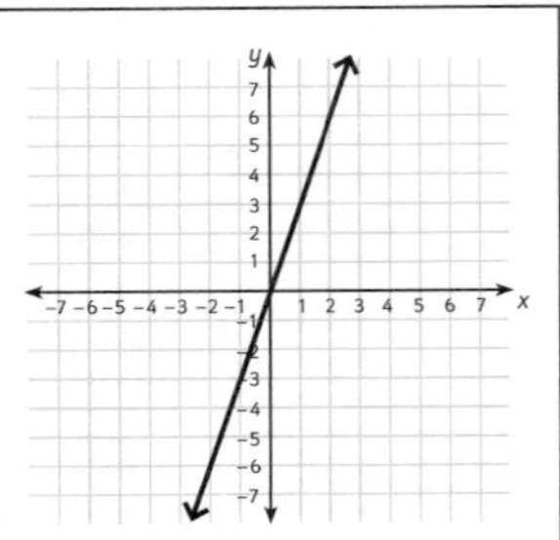

2.

x	y
1	−1
2	−2
3	−3
4	−4

$y = -x$

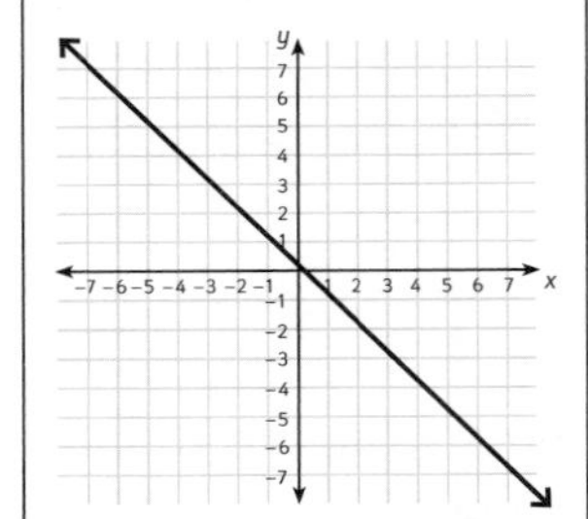

382 Unit 9 • Lesson 13

Problem Solving:
▶ The Point Where Functions Intersect on a Graph

Where do two functions meet?
(*Student Text*, pages 766–767)

Explain
Use page 766 in the *Student Text* to discuss how graphs of functions can be used to help us make important comparisons in everyday functions. Tell students that quite often, we are interested in where two functions meet. This helps us decide which function represents the better situation.

Demonstrate
- Have students look at **Example 1**. In this example, we demonstrate two different payment plans for buying a car.
- Read through the scenario and payment plans. Then explain to students that we can use algebra to find out where the two lines meet by making the functions equal to each other.
- Show how we start by writing the functions. We determine what is changing and what is staying the same.
- Point out that in Plan 1, the $500 stays the same and the number of months we pay $100 changes. So our function is $\boldsymbol{y = 100x + 500}$.
- Then point out that in Plan 2, we pay $150 per month. The number of months we pay changes. So our function is $\boldsymbol{y = 150x}$.
- Point out that $\boldsymbol{150x = 100x + 500}$ because the expressions from the two plans each equal y.

Where do two functions meet?

There are times when linear functions help us make important decisions. This often happens when we are given a choice and we can't decide what to do. Example 1 shows what different payment plans mean when we buy a used car. We use algebra to figure out the point where the plans cross.

Example 1

Use equations and a graph to solve the problem.

Problem:

Garrison Motors offers two payment plan choices when you buy a used car.

Plan 1: Pay $500 down and make payments of $100 per month.

Plan 2: Just pay $150 per month.

At what point will you have paid the same amount of money?

We begin by writing the two functions.

Plan 1: What is changing and what is the same?

When we pay $500 up front, that stays the same. What is changing is the number of months that we pay $100. The function for Plan 1 is $y = 100x + 500$.

Plan 2: What is changing and what is the same?

The only thing that is happening in Plan 2 is change. Nothing is staying the same. We pay $150 per month. The number of months that we pay changes. The function for Plan 2 is $y = 150x$.

We use algebra to figure out where the functions cross.

If $y = 100x + 500$ and $y = 150x$, that means $150x = 100x + 500$ because both of these expressions equal y.

- Remind students of the activity they did to introduce today's lesson. When two expressions equal the same number, we can rewrite them, as we did here.

Where do two functions meet?
(continued)

Demonstrate

- Continue going over Example 1 on page 767 of the *Student Text*.
- Go over all of the algebraic steps and be sure students understand the justification for each to see that $x = 10$, which is 10 months.
- Explain to students that we can also solve the problem by graphing the two functions and finding where their lines intersect.
- Have students look at the graph to see that the two functions cross at 10 months on the x-axis.

Now we solve the problem using the rules and properties in our Algebra Toolbox.

$$150x = 100x + 500$$
$$150x + -100x = 100x + -100x + 500$$
$$50x = 0 + 500$$
$$50x = 500$$
$$\frac{50}{50}x = \frac{500}{50}$$
$$1x = 10$$
$$x = 10 \text{ or } 10 \text{ months}$$

Here is the graph with the two functions. The two functions cross at 10 months on the x-axis.

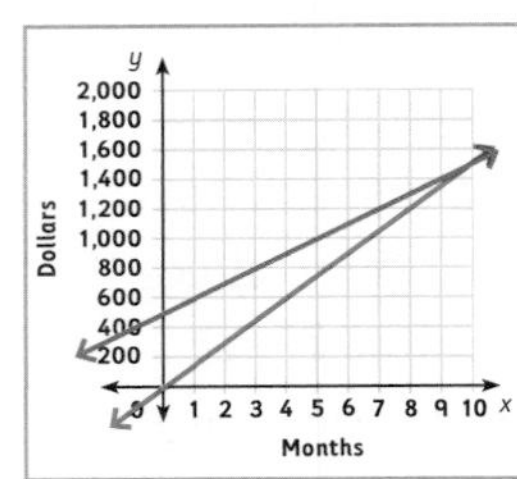

Problem-Solving Activity Turn to ***Interactive Text***, page 383.

Reinforce Understanding Use the ***mBook Study Guide*** to review lesson concepts.

Problem-Solving Activity
(*Interactive Text*, page 383)

Have students turn to page 383 in the *Interactive Text*, which provides students an opportunity to practice finding where two functions intersect.

Students solve the problems involving two functions by first solving them algebraically, then graphing the lines and seeing where the lines intersect.

Monitor students' work as they complete the activity.

Watch for:

- Can students write the equations and solve them algebraically for finding where the two functions meet?
- Can students draw the two graphs and see where the lines intersect?
- Can students see that the answers should be the same? Are the answers the same? Is the answer correct?

Reinforce Understanding

Remind students that they can review lesson concepts by accessing the online *mBook Study Guide*.

Lesson 13 | Problem-Solving Activity

Name ______________________ Date ______________

Problem-Solving Activity
The Point Where Functions Intersect on a Graph

Write two functions to solve each problem. Use algebra to find where the two functions cross on the graph. Then plot the functions on a graph to see where they intersect.

1. Garrison Motors has two plans for buying new cars.

   Plan 1: You pay $450 per month.

   Plan 2: You pay $1,000 down and pay $250 per month.

   What are the two functions?

   $y = 450x$; $y = 250x + 1{,}000$

   How many months before you pay the same amount with both plans?

   5 months

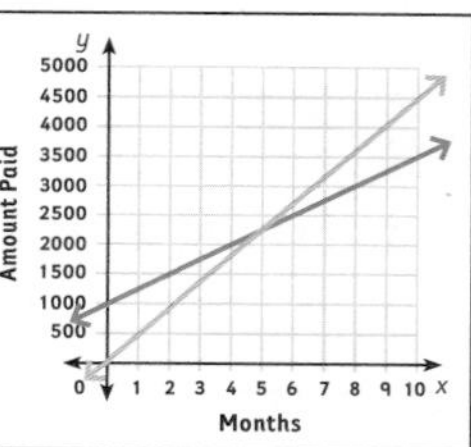

2. Raul is getting a summer job delivering pizza. He has done it before, and he has to choose between two different companies. Bonzo Pizza will pay him $10 a day and $3 for every pizza he delivers. Too Hot to Eat Pizza will pay him $5 for every pizza he delivers.

   What are the two functions?

   $y = 10x + 3$; $y + 5x$

   At what point will he make the same amount of money?

   After he delivers 5 pizzas.

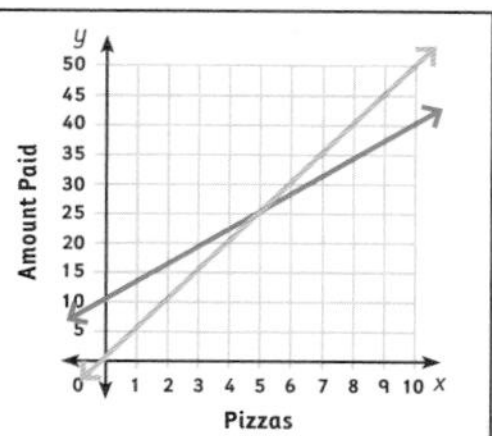

Unit 9

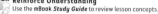

mBook Reinforce Understanding
Use the mBook *Study Guide* to review lesson concepts.

Unit 9 • Lesson 13 383

Homework

Go over the instructions on pages 768–769 of the *Student Text* for each part of the homework.

Activity 1

Students create x/y tables from graphs of lines.

Activity 2

Students write the equation for the function that is represented in the x/y tables.

Homework

Activity 1

For each of the graphs, create an x/y table.

1.

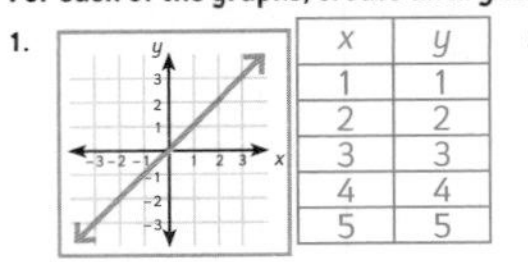

x	y
1	1
2	2
3	3
4	4
5	5

2.

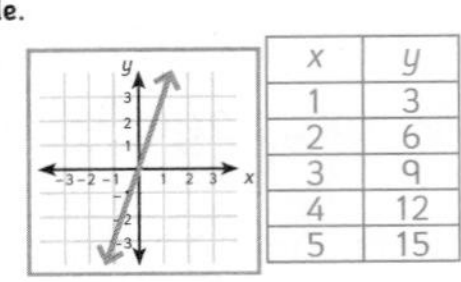

x	y
1	3
2	6
3	9
4	12
5	15

3.

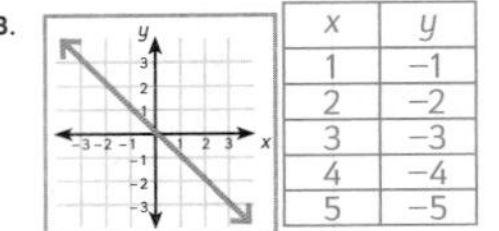

x	y
1	−1
2	−2
3	−3
4	−4
5	−5

4.

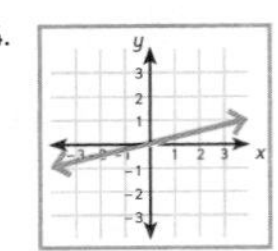

x	y
1	$\frac{1}{4}$
2	$\frac{1}{2}$
3	$\frac{3}{4}$
4	1
5	$1\frac{1}{4}$

Activity 2

For each of the x/y tables, write an equation that represents the function.

1.

x	y
2	4
3	6
10	20
100	200

$y = 2x$

2.

x	y
4	2
6	3
20	10
200	100

$y = \frac{1}{2}x$

3.

x	y
5	−5
10	−10
100	−100
0	0

$y = -x$

4.

x	y
16	4
100	25
32	8
4	1

$y = \frac{1}{4}x$

Homework

Go over the instructions on page 769 of the *Student Text* for each part of the homework.

Activity 3

Students tell the point where two lines intersect on a graph.

Activity 4 • Distributed Practice

Students solve one- and two-step equations.

Homework

Activity 3

Look at each of the graphs. They show the relationship between two functions. Tell the point where the two functions intersect.

1. 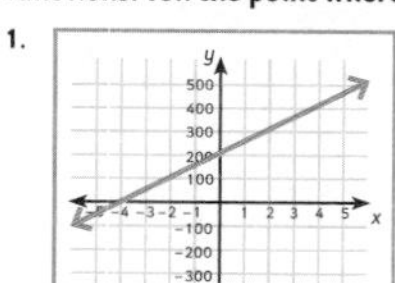

What are the coordinates of the point where the two functions intersect? (4, 400)

2. 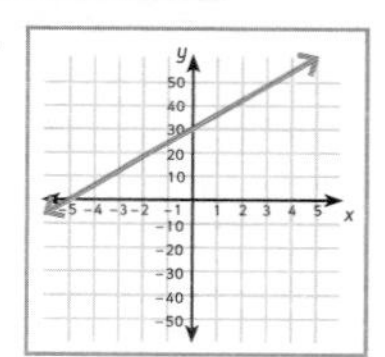

What are the coordinates of the point where the two functions intersect? (5, 30)

3. 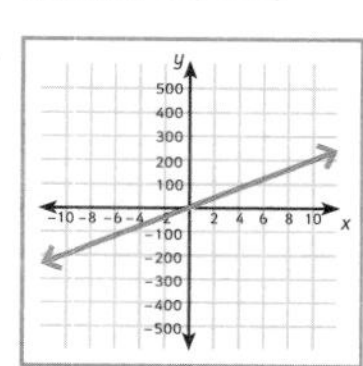

What are the coordinates of the point where the two functions intersect? (10, 200)

Activity 4 • Distributed Practice

Solve.

1. $3x + 4 = 12$ $2\frac{2}{3}$
2. $-56 = -8x$ 7
3. $4x + 7 = 15$ 2
4. $-27 = 9 + -4x$ 9
5. $90x = 180$ 2
6. $-15 = 12 + 3x$ −9
7. $-48x = -46 - 2x$ 1
8. $x + 17 = 34$ 17

Lesson 14 ▸Creating an Equation From a Graph

Problem Solving: ▸Using a Function to Find the Best Deal

Lesson Planner

Skills Maintenance

Finding the Intersecting Points

Building Number Concepts:

▸ Creating an Equation From a Graph

Students learn to write the equation from the graph without creating a table first. We look at functions with positive and negative slopes, and functions that have a y-intercept other than 0.

Objective

Students will create equations from a graph.

Problem Solving:

▸ Using a Function to Find the Best Deal

Students learn that we often use algebra or graphs of lines to see where two functions meet to find the better deal in a problem-solving situation. We look at a real-world situation of a pizza delivery person, and compare which company would pay him more in a day.

Objective

Students will use functions to figure out the best deal.

Homework

Students tell the slope by looking at rise and run of a line on a graph, tell the y-intercept by looking at a graph of a line, and look at a graph of a line and tell the equation that represents it. In Distributed Practice, students solve one- and two-step equations, as well as apply rules for performing operations on integers.

Lesson 14 | Skills Maintenance

Name ______ Date ______

Skills Maintenance
Finding the Intersecting Points

Activity 1

Look at the graphs. Write the coordinates of the point where the two functions meet.

1.

The two lines intersect at the point (8, 6).

2.

The two lines intersect at the point (4, −1).

384 Unit 9 • Lesson 14

Skills Maintenance

Finding the Intersecting Points

(*Interactive Text*, page 384)

Activity 1

Students tell the coordinates of the point where the graphs of two functions intersect.

Building Number Concepts:
▶ Creating an Equation From a Graph

How do we figure out the equation of a function from a graph?

(*Student Text*, pages 770–774)

Connect to Prior Knowledge

Begin by asking students if they would rather pay $1,200 for a car all at once or $100 a month for a year with no interest. Which is the better deal? Give students an opportunity to grapple with the problem before discussing possible answers.

Listen for:

- A discussion about the plans costing the same.
- One advantage of the second option is smaller, more manageable payments each month.

Tell students that people have to make decisions and comparisons about financial deals all the time in the real world.

Link to Today's Concept

In today's lesson, we learn how to use algebra to help us find the better deal.

Demonstrate

Engagement Strategy: Teacher Modeling

Demonstrate how to create equations of a function from a graph in one of the following ways:

mBook: Use the *mBook Teacher Edition* for pages 770–771 of the *Student Text*. m

Overhead Projector: Reproduce the equations on Transparency 17, and modify as discussed.

Lesson 14 | ▶Creating an Equation From a Graph
Problem Solving:
▶Using a Function to Find the Best Deal

▶Creating an Equation From a Graph

How do we figure out the equation of a function from a graph?

In the last lesson, we created an x/y table using the coordinates on a graph. We could then write the equation. But we can write the equation from the graph without creating a table first. How do we look at a line on a coordinate graph and figure out its equation? Just think about the two parts to a linear equation—the slope and the y-intercept.

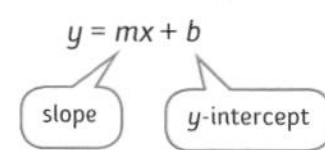

Example 1 shows a line on a coordinate graph. The line goes through the origin. That means the value for b is 0, so all we look at is $y = mx$. We figure out m (or slope) by using rise over run. We begin by looking at two points on the line, (1, 2) and (2, 4). From these two points, we find the rise and run for computing the slope.

770 Unit 9 • Lesson 14

Board: Copy the equations and graphs on the board, and modify as discussed.

- Explain that we can find the equation of a function from a graph and finding slope and y-intercept.
- Review $\boldsymbol{y = mx + b}$, and remind students that m is the slope and b is the y-intercept. m
- Explain that we can find slope by analyzing a graph to find rise over run. To find the y-intercept, we look at the place where the line intersects the y-axis.

How do we figure out the equation of a function from a graph? *(continued)*

Demonstrate

- Go over **Example 1**. Have students look at the graph. Point out that we begin by looking at two points on the line: **(1, 2)** and **(2, 4)**, to find the rise and run.
- Point out that the rise equals 2 and the run equals 1.
- Explain that we calculate the slope as rise over run. In this case, the rise over run is $\frac{2}{1}$, or **2**. So the slope is 2.
- In this example, the slope is positive and the line intersects at the point (0, 0). This means the y-intercept is 0. We can also say that there is no y-intercept.
- Now that we know the slope, we write the equation as $y = 2x + 0$, or just $y = 2x$.

Lesson 14

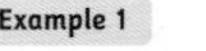

Example 1

Use the graph to write an equation for the function.

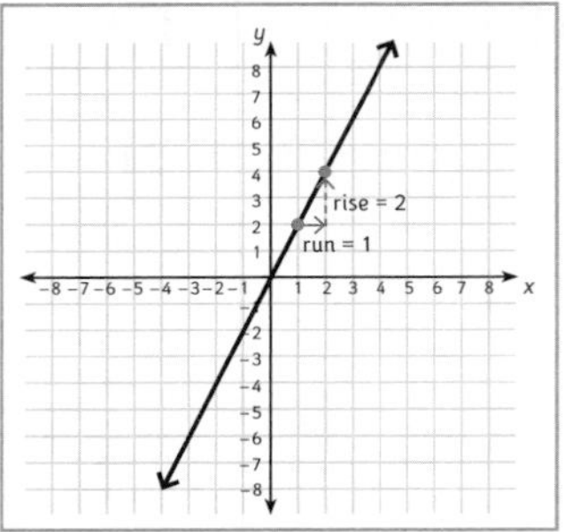

$\frac{\text{Rise}}{\text{Run}} = \frac{2}{1}$ or 2

The slope = 2

The graph goes through the origin (0, 0), so we know the y-intercept is zero.

The equation for the function is $y = 2x + 0$ or just $y = 2x$.

Demonstrate

- Tell students that we can also figure out how to write functions with negative slopes by looking at a graph. We need to pay attention to the direction we are moving.
- Have students turn to **Example 2** on page 772 of the *Student Text*. In this example, the function has a negative slope and the line intersects the y-axis at the point (0, 0).
- Tell students that we look at the two points **(−2, 1)** and **(−5, 2)** in Quadrant II on the graph.
- Point out the ways we can tell it is a negative slope. One thing we notice is that it is in Quadrants II and IV. Another thing is that the rise goes down and not up. This can be confusing to students because of the term rise. Be sure they understand that the rise just means the difference in the vertical aspect of the line.
- Show students how to find the slope using rise over run to get $\frac{\mathbf{1}}{\mathbf{-3}}$, or $-\frac{\mathbf{1}}{\mathbf{3}}$. This means the slope is $-\frac{1}{3}$.
- Explain that the equation for this function is $\boldsymbol{y = -\frac{1}{3}x + 0}$, or just $\boldsymbol{y = -\frac{1}{3}x}$.

We can also figure out how to write functions with negative slopes just by looking at the graph. In this case, we have to pay attention to the direction we are moving. In Example 2, we look at the two points (−2, 1) and (−5, 2), which are in Quadrant II on the graph.

Example 2

Use the graph to write an equation for the function.

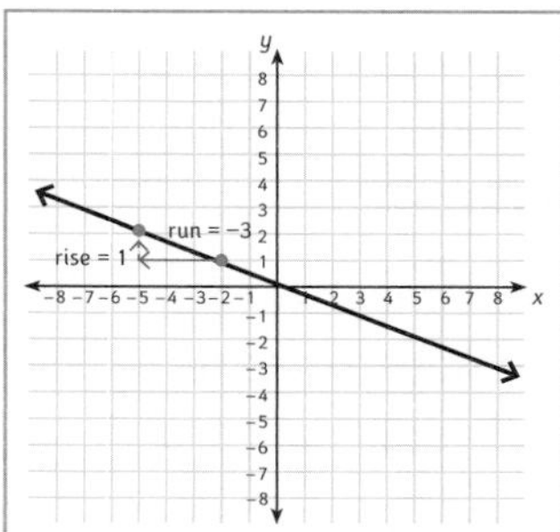

The run is going in the negative direction. We see this on the x-axis.

$\frac{\text{Rise}}{\text{Run}} = \frac{1}{-3}$ or $-\frac{1}{3}$

The slope $= -\frac{1}{3}$

The graph also goes through the origin (0, 0), so the y-intercept is zero.

The equation for this function is $y = -\frac{1}{3}x + 0$ or just $y = -\frac{1}{3}x$.

How do we figure out the equation of a function from a graph? *(continued)*

Demonstrate

- Tell students that it is important to be able to write equations for functions that have y-intercepts that are not zero.
- Turn to page 773 of the *Student Text* to go over **Example 3**, which demonstrates a function where the y-intercept is not zero.
- Tell students that we use the points **(1, 3)** and **(2, 4)** to find the rise and run.
- Be sure students see that the rise over run is $\frac{1}{1}$, so **the slope is 1**. This is written with no coefficient in front of the x.
- Point out that the line crosses the y-axis at the point **(0, 2)**. This means that **the y-intercept is 2**. Be sure students understand how this translates into the equation $y = x + 2$.

It's also important to be able to write an equation for a function that has a y-intercept other than 0. Example 3 shows a line that intersects the y-axis at the point (0, 2). That means the value for b is 2. Now we use rise over run to figure out the slope. Once again, we look at two points on the graph, (1, 3) and (2, 4). These two points are in Quadrant I.

Example 3

Use the graph to write an equation for the function.

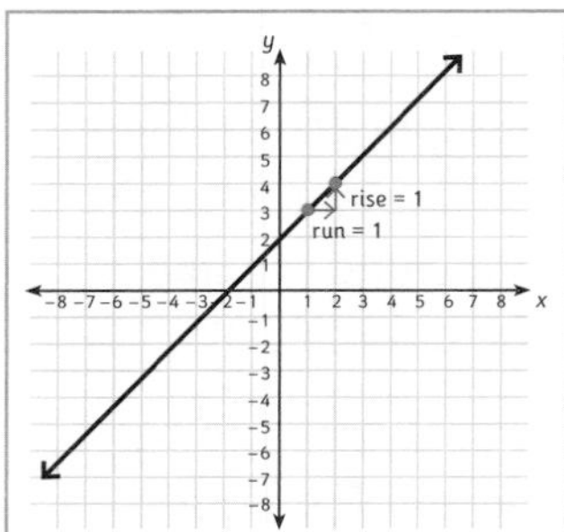

$\frac{\text{Rise}}{\text{Run}} = \frac{1}{1}$ or 1

The slope = 1

The line crosses the y-axis at the point (0, 2). This means that the y-intercept for this function is 2, or that $b = 2$.

The equation for the function is $y = x + 2$.

Demonstrate

- Have students turn to the page 774 of the *Student Text* to go over **Example 4**.
- In this example, the slope is negative and the line crosses at the point (0, −6). Be sure students see how this results in the equation $y = -\frac{3}{2}x - 6$. Tell students you can write this equation as either $y = -\frac{3}{2}x + -6$ **or** $-\frac{3}{2}x - 6$.

Check for Understanding
Engagement Strategy: Pair/Share

Have students pair with another student. Ask them to summarize how to write an equation of a function using a graph.

Listen for:

- *Look at two points to find the rise over run. Remember to think about what direction we are moving in.*
- *Calculate the slope using the rise and run.*
- *Find the y-intercept by finding where the graph crosses the y-axis.*
- *Substitute the values into y = mx + b form.*

When pairs have finished, have volunteers share their summaries with the class.

In Example 4 we have a function with a negative slope and a y-intercept other than 0. In this function, the line goes through the y-axis at the point (0, −6). This means $b = -6$.

Next, we find the slope, or m. We again look at two points to find the slope, (−1, −4) and (−3, −1). The two points are found in Quadrant III this time. These points are interesting because even though they each have two negative coordinates, the rise is going up so it is positive. To go from −4 to −1 we add 3: −4 + 3 = −1. That is why the rise is a positive number.

Example 4

Use the graph to write an equation for the function.

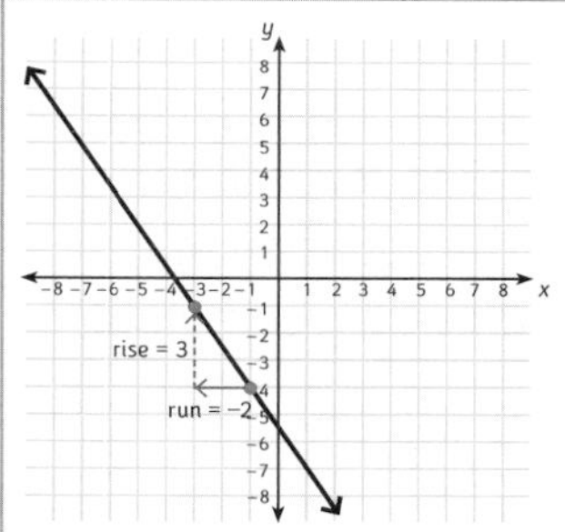

We are going the negative direction with run. We see on the x-axis that we are moving to the left, or in a negative direction, two units.

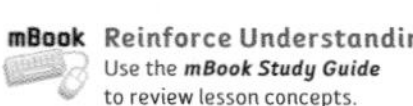

The graph crosses the y-axis at the point (0, −6), so the y-intercept, or b, is −6.

The equation for this function is $y = -\frac{3}{2}x + -6$ or $-\frac{3}{2}x - 6$.

Apply Skills Turn to *Interactive Text*, page 385.

mBook Reinforce Understanding Use the *mBook Study Guide* to review lesson concepts.

Apply Skills
(*Interactive Text*, page 385)

Have students turn to page 385 in the *Interactive Text*, which provides students an opportunity to practice analyzing lines on a coordinate graph.

Activity 1

Students look at the graph of a function and tell the slope, the y-intercept, and the equation of the line. Monitor students' work as they complete the activity.

Watch for:

- Can students determine the slope by looking at the rise and the run of the line on the graph?
- Can students determine the y-intercept by looking at the place where the line crosses the y-axis?
- Can students write the equation based on the slope and y-intercept information they found for the graph?

mBook Reinforce Understanding

Remind students that they can review lesson concepts by accessing the online *mBook Study Guide*.

Lesson 14 | Apply Skills

Name ______________________ Date ______________

Apply Skills
Creating an Equation From a Graph

Activity 1

Look at each of the graphs. Analyze the line and find the slope, y-intercept, and equation in $y = mx + b$ form.

1.

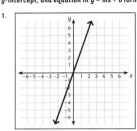

What is the slope? 3
What is the y-intercept? 0
What is the equation? $y = 3x$

2.

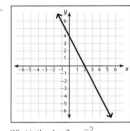

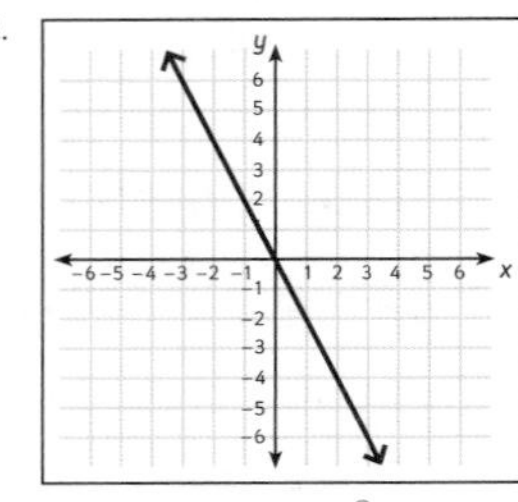

What is the slope? -2
What is the y-intercept? 0
What is the equation? $y = -2x$

3.

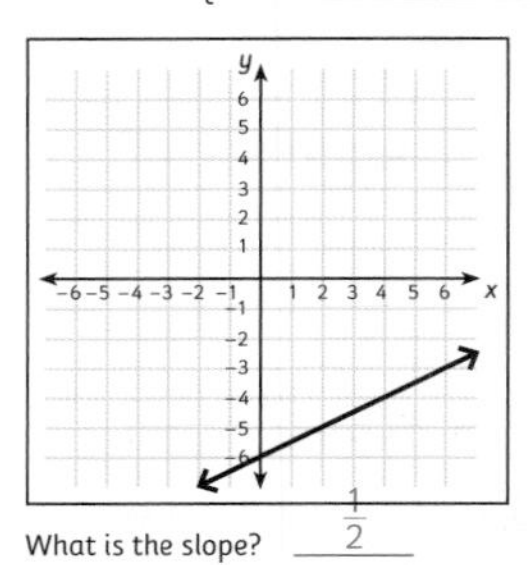

What is the slope? $\frac{1}{2}$
What is the y-intercept? -6
What is the equation? $y = \frac{1}{2}x - 6$

4.

What is the slope? -2
What is the y-intercept? 4
What is the equation? $y = -2x + 4$

Unit 9 • Lesson 14 385

Unit 9

Problem Solving:
▶ Using A Function to Find the Best Deal

How do functions help us figure out the best deal?

(*Student Text*, pages 775)

Connect to Prior Knowledge

Have students turn to the material on page 775 of the *Student Text*. Remind students about the ways we compared functions in the last lesson: We made the equations equal or looked at the graphs to see where the lines intersected.

Link to Today's Concept

Tell students that in today's lesson, we compare functions to find the better deal.

Demonstrate

- Have students look at **Example 1**. In this example, Raul applied for jobs at two different pizza places. Bonzo Pizza will pay him \$10 a day and \$3 for every pizza he delivers, and Too Hot to Eat Pizza will pay him \$5 for every pizza he delivers.
- Tell students that we make a decision based on this information about what is the best deal. That is, which company will pay more in a day?
- Show how we solve the problem using algebra by setting up the functions for each company.
- Point out that we can set up the equation as $\mathbf{5x = 3x + 10}$ because both functions equal y. Tell students that ***y* equals the amount of money** Raul will make in a day, and ***x* equals the amount of pizzas he will deliver**.
- Walk through the algebraic steps to find that $\mathbf{x = 5}$, which is five pizzas.

Lesson 14

▶Problem Solving: Using a Function to Find the Best Deal

How do functions help us figure out the best deal?

Raul works in pizza delivery. He had to choose between two different companies to work for. Let's see which company would pay him more in a day.

Example 1

Solve the problem by finding the intersection of the functions.

Problem:

Raul has to choose between two companies to work for.

Bonzo Pizza will pay him \$10 a day and \$3 for every pizza he delivers. Too Hot to Eat Pizza will pay him \$5 for every pizza he delivers. Which company will pay more in a day?

We solve the problem using algebra.

- Let x = pizzas delivered and y = total pay
- The function for Bonzo Pizza is $y = 3x + 10$
- The function for Too Hot to Eat Pizza is $y = 5x$

$$5x = 3x + 10$$
$$5x + -3x = 3x + -3x + 10$$
$$2x = 0 + 10$$
$$2x = 10$$
$$\frac{2}{2}x = \frac{10}{2}$$
$$1x = 5$$
$$x = 5 \text{ or } 5 \text{ pizzas}$$

Look at the graph for the two linear functions. After six pizzas Raul is earning more working at Too Hot to Eat. By following the lines, we see that working at Too Hot to Eat pays more if Raul delivers more than five pizzas per day.

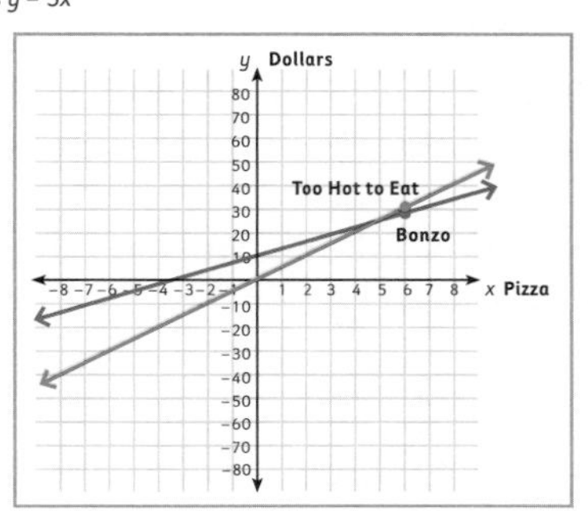

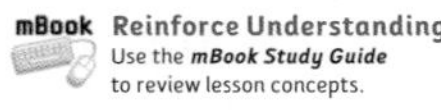

Problem-Solving Activity Turn to *Interactive Text*, page 386.

mBook Reinforce Understanding Use the *mBook Study Guide* to review lesson concepts.

- Have students look at the graph for the two functions to see that after delivering six pizzas, Raul is earning more working at Too Hot to Eat.
- Help students go through the analysis of this problem and come to the conclusion that Too Hot to Eat Pizza is the better deal if Raul delivers more than five pizzas a day. Be sure students understand each of the steps and the justification for each as you work through this example.

Lesson 14

Problem-Solving Activity
(*Interactive Text*, page 386)

Have students turn to page 386 in the *Interactive Text*, which provides students an opportunity to practice these concepts on their own.

Students use what they know about writing functions to find the job or activity that is the better deal. They need to use algebra to find out where the two functions cross on the graph. Then they plot the two functions on the graph and use this information to answer the questions.

Monitor students' work as they complete the activity.

Watch for:

- Can students solve the equations algebraically?
- Can students plot the functions on a graph to determine where they intersect?
- Can students answer the questions based on the graph and algebra?

mBook Reinforce Understanding

Remind students that they can review lesson concepts by accessing the online *mBook Study Guide*.

Lesson 14 | Problem-Solving Activity

Name ______________________ Date ______________________

Problem-Solving Activity
Using a Function to Find the Best Deal

Find the job or activity that is the best deal. Write functions from each of the word problems, then plot them on the graph.

1. Mindy has the choice of two different jobs at Thompson's Manufacturing. She wants the job that will pay her the most money per week. Her choices are:
   a. Work as a receptionist answering phones. She gets a base pay of $50 per week and $8 per hour.
   b. Work in shipping packing boxes. She gets a base pay of $10 per hour.

   Mindy can only work 40 hours per week. At what point will she make the same amount for both jobs? Which job should she take if she wants to make the most money per week?

   25 hours until she makes the same amount; she should pack boxes

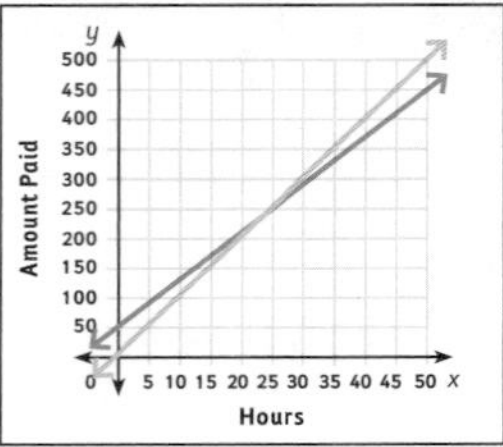

2. Rachel volunteered to walk on Sunday for people with cancer. She wants to raise as much money as she can. She has to choose between two ways to raise money.
   a. She gets $20 just to do the walk and $2 for every mile she walks.
   b. She gets $3 for every mile she walks.

   How far does Rachel have to walk before she raises the same amount of money?

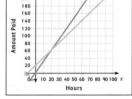

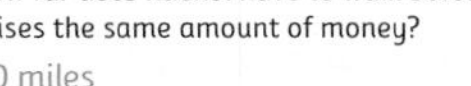

   20 miles

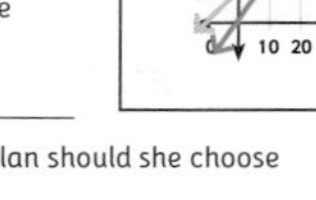

   Let's say Rachel can walk 15 miles. Which plan should she choose in order to raise the most money?

   Plan A

386 Unit 9 • Lesson 14

Homework

Go over the instructions on pages 776–777 of the *Student Text* for each part of the homework.

Activity 1

Students tell the rise, run, and slope by looking at a function on a graph.

Activity 2

Students find the y-intercept by looking at a line on a coordinate graph.

Lesson 14

Homework

Activity 1

Answer the questions for each of the graphs.

1\.

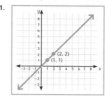

(a) What is the rise? 1
(b) What is the run? 1
(c) What is the slope? 1

2\.

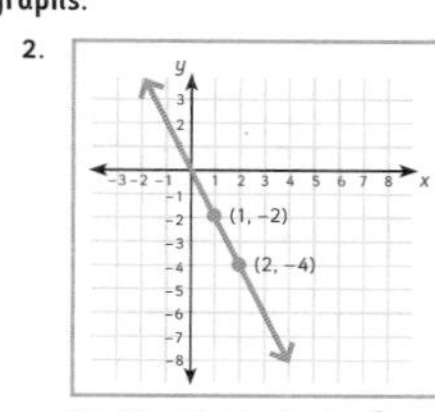

(a) What is the rise? −2
(b) What is the run? 1
(c) What is the slope? −2

Activity 2

Answer the questions for each of the graphs.

1\.

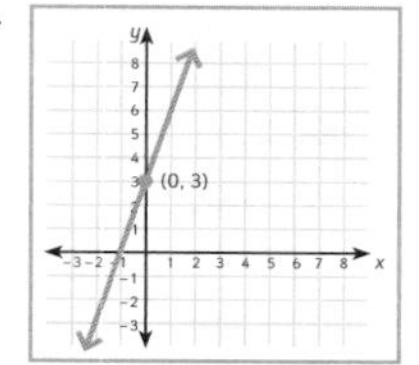

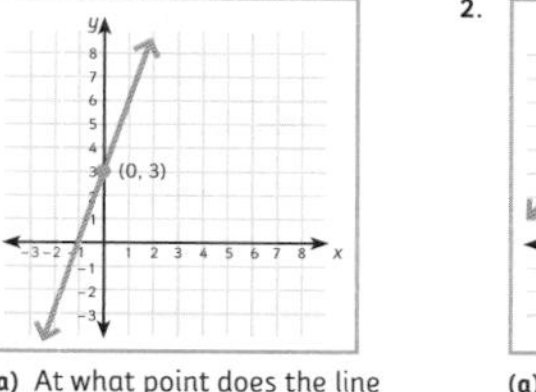

(a) At what point does the line cross the y-axis? 3
(b) What is the y-intercept? (0, 3)

2\.

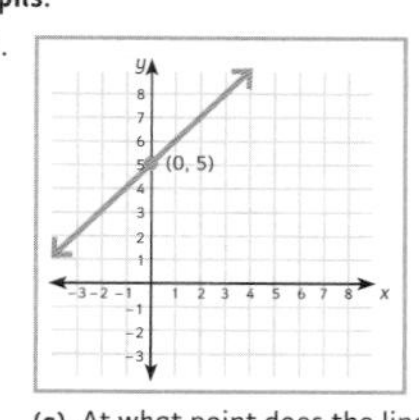

(a) At what point does the line cross the y-axis? 5
(b) What is the y-intercept? (0, 5)

776 Unit 9 • Lesson 14

Homework

Go over the instructions on page 777 of the *Student Text* for each part of the homework.

Activity 3

Students look at graphs of lines and find the equation of the function that represents each.

Activity 4 • Distributed Practice

Students solve one- and two-step equations, and apply rules for performing operations on integers.

Lesson 14

Homework

Activity 3

Write the equation for the function shown in each graph by finding the slope and intercept.

1. What is the equation for this graph? $y = -3x$

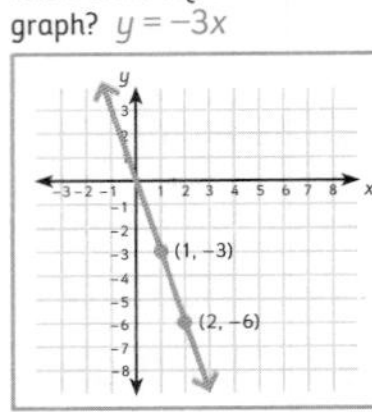

2. What is the equation for this graph? $y = x + 1$

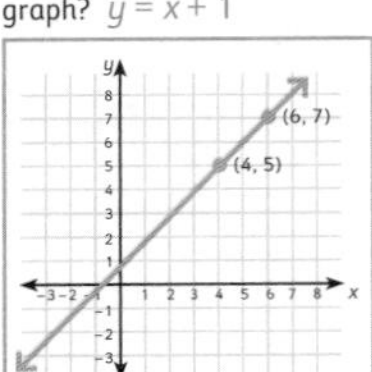

3. What is the equation for this graph? $y = 2x + 1$

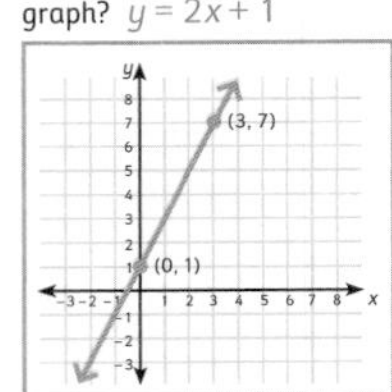

Activity 4 • Distributed Practice

Solve.

1. $3x = 4x + 2$ -2
2. $5x + 3 = 2x + 2$ $-\frac{1}{3}$
3. $x + 7 = -2x + 5$ $-\frac{2}{3}$
4. $5 - x = 3x + -5$ $2\frac{1}{2}$
5. $2x + 10 = -10 + -4x$ $-3\frac{1}{3}$
6. $-4x = -3x + 4$ -4
7. $-2x - 2 = 2 + -x$ -4
8. $4 - x = 5 + x$ $-\frac{1}{2}$

Lesson 15 | Unit Review ▶Introduction to Functions

Problem Solving: ▶Working With Coordinate Graphs

Lesson Planner

Vocabulary Development

function
systematic relationship
independent variable
dependent variable
slope
run
rise
positive slope
negative slope
rate of change
***y*-intercept**
linear functions
zero slope

Skills Maintenance

Substitution

Building Number Concepts: ▶ Introduction to Functions

Functions are a key idea that students need to learn as they begin their study of algebra. Functions show a systematic relationship between two variables. Another way to think about functions is that the variable y depends upon x. Functions are systematic relationships between two variables that help us make predictions.

Problem Solving: ▶ Working With Coordinate Graphs

The main focus of the unit is on linear functions. Plotting a function on a graph helps students understand concepts like direct and inverse relationships, as well as rate of change. We can create a function using symbols based on the line on a graph by figuring slope and seeing where the line intercepts the y-axis. We can determine the placement of the line on the coordinate graph by looking at the sign of the slope.

Name ______________________ Date ______________________

Skills Maintenance
Substitution

Activity 1

Substitute the value of the variable and solve.

1. Solve $y = 3x$ if $x = 5$. $y = 15$
2. Solve $y = 2x$ if $x = 1$. $y = 2$
3. Solve $y = 5x$ if $x = 5$. $y = 25$
4. Solve $y = x + 4$ if $x = 1$. $y = 5$
5. Solve $y = 7x + 23$ if $x = 7$. $y = 72$
6. Solve $y = -3x + 5$ if $x = 4$. $y = -7$
7. Solve $y = 4x - 10$ if $x = -2$. $y = -18$
8. Solve $y = -9x - 10$ if $x = -3$. $y = 17$

Unit 9

Skills Maintenance

Substitution

(*Interactive Text*, page 387)

Activity 1

Students substitute the value of the variable in an algebraic equation and solve.

Building Number Concepts:
▶ Introduction to Functions

What is so different about functions?
(*Student Text*, pages 778–781)

Discuss

Begin by having students think about a simple situation. Have them imagine that they are slowly squeezing an empty soda can. Get them to imagine at first that they are barely squeezing the can and then slowly applying more and more pressure.

Ask:

> **What would happen to the can as you increased the pressure? What is the relationship between the pressure and the dent in the can?**

Listen for:

- *The sides get more dented.*
- *The more you squeeze the can, the more the can dents.*

Discuss how a simple, everyday relationship like this can be described as a functional relationship. All you need is numbers for the amount of pressure and related numbers that describe how much the can would dent.

Demonstrate

- Turn to *Student Text*, page 778, and go over the material at the top of the page and review the function $y = mx + b$.
- Review the terms independent variable and dependent variable and their role in functions.
- Remind students that word problems and tables show us systematic relationships and help us make predictions.

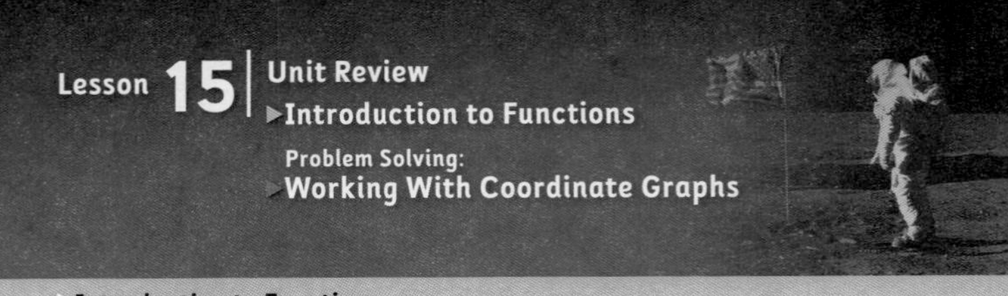

▶Introduction to Functions

What is so different about functions?

We study functions when we learn about algebra. It is easy to mix functions and algebra together, but functions have important properties that need to be understood by themselves.

Functions show systematic relationships between two variables, x and y.

In the function $y = mx + b$, we say that the value of y depends upon what is in $mx + b$.

Word problems and tables of numbers are one way to understand how functions are all around us. Both word problems and tables show systematic relationships and help us make predictions.

Review 1

How do word problems and tables help us understand functions?

Problem:

Two clubs at Freemont High School are having a water balloon fight. They are doing this to raise money for charity. Both sides have catapults that launch water balloons. When we pull back on the catapult, the balloon flies out of the bucket. Based on the data the teams collected, what is the relationship between how far the catapult is pulled back and the distance the balloon travels?

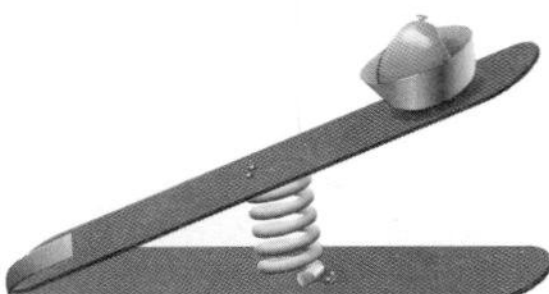

778 Unit 9 • Lesson 15

- Look at **Review 1**. Read through the problem with students. Make sure that they understand the context of the problem, including the context of a catapult.

Demonstrate

- Continue with Review 1 on page 779 of the *Student Text*. Review the data in the table, and make sure that students understand how the relationship between the amount you pull the catapult back and the distance the water balloon travels.
- Explain how the function $y = 2x$ is based on the relationship between the data in the table.
- Also stress that this table creates the basis for making predictions. For example, if you were to pull the catapult back 30 inches, the balloon would travel 60 feet.

Discuss

Remind students that when we work with word problems that involve functions, we need to think about the parts of the problem that stay the same and the parts that are changing.

Ask:

What parts of the catapult problem change, and what parts stay the same?

Listen for:

- *The amount we pull back on the catapult changes.*
- *The distance the balloon travels changes.*
- *Nothing stays the same.*

Amount We Pulled Back on Catapult (in inches)	Distance Traveled (in feet)
5	10
10	20
15	30
20	40

What is the relationship?

The more we pull back on the catapult, the farther the water balloon flies.

What is the function?

We multiply the number in the first column by 2 to get the number in the second column.

Let y = the distance traveled and x = the amount we pull back on the catapult.

$$y = 2 \cdot x \text{ or } y = 2x$$

In the catapult example, the distance the balloon travels depends on how far we pull back the catapult. We use the function to make predictions. If we pull back the catapult 30 inches, the balloon should go 60 feet.

Word problems that involve functions also require us to think about what parts of the problem are changing and what parts are staying the same. In the catapult problem, the amount we pull back on the catapult is always changing, and the distance the balloon travels always changes. Nothing is the same. There are a lot of cases where we have to determine what is changing and what stays the same so that we can write the function correctly.

What is so different about functions? *(continued)*

Demonstrate

- Turn to page 780 of the *Student Text* to look at **Review 2**. This example emphasizes how functions can involve two concepts: (1) what is changing and (2) what is staying the same.
- Discuss the cell phone problem in Review 2. Make sure students see that the minimum bill every month is **$58**. That will not change.
- Also make sure that they see what changes is the number of minutes, not the $0.10 per minute.
- Show how we write the function $y = 0.10x + 58$ with the information.

Lesson 15

Review 2

How do we decide what is changing and what stays the same?

Problem:

Most cell phone plans have a basic monthly fee and then there are additional charges for extra minutes that you use. Celia has a plan where she pays $58 per month for 500 minutes and then $0.10 per additional minute used.

What stays the same? The monthly charge of $58 per month.

What changes? How many minutes more than 500 she talks in a month.

What is the relationship?

Celia's monthly bill depends upon her monthly charge plus the amount for overtime minutes.

Let's say that last month Celia talked 560 minutes. That is 60 minutes more than the 500 she gets.

What is the function?

Let y = the total bill and x = the number of minutes more than 500.

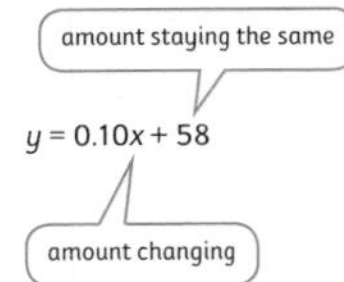

Demonstrate

- Turn to page 781 of the *Student Text* and continue going over Review 2.
- Work through computation when we substitute 60 for x in the function to get $y = 64$. This means that **Celia's bill for the month is $64**.
- Explain that we can use the function to make predictions about Celia's bill depending on how long she talked on the phone during the month.
- Remind students that the rate of change is called the slope.

What is the solution to the problem?

We substitute the extra 60 minutes into our function to find Celia's total bill.

$$y = 0.10x + 58 \quad (x \leftarrow 60)$$

$y = 0.10 \cdot 60 + 58$

$y = 6 + 58$

$y = 64$

Celia's bill for the month is $64.

We can also use this function to make predictions about how much Celia's bill would be if she talked even longer on the phone that month.

The rate of change in a function is called the slope.

Apply Skills
Turn to ***Interactive Text***, page 388.

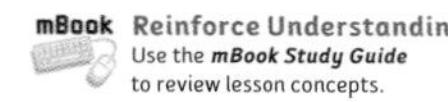

Reinforce Understanding
Use the ***mBook Study Guide*** to review lesson concepts.

Unit Review: Introduction to Functions

(*Interactive Text*, page 388)

Have students turn to page 388 in the *Interactive Text*, which provides students an opportunity to review these skills on their own.

Activity 1

Students look at a table of data, then write a function based on the table.

Activity 2

Students read word problems, then write a function based on the information.

Monitor students' work as they complete the activities.

Watch for:

- Are students able to see the multiplicative relationship in the *x*/*y* tables?
- Do students add extra elements to their functions, such as a *y*-intercept?
- Do students have difficulties reading the word problems and then finding what is changing and what is staying the same?

Once students have finished, discuss any difficulties that you noticed.

mBook **Reinforce Understanding**

Remind students that they can review unit concepts by accessing the online *mBook Study Guide*.

Lesson 15 | Unit Review

Name ______________________ Date ______________________

Unit Review
Introduction to Functions

Activity 1

Write a function based on each table of data.

1.

x	y
9	27
2	6
5	15
4	12

Function $y = 3x$

2.

x	y
−3	3
4	10
−10	−4
2	8

Function $y = x + 6$

Activity 2

Write a function for each word problem.

1. The water bill for your house depends on how much water you use. You probably use a lot more in the summer. The water company has a basic charge of $20 per month plus $3 for every hundred gallons that you use. $y = 3x + 20$

2. Campino's Go-Cart Track is a place for serious go-cart drivers. If you want to drive a lot, Campino has a special rate. It's $10 a week plus $3 a race. You can race as many times as you want during the week. Leo loves go-carts and spent $43 last week at Campino's. How many races was she in? $y = 3x + 10$

388 Unit 9 • Lesson 15

Problem Solving:
▶ Working With Coordinate Graphs

What do functions look like on a coordinate graph?

(*Student Text*, pages 782–784)

Discuss

Turn to page 782 of the *Student Text* and review the formula for linear functions. Remind students that m represents the slope and b represents the y-intercept. Remind students that we use this formula to plot a line on a graph.

Discuss the simplest function where the y-intercept is 0, and how this affects the formula.

Demonstrate

- Have students look at **Review 1**. Review how we use slope to compare functions.
- Have students look at the coordinate graph and remind them that the greater the number for the slope, the greater the rate of change. In this case, a car going faster is going more miles in the same time than the slower cars.

Lesson 15

▶Problem Solving: **Working With Coordinate Graphs**

What do functions look like on a coordinate graph?

We learned about functions on coordinate graphs that involve straight lines. These are linear functions. There is a specific formula for plotting the lines for these functions on a coordinate graph.

Formula for linear function:

$$y = mx + b$$

slope | y-intercept

We use this formula to plot a line on a graph. The simplest function is one where the y-intercept is the origin. This means the value for b is zero and we don't need to write it as part of our function.

The slope of a function tells us how quickly the function is increasing or decreasing. On a graph, we can find the slope by taking the rise over the run.

Review 1 shows different functions that go through the origin. They all show the different rates a car travels.

Review 1

How do we use slope to compare functions?

The bigger the number in front of x, the steeper the slope. The graph with the steepest slope has the greatest rate of change. That means the car going 60 miles in one hour is changing more (or going more miles) than the cars going 40 or 50 miles in one hour.

The steeper the slope, the greater the rate of change.

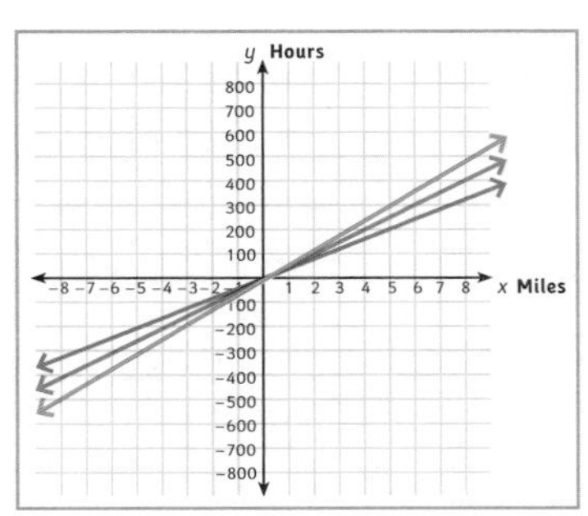

782 Unit 9 • Lesson 15

What do functions look like on a coordinate graph? *(continued)*

Demonstrate

- Turn to page 783 of the *Student Text* to look at **Review 2**, which shows how a table of data can be created based on a function.
- Explain that we can do this by substituting a small range of values for x into our formula. For example, we substitute 0 for x to get a y value of -2.
- Tell students that we use the table we created to graph the line of the function. Each row of x/y values serves as a coordinate point that we can plot on the graph.
- Explain that this is a relatively easy way to create a table and a graph.

We use a formula to graph a line.

Review 2

How do we graph a function?

$y = 3x - 2$

We create an x/y table based on this function. We substitute values for x to get values for y.

x	y
0	−2
1	1
2	4

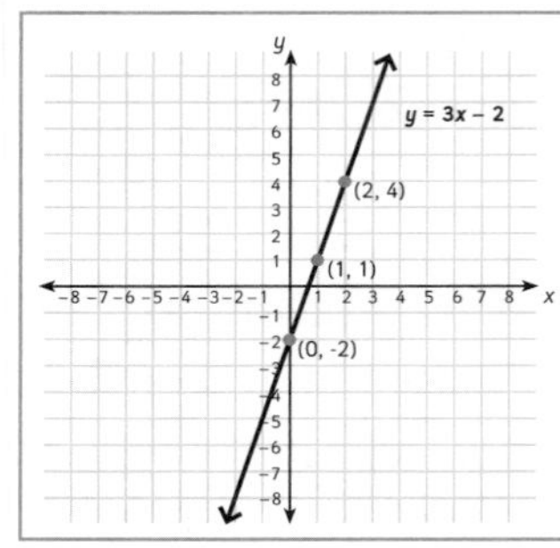

We can use the graph to write an equation. We need to remember "rise over run." Review 3 shows how to figure out the slope of the line using rise over run. Then we look for the place where the line crosses (or intercepts) the y-axis.

Demonstrate

- Turn to page 784 of the *Student Text* to look at **Review 3**.
- Tell students that we can reverse the process and look at the line on the graph to write the function.
- Review how to calculate rise over run. It is easy for students to miscalculate if they do not attend to the starting and ending points for the rise and run.
- Review the importance of paying attention to what direction we are moving in and how this is related to negative slope, positive slope, and zero slope.
- Remind students that we find the y-intercept by looking to see where the line crosses the y-axis.
- Then show students how we substitute the values for the slope and y-intercept into the formula. In this case, we have a **slope of 3** and a ***y*-intercept of 1**, so the function is $y = 3x + 1$.

Review 3

How do we use a graph to write the equation for a function?

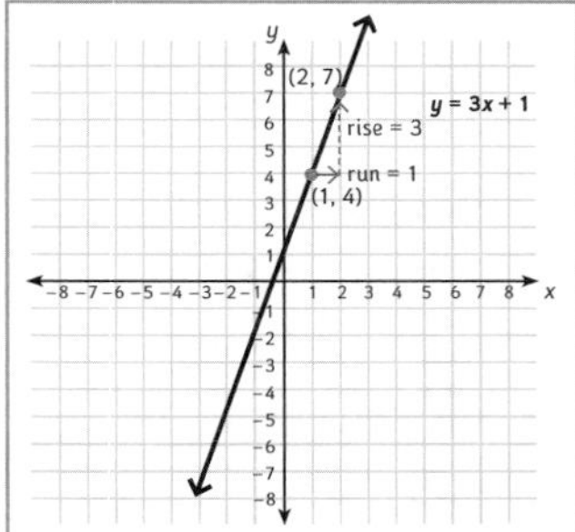

First we find rise over run. The rise is 3 and the run is 1, so our slope is $\frac{3}{1}$ or 3.

Find where the line crosses the y-axis. It crosses at 1.

Substitute the values for slope and y intercept into the formula.

$$\begin{matrix} & & 3 & & 1 \\ & & \downarrow & & \downarrow \\ y & = & m & x + & b \end{matrix}$$

The equation for the function is $y = 3x + 1$.

How do we make decisions based on functions?

Demonstrate

- Turn to page 785 of the *Student Text*, and review with students how functions on graphs can be much more than just lines. They can be important tools for making decisions, and they can help us make important decisions in the real world.
- Explain that for example, we can use them when we buy products, take out loans, or buy services where there are monthly charges, such as cell phone plans.
- Discuss the problem in **Review 1**, which shows what happens at the intersection of two functions.
- Read through the problem and go over how to write the functions for each plan.
- Work through the computations to see that $x = 2$, or **2 months**.
- Have students look at the graph to see the way the two functions cross the y-axis at different points but eventually meet.
- Describe how the intersection point shows that the amounts paid for each plan are the same. We know this by looking at tic marks on the x- and y-axes. At two months on the x-axis and $600 on the y-axis, Chantrelle would have paid the same amount of money.
- You may also want to point out that at three months, Chantrelle will have paid more money to the furniture store using the $300 a month plan than the other plan. This means she will pay for the furniture faster using this plan.

How do we make decisions based on functions?

One of the ways that we can use functions is to make comparisons. When we graph two linear functions, it is often possible to find where the two functions intersect. This is especially useful if we are comparing two plans that involve money.

Review 1

What happens at the intersection of two functions?

Problem:

Chantrelle needs to buy new furniture for her apartment. When she goes to the furniture store, they offer her two payment plans. When will she have paid the same amount?

Plan 1: Pay $400 down and $100 per month.

Plan 2: Pay $300 per month.

We use what we know about functions and algebra to answer this question.

What are the functions?

Plan 1: $y = 100x + 400$

Plan 2: $y = 300x$

They both equal y, so:

$$300x = 100x + 400$$
$$300x + -100x = 100x + -100x + 400$$
$$200x = 0 + 400$$
$$200x = 400$$
$$\frac{200}{200}x = \frac{400}{200}$$
$$1x = 2$$
$$x = 2$$

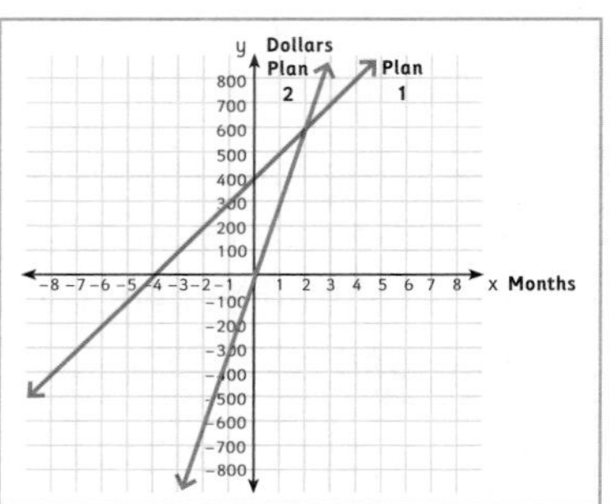

At 2 months, Chantrelle would have paid the same amount of money regardless of the plan she selects. After that, she is paying more money per month if she chose Plan 2 (paying $300 per month).

Demonstrate

- Then turn to *Student Text*, page 786, and go through **Review 2**. This demonstrates how comparing functions on a graph also lets us figure out the better deal.
- Read through the problem in Review 2 and make sure students understand the context of comparing the price and amount of time it takes for a painting company to paint a house.
- Work through the choice of two different house painting companies. Stress how each company's information represents a function, and how we can make an algebraic equation to find out where the two functions meet.
- Show how to use the information from the problem to write the functions for **Bid 1:** $y = 30x + 200$, and **Bid 2:** $y = 40x$. Remind students to think about what is changing and what stays the same.
- Work through the computations to get $x = 20$, which represents hours. Then have students look at the functions on the graph.
- Show students that after they intersect at 20 hours, they should see that Bid 2 is more expensive.

Functions help us make decisions. We use functions to figure out what happens in the long run. Which choice is the better deal? Which job pays more money? These are just a few of the questions we can answer when we compare functions.

Review 2

How do we use functions to make comparisons?

Problem:

You are going to hire a company to paint your house. You get bids from two companies. Which one should you choose based on price alone?

Bid 1: TriFlex Painting will charge you $200 for paint and $30 per hour.

Bid 2: Randall's Painting will charge you $40 per hour, with no charge for the paint.

You can make a decision on which company you want if you have a good idea of how long it will take to paint your house. We can use algebra and graphs to answer the question.

What are the functions?

Bid 1: $y = 30x + 200$

Bid 2: $y = 40x$

We find out when they will cost the same using algebra.

$$40x = 30x + 200$$
$$40x + -30x = 30x + -30x + 200$$
$$10x = 0 + 200$$
$$10x = 200$$
$$\frac{10}{10}x = \frac{200}{10}$$
$$x = 20$$

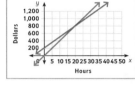

You will pay the same amount if the job takes 20 hours.

If the job takes more than 20 hours, it will cost you more to choose Bid 2 ($40 per hour).

Problem-Solving Activity Turn to ***Interactive Text***, page 389.

Reinforce Understanding Use the ***mBook Study Guide*** to review lesson concepts.

Unit Review: Working With Coordinate Graphs

(*Interactive Text*, pages 389–390)

Have students turn to pages 389–390 in the *Interactive Text*, which provide students an opportunity to review these skills on their own.

Activity 1

Students create an *x*/*y* table based on the provided function. Then they plot the function on the coordinate graph.

Activity 2

Students answer questions about functions.

Activity 3

Students decide which scenario gives them the best deal. They create functions, then plot them on the coordinate graph and label the point where the two lines intersect.

Watch for:

- Can students accurately plot points on a graph?
- Do students have a good understanding of the number for slope in a function and its steepness on a graph?
- Do students have difficulty reading and understanding the word problems?
- Do students construct an algebra equation that lets them find when the functions intersect?

Once students have finished, discuss any difficulties that you noticed.

mBook **Reinforce Understanding**
Remind students that they can review unit concepts by accessing the online *mBook Study Guide*.

Name ______________________ Date ______________

Unit Review
Working With Coordinate Graphs

Activity 1

Create an *x*/*y* table based on the function. Then plot the function on the coordinate graph.

$y = 2x - 3$ Answers will vary. Sample answer:

x	*y*
4	5
5	7
6	9
7	11
8	13

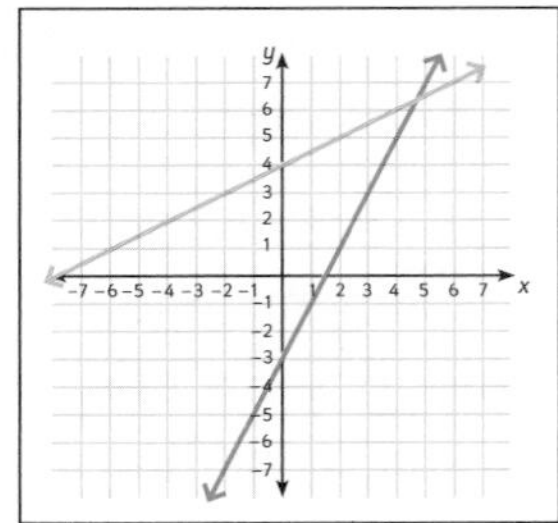

Draw the lines for this function on the coordinate graph: $y = \frac{1}{2}x + 4$.

Where do the two lines meet? Between (4, 6) and (5,7).

Activity 2

Answer the questions about each function.

1. Which line is steeper?
   (a) $y = 2x + 3$
   (b) $y = \frac{1}{2}x + 3$
   (c) $y = 3x + 2$ (circled)
   (d) $y = x + 5$

2. Which line is steeper?
   (a) $y = 4x$ (circled)
   (b) $y = \frac{3}{4}x$
   (c) $y = x + 6$
   (d) $y = \frac{1}{2}x + 10$

Unit 9

Name ______________________ Date ______________

Activity 3

Use algebra to answer the questions. Decide which scenario will give you the best deal. Then graph the functions for each problem on a coordinate graph and label the point where they intersect.

1. Your family decides it needs new carpet in the entire house. You can pay for the carpet and the work to install it in two ways:
   a: Pay $50 per month.
   b: Pay $100 down and $25 per month.
   When will you pay the same amount?
   4 months
   What plan is the better deal?
   Plan 2

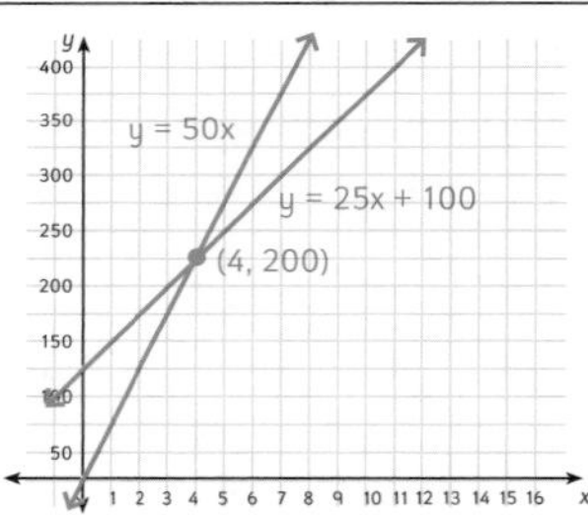

2. You want to make as much money as you can in your summer job. You have two jobs to choose from. Each job will pay you by the week.
   a: You can work on the factory floor for $10 an hour.
   b: You can work on the night shift cleaning floors. You make $30 per week as a base pay and $8 per hour.
   When will you make the same amount of money?
   15 hours
   Which job should you take?
   Working on the factory floor.

(16,150)
y = 8x + 30
y = 10x

Assessment Planner

Students	Assess	Differentiate		Assess
	Day 1	Day 2	Day 3	Day 4
All	End-of-Unit Assessment *Form A*			Performance Assessments Unit 10 Opener
Scored 80% or above		Extension	Extension	
Scored Below 80%		Reinforcement	Retest	

Assessment Objectives

Building Number Concepts:

▶ Introduction to Functions

- Use word problems and tables to think about functional relationships
- Interpret the slope and y-intercept of a function in a real-world situation
- Use a function to make predictions in a real-world situation

Problem Solving:

▶ Working With Coordinate Graphs

- Graph linear functions on a coordinate graph
- Convert functions between representations (tables, graphs, and equations)
- Interpret the intersection of two functions in a real-world situation

Monitoring Progress: ▶ Unit Assessments

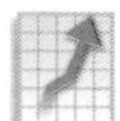

Assess
End-of-Unit Assessment

- Administer End-of-Unit Assessment Form A in the *Assessment Book*, pages 83–84.

Differentiate

- Review End-of-Unit Assessment Form A with class.
- Identify students for Extension or Reinforcement.

Extension
For those students who score 80 percent or better, provide the On Track! Activities from Unit 9, Lessons 11–15, from the *mBook Teacher Edition*.

Reinforcement
For those students who score below 80 percent, provide additional support in one of these ways:

- Have students access the online tutorial provided in the *mBook Study Guide*.
- Have students complete the Interactive Reinforcement Exercises for Unit 9, in the *mBook Study Guide*.
- Provide teacher-directed reteaching of unit concepts.

Retest
Administer End-of Unit Assessment Form B from the *mBook Teacher Edition* to those students who scored below 80 percent on Form A.

Assess
Performance Assessments

- Guide students through the Performance Assessment Model on *Assessment Book*, page 85. Then, administer the Performance Assessments on pages 86–87.

Name ______________________ Date ______________________

Form A

Monitoring Progress
Introduction to Functions

Part 1

Write the functions based on the data in the *x*/*y* tables.

1. $y = 4x$

x	y
4	16
2	8
10	40
5	20

2. $y = \frac{1}{2}x$

x	y
8	4
20	10
6	3
12	6

3. $y = x - 5$

x	y
9	4
4	−1
12	7
5	0

Part 2

Write a function for the word problems.

1. The gas station lets you get gas and a car wash. The gas is $4 per gallon and it is an extra $10 for the car wash.
   $y = 4x + 10$

2. The Movie Club charges $10 to be a member and $2 for each movie that you rent.
   $y = 2x + 10$

Part 3

Create an *x*/*y* table based on the function.

1. $y = 3x - 1$

x	y
1	2
2	5
3	8
4	11

2. $y = -2x + 1$

x	y
1	−1
2	−3
3	−5
4	−7

3. $y = 5x + 4$

x	y
1	9
2	14
3	19
4	24

Unit 9

Monitoring Progress
Working With Coordinate Graphs

Part 3

Answer the questions about lines.

1. Which line is steeper? A
   (a) $y = 4x - 2$ (b) $y = 2x + 3$
   (c) $y = \frac{1}{3}x + 2$ (d) $y = x - 5$

2. Which line is steeper? D
   (a) $y = 2x$ (b) $y = 3x$
   (c) $y = 3x + 6$ (d) $y = 4x$

3. Which function goes with the graph? D
   (a) $2x + 2$
   (b) $2x - 2$
   (c) $2x + 1$
   (d) $-2x - 1$

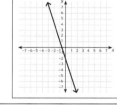

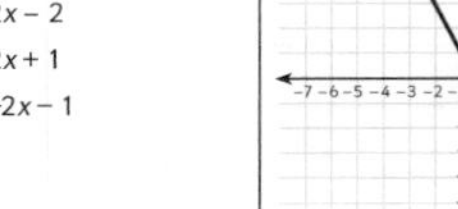
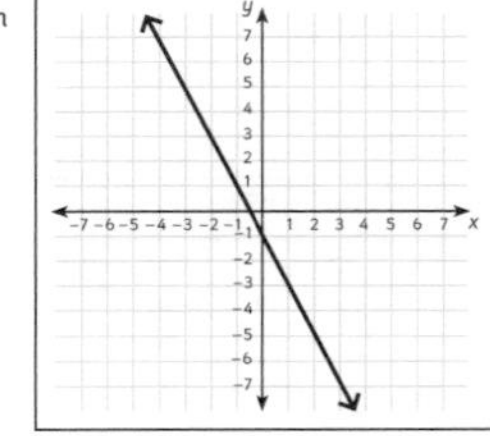

Part 4

Use algebra to answer the problems.

1. You want to buy a new motorcycle. There are two ways to buy it.
   Plan 1: You pay $50 per month.
   Plan 2: You pay $100 down and $25 per month.
   At what point will you pay the same amount? 4 months

2. You want to make as much money as you can working after school. You have two jobs to choose from. Each job will pay you by the hour.
   Job 1: You can work in a convenience store for $7 an hour.
   Job 2: You can work in a restaurant for $10 the day you start plus $5 per hour.
   How many hours will it take until you make the same money?
   5 hours

Name ______________________ Date ______________________

Form B

mBook

Monitoring Progress
Introduction to Functions

Part 1

Write the functions based on the data in the *x*/*y* tables.

1. $y = 7x$

x	y
3	21
2	14
10	70
5	35

2. $y = \frac{1}{2}x$

x	y
10	5
30	15
8	4
20	10

3. $y = x - 2$

x	y
6	4
1	−1
9	7
2	0

Part 2

Write a function for the word problems.

1. The gas station lets you get gas and a car wash. The gas is $3 per gallon, and it is an extra $5 for the car wash.
   $y = 3x + 5$

2. The Movie Club charges $15 to be a member and $1 for each movie that you rent.
   $y = x + 15$

Part 3

Create an *x*/*y* table based on the function.

1. $y = 2x + 2$

x	y
−1	0
0	2
1	4
2	6

2. $y = -3x - 1$

x	y
−1	2
0	−1
1	−4
2	−7

3. $y = 4x + 2$

x	y
−1	−2
0	2
1	6
2	10

Name ______________________ Date ______________________

Monitoring Progress
Working With Coordinate Graphs

Part 3

Answer the questions about lines.

1. Which line is steeper? A
   (a) $y = 6x - 1$ (b) $y = 4x + 10$
   (c) $y = \frac{1}{4}x + 12$ (d) $y = x - 7$

2. Which line is steeper? D
   (a) $y = 3x$ (b) $y = 5x$
   (c) $y = 5x + 3$ (d) $y = 6x$

3. Which function goes with the graph? A
   (a) $-3x - 2$
   (b) $3x + 2$
   (c) $x + 1$
   (d) $-x - 1$

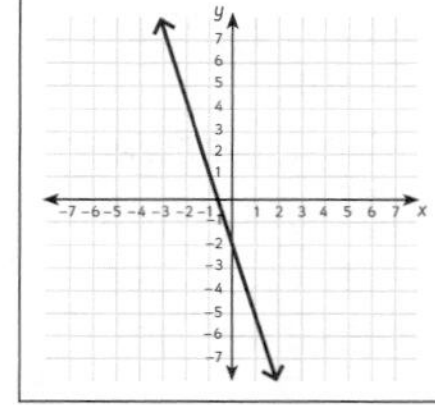

Part 4

Use algebra to answer the problems.

1. You want to buy a motorcycle. There are two ways to buy it.
   Plan 1: You pay $45 per month.
   Plan 2: You pay $75 down and $30 per month.
   At what point will you pay the same amount? 5 months

2. You want to make as much money as you can working after school. You have two jobs to choose from. Each job will pay you by the hour.
   Job 1: You can work in a convenience store for $10 an hour.
   Job 2: You can work in a restaurant for $10 the day you start plus $8 per hour.
   How many hours will it take until you make the same money? 5 hours

Name ______________________ Date ______________________

Monitoring Progress
Practice Problem 3-9

Solve the Problem

There are two ways to play games at Play Now. One option is to pay \$4 an hour plus \$1 per game. The other option is to pay \$3 per game. The graph shows the functions for the two choices. Which pair of equations go with the graph?

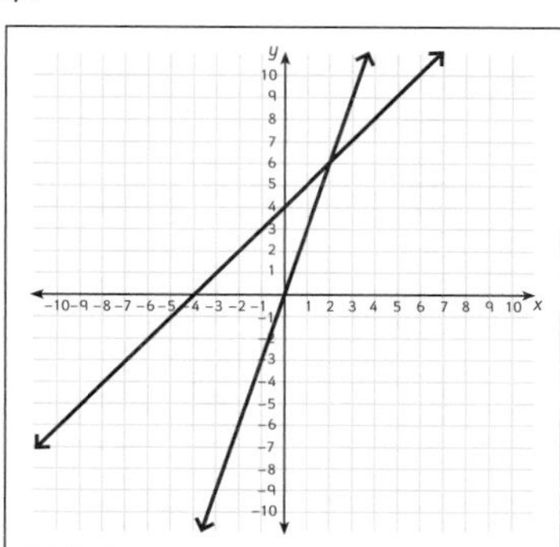

(a) $y = x + 4$ and $y = 3x$

(b) $y = x + 3$ and $y = 4x + 1$

(c) $y = 8x$ and $y = 8x + 1$

(d) $y = 8x$ and $y = 8x + 4$

(The answer is a.)

Monitoring Progress
Problem 3-9-A

Solve the Problem

Fastwave Music and Video offers two plans for downloading movies off of its Web site. With the first plan, you pay \$8 to join and \$1 per movie. The second plan lets you download songs for \$2 per movie. The graph shows the functions for the plans. Which pair of functions are shown on the graph?

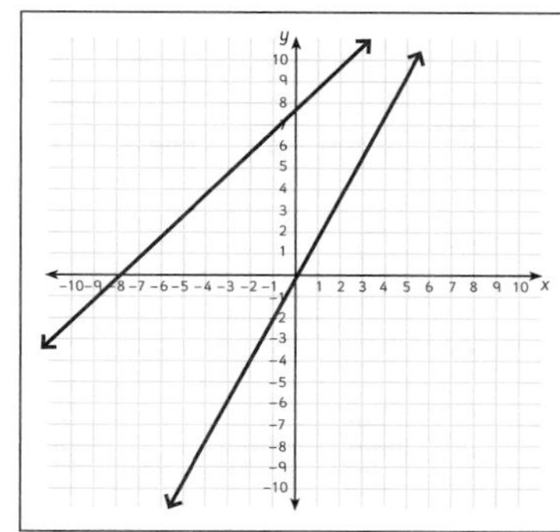

(a) $y = x + 2$ and $y = x + 8$

(b) $y = 8x$ and $y = x + 2$

(c) $y = 8x$ and $y = 2x + 8$

(d) $y = 2x$ and $y = x + 8$

Name ______________________ Date ______________________

Monitoring Progress
Problem 3-9-B

Solve the Problem

Fastwave Music has become so popular that it has decided that it can charge more for movie downloads. Starting in May, it will offer two plans.
Plan 1: Pay \$5 to join and \$2 per movie
Plan 2: Pay \$4 per movie
Write the function for each plan.
Plan 1 $y = 2x + 5$ **Plan 2** $y = 4x$
Draw each function on the graph.

If I want to download six movies per month, which plan is the better deal? Explain your answer.

Answers will vary. Sample answer: If you pay five dollars and then \$2 per movie for six, that's only \$17. If you pay \$4 per movie, six movies cost \$24.

Unit 10 Square Roots and Irrational Numbers

Problem Solving: Nonlinear Functions

The sum of the square roots of any two sides of an *isosceles triangle* is equal to the square root of the remaining side.

Unit Opener: Background Information

With students, read through the Unit Opener of *Student Text*, pages 787–788, then share some additional information about the Scarecrow and the Pythagorean theorem.

- An isosceles triangle is a triangle that has two equal sides. A right triangle has 1 angle of 90 degrees. The Scarecrow's irrational statement, made at the end of the 1939 film, *The Wizard of Oz*, is similar to the Pythagorean theorem, but the words *isosceles* and *square root* are incorrect. It is not known whether the scriptwriters intentionally wrote this statement incorrectly or whether the actor, Tony–award-winning Ray Bolger, altered it as a joke. Was he challenging the audience to listen and think carefully?
- The Pythagorean theorem is one of the most important theorems in geometry. It states that adding the squares of two lengths of a right triangle (a and b) equal the square of the hypotenuse (the side opposite the right angle), or $a^2 + b^2 = c^2$. This theorem is is used to determine the length of the third side of a right triangle. More than a thousand years before Pythagoras generalized and popularized this principle, the ancient Egyptians used it in their buildings, as did the Chinese and the Babylonians.

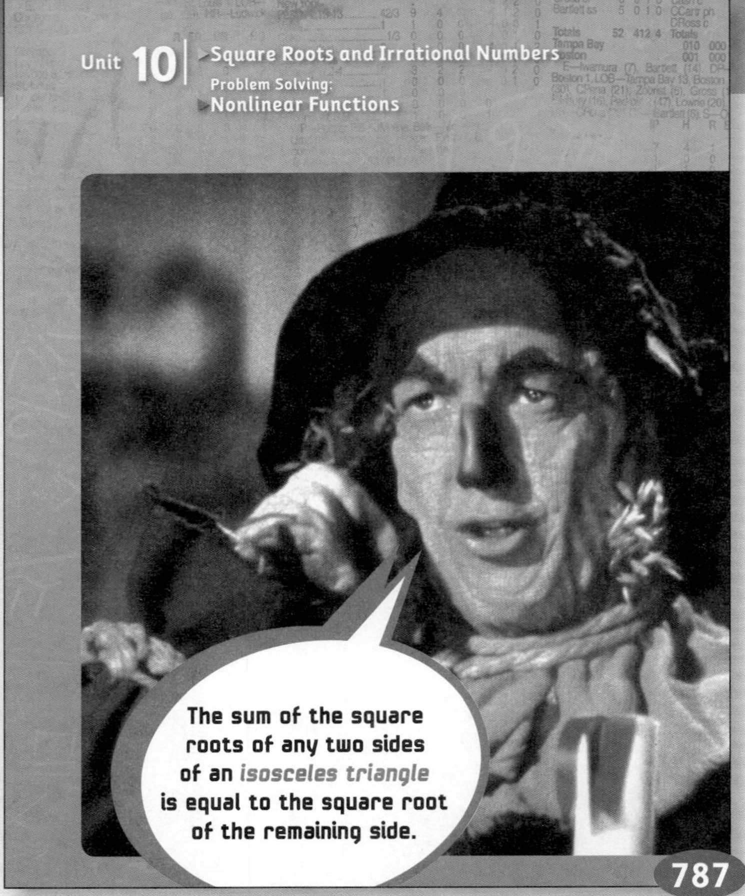

Unit 10 Building Number Concepts: Square Roots and Irrational Numbers
Problem Solving: Nonlinear Functions

Building Number Concepts	Problem Solving
• Solve algebraic equations, and estimate answers involving square roots • Use the Pythagorean theorem to find the lengths of sides of right triangles • Identify and use irrational numbers	• Tell whether a function is linear or nonlinear given a table, equation, or graph • Graph nonlinear functions on a coordinate graph • Understand the role of the coefficient in a nonlinear function

Overview

Squared numbers and square root numbers play an essential role in secondary mathematics, particularly in solving algebraic equations. This unit introduces square roots through the Pythagorean theorem and then continues to a discussion of irrational numbers. We address properties of irrational numbers and methods for estimating square roots based on perfect square numbers.

Unit Vocabulary

Pythagorean theorem
hypotenuse
square root
radical sign
perfect square numbers
irrational numbers

The Problem Solving strand provides a contrast to the previous unit on linear functions. Students see the role of squared numbers and their effect on the shape of a line, transforming straight-lined linear functions into various kinds of curved lines.

Unit Vocabulary

dependent variable
independent variable
parabola

Building Number Concepts:
Square Roots and Irrational Numbers

Key Questions That Guide Student Understanding

- *How do square roots improve our number sense?*

Enduring Understandings for Square Roots and Irrational Numbers

A simple understanding of square roots is that they are an undoing process of squared numbers; however, square roots are actually more complicated. There are two square roots for a positive integer, one positive and the other negative. This concept helps students connect to integer rules for multiplication (i.e., a negative number times a negative number yields a positive number).

The square roots of positive integers reveal an important pattern. Most square roots are irrational numbers: decimal numbers that do not terminate or repeat.

Finding a square root that is an irrational number without a calculator involves good number sense. Students can draw on their knowledge of perfect square numbers or a mental or actual number line to approximate where a square root should be.

Tools for Understanding Square Roots and Irrational Numbers

Using Models

Geometry is traditionally used to help students understand the Pythagorean theorem. The right triangle and associated squares for each side demonstrate how the sum of the squared sides equals the square of the hypotenuse. This framework provides an entry to understanding square roots and irrational numbers.

Number lines make a good complement to understanding irrational numbers. Students can estimate the location of square roots on the number line in relation to perfect squares.

Problem Solving:
▶Nonlinear Functions

Key Questions That Guide Student Understanding

- *How does a change in symbols affect the shape of a line?*

Enduring Understandings for Nonlinear Functions

Linear functions, which can be graphed as straight lines, are just one kind of functional representation. As we move into secondary mathematics, lines take on different shapes depending on the presence of a square (or higher) variable.

Squaring the x-variable in a function is the first step in creating a curved line, or parabola. Changing the constant in front of the variable enables us to manipulate the shape and direction of a parabola. Subtle changes in functions can have dramatic effects on the shape and direction of lines on a coordinate graph. Comprehension of functions in secondary mathematics relies on such subtle manipulation as reflected by changes in a graph.

Tools for Understanding Nonlinear Functions

Using Graphs

The last unit showed what linear functions look like on a coordinate graph. We connect this topic to squared numbers to extend student understanding of functions. In changing the exponent and the coefficient for the x-value, we change the shape and direction of the line on the graph. Squared x-values in this unit are either U-shaped or, in the case of $y = x^3$, vertical lines curved near the point of origin.

Building Number Concepts:
Square Roots and Irrational Numbers

Lesson	Lesson Objectives—Students will:
1	• Analyze the relationship between the sides of a right triangle using the Pythagorean theorem.
2	• Find the length of one side of a right triangle using squares and square roots.
3	• Find the length of sides of a right triangle using the Pythagorean theorem.
4	
5	• Find irrational numbers by taking the square roots of different numbers.
6	
7	• Evaluate expressions with a radical sign.
8	• Use algebraic properties to solve problems with square roots.
9	• Use number sense and the number line to estimate square roots.
10	• Review Square Roots and Irrational Numbers concepts.
Unit Assessments	End-of-Unit Assessment Performance Assessment

Problem Solving:

Nonlinear Functions

Lesson Objectives—Students will:	Assessment
• Analyze and graph nonlinear functions.	
	Quiz 1
• Learn how negative numbers and negative coefficients affect nonlinear functions.	
• Explain how the coefficient in front of the *x*-variable changes the shape of the graph of a nonlinear function.	
• Examine the graphs of other nonlinear functions.	
• Review Nonlinear Functions concepts.	Unit Review
	End-of-Unit Assessment Performance Assessment

Lesson 1 ▶The Pythagorean Theorem

Lesson Planner

Vocabulary Development

Pythagorean theorem
hypotenuse

Skills Maintenance

Substitution

Building Number Concepts:

▶ The Pythagorean Theorem

Students read about the relationship between squares, rectangles, and triangles to understand the Pythagorean theorem. Students learn that the Pythagorean theorem is a proven strategy for finding the missing length of a side, or the hypotenuse, of a right triangle. The formula is $a^2 + b^2 = c^2$, where a and b are the sides of the triangle, and c is the side opposite the 90-degree angle, or the hypotenuse.

Objective

Students will analyze the relationship between the sides of a right triangle using the Pythagorean theorem.

Homework

Students find the areas of the square, rectangle, and triangle, tell if statements are true or false about properties of shapes and change the wording of false statements to make them true, and prove the Pythagorean theorem works for the two triangles. In Distributed Practice, students practice creating *x/y* tables to represent functions.

Lesson 1 | Skills Maintenance

Name ______________________ Date ______________________

Skills Maintenance
Substitution

Activity 1

Solve the equations by using substitution.

1. Solve $y = 3x + 2$ if $x = 8$. $y = 26$
2. Solve $y = -x - 3$ if $x = 6$. $y = -9$
3. Solve $y = 2x - 4$ if $x = 5$. $y = 6$
4. Solve $y = -4x + -12$ if $x = 7$. $y = -40$

Unit 10

Unit 10 • Lesson 1 391

Skills Maintenance

Substitution

(*Interactive Text*, page 391)

Activity 1

Students substitute values for variables and solve equations.

Building Number Concepts: The Pythagorean Theorem

What is the relationship between squares, rectangles, and triangles?

(*Student Text*, pages 789–792)

Connect to Prior Knowledge

Begin by asking students to provide the area formulas for a **2 by 2 square**, a **2 by 5 rectangle**, and a **triangle** with a **height of 4 and base of 5**.

Listen for:

- *The area of a square is base times height. Two times 2 is 4 square inches.*
- *The area of a rectangle is base times height. Five times 2 is 10 square inches.*
- *The area of a triangle is $\frac{1}{2}$ times base times height. One half of 5 times 4 is 10 square inches.*

Link to Today's Concept

Tell students that understanding the area of squares and rectangles helps us understand the area of triangles. In today's lesson, we see how the area of triangles is related to the area of squares and rectangles.

Demonstrate

Engagement Strategy: Teacher Modeling

Demonstrate finding the area of the shapes in one of the following ways:

mBook: Use the *mBook Teacher Edition* for *Student Text*, pages 789–792. **m**

Overhead Projector: Reproduce the shapes and area formulas on a transparency, and modify as discussed.

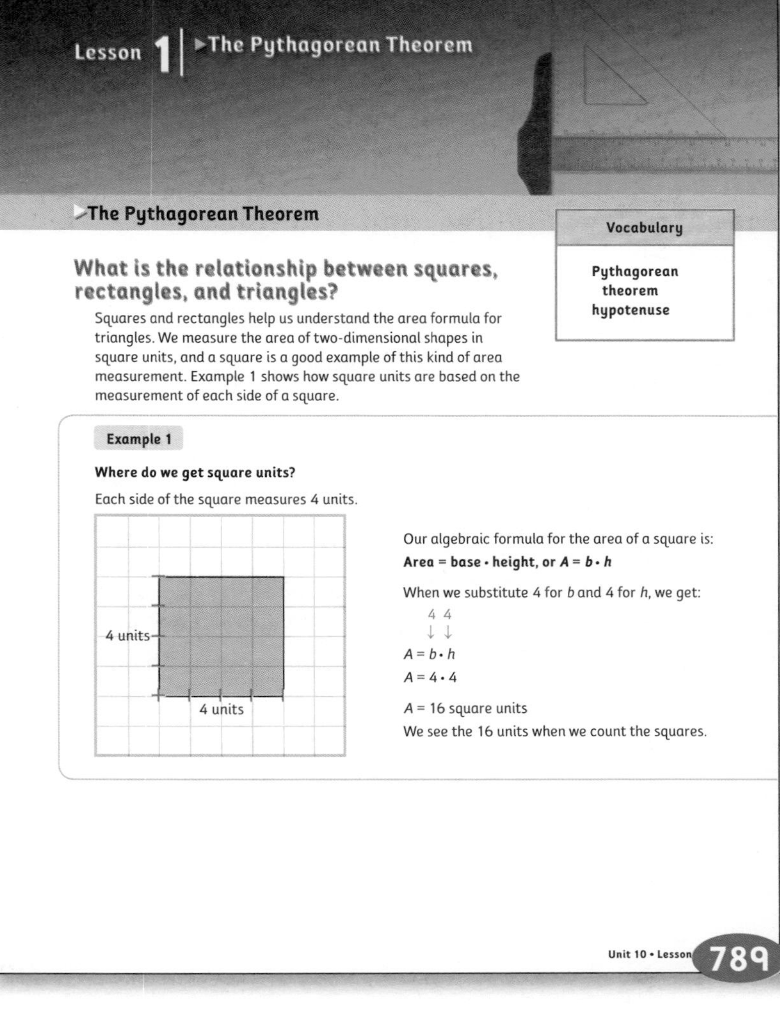

Lesson 1 The Pythagorean Theorem
The Pythagorean Theorem
Vocabulary
Pythagorean theorem
hypotenuse
What is the relationship between squares, rectangles, and triangles?
Squares and rectangles help us understand the area formula for triangles. We measure the area of two-dimensional shapes in square units, and a square is a good example of this kind of area measurement. Example 1 shows how square units are based on the measurement of each side of a square.
Example 1
Where do we get square units?
Each side of the square measures 4 units.
4 units
4 units
Our algebraic formula for the area of a square is:
Area = base • height, or A = b • h
When we substitute 4 for b and 4 for h, we get:
4 4
A = b • h
A = 4 • 4
A = 16 square units
We see the 16 units when we count the squares.
Unit 10 • Lesson 1 789

Board: Copy the shapes and area formulas on the board, and modify as discussed.

- Discuss how square units are based on the measurement inside a square. Demonstrate how to find the area of the square in **Example 1**. **m**

What is the relationship between squares, rectangles, and triangles? *(continued)*

Demonstrate

- Continue looking at the square from Example 1.
- Remind students that we can count the squares to confirm our answer of 16 square units. m
- Next show students that a square is made of two triangles in **Example 2**. Point out that each triangle is one-half the square. m
- Demonstrate how the area formula of a square helps us derive the area formula of a triangle. m

Our area formula for triangles makes sense based on what we know about the area of a square. We simply make two triangles out of the square by drawing a diagonal from one vertex of the square to the opposite vertex. Example 2 shows how we find the area formula of a triangle.

Example 2

How do we find the area of a triangle?

The square is divided into two congruent triangles.

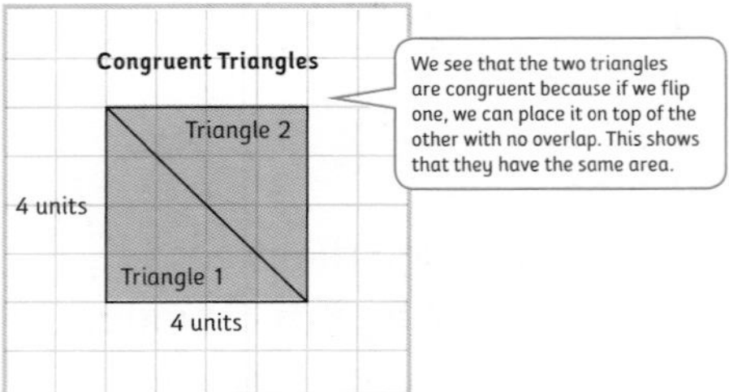
Congruent Triangles
Triangle 2
Triangle 1
4 units
4 units
We see that the two triangles are congruent because if we flip one, we can place it on top of the other with no overlap. This shows that they have the same area.

This means the area formula for a triangle is:

Area = $\frac{1}{2}$ · base · height, or $A = \frac{1}{2} \cdot b \cdot h$

$$A = \frac{1}{2} \cdot \underset{\uparrow 4}{b} \cdot \underset{\uparrow 4}{h}$$

$A = \frac{1}{2} \cdot 4 \cdot 4$

$A = \frac{1}{2} \cdot 16$

$A = 8$ square units

Demonstrate

- Continue looking at the triangles in Example 2. Show how to count squares in the triangle to confirm our answer. m
- Next look at **Example 3**. Explain that the same thinking applies to the area of rectangles. Walk through finding the area of the rectangle. m

Counting the square units in each triangle also confirms that the area of Triangle 1 = $\frac{1}{2} \cdot b \cdot h$, or 8 square units.

Congruent Triangles in a Square

Area = 8 square units

The same kind of thinking applies to triangles and rectangles. It is easy to see how we get the area formula for a triangle from the area of a rectangle.

Example 3

How are the areas of rectangles and triangles related?

Rectangle

3 units

5 units

Area of a rectangle = $b \cdot h$

$A = b \cdot h$ (5 → b, 3 → h)

$A = 5 \cdot 3$

$A = 15$ square units

What is the relationship between squares, rectangles, and triangles?
(*continued*)

Demonstrate

- Continue looking at Example 3.
- Point out that a rectangle is also made up of triangles. Make sure students understand that the area of the triangle is one half the area of the rectangle. m
- Finally, show the other types of triangles, and point out that the area formula for all triangles is $A = \frac{1}{2} \cdot b \cdot h$. m

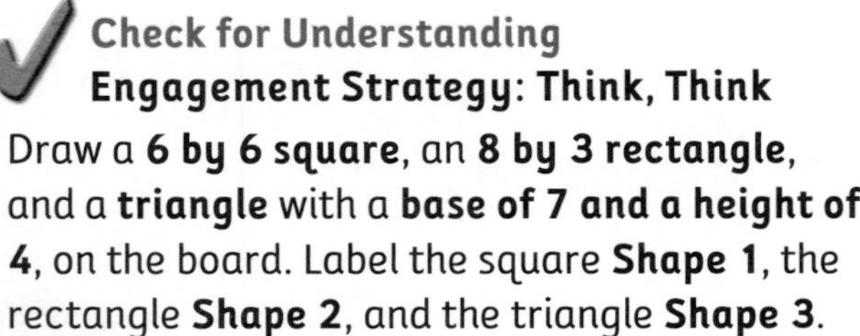

Check for Understanding
Engagement Strategy: Think, Think

Draw a **6 by 6 square**, an **8 by 3 rectangle**, and a **triangle** with a **base of 7 and a height of 4**, on the board. Label the square **Shape 1**, the rectangle **Shape 2**, and the triangle **Shape 3**.

Tell students that they will substitute the numbers into the area formula to find the area of each shape. Have students listen for their names, and have them give you the area for a shape when you call on them. Allow students time to think of their answer for each shape and then call on a student by name. If correct, congratulate the student.

Ask:

What is the area of Shape 1? (*36 square units*)

What is the area of Shape 2? (*24 square units*)

What is the area of Shape 3? (*14 square units*)

Lesson 1

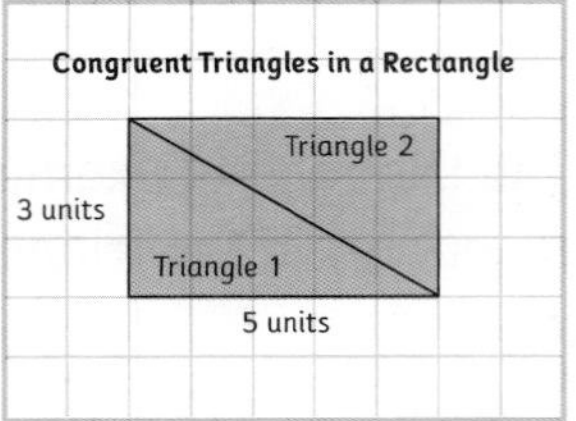

The area of Triangle 1 is $\frac{1}{2}$ the area of the rectangle. We see that the formula for the area of the triangle remains the same.

Area of a triangle = $\frac{1}{2} \cdot b \cdot h$

5 3
↓ ↓

$A = \frac{1}{2} \cdot b \cdot h$

$A = \frac{1}{2} \cdot 5 \cdot 3$

$A = \frac{1}{2} \cdot 15$

$A = 7\frac{1}{2}$ square units

The triangle in Examples 2 and 3 are right triangles because one angle measures 90 degrees. However, the area formula applies to any triangle.

The formula $A = \frac{1}{2} \cdot b \cdot h$ works for all triangles.

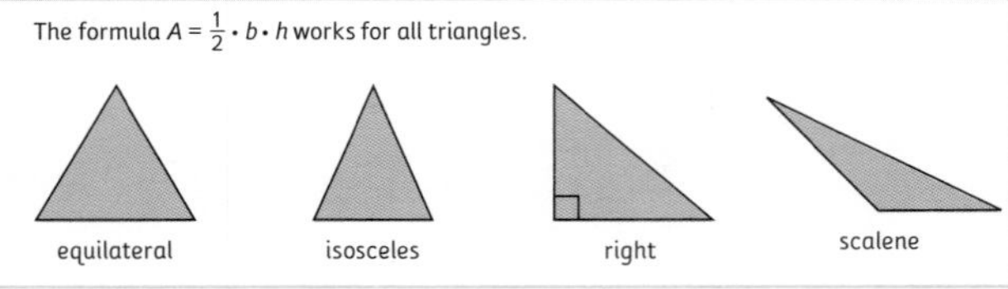

What is the relationship between sides of squares and rectangles?

(*Student Text*, page 793)

Demonstrate

- Turn to page 793 of the *Student Text*, and go over the rules about sides of squares and rectangles.
- Tell students that the rule for squares is that their sides are all the same length.
- Tell students that the rule for rectangles is that opposite sides are equal.
- Have students look at the pictures for a clear, visual representation of these rules.

What is the Pythagorean theorem?

(*Student Text*, pages 793–795)

Demonstrate

- Tell students that there is a special rule for understanding the relationship between the lengths of the sides of a right triangle. Explain that we use the **Pythagorean theorem** to look at this relationship.
- Tell students that the formula works for right triangles, and we use it to figure out the length of the **hypotenuse**, the side opposite the right triangle. Discuss each part of the triangle on the diagram.

Lesson 1

What is the relationship between sides of squares and rectangles?

We can see a clear relationship between the different sides of a square or a rectangle if we think about the properties of these two shapes. All sides of a square are equal in length. The opposite sides of a rectangle are equal in length.

Relationship Between the Sides of Squares and Rectangles

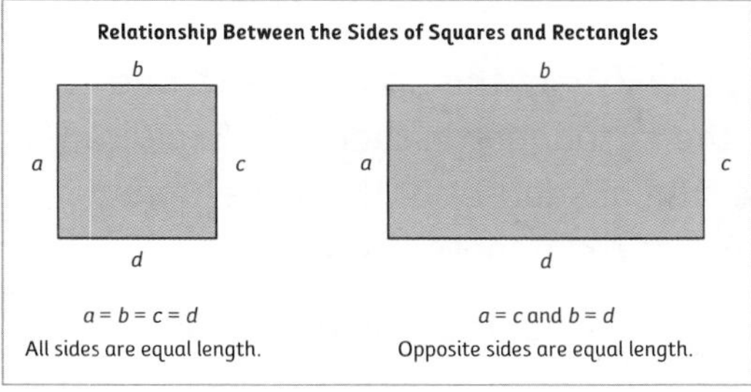

$a = b = c = d$
All sides are equal length.

$a = c$ and $b = d$
Opposite sides are equal length.

What is the Pythagorean theorem?

There is a special relationship between the sides of a right triangle that is a bit more complicated. We can use the **Pythagorean theorem** to see this relationship. This formula only works for right triangles. We generally use it to figure out the length of the hypotenuse. The **hypotenuse** is the side opposite the right angle.

Right triangle

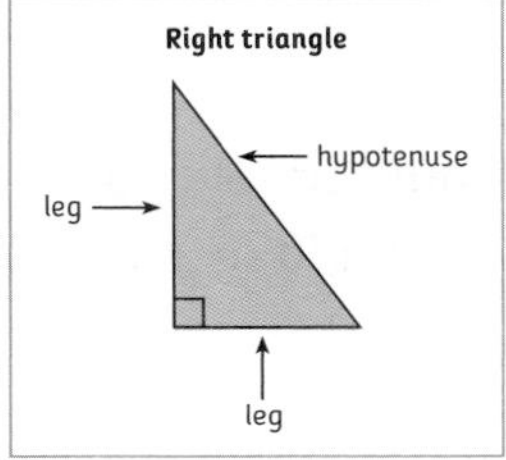

In a right triangle, the sides that form the right angle are called legs.

Unit 10 • Lesson 793

What is the Pythagorean theorem?
(continued)

Demonstrate

- Turn to page 794 of the *Student Text,* and go over the Pythagorean theorem. Explain that the sum of squares of the sides equals the square of the hypotenuse.
- Point out the formula for the theorem: $\boldsymbol{a^2 + b^2 = c^2}$.
- Use **Example 1** to demonstrate how the formula shows that the Pythagorean theorem works. Walk through the substitution to show that $\mathbf{12^2 + 5^2 = 13^2}$, or **144 + 25 = 169**.
- Point out that the formula simplifies to **169 = 169**; therefore, the formula $\boldsymbol{a^2 + b^2 = c^2}$ is true for this triangle.

Check for Understanding
Engagement Strategy: Look About

Draw a right triangle with a **base of 6**, a **height of 8**, and a **hypotenuse of 10** on the board ($6^2 + 8^2 = 10^2$, $36 + 64 = 100$, $100 = 100$). Tell students that they will show that the Pythagorean theorem works for the triangle with the help of the whole class. Students should copy the formula and show their work in large writing on a piece of paper or a dry erase board. When students finish their work, they should hold up their answer for everyone to see.

If students are not sure about the answer, prompt them to look about at other students' solutions to help with their thinking. Review the answers after all students hold up their solutions.

Lesson 1

The Pythagorean Theorem

The Pythagorean theorem tells us that the sum of the squares of the legs of a right triangle is equal to the square of the hypotenuse. In the Pythagorean theorem, we label the legs of the triangle *a* and *b*. The hypotenuse is *c*. This helps us write the formula for the theorem.

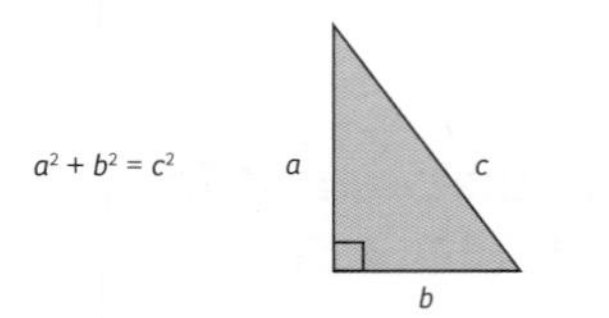

We can show that the Pythagorean theorem works by substituting numbers into the formula.

Example 1

Show that the Pythagorean theorem is true for this triangle.

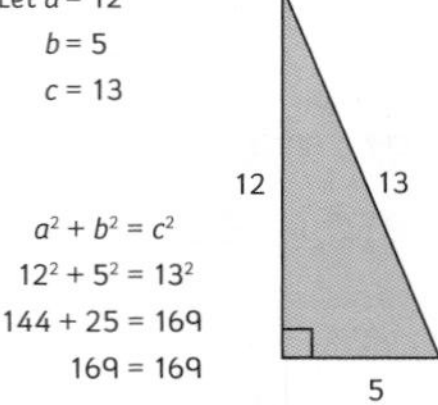

We see that the formula, $a^2 + b^2 = c^2$, is true for this triangle.

794 Unit 10 • Lesson 1

Demonstrate

- Tell students we can prove that the Pythagorean theorem works using a simple drawing. Have students look at the drawing on *Student Text*, page 795.
- Remind students that the theorem tells us that we square each side of the triangle. The sum of the two squares of the sides is equal to the square of the hypotenuse. Point out that in the drawing there is a square on each side of the triangle.
- Explain that if we add the areas of the small and medium squares in the drawing, they should equal the area of the large square: **25 + 144 = 169**. When we add 25 and 144, we find their sum to be 169: **169 = 169**.
- Tell students that we know the Pythagorean theorem is true for this triangle.

Check for Understanding
Engagement Strategy: Look About

Draw a right triangle on the board. Label the **base 4**, the **height 3**, and the **hypotenuse 5**. Tell students they will check that the lengths of the sides are correct using the Pythagorean theorem and the help of the class (*16 + 9 = 25, 25 = 25*). Direct students to draw the triangle and the squares on each side of the triangle, as shown on *Student Text*, page 795. Students should show their work in large writing on a piece of paper or a dry erase board. When students finish their work, they should hold up their answers for everyone to see.

If students are not sure about the answer, prompt them to look about at other students' work to help with their thinking. Review the answers after all students hold up their solutions.

Lesson 1

We can prove that the Pythagorean theorem works using a simple drawing. Remember that the theorem tells us that we square each side of the triangle. We draw a square on each side to show this.

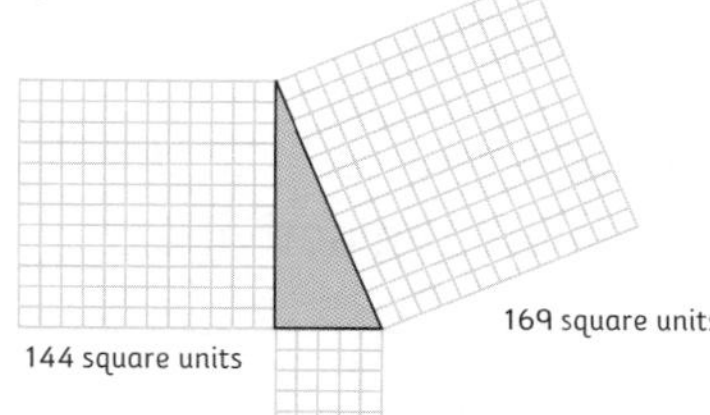

Remember the theorem: the sum of the squares of the legs of a right triangle is equal to the square of the hypotenuse. This means that if we add the areas of the small and medium squares, they should equal the area of the large square.

25 + 144 = 169
169 = 169

The numbers are the same. We see that the formula $a^2 + b^2 = c^2$ is true for this triangle.

Apply Skills
Turn to ***Interactive Text***, page 392.

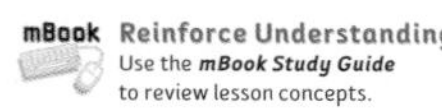
Reinforce Understanding
Use the ***mBook Study Guide*** to review lesson concepts.

Unit 10 • Lesson 795

Apply Skills
(*Interactive Text*, pages 392–394)

Have students turn to pages 392–394 in the *Interactive Text*, and complete the activities.

Activity 1

Students find the areas of three shapes: a rectangle, a square, and a triangle.

Activity 2

Students identify the types of triangles.

Activity 3

Students look at the picture of the three squares forming the right triangle and answer the questions that follow it.

Monitor students' work as they complete the activities.

Watch for:

- Can students apply the area formulas to find the area of each shape?
- Can students identify the different types of triangles?
- Can students make the connection between the sides of the squares and the sides of the triangle?
- Can students test the values in the Pythagorean theorem to demonstrate that they work?
- Can students draw the triangles to test the Pythagorean theorem?

mBook **Reinforce Understanding**
Remind students that they can review lesson concepts by accessing the *mBook Study Guide.*

Lesson 1 | Apply Skills

Name ______ Date ______

Apply Skills
The Pythagorean Theorem

Activity 1

Find the areas of the shapes by substituting the dimensions into the area formulas.

1. Area of a Rectangle = base • height
   4, 8
   What is the area of the rectangle?
   32 square units

2. Area of a Square = base • height
   5, 5
   What is the area of the square?
   25 square units

3. Area of a Triangle = $\frac{1}{2}$ (base • height)
   4, 8
   What is the area of the triangle?
   16 square units

Activity 2

Match the type of triangle with its picture.

1. d — (a) Scalene
2. c — (b) Right
3. b — (c) Isosceles
4. a — (d) Equilateral

392 Unit 10 • Lesson 1

Lesson 1 | Apply Skills

Name ______ Date ______

Activity 3

Prove that the Pythagorean Theorem works using the area of squares. We will change the area formula for squares slightly. You can see that both formulas give you the same area. Look at the model then at the triangle and squares. Then answer the questions about the sides of the triangle.

	Two Ways to Think About the Area of Squares	
	Traditional formula $A = b \cdot h$	New formula $A = s^2$
Model	h, b	s, s

We can show that the Pythagorean Theorem works by drawing squares onto each side of a right triangle as shown. Think about how the area of those squares helps prove the Pythagorean Theorem.

a, b, c

1. What do we know about each of the sides of the right triangle based on the three squares?
   Answers may vary. Sample answer: Each side is a different length.
2. What do squared units have to do with the Pythagorean Theorem?
   Answers may vary. Sample answer: The sum of the squared shorter sides of the triangle is equal to the square of the hypotenuse (longest side).
3. If the measurements of the sides of a right triangle are as follows: a = 3, b = 4, and c = 5, does this demonstrate that the Pythagorean Theorem works?
   Answers may vary. Sample answer: Yes, because $3^2 + 4^2 = 5^2$.

Unit 10

Unit 10 • Lesson 1 393

Homework

Go over the instructions on page 796 of the *Student Text* for each part of the homework.

Activity 1

Students find the areas of the square and the triangle.

Activity 2

Students tell if statements are true or false about properties of shapes. If they are false, then students change the wording to make a true statement.

Activity 3

Students prove the Pythagorean theorem works for the two triangles.

Activity 4 • Distributed Practice

Students create x/y tables for each of the equations of functions.

Activity 1

Find the area of the shapes.

1. What is the area of this square? Use the formula $A = s^2$.

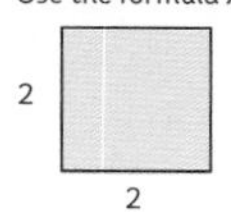

4 square units

2. What is the area of this triangle? Use the formula $A = \frac{1}{2} \cdot b \cdot h$.

6
4

12 square units

Activity 2

Write whether each of the statements about the properties of shapes is true or false. If the statement is false, rewrite it to make it true.

1. All the sides of a rectangle are always the same length.
   False. The sides of a rectangle are not always the same length.
2. All the sides of a square are always the same length.
   True
3. All the sides of a triangle are always the same length.
   False. All the sides of a triangle are sometimes the same length.
4. The area of a triangle is half of the area of a rectangle if it has the same base and height. True
5. The area of a square is half the area of a rectangle if it has the same base and height. False. The area of a square is the same as a rectangle if it has the same base and height.

Activity 3

Prove the Pythagorean theorem works for these triangles.

1.

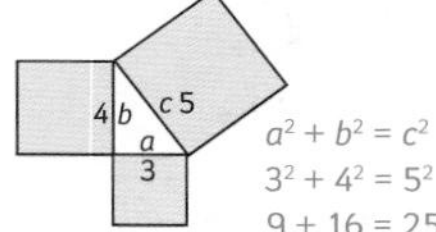

$a^2 + b^2 = c^2$
$3^2 + 4^2 = 5^2$
$9 + 16 = 25$
$25 = 25$

2.

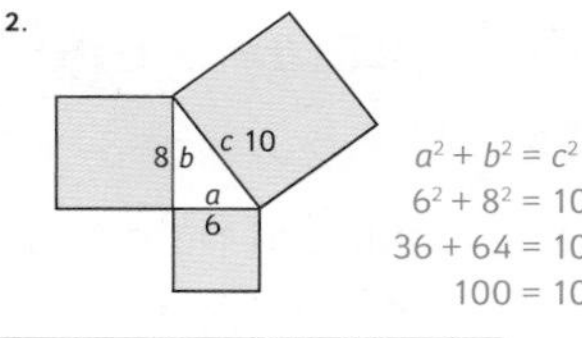

$a^2 + b^2 = c^2$
$6^2 + 8^2 = 10^2$
$36 + 64 = 100$
$100 = 100$

Activity 4 • Distributed Practice

Create x/y tables for each of the following functions.

1. $y = 3x$
2. $y = -x$
3. $y = \frac{1}{2}x$

See Additional Answers below.

Additional Answers

Activity 4

1.

x	y
1	3
2	6
3	9
4	12
5	15

2.

x	y
1	−1
2	−2
3	−3
4	−4
5	−5

3.

x	y
1	$\frac{1}{2}$
2	1
3	$1\frac{1}{2}$
4	2
5	$2\frac{1}{2}$

Lesson 2 ▶Square Numbers and Square Roots

Lesson Planner

Vocabulary Development

square root
radical sign

Skills Maintenance

Square Numbers

Building Number Concepts:

▶ Square Numbers and Square Roots

We continue looking at right triangles and the Pythagorean theorem to find the length of the side of a right triangle, given the lengths of the other two sides. Students learn about the relationship between square numbers and square roots. Square roots are the way to unsquare a number. A square root has both a positive and a negative answer.

Objective

Students will find the length of one side of a right triangle using squares and square roots.

Homework

Students tell the square roots of perfect squares, solve square roots of nonperfect squares, and find the length of missing side c using the Pythagorean theorem. In Distributed Practice, students write equations for functions from data found in *x/y* tables.

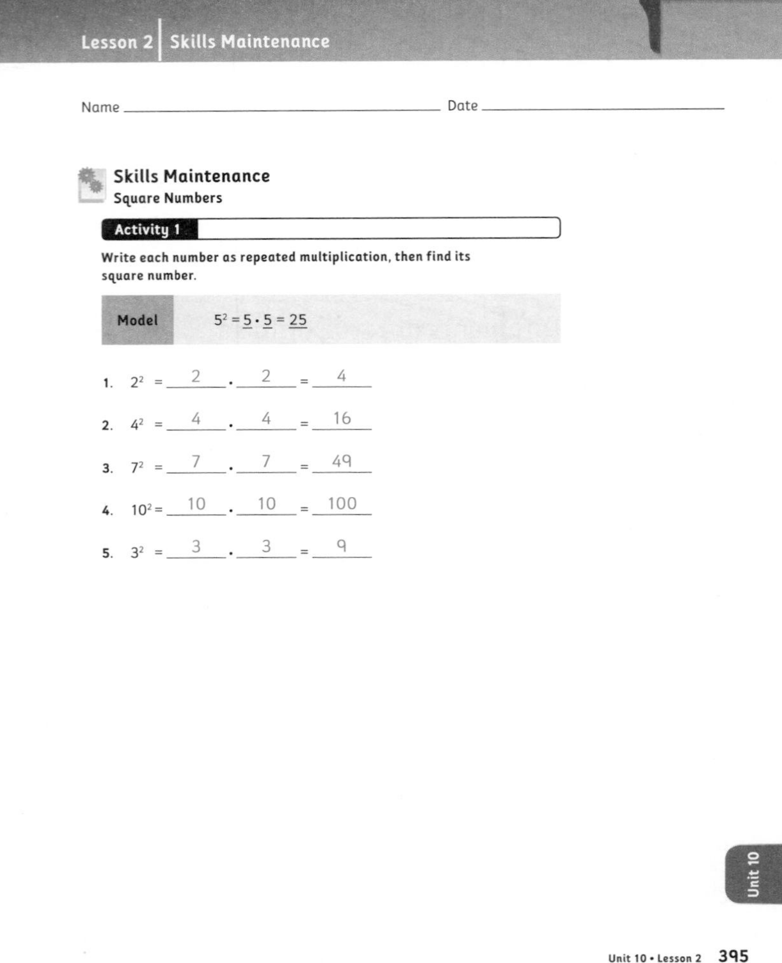
Lesson 2 | Skills Maintenance

Name ______ Date ______

Skills Maintenance
Square Numbers

Activity 1

Write each number as repeated multiplication, then find its square number.

Model $5^2 = 5 \cdot 5 = 25$

1. $2^2 = 2 \cdot 2 = 4$
2. $4^2 = 4 \cdot 4 = 16$
3. $7^2 = 7 \cdot 7 = 49$
4. $10^2 = 10 \cdot 10 = 100$
5. $3^2 = 3 \cdot 3 = 9$

Unit 10

Unit 10 • Lesson 2 395

Skills Maintenance

Square Numbers

(*Interactive Text*, page 395)

Activity 1

Students square numbers by writing them as repeated multiplication and solving them.

Building Number Concepts: Square Numbers and Square Roots

How do we find the length of the side of a right triangle?

(*Student Text*, pages 797–798)

Connect to Prior Knowledge

Begin by reminding students of the Pythagorean theorem from the previous lesson. Write it on the board or overhead or have a volunteer write it. Tell students that the squares in the problem present a little bit of difficulty. We are used to starting with a number and squaring it to get the answer. In these types of problems, we sometimes start with a number that has to be unsquared. Tell students that some numbers are easy to unsquare. List some on the board and have students unsquare them:

100 (*10*) **25** (*5*) **49** (*7*) **64** (*8*) **16** (*4*) **36** (*6*)

Link to Today's Concept

Tell students that in today's lesson, we learn about a formal way for unsquaring numbers and learn some important properties about this process.

Demonstrate

Engagement Strategy: Teacher Modeling

Demonstrate how the Pythagorean theorem works in of the following ways:

mBook: Use the *mBook Teacher Edition* for *Student Text*, pages 797–798.

Overhead Projector: Reproduce the triangles and formula on a transparency, and modify as discussed.

Board: Copy the triangles and formula on the board, and modify as discussed.

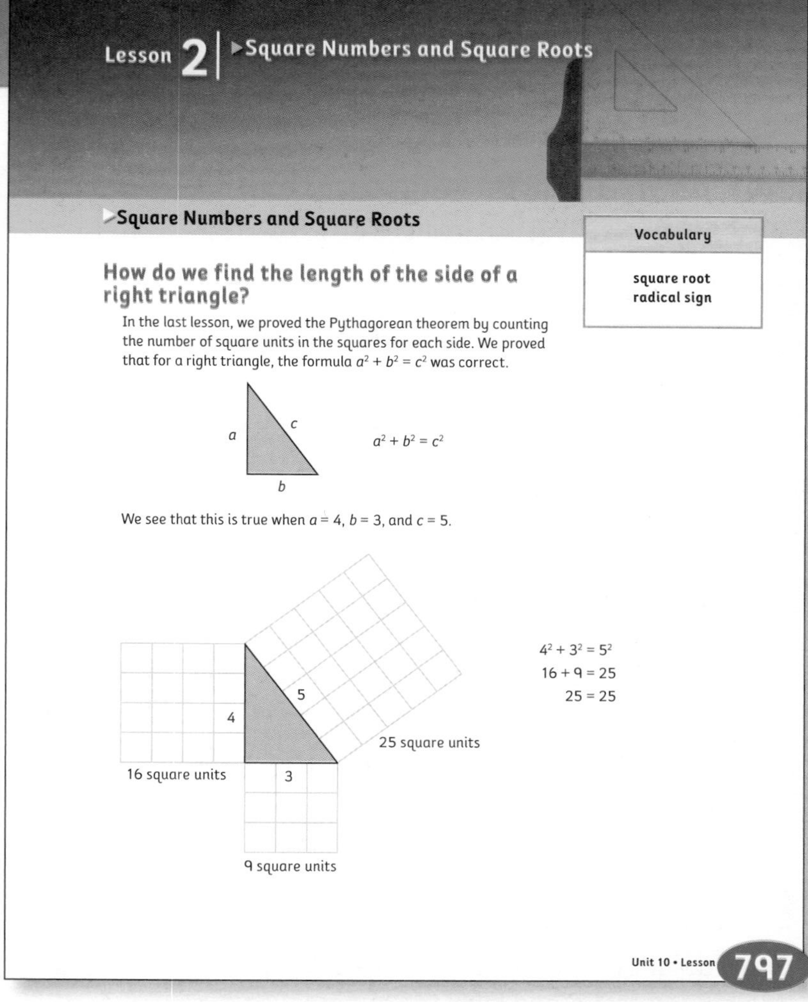

Lesson 2 ▸Square Numbers and Square Roots

▸Square Numbers and Square Roots

How do we find the length of the side of a right triangle?

In the last lesson, we proved the Pythagorean theorem by counting the number of square units in the squares for each side. We proved that for a right triangle, the formula $a^2 + b^2 = c^2$ was correct.

Vocabulary
square root radical sign

We see that this is true when $a = 4$, $b = 3$, and $c = 5$.

- Have students look at the triangles. Remind them of the formula $a^2 + b^2 = c^2$. Walk through each step of substituting the values into the formula to show that the Pythagorean theorem is true for this triangle.

How do we find the length of the side of a right triangle? *(continued)*

Demonstrate

- Next turn to page 798 of the *Student Text,* and go over **Example 1**.
- Point out that in this example, we know the lengths of two of the sides but not the third side.
- Demonstrate how we can use the Pythagorean Theorem to find the length of the third side. Start by substituting the 8 and 6 for *a* and *b*. Then walk through the formula until you get to $100 = c^2$.
- Remind students that $10 \cdot 10 = 100$. So the length of the side is 10.

Check for Understanding

Engagement Strategy: Think Tank

Draw a right triangle and label one side **9**, the other side **12**, and label the hypotenuse ***c***. Distribute strips of paper to students and have them write their name on them. Tell students to use the Pythagorean theorem to find the length of the hypotenuse ($c = 15$). Have students write their answer on the strip of paper, and collect the strips in a container. Draw a strip from the container, and share the answer with the class. If correct, congratulate the student. Invite the student to walk through the solution with the class.

We use this formula to find the missing length of any one side of a right triangle. Let's suppose that we do not know the length of the hypotenuse of this triangle.

Example 1

Use the Pythagorean theorem to find the length of the hypotenuse.

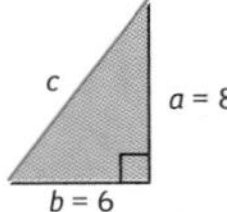

We substitute the numbers for the variables in the formula for the Pythagorean theorem.

$$a^2 + b^2 = c^2 \quad (a = 8,\ b = 6)$$
$$8^2 + 6^2 = c^2$$
$$64 + 36 = c^2$$
$$100 = c^2$$

At this point, we can use our number sense to find *c*. We know $c^2 = c \cdot c$ and $100 = 10^2$, or $10 \cdot 10$. So $c = 10$.

Number sense tells us this is correct.

The length of the hypotenuse is 10.

What is the relationship between square numbers and square roots?

(*Student Text*, page 799)

Demonstrate

- Have students turn to page 799 of the *Student Text*, and read the material at the top of the page.
- Explain to students that we need a formal way to unsquare numbers when we use the Pythagorean theorem. We know that $3^2 = 9$ and $2^2 = 4$, but we need a way to unsquare 9 and get 3 or unsquare 4 and get 2.
- Explain that we do this with **square roots**. Explain that a square root is the number multiplied by itself to get a square number. Show students we use the symbol $\sqrt{\ }$ to indicate square root. Explain that it is sometimes called a **radical sign**.
- Next tell students that a unique property of square roots is that they actually have two answers when we solve them. They can be positive or negative. Go over **Example 1**.
- Show students that not only does $5 \cdot 5 = 25$, but also $-5 \cdot -5 = 25$. When we unsquare 25, we have to remember that there are two possible values that we could get for our answer.
- Walk through all the square roots in Example 1 with students, pointing out the positive and negative square roots. Remind students of the rule that when we multiply two negative numbers, we get a positive number.

Lesson 2

What is the relationship between square numbers and square roots?

It is not always easy to find the length of the hypotenuse using number sense as we did in the previous example. What we need to do is find the **square root** of a number. A square root is a number that, when multiplied by itself, becomes a square number.

100

We start with the square number 100. To find the square root of the number, we ask, "What number squared will give me this number?" In this case, the square root is 10.

$10^2 = 100$

When we want to show square roots, we write problems this way:

$\sqrt{100} = 10$

The $\sqrt{\ }$ sign over the 100 is called the **radical sign**.

The next example shows a surprising fact about square numbers and square roots.

As we can see, all numbers have a positive and negative square root. This makes sense when we think about the rule for negative numbers—a negative number times a negative number is a positive number.

Example 1

Use what we know about square numbers to find the square roots.

Square Number	Square Roots
$5 \cdot 5 = \mathbf{25}$ $-5 \cdot -5 = \mathbf{25}$	$\sqrt{\mathbf{25}} = 5$ and -5
$7 \cdot 7 = \mathbf{49}$ $-7 \cdot -7 = \mathbf{49}$	$\sqrt{\mathbf{49}} = 7$ and -7
$3 \cdot 3 = \mathbf{9}$ $-3 \cdot -3 = \mathbf{9}$	$\sqrt{\mathbf{9}} = 3$ and -3
$20 \cdot 20 = \mathbf{400}$ $-20 \cdot -20 = \mathbf{400}$	$\sqrt{\mathbf{400}} = 20$ and -20

Unit 10 • Lesson 799

How do we solve square roots that are not perfect squares?

(*Student Text*, page 800)

Demonstrate

- Turn to page 800 of the *Student Text*, and read through the material with students.
- Tell students that we can find square roots on the calculator as well.
- Demonstrate how to input the information on a calculator to get the square root. Have students get out their calculators. Circulate around the room, pointing out the key on the calculator that stands for square root.
- Explain that not all numbers are perfect squares. This means that not all square roots are integers. Tell students that, in fact, it is more common to not have a perfect square.
- Have students try some of the problems on the page. Tell students that the numbers are rounded so they might look different (e.g., shorter) than the number that is on their calculators.
- Next explain that the calculator only gives the positive answer, but like we found with perfect squares, these numbers also have two answers, one positive and one negative.

Check for Understanding

Engagement Strategy: Pair/Share

Divide the class into pairs. Have each partner write down three numbers. Have partners exchange papers and use their calculators to find the square root of the numbers. Have students write their answers on a piece of paper. When partners finish, have them exchange papers again and use their calculators to check the answers.

Lesson 2

How do we solve square roots that are not perfect squares?

Not all numbers have integers as square roots. When we try to find the square root of most numbers, our answer is often a decimal number. Usually we just enter a number and press the √ button on a calculator to find a square root. Here are some examples of square roots that are not integers. We have rounded the decimal number to the hundred-thousandths place.

Square Roots That are Decimal Numbers
$\sqrt{3}$ = 1.73205 and −1.73205
$\sqrt{10}$ = 3.16228 and −3.16228
$\sqrt{6}$ = 2.44949 and −2.44949
$\sqrt{150}$ = 12.24745 and −12.24745

Although we have been talking about both positive and negative square roots, when we use a calculator to compute the square root of a number, it is only shown as a positive number. For most applications of square roots, including the formula for the Pythagorean theorem, this is all we need. When we measure the length of something, it is always a positive number.

Apply Skills
Turn to *Interactive Text*, page 396.

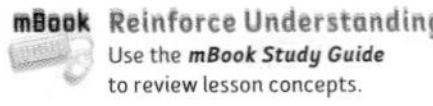

Reinforce Understanding
Use the *mBook Study Guide* to review lesson concepts.

800 Unit 10 • Lesson 2

Watch for:

- Students input the numbers correctly into the calculator.
- Students write down both the positive and negative square root as the answer.

Apply Skills

(*Interactive Text*, pages 396–398)

Have students turn to pages 396–398 in the *Interactive Text*, and complete the activities.

Activity 1

Students find the square root of some common perfect square numbers. Monitor students' work as they complete the activity.

Watch for:

- Can students identify the square root of each of the numbers?
- Did students remember that there is a negative answer as well as a positive one?

Activity 2

Students find the missing side length of different shapes. They are to use their knowledge of square roots and the Pythagorean theorem. Remind students that lengths can never have a negative measurement, so all the values in these problems are positive. Monitor students' work as they complete the activities.

Watch for:

- Can students set up the problem correctly using the Pythagorean theorem?
- Can students compute the length of the missing side using the calculator of nonperfect squares?
- Can students check the answer by substituting all the values into the formula and determining if the left side of the equation equals the right?

Lesson 2 | Apply Skills

Name ______________________ Date ______________

Apply Skills
Square Numbers and Square Roots

Activity 1

Find the square root of each number. Remember to include negative numbers. Round decimal numbers to the nearest hundredth.

Model $\sqrt{100}$ $+10$ or -10

1. $\sqrt{49}$ $+7$ or -7
2. $\sqrt{64}$ $+8$ or -8
3. $\sqrt{16}$ $+4$ or -4
4. $\sqrt{1}$ $+1$ or -1
5. $\sqrt{63}$ $+7.94$ or -7.94
6. $\sqrt{81}$ $+9$ or -9
7. $\sqrt{121}$ $+11$ or -11
8. $\sqrt{14}$ $+3.74$ or -3.74

Activity 2

Find the square roots of sides for different shapes. Be sure to remember these two formulas:

Area of a square

$A = s^2$

Pythagorean Theorem

$a^2 + b^2 = c^2$

Do not use a calculator in this exercise. Remember what you know about numbers and square numbers. For example, if you see a number like 25, you know that it is the same as 5 • 5. That means the square root of 25 is 5. If the number is not one that you know well, just write the square root symbol.

396 Unit 10 • Lesson 2

Lesson 2 | Apply Skills

Name ______________________ Date ______________

1. What is the length of side *a*? $\sqrt{100} = 10$; $a = 10$

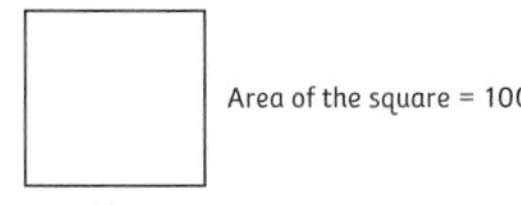

2. What is the length of side *c*? $7^2 + 5^2 = c^2$; $c = \sqrt{74}$

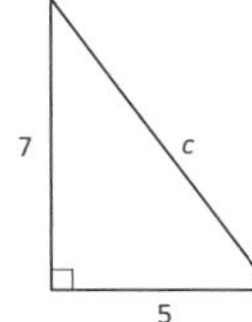

3. What is the length of side *d*? $3^2 + 4^2 = d^2$; $d = \sqrt{25} = 5$

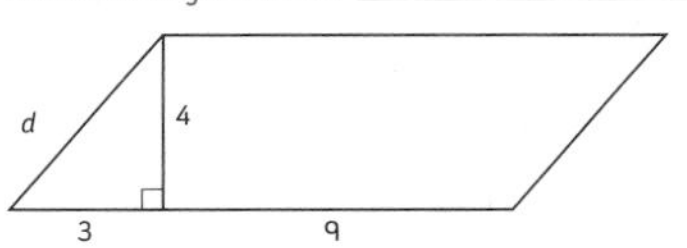

Unit 10

Unit 10 • Lesson 2 397

mBook **Reinforce Understanding**
Remind students that they can review lesson concepts by accessing the online *mBook Study Guide.*

Name ______________________ Date ______________________

4. What is the length of side r? $3^2 + 4^2 = r^2$; $r = \sqrt{25} = 5$

5. What is the length of side m? $10^2 + 3^2 = m^2$; $m = \sqrt{109}$

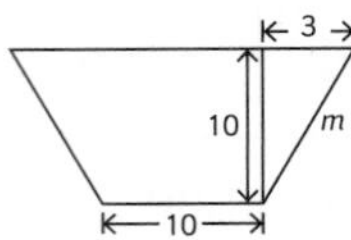

6. What is the length of side b? $8^2 + 6^2 = b^2$; $b = \sqrt{100} = 10$

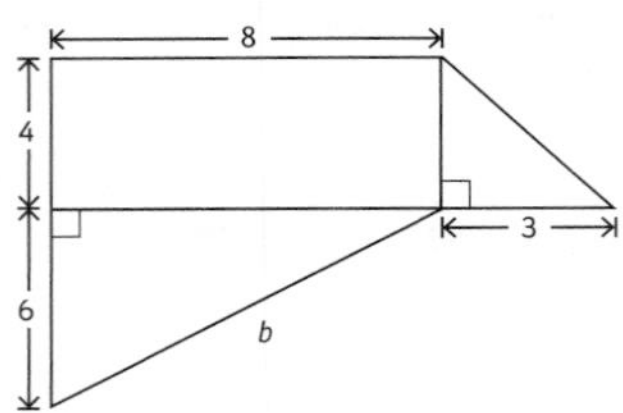

mBook Reinforce Understanding
Use the **mBook** ***Study Guide*** to review lesson concepts.

Homework

Go over the instructions on pages 801–802 of the *Student Text* for each part of the homework.

Activity 1

Students tell the square roots of perfect squares. Remind students to include both the positive and negative answers for these.

Activity 2

Students solve square roots of nonperfect squares. Tell students they will need to use a calculator for this section. Remind them that there is a negative answer as well that will not show up on their calculators. Also, tell them to round the numbers to the nearest tenths place.

Activity 3

Students find the length of the hypotenuse using the Pythagorean theorem.

Lesson 2

Homework

Activity 1

Find the square root of the perfect square numbers. Remember the negatives.

1. $\sqrt{25}$ 5 and −5
2. $\sqrt{49}$ 7 and −7
3. $\sqrt{64}$ 8 and −8
4. $\sqrt{100}$ 10 and −10
5. $\sqrt{1}$ 1 and −1

Activity 2

Find the square root of these nonperfect square numbers. Use a calculator. Round the answer to the nearest tenth.

1. $\sqrt{82}$ 9.1
2. $\sqrt{5}$ 2.2
3. $\sqrt{50}$ 7.1
4. $\sqrt{17}$ 4.1
5. $\sqrt{26}$ 5.1

Activity 3

Find the length of the hypotenuse in each triangle. Use the Pythagorean theorem and a calculator. Round your answers to the nearest tenth.

1. What is the measure of side *c*?

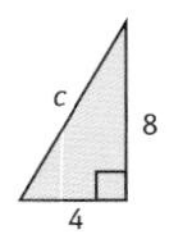

8.9

2. What is the measure of side *c*?

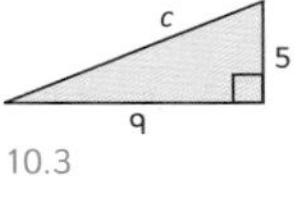

10.3

3. What is the measure of side *c*?

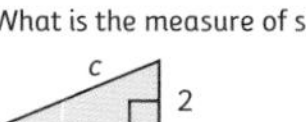

5.4

4. What is the measure of side *c*?

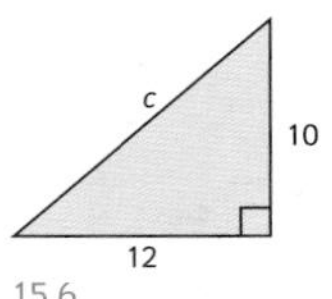

15.6

Unit 10 • Lesson 2 801

Homework

Go over the instructions on page 802 of the *Student Text* for each part of the homework.

Activity 4 • Distributed Practice

Students write equations for functions from data found in *x*/*y* tables.

Homework

Activity 4 • Distributed Practice

Write an equation for each of the functions using the data found in the *x*/*y* tables.

1. What is the equation for this function? $y = 2x$

x	y
1	2
2	4
3	6
4	8

2. What is the equation for this function? $y = \frac{1}{3}x$

x	y
9	3
12	4
15	5
18	6

3. What is the equation for this function? $y = 6x$

x	y
1	6
2	12
3	18
4	24

4. What is the equation for this function? $y = \frac{1}{2}x$

x	y
50	25
40	20
30	15
20	10

Lesson Planner

Skills Maintenance

Square Roots

Building Number Concepts:

▶ Applying the Pythagorean Theorem

Students continue practicing the Pythagorean theorem. So far we have used the Pythagorean theorem to find the length of the hypotenuse. In this lesson, we use the Pythagorean theorem to find lengths of the other sides of a right triangle. We then see how the Pythagorean theorem applies to many real-world applications. We again use a picture to help set up a problem when using the Pythagorean theorem.

Objective

Students will find the length of sides of a right triangle using the Pythagorean theorem.

Homework

Students solve square roots, solve for the missing part of the right triangle, and solve real-world applications using the Pythagorean theorem. In Distributed Practice, students tell the equation of the function by looking at its graph.

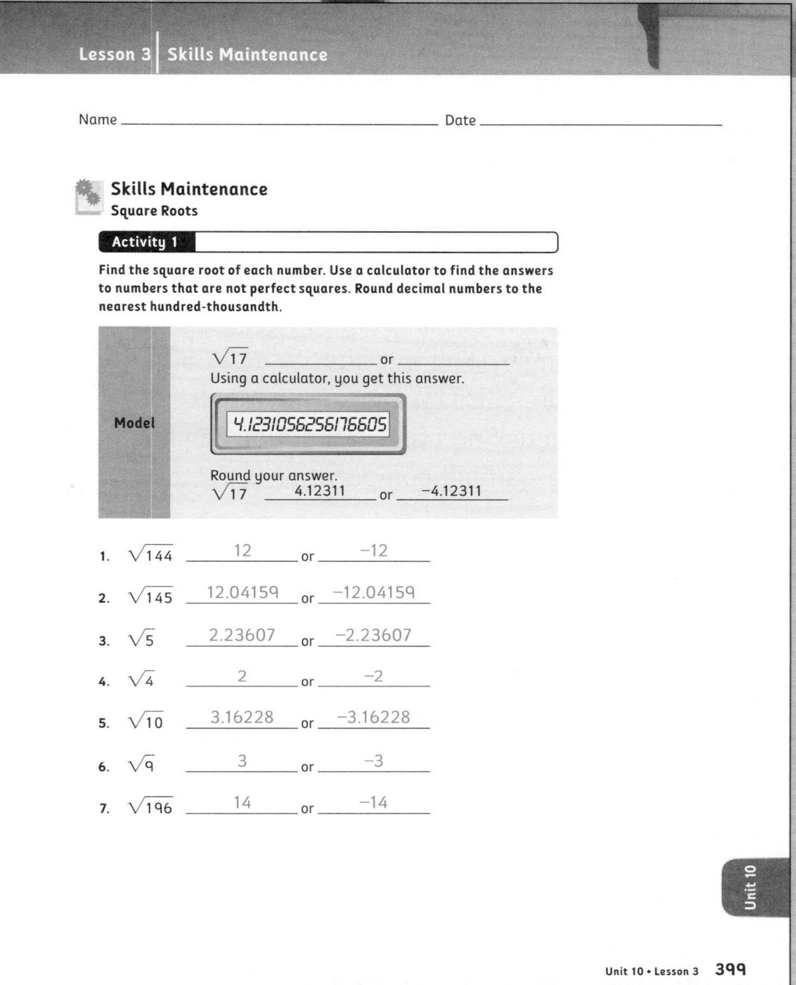

Lesson 3 | Skills Maintenance

Name ______________________ Date ______________________

Skills Maintenance
Square Roots

Activity 1

Find the square root of each number. Use a calculator to find the answers to numbers that are not perfect squares. Round decimal numbers to the nearest hundred-thousandth.

Model

$\sqrt{17}$ ________ or ________

Using a calculator, you get this answer.

4.1231056256176605

Round your answer.

$\sqrt{17}$ 4.12311 or −4.12311

1. $\sqrt{144}$ 12 or −12
2. $\sqrt{145}$ 12.04159 or −12.04159
3. $\sqrt{5}$ 2.23607 or −2.23607
4. $\sqrt{4}$ 2 or −2
5. $\sqrt{10}$ 3.16228 or −3.16228
6. $\sqrt{9}$ 3 or −3
7. $\sqrt{196}$ 14 or −14

Unit 10

Unit 10 • Lesson 3 399

Skills Maintenance

Square Roots

(*Interactive Text*, page 399)

Activity 1

Students solve square roots by hand if they are perfect squares and use a calculator if the squares are nonperfect. Remind students to give both the positive and the negative answer.

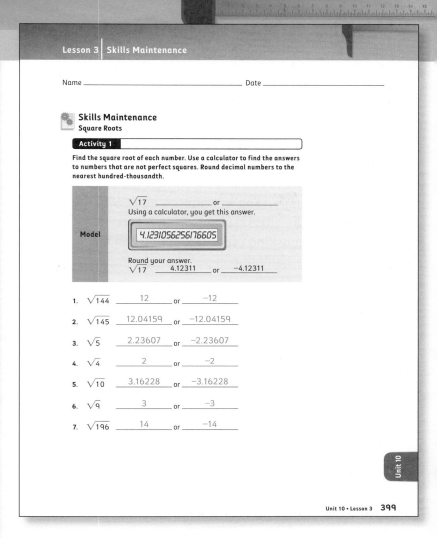

Building Number Concepts:
▶ Applying the Pythagorean Theorem

How do we find the lengths of other sides of a right triangle?

(*Student Text*, pages 803–804)

Connect to Prior Knowledge

Begin by asking for three student volunteers. Position the students in the room so that they form a right triangle. (You will want to mark off the triangle before class by measuring it and marking it with masking tape so that you can be assured of whole-number computations.)

Measure the distance between Student A and Student B using a yard stick. Record this measurement on the board or overhead. This represents the base of your triangle. Next measure the distance from Student A to Student C. This represents the height of your triangle. Record this measurement.

Next tell students that we will use the Pythagorean theorem to find the distance between Student B and Student C. Record the answer. Then use the yard stick to actually measure the distance and check the answer.

Link to Today's Concept

Tell students that in today's lesson, we look at many different uses of the Pythagorean theorem. It is important that they realize math concepts are found in real-world computations.

Demonstrate

Engagement Strategy: Teacher Modeling

Demonstrate finding the length of a side of the right triangles in one of the following ways:

mBook: Use the *mBook Teacher Edition* for *Student Text*, pages 803–804. m

Lesson 3 | ▶Applying the Pythagorean Theorem

▶Applying the Pythagorean Theorem

How do we find the lengths of other sides of a right triangle?

We have learned how to find the length of the hypotenuse of a right triangle by using the Pythagorean theorem. We use algebra to find the length of any one of the sides of a right triangle if we know the length of the other two sides.

In Example 1, we will use the length of the hypotenuse and one leg to find the length of the other leg. We will use algebra to find the length of the unknown side in each triangle.

Example 1

Use the Pythagorean theorem to find the missing lengths.

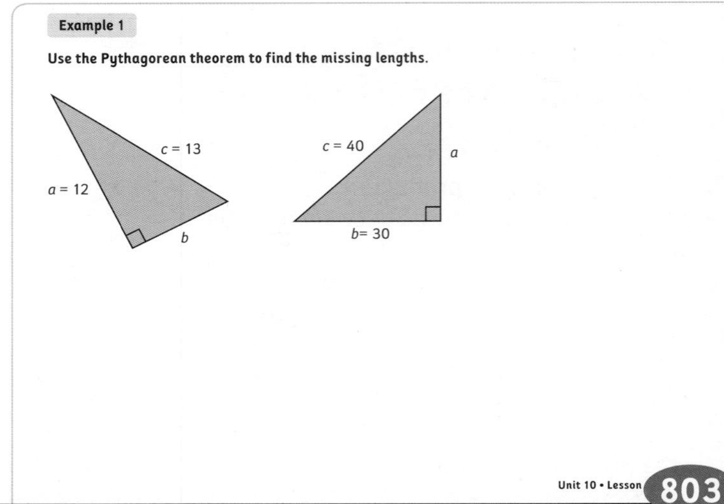

Unit 10 • Lesson 3 803

Overhead Projector: Reproduce the triangles and formulas on a transparency, and modify as discussed.

Board: Copy the triangles and formulas on the board, and modify as discussed.

- Tell students that we have shown in other examples that we can find the length of the hypotenuse using the Pythagorean theorem. Tell them that we can also find the lengths of either of the other two sides if we know one of the other sides and the hypotenuse. m
- Have students look at the triangles in **Example 1**. Point out that one of the triangles is missing side *a*, and the other is missing side *b*.

Demonstrate

- Continue going through Example 1.
- Start with Triangle 1. Show the steps of applying the Pythagorean theorem. Go through each step carefully, and the justification for each step.
- Point out that we know the values of one side and the hypotenuse. Demonstrate how to substitute the values into the formula. m
- Walk through the rest of the steps to solve for *b*. The answer is $b = 5$. m
- Repeat with Triangle 2, this time pointing out that we do not know the length of side *a*. Walk through the substitution and the computation to solve for *a*. The answer is $a = 26.46$. m
- Remind students at the end that we do not need to worry about the negative answer in this case because measurements are never negative.

Pythagorean theorem: $a^2 + b^2 = c^2$

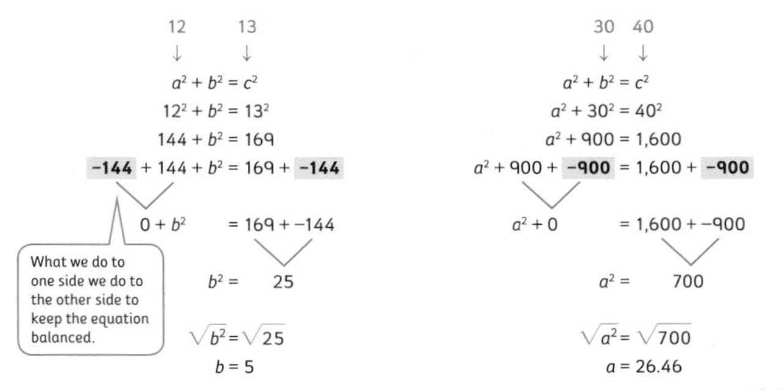

12 13

$a^2 + b^2 = c^2$

$12^2 + b^2 = 13^2$

$144 + b^2 = 169$

$-144 + 144 + b^2 = 169 + -144$

$0 + b^2 = 169 + -144$

$b^2 = 25$

$\sqrt{b^2} = \sqrt{25}$

$b = 5$

What we do to one side we do to the other side to keep the equation balanced.

30 40

$a^2 + b^2 = c^2$

$a^2 + 30^2 = 40^2$

$a^2 + 900 = 1{,}600$

$a^2 + 900 + -900 = 1{,}600 + -900$

$a^2 + 0 = 1{,}600 + -900$

$a^2 = 700$

$\sqrt{a^2} = \sqrt{700}$

$a = 26.46$

Remember that the square root of a number can be either positive or negative. Notice that we only used the positive square root in these answers. This is because we only use positive numbers when we talk about the length of a side of a triangle.

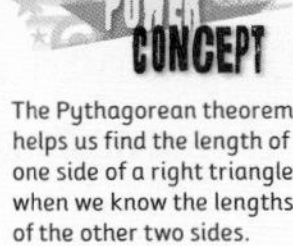

The Pythagorean theorem helps us find the length of one side of a right triangle when we know the lengths of the other two sides.

Discuss

Call students' attention to the Power Concept, and point out that it will be helpful as they complete the activities.

The Pythagorean theorem helps us find the length of one side of a right triangle when we know the lengths of the other two sides.

Check for Understanding

Engagement Strategy: Look About

Draw a right triangle with the following dimensions: ***a* = 10** and ***c* = 20**. Label the other side ***b***. Tell students that they use the Pythagorean theorem to find the length of the missing side with the help of the whole class ($b = 17.32$). Have students round their answers to the nearest hundredth. Students should show their work in large writing on a piece of paper or a dry erase board. When students finish their work, they should hold up their answer for everyone to see.

If students are not sure about the answer, prompt them to look about at other students' solutions to help with their thinking. Review the answers after all students hold up their solutions.

How do we use the Pythagorean theorem in sports?

(*Student Text*, pages 805–808)

Demonstrate

- Turn to page 805 of the *Student Text*. Explain to students there are many applications where we use Pythagorean theorem.
- Explain that sports are a big venue for this concept.
- Point out the shape of a baseball field. If we look at home plate and the three bases, they form a square. If we cut that in half, we have two right triangles.
- Read the problem together, and make sure students understand that baseball players think about the length of the sides of the triangle (i.e., the distance between bases) and the length of the hypotenuse (i.e., the distance from the catcher to second base) when thinking about throwing a player out at second base.
- Make sure students understand that these distances make up the sides of a right triangle, and we use the Pythagorean theorem to figure out these lengths.

How do we use the Pythagorean theorem in sports?

The Pythagorean theorem is surprisingly useful in many everyday applications, especially in sports. A very simple example is baseball. Suppose there is a runner on first base and one on second base. Both runners try to steal when the next pitch is thrown. Let's say that one runner is just as fast as the other runner. Where would it be faster to throw the ball to get one of the runners out? Should the catcher throw it to second base or third base?

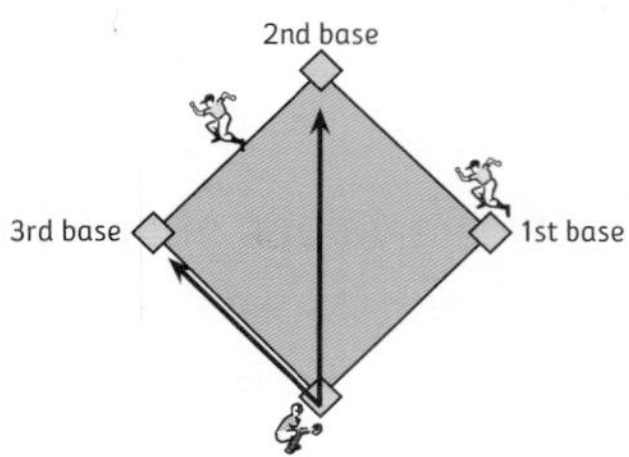

We need to think about baseball diamonds in order to answer the question.

- First, diamonds in baseball are actually squares. Each base is on a vertex, and the angles measure 90 degrees. If we cut the square in half, we have two right triangles.
- Second, if we look at the triangle on the left in Example 1, there is a right angle at third base. We also know that the distance between each base is 90 feet.

We can solve the problem using the Pythagorean theorem.

Demonstrate

- Turn to page 806 and go over **Example 1**, which shows a baseball situation that involves the Pythagorean theorem.
- Point out to students that the catcher is trying to figure out if he should throw the ball to third base or to second base. This involves finding the distance between home plate and second base (variable a in the formula) and the distance between home plate and third base (variable b).
- Point out that we know the distance between bases is 90 feet, so we know the dimensions of two sides of the triangle. Demonstrate substituting these dimensions in for a and b in the Pythagorean theorem to find the length of the hypotenuse, or the distance from home plate to second base.
- Complete the computation to find the distance from home plate to second base.
- Explain to students that the distance from home plate to third base is 90 feet, which is shorter than the distance from home plate to second base, 127.28 feet. This means that the catcher would have a better chance at throwing the runner out at third base than at second base because it is a shorter distance to throw.

Example 1

Use the Pythagorean theorem to find the distance from home plate to second base.

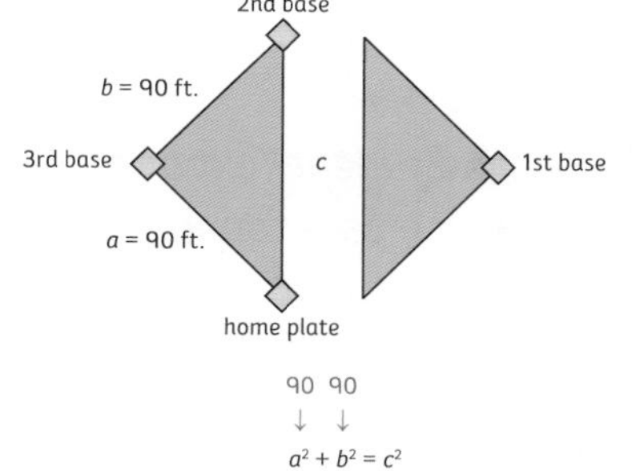

$$\begin{aligned} &\;\;90 \;\; 90 \\ &\;\;\downarrow \;\;\; \downarrow \\ a^2 + b^2 &= c^2 \\ 90^2 + 90^2 &= c^2 \\ 8{,}100 + 8{,}100 &= c^2 \\ 16{,}200 &= c^2 \\ \sqrt{16{,}200} &= \sqrt{c^2} \\ 127.28 &= c \end{aligned}$$

The distance from home plate to second base is 127.28 feet or about 127 feet.

The catcher should throw the ball to third base because it is a shorter distance. It is only 90 feet instead of 127 feet.

How do we use the Pythagorean theorem in sports? *(continued)*

Demonstrate

- Turn to page 807 of the *Student Text* and go over **Example 2**, which uses tennis as a venue for the Pythagorean theorem.
- Go over the problem carefully and be sure students understand which part of the tennis court is associated with which part of the right triangle.
- Have students look at the diagram of the tennis court and make sure they understand that 78 and 27 represent sides *a* and *b* in the formula.
- Substitute the values into the formula and walk through the steps to solve for the hypotenuse, *c*.
- Explain that when the players hit the ball from one corner of the tennis court to another (the length of the hypotenuse), the ball has a better chance of staying in bounds because there is more room to hit the ball.

We can use the same kind of thinking to understand why tennis players hit a ball from one corner of a tennis court to the other. They do this because the ball has a better chance of staying in the court if hit diagonally. We see this in Example 2.

Example 2

Use the Pythagorean theorem to find the distance diagonally across a tennis court. Then compare that distance to the length of the court.

When players play from the middle, they only have 78 feet. When they hit the ball across court, they have more room to hit the ball.

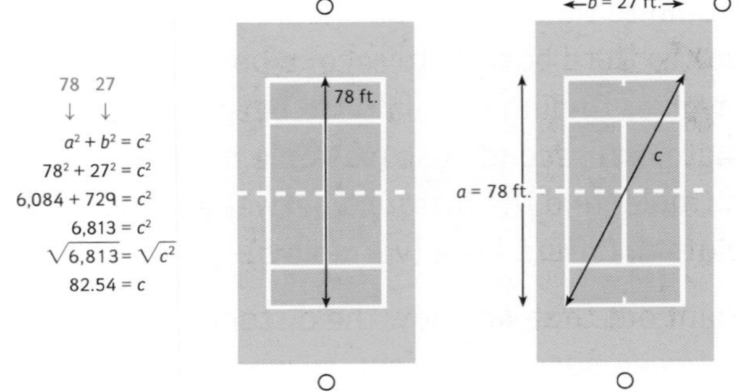

There is about 82 feet to hit the ball inside the court when we hit across a diagonal. That is 4 feet more than when players are hitting from the middle of the court.

Demonstrate

- Turn to page 808 of the *Student Text* and go to **Example 3**, which shows right triangles on a soccer field.
- Tell students that we use the Pythagorean theorem to determine the answer to this problem as well.
- Go over the steps carefully. Be sure students understand the reasoning behind each step. Also be sure they associate the appropriate part of the soccer field with the corresponding part of the right triangle.
- Demonstrate how to find the distances that the ball travels on the field. Make sure students understand which distances are shorter for the ball to travel.

Check for Understanding
Engagement Strategy: Look About

Tell students they will apply the Pythagorean theorem to an example in sports with the help of the whole class. Tell students that a soccer player is standing **15 yards** from the goal. She wants to know what the distance from the goal would be if she kicked the ball **20 yards** over to the left (*25 yards*). Have students draw the right triangle and find the distance to the goal in large writing on a piece of paper or a dry erase board. When students finish their work, they should hold up their answer for everyone to see.

If students are not sure about the answer, prompt them to look about at other students' solutions to help with their thinking. Review the answers after all students hold up their solutions.

Finally, soccer players often take penalty kicks during a game. The greater the distance that the ball travels, the better chance there is to block the ball. It is a shorter distance in front of the goal than it is off to the side.

Example 3

Use the Pythagorean theorem to find the distance the soccer ball travels in each situation.

The player kicks 20 yards centered in front of the goal.
Another player kicks from 30 yards to the left.

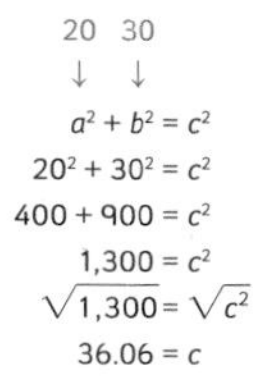

$$a^2 + b^2 = c^2$$
$$20^2 + 30^2 = c^2$$
$$400 + 900 = c^2$$
$$1{,}300 = c^2$$
$$\sqrt{1{,}300} = \sqrt{c^2}$$
$$36.06 = c$$

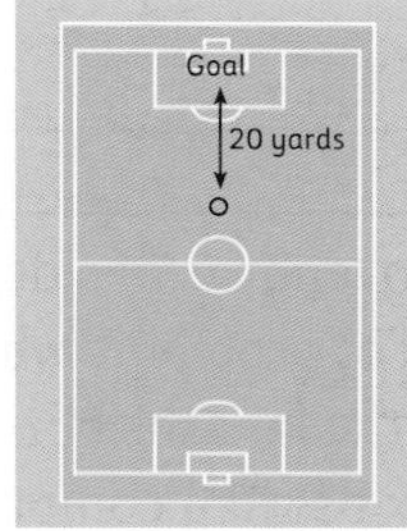

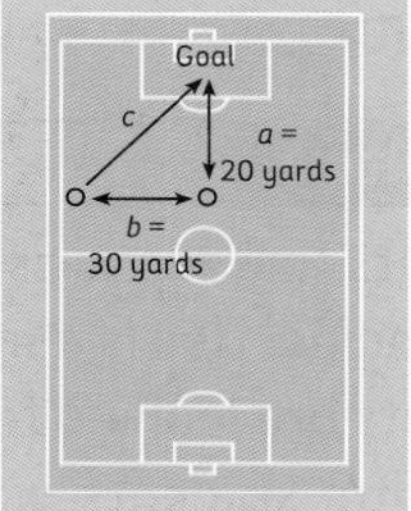

The player near the sideline kicks the ball 36 yards instead of 20 yards. That is an extra 16 yards.

Distance makes a difference when playing sports. Most of the time coming from an angle means that we will have to hit, kick, throw, or shoot the ball farther. With tennis, more distance means the ball has a better chance of staying in the court. With soccer and baseball, it means that we will have to kick or throw the ball farther.

Apply Skills Turn to *Interactive Text*, page 400.

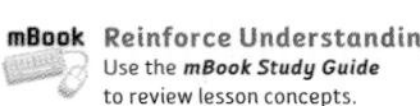

Reinforce Understanding Use the *mBook Study Guide* to review lesson concepts.

Apply Skills

(*Interactive Text*, pages 400–403)

Have students turn to pages 400–403 in the *Interactive Text*, which provides students an opportunity to practice using the Pythagorean theorem.

Activity 1

Students find the missing lengths of sides of triangles. This is a mix of problems where students are looking for the lengths of *a*, *b*, or *c*. Monitor students' work as they complete the activity.

Watch for:

- Can students solve the Pythagorean theorem for another side besides *c*?
- Can students use the concept of square root effectively in solving the problems?

Lesson 3 | Apply Skills

Name ____________________ Date ____________________

Apply Skills
Applying the Pythagorean Theorem

Activity 1

Use the Pythagorean Theorem to find the missing lengths of the sides of right triangles. You may need to find the length of side *a*, *b*, or *c*. If your answer is not a perfect square, leave the square root as your answer.

1. What is the length of side *a*? 3
   Show your work here.
   $a^2 + b^2 = c^2$
   $a^2 + 4^2 = 5^2$
   $a^2 + 16 = 25$

   a = ? c = 5 b = 4

2. What is the length of side *b*? $\sqrt{17}$
   Show your work here.
   $a^2 + b^2 = c^2$
   $8^2 + b^2 = 9^2$
   $64 + b^2 = 81$

   b = ? a = 8 c = 9

3. What is the length of side *c*? 10
   Show your work here.
   $a^2 + b^2 = c^2$
   $6^2 + 8^2 = c^2$
   $36 + 64 = c^2$

   a = 6 c = ? b = 8

400 Unit 10 • Lesson 3

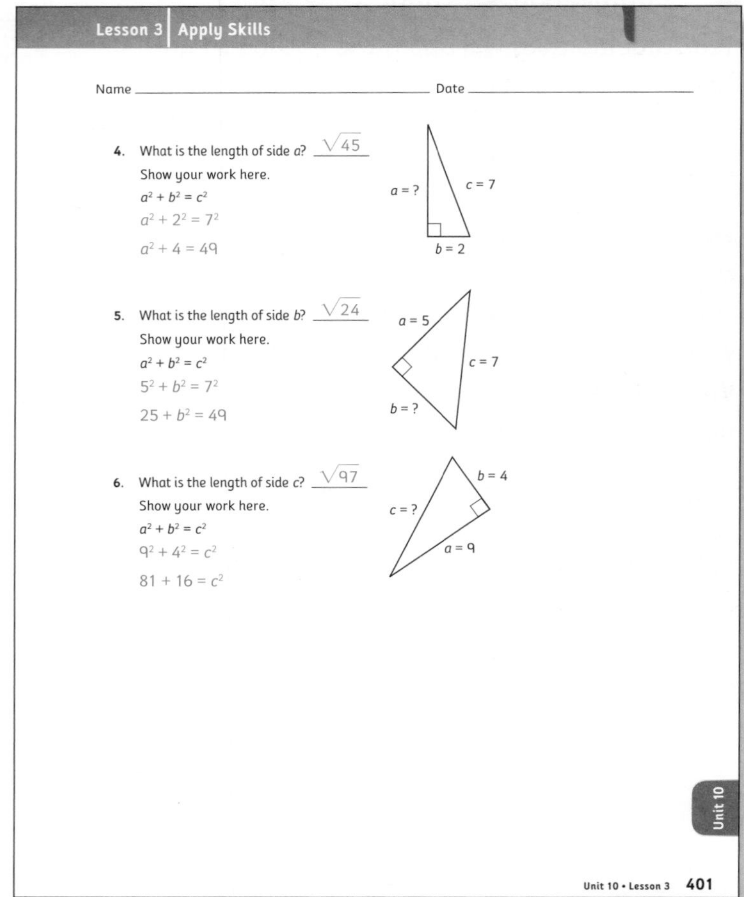
Lesson 3 | Apply Skills

Name ____________________ Date ____________________

4. What is the length of side *a*? $\sqrt{45}$
   Show your work here.
   $a^2 + b^2 = c^2$
   $a^2 + 2^2 = 7^2$
   $a^2 + 4 = 49$

   a = ? c = 7 b = 2

5. What is the length of side *b*? $\sqrt{24}$
   Show your work here.
   $a^2 + b^2 = c^2$
   $5^2 + b^2 = 7^2$
   $25 + b^2 = 49$

   a = 5 c = 7 b = ?

6. What is the length of side *c*? $\sqrt{97}$
   Show your work here.
   $a^2 + b^2 = c^2$
   $9^2 + 4^2 = c^2$
   $81 + 16 = c^2$

   b = 4 c = ? a = 9

Unit 10

Unit 10 • Lesson 3 401

Activity 2

Students solve four sports problems involving right triangles using the Pythagorean theorem. Monitor students' work as they complete the activity.

Watch for:

- Can students associate the base, height, and hypotenuse of the right triangle with the application problem?
- Can students identify which part of the Pythagorean theorem they are solving?
- Can students solve the problem successfully using the Pythagorean theorem?

mBook Reinforce Understanding

Remind students that they can review lesson concepts by accessing the *mBook Study Guide*.

Name ______________________ Date ______________

Activity 2

Use what you know about the Pythagorean Theorem to solve the problems. Round decimal numbers to the nearest tenth. Think about why the distance is important for each sport.

1. In football, teams can score points by kicking a field goal. When a player kicks a field goal, it is a lot easier (and shorter) if he is straight in front of the goal post. How far is it if he kicks the field goal from near the sidelines?

   $15^2 + 50^2 = c^2$ $c = 52.2$ yards

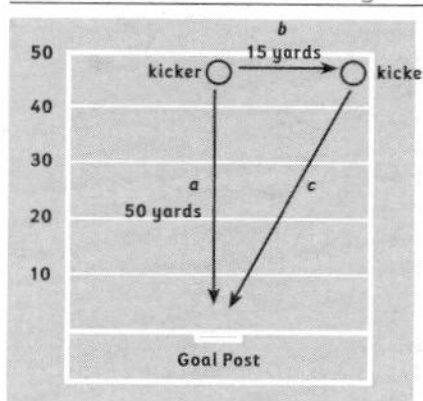

2. A quarterback doesn't have to throw the ball as far from the middle of the field than from the sideline. A longer throw means there is more a chance the ball will be intercepted by the other team. How far does the quarterback throw the ball from the sidelines?

   $20^2 + 30^2 = c^2$ $c = 36.06$ yards

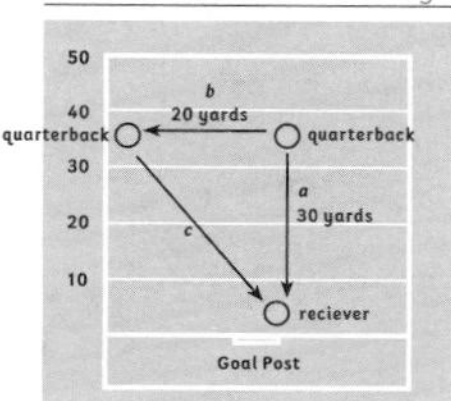

Name ______________________ Date ______________

3. A basketball player shoots a three-point shot straight at the basket. This is a distance of about 20 feet. If the player moves 15 feet to the right, it is a much longer shot. How far is the longer shot?

   $20^2 + 15^2 = c^2$ $c = 25$ feet

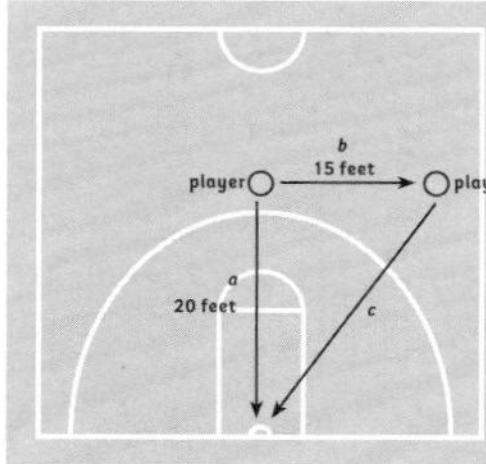

4. A golfer does not have to hit the ball as far is she is in front of the pin on the green. If she is off to the side, the shot is farther. How far is it to hit the shot from the side?

   $30^2 + 200^2 = c^2$ $c = 202.24$ yards

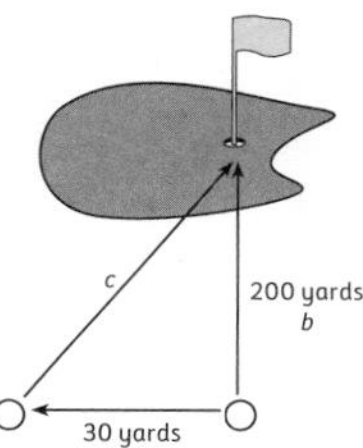

mBook Reinforce Understanding
Use the **mBook *Study Guide*** to review lesson concepts.

Unit 10

Homework

Go over the instructions on pages 809–810 of the *Student Text* for each part of the homework.

Activity 1

Students find the square root of each number.

Activity 2

Students solve for the missing length of the right triangle.

Homework

Activity 1

Solve the square roots. Use a calculator and round the answer to the nearest tenth. Remember the negatives.

1. $\sqrt{47}$ ±6.9
2. $\sqrt{55}$ ±7.4
3. $\sqrt{65}$ ±8.1
4. $\sqrt{82}$ ±9.1
5. $\sqrt{101}$ ±10.0
6. $\sqrt{75}$ ±8.7

Activity 2

Using the Pythagorean theorem, find the missing parts of the right triangle.

1. What is the measure of side c? 12.65

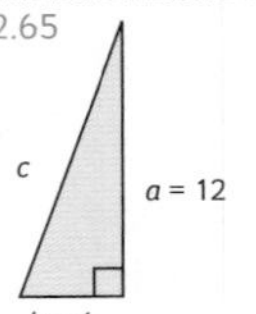

2. What is the measure of side a? 3.4

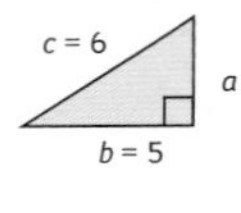

3. What is the measure of side b? 3

c = 5, a = 4, b

Activity 3

Students solve real-world applications using the Pythagorean theorem.

Activity 4 • Distributed Practice

Students tell the equation of the function by looking at its graph.

Lesson 3

Homework

Activity 3

Solve the application problems using the Pythagorean theorem.

1. What is the length of the diagonal across the doubles match tennis court? 85.9 ft.

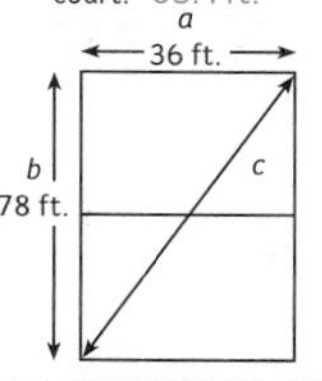

2. How far does the catcher throw from home plate to second base? 91.9 ft.

3. How far is it from Golfer X to the flag? 101.9 yards

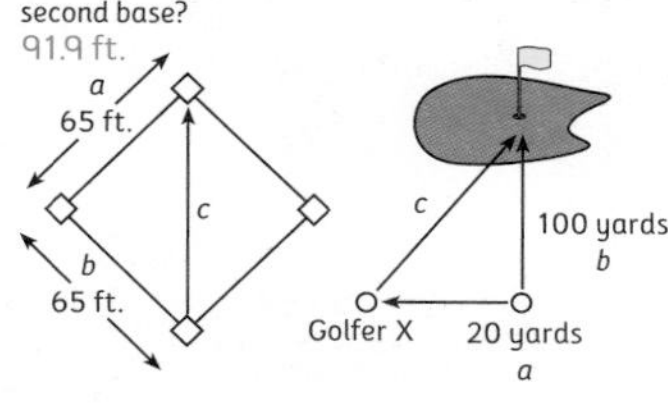

Activity 4 • Distributed Practice

Look at the graph for each function and write its equation.

1. 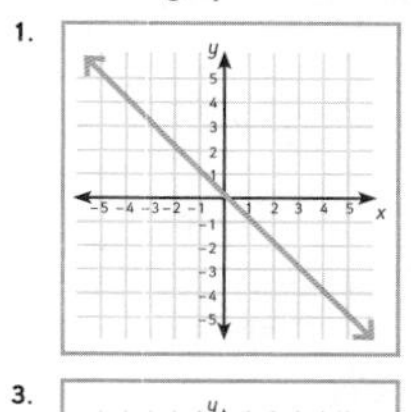 $y = -x$

2. 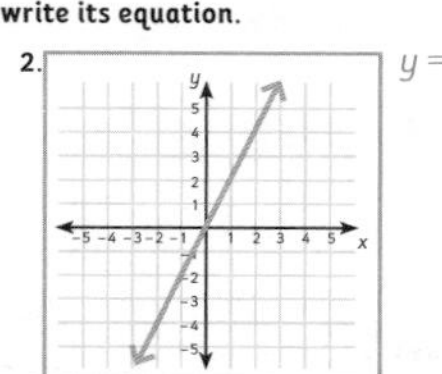 $y = 2x$

3. 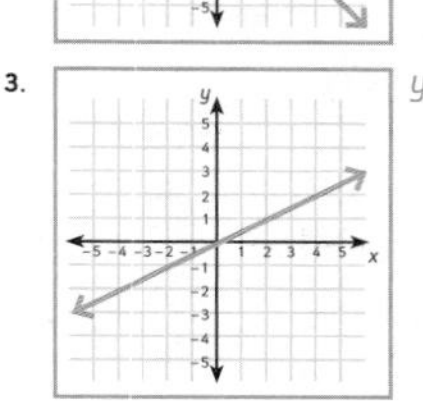 $y = \frac{1}{2}x$

Lesson 4 | Problem Solving: Nonlinear Functions

Lesson Planner

Vocabulary Development

dependent variable
independent variable

Skills Maintenance

Using the Pythagorean Theorem

Problem Solving: ▶ Nonlinear Functions

Students learn the difference between linear and nonlinear functions. One key feature of a nonlinear function is that it has an exponent associated with the *x* term. Also the graph of a nonlinear function is not a straight line but rather a curved line.

Objective

Students will analyze and graph nonlinear functions.

Homework

Students create *x*/*y* tables for linear and nonlinear functions, complete the graphs of nonlinear functions using their knowledge of symmetry, and answer multiple-choice questions about the differences between linear and nonlinear functions. In Distributed Practice, students write an equation for each written description of a function.

Lesson 4 | Skills Maintenance

Name ______________________ Date ______________________

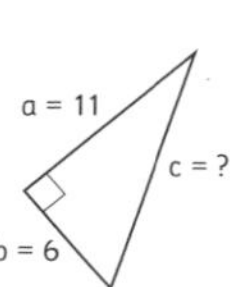

Skills Maintenance
Using the Pythagorean Theorem

Activity 1

Use the Pythagorean Theorem to find the length of the missing side for each right triangle. Round decimal numbers to the nearest tenth.

1. What is the length of side *a*? 6.9
   Show your work here.
   $a^2 + b^2 = c^2$
   $a^2 + 4^2 = 8^2$
   $a^2 + 16 = 64$
   $a^2 = 48$

2. What is the length of side *b*? 6.6
   Show your work here.
   $a^2 + b^2 = c^2$
   $10^2 + b^2 = 12^2$
   $100 + b^2 = 144$
   $b^2 = 44$

3. What is the length of side *c*? 12.5
   Show your work here.
   $a^2 + b^2 = c^2$
   $11^2 + 6^2 = c^2$
   $121 + 36 = c^2$
   $c^2 = 157$

404 Unit 10 • Lesson 4

Skills Maintenance

Using the Pythagorean Theorem
(*Interactive Text*, page 404)

Activity 1

Students apply the Pythagorean theorem to find the length of the missing side. Students use calculators for this activity.

Problem Solving: ▶ Nonlinear Functions

What is the difference between linear and nonlinear functions?

(*Student Text*, pages 811–813)

Connect to Prior Knowledge

Begin by writing the function $x = y$ on the board. Ask students what the independent variable and dependent variables are. Remind students that this is a linear function. That means the graph is a straight line, and there is a systematic relationship between x and y.

Listen for:

- *The independent variable is x. Its value does not depend on the value of y.*
- *The dependent variable is y. Its value depends on the value of x.*

Link to Today's Concept

Tell students that in today's lesson, we look at nonlinear functions. One of the key features of this type of function is that there is an exponent associated with the x term. Tell students it can be any exponent.

Demonstrate

Engagement Strategy: Teacher Modeling

Demonstrate the difference between linear and nonlinear functions in one of the following ways:

mBook: Use the *mBook Teacher Edition* for *Student Text*, pages 811–812. m

Overhead Projector: Reproduce the tables on Transparency #17, and modify as discussed.

Board: Copy the tables and graphs on the board, and modify as discussed.

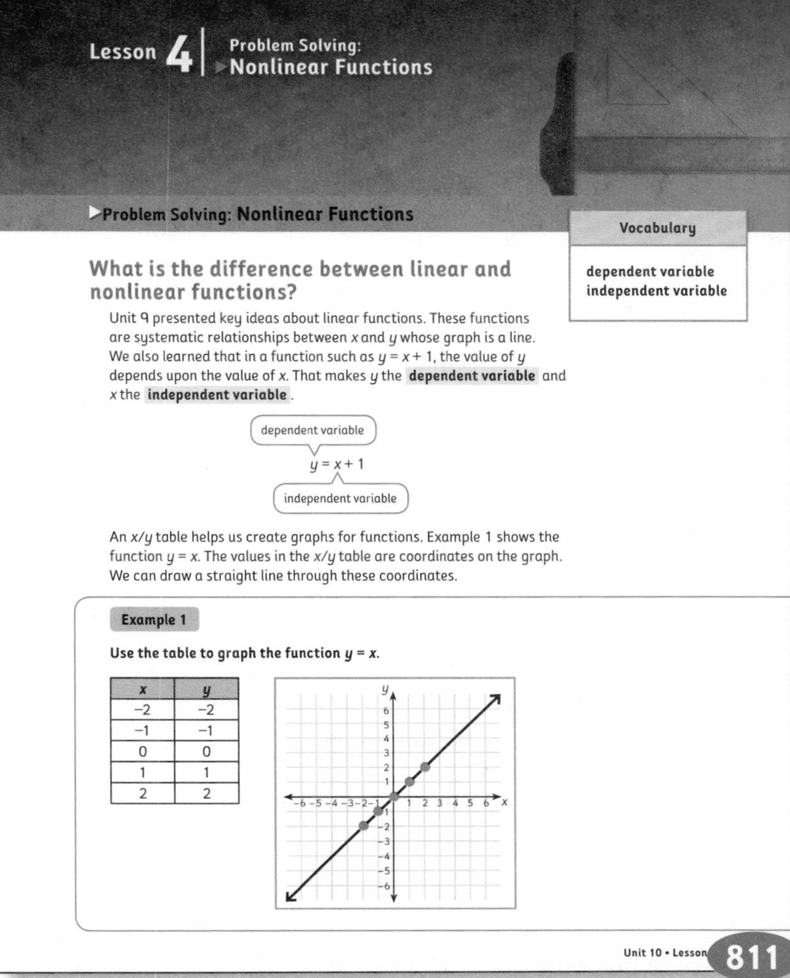

Lesson 4 | Problem Solving: ▶Nonlinear Functions

▶Problem Solving: Nonlinear Functions

Vocabulary

dependent variable
independent variable

What is the difference between linear and nonlinear functions?

Unit 9 presented key ideas about linear functions. These functions are systematic relationships between x and y whose graph is a line. We also learned that in a function such as $y = x + 1$, the value of y depends upon the value of x. That makes y the **dependent variable** and x the **independent variable**.

An x/y table helps us create graphs for functions. Example 1 shows the function $y = x$. The values in the x/y table are coordinates on the graph. We can draw a straight line through these coordinates.

Example 1

Use the table to graph the function $y = x$.

x	y
−2	−2
−1	−1
0	0
1	1
2	2

Unit 10 • Lesson 4 811

- Review with students that linear functions are systematic functions between x and y. The value of y depends on the value of x. m
- Review the linear function $y = x$ in **Example 1**. Remind students of the three different ways to represent the function: an equation, an x/y table, and a graph. m

What is the difference between linear and nonlinear functions? *(continued)*

Demonstrate

- Turn to page 812 of the *Student Text*, and continue the discussion of the differences between linear and nonlinear functions.
- Remind students that in linear functions the dependent variable changes by the same amount.
- Explain to students that with nonlinear functions, the dependent variable does not change by the same amount each time. Explain that this happens when the x variable has an exponent.
- Go over **Example 2** with students, and point out the exponent in $y = x^2$. m
- Next walk through completing the x/y table to show how the y value changes when the x value has an exponent. Start with −2. The number −2 squared is 4. m
- Repeat with the numbers −1, 0, 1, and 2, and complete the table. m
- Help students notice that the values do not increase by the same amount each time. Explain that this makes it more difficult to predict the next number. m
- Explain to students that nonlinear functions can have any exponent.

Discuss

Call students' attention to the Power Concept, and explain that it will be helpful as they complete the activities.

POWER
CONCEPT

In a nonlinear function, the values for the dependent variable do not increase by the same amount each time.

One difference between linear and nonlinear functions is that the value of the dependent variable does not change by the same amount each time in a nonlinear function. This happens when the x-variable has an exponent. Example 2 shows a function where y is the x-value squared. Look carefully at how this affects the y-values in the table.

Example 2

Create a table for the function $y = x^2$.

Let's see how the exponent changes the y-values in the table.

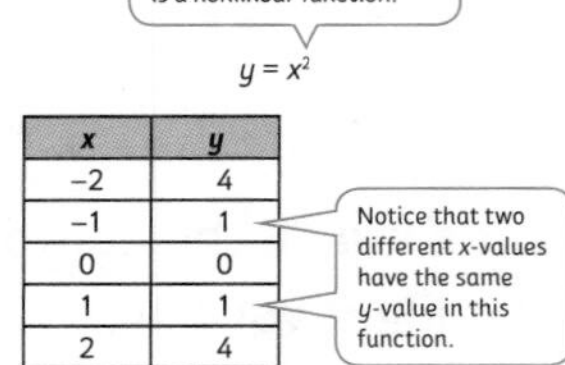
The exponent tells us this is a nonlinear function.
y = x²

x	y
−2	4
−1	1
0	0
1	1
2	4

Notice that two different x-values have the same y-value in this function.

We substitute the value of x into $y = x^2$. When we substitute −2 for x, we get $y = (-2)^2$ or $y = 4$. We use the same process to complete the rest of the table.

POWER CONCEPT

In a nonlinear function, the values for the dependent variable do not increase by the same amount each time.

Notice that the y-values do not increase by the same amount each time. This is one of the differences between linear and nonlinear functions. This makes it more difficult to predict what number will come next.

Nonlinear functions may have different exponents, not just squares. We may have x^3, x^4, x^5, etc., as our variable term.

Demonstrate

- Tell students that when we work with exponents, we should use a calculator to compute values. Explain that many calculators have a y^x key. This helps us find any number to any power.
- Turn to page 813 of the *Student Text* and go through **Example 3**.
- Have students look at the function $y = x^3$. Walk through the steps of substituting values in for x and completing the table with values for y.
- Demonstrate how to punch the keys in the calculator.

Check for Understanding

Engagement Strategy: Think, Think

Write the function $y = x^5$ on the board, and draw an x/y table with the values of 0 through 5 in the first column. Have students take out their calculators. Tell students that they will substitute x values into function to find each y value. Call out a number in the table, and have students use their calculator to compute the y value. Have students listen for their name as you call out each number. Allow students time to compute their answer for each x value and then call on a student by name. If correct, record the answer in the x/y table on the board.

x	y
0	0
1	1
2	32
3	243
4	1,024
5	3,125

When we are working with exponents, we should use a calculator to compute these values. Many calculators have a y^x key. This is the key we use to find a power of something. For instance, if we are solving 2^5, we would enter 2, y^x, and then 5. The result is 32. If we multiply $2 \cdot 2 \cdot 2 \cdot 2 \cdot 2$, we would get the same result.

Example 3 shows an x/y table for a nonlinear function with an exponent other than 2.

Example 3

Create a table for the function $y = x^3$. Use a calculator to find the y-values.

$y = x^3$

x	y
0	0
1	1
2	8
3	27
4	64

We substitute each value for x into the function to find the y-values.

To find the value of y when x is 2, we would press these keys on the calculator:

What do nonlinear functions look like on a graph?

(*Student Text*, page 814)

Demonstrate

- Turn to page 814 of the *Student Text*. Tell students that another key feature of the nonlinear function is the way it appears on a graph.
- Remind students that a linear function graphs as a straight line.
- Go over **Example 1**, which shows the function $y = x^2$; the x/y table, including 0 and positive values; and the graph of the function.
- Remind students that we first looked at this function in Example 2 when we looked at its x/y table. Now we look at its graph.
- Point out that the line curves between 0 and 1 on the x-axis of the coordinate graph.
- Point out both sides of the graph, with the negative x values on the left and the positive x values on the right.
- Be sure to point out that two x values (e.g., –1 and 1) both result in the same y value. Explain that this is what causes the graph to curve.

What do nonlinear functions look like on a graph?

We learned that the y-values do not increase by the same amount each time in a nonlinear function. This tells us that the graph of the function will not be a straight line.

The shape of the line changes just by squaring the x. Let's look at an example.

Example 1

Use the table to graph the function $y = x^2$.

$y = x^2$

x	y
−2	4
−1	1
0	0
1	1
2	4

The line for a nonlinear function is a curve—not a straight line.

The graph of a nonliner function will always have at least one curve. It is never a straight line.

Problem-Solving Activity
Turn to ***Interactive Text***, page 405.

mBook Reinforce Understanding
Use the ***mBook Study Guide*** to review lesson concepts.

Problem-Solving Activity

(*Interactive Text*, pages 405–406)

Have students turn to pages 405–406 in the *Interactive Text*. First students create *x*/*y* tables for nonlinear functions. Tell students to be careful solving the power and use a calculator if necessary.

Next students create an *x*/*y* table with *x* values, including positives, negatives, and 0. Then they graph the function on a coordinate graph. Finally they answer questions based on observations of the table and graph.

Monitor students' work as they complete the activities.

Watch for:

- Can students accurately solve the power in the equation?
- Can students adjust their thinking for the equations that have additional computations beyond the power, such as $x^2 + 1$?
- Can students graph the function on the coordinate graph?
- Do students notice that each of the *y* values, except 0, has two *x* values linked to it?

A key discussion with nonlinear functions is the fact that two *x* values (e.g., −1 and 1) both result in the same *y* value. Another important discussion is that this is what causes the graph to curve. Finally emphasize the idea of symmetry on the graph.

Reinforce Understanding

Remind students that they can review lesson concepts by accessing the *mBook Study Guide.*

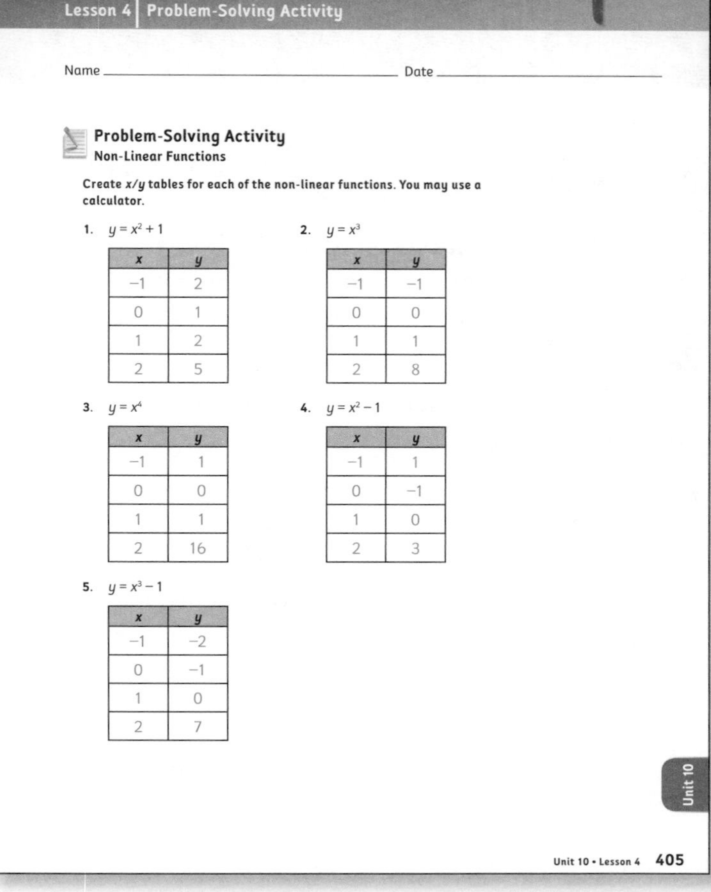

Lesson 4 | Problem-Solving Activity

Name ______ Date ______

Problem-Solving Activity
Non-Linear Functions

Create *x*/*y* tables for each of the non-linear functions. You may use a calculator.

1. $y = x^2 + 1$

x	*y*
−1	2
0	1
1	2
2	5

2. $y = x^3$

x	*y*
−1	−1
0	0
1	1
2	8

3. $y = x^4$

x	*y*
−1	1
0	0
1	1
2	16

4. $y = x^2 - 1$

x	*y*
−1	1
0	−1
1	0
2	3

5. $y = x^3 - 1$

x	*y*
−1	−2
0	−1
1	0
2	7

Unit 10

Unit 10 • Lesson 4 405

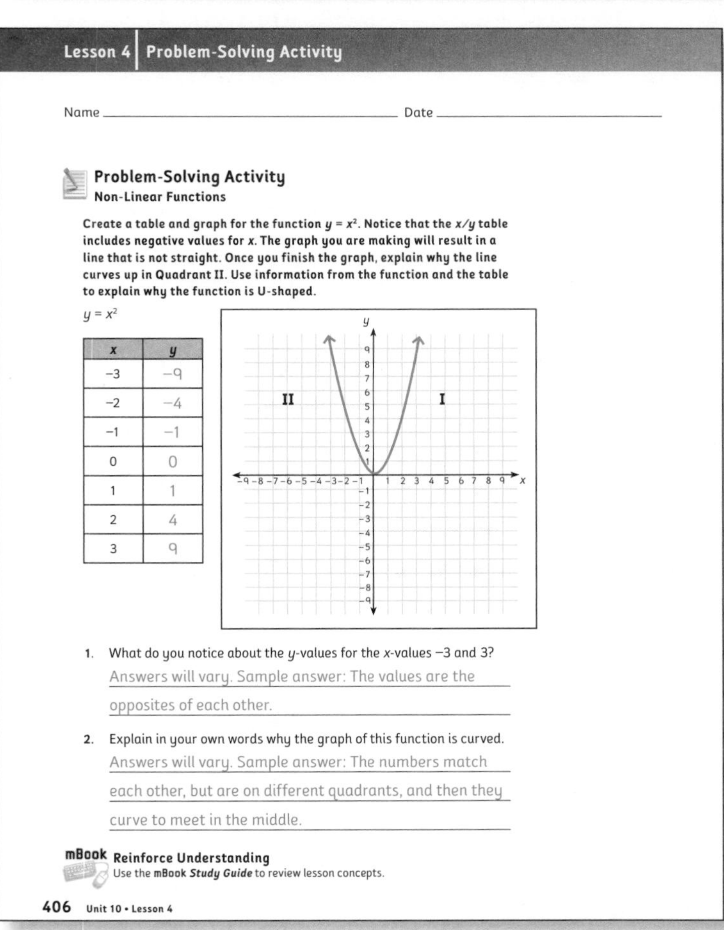

Lesson 4 | Problem-Solving Activity

Name ______ Date ______

Problem-Solving Activity
Non-Linear Functions

Create a table and graph for the function $y = x^2$. Notice that the *x*/*y* table includes negative values for *x*. The graph you are making will result in a line that is not straight. Once you finish the graph, explain why the line curves up in Quadrant II. Use information from the function and the table to explain why the function is U-shaped.

$y = x^2$

x	*y*
−3	−9
−2	−4
−1	−1
0	0
1	1
2	4
3	9

1. What do you notice about the *y*-values for the *x*-values −3 and 3?
Answers will vary. Sample answer: The values are the opposites of each other.

2. Explain in your own words why the graph of this function is curved.
Answers will vary. Sample answer: The numbers match each other, but are on different quadrants, and then they curve to meet in the middle.

mBook **Reinforce Understanding**
Use the mBook *Study Guide* to review lesson concepts.

406 Unit 10 • Lesson 4

Homework

Go over the instructions on pages 815–816 of the *Student Text* for each part of the homework.

Activity 1

Students create x/y tables for linear and nonlinear functions.

Activity 2

Students complete the graphs of nonlinear functions using their knowledge of symmetry.

Additional Answers

Activity 1

1.

x	y
−2	1
−1	2
0	3
1	4
2	5

2.

x	y
−2	4
−1	1
0	0
1	1
2	4

3.

x	y
−2	1
−1	0
0	−1
1	−2
2	−3

4.

x	y
−2	−8
−1	−1
0	0
1	1
2	8

Lesson 4

Homework

Activity 1

Create x/y tables for the functions. Include these x values: −2, −1, 0, 1, and 2.

1. $y = x + 3$ 2. $y = x^2$ 3. $y = -x - 1$ 4. $y = x^3$

See Additional Answers below.

Activity 2

Use your knowledge of nonlinear functions and symmetry to complete the graphs.

1. Complete this graph for the function $y = x^2$.

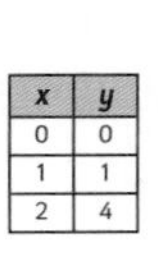

x	y
0	0
1	1
2	4

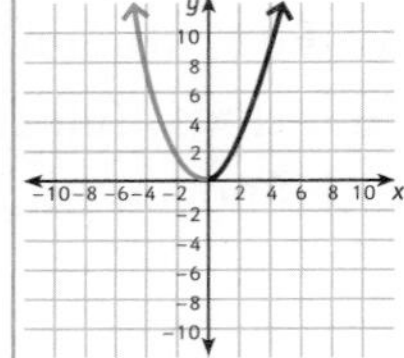

2. Complete this graph for the function $y = 2x^2$.

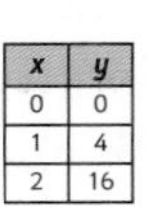

x	y
0	0
1	4
2	16

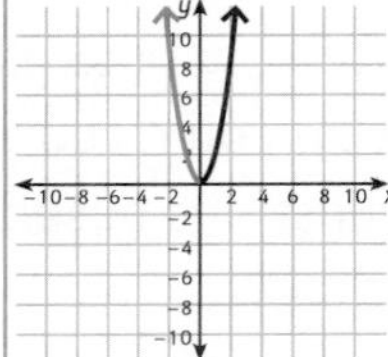

3. Complete this graph for the function $y = x^3$.

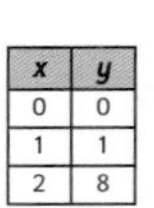

x	y
0	0
1	1
2	8

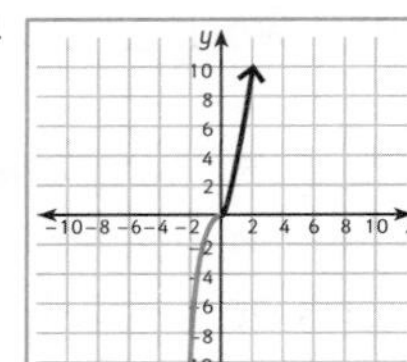

Unit 10 • Lesson 815

Activity 3

Students answer multiple-choice questions about the differences between linear and nonlinear functions.

Activity 4 • Distributed Practice

Students write an equation for each written description of a function.

Lesson 4

Homework

Activity 3

Choose the correct multiple choice answer.

1. One of the key differences between nonlinear and linear functions is how they are graphed. The way they are different is:
   (a) They are lines that go in different directions.
   (b) One is a line and one is a curve.
   (c) They are curves that curve in different directions.
2. Another key difference between nonlinear and linear functions is in the equation. The way they are different is:
   (a) One has an exponent and the other does not.
   (b) One has a slope and the other does not.
   (c) One has a y-intercept and the other does not.
3. In the function $y = x^2$, we see something different in the x/y table. What is it?
   (a) Two of the x/y values are the same.
   (b) Two y-values have the same x-value.
   (c) Two x-values have the same y-value.

Activity 4 • Distributed Practice

Write an equation for each of the functions using $y = mx + b$.

1. The cost of blueberries is $3 per pound. $y = 3x + 0$
2. The daily cost of the rental car is $0.10 per mile plus a base fee of $25. $y = .10x + 25$
3. The price of gas is $4 per gallon. $y = 4x + 0$

Lesson 5 | Properties of Irrational Numbers

Monitoring Progress: Quiz 1

Lesson Planner

Vocabulary Development

perfect square numbers
irrational numbers

Skills Maintenance

Finding Square Roots

Building Number Concepts: Properties of Irrational Numbers

We start the lesson by looking at different rational numbers. We look at decimal numbers, fractions, and integers. In today's lesson, students learn that when we solve square roots, they often result in irrational numbers, or decimal numbers that do not terminate and do not repeat. It is sufficient to round irrational numbers to the nearest tenths or hundredths place when we work with these numbers in everyday situations.

Objective

Students will find irrational numbers by taking the square roots of different numbers.

Monitoring Progress: Quiz 1

Distribute the quiz, and remind students that the questions involve material covered over the previous lessons in the unit.

Homework

Students find the square root, tell if the numbers are integers, rational numbers, or irrational, and find the square roots between 20 and 30 and answer questions about them. In Distributed Practice, students create *x*/*y* tables for each of the functions shown in graphs.

Lesson 5 | Skills Maintenance

Name ______________________ Date ______________________

Skills Maintenance
Finding Square Roots

Activity 1

Find the square root of each number. Use a calculator to find the numbers that are not perfect squares. Round to the nearest hundredth. Don't forget to include the negative numbers.

1. $\sqrt{49}$ 7 or −7
2. $\sqrt{50}$ 7.07 or −7.07
3. $\sqrt{64}$ 8 or −8
4. $\sqrt{65}$ 8.06 or −8.06
5. $\sqrt{74}$ 8.60 or −8.60
6. $\sqrt{81}$ 9 or −9

Unit 10

Unit 10 • Lesson 5 407

Skills Maintenance

Finding Square Roots

(*Interactive Text*, page 407)

Activity 1

Students solve square roots. They should round to the nearest hundredths place.

Building Number Concepts:
▶ Properties of Irrational Numbers

What are rational numbers?
(*Student Text*, pages 817–818)

Connect to Prior Knowledge

Begin by having students get out their calculators. Ask them to select any two whole numbers (not 0). Then tell them to divide the smaller number by the larger number. Have them write their answer on a sheet of paper and label it 1. Next have students select another whole number randomly (not 0). Have students enter that number in their calculators and find its square root. Have them write that number on their paper and label it 2.

Link to Today's Concept

Tell students that we learn about different kinds of numbers called **irrational numbers** in today's lesson. Tell them to hold on to this paper with their answers and we discuss them later in today's lesson.

Demonstrate

Engagement Strategy: Teacher Modeling

Demonstrate calculating rational numbers and square roots in one of the following ways:

mBook: Use the *mBook Teacher Edition* for *Student Text*, pages 817–818. m

Overhead Projector: Reproduce the numbers $\frac{24}{8}$, $\frac{3}{8}$, and $\frac{7}{11}$ and the table on a transparency, and modify as discussed.

Board: Reproduce the numbers $\frac{24}{8}$, $\frac{3}{8}$, and $\frac{7}{11}$ and the table on the board, and modify as discussed.

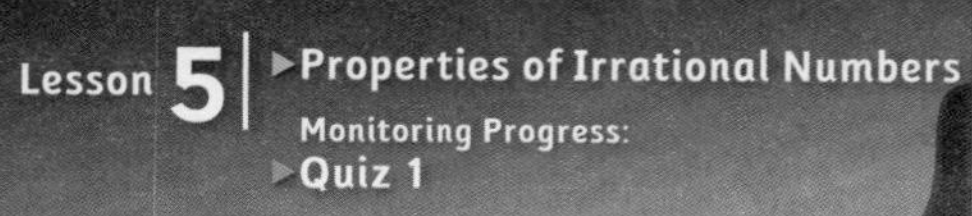

▶ Properties of Irrational Numbers

Vocabulary

perfect square numbers
irrational numbers

What are rational numbers?

One way to change a simple fraction into an integer or a decimal number is to divide the denominator into the numerator. When we do this, we either get an integer, a decimal number that ends (or terminates), or a pattern in the decimal number place that repeats itself. They are all rational numbers.

Rational Numbers	
When we divide the numerator by the denominator . . .	**the resulting number is a rational number**
$\frac{24}{8} = 3$	an integer
$\frac{3}{8} = 0.375$	a decimal number that terminates
$\frac{7}{11} = 0.63636363\ldots$	a repeating pattern of decimal numbers

Something different happens when we compute the square root of a number. When we use a calculator or a spreadsheet to find the square root of a number, we usually get a long decimal number. Example 1 shows what kind of numbers we get when we find the square root of the numbers 1 through 10.

Unit 10 • Lesson 817

- Explain that dividing a numerator by its denominator results in a rational number. m
- Point out that $\frac{24}{8}$ results in an integer. m
- Next point out that the number $\frac{3}{8}$ results in a rational number that terminates. m
- Finally, point out the number $\frac{7}{11}$, which results in a repeating, nonterminating rational number. m

What are rational numbers? *(continued)*

Demonstrate

- Turn to page 818 of the *Student Text,* and go over **Example 1**.
- Tell students that there is a different kind of number that we have not yet studied. Explain that they have seen these kinds of numbers with certain square roots we have solved.
- Go over Example 1, and point out the numbers that are irrational numbers. Tell students that these numbers were rounded. If we look at these numbers on the calculator, we see even more decimal places with no repeating pattern.
- Go through each of the calculations with students. Have students solve some of these on their calculators, such as $\sqrt{2}$, $\sqrt{3}$, and $\sqrt{5}$, so they can see this. m
- Finally, re-emphasize the need to round these numbers when we work with them in problems to make sense of them. Point out that it is common to round these to tenths or hundredths so that we can work with them in problems.
- Remind students that any place-value position to the right of the hundredths place represents a very, very, very small number. That is why we are not altering the number by all that much when we round it.
- Next collect student data from the introductory activity. Ask students to look at answer number 2 on their papers. Again go through each type, and ask for examples from students to add to the list of examples on the board for each type of number. Compare the number of answers that are irrational to the other answers.

Example 1

What are the square roots of these numbers?

Number	Square Roots
1	1 and −1
2	1.4142 and −1.4142
3	1.7321 and −1.7321
4	2 and −2
5	2.2361 and −2.2361
6	2.4495 and −2.4495
7	2.6458 and −2.6458
8	2.8284 and −2.8284
9	3 and −3
10	3.1623 and −3.1623

The numbers 1, 4, and 9 are perfect square numbers.

Numbers like 1, 4, and 9 are called **perfect square numbers** because their square roots are integers. As we can see, most of the square roots are decimal numbers. The decimal numbers have been rounded to the ten-thousandths place. They are not rational numbers.

Build Vocabulary

Explain to students that numbers like 1, 4, and 9 are **perfect square numbers** because their square roots are integers.

What are irrational numbers?
(*Student Text*, page 819)

Demonstrate

- Turn to page 819 of the *Student Text*, and read the material. Explain that most square roots are nonrepeating, nonterminating irrational numbers.
- Show students the square root of **2**. Explain that the decimal number does not end, and there is no pattern in the decimal numbers.
- Use **Example 1** to demonstrate how to round irrational numbers. Explain that we have to round square roots when we use them because the numbers repeat without terminating.
- Explain to students that for square roots, we usually round the number to the tenths or hundredths place. Remind students of the rules for rounding.
- Walk through each of the examples of rounding to the tenths and the hundredths places in the chart.

Check for Understanding
Engagement Strategy: Think Tank

Write $\sqrt{11}$ on the board. Distribute strips of paper to students and have them write their name on them. Have students use their calculator to find the square roots of the number and round the answer to the nearest hundredths place (*3.32, −3.32*). Have them write their answers on the strip of paper. Collect the strips into a container, and draw one. Read the answer out loud, and record the answer on the board. Make sure that the student's answer has a positive and a negative square root.

Lesson 5

What are irrational numbers?

If we use a calculator or a spreadsheet to calculate square roots, we will also find something else—the decimal numbers for square roots do not end and they do not repeat themselves in a pattern. When a decimal number does not end and does not have a pattern, we call that number an **irrational number**.

We see this with the square root of 2.

$$\sqrt{2} = 1.4142135623731...$$

The decimal number does not end, and there is no pattern to the decimal numbers.

All of this means that we have to round square roots when we use them. We usually round the decimal number to the tenths or hundredths place. Remember to use rounding rules. Example 1 shows some positive square roots.

Example 1

Round these irrational numbers to the nearest tenths and hundredths place.

		Rounded to the Tenths Place	Rounded to the Hundredths Place
$\sqrt{2}$ =	1.4142	1.4	1.41
$\sqrt{3}$ =	1.7321	1.7	1.73
$\sqrt{5}$ =	2.2361	2.2	2.24

Apply Skills
Turn to *Interactive Text*, page 408.

Monitoring Progress
Quiz 1

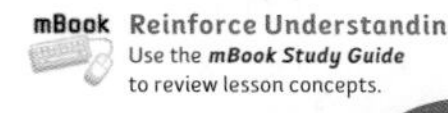
Reinforce Understanding
Use the *mBook Study Guide* to review lesson concepts.

Unit 10 • Lesson 819

Apply Skills
(*Interactive Text*, page 408)

Have students turn to *Interactive Text*, page 408, and complete the activities.

Activity 1

Students circle the irrational numbers and write how they can tell the difference between irrational numbers and rational numbers.

Activity 2

Students find the square root of several numbers. Some will be integers, and some will be irrational numbers. Tell students they can use a calculator, and they need to round the answer. Also tell them to remember the negative answers.

Monitor students' work as they complete the activities.

Watch for:

- Can students find the square root of each number?
- Can students round the irrational results to the nearest tenth?
- Did students remember to include the negative values?

mBook Reinforce Understanding

Remind students that they can review lesson concepts by accessing the *mBook Study Guide*.

Lesson 5 | Apply Skills

Name ______________ Date ______________

Apply Skills

Properties of Irrational Numbers

Activity 1

Circle the numbers that are irrational numbers in the list. Then explain how you can tell irrational numbers from rational numbers.

($\sqrt{13}$) 4.2 $\sqrt{4}$ −3 $-\frac{1}{4}$ 5 ($\sqrt{5}$) −2.1 $\frac{2}{3}$

How can you tell irrational numbers from rational numbers?

Answers may vary. Sample answer: You can tell that a number is irrational when there is a long decimal that doesn't end and doesn't have any kind of pattern.

Activity 2

Find the square roots of each number. You may use a calculator. Round the irrational numbers to the nearest tenth. Remember to include the negative numbers.

Number	Square Roots	Number	Square Roots
$\sqrt{9}$	3 and −3	$\sqrt{10}$	3.2 and −3.2
$\sqrt{11}$	3.3 and −3.3	$\sqrt{13}$	3.6 and −3.6
$\sqrt{16}$	4 and −4	$\sqrt{20}$	4.5 and −4.5
$\sqrt{25}$	5 and −5	$\sqrt{27}$	5.2 and −5.2
$\sqrt{30}$	5.5 and −5.5	$\sqrt{33}$	5.7 and −5.7
$\sqrt{36}$	6 and −6	$\sqrt{40}$	6.3 and −6.3
$\sqrt{45}$	6.7 and −6.7	$\sqrt{49}$	7 and −7
$\sqrt{50}$	7.1 and −7.1	$\sqrt{55}$	7.4 and −7.4
$\sqrt{64}$	8 and −8	$\sqrt{69}$	8.3 and −8.3

mBook **Reinforce Understanding**
Use the **mBook** ***Study Guide*** to review lesson concepts.

408 Unit 10 • Lesson 5

Monitoring Progress:
▶ Quiz 1

Assess
Quiz 1

- Administer Quiz 1 Form A in the *Assessment Book*, pages 89–90. (If necessary, retest students with Quiz 1 Form B from the *mBook Teacher Edition* following differentiation.)

Students	Assess	Differentiate
	Day 1	Day 2
All	Quiz 1 *Form A*	
Scored 80% or above		Extension
Scored Below 80%		Reinforcement

Differentiate

- Review Quiz 1 Form A with class.
- Identify students for Extension or Reinforcement.

Extension

For those students who score 80 percent or better, provide the On Track! Activities from Unit 10, Lessons 1–5, from the *mBook Teacher Edition.*

Reinforcement

For those students who score below 80 percent, provide additional support in one of the following ways:

- Have students access the online tutorial provided in the *mBook Study Guide.*
- Have students complete the Interactive Reinforcement Exercises for Unit 10, Lessons 1–4, in the *mBook Study Guide.*
- Provide teacher-directed reteaching of unit concepts.

Name ______ Date ______

Form A

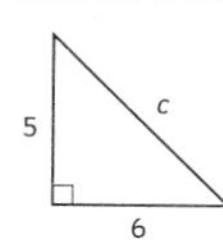

Monitoring Progress
Pythagorean Theorem

Part 1

Use your calculators to find the lengths of the missing sides. Round to the nearest tenth.

1. $c = 7.8$

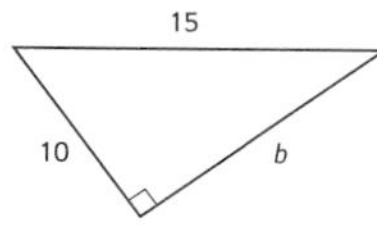

2. $b = 11.2$

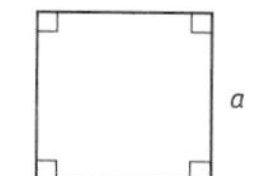

3. This figure is a square. Area = 30 square units $a = 5.5$

a

Part 2

Answer the questions about square roots.

1. Fill in the square roots. Round to the nearest tenth.

Number	Square Roots
64	8
50	7.1
100	10
200	14.1
500	22.4
1,600	40

2. What is one big difference between the square roots of 25 and 26?

Answers may vary. Sample answer: 25 has a perfect square, and 26 is a very long decimal number.

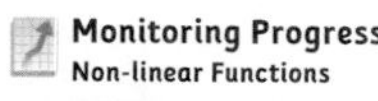

Monitoring Progress
Non-linear Functions

Part 3

Answer the questions about non-linear functions.

1. Fill in the y values in the x/y table for this function. Then circle the graph that goes with the function.

$y = x^2$

x	y
−5	25
−4	16
−3	9
−2	4
−1	1
0	0
1	1

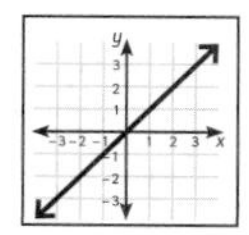

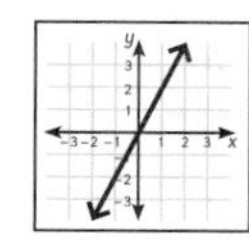

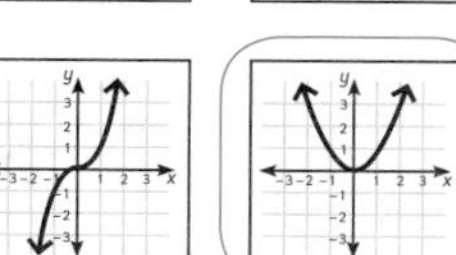

Name ________________ Date ________________

Form B

mBook

Monitoring Progress
Pythagorean Theorem

Part 1

Use your calculators to find the lengths of the missing sides. Round to the nearest tenth.

1. $c = 11.3$

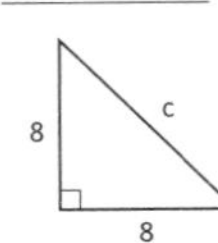

2. $b = 10.7$

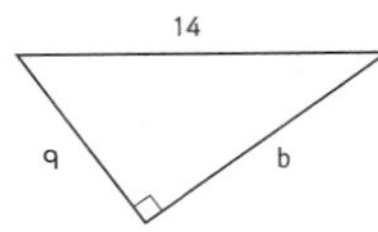

3. This figure is a square. Area = 35 square units $a = 5.9$

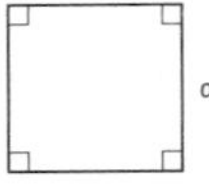

Name ________________ Date ________________

Part 2

Answer the questions about square roots. Round to the nearest tenth.

1. Fill in the square roots.

Number	Square Roots
36	6
49	7
90	9.5
160	12.6
250	15.8
2,500	50

2. What is one big difference between the square roots of 36 and 40?
Answers may vary. Sample answer: 36 has a perfect square, and 40 is a very long decimal number.

Monitoring Progress
Non-linear Functions

Part 3

Answer the questions about non-linear functions.

1. Fill in the y values in the x/y table for this function. Then circle the graph that goes with the function.

$y = x^2$

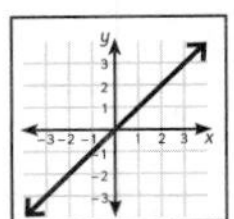

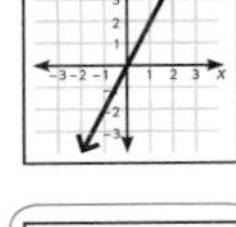

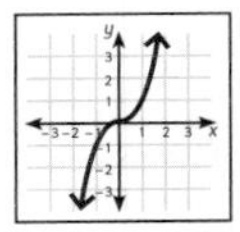

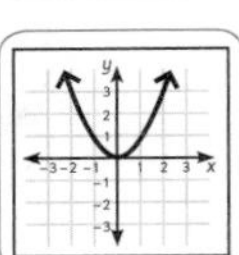

x	y
−6	36
−4	16
−2	4
−1	1
0	0
1	1
3	9

Homework

Go over the instructions on pages 820–821 of the *Student Text* for each part of the homework.

Activity 1

Students find the square root. Tell them they are to use a calculator and round irrational answers to the nearest tenth. Remind them there are negative values that we need to remember as well.

You might introduce the notation ± at this point. We avoided it because want to make it very clear to students that these two values are unique entities. We have now done a significant amount of practice with this.

Activity 2

Students tell if the numbers are integers (IN), rational numbers (R), or irrational (IR).

Activity 3

Students find the square roots between 20 and 30 and answer questions about them.

Lesson 5

Homework

Activity 1

Solve the square roots. Remember the negatives. Use your calculator and round to the nearest tenths place.

1. $\sqrt{9}$ ±3.0
2. $\sqrt{10}$ ±3.2
3. $\sqrt{4}$ ±2.0
4. $\sqrt{11}$ ±3.3
5. $\sqrt{2}$ ±1.4
6. $\sqrt{17}$ ±4.1

Activity 2

For each of the numbers, tell if it's an integer (IN), a rational number (R), or an irrational number (IR). Use the letter abbreviations.

1. 3.4 R
2. −4 IN
3. $\sqrt{5}$ IR
4. 0.1111111111111111111111... R
5. 2.2360679774997896964091736687313... IR
6. $\frac{2}{3}$ R
7. 0.375 R
8. 0.428571428571428571428571428571 42... R

Activity 3

Find the square roots of the numbers between 20 and 30 and answer the questions.

1. How many of the square roots between 20 and 30 are integers? What are they? One; 25
2. How many of the square roots between 20 and 30 are rational numbers? What are they? One; 25
3. How many of the square roots between 20 and 30 are irrational numbers? What are they? All but 25

820 Unit 10 • Lesson 5

Homework

Go over the instructions on page 821 of the *Student Text* for each part of the homework.

Activity 4 • Distributed Practice

Students create *x*/*y* tables for each of the functions shown in graphs.

Homework

Activity 4 • Distributed Practice

Create an *x*/*y* table for the functions shown in the graphs.

1.

x	y
−2	−6
−1	−3
0	0
1	3
2	6

2.

x	y
−2	4
−1	2
0	0
1	−2
2	−4

3.

x	y
−3	3
−1	1
0	0
2	−2
4	−4

Lesson 6 | Problem Solving: The Direction of Nonlinear Functions

Lesson Planner

Vocabulary Development

parabola

Skills Maintenance

Finding Square Roots

Problem Solving:

▶ The Direction of Nonlinear Functions

Students learn the name for one type of nonlinear function, the parabola. We use our integer rules to examine what happens when x is negative in a nonlinear function. We look at the function $y = -x^2$ and see that there is an implied coefficient of −1. Students learn that a negative coefficient in an exponential function affects the location and direction of its graph.

Objective

Students will learn how negative numbers and negative coefficients affect nonlinear functions.

Homework

Students solve equations using substitution, create x/y tables for exponential functions, and tell if the function has a negative coefficient or a positive coefficient by looking at the graph. In Distributed Practice, students create x/y tables for each of the equations of functions.

Lesson 6 | Skills Maintenance

Name ______________ Date ______________

Skills Maintenance
Finding Square Roots

Activity 1

Solve the square roots. Use your calculator to find the numbers that are not perfect squares. Round your answers to the nearest tenth. Remember to include the negative numbers.

1. $\sqrt{89}$ 9.4 and −9.4
2. $\sqrt{95}$ 9.7 and −9.7
3. $\sqrt{100}$ 10 and −10
4. $\sqrt{112}$ 10.6 and −10.6
5. $\sqrt{121}$ 11 and −11
6. $\sqrt{136}$ 11.7 and −11.7
7. $\sqrt{141}$ 11.9 and −11.9
8. $\sqrt{144}$ 12 and −12

Unit 10 • Lesson 6 409

Skills Maintenance

Finding Square Roots

(*Interactive Text*, page 409)

Activity 1

Students solve square roots. Tell students they can use a calculator, and they are to round their answers to the nearest tenths place. Remind them to include the negative solutions as well.

Problem Solving:
▶ The Direction of Nonlinear Functions

What happens when *x* is negative?
(*Student Text*, pages 822–824)

Connect to Prior Knowledge
Draw a coordinate graph on the board and ask students to explain how we graph $y = x$. Have a volunteer draw the linear function as students discuss the process. Point out that the straight line on the graph is called a linear function. Remind students of how we made function tables for nonlinear functions. The y values in these tables did not seem predictable.

Link to Today's Concept
In today's lesson students learn to graph nonlinear functions.

Build Vocabulary
Have students turn to page 822 of the *Student Text*, and review the graph of the function $y = x^2$. Tell students that the curve is called a **parabola**.

Demonstrate
Engagement Strategy: Teacher Modeling

Demonstrate the effect on a linear function when x is negative in one of the following ways:

mBook: Use the *mBook Teacher Edition* for *Student Text*, pages 822–823. m

Overhead Projector: Reproduce the table on Transparency 17, and modify as discussed.

Board: Copy the table and graph on the board, and modify as discussed.

- Remind students that we looked at the graph of the function $y = x^2$. Now we look at what happens when x is negative. m

Lesson 6 | Problem Solving: ▶The Direction of Nonlinear Functions

▶Problem Solving: The Direction of Nonlinear Functions

What happens when *x* is negative?

In Lesson 4, we saw the graph of the function $y = x^2$. The graph was a curve. This curve is called a **parabola**. Let's look at our parabola and the table again to see how x^2 makes the parabola.

Vocabulary
parabola

$y = x^2$

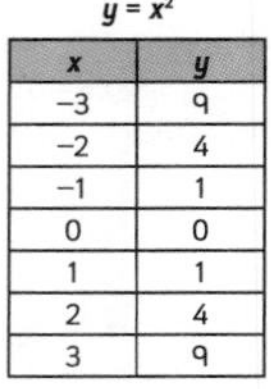

x	y
−3	9
−2	4
−1	1
0	0
1	1
2	4
3	9

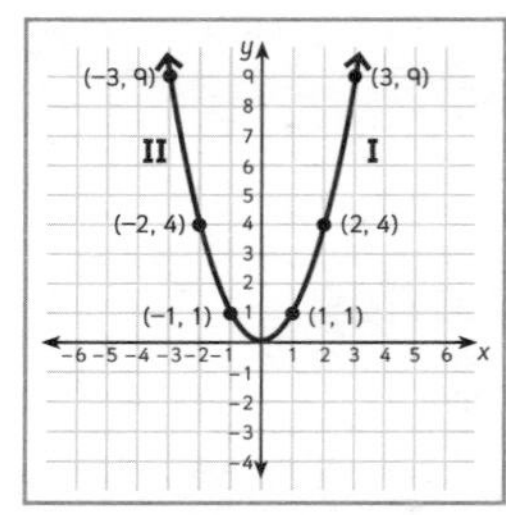

The parabola is in Quadrants I and II. This is because when we substitute any value for x in x^2, we get a positive output. Our Integer Rules help us understand why this happens.

Integer Rules
- When we substitute a positive value for x, we are multiplying a positive times a positive. The answer is positive.
- When we substitute a negative value for x, we are multiplying a negative times a negative. The answer is positive.

That means the y-values for this function will always be positive.

822 Unit 10 • Lesson 6

- Show students that when x is −3, y equals 9 because −3 times −3 is 9. So the coordinates are (−3, 9). Point out the point on the graph. m
- Repeat the process for the rest of the values to complete the parabola. m
- Point out to students that the y values are all positive or 0 and that the graph appears in Quadrants I and II. m
- Next discuss with students why this happens. Remind them of the integer rule PASS. You always get a positive answer when you multiply two numbers with the same sign. The product of two negatives is a positive. So for this function, the y values are always positive. m
- Next, tell students that $y = x^2$ is just one type of exponential function. There are others.

Demonstrate

- Explain that it is important to think about what happens when we work with negative numbers, especially as functions become more complicated.
- Go over **Example 1**, where we point out $y = x^3$, $y = x^4$ and $y = x^5$ and why the y values of these functions are either positive or negative. m
- Point out the problems where we end up finding the product of two numbers with the same sign and those where we find the product of two numbers with different signs.

Discuss

Call students' attention to the Power Concept, and point out that it will be helpful as they complete the activities.

In an equation such as $y = x^n$:

- When n is odd, a negative value for x will give a negative value for y.
- When n is even, a negative value for x will give a positive value for y.

Functions can get complicated, and it is important to think about what is happening when we work with negative numbers. Example 1 shows what happens when we substitute a negative number into functions with different exponents. Notice that if the exponent is odd, the result is a negative number.

Example 1

Substitute a negative integer for x in each function.
Let $x = -2$.

Remember to use the Integer Rules from the Algebra Toolbox.

Function	Multiplication	Result
$y = x^2$	$-2 \cdot -2 =$ (same signs)	4
$y = x^3$	$-2 \cdot -2 \cdot -2 =$ $4 \cdot -2 =$ (different signs)	−8
$y = x^4$	$-2 \cdot -2 \cdot -2 \cdot -2 =$ $4 \cdot -2 \cdot -2 =$ $-8 \cdot -2 =$ (same signs)	16
$y = x^5$	$-2 \cdot -2 \cdot -2 \cdot -2 \cdot -2 =$ $4 \cdot -2 \cdot -2 \cdot -2 =$ $-8 \cdot -2 \cdot -2 =$ $16 \cdot -2 =$ (different signs)	−32

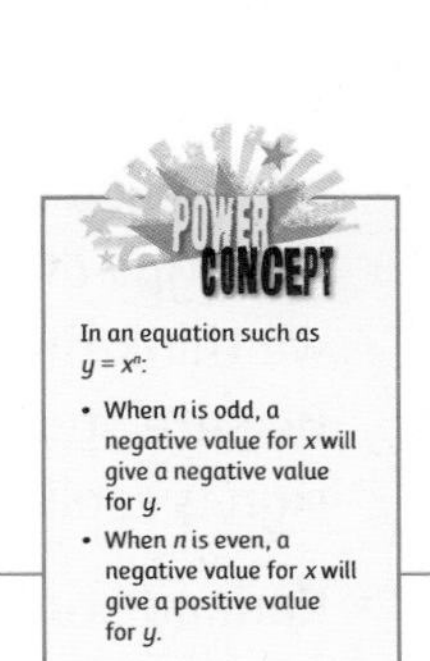
In an equation such as $y = x^n$:
- When n is odd, a negative value for x will give a negative value for y.
- When n is even, a negative value for x will give a positive value for y.

Check for Understanding

Engagement Strategy: Think, Think

Ask students the following questions. Write the functions on the board, if necessary. Tell them that you will call on one of them to answer a question after you ask it. After each question, allow time for students to think of the answer. Then call on a student.

Ask:

If $y = x^4$ and $x = -2$, will y be a positive number or a negative number? (*positive*)

If $y = x^6$ and $x = -2$, will y be a positive number or a negative number? (*positive*)

If $y = x^7$ and $x = -2$, will y be a positive number or a negative number? (*negative*)

What happens when x is negative?

(continued)

Demonstrate

- Tell students that the coefficient in front of the x term might also affect our answers. Remind students that the order of operations tells us to do the exponent first.
- Go over **Example 2** on page 824 of the *Student Text*.
- Explain that in the function $y = -x^2$, we have an implied coefficient of –1. Point out that this type of function can be tricky because we think the negative sign goes with the x. Be sure students remember the negative sign is really the implied coefficient **–1**.
- Remind students that according to the PEMDAS rules, we solve the power first to get 9 and then multiply by –1. So $y = -9$.
- Then look at the function $y = -2x^3$, where we have an explicit coefficient of –2. Walk through the computations when we substitute –3 for x.
- Remind students of the PEMDAS rules: We solve the power first to get **–27**.
- Then explain that after solving the power, we multiply by –2. Point out that a negative times a negative is a positive, so $y = 54$.
- Reiterate that it is very important to use PEMDAS. We must solve the power first before we multiply.
- Point out that the negative coefficient changes the output for the functions. In the first case, a positive input gave a negative output. In the second case, a negative input gave a positive output.

Lesson 6

Another important thing to consider when working with functions is whether the exponent has a negative coefficient. Remember that the negative sign in front of the x^2 in the function $y = -x^2$ is actually an invisible coefficient. It is –1.

Example 2

Determine how a negative coefficient changes the output of a function.

Function

$y = -x^2$

The equation $y = -x^2$ is the same as $y = -1 \cdot x^2$.

Let $x = 3$.

3

↓

$y = -x^2$

$y = -1 \cdot 3^2$

$y = -1 \cdot 9$

$y = -9$

Function

$y = -2x^3$

The equation $y = -2x^3$ is the same as $y = -2 \cdot x^3$.

Let $x = -3$.

–3

↓

$y = -2x^3$

$y = -2 \cdot (-3)^3$

$y = -2 \cdot -27$

$y = 54$

ALGEBRA TOOLBOX

PEMDAS
Remember to use the PEMDAS rules from the Algebra Toolbox to work these kinds of problems. Always work the exponent before you do multiplication.

The negative coefficient changes the output for the function. A positive input into $y = -x^2$ gave a negative output instead of a positive output. A negative input into $y = -2x^3$ gave a positive output instead of negative output.

824 Unit 10 • Lesson 6

Check for Understanding

Engagement Strategy: Pair/Share

Divide students into pairs. Write the following function on the board:

$$y = -3x^3$$

Assign each partner either the value for $x = 2$ or $x = -2$. Have each partner solve for y using the assigned value of x (*when $x = 2$, $y = -24$; when $x = -2$, $y = 24$*). Then have students compare answers to see that when $x = 2$, y is negative, and when $x = -2$, y is positive. Review the answers with the class.

How does a negative coefficient affect the graph of a nonlinear function?

(*Student Text*, page 825)

Demonstrate

- Have students turn to the material on page 825 of the *Student Text*, and tell students that a parabola can appear in different quadrants of the coordinate graph. It all depends on the coefficient of the function.
- Go over **Example 1**. In this example, we compare the graphs of the functions $y = 4x^2$ and $y = -4x^2$.
- Go over the x/y table for each function, and make sure students understand how the value of y was calculated and why the value is positive or negative.
- Have students look at the graphs and point out that the graph with the positive coefficient appears in Quadrants I and II, and the graph with the negative coefficient appears in Quadrants III and IV. It is important for students to see that the parabola changes directions on the graph as a result of the sign of the coefficient.

Discuss

Call students' attention to the Power Concept and point out that it will be helpful as they complete the activities.

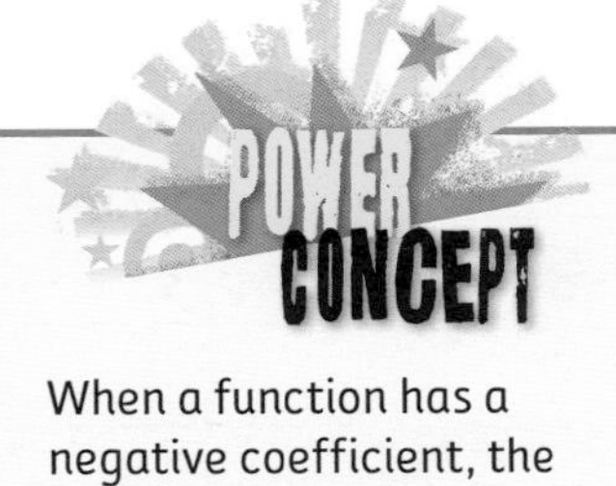

When a function has a negative coefficient, the graph is reflected over the x-axis.

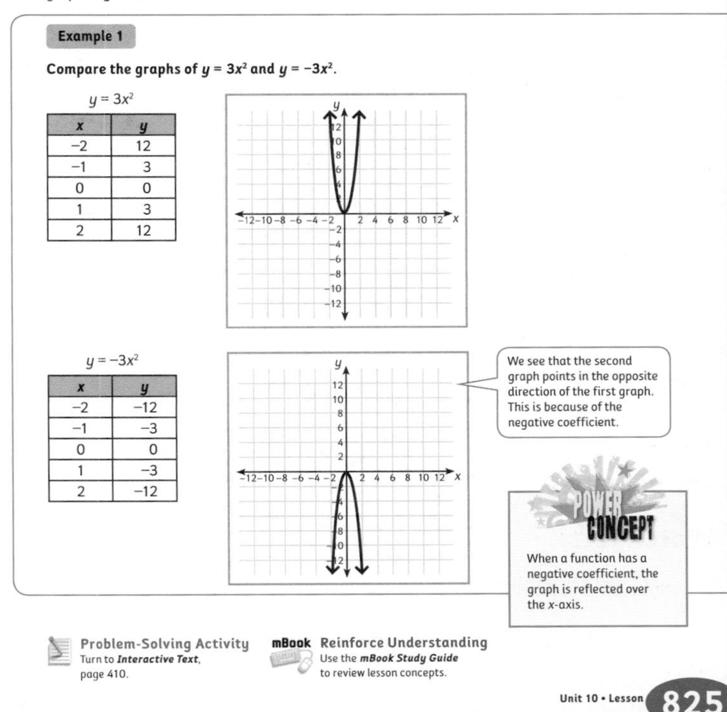

Lesson 6
How does a negative coefficient affect the graph of a nonlinear function?
Now that we know how to find y-values for nonlinear functions, let's see what the functions look like on a coordinate graph. Example 1 shows two parabolas. The first is the graph of y = 3x², and the second is the graph of y = −3x².
Example 1
Compare the graphs of y = 3x² and y = −3x².
y = 3x²
x | y: −2 12; −1 3; 0 0; 1 3; 2 12
y = −3x²
x | y: −2 −12; −1 −3; 0 0; 1 −3; 2 −12
We see that the second graph points in the opposite direction of the first graph. This is because of the negative coefficient.
POWER CONCEPT
When a function has a negative coefficient, the graph is reflected over the x-axis.
Problem-Solving Activity Turn to Interactive Text, page 410.
mBook Reinforce Understanding Use the mBook Study Guide to review lesson concepts.
Unit 10 • Lesson 825

Problem-Solving Activity

(*Interactive Text*, pages 410–412)

Have students turn to pages 410–412 in the *Interactive Text*, and complete the activities.

First students create *x*/*y* tables for the exponential functions. Remind students to solve the power first and then multiply by the coefficient.

Then students create tables and graphs and answer question about the functions $y = x^2$ and $y = -x^2$.

Monitor students' work as they complete the activities.

Watch for:

- Can students solve the power correctly?
- Do students remember to multiply by the coefficient after solving the power?
- Can students find the correct *y* value?
- Can students create the graphs for both functions?
- Can students write about the differences in the tables and graphs?

Lesson 6 | Problem-Solving Activity

Name ______________________ Date ______________

Problem-Solving Activity

The Direction of Non-Linear Functions

Create an *x*/*y* table for each of the functions. Remember to use the rules from PEMDAS. Solve the exponent before you multiply by the coefficient.

1. $y = \frac{1}{2}x^2$

x	y
−2	2
−1	0.5
0	0
1	0.5
2	2

2. $y = -x^2$

x	y
−2	4
−1	1
0	0
1	−1
2	−4

3. $y = -2x^2$

x	y
−2	−8
−1	−2
0	0
1	−1
2	−8

4. $y = -2x^2 + 1$

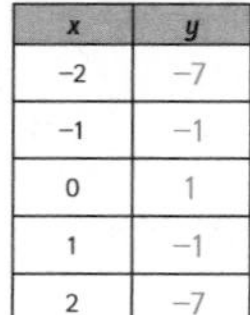

x	y
−2	−7
−1	−1
0	1
1	−1
2	−7

410 Unit 10 • Lesson 6

Lesson 6 | Problem-Solving Activity

Name ______________________ Date ______________

Problem-Solving Activity

The Direction of Non-Linear Functions

Create a table and graph for the functions $y = x^2$ and $y = -x^2$. After you create them, answer the questions about the two functions.

$y = x^2$

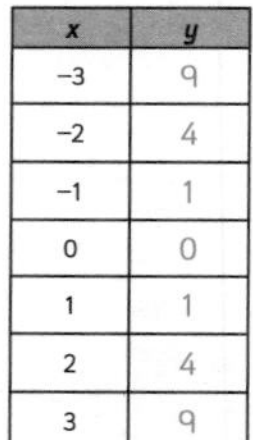

x	y
−3	9
−2	4
−1	1
0	0
1	1
2	4
3	9

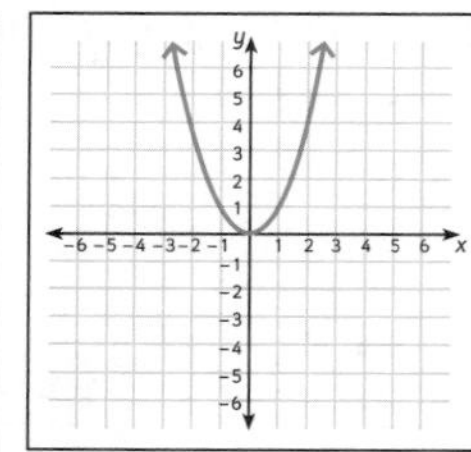

$y = -x^2$

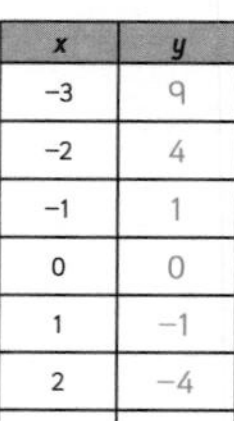

x	y
−3	9
−2	4
−1	1
0	0
1	−1
2	−4
3	−9

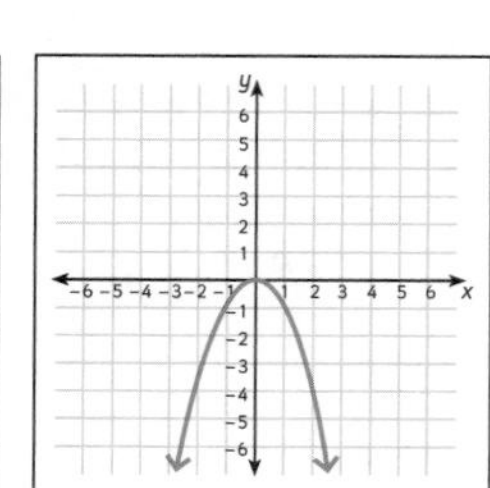

Unit 10

Unit 10 • Lesson 6 411

mBook **Reinforce Understanding**
Remind students that they can review lesson concepts by accessing the online *mBook Study Guide*.

Name ______________________ Date ______________________

1. How do the tables differ for the two functions? Give examples.
Answers will vary. Sample answer: The two tables are different because of the amount of negatives there are. Because the second equation has a negative, it makes half of the numbers in the table negative.

2. How do the graphs differ for the two functions? Give examples.
Answers will vary. Sample answer: The first is in Quadrants I and II and the second is in Quadrants III and IV.

3. Explain how the coefficient affects the tables and graphs of the functions.
Answers will vary. Sample answer: Because the second equation has a negative coefficient, it creates a parabola in the graph and negative numbers in the table.

mBook **Reinforce Understanding**
Use the **mBook** ***Study Guide*** to review lesson concepts.

Homework

Go over the instructions on page 826 of the *Student Text* for each part of the homework.

Activity 1

Students solve equations using substitution.

Activity 2

Students create *x*/*y* tables for exponential functions. Be sure they use the *x* values −2, −1, 0, 1, and 2.

Activity 3

Students tell if the function has a negative coefficient or a positive coefficient by looking at the graph.

Activity 4 • Distributed Practice

Students create *x*/*y* tables for each of the equations of functions.

Lesson 6

Homework

Activity 1

Solve the equations using substitution.

1. $y = x^2$ for $x = -1$ 1
2. $y = -x^2$ for $x = -1$ 1
3. $y = 2x^2$ for $x = -3$ 18
4. $y = -2x^2$ for $x = -3$ −18
5. $y = 3x^2$ for $x = -2$ 12
6. $y = -3x^2$ for $x = -2$ 36

Activity 2

Create *x*/*y* tables for the functions. Use the *x*-values −2, −1, 0, 1, and 2.

1. $y = x^2$
2. $y = -x^2$
3. $y = -2x^2$
4. $y = 2x^2$
5. $y = -\frac{1}{2}x^2$
6. $y = \frac{1}{2}x^2$

See Additional Answers below.

Activity 3

Look at the graphs of functions and tell if the function has a negative coefficient or a positive coefficient.

1. 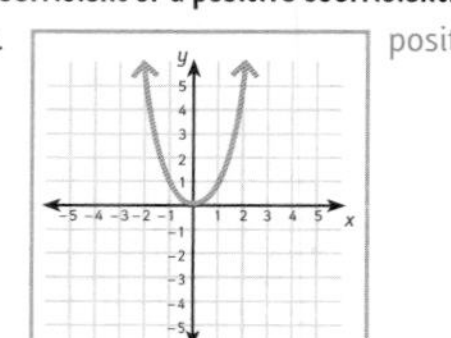 positive

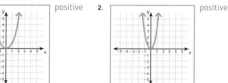

2. positive

3. 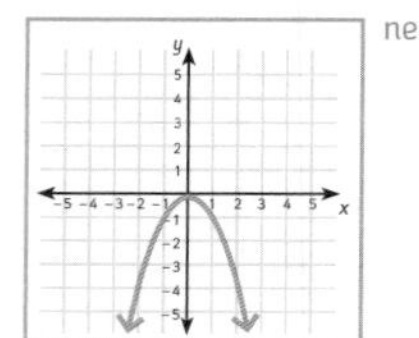 negative

4. 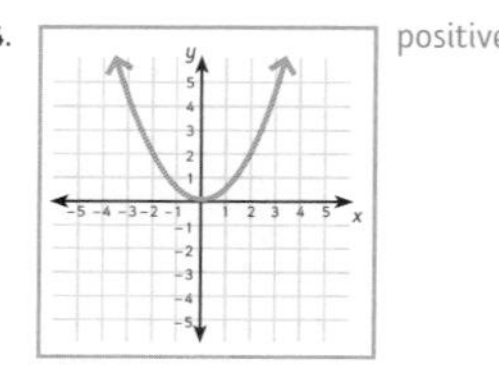 positive

Activity 4 • Distributed Practice

Create an *x*/*y* table for each of the functions using the equations.

1. $y = 3x + 2$
2. $y = -x - 1$
3. $y = -2x + 5$

See Additional Answers below.

826 Unit 10 • Lesson 6

(*Additional Answers continue on Appendix, page A2.*)

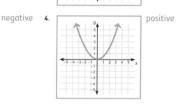

Lesson 7 | The Radical Sign and Evaluating Numeric Expressions

Problem Solving: Changing the Shape of a Nonlinear Function

Lesson Planner

Skills Maintenance

Non-linear Functions

Building Number Concepts:

▶ The Radical Sign and Evaluating Numeric Expressions

Students learn the name for the radical sign and learn that it is a type of grouping symbol, like parentheses and brackets. Students add this symbol to their PEMDAS rules and learn that anything under the radical is solved first.

Students learn that expressions with radicals break into two different expressions because of the ± symbol, resulting in two answers.

Objective

Students will evaluate expressions with a radical sign.

Problem Solving:

▶ Changing the Shape of a Nonlinear Function

We looked at how the graph of a nonlinear function can change direction according to a negative or positive coefficient. Today we look at how the shape of a nonlinear function can change depending on the coefficient in front of the *x* variable.

Objective

Students will explain how the coefficient in front of the *x* variable changes the shape of the graph of a nonlinear function.

Homework

Students solve radicals and expressions involving radicals and match functions with parabolas. In Distributed Practice, students graph functions.

Name ______________________ Date ______________________

Skills Maintenance
Non-Linear Functions

Activity 1

Create x/y tables for the non-linear functions. Remember to use PEMDAS and solve the exponent first. The x-values are filled in for you.

1. $y = -2x^2$

x	y
−2	−8
−1	−2
0	0
1	−2
2	−8

2. $y = 5x^2$

x	y
−2	20
−1	5
0	0
1	5
2	20

3. $y = -x^2$

x	y
−2	−4
−1	−1
0	0
1	−1
2	−4

Unit 10

Skills Maintenance

Non-linear Functions

(*Interactive Text*, page 413)

Activity 1

Students create x/y tables for nonlinear functions.

Building Number Concepts:
▶ The Radical Sign and Evaluating Numeric Expressions

How do we use algebra to solve problems with square roots?
(*Student Text*, pages 827–829)

Connect to Prior Knowledge

Begin by reminding students about PEMDAS. The first letter in the acronym stands for Parentheses. Tell students that parentheses are just one type of grouping symbol. See if students can think of others. Have them come up to the board or overhead and write them. Here are some samples:

Brackets [ ] Braces { }

Link to Today's Concept

Tell students that in today's lesson, they learn one more grouping symbol.

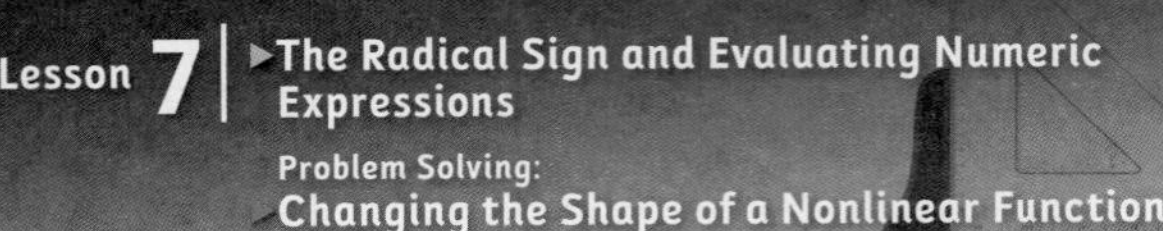

Lesson 7 ▶The Radical Sign and Evaluating Numeric Expressions

Problem Solving: Changing the Shape of a Nonlinear Function

▶The Radical Sign and Evaluating Numeric Expressions

How do we use algebra to solve problems with square roots?

We have found the square roots of numbers using either number sense or a calculator. We use number sense when the number is a perfect square number, such as 25 or 36.

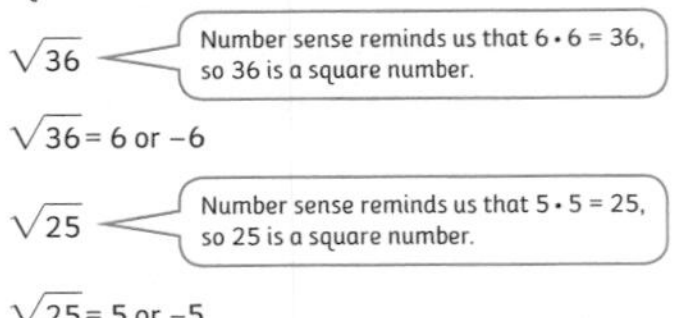

Number sense reminds us that 6 • 6 = 36, so 36 is a square number.
Number sense reminds us that 5 • 5 = 25, so 25 is a square number.

$\sqrt{36}$

$\sqrt{36} = 6$ or -6

$\sqrt{25}$

$\sqrt{25} = 5$ or -5

Sometimes we are given problems that have numeric expressions under the radical sign. The radical is the name of the square root symbol. When we solve this, we need to think about our rules for order of operation, PEMDAS.

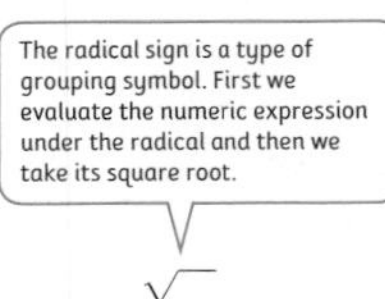

The radical sign is a type of grouping symbol. First we evaluate the numeric expression under the radical and then we take its square root.

$\sqrt{}$

Remember that parentheses are always solved first. We extend this rule to any type of grouping symbol.

PEMDAS
Remember to use the PEMDAS rules from the Algebra Toolbox to work these kinds of problems. Always work the exponent before you do multiplication.

Unit 10 • Lesson 827

Demonstrate

Engagement Strategy: Teacher Modeling

Demonstrate how to solve problems with a radical sign in one of the following ways:

mBook: Use the *mBook Teacher Edition* for *Student Text*, pages 827–828. m

Overhead Projector: Reproduce the problems on a transparency, and modify as discussed.

Board: Copy the problems on the board, and modify as discussed.

- Show the radical sign: $\sqrt{}$. Explain that in some problems we have to evaluate the expression under the radical before we find the square root. m
- Review how to find square roots. Remind students that we have been solving them using mental math.
- Discuss the example $\sqrt{36}$. Walk through the steps to find that $\sqrt{36} = 6$. Remind students that it is helpful to think about the problem in reverse. What number times itself is 36? This requires number sense about square numbers. m
- Repeat with $\sqrt{25}$. m
- Next tell students that sometimes there is a numeric expression under the radical. We have to solve that first and then take the square root. We can think of the radical as another type of grouping symbol. Remind students that in PEMDAS, we solve parentheses first. This applies to any grouping symbols.

Demonstrate

- Look at **Example 1**. This demonstrates two problems that require us to evaluate the expression under the radical first and then find its square root.
- Have students look at the first problem $\sqrt{2 \cdot 8}$. Go though each step carefully, reminding students of the order of operations. When you get to $\sqrt{16}$, point out that the answer is ± 4. Make sure students understand that this means the answer is **+4 and −4**. m
- Then go over the second problem $\sqrt{30 \div 5}$ in the same way. When you get to $\sqrt{6}$, point out that we use a calculator. Again make sure students understand that the answer is **+2.45 and −2.45**. m
- Notice one of the problems could be solved using number sense, and the other required a calculator. Tell students to round their calculator answers so that they make sense.

Example 1 shows this situation. We use the symbol ± when there is a positive and negative answer.

Example 1

Use PEMDAS to solve problems that have a radical sign.

Problem 1

$\sqrt{2 \cdot 8}$	←	The problem.
$\sqrt{2 \cdot 8}$	←	Evaluate the expression under the radical first.
$\sqrt{16}$	←	Find the square root using mental math.
$\sqrt{16} = \pm 4$	←	The answer is +4 and −4.

Problem 2

$\sqrt{30 \div 5}$	←	The problem.
$\sqrt{30 \div 5}$	←	Evaluate the expression under the radical first.
$\sqrt{6}$	←	Find the square root using a calculator.
$\sqrt{6} = \pm 2.45$	←	The answer is +2.45 and −2.45.

We might also have a case where the radical is just part of a larger expression. In this case, it's especially important to remember PEMDAS.

We also need to realize that we have two expressions to evaluate. Given the fact that the square root can be positive or negative, we have to solve for both. Example 2 demonstrates this situation.

Explain

Next tell students that radicals can be part of a more complex expression with more than one operation. When this is the case, we again turn to our PEMDAS rules. It is important to point out that any time we have a radical involved in a problem, we end up solving two different expressions. This is because of the ± symbol. When we take the square root of something, we get two answers. We have to finish evaluating the expression for both possible answers.

How do we use algebra to solve problems with square roots? *(continued)*

Demonstrate

- Turn to page 829 of the *Student Text* to discuss **Example 2**, which demonstrates more complex expressions.
- Go over the first problem carefully, reminding students of PEMDAS rules. We first solve what is under the radical sign, **2 • 8**, and then find the square root.
- Note the step where we write the two different expressions. Point out that when we find the square root, we have two answers: +4 and −4. So we must write two expressions. Note that the two answers to the problem are **6** and **−2**.
- Go over the second problem in the same way. Again, remind students that the rules of PEMDAS tell us that we must solve what is under the radical sign first.
- Point out that when we find the square root, we have two answers: **+2.45** and **−2.45**. This means that we write two different expressions and get two answers: **9.35** and **−5.35**.

Check for Understanding
Engagement Strategy: Think Tank

Write the problem $\mathbf{4 \cdot \sqrt{5 \cdot 5} + 6}$ on the board. Distribute strips of paper and have students write their names on the papers. Tell students to find all the solutions to the expression (*26* and *−14*). Remind students to use PEMDAS. When students finish, collect the papers in a container. Draw an answer, and read it aloud. If it is correct, congratulate the student, and invite the student to explain the solutions.

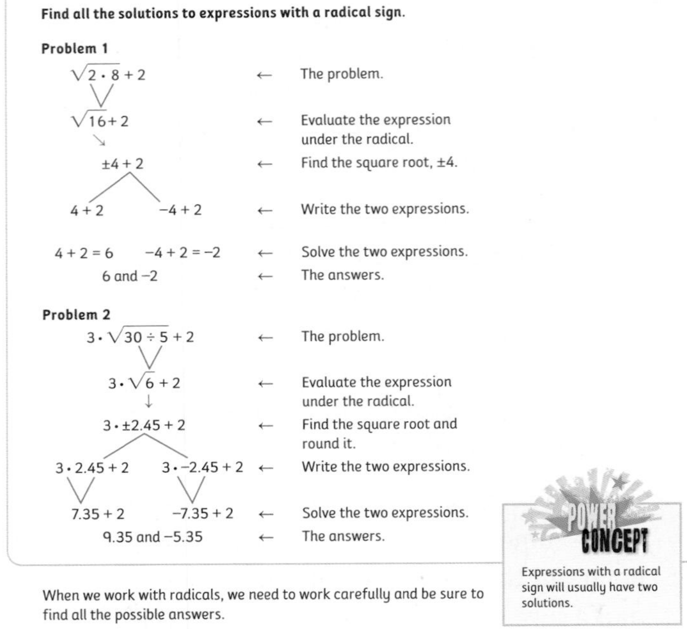

Example 2

Find all the solutions to expressions with a radical sign.

Problem 1

$\sqrt{2 \cdot 8} + 2$	←	The problem.
$\sqrt{16} + 2$	←	Evaluate the expression under the radical.
$\pm 4 + 2$	←	Find the square root, ±4.
$4 + 2$ $-4 + 2$	←	Write the two expressions.
$4 + 2 = 6$ $-4 + 2 = -2$	←	Solve the two expressions.
6 and −2	←	The answers.

Problem 2

$3 \cdot \sqrt{30 \div 5} + 2$	←	The problem.
$3 \cdot \sqrt{6} + 2$	←	Evaluate the expression under the radical.
$3 \cdot \pm 2.45 + 2$	←	Find the square root and round it.
$3 \cdot 2.45 + 2$ $3 \cdot -2.45 + 2$	←	Write the two expressions.
$7.35 + 2$ $-7.35 + 2$	←	Solve the two expressions.
9.35 and −5.35	←	The answers.

POWER CONCEPT

Expressions with a radical sign will usually have two solutions.

When we work with radicals, we need to work carefully and be sure to find all the possible answers.

Apply Skills
Turn to *Interactive Text*, page 414.

mBook Reinforce Understanding
Use the *mBook Study Guide* to review lesson concepts.

Unit 10 • Lesson 829

Discuss

Call students' attention to the Power Concept, and point out that it will be helpful as they complete the activity.

Expressions with a radical sign will usually have two solutions.

Apply Skills

(*Interactive Text*, page 414)

Have students turn to page 414 in the *Interactive Text*, and complete the activity.

Activity 1

Students evaluate expressions involving radicals. Tell them to remember the PEMDAS rules. Remind students that they have two expressions to evaluate whenever a radical is involved. Monitor students' work as they complete the activity.

Watch for:

- Can students use the rules of PEMDAS and evaluate the expression in the correct order?
- Can students use a calculator and round when necessary and use mental math when necessary?
- Can students write the two expressions that lead to the answers?
- Can students come up with the correct two answers to the problem?

mBook **Reinforce Understanding**

Remind students that they can review lesson concepts by accessing the online *mBook Study Guide*.

Lesson 7 | Apply Skills

Name ______________________ Date ______________________

Apply Skills

The Radical Sign and Evaluating Numeric Expressions

Activity 1

Solve the radicals in each expression. Remember to use the rules of PEMDAS. Be sure to consider ± symbols in your answers.

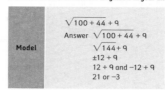

Model	$\sqrt{100+44}+9$ Answer $\sqrt{100+44}+9$ $\sqrt{144}+9$ $\pm12+9$ $12+9$ and $-12+9$ 21 or -3

1. $\sqrt{24+12}$ ____ ±6 ____
2. $\sqrt{56+8}$ ____ ±8 ____
3. $\sqrt{86-5}+2$ ____ 11 or −7 ____
4. $3\cdot\sqrt{37+12}$ ____ ±21 ____
5. $2\cdot\sqrt{4+5}+5$ ____ 11 or −1 ____

414 Unit 10 • Lesson 7

Problem Solving:
▶ Changing the Shape of a Nonlinear Function

How does changing the coefficient change the shape of a nonlinear function?

(*Student Text*, pages 830–831)

Connect to Prior Knowledge

Remind students that the sign of the coefficient in front of the x makes the graphs appear in different quadrants facing different directions.

Link to Today's Concept

In today's lesson we see that the coefficient in front of the x also affects the shape of the graph.

Demonstrate

- Have students look at the tables and graphs in **Example 1** on *Student Text*, page 830. Show students how we can make the parabola wider or narrower depending on the size of the coefficient.
- Have students look at the table and graph for the function $\boldsymbol{y = \frac{1}{3}x^2}$. Make sure students understand how we calculate the y values and how the x/y values correspond to the plotted points on the graph.
- Then have students look at the table and graph for the function $\boldsymbol{y = x^2}$. Remind students that in this case, we have an invisible coefficient of 1, which is bigger than the coefficient in the previous function. Discuss the table and graph in the same way.
- Point out that the parabola of $y = x^2$ is narrower than the parabola for $y = \frac{1}{3}x^2$.

Lesson 7

▶Problem Solving: Changing the Shape of a Nonlinear Function

How does changing the coefficient change the shape of a nonlinear function?

In the last lesson, we looked at how a negative coefficient changes the direction of a nonlinear function. We can also change the shape of a nonlinear function by changing the coefficient in front of the x-variable. Look at the three functions in Example 1.

Example 1

Compare the graphs of the functions.

$y = \frac{1}{3}x^2$

x	y
−3	3
−2	$\frac{4}{3}$
−1	$\frac{1}{3}$
0	0
1	$\frac{1}{3}$
2	$\frac{4}{3}$
3	3

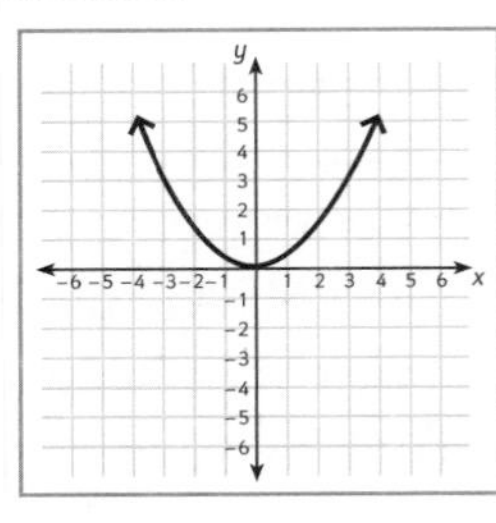

$y = x^2$

x	y
−3	9
−2	4
−1	1
0	0
1	1
2	4
3	9

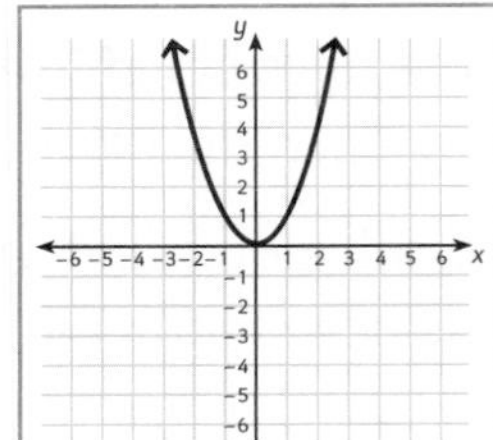

Demonstrate

- Turn to page 831 of the *Student Text*, and continue going over Example 1. Go over the table and graph for the function $y = 3x^2$ in the same way.
- Ask students to make observations about the graphs and the relationship to the coefficients.

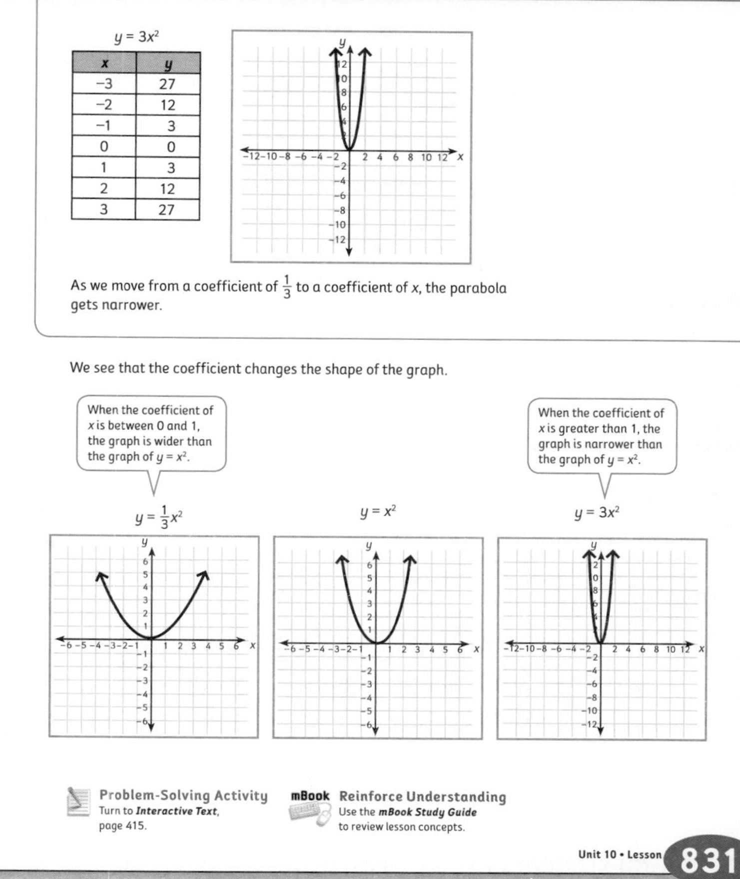

$y = 3x^2$

x	y
−3	27
−2	12
−1	3
0	0
1	3
2	12
3	27

As we move from a coefficient of $\frac{1}{3}$ to a coefficient of x, the parabola gets narrower.

We see that the coefficient changes the shape of the graph.

When the coefficient of x is between 0 and 1, the graph is wider than the graph of $y = x^2$.
When the coefficient of x is greater than 1, the graph is narrower than the graph of $y = x^2$.
$y = \frac{1}{3}x^2$
$y = x^2$
$y = 3x^2$

Problem-Solving Activity Turn to *Interactive Text*, page 415.

mBook Reinforce Understanding Use the *mBook Study Guide* to review lesson concepts.

Listen for:

- *The bigger the coefficient of x, the narrower the parabola.*
- *The smaller the coefficient of x, the wider the parabola.*

- Be sure students see how the graphs are the same and how they are different.
- Summarize what happens to the graph when the coefficient changes. When the coefficient is between 0 and 1, the graph is wider. When it is greater than 1, the graph is narrower.

Check for Understanding

Engagement Strategy: Think, Think

Ask students the following questions about the following functions: $y = 5x^2$, $y = \frac{1}{2}x^2$, and $y = x^2$. Tell them that you will call on one of them to answer a question after you ask it. Tell them to listen for their names. After each question, allow time for students to think of the answer. Then call on a student.

Ask:

Which parabola will be the widest? ($y = \frac{1}{2}x^2$)

How do you know? (*It has the smallest coefficient.*)

Which parabola will be the narrowest? ($y = 5x^2$)

How do you know? (*It has the biggest coefficient.*)

Problem-Solving Activity
(*Interactive Text*, pages 415–416)

Have students turn to pages 415–416 in the *Interactive Text*, which provides students an opportunity to practice these concepts on their own.

Students create tables and graphs for two exponential functions. Then they answer questions about the functions.

Monitor students' work as they complete the activity.

Watch for:

- Can students see how the negative coefficient affects the graph?
- Can students see how the change in the size of the coefficient (both still negative) affects the graph?
- Can students explain similarities and differences between the two functions?

mBook **Reinforce Understanding**
Remind students that they can review lesson concepts by accessing the online *mBook Study Guide*.

Name ____________________ Date ____________________

Problem-Solving Activity
Changing the Shape of a Non-Linear Function

Activity 1

Create a table and graph for the functions $y = -\frac{1}{2}x^2$ and $y = -2x^2$. After you create the tables and the graphs, answer the questions.

$y = -\frac{1}{2}x^2$

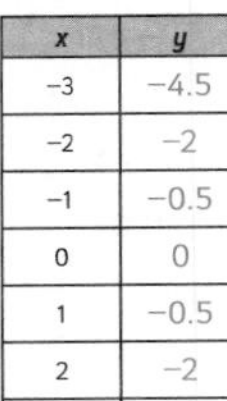

x	y
−3	−4.5
−2	−2
−1	−0.5
0	0
1	−0.5
2	−2
3	−4.5

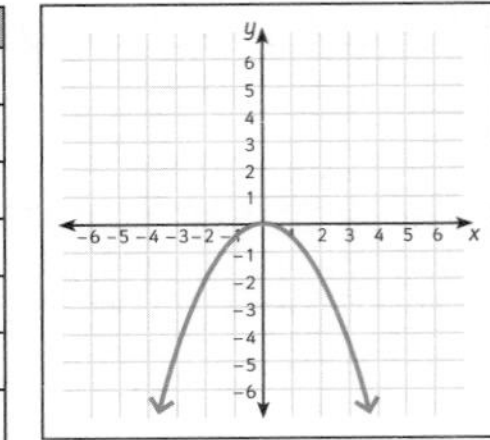

$y = -2x^2$

x	y
−3	−18
−2	−8
−1	−2
0	0
1	−2
2	−8
3	−18

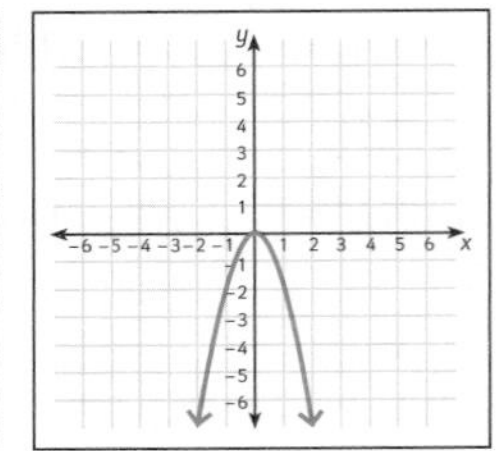

Unit 10

Name ____________________ Date ____________________

1. How are the tables different for the two functions?
   Answers will vary. Sample answer: The tables only differ in the size of *y*.

2. How are the graphs different for the two functions?
   Answers will vary. Sample answer: The first graph has a wider parabola than the second graph.

3. Explain the impact of a negative coefficient on a parabola. Explain the impact of different-sized negative coefficients on a parabola.
   Answers will vary. Sample answer: The negative coefficient eliminates the parabola because the graph goes up and down in one quadrant. The size only affects the size of the line.

mBook Reinforce Understanding
Use the **mBook *Study Guide*** to review lesson concepts.

Homework

Go over the instructions on page 832 of the *Student Text* for each part of the homework.

Activity 1

Students solve the radicals using PEMDAS.

Activity 2

Students solve the expressions involving radicals using PEMDAS.

Activity 3

Students match the function with its parabola. Tell them to use their knowledge of the properties of parabolas to help them think about the equation.

Activity 4 • Distributed Practice

Students draw graphs of the functions given to them as equations.

Homework

Activity 1

Solve the expressions. Remember to use PEMDAS. Use a calculator if necessary and round to the nearest tenths place.

1. $\sqrt{2+4}$ ±2.4 2. $\sqrt{3+13}$ ±4 3. $\sqrt{55-6}$ ±7 4. $\sqrt{7+3}$ ±3.2

Activity 2

Solve the expressions involving radicals. Remember to use PEMDAS. Be sure to find all of the solutions.

1. $\sqrt{2+4}+9$ 11.4 and 6.6
2. $2 \cdot \sqrt{3+13}$ 8 and −8
3. $3 \cdot \sqrt{55-6}+2$ 23 and −19
4. $-3 \cdot \sqrt{7+3}-8$ 1.6 and −17.6

Activity 3

Match the functions with their graphs. Use the letters next to the parabolas to identify them.

1. $y=-\frac{1}{2}x^2$ A
2. $y=3x^2$ D
3. $y=-3x^2$ B
4. $y=\frac{1}{2}x^2$ C

A

B

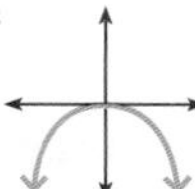

C

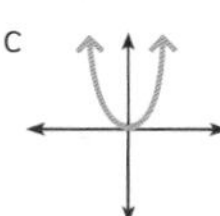

D

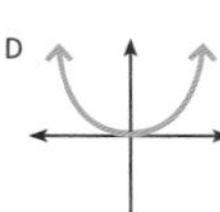

Activity 4 • Distributed Practice

Draw the graph for each of the functions.

1. $y=3x$ 2. $y=-x$ 3. $y=2x+-1$

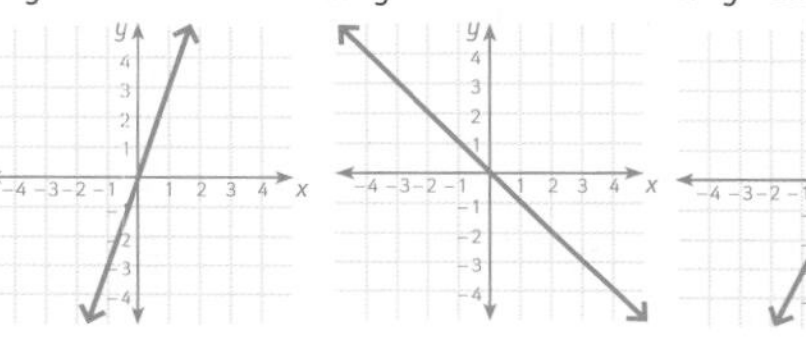

Lesson 8 ▶The Radical Sign and Algebraic Equations

Problem Solving: ▶Other Nonlinear Functions

Lesson Planner

Skills Maintenance

Squaring Numbers

Building Number Concepts:

▶ The Radical Sign and Algebraic Equations

Students learn that we can use algebraic properties to solve equations involving radicals. Properties of equality, for instance, are helpful in solving problems with radicals by helping to eliminate the radical on one side of the equation.

Objective

Students will use algebraic properties to solve problems with square roots.

Problem Solving:

▶ Other Nonlinear Functions

Students already know that there are many types of exponential functions. Today we look at the graphs of other exponential functions, specifically the function $y = x^3$. We compare the graph of this function to the graph of parabolas that students have seen.

Objective

Students will examine the graphs of other nonlinear functions.

Homework

Students square the numbers, solve the equations with radicals by squaring both sides first, and match the graph with the equation of its function. In Distributed Practice, students write word problems for functions given their equations.

Lesson 8 | Skills Maintenance

Name ______________________ Date ______________________

Skills Maintenance
Squaring Numbers

Activity 1

Square each of the numbers. You may use a calculator.

1. 2^2 4
2. 1.2^2 1.44
3. $\left(\frac{1}{2}\right)^2$ 0.25
4. $(4 + 2)^2$ 36
5. 2.8^2 7.84

Unit 10

Unit 10 • Lesson 8 417

Skills Maintenance

Squaring Numbers

(*Interactive Text*, page 417)

Activity 1

Students practice squaring numbers.

Building Number Concepts: ▶ The Radical Sign and Algebraic Equations

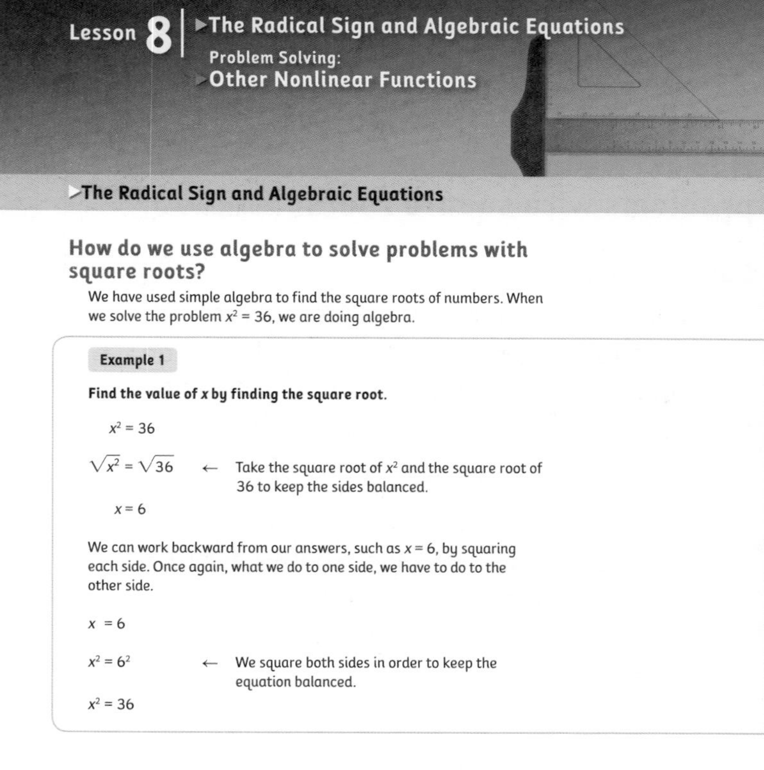
Lesson 8 ▶The Radical Sign and Algebraic Equations
Problem Solving: ▶Other Nonlinear Functions

▶The Radical Sign and Algebraic Equations

How do we use algebra to solve problems with square roots?

We have used simple algebra to find the square roots of numbers. When we solve the problem $x^2 = 36$, we are doing algebra.

Example 1

Find the value of x by finding the square root.

$x^2 = 36$

$\sqrt{x^2} = \sqrt{36}$ ← Take the square root of x^2 and the square root of 36 to keep the sides balanced.

$x = 6$

We can work backward from our answers, such as $x = 6$, by squaring each side. Once again, what we do to one side, we have to do to the other side.

$x = 6$

$x^2 = 6^2$ ← We square both sides in order to keep the equation balanced.

$x^2 = 36$

Unit 10 • Lesson 833

How do we use algebra to solve problems with square roots?

(*Student Text*, pages 833–834)

Connect to Prior Knowledge

Begin by reminding students about the doing and undoing relationship between squares and square roots. Put the following on the board or overhead:

5^2 $\sqrt{25}$

4^2 $\sqrt{16}$

2.4^2 $\sqrt{5.76}$

Ask students to describe the relationship.

Listen for:

- A discussion about squaring and unsquaring.

Link to Today's Concept

Tell students that we are going to use this relationship in today's lesson to help us solve problems more simply.

Demonstrate

Engagement Strategy: Teacher Modeling

Demonstrate how to use algebra to solve problems with square roots in one of the following ways:

mBook: Use the *mBook Teacher Edition* for *Student Text*, pages 833–834. m

Overhead Projector: Reproduce the equations on a transparency, and modify as discussed.

Board: Copy the equations on the board, and modify as discussed.

- Show the problem $\boldsymbol{x^2 = 36}$, and remind students that we used simple algebra to solve problems like these. m
- Show students how we take the square root of each side or unsquare each side, and we get the answer $\boldsymbol{x = 6}$. m
- Point out that we can do the opposite with the expression $x = 6$. We can square both sides and get the original equation, $\boldsymbol{x^2 = 36}$. m

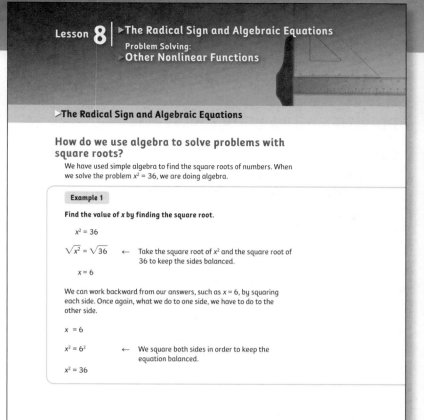

How do we use algebra to solve problems with square roots? *(continued)*

Demonstrate

- Tell students that what we just did is a good tool for getting rid of the radical in an equation. Explain that it is more difficult to solve an equation with a radical, so it is to our advantage to try to get rid of it.
- Direct students' attention to **Example 2**, which shows how we square both sides to get rid of the radical. Remind students that the properties of equality allow you to do the same thing to both sides of the equation, and it stays equal.
- Show the problem $\sqrt{x + 2} = 5$. Show how we square both sides, which gets rid of the radical. Then point out that the rest of the problem is then solved like we would solve any other algebraic equation, using the same rules and properties. Go over each step carefully. m
- Be sure students understand each of the steps and the justification of each step.
- Finally, be sure students see how we check the answer at the end by substituting it back into the original problem with the radical. m

Check for Understanding
Engagement Strategy: Look About

Write the problem $\sqrt{x + 4} = 2$ on the board ($x = 0$). Tell students that they will solve the equation with the help of the whole class. Students should write their solutions in large writing on a piece of paper or a dry erase board. When students finish their work, they should hold up their answer for everyone to see.

Lesson 8

Now that we know how to work with square numbers and radical signs, we can put both of these ideas together and solve equations like the one in Example 2.

Example 2

Solve the equation by squaring both sides.

$\sqrt{x+2} = 5$

$\left(\sqrt{x+2}\right)^2 = 5^2$ ← We square both sides to keep the equation balanced.

$x + 2 = 25$ ← When we square a square root, we remove the radical.

$x + 2 + -2 = 25 + -2$

$x + 0 = 25 + -2$

$x + 0 = 23$

$x = 23$

Check to see if this is correct by substituting 23 for x in the original equation.

23 ↓

$\sqrt{x+2} = 5$

$\sqrt{23+2} = 5$

$\sqrt{25} = 5$

$5 = 5$

The answer 23 is correct.

Apply Skills Turn to ***Interactive Text***, page 418.

mBook Reinforce Understanding Use the ***mBook Study Guide*** to review lesson concepts.

If students are not sure about the answer, prompt them to look about at other students' solutions to help with their thinking. Review the answers after all students have held up their solutions.

Apply Skills
(*Interactive Text*, page 418)

Have students turn to page 418 in the *Interactive Text*, and complete the activity.

Activity 1

Students solve algebraic equations involving radicals by squaring both sides to get rid of the radical. Monitor students' work as they complete the activity.

Watch for:

- Can students correctly square each side?
- Can students solve the algebraic equation using appropriate rules and properties once the radical has been removed?
- Can students check the answer by substituting the value for the variable back in the original equation?

mBook **Reinforce Understanding**
Remind students that they can review lesson concepts by accessing the online *mBook Study Guide*.

Lesson 8 | Apply Skills

Name ______________________ Date ______________________

Apply Skills
The Radical Sign and Algebraic Equations

Activity 1

Use algebra and properties of square roots to solve the each expression.

Model

$\sqrt{x+3} = 6$ $\underline{x = 33}$

Answer: $\left(\sqrt{x+3}\right)^2 = 6^2$ Square both sides.

$x + 3 = 36$ Remove the radical on the left.

$x = 33$ Solve.

Check the answer: $\sqrt{33+3} = 6$

$\sqrt{36} = 6$ TRUE

1. $\sqrt{x+2} = 4$ $\underline{x = 14}$
   Show your work here.
   $x + 2 = 16$
   $-2 = -2$

2. $\sqrt{2x+2} = 2$ $\underline{x = 1}$
   Show your work here.
   $2x + 2 = 4$
   $2x = 2$

3. $\sqrt{4x-1} = 1$ $\underline{x = \frac{1}{2}}$
   Show your work here.
   $4x - 1 = 1$
   $4x = 2$
   $x = \frac{2}{4}$

4. $\sqrt{x-3} = 3$ $\underline{x = 12}$
   Show your work here.
   $x - 3 = 9$
   $x = 12$

5. $\sqrt{14+2} = x$ $\underline{x = 4}$
   Show your work here.
   $\sqrt{16} = x$
   $4 = x$

418 Unit 10 • Lesson 8

Problem Solving: ▶ Other Nonlinear Functions

What happens to the graph when our function is $y = x^3$?

(*Student Text*, pages 835–837)

Connect to Prior Knowledge

Remind students that the graph of a function with x^2 in it is a parabola as seen at the top of page 835 of the *Student Text.*

Link to Today's Concept

Tell students that there are different kinds of exponential functions. Explain that they have different kinds of graphs. In today's lesson, we explore functions with x^3.

Demonstrate

- Draw a blank coordinate graph on the board or overhead, and label the quadrants. Ask students to tell you the values of the coordinates in each quadrant. Write them on the coordinate graph.
- Next remind students of our discussion about the exponents being odd or even and that an odd exponent results in negative y values for negative x values. This means that the negative x values in the function $\boldsymbol{y = x^3}$ will result in negative y values.
- Have students think about what that means in terms of differences in the graphs between $\boldsymbol{y = x^3}$ and $\boldsymbol{y = x^2}$. To do this, they need to think about where on a coordinate graph the x and y values are both negative. This occurs in Quadrant III.
- Tell students that positive x values result in positive y values in $y = x^3$. Ask students to think about where the x and y values are both positive on a coordinate graph. It is in Quadrant I.

▶Problem Solving: Other Nonlinear Functions

What happens to the graph when our function is $y = x^3$?

The only kind of graph with a curve we have seen in this unit has been one with a parabola. This is because the x in our functions has been squared. The function $y = x^2$ is a common example.

The Graph for the Function $y = x^2$

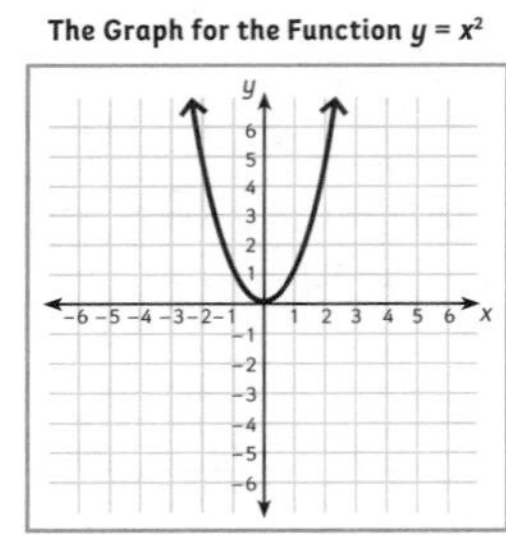

When we change the function to $y = x^3$, it seems like a small change. However, it makes a big difference when we look at the graph. Suddenly the shape of the line is entirely different. If we look at the x/y table, the change makes sense. The exponent is an odd number, so when we multiply three negative numbers together we get a negative answer or product.

Example 1

Graph the function $y = x^3$.

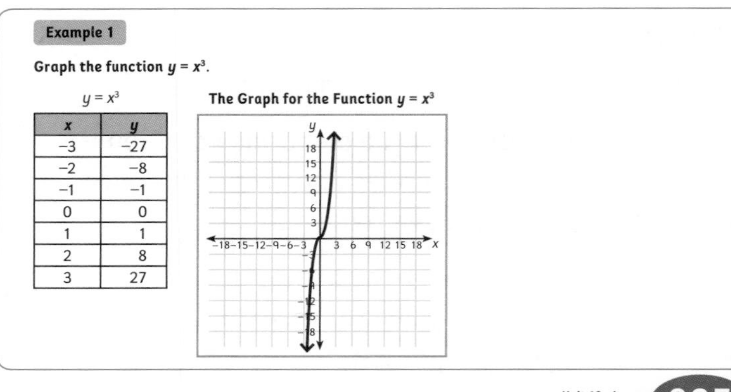

$y = x^3$

x	y
–3	–27
–2	–8
–1	–1
0	0
1	1
2	8
3	27

- Have students look at **Example 1**, which demonstrates the table and graph for the function $y = x^3$. Be sure students understand the connection between the x values, the function that has an exponent of 3, and the y values. Discuss how all these factors affect the graph of the function.

Demonstrate

- Turn to page 836 of the *Student Text* to review the different ways we looked at nonlinear graphs in this unit. Remind students that the *x*-values of the functions all had an exponent.
- Go over the *x*/*y* table and graph for the function $\boldsymbol{y = x^2}$. Remind students that squaring the *x* changes what was a straight line into a curve, or a parabola.
- Then go over the *x*/*y* table and graph for the function $\boldsymbol{y = -x^2}$. Remind students that a negative coefficient in front of *x* changes the orientation of the parabola: It turns it upside down.

As we explore mathematics, we will learn about more nonlinear graphs. This is a summary of the different ways we have looked at nonlinear graphs in this unit. Each one is based on a function where the *x*-value has an exponent.

Squaring the *x* changes what was a straight line into a curve called a parabola.

$y = x^2$

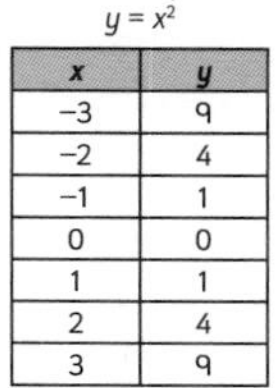

x	*y*
−3	9
−2	4
−1	1
0	0
1	1
2	4
3	9

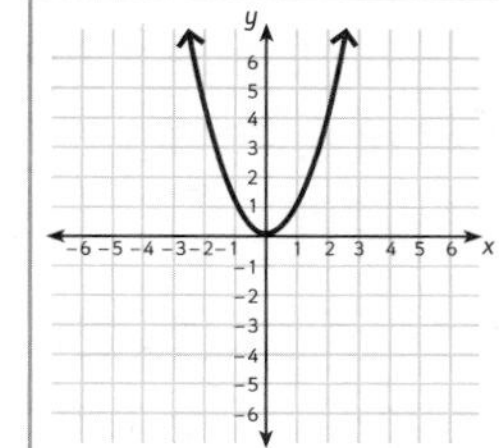

The negative coefficient in front of *x* turns the parabola upside down. It changes the direction of the function.

$y = -x^2$

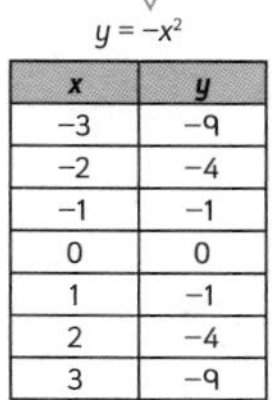

x	*y*
−3	−9
−2	−4
−1	−1
0	0
1	−1
2	−4
3	−9

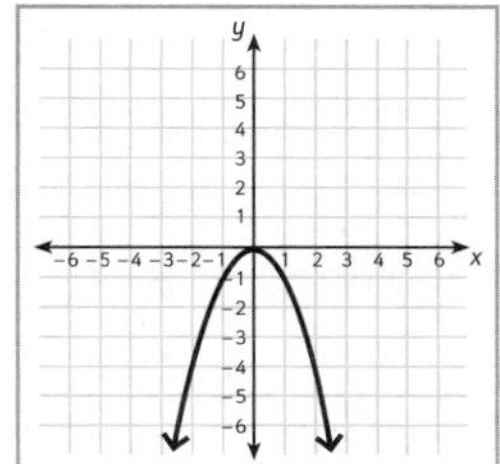

What happens to the graph when our function is $y = x^2$? *(continued)*

Demonstrate

- Turn to page 837 of the *Student Text* to continue reviewing the different ways we looked at nonlinear graphs.
- Go over the *x*/*y* table and graph for the function $y = \frac{1}{2}x^2$. Remind students that changing the constant, or the coefficient in front of the *x*, changes the shape of the functions.
- Remind students that a smaller constant results in a wider parabola. A bigger constant makes the shape steeper.
- Finally, go over the *x*/*y* table and graph for the function $y = x^3$. Again point out that changing the exponent changes the graph significantly.

Changing the constant or coefficient in front of the *x* changes the shape of the function. Smaller constants make the shape of the parabola wider. Bigger constants make the shape steeper.

$y = \frac{1}{2}x^2$

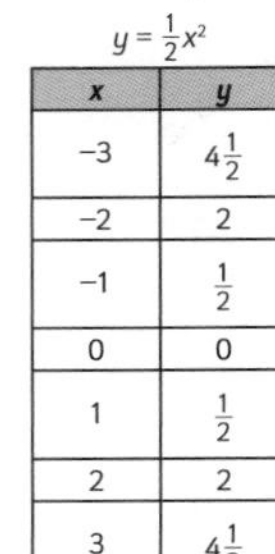

x	*y*
−3	$4\frac{1}{2}$
−2	2
−1	$\frac{1}{2}$
0	0
1	$\frac{1}{2}$
2	2
3	$4\frac{1}{2}$

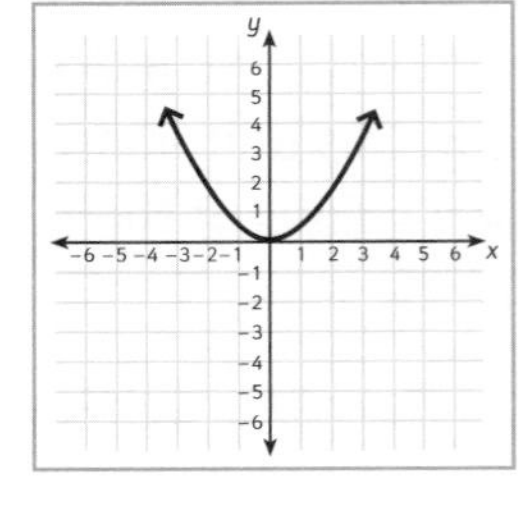

By changing x^2 to x^3, the graph changes significantly.

$y = x^3$

x	*y*
−3	−27
−2	−8
−1	−1
0	0
1	1
2	8
3	27

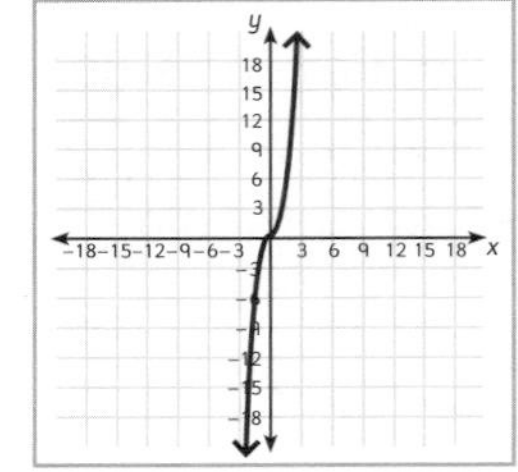

Problem-Solving Activity Turn to ***Interactive Text***, page 419.

mBook Reinforce Understanding Use the ***mBook Study Guide*** to review lesson concepts.

Problem-Solving Activity
(*Interactive Text*, page 419)

Have students turn to page 419 in the *Interactive Text*. Students match the equation of the function with the graph. They do this by circling the correct graph. Then they write why they chose this graph.

Monitor students' work as they complete the activity.

Watch for:

- Can students identify the correct graph that matches the function?
- Can students explain how they knew this was the correct graph?

Be sure to go over student responses. Listen for discussions about the direction of the graph, positive and negative coordinates of points on the graph, location in various quadrants on the coordinate graph, coefficients of the *x* terms, exponents, and linear versus nonlinear features and attributes.

mBook Reinforce Understanding
Remind students that they can review lesson concepts by accessing the online *mBook Study Guide*.

Lesson 8 | Problem-Solving Activity

Name ______________________ Date ______________

Problem-Solving Activity
Other Non-Linear Functions

Match the function with the correct graph and circle the answer. Write a sentence explaining your answer.

1. Circle the graph for this function $y = 3x^2$.

(a)
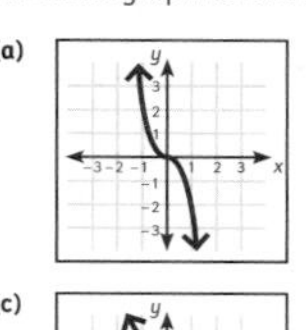
(b)
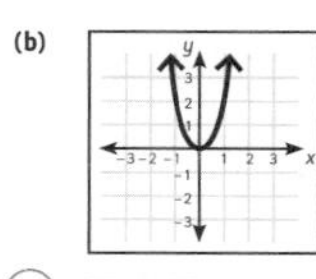
(c)
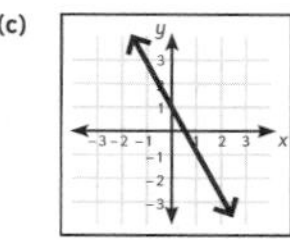
(d)
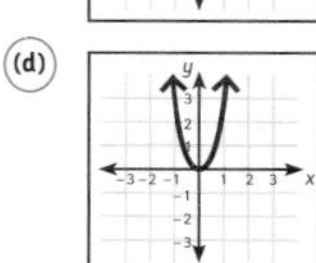

Answers will vary. Sample answer: The positive coefficient make the function open up.

2. Circle the graph for this function $y = -2x^2$.

(a)
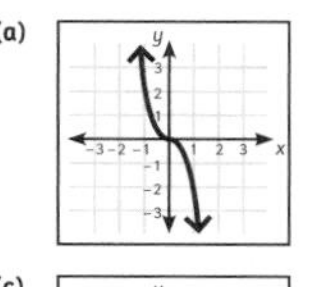
(b)
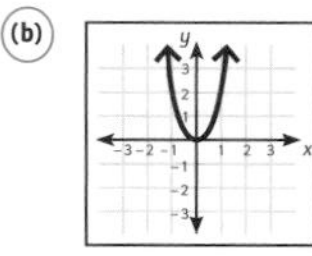
(c)
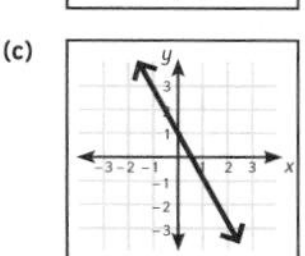
(d)
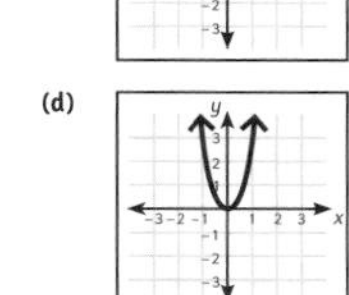

Answers will vary. Sample answer: The negative coefficient makes the parabola opendowneard.

Unit 10

Unit 10 • Lesson 8 419

Homework

Go over the instructions on pages 838–839 of the *Student Text* for each part of the homework.

Activity 1

Students square the numbers.

Activity 2

Students solve the equations with radicals by squaring both sides first.

Activity 3

Students match the graph with the equation of its function.

Lesson 8

Homework

Activity 1

Square the numbers.

1. 5^2 25
2. $\left(\frac{1}{3}\right)^2$ $\frac{1}{9}$
3. x^2 when $x = -2$ 4
4. $(5 + 2)^2$ 49
5. 3.3^2 10.89

Activity 2

Solve the equations involving radicals. Remember, you can square each side to make the solution easier.

1. $\sqrt{x+1} = 2$ 3
2. $\sqrt{2+x} = 4$ 14
3. $\sqrt{x-4} = \sqrt{9}$ 13
4. $\sqrt{2x+1} = 3$ 4
5. $\sqrt{4x+2} = 5$ $5\frac{3}{4}$

Activity 3

Select the graph that matches each of the equations for functions. Use the letter next to the graph to identify it.

1. $y = x^2$ b
2. $y = \frac{1}{2}x$ e
3. $y = x^3$ d
4. $y = 2x$ a
5. $y = -2x^2$ c

(a)

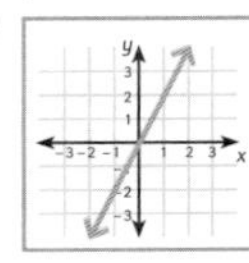

(b)

(c)

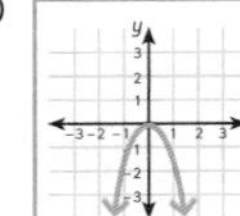

(d)

(e)

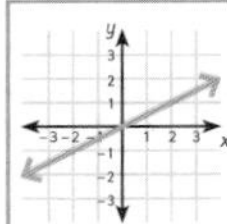

838 Unit 10 • Lesson 8

Activity 4 • Distributed Practice

Students write word problems for functions given their equations.

Lesson 8

Homework

Activity 4 • Distributed Practice

Represent the functions given as equations using words. There are many different applications you can use. Some examples are car rentals, price per pound, cost per gallon, or dollars per hour.

1. Write a word statement for the function $y = 4x$.
   Answers will vary. Hamburger costs $4 per pound.
2. Write a word statement for the function $y = x$.
   Answers will vary. Frankie's supporters would pay a dollar for every mile she walked.
3. Write a word statement for the function $y = 0.10x + 100$.
   Answers will vary. The magazine paid $100 per article plus $.10 for every word written.

Lesson 9 ▸ Using Number Sense With Square Roots

Lesson Planner

Skills Maintenance

Solving Square Roots

Building Number Concepts:

▸ Using Number Sense With Square Roots

Even though we typically solve square roots with a calculator, it is important to build number sense about them. Students learn how to narrow down the location of a square root of a nonperfect square between lower and higher perfect squares. We use a number line to estimate square roots.

Objective

Students will use number sense and the number line to estimate square roots.

Homework

Students tell the perfect squares above and below the number, estimate the square roots, and answer true and false to questions about estimates for square roots. In Distributed Practice, students create *x*/*y* tables for each description of a function.

Lesson 9 | Skills Maintenance

Name ______ Date ______

Skills Maintenance
Solving Square Roots

Activity 1

Use a calculator to solve the square roots. Round your answers to the nearest tenth.

1. $\sqrt{32}$ ± 5.7
2. $\sqrt{48}$ ± 6.9
3. $\sqrt{62}$ ± 7.9
4. $\sqrt{80}$ ± 8.9
5. $\sqrt{99}$ ± 9.9

420 Unit 10 • Lesson 9

Skills Maintenance

Solving Square Roots

(*Interactive Text*, page 420)

Activity 1

Students solve square roots. Remind them to round their answers to the nearest tenths place.

Building Number Concepts: ▶ Using Number Sense With Square Roots

What are good estimates of square roots?

(*Student Text*, pages 840–841)

Connect to Prior Knowledge

Begin by playing a game with students called Guess My Number. Tell them that you are going to think of a number between 0 and 100. They are to guess your number, and you respond higher or lower until they guess your number.

Link to Today's Concept

Tell students that today's lesson involves a process like this to gain number sense about square roots. The process is called interpolation.

Demonstrate

Engagement Strategy: Teacher Modeling

Demonstrate how to use interpolation to estimate square roots in one of the following ways:

mBook: Use the *mBook Teacher Edition* for *Student Text,* pages 840–841. m

Overhead Projector: Display Transparency 6, and modify as discussed.

Board: Copy the number lines on the board, and modify as discussed.

- Tell students that most people do not have very good number sense about square roots. There are several reasons for this. One reason is that we normally use calculators to solve them. This is just a series of pushing buttons, and we do not get a clear sense of what is happening behind the scenes.

Lesson 9 | ▶Using Number Sense With Square Roots

▶Using Number Sense With Square Roots

What are good estimates of square roots?

It's difficult to have good number sense about square roots if we just use a calculator to compute our answer. In some ways, the square root button makes things too easy. Part of the problem is since most square roots are irrational numbers, we see a long string of decimal numbers. We don't think about where the square number is on the number line. We also lose our ability to find a good estimate of a square root if we are only using a calculator.

We can begin building our number sense by thinking about square roots and perfect square numbers. Let's say that we need to find the square root of 10. We begin by thinking about the perfect squares that are near 10.

Example 1

Find $\sqrt{10}$ without using a calculator.

The number line helps us think about the answer to this problem.

3   4

$\sqrt{9}$ $\sqrt{10}$ $\sqrt{11}$ $\sqrt{12}$ $\sqrt{13}$ $\sqrt{14}$ $\sqrt{15}$ $\sqrt{16}$

The number line shows us that $\sqrt{10}$ is between 3 and 4. It is also closer to 3.

840 Unit 10 • Lesson 9

- Explain that another reason is that the answer to most square root problems is an irrational number presented as a long string of decimal places. These numbers, although usually quite small, seem large to us just because they are made up of so many numerals. Tell students as example is **0.99999999999999999999999999**.
- Tell students that a good place to begin building number sense about square numbers is with perfect squares.
- Go over **Example 1**. Point out to students that we are building number sense about $\sqrt{10}$. We do this by thinking of the square numbers directly above it and below it. We use a number line to think about this. m

What are good estimates of square roots? *(continued)*

Demonstrate

- Remind students that there are many decimal numbers in between 3 and 4, such as 3.1, 3.2, 3.3, . . . , 3.9.
- Continue with Example 1. Point out to students that the square number below $\sqrt{\mathbf{10}}$ is $\sqrt{\mathbf{9}}$, which is the whole number 3, and the square number above $\sqrt{10}$ is $\sqrt{\mathbf{16}}$, which is the whole number 4. We can see this on the number line. Tell them that this means $\sqrt{10}$ is somewhere between **3** and **4**. m
- Tell students to look at the number line and try to get a sense of where $\sqrt{10}$ falls between the whole numbers 3 and 4. Point out that because 10 is closer to $\sqrt{9}$ than it is to $\sqrt{16}$, we know that it is closer to that end of the number line. We can make a good estimate that $\sqrt{10}$ is about **3.1** or **3.2**. m
- Have students calculate $\sqrt{10}$ with their calculators to see that the calculator answer is **3.162**. Point out that the estimate is fairly close. m

How do we find more exact square roots?

(*Student Text*, pages 841–842)

Demonstrate

- Tell students we can get an even closer estimate of square roots if we look at rational numbers. Direct students' attention to **Example 1** at the bottom of the page. In this example, we are estimating $\sqrt{\mathbf{21}}$.

Lesson 9

A good estimate for $\sqrt{10}$ on the number line is that it is between 3 and 4, but it is much closer to 3. We can use decimal numbers to make an even closer estimate of $\sqrt{10}$.

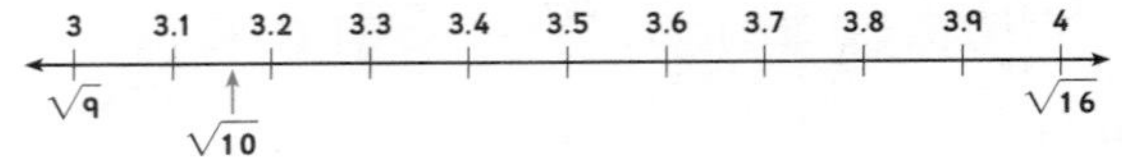

A more exact estimate of $\sqrt{10}$ would be 3.1 or 3.2.

Here is the calculator answer:
$\sqrt{10} = 3.162$

Our estimate was fairly close.

How do we find more exact square roots?

We just used a number line and perfect squares to find a good estimate of a square root. We can take this one step further. We can use a calculator to get an even more precise estimate of the square root of numbers. All we do is use the calculator for our multiplication.

Example 1

Use a calculator to estimate $\sqrt{21}$.

Find the value of $\sqrt{21}$.

STEP 1

Think about perfect squares we know above and below $\sqrt{21}$.

The perfect square below $\sqrt{21}$ is $\sqrt{16}$. We know $\sqrt{16} = 4$.

The perfect square above $\sqrt{21}$ is $\sqrt{25}$. We know $\sqrt{25} = 5$.

Unit 10 • Lesson 841

STEP 1

- Explain that the first step is to think about the perfect squares that surround $\sqrt{21}$. They are $\sqrt{\mathbf{16}}$ and $\sqrt{\mathbf{25}}$.

Demonstrate

- Have students turn to page 842 of the *Student Text*. Continue working through the steps in example 1.

STEP 2

- Point out the number line. Tell students we know the answer is somewhere between **4** and **5**, about in the middle, or **4.5**.

STEP 3

- Next tell students that we can get even closer by squaring the decimal numbers. Start with $\mathbf{4.5^2}$, or 4.5 times 4.5. It is **20.25**. Tell students that because this number is too low, we will try $\mathbf{4.6^2}$, or 4.6 times 4.6. It is **21.16**. Tell students that this number is just a little too high.
- Ask students if there is a number in between 4.5 and 4.6. Remind them that if we add another decimal place, we get a number in between.
- Next we try $\mathbf{4.58^2}$. Point out that this decimal number is just less than 4.6: $\mathbf{4.58^2 = 20.98}$.
- Tell students that we now have an estimate that is pretty close. We can keep adding decimal places to get even more exact but because $\sqrt{21}$ is irrational, we may never find the exact number.
- Have students find the square root using a calculator: $\sqrt{21}$ = **4.582575694955840006588047193728**.
- Point out the fact that the first three digits, **4.58**, are really all we need to check our estimate. It is very close.

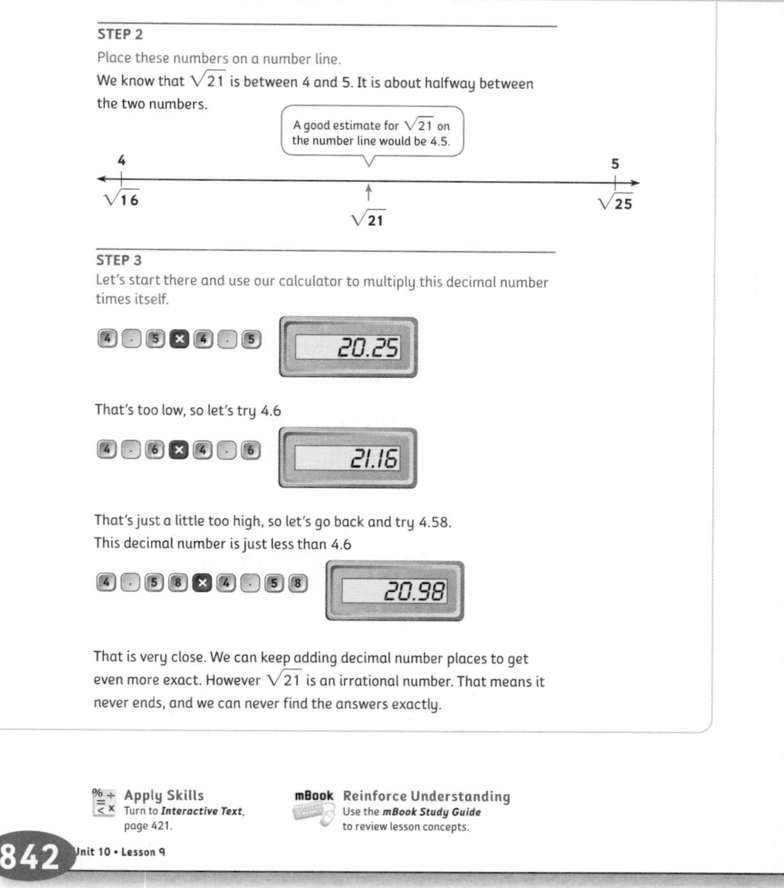

STEP 2

Place these numbers on a number line.

We know that $\sqrt{21}$ is between 4 and 5. It is about halfway between the two numbers.

STEP 3

Let's start there and use our calculator to multiply this decimal number times itself.

That's too low, so let's try 4.6

That's just a little too high, so let's go back and try 4.58.

This decimal number is just less than 4.6

That is very close. We can keep adding decimal number places to get even more exact. However $\sqrt{21}$ is an irrational number. That means it never ends, and we can never find the answers exactly.

Apply Skills
Turn to *Interactive Text*, page 421.

mBook Reinforce Understanding
Use the *mBook Study Guide* to review lesson concepts.

Check for Understanding

Engagement Strategy: Think Tank

Write the $\sqrt{8}$ on the board. Tell students that they will use good number sense and a number line to estimate the answer as close as possible. Distribute strips of paper and have students write their names and closest estimate without checking the answer on the calculator. When students finish, collect the strips in a container and draw out an answer. Have students check how close the estimate is to the calculator answer (*2.828427125*). Keep drawing out answers to see who gets the closest estimate.

Reinforce Understanding

If students need further practice, have them estimate the following. Answers should be close to given calculator answers.

$\sqrt{13}$ (*3.605551275*)

$\sqrt{29}$ (*5.385164807*)

Apply Skills

(*Interactive Text*, page 421)

Have students turn to page 421 in the *Interactive Text*, and complete the activity.

Activity 1

Students use the process of interpolation to estimate the square root of nonperfect squares using perfect squares as benchmarks. Monitor students' work as they complete the activity.

Watch for:

- Can students identify the upper- and lower-benchmark perfect squares?
- Can students use these benchmarks to estimate an answer?
- Can students compute the square root on the calculator and compare it to the estimate?

mBook Reinforce Understanding

Remind students that they can review lesson concepts by accessing the online *mBook Study Guide*.

Lesson 9 | Apply Skills

Name ______________ Date ______________

Apply Skills

Using Number Sense With Square Roots

Activity 1

Estimate the square roots. Use perfect squares to narrow down the location between two whole numbers. Compute the multiplication and square root on a calculator and compare them to find your estimate.

1. Estimate $\sqrt{32}$. It is between $\sqrt{25}$ and $\sqrt{36}$. Put the numbers on the number line:

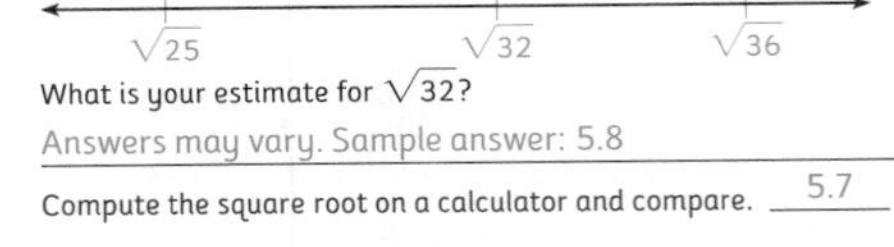

What is your estimate for $\sqrt{32}$?

Answers may vary. Sample answer: 5.8

Compute the square root on a calculator and compare. 5.7

2. Estimate $\sqrt{51}$. It is between $\sqrt{49}$ and $\sqrt{64}$. Put the numbers on the number line:

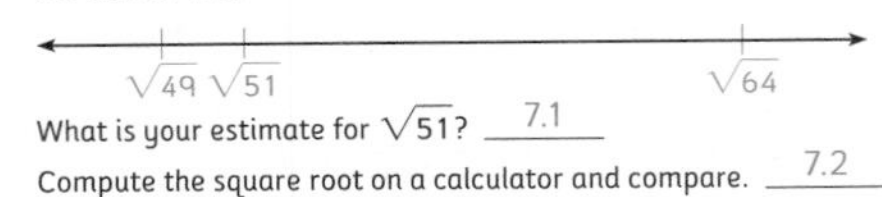

What is your estimate for $\sqrt{51}$? 7.1

Compute the square root on a calculator and compare. 7.2

3. Estimate $\sqrt{12}$. It is between $\sqrt{9}$ and $\sqrt{16}$. Put the numbers on the number line:

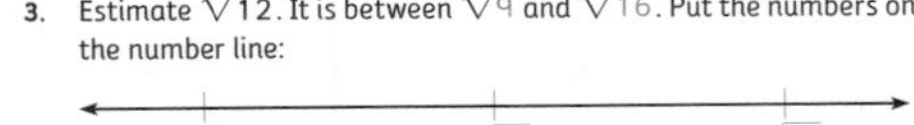

What is your estimate for $\sqrt{12}$? 3.5

Compute the square root on a calculator and compare. 3.5

4. Estimate $\sqrt{80}$. It is between $\sqrt{64}$ and $\sqrt{81}$. Put the numbers on the number line:

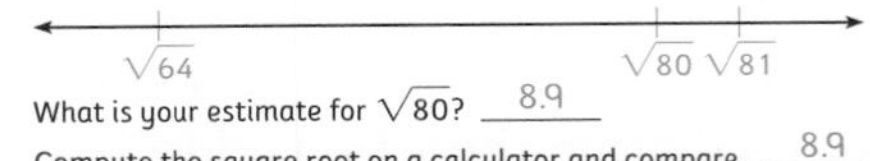

What is your estimate for $\sqrt{80}$? 8.9

Compute the square root on a calculator and compare. 8.9

Unit 10

Unit 10 • Lesson 9 421

Homework

Go over the instructions on page 843 of the *Student Text* for each part of the homework.

Activity 1

Students tell the perfect squares above and below the numbers.

Activity 2

Students estimate the answers using interpolation.

Activity 3

Students answer true and false to questions about estimates for square roots.

Activity 4 • Distributed Practice

Students create *x*/*y* tables for each description of a function.

Homework

Activity 1

Tell the perfect squares you would use above and below each of the numbers if you were estimating the square root.

1. $\sqrt{20}$ is between $\sqrt{?}$ and $\sqrt{?}$ 16 and 25
2. $\sqrt{90}$ is between $\sqrt{?}$ and $\sqrt{?}$ 81 and 100
3. $\sqrt{40}$ is between $\sqrt{?}$ and $\sqrt{?}$ 36 and 49
4. $\sqrt{30}$ is between $\sqrt{?}$ and $\sqrt{?}$ 25 and 36
5. $\sqrt{5}$ is between $\sqrt{?}$ and $\sqrt{?}$ 4 and 9

Activity 2

Estimate the square roots.

1. $\sqrt{105}$ 10.2
2. $\sqrt{88}$ 9.4
3. $\sqrt{39}$ 6.2
4. $\sqrt{2}$ 1.4
5. $\sqrt{55}$ 7.4

Activity 3

Use estimation and answer true or false.

1. A good estimate for $\sqrt{28}$ is 14. False
2. A good estimate for $\sqrt{57}$ is 7.5. True
3. A good estimate for $\sqrt{68}$ is 9. False
4. A good estimate for $\sqrt{14}$ is 2.4. False
5. A good estimate for $\sqrt{7}$ is 2.6. True

Activity 4 • Distributed Practice

Represent the functions given in words using *x*/*y* tables.

1. The cost of gas is $3.50 per gallon.
2. The rental car cost $25 per day.
3. Britt makes $10 per hour.

See Additional Answers below.

Additional Answers

Activity 4

1.

X	y
1	3.50
2	7.00
3	10.50
4	14.00
5	17.50

2.

X	y
1	25
2	50
3	75
4	100
5	125

3.

X	y
1	10
2	20
3	30
4	40
5	50

Lesson 10 | Unit Review ▶Square Roots and Irrational Numbers

Problem Solving:
▶Nonlinear Functions

Lesson Planner

Vocabulary Development

Pythagorean theorem
hypotenuse
square root
radical sign
perfect square numbers
irrational numbers
dependent variable
independent variable
parabola

Skills Maintenance

Exponents and Repeated Multiplication

Building Number Concepts:
▶ Square Roots and Irrational Numbers

Square roots are an important part of higher mathematics. On some occasions, we have perfect square numbers. The square root of a number is both positive and negative because of integer multiplication. Most of the time, however, the square root is an irrational number. The Pythagorean theorem is a common application of squared numbers and square roots. The Pythagorean theorem helps us find the length of an unknown side of any right triangle.

Problem Solving:
▶ Nonlinear Functions

This final unit shows students that functions do not have to be linear. Nonlinear functions in this unit have exponents with the *x* value. This topic also extends the role of the squared number, showing how it turns a straight line into a curve. The parabola is a key idea for the first part of the unit. By changing the constant, we can change the direction and/or the shape of the parabola.

Lesson 10 | Skills Maintenance

Name ______________ Date ______________

Skills Maintenance
Exponents and Repeated Multiplication

Activity 1

Rewrite each of the problems with exponents as repeated multiplication. Then use your calculator to solve.

Model	2^5 $2 \cdot 2 \cdot 2 \cdot 2 \cdot 2 = 32$

1. 3^4 $3 \cdot 3 \cdot 3 \cdot 3 = 81$
2. 4^2 $4 \cdot 4 = 16$
3. 5^3 $5 \cdot 5 \cdot 5 = 125$
4. 2^6 $2 \cdot 2 \cdot 2 \cdot 2 \cdot 2 \cdot 2 = 64$
5. 1^9 $1 \cdot 1 \cdot 1 \cdot 1 \cdot 1 \cdot 1 \cdot 1 \cdot 1 \cdot 1 = 1$

422 Unit 10 • Lesson 10

Skills Maintenance

Exponents and Repeated Multiplication
(*Interactive Text*, page 422)

Activity 1

Students rewrite each problem with exponents as repeated multiplication. Then they use a calculator to solve.

Building Number Concepts: ▶ Square Roots and Irrational Numbers

Why is a square root important?
(*Student Text*, pages 844–847)

Discuss

Begin by drawing a square on the board or overhead. Write near the square **Area = 25 square units.** Tell the students it is a square and ask them what the length of each side is.

Listen for:

- *5 units*

Next, erase the 25, and write 20 square units and ask the same question.

Listen for:

- *Square root of 20*
- *Not a whole number*

Discuss how even the easiest problems such as this are not that easy to solve. Remind students that they worked area problems for a long time, but usually they are given the lengths of the sides or base and height and then we calculate area. Working backward like this reminds us that we cannot always measure distance in whole numbers or even simple decimal numbers.

Remind students of the term exponent, and discuss its relationship to what we looked at in this unit.

Demonstrate

- Look at **Review 1** and point out the equation $\mathbf{2x^2 + 1 = 29}$. Work through each of the steps to solve the equation.
- Make sure students understand that they can use all the rules and properties from their toolbox to solve equations involving squared numbers and those with square roots.
- Explain to students that when they need to take the square root of an expression like x^2, they need to use the same kind of thinking that they do when they add a negative number to each side of the equation or multiply each side by a reciprocal. In other words, they take the square root of the expressions on each side of the equation.

Lesson 10 | Unit Review
▶Square Roots and Irrational Numbers
Problem Solving:
▶Nonlinear Functions

▶Square Roots and Irrational Numbers

Why is a square root important?

In secondary mathematics, we spend a lot of time working with numbers that have exponents. Many times, these are square numbers like the one shown in the algebraic equation. Solving for *x* means that we need to find a square root.

Review 1

How do we use square roots to solve equations?

$$2x^2 + 1 = 29$$
$$2x^2 + 1 + -1 = 29 + -1$$
$$2x^2 = 28$$
$$\frac{1}{2} \cdot 2x^2 = 28 \cdot \frac{1}{2}$$
$$\frac{2}{2}x^2 = \frac{28}{2}$$
$$x^2 = 14$$
$$\sqrt{x^2} = \sqrt{14}$$
$$x = 3.74$$

One formula that helps us find the square root of a number is the Pythagorean theorem. Most of the time, the hypotenuse of a right triangle does not have an exact integer length. Square roots allow us to find the length of the hypotenuse.

844 Unit 10 • Lesson 10

Why is a square root important? *(continued)*

Demonstrate

- Next have students turn to page 845 of the *Student Text* to go over **Review 2**, which reminds students of the formula for the Pythagorean theorem. Like the square problem in the opening activity, the theorem, as well as the idea of square roots, helps us figure out the length of an unknown side.
- Point out the substitution of **6** and **4** into the formula, and walk through the computations to find that $c = 7.21$.
- Remind students that the unknown side does not always have to be the hypotenuse.
- Remind students of the importance of good number sense when working with square roots. Point out that we can think of our multiplication facts and our integer rules to find square roots of numbers.

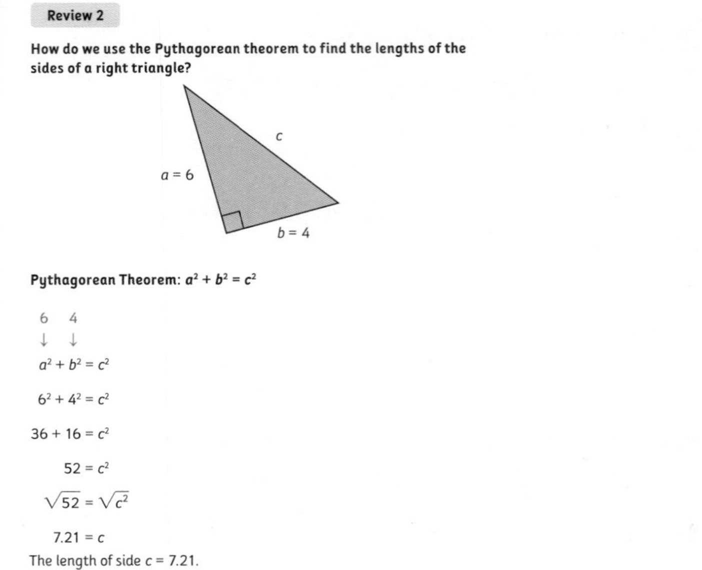

Lesson 10
Review 2
How do we use the Pythagorean theorem to find the lengths of the sides of a right triangle?
c
a = 6
b = 4
Pythagorean Theorem: $a^2 + b^2 = c^2$
6 4
↓ ↓
$a^2 + b^2 = c^2$
$6^2 + 4^2 = c^2$
$36 + 16 = c^2$
$52 = c^2$
$\sqrt{52} = \sqrt{c^2}$
$7.21 = c$
The length of side $c = 7.21$.
Unit 10 • Lesson 1
845

Demonstrate

- Have students turn to page 846 of the *Student Text*. It is important to review the fact that there are two square roots of positive integers.
- Have students look at the table in **Review 3** where we show perfect square numbers and their positive and negative roots. Ask students why a positive and a negative number are possible.

Listen for:

- *A number times itself makes a perfect square number. That means the first number you multiply is the square root.*
- *When you multiply a negative times a negative number, you get a positive number.*

- Finally, move on to a discussion of irrational numbers with **Review 4**. Ask students what the properties are of irrational numbers and how they relate to square roots.

Listen for:

- *Most square roots are irrational numbers.*
- *Irrational numbers don't end, and they don't have repeated patterns.*

We need to do more than use a calculator in order to work with square roots. We still need good number sense. We can find some square roots just by noticing that the number is a perfect square number. If we think of our multiplication facts and what we know about multiplying two negative numbers, we can find the square roots for that number.

Review 3

What are some perfect square numbers and their square roots?

Perfect Square Number	Square Roots
4	2 and −2
16	4 and −4
81	9 and −9
100	10 and −10

Most of the time it isn't this easy. When we use a calculator to find the square root of a number such as 15, we notice it's a decimal number with a long string of decimal places.

Review 4

What are irrational numbers?

Numbers like $\sqrt{15}$ do not end and they do not follow a pattern.

$\sqrt{15} = 3.872983...$

These square roots are irrational numbers, or decimal numbers that do not terminate or repeat.

We can still use good number sense to find square roots by remembering that perfect square numbers are around a number like 15.

Why is a square root important? (*continued*)

Demonstrate

- Move to page 847 of the *Student Text* to look at **Review 5**.
- Remind students that although calculators are always helpful, we can still use our number sense to make good estimates of square roots.
- As Review 5 indicates, the perfect square numbers that surround a target number like 15 are our starting point.
- Explain that number lines on paper or mental number lines can give us a sense of which perfect square the target number is closest to. We can use this information to estimate what the square root is.
- Demonstrate finding an estimate of $\sqrt{15}$ by using the number line. Point out that we know it is between the perfect square numbers of $\sqrt{9}$ and $\sqrt{16}$ but much closer to $\sqrt{16}$.
- Remind students that we can use decimal numbers to make a closer estimate. We can check against the calculator answer of **3.87** to see that our estimate of 3.8 or 3.9 is close.

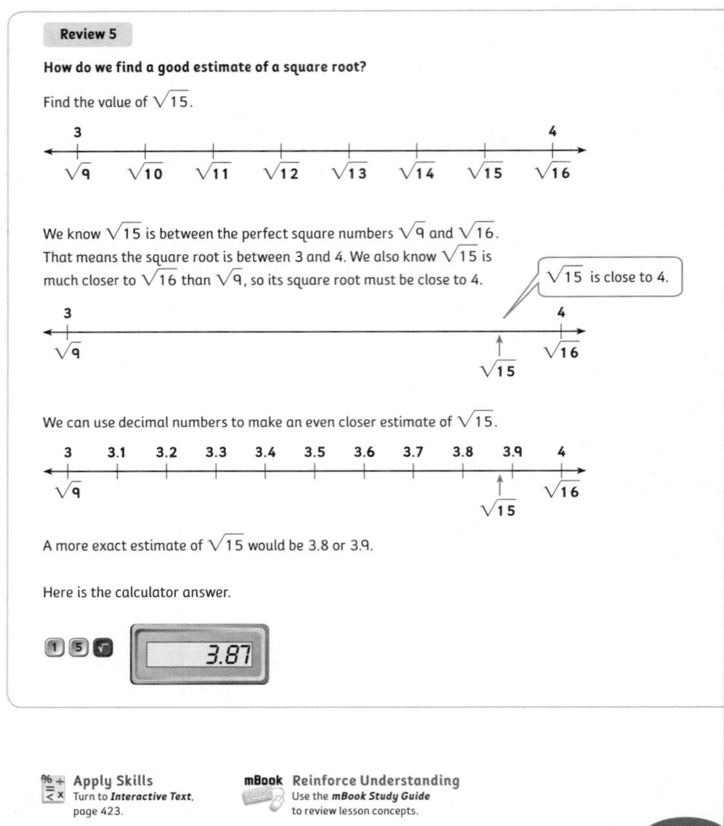

Lesson 10
Review 5
How do we find a good estimate of a square root?
Find the value of $\sqrt{15}$.
3
4
$\sqrt{9}$ $\sqrt{10}$ $\sqrt{11}$ $\sqrt{12}$ $\sqrt{13}$ $\sqrt{14}$ $\sqrt{15}$ $\sqrt{16}$
We know $\sqrt{15}$ is between the perfect square numbers $\sqrt{9}$ and $\sqrt{16}$. That means the square root is between 3 and 4. We also know $\sqrt{15}$ is much closer to $\sqrt{16}$ than $\sqrt{9}$, so its square root must be close to 4.
$\sqrt{15}$ is close to 4.
We can use decimal numbers to make an even closer estimate of $\sqrt{15}$.
3 3.1 3.2 3.3 3.4 3.5 3.6 3.7 3.8 3.9 4
A more exact estimate of $\sqrt{15}$ would be 3.8 or 3.9.
Here is the calculator answer.
3.87
Apply Skills
Turn to *Interactive Text*, page 423.
mBook Reinforce Understanding
Use the *mBook Study Guide* to review lesson concepts.
Unit 10 • Lesson 1
847

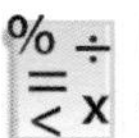

Unit Review: Square Roots and Irrational Numbers

(*Interactive Text*, pages 423–425)

Have students turn to pages 423–425 in the *Interactive Text*, and complete Activities 1–5.

Activity 1

Students use calculators to find square roots. They round their answers to the nearest hundredths place.

Activity 2

Students solve equations involving exponents.

Activity 3

Students find the value of x in equations involving exponents and radicals.

Activity 4

Students estimate square roots using number lines.

Name ______ Date ______

Unit Review

Square Roots and Irrational Numbers

Activity 1

Use a calculator to find the square roots for the numbers in the table. Round your answer to the nearest hundredth.

Number	Square Roots
20	4.47
32	5.66
45	6.71
61	7.81

Activity 2

Solve the equations with square roots. Remember that anything to the 0 power is 1.

1. $2^2 + 2^3$ 12
2. 3^0 3
3. $4^2 + 4^2$ 32
4. $3^0 + 2^2$ 7
5. $2^0 + 2^3$ 10
6. $100^0 + 2^2$ 104
7. $2^2 + 5^0$ 9
8. $3^2 + 3^0$ 12

Activity 3

Find the value of x.

1. $\sqrt{3 + x} = 4$ $x =$ 13
2. $x^2 = 64$ $x =$ 8
3. $x^2 + 9 = 25$ $x =$ 4
4. $\sqrt{4x} = 8$ $x =$ 16
5. $2x^2 = 50$ $x =$ 5

Unit 10

Name ______ Date ______

Activity 4

Use what you know about square numbers to estimate the number in each problem. Use the number line to show how you figured out your answer.

1. $\sqrt{20}$

   Show the perfect square numbers around 20 and where $\sqrt{20}$ would be on the number line.

   16 20 25

   What is your estimated answer of $\sqrt{20}$? 4.5

2. $\sqrt{27}$

   Show the perfect square numbers around 27 and where $\sqrt{27}$ would be on the number line.

   25 27 36

   What is your estimated answer of $\sqrt{27}$? 5.2

3. $\sqrt{35}$

   Show the perfect square numbers around 35 and where $\sqrt{35}$ would be on the number line.

   25 27 36

   What is your estimated answer of $\sqrt{35}$? 5.9

Activity 5

Students find the missing side length of right triangles using the Pythagorean theorem.

Monitor students' work as they complete the activities.

Watch for:

- Are students able to read square roots from their calculators and round numbers to the nearest hundredth?
- Do students remember the Pythagorean theorem and how to apply it to an unknown side?
- Do students have a good sense of perfect square numbers, and do they know where the target number is in relation to these square numbers? Do they transfer this relationship to square roots?

Once students finish, discuss any difficulties that you noticed.

Reinforce Understanding

Remind students that they can review lesson concepts by accessing the online *mBook Study Guide*.

Name ______________________ Date ______________________

Activity 5

Find the missing side length for each of the right triangles using the Pythagorean Theorem. Round to the hundredth.

1. What is the length of side *a*? 3.61
   Show your work here.

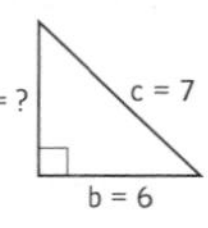

2. What is the length of side *b*? 4.36
   Show your work here.

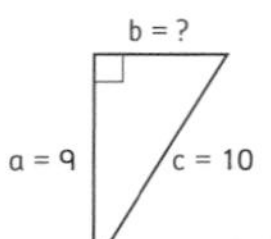

3. What is the length of side *c*? 11.18
   Show your work here.

a = 10
c
b = 5

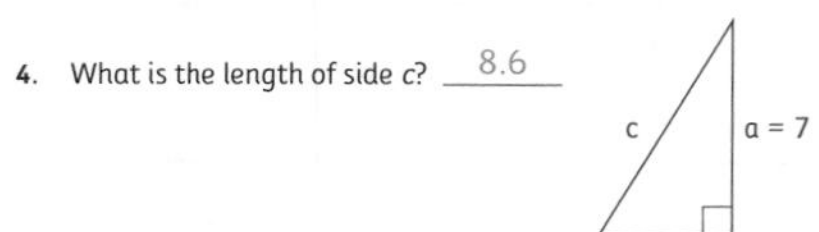

4. What is the length of side *c*? 8.6

c
a = 7
b = 5

5. What is the length of side *a*? 8

c = 10
a
b = 6

Unit 10

Problem Solving:
▶ Nonlinear Functions

What is the difference between linear and nonlinear functions?

(*Student Text*, pages 848–851)

Discuss

Turn to page 848 of the *Student Text*. Begin by reviewing the equation for linear functions, $\boldsymbol{y = mx + b}$, stressing the key vocabulary of slope and y-intercept. Also emphasize that the y-intercept is constant although the mx portion of the expression changes because of the fact that we substitute values for x.

Demonstrate

- Move to **Review 1**, and go over the values in the x/y table. Remind students that we can use these values to create a graph.

Lesson 10

▶Problem Solving: Nonlinear Functions

What is the difference between linear and nonlinear functions?

The linear functions that we studied in Unit 9 are based on a special equation. The key parts of the equation are slope and y-intercept.

Equation for a Linear Function

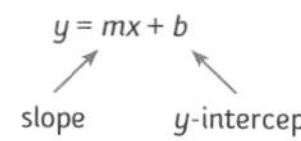

When we substitute values into the equation, we can create a line on a coordinate graph. It is important to notice that the y-intercept is constant. It does not change. It is the mx part of the equation that changes. That is because we are substituting different values for x.

Review 1

What does a linear function look like on a graph?

Let $b = 3$

Let $m = 2$

We can substitute these values from our x/y table to create a graph.

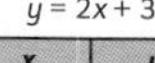

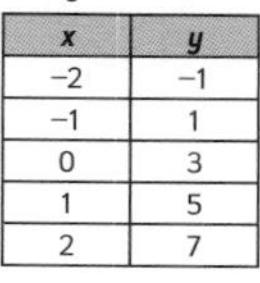

x	y
−2	−1
−1	1
0	3
1	5
2	7

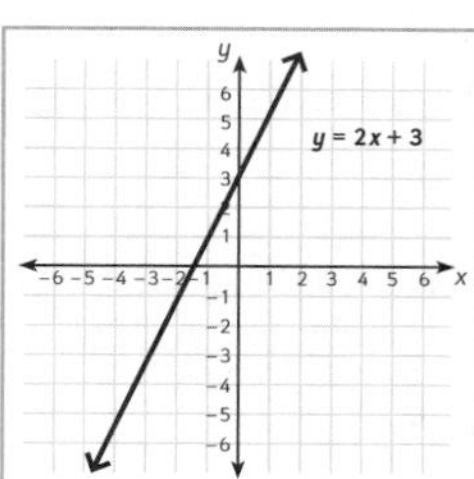

848 Unit 10 • Lesson 10

What is the difference between linear and nonlinear functions? *(continued)*

Demonstrate

- Have students turn to page 849 of the *Student Text*. Remind them of the integer multiplication rule: A negative times a negative is always positive.
- Move to **Review 2**, which shows why the y values in the nonlinear function $\boldsymbol{y = x^2}$ are never negative.
- Go over the x and y values in the table and then review the graph.
- Stress the role of the exponent in changing a straight line into a curve, and in this case, the result is a parabola.

The nonlinear functions that we studied in this unit have exponents as part of the equation. When x is squared or when it has a higher exponent, the shape of the line changes from a straight line to a curve. This makes sense when we look at a simple x/y table for the function $y = x^2$. In this case, the value of y is never negative because x is always squared. A negative number times a negative number is always positive.

Review 2

What does a nonlinear function look like on a graph?

$y = x^2$

x	y
−3	9
−2	4
−1	1
0	0
1	1
2	4
3	9

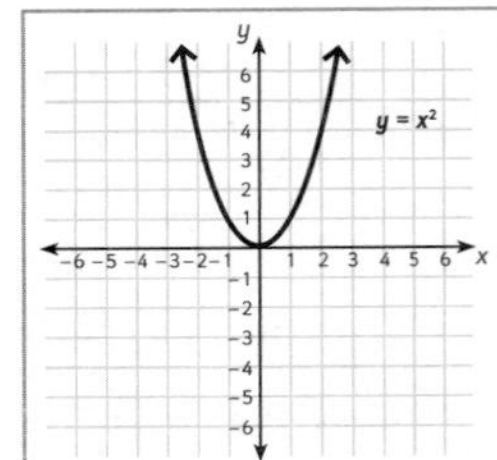

We can change the shape and direction of a nonlinear function by changing the coefficient in front of the x-variable. We can make the parabola wider or thinner depending upon how large the coefficient is. Negative coefficients make the parabola point down.

Demonstrate

- Turn to page 850 of the *Student Text* to look at **Review 3**. Remind students of the role of a constant in simple nonlinear functions.
- Point out that, as the example shows, when we vary the constant, we can change the shape of the parabola.
- Remind students that when we change the coefficient to $\frac{1}{2}$, the parabola becomes wider as we see in the function $\boldsymbol{y = \frac{1}{2}x^2}$.

Review 3

How can we change the direction and shape of a nonlinear function?

Begin with a simple nonlinear function.

$y = x^2$

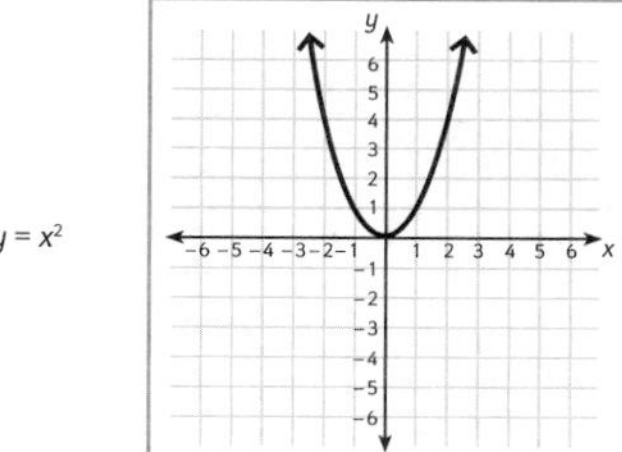

Change the shape by making the coefficient $\frac{1}{2}$. This makes the parabola wider.

$y = \frac{1}{2}x^2$

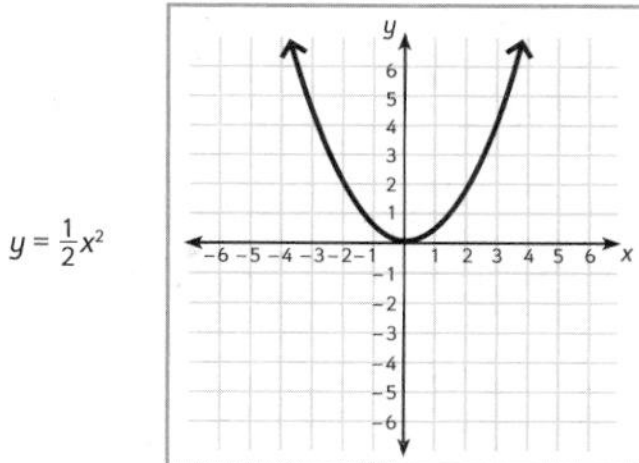

We can make the parabola steeper by changing the coefficient from $\frac{1}{2}$ to 3.

What is the difference between linear and nonlinear functions? *(continued)*

Demonstrate

- Continue with Review 3 on page 851 of the *Student Text.*
- Have students look at the graphs for the functions $y = 3x^2$ and $y = -3x^2$.
- Remind students that by using a negative constant, we can invert the direction of the parabola.

$y = 3x^2$

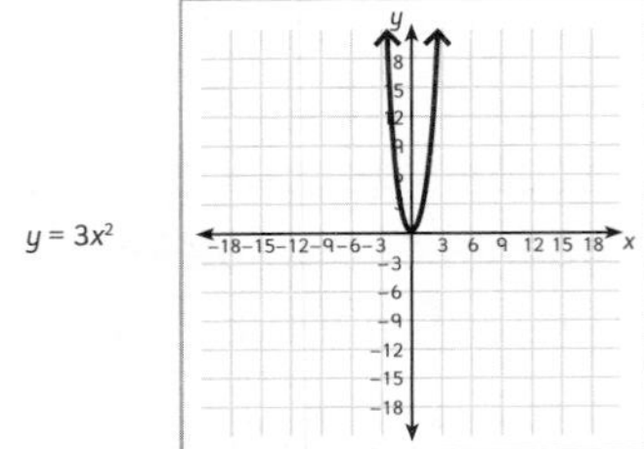

Finally, we can flip over the parabola by making the coefficient negative.

$y = -3x^2$

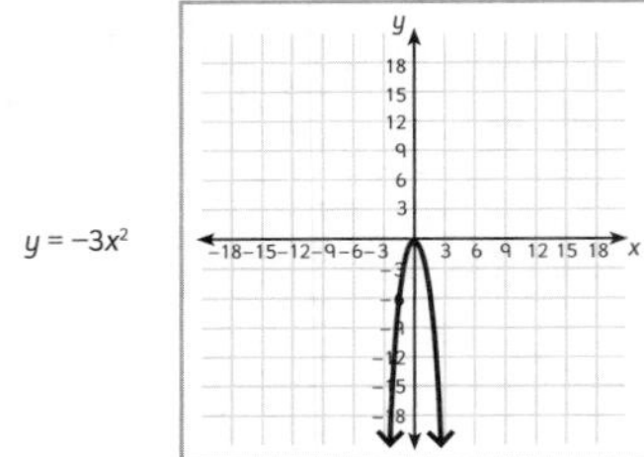

What are other nonlinear functions?
(*Student Text*, page 852)

Demonstrate

- Finally, turn to page 852 of the *Student Text* to review another type of nonlinear function, $\boldsymbol{y = x^3}$.
- Have students look at the graph, and point out that the graph is in Quadrants I and III.

What are other nonlinear functions?

We learned about another nonlinear function, $y = x^3$. This function is different from $y = x^2$.

Review 1

What does the function $y = x^3$ look like?

Look at the graph of $y = x^3$.

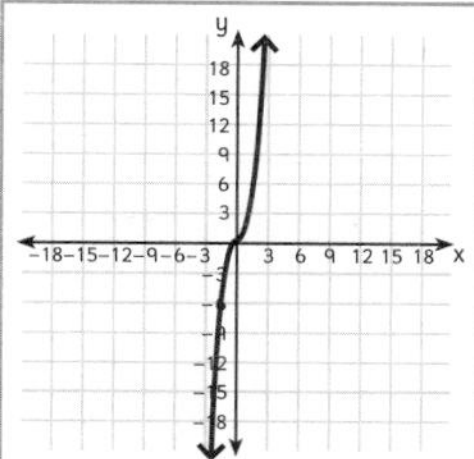

This graph is very different from the graph of $y = x^2$. We see that the graph is in Quadrants I and III, and that it is narrower than the graph of $y = x^2$.

We will learn about other nonlinear graphs as we continue to study mathematics.

Problem-Solving Activity
Turn to ***Interactive Text***, page 426.

mBook Reinforce Understanding
Use the ***mBook Study Guide*** to review lesson concepts.

Unit Review: Nonlinear Functions

(*Interactive Text*, pages 426–428)

Have students turn to pages 426–428 in the *Interactive Text*, and complete Activities 1–3.

Activity 1

Students graph linear functions using the *x* and *y* values in tables.

Activity 2

Students complete the table by filling the *y* values into the table. Then they graph the nonlinear function.

Activity 3

Students complete the tables by filling the *x* and *y* values into the table using the functions. Then they identify the corresponding graph.

Monitor students' work as they complete the activities.

Watch for:

- Can students complete tables accurately based on the functions?
- Can students appropriately select graphs based on tables?
- Do students know how to apply exponential growth?

Lesson 10 | Unit Review

Name ________________ Date ________________

Unit Review
Non-Linear Functions

Activity 1

For each of the *x/y* tables, write the linear function using an equation. Then graph the function.

1.

x	y
1	3
2	6
3	9
4	12
5	15

What is the function? $x \cdot 3 = y$

2.

x	y
1	4
2	8
3	12
4	16
5	20

What is the function? $x + 4 = y$

426 Unit 10 • Lesson 10

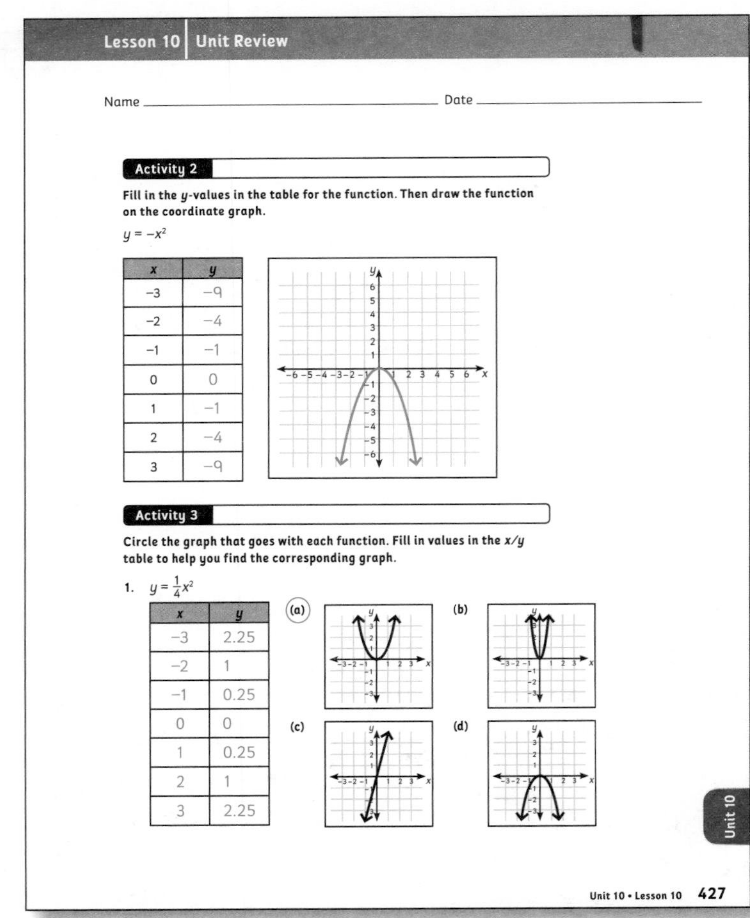

Lesson 10 | Unit Review

Name ________________ Date ________________

Activity 2

Fill in the *y*-values in the table for the function. Then draw the function on the coordinate graph.

$y = -x^2$

x	y
−3	−9
−2	−4
−1	−1
0	0
1	−1
2	−4
3	−9

Activity 3

Circle the graph that goes with each function. Fill in values in the *x/y* table to help you find the corresponding graph.

1. $y = \frac{1}{4}x^2$

x	y
−3	2.25
−2	1
−1	0.25
0	0
1	0.25
2	1
3	2.25

(a) (b) (c) (d)

Unit 10

Unit 10 • Lesson 10 427

Once students finish the activities, discuss any difficulties that you noticed.

mBook **Reinforce Understanding**
Remind students that they can review lesson concepts by accessing the online *mBook Study Guide*.

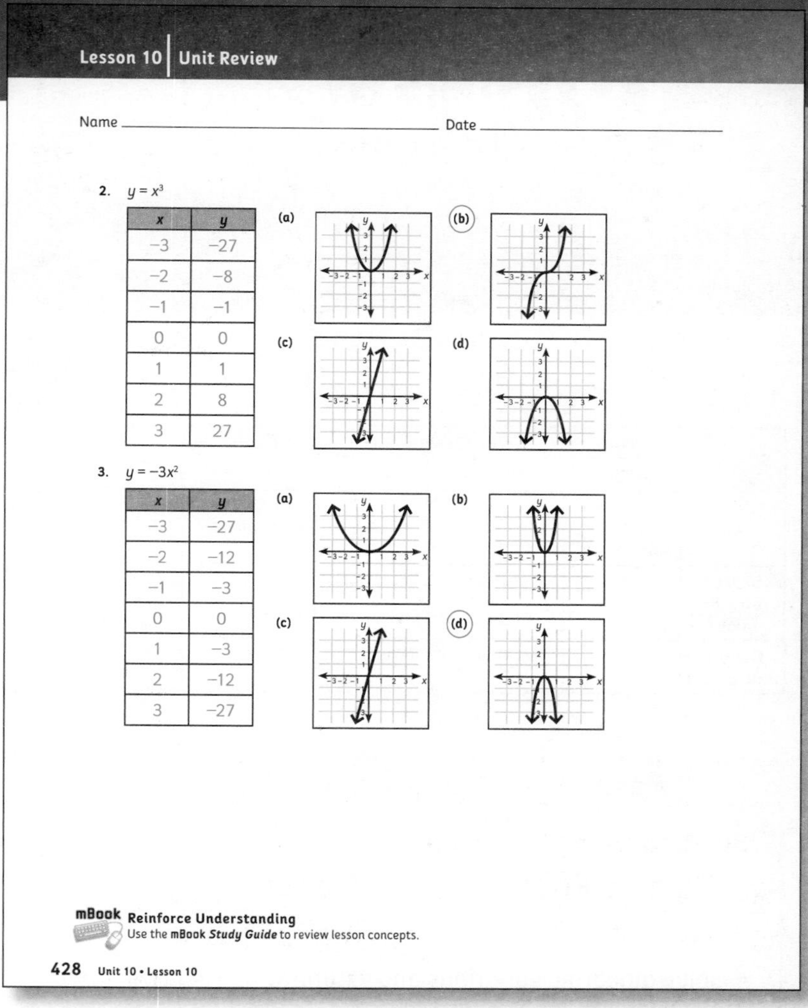

Name ______________________ Date ______________

2. $y = x^3$

x	y
−3	−27
−2	−8
−1	−1
0	0
1	1
2	8
3	27

(a) (b) (c) (d)

3. $y = -3x^2$

x	y
−3	−27
−2	−12
−1	−3
0	0
1	−3
2	−12
3	−27

(a) (b) (c) (d)

mBook **Reinforce Understanding**
Use the mBook *Study Guide* to review lesson concepts.

Assessment Planner

Students	Assess	Differentiate		Assess
	Day 1	Day 2	Day 3	Day 4
All	End-of-Unit Assessment *Form A*			Performance Assessments
Scored 80% or above		Extension	Extension	
Scored Below 80%		Reinforcement	Retest	

Assessment Objectives

Building Number Concepts:

▶ Square Roots and Irrational Numbers

- Solve algebraic equations and estimate answers involving square roots
- Use the Pythagorean theorem to find the lengths of sides of right triangles
- Identify and use irrational numbers

Problem Solving:

▶ Nonlinear Functions

- Tell whether a function is linear or nonlinear given a table, equation, or graph
- Graph nonlinear functions on a coordinate graph
- Understand the role of the coefficient in a nonlinear function

Monitoring Progress: ▶ Unit Assessments

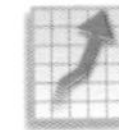

Assess
End-of-Unit Assessment

- Administer End-of-Unit Assessment Form A in the *Assessment Book*, pages 91–93.

Differentiate

- Review End-of-Unit Assessment Form A with class.
- Identify students for Extension or Reinforcement.

Extension
For those students who score 80 percent or better, provide the On Track! Activities from Unit 10, Lessons 6–10, from the *mBook Teacher Edition.*

Reinforcement
For those students who score below 80 percent, provide additional support in one of these ways:

- Have students access the online tutorial provided in the *mBook Study Guide.*
- Have students complete the Interactive Reinforcement Exercises for Unit 10, in the *mBook Study Guide.*
- Provide teacher-directed reteaching of unit concepts.

Retest
Administer End-of Unit Assessment Form B from the *mBook Teacher Edition* to those students who scored below 80 percent on Form A.

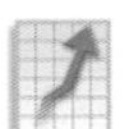

Assess
Performance Assessments

- Guide students through the Performance Assessment Model on *Assessment Book*, page 95. Then, administer the Performance Assessments on pages 96–97.

Name ______________________ Date ______________________

Form A

Monitoring Progress
Square Roots and Irrational Numbers

Part 1

Answer the questions about square roots.

1. Write the square roots for these numbers. Do not use a calculator.

Number	Square Roots
49	7
25	5
81	9
64	8

2. Use a calculator to find the square roots for these numbers. Round your answer to the nearest hundredth.

Number	Square Roots
24	4.90
40	6.32
54	7.35
82	9.06

Part 2

Use the Pythagorean theorem to solve. Round your answer to the nearest hundredth.

1. What is the length of side b? 8.94

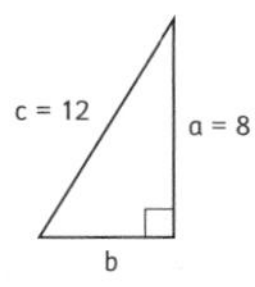

2. What is the length of side c? 8.6

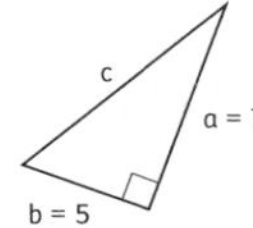

Part 3

Find the value of *x*.

1. $\sqrt{x} - 8 = 5$ 33
2. $x^2 = 64$ 8
3. $x^2 - 3 = 22$ 5
4. $\sqrt{4x} = 8$ 16
5. $\sqrt{4x^2} = 6$ 3

Unit 10

Part 4

Find a good estimate of the square root of the number. Use the number line to show how you figured out your answer.

1. $\sqrt{20}$ Answers will vary. Answers should be around 4.47

Show the perfect square numbers around 20.

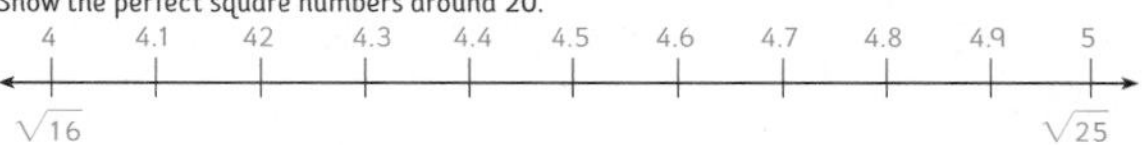

Show where $\sqrt{20}$ would be on the number line here.

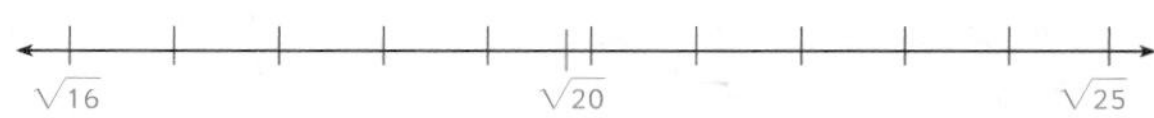

2. $\sqrt{8}$ Answers will vary. Answer should be around 2.83

Show the perfect square numbers around 20.

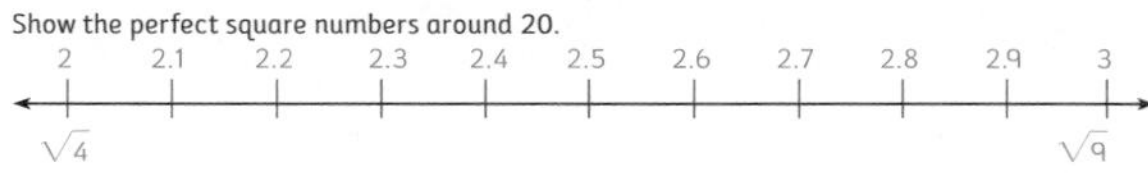

Show where $\sqrt{8}$ would be on the number line here.

3. $\sqrt{57}$ Answers will vary. Answer should be around 7.55

Show the perfect square numbers around 57.

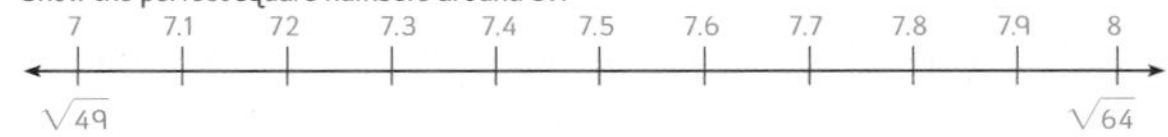

Show where $\sqrt{57}$ would be on the number line here.

Name ______________________ Date ______________________

Monitoring Progress
Non-linear Functions

Part 5

Fill in the *y* values in the table for this function. Then draw the function.

1. $y = x^2$

x	y
−2	4
−1	1
0	0
1	1
2	4

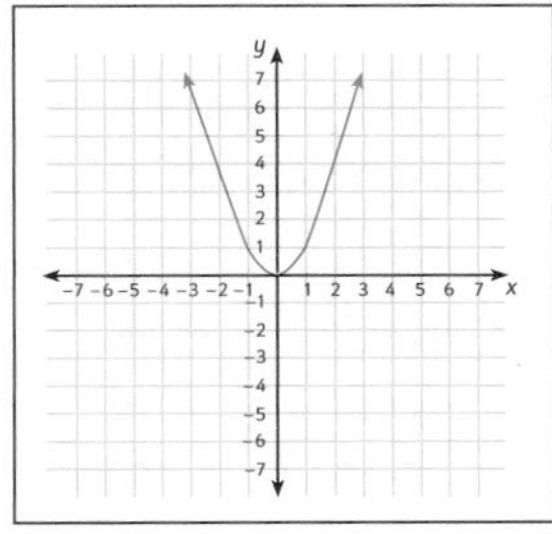

Part 6

Circle the graph that shows the function. Fill in the *y* values in the *x/y* table.

1. $y = \frac{1}{2}x^2$

x	y
−6	18
−4	8
−2	2
0	0
2	2
4	8

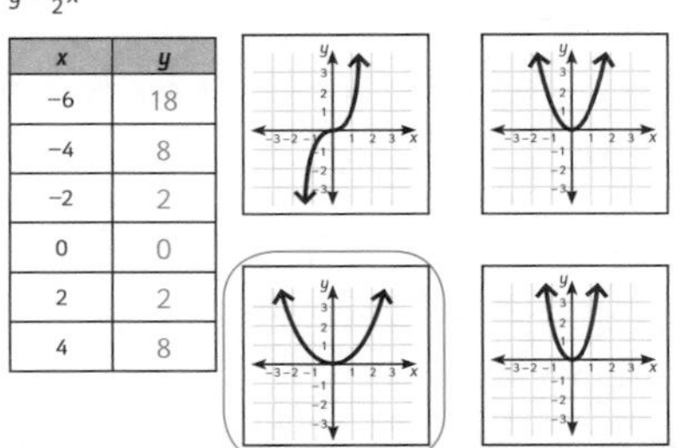

Unit 10

Name ______________________ Date ______________________

Form B

mBook

Monitoring Progress
Square Roots and Irrational Numbers

Part 1

Answer the questions about square roots.

1. Write the square roots for these numbers. Do not use a calculator.

Number	Square Roots
36	6
16	4
100	10
25	5

2. Use a calculator to find the square roots for these numbers. Round your answer to the nearest hundredth.

Number	Square Roots
21	4.58
37	6.08
44	6.63
72	8.49

Part 2

Use the Pythagorean theorem to solve. Round your answer to the nearest hundredth.

1. What is the length of side *b*? 7.14

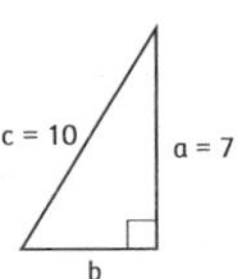

2. What is the length of side *c*? 7.21

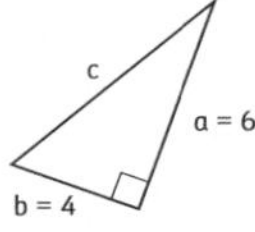

Part 3

Find the value of *x*.

1. $\sqrt{x} - 10 = 5$ 225
2. $x^2 = 81$ 9
3. $x^2 - 5 = 31$ 6
4. $\sqrt{6x} = 8$ 10.67
5. $5x^2 = 125$ 5

Name ________________ Date ________________

Part 4

Find a good estimate of the square root of the number. Use the number line to show how you figured out your answer.

1. $\sqrt{32}$ Answers will vary. Answers should be around 5.6

Show the perfect square numbers around 32.

Show where $\sqrt{32}$ would be on the number line here.

2. $\sqrt{12}$ Answers will vary. Answer should be around 3.46

Show the perfect square numbers around 12.

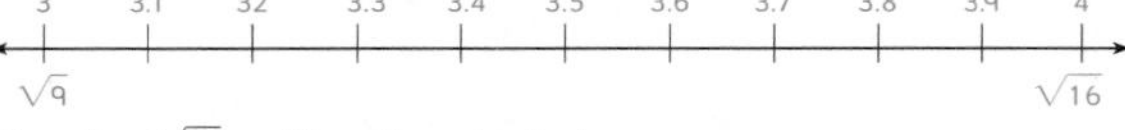

Show where $\sqrt{12}$ would be on the number line here.

3. $\sqrt{47}$ Answers will vary. Answer should be around 6.86

Show the perfect square numbers around 47.

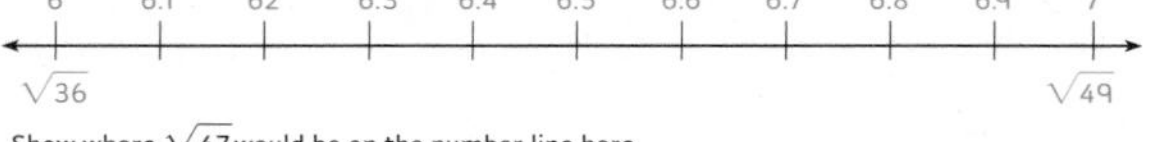

Show where $\sqrt{47}$ would be on the number line here.

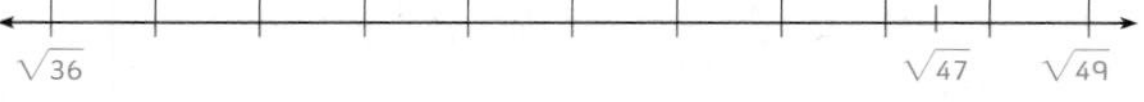

Name ________________ Date ________________

Monitoring Progress
Non-Linear Functions

Part 5

Fill in the y values in the table for this function. Then draw the function.

1. $y = x^2$

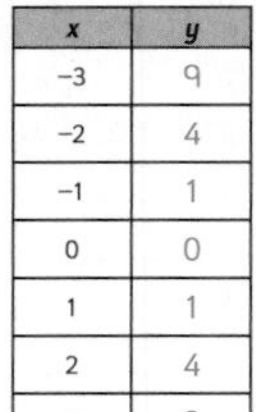

x	y
−3	9
−2	4
−1	1
0	0
1	1
2	4
3	9

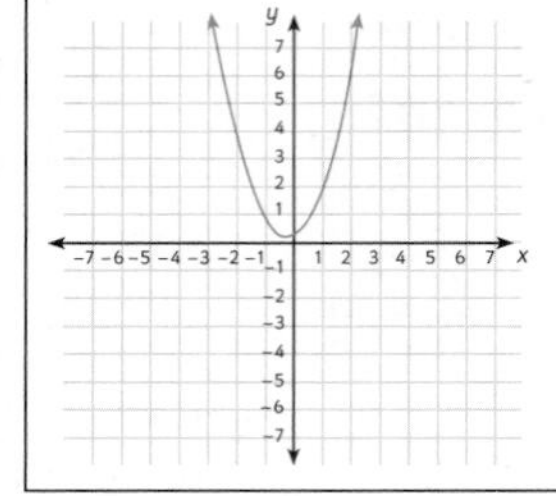

Part 6

Circle the graph that shows the function. Fill in the y values in the x/y table.

1. $y = \frac{1}{2}x^2$

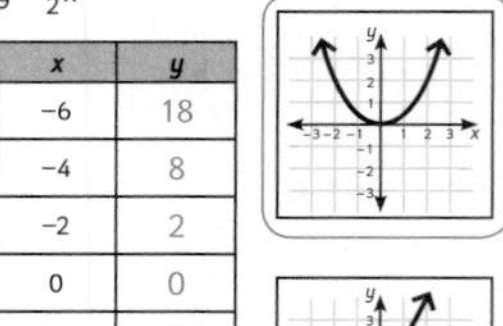

x	y
−6	18
−4	8
−2	2
0	0
2	2
4	8
6	16

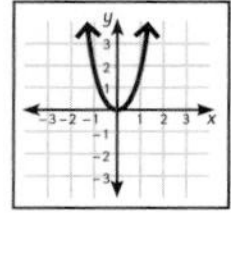

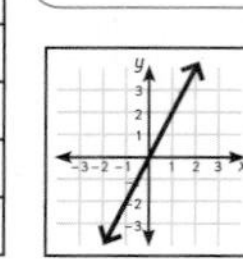

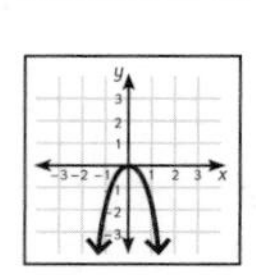

Name ________________ Date ________________

Monitoring Progress
Practice Problem 3-10

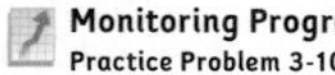

Solve the Problem

The picture shows a rocket that can be launched into space. The rocket carries 500 pounds of rocket fuel. Remember, this symbol ∟ means it is a right angle.

What is the measure of side a?

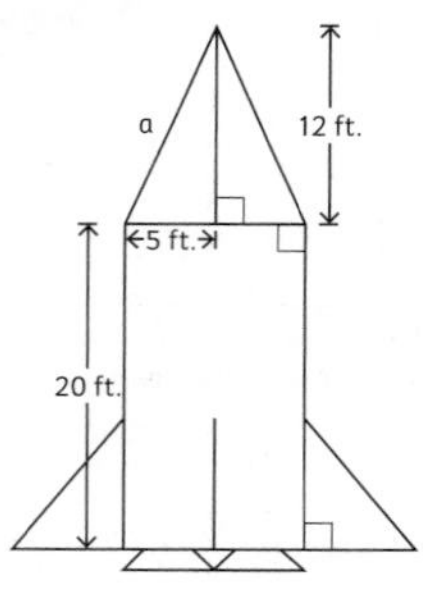

(a) 5 feet
(b) 13 feet
(c) 20 feet
(d) 500 feet

(The answer is b.)

Monitoring Progress
Problem 3-10-A

Solve the Problem

What is the measure of side d?

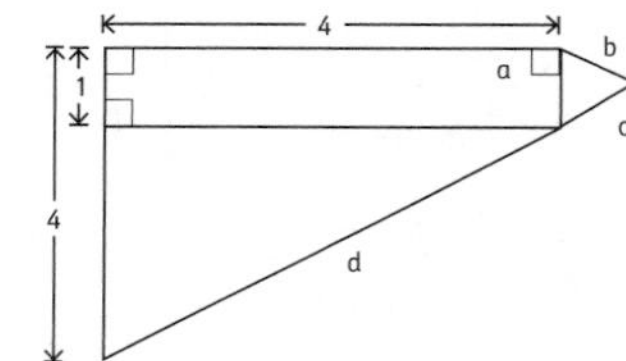

(a) 3.5 units
(b) 4 units
(c) 5 units (circled)
(d) 6.5 units

Name ______________________ Date ______________________

Monitoring Progress
Problem 3-10-B

Solve the Problem

Use your calculator to find the measure of side m.

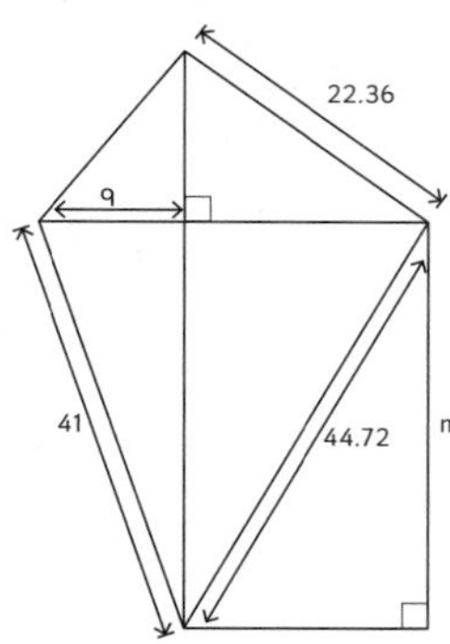

Explain Your Thinking

Explain how you found your answer.

40. Sample answer: To find the height I subtracted $41^2 - 9^2$. Then I took the square root of that number to find the line parallel to *m*. Since they were the same length I knew *m* was also 40.

Appendix

Additional Homework Answers
Student Text, page 729

Unit 9

Lesson 7—page 729

Activity 3

1.

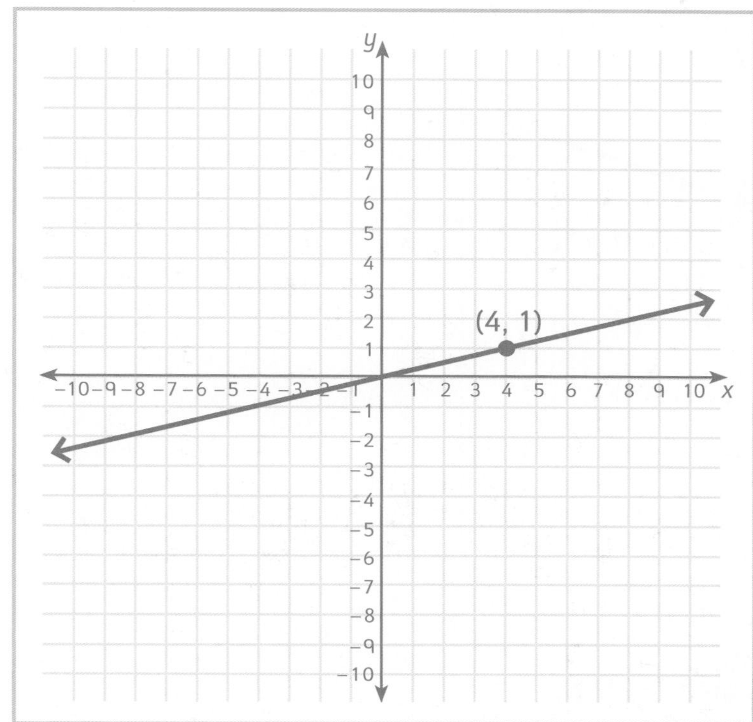

2.

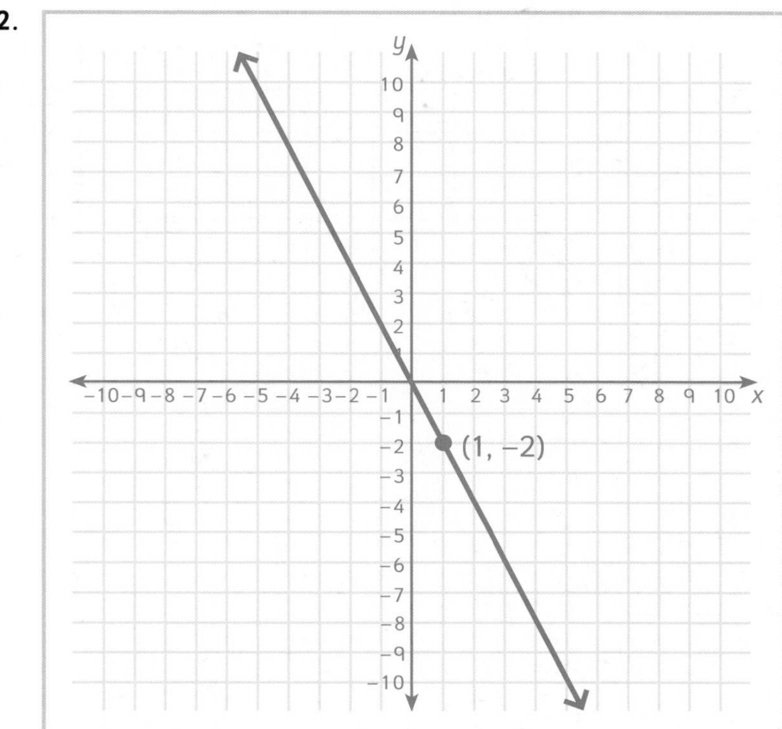

Additional Homework Answers
Student Text, pages 729 and 826

3.

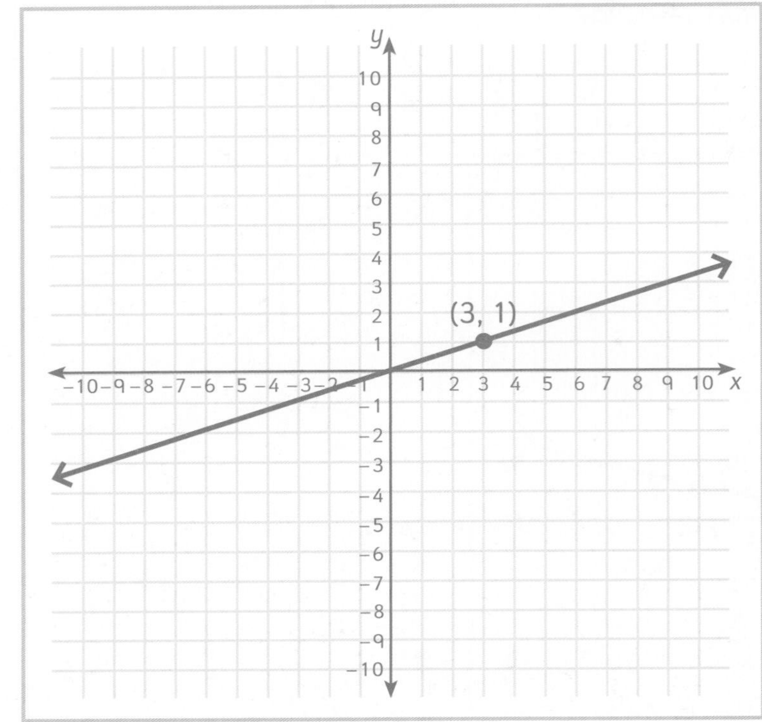

Unit 10

Lesson 6—page 826

Activity 2

1.

x	y
−2	4
−1	1
0	0
1	1
2	4

2.

x	y
−2	−4
−1	−1
0	0
1	−1
2	−4

3.

x	y
−2	−8
−1	−2
0	0
1	−2
2	−8

4.

x	y
−2	8
−1	2
0	0
1	2
2	8

5.

x	y
−2	−2
−1	$-\frac{1}{2}$
0	0
1	$-\frac{1}{2}$
2	−2

6.

x	y
−2	2
−1	$\frac{1}{2}$
0	0
1	$\frac{1}{2}$
2	2

Activity 4

1.

x	y
−1	−1
0	2
1	5
2	8

2.

x	y
−1	0
0	−1
1	−2
2	−3

3.

x	y
−1	7
0	5
1	3
2	1

Glossary

3-D An object having length, width, and height (p. 568)

A

absolute value The distance of a number from zero on a number line (p. 593)

additive Involving addition (p. 710)

algebraic expression An expression that contains a variable (p. 563)

arc Part of the circumference of a circle (p. 777)

associative property Property that allows us to regroup numbers in addition and multiplication without changing the answer (p. 633)

attributes The different features of a shape (p. 571)

B

balanced When the expression on one side of an equation equals the expression on the other side (p. 773)

base The face at the top and bottom of a 3-D shape (p. 569)

benchmark A standard by which something can be measured or judged (p. 86)

bisect Split in half (p. 788)

box-and-whisker plots A kind of graph that helps us understand how all the data are distributed from high to low (p. 64)

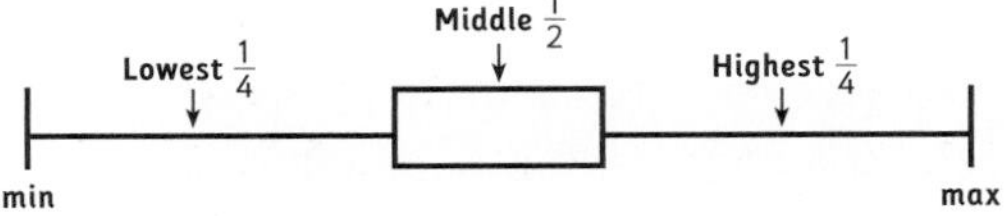

C

coefficient A number that is being multiplied by an unknown quantity; represents the number of variables, for example, $3m + 1$, 3 variables (p. 615)

common denominator Denominators that are the same (p. 20)

commutative property for addition Property that allows us to move numbers around when we add them (p. 190)

consecutive numbers Numbers that are next to each other on the number line (p. 701)

constructions The drawing of geometric items (p. 788)

coordinate graph A graph where points are plotted using x- and y-coordinates (p. 1049)

coordinates Dots showing location on a graph (p. 1049)

cubic inches Unit for measuring volume (p. 683)

cubic units How volume is measured; the basic unit of measurement for a 3-D object (p. 684)

D

data A collection of facts from which conclusions are drawn (p. 1075)

dependent variable A variable in a logical or mathematical expression whose value depends on the independent variable (p. 1084)

depth An additional dimension for a 3-D object (p. 568)

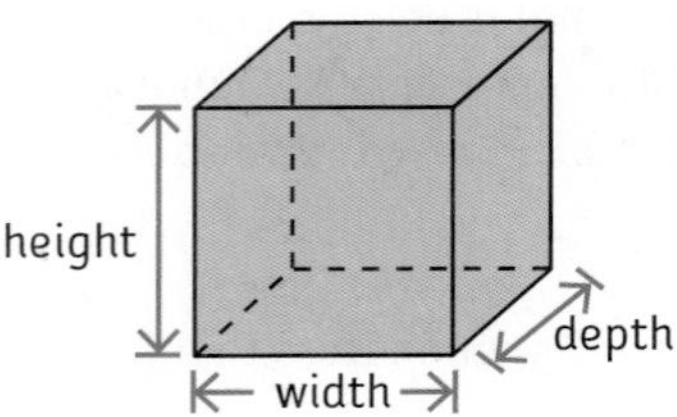

direct relationship A relationship that when one variable increases or decreases, the other variable does the same (p. 118)

distributive property Property that allows us to distribute a term over a quantity; $a(b + c) = ab + ac$ (p. 727)

double inequality An inequality that shows a range with an upper boundary and a lower boundary (p. 406)

E

edge Where the faces of a 3-D shape come together (p. 569)

equation A math statement that shows that one expression is equal to another expression (p. 773)

evaluating the expression When the expression is solved (p. 563)

even number Any number that can be divided by 2 with no remainder (p. 520)

expression A math statement that does not have an equals sign or an inequality symbol (p. 563)

F

face The flat side of a shape (p. 569)

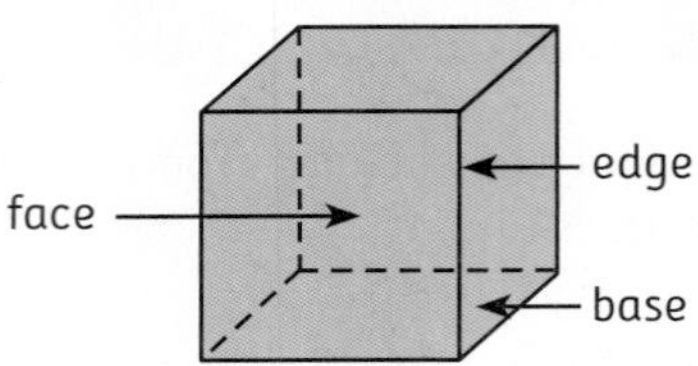

function A systematic relationship between two variables (p. 1045)

G

guess and check A strategy used to find the pattern of the output (p. 503)

H

height One of the dimensions of a 3-D object (p. 568)

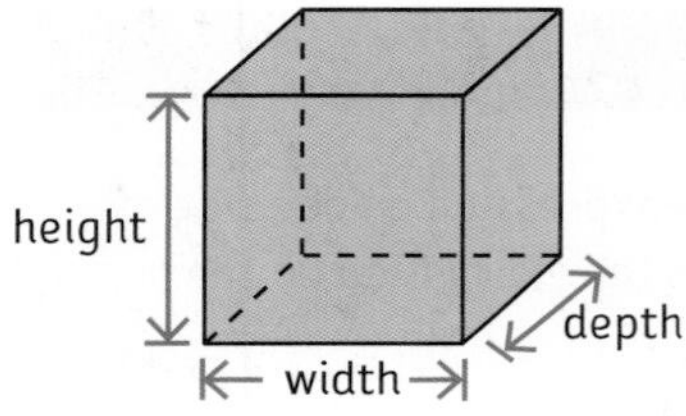

hypotenuse The side opposite the right angle (p. 1207)

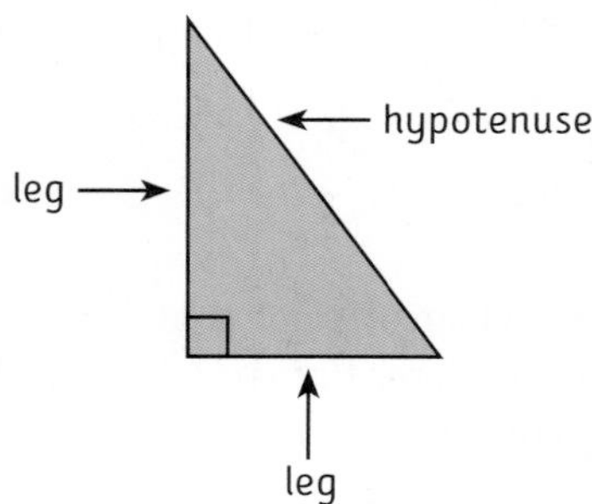

I

implied coefficient An invisible coefficient, always 1 or -1 (p. 616)

independent variable A variable whose values are independent of changes in other variables (p. 1084)

indirect relationship A relationship that when the value of one variable goes up, the value of other variable in the relationship goes down (p. 128)

inequality A statement involving two expressions where one expression is greater than or less than the other (p. 347)

input The number going into a function (p. 503)

integers Numbers that include only positive and negative whole numbers and zero (p. 592)

irrational numbers Decimal numbers that never end but do not repeat (p. 87, 1241)

L

least common denominator The smallest number that two different denominators can divide into evenly (p. 23)

linear function A function that has a constant rate of change and can be modeled by a straight line (p. 1095)

line of best fit A line placed through a scatter plot to clearly view the direction of the points (p. 137)

line segment Part of a line that has end points and a definite length (p. 777)

M

maximum The greatest number in the data set (p. 15)

mean The average of a set of data (p. 15)

median The middle number in a set of data (p. 33)

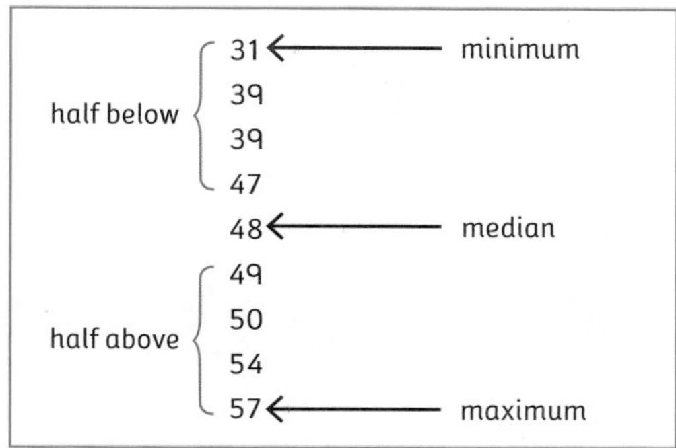

midpoint The middle point of a line segment (p. 777)

minimum The smallest number in a set of data (p. 15)

mixture The whole, or the total, amount (p. 506)

mode The number that appears the most in a data set (p. 15)

multiplicative Involving multiplication (p. 710)

N

negative slope The slope of a graph that decreases from left to right (p. 1112)

number grid A table of consecutive numbers (p. 701)

number term Part of an algebraic expression that includes only numbers (p. 613)

numeric expression When an expression has only numbers (p. 563)

O

odd number Any number that does have a remainder when divided by 2 (p. 520)

order of operations Rules that were created so that people can agree on one correct answer (p. 564)

outlier Extreme numbers in a data set (p. 47)

output The number going out of a function (p. 503)

P

parabola The graph, or curve, of the function $y = ax^2$ (p. 1250)

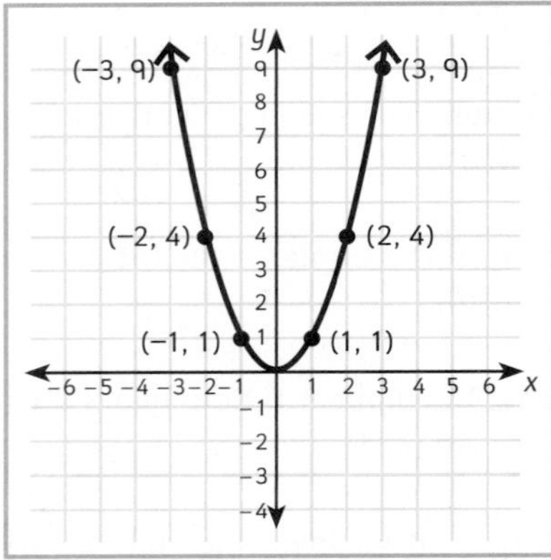

parallel Lines that do not intersect or meet (p. 779)

PASS Rule **P**ositive **A**nswers **S**ame **S**ign

1. When we multiply two negative numbers, the answer is positive
2. When we multiply a negative by a positive, the answer is negative
3. When we divide a negative by a negative, the answer is positive
4. When we divide a positive number by a negative number, the answer is negative
5. When we divide a positive by a positive, the answer is positive (p. 671)

perfect square number An integer that can be written as the square of some other integer; in other words, it is the product of some integer with itself (p. 1242)

perpendicular A straight line at a right angle to another straight line (p. 777)

point of origin Where the x- and y-axes cross (0, 0) (p. 1049)

positive slope The slope of a graph that increases from right to left (p. 1111)

prime number A number that is only divisible by 1 and itself (p. 520)

proof The steps followed when making an inference to justify the solution to a problem (p. 984)

proper fraction A fraction where the numerator is less than the denominator (p. 30)

property of equality When we do something to one side of the equation, we do the same thing to the other side (p. 804)

property of opposites Tells us that any number plus its opposite equals zero (p. 634)

proportion Two or more ratios that are equal (p. 232)

Pythagorean theorem Formula for the length of the hypotenuse, telling us that the sum of the squares of the legs of a right triangle is equal to the square of the hypotenuse (p. 1207)

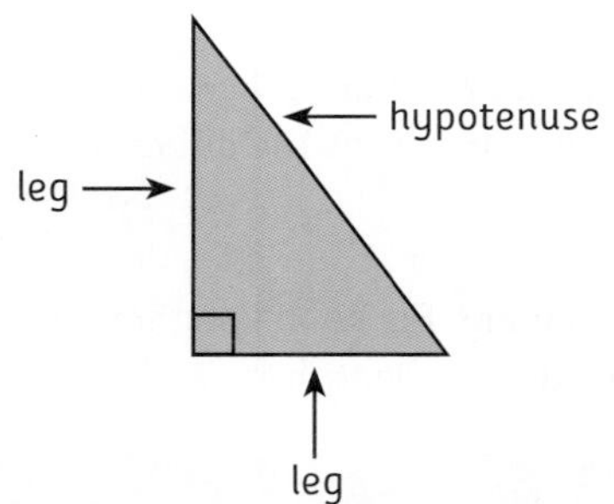

R

radical sign The $\sqrt{}$ sign over the number squared (p. 1215)

range The difference between the biggest number and the smallest number in a data set (p. 15)

rate A comparison of numbers that are measured in different units (p. 353)

rate of change The speed at which a function is increasing or decreasing (p. 1120)

ratio The comparison of two numbers (p. 211)

rational number Any number that can be expressed as a fraction (p. 72)

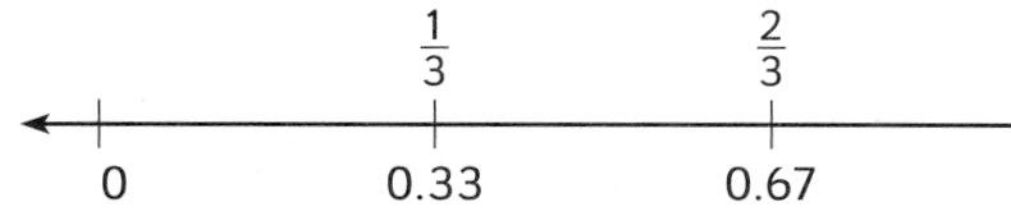

ray A line that extends in only one direction (p. 348)

reciprocal The inverse of the coefficient (p. 62, 820)

repeating decimals Fractions that when turned into a decimal produce a repeating pattern (p. 87)

right angle An angle of 90 degrees (p. 777)

rise The vertical movement on the graph (p. 1103)

run The horizontal movement on the graph (p. 1103)

S

scatter plot A data analysis tool that shows the relationship between two variables (p. 99)

slant height The height of a face of a pyramid or cone (p. 626)

slope The steepness, or slant, of a function (p. 1102)

square root A number that when multiplied by itself equals a given number (p. 1215)

$$\sqrt{100} = 10$$

substitution Replacing a variable with a number value (p. 202)

supplementary angles Angles that add up to 180 degrees (p. 826)

surface area The sum of all the areas of the surfaces of a 3-D shape (p. 602)

systematic relationship The change in one variable leads to a predictable change in another variable (p. 1056)

T

transitive property Property that says if $a = b$ and $b = c$, then $a = c$ (p. 984)

transversal A line that cuts across two parallel lines (p. 985)

U

unit rate How much of something is in one unit (p. 355)

V

variable term Part of an algebraic expression that contains a variable (p. 613)

volume The amount of 3-dimensional space inside an object (p. 675)

W

word statement Uses words to describe a relationship (p. 361)

width One of the dimensions of a 3-D object (p. 568)

X

***x*-axis** The horizontal axis of the graph (p. 1049)

***x*-coordinate** The *x* portion of the coordinate (p. 1049)

Y

***y*-axis** The vertical axis of the graph (p. 1049)

***y*-coordinate** The *y* portion of the coordinate (p. 1049)

***y*-intercept** The point where the graph of a function or relation intersects the *y*-axis of the coordinate graph (p. 1129)

Z

zero slope The slope of a horizontal line (p. 1143)

Index

D

E

F

O

P

W

X

Y

Z

Photo and Illustration Credits

PHOTO CREDITS

Unit 1 1 Batter © Rick Friedman/Corbis. Hitter ©istockphoto.com/Robert Kelsey. Softball and glove ©Jupiter Images.

Unit 2 Thumbprint (large) ©istockphoto.com/Nathan Fabro. Handprint ©istockphoto.com/omergenc. Eyeball ©istockphoto.com/Paul Kline. DNA ©istockphoto.com/Luis M. Molina. Chemist ©istockphoto.com/Laurence Gough. Thumbprint (small) ©istockphoto.com/appleuzr.

Unit 3 Geese ©istockphoto.com/Kevin Miller. Geese silhouette ©istockphoto.com/Gord Horne. Sky ©istockphoto.com/konradlew. Snow geese ©istockphoto.com/Ken Canning. Wetlands ©istockphoto.com/John Anderson. Birds ©istockphoto.com/Rob Pavey.

Unit 4 Ant with leaf ©istockphoto.com/Mark Evans. Elephant seal ©istockphoto.com/Nancy Nehring. Boy ©Jupiter Images. Car ©istockphoto.com/Crisian Lupu. Girl (two hands) ©Jupiter Images. Linemen ©istockphoto.com/George Peters. Girl (one finger) ©Jupiter Images.

Unit 5 Teens with 3D glasses ©istockphoto.com/Bob Ingelhart. Popcorn ©istockphoto.com/Amanda Rohde. Giza pyramids ©istockphoto.com/Volker Kreinacke. Montreal Biosphere ©istockphoto.com/Dan Moore. Modern houses ©istockphoto.com/LyaC. Los Angeles hotel towers istockphoto.com/Daniel Stein. 3D glasses ©istockphoto.com/Florian Röbig.

Unit 6 Woman ©istockphoto.com/Michael Krinke. Milk glass (first) ©istockphoto.com/Ina Peters. Milk glass (second) ©istockphoto.com/Sergey Mironov. Cow ©istockphoto.com/Michael Krakowiak. Milk churn ©istockphoto.com/Rtimages. Dairy silos ©istockphoto.com/steverts. Milk truck ©istockphoto.com/Nancy Brammer. Farm ©istockphoto.com/Aimin Tang. Rural road ©istockphoto.com/Maksym Dyachenko. Milk gallon ©istockphoto.com/DNY59.

Unit 7 Snowboarder ©istockphoto.com/Bob Ingelhart. Chairlift and mountains ©istockphoto.com/Superseker. Snowboarders standing ©istockphoto.com/Eric Belisle. Snowboarders sitting ©istockphoto.com/Denis Pepin. Snowboard jump ©istockphoto.com/Eugeny Shevchenko.

Unit 8 Tire tracks ©istockphoto.com/Jeff Chevrier. Stairs ©istockphoto.com/Mike Panic. Bridge ©istockphoto.com/javarman3. Construction ©istockphoto.com/Michael Braun. Freeway ©istockphoto.com/Maciej Noskowki. Roller coaster ©istockphoto.com/Paul Erickson. Barn door ©istockphoto.com/Jim Jurica. Field ©istockphoto.com/Rene Mansi. Rails ©istockphoto.com/fontmonster. Girl ©istockphoto.com/Justin Horrocks. Boy ©istockphoto.com/Eric Simard. Hatch marks ©istockphoto.com/Dietmar Klement.

Unit 9 Earth from moon, Apollo command and service modules, footprint courtesy of NASA. Lunar module ©istockphoto.com/P. Wei. Rocket man ©Fabrice Coffrini/AFP/Getty Images. Hand and pencil ©istockphoto.com/Yenwen Lu. Buzz Aldrin and flag on moon courtesy of NASA.

Unit 10 Scarecrow THE WIZARD OF OZ ©Turner Entertainment Co. A Warner Bros. Entertainment Company. All Rights Reserved. Movie projector ©istockphoto.com/Michael Kurtz. Boy ©istockphoto.com/Frances Wicks. T-square and triangle ©istockphoto.com/Joan Loitz.

ILLUSTRATION CREDITS

Unit 2 Cybermap ©istockphoto.com/Emrah Türüdü.

Unit 3 Globe ©istockphoto.com/zbruh.

Unit 4 Cartoon CALVIN AND HOBBES © 1986 Watterson. Dist. by UNIVERSAL PRESS SYNDICATE. Reprinted with permission. All rights reserved.

Unit 8 Airplane ©Jupiter Images.

Unit 9 Apollo 11, astronaut, moonscape illustrations based on photos courtesy of NASA.